BUSINESS MARKETING
A Global Perspective

BUSINESS MARKETING
A Global Perspective

H. Michael Hayes
University of Colorado at Denver

Per V. Jenster
Copenhagen Business School

Nils-Erik Aaby
University of Colorado at Colorado Springs

IRWIN

Chicago • Bogotá • Boston • Buenos Aires • Caracas
London • Madrid • Mexico City • Sydney • Toronto

Copyright © 1996 Richard D. Irwin, a Times Mirror Higher Education Group Inc. company.

Publisher: William H. Schoof
Production Manager: Bob Lange
Marketing Manager: Michael Campbell

Design and project management provided by
Elm Street Publishing Services, Inc.

Compositor: Elm Street Publishing Services, Inc.
Typeface: 10/12 New Caledonia
Printer: R. R. Donnelley & Sons Company

Library of Congress Cataloging-in-Publication Data
Hayes, H. Michael.
    Business marketing: a global perspective / H. Michael Hayes, Per V. Jenster,
    Nils-Erik Aaby.
        p.   cm.
    Includes bibliographical references and index.
    ISBN 0-256-15976-9
    1. Industrial marketing. 2. Export marketing. I. Aaby, Nils-Erik. II. Jenster,
    Per V. III. Title.
HD5415.1263.H39 1995
658.8—dc20   95-49443

Printed in the United States of America
1 2 3 4 5 6 7 8 9 0 DOC 9 8 7 6

Preface

Our Objectives for the Book

If we were asked to establish one overriding objective for this book, it would be that each student who uses it would come to share our fascination with and love of business marketing. Admittedly, we are biased by our personal experiences. Much of Michael Hayes's career was spent with General Electric in a wide variety of sales and management assignments that encompassed a broad range of products and services sold to industrial organizations, governments, and institutions. Per Jenster's experience includes international product and sales management and extensive consulting to business organizations. He was also in charge of the Industrial Marketing Program offered by the International Institute of Management Development (IMD) in Lausanne, Switzerland. In addition to academic work, Nils-Erik Aaby has extensive experience in business marketing in Europe with Elopak and IBM.

Few aspects of business are as complex and intellectually challenging as business marketing. How organizations buy, with multiple influences in the customer's organization interacting with others in the organization and with suppliers, is in and of itself a fascinating study of human behavior. The relationship between buying and selling organizations, with both cooperating and conflicting objectives, is not only complex but dynamic as firms adapt their strategies to changing circumstances. In formulating marketing strategy, marketers are faced with an almost infinite array of product–market choices. Product or service customization is the norm. Markets can be segmented horizontally, vertically, or both. With few exceptions, goods and services for business markets travel easily across country borders, expanding market choices but requiring further consideration of customization.

This complexity leads to our second and broader objective, which is to develop the student's ability to formulate implementable business marketing strategies. We believe this has three dimensions. The first is the ability to understand the complexity of business marketing situations in a global context. The second is the ability to formulate good strategies, recognizing that there is no one "right" strategy but rather that the key to strategy determination is the selection of the best strategy from a number of competing alternatives. The third is an appreciation of the issues that must be managed in order to implement the chosen strategy.

The Scope of the Book

The structure of the book reflects our belief that these objectives are best accomplished through rigorous analysis of a large number of business marketing situations, guided by certain fundamental concepts and leavened by an exposure to marketing literature that reports on recent empirical research and conceptualizations. Again, we are biased. Our experience in researching, writing, and teaching cases to MBA students, undergraduate students, and executives has led us to conclude that, short of the opportunity for hands-on experience of real-world analysis, one of the best ways to acquaint the student with the complexity and intellectual challenge of business marketing is through the analysis of cases. Clearly, no reasonable set of cases can fully encompass all possible marketing situations. Still further, we recognize that the historical nature of cases precludes the opportunity to consider immediately contemporaneous situations. The cases we have selected, however, are current, comprehensive, and broad ranging, and we have included cases set in many countries. Their study will assist the student's development of analytical skills that can then be applied to many other situations. Their study will also assist the student's discovery of basic concepts that will generalize to other situations.

Most of the cases we have included deal with many aspects of marketing situations. The Rogers, Nagel, Langhart case, for instance, which we identify in Chapter 1, also involves segmentation issues addressed in Chapter 6. The Du Pont case, which we identify in Chapter 2, also involves marketing communication issues addressed in Chapters 9 and 10. Depending on the course design of a particular instructor, the cases may be used with chapters other than those where we have first identified them.

Our objective for the text material is to provide the student with basic frameworks or ways to think about business marketing situations. Some of these are fundamentals that have stood the test of time. Others have been developed from the extensive and ongoing research in the field or have been adapted from research in some of the basic social sciences. We have avoided extensive comparisons of business marketing to consumer goods marketing on the premise that business marketing merits its own and separate treatment. As is inevitable with any textbook, some aspects of the subject are treated only modestly, and we expect that the text will be supplemented by the instructor and, where appropriate, by the students' own experiences.

The readings we have included represent only a fraction of the wealth of recent research into business marketing, and we recognize that others might have selected a very different set of readings. Our selection was guided by three considerations. First, we looked for readings that complemented, or supplemented, the text material. Second, we looked for readings that are representative of current research and thinking with respect to business marketing, not only for their intellectual contributions but to encourage the student to do further reading in the field. Third, we selected readings from a wide range of journals with international applications in mind.

The Context of Business Marketing

Historically, there has been a tendency to equate business marketing with heavy smokestack industries. Early textbooks tended to focus on products for large, capital-intensive industries and gave minimum attention to services. Today, the scope of business marketing is much broader. Steel companies still buy heavy rolling mills, and electric utilities still buy turbine generators and large transformers, but new products and new industries have emerged as major elements of business marketing. Computers, once sold only to large organizations, are now sold to thousands of organizations, both large and small. The hospital industry has emerged as a major purchaser, not just of health care equipment, but of all the other products and services necessary to the functioning of a large industry. Attention to services, once of concern principally as an adjunct to related products, is increasing both because of the importance of services in their own right and as they are being unbundled from their related products. The dynamic nature of corporate organizations suggests that this broadening of scope will continue as new products and services are developed, as new industries emerge, and as firms focus on their core competencies and use external suppliers for many products or services that once were produced in-house. No textbook can enumerate all the possible products or services that are part of business marketing or treat all their idiosyncrasies. For the student it is important, therefore, to recognize that using this book in the study of business marketing is just a starting point for learning about a fascinating field.

The global dimension of business marketing adds to its excitement and intellectual challenge. Goods and services for business markets have always traveled easily across country borders. Statistics about the large U.S. merchandise trade deficit mask the fact that in 1993 the United States exported $288 billion of capital goods and industrial supplies, more than 65 percent of total merchandise exports, and ran a favorable balance of payments of $42.1 billion. Similarly, with perhaps the exception of automobiles and consumer electronics, the exports of most other industrialized countries are heavily weighted toward business markets. While not all firms may elect to pursue markets outside of home country boundaries, few producers of business products and services can ignore their consideration. In the text material and by our selection of cases and readings, we have attempted to demonstrate the importance of such consideration and to provide the necessary understanding for it.

For the student pursuing a career in business marketing, we hope our book will materially assist in ensuring a rewarding career. For those who pursue other careers, we believe that the analytical skills and concepts developed in the course of studying this book will apply to a broad range of marketing situations. In either case, we hope you find the study of the subject as fascinating as we do.

Features of the Book

Several features of the book merit special mention.

- Unique to business marketing books our book includes, in one volume, text that presents major concepts, readings that introduce the student directly to a considerable body of business marketing research, and comprehensive cases, many of which have an international dimension.
- A global perspective is integrated throughout the text. Our basic premise is that marketing concepts are fundamentally international. We elected, therefore, to integrate international aspects of marketing as extensions of fundamental concepts where appropriate rather than to have separate international sections. We extended this premise to the readings, many of which deal with international issues, and to the cases, 17 of which have international dimensions.
- The book has a strong strategic and managerial orientation. The first five chapters establish the context of marketing planning and include corporate and business planning and a separate chapter on industry analysis. The remaining chapters address segmentation and product, pricing, and communication and distribution decisions.

Ancillaries

The *Instructor's Manual*, prepared by Per V. Jenster and H. Michael Hayes, is intended to provide guidance and support for using *Business Marketing: A Global Perspective*. The manual includes suggestions for use of the chapter readings, a sample class syllabus that may be tailored by the instructors to their particular needs, and comprehensive teaching notes for each case.

The *Test Bank*, developed by Dr. Gopal R. Iyers of City University of New York, contains more than 650 true/false, multiple-choice, and short answer questions. A rationale for each answer is also included.

Acknowledgments

Few textbooks are the work of just the authors, and our book is no exception. We first want to express our sincere appreciation to Bill Schoof, who gave us the opportunity to develop a different approach to a business marketing textbook and whose advice and counsel during the development of the book were invaluable.

We are especially indebted to Barbara Campbell, our project editor at Elm Street Publishing Services, who, together with Peter Kilander, Melissa Morgan, Nancy Moudry, Betsy Webster, Kelly Spiller, and Abby Westapher, did marvels in editing and polishing the text and kept us on track and on schedule when it frequently appeared an impossible task.

We extend our gratitude to Gopal Iyer at City University of New York for his work in developing the Test Bank.

We sincerely thank the reviewers, whose valuable input helped to shape the text: Larry Anderson, Long Island University; Jill Kapron, University of Wisconsin—Madison; Elliot Maltz, University of Southern California; and Bradley S. O'Hara, Southeastern Louisiana University.

Case Contributors

Kenneth L. Bernhardt, *Georgia State University*
Thomas V. Bonoma, *Harvard University*
Jonathan Guiliano and Cornelius A. deKluyver, *University of Virginia*
Constance M. Kinnear, *University of Michigan*
Thomas J. Kosnik, *Harvard University*
Michael Leenders, *University of Western Ontario*
Gordon H. G. McDougall, *Wilfrid Laurier University*
James E. Nelson, *University of Colorado at Boulder*
Robert A. Peterson, *University of Texas at Austin*
Jeffrey J. Sherman and Benson P. Shapiro, *Harvard University*
Douglas Snetsinger and Susan Spencer, *University of Toronto*
Dominique Turpin, *International Institute for Management Development*

We are indebted to the University of Colorado at Denver and the University of Colorado at Colorado Springs for the encouragement given to Michael Hayes and Nils-Erik Aaby to undertake this task and to the International Institute of Management Development (IMD) and its outstanding faculty for their generous support of the case writing work of Per Jenster. Without their support this book would not have been possible.

Lastly, but most importantly, we are indebted to our families who supported us throughout the writing of this book: to Neola; to Nancy, Danielle, Carl Christian, and Allison; and to Mary Jane and the boys.

H. Michael Hayes
Per V. Jenster
Nils-Erik Aaby
January 1996

About the Authors

H. Michael Hayes is Professor of Marketing and Strategic Management at the University of Colorado at Denver. He holds a B.S. in Electrical Engineering from the University of New Mexico and a Ph.D. in Business Administration from the University of Michigan. He teaches and conducts research in the areas of business marketing, international marketing, sales force management, and strategic management. His research articles on business marketing have appeared in *Industrial Marketing Management*, the *Journal of Purchasing and Materials Management*, and *Business Horizons*. He serves on the Editorial Review boards of *Industrial Marketing Management* and the *Journal of Strategic Change*, is currently the Director of the Master of Science in International Business Program at the University of Colorado at Denver, and serves as the External Examiner for the MBA program at Trinity College, Dublin. In addition to his academic experience, he has extensive experience in industry as an industrial sales engineer, district manager, and manager of executive education for General Electric.

Per V. Jenster is Director of Company Programs at the Center for International Management & Industrial Development, Lausanne, Switzerland, and Visiting Professor at the Copenhagen Business School. He was previously Professor at the International Institute for Management Development (IMD), Lausanne, Switzerland, where he was Director of IMD's Managing Industrial Market Strategy program. He holds a Cand. Oecon. from the University of Arhus (Denmark) and a Ph.D. in Strategic Management and Information Systems from the University of Pittsburgh. He has published more than 55 articles, books, and case studies. He has extensive consulting experience and serves on the boards of several companies.

Nils-Erik Aaby is Associate Professor of Marketing and International Business at the University of Colorado at Colorado Springs. He holds a B.S. in Business Administration and an MBA from the University of Wyoming and a Ph.D. in Marketing from the University of Nebraska. He teaches and conducts research in international marketing strategy and international business. His research articles have appeared in the *European Journal of Marketing*, the *Journal of Advertising*, the *Journal of Business and Industrial Marketing*, and the *Journal of Professional Services Marketing*. In 1990 he was the co-recipient of the Hans B. Thorelli Award for the Outstanding Article in the *International Marketing Review*. In addition to his academic and consulting experience, he has more than 10 years of industry experience as Marketing Manager–Europe for the Elopak Group and Marketing and Business Development Manager in Europe with IBM.

Brief Contents

Contents

Chapter 9   **Communicating with Business Customers:
Personal Selling   337**

Chapter 10   Communicating with Business Customers: Beyond Personal Selling   386

Chapter 11   Business Distribution Management   419

A Collection of 24 Cases

Chapter 1

An Overview of Business Marketing

More than half the world's economic activity consists of exchanges between organizations. Most of these organizations are commercial enterprises that exist to provide products or services to other organizations or to an ultimate consumer. Others are government entities or not-for-profit institutions such as schools or hospitals, that also provide products or services to others. The term *business marketing* has evolved to indicate the marketing of any product or service to organizations that produce products and services for others. We define *business marketing* as the marketing of products and services to commercial enterprises, governments, and other not-for-profit institutions for use in the products and services they, in turn, produce.

This book is about the formulation and implementation of business marketing strategies. We begin by providing an overview of the territory we plan to cover and the basic premises, logic, and structure of the book.

The Nature of Business Marketing

The issues business marketers face are significantly different from those faced by marketers of consumer products or services. The fundamentals are similar; that is, all marketers are concerned with the selection of target markets, segmentation within these markets, and decisions regarding product, promotion, pricing, and distribution. The context within which these decisions are made varies enormously between business and consumer marketing, which justifies a separate study of business marketing.

The nature of organizational buying, characterized by multiple influences, professional buyers, and long-term relationships, is very different from that of

1

consumer buying. Because organizations buy in order to achieve organizational purposes, there is more emphasis on functionality. As a result, most products and services produced to meet the needs of organizations can be sold in many countries. The critical decision of market selection has the horizontal dimension of consumer goods marketing plus a vertical dimension. Horizontally, for instance, business marketers can select customers on the basis of the industry, the size of an organization, or the nature of the purchasing practice. Vertically, they can target component manufacturers, equipment manufacturers, or end users. Products (a word we use frequently to include both products and services) are often custom built, and, in many instances, new product ideas come from customers. Promotion relies heavily on personal selling, hence managing the sales force in orchestrating organizational resources to satisfy customer needs is a major concern. Price determination is heavily influenced by the prevalence of both sealed bidding and negotiation with skilled professionals. Distribution decisions must take into account the high degree of specialization among distributors, the relationships distributors have established with end customers, and the complex set of tasks performed by industrial distributors.

Business Marketing Strategy

At the heart of business marketing is the formulation of strategy. Strategy must take into account the nature of demand for the particular product or service, the industry in which the firm competes, and events and trends in the broader external environment. Marketing strategy, however, is not conceived in an organizational vacuum. Its purpose is to assist the firm to achieve its objectives. It must consider the capabilities and aspirations of the firm, and it must work closely and in harmony with other functional strategies. In Chapter 2 we discuss a number of marketing strategy concepts and analytical frameworks and emphasize the relationship between marketing strategy and business and corporate strategy.

But even the most brilliantly formulated marketing strategy can fail if it is not executed properly. Marketing strategy, therefore, must take into account the organization's ability to implement it. As we discuss throughout the text, and particularly in Chapters 9 and 10 on communicating with customers, the individuals who are to be involved in executing marketing strategy should also be involved in its development, both for the knowledge they contribute and to ensure they have a sense of ownership in the strategy.

Business Markets

It is estimated that half or more of manufactured products are sold to organizations and that, in total, more products and services are involved in sales to business buyers than to consumers. In the United States there are some 13 million organizations that buy products and services. Many of these organizations are links in a chain leading from raw materials to finished products. In the automotive industry, for instance, equipment manufacturers supply the steel industry with the necessary machinery to mine coal and iron ore and to convert the ore to steel. Steel suppliers supply their steel directly to car manufacturers and to a host of component manufacturers that also supply the car manufacturers. Suppliers of a wide range of services, from accounting to medical insurance to specialized consulting, provide their services at all levels in the chain. In a world economy in excess of $20 trillion, as shown in the table below, the market for business goods and services is enormous.

While the sheer size of business markets indicates their importance, the diversity of business markets indicates the complexity of establishing appropriate marketing strategies to serve them. Organizations buy and sell an incredible array of goods and services: some are familiar, such as computers or architectural services; others are less familiar, such as insulation for spacecraft or remote diagnostics for maintaining sophisticated machine tools.

Business markets are frequently contrasted with consumer markets to make the point that business markets have fewer buyers, larger buyers, and geographically concentrated buyers and that close relationships exist between suppliers and customers. These generalizations tend to oversimplify the nature of business markets. Some industries are, indeed, almost totally comprised of large players. For example, the tire manufacturing industry is dominated by Goodyear in the United States, Michelin in France, and Bridgestone in Japan; the aircraft manufacturing industry is dominated by Boeing and McDonnell Douglas in the United States and Airbus in Europe; and the mainframe computer industry is dominated by IBM worldwide. But other industries are comprised of thousands of small firms, with no one firm having more than a small share of the market. An example is the furniture manufacturing industry, with more than 11,000 competing firms just in the United States. Still other industries have both large and small players; for example, the accounting industry has the Big 6 firms that dominate the large corporation market worldwide and

Gross Domestic Product (GDP): 1993 (in 1988 Billions of U.S. $)

Developed Economies	*13,878*
United States	5,291
European Union	5,230
Japan	3,357
Economies in Transition	*1,501*
Eastern Europe	436
Former Soviet Union	1,065
Developing Countries	*3,943*
Total	19,322

Source: *World Economic and Social Survey: 1994,* New York: United Nations, 1994, p. 259.

many small, sometimes one-person, practices that serve the needs of medium and small clients.

Some business market customers are indeed large. The motor vehicle industry in the United States, for instance, which spends up to 60 percent of its sales revenues (some $68 billion in 1993) on purchased materials, includes such giants as General Motors and Ford. Other customers are as small as the one-person CPA (Certified Public Accountant) office that purchases perhaps $10,000 per year of equipment and supplies.

In some industries customers are geographically concentrated, as in the steel industry, which has major clusters of customers near Pittsburgh in the United States and in the Ruhr region in Germany. In other industries customers are widely dispersed, particularly service businesses and local governments.

The variations in industry composition, size of customers, and geographic concentration suggest the variety of options business marketers must consider in selecting a particular target market or in electing to serve multiple markets.

The relationships between suppliers and customers and the nature of purchasing practices also vary in business markets. Some customers prefer and nurture long-term relationships with suppliers. Such customers believe suppliers have much more to offer than just availability and price. Other customers aggressively pursue low prices; they use a wide variety of purchasing tactics, including a willingness to change suppliers frequently. Again, this variation suggests the variety of options available to suppliers. Some suppliers elect to serve only customers who prefer long-term relationships. Others target only customers who pursue low prices because of volume considerations or favorable cost structures. Still others target both segments, despite the complexity of doing so.

The nature of the contract and forms of payment also vary. Most exchanges in business markets involve purchases where payment is made in cash on receipt of goods or services, but rental and lease arrangements are also common. General Electric, for instance, the world's largest owner of passenger aircraft, leases its aircraft to airlines. Transactions often involve some form of barter, where payment is made in goods; or offset, where payment is made in cash but the supplier also guarantees to purchase a certain amount of other goods from the customer over a set period in the future. While rentals, leases, barter, and offset can expand the firm's opportunity set, the pursuit of these arrangements cannot be undertaken without considering the requirements for special competencies.

Despite the variation in business markets, there is a common theme: purchasing organizations buy only to accomplish their objectives or strategy. This significantly influences the nature of demand in business markets in four ways. First, demand is derived; that is, demand for business goods and services is ultimately derived from demand for consumer goods. If demand for consumer goods changes, so will demand for business goods and services. For example, the number of mufflers automobile manufacturers buy is dictated by the number of cars they make to satisfy customer demand. Second, demand is relatively price inelastic for many product categories. Substantial cuts in the price of mufflers does not motivate automobile manufacturers to purchase more mufflers than needed for the cars they produce. While this is true for mufflers, it should be noted that it might not be true when the cost of the component part or raw material represents a substantial portion of the cost of the finished product. A substantial reduction in the price of steel, for instance, if passed along to consumers in the form of lower car prices, might be expected to increase the sale of cars and, hence, of steel as well. Third, demand is highly price cross-elastic. Even though the automobile industry does not buy more mufflers than it needs, all else being equal, the low-priced supplier will enjoy the largest share of the available business. Fourth, demand for many goods and services sold to organizations tends to be volatile. This is particularly true for long-delivery-cycle equipment and in industries where capacity is added in large increments, as is the case for turbine generators or for heavy steel mill machinery. Orders for such equipment tend to diminish at the bottom of a business cycle, whereas many orders are placed when economic prospects are favorable. In broad terms, therefore, business marketing strategy must take into account not only the immediate customer but, as we discuss further in Chapter 4, also the customer's customer.

Historically, with the possible exception of tourism, international markets have been more important for industrial and commercial goods and services than for consumer products. There are exceptions, of course, but as a general rule technical functionality has crossed national borders more easily than have features that must meet local consumer preferences. Edison's first commercial power plant, for instance, was installed in London in 1882, six months before one was installed in the United States. More recently, Compaq Computer built a plant in Scotland to serve the European market before it had sold its first computer in the United States.

In recent years, world trade has been expanding at a greater rate than the growth in world economic output. As reported in the *World Economic and Social Survey: 1994,* increases in world output were estimated at 2.5 percent for 1994 and 3 percent for 1995, whereas world trade was estimated to increase 6 percent in 1994 and 6.5 percent in 1995. In this environment of expanding trade, the U.S. trade deficits in recent years have tended to mask both the positive contribution of capital goods, industrial supplies, and services to the trade balance and their relative importance as components of international trade. As shown in Table 1.1, in 1993, when the overall U.S. trade balance showed a deficit of $118.5 billion, exports of capital goods and industrial supplies were $288.3 billion compared to imports of $246.2 billion, resulting in a positive contribution of $42.1 billion, and services made a positive contribution of $55.7 billion. And capital goods and industrial supplies represented 65 percent of total exports.

Even so, until recently most firms have treated international business markets as something outside of the mainstream of their organizational activities. During the last two decades, however, recognizing this growth of world trade, an increasing number of firms have realized that consideration of international

TABLE 1.1
Selected U.S. Trade Statistics: 1993

Category	Exports	Imports	Total	Balance
Capital goods	$183.0	$152.7	$335.7	$30.3
Consumer goods	53.4	133.9	187.3	-80.5
Auto. vehicles and parts	51.4	100.4	151.8	-49.0
Food and beverage	40.8	27.4	68.2	13.4
Petroleum	6.6	51.1	57.7	-44.5
Other industrial supplies	105.3	93.5	198.8	11.8
Total	440.5	559.0	999.5	-118.5
Total merchandise (Census basis)	464.8	580.5	1045.3	-115.7
Current account total	753.9	863.1	1617.0	-109.2
Merchandise trade less military	456.8	589.2	1046.0	-132.4
Service	186.8	131.1	317.9	55.7
Investment	110.3	110.3	220.6	.0
Capital plus industrial supplies	288.3	246.2	534.5	42.1
Capital plus industrial supplies, % of total	65%	44%	53%	

Source: *Business America,* March 1994, pp. 29–30.

market opportunities should be on a par with consideration of domestic market opportunities.

As we will discuss in Chapters 2, 3, 4, and 5, understanding business markets requires a good understanding of marketing concepts, good situation analysis, and a good marketing intelligence system. In this book we take the view that the fundamentals of marketing decision making are not restricted by national borders. While it is not imperative that every firm target markets in more than one country, we contend that decisions on market selection must be based on a comprehensive understanding of market opportunities, and this can only come from analysis that crosses country borders with respect to customers, competitors, and industry trends and characteristics.

Business Products and Services

In addition to the characteristics of business markets presented above, business marketing strategy is also influenced by the characteristics of goods and services, irrespective of the target market. A number of classification schemes have been developed to identify the nature of these goods and services as a basis for understanding the nature of the purchasing process for them and thus for developing marketing strategy. Most classification schemes include the following categories.

Raw Materials. This category includes farm products, mining and mineral products, coal, and iron ore. These products tend to be commodities, giving suppliers few opportunities to differentiate their products from others based on product characteristics. Continuity of supply, however, is critical and customers often enter into long-term contracts with suppliers to ensure supply and to protect against the price fluctuations characteristic of commodities.

Manufactured Materials. As with raw materials, this category includes some manufactured products that are also essentially commodities, such as sulfuric acid, or semifinished food products, such as dough sold to bakeries. It also includes proprietary manufactured materials such as DuPont's Nylon®, GE's Lexan®, or Elopak's Pure-Pak® containers for milk and fruit juices. Suppliers of proprietary materials have significant opportunities to differentiate their products, and branding is an important element of marketing strategy. In many instances, market development is a major concern, both with the purchasing customer and the ultimate user.

Components. This category includes such products as small motors used in appliances and microprocessors used in personal computers. Components can lose their identity in the finished product. Few buyers of appliances, for instance, know the make of the electric motor used in their appliances. In such cases, product performance is important, but there is little or no opportunity to build end-user preference. In other cases, the component may be well known. For example, in the personal computer industry Intel has extensively advertised its microprocessors to end users, with the expectation that end-user preference for Intel products will influence the computer manufacturer to use them. In both situations, continuity of supply and quality are critical. Price relative to competitors is important but less so where end-user preference can be developed. Absolute price also may be important if the component has a significant influence on the price of the end product in a price-sensitive market.

Construction. This category includes buildings and other structures such as oil drilling rigs, processing plants, and pipelines. These products are usually provided by heavy engineering contractors, based on a design of an architect or consulting engineer or, particularly in the case of processing plants or pipelines, on a design of the contractor. Contractors also purchase a wide variety of products needed for their construction projects. Key considerations are the ability of the contractor to deliver a well performing facility on time and within budget.

Capital Goods. This category includes a wide variety of products ranging from heavy or fixed equipment (turbine generators or mainframe computers) to factory equipment (lift trucks or hand tools) to office equipment (photocopiers or stand-alone personal computers). Heavy or fixed equipment and some factory equipment is carried on the books as plant and equipment and depreciated over a period of years. Price is important, but long-term functionality and service are critical because these products become the heart of the manufacturing process. Less expensive or portable products are frequently expensed in the year of their purchase, reflecting their shorter lives. Functionality is still important, but price and availability tend to dominate the purchasing decision.

Maintenance, Repair, and Operating (MRO) Supplies. This category includes the wide variety of products needed to run offices and factories, such as parts for capital goods, small tools for manufacturing facilities, paint for buildings, and stationery for offices. These products are inexpensive on an individual basis, but total expenditures for them are significant. Price, therefore, is a major consideration, as is availability.

Services. Organizations purchase a broad range of services. Some services are directly related to a product and are provided either pre- or postsale. These services can be complex, for example, the servicing of sophisticated machine tools or computers, or relatively simple, as in the case of photocopier repair. When products are introduced, the service is usually packaged with the product. As the product matures, the service may be separated from the product and is frequently sourced from an independent provider rather than the product manufacturer. Other services are essentially independent of a product. They can be complex (legal, architectural, or consulting services), or simple (janitorial services). Firms usually choose providers of routine services from a number of potential suppliers, and price often is their predominant selection criterion. For more sophisticated services, the selection process is usually complex, taking into account a number of criteria, and decisions are made at high levels in the organization.

The Approach of the Book

We wrote this book for students who have been exposed to the broad fundamentals of marketing, either through previous coursework or through extensive work experience. We emphasize improving the student's ability to analyze business marketing situations and to develop appropriate plans or courses of action. Business marketing can be studied in a number of ways. Our approach relies

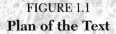

FIGURE 1.1
Plan of the Text

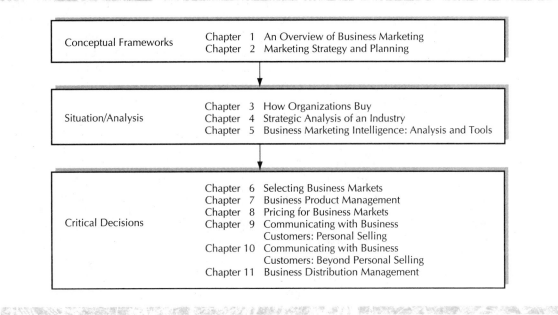

Conceptual Frameworks	Chapter 1 An Overview of Business Marketing Chapter 2 Marketing Strategy and Planning

Situation/Analysis	Chapter 3 How Organizations Buy Chapter 4 Strategic Analysis of an Industry Chapter 5 Business Marketing Intelligence: Analysis and Tools

Critical Decisions	Chapter 6 Selecting Business Markets Chapter 7 Business Product Management Chapter 8 Pricing for Business Markets Chapter 9 Communicating with Business Customers: Personal Selling Chapter 10 Communicating with Business Customers: Beyond Personal Selling Chapter 11 Business Distribution Management

heavily on case analysis, which is supplemented by textual coverage of major concepts and an extensive number of readings that elaborate on those concepts.

Textual Material

The text provides good coverage of concepts fundamental to business marketing without overwhelming students with detail. It is organized in three sections, as shown in Figure 1.1. Chapters 1 and 2 present the conceptual framework within which business marketing analysis and decision making take place. Chapters 3, 4, and 5 provide the necessary background for situation analysis by focusing on understanding the industry, the customer, and the process of acquiring information. Chapters 6 through 11 cover the five key areas of marketing decision making. While we emphasize the decisions that form the basis of strategy, implementation is also a key theme that runs throughout these chapters.

Ethics is another theme incorporated throughout the book. We believe it is important for students to appreciate the nature of ethical issues business marketers face and to consider how they might deal with such issues. We have included a number of short descriptions of situations that encourage discussion of the ethical aspects of a variety of business marketing decisions. In addition, we have included one comprehensive case (Lussman-Shizuku Corporation) that gives students the opportunity to discuss a complex situation in a Japanese firm.

Case Analysis

The use of cases merits special mention. Case analysis and discussion acquaint students with the unstructured, messy problems that characterize the real world of business marketing and sharpen their analytical ability. Students will discover, for instance, that it is frequently not clear what the problem is, or that what appears to be the problem is in fact not the real problem. In many instances they will learn to deal with the frustration at the lack of information available for decision making, as do real-world managers. From other cases, students will learn to deal with the anomaly of organizational success in the face of questions as to managerial competence.

The cases are accounts of actual situations in which managers were confronted with problems or issues requiring decisions or action. Most cases deal with recent situations. We point out, however, that many of the issues firms face today—for example, how to organize the field sales force—are not new issues. The time frame of a case, therefore, is not as important as the issue(s) with which it deals.

Many cases in this book deal with more than one issue. Analysis of the Leykam Mürztaler case, for instance, requires consideration of distribution, communication, and branding decisions. Each chapter includes a brief outline of the cases most closely associated with that chapter, but most likely there will be considerable variation in how instructors actually assign the cases.

Analysis and discussion of the situations described in the cases provide the opportunity for a number of learning outcomes, including:

- Improvement of the student's understanding of the nature of business marketing, particularly with respect to how and why organizational customers buy and how firms compete within their industries.
- Enhancement of the student's ability to analyze a wide variety of business marketing situations and to make appropriate recommendations for action.
- Development of the student's ability to learn inductively; that is, to develop general principles from the study of one situation that will apply in other situations.

The last outcome merits further consideration. As David Kolb has observed, most managerial learning comes from experience.[1] That is, managers act, observe the consequences of their action, and make a conclusion about the appropriateness of their action. This, in turn, guides future actions. In other words, managers learn inductively, as much from their own experience as from the experience or teaching of others. In the main, this learning takes place without extensive reflection. Few managers write down the principles on which they base their actions, yet most develop heuristics, or rules of thumb, that guide them in a wide variety of situations. One of the reasons cases are so popular in executive programs is that they provide similar opportunities for managers to develop new heuristics, or to validate the applicability of existing heuristics, in an environment of comment by other seasoned managers. In the academic classroom, cases give students the opportunity to start the process of learning from experience, to consider how personal heuristics are developed and how to validate them, either against research results or the instructor's experience. Depending on the experiences of the class members, there may also be the opportunity to further develop or validate them against the comments of other students. In sum, by putting students in the position of managers, case analysis and discussion can bring students much closer to the realities of organizational life and managerial decision making.

Readings

We selected readings that reinforce and elaborate on important text concepts and expose students to the current literature of business marketing. We hope this exposure to business marketing literature will encourage students to read the literature as a permanent part of their life-long approach to learning about this complex and ever-changing subject.

Summary

All marketers are faced with certain fundamental issues, including target market selection, market segmentation, and decisions about product, price, promotion, and distribution. The nature of business marketing, however, with its emphasis on selling to organizations rather than to individual consumers, the size of business markets, and the wide variety of strategic choices available to business marketers, merits specialized consideration. Organizations buy only to accomplish their objectives or strategy, and the buying process is characterized by multiple influences. Business marketers must understand the forces that give rise to organizational demand and must be able to analyze complex organizational buying processes. The size of business markets is enormous, comprising more than half the world's economic activity. The diversity of these markets presents business marketers with a wide array of strategic choices with respect to both horizontal and vertical market selection, which should take into account international as well as domestic opportunities.

A variety of classification schemes has been developed to assist in the analysis of business markets. One scheme classifies business products in terms of raw materials; manufactured materials; components; construction material; capital goods; maintenance, repair, and operating supplies; and services. Each category suggests variations in marketing strategy and its implementation. Throughout the text we introduce other classification schemes that suggest similar variations in marketing strategy. In the final analysis, however, marketing strategies and their implementation must take into account the unique situation of the firm with respect to its competencies, its opportunities, and the values of its management.

Overview of Chapter Cases

✸ The Rogers Nagel Langhart case describes how a leading architectural firm in Denver is challenged with developing a marketing orientation in an industry that has ignored or actively avoided marketing. It provides the opportunity to consider product market selection, the organization of marketing activities, and what a marketing orientation means in a service business.

✸ The Toro Industrial Flavors case describes how a small Norwegian firm made the transition from consumer to business markets and presents the requirements for successfully pursuing international opportunities in the industrial flavors business.

Endnotes

1. David A. Kolb, "Four Styles of Managerial Learning," in David A. Kolb, Irwin M. Rubin, and James M. McIntyre, eds., *Organizational Psychology: A Book of Readings,* 2nd ed. (Englewood Cliffs, NJ: Prentice-Hall, Inc., 1974), 27–34.

B. Charles Ames

Trappings versus Substance in Industrial Marketing

*While executives are quick to say that they understand and believe in
the marketing concept, their actions show otherwise.*

Creating and supporting a marketing organization, adopting new administrative mechanisms, and increasing one's marketing expenditures—important as these trappings may be—are moves that by themselves do not guarantee marketing success. Unless there is also a change in attitude throughout the company, real results cannot be gained. In this article, the author discusses the fundamental principles that go beyond the trappings to ensure substantive marketing for industrial companies. ✳

The case for stronger marketing can be made almost any time for any company. But I believe it is especially timely now to dig into the question of what it takes to make marketing a more powerful force in industrial companies. I submit that industrial companies everywhere will find themselves faced with a more challenging business environment in the 1970's than at any time in the past.

To start with, more and more companies are attempting to tap foreign markets, and this interest in worldwide expansion is intensifying competition on almost every front. Thus companies are being forced to develop increased marketing skills to meet competitors they have never had to contend with before.

In addition to fighting the inroads of new and tougher competition, marketing skills will become increasingly important to the job of capitalizing on technology. Industry has had far more failures than successes in this area in the past; and with the continuing acceleration of technological innovation, the job of moving profitably from the laboratory to the marketplace will become even more difficult.

And, at least domestically, added marketing strength will be needed to tap new sources of profit growth so as to reduce reliance on growth through acquisition and merger. For unless there is a dramatic shift in the thinking of the Justice Department, this avenue to growth, which has been so popular in recent years, is likely to be partially blocked in the years ahead.

Few will quarrel with these facts of business life, and certainly in this day and age no one quarrels with the marketing concept. In fact, it would be hard to get anyone to argue against the idea that gearing the business to be responsive to consumer needs—which is a simple but meaningful description of what marketing is all about—is not only sensible but the only way to run the business.

Over the past several years, I have worked with a good cross section of large industrial companies—that is, companies that sell to other manufacturers rather than to the consuming public. I

At the time this article was written, Mr. Ames was a Director of McKinsey & Company, Inc. and Managing Partner in the firm's Cleveland office. He is the author of "Payoff From Product Management," *HBR*, November–December 1963, and "Marketing Planning for Industrial Products," *HBR*, September–October 1968. *Source:* Reprinted by permission of *Harvard Business Review*, "Trapping vs. Substance in Industrial Marketing," by B. Charles Ames, (July–August 1970). Copyright © 1970 by the President and Fellows of Harvard College; all rights reserved.

have noticed that top executives increasingly stress the importance of stepping up marketing effectiveness as a means of becoming more competitive and accelerating profit growth. Despite their conviction that marketing is important, many of these executives are disappointed with their marketing efforts so far. To quote one president:

"I can't really say that the marketing concept has made much of a contribution so far, and I don't know what to do about it. Our sales and administrative costs are up because of staff additions and higher salaries in the marketing department, but we really don't operate any differently now than we did before we started talking about marketing."

And, in the words of another industrial-based corporate president:

"Our marketing effort has been a total waste. All we've gained is an expensive marketing staff with hairbrained ideas about advertising and promotion. Most recently, we spent $600,000 on an advertising campaign in the top journals, and our sales haven't increased at all. I'm not even sure our customers read the magazines we've been pouring advertising money into."

I could cite a string of similar examples, but these two make my point. Only in a very few industrial companies can executives honestly say they are happy with what marketing has done for them— and support this belief with concrete evidence of improved results. No one I know has any thoughts about giving up on marketing; the concept is too sound. But certainly many executives are perplexed about what they need to do to achieve the improvement that they want.

For a checklist of questions that are a good test of how substantive your company's marketing efforts are, see Table 1.

My hope is that this article will shed some light on the roadblocks which have prevented industrial companies from getting the payoff they should from marketing, as well as present some ideas on how to clear these obstacles out of the way.

Where Marketing Fails

As I see it, marketing has not measured up to expectations in many industrial companies because management has concentrated on what I call the "trappings" of marketing rather than the substance. Let me explain what I mean by trappings. When most executives talk about what their companies have done to become more marketing-oriented, they usually point to such things as:

- Declarations of support from top management—speeches, annual reports.

- Creation of a marketing organization—appointment of a marketing head and product or market managers, transfer to marketing of the product development and service functions, establishment of a market research function, salesmen reassigned around markets, advertising function strengthened.

- Adoption of new administrative mechanisms—formal marketing planning approaches, more and better sales information, reporting system restructured around markets.

- Increased marketing expenditures—staffing, training and development, advertising, research.

I do not mean to imply that these moves are useless, but by themselves they are no guarantee of marketing success. The kind of change that is needed is a fundamental shift in thinking and attitude throughout the company so that everyone in every functional area places paramount importance on being responsive to market needs. This is why I maintain that the typical organizational and administrative steps taken in most companies are trappings; they fail to accomplish this shift in attitude. And without this shift in attitude—companywide—the most highly developed marketing operation cannot produce any real results.

Why have so few companies gone beyond the trappings and achieved the change in attitude that ensures substantive marketing? I do not pretend to have all the answers, but my experience suggests that frequently one or more of these situations exist:

TABLE 1
Marketing Orientation Checklist

These questions are a good test of how substantive your company's marketing efforts are. If you have trouble answering any of them, this article deserves careful study.

1. Can you describe at least three feasible strategic focuses that have been evaluated and seriously considered for each of your product/market businesses?

2. Can you cite specific steps your marketing department has taken over the past three years that effectively blocked the competitive threat of international as well as domestic competitors?

3. Can you cite changes in the specifications or characteristics of your product/service package that are linked directly to the identification of changing needs in specific customer segments?

4. Is there an effective interchange of ideas among your marketing, operating, and financial functions—in both the development of product/market strategy and the execution of it? Is top management actively involved in this process?

5. Do you have an organized channel of communication to ensure that the views of those men working most closely with the customers are taken into account in identifying product needs and opportunities?

6. Do you have a clear picture of the relative profit contribution from sales of individual items to all of your customer/channel segments?

7. Have you, within the last 12 months, evaluated—and made a conscious decision whether to drop or retain—those products and customers that account for less than 10% of sales and profits?

8. Have you made a comparison of your economics with those of your competitors, as well as a comparative value analysis of all individual items where you compete head-to-head?

9. Are your marketing organization and your planning and control system designed around end-use market characteristics?

10. Can you honestly say that four out of every five of the men filling your top marketing positions are serious candidates for future general management jobs?

- In a surprising number of cases, management does not fully understand the marketing concept as it applies to industrial companies.

- In many other cases, management understands the implications of the marketing concept but has not committed itself to the actions and decisions needed to reinforce it.

- In almost every case, management has failed to install the administrative mechanisms necessary for effective implementation of the concept.

In this article I propose to discuss each of these situations in turn, illustrating the kinds of problems they can cause and pointing out how some companies succeed in building substance into their marketing.

Understanding the Concept

When I say that in many cases management does not understand how the marketing concept applies to industrial companies, you may think I am imagining things. But time and time again, I have found evidence that this contention is valid. For while most executives are quick to say that they understand and believe in the marketing concept, many of their actions and decisions show otherwise.

Key Dimensions

To prove my point, I shall start out by defining what marketing in the industrial world is not. It is not, as many believe, simply a departmental operation set up to handle advertising, promotion, merchandising, and selling, as might be the case in a consumer-goods company. Nor does it *necessarily* mean striving for the greatest short-term profit contribution, going all out for volume, or seeking to serve everyone in the market.

Rather, marketing in the industrial world is a total business philosophy aimed at improving profit performance by identifying the needs of each key customer group and then designing and producing a product/service package that will enable the company to serve selected groups more effectively than does its competition.

This definition is admittedly a mouthful, but it reveals four key dimensions to industrial marketing: (1) aiming for improved profit performance; (2) identifying customer needs; (3) selecting customer groups for whom the company can develop a competitive edge; and (4) designing and producing the right product/service package or packages. Let me enlarge on each point.

1. *Aiming for improved profit performance:* Too many industrial companies talk a good game of marketing and profit orientation, but a close look at how they make decisions reveals that volume is still the swing consideration. Many of these companies would actually have a better profit picture if they gave a lower priority to volume, even if it meant scaling back the business.

2. *Identifying customer needs:* There are still many equipment manufacturers who know substantially all there is to know about their own technology and virtually nothing about how their customers really operate and make money. Many of these manufacturers spend millions developing labor-saving machinery for the least costly parts of their customers' production process, or they design costly features into their products without considering the value of such features to their customers—and then wonder why their sales departments are not able to sell the products.

3. *Selecting customer groups for emphasis:* We all know of companies that strive to be all things to all customers. These companies that take a shotgun approach to the market inevitably end up with a houseful of marginal product items and a long list of unproductive customers who generate a small fraction of sales and an even smaller fraction of profits. It is not surprising that more selective companies earn better profits, for they concentrate their limited resources on filling specialized product needs for customers who will pay for value.

4. *Designing the product/service package:* All of us have heard horror stories about companies that failed in the marketplace because they tried to sell a Cadillac when the trade wanted a Model A Ford. Actually, the analogy is somewhat misleading. A company does not have to be this far off the mark with its product/service package to be a marketing flop in the industrial world. For the buying decision hinges on minor differences, and a company is in trouble whenever competition has a product/service package that matches the customer's needs just a little better.

From all this, one conclusion is clear: marketing in the industrial world is much more a general management responsibility than it is in the consumer-products field. For in a consumer-goods company major changes in marketing strategy can be made and carried out within the marketing department through changes in advertising emphasis or weight, promotion emphasis or type, package design, and the like.

In an industrial company, on the other hand, changes in marketing strategy are more likely to involve capital commitments for new equipment, shifts in development activities, or departures from traditional engineering and manufacturing approaches, any one of which would have companywide implications. And, while marketing may identify the need for such departures, general management must make the decision on the course the company will take to respond to the market—and it must provide the follow-through to ensure that this course is pursued in every functional area.

Now that industrial marketing has been defined as a total business philosophy, it should be easy to distinguish those executives who understand the concept from those who do not. In short, the president who consciously frames his total business strategy in response to market needs shows that he understands the marketing concept, whether or not he has the trappings discussed earlier. (In fact, I can think of a couple of companies without formal marketing departments that are as marketing-oriented as any I know.)

Conversely, the president who merely enlarges his marketing department, or who continually spurs his salesmen on to find new customers of any sort, or who indiscriminately adds more products to his line, does not understand the concept in the industrial context.

Commitment to Action

Understanding the marketing concept is one thing, following through with the commitment to make the tough decisions that are frequently involved is quite another. Many companies stumble badly here. Companies with a superior marketing effort, on the other hand, repeatedly demonstrate their commitment to follow the marketing concept by their willingness to require cooperation from all functions, to invest for long-term goals, and to face up to deficiencies in product, price, or service.

Require Functional Cooperation

A willingness to require—and force, if necessary—all functions to make the changes needed to be responsive to market needs is the first form of commitment top management must make. In many cases, doing this is more difficult than one might think.

Here is an example that shows how hard it can be:

❑ In one capital-goods company, management had historically focused on selling the largest, highest powered, most maintenance-free units possible, with the thought that this approach favored the company's manufacturing economics. However, user needs had shifted toward smaller, less costly units without the rugged engineering characteristics required for maintenance-free operation.

Since this trend was clear, and the company was losing market position, marketing had recommended a major redesign of the product line. However, the company's manufacturing and engineering executives, who were acknowledged industry experts, argued convincingly that the current product design and cost structure were still superior to any competitor's, and all that was needed was a better selling effort.

Faced with these conflicting points of view, top management decided to stick with the original product concept and put pressure on the marketing group for a more aggressive selling effort. It was not until the company lost substantial market share and its entire profit structure was threatened that the president could bring himself to fly in the face of the expert opinion of his engineering and manufacturing executives and force the redesign through.

Now that he has, things are looking up. In a situation like this, it is unrealistic, of course, to expect a dramatic turnaround. But the early reactions of the market are encouraging, and the management team is now convinced that it is on the right track.

This example is not uncommon. I have run into many similar situations where management had to overcome a long-standing preoccupation with operating objectives that crippled the marketing effort—objectives such as "get maximum engineering content into the units," "keep the plant loaded," "increase the value added," or "move tonnage."

You may wonder why these attitudes are so hard to overcome, but it is understandable when you consider that the product concept in many industrial companies is actually the origin and chief reason for success of the enterprise. Management is naturally reluctant to move away from a product concept that has been demonstrably superior.

Also, remember that marketing recommendations lack the precision of technical data. Typically, top management is confronted with hard numbers from manufacturing and engineering—material costs, production costs, installation costs, and so on—while marketing must make its case on the basis of forecasts and judgments. Of course, these forecasts are quantified, too, but they can never be stated with as much precision as the historical performance data submitted by manufacturing and engineering.

Consider the example just discussed. Tradition won out over change because marketing was unable to nail down and quantify the shift in user preferences for smaller, less costly units before serious damage was done.

Finally, most of the general management executives I have talked to had a technical background themselves, and frequently tended to assess their products from a technical rather than a user point of view. Trying to convince these executives that a technically inferior product is what the market wants is next to impossible.

Thus, if I have learned one thing from my work with industrial companies, it is this: the task of shifting a company that has been traditionally dominated by engineering and manufacturing considerations to one that is truly marketing-oriented is enormous. It takes a lot of effort on the part of marketing executives to ensure that their proposals are carefully thought through, solidly documented with market and economic facts, and show an understanding of their impact on operating functions. And it also requires top management understanding of the obstacles just discussed, as well as active support with both actions and words, to successfully make the transition.

Invest for the Long Term

Another commitment management must make is a willingness to invest to achieve longer term goals. The idea of investing to strengthen one's marketing position is accepted and practiced every day in consumer-goods companies—even though these investments commonly have a relatively long payback period. For some reason, this idea does not seem to be acceptable or even considered in most industrial companies.

Yet one could argue that an investment point of view is more critical in industrial companies than in consumer package-goods companies because of the long time frame attached to the design, make, and sell cycle for any new product. Designing performance or cost improvements into an already proven product is a long, hard job. Then, developing the test or performance data to prove these advantages takes even more time.

Finally, it is understandably difficult to get an industrial customer to even try a new or different piece of equipment that may cost thousands of dollars and, more important, affect his entire production process. Thus it can take years to gain full customer acceptance and build a solid market base for a product/service innovation in the industrial world.

Despite these considerations, management in many industrial companies is reluctant to look at increased expense for product development, testing, or launching as an investment, or to take any actions to build a stronger market position if they cut into short-term profits.

Only recently, I encountered a situation which illustrates an all-too-common point of view:

❏ One company had committed over a million dollars to the development of several new products to make its line more competitive. It had also invested heavily in manufacturing equipment to get the new products ready for the market. When plans for market introductions were being made, the marketing director requested a budget increase to set up a specialized sales group to introduce these new products. He pointed out that although the added costs of a specialized sales group would not be recovered during the first year or so, by the end of two years the added volume would more than cover the cost of this group.

Initially, the division manager balked at the budget increase, claiming it would cut too deeply into short-term profits. It took a lot of effort, but the marketing director finally convinced him this was shortsighted by saying, "If we don't get these products established this year, we will lose the slim lead time we have in the market—and the $2 million that we sank into development and equipment will be down the drain."

Unhappily, only rarely does marketing succeed in getting the breathing room it needs to make a substantive contribution, as it did in this company. I have seen cases where division management's overriding emphasis on the short term prevented new products from being developed or effectively launched when they were clearly needed. I have also seen others where division managers resisted the weeding out of marginal products or customers so that the mix could be upgraded, when this was clearly the right move to make.

In all of these cases, it is clear that the actions needed to be responsive to the market were blocked—because it would have led to a temporary drop in profits—without regard for the longer term impact.

Actually, very few of the industrial executives I know are particularly sympathetic to the idea of investing marketing dollars for a longer term payoff, though they are perfectly willing to think in these terms when it comes to a capital proposal for new plant or equipment. As we have seen, there are executives who can be convinced that this approach can pay off. But until more industrial executives start to think naturally in these terms, the marketing concept operates under a serious constraint.

Face up to Deficiencies

Management must also demonstrate its commitment to the marketing concept by a willingness to squarely face up to critical deficiencies in product, price, or service. These disadvantages are tough enough to overcome in any business, but they are impossible to overcome in the industrial world, for deficiencies cannot be glossed over when some steely eyed engineer or purchasing agent typically makes or controls the buying decision. Unlike the housewife, the industrial buyer, since his decisions are usually based on economic and engineering considerations, is largely unaf-

fected by the emotional appeals of advertising, packaging, and merchandising.

You may think that I am belaboring the obvious by making this point. Let me assure you I am not. For management has a natural tendency to view its products through rose-colored glasses, and to conclude that any advantages claimed for competitors' products are exaggerated or insignificant or that competition is "giving the business away" or that it has a "cheaply engineered" or "shoddily manufactured" line if it is sold at a lower price.

I saw a good example of this in one company, which started to lose business because management would not face up to the fact that its product was inferior to its competitors' in terms of both price and performance characteristics. This was the situation:

❏ The company had been losing its share of market in one of its major product lines for several years. During this period, three different product managers had been making the point that competitor changes in product and price had made it impossible to compete with this line as currently designed and priced. They then went on to recommend a redesign program to take cost out of the line and to add certain product features. At the same time, they proposed a lower price structure to make the line more competitive.

Top management executives, including the vice president of marketing, reacted negatively. They simply could not accept the fact that their product line, which had been a long-time winner, was that far out of position. Instead, they blamed the product managers for not having a good grasp of the business and for not being imaginative in their recommendations to rebuild market share.

It was not until a new division general manager came on the scene that this position was reversed. He took a fresh, unprejudiced look at his company's product as compared with the competition. The conclusion that he reached was that the product managers had been right, and no amount of "more aggressive selling," "creative merchandising," or any other so-called marketing activity could overcome the basic competitive disadvantages of this product.

Admittedly, decisions like those suggested in the foregoing examples are frequently very difficult to make, and I do not mean to pass over them lightly. Nor do I mean to imply that a company must always do things differently or always suffer a short-term profit loss in order to successfully follow the marketing concept.

I do mean, however, that decisions like these must be made if that is what it takes to be responsive to the market. Management cannot allow emotional ties to what has been done in the past to overrule market considerations. Otherwise, as the marketing manager in one company suggested, "Management does a lot of talking about following the marketing concept, but in reality it's a joke."

Implementing the Concept

The third reason companies have not succeeded in getting positive results from marketing is ineffective implementation. As I see it, the three ingredients essential to proper implementation of the marketing concept are (1) qualified people, (2) reliable market and economic information, and (3) planning to ensure the right strategic focus for the business. I know a number of company presidents who are vitally interested in making marketing the cutting edge of the business, but who are frustrated in this attempt because of deficiencies in these areas.

Seek Qualified People

It takes superior knowledge of the market and the economics of the business, along with a healthy dose of good business judgment, to be an effective marketing executive in the industrial world. Without these characteristics, the marketing executive cannot command the respect of the other functional executives that will induce them to follow marketing's lead. Yet I submit that many companies have staffed key marketing positions (e.g., marketing head, product manager, market manager) with men who clearly do not have any of these qualities.

Where does management go wrong? In some cases, the problem stems from management's tendency to equate marketing with aggressive selling and thus to look only to the sales department for men to move into these positions. Many of these men are simply not able to develop a total company perspective, and their sales or volume orientation tends to dominate their marketing recommendations and decisions. As you would expect, with this point of view, they quickly lose the respect of other functional and top management executives, and they have no chance to influence major decisions.

In other cases, management turns to the outside in a search for men with a ready-made bag of marketing skills that will make their company marketing-oriented overnight. But except in rare cases, these men perform well below expectations, for they typically come equipped with skills that are not really applicable. There is no accepted bag of skills in industrial marketing that is readily transferable from one situation to another as there is in consumer-goods marketing, where basic advertising and promotion skills are applicable to a wide range of situations.

As I discussed earlier, success in industrial marketing depends on skills related to a specific industrial situation. It requires a comprehensive understanding of the particular market and of the economic aspects and operating characteristics of the business. And it requires mature business judgment to achieve a balance among functional considerations (i.e., product design, manufacturing cost, selling price alternatives) and between long- and short-term interests, and then to come up with sound recommendations for achieving maximum profit growth.

In effect, the industrial marketing executive must be an embryo general manager, and this is what the best marketing companies look for in staffing their key marketing positions. There is no magic in the way they get these men. They have no special recruiting sources, no extraordinary training or development programs; they do not pay excessive salaries, though they make sure salaries are fully competitive.

What these companies do is very basic. They are aware that marketing men are attracted to a company in which the marketing function receives top priority. They therefore make certain that the marketing function is set up in the organization as the lead function, and they see to it that everyone understands its role.

This means the marketing department has the responsibility to identify the changing needs of the market and the opportunities these represent for the company. It means also that the marketing department is expected to translate the market requirements into the actions needed by the other principal functions of the company (e.g., R&D, engineering, manufacturing, finance) to capitalize on these opportunities.

When I say that marketing is the lead function of the company, I do not mean by this that marketing is organizationally superior to the other functions. Its role is to show the way to the marketplace, and the role of the other functions is to follow this lead and get the company firmly established in the marketplace.

In addition, successful marketing companies are careful not to overlook sources which might provide high-potential candidates. They seek able men who have the necessary qualities—or the potential to develop them—without regard for their functional background. I have seen many cases where men from the financial, engineering, or manufacturing end of the business developed into marketing executives fully as effective as those who came up the sales route.

Finally, these companies recognize that there is no way to short-cut the development of their marketing executives. Whether they are home-grown or imported, they must be given both the time and the opportunity to learn about the total dynamics of the business. The importance of this broad-gauged understanding of the total business cannot be overemphasized, for it is the knowledge foundation that permits the good marketing executive to make the kind of balanced decisions and recommendations that will ensure for marketing its rightful role as the lead function of the business.

Get Reliable Information

Even men with the highest qualifications cannot operate effectively without reliable information. Yet many marketing executives complain that they

simply do not have access to the kind of information necessary to make intelligent marketing plans and decisions. Their complaints, which relate to both market data (e.g., market share, sales to end-user segments) and cost and profit information, could be overcome with relative ease, for the raw data is almost always available somewhere in the company.

The trouble is that it typically is not ordered in a way which is useful to marketing executives. In the case of cost and profit data, accountants usually design the information structure for external reporting and for manufacturing and cost control. Thus it is not geared to nail down the profit consequences of selling individual items or various mixes to different channels. And all too often market data are fragmented and incomplete. Here marketing executives must shoulder most of the blame, for they simply have not done the job necessary to define the information they need and how it should be drawn together.

In one company I worked with, the case for good information was made dramatically. Marketing management wanted to weed out some of the marginal items in the line to reduce inventory costs and free sales time for more profitable items. Figure 1A shows the picture the managers developed using the profit information available to them—gross margin. On the basis of this analysis, they decided to cut out several low-margin items, such as Fiber B.

Fortunately, before any items were dropped, a plant controller made a special analysis to determine the variable contribution per machine-hour that each item generated—that is, the profit each product contributed for the amount of plant capacity it used. His analysis, shown in Figure 1B, revealed a different picture from the gross margin comparisons and caused everyone to wonder if they were on the right track.

Then the division controller decided to look even deeper and made another special analysis to factor in the selling costs. As Figure 1C shows, once selling costs were considered, what initially were thought to be the low-profit items were actually the most profitable. Complete information resulted in a conclusion just the reverse of the original one. Now

FIGURE 1
Dramatic Example of the Case for Good Information

A. Traditional gross margin information leads to one conclusion.

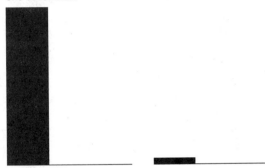

Fiber A   Fiber B

B. Examination of contribution per machine-hour shows a different picture.

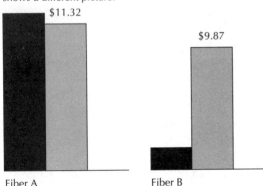

Fiber A   Fiber B

C. Analysis of selling costs reverses original conclusion.

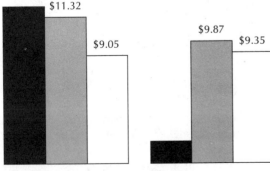

Fiber A   Fiber B

the company has completely recast its information structure so that its marketing executives get this kind of information as a matter of course.

Many companies with successful marketing records have made similar revisions in their information structure. This does not mean that they have abandoned the information necessary for external reporting or effective manufacturing control. Rather, they have added to their information structure data that enables their marketing executives to make fact-based decisions on products, channels, markets, and customers.

Do Strategic Planning

Virtually all of the companies I have worked with regard planning as a key ingredient in their marketing effort. Many of them are quick to admit, however, that their efforts to do a good job of planning are not nearly as effective as they should be, and they cite this shortcoming as one of the chief reasons that the marketing concept has not really taken hold. I think they are right. For soundly conceived market-oriented plans are the framework that keeps all the company functions operating around the marketing concept.

Planning, of course, is a broad and complicated subject in itself, and I have covered it in detail elsewhere.[1] It is clear, however, that the reason many companies have difficulty with their planning is that they pattern their efforts after companies in the consumer-goods field. Specifically, they tend to regard marketing as a discrete function, and they develop discrete marketing plans.

While this approach makes sense in the consumer-products field, where the key volume and profit-making activities are within the marketing department (i.e., advertising, merchandising, promotion), it does not make sense in an industrial company, where activities outside the marketing function (e.g., manufacturing, engineering, technical service) typically control success or failure in the marketplace.

---

[1]   See my article, "Marketing Planning for Industrial Products," *HBR*, September–October, 1968, p. 100.

Companies that do a superior job of marketing concentrate their planning efforts on making sure they have the right strategic focus for their business. Reviewing the strategic focus is time well spent in an industrial company. For one thing, it is all too easy to develop "marketing myopia"[2] in the industrial world and allow the need to "load the plant" or "increase engineering content" to override indications that present customer needs are changing or additional customer needs exist.

Because of this pitfall, in many companies the thinking of management is constrained by existing products and technology; opportunities to gain a competitive edge in present markets, develop new markets, or enter related markets go unnoticed. Moreover, the velocity of technological change and the consequent impact of this change on the competitive structure, on customer acceptance of existing products, and on new market opportunities can readily obsolete a strategic focus that was once highly successful.

The experience of a motor manufacturer I worked with shows how a shift in strategic focus can create vast differences in market potential and ultimately change the entire character of the business. Here is the picture:

❑ The company had traditionally held a 25% to 30% share of a market that was worth about $400 million and was growing at about 5% a year. Recognizing that it would probably have cut into its margins to capture a larger share from competitors, management took a hard look at how the market might be defined differently to expand the opportunity.

The first step was to include the drive linkage and systems that were powered directly from their motors. This more than doubled the potential market for this company and opened up a whole range of new product opportunities.

Management then shifted its view of the market to include the whole field of automation. As management defined automation, this shift in focus gave the company a market to work with of

some $2 billion—8 to 10 times the size of its original market opportunity. More important, the automation market is growing over 10% a year, or twice as fast as the motor market alone.

In recent months, the president of this company has said repeatedly, "It took us a long time to define our market in the right way, but once we did, the door was open for a whole stream of new product businesses that we wouldn't even consider before. Getting the right product/market focus has contributed to our accelerated growth and profits more than anything else."

In companies that take this approach to planning, the marketing department, of course, plays the lead role in defining market needs and opportunities, as well as in determining what it takes to serve various markets or segments. From this point on, however, planning becomes a collaborative effort, with all of the key functions contributing their points of view in a series of face-to-face emphasis on the planning system—that is, on such components as format, techniques, and lengthy writing assignments.

Naturally, the recommended plan gets the inputs and final stamp of approval from top management before it becomes an operating blueprint for the business. This approach—based on a continuous dialogue between key managers rather than on the completion of forms by function heads working in isolation—ensures the kind of balancing between functions, and between long- and short-term interests, that is required to make the marketing concept work.

Conclusion

There is nothing particularly sophisticated about the marketing concept as it applies to the industrial world. Nor is there anything conceptually difficult about what it takes to build substance into industrial marketing as opposed to simply having the trappings.

What it takes is total company involvement—from the top down—in the marketing effort and

---

[2] See Theodore Levitt, "Marketing Myopia," *HBR*, July–August 1960, p. 45.

management willingness to depart from traditional practices if this is what is required to be responsive to the market.

When I say there is nothing particularly sophisticated about the marketing concept, I do not mean to minimize the task of shifting an operations-oriented company to one that is market-oriented. As I have said, it is a tough job. It takes time—probably several years—and a lot of effort. Proof of the difficulty lies in the fact that only a few companies have done the job well.

For those few that have been successful, however, the time and effort involved have been well spent. For their responsiveness to the market will give them a competitive advantage that is certain to accelerate their profit growth in the years ahead.

My experience suggests that while most companies will agree with the fundamental principles I have discussed, only a few really live by them. And, in my judgment, this is what separates the successful from the unsuccessful companies in industrial marketing.

Frank V. Cespedes

Industrial Marketing: Managing New Requirements

In most industrial firms, marketing efforts encompass three groups: product management, sales, and customer service units. Managers have devoted much attention to managing effectively within each unit but not to coordinating across the units. The author discusses why managing these marketing interfaces is increasingly important and complex at industrial firms, the interdependencies and organizational barriers that affect their joint activities, and the strengths and vulnerabilities of initiatives aimed at improving links among the marketing groups. ✳

An industrial products firm recently held a meeting for senior managers to discuss marketing strategy and implementation. An outside facilitator, who led a discussion about improving marketing effectiveness, encouraged participants to list the key issues facing the firm. The blackboard in the meeting room was soon field with two lists:

Salespeople say:

- "Marketing people do not spend enough time in the field. They don't take specific customer complaints seriously enough. Marketing needs to establish a system for better field communications."

- "Marketing should be more demanding with R&D and manufacturing to alter product designs and production schedules."

- "Biggest frustration to our sales reps is lack of timely information."

- "Sales reps' compensation should not be penalized for price erosion. . . . That's a product issue out of our control."

At the time this article was written, Frank V. Cespedes was an associate professor at the Harvard Business School. *Source:* Reprinted from "Industrial Marketing: Managing New Requirements" by Frank B. Cespedes, *Sloan Management Review,* Spring 1994, pp. 45–60, by permission of publisher. Copyright © 1994 by the Sloan Management Review Association. All rights reserved.

Marketing people say:

- "Salespeople are always asking for information that they have already received. We spend much effort gathering and writing up product and competitive information, send out that information, and reps call a week later for the same information. . . . This takes time away from other important tasks we have."

- "We are underresourced: too many chiefs and not enough implementation people."

- "Our success depends on fulfilling customer expectations for tomorrow, not just today."

- "Sales is happy to criticize, rather than accept responsibility and suggest constructive improvements."

These comments reflect the changing tasks these managers face. Salespeople in this firm need more information, more often, from more marketing managers, as sales tasks involve more customized product-service packages at accounts. Conversely, marketing's complaints about "too many chiefs and not enough implementation people" reflect a situation in which product managers must work with more functional areas (and especially with field sales and service), even as cost-reduction pressures shrink staff support resources. Also, while sales generates more customized orders and complains about marketing's seeming inability to alter product designs and production schedules, marketing managers respond that "our company now has highly automated manufacturing operations, making design and other product changes a complex process." Hence, marketing rightly evaluates these requests with more than sales' often account-specific specifications in mind.

Especially for industrial firms, these interactions can be costly. Studies indicate that as many as one-half of new industrial products fail to meet business goals and consistently point to the management of the product launch—and, in particular, the hand-off from product management to sales and service groups—as key to new product success or failure.[1] But little effort has been made to identify the dimensions of required coordination among these marketing groups, organizational factors that affect their interactions, or how managers can usefully diagnose relevant options.

This article focuses on the interface between sales and service, and especially between sales and product management. Based on research at computer, telecommunications, and medical equipment firms (see the Appendix for details of the study), it first discusses why managing marketing interfaces is increasingly important and complex at many industrial firms. It then outlines typical interdependencies and organizational barriers that affect the planning and execution of these activities. It concludes by evaluating the strengths and vulnerabilities of initiatives aimed at improving links between the marketing groups.

New Marketing Requirements

Factors affecting the marketing units include changes in what many industrial firms sell (the nature of the product offering), to whom they sell it (market fragmentation), how they sell it (supply chain management requirements), and under what product life-cycle conditions they sell it.

Nature of the Product Offering

Industrial marketing programs increasingly involve a combination of tangible products, service support, and ongoing information services both before and after the sale.[2] Development and execution of such programs require the participation of the various marketing groups responsible for managing product, service, and actual sale.

A salient example is "systems integration" in the computer business. Many computer vendors are positioning themselves as a single point of contact for integrated systems, with the vendor (often with third parties) providing a combination of hardware, software, training, and other services tailored to the customer's business goals. In effect, the seller acts as a general contractor in managing system design, installation, maintenance, and, in some cases, ongoing operation of installed systems. The seller's offering to customers is ultimately the ability to coordinate its own product, sales, and service activities smoothly. One executive noted, "The real product is our company itself, and most of my job is to act as an information broker: I try to make my company transparent to the customer and the customer's requirements transparent to relevant product and service units in my company."

Similar requirements now face firms in many industrial markets. At medical equipment firms, group purchasing arrangements among hospitals have increased buyers' knowledge of terms and conditions among potential suppliers. An executive explained how this affected suppliers' marketing programs:

> Basic services in our business now include on-time delivery, damage-free goods, and effective order-inquiry routines. Value-added services in our business include custom-designed product labeling, customized quality programs, dedicated order-entry specialists, extended warranty plans, and new services in areas such as waste management and safety programs. Value-added services build the relationship and sustain our pricing structure; and we've found that cost-effective development and provision of these services require a multifunctional approach among product, sales, and service personnel in different divisions.

For the customer, these services are growing portions of the value added by a supplier. For the supplier, closer product-sales-service linkages are more important as its offer in the marketplace becomes a changing product-service-information mix that must reflect more segmented opportunities.

Market Fragmentation

Phrases like "micro-marketing" and "mass customization" have become perhaps too familiar in recent years. Managers risk losing sight of what is competitively distinctive about these developments versus what is fundamentally old wine in new bottles.

What is *not* new is that fact of customer differences and niche marketing. Industrial product applications have long been tailored to various customer groups that employ the same core product for different uses. What *is* new is the extent and necessity of such segmentation due to the tools now available for tracking differences in many markets. Commercial customers are more diverse in terms of vertical applications and geography, yet more able (via their internal information systems) to coordinate purchasing requirements across heretofore separate buying centers. Conversely, the sellers' information search costs associated with locating these differences are also lower and, in many product categories, worth more to the industrial marketer in a slow-growth economy.

A manager at a telecommunications firm noted, "We can no longer target broad industry categories for our products. Value and profits no longer reside, for example, in 'financial service' applications, but in more specific products aimed at commercial banks versus brokerage firms versus community financial institutions." Similarly, a computer executive described a market evolution common to many other industrial businesses:

Twenty years ago, we provided the hardware and the specifications for a broad application, and the customer's MIS department provided the specific solution. But, over the past two decades, the industry has grown and fragmented. At each stage of the value chain, specialists have arisen, while buying is more influenced by end users at accounts. Segmentation becomes more important.

In responding to more diverse segments, product variety often expands significantly. Most of the firms I studied increased the number of items they assigned to product managers by 50 percent or more during the past decade—findings in keeping with studies of product variety in other industrial markets.[3] This affects sales and service requirements as well as the need for links among product, sales, and service groups. Managers noted headquarters' difficulty in responding to market fragmentation on a centralized basis. Field sales and service personnel are often *better* informed about customer requirements (and an account's willingness to pay for an application or line extension) than upper management or headquarters product managers can be. But field personnel, responding to local conditions, are often less able to ensure scale economies or consistency in company dealings across segments. One executive commented, "Our central marketing issue is simply stated and difficult to manage: we need to decentralize and empower lower levels in the organization while maintaining a coordinated customer interface."

Supply Chain Management

Competitive bidding has historically dominated buyer–seller negotiations for many industrial products. The buyer's primary objective was to minimize nominal price by working with a large vendor base (to ensure supply continuity and increase buyer power), making frequent shifts in the amount of business it gives to each supplier (to limit supplier power and signal "discipline"), and conducting arm's-length, transaction-oriented negotiations through annual contract renewals and rebidding.[4] But total quality concepts focus on ways to reduce reject rates, improve cycle times, and decrease inventory throughout the supply chain. From this

TABLE 1
Customers' Cost-in-Use-Components

Acquisition Costs	+	Possession Costs	+	Usage Costs	=	Total Cost-in-Use
Price		Interest cost		Field defects		
Paperwork cost		Storage cost		Training cost		
Shopping time		Quality control		User labor cost		
Expediting cost		Taxes and insurance		Product longevity		
Cost of mistakes in order		Shrinkage and obsolescence		Replacement costs		
Prepurchase product evaluation costs		General internal handling costs		Disposal costs		

perspective, the cost and time for monitoring many suppliers of a product—largely "hidden" costs in the competitive bidding model—become visible and significant, while the means for improving information and product flows along the supply chain often motivate closer relations with fewer supply sources. Major industrial customers such as Allied-Signal, Ford, GM, Motorola, Texas Instruments, and Xerox have cut the number of suppliers they use by 20 percent to 90 percent during the past decade and have demanded new supply-chain arrangements from those they continue to do business with.[5]

One goal is to optimize the total cost in use of doing business with a vendor. Customers' cost-in-use components fall into three groups (see Table 1). Supply chain initiatives seek to lower these costs and increase the vendor's ability to develop and sustain value-based pricing policies that reflect total system benefits for customers. Implementation of this concept affects companies in at least two ways. First, this sales strategy emphasizes customizing product mix, delivery, handling, and other supply-chain activities to customers' operating characteristics. This increases the required interactions between the vendor's product and sales personnel.

Second, this approach requires closer coordination of sales and service, since important account management tasks involve just-in-time delivery, special field-engineering resources, and order-fulfillment factors that service units often execute. For example, a service executive explained how this approach places more pressure on the accuracy of sales forecasts, "Inaccurate forecasts mean greater transportation, warehousing, and inventory carrying costs. So it make sense that we be involved in administering the forecasts. I don't think of them as forecasts anymore; it's a management planning tool." Further, key elements of service in industrial markets often vary by type of customer and, for a customer, across different phases of the order cycle and account relationship.[6] Understanding these differences and activating relevant alignments along the vendor's supply chain become part of the selling process. This places more emphasis on product-sales-service coordination in order to design products with supply-chain requirements in mind.

Product Life Cycles

As in many other markets, product life cycles at the companies I examined had shortened in recent years.[7] A computer executive commented, "Until the 1980s, our business was like the old automobile business—five-year model changes. Product management utilized these time horizons and then performed basic market research, did relevant financial

FIGURE 1
A Continuum of Marketing Tasks

Product Management	. . .	Sales Management	. . .	Customer Service

- Market research
  - Competitive analysis
    - Product development
      - Product positioning
        - Advertising consumer communications
          - Packaging
            - Promotions
              - Pricing
                - Account selection
                  - Personal selling
                    - Channel management
                      - Account management
                        - Applications development
                          - Physical distribution
                            - Installation merchandising
                              - After-sale service(s)

projections, and worked to get other functions to buy into a product plan. [But] market changes make the results obsolete way before the end date." At telecommunications firms, deregulation and merging of voice and data technologies have had a similar impact on product life cycles, while hospital cost-control legislation and new safety concerns have accelerated life cycles for medical products.

These developments have made the notion of "time-based competition" common in the management literature of the 1990s, which emphasizes faster product development and linked manufacturing-distribution systems. But there has been little attention paid to the impact on downstream marketing activities, where responsibility for the customer's implementation of these initiatives still resides. One computer firm decreased product development cycles by 67 percent between 1986 and 1990. But for the salespeople, the new prod-

ucts meant learning new technologies, establishing relationships with different decision makers in reseller and end-user organizations, confronting different buying processes, seeking more information and support from product managers and service personnel—in short, developing new ways of marketing that were perceived as "alien" to traditional revenue-generation routines. The firm eventually realized that there is limited utility in shortening product-development cycles and investing millions in flexible manufacturing if the firm's marketing system cannot handle or (as in some companies) actively resists a greater variety of products, services, and segments.

Hence, even as other factors increase the amount of required coordination among these marketing groups, shorter product life cycles decrease the time available for establishing and assimilating the relevant coordination mechanisms.

Market Requirements and Marketing Interdependencies

Market changes require changes in marketing programs. But without understanding the issues that traditional organizational alignments generate, change is less likely to be purposeful. Figure 1 indicates tasks often associated with product, sales, and customer service groups at industrial firms. Where the responsibility for each task resides varies among companies. Together, however, these groups are responsible for tasks that move from market and competitive analysis, through the activities associated with the marketing mix (product policy, pricing, promotion, and distribution), to the provision of pre- and post-sale services. As Figure 1 suggests, these tasks are best viewed as a continuum of activities where one unit has primary responsibility for tasks whose achievement is affected by another group's plans and actions.

Inherent in this alignment is the interlinked nature of their responsibilities. Figure 2 emphasizes the mutual dependencies and information flows. The product market, supply chain, and life cycle factors discussed above make the timely exchange of this information more complex *and* more crucial for marketing effectiveness. But most industrial firms differentiate these activities so that expertise in (and accountability for) some subset of the continuum outlined in Figure 1 can be developed and maintained. In the firms I studied (as at other industrial firms), product managers' core responsibilities included creating strategies, developing plans, and managing budgets and programs for one or more of the firm's products.[8] Field sales was responsible, in varying proportions, for five types of activities: contacting customers directly, working with orders, working with resellers, servicing the product and/or account, and managing information to and from the seller and buyer. Customer service personnel were involved in pre- and post-sale activities that affected product programs and sales tasks (e.g., product demonstrations, installation, customer training, field repair, and inventory management services).

FIGURE 2
Typical Interdependencies along the Continuum

Product Management . . . Field Sales . . . Customer Service

Market strategies and plans
Market research data and analysis
Product literature, displays, etc.
Pricing analyses and policies

Sales forecasts and results
Customer feedback on:
• Current products
• New products
Information on:
• Buying behavior
• Competitive activity

Sales strategies and plans
Account-specific goals and activities
Formal sales terms and conditions
"Promises" made during selling process

Pre-sale service support:
• Demonstrations
• Order fulfillment
• Installation
Post-sale service support:
• Customer training
• Maintenance, repair, warranty
• Merchandising support

What issues affect the daily give-and-take between marketing groups with more interdependencies yet distinct roles in customer-contact efforts? My research indicates that three factors are especially important: (1) the layering of priorities that characterizes each group's *hierarchy of attention;* (2) *measurement systems* that help to enforce these priorities; and (3) *information flows* that affect the data each unit tracks, the role of the data, and the measurements that influence each unit's priorities.

Hierarchies of Attention

The marketing units differed in their priorities and the resource allocation patterns that flowed from these priorities. These are differences in their "hierarchy of attention"—i.e., what each group takes for granted as part of its daily work versus what it considers as nice to have or discretionary in its allocation of attention and effort.[9] In particular, product management's focus on its assigned products often clashes with sales' and service's responsibilities for multiple products at multiple accounts. One result is explicit conflict partly due to implicit disagreements about what constitutes "success" in performing a marketing activity. Managers in each area may agree that success is ultimately defined by "the customer." But the groups that are jointly responsible for customer satisfaction perceive the customer differently.

Consider product introductions. At a telecommunications firm, one product group ran a promotional blitz to generate field enthusiasm for its product. But another product manager noted that, due to this campaign, "I just can't compete for sales reps' attention," and redirected her efforts to telemarketing and reseller channels—distribution components not prominent in her original plans and where channel support required redesigning many product features. At a computer firm, product and sales managers typically disagreed about the timing of new product announcements. Sales preferred delaying announcements as long as possible because, as one sales executive explained, "Once a new product announcement is made, customers stop buying the current generation of products while they evaluate the new technology. The result can be stalled sales and quota-crushing delays." But product managers preferred to announce new products as early as possible to build customer attention and train service personnel well in advance of actual introduction.

These marketing units also differed in their time horizons. In each firm, ongoing product-line development was a key product management responsibility, and, as a product manager at a medical equipment firm noted, "Crucial development decisions must be made years before introduction, and the consequences of those decisions linger for years afterward. Meanwhile, budgeting procedures at the customers contacted by sales and service rarely allow them to look long term in assessing their needs." Moreover, product managers implicitly competed for the firm's available development resources. This provided an incentive to "stretch" a proposed product's applicability across multiple segments to justify budget requests and drive development resources in one direction—a finding consistent with previous studies of marketing budgeting procedures.[10]

With their focus on specific accounts, however, sales personnel had different time horizons and priorities. Even as product managers tried to stretch a product's applicability across customer groups as part of the selling firm's capital budgeting process, sales managers often tried to specify product requirements more narrowly in terms of buying processes at assigned accounts. A common result was the complaint of one sales manager at a medical products firm, "Salespeople know customer interests [but] we sometimes introduce products that product managers are successful in attaining from other functions, not what my customer wants."

Measurement Systems

Quotas, performance appraisals, and bonuses for salespeople at the companies I studied focused primarily on sales volume. Product management measures focused on annual profit contribution for assigned products. Customer service metrics varied but typically involved both "customer satisfaction" (measured via customer surveys and/or customer retention) and cost efficiencies in providing relevant services. These varying metrics raise a number of issues at marketing interfaces.

In four firms, multiple product groups went to market via a pooled salesforce. The firms apportioned selling expenses to product units during the marketing planning process. A manager explained, "P&L product managers view the apportionment as a fixed cost [during the relevant budgeting cycle], and then push for as much sales attention as possible to their product line." An example is a computer firm, where profit and pricing responsibility resided with each product group, while sales earned credit toward quotas and bonuses via a point system based on sales volume of individual products at list price (i.e., before netting out any discounts granted to customers). During annual negotiating sessions, sales managers and product managers set product point allocations. One executive described the process:

> Product managers essentially lobbied [sales] to place more points on their particular product line in the annual sales compensation plan, and the negotiations usually centered on the allowable price discounts. Since the larger, better established lines had more room to move in this regard, the tendency was to place disproportionate emphasis on established hardware products and less on newer products, especially software and services. We know something was wrong when for three years running, 75 percent of field reps made their point targets while the corporation missed its annual revenue and profit goals.

Another issue concerns the impact of different measurement systems on account-management tasks. Every company in this sample had established a key account program for cross-selling at important customers. But prevailing metrics often made it difficult for account managers to orchestrate the selling company's product and pricing package. An executive explained:

> Sales and product see the world differently: a customer might be interested in a package of products, yet each product unit is primarily interested in its product line and resistant to altering price or terms and conditions for the sake of the package. But industrial customers are looking for productivity improvements and a vendor provides those improvements with a system, not individual products.

Conversely, salesforce metrics affect product development and service requirements. At a computer firm that sells mainframe and mid-range systems, an executive in the mid-range business explained the impact of revenue-based sales com-

pensation policies on product policy. The firm sold mainframes through the direct salesforce, while mid-range systems required comarketing efforts between direct and reseller channels. To generate more field attention for its line, mid-range product management had for years skewed development priorities toward larger, higher-priced systems that provided more revenue for direct selling efforts. But one result was that, as a manager remarked, "We neglected the growing low end of this market, left ourselves open to more competitors, and generated pre-and post-sale service requirements that exceeded our resellers' capabilities."

Information Flows

The marketing units also differed in the types of data each unit tracked, the role and use of that data, and (in the majority of the firms I studied) the hardware and software systems for disseminating information among the groups.

Product managers viewed data about pertinent products and markets (defined as segments across geographical boundaries) as their highest information priorities. Sales managers sought data about geographically defined markets and specific accounts and resellers within those markets. Service managers needed data about both products and accounts but in different terms from the data categories most salient to product and sales units. As in many companies, accounting systems tracked costs and other information primarily by product categories, rather than customer or channel categories. One result was often a gap between the aggregate data most meaningful to product planning activities and the disaggregate data meaningful to account- or region-specific sales and service activities.[11]

How these marketing units used the information also differed. Product managers need detailed data relevant to product development, costing, and pricing decisions. They make formal presentations a part of their firms' planning processes, more so than sales or service managers do. Hence, compatibility with the *selling* firm's budgeting and planning vocabulary is an important criterion of useful data for product managers. By contrast, compatibility with multiple *buying* vocabularies and data categories are more important to sales managers. Also, the less formal and often time-constrained context of sales calls means that "a few key points" are an important criterion of useful information for sales personnel. Service's responsibilities make detailed data about product specifications and delivery requirements important. But in contrast to priorities in product or sales units, compatibility with customers' technical or logistical vocabularies are the criteria for useful service information.

These differing data uses can create organizational "transmission problems." Across the companies I studied, the most common field complaint about information flows was the lack of timely information. One sales manager explained, "'Timely' means data relevant to current selling efforts. The information is not useful if it arrives too late to be used in our customers' budgeting cycles." Product managers in the firm provided the complementary perspective, "We spend considerable effort gathering and writing up product and competitive information, send out that information, and reps call a week later for the same information. [For product managers], this takes time away from other important things." Such comments reflect different cycles of information use. Industrial product managers must typically gather and present data to and from a variety of internal departments. At one company, charting a product's competitive price and share for annual planning purposes meant soliciting data from more than twenty countries as well as finance, warehousing, and sales departments. By contrast, the timing of sales' and service's information needs is irregular, less capable of being scheduled, and generated (in sales' eyes at least) by an "urgent" customer need.

Finally, information technology also affected marketing interactions and output. At most of the companies in my sample, the hardware and software used for disseminating information among the units had become fragmented. Meanwhile, cus-tomer activities required the integration of data captured by multiple, often technically incompatible systems. For example, at the telecommunications firms, competition for commercial customers increasingly focused on developing and selling network applications. In both firms, software and marketing expenses began to surpass annual facilities expenses. But both firms also encountered the following situation: their product, sales, and service units used different information systems and means to categorize expense data, resulting in a number of inconsistent and money-losing bids for commercial business. At a computer firm where sales and product units utilized different information systems, salespeople candidly admitted that they often shaped orders to *avoid* cross-product orders because of the time-consuming internal interactions involved. In turn, this limited the company's presence in important systems integration markets.

More generally, fragmented information systems mean that the groups meet to discuss customer-related issues on a reactive rather than proactive basis, and each group arrives with ideas based on different data sources. In practice, it is difficult to coordinate under such circumstances.

Competency Traps

The traditional alignment of industrial marketing roles and responsibilities assumes a sequential process in which sales and service execute product management's plans (see Table 2). But market developments are changing their coordination requirements. As outlined in Figure 3, there is a "domino effect" inherent in the market factors discussed earlier in this article, which place more emphasis on a firm's ability to customize product-service packages for more diverse customer groups. This places more value on the ability to generate and maintain timely segment- and account-specific knowledge throughout the marketing organization. In turn, this places new requirements on field sales and service systems because, in most industrial firms, this is where primary responsibility for

TABLE 2
Typical Differences among Marketing Groups at Industrial Firms

	Product Management	Field Sales	Customer Service
Hierarchy of Attention			
	Operate across geographies, with specific product responsibilities.	Operate within geographical territories, with specific account responsibilities.	Operate within geographies, with multiple product and account responsibilities.
Time Horizons Driven by:	Product development and introduction cycles.	Selling cycles at multiple accounts.	Product installation/maintenance.
	Internal budgeting processes.	External buying processes.	Field service processes.
Measurement Systems			
	Performance measures based on profit-and-loss market-share metrics.	Performance measures based primarily on annual, quarterly, or monthly sales volume.	Measures vary, but typically "customer satisfaction" and cost efficiencies.
Information Flows			
Data Priorities:	Aggregate data about products and markets (defined in terms of segments).	Disaggregate data about geographical markets, specific accounts, and pertinent resellers.	Disaggregate data about product usage at accounts.
Key Data Uses:	Role of data makes compatibility with seller's planning and budgeting categories a criterion of useful information.	Role of data makes compatibility with buyers' categories a criterion of useful information; "timely" data as a function of varied selling cycles at assigned accounts.	Role of data makes compatibility with relevant technical vocabularies a criterion of useful information.

customer access and information exchange resides.

In many companies, the result is a misfit between market developments and the organizational capabilities needed for effective marketing. Product, sales, and service units must synchronize their activities in a context in which each unit's window on the external environment, its metrics and time horizons, and its information flows differ. Each unit adopts routines that accelerate the performance of its own subset of customer-contact responsibilities. Provided these routines support using procedures with the highest potential for cus-tomer satisfaction, this specialization is advantageous. But in most busy organizations, the routines themselves soon are treated as fixed. The result is too often a series of "competency traps" in which each group is unwittingly "fighting the last war"— i.e., developing and executing marketing programs relevant to a previous stage of product-market competition.[12] Further, each unit's established procedures keep the firm from gaining experience with new procedures. Our alignments may be more appropriate to changing market conditions. But competency is associated with the information

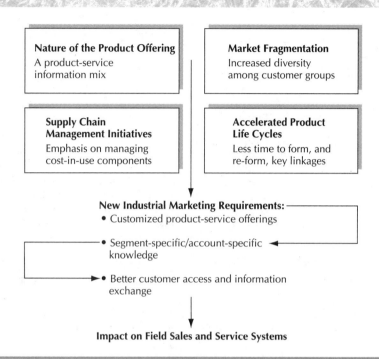

FIGURE 3
"Domino Effect" of Market Factors

flows supporting the metrics that complement the hierarchy of attention at each marketing unit.

Managing New Requirements

How can managers avoid competency traps? How can they think about the options involved in coordinating these marketing units? A first step is to recognize the organizational issues that typically impede coordination among the groups. Because integrating their activities takes time and resources, however, the next step involves choices about where and how to attempt links along the continuum of tasks outlined in Figure 1.

At the companies I studied, major initiatives fell into three categories: an emphasis on headquarters *structural* devices, such as formal liaison units; changes in field marketing *systems,* such as

multifunctional account teams; and alterations in broader management *processes,* including new career paths and training programs. These categories are neither exhaustive nor mutually exclusive. Most firms utilized a variety of linkage mechanisms among, and in addition to, those discussed here. Moreover, the initiatives are themselves interdependent: new headquarters structures without supporting field implementation systems, or new account-management systems without the appropriate human resources and wider organizational processes, have limited impact. But these initiatives were the most widely used, and, at different firms, each frequently represented the "platform" on which management hoped to build complementary mechanisms for improving product-sales-service integration. Further, the emphasis on the set of initiatives differed for companies in different business environments. Next I evaluate the environment, benefits, and key issues associated with each approach.

Liaison Units

One dimension along which industrial firms differ is the relative complexity of product technology and how dynamic the technology is. When product technology is complex and fast-changing, coordinating mechanisms need to ensure that product, sales, and service units work together on aspects of marketing plans and programs while maintaining distinct expertise in product development and account management tasks. In my sample, the computer firms dealt with the most complex and fast-changing technology. In these firms, product development required concentrated technical expertise and sales or customer input far in advance of introduction, while effective product introductions required sales and service to identify the specific product-service combinations that compose a customer solution in the filed.

In these firms, formal liaison units were common. Located at headquarters, their focus was on "upstream" interactions between product management and field sales and service units in developing marketing plans and during the introduction phase of product programs. One executive explained:

> We must accelerate our time to market. Also, customers want integrated solutions. That means forging closer working relationships between our labs, field sales, and product management groups to make sure customer requirements and known early in product development. Differences must be resolved more quickly, and [the liaison units] are intended to expedite this process and surface any problems earlier in the development-to-introduction cycle.

One benefit of establishing such units is that they signal the importance of product-sales-service collaboration in companies where these activities have traditionally been in separate departments, each with its own hierarchy of attention. Without a dedicated liaison unit, informal methods of managing their interactions are often too time-consuming (in a rapidly changing marketplace) or simply ineffective because other units view attempts by product, sales, or service personnel to alter their plans as inappropriate infringements on their domain. This is true whether or not the company conforms to popular conceptions of bureaucracy. An executive at a computer firm known for its informal culture of empowerment noted:

> We are a company with few official channels. But when product managers tried to alter sales plans, or when a sales vice president lobbied for a product modification, they were seen as meddling in the other group's business and without understanding the tradeoffs involved. Important changes weren't made even though more people spent more time in meetings. Despite our distaste for structure, we found we needed an official liaison group.

Usually staffed by sales as well as product personnel, liaison units also help to shape product plans and promotions with field realities in mind. They provide a specific decision-making mechanism in an environment where important tradeoffs and marketing information increasingly reside at the interfaces *among* product, sales, and service groups, rather than *within* each area. At one firm, the liaison unit had a limited budget to fund the development priorities that field groups identified. The unit head explained how this affected product-sales interactions:

> In a technically complex category, each product unit works for years on its line, and the natural tendency is to provide the state-of-the-art configuration. But the result is often a product with costs too high to support a competitive price or too late to capture important first-mover advantages. Our role is to increase the market tension in the development process.
>
> For example, we believed a new low-end product, at a certain price point, would be an important addition to our line. We then informed the relevant product manager that her group could have $X million and a certain time frame to spend on this project. She responded with a figure of $2X million and a longer development schedule, and our response was

that we would take our funds to another product group to get the work done. Her reaction was, "We'll look again at our assumptions and get back to you." We finally compromised on the time and money involved. The process forces a healthy prioritization of time and resources.

Another benefit is that liaison units can make increasingly segmented customer requirements salient earlier, and higher, in planning processes. Some managers stressed an analogy with quality initiatives: such units, an executive commented, help to "make visible issues that cut across product and sales groups, just as quality circles helped to build awareness of the cross-functional requirements of quality management." A manager in one liaison unit explained that, at planning sessions, "My role is to inject industry or other vertical market applications criteria into what would otherwise be investment decisions guided by product categories." Another liaison unit altered traditional product development processes to take explicit account of the interplay between product features and the requirements of selling and servicing customers through indirect distribution channels.

Liaison units represent another management layer with attendant costs in salaries, support systems, and overhead. As a result, such units require a critical mass in the firm's product portfolio and sales base to be economically viable. Thus, they tend to be established in larger companies where the additional management layer can be a mixed blessing for speedy marketing decision making.

Further, liaison units usually face a constant challenge from line managers in product, sales, and service, who often perceive them as staff interlopers rather than integrators. In practice, these units tend to be the focus of many contentious negotiations. This may be inherent in their role, which must balance consistent product strategies with customized channel and service requirements—or, as one liaison manager commented, "We sit in the middle between product management's development and manufacturing concerns and the field's selling and service concerns, and we don't 'own' resources on either side. So, information, personal

relations, and judicious use of top management become paramount management tools."

To develop credibility and influence, these units need managers with broad organizational contacts and current knowledge of changing product and field realities. This presents a staffing challenge in many industrial firms. Experienced managers are often reluctant to take a position with no direct line authority. And, to keep contacts and knowledge current, these units typically rotate personnel frequently. The head of one liaison unit noted:

> In staffing, you need a balance between "short-timers" and "long-termers." Rotating twelve- to eighteen-month assignments keep our field contacts and information current; on the other hand, our development process is lengthy, and it takes time and continuity [to] understand the product strategy, develop trust in the development groups, and master the complexity of product introductions. My staff is about 80 percent short-timers and 20 percent long-termers.

This is a difficult balance to achieve, and the danger with this amount of rotation is that other managers will see those in the liaison unit as "always learning what their job is." But, when balance is achieved, those units provide a way to capture and disseminate learning about important marketing-interface activities and to combine one group's product-technology perspectives with others' channel-account perspectives.

Multifunctional Account Teams

Another important dimension distinguishing industrial firms is their coordination requirements for managing customer relationships. At one end of a spectrum, a firm may sell one product with one application to an account. At the other end are companies selling multiple products with multiple applications among multiple sites of an account, each interdependent in terms of the vendor's selling and/or service activities. In the latter situation, important account management tasks require the alignment of multiple areas of expertise at both the buyer and the seller.

The medical products firms in my sample encountered this requirement at multihospital chains and group purchasing organizations (GPOs). Both are intended to increase buyer power, and, during the past decade, most U.S. hospitals have established affiliations with chains or GPOs. These organizations purchase across the seller's product line and choose vendors on the basis of specialized services in addition to price (e.g., logistical support, special order-entry systems, or ongoing reports about product usage in various hospital departments). In providing these services, the medical products suppliers in my study instituted multifunctional account teams for selected customers.

These teams comprise individuals from product marketing, sales, service, and often manufacturing, logistics, MIS, and other functions. Unlike the liaison units described above, the focus is rarely on product development activities but, rather, on interactions for cost-effective implementation of services that cut across the seller's product groups, sales territories, and business units. Hence, this approach differs from traditional account-management programs in two ways. First, the nature of buyer–seller exchange places a premium on effective supply chain management, and the team's primary responsibility involves reducing the spectrum of cost-in-use components outlined in Table 1. One executive commented:

> Traditional account management—where a salesperson coordinates the seller's resources—works when you're providing a solution for a customer in a discrete functional area. That's project management, and good salespeople are good project managers. But in our industry, the value added is in providing solutions that cut across our customers' functions and our own product, selling, distribution, and service activities. That's program management and requires a different approach.

Second, because of this emphasis, the account manager in such situations is not necessarily someone from sales, because core tasks involve integration of product bundles, pre-and post-sales services, stocking and other logistics arrangements, and ongoing information exchange about evolving product use and applications. At one firm, the manager of a multifunctional team for a buying group was a finance executive, partly because new MIS and distribution links between the buyer and seller make payment terms a way to increase sales to this account *and* a way to protect the seller's pricing structure in response to increasingly cost-conscious buyers.

One benefit of this coordinating mechanism is that it can focus information flows on the ultimate source of revenues and profits: the customer. The multifunctional team becomes a way of dealing on an account-specific basis, with the information "transmission problems" noted earlier. At industrial firms, product managers typically have the product-profitability data, knowledge of planned product introductions, and other information necessary to customize profitably a company's product-service package. But sales and service personnel have the accrued local knowledge necessary to know what specific customers value in each area of supply-chain activity. This approach facilities exchange of information at the account level.

Another benefit is the impact on business planning. Salespeople at major customers are often the first to recognize emerging market problems and opportunities. But they often lack the means to respond with more than tactical (usually, price-sensitive) programs. One reason is that, without this approach, sales efforts lack the cross-functional perspective required to manage cost in use. Also, with traditional account-management systems, sales and service efforts on behalf of individual product groups hamper the vendor's ability to track and manage its true marketing costs at an account, while obscuring the service value that it often *does* provide to customers that purchase across the product line. A senior executive at a medical products firm commented:

> Traditionally, we categorized customers by the amounts bought from different product groups. That's the way we were organized, but not the way markets act. Our total costs and benefits with a hospital or GPO were large but "hidden" because sales were spread across product groups. We have the broadest line in the category (which facilitates cus-

tomer ordering and usage), a broad distribution net-work (which makes inventory management easier to handle and plan), and our sales and service personnel provide extensive end-user training and other services not explicitly costed out in our contracts. Accounts will focus on price and ignore these services unless there's a coordinated approach on our part.

Key issues in managing multifunctional teams are team staffing, decision-making processes, and account selection. This approach may spur integration at the account level, but wider functional reporting relationships usually remain intact. Hence, when resources are allocated, the lines of authority are often unclear. One firm required more than a dozen senior executive signatures to approve team initiatives with accounts. Another firm allocated account-team funding by product group, raising concerns in each group about "who works for whom" when account behavior and product-group goals did not coincide. One manager remarked:

When we established a multifunctional partnership with [account Z], people here were thrilled. But that account recently decided to source one of our product categories from a competitor. That product group is outraged. "Partnering" often connotes across-the-board agreements to many managers, and that's unrealistic. We have many common goals and conflicts with this account. And the tradeoffs differ for individual product and sales units in our firm.

Multifunctional teams also raise human resource challenges. Team members from different functions rotate even as the team seeks to build continuity and relationships with customers. Product, service, and other personnel often resist what they see as a "sales" assignment. Conversely, many salespeople, accustomed to working on their own, often lack the skills and temperament for operating in teams.

Finally, this approach generates many transaction-specific investments for sellers. Some firms require major IS investments to provide on-line order entry, automated stock replenishment, and other supply-chain services to accounts. One manager explained:

Which customers *don't* become multifunctional partners? That's a tough issue. Inevitably, other accounts want the customized services that account X is getting. And if we don't give that service, one of our competitors will. Also, many of the product-sales-service linkages required to implement the concept are specific to an account, and the benefits for individual product and sales units in our company differ widely by account. I'm not sure the customer incurs the same switching costs we do.

These factors ultimately emphasize the importance of rigorous account selection in linking functions. The successful multifunctional teams at these firms shared certain characteristics: (1) initiation of the approach at top levels of both buyer and seller firms; (2) a buyer who buys across the seller's product line; and (3) customers seen as influential and leading edge in some aspect of product applications or supply-chain management, so that the seller's investments yielded benefits at other accounts.

Career Paths and Training Programs

In many high-tech industrial firms, career paths in product management and sales diverge sharply. Product managers have undergraduate technical degrees, are increasingly recruited from MBA programs, and rotate among product lines as preparation for a potential general management position. Salespeople usually have much less technical training and their career paths keep them in a given sales territory for some time so the account relationships are not severed. Rarely do the twain meet. In other industrial firms, career paths in sales versus service are the mirror image of the product-sales situation in high-tech firms. Sales is the "fast track" up the management hierarchy, while service personnel accrue "time in territory" experience with end users and distributors.

Hence, beyond changes in structure and account teams, companies have tried to develop managers experienced on "both sides" of marketing interfaces. In my sample, this was especially true at telecommunications firms, for reasons related to their business environment. During the 1980s, after the development of fiber optics and new network software, these firms provided many new voice/data/messaging service combinations. The same software also allowed commercial customers to track patterns of telecommunications use in their organizations more easily and precisely. The result was to increase dramatically the range of potential product-market applications and shift the basis of competition to product packages tailored to customer specifications that differ by industry, size of company, and region. One executive explained:

> A key company asset is the shared network, and that means headquarters product management must understand the interrelationships implicated by each product introduction or modification. The complexity of this increases as software-based services become a bigger part of the products we offer. Similarly, in a high fixed-cost service operation, sales and service personnel confront a quickly expanding product line and must deal with more groups in pre- and post-sales activities that affect our shared asset.

Thus, coordinating mechanisms in these firms must address a situation in which adapting a core asset requires local knowledge that is unavailable (or too costly to gather and keep current) at headquarters levels, but in which using shared resources efficiently also requires central oversight to ensure that field activities support companywide operating and marketing objectives (e.g., capacity utilization and consistent product positioning and pricing).

To address this situation, the telecommunications firms have altered career tracks to provide more cross-functional mobility for product, sales, and service managers. This includes expanding the length and type of field sales exposure required for product management positions and creating new positions. One firm established field marketing specialists (FMS), mid-level product and sales managers who, after eighteen to twenty-four months in this position, were slotted for senior line positions in the core product or sales organization. Unlike the liaison units described earlier, FMSs are assigned to field regions, but, unlike the multifunc-

tional account team initiatives, their focus is on a subset of the firm's product line, not on a specific customer. FMSs have two roles: (1) to increase learning (and comfort level) with new selling and service requirements (FMSs work with sales and service managers on applications identification, product demonstrations, and installation) and (2) to coordinate these field activities with headquarters product units. FMSs are a way for a product group to "sell" field managers on a new initiative. Conversely, FMSs negotiate with product groups for the product modifications and engineering resources needed locally.

At another telecommunications firm, the customer service engineers (CSEs) were at customer locations more frequently than the salespeople and were important to customer retention and revenue growth in the installed base. Yet, an executive explained, "CSEs are technical people who don't like to think of themselves as selling, even though that's what they're implicitly doing. Conversely, many sales reps worry about account control; their attitude is, 'No one can do this at my account, as well as I can.'" The company now provides joint training for salespeople and CSEs and has realigned its reward system to provide a new-revenue bonus that sales and service personnel at an account share. In addition, sales and service reps now evaluate each other on a questionnaire that ranks performance in such areas as "quick response" and "contribution to customer satisfaction." Customers complete these questionnaires, managers to whom the sales and service reps report review them, and sales and service personnel assigned to the same account meet biannually to explain their evaluations. A manger noted, "These discussions are a considerable benefit in a business where, for good logistical reasons, the sales rep is dedicated to a select group of accounts, but these customers are among dozens that clamor for the service rep's attention."

One benefit of these initiatives is better awareness of another unit's operating conditions, constraints, and contributions. Managers with product and sales experience, for example, are more likely to develop marketing programs that reflect their reciprocal requirements. One interviewee, who became a product manager after a decade in sales, noted, "In sales, I had no appreciation for what product marketing does. In sales, there are identifiable wins and losses, but 80 percent of product management is invisible to salespeople—and essential to effective selling."

More generally, these assignments help to build what an observer called the "thick informal networks one finds wherever multiple leadership initiatives work in harmony. . . . Too often these networks are fragmented: a tight network exists inside the marketing group and inside R&D but not across the two departments.[13] Similarly, a study of multinational firms found that cross-country career paths create a "verbal information network . . . which results in [coordination] that is personal yet decentralized," allowing local discretion within the context of companywide policies.[14] Likewise, product-sales-service career paths provide bridges across the differing information flows described earlier and complement any formal liaison positions. With training programs, these assignments can also develop what one executive called "system savvy. Most managers are 'good citizens' who want to do what is right for the firm, not just their area. But they're often unaware of the impact of their decisions on other parts of an interdependent business system. Our joint training programs and career rotation aim at disseminating this savvy."

However, the management issues raised by this approach are formidable. In many industrial firms, joint training programs usually entail *additional* training beyond the still-required functional training in product management, sales, and service tasks. So, beyond incremental expenses, therefore, people are spending more time in training and less on "core" activities; some firms view this as unnecessary or infeasible in a cost-conscious environment in which they are not adding marketing personnel.

Similarly, these career paths entail multiyear time horizons for the company and the individuals involved plus a willingness to assume inherent career risks, since most managers have risen to their positions by acquiring functional expertise. Cross-functional career paths tend to build skill bases that are more company-specific than do functionally oriented careers. In Japanese firms, while cross-functional rotations and training programs are common, they are traditionally complemented by "lifetime employment" patterns, promotions based on seniority, and, historically, social pressures on managers who seek to switch employers. As a result, Japanese firms have had more assurance that a competitor will not reap returns on long-term investments in cross-functional careers, while individual managers have less incentive to develop a career via expertise in one area and more incentive to develop cross-functional skills at a single firm.[15] These wider corporate and social conditions rarely pertain at Western companies. Hence, at the firms I studied, training and career path initiatives were limited to a few managers who often encountered obstacles because most careers in their organizations proceeded according to a different paradigm.

Conclusion

Firms utilize other initiatives in addition to those I discuss here. Managers interested in improving linkages among product, sales, and service units should not focus on identifying only one preferred approach. Rather, after analyzing how market factors affect marketing interdependencies in their firms, managers should focus on those areas and actions that, within their business context, are likely to provide the best returns on time-consuming and expensive coordination efforts.

Table 3 summarizes the focus, environment, and key management issues associated with each initiative I discuss. By highlighting the implementation issues, Table 3 emphasizes an important challenge facing firms in this aspect of their marketing efforts. "Coordination" is a value-laden term with positive connotations. Especially before making tradeoffs and allocating resources, managers' espoused support for coordination is now the "politically correct" attitude. But, as this article indicates, coordination comes at a cost, and each

TABLE 3
Coordinating Mechanisms in Different Marketing Environments

	Formal Liaison Units	Multifunctional Account Teams	Career Paths and Training Programs
Focus	Facilitate product-sales-service interactions in the development of product marketing plans and during product introduction.	Product-sales-service interactions concerning specialized services at key accounts.	Product-sales and sales-service interactions concerning various customization activities of shared assets.
Most Common Marketing Environment			
Product:	Complex, fast-changing technology; long lead times between product development and actual introduction to market(s).	Importance of cost-in-use and supply chain management activities in purchase criteria for multiple product offerings from vendor.	Product value and pricing tied to applications tailored to different customer groups; applications development/installation requires adaptation of a core asset.
Market:	Multiple products flowing through common channels of distribution.	Large, multilocation accounts that generate many transaction-specific investments by the seller.	Headquarters product marketing programs require ongoing modifications and local field sales and service knowledge of varied segments; efficient use/positioning of shared asset requires central oversight of local field activities.
Key Management Issues	Costs, credibility, and staffing of liaison units.	Account selection criteria, accountability, impact of wider organizational processes on staffing and decision making.	Costs, time, and impact on individual managers.

approach is implicitly a choice about the kinds of ongoing issues a firm must monitor and manage.

Further, the conflicts I discuss partly reflect the continuing need for specialized expertise in each marketing unit. Such expertise is important for achieving the in-depth knowledge, scale and scope economies, and ongoing efficiencies in each unit that remain important aspects of industrial marketing efforts. Hence, the goal in managing new marketing requirements should not be to erad-icate differences between these groups or to assert that "everybody is responsible for customer satisfaction." In most busy organizations, what everyone is responsible for in theory, nobody is responsible for in practice. Rather, the managerial issue is how to link, efficiently and effectively, knowledge, resources, and varying sources of customer value that are necessarily located *across* different marketing units in many industrial firms. In considering the initiatives I discuss, managers must keep this distinction in mind, while recognizing that, without appropriate linkages among these groups, their firms increasingly encounter two other types of costs.

One cost is fragmentation at the company-customer interface. The market factors outlined in Figure 3 mean that effective marketing management at industrial firms requires developing and executing customer solutions across internal product, sales, and service units. But the differences outlined in Table 2 tend to direct funding, time, attention, and efforts within, rather than across, these units. The result is too often a partial solution, with limited customer value and usually negative competitive consequences.

The other cost is more subtle. The issues discussed in this article rarely mean total paralysis in interactions among product, sales, and service units. Managers needing to "get product out the door" will forge agreements sooner or later. But the nature of these agreements is unlikely to maximize customer value, and the process itself can be harmful. One executive, commenting on interactions between product and sales managers in her company, articulated the implicit cost, "We spend so much time bargaining, and the result is that we often unintentionally reward managers for their negotiating skills, not for problem solving or customer-oriented performance."

Appendix

The study involved 125 personal interviews at six industrial firms: two computer firms, two telecommunications companies, and two medical equipment suppliers. At participating companies, the focus was on business units where product management, sales, and customer service activities are primary responsibilities of various managers within the business unit's marketing function. In 1992, sales of these business units ranged from $100 million to more than $1 billion.

At each company, I conducted interviews with managers, on both sides of each sales interface and, when present, with formal liaison managers between sales and product management or service units, as well as selected managers in areas such as R&D, MIS, and market research. Other data included internal company documents that interviewees supplied, personal observation while attending company meetings, and customer calls with field sales and service personnel.

The unstructured interviews averaged ninety minutes. Interviewees received a list of the research question in advance. Thus, most interviews focused on one or more of the following questions (depending on the responsibilities of the interviewee): (1) What are the major issues facing your area in interactions with product management/sales/service?; (2) What factors determine the relative importance of coordination with each group, the tasks that must be coordinated, and the kinds of conflicts or opportunities that arise?; (3) What mechanisms exist in your firm for managing these joint tasks?; (4) In practice, how do things most often "get done" at these sales interfaces—i.e., what are the informal as well as formal means for managing interactions across these marketing units?

References

1. For pertinent studies of industrial product introductions, see: J. Choffray and G. Lilien, "Strategies behind the Successful Industrial Product Launch," *Business Marketing* 17 (1984): 82–94; R. Cooper and E. Kleinschmidt, "New Product Processes at Leading Industrial Firms," *Industrial Marketing Management* 20 (1991): 137–147; J. Konrath, "Why New Products Fail," *Sales & Marketing Management* 144 (1992): 48–56; and V. Mahajan and J. Wind, "New Product Models: Practice, Shortcomings, and Desired Improvements" (Cambridge, Massachusetts: Marketing Science Institute, Report 91-125, 1991).

2. Developments tending toward a merging of manufacturing and service businesses have been discussed from various perspectives. For example, see: J. Gershuny and I. Miles, *The New Service Economy* (London: Pinter, 1983); M. Piore and C. Sabel, *The Second Industrial Divide* (New York: Basic Books, 1984); J.B. Quinn et al., "Technology in Services: Rethinking Strategic Focus," *Sloan Management Review,* Winter 1990, pp. 79–87; and R. Norman and R. Ramirez, "From Value Chain to Value Constellation, " *Harvard Business Review,* July–August 1993, pp. 65–77.

3. For data concerning product variety, see: S. Wheelwright and K. Clark, *Revolutionizing Product Development* (New York: Free Press, 1992), chapter 1.

4. E.R. Corey, *Procurement Management: Strategy, Organization, and Decision Making* (Boston: CBI Publishing Company, 1978).

5. J. Emshwiller, "Suppliers Struggle to Improve Quality as Big Firms Slash Their Vendor Rolls," *Wall Street Journal,* 16 August 1991, p. B1.

6. For more on this topic, see: F. Cespedes, "Once More: How Do You Improve Customer Service?" *Business Horizons,* March–April 1992, pp. 58–67. For an excellent discussion of wider cross-functional issues implicated in supply-chain initiatives, see: H. Lee and C. Billington, "Managing Supply Chain Inventory: Pitfalls and Opportunities, *Sloan Management Review,* Spring 1992, pp. 65–73.

7. For data concerning product life cycles in various industrial product categories, see: C.J. Easingwood, "Product Life Cycle Patterns for New Industrial Products," *R&D Management* 18 (1988) 22–32; and C.F. von Braun, "The Acceleration Trap," *Sloan Management Review,* Fall 1990, pp. 49–58.

8. For data on responsibilities of industrial product and sales personnel, see: R. Eccles and T. Novotny, "Industrial Product Managers: Authority and Responsibility," *Industrial Marketing Management* 13 (1984): 71–76; and W. Moncrief, "Selling Activity and Sales Position Taxonomies for Industrial Sales Forces," *Journal of Marketing Research* 23 (1986): 261–270.

9. What I here call "hierarchies of attention" is analogous to what some have labeled organizational "routines" or "thought worlds": the patterns of activity that characterize different subgroups in a firm, that shape the assumptions and marketplace interpretations of each group, and that in turn become the "genes" of a firm's repertoire of capabilities.

For a discussion of organizational routines see:

   R. Nelson and S. Winter, *An Evolutionary Theory of Economic Change* (Cambridge, Massachusetts: Harvard University Press, 1982), chapter 5. For a discussion of the various "thought worlds" that characterize groups typically involved in industrial product development activities, see: D. Dougherty, "Interpretive Barriers to Successful Product Innovation in Large Firms, *Organization Science* 3 (1992): 179–202.

10. See M. Cunningham and C. Clark, "The Product Management Function in Marketing," *European Journal of Marketing* 9 (1975): 129–149; and N. Piercy, "The Marketing Budgeting Process," *Journal of Marketing,* October 1987, pp. 45–59.

11. For a discussion of the gaps between accounting data and the types of information sought by managers in various functional areas, see: S.M. McKinnon and W.J. Bruns, Jr., *The Information Mosaic* (Boston: Harvard Business School Press, 1992).

12. B. Levitt and J.G. March, "Organizational Learning," *Annual Review of Sociology* 14 (1988): 319–340.

13. J.P. Kotter, *A Force for Change* (New York: Free Press, 1990), p. 92.

14. A. Edstrom and J.R. Galbraith, "Transfer of Managers as a Coordination and Control Strategy in Multinational Organizations," *Administrative Science Quarterly* 22 (1977): 251.

15. See M. Aoki, "Ranking Hierarchy as an Incentive Scheme," in *Information, Incentives, and Bargaining in the Japanese Economy* (Cambridge, England: Cambridge University Press, 1988), chapter 3; and K. Koike, "Skill Formation Systems: Japan and U.S.," in *The Economic Analysis of the Japanese Firm,* ed. M. Aoki (New York: North-Holland Press, 1984), pp. 63–73.

Chapter 2

Marketing Strategy and Planning

There is only one valid definition of business purpose: to create a customer. Markets are not created by God, nature, or economic forces but by the people who manage a business. The want a business satisfies may have been felt by customers before they were offered the means of satisfying it. . . . but it remained a potential want until the action of business people converted it into effective demand.[1]

The marketing concept holds that the purpose of a business is—or should be—to satisfy the wants and needs of its customers better than its competitors and at a profit. This requires the collective efforts of all people in the organization. Guiding these collective efforts is the role of business strategy. Marketing strategy may guide the development of business strategy, but it must also support it and work in harmony with other functional strategies.

Typically business strategies establish broad business objectives, indicate the scope of the business in terms of products and markets, and identify the principal technologies and source of competitive advantage. The components of business strategy are usually the functional strategies. These include a marketing strategy, which deals with target markets and the actions necessary to reach them effectively; a manufacturing strategy, which deals with make or buy decisions, plant size, and manufacturing processes; a research and development or engineering strategy, which addresses such issues as basic or applied research and fields of technology; a financial strategy, which deals with methods of financing, financial terms, credit risks, and working capital requirements; and a human resources strategy, which addresses skill requirements, size and nature of the work force, and people management systems.

Depending on the nature of the business, the business strategy may include other dimensions. Marketing strategy, however, lies at the heart of business strategy. More than any other strategy, it is concerned with the external environment, thus providing guidance on markets to be served and products to be produced—the fundamental business decisions. These business decisions

45

can only be made in the context of the resources of the firm and its collective skills and abilities. Marketing strategy, therefore, must be as concerned with the capabilities of the firm as it is with customers, competitors, and other elements of the external environment.

This chapter is principally concerned with marketing strategy. Because of its relationship to business and corporate strategy, we first introduce a number of key strategy concepts and discuss the relationship between marketing, business, and corporate strategy. We then describe the major planning concepts and tools firms use to guide the formulation of corporate and business strategy and that establish the context within which marketing strategy is developed. We then present the specifics of marketing strategy and the marketing planning process.

Key Strategy Concepts

Strategy is an elusive term used in many ways. There are corporate, business, and functional strategies. There are growth, diversification, harvest, and turn-around strategies to name a few. Regardless of usage, three key concepts of strategy should be kept in mind. First, the concept of strategy implies a fit or match between opportunities and threats in the external environment and the capabilities of the firm. Examples abound of firms that failed to recognize the importance of fit. A major European manufacturer of expensive plumbing supplies, for instance, decided to introduce an inexpensive product line to compete more effectively in southern European markets. The new product line, however, turned out to be as expensive as its existing products. The company learned that the design and manufacturing skills required for inexpensive products were very different from those associated with its successful expensive products. Thus, marketing strategy must go beyond consideration of customer wants and needs, competitor actions, and other elements of the external environment; it must also take into account the capabilities and resources of the firm in all functional areas.

Second, the term *strategy* is sometimes used in a broad sense to convey both objectives and courses of action. Andrews, in his classic work on strategy, defined it as "the pattern of major objectives, purpose, or goals and essential policies and plans for achievement of those goals, stated in such a way as to define what business the company is in, or is to be in, and the kind of company it is, or is to be."[2] Others separate courses of action from objectives. Corey defines an objective as a desired end and strategy as a plan for achieving it.[3] We prefer the broader definition, but, regardless of the definition, it is important to recognize the linkage between objectives and action. Too frequently firms establish objectives without identifying the specific action needed for their attainment. For example, a major U.S. supplier of chemical analysis equipment established a sales growth objective of 15 percent in a market that was growing at the rate of 10 percent. But the company made no provision either for an increase in promotional expenditures or for specific direction of the sales force on ways to achieve such growth. Not surprisingly, the objective was not achieved. Third, beyond linking objectives and action, it is important to recognize that marketing objectives must support business objectives. It makes little sense, for instance, to establish sales growth objectives that can be achieved only at the expense of profit objectives.

Strategic Planning

Marketing strategy is normally developed in connection with the firm's strategic planning process. This process varies from one organization to another. In some organizations strategies are the result of a very formal process, with well defined planning structures and procedures and extensive planning documents. In other organizations strategies are the result of ad hoc processes, with little or no effort to formally record the strategy in written documents. To the extent that strategic planning processes share a common characteristic, it is the frequency with which they are changed or modified. When strategic planning first became popular in the early 1970s, the tendency was to set up separate planning components charged with the responsibility for development of comprehensive strategic plans; the plans were then given to operating components for execution. Many planning components then evolved into large bureaucracies isolated from the operating components. Another tendency was to prepare plans on an annual basis geared to the development of an annual budget rather than to the strategic requirements of the firm. Plans tended to be inflexible, and opportunities for change were considered only during the next annual planning cycle.

During the 1980s, growing disenchantment with the results of strategic planning led to a significant shift away from separate planning components. Planning, it was concluded, was better done by line managers responsible for execution of the plans. Strategic planning components were either abolished or changed. At Intel, for example, the principal responsibility of the vice president for strategic planning was not to develop strategic plans but to assist the planning process of line managers and to ensure appropriate corporate reviews. Planning calendars were also changed. Firms in dynamic industries, particularly high-tech businesses, reviewed strategies quarterly, semiannually, or as events dictated. Firms in less dynamic industries found that strategic plans could span longer time horizons. Plans became more flexible. Changes in strategy did not have to wait for a formal planning review as strategies could be modified as circumstances changed.

Changes in the nature of strategic planning have increased the importance of marketing planning and the marketing planning process. In a Conference Board survey of marketing planning practices, over 60 percent of the respondents indicated they expected more emphasis on marketing plans in

TABLE 2.1
The Relationship of Corporate, Business, and Marketing Strategy

	Corporate Strategy	Business Strategy	Marketing Strategy
Scope:	Ultimate destiny of the firm.	Plans the war.	Plans the battle.
Basic Questions:	What businesses should we be in, how do we allocate responsibility for results, how do we allocate resources, how do we organize?	What products, for what markets, with what competitive advantage?	What product variations, for what segments, at what prices, with what communication, and what distribution?
Objectives:	Current and future ROI and ROE,° earnings per share, stock price, contributions to other stakeholders.	Broad in terms of the total business, with specific $ profit or ROI targets.	Narrow in terms of segments, with specific volume and contribution targets.
Planning Horizon:	Longest term.	Long term.	Medium term.
Resources Allocated to:	Business units.	Engineering, manufacturing, and marketing.	Product planning, promotion, and distribution.
External Focus:	Comprehensive, macro in nature.	Comprehensive, essentially macro in nature but in the context of the business.	Sharply focused on customers, competitors, channels, and laws affecting marketing.
Major Concerns:	Capitalizing on synergies, adding value.	Formulation of overall strategy, functional integration.	Formulation and implementation, management of marketing activities, and functional relations.

°ROI (return on investment), ROE (return on equity).

the future. In fact, some 10 percent of the respondents indicated that formal marketing planning was new to their organizations within the last five years.[4] The study also found that one of the most significant changes in the planning process was that firms were making a much more deliberate effort to mesh the marketing plan with the overall plan for the business.

Strategy at Three Levels

Most firms originate with a single good or service targeted at a single market. Some firms remain focused on their original products and markets. Lincoln

Electric, for example, has focused on manufacturing welding equipment for manufacturing industries and the construction industry for almost 100 years. For such firms, business and corporate strategy are synonymous. In these situations, marketing strategy is concerned with supporting just the business strategy. Other firms expand by offering new products or pursuing new markets, either organically (i.e., through internal growth) or by merger or acquisition. The result is a corporation made up of many businesses, generally called strategic business units (SBUs). The BOC Group (see the Ohmeda Monitoring Systems case) is a classic example, with its diverse health and industrial gas businesses. In multibusiness corporations marketing strategy also needs to take corporate strategy into account.

In broad terms the relationships between corporate, business, and marketing strategies are shown in Table 2.1. The key question for corporate strategy is "What businesses should we be in?" During the 1960s and 1970s the trend was toward broadly diversified businesses, or conglomerate corporations. Implicit in this trend was the view that management skills were generic, easily transferable from one business to another. During the 1980s the trend reversed. Many firms found diversification into unrelated businesses unprofitable. Many acquired businesses were divested. The new view of management skills was that firms should "stick to their knitting." In the broadly diversified corporation the role of corporate-level marketing was minimal, restricted primarily to the identification of emerging market opportunities. In corporations with more closely related businesses the role of corporate-level marketing expanded, with emphasis on coordinating the marketing efforts of the businesses and on developing a corporate position. At Honeywell, for instance, corporate marketing led the effort to coordinate the work of Honeywell's several sales forces, many of which called on the same customers. It also developed an overall positioning strategy for all Honeywell businesses that emphasized creating partnerships with customers with the advertising theme "Together We Can Find the Answers."

The key questions for business strategy are "What products, for what markets, and with what competitive advantage?" These decisions are made at the business level, based on inputs from all functional areas. While marketing strategy is at the heart of business strategy, in operational terms it must support business strategy and direct the marketing efforts of the business to achieve business objectives. In multibusiness firms it must also support corporate marketing efforts.

As marketing strategy becomes more closely integrated with business and corporate strategies, it must take into account the planning tools and concepts used to assist in the their formulation. In the following sections we describe a number of planning tools and concepts, which can also be useful in developing marketing strategy.

Corporate Strategy

As multibusiness corporations emerged or grew, questions arose about how corporate managers could understand diverse businesses with respect to a host

FIGURE 2.1
Growth-Share Matrix

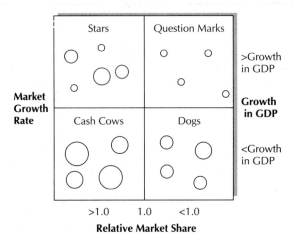

of business decisions. Traditional measures of return on investment (ROI) and return on sales (ROS) were good indicators of past performance but not necessarily of future potential. For example, these measures did not provide a basis for agreement of future results. In particular, they did not indicate those businesses in which the corporation should continue to invest and those in which it was time to reap the rewards of past investment. An approach was needed that would provide corporate managers with a better way of understanding the strategic situation of each business, of assessing its future potential on dimensions other than past profitability, and of having at least a generic sense of appropriate strategies for businesses with which they were not intimately familiar. This need led to the development of several planning approaches based on the concept of managing the businesses as a portfolio in order to optimize the overall results of the corporation. We briefly describe the two most widely used portfolio approaches and their implications for marketing strategy.

The Growth–Share Matrix

First proposed by the Boston Consulting Group (BCG), the growth-share matrix approach holds that the corporation should manage its portfolio of businesses to optimize the firm's cash flow. The matrix is depicted in Figure 2.1. Businesses are positioned on the matrix on the basis of sales growth and market share. The general concept is that businesses in the high-growth category are in the growth phase of the product life cycle and businesses in the low-growth category are considered mature. However, there is nothing sacred about the dividing line. In Figure 2.1 we show the dividing line as growth in gross domestic product (GDP) on the premise that markets growing faster than the growth in GDP are not yet saturated and can be considered growth markets. Some early examples established the dividing line at 10 percent, roughly the sum of inflation at the time and the growth in GDP. Many firms, however, establish their own dividing lines, and others omit the dividing line and use a continuous scale for positioning their businesses. The key point is that growth rate is an indicator of a business's need for cash to fund continued growth.

Market share is generally considered relative to the firm's largest competitor. The dividing line between high- and low-share companies is usually placed at 1.0 or 1.5. But again, there is nothing sacred about the dividing line, and in many instances the dividing line has a different value for high- and low-growth businesses, based on the assumption that relative market share is less important when a business matures. The key point is to recognize the extent that differences in market share affect cumulative volume and, hence costs. The size of the circles on the matrix indicates the relative revenue of the business to show the impact of individual businesses on the cash flow of the firm.

Two premises underlie the growth-share approach. The first is that high relative market share is the key to low relative costs, giving the firm a source of competitive advantage. This is based on the experience, or learning curve, concept, which holds that cumulative volume leads to predictable decreases in cost. The firm that maintains a dominant market share will, therefore, have the greatest cumulative volume and the lowest cost. The second premise is that the portfolio of businesses should be managed to optimize cash flow by using mature businesses to supply the cash needed to fund new ventures that have the potential of generating surplus cash in the future.

The widespread use of the growth-share approach attests to its many appealing characteristics. Using cash flow as a way to manage a portfolio is intuitively appealing. The two-dimension classification scheme is easy to learn and apply. Because it quickly conveys the broad strategic situation of a business and suggests the nature of the business's objectives and the ways to accomplish them, the matrix facilitates discussions between corporate and business management about future strategies. We briefly describe the four classifications and their associated generic marketing strategies.

Stars. These are high-growth, high-share businesses that produce high profit margins. Because stars need cash for reinvestment in the business to sustain growth, there is little cash flow in or out of the business. Generic prescriptions for the marketing strategy of stars include:

- Protect or grow share.
- Make constant product improvements.
- Improve market coverage.
- Consider price reductions.
- Focus on sources of growth.

Cash Cows. These low-growth, high-share businesses are expected to produce high profit margins. Investment for growth is not necessary, so there is a large cash flow above the needs of the business that can be used to fund question marks, R&D, acquisitions, dividends, or other corporate ventures. Generic prescriptions for the marketing strategy of cash cows include:

- Maintain market share or dominance.
- Maintain price leadership.

Question Marks. These low-share, high-growth businesses have low profit margins and need externally supplied cash to grow. Future potential may justify an infusion of cash to fund continued growth. Generic prescriptions for the marketing strategy of question marks include:

- Invest to gain share.
- Grow share in a niche with an eye on the whole market.
- Abandon the business if potential returns are not attractive.

Dogs. These low-share, low-growth businesses have low profit margins. Cash is not needed as growth is not expected and the businesses are unlikely to generate cash for other purposes. Generic prescriptions for the marketing strategy of dogs include:

- Stay focused on a specialized niche.
- Look for price improvement opportunities.
- Position the business for sale or liquidation.

Despite its widespread use, the growth-share approach has drawbacks. The dividing lines are arbitrary and can be used inappropriately. Market share is frequently difficult to calculate and can be significantly influenced by the definition of the market. The experience effect is not uniformly applicable to all industries. In many instances, large portions of a manufacturer's costs may be determined by suppliers, and the manufacturer's own experience may only slightly affect total costs. Still further, empirical evidence indicates substantial performance variation within the various categories. Many businesses categorized as dogs, for example, have performed very well. There are also concerns about the unit of analysis. Many business units are comprised of smaller businesses. Classification of composite business units may obscure very different situations for the smaller businesses that make them up. Consideration of just cash flow may fail to account for possible synergies between businesses. Finally, there is concern that the approach does not take into account the motivations of managers and that some of the labels may actually demotivate managers.

Overall, a major concern is that the approach is simplistic and does not fully consider the totality of a firm's strategic situation. This concern lead to the

FIGURE 2.2
The Investment Priority Matrix

Industry Attractiveness

	High	Medium	Low	
	Aggressively invest for growth in market position, volume, and profit	Invest to protect market position and to improve profitability	Invest to exploit position and to improve profits	Strong
Business Position	Invest to improve market position and profitability	Invest to hold position and improve profitability	Invest only to harvest position, contain risk, and reduce drag	Medium
	Invest for profit improvement, not for better market position	Invest minimally, contain risk, and reduce drag on the company	Prepare for probable exit, divestiture, liquidation, or slow winddown	Weak

development of another approach by McKinsey and General Electric, variously described as the Stop Light matrix, the industry attractiveness–business position matrix or, to use GE terminology, the Investment Priority Matrix.

Investment Priority Matrix

This approach, illustrated in Figure 2.2, focuses on establishing priorities for investment in the businesses that make up the corporation's portfolio. Businesses are positioned on the matrix on the basis of business position and industry attractiveness. As with the BCG approach, businesses are represented by circles whose size indicates the relative revenue of the businesses.

Business position is a composite assessment of market share and other factors such as size, profitability, skills of the firm, customer relations, distributor relations, or patent positions. Industry attractiveness is a composite assessment of industry growth and other factors such as industry profitability, competitive intensity, ability of the industry to pass cost increases to customers, or government regulation.

To assign a business to a particular category, some firms establish weights for appropriate factors and then assess a particular business, using a scale of 1 through 5, where 5 is very favorable and 1 is very unfavorable. The following example shows the method using an illustrative set of factors. In actual practice, many more factors might be involved. The scores are used to assign a business to a particular cell on the matrix.

Business Position	Weight	Score	Weighted Score
Skills of the firm	.25	4.0	1.00
Customer relations	.15	3.0	.45
Distributor relations	.10	2.0	.20
Profitability	.15	3.0	.45
Patent position	.20	2.0	.40
Market share	.20	2.5	.50
Total Score			3.00

Industry Attractiveness	Weight	Score	Weighted Score
Growth	.30	3.0	.60
Industry profitability	.30	2.5	.75
Competitive intensity	.15	4.0	.60
Ability to raise prices	.15	1.0	.15
Regulation	.10	1.0	.10
Total Score			2.20

Strategy prescriptions for the various cells of the Investment Priority matrix are generally couched in terms of investment objectives, as shown in Figure 2.2. Less prescriptive than the growth-share approach, the objectives still provide an overall sense of direction for marketing strategy.

As with the growth-share approach, the widespread use of the Investment Priority approach also attests to its many appealing characteristics. It overcomes the objection that market share and growth do not fully capture the strategic situation of a business. It allows for assessment of the future attractiveness of an industry. Because it does not focus just on growth and market share, it is somewhat more flexible with respect to the unit of analysis. It avoids the use of demotivating labels. Once a business has been classified, corporate management or staff can track whether the business is investing as its classification prescribes.

Despite its appealing characteristics, there are concerns about the Investment Priority approach. Choice of the dimensions on which industry attractiveness and business position are evaluated, as well as the evaluations themselves, are subjective decisions. Inevitably there are arguments between the business unit and corporate as to how the business should be classified. While broad investment objectives are specified, there is little in the way of definitive prescriptions for strategy. Finally, the unit of analysis may be a problem. At GE, for instance, at a time when sales were about $25 billion, 39 businesses had been designated as SBUs and were classified using the Investment Priority matrix. EG&G, on the other hand, a U.S. manufacturer of technical products with sales of some $600 million, had designated 101 components as business elements (their term for an SBU), with responsibility for strategic planning. In the GE case, many SBUs whose plans were reviewed at the corporate level included smaller components that other firms would have designated as SBUs.

Implications for Marketing

The foregoing is not intended to be a comprehensive description of portfolio approaches.[5] Rather, it is intended to provide understanding of a key situational aspect marketers must consider as they formulate and implement marketing strategy. Not all firms use portfolio approaches. Some firms tried and then abandoned them, disappointed for some of the reasons given above. Other firms downsized their large strategic planning staffs, eliminating some of the expertise necessary to manage a portfolio approach. The key point is that in most corporations, SBUs are not free to choose their strategies independent of the corporate situation. One business may believe it has enormous opportunities to exploit if corporate managers would free it from the burden of current profit responsibility. Another SBU may believe it deserves one more opportunity to turn the business around after several years of disappointing profit results. Finally, even if a business is classified as a star or in the upper left cell of the Investment Priority matrix, the strategy prescriptions for the classifications are only guides. It is still the corporate prerogative to decide on the level of investment or reinvestment in the business, taking into account other circumstances. In short, the objectives corporate assigns to the business become the strategic reality for marketing.

Although developed principally for use at the corporate level, portfolio approaches also apply at the product level, so they can be directly used for marketing planning. As we discuss in the product life cycle (PLC) section, the growth-share matrix has much in common with the product life cycle. Using the growth-share matrix to visually display products quickly conveys the mix of products in the marketing portfolio and indicates if the balance in the various categories is appropriate. The Investment Priority matrix can be used to assess the strength of a product's position and its future market attractiveness to help make decisions about the allocation of marketing resources.

Planning at the Business Level

Interest in strategic planning has led to the development of planning tools applicable at the business level as well as the corporate level. Four are of particular interest to those in marketing.

Product–Market Expansion Matrix

For most firms, growth in sales and profits is a basic objective. Fundamental to achieving this objective are decisions about what markets to serve and what

FIGURE 2.3
Product–Market Expansion Matrix: Strategic Choices for Growth

Products

		Existing	New
Markets	Existing	Market Share Strategy	Product Development Strategy
	New	Market Development Strategy	Diversification Strategy

products to make. These decisions must be made in the context of the firm's strengths, weaknesses, and competitive advantage. According to Ansoff, who first proposed what has come to be known as the product–market expansion matrix, there are four fundamental choices, as shown in Figure 2.3.[6]

The firm can continue to serve existing markets with existing products. If these markets are growing at a rate that meets the firm's growth objective, then the growth objective is achieved by maintaining market share. Market growth rates below the firm's growth objective require the firm to increase its market share. Competitive position with regard to cost, product features, or both is key to success. Monitoring the firm's position with respect to competitors is a critical activity.

When competitive rivalry rules out a market share strategy, product development or market development strategies are the logical alternatives. The choice depends on the skills of the firm and, particularly, the degree of change the firm is capable of managing. Product development strategy focuses on existing markets. It requires a good understanding of existing market needs and product development processes that effectively link marketing to R&D and manufacturing.

Market development strategy suggests that an organization is capable of handling considerable change. New markets require learning new purchasing practices or new uses for products and the establishment of new relationships with distributors and customers. Some market development strategies may require only modest changes, involving principally the field sales force. This was the case for the European subsidiary of a U.S. chemical manufacturer when it shifted its attention from large customers who bought on price to small customers for whom application service was more important. In other instances, extensive change is required, as was the case for MacTec, a Swedish manufacturer of water measurement equipment, when it considered expansion from European to U.S. markets.

Diversification is the most difficult growth strategy, combining both the necessity to develop new products and learn new markets simultaneously. The degree of difficulty can be somewhat reduced through diversification closely related to existing products and markets, as was the case when Texas Instruments started producing personal computers. Nevertheless, most diversification strategies essentially start new businesses and should be viewed in that light.

The Profit Impact of Market Strategy (PIMS)

Despite similar positions on the portfolio matrixes or similar strategic choices for growth, profitability of firms varies enormously. In the 1960s, GE launched an investigation to determine if the variation in the performance results of its some 150 businesses was attributable solely to the skills of its managers or if some of the variation could be explained by situational variables or specific patterns of managerial decisions. Subsequently the investigation was moved to the Marketing Science Institute and then to the Strategic Planning Institute where investigations continue. The initial study, headed by Dr. Sidney Schoeffler, found that there were certain factors that explained as much as 70 percent of the variation in ROI, used as the principal measure of business performance. The factors, generally grouped in three main categories, are those associated with:

- The market environment (e.g., market growth rate, importance of the product to end users, marketing expenditures).
- Competitive position (e.g., relative quality, market share, patent protection).
- The capital and production structure (e.g., investment intensity, capacity utilization, vertical integration).

Extensive background on PIMS, its development, and its findings is given in the Van Moppes-IDP Limited case that considers if, and how, a firm might use PIMS to develop business and marketing strategy. To date, over 3,000 businesses have participated in PIMS. Some have used PIMS as a tool for corporate management to analyze proposed business strategies and compare, for instance, profit forecasts against actual profit results of businesses in similar situations. Others have used PIMS at the business-unit level to help develop business or marketing strategies. Still others, as in the case of Van Moppes-IDP, have used PIMS more broadly as a way of considering how to organize components of the business or of focusing attention on critical areas of the business.

Beyond the businesses that have actually participated in PIMS, both by providing data and comparing their own business performance to the performance of other businesses in the PIMS data base, academic researchers have used the data base extensively. Their findings have been reported in numerous journals and have served as broad guidelines for many strategic decisions and as the basis for many strategic planning models. Much of this research is summarized in *The PIMS Principles.*[7]

Although widely used, PIMS has been criticized considerably both for its methodology and use. Businesses in the data base tend to be large and relatively sophisticated. While some of their products may be new, the overall product mix is generally well beyond the introductory stage of the product life cycle. These characteristics have raised questions about the generalizability of the findings. Data are self-reported and some data require subjective assessments, which may result in biased reporting. Other criticism points to problems with some of the statistical analyses. Users of PIMS have been criticized for looking for simplistic answers to complex problems or for assuming that PIMS would develop a complete business strategy.

Despite criticisms about its methodology and use, the PIMS data base is the largest single strategic data base available to managers and researchers. As with other tools developed to assist in the formulation of strategy, when used with care and understanding PIMS can provide valuable insights into the development of business and marketing strategies.

The Product Life Cycle

The concept of the product life cycle (PLC) is familiar to most marketers. In brief, it holds that most products go through four stages. In the first stage the product is introduced. If the introduction is successful, the product experiences rapid sales growth in the second stage, up to the point that the market starts to saturate. Once saturation occurs, the product enters the mature stage, where growth slows to parallel the overall growth of the economy. In the fourth stage, decline is expected, principally because new or different products are introduced that better meet customer wants and needs.

Marketing strategies appropriate in one stage of the PLC are not likely to be appropriate in other stages. Table 2.2 lists some traditional prescriptions for marketing strategy in each stage of the PLC. Note the similarities between stages of the PLC and cells of the growth-share matrix and their marketing strategy prescriptions. The strategy prescriptions represent the average experiences of many firms, hence they are useful as guides for strategy. But note that they are generic. In a sense, they are prescriptions one might make if one knew nothing else about the situation. Consider, for instance, the standard prescription to price high in the growth stage of the PLC. As we will see in Chapter 7, this is the standard skimming price strategy, which is appropriate in certain circumstances. In other circumstances a low price or penetration strategy might be more appropriate. Similarly, the standard prescription in the decline stage of the PLC is to cut back on promotion spending. In many instances this action will accelerate the sales decline whereas higher expenditures on promotion might have extended the PLC. Like the strategy prescriptions associated with the growth-share matrix, the PLC prescriptions for marketing strategy are start-

TABLE 2.2

Market(ing) Elements over the Product Life Cycle

Element	Stages of the PLC			
	Introduction	**Growth**	**Maturity**	**Decline**
Objective	Establishment	Penetration	Defense	Harvest
Customers	Innovators	Early adopters	Mass market	Laggards, specials
Competitors	Few	Many	Some	Few
Profits	Negative	Peak	Declining	Low
Price	High	High/medium	Medium	Low
Distribution	Exclusive	Selective	Intensive	Selective
Promotion focus	Concept/ trial	Brand/ features	Value/ different-iation	Special applications
Promotion cost	Medium	Large	Moderate	Small
Service	Low	High	Moderate	Low

ing points for strategy formulation. The PLC, like other planning tools, should be used to assist in formulating strategy, not in specifying it.

International Product Cycle

In the mid-1960s, the international product cycle (IPC) was proposed as a way of explaining firms' export activities.[8] According to the IPC, new products go through the introductory and growth stages of the PLC in countries with many scientists and engineers (i.e., inventors) and with affluent customers. The IPC suggested the largest percentage of new products would be introduced in the United States, the country with the most scientists and engineers and the highest per capita income. Products in the maturity stage would then be exported to other countries, first to other developed countries and then to less developed countries. Finally, during the maturity stage there would be a shift of manufacturing to less developed countries.

The IPC is useful in pointing out that marketing strategies need to take into account the stage of the PLC in a given market. But firms often do not have the luxury of leisurely introducing their product in the home market and then exporting it to other markets at a later date. Increasingly, the nature of global competition and global customers requires simultaneous introduction of new products in many markets. In addition, meeting the needs of increasingly demanding customers may favor locating manufacturing facilities close to customers rather than in a less developed country with lower labor costs.

Marketing Strategy and the Marketing Plan

Marketing strategy should have two purposes: (1) to provide broad guidance to the development of business strategy, and (2) to guide and direct marketing activities. We define *marketing strategy* as customer-focused objectives that guide and support the business strategy and decisions and actions with respect to target customers, price, product, promotion, and distribution necessary to accomplish the objectives. More comprehensively, marketing strategy should answer the following questions:

- What are our objectives? That is, what are we trying to accomplish?
- What customers should we target?
- What is our product, from the customer's perspective, what role does it play, and how should it be positioned?
- What price should we charge?
- How should we communicate about our product to targeted customers?
- How should we distribute our product?
- What information do we need about the external environment and reaction to our marketing efforts?
- What options did we consider in formulating our marketing strategy?
- What are the critical actions necessary for accomplishment of our strategy?
- What are the critical assumptions on which our strategy is predicated?
- How will we coordinate with the rest of the organization?

The answers to these question should be found in the marketing plan. Good marketing plans are simply written statements of the marketing strategy for a given time period. The format of marketing plans can vary enormously. Some plans are comprehensive and include all the firm's products and served markets. Other plans are more sharply focused either on a limited set of products or on a specific market. In both cases, the plan usually includes the situation analysis on which it is based.

Elements common to most marketing plans are shown in Table 2.3. All plans should convey the objectives to be accomplished and the way in which they are to be accomplished. Credibility of the plan is enhanced by including a discussion of the various options considered before choosing the option selected and by stipulating key assumptions and critical actions.

The Marketing Planning Process

We define *marketing planning* as a flexible process whose purpose is to develop or modify marketing strategies and that interacts with, or is integrated into, the processes by which business strategies and other functional strategies are developed.

TABLE 2.3
Contents of a Comprehensive Marketing Plan*

Objectives

The volume to be sold (in dollar amounts and/or in units) and market share.

Profit contribution (in dollar amounts or in margins).

Nonfinancial objectives (e.g., image, key relations, new accounts, etc.).

Target Customers

Who they are.

Where they are.

What their characteristics are.

What segments are served (if any).

Product

A description of the basic product plus service, packaging, warranties, etc.

Position. What the product is expected to do for the customer. How it relates to competitive products.

Role. What the product is expected to do for the firm, beyond simply contributing to profit (e.g., cash cow, lead into new markets, defend against a competitive attack).

The branding strategy.

Distribution

Direct or through distribution.

Use and role of agents.

If through distribution, then:

Types of wholesalers.

Channel length or number of levels.

Exclusive or selective.

Role for each type and level of wholesaler.

Key functions or activities.

Margins and other motivating mechanisms.

Promotion

The nature of the promotional effort, with particular attention to the role of the sales force.

The targets of the promotional effort.

The promotional mix: relationship between personal selling, advertising, sales promotion, and publicity.

The role of distribution (if used) in the promotional effort.

The promotional budget.

(continued)

TABLE 2.3 *(continued)*

Price

The overall price policy including relationship to competition, variation in prices, responsibility for setting prices, etc.).

Specific price to end-users.

Discount structure to end users and intermediaries.

Contingencies

Contingencies that might occur.

Action to be taken.

Event(s) that will trigger contingency actions.

Market Research

Additional market research needed before the plan is implemented.

Research needed after the plan is implemented to ensure it is on track.

Other Options Considered

The plan should identify critical assumptions and actions critical to success.

*Note: Many plans also include the situation analysis, which is the foundation on which the plan is developed. Here we only list the objectives of the plan and their principal means of achievement.

External and internal situation analysis is essential to the marketing planning process. The customer is key, but competitors, the industry and its structure, the nature of distribution channels, and environmental trends all shape the context within which marketing strategy is developed. The concept of strategy as a match between the external environment and the firm's capabilities emphasizes the need for internal analysis. Table 2.4 identifies specific areas for analysis, which are discussed in subsequent chapters. The key to situation analysis is to continually ask what the implications are for the marketing program. For example, if the buying decision is made by a group, how can promotion reach all the buying influences? If customers vary extensively in their purchasing practices, will it be necessary to develop more than one marketing program?

The analysis should lead to the development of key problems and opportunities facing the firm that relate to the specific issues or decision questions faced by management. These need to be considered in the context of the skills of the firm. The emergence of a corporate personal computer market was a greater opportunity for IBM, with its direct corporate contacts, than for Apple, with its strong commitment to sell through distributors. Such analysis enables assessment of the overall situation—is it very favorable, somewhat favorable, neutral, somewhat unfavorable, or very unfavorable?—and should help identify key issues the marketing program needs to address.

> **TABLE 2.4**
> **Situation Analysis for Marketing Planning**
> *Areas for Investigation*

External Analysis

The Customer

It is important to develop an explicit view of the motivations of the customer(s), the nature of the purchase decision process for the goods or services under investigation, and the degree to which these vary between customers or groups of customers. Often it will also be important to extend analysis to the customer's customers.

The Market

Here we are concerned with the overall size of the market, both current and future, and with the size of segments that vary in motivations, the nature of the buying processes, or other dimensions that would either rule out some customers or require modifications in marketing strategy.

The Industry

Marketing strategy must take into account the salient characteristics of the industry in which the firm will compete. It must, for instance, take into account the extent of competition, the positions of competitors, their current strategies or possible initiatives, and possible reaction(s) to the firm's strategic or tactical moves. It must also consider how the industry fits in the business system, where value is added, and trends in the industry.

Distribution Structure

Few aspects of the external situation are more critical to the success of a marketing plan than good distribution. Analysis needs to take into account the structure of distribution channels, the likelihood of availability of distributors to the firm, the nature of relations with distributors, and so on.

(continued)

Design of the planning process involves consideration of a number of questions.

- Who is responsible for the plan?
- Who should review or approve the plan?
- How should marketing planning relate to the strategic planning process?

In most industrial firms, marketing planning is a team effort. Primary responsibility for the marketing plan usually falls on one person, the marketing manager, the vice president of marketing, or a product manager. One person can develop the plan, with inputs from others, or it can be developed by a task force or standing planning committee.

TABLE 2.4 *(continued)*

Product Life Cycle

Marketing strategies should change over the product life cycle. While the exact stage of the PLC cannot be estimated with certainty it is useful to compare proposed changes in strategy with generic prescriptions for various stages of the PLC.

Environmental Climate

A wide variety of external events can influence customer or competitor behavior or the firm's own situation. Categories for analysis include technology, the political situation, the economic situation, and social trends. Events need to be classified as favorable, thus providing additional opportunities, or unfavorable, thus representing threats to be defended against.

Internal Analysis

Skills of the Firm

Marketing strategy must take into account the ability of the firm to implement the chosen strategy and to defend itself against initiatives of competitors. This goes beyond the marketing skills of the firm; it also includes engineering skills, manufacturing skills, overall management skills, and other organizational capabilities.

Financial Resources of the Firm

Marketing strategies must be financed. Most often, funds must be committed to marketing activities considerably in advance of revenues. Marketing strategy must assess the extent of resources and the degree to which they will be made available to fund marketing expenses.

Corporate or Business Strategy

Marketing strategy must take into account and support overall business strategy. Business strategy, in turn, must take into account and support overall corporate strategy. Overall objectives, sources of competitive advantage, and the assigned role of the business within the corporate portfolio can significantly influence marketing strategy.

This table draws heavily on the Marketing Planning Outline developed by Professor James R. Taylor and his colleagues at the University of Michigan Business School, and his work in this area is gratefully acknowledged.

An interesting aspect of planning is the location of responsibility for gathering planning information. As described in the Quest International case, responsibility can be centralized either in a formal market research function or a marketing management information system (MMIS) function. Alternatively, it can be decentralized to the various product or market managers. As businesses expand, the skill required to manage large data bases and information systems argues for centralization. But because managers of centralized functions frequently are remote from the daily information needs of product or market managers and may be remote from the field sales force, a prime source of information, the information gathering processes they develop and their analysis of data may not adequately respond to the realities of the market situation.

TABLE 2.5
Strategic Planning at GE

The marketing manager is the most significant functional contributor to the strategic planning process, with leadership roles in defining the business mission; analysis of the environmental, competitive, and business situation; developing objectives, goals, and strategies; and defining product, market, distribution, and quality plans to implement the business's strategies. This involvement extends to the development of programs and operating plans that are fully linked with the strategic plan.

Source: From a speech by Steve Harrell, a GE strategic planning manager, given at the American Marketing Association's Summer Educators' Meeting, Chicago, August 5, 1980.

Increasingly, marketing plan approval takes place at the level of the SBU general manager or at a higher level. In some instances, as in the case of the Norton Co., a U.S. manufacturer of abrasive materials, the marketing plan is reviewed as part of the SBU plan at several reviewing levels. In other instances, as in the case of Perkin-Elmer, a U.S. manufacturer of high-tech equipment, advisory boards with specialized knowledge of selected target markets may review and comment on plans before they are submitted for approval.

The extent to which marketing planning is part of the business planning process varies considerably. An example of extensive involvement is shown in Table 2.5. A high degree of involvement usually is the result of a top-down, bottom-up planning process. With many exceptions, this is done on an annual basis. Early in the planning year, the business or function receives planning assumptions and broad objectives. Planning assumptions might include economic forecasts, exchange rate forecasts, or political risk assessments. Assumptions can be more specific, as would be the case for Ohmeda Monitoring Systems where, for example, policy decisions with regard to national health expenditures are critical to planning. Objectives invariably include profit expectations and may also include productivity targets or other performance measures. Of particular interest to marketing may be the identification of new and potentially attractive target markets.

Within the context of established corporate objectives and planning assumptions, business objectives and assumptions are then established by the SBU manager. Depending on how the SBU is organized, functional or other managers then initiate the planning process within their components. Key to this planning effort is the development of plans that support the business objectives and coordinate with other components.

Where planning is done on an annual basis, component plans are usually integrated into a business plan in the middle of the planning year. Subsequent steps in the planning process will include a higher level review, with either approval or modification. The approved strategic plan then becomes the basis for establishing the financial plan for the business. Depending on the degree to which combined financial plans of all the SBUs meet corporate objectives, there is either approval or renegotiation of financial objectives for individual SBUs. The final combination of financial plans becomes the corporate budget for the next year.

Summary

Marketing planning is not isolated from other activities of the organization. Rather, it takes place within the context of corporate and business planning and objectives. In broad terms, marketing planning needs to recognize three key concepts: the importance of the match between opportunities and organizational competence, the importance of linking actions to objectives, and the need for marketing objectives that support business objectives.

A number of tools or analytical frameworks have been developed to assist corporate planning. Two frequently used tools are the growth-share matrix and the Investment Priority matrix. Marketers should understand how these and other planning tools are used and how their use may influence marketing plans. Additional tools developed to assist business and marketing planning include the product–market expansion matrix, PIMS, the PLC, and the IPC. Marketers can use these tools as guides to assist in the planning process, which also must take into account the unique situation of the individual firm.

Although marketing planning needs to consider corporate and business planning and objectives, its principal focus must be on understanding the external situation—customers, the competitors, and the industry within which the firm competes. Good situation analysis is imperative, starting with how and why customers buy. The marketing plan can take many forms, but all plans should clearly convey the marketing objectives, the target market, and the critical decisions or policies on product, price, promotion, and distribution, as well as key assumptions and anticipated contingencies.

In subsequent chapters, we will address more extensively areas for analysis and options for market selection, price, promotion, product, and distribution strategies.

Overview of Chapter Cases

✻ The Van Moppes-IDP case describes a British manufacturer of ultra-hard cutting tools considering the use of PIMS as a way to enhance its ability to focus on markets and improve quality. It provides the opportunity to assess the value and use of a major strategic planning tool.

✻ The E.I. Du Pont de Nemours & Co. case describes the situation facing the marketing director for a Du Pont division in developing next year's marketing plan. It provides the opportunity to consider the financial aspects of marketing planning and the nature of the marketing planning process.

Endnotes

1. Peter F. Drucker, *People and Performance: The Best of Peter Drucker on Management* (New York: Harper & Row, Publishers, Inc., 1977), 89–90.
2. Kenneth R. Andrews, *The Concept of Corporate Strategy* (Homewood, IL: Dow Jones-Irwin, Inc. 1971).
3. E. Raymond Corey, *Industrial Marketing: Cases and Concepts* (Englewood Cliffs, NJ: Prentice-Hall, Inc., 1983), 2.
4. For an excellent review of marketing plans, see Howard Sutton, *The Marketing Plan in the 1990s* (New York: The Conference Board, 1990).
5. For a comprehensive discussion, see Derek Abell and John Hammond, *Strategic Market Planning* (Englewood Cliffs, NJ: Prentice-Hall, Inc. 1979).
6. Igor Ansoff, "Strategies for Diversification," *Harvard Business Review*, September–October 1957, 113–124.
7. Robert D. Buzzell and Bradley T. Gale, *The PIMS Principles* (New York: The Free Press, 1987).
8. Vernon, Raymond, "International Investment and International Trade in the Product Cycle," *Quarterly Journal of Economics* (May 1966).

Todd M. Helmeke

Strategic Business Unit Market Planning
An Industrial Case History

Since the late 1960s numerous large, diversified corporations have built their strategic planning programs around the concept of the Strategic Business Unit (SBU). By concentrating on the SBU, an entity that markets similar products to one or more markets with similar characteristics, they sharpened their focus on the individual strategies which combine to form the overall corporate thrust in its served markets.

Borg-Warner has employed strategic planning at the SBU level since 1974. In this article, we'll examine how one SBU, the domestic operations of the Mechanical Seal Division of Borg-Warner Industrial Products, devised its strategy for a specific market, harnessing a well-known matrix approach to planning at an operating level. The approach provides better analysis of served markets and allows managers to create more market-sensitive strategies and tactics.

A mechanical seal is a precision device used to control leakage in rotating machinery, such as centrifugal pumps. B-W sells its mechanical seals primarily to petroleum refineries, pipelines, petrochemical and chemical processing plants, and electric power utilities. As a product category, its greatest competition is packing materials used in lieu of mechanical seals.

The Planning Discipline

Planning forces a company to formally state its perceptions about the nature, scope, potential, and major trends in a market. It explicitly examines the strengths, weaknesses, strategies, and market positions of the company itself and its primary and secondary competitors. And it prescribes the objectives of the SBU as well as the strategies to achieve them. The planning process builds a management team consensus behind the SBU's strategies and tactics.

In recent years, however, strategic planning has been getting some bad publicity, much of it deserved. In short, the glamorous growth years of the 1960s produced legions of corporate staff planners divorced from the day-to-day world of line operations. Armed with popular planning models, those professional planners dictated to individual corporate SBUs from on high. And much as an investor studies the fundamentals of each stock in his portfolio, the planners had their bloodless formulas and numbers to apply to each SBU in the corporate "portfolio." They rarely were close enough to the realities of the marketplace and individual SBU competitive environments.

Corporate operating managers share some of the blame, of course, for letting staff planning get out of hand. Coping with day-to-day problems and unwilling to take more than a short-term approach to planning, top management justifiably grew impatient with their inability to devise systematic strategies.

But fast-changing markets and less economic certainty in the 1980s have tarnished the professional planner's badge at many corporations. Top management learned that planning divorced from first-hand knowledge of marketplaces produced stilted and unresponsive strategies that were often wrong.

Todd M. Helmeke launched his Vista Strategies consulting firm in San Diego in 1984. He had been director of business development and marketing at Borg-Warner Industrial Products, Long Beach, Cal. *Source:* Reprinted with permission from the 1984 issue of *Business Marketing.* Copyright, Crain Communications, Inc.

FIGURE 1
Marketing Planning Cycle

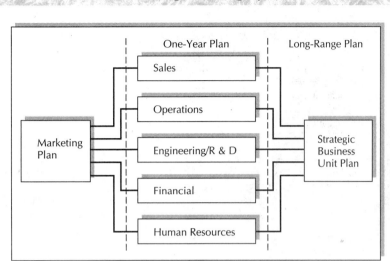

It's not that the decision frameworks employed by full-time planners necessarily didn't work. It's because the judgment and experience that go into a good plan cannot be replaced by formulas alone. Hence the corporate imperative nowadays is to put planning back in the hands of operating management.

Borg-Warner always has put operations people in charge of planning. The company never had a central planning staff at the corporate level which dictated strategies to operating levels of the organization.

As a result, Borg-Warner has been able to use systematic approaches such as the market attractiveness/business strength matrix popularized by the Boston Consulting Group, as we'll discuss below. But the company has kept the process where it works best, in the hands of SBU operating managers who are close to their markets and the competition. And having devised their own plans, they have a definite stake in implementing them successfully.

Another word about marketing strategy planning is in order. Marketing planning and sales planning are two different things, although many companies confuse the two. The difference is analogous to the difference between a sprinter and a marathon runner.

Sales planning is the sprint, designed to get fast results over a short distance. But marketing planning is like the long-distance run. The task requires more time and encounters more obstacles, but it takes one a lot farther. It aims at long-range business objectives and strategies to cope with the characteristics of a changing market.

Unfortunately, many marketing executives substitute sales planning for what should be marketing planning. They examine existing markets for their existing products, and ask how they will *sell* to them. They collect sales forecasts for each product and parcel those into sales quotas. They budget for sales expenses, marketing communications, and the other costs necessary to ensure a specified level of sales over a given period. Then they hand the data

FIGURE 2
Overview of Marketing Planning Process

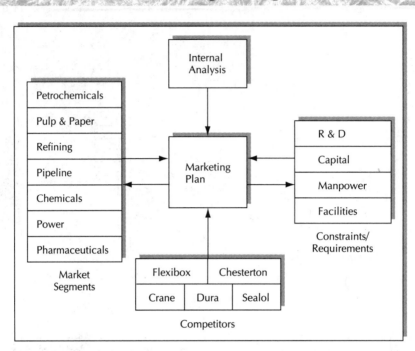

up to corporate management where analysts calculate *pro forma* income and cash flow statements.

Without sales planning, of course, the entire organization would be doing business blindly. But sales planning is only a part of market planning. In its long-term view, marketing must account for trends—including the opportunities for new products in new markets where the company has or can acquire strength. Most of all, it asks, "What do customers need? What *should* we sell?"

Developing the Plan

Conceptually, the SBU planning process at Borg-Warner companies is a three-step process as shown in Figure 1. The marketing plan feeds information into the various elements of the one-year plan—sales, operations, engineering/R&D, finance, and human resources—which in turn feed into the long-range SBU plan. All three plans are interrelated, with the marketing plan providing much of the basic data used in the one-year and SBU plans.

The process is continuous and interactive, however, as depicted in Figure 2. After management has established the SBU long-term mission, or goal, market research provides detailed analyses of: (1) the opportunities available in each of the market segments served; and (2) the threats created by the strategies of competitors.

Next, an internal analysis of the firm's own business strengths and weaknesses is prepared. Then, management assesses the SBU's capital, manpower, facilities, and R&D constraints in order to define the parameters of affordable growth.

It's a dynamic process, for as changes occur internally and externally in served market segments and in the strategies of competitors, they are reflected in the marketing plan. And the process repeats,

FIGURE 3
1983 Pulp and Paper Industry Environment

- Overall capacity growth will be moderate—2 percent, 1983, and 1½ percent, 1984.
- Good growth market as industry that was packing oriented is now moving to mechanical seals.
- Energy, environmental, and simplified maintenance concerns are providing a basis for long-term penetration in the U.S.
- U.S. end-users are now familiarizing themselves with mechanical seals.
- Approximately 20–25 percent of all new pumps now are purchased with mechanical seals.

the marketing plan feeding new information to various functions within the business, which in turn feed information to the long-range SBU plan.

Note too that the process involves line operating managers at every step. Yet their involvement is a disciplined approach. That's crucial, lest managers lose sight of the long-term picture amid their day-to-day crises and short-term opportunities.

Marketing Plan Structure

Structuring the plan is an important part of maintaining discipline. For example, our marketing plans use a six-step approach:

1. Formulating the mission/goal statement.
2. Preparing a detailed market analysis, including competitor strengths, weaknesses, and strategies; and economic, legislative, and regulatory trends affecting the company, its customers, and/or its competitors.
3. Analyzing the SBU's international business strengths and weaknesses, including its products, distribution, pricing, and promotion programs.
4. Following completion of the first three steps, formulating the marketing objectives, the strategies, and the implemental tactics essential to the plan.

5. Examining the human and financial resources required to accomplish the objectives. If there are shortfalls in resource allocation—as is usually the case—the objectives, strategies, and tactics must be reviewed and pared down to fit the available resources.
6. Comparing the revised objectives to the long-term mission/goal statement to ensure that the objectives are compatible with the company's long-term direction and the opportunities that exist or will occur in the marketplace.

Single-Market Example

To examine the process in more detail, here's how the Mechanical Seal Division developed its 1983 plan for one of its markets, the domestic pulp mill industry.

The first step examines the business environment.

Key points, summarized in Figure 3, help to focus attention on the probable effects economic trends and environmental factors and regulations may have on the division's future share of the market.

Figure 4 summarizes the key points in the next step of the process: preparing the market profile. The actual profile statement in a plan is much more detailed, of course, in discussing subjects such

FIGURE 4
U.S. Pulp Mill Market Profile

- 248 pulp mill sites
- 65% in southern United States
- 1982 estimated market shares

Chesterton	12.0%
John Crane	6.0%
Durametallic	3.5%
Borg-Warner	0.1%
Sealol	3.5%
Packing	74.9%

FIGURE 5
Pulp and Paper Market Segments

Segments	Characteristics	BWMS Product Coverage
Severe services	Heat transfer	Uniseal I & II
	Coatings	BXRH, BX
	Corrosives: Caustic chlorine and acids	
	Liquor, digestors	
	Temperatures to 500 F	
	Low pressures to 250 PSI (max.)	
General services	Fuel oil, white water on paper machine	Uniseal I
	Stock pumps	BX, Q, QB
	Some abrasives, solids	
	Temperatures below 250 F	
	Pressures 0 to 200 PSI	
Off-stream services	Water services	Q

as the number of plants, major geographic concentrations, the market share of each primary competitor, and the production level of the industry.

But that's still only a start. The next step segments the market for the division's products, listing segment characteristics and the product coverage the SBU (BWMS) provides. As Figure 5 shows, the division's two most important segments are severe and general service applications, while "off-stream" services are a comparatively smaller third segment.

The Matrix Approach

The question then becomes, which segment or segments deserve the most emphasis strategically? The answer depends on two considerations:

• Each segment's relative attractiveness. It's a function of sales potential, growth, competition, pricing sensitivity, unmet needs, and the product penetration/usage in each segment of the market.

Properly prepared, the tabular analysis offers invaluable help in understanding the market and in formulating strategies for attaching competitors while better satisfying customer needs. Figure 6 illustrates the Mechanical Seal Division's main conclusions on those points.

• Company strengths and weaknesses in serving each segment, relative to competitors. The analysis requires a candid analysis of such business factors as product coverage, pricing, coverage of market, service facilities, advertising and sales promotion, and company reputations. Figure 7 shows key Borg-Warner considerations.

Borg-Warner summarizes the implications of those data on a nine-cell market attractiveness/business strength matrix, as shown in Figure 8. Business strengths are measured from right to left on the horizontal axis of the matrix and are based on several factors, heavily weighted by market

FIGURE 6
Pulp Mill Market Analysis of Market Attractiveness Factors

	Severe Services	General Services	Off-Stream Services
Size and Potential	$8.5MM	$14.2MM	$5.6MM
Growth	10%	5%	3%
Competition	Users becoming oriented to mechanical seals Chesterton and Crane are strong Durametallic and Sealol a factor		Primary packing suppliers
Price	Of some importance	Important; some price resistance to mechanical seals	Price resistant to mechanical seals
Unmet Needs	Orientation to benefits of mechanical seals Training on seal application and specification, installation, and maintenance		No unmet needs perceived
Percent Sealed	25% to 30%	10% to 15%	0 to 1 %

FIGURE 7
Pulp Mill Market Analysis of Business Strength Factors

	A Services	B Services	C Services
Product	Fair coverage with bellows seals in liquor and slurry services	Limited coverage with spring seal products	No coverage
Price	Competitive with other seal manufacturers Mechanical seals generally not perceived competitive with packing		
Place	Present offices and facilities provide very limited coverage of market		
Service	Substantial sales coverage gap; good capability, low level of commitment; limited to select few accounts		
Advertising Promotion	Poor; case histories under development		
Reputation	Generally unknown; limited to select few accounts Market recognizes suppliers with both seal and packing products		

FIGURE 8
U.S. Pulp Mill Market Analysis of Present BWMS Market Positon

FIGURE 8
U.S. Pulp Mill Market Analysis of Present BWMS Market Positon

Business Strengths

High | Medium | Low

Market Attractiveness — High / Medium / Low

Applications:
(A)–Severe services
(B)–General services
(C)–Off-stream services

Segment	1982 Market Potential	BWMS Product Coverage	1982 BWMS Market Share
A	$ 8.5MM	BXRH, BX, UNISEAL I & II	0.5%
B	14.2MM	BX, UNISEAL I, QB, Q	.0%
C	5.6MM	Q	–
	$28.3MM*		0.1%

*Excludes OEM market potential

share. Market attractiveness reads from bottom to top on the vertical axis and is also based on several factors, especially real market growth. Each square represents a portion of the potential of the market in each area.

Accordingly, the greater a firm's business strengths in serving a market and the more attractive the market, the closer the firm will be positioned toward the upper-left-hand corner of Figure 8.

The matrix approach is a relatively easy, and conceptually attractive, way to summarize a company's or SBU's current position, and where it has opportunity to grow. As a key feature of strategic planning theory developed by the Boston Consulting Group and General Electric in the mid-1960s, its appeal is obvious. That helps to explain why BCG modeling and its spin-offs enraptured planners throughout the 1970s, whether or not they used it correctly.

In the example here, BWMS' strengths in all three segments—"A" (severe services), "B" (general services), and "C" (off-stream services)—were very low on both dimensions of the matrix.

Figure 9 shows the strategy BWMS chose to improve its position in the pulp mill market, particularly through an aggressive approach to segment "A." Although "A" is not the largest segment, it's the fastest growing and it's the segment in which BWMS has the most presence. On the matrix, "A" enclosed in a square is positioned higher and to the left of the circled "A" to indicate the objective of increased share in the severe services segment.

At the same time, BWMS decided to accept its no-share position in the unpromising segment "C," and maintain moderate expansion strategies in the "B" segment.

Following Up

This detailed, logical approach to marketing planning, beginning with the market environment and concluding with the strategy matrix, provides essential information about each of the division's markets. It sows the seeds of strategic planning and

FIGURE 9
U.S. Pulp Mill Market Strategy

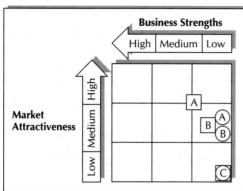

- Concentrate on liquor, acid slurry, and stock services.
- Develop case histories.
- Define market segments and applications.
- Increase market penetration through introduction of UNISEAL I and II with stocking distributors.

FIGURE 10
Marketing Objectives

		1978	1979	1980	1981	1982	1983
1.	Net Sales	$	$	$	$	$	$
2.	Margin %	%	%	%	%	%	%
3.	Mrkt Seg. Sales						
	Chemical	$	$	$	$	$	$
	Pulp & Paper	$	$	$	$	$	$
	OEM	$	$	$	$	$	$
	Refining	$	$	$	$	$	$
4.	Market Share						
	Chemical	%	%	%	%	%	%
	Pulp & Paper	%	%	%	%	%	%
	OEM	%	%	%	%	%	%
	Refining	%	%	%	%	%	%

FIGURE 11
Marketing Strategy, Pulp and Paper

A.   **Strategy Summary**

Promote technology and service in B service segments, refrain from price competition, emphasize cost effectiveness, technology, and service:

- Energy savings
- Environmental control
- Reduced maintenance and labor

- Standardization and safety
- Features of bellows seal technology
- Emergency repair and manufacturing

B.   **Central Engineering Departments and A&E Accounts**

- Conduct technical presentations
- Conduct plant/unit surveys

- Provide a trouble-shooting seminar
- Provide installation assistance

C.   **Identify Target Accounts**

- **Central Engineering**

  Georgia Pacific
  Weyerhauser
  International Paper

- **A&E Firms**

  Fluor
  Foster Wheeler
  C.F. Braun
  Brown and Root
  Bechtel

D.   **Plant Engineering and OEM Sales Office Strategy**

- Promote regular visits to service centers by customers

---

provides fertile ground for them to take root among operating managers.

Of course, all objectives for all markets must be quantified on a time dimension. Figure 10 provides a format for listing sales, market share, and profit margin objectives for the SBU, and sales and share objectives for individual markets. (OEM's include the manufacturers of centrifugal pumps, agitators, and compressors.) For competitive reasons, actual BWMS data aren't shown.

Figure 11 shows the approach used to clarify the strategy decided upon by the management team for each major market. The overall strategy is summarized and broken down into its various elements and influence factors. In this example, the strategies focus on decision-making segments such as central engineering departments at target pulp producers, and design engineering firms (A&Es).

The final step in the marketing planning process establishes the tactics that will be used by the SBU to implement its strategies and achieve its objectives. Figure 12 shows how the tactical plan is time-phased. The responsibilities of each affected department are clearly defined.

In 1983, the first year affected by the plan described above, BWMS increased its pulp mill market share by a factor of 10, moving from 0.1 percent to 1 percent.

By the division's estimate, the 1983 market shares of other competitors listed in Figure 4 were:

Chesterton: 13.3 percent
John Crane: 7.8 percent
Durametallic: 3.8 percent
Sealol: 4.0 percent
Packing instead of mechanical seals: 70.1 percent

FIGURE 12
Tactics/Action Plans, Pulp and Paper

	Customers				Respons.			Time Sch.		
	MAJOR	MINOR	OEMs	A&Es	DEPT.	DUE DATE	MAN HRS.	JAN.	FEB.	MAR.
A. Educational Programs for District Managers and Sales Engineers										
1. ANSI standards catalog for BX and QS seals				X						
2. Product literature	X									
3. Seal systems description, drawings	X		X	X				X →		
4. Educational brochures on pulp and paper industry	X	X		X					X →	
5. Define product policy	X							X →		
B. Sales Calling and Coverage										
1. Determine additional sales and distribution needs.	X	X								
2. Establish criteria for distributors.										
3. Define target accounts.	X	X								
4. Conduct plant surveys.	X									
5. Establish plan for developing rapport with key OEM offices located near target accounts.			X							X

Keys to Success

To be successful, the marketing planning process described above must have the full support of management. Furthermore, to rigorously go through the reiterative planning process requires:

- The services of a full-time marketing professional to direct market research and be the catalyst for planning activities.
- The active participation of operating management in marketing planning. At the Mechanical Seal Division, the management team spends eight to 10 days a year reviewing and discussing the marketing plan. That is done in a collegial atmosphere, with the involvement of all major functional areas—manufacturing, human resources, engineering, finance, sales, and, of course, marketing.
- Approval for market research expenditures on an "as-needed" basis to unearth the facts about, and understand the trends within, each of the served markets.

But marketing planning must have a payback. It must produce favorable financial results to justify the considerable investments in time and money required to do it well.

Long-range market planning at the SBU level was inaugurated in 1976 at the Mechanical Seal Division. By 1981, division sales had doubled. In the past two years they have continued to increase.

Those results can be traced, in part at least, to the division's diligent marketing planning program.

Donald L. McCabe
V. K. Narayanan

The Life Cycle of the PIMS and BCG Models

The information revolution has reshaped the way corporations are managed in the 1990s. Traditional strategic planning models, once the mainstay of corporate planners, are now considered by many to be fads or fashions whose day has come and gone. However, the research discussed here suggests that such a view may do a great disservice to strategy models. A survey of America's largest corporations reveals that many organizations have been reluctant to discard the tools that are viewed historically as integral to their success. Indeed, strategic planning models seem likely to survive the complex world of the 1990s and beyond.

When Tom Peters published *Thriving On Chaos* [1], many felt his dramatic predictions of the fundamental changes facing U.S. corporations were extreme. Less than five years later, however, it appears he may have underestimated both the intensity and complexity of those changes. Aggressive global competitors have brought a new set of rules to the game. Accelerating technological change has dramatically shortened typical product life cycles. The information revolution has reshaped the way corporations can be managed.

Amid this frenzied change, it is not surprising that strategic planning models, only recently darlings of the corporate suite, have come in for their share of criticism. Whether it be Tom Peters telling us that there is no such thing as "a good strategic plan" or Henry Mintzberg suggesting that strategic planning is a "grand fallacy" [2], one not need look far to discover that many management "experts" have abandoned ship.

At the time this article was written, Donald L. McCabe was Associate Professor at the Graduate School of Management, Rutgers University, Newark, New Jersey. V. K. Narayanan was Professor at the University of Kansas School of Business in Lawrence, Kansas. Reprinted by permission of the publisher from *Industrial Marketing Management 20*, 347–352 (1991). © Elsevier Science, Inc., 1991.

Yet the evidence from management practitioners is mixed. Although it may be easy for some to debunk these models as fads or fashions whose day has come and gone, we think this does the models a disservice. Such a simplistic response not only runs the risk of losing the valuable insights that these models still provide, but it also fails to focus on developing solutions to the new planning dilemmas corporations face. The research described here suggests that many companies are reluctant to discard the techniques that were historically integral to their success. Indeed, strategic planning models may well survive the complex world of the 1990s, and beyond.

The Life Cycle of Strategic Planning Models

In the 1960s, strategic planning models were introduced with regularity as new planning problems were identified and firms searched for ways to manage these uncertainties. General Electric (GE) provides the classic example, having played a significant role in the development of the growth-share matrix, the PIMS model, and others. These models entered a rapid growth phase when their use expanded not only within the firms developing them, but in many cases throughout major segments of the Fortune 500 and beyond. For example, by 1979 the Strategic Planning Institute reported that over 250 firms were among its membership and employing the PIMS principles in the management of their businesses [3]. However, by the early 1980s it was clear that PIMS and other classic strategic planning models had reached maturity; not only had the adoption rate of these models abated, there was also evidence of a decline in total use [4]. Some corporations discarded the models as irrelevant in an era of increasing uncertainty and complexity. Others greatly reduced their role in the overall planning process. As new problems arose, the "old" models were simply pushed into the background. Consequently, it became fashionable for both business journalists and academics to debunk these models.

However such "model bashing" may have been unwarranted, as we actually knew very little about the adoption and use of strategy models by individual corporations and industries. Most discussions in academic and practitioner forums relied on anecdotal data, and this paucity of empirical evidence limited our ability to assess accurately the impact of current practice and to prescribe directions for the future. We hope to shed some light on these issues by studying the adoption and use of three of the most popular early strategy models—PIMS and the BCG and GE portfolio models—through a survey of senior corporate planning executives, augmented by publicly available data about the performance of their organizations. These executives were queried with four objectives in mind:

1. Comparative profiles of adopters and non-adopters of strategy models.
2. The diffusion pattern of these models (e.g., across different industries).
3. The "de-adoption" pattern of these models and the practical meaning of the decision to discontinue their use.
4. Performance implications flowing from the use of the models.

The Survey

The data generated in this study are part of a large research project which gathered data on corporate planning techniques using a structured questionnaire which was mailed to 1,000 of the largest U.S. corporations. This group included industrial, transportation, and utility companies, but did not include any financial organizations. The questionnaire was addressed to the senior planning officer in each organization and requested data of the firm's use of selected strategic planning models. The data were augmented by firm-specific data drawn from the COMPUSTAT data tapes.

Responses were received from a total of 248 organizations (24.8 percent). Completed questionnaires were received from 227 organizations (22.7 percent) and an additional 21 organizations responded to explain that corporate policy precluded participation or that there was no one who could provide accurate historical information on the use of strategic planning models within the organization.

A comparison of respondents and non-respondents showed that responding firms were significantly larger (mean sales $4.7 billion; $P < 0.001$) than nonrespondents (mean sales $2.7 billion) but there were no significant differences in terms of industry membership. Respondents came from a broad cross-section of industries and in only three cases—utilities (18.5 percent), chemical and allied manufacturers (9.3 percent), and foods and allied products (6.6 percent)—did any two-digit SIC code account for more than 5 percent of our final sample. The data drawn from the survey were straightforward: whether any of the models were ever utilized by the organization; the year of adoption and termination (if no longer used); and the level at which they were used in each organization (corporate, divisional, or both).

Data for measures of individual firm size, financial performance, and growth rate were generated from the COMPUSTAT tapes and, where available, mean values for the 20-year period from 1968 to 1987 were employed to operationalize these measures.

Total assets were used to measure size and two different measures of financial performance were employed: return on assets (net income divided by total assets) and return on total equity. In addition to mean performance data for the 1968–1987 period, mean performance for the 5-year periods immediately preceding and following the adoption of a strategic planning model by a specific firm was calculated for intrafirm comparisons to be described later. Growth in total assets for the 20-year period from 1968 to 1987, as well as growth rates for the 5-year periods preceding and following the adoption of a strategic planning model, were also calculated.

COMPUSTAT data for the 20-year period studied was available for only 109 of the 227 respondents. The remaining 118 organizations were private; were divisions of larger corporate entities; lacked complete financial data due to mergers, start-ups, etc.; or were not included in the COMPUSTAT data base. Unless otherwise specified, the sample used in all financial analyses discussed here consisted of these 109 organizations with mean 1987 sales revenues of $8.78 billion, clearly a sample of the country's corporate giants.

Findings

Differences between Users and Nonusers

Two major findings stand out when the profiles of users and nonusers are compared:

- Organizational size is positively related to the use of strategy models: firms using one or more of the models studied here ($n = 61$) had mean assets of $5.65 billion over the 20-year period studied; nonusers ($n = 48$) had mean assets of only $2.38 billion ($P < 0.05$).

- There were no significant differences in either the growth of total assets or financial performance (return on assets) between users and nonusers in the 20-year period studied.

Performance Implications

An exploratory analysis of the performance implications of the use of strategy models was conducted by comparing the intrafirm performance of model users for comparable 5-year periods before and after adoption of a specific strategy model. There were no significant differences between the pre-adoption and postadoption periods on either of our return measures. However, comparisons of intrafirm differences in growth rates were surprising. Not only did we find the relationship between the use of strategy models and growth in assets to be negative, but it was statistically significant for two of the models ($P < 0.10$).

Further analysis paired comparably-sized (based on total assets) user and nonuser firms from the same industry (based on two-digit SIC numbers) and compared the growth and financial performance of these pairs. It was possible to construct 20 such pairs of user and nonuser firms. Comparison of financial performance criteria for these pairs revealed no significant differences between users and nonusers. We also found no statistically significant differences in growth measures when we controlled for industry differences.

We also looked at differences between users that have continued to use a particular strategy model and those who eventually abandoned that model. As shown in Table 1, a clear minority of firms were adopters of any given model and at least

TABLE 1

Comparison of Number of Nonusers, Continuing, and Former Users, by Model

Planning Model	Nonusers (%)	Users (%)	
		Continuing	Former
BCG Matrix	137 (60)	35 (16)	55 (24)
GE Portfolio	185 (82)	21 (9)	21 (9)
PIMS	155 (68)	24 (11)	48 (21)

FIGURE 1
Product Life Cycle Strategic Planning Models

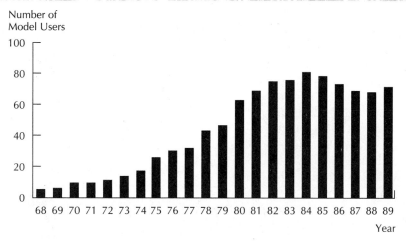

half of the adopters in each case no longer use the model. In addition, analysis of the COMPUSTAT data shows that there are no significant differences between those who continue to use any of the planning models and those who abandoned them.

The Time Period of Adoption

Figure 1 presents consolidated data on the year of adoption and, where appropriate, the year of abandonment of each model by individual firms, producing a histogram of the number of current users on a year-by-year basis. As shown, usage increased throughout the 1970s and declined in the 1980s. (Companies continuing to use individual models today are generally firms which adopted them relatively later than noncontinuing users.) These findings suggest that the high point of utilization of these models has passed. Not only has the rate of adoption decreased substantially for all models, it has been surpassed by the rate at which individual models are abandoned.

Discussion

The results of this survey suggest that

- Larger firms adopted strategy models earlier than smaller firms.
- The high point of their use in strategic planning is over.
- Performance improvements cannot be attributed to the use of these models.

Of course, for many practitioners and scholars, this may appear to confirm what they knew all along.

But simply taking these results at face value does not tell the whole story. In particular, we are concerned by the rush in both the popular press [5] and the academic literature [6] to dismiss the PIMS and portfolio models as outdated tools in the arsenal of corporate strategic planners, a fad whose time has passed. Although the data clearly show declining usage of these models, the data also show that nearly 30 percent of the firms surveyed currently use one or more of the models. Perhaps the most interesting results of the survey are that

- The models continue to be adopted, albeit at a slower rate.
- The principles embodied in the models are still integral to many corporate planning systems.

Recent Adoptions

An examination of the 14 respondents in our sample (6 percent) currently using one or more of the models studied here who adopted those models within the last five years is revealing. Three of these companies are Baby Bell entities obviously facing new competitive challenges; two are utilities with new competitive opportunities available to them in the face of a changing regulatory environment; three are undergoing major strategy reformation; three are smaller growth-oriented companies just reaching a size where formal planning models may make more sense; and one is a returning user of the PIMS model. Thus it appears the models are being used by firms experimenting with new approaches to planning, either for the first time or in an attempt to breathe new life into an outdated system.

Such findings suggest that rumors of the death of PIMS and portfolio models have been greatly exaggerated. New adoptions still occur among large corporations for valid reasons. Indeed, our data on recent adopters suggest that the future of these early strategic planning models may lie with two major groups:

1. Companies who have relatively young planning systems (e.g., smaller growth-oriented firms which have reached a threshold size).
2. Larger firms facing renewed competitive pressures with which their current planning systems can no longer cope.

One could hypothesize that new adopters might include a third segment—firms who are returning to basics as part of a strategic relearning process.

Institutionalization of Models

Open-ended responses to our survey highlight the value that many planners continue to place on the fundamental principles embodied in these models. Our data suggest that these principles are still integral to many corporate planning processes, including the processes of many companies who no longer count themselves as formal users of the models.

Portfolio Models. A major food retailer, a diversified chemical company, manufacturers of a variety of industrial products, a major construction company, and many others who have abandoned formal portfolio models note that the principles and concepts which comprise the underlying logic of these models are still relevant to and at least implicitly incorporated in the planning process. A major, diversified electronics company discontinued using the portfolio models in 1981 but replaced them with a value-based portfolio approach, which is still used today. Similar transitions were reported by two major food companies and the chemical division of a major oil company. In addition, nine companies who reported using a portfolio model other than the BCG or GE approaches were not considered as users in this analysis; seven of these companies continue to use those models today.

Thus even though the formal use of portfolio models is on the decline in our sample, almost one in four of the companies surveyed (24 percent) continue to use an explicit portfolio model and perhaps as many as another one in four use portfolio logic implicitly in their planning. The point is that, even though our data confirm the popular belief that the actual use of portfolio models is declining, they also show that portfolio logic is still an important element of many strategic planning processes—often in the form of an updated portfolio model (typically with some stockholder-value–based dimension, e.g., Alcar), but just as often as an implicit element of the process.

PIMS. We observe a similar, but perhaps less pervasive, trend in the case of PIMS. First, our survey uncovered some of the cynicism about the formal model which has fueled the fervor of those ready to bury it [5,6]. A quote from vice president for strategic planning and development for a major division of a multibillion dollar conglomerate which has never explicitly used the model captures the essence of this sentiment: "these programs/concepts should be implicit in any intelligent corporate planning...these programs are just common sense guides." In addition, several former users—including a major engineering firm and a large consumer products company—have concluded that the PIMS approach no longer fits their particular competitive situation since it cannot "simulate our major business well."

Yet a number of companies who have abandoned the formal model continue to use the principles of the model conceptually in their planning process. A common view is that of the vice president for finance and business development at a large hotel chain who commented that although these models do not capture the "dynamics of today's economy," their logic remains an important element in the overall planning process.

As in the case of portfolio models, the claims regarding the death of PIMS models are vastly exaggerated. One in 10 of our respondents (10 percent) continue to use the model as a formal planning tool, while another 5 to 10 percent suggest that they implicitly employ the logic of the PIMS model as a planning guide. The current popularity of *The PIMS Principles* [7] suggests that the latter group may indeed be larger.

Conclusion

Clearly, corporate planners and managers have learned that no single planning technique can serve all businesses in all contexts. Our concern is that this should not—and based on our data does not—mean that there is no place for the pioneering models of the strategic planning revolution in today's highly competitive global environment. However, it does confirm that none of these models is the panacea that may of their proponents touted them to be in the 1970s.

Essentially, the profile of recent adopters and the continuing abandonment by many users suggest that these models represent but one step in the evolution of strategic planning within a corporation. Although no longer leading edge, they are a routine part of many sophisticated planning systems. In many cases, they are being displaced by newer models which incorporate the fundamental elements of the early models but which also respond to the changing competitive environment. As every good corporate planner knows, this life cycle evolution is predictable and healthy.

While this maturation is inevitable and desirable, the key may be not to forget the basics—although they aren't enough in today's highly competitive, global markets, they still have something to teach us. Many proponents of early strategic planning models sowed the seeds of their own destruction by putting all of their planning eggs in one basket. They probably would have done better to heed the advice of Sid Schoeffler, a PIMS pioneer, which still makes sense 20 years later. Don't ignore the findings and implications of models such as PIMS simply because they don't make immediate sense in your competitive environment, but don't take them on blind faith either. A 1990s reinterpretation of this advice might be, don't ignore the findings and implications of PIMS or portfolio models because they seem basic or trivial in today's competitive environment; instead, build on them until you have a planning system which does make sense in the increasingly competitive world of the 1990s.

References

1. Peters, Tom, *Thriving On Chaos*. Alfred A. Knopf, Inc., New York, 1987.

2. Mintzberg, Henry, *Mintzberg On Management*. The Free Press, New York, 1989.

3. The Strategic Planning Institute. *PIMS–79 Working Papers*. The Strategic Planning Institute. Cambridge, Massachusetts, 1979.

4. Kiechel, Walter, "Oh Where, Oh Where Has My Little Dog Gone? Or My Cash Cow? Or My Star?"

Fortune 104: 148–154 (1981).

5. Byrne, J.A., "Business Fads: What's In and Out," *Business Week* 52–61 (January 20, 1986).

6. Gluck, F.W., "A Fresh Look at Strategic Management," *Journal of Business Strategy* 6:4–19 (1985).

7. Buzzell, R.D., and Gale, B.T., *The PIMS Principles: Linking Strategy to Performance*. The Free Press, New York, 1987.

Chapter 3

How Organizations Buy

W hy do organizations buy, and how? Answers to these questions are fundamental prerequisites to market selection and to the development and implementation of marketing strategy. In this chapter we identify the key aspects of organizational buying and describe the nature of professional purchasing. We then discuss approaches developed for analyzing organizational buying. Finally, we present implications for marketing strategy.

Buyer Behavior: An Overview

In most organizations, the signed purchase order is the culmination of a complex process. This process usually involves a number of individuals. Their individual and collective decisions are influenced by organizational factors such as the nature and purpose of the organization, its policies, and organizational structure; and by personal factors such as individual values, perceptions, skills, and interpersonal relations both within and outside of the organization. Marketing strategy needs to consider the following key characteristics of the buying process.

Derived Demand

The starting point for understanding organizational buying is to recognize that an organization's demand for products and services is derived from the activities involved in supplying its customers. That is, businesses buy only as required to meet the needs of their customers. For raw materials and components that directly enter the product, demand closely parallels fluctuations in demand in the final market. Demand for maintenance, repair, and operating (MRO) items and some services, particularly those closely associated with the production process, also closely tracks demand in the final market. Suppliers need to forecast short-term demand for their customers' goods or services, as determined by both short-term economic activity and competitive position. In some instances, suppliers have opportunities to work with customers to stimulate demand in the final market. For example, aluminum manufacturers and beverage firms have jointly promoted the benefits of aluminum as a can material to consumers. In other instances, a supplier may work exclusively with one customer, giving that customer an advantage over competitors.

For capital goods and more complex services, demand is more likely to be based on customer requirements determined by long-term demand, replacement needs, or other circumstances not related to immediate levels of economic activity. Demand for machine tools or consulting engineering services, for example, is tied to plant expansion or modernization. Often capacity expansion is made in large increments, lengthening the period between purchases of associated goods and services. For suppliers this may entail forecasting long-term requirements to justify maintenance of readiness to serve or maintenance of customer relationships in the absence of orders for long periods of time. Demand for some services, such as investment banking or consulting services associated with mergers and acquisitions, may be determined by strategic moves of the firm not directly related to economic activity. Although difficult to forecast, it is still important for providers of such services to maintain relationships so they are positioned to capitalize on opportunities as they arise.

While the extent of demand for products and services is determined by the demand for the customer's products, the nature of demand is shaped by the customer's overall business strategy. For example, a customer's decision to enter foreign markets may significantly change requirements for the supplier's product. When U.S. manufacturers of large refrigerant compressors established plants in Europe, A.O. Smith, a U.S. manufacturer of electric motor components for compressors, established a manufacturing plant in Ireland to shorten the supply line, facilitate customer contact, and better meet European voltage and frequency requirements. Similarly, the customer's decision to change the technological base of a product, such as when GE's radar business decided to change from analog to digital electronics, may have profound implications for a component supplier. The monitoring of customer strategies, particularly of key customers, is of critical importance to suppliers.

Multiple Buying Influences

In Chapter 1 we identified multiple buying influences as a key aspect of business buying. Functional requirements for products are usually determined by those in engineering, R&D, or manufacturing, but they may also be determined by those in marketing, as illustrated in the Grasse Fragrances case. Delivery requirements are usually determined by individuals in manufacturing, but they also may be determined by those in marketing. Policies regarding relationships with suppliers and the nature of the purchase decision-making process are usually determined by individuals in the purchasing department, but they are frequently influenced by those in other functions and by upper management.

Although multiple buying influences exist, the degree of influence exerted and the involvement of various individuals in specific purchasing decisions varies enormously. As we discuss later in more detail, some purchases are relatively routine, such as highly standardized components purchased repetitively, and the purchase decision may be made by one individual at a relatively low level. Other purchases may be the culmination of long, extensive investigations, such as the acquisition of a large computer or the selection of an architect for a major building, with the CEO making the final decision.

Often the purchasing decision may be influenced by those outside of the buying organization. Architects and consulting engineers involved in plant expansions usually specify equipment characteristics and have at least some say in equipment approval. Specialists may be hired to assist the firm in purchases beyond its normal area of competence. In the paper industry the printer's purchasing decision may be influenced by the advertising agency or by the printer's customer, as described in the Leykam Mürztaler case.

Long-Term Relationships[1]

A key characteristic of business marketing is the recognition by both buyers and sellers of their mutual dependency. From the seller's standpoint, with relatively few customers, this emphasizes the importance of repeat orders. How well the supplier performs on current orders is a major determinant of future business. But the relationship goes beyond merely ensuring repeat business. Customers, for instance, can be a major source of new product ideas, and buyers and sellers can collaborate on joint market development activities.[2] From the buyer's standpoint, it is critical to have highly qualified suppliers capable of supplying the firm's current and future requirements economically and reliably.

The exact nature of the relationship between buyers and sellers varies. It may be close, with a high degree of trust and information sharing. Or it may be at arm's length, guided by formal processes and rules. With many exceptions, the norm in the United States leans more toward reliance on rules and contractual terms, whereas in much of the rest of the world, particularly Japan, southern Europe, and Latin America, there is more reliance on personal relationships, developed over long periods of time.

While the interdependency of buyers and sellers may be apparent, what may not be apparent is the extent of attention by those in purchasing to the management of the buyer–seller relationship. In fact, managing the relationship is one of the major objectives of the purchasing function.[3] In most firms, the development of comprehensive purchasing strategies, including searching for and qualifying suppliers, is a highly active process, usually led by those in the purchasing function.

Make versus Buy

Organizations often have the option to make rather than buy both goods and services. A classic example is found in the beverage can industry, where large beverage firms can make some or all of their cans and are able to use the credible threat of self-manufacture to put extreme price pressure on can suppliers. Services, with their relatively low capital requirements, are even more vulnerable to the threat of self-provision. Except for the most specialized services, such as investment banking or some accounting services required by law to be externally provided, even small firms can elect to provide a host of services internally.

Historically, firms have elected the make option, or provide internally, to ensure continuity of supply, to achieve cost savings, to ensure quality, or some combination of all three. Today there is a trend to more external sourcing for goods and services. GE, for instance, in equipping its new washing machine manufacturing plant in Kentucky, established a policy that the only certain in-house manufacturing activity would be final assembly. All other manufacturing activities had to be justified on a value-added basis or they were to be purchased externally. This trend is encouraged by concepts of the "hollow corporation," envisioned as a small core of activities surrounded by a network of external suppliers, or the "virtual corporation," envisioned as an organization that constantly changes its form as it responds to changes in its external environment.

Several factors are responsible for this trend. Carefully qualified suppliers are demonstrating they can ensure continuity of supply and quality of a good or service at least at the same level as those produced internally. Specialized suppliers not only may have cost advantages over internally produced components or services, but their use may free up capital needed for the core business. For example, Emery Worldwide's new operation, Global Logistics, expanded its transportation services to include warehousing of raw materials and finished goods for customers, taking material into inventory, maintaining inventory records, and reordering when inventory gets low. Federal Express provides a similar global logistics process for National Semiconductor Corporation that will give National a two-business-day delivery service to all its customers worldwide. Finally, external suppliers are frequently more responsive to the needs of the business than is an internal component.

Reciprocity

Many businesses do business with each other. Raw material suppliers, for instance, buy capital goods from firms that buy their raw materials. Equipment manufacturers buy components from firms and then attempt to sell their equipment to those firms. This has the potential of creating "You buy from me, I'll buy from you" agreements. In the United States, reciprocity is legal as long as it is not enforced through coercive power by one of the parties and does not substantially lessen competition. But even when it is legal, there is concern that purchasing decisions involving reciprocity may fail to take into account product quality, supply reliability, and other important attributes. Efforts to use reciprocity as a selling tool have the potential to alienate those in the customer's organization for whom product performance or price are of prime importance.

Competing with Customers

Suppliers may discover they are competing with their customers. Aluminum companies sell aluminum to can manufacturers and also make cans in direct competition with them. Siemens, a large manufacturer of electrical switchboards that use internally produced components, also sells these components to switchboard manufacturers with whom it competes. Multiproduct firms can compete with customers less directly. One GE business sells equipment used for testing jet engines to Pratt and Whitney. Another GE business competes with Pratt and Whitney to sell jet engines to the aircraft industry. For suppliers and buyers this raises a number of interesting questions—To what extent can the supplier's representatives be taken into the buyer's confidence with regard to future requirements? Which customer, internal or external, is favored in times of short supply?

Organization of the Purchasing Function

In large enterprises, purchasing can be centralized, decentralized, or a combination of both. The electronic businesses of GTE, for instance, with plants throughout the United States, established local purchasing departments for needs unique to each plant. But requirements common to several plants were combined and annual negotiations were held with suppliers to establish blanket purchasing contracts against which local plants could draw. In such situations, service to the local plant becomes an issue, as we discuss in Chapter 9.

International Aspects

The growth in international sourcing is closely related to the growth in exports and world trade. According to Monczka and Trent, international sourcing strategy progresses through four phases: (1) domestic sourcing, (2) foreign sourcing based on competitive need, (3) foreign sourcing as part of a sourcing strategy, and (4) coordinated global sourcing for competitive advantage.[4] Many aspects of a coordinated global sourcing strategy are simply logical extensions of a domestic strategy that seeks qualified suppliers who can reliably supply goods and services at the lowest possible price. For marketing strategy it is important to recognize the similarities and differences of domestic and international sourcing.

    The principal factors influencing the buying decision remain constant. Quality, availability, price, assurance of supply, and service are key considerations regardless of country of manufacture. On the other hand, the nature of buyer–seller relationships, product standards, language, country laws, and currency denomination may vary. The formal relationships between buyers and sellers in the German-speaking countries of Germany, Austria, and parts of Switzerland are in sharp contrast to the relatively relaxed relationships in Scandinavian countries. Except in the United States, the metric system is the world standard. The International Organization for Standards (ISO) is attempting to coordinate technical standards on a worldwide basis, but many standards still vary by country or region. English, frequently described as the language of business, is not the language customers in non-English-speaking countries prefer for business discussions. In France, for instance, the regional manager for ALCOA, having made an initial contact with an important customer who spoke fluent English, was told that all future conversations must be in French if ALCOA expected to do any business with the firm. The reliance on legal contract language in the United States is in sharp contrast with the reliance on personal relationships in Japan, countries in the Middle East, southern Europe, and Latin America. The legal system in the United States, the United Kingdom, and other common law countries is substantially different from the system in France, Germany, and other code law countries, significantly influencing contract formation and the location for resolution of disputes, should they arise. Finally, currency denomination for payment is always a contentious issue, raising questions of convenience and exposure to risks associated with currency fluctuation.

Professional Buyers

With some firms spending as much as half or more of sales revenues on the purchase of materials and services, it should be clear that purchasing decisions have a major impact on the firm's performance in operational and financial terms. There has been concern, however, that firms have not assigned professional buyers an appropriate role in the purchasing process.[5] Often, decisions regarding capital equipment may be made by those in engineering or manufacturing, based principally on functionality, with inadequate attention to price, terms, or other considerations. Similarly, decisions regarding raw materials, components, or services may be made by those in manufacturing, based principally on reliability of supply, with inadequate attention to price, terms, or other considerations. Although there is considerable basis for these concerns, there is a long-term trend toward giving professional buyers in the purchasing department a more influential role in defining the purchasing process and making the purchasing decision. At least in part this is due to the efforts in the United States of the education programs of the National Association of Purchasing Management (NAPM), which are designed to improve the competence of purchasing professionals. In 1975, NAPM inaugurated a certification program that to date has qualified some 23,000 Certified Purchasing Managers (CPMs). Similar organizations operate in most other industrial countries, and are linked by the International Federation of Purchasing and Material Management (IFPMM). In Japan, the counterpart of NAPM is the Japan Material Management Association (JMMA). In the following section we address the role of professional purchasing more extensively.

Professional Purchasing

Most organizations have a professional purchasing function staffed by well-trained, experienced individuals whose responsibility is to ensure the organization buys wisely. Once assigned primary responsibility for relatively mundane purchases, increasingly those in purchasing are playing a significant role in purchases of a wide variety of equipment. An extreme example is the 1992 appointment by General Motors of José Ignacio López de Arriortúa as its purchasing czar. Backed by GM's new CEO John F. Smith, Jr., López combined 27 separate purchasing divisions into one to increase the leverage of GM's enormous purchasing clout. Despite concerns about buyer–seller relationships, López demanded double-digit percentage price cuts from suppliers, shared proprietary supplier information with competitors, and shaved some $4 billion from the cost of GM's purchases.

As the scope of purchasing has increased, so has the influence of those in purchasing on the overall purchasing process. A leading purchasing textbook identifies the following objectives for purchasing management:[6]

1. To support company operations with an uninterrupted flow of materials and services.
2. To buy competitively.
3. To buy wisely.
4. To keep inventory investment and inventory losses at a practical minimum.
5. To develop reliable and effective sources of supply.
6. To develop good relationships with the vendor community and good continuing relationships with suppliers.
7. To achieve maximum integration with the other departments of the firm.
8. To administer the purchasing function in a professional, cost-effective manner.

To meet these objectives, the purchasing function is becoming more proactive in its internal and external relationships. Of particular interest to those in marketing are the policies promulgated by purchasing departments with respect to acquisition and evaluation of proposals and, more generally, buyer–seller relationships.

Acquisition and Evaluation of Proposals

The normative or commonly prescribed approach to the acquisition of proposals is to describe requirements in sufficient detail such that qualified suppliers can respond with quotes or bids that can be evaluated, with the award going to the lowest or best bidder. Subject to meeting certain constraints, it is generally felt that this competitive bidding process is efficient and results in competitive prices for the buyer. The constraints are that the dollar value of the purchase must be large enough to justify the bidding expense; that specifications must be clear; that there must be an adequate number of sellers willing to quote; that sellers must be qualified and want the order; and that there is sufficient time for obtaining and evaluating quotes or bids.

Evaluation processes are becoming more formal and sophisticated. Prospective suppliers may be evaluated with respect to technical or production capability, quality control, managerial capability, financial condition, and service capacity. For relatively standard products or low-dollar-value purchases the evaluation may be based on catalogs, financial reports, or other readily available data. For complex or high-dollar-value purchases the evaluation may include visits to the facilities of two or three suppliers. Table 3.1 illustrates how potential suppliers might be evaluated. Current suppliers may also be evaluated, either for continuation or for making a particular purchasing decision. Table 3.2 shows how Chrysler Corporation grades suppliers of electronic components.

When actual bids or quotations are being evaluated, factors used to evaluate prospective suppliers or the performance of existing suppliers can be combined with factors specific to the individual transaction to assist in making the purchase award. The purchasing department will often ask the engineering or operating departments to make an economic evaluation of competing proposals that will be used in combination with the price and evaluation of other factors to make the final determination of the best proposal.

Competitive bidding must be perceived as fair by suppliers. Two policies are prescribed to achieve fairness: (1) buyers must be willing to do business with every vendor from whom a bid is solicited, and (2) buyers must give a reasonable explanation to unsuccessful bidders why they did not receive the award. These requirements may seem simple, but they are difficult to put into practice. Suppliers are not all equal. Buyers may prefer certain suppliers for legitimate reasons. Some evaluation criteria are subjective and sellers may not accept the buyer's evaluation. Discussion of price, even after the fact, may be seen as closely related to negotiation. As a result, many buyers avoid disclosure of details of their evaluation criteria or of their bid analyses.

While competitive bidding is the normative approach, there are extensive variations in purchasing approaches. When there is only one supplier, some form of negotiation is required. Many buyers insist on receiving cost

TABLE 3.1
Evaluating Prospective Suppliers

Factor	Maximum Score	Score Supplier A	Supplier B
Technical competence	15	12	10
Production capacity	20	15	12
Quality control	20	15	18
Managerial capability	10	7	8
Financial condition	10	8	7
Prepurchase service	10	7	9
Postpurchase service	15	7	11
Total	100	71	75

TABLE 3.2
How Chrysler Grades Suppliers

Supplier Rating Chart:

Supplier Name: _____   Commodity: _____

Shipping Location: _____   Annual Sales Dollars: _____

	5 Excellent	4 Good	3 Satisfactory	2 Fair	1 Poor	0 N/A
Quality 40%						
Supplier defect rates _____						
SQA program conformance _____						
Sample approval performance _____						
Responsiveness to quality problems _____						
Overall rating _____						
Delivery 25%						
Avoidance of late or overshipments _____						
Ability to expand production capacity _____						
Engineering sample delivery performance _____						
Response to fluctuating supply demands _____						
Overall delivery rating _____						
Price 25%						
Price competitiveness _____						
Absorption of economic price increases _____						
Submission of cost savings plans _____						
Payment terms _____						
Overall price rating _____						
Technology 10%						
State-of-the-art component technology _____						
Sharing research development capability _____						
Capable and willing to provide circuit design services _____						
Responsiveness to engineering problems _____						
Overall technology rating _____						

Buyer: _____   Date: _____

Comments: _____

Source: Courtesy of Chrysler Corporation.

information from the supplier and this may become a matter for negotiation. When the value of the order is small or when the time to place the order is important, buyers may elect to place the order noncompetitively or on the basis of informal quotations. Even when there are many suppliers, a firm may elect to do business with only one supplier. This is frequently the case when the buyer has adopted just-in-time manufacturing (JIT) and has established stringent performance expectations of the supplier. Hewlett-Packard, for instance, told its prospective JIT suppliers that one of its expectations of selected suppliers would be continuing price reductions.

When there are many potential suppliers, some firms choose to split their business between two or more of the lowest bidders to ensure continuity of supply. In another approach called stimulated competition, the buyer uses the original bids as a starting point for extensive discussions with suppliers on ways for them to reduce costs and thus reduce their bid price. Purchasing approaches within the firm may also vary, with sole source used for some purchases and competitive bids or stimulated competition for others.

Buyer–Seller Relationships

We previously stated that long-term relationships, sometimes stretching over decades, are a key characteristic of business marketing. A simplistic view of these relationships assumes that the principal, and sometimes only, contact between firms is by those in sales and purchasing. In fact, in many situations there is extensive contact between various members of buying and selling organizations. For example, specifying engineers frequently talk directly to design engineers, management representatives in both organizations interact in business and social situations, and order expediters talk to order processors or production staff.

These interactions suggest the need for formalizing buyer–seller relationships. Many firms have established written purchasing policies that attempt to describe the desired relationship. But given the complexities of most relationships, many policies governing them are informal and represent the views not only of those in purchasing, but also the views of other functions and top management. Recognizing these complexities is key to the development and implementation of marketing strategy.

Just-In-Time (JIT) Manufacturing

JIT is an approach to manufacturing based on the concept of achieving quality improvement and cost reduction by delivering parts and materials to the production process at the moment they are needed. Originated in Japan by the Toyota Manufacturing Company, JIT was adopted by firms throughout the world during the 1980s. It has significantly changed purchasing and buyer–seller relations.

The JIT concept is designed to reduce or eliminate parts and materials inventories and significantly improve product quality. For purchasing this has meant a major change in the approach to suppliers. At the heart of this change is the close integration of production of the buyer and suppliers, which is usually accompanied by a switch from several suppliers to one, or at most a few. Extensive sharing of information is required to facilitate rapid adjustment by suppliers to precisely meet the buyer's schedule of requirements. Suppliers are held to higher quality standards to eliminate the buyer's requirement for incoming material inspections. JIT suppliers are generally chosen for long periods of time as the degree of required integration militates against frequent changes in suppliers. In many instances this closer integration leads to a partnership in which suppliers assume responsibility for innovations in design, based on their greater insight into buyer needs. As previously indicated, it is usually expected that suppliers' costs will improve due to increased volume and increased certainty of orders, leading to the requirement that suppliers continually reduce prices.

For those in purchasing, the move to JIT presents several challenges. Dependency on fewer suppliers makes supplier selection and management of the relationship more critical than ever. Even carefully selected suppliers may be more interested in the increased volume than in the changes necessary to operate as effective JIT suppliers. As one industry representative said, "The easy one-half of the job of implementing JIT is doing it inside. The tough one-half is doing it with suppliers."[7] Supplier training, therefore, is a required part of the move to JIT, and the primary responsibility for this training rests with the purchasing department.

Not all firms successfully convert to JIT manufacturing. A major GE facility, which had moved to JIT and close partnerships with a number of its suppliers, concluded that further reductions in the price of materials and components could only be achieved by going back to many suppliers competing vigorously for each order. Many suppliers are unwilling to adopt the JIT philosophy necessary to be a successful JIT supplier. Others find it difficult to simultaneously supply both JIT and non-JIT customers. It is clear, however, that a good understanding of how JIT works and what customers expect of a JIT supplier is becoming important for an increasing number of firms.

The Battle of the Forms

Most of the discussion leading up to placing an order focuses on product specification, price, and delivery. Frequently overlooked are the general terms and conditions stipulated by buyers and sellers and included on the back of most purchase orders or quotation letters. These terms and conditions may state some relatively mundane requirements, such as the number of copies of invoices, but they also address the matter of responsibility in the event of failure of either party to perform. Inevitably these terms and conditions create conflict. Sellers attempt to limit their risk, particularly with regard to warranty provisions and possible failure to honor all aspects of the contract. Buyers, on the other hand, seek to hold sellers to the highest level of responsibility. The most contentious issues are *fitness for purpose* and *merchantability*, dealing with the

question of what is warranted; *cover,* dealing with the rights of the buyer to pro-
cure a product from an alternative source in the event of late delivery; and
damages, dealing with the obligations of the seller to reimburse the buyer for
costs resulting from product failure.

In the United States conflict over these issues has given rise to a phenomenon unique to business marketing, usually referred to as the "Battle of the
Forms," in which buyers and sellers strive to make *their* terms and conditions the
basis for the contract. In the exchange of quotation letters, purchase orders,
and order acknowledgments, each party insists on its terms and conditions. In
previous years, this resulted in what was called the "Last Shot Doctrine," which
held that, unless objected to, the terms in the last document to be sent formed
the basis of the contract. The Uniform Commercial Code (UCC), adopted by
most states during the 1950s, negates the Last Shot Doctrine and provides that
in the event of conflict between the parties' terms, the basis for the contract shall
be those terms on which there is agreement *plus* the provisions of the UCC on
those matters where there is silence or disagreement. In general, these provisions tend to favor the buyer. In particular, the UCC's treatment of fitness for
purpose, merchantability, cover, and damages is unacceptable to most suppliers.

The situation becomes more complicated when doing business across
national borders. Not only are desires of the contracting parties likely to differ
substantially, but there also is the question of legal jurisdiction in case of dis-
pute. To address this matter, the United Nations developed the Convention on
Contracts for the International Sale of Goods (CISG), which has many similarities to the UCC. If the buyer and seller are located in countries that have rati-
fied the convention (now including the United States and many countries in
Europe and Asia), then most contracts involving the sale and purchase of goods
will be governed by provisions of the CISG.

Inasmuch as the vast majority of contracts are completed without significant problems, the importance of terms and conditions is frequently ignored.
Few in marketing are expert in matters of contract law. Trying to reach agreement on specific terms may be contentious and time consuming. As a result,
sellers tend to give them little attention unless some event has occurred to
expose them to unanticipated liability. Purchasing agents, however, are constantly reminded of their importance, through seminars and the considerable
attention they are given in the trade press, and are likely to give them relatively high priority. While it is beyond the scope of this text to deal with all the complexities of either the UCC or the CISG, it is important for business marketers
to recognize their importance and to take appropriate steps to ensure that they
can live with the legal provisions of contracts as well as with the more familiar
matters of product specifications, price, and delivery.

Purchasing Trends

There is little question that the role of the purchasing function is changing. The
introduction to a recent book on purchasing asserted that "the revolution in
purchasing is challenging the traditional thinking that has dominated business

for the last twenty years. The adversarial relationship between buyers and suppliers is evolving into a new partnership, based on long-term business goals. Companies are now leveraging the role of purchasing to achieve competitive advantage in supplier quality, product delivery and new product development."[8] The importance of purchasing to the organization is indicated in a recent survey that found that two-thirds of CEOs and presidents now view the function as very important to the overall success of their firms.[9]

The exact nature of change will be determined both by those in purchasing and by the strategic situation of the firm. Growing professionalism of those in purchasing has the potential to expand their role and enable them to become involved in quality and customer satisfaction efforts and, more generally, in strategic planning. Purchasers will pursue partnerships with suppliers in situations where they can make unique contributions in areas such as product development or JIT manufacturing. In other instances, purchase price considerations will be predominant, as at General Motors, and suppliers can expect to face extreme bidding or negotiation pressure. While individual firms will differ in their approaches, the common theme will be increased proactivity by those in purchasing.

Buyer Behavior: Analytical Frameworks

The foregoing discussion suggests the complexity of the organizational buying process. In this section we introduce two models that are particularly useful in its analysis and in the development of marketing strategy.

The BUYGRID Model

To fully understand organizational buying behavior requires identification of the steps in the buying process and recognition of how these steps may vary, depending on the specific buying situation. A widely used study has identified eight steps, or buy phases, as shown in Table 3.3, and three categories of buying situations, or buy classes—new task, modified rebuy, and straight rebuy.[10]

New task buying involves a requirement or problem that has not arisen before. There is little past experience to draw on, and a great deal of information is needed. The buyer seeks alternative ways of solving the problem and considers alternative suppliers. New task buying occurs relatively infrequently but represents an opportunity for suppliers to get in on the ground floor and establish a position for subsequent purchases. All buy phases are involved in new task situations. Problem recognition can come from within or outside the firm. Determining and describing the characteristics and required quantity of the needed item involves many individuals within the firm. Opportunities may exist for suppliers to assist the process. The search for suppliers, and their qualification, is extensive. This is usually the last opportunity for a supplier to become established as a prospective bidder. Proposal solicitation and supplier selection involve many buying influences in the firm, all of whom need to be contacted by the supplier. The ordering routine goes beyond

TABLE 3.3
The BUYGRID Framework

Buy Phases	Buy Classes		
	New Task	Modified Rebuy	Straight Rebuy
Anticipation or recognition of a problem (need) and a general solution	Yes	Maybe	No
Determination of characteristics and quantity of needed item	Yes	Maybe	No
Description of characteristics and quantity of needed item	Yes	Yes	No
Search for and qualification of potential sources	Yes	Maybe	No
Acquisition and analysis of proposals	Yes	Maybe	Maybe
Evaluation of proposals and selection of suppliers	Yes	Maybe	Maybe
Selection of an order routine	Yes	Yes	Yes
Performance feedback and evaluation	Yes	Yes	Yes

Source: Modified from Patrick J. Robinson and Charles W. Faris, *Industrial Buying and Creative Marketing* (Boston: Allyn & Bacon, Inc., 1967), 14, to indicate the likelihood of activity in the various buy classes.

merely placing an order; it involves a wide variety of follow-up activities. Finally, the buyer assesses supplier performance and uses the assessment as a basis for placing future orders.

In the straight rebuy situation the routine is far simpler. The buyer has specified the product and has qualified suppliers. All that is required is solicitation of proposals that focus on price and delivery, with some form of performance review following the receipt of the good or service. The objective of qualified suppliers is to stay qualified. The objective of nonqualified suppliers is to provide evidence to the buyer to justify moving to a modified rebuy situation.

Modified rebuy situations can arise out of either new task or straight rebuy situations. Following a new task purchase, some modifications may need to be made with respect to future purchases. The objective of qualified suppliers is to stay qualified and, perhaps, influence specifications so they achieve a competitive advantage. In some instances, previously nonqualified suppliers may have the opportunity for reconsideration. Alternatively, poor performance by suppliers in straight rebuy situations or evidence of special qualifications of new suppliers may also lead to modified rebuy situations.

An Organizational Model of Buying Behavior[11]

Although the BUYGRID framework identifies the phases in the buying process and indicates how phases may vary depending on the buying situation, it does not address the interrelationship of organizational factors and individual factors that influence the decision-making process. Webster and Wind developed an excellent framework for better understanding and analyzing these interrelationships. They propose thinking about the individuals involved in any buying decision as belonging to a *buying center*[12]. They further propose that buying behavior is a function of the *individual characteristics* of those who make up the particular center, plus what they call *group factors, organizational factors,* and *environmental factors.* Finally, they propose that each of these four factors can influence the buying decision through a set of variables relating to the buying *task* and through a set of variables not directly related to the task at hand (*nontask*). Insights into the decision-making process within a particular buying center can be developed by identifying each of its determinants, for both task and nontask variables. A brief example of such use is shown in Table 3.4.

The starting point for analysis is to identify the individuals in the buying center. Webster and Wind define the *buying center* as that group of individuals who collectively interact in order to accomplish the objectives of the specific buying task. Roles within the center vary. Purchasing agents may select suppliers within certain parameters of delegated authority. Specifiers define required features and characteristics. Users influence specifications and supplier selection based on projected needs and past experience. Gatekeepers (e.g., receptionists, secretaries, librarians, and, sometimes, purchasing agents) control the flow of information or access to others in the center.

Within the center, the locus of influence may vary substantially. In some instances, all members of the center have equal say and influence. Increased product complexity, however, may shift the influence to individuals in the engineering function. Strong personalities may exercise influence disproportionate to their functional expertise, as when the purchasing manager overrules an engineering recommendation despite product complexity. Political aspects can shift the locus of influence, as when top management takes special interest in a large purchase perceived to have implications outside the organization. Finally, the number of individuals in the center may vary. In new buy situations, the center includes many influences; in a straight rebuy, the center may include only individuals in purchasing.

TABLE 3.4

A Classification of Determinants of Organizational Buying Behavior

Source of Influence	Task Variables	Nontask Variables
Individual factors	Desire for low price, short delivery, total cost, etc.	Desire for close personal relations, ego enhancement, cost, etc.
Group factors	Procedures to set specifications, buying committee processes	Off-the-job interactions among group members
Organizational factors	Policies with respect to quality, bidding procedures	Policies regarding community relations
Environmental factors	Expected trends in business conditions	Political factors in an election year

Source: Modified from Frederick E. Webster, Jr. and Yoram Wind, *Organizational Buying Behavior* (Englewood Cliffs, NJ: Prentice-Hall, Inc., ©, 1972), 29. Reprinted by permission of Prentice-Hall, Inc., Upper Saddle River, NJ 07458.

Business purchasing is characterized as a rational process and hence unemotional. In fact, the behavior of *individuals* in the buying center is very much influenced by their personal needs, goals, habits, past experience, information, and attitudes. Buying center members form a *group* whose previous interactions and social experiences establish a set of shared values and patterns of communication that direct and constrain the behavior of individuals in the group. *Organizational factors* such as objectives, policies, procedures, structure, and reward systems define the formal organization as an entity and significantly influence the buying process at all stages. Finally, *environmental factors*, including the influence of market stimuli and technical, political, and economic characteristics of the society influence the organization, its members, and its patterns of interaction.

These four factors are, in turn, influenced by task and nontask variables. Task variables relate directly to the objectives of the buying task. Examples include an individual's desire to obtain the lowest price, meetings to set product specifications, company policies on product quality, and expected trends in business conditions. Nontask variables include personal values of a religious nature, off-the-job interactions among company employees, company policies on community relations, and social or political trends.

Implications for Marketing

We conclude this section by reiterating the importance of understanding organizational buyer behavior. Marketing strategy must consider the wide variation in customer situations and purchasing practices. Sales representatives may have the opportunity to influence the nature of purchasing practices, particularly with respect to evaluation approaches. As we discuss in Chapter 6, the nature of purchasing practices is usually a key segmentation variable. In many cases, market research will focus on just a few customers but must ensure inclusion of the views of the many individuals who make up a buying center or decision-making unit. Product, price, and distribution decisions and overall promotion strategy will be determined, in large part, by the purchasing practices of the targeted market segment. The customer's strategic situation may indicate opportunities for joint market development activities.

While formulation of marketing strategy needs to assess a variety of customer situations, implementation of strategy, usually the responsibility of the field sales force, needs to be based on in-depth understanding of each assigned account. As we discuss in Chapter 9, the ability of individual salespersons to diagnose and understand the decision-making process for each account is critical to sales success.

Summary

Understanding how organizations buy is a fundamental prerequisite to the development of marketing plans and their implementation. Such understanding must take into account the key aspects of organizational buying behavior: derived demand, multiple buying influences, long-term relationships, the customer's ability to make or buy, the possibility of competing with one's customers, the various ways in which the purchasing function may be organized, and the growth in international sourcing. It must also consider the growth in professionalism of the purchasing function and the increasing influence of those in purchasing or buying decisions. A number of models have been developed to assist in analyzing organizational buying behavior. Two models particularly useful for marketers in developing marketing plans for understanding how individual customers buy are the BUYGRID model and the organizational model of buying behavior developed by Webster and Wind.

Overview of Chapter Cases

✳ The DIPROD case describes the dilemma of a relatively new buyer considering four very different bids for a large annual chemical contract. The firm has well-defined purchasing objectives and a statement of its purchasing policies that was given to all new suppliers. The case provides the opportunity to consider the purchasing decision from the perspective of the buyer and the implications of the decision-making process for marketing strategy.

Endnotes

1. In the readings we have included "The Development of Buyer–Seller Relationships in Industrial Markets" by David Ford, which discusses some of the basic concepts developed by the IMP (Industrial Marketing and Purchasing) group in Europe. An outstanding collection of work of this group is contained in *Understanding Business Markets: Interaction, Relationships and Networks,* ed. David Ford (San Diego: Academic Press, Inc., 1990).

2. See, for instance, Cornelius Herstatt and Eric von Hippel, "FROM EXPERIENCE: Developing New Product Concepts Via the Lead User Method: A Case Study in a Low-Tech Field," *Journal of Product Innovation Management* 9 (1992): 213–221.

3. See, for instance, Lars-Erik Gadde and Hakan Hakansson, *Professional Purchasing* (New York: Routledge, 1993).

4. R.M. Monczka and R.J. Trent, "Global Sourcing: A Development Approach," *International Journal of Purchasing and Materials Management* (Spring 1991): 2–7.

5. Michael E. Heberling, "The Rediscovery of Modern Purchasing," *International Journal of Purchasing and Materials Management* (Fall 1993): 47–53.

6. Donald W. Dobler et al., *Purchasing and Materials Management: Text and Cases* (New York: McGraw-Hill, Inc., 1990).

7. Charles O'Neal and Kate Bertrand, *Developing a Winning J.I.T. Marketing Strategy: The Industrial Marketer's Guide* (Englewood Cliffs, NJ: Prentice-Hall, Inc., 1991), 13.

8. John E. Schorr, *Purchasing in the 21st Century* (Essex Junction, VT: Oliver Wight Publications, Inc., 1992).

9. William A. Bales and Harold E. Fearon, "CEOs'/Presidents' Perceptions and Expectation of the Purchasing Function," Center for Advanced Purchasing Studies, May 1993.

10. Patrick J. Robinson and Charles W. Faris, *Industrial Buying and Creative Marketing* (Boston: Allyn & Bacon, Inc., 1967).

11. This section draws heavily on Frederick E. Webster, Jr. and Yoram Wind, *Organizational Buying Behavior* (Englewood Cliffs, NJ: Prentice-Hall, Inc., 1972).

12. Most other models refer to the buying center as the decision-making unit (DMU), and elsewhere we will use this terminology.

Michael E. Heberling

The Rediscovery of Modern Purchasing

Much has been written about the emerging importance and recognition of the purchasing function by senior management. Firms are adopting a number of new purchasing strategies as a means to counter increased competition from both domestic and international firms. These include things such as quality purchasing, profit purchasing, strategic purchasing, and just-in-time purchasing. However, a review of the purchasing function over the past 75 years shows that many of the "new" ideas are not really new. They simply have been rediscovered. The relationship of purchasing with senior management during this period has been cyclical. Purchasing becomes important when management views its role in terms other than simply obtaining materials at low prices. This usually occurs during periods of market instability. Finally, a review of early purchasing data reveals that the relationship of purchases to wages and salaries was not significantly different then from that which exists today. ✳

Introduction

The purchasing function should play a major role in corporate strategic planning. After all, purchases are known to make up a major portion of the cost of goods sold for many industries. In manufacturing, for example, purchases average 63 percent of a firm's revenues. As shown in Figures 1a and 1b, the percentages for purchases are even greater in the wholesale (86%), retail (78%), and utility (86%) industries.[1] In spite of these high percentages, senior management historically has given the purchasing function only cursory attention. Consider the following statement that appeared in a recent research report.

At the time this article was written, Lt. Col. Michael E. Heberling was Head of the Graduate Acquisition Management Department at the Air Force Institute of Technology in Wright-Patterson AFB, Ohio. Colonel Heberling received his Ph.D. degree in purchasing and materials management from Michigan State University. *Source:* Reprinted with permission from the publisher, the National Association of Purchasing Management, "The Rediscovery of Modern Purchasing," by Michael E. Heberling, *International Journal of Purchasing and Materials Management*, Fall 1993, Volume 38, Number 4, pp. 48–53.

A careful review of the purchasing management literature shows that the importance of the purchasing function in corporate performance has not been fully recognized in the United States. Traditionally, purchasing has been treated as a lower level operating function that has little to do with overall corporate competitive strategy.[2]

In this century, when senior management has taken an active interest in the purchasing function, it has more than likely been during a period of intense business upheaval. The following situations fall into this category: (1) war, (2) supply shortages, (3) high interest rates, and (4) intense competition. Unfortunately, the elevated interest in purchasing by senior management is usually ephemeral. Hence, the importance of purchasing in many firms has been cyclical over the past 75 years—importance fades into obscurity, then is followed by rediscovery.

Management and the Purchasing Function

Today, the purchasing function is once again in the forefront of corporate attention, due largely to

FIGURE 1a
Expenditures by Industry, 1982

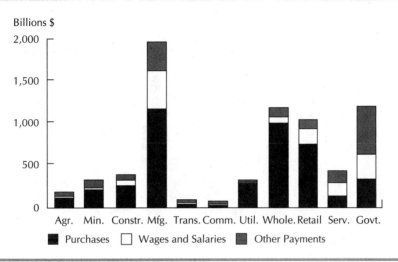

the pressure of intense foreign competition. To meet this challenge, management is directing its attention to several critical purchasing strategies. These include:

Quality Purchasing. Too often the question of price is the determining factor in buying. Little consideration is given to other phases of the transaction. The buyer must consider price and quality together. For one's special and particular needs, the highest quality may be the cheapest.

Profit Purchasing. This country has traditionally solved the problem of getting more profit by making more sales. Conservation of natural resources and competition have forced a realization. An increase in advertising and marketing will not increase profits in proportion to the increase in expenses; hence, the need for reducing costs.

Strategic Purchasing. The purchasing department makes a large proportion of the expenditures for a business. The success of a business is a function of the amount of thought given to this department and the judiciousness with which the purchases are made. The success or failure of a business may be the direct result of good or bad buying.

Just-In-Time Purchasing. The buying function should furnish the goods and materials at the time and in the quantity required. Buying at inopportune times or in excess of requirements is liable to entail severe losses. An accumulation of goods and supplies beyond what is required means the following losses are incurred: depreciation, insurance, value of space occupied, and loss of interest on investment.

While the above topics are current, the discussions that follow them are not. In fact, all the narratives come from the book, *Purchasing, Its Economic Aspects and Proper Methods,* written by H.B. Twyford in . . . 1915![3]

Twyford was not alone in establishing purchasing fundamentals. Clifton Field made similar contributions to the purchasing profession in his 1917 book, *Retail Buying.* Field began his book with a very simple premise: "Goods well bought are half sold." This old adage, even in 1917, simply meant that carelessness or inefficiency in buying will complicate the selling function.

According to Field, "It doesn't matter whether the buying is done entirely by a proprietor

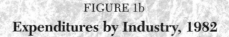

FIGURE 1b
Expenditures by Industry, 1982

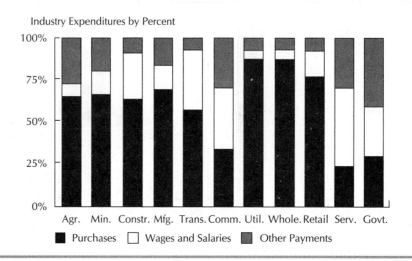

Industry Expenditures by Percent

■ Purchases   □ Wages and Salaries   ▨ Other Payments

or by a staff of a hundred or more buyers; the methods of good buying are fundamental."

Field's buying principles include the following:

1. *Know your customer.* To do an effective job, you must make sure that you know your customers' requirements.

2. *Know your competition.* Every buyer realizes that his or her firm is not the only merchant in the field. The competition largely regulates the selling price. Buying should be done in such a way so as to protect profits. Knowing what the competition is doing is as important as understanding the operations within your own firm.

3. *Know the buying market.* The buyer's knowledge of the market should be wide, specific, and as detailed as possible. The buyer should not only know the manufacturers and all the other supply channels, but should understand the level of reliance that can be placed on each. Answers to the following questions should be available: Where are the highest quality grades? Where can you find the cheap lines? How do the various firms stand on

deliveries? Which firms can you trust to fill emergency orders?

4. *Know what you are buying.* A buyer should have a technical knowledge of the raw materials and a familiarity with the manufacturing process. Also, the buyer should know the latest improvements in manufacturing methods as well as who the progressive manufacturers are. This approach provides an almost unfailing guide to buying quality goods at cheaper prices.

5. *Know the best system to store records.* The buyer who is systematic about his or her business can buy more intelligently. A thorough, though simple, system of invoicing, stock keeping, inventory, and record of demands is always essential. The buyer who devises and then uses such a system is laying the foundation for future progress. (It should be noted that although the concept that Field discusses still applies, today it would more likely be called a purchasing management information system (PMIS).

6. *Know people.* Much of a buyer's success is in proportion to his or her knowledge of the condi-

tions within and outside the firm. Understanding human nature enhances the success of any buyer.[4]

It is noteworthy that these purchasing fundamentals were written in 1917. They could easily serve as guidelines for a modern purchasing organization. The works of Twyford and Field clearly illustrate the existence of relevant purchasing principles well over 70 years ago. The real issue, however, is why did these basic tenets of purchasing repeatedly fall into disuse only to be rediscovered again and again? A review of purchasing history helps to provide some insight. Fearon wrote in 1968:

> . . . it is important to understand how the purchasing function has developed to the level and position it occupies today. A knowledge of what has happened in the past often will give one a keen insight into the problems of today and a better picture of what may occur in the future.[5]

A review of purchasing history in the first part of this century shows surprising similarities to the present.

The Beginnings of Modern Purchasing: 1910–1919

Although purchasing has always been an important function in business, little was done to formalize its role until the second decade of this century. One of the first books on purchasing was *The Supply Department*, published in 1911.[6]

In 1913, an article appearing in *Iron Age* suggested the need for a professional purchasing organization. This group "would serve to promote the interests of purchasing agents." One objective would be the publicity of their activities.[7]

In 1915, three significant events took place:

1. The founding of the National Association of Purchasing Agents, which is now the National Association of Purchasing Management (NAPM).

2. The publishing of the first purchasing periodicals.

3. The first offering of a college course in purchasing.

The flurry of purchasing activity during this decade may have been in large part the result of World War I. Although the United States did not enter that war until 1917, domestic firms had been supplying materials to the allied powers since 1914.[8]

The war put significant strains on purchasing departments across the country. This was due to a combination of the expanded production levels[9] and supply shortages caused by emergency restrictions placed on many commodities.[10] Consequently, top management began to focus on the buying function as a direct consequence of World War I.[11]

The 1920s

During the twenties, businesses were not subject to the pressures of material shortages or rapidly rising material costs as was the case in the previous decade. Relieved of these anxieties, management lost interest in the importance of the purchasing function.[12] This apathy may explain why the Harvard Business School decided to drop its purchasing course in 1922.[13]

A review of the 1929 census of manufacturers provides some insight into the purchasing function of the twenties:

- Materials represented the largest single item of cost for the average manufacturer (54.7%).

- 82.6 percent of the raw materials were of domestic origin.

- There were growing numbers of specialized purchasing officials in corporate materials organizations.[14]

Figure 2 was taken from the May 15, 1925, issue of the *Purchasor*. It shows a breakout of "all manufacturing" costs, categorized by materials, wages, and the balance (or remainder of cost). There are also nine specific manufacturing industries shown: (1) steel works, (2) coke, (3) slaughtering and meat packing, (4) cement, (5) motor vehicles, (6) silk goods, (7) furniture, (8) glass, and (9) jewelry. All ten graphs show similar data for selected years form 1899 to 1923. This data came from the *Monthly Review* of the New York Federal

FIGURE 2
Total Value of Manufactured Goods (1899–1923)

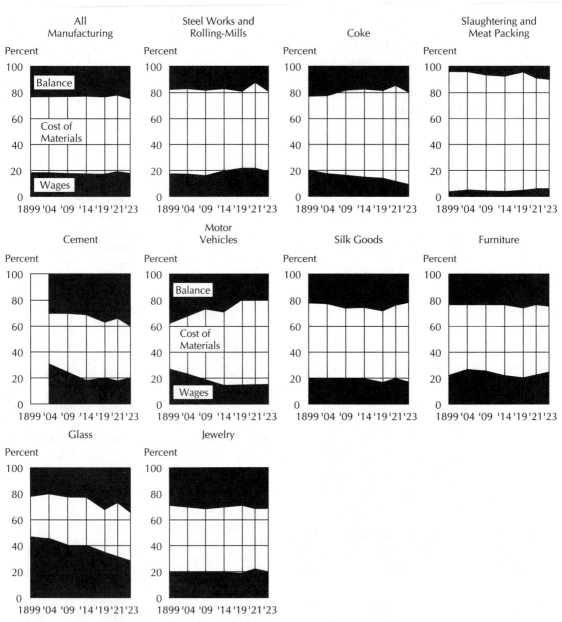

Percentages of total value of manufacturing products represented by wages and cost of materials.
Balance represents percentage remaining for interest, dividends, taxes, selling, expenses, etc.

Source: *The Purchasor*, May 15, 1925, adapted from *The Monthly Review*, published by the New York Federal Reserve Bank.

TABLE 1

Selected Manufacturing Cost Comparisons as a Percentage of Total Costs, 1923 and 1982

Type of Manufacturing	(SIC Code)	Materials		Labor°		Balance	
		1923	1982	1923	1982	1923	1982
Meat Packing Plants	2011	83%	80%	8%	7%	9%	13%
Furniture	25XX	46	42	25	30	29	28
Glass	3211	37	30	28	34	35	26
Cement/Concrete	3273	41	55	19	21	40	24
Steel Mills	3312	66	50	20	33	16	17
Motor Vehicles	3711	66	77	15	14	19	9
Jewelry	3911	48	55	20	20	32	25
Total Manufacturing	20-39	58%	51%	19%	21%	23%	28%

°Labor figures include fringe benefits and labor overhead support costs.

Reserve Bank. The following quotation comes from the article that accompanied the charts.

> These charts serve to emphasize the fact that losses or profits are greatly influenced by the ability to buy right. A savings of one percent in the cost of materials means more than the same percentage of savings on other items of cost.[15]

How different was the purchasing environment of the twenties when compared with more recent data? Using 1982 census data, it was possible to compare eight of the ten charts; the year 1923 was selected for comparison. Unfortunately, background information, such as the size of the data base, did not accompany the 1925 article.

The use of 70-year-old secondary data on purchasing presents a number of problems. For example, the use of cost of *materials* is not the best indicator of *total purchases*. In the case of the glass industry, materials make up only 52 percent of the total purchases, and energy purchases make up 24 percent of the total glass purchases. When all purchases are taken into account, total purchases represent 58 percent of the total glass industry costs in 1982.[16] This total purchase cost figure is 28 percentage points higher than the purchase cost for materials alone. The same problem exists for each

of the other seven types of manufacturing listed in Figure 2.

As stated at the beginning of this article, purchases in manufacturing made up 63 percent of the total cost, when *all* purchases are included. Table 1 shows 51 percent because it considers only the cost of *materials* and not the cost of other types of purchases.

However, the most striking piece of information in Table 1 is the absence of any significant change in the percentage of labor costs over the period of 60 years. This information refutes a rather common assumption in the purchasing field that, *in this century, labor costs have gone down and purchase costs have gone up as a percent of total costs.*

There are several possible explanations for this apparent inconsistency:

1. The number and percentage of hourly manufacturing workers has, in fact, gone down, but this has been offset by more salaried and support (or "overhead") labor costs.

2. The number and percentage of hourly manufacturing workers has gone down, but hourly and salaried workers are paid proportionately more than their 1920 counterparts, especially

when fringe benefits, such as social security, are included.

3. Both of the previous explanations are correct. That is, there are fewer hourly workers and more "overhead" workers, and both sets of workers receive far more lucrative fringe benefits than did those workers of the 1920s.

The 1930s

Ironically, the depression had little impact on the role or importance of purchasing. During this period, there were no material shortages, no rapidly rising material costs, nor was there intense foreign competition. This may explain why there were so few purchasing initiatives, either by practitioners or by academics.[17]

One important exception was the research done by Howard T. Lewis, a professor of marketing at the Harvard Business School. The focus of Lewis's work was on purchasing done by industrial organizations. He felt that industrial purchasing was a specialized function because of the knowledge and judgment needed to:

1. Anticipate the requirements of users.

2. Interpret price trends and market conditions.

3. Locate and determine reliable sources.

4. Negotiate wisely with suppliers.

To Lewis, the purchasing function was extremely important to the firm. This was especially true because of the large percentage of total cost outlays represented by purchases. In addition, he thought that the purchasing function played a critical role in the success of an organization in the sense that purchasing performance directly impacts profit through cost reduction, quality control, pricing policies, and customer goodwill.[18]

Lewis's interpretation of the importance of the purchasing function is of interest for two reasons. First, he reaches his conclusions independent of any previous purchasing research. His conclusions were the result of research done on the purchasing function in a number of large industrial settings. The second point is that Lewis's conclusions are remark-

ably similar to those that Twyford and Field reached 20 years earlier. It appears that Professor Lewis had simply rediscovered purchasing.

World War II

The conditions that advanced purchasing (albeit temporarily) during World War I were nearly the same 25 years later during the second World War. Again, the United States was a major supplier of war supplies and equipment years before its actual entry into the war. This time, however, the sheer size of the supply problems elevated the importance of the procurement function in the eyes of senior management.[19]

Purchasing becomes important when management views its role in terms *other than simply getting supplies at the lowest price*. This situation is apparent in Culliton's description of the purchasing function during World War II:

> In any business producing national defense goods, the procurement problem remains, as always, one of getting the things that are needed, when they are needed, and at reasonable cost. The concept of what is reasonable cost may well have changed under the present pressure to produce, since the most important objective of procurement has probably become that of *getting* what is needed.[20]

The 1950s and 1960s

The 1950s saw wide swings in economic activity. This precipitated three recessions in the decade and focused a great deal of attention toward cost-cutting efforts on purchased supplies.[21] Purchasing was increasingly being recognized as a major contributor to the profitability of the firm,

In this time frame, not only were there new developments in purchasing itself, but management was taking a new attitude toward the purchasing function. Messner notes that it took a war, or actually several of them (World War II, Korea, and Vietnam) to force greater recognition of the importance of purchasing.

Management was finally appreciating the people who control 15 to 20 percent of the income dollars in service industries and up to 60 to 70 percent in manufacturing industries. The people in purchasing should be trained professionals on a par with those in production, engineering, and finance.[22]

The 1970s and 1980s

Management once again took a major interest in the purchasing function during the two decades of the 1970s and 1980s. The oil embargo of 1973–74 triggered near economic chaos. The seventies and early eighties were characterized by soaring prices and shortages in materials. Purchasing managers played a major role in keeping their organizations solvent. A number of important lessons resulted from that experience. These included:

1. The need for more and better purchasing planning.
2. The uncertainty of a long-range supply of some critical materials.
3. The need for an intensive search for substitutes and alternatives.
4. The need for the purchasing function to take on global perspectives.[23]

Heinritz and Farrell note that none of the above lessons were actually new. However, the turbulent economic conditions of supply shortages and foreign competition had simply forced management, once again, to rediscover the importance of the purchasing function. They conclude that management had simply become indifferent to the potential inherent in scientific purchasing.

There were also a number of outside forces that would directly affect the purchasing department during this period. Government and private sector efforts to increase minority business participation, occupational safety and health requirements, and environmental regulations added to the already complex purchasing problems of the seventies and eighties.[24]

Conclusion

Even though purchasing makes up the most significant portion of the cost of goods sold in many industries, historically this fact has not registered with management. Consider the following two statements:

> One can find plenty of books devoted to the problem of reducing labor costs, but comparatively little literature can be found on the subject of scientific methods of buying. (*H.B. Twyford, 1915*)

> Management properly gives close and continuous attention to labor costs.... The material item is sometimes taken for granted, as if it were a fixed cost and nothing could be done about it. (*Heinritz and Farrell, 1981*)

Today, the marketplace presents many challenges for the business community and for the purchasing function. Perhaps the most notable recent change for business has been the increase in international competition. In response, businesses have adopted a global perspective in all of their operations. This includes foreign markets as well as foreign sources of supply. This strategy is probably the most significant change that has occurred in the purchasing function during this century.

This intense foreign competition may help to establish purchasing as a permanent rather than an ephemeral strategic function. After 15 years of almost continuous senior management attention, the purchasing function may have finally broken out of its historic obscurity/rediscovery cycle.

Corporate leaders are no longer viewing purchasing as an isolated cost generating function. Successful companies are turning to purchasing for competitive advantage. Purchasing is becoming an integral part of a strategic cross-functional team.

References

1. Michael E. Heberling, Joseph R. Carter, and John H. Hoagland, "An Investigation of Purchases by American Businesses and Governments," *International Journal of Purchasing and Materials Management*, vol. 28, no. 4 (Fall 1992), p. 41.

2. Charles A. Watts, Kee Young Kim, and Chan J. Hahn, "Linking Purchasing to Corporate Competitive Strategy," *International Journal of Purchasing and Materials Management*, vol. 28, no. 4 (Fall 1992), pp. 2–3.

3. H.B. Twyford, *Purchasing—Its Economic Aspects and Proper Methods* (New York: D. Van Nostrand, 1915), pp. 4–19.

4. Clifton, C. Field, *Retail Buying* (New York: Harper, 1917), pp. 3–12.

5. Harold E. Fearon, "Historical Evolution of the Purchasing Function," *Journal of Purchasing and Materials Management* (25th Anniversary, 1989), p. 71.

6. William A. Messner, *Profitable Purchasing Management: A Guide for Small Business Owners/Managers* (New York: AMACOM, 1982), p. 2.

7. Gary J. Zenz, *Purchasing and the Management of Materials* (New York: John Wiley, 1981), p. 2.

8. William A. Messner, op. cit.

9. J.H. Westing, I.V. Fine, and G.J. Zenz, *Purchasing Management Materials in Motion* (New York: John Wiley, 1969), p. 6.

10. Ibid.

11. Henry G. Hodges, *Procurement: The Modern Science of Purchasing* (New York: Harper & Brothers, 1961), p. 1.

12. Ibid.

13. Howard T. Lewis, *Problems in Industrial Purchasing* (New York: McGraw-Hill, 1939), p. vii.

14. U.S. Bureau of the Census, *Materials Used in Manufactures: 1929* (Washington, DC: U.S. Government Printing Office, 1933), pp. 43–44.

15. J.W. Osborne, "The Importance of Ability in Purchasing," *Purchasor,* May 15, 1925, p. 133.

16. Michael E. Heberling, *Purchases by American Businesses and Governments: Types and Dollar Magnitudes by Industries.* Doctoral dissertation, Michigan State University, Graduate School of Business Administration, 1991, pp. 186 and 190.

17. Harold E. Fearon and John H. Hoagland, "Purchasing Research in American Industry." Unpublished document, Michigan State University, p. 8.

18. Lewis, op. cit., p. vi.

19. Hodges, op. cit., p.1.

20. James W. Culliton, *Make or Buy* (Boston: President and Fellows of Harvard College, 1942), p. vi.

21. Zenz, op. cit., p. 2.

22. Messner, op. cit., p. 4.

23. S.F. Heinritz and P.V. Farrell, *Purchasing Principles and Applications* (Englewood Cliffs, N.J.: Prentice Hall, 1981), p. vi.

24. Ibid.

D. Ford

The Development of Buyer–Seller Relationships in Industrial Markets*

Introduction

It has frequently been noted that buyer–seller interdependence is a crucial characteristic of industrial marketing[1], i.e. that industrial firms establish buyer–seller relationships which are often close, complex and frequently long-term. Despite this, the nature of these relationships has, until recently, received scant attention in the literature.[2] Instead, marketing writers have been more concerned with analysis of the (albeit complex) process by which buying firms arrive at individual purchase decisions, and the ways in which the seller can influence this process in its favour.

This paper examines the nature of buyer–seller relationships in industrial markets by considering their development as a process through time. It is based on ideas generated from the IMP project[3] and is particularly concerned with the following factors:

- What is it that makes a buyer establish and develop relationships with one or a few suppliers, as an alternative to "playing the market"?

- How do the relationships between buying and selling firms change over time? What are the factors which aid or hinder the development of close relationships? Which of these are within the control of the two companies?

*The author acknowledges the contribution of Anna Lawson who read earlier drafts of this article.

Reprinted with permission from *European Journal of Marketing*, Vol 14, No 5/6, pp. 339–354. Copyright © 1980 MCB University Press Limited.

- What are the implications of close buyer–seller relationships for the two organizations involved? What problems can they lead to? How are the day-to-day dealings between the companies affected by, and how do they affect, the overall relationship?

Theoretical Basis

Buyer–seller relations can be examined with reference to the interaction approach as developed by the IMP group[4] as well as concepts drawn from the "New Institutionalists" within economics.[5]

The Interaction Approach

This sees buyer–seller relationships taking place between two *active* parties. This is in contrast to the more traditional view of marketing which analyses the *reaction* of an aggregate market to a seller's offering. The interaction approach considers that either buyer or seller may take the initiative in seeking a partner. Further, both companies are likely to be involved in adaptations to their own process or product technologies to accommodate each other. Neither party is likely to be able to make unilateral changes in its activities as buyer or seller without consultation, or at least consideration, of the possible reactions of their individual opposite numbers. Thus, industrial marketing and purchasing can properly be described as the "management of buyer–seller relationships."

The Nature of Relationships

Not all of the dealings between industrial buying and selling firms take place within close relationships.

There are clear differences between the supply of paper clips and automotive components, or lubricating oil and factory buildings. The product and progress technologies of the two companies are important factors in determining the nature of buyer–seller relations. Also important are the buyer and seller market structures which exist and hence the availability of alternative buyers and sellers.

Companies will develop close relationships rather than play the market, where they can obtain benefits in the form of cost reduction or increased revenues. These benefits are achieved by tailoring their resources to dealing with a specific buyer or seller, i.e. by making "durable transaction specific investments."[6] These investments mark major *adaptations* by a company to the relationship. By definition, they are not marketable, or at least their value in other transactions is less than in the specialised use for which they were intended. Therefore these adaptations mark a *commitment* by the buyer or seller to the relationship. They can be seen most clearly in such things as a supplier's development of a special product for a customer, a buyer's modification of a production process to accommodate a supplier's product or the joint establishment of a stock facility in a neutral warehouse. On the other hand, companies can be involved in "human capital investments,"[7] i.e. alterations in procedures, special training, or allocation of managerial resources. These human adaptations produce savings by the familiarity and trust which they generate between the parties.

Overall Relationships and Individual Episodes

The complexity of buyer–seller relations and the importance of mutual adaptations means that the analysis of relationships must be separated between the overall relationship itself and the individual *episodes* which comprise it. Thus, each delivery of product, price negotiation or social meeting takes place within the context of the overall relationship. Each episode is affected by the norms and procedures of the relationship as well as the atmosphere of co-operation or conflict which may have been established. Additionally, each episode affects the overall relationship and a single episode can change it radically, e.g. a relationship can be broken off "because" of a single failure in delivery. In fact, this failure is more likely to be the culminating episode in a worsening relationship. Thus, only a partial analysis of buyer–seller relations is achieved by researching individual episodes, e.g. a particular buying decision. On the other hand, an incomplete picture is obtained by examining the overall atmosphere of a relationship, for example in terms of power and dependency. Thus it is important to analyse both individual episodes and the overall relationship, as well as to understand the interaction between the two.[8]

The Development of Buyer–Seller Relationships

This article is less concerned with the reasons for the choice of buyer or seller partners (although this is acknowledged as a question of considerable importance!). Instead, it analyses the process of establishment and development of relationship over time by considering five stages in their evolution. We should also note that the process described here does not argue the inevitability of relationship development. Relationships can fail to develop or regress depending upon the actions of either party or of competing buyers or sellers. Throughout the examination, the bilateral nature of relationships will be stressed, particularly the similarity of the buyer's and seller's activities. The five stages are illustrated in Table 1. Throughout the analysis we consider the variables of Experience, Uncertainty, Distance, Commitment and Adaptions.

Stage 1: The Pre-relationship Stage

Previous authors have stressed the *inertia* of buying companies, when it comes to seeking new sources of supply.[9] Buyers may continue with existing sources with relatively little knowledge or evaluation of the wider supply markets available to them. We will take as our starting point the case of a company which has grown to rely on a main supplier for

TABLE 1
The Development of Buyer–Seller Relationships in Industrial Markets — Summary

1 Pre-relationship stage	2 Early stage	3 Development stage	4 Long-term stage	5 Final stage
Evaluation of new potential supplier	Negotiation of sample delivery	Contract signed or delivery build-up	After several major purchases or large scale deliveries	In long-established stable markets
Evaluation initiated by:	Experience			
Particular episode in existing relationship	Low	Increased	High	
General evaluation of existing supplier performance	Uncertainty			
Efforts of non-supplier	High	Reduced	Minimum development of institutionalization	Extensive institutionalization
Other information sources	Distance			
Overall policy decision	High	Reduced	Minimum	
				Business based on Industry Codes of Practice
Evaluation conditioned by:		Actual: increased	Actual: maximum	
Experience with previous supplier	Commitment	Perceived: demonstrated by informal adaptations	Perceived: reduced	
Uncertainty about potential relationship	Actual: low Perceived: low			
"Distance" from potential supplier	Adaptation	Increasing formal and informal adaptations Cost-savings increase	Extensive adaptations Cost-savings reduced by institutionalization	
Commitment	High investment of management time			
Zero	Few cost-savings			

a particular product purchased on a regular basis, as in the case of equipment, or continuously as with a component.

In these circumstances a decision to evaluate a potential new supplier can be the result of a particular episode in an existing relationship. For example, a UK producer of consumer durables started to evaluate alternative suppliers following a major price increase by a company, which had until then supplied all its requirements for a certain product.

Other reasons which may cause evaluation of new potential suppliers include: a regular vendor analysis in which the performance and potential of existing suppliers is assessed; the efforts of a non-supplying company to obtain business, perhaps based on a major change in its offering, e.g. a new product introduction; some change in requirements or market conditions experienced by the buyer, e.g. a UK car manufacturer began evaluating overseas sources for windscreens following the move towards tempered glass for which there was a European capacity shortage.

Alternatively, the evaluation of potential suppliers can be the result of a general policy. For example, widespread industrial troubles in the UK in 1974 ("the three-day week") caused one manufacturer to adopt the policy of obtaining approximately 40% of its components from overseas. It then started a search to find and evaluate potential sources of supply to carry out this policy.

A company's evaluation of a potential new supplier will take place without any commitment to that supplier at this stage. The evaluation will be conditioned by three factors: experience, uncertainty, and distance. Experience in existing and previous relationships provides the criteria by which the potential and performance of a new partner will be judged—a partner of which the company has no experience. The buyer will face uncertainty about the potential costs and benefits which are likely to be involved in dealing with a new supplier. The costs can be separated into those involved in making a change to a particular partner, e.g. in a buyer modifying its own product to suit that of a new seller. Additionally, there are the opportunity costs involved in the continuing relationship, when compared with alternative partners, e.g. in a buyer having to accept less frequent deliveries.

The distance which is perceived to exist between buyer and seller has several aspects:

- *Social distance:* the extent to which both the individuals and organizations in a relationship are unfamiliar with each others' ways of working.
- *Cultural distance:* the degree to which the norms, values or working methods between two companies differ because of their separate national characteristics.
- *Technological distance:* the differences between the two companies' product and process technologies.
- *Time distance:* the time which must elapse between establishing contact or placing an order, and the actual transfer of the product or service involved.
- *Geographical distance:* the physical distance between the two companies' locations.

Technological distance is likely to be great in evaluations for the purchase of innovative products. Social distance will be considerable in all new relationships as the companies know little of each other. This is combined with large cultural and geographical distance when the companies are dealing across national boundaries.[10] Finally, the companies will be considering a purchase which is unlikely to take place for considerable time, with consequent apprehension that it will not come to fruition as desired.

We can now see the effects of these variables of Experience, Uncertainty, Distance and Commitment in the early stages of dealings between the companies.

Stage 2: The Early Stage

This is the time when *potential* suppliers are in contact with purchasers to negotiate or develop a specification for a capital goods purchase. This stage can also involve sample delivery for frequently purchased components or supplies. The stage can be characterized as follows.

Experience. At this early stage in their relationship, both buyer and seller are likely to have little experience of each other. They will only have a restricted view of what the other party requires of them, or even of what they hope to gain from the relationship themselves. No routing procedures will have been established to deal with issues as they arise, such as sample quality, design changes, etc. These issues can only be resolved by a considerable investment of management time at this stage. This investment of human resources is likely to proceed any investment in physical plant.

Uncertainty. Human resource investment will be made at a time of considerable uncertainty, when the potential rewards from the relationship will be difficult to assess and the pattern of future costs is undetermined.

Distance. There will have been little opportunity to reduce the distance between the parties at this early stage in their dealings.

Social Distance. There will be a lack of knowledge between buyer and seller companies as well as an absence of personal relationships between the individuals involved. This will mean that many of the judgments made of each company will be on their reputation, as a substitute for experience of their abilities.

Geographical–Cultural Distance. Geographical distance is, of course, beyond the control of the seller except in so far as it can be reduced by the establishment of a local sales office or by sending staff out to the customer on a residential basis. Cultural differences can only be reduced by employment of local nationals. The lack of social relationships means that there is nothing to reduce the effects of geographical and particularly cultural distance. This can result in a lack of trust between the companies. For example, a supplier may believe that he is simply being used as a source of information and that the customer has no intention of placing major orders or building a relationship. Further, the distrust of an individual supplier can cause a purchaser to place emphasis on cultural stereotypes—e.g. a customer may attach importance to the alleged "discipline" of German suppliers, as opposed to a lack of faith in "undisciplined" British suppliers.

Technological Distance. Inexperience of a supplier's product will emphasize any differences which may exist between the product or process technologies of the two companies.

Time Distance. In the early stage of a relationship, companies are likely to be negotiating about agreements or transactions which may only come to fruition at some considerable time in the future. This maximizes the buyer's concern about whether he will receive the product in the form specified and at the promised price and time. Similarly, the seller will be concerned as to whether orders being discussed will ever materialize in the way it expects.

Commitment. Both companies will be aware of the risks involved and will have little or no evidence on which to judge their partner's commitment to the relationship. In fact, it is likely that the actual commitment of both parties will be low at this time. Thus, perceptions of the likely commitment of the other company are strongly influenced by factors outside the relationship such as the number and importance of its other customers or suppliers.

The actions of seller and buyer in the future will be influenced by their initial assessment of the performance and potential of their partner. Their judgment of the place and importance of this relationship within the company's portfolio of suppliers or clients will also be important. Thus, a U.S. engineering manufacturer clearly separates those "development suppliers" from others, very early in their dealings. It is these suppliers who receive the customer's investment of time, money and expertise to build the relationship. It may be that one of the partners may seek to develop the relationship, while the other remains passive. Also, efforts at development may founder, either because of the unwillingness of the partner or the incompetence of the initiator in overcoming the problems inherent in the early stages of a relationship.

We can now consider the development of a relationship beyond the early stage in terms of the tasks of building experience, increasing commitment and the associated reduction in uncertainty and distance.

Stage 3: The Development Stage

The development stage of a relationship occurs as deliveries of continuously purchased products increase. Alternatively, it is the time after contract signing for major capital purchases. Staged deliveries may be being made or the supplier may have started work on the item. Both buyer and seller will be dealing with such aspects as integration of the purchased product into the customer's operations or pre-delivery training, etc.

Experience. The development stage is marked by increasing experience between the companies of the operations of each other's organizations. Additionally, the individuals involved will have acquired some knowledge of each other's norms and values.

Uncertainty. The uncertainties which exist for both parties in the relationship will have been reduced by experience. In particular, the adaptations required to meet the wishes of the partner company will have become more apparent and the costs involved in these adaptations will also become clearer. Each company will be better able to judge the adaptations to meet its own requirements. These include those made by itself and those which it should require from its partner.

Distance.

Social Distance. This is reduced by the social exchange which takes place between the companies. As well as increasing their knowledge of each other, these personal relations establish trust between individuals. Nonetheless, this trust cannot be based upon social relationships alone. It also requires personal experience of the other company's satisfactory performance in exchange of product or services and finance.

Geographical and Cultural Distance. The reduction in social distance also contributes to a lessening of the effects of geographical and cultural distance. However, in a relationship between companies in different countries, it is possible that the seller company may reduce geographical and cultural distance through the establishment of a local office and employment of local nationals as business builds up.

Technological Distance. The adaptations which companies make to suit each other reduce the technological distance between them. Thus, their respective products, production and administrative processes become more closely matched with each other. This produces consequent savings for one or both parties.

Time Distance. The experience of transactions means that the time distance between negotiation and delivery is eliminated in the case of continually delivered products. However, in the case of irregular purchases of, for example, capital goods, then each cycle of order and delivery can be marked by similar time distances. Nevertheless, the importance of this distance decreases as the companies' mutual experience and trust of each other builds up.

Commitment. Much of a company's evaluation of a supplier or customer during the development of their relationship will depend on perceptions of their commitment to its development. Efforts to reduce social distance are one way for the supplier to demonstrate commitment. Commitment can also be shown in other ways.

It can be indicated by "adapting" to meet the needs of the other company, either by incurring costs or by management involvement. It is useful to separate these adaptations into *formal* adaptations which are contractually agreed between the companies and *informal* adaptations which may be arranged subsequently, to cope with particular issues which arise as the relationship develops. It is possible that the formal adaptations between companies may be dictated by the nature of the industry, e.g. that special products must always be developed for individual customers. On the other hand, a supplier's informal adaptations beyond the terms of a contract are often an important indicator of commitment.[11] For example, one large UK buying organization lists a major criterion in assessing the commitment of suppliers to be their "flexibility," for example in arranging a rapid increase in supply to cope with a sudden demand change.

In the international context, a company can demonstrate its commitment to a general market. This can be done by setting up a sales or buying office in that market. For example, a UK manufacturer and a French company had not progressed beyond the stage of exchanging "letters of intent" to buy. This was despite being in contact with each other for over two years. It was clear that the buyer doubted the supplier's commitment to it or the market, because of its unwillingness to establish a French office or assign specific personnel to the relationship during its development.

Finally, a company can emphasize commitment to a relationship by the way it organizes its contacts with its partner. This includes both the status of personnel involved and the frequency of contact. For example, a British buyer of packaging machinery formed an unfavorable impression of the commitment of a Swedish supplier because of the lack of seniority of the people with which it had to deal and their slow speed of response in their contacts.

The process of development of an inter-company relationship is associated with an increasing level of business between the companies. Over time, many of the difficulties existing in the early stages of a relationship are removed through the processes we have described in the development stage. However, development does not continue indefinitely. The relationship can be discontinued by either party on the basis of their assessment of its potential, the performance of the other party, or of the actions of outsiders. Even if this does not occur, the character of a relationship will change gradually. The changes which slowly develop are of vital significance to both buying and selling firms and we now turn to their description.

Stage 4: The Long-Term Stage

It is not possible to put a timetable on the process by which a relationship reaches the long-term stage. This stage is characterized by the companies' mutual importance to each other. It is reached after large-scale deliveries of continuously purchased products have occurred or after several purchases of major unit products.[12]

Experience. The considerable experience of the two companies in dealing with each other leads to the establishment of standard operating procedures, trust, and norms of conduct. For example, a UK supplier of components to a German truck producer has arrangements for deliveries against three-month "firm" and six-month "tentative" orders. Prices are negotiated on an annual basis with an effective date of 1 January… "although we often don't get round to firming them up until well in the spring, so we just apply them retrospectively." Similarly, a UK producer of marine diesel engines will start construction of an individual unit costing up to £100 000 on the basis of a verbal order from a main customer. Formal orders often follow much later.

Uncertainty. Uncertainty about the process of dealing with a particular partner is reduced to a minimum in the long-term stage. Paradoxically, this reduction in uncertainty can create problems. It is possible that routine ways of dealing with the partner will cease to be questioned by this stage. This can be even though these routines may no longer relate well to either parties' requirements. We refer to this phenomenon as *institutionalization*. For example, discount structures may have become unrelated to developing delivery patterns, product variety may involve increased production costs for the seller whilst the buyer may be able to use a much narrower range of product.

These institutionalized patterns of operation make it difficult for a company to assess its partner's real requirements and so it may appear less responsive or uncommitted to the relationship. Institutionalized practices may also allow a company to drift into overdependence on a partner or incur excessive costs in its dealings. One company may exploit the other's institutionalized practices and lack of awareness and hence reduce its own costs at the expense of the partner. Finally, institutionalized practices of one relationship can affect a company's whole organization and hence its development of other relationships. For example, a supplier of high-grade alloys had become very heavily involved with a large domestic customer. It then attempted to transfer its experience with this customer to others in different market segments overseas. So many aspects and operations within this relationship had become institutionalized, or taken for granted, that the supplier was unable to modify its procedures to suit new customers.

Distance.
Social Distance. This is also minimized in the long-term stage. There are three particular features to the close relationship established by this stage.

Firstly, an extensive contact pattern will have developed between the companies. This may involve several functional areas and its aim will be to achieve an effective matching and adaptation of the systems and procedures of both supplier and customer. However, in the long-term stage the interactions by the different functions may become separated. For example, the technical problem solving between a supplier and its customers can become quite separate from the commercial transactions which take place. This can lead to problems of co-ordination and control if different departments are not to work in conflict with each other. For example, a German engineering company had 40 of its staff in constant contact with 12 people in a UK supplier. In view of this, the customer appointed a section head to "manage" the relationship. It was his responsibility to ensure that all of the separate interactions with the supplier were mutually compatible and in line with the overall policy of the buying company.

Secondly, strong personal relationships will have developed between individuals in the two companies. The strength of these can be seen by the extent of mutual problem solving and informal adaptations which occur. However, it may be difficult for an individual to separate these personal relations from the business relation. Difficulties can arise when company interests are subordinated to those of the personal relationships. This has its most extreme form in the phenomenon of "side-changing" where individuals act in the interests of the other company and against their own, on the strength of their personal allegiances.

Thirdly, in the long-term stage, companies may become personified in an individual representative. Indeed, it may be the seller's policy to identify closely a relationship with the person of their local representative. This may be of value in establishing a presence in an overseas market. However, it inevitably involves problems if this individual has to be replaced or acts in his own interests rather than those of the company. For example, a UK exporter of machinery had to re-negotiate spares prices charged to its main French customer. These had previously been fixed by the supplier's local representative at a very low level. This had been done because the representative was greatly concerned about the effects of losing this business on his own position.

Technological Distance. Successive contracts and agreements between the companies lead to exten-

sive formal adaptations. These closely integrate many aspects of the operations of the two companies. This close integration is motivated by cost reduction for both companies as well as increased control over either their supply or buyer markets. De Monthoux has emphasized the barriers to the entry of other companies to which this close integration leads.[13]

Commitment. By the long-term stage, both seller and buyer companies' commitment to the relationship will have been demonstrated by the extensive formal and informal adaptations which have occurred. Nevertheless, the seller company faces two difficulties over commitment at this stage.

Firstly, it is likely to be difficult for a company to balance the need to demonstrate commitment to a client against the danger of becoming overly dependent on that client. This was expressed by a UK supplier faced with a major customer as follows: "We want them to think they are still important to us. At the same time we also want them to believe that they must work for our attention in competition with other customers."

Secondly, a customer's perception of a supplier's commitment to a relationship may differ from the actual level. This is because the required investment of resources has largely been incurred before the long-term stage is reached. It is also possible that the level of business between the companies has stabilized. Thus, paradoxically, when a supplier is at his most committed to a long-term and important client, he may *appear* less committed than during the development stage.

We have now come "full circle" in the description of relationship development. We have reached that stable situation before evaluation of potential new suppliers which was our starting point. In this, a company may continue with existing sources of supply or customers with little knowledge or evaluation of the available supply or customer markets. However, before concluding, it is worthwhile to mention a final stage which buyer–seller relationships may enter.

Stage 5: The Final Stage

This stage is reached in stable markets over long periods of time. It is marked by an extension of the institutionalization process to a point where the conduct of business is based on industry codes of practice. These may have relatively little to do with commercial considerations, but correspond more to a "right way to do business," e.g. the avoidance of price cutting and restrictions on changes in the respective roles of buyer and seller. It is often the case that attempts to break out of institutionalized patterns of trading in the final stage will be met by sanctions from other trading partners or the company's fellow buyers or sellers.[14]

Marketing Implications

We have described how the development of buyer–seller relationships can be seen as a process in terms of:

- The increasing experience of the two companies;
- The reduction in their uncertainty and the distance between them;
- The growth of both actual and perceived commitment;
- Their formal and informal adaptations to each other and the investments and savings involved.

We can now turn to some of the implications of this process for the marketing company. The most obvious implication is that a company cannot treat its market in some overall way. Not only must it segment that market according to the different requirements of companies, it must also see its potential market as a network of relationships. Each of these must be assessed according to the opportunity they represent and how the relationship can be developed. The company's marketing task then becomes the establishment, development and maintenance of these relationships, rather than the manipulation of a generalized marketing mix. Further, this management of relationships must take place with regard to the company's skills and the costs involved, as well as the allocation of its

resources between different relationships according to the likely return.

Establishing Relationships

The existing relationships between buying and selling companies in an industrial market are a powerful barrier to the entry of another company. The barrier consists of the inertia in existing relationships, the uncertainties for the customer in any change of supplier, the distance which exists between user and a potential seller, and the lack of awareness or information about possible alternative partners. These factors are particularly significant in the case of overseas purchases,[15] where buyers may form stereotypes of national characteristics.

The marketer should be involved in the following activities to overcome these problems:

Market Analysis. An analysis is required, which goes beyond determining which markets or sectors to enter. This analysis must examine the relationships held by potential customers and existing competitors. Customers may be categorized into those with long-established supplier relationships for the product, or those in the development or early stages. It is difficult to generalize at which stage relationships are easiest to break into, although different approaches will be required depending on this stage. Thus, a potential customer in the early stages of a relationship with a supplier may be facing problems which require considerable management involvement. This may mean that the company is in a position to evaluate alternatives and is aware of the inadequacies of its existing relationship. In contrast, a company which has begun to adapt and become committed to a supplier, may be unwilling to face further uncertainty by considering a change. Thus, in the case of a satisfactorily developing or long-term relationship, it is likely that a new supplier will only be considered if there is some failure or particular inadequacy in an existing supplier. For example, we have pointed out that a buyer's perception of a supplier's commitment can decrease in the long-term stage and that problems may arise through institutionalized practices.

The analysis we refer to will indicate the required approach to different potential customers. Breaking into existing, early-stage relationships may involve emphasis on a broad range of factors, e.g. product specification, prices and delivery. Also, the approach may be to the senior management which is likely to be involved at this stage. The approach to customers with more established relationships involves determining the *specific* problems they are facing. Also, the seller must examine whether an attempt to solve these problems is within its capabilities. The company must question whether the adaptations it must make will provide adequate returns. Finally, it must tailor its approach to the individuals within the customer who are in the areas of the relationship where problems have arisen.

Developing Relationships. We have discussed the importance of commitment and distance reduction in the development of relationships. Those involve a supplier in human and capital costs—in an overall market. It is worth noting that commitment to a market normally involves investment, in the form of local offices, etc., *before* business has developed. This contrasts with the attitudes of many industrial exporters who seem only prepared to invest in a sales or serve operation *after* sales have been achieved.

The development of relationships can also be considered as a problem of strategy and organization. We must distinguish between the "strategic management" of relationships and the "operational management" of a single relationship. Strategic management involves the assessment of any one relationship within the company's strategy in a particular market or markets. Further, strategic management covers a portfolio of relationships. It is concerned with the interplay between them, their respective importance and the consequent resource allocation between them. It is difficult for those people involved in detailed interaction with a customer to see the relationship in perspective or to see the possible effective of institutionalization on it. It is because of this, that the strategic management function should be carried out by marketing staff who are not involved in the day-to-day operation of relationships.

A company's marketing structure should also follow from the nature of its relationships. A functional organization within marketing may be appropriate for a firm with a large number of small clients. However, the complexity of the interaction with major clients emphasizes the importance of co-ordination of all aspects of a company's dealings with a client. There is a clear role for a "relationship manager" as in the German buying company referred to earlier. This is someone of sufficient status to co-ordinate all aspects of the company's relationships with major clients at the operational level. This individual is the major "contact man" for the company. He takes overall responsibility for the successful development of a relationship. This is based on his assessment of appropriate resource allocation to that relationship and his orchestration of the interactions between *all* functions—product development, production, sales, quality, and finance, etc. This requires more than the kind of authority usually given to an industrial salesman or "key account executive." In fact, the relationship manager should be independent of those departments which he co-ordinates in managing his portfolio of important relationships. Relationship management is most likely to be seen in operational form in industrial export marketing. Paradoxically, the limited resources often allocated by the seller company to export business mean that one man is involved directly or indirectly in all contacts— hence providing effective co-ordination. The relationship manager has a vital function in the case of irregularly purchased products, e.g. capital equipment. In this case, there is a clear need to *maintain* the relationship between purchase opportunities, either using sales staff or by his own contact.

Our research indicates that industrial companies are more likely to invest marketing resources at the operational than at the strategic level, perhaps because of their more immediately apparent results. This means that many companies are better staffed in the sales areas than under such designations as market planning or market development managers. Thus, staff are often pulled between the separate tasks of day-to-day operations and longer-term strategic planning. Under these circumstances it is not surprising that strategic planning is inadequately covered in the company.

Maintaining Relationships. We have noted that perhaps the most significant aspect of long-term relationships is the problem of institutionalization. This can make a seller unresponsive to the changing requirements of its customers. The separation of operational and strategic management within the company's marketing is the key to reducing these problems. Strategic management includes a company's market analysis and points to differences in market sector and customer characteristics. Hence, it reduces the danger of transferring inappropriate marketing practices from one market to another. Strategic management involves a re-examination of the company's existing operations to see if they continue to be relevant to particular client relationships and market conditions. Finally, strategic management determines the resource allocation between different relationships according to their potential and stage of development. The over-emphasis on operational marketing within many companies means that they do not have the staff or . the time to re-examine those activities which have been taken for granted in the company's long-term relationships.

Final Remarks

In conclusion, it is important to emphasize that companies should examine their existing relationships whether home or overseas to see which of the stages described here they fall into. This examination should be a preliminary to an assessment of each relationship, as follows:

1. What is the likely potential of this relationship?

2. What resources are required to fulfill this potential?

3. Where do the threats to this development come from?

4. Where does this relationship fit within the context of the company's overall operations and resource allocation in that market?

5. Are the current efforts devoted to the relationship appropriate to this overall strategy?

6. Are we over-committed to this customer?

7. Finally, are our ways of dealing with this customer appropriate both to its needs and our strategy or are they dealings based on habit or history?

References and Notes

1. For example: Webster, F.E. *Industrial Marketing Strategy.* Wiley, New York (1979).

2. Exceptions include: de Monthoux, P.B.L.G. Organizational mating and industrial marketing conservation—some reasons why industrial marketing managers resist marketing theory. *Industrial Marketing Management*, **4**, 25–36 (1975); Blois, K.J. Vertical quasi-integration. *Journal of Industrial Economics*, **XX**, July, 253–72 (1972); Håkansson, H. and Wootz, B.A. framework for industrial buying and selling. *Industrial Marketing Management*, **3**, 28–39 (1979).

3. For details see: Cunningham, M.T. International marketing and purchasing of industrial goods: features of a European research project. *European Journal of Marketing*, **14**(5/6), 322–338, (1980).

4. *Ibid.*

5. See for example: Williamson, O.E. *Markets and Hierarchies: Analysis and Anti-Trust Implications.* Free Press, New York (1975).

6. Williamson, O.E. Transaction cost economics: the governance of contractual relations. *Journal of Law and Economics*, **22**(2), October, 232–62 (1979).

7. *Ibid.*

8. For a discussion of the methodological implications of analysis of episodes and relationships see: Ford, I.D. A methodology for the study of inter-company relations in industrial market channels. *Journal of the Market Research Society*, **22**(1), 44–59 (1980).

9. See for example: Cunningham, M.T. and White, J.G. The determinants of choice of supply. *European Journal of Marketing*, **7**(3), 189–202 (1973).

10. For use of a similar concept of distance in international business see: Johansson, J. and Wiedersheim-Paul, F. The internationalization of the firm—four Swedish case studies. *Journal of Management Studies,* October, 305–22 (1975). For an attempt to analyze the effect of distance on purchase behaviour see: Håkansson, H. and Wootz, B. Supplier selection in an international environment—an experimental study. *Journal of Marketing Research,* **XII**, 46–51 (1975).

11. Suppliers' informal adaptations are often referred to in the purchasing literature as "Supplier Value Added".

12. This does not mean that a single supplier has been responsible for all of a customer's requirements of a continuously purchased product or every purchase of a major item.

13. de Monthoux, *op cit.*

14. For further discussion of institutionalized practices in long-established markets see: Ford, I.D. Stability factors in industrial marketing channels. *Industrial Marketing Management,* **7**, 410–27 (1978).

15. See: Håkansson, H. and Wootz, B. Supplier selection in an international environment. *Journal of Marketing Research,* **XII**, February, 46–51 (1975).

Chapter 4

Strategic Analysis of an Industry

The focus of marketing strategy is on effectively meeting the wants and needs of carefully selected customers. But this is not enough. To be successful, a firm must meet these wants and needs more effectively than its competitors do. One of the goals of marketing strategy, therefore, must be to develop or exploit the firm's competitive advantage. Marketers must not only know how organizations buy, they must also take into account strategies of competitors and the complex interaction of competitive rivalry. Understanding this complex interaction and developing inferences for the development of marketing strategies is the goal of industry analysis.

The conventional approach to industry analysis is to consider the firms that compete with each other and how this competition, or rivalry, is influenced by external forces. Another approach is to consider the principal activities required in producing a good or service in its final form and then to develop an understanding of the role of each activity. Alderson, a pioneering marketing academic, argued for this approach through analysis of what he called the transvection chain; that is, all the transactions and transformations that take place going from raw materials to the ultimate good or service purchased by the final customer.[1] More recently, concepts such as "deconstructed" firms, "value-adding partnerships," and "virtual corporations" have been introduced, which focus attention on subsets of value-adding functions and the coordinated relationships necessary between firms to provide the total value-chain activities needed for a market offering.[2] Many of these concepts are included in what has come to be called business system analysis.

123

In this chapter we first provide the conceptual underpinnings of industry and business system analysis. We then outline a multistep approach to a marketing-strategy-oriented analysis that combines concepts of industry and business system analysis.

Industry Analysis

Market and industry analysis are closely related. In fact, some economists use the term *market* to include both buyers and sellers. For business marketers, however, it is important to distinguish between the two. Market analysis is concerned with discerning wants and needs of customers and how they buy to satisfy those needs. Industry analysis, on the other hand, is concerned with how to satisfy these needs better than competitors do.

The term *industry* tends to be used in many ways. Used broadly, it might include a variety of firms providing a wide array of goods and services. The telecommunications industry, for instance, includes local providers of voice and data service, long-distance providers of voice and data service, hardware suppliers of such products as digital switches for central office use or commercial institutions, and hardware suppliers of a wide variety of other products such as fiber optic cables, handsets, and, increasingly, personal computers and software. In some instances these goods and services are provided exclusively to organizations; in others they are provided exclusively to individual consumers, and in still others they are provided to both. Surrounding these goods and services associated with the telecommunications industry is a host of other firms who are major suppliers to the industry, such as contractors or providers of vehicles or maintenance equipment.

For some purposes it is useful to analyze an industry defined in broad terms. Growth of the overall industry, for instance, influences the available business for all firms and may determine significant investment decisions. Technology developments in one segment may have implications for those in another, even if the two segments do not compete with one another. Data compression techniques, for instance, are of interest to both providers of data transmission services and manufacturers of digital switches and other forms of computers. Defining an industry in broad terms, however, does not focus on immediate competitors—those with whom a given firm may compete for customers.

For this purpose we borrow, with modification, from Kotler[3] and Porter[4] and define an **industry** as *a group of firms that offers goods or services that are reasonably close substitutes for one another*. It should be noted that the analysis should focus on competitors at the business level. General Electric, for instance, does not compete in the marketplace as a corporate entity. Rather, its medical equipment business competes with the medical equipment business of Siemens, its light bulb business competes with Phillips' light bulb business, and so forth. Similarly, IBM's personal computer business competes most directly with firms such as Dell, Compaq, and Apple, whereas its mainframe business competes most directly with firms such as Amdahl, Bull, or Cray Research. The precise definition of the group will vary as a function of the purposes of the analysis. These might include:

- Identification of potential competitors.
- Identification of market niches not currently being served by other players.
- Anticipation of attacks by competitors on customer positions.
- Identification of competitors' weaknesses for potential attack.
- Learning successful strategies or skills from competitors.
- Identification of opportunities to cooperate with competitors.

In the accounting industry, for instance, the Big 6 seldom compete with small, local firms. They might, however, decide to identify and follow medium-size firms that have the potential to grow to a national or international scale or that have the capability to attack certain Big 6 customers. Similarly, manufacturers of electromechanical calculators such as Marchant would have been well advised to include manufacturers of electronic calculators, such as Sharp, as potential competitors. It is interesting to note that apparently they did not, in part because Sharp did not have extensive service facilities. What was not recognized was that electronic calculators would not require the level of service required by electromechanical calculators.

Definition of the group may also depend on the circumstances of the firm. At one time, a U.S. manufacturer of turbine generators might have identified only other U.S. manufacturers of turbine generators (such as GE, Westinghouse, and Allis-Chalmers) as comprising the turbine generator industry, although non-U.S. manufacturers might have been included if it was felt they were credible potential competitors. Today, the industry is global, and any industry definition of the group must include Asea Brown Boveri (ABB) of Switzerland, Siemens of Germany, and Hitachi of Japan.

Complete industry analysis, then, and the accompanying examination of competitive behavior, allow managers to gain a better understanding of the playing field on which a group of firms competes. Without such analysis, it is impossible to explain performance differences or discover opportunities for advantage between firms competing in the same industry. In addition, without such analysis accurate assessment of a firm's own strengths and weaknesses is difficult, as these strengths and weaknesses take on meaning in relationship to competitors.

Approaches to Industry Analysis

A number of frameworks have been developed to facilitate industry analysis. Scherer developed a model of industrial organization analysis designed to facilitate understanding of the basic conditions underlying demand and supply that influence industry structure which, in turn, influences industry conduct.[5] Perhaps most popular is the five forces model developed by Porter which examines rivals and how their strategies interact, influences of the power of buyers, the power of suppliers, the threat of substitutes, and the potential entry of others into the industry.[6]

Rivalry

At the heart of Porter's model are the firms that compete with one another for customer patronage. As we describe in Chapter 5, a major objective of marketing intelligence is to develop an understanding of these competitors and their strategies, strengths and weaknesses, possible aggressive moves, or vulnerability to attack. Within the industry we may find competitors with significantly different strategies. Some may concentrate on cost reductions, making possible aggressive pricing strategies. Texas Instruments, for instance, has long favored this approach to its semiconductor business. Others, such as Intel, may emphasize functionality, with relatively higher prices. For analytical purposes it is useful to identify competitors who appear to be following similar strategies directed at a given target market. We do this by using strategic group mapping.

Strategic Group Mapping. The purpose of strategic group mapping is to facilitate making strategic decisions, taking into account how the firm's strategy interacts with the strategies of rivals. In some industries all or most competitors may follow the same strategy. In commodity businesses, for instance, there may be little opportunity for product differentiation, and economies of scale may require that all firms pursue all possible markets. In such cases all firms will be in one strategic group. In most instances, however, there are considerable degrees of freedom with respect to strategic decisions, and competitors will follow different strategies. While each strategy is unique, competitors may be evaluated on major dimensions and then assigned to a strategic group consisting of firms following similar strategies. In the robotics industry, for instance, one key decision was which applications to target. Another decision was the extent to which systems integration services should be offered. Using these two dimensions, a map can be constructed, as shown in Figure 4.1, and used to visualize the consequences of actual or potential strategic moves of various players or to visualize potential strategic opportunities. Depending on the strategic question, maps can be constructed using other dimensions. In the robotics industry, for instance, one dimension might be the target industries.

Beyond the general insights this approach develops, such maps can be used to consider how rivalry might change, depending on strategic choices made by various players. In some instances significant barriers may exist between strategic groups. Distribution patterns, in particular, are difficult to change, at least in the short run. Other barriers may exist as a result of required key success factors, as we discuss later. In other instances, changing strategy may be less difficult, suggesting opportunities for offensive moves or the need to prepare for defenses against competitors' offensive moves.

FIGURE 4.1
Strategic Groups in the Worldwide Robotics Industry

Principal Approach

	Hardware	Hardware and Systems Integration	Systems Integration
Welding	Nachi-Fujikoshi Cloos Yasakawa Cincinnati-Milacron	Kawasaki KUKA	
Principal Application — Multiple Applications	Fanuc	GM Fanuc ASEA Robotics	Thyssen Ingersoll Rand Budd
Material Handling/ Assembly		Prab	

Estimated positions of principal players in the industry, based on "The Worldwide Robotics Industry 1987," IMD Case GM415.

Bargaining Power of Buyers and Suppliers

In some industries, such as can manufacturing, large buyers and suppliers are the norm. The threat of self-manufacture of cans by large beverage producers puts severe constraints on a can manufacturer's ability to increase its prices. Can manufacturers usually need the steel or aluminum supplier more than the supplier needs the firm, and large suppliers may have the capability to forward integrate, as in the case of aluminum cans, making them less responsive to the needs of the firm. Competing in industries where there is such homogeneity of suppliers and buyers severely limits the strategic choices the firm can make.

On the other hand, in many industries buyers and suppliers are heterogeneous, facilitating a much greater range of strategic options. Some firms may elect to sell to large, powerful buyers because the volume of available business is sufficiently attractive to offset the ability of the buyer to negotiate low prices. Such is the case with the steel manufacturers supplying the automobile industry. Other firms may elect to serve only customers for whom their product represents a small percentage of total purchases, thus reducing the buyer's incentive to aggressively negotiate for low prices. The Dexter Corporation, for instance, produces highly specialized materials such as a film used to coat the interior of beer cans. The film represents only a small percentage of the total cost of a can yet has important functional characteristics, so Dexter can pass on price increases relatively easily.

Potential New Entrants and Possible Substitutes

While the firm is most focused on its customers and competitors, it must also take into account the potential entry of new competitors as well as the possibility of substitutes. Industries with high profit margins and low barriers to entry are obviously attractive targets for new players. For the firms within these industries, this requires consideration of the extent to which barriers to entry can be created and the extent to which opportunities to raise prices should be forgone. Some barriers are structural, such as capital requirements, and cannot easily be influenced by the firm. Others, such as patents and switching costs, are under control of the firm and are potential elements of the firm's strategy. Pricing decisions not only need to take into account their deterrent effect on potential entrants but also the potential substitutes for the firm's product. For example, engineered plastics producers supplying material for automobile bumpers must consider the cost of potential substitute materials such as steel or aluminum.

The Business System

Porter's approach considers the industry in terms of firms that compete with one another and how their rivalry, and thus firm profitability, is influenced by four external forces. Business system analysis takes a different perspective. As Gilbert and Strebel have argued, "Many definitions of a company's business, or of its industry, have been too narrow: there is more to its business than a product, a process, and a market; there is in fact an entire chain of activities, from product design to product utilization by the final customer, that must be mobilized to meet certain market expectations."[7]

Gilbert and Strebel cite the example of the personal computer industry where the business system includes a wide range of activities: product design, component manufacturing, different stages of assembly, software development, marketing, selling, distribution, service and support to the customer, and the utilization of the product by the customer. They point out that each of these activities is expected to add value to the product so that it meets the needs of the customer. The search for competitive advantage requires an understanding of these activities and the relative value added by each. Hence, Gilbert and Strebel argue that rather than considering the company as competing in an industry, it should be seen as competing within a business system, where it is competing with other companies on the activities of design, component manufacturing, assembly of specific configurations, software development, marketing,

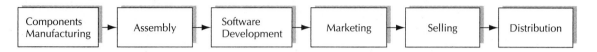

FIGURE 4.2
The Business System for the Personal Computer Industry

Source: Adapted from Xavier Gilbert and Paul Strebel, "Developing Competitive Advantage" in *The Strategy Process*, 2d ed., eds. Henry Mintzberg and James Brian Quinn (Englewood Cliffs, NJ: Prentice-Hall, Inc., 1991).

selling, distribution, and service to the customer. The business system for the personal computer industry might be mapped as shown in Figure 4.2.

The logic of business system analysis is based on the notion that competitive advantage is derived from offering higher perceived value, lower delivered cost, or both, than competitors. Achieving these objectives requires that all activities in the chain be coordinated. If, for instance, low delivered cost is viewed as the critical competitive parameter, then all the activities in the chain, including selling and distribution, must be managed toward this aim, even if the firm itself does not have direct control of a particular activity. Dell Corporation, a direct marketer of personal computers, is a classic example of a firm that matches low-cost manufacturing, done by others, with its low-cost selling and distribution.

Key Success Factors and Competitive Advantage

Of the many understandings developed through industry and business system analysis, few are more important than key success factors and sources of competitive advantage. These are often misunderstood and used interchangeably. Although related, they are, in fact, two very different things.

Key success factors are activities that must be done well or resources that must be thoroughly controlled to ensure that a strategy has the potential to succeed. In other words, key success factors are those activities or resources necessary for *any and all* firms that elect a particular strategy focusing on a particular target market. As such, they do not necessarily lead to competitive advantage. Because they are associated with a particular strategy, key success factors vary from one strategic group or one industry to another. As we see in the Grasse Fragrances case, players in the fragrances industry who have targeted large, multinational customers must have market research capability to assess how a particular fragrance might enhance a customer's product offering. Firms lacking the capability would not be considered as potential suppliers. Firms having the capability might have a competitive advantage, but only if the capability enabled the firm to meet customer needs more effectively than its competitors. Other key success factors include the ability to develop and manufacture a wide variety of fragrances and a worldwide sales force staffed with salespersons who can operate in sales teams. In the pharmaceutical industry, on the other hand, key success factors include the ability to develop patentable products, the ability to work with the medical industry and regulators to gain their approval, and local sales forces that can introduce new products to medical practitioners. In both industries, other capabilities such as advertising might be desirable, but not having them would not preclude a player from participating in the industry. In short, in identifying key success factors for a particular strategy, it is important to keep in mind that the activities assessed be industry-relevant and that the key success factors be strategy-relevant.

In contrast with a key success factor, which is mandatory to be a player in a particular industry, competitive advantage refers to some aspect of the firm's situation that enables it to meet customers' wants and needs better than its competitors. Competitive advantage can derive from a key success factor, as might be the case with a pharmaceutical firm whose sales force can introduce new products more quickly than can its competitors and so establish preemptive positions, or whose research and development efforts lead to products with strong patent positions. It can also derive from some aspect of the firm's position developed over time. For many years, its name gave IBM a competitive advantage over smaller and lesser known rivals that, in many instances, offered more functionality than did IBM and equaled IBM in service and reliability.

Although competitive advantage is frequently described in terms of a particular activity, resource, or position, such as new product development capability, access to financing, or a highly regarded brand name, it takes on meaning only if it is translated into superior performance in the marketplace, as perceived by the customer. Hewlett-Packard, for instance, has established an enviable record on college campuses, which enables it to recruit some of the best engineering graduates. As a result, Hewlett-Packard has an outstanding engineering competence. Even so, this is a competitive advantage only if it provides the customer with demonstrably superior products or services. Similarly, while many firms pursue, and achieve, low cost in order to develop competitive advantage, it is a competitive advantage only if customers actually see lower prices or favorably evaluate the firm for its past pricing moves, or if the firm's low cost dissuades competitors from aggressive pricing moves.

Two important aspects of competitive advantage need to be kept in mind. First is the need for realistic appraisal of the firm's situation. It is the authors' experience that competitive advantage is frequently overestimated, either through failure to think in customer terms or because of the lack of good marketing intelligence. Second is the difficulty of sustaining a particular competitive advantage. For example, experience effects associated with low cost tend to erode in mature industries and can be frequently avoided. Broad product lines, which make it easier for the customer to do business with one rather than several firms, may be difficult for one sales force to represent, particularly as products become more complex. Favorable evaluation of brand names, associated with past service or products, can erode, even with careful nurturing. This does not suggest that firms should not pursue competitive advantage.

Rather it emphasizes the importance of realistically appraising how the firm compares to its competitors and the need to pursue competitive advantage on an ongoing basis.

Industry Life Cycle

The concept of industry life cycle is closely related to the product life cycle discussed in Chapter 2. Porter points out that the product life cycle is the grandfather of concepts for predicting the probable course of industry evolution.[8] There are, however, some important differences, particularly with respect to time horizons and focus. Industries, like products, go through the stages of introduction, growth, maturity, and decline. Generally they do so at a slower rate than do individual products. The personal computer industry, for instance, is now some 16 years old and is still in the growth stage. Within the industry, however, product life cycles are shortening dramatically. Some products have already gone through all four stages and are no longer produced. As discussed in Chapter 2, the principal focus of product life cycle analysis is on the market and its response to marketing strategy. The principal focus of industry life cycle analysis is on competitors and their behavior. In terms of Porter's five forces model, Hill and Jones argue that industry evolution has major implications with respect to potential competitors and rivalry, as shown in Figure 4.3.[9]

Competitors' behavior, of course, is influenced by characteristics of the market. It is also influenced by structural shifts such as changes in capital intensity, technological changes that may impact product designs, changes in manufacturing processes, and so forth. In analyzing an industry from a life cycle

FIGURE 4.3
Competitive Rivalry over the Life of an Industry

		Stage of Industry Evolution				
		Embryonic	Growth	Shakeout	Maturity	Decline
Competitive Features	Price Competition	Low	Low	High	Normally low to medium, can be high	May vary from low to high
	Brand Loyalty	Low	Low	High	High	Generally high
	Overall Rivalry	Low	Low	High	Medium, can be high	May vary from low to high

Source: Modified from Charles W.L. Hill and Gareth R. Jones, *Strategic Management Theory: An Integrated Approach*, 2d ed., 89. Copyright © 1992 by Houghton Mifflin Company. Used with permission.

standpoint, the focus of the analysis is on the basis of competition and how it is changing and on the development of opportunities for competitive advantage.

Conducting the Analysis

We have previously indicated the importance of identifying the purpose of a particular industry analysis. All analyses should answer three general sets of questions:

- Is the industry attractive? Why, or why not? Attractive industries tend to be high growth, with high barriers to entry, capacity added in small increments, high profit margins, and suppliers and buyers with relatively low bargaining power.
- If the industry is attractive, what are the economic structures of the different activities in the industry? How might changes threaten the economic structure of each activity? If the industry is not attractive, what opportunities exist to improve its attractiveness? What changes are likely to occur?
- What are the main competitors' strategies now, and what are they likely to be in the future? Are there different groupings of companies that seem to be competing in a similar way? What are the differences, if any, in the profitability among strategic groups and among firms within the groups, and why? What are the key success factors associated with each strategic group?

Structuring the Industry Analysis Process

We suggest the following six-step process for conducting a complete industry analysis.

1. Establish the purpose and scope of the analysis.
2. Profile the industry.
3. Map the business system, both in terms of strategic groups and an activity chain.
4. Analyze strategic groups.
5. Analyze key activities.
6. Develop implications for marketing strategy.

Establishing the Purpose and Scope of the Analysis

The starting point for analysis is often a business issue or challenge such as declining margins, unsatisfactory asset turnover, market share deterioration, changing technology, emergence of new competitors or novel moves by old foes into new markets or segments, changing customer needs, environmental threats, or regulatory modifications. As with any other analytical exercise, the analysis should start by specifying the exact purpose of the task. The clarification of the purpose should also include attention to whom and in what form the analysis is to be presented.

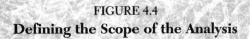

FIGURE 4.4
Defining the Scope of the Analysis

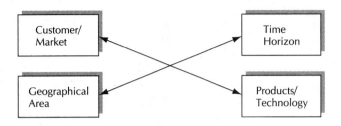

The statement of purpose helps in defining the scope of the analysis. Because the analysis is often conducted by a team of people, it is necessary to specify what should and should not be included in the analytical task. We have found it useful to define the scope in terms of the four broad dimensions given in Figure 4.4. The following are illustrations of how the dimensions may be used to focus the scope of the analysis.

Who	Customer needs/market served: (end user groups/end users served)	Hotel, restaurant, and catering markets
What	Product/technology/services:	Cooking stoves and ventilation systems
Where	Geographic area:	Nordic countries
When	Time horizon:	Analysis to cover the period from 1985 through 1997

Profiling the Industry

We profile the industry by first answering two sets of questions. Using the five forces model as a starting point, the first set of questions is:

- Who are the competitors? This should include both those that compete directly as well as those that are sufficiently close competitors that their strategies need to be taken into account as the firm formulates its marketing strategy.

- Who are the buyers, suppliers, potential entrants, and possible substitutes, and what are their major characteristics?

- What is the size of the industry, and what is its growth rate in physical units and dollar value?

- What are the key characteristics of the industry, in terms of its technologies, its capital structure, its manufacturing processes, and its position in the industry life cycle?

Then, using the business systems approach, the second set of questions is:

- What are the key activities that define the industry, regardless of who performs them, and what are the key cost elements?

Finally, its useful to think about an industry in a historical context. This enhances understanding of the changes that have occurred in the past and provides a basis for anticipating changes in the future. Plotting historical data such as growth rates, cyclical volume changes, seasonal fluctuations, profit margin changes, asset turnover fluctuations, technological breakthroughs, degree of vertical integration, and acquisition and merger patterns, gives clues to changes that have driven industry performance. Questions to ask include:

- What have been the key developments in production? For example, have manufacturing patterns shifted by volume or value or by country or trade area?
- How have patterns of international trade changed? For example, how have imports, exports, or the balance of trade changed?
- How have patterns of distribution changed? For example, how have the structure of distribution, logistics, inventory levels, etc. changed?
- How have consumption patterns changed? For example, what categories have increased or decreased? What about country or regional variations?
- Has the number of industry participants changed? Has it increased or decreased, and why?

Mapping the Strategic Groups and the Business System

One or more maps of strategic groups should be developed, plotting the firms identified as competitors on appropriate dimensions. Generally, the dimensions represent major possible strategic choices or options on which firms in the industry can build their strategies. Options include competing on cost or features, targeting domestic or multinational markets, selling direct or going through distribution, and offering broad or narrow product lines. For multinational firms the dimensions might also include options with regard to standardized or differentiated products and home country or dispersed manufacturing facilities.

The business system should be mapped on the basis of the five or six key activities necessary to meet expectations of the final customer. This map should take into account that some players will be involved in many activities, integrating either forward or backward, and others may be involved in only one or a few activities.

Analyzing the Strategic Groups and the Individual Players

The purpose of mapping competitors into strategic groups is to develop insights into the broad positions of the various players, the key success factors, the possible sources of competitive advantage, the potential moves of the players, and the barriers to mobility. For individual competitors the analysis needs to evaluate their strengths and weaknesses, their sources of competitive advantage, their vulnerability and likely responses to attack, and their possible aggressive moves.

Analyzing the Key Activities

Key activities are considered in detail for three reasons: (1) to develop an understanding of how and where value is added in the business system, (2) to provide a detailed framework within which to assess a firm's strengths and weaknesses relative to its competitors' activities, and (3) to develop insights for appropriate coordination of key activities in ways that will provide customers with the greatest value at the lowest possible cost. For each activity opportunities to decrease costs and increase value need to be evaluated. Similarly, it is necessary to examine threats that may increase costs and decrease value. These opportunities and threats should be consolidated into an integrated view that gives a complete picture of the industry. Starting the analysis with the most downstream activity ensures that the analysis takes place from the perspective of both the customer and the customer's customer.

Developing Implications for Marketing Strategy

The key purpose of the previous steps is to develop insights that will guide the formulation of marketing strategy and reveal opportunities for improving the internal operations of the firm. At a minimum, the analysis should sharpen insights with respect to:

- Key success factor requirements for a particular strategy.
- Sources of competitive advantage.
- Unserved, or underserved, market segments.
- Implications of market selection with regard to the negotiating power of buyers.
- Feasibility of various strategic options.
- Profit potential of various strategic options.
- Strengths and weaknesses of competitors and their offensive and defensive profiles.
- Strengths and weaknesses of the firm.
- Opportunities for integration or divestiture of key activities.
- Potential competitors.

Summary

Good marketing strategies require an understanding of the industry within which the firm competes, with particular emphasis on immediate competitors and the forces that may influence their behavior. They also require understanding where and how value is added in the business system. Industry analysis, a fundamental part of strategic marketing decision making, is closely related to market analysis, and in many instances the two overlap. It is, nevertheless, a very different form of analysis, with different questions and approaches. The specific issues or problems that dictate the nature of the analysis are related to the specific company situation. The analysis itself often uncovers additional important issues the company needs to address in selecting and implementing a certain market strategy.

Overview of Chapter Cases

❋ The World Flavor Industry case describes the industry in the late 1980s and the changes the industry was experiencing. It provides the opportunity to consider the strategic options for players in the industry as well as presents background information for the Toro Industrial Flavors case.

❋ The Japanese Construction Industry—1992 case describes the industry at a time of tremendous strategic upheaval. It provides the opportunity to consider how industry changes affect the role of sales and marketing.

❋ The West European Car Rental Industry case describes the industry in 1991. It provides the opportunity to analyze the structure of the industry, to consider the external forces influencing the industry, and to learn from the U.S. experience.

Endnotes

1. Wroe Alderson, *Marketing Behavior and Executive Action, 1957* (Homewood, IL: Richard D. Irwin, Inc. 1957).
2. See, for instance, James C. Anderson, Håkan Håkansson, and Jan Johanson, "Dyadic Business Relationships within a Business Network Context," *Journal of Marketing* (October 1994): 1–15, who argue that analysis of dyadic relationships must take into account suppliers, customers' customers, and a host of other ancillary firms.
3. Philip Kotler, *Marketing Management, Planning, Implementation and Control* (Englewood Cliffs, NJ: Prentice-Hall, Inc., 1994), 225.
4. Michael E. Porter, *Competitive Strategy* (New York: The Free Press, 1980), 5.
5. F.M. Scherer, *Industrial Market Structure and Economic Performance*, 2d ed. (Boston: Houghton Mifflin, 1989), 4.
6. Porter, *Competitive Strategy*, 4.
7. Xavier Gilbert and Paul Strebel, "Developing Competitive Advantage," in *The Strategy Process*, 2d ed., eds. Henry Mintzberg and James Brian Quinn (Englewood Cliffs, NJ: Prentice-Hall, Inc., 1991), 82–93.
8. Porter, *Competitive Strategy*, 157.
9. Charles W.L. Hill and Gareth R. Jones, *Strategic Management Theory* (Boston: Houghton Mifflin Company, 1992), 85–92.

Per V. Jenster
Peter Barklin

The Noble Art and Practice of Industry Analysis

The purpose of strategic marketing in any organization is through a thorough analysis of the firm's market opportunities and challenges, to determine the optimal way in which the firm can channel resources to increase the value for its share holders.

Therefore, the starting point for any strategic marketing problem is to solve business problems of strategic importance. Although much has been written on strategic marketing models, little has been written on how to actually carry out the work leading to a conclusive analysis.

This article takes the point of view of a management team undertaking a strategy development process. It investigates the practical work the strategic market analyst should go through to arrive at useful results.

As a generic prescription, the strategic market analysis is divided into three parts:

- Overview of the general market.
- Driving forces which impact industry relevant activities serving customer segments; we call this transvection process, the 'business system'.[1]
- Competitive dynamics, including analysis of players and the different ways of competing profitably.

Following this 'road map' in the analytical process, there are three key sets of questions which must be answered:

1. Is the industry attractive? Why or why not?
2. If attractive, how do the economics work, and what issues threaten attractiveness? If not attractive, which opportunities exist to improve attractiveness?
3. Which strategy can competitors pursue?

In order to illustrate this approach, we will use the European soft drinks industry as a practical example. In addition to this methodology, we will also summarize how data can be gathered from a wide variety of sources, and explain some of the specific data gathering techniques and sources used in the process.

Step 1

Determining the Current Attractiveness of the Industry

An industry's attractiveness depends on a specific company's point of view. A capital rich, but slowly growing corporation may look for capital intensity (to keep competition out) and absolute size (to be worth the effort). A smaller entrepreneurial company may look for requirements of special skills and emerging technologies (that the company masters). With only a few exceptions, all companies seek profitability and growth.

The criteria described in Table 1 can be used as a checklist. The list is not complete but provides a good starting point for your analysis. The further you go down this list, the more the

---

[1] Originally developed and used by consultants, such as McKinsey & Co., this approach to studying industries has gained popularity also amongst academics. At IMD, scholars such as Professors Bouvard, Boscheck, Gilbert, Kubes, and Strebel have further developed the academic side of business system analysis.

At the time this article was written, Per V. Jenster was a professor at IMD, Lausanne, Switzerland, and Peter Barklin was a partner, The Senior Management Company, London. "The Noble Art and Practice of Industry Analysis" by Per V. Jenster and Peter Barklin, *Journal of Strategic Change*, Vol. 3, 107–118, 1994. © 1994 John Wiley & Sons, Ltd. Reproduced by permission of John Wiley & Sons, Ltd.

TABLE 1
Factors Indicating Level of Industry Attractiveness

Profitability	The financial return on capital to competitors in the industry
Growth	The opportunity to grow businesses organically by keeping up with basic demand
Size	The industry must be large enough to be significant to 'serious players'
Customer/Risk	The more customers the less risk
Barriers to Entry/Exit	The difficulty for new competitors to enter the industry or old ones to leave
Capital Intensity	The relative amount of capital required to support revenue

criteria tend to be determinants influencing profitability and growth—the most critical factors. Arguably, the shortest possible list includes only profitability and growth. After all, who would not be happy to compete in a highly profitable and strongly growing industry?

The soft drinks industry has been very profitable and consistently so (Figure 1). The industry has also been growing very fast compared with most other related industries. Ask now 'So what?'. Maybe the industry is very profitable, because it is growing so fast? Or are there other explanations? Are all product categories equal in development (see Figure 2)? Can it continue to grow at these rates? The industry is clearly very attractive, but are there any threats to this?

Let us first examine the prospects for future growth. While this type of analysis should never be turned into a forecasting exercise, it is clearly useful to assess the likelihood of future growth. Ideally, you want to identify the growth driver(s), the

factor(s) determining why growth is so high and then try to explain growth prospects through an understanding of the driver.

The question to follow, then, must be *what is driving growth?* At this stage of the analysis you may not even have a clearly articulated hypothesis, and the best advice is therefore to turn to industry experts or veterans. Simply start to place telephone calls to people in the industry asking:

Why has demand for soft drinks grown so rapidly?

In this case, we listened to as many different answers as the 20 people we interviewed.[2] Typical answers were:

The changing lifestyle of consumers, the ease-of-use of the product, the advertising we do, the Americanization of our society, and our ability to develop products consumers want.

How can these influences be quantified—let alone be predictors for the future? They cannot. While they may all be true, you will have to find some tangible benchmark against which to judge future growth. We were able to identify three such pieces of 'hard data'.

Firstly, growth in consumption of soft drinks has historically been at the expense of other drinks (Figure 3). The underlying growth driver is not just population growth, but a trend explained by various changes in consumption habits, driving consumers away from traditional beverages and over to soft drinks.

Secondly, it appears that there is a relationship between national wealth and consumption of soft drinks (Figure 4). The richer the country, the higher the consumption per capita.

Thirdly, while European consumption averages 200 litres per capita per year and is still growing, U.S. consumption averages 300 litres per capita per year and is stagnant. What is more, U.S. consumption seems to be on a different relationship 'curve' between national wealth and consumption.

We then *hypothesized* that all the factors affecting consumption in Europe had already been 'discounted' in the per capita consumption in the U.S.

---

[2]This is also a good illustration of how an unaware analyst, by applying this structured approach, can actually 'add value' through highlighting different perspectives to decision makers who have spent a lifetime in an industry.

FIGURE 1
Return on Capital (Profit before Tax/Capital) Employed

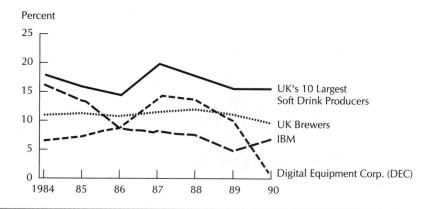

Source: Market reports, annual reports.

FIGURE 2
European Market for Soft Drinks

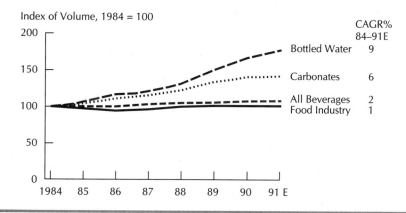

Source: Euromonitor, Canadean.

Using this information, we can start building scenarios for future growth of European industry. If we believe that the relationship between consumption and gross domestic product (GDP) per capita will continue to be true and that the U.S. market represents the highest possible consumption per capita and the U.S. market is saturated, then it is easy to calculate how much growth there is left in the European market. It works out to approximately 6 years at present growth rates, assuming Europe will reach the full U.S. level. To 'close half the gap', Europe has 3

FIGURE 3
Consumption of All Beverages in Western Europe

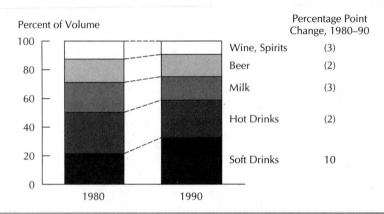

Source: Canadean.

FIGURE 4
Soft Drinks Consumption *versus* GDP

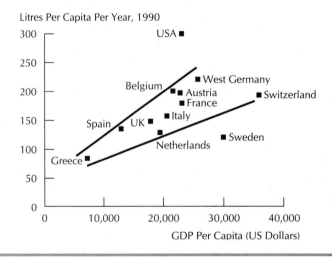

Source: *The Economist,* Key Note Report.

years of high growth left. The calculation is illustrated in Figure 5.

Without attempting to make exact predictions, we have built a likely growth scenario; that the European soft drink market has about 3–6 years

of high growth left. Regardless of exactly when growth slows, the issues of strategic importance are:

1. How will slower growth change the ways of competition in the industry?

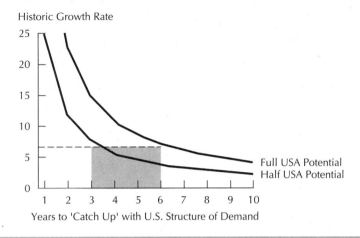

FIGURE 5

Relationship between Annual Growth Rate of and Demand for Soft Drinks

Source: SMC analysis assuming no growth in the U.S.A.

2. What will that mean to profitability?

3. Which actions can competitors take to prepare themselves?

In other words, we need to dig deeper into the dynamics of the industry in order to understand exactly how economic value is created and what changes are happening to threaten and to provide opportunities.

Step 2

Analysing the Business System

The vehicle we chose to do more detailed analysis has been termed the 'business system' (an old consulting tool, popularized by academics). It very simply consists of the chain of the major relevant activities necessary to develop, produce, market, and distribute products to end users. Once you have mapped out the chain, you have an analytical tool that will help ensure that no activity within the playing field is forgotten. Figure 6 shows the business system for the soft drinks industry.

As one examines each of the boxes of the business system, it should be kept in mind that

costs are added to the final product at each step of the way.[3] These costs can be accounted for (the number on top of the boxes indicates how much COST is added at each stage–shown as a percentage of price paid by the consumer). Ask:

What is happening to influence the size and variations of the costs?

Consumers are generally ignorant of the physical activities of bringing a product to market and only perceive the final attributes of the product/service bundle. Each competitor must manage the business system to create as much perceived value as possible, while incurring as little cost as possible. Ask:

Is the cost added at each stage justified by the value perceived by the customer, and what is the opportunity at each stage to create more perceived value at the same, or lower, cost?

Changes happening in each of the 'boxes' must be analyzed, and the impact on the industry as a whole considered. The strategic importance of

---

[3]It should be remembered that 'costs' are distinctly different from the 'value' created in the eyes of the customer. This is one reason why we prefer not to use the term 'the value chain'.

FIGURE 6
Business System for the Soft Drinks Industry

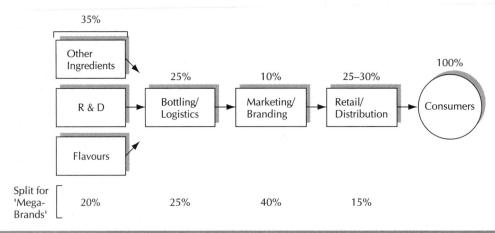

each issue should be evaluated so that issues not affecting value creation can be disregarded.

Usually, you will start by analyzing the 'consumers box'. For the soft drinks industry, we have already identified the threat to continued growth. Whenever you analyze food-based industries the health trend is likely to appear. The soft drinks market has been a high differential growth in DIET (low-calorie) products. But what is the strategic impact of this trend? We would argue that when (some) consumers demand sugar-free drinks, competitors simply have to respond by launching sugar-free drinks. **Doing so is not a strategic decision**—merely a response to a change in what customers want!

What then is a strategic issue? For European soft drinks customers, the most important issue is that they keep demanding more but will probably only do so for another 3–6 years. That is the issue which the strategy must address, as it is likely to significantly change the rules of competition!

Without dealing with each strategic issue in great detail, here is a list of the most important ones this business system analysis uncovered:

• The issue of private labels in the retail sector. For some products, mainly low-growth prod-

ucts, the share of private labels has grown to over 90%, posing a powerful threat to producers. If private branding of soft drinks really takes off, there will be pressure on margins, advertising will become less important, and hence require different competitive strategies.

• General concentration in distribution is intensifying, especially in Northern Europe, giving retailers additional power. The strategy must address how to secure retail distribution as chains become less dependent on choice of brands, more dependent on private labels and more powerful in deciding who should be their favoured suppliers.

• As margins come under pressure, competitors will seek to improve profits through more efficient operations. For producers of branded products this means focusing on marketing expenses as these represent the largest part of their cost structure. Producers who do not rely solely on branded products must focus primarily on production and cost of logistics. The pressure to operate more efficiently can be responded to by traditional cost cutting and by increasing the scale of operations.

TABLE 2
Apparent Competitive Strategies

	Type 1: 'Megabranders'	Type 2 'Premiums'	Type 3 'Low-cost Producers'
Anticipation of Lower Growth	Expansion in developing areas such as China, South-East Asia, and Eastern Europe	Segment/niche focus	Price competitiveness
Threat of Private Labels and Brands	Reinforce own branding	Segment/niche focus	Subcontracts to owners of own brands
Growing Retailer Power	Securing HoReCa through acquisitions and alliances Stimulates consumer demand through 'pull' advertising	(not observed)	Tries to secure long-term contracts
Pressure to be More Efficient	Pesistent cost-focus culture. Outsourcing and contracting	(not observed)	Low-cost focus in raw materials, processing, and marketing
Strong Branding through Marketing	'Mainstream' pricing through life-style advertising	Premium pricing through image of health/life-style	Cost focus. No branding, only selling
Merger Activity	Acquires bottlers around the world	(not observed)	(not observed)

Source: GENSTRAT GGM.

- In the branding function of the industry activity chain there has been a lot of takeover activity. This has happened in the belief that there are economies of scale to be achieved, a belief which is probably true (Table 2). This trend could easily intensify, especially when demand and hence organic company growth slows down.
- Competitors must consider what would happen if their relative cost position becomes eroded by other competitive activities to create scale.

At this stage of the analysis, you have now created a good helicopter view of the trends in the industry. To summarize, the industry is very profitable and rapidly growing but over the next 3–6 years growth will probably slow down. Margins will

probably come under pressure because of the private label threat and the growing power of retailers due to concentration. The best players in the industry should respond by becoming more efficient which, in addition to traditional cost reduction measures, could lead to merger and takeover activity in order to take advantage of economies of scale.

So, if the above represents the issues and general trends in the industry, what then should a company do to compete successfully and profitably? Which competitive strategy should be pursued? Are alternative strategies equally viable?

The answer, of course, depends on specific, company-related factors that are unique to each competitor. An industry analysis should therefore not seek to answer that question for individual

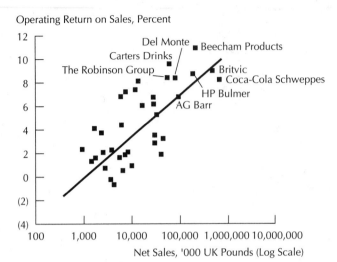

FIGURE 7

UK Soft Drinks Manufacturers 1990/91

Source: ICC Business Ratios Ltd.

competitors. Rather, it should identify generic strategies that could be pursued by types of competitors. Strategies must then be 'fine-tuned' at later stages in the strategic process involving detailed company analysis.

Step 3

Competitor Analysis

We believe it is critical to study existing ways of competition by examining activities and results of the industry's competitors and their evolution. In doing so, one should focus on how the key issues identified earlier are addressed by the various competitors.

Analyzing competition is an exhaustive and time-consuming process. First, one must understand the 'apparent' strategy followed by each competitor. Then the analyst must assess the degree of success each competitor has achieved.

The apparent strategy describes how the competitor addresses each of the key issues we identified in the business system analysis. After a

thorough analysis of all competitors, one should try to group them into meaningful clusters as we did for the soft drinks industry (Figure 7). 'Mega-branders' are the very large brand based companies such as The Coca-Cola Company and Pepsio. 'Premiums' sell specialized brands, typically with health and/or sports claims. 'Low-cost producers' sometimes have their own brands, but are primarily producing for retail chains' own labels. There is a fourth group that appears to be 'doing everything'; the companies in that group pursue very confusing strategies. An analysis of performance success shows that these companies are not very profitable and in some cases even loss-making.

We prefer to conduct a performance assessment which includes: (1) market performance, (2) operational performance, and (3) financial performance. It should be carried out in order to deepen the understanding and assessment of the success of each of the above strategies.

a. Market performance must include an assessment of absolute size and development in market share, growth relative to the total market, price realization, product range, consumer awareness, and relations to distribution channels.

b. Operational performance looks at productivity, capacity utilization, and other internal factors such as organization and management.

c. Financial performance includes study of key indicators. In the soft drinks industry, it seems more to be a function of size than of strategy. All categories, 'megabranders', 'premiums', and 'cost producers', are making healthy profits. Companies without clear strategies are not very profitable which is hardly surprising—this is the case in most industries we have analyzed.

At this stage of the analysis, you may find information that contradicts your initial hypothesis. If, for example, we had found that some competitors were addressing issues that we had not anticipated, we would have had to go back to the business system analysis and, maybe, completely revise our earlier conclusions. Fortunately, that did happen in this case.

Generating Strategic Options and Generic Strategies

In the final phase of the industry analysis, you should also apply 'wisdom' based on your findings in the preceding two parts. You need to make sense of the generic strategies in a way that will help you check consistency and spell out the actions of individual competitors in the context of the industry as a whole.

For this you need a framework. Clearly, many frameworks exist in books written on this subject, and there is no guide to help you pick the right one. Sometimes you can borrow from similar situations, other times you need to develop one from scratch. Our analysis uses the so-called HPV-LDC diagram, an analytical tool refined at IMD.

As mentioned earlier, customers trade-off perceived value of a product against its cost. Fortunately, not all customers make the same trade-offs so they can be grouped into segments. To illustrate, one group of customers is willing to pay a higher price for drinks with a health claim.

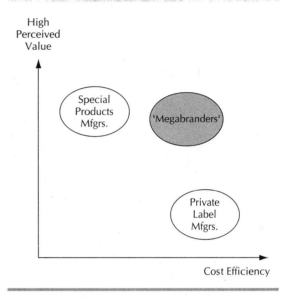

FIGURE 8
Organic Growth Strategies

Others simply go for the lowest price. Still others may be somewhere in between.

Figure 8 shows two viable strategies. The 'premium' companies (illustrated by the upper left circle) are able to create high-perceived value, although at a relatively high cost. These firms are still able to maintain attractive margins. Because there are customers willing to pay a premium price for that company's products, the company is able to make good profits following this strategy.

In contrast, 'low-cost producers' (illustrated by the lower right circle) focus primarily on costs, and may not be highly regarded for product quality, innovation, etc. However, because of the low-cost position, the company can sell products at cheaper prices, thus attracting a particular consumer segment. Although prices are low, so is the cost position gained through volume advantages, providing healthy margins with good profits as a result.

The megabrand companies such as Coca-Cola and PepsiCo are probably positioned somewhere between our two focused companies. Coca-Cola and PepsiCo may not have the lowest possible unit costs (because of large marketing expenses) and their perceived value may not be the highest in the industry (because others can emphasize specific product attributes such as health/sports), but because they can be almost as cost-efficient and deliver almost as high value as the best in the industry, they are able to sell at high prices leading to very high profitability, and as the customer segment is so large, this leads to large absolute size (Figure 8)!

The megabranders are almost outpacing competition but as long as focused competitors can find ways to create more value or produce at lower costs, they still can make money in their segments.

As our competitor analysis showed, it is the unfocused businesses—companies trying to be everything to everybody—that are in trouble (Figure 9). Because of scale disadvantages, nobody will be able to do what megabranders do.

Trying to create 'branded value' will definitely lead to higher costs. Trying to compete on price at the same time will lead to lower gross margins. In total, profits will be eroded and survival will be high on the company's agenda.

Growth through Acquisition

As organic growth in existing markets slows down, competitors will seek to grow through entry into other markets through acquisition of competitors upstream and downstream in the business system.

Let us examine some 'alternative' growth strategies, as these will affect every competitor— even the one who chooses not to pursue them (they may get their relative cost position eroded). Figure 10 shows the business system once again and looks particularly at the strategies followed by megabranders. The activities of megabranders should be interesting, not only for the ideas they can provide, but also because their actions are likely to affect the industry.

As market growth slows down Coca-Cola's and PepsiCo's traditional markets, these companies repeat their successes in emerging geographical

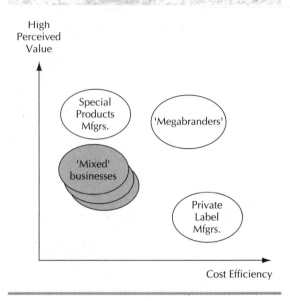

FIGURE 9
Organic Growth Strategies

markets throughout the world, leveraging off their core marketing skills. We have already discussed this 'option' which need not be acquisition-led.

The business system in Figure 10 can used to think about possible directions the 'megabranders' can take when making acquisitions. PepsiCo is probably the best example of a 'megabrander' trying to control distribution, simply by buying restaurant chains. PepsiCo and Coca-Cola are both very actively running 'armies' of vending machines.

Coca-Cola has begun to buy into its own bottling licensees in some highly developed European markets, and indications are that PepsiCo will be pursuing a similar strategy. The cost structure suggests that Coca-Cola potentially can capture another 25% of the retail revenue for its sales, which in itself is a growth opportunity. The real question is:

Does Coca-Cola plan any restructuring opportunities such as mergers, closures, etc. that could threaten other competitors on both cost structure and access to distribution?

FIGURE 10
Acquisition Growth Strategies of MegaBranders

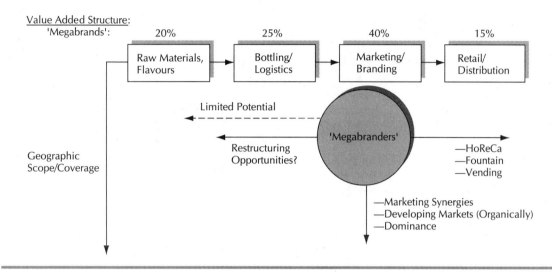

Opportunities for Nationally Based Competitors

Figure 11 shows the business system for nationally based competitors. There is evidence that mergers have already taken place between nationally based (smaller) competitors, and the number of competitors in the marketplace has certainly gone down.

Before thinking about growth through acquisition, the smaller player must be clear on which organic growth strategy he wants to pursue. How else can a company's strategy be consistent?

The 'low-cost producer' can think about further defending and improving his cost position through consolidation by acquisition of scale and subsequent realization of synergy potential in production, sourcing, logistics, and administration. It may even be possible to build a transport shield within a geographical area by building a dominant position in that area.

The nationally based 'low-cost producer' is probably too small to acquire distribution outlets but may seek to establish alliances with retailers by creating value for the retailer at low cost to the competitor.

The 'premiums' rely on marketing and may be able to exploit their brand names in a wider geographical area, thus achieving synergies by spreading expensive selling costs over a larger revenue base.

In addition, as we have shown, companies focused on specially branded products have an equally strong need to keep costs down, so most of the elements of low-cost strategies will apply to them as well.

Summary

The European soft drinks industry is currently very profitable and demand for such products is growing. However, growth is not expected to continue at these high rates forever, and when growth slows, competitors will be exposed to a number of issues that will put pressure on their margins and threaten their sales volume.

Every competitor should start preparing for these structural changes by first deciding which

FIGURE 11

Acquisition Growth Strategies of National Competitors

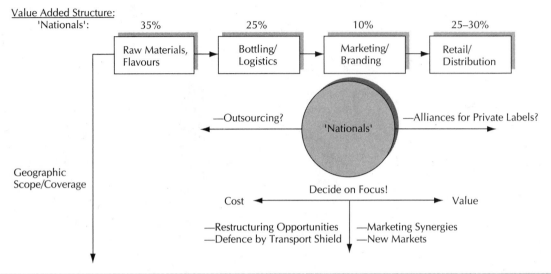

organic strategy to pursue and second considering how to respond to a likely wave of mergers and acquisitions.

The analytical process competitors should undertake (in continuation of this industry analysis) is:

i. Refine and expand this industry analysis to include the geographical area in which they compete.

ii. Perform in-depth analyses of each competitor within that area.

iii. Analyze in-depth, their own company in order to decide which strategy is the right one given that company's situation.

iv. Formulate action plans and start implementation immediately. The advantage of being the 'first mover' often determines the difference between success and failure, and the opportunity to move first will not reappear.

Conclusions

As mentioned in the beginning of this article, a strategic marketing analysis is the starting point for phases in a, say, strategy development project. What follows must consider the situation of the specific company as an integral part of the strategy process; its strengths and weaknesses as well as its general position in the marketplace.

This follow-on phase often uncovers important issues the company needs to address before it can implement a certain market strategy. This is because few companies are perfectly positioned to the realities of the market segment(s) it chooses to serve. These issues represent specific decisions that need to be taken in areas as diverse as marketing, product development, production, finance, and general management. Examples of such issues are organizational adequacy, depth/width of product range, pricing policy, choice of distribution channels, structure of capitalization, and even ownership decision.

It is the hope of the authors that this article will help initiate the strategic process and that it in turn will help management make better choices.

Pankaj Ghemawat

Sustainable Advantage

"If a man . . . make a better mouse-trap than his neighbor, tho' he build his house in the woods, the world will make a beaten path to his door." Attributed to one of Emerson's lectures in the nineteenth century, these words seem to have anticipated the exhortations of the twentieth: manage for uniqueness, develop a distinctive competence, create competitive advantage.

But that's not all Emerson had to say about investment in better mousetraps: he also remarked, "Invention breeds invention." What will restrain rivals from imitating or even improving on an invention? That question preoccupies the real mousetrap industry as it staggers from imported copies of its innovative glueboards and repeating traps.

That question is also central to competitive strategy. Strategists insist that for outstanding performance, a company has to beat out the competition. The trouble is that the competition has heard the same message. Deadlocks ensue. Look at the cross-industry findings about three competitive hot spots:

1. Product innovation. Competitors secure detailed information on 70% of all new products within a year of their development. Patenting usually fails to deter imitation. On average, imitation costs a third less than innovation and is a third quicker.[1]

At the time this article was written, Mr. Ghemawat was an assistant professor of business administration at the Harvard Business School, where he taught courses on industry and competitive analysis. His research and consulting focus on competitive dynamics and strategic investments. This was his second article for HBR. Reprinted by permission of *Harvard Business Review*, "Sustainable Advantage," by Pankaj Ghemawat, (September–October 1986). Copyright © 1986 by the President and Fellows of Harvard College; all rights reserved.

2. Production. New processes are even harder to protect than new products. Incremental improvements to old processes are vulnerable too—if consultants are to be believed, 60% to 90% of all "learning" ultimately diffuses to competitors. Production often blurs competitive advantage: recent studies show that unionized workers pocket two-thirds of the potential profits in U.S. manufacturing.[2]

3. Marketing. Nonprice instruments are usually ascribed more potency than price changes, partly because they are harder to match. Rivals often react to a particular move, however, by adjusting their entire marketing mix. Such reactions tend to be intense; limited data on advertising suggest that the moves and countermoves frequently cancel out.[3]

In principle, threats like these have always been part of doing business. In practice, they have multiplied with the intensification of domestic and international competition. How should a business cope with such competitive pressure? For guidance, we can turn from cross-industry findings to cases.

Keeping the Edge

This study of sustainable success grew out of a sample of 100 businesses that far outperformed their industries in the recent past. Not all of them promise to be as successful in the coming decade. The vulnerable ones have a lesson to impart.

Analog Devices, which focuses on specialized applications for analog semiconductors, has invested countercyclically to cash in on business upturns. The results: 80% faster growth and 50% higher profitability than the rest of the semiconductor industry. But existing competitors seem set to copy

149

Analog's investment policy, and new ones—notably the Japanese—are invading its profitable niches.

Nike's leadership in athletic shoes was built on cheap Far Eastern labor and massive investments in product development and marketing. Over the last five years, Nike averaged thrice the profitability and four times the growth of the rest of the U.S. shoe industry. But competitors are busy cloning its strategy. Reebok International, for one, sources 95% of its shoes from South Korea, spends heavily on product styling, and has won endorsements from rock stars as well as athletes. Reebok's sales and profits expanded fivefold in 1985, while Nike's actually declined.

Piedmont Aviation's hubs at Baltimore, Charlotte, and Dayton tie together dozens of small and mid-sized cities. Since the major airlines had neglected these routes, Piedmont grew three times as fast as the rest of the industry and was six times as profitable. But others are now muscling in: People Express has started to encroach, and American Airlines' planned hub at Raleigh will hurt Piedmont's operations out of Baltimore and Charlotte.

Analog Devices, Nike, and Piedmont are very different from one another, yet they face the same threat: copying by competitors. Their competitive advantages are insecure, or contestable, because each can be duplicated. These examples also show that some success stories do revolve around contestable advantages: all of a company's competitors may be stupid some of the time. But can you count on your competitors being stupid *all* of the time? The historical record suggests otherwise. That is why sustainable advantages—advantages anchored in industry economics—command attention.

The literature on strategy is crammed with accounts of why a sustainable competitive advantage is A Good Thing To Have. But all those accounts beg two key questions. Which advantages tend to be sustainable, and why?

Sustainable advantages fall into three categories: size in the targeted market, superior access to resources or customers, and restrictions on competitors' options. Note that these advantages are nonexclusive. They can, and often do, interact. The more of them, the better.

Benefits of Size

Size advantages exist because markets are finite. If a business can commit to being large, competitors may resign themselves to remaining smaller. What holds them back is the fear that if they matched the leader's size, supply might exceed demand by enough to make the market unprofitable for everyone.

Commitment to being large means making durable, irreversible investments. To exploit commitment opportunities, a business must be able to preempt its competitors. Caveat preemptor: firstmovers have to be especially wary of environmental changes that can erode the value of their early investments.

Size is an advantage only if, net net, there are compelling economies to being large. Such economies have three possible bases: scale, experience, and scope.

Scale economies usually summon up a vision of a global factory running flat out. But it is important to remember that scale can work on a national, regional, or even local level, and that its effects need not be confined to manufacturing.

Wal-Mart, the discount merchandiser, illustrates the power of local and regional scale economies. Historically, it focused on small Sunbelt towns that its competitors had neglected. Most of these towns could not support two discounters, so once Wal-Mart made a long-lived, largely unrecoverable investment to service such a town, it gained a local monopoly. The company reinforced this advantage by wrapping its stores in concentric rings around regional distribution centers. By the time competitors realized that this policy cut distribution costs in half, Wal-Mart had preempted enough store sites to render competing regional warehouses unviable. Now you know why Sam Walton was one of the richest men in America.

The Wal-Mart story also shows the limits to scale economies. Kmart and other discounters are beginning to enter some of Wal-Mart's larger locations. The problem ironically, is market growth:

because of the boom in the Sunbelt, some of these towns can now accommodate two discounters. And even the warehousing advantages look insecure in the regions into which Wal-Mart is expanding; it probably won't be able to blanket these areas with stores before competitors move in.

Experience effects are based on size over time, rather than size at a particular point in time. If you think about it, experience is a kind of irreversible, market-specific investment. While it is usually cited in the context of the experience curve—the inverse relation between cumulative production and average cost—its ambit is actually much broader. For example, experience has been shown to increase the operating reliability of processing plants, the success rate of product introductions, and the marketability of high-tech products.

Experience effects—especially experience curves—have come under heavy fire recently because they were oversold in the 1970s. Yet some companies *have* parlayed them into competitive success. Take Lincoln Electric's experience in the electric welding industry. Even since John Lincoln developed the portable arc welder in 1895, Lincoln Electric has out-raced its competition down the experience curve. In its ninth decade it still commands a 7% to 15% cost advantage over its four largest rivals.

Lincoln is an object lesson about when and how to exploit experience effects. As the product pioneer it had a first-mover advantage; and that lead has proved durable because of the incrementalism of technological change. Lincoln has also kept its experience proprietary by integrating backward, customizing its production machinery, and holding annual worker turnover under 3%. Finally, it has continued to invest in experience by sharing cost reductions with customers. Competitors complain publicly that they have trouble matching Lincoln's prices, let alone undercutting them.

Scope economies are derived from activities in interrelated markets. If they are strong, a sustainable advantage in one market can be used to build sustainability in another. The term scope economies isn't just a newfangled name for synergy; it actually defines the conditions under which

synergy works. To achieve economies of scope, a company must be able to share resources across markets, while making sure that the cost of those resources remains largely fixed. Only then can economies be effected by spreading assets over a greater number of markets.

Cincinnati Milacron, the largest U.S. machine tool manufacturer, shows how companies can capitalize on scope economies. For the last two decades it has led the U.S. machine tool industry in both R&D and the size of its sales and service networks—activities that account for a third of the value added by the industry. In the 1980s it has pushed hard into robotics, with good reason. Its cumulative R&D experience gives the company such a big lead in the machine tool segment that no domestic challenger can rationally commit to matching its R&D, sales-force, or service expenditures. Furthermore, the technologies and customers for its computerized, numerically controlled machine tools overlap with those for robotics. And the company's R&D, sales, and service activities are all very volume sensitive, which slashes the incremental costs of moving into robotics. These factors make it a formidable contender in the industry.

A company pursuing a sustainable scope advantage cannot afford to run its businesses as isolated units. Activities have to be coordinated and allowances must be made for contributions from one business to the success of another. This makes scope economies especially hard to implement.

Access Advantages

Preferred access to resources or customers can award a business a sustainable advantage that is independent of size. The advantage persists because competitors are held back by an investment asymmetry: they would suffer a penalty if they tried to imitate the leader.

Access will lead to a sustainable advantage if two conditions are met: it must be secured under better terms that competitors will be able to get later, and the advantage has to be enforceable over the long run. Enforceability can come from ownership, binding contracts, or self-enforcing mechanisms such as switching costs. Without enforceability, the terms of access shift in line with overall market conditions, wiping out any competitive differences.

Enforceability can be a two-edged sword, however. The risk of pursuing sustainable access advantages is that they may saddle a business with worse terms than those available to its rivals.

Know-how. Superior access to information may reflect the benefits of scale or experience. Boeing, for instance, has acquired superior know-how about commercial jet aircraft through billions of dollars of cumulative investments in R&D. More often, though, sustainability hinges on hidden know-how—what your rivals don't see. For example, IBM's size and the complexity of its operating environment make it hard for competitors to figure out exactly what makes it tick. If the cost of surmounting that kind of informational barrier exceeds the payoffs, rivals may not even attempt imitation.

Consider Du Pont's preemption of all the capacity expansion in the U.S. titanium dioxide industry in the 1970s. Thanks to a production process based on low-cost feedstock, Du Pont enjoyed a 20% cost advantage over competitors' processes. Mastering the cheaper feedstock technology was a black art—it could be accomplished only by investing $50 million to $100 million and several years of testing time in an efficiently scaled plant. The cost and risk of this alternative kept Du Pont's competitors from trying to imitate its demonstrably superior technology.

An obvious but important point: know-how must be kept secret if it is to yield an advantage. Many high-tech and service companies have been devastated by the defection of key personnel in whom their know-how is vested. The Boston Consulting Group, for instance, has suffered more than a dozen spin-offs, eroding its competitive advantage in management consulting and its client base. Other sources of leaks include suppliers, customers, reverse engineering, and even patent documents.

Inputs. Tying up inputs will lead to a sustainable advantage only if the commodity's supply is bounded and the company has the right to use it on favorable terms. Boundedness here is interpreted broadly: it may imply either a strictly limited supply of the input or a supply that is elastic but of varying quality. In both cases, the supply of the preferred input is limited; as a result, tying it up can be very profitable.

Research method

I have drawn many of my examples from research reports prepared by MBA students for the Industry and Competitive Analysis (ICA) course at the Harvard Business School. Constraints of space preclude individual citations; I should, however, emphasize the collective contribution of ICA students to this article.

In fall 1984 and 1985, we asked our students to analyze companies identified as outstanding performers in their industries. The purpose was threefold: to understand the sources of competitive advantage on which these companies relied, to determine why the advantages had proved sustainable, and to assess their future security.

Our students submitted reports on well over 150 companies. Some, obviously, dealt with companies that had been canonized publicly; many others, however, were unfamiliar to the ICA teaching group.

Even more important, the quality of the reports surpassed our expectations. Taken together, they suggest answers to some of the most fundamental questions about strategy formulation. To give these reports the broader circulation they deserve, Douglas Anderson, Michael Porter, and I are editing 20 of them for publication. The compendium will be available in 1987.

This description covers a wide range of phenomena. Courtaulds' 10% to 15% cost advantage over its competitors in the viscose industry can be traced to its backward integration into dissolving pulp, which accounts for a third of the finished product's cost. Courtaulds gets its pulp from a well-located subsidiary for half what its competitors pay. James River Corporation has averaged a 24% ROE by buying obsolete commodity paper machines at fire-sale prices and converting them to specialty products, a stratagem that has held its assets-to-sales ratio to two-thirds the industry average. In diamonds, the Central Selling Organization (controlled by De Beers) has built up its marketing muscle by tying up contracts to market 80% of the western hemisphere's supply.

Companies can also secure preferred access through their reputations or established relationships. In the record industry, for example, CBS has attracted promising artists because of its reputation for being able to take them to the top—at least partially a self-fulfilling prophecy.

Access advantages are vulnerable to shifts in input availability or prices. Courtaulds' cost advantage in dissolving pulp will wither as infrastructural development opens up more tropical and subtropical forests. And James River's competitors, particularly Hammermill, have begun to bid up the prices of the second-hand paper machines that it traditionally bought for a song. This constrains James River's growth, even though its cheap asset base will prop up profitability for years to come.

Markets. In many ways, preferred access to markets is the mirror image of preferred access to inputs. But access to markets relies less on vertical integration or contracts and more on self-enforcing mechanisms such as reputation, relationships, switching costs, and product complementarities.

That is not to say that vertical integration and contracts are entirely missing from the picture. Tele-Communications' strategy in cable television systems shows otherwise. While competitors outbid each other in their scramble to secure big franchises, Tele-Communications concentrated on acquiring small, contiguous systems in areas that were poorly served because they were hard to get to or far from large population centers. Tele-Communications' current network faces no serious threats from substitutes or competitors, limits its exposure to the whims of any one regulatory authority, and allows the company to spread the costs of its microwave common-carrier network over several communities.

Still, self-enforcing mechanisms for market access crop up far more frequently. Let us look at just two examples. Tandem, which pioneered expandable, fault-tolerant computers for processing transactions, has gained preferred access to

demand for upgrades and replacements because changeovers from one system to another are very costly. And Borden's brand of processed lemon juice, ReaLemon, attained a 50% premium over identical competing brands because as the pioneer, it benefited from consumer risk-aversion: lemon juice doesn't cost very much and you don't buy it very often, so why take a chance with an untried brand?

You have probably already figured out that market access advantages are very sensitive to customer preferences. Even slight, apparently innocuous shifts in preferences can weaken an entrenched brand, dispel accumulated switching costs, or undercut long-standing relationships.

Exercising Options

Sometimes the sustainability of an advantage cannot be pinned on either size or access. Instead, competitors' options may differ fundamentally from yours, hamstringing their ability to imitate your company's strategy. Rivals may be frozen into their current positions for several reasons:

Public Policy. Government intervention always affects the workings of markets; that is its avowed purpose. Sometimes its actions percolate so far as to affect competitive positions within an industry. The examples are familiar: patents (try to) protect innovators from imitators, antitrust laws prevent large businesses from being as aggressive as smaller competitors, some companies get handouts while others do not. The lesson, strategically, is that a company that is on the right side of public policy can exploit its position to build sustainability against companies that are not.

Heileman Brewing exemplifies both the leverage from this source of sustainability and its limits. The shakeout in the U.S. brewing industry during the 1970s endangered many small, regional brewers. Antitrust laws prevented the national brewers—Anheuser-Busch, Miller, and Schlitz—from acquiring them. Heileman, then one of the larger regional brewers, faced no such constraints. It grew throughout the decade by buying out numerous smaller brewers lock, stock, and barrel.

These cheap assets fed right through to the bottom line: with an average ROE of 29% over the last five years, Heileman is still ahead of its competitors. But the bloom on this particular strategy is fading. By 1982, Heileman's market share had tripled, and the Justice Department blocked its proposed acquisitions of Schlitz and Pabst. Other takeovers by Heileman are improbable.

Remember that what the government gives, the government can take away. Treat an advantage based on public policy as sustainable only if you are sure you will continue to be on the right side. If not, try a different route.

Defense. A business can also sustain an advantage if its competitors are restricted by past investments. If imitation threatens the cash flow from those investments, disadvantaged competitors may rationally stay put and defend them, thereby giving the innovator an opportunity to take the lead.

Examples of defensiveness are legion. Bic used its 19-cent Crystal to wrest leadership from Gillette in the U.S. pen market in the 1950s, when Bic's aggression went unmatched because Gillette did not want to decimate the sales of its more expensive Paper Mate line. In plain-paper copying, a number of competitors successfully attacked Xerox in the 1970s. Recognizing that its multibillion-dollar rental base was becoming obsolete, Xerox milked it by dragging its feet on price cuts and product innovation—even though these lags caused its share of new placements to fall from nearly 100% in 1972 to 14% by 1976.

Time often erodes defensiveness, however, as it depreciates the value of past investments. In 1970, Gillette introduced a low-priced line of Write Bros. pens to arrest Bic's advance. And since 1977, Xerox has restored its share of new copier placements to the 40% to 50% range by matching competitors' prices and product features.

Response Lags. The final restriction on rivals' options comes from response lags. One business can be every bit as efficient as another in terms of potential size or access without being equally prepared to make a specific move. In that event, the nimbler of the two can count on a lag in its competitor's response, or a period of sustainability.

The longer the response lag the better, as existing advantages stretch out and opportunities to create new ones multiply. Lag times vary enormously, of course, but I can make some broad generalizations. Responses to most pricing moves come in weeks if not days, while responses to nonprice competition and to R&D usually take a few years. And it may take a decade or more to match a competitor's scope economics or superior organization.[4]

Kodak vividly illustrates how you can sustain a lead by exploiting competitors' response lags. In the late 1950s, Du Pont and Bell & Howell formed a joint venture to challenge Kodak's dominance of the color film market. They found product development exasperating, however, because each time they improved their film, Kodak seemed, as if by magic, to make its film even better. When the Du Pont–Bell & Howell film was finally ready, Kodak administered the coup de grace by introducing the vastly superior Kodachrome II slide film. The competing entry never reached the market.

Guidelines for Strategy

I have outlined a set of factors that affect the sustainability of competitive advantages. How should these factors—and the broad notation of sustainability—be integrated into strategy formulation? Here are several points to remember:

1. Managers cannot afford to ignore contestable advantages. For one thing, even moves that offer ephemeral advantages may be worth making, if only to avoid a competitive *disadvantage*. For another, some contestable advantages may survive uncontested: disadvantaged competitors may be tied up trying to meet their profit targets, constrained by their corporate strategies, or just ineptly managed.

2. The distinction between contestable and sustainable advantages is a matter of degree. Sustainability is greatest when based on several kinds of advantages rather than one, when the advantage is large, and when few environmental threats to it exist.

3. Not all industries offer equal opportunities to sustain an advantage. First-mover advantages tend to be most potent in industries characterized by durable, irreversible, market-specific assets, either tangible or intangible. Industries that evolve gradually offer more room to sustain advantages than those that are regularly rocked by drastic changes in technology or demand. And sustainability is more accessible in industries with more than one dominant strategy because competitors may not have the same options you do.

4. To create a sustainable advantage, you must either be blessed with competitors that have a restricted menu of options or be able to preempt them. Propitious times to preempt occur when an industry is undergoing wrenching changes in technology, demand patterns, or input availability. Scan the environment actively. If you notice any changes, see whether they play to your particular strengths.

Ultimately, the search for sustainability involves a series of decisions about the degree to which you are willing to commit your business to a particular way of doing things. You have to pick the relative emphasis you are going to place on two things: commitment to competing a particular way and retaining the flexibility to compete effectively in other ways.

References

1. Edwin Mansfield, "How Rapidly Does New Industrial Technology Leak Out?" *Journal of Industrial Economics,* December 1985, p. 217, Richard C. Levin et al., "Survey Research on R&D Appropriability and Technological Opportunity, Part I," Yale University Working Paper (New Haven: July 1984); and Edwin Mansfield, Mark Schwartz, and Samual Wagner, "Imitation Costs and Patents: An Empirical Study," *Economic Journal,* December 1981, p. 907.

2. Michael A. Salinger, "Tobin's q., Unionization, and the Concentration-Profits Relationship," *Rand Journal of Economics,* Summer 1984, p. 159; and Thomas Karier. "Unions and Monopoly Profits," *Review of Economics and Statistics,* February 1985, p 34.

3. M.M. Metwally, "Advertising and Competitive Behavior of Selected Australian Firms," *Review of Economics and Statistics,* November 1975 p. 417; Jean-Jacques Lambin, *Advertising, Competition,* and *Market Conduct in Oligopoly Over Time* (Amsterdam: North-Holland, 1976); and Jeffrey M. Netter, "Excessive Advertising: An Empirical Analysis," *Journal of Industrial Economics,* June 1982, p. 361.

4. See, for example, David J. Teece, "The Diffusion of an Administrative Innovation," *Management Science,* May 1980, p.464.

Editors Note: Additional references are available from the author.

Xavier Gilbert
Paul Strebel
IMEDE

Developing Competitive Advantage

Different industries offer different competitive opportunities and, as a result, successful strategies vary from one industry to another. Identifying which strategies can lead to competitive advantages in an industry may be done in three main steps:

1. Industry Definition: This involves defining the boundaries of the industry, learning its rules of the game, and identifying the other players.
2. Identification of Possible Competitive Moves: Competitive moves exploit the possible sources of competitive advantages in the industry. Their degree of effectiveness evolves with the industry life cycle and is influenced by the moves of other competitors.
3. Selecting among Generic Strategies: Successful strategies rely on a sequence of competitive moves. There are only a few such successful sequences corresponding to different industry situations.

We shall discuss each of these steps in turn.

Industry Definition

The arena of competition within which an industry member should fight will be described in terms of its boundaries, its rules of the game, and its players.

Identifying the Boundaries of the Industry

In identifying what constitutes the industry, we

Source: Original article by Xavier Gilbert and Paul Strebel, International Institute for Management Development. This edited version is reproduced by special permission of the authors and H. Mintzberg and J. Quinn for *The Strategy Process*, Prentice-Hall, 1990.

must take into account all the activities that are necessary to deliver a product or service that meets the expectations of a market. In this regard, many definitions of a company's business, or of its industry, have been too narrow: there is more to its business than a product, a process, and a market; there is in fact an entire chain of activities, from product design to product utilization by the final customer, that must be mobilized to meet certain market expectations.

The most commonly accepted term to designate this chain of activities is the *business system.* The concept, or some variation of it, has been used frequently under different names, such as "industry dynamics" or "value chain"; the term "business system" was coined in the seventies by the consulting firm McKinsey & Company, from whom we borrow it. Some examples will illustrate why it is important to take into account the entire chain of activities represented by the business system when deciding how to compete.

The first example is provided by the personal computer industry (Exhibit 1). The business system of the personal computer industry includes a wide range of activities: product design, component manufacturing, different stages of assembly, software development, marketing, selling, distribution, service and support to the customer, and the utilization of the product by the customer. Each of these activities is expected to add value to the product so that it meets the needs of the customer. A view of all the activities necessary to serve customer expectations, as provided by the industry's business system, is thus the starting point of industry analysis.

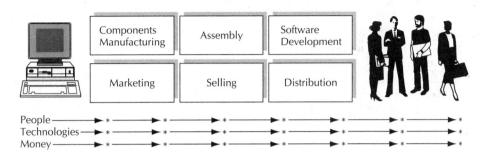

EXHIBIT 1
The PC Industry

Different competitors have made different choices with respect to how these activities should be dealt with. Some have designed their product around the "IBM industry standard" in order to have access to software, while others have been using a proprietary operating system. Some are designing their own components, while others are finding sources for them outside. Some have selectively authorized dealers to sell their products, while others use mass-retailing channels and others again sell directly to the final customer. This shows that there may be different ways to use the activities in the business system to provide value to the final customer.

Rather than considering the company as competing *in an industry*, it should thus be seen as competing *within a business system*, in the same way as a chess player uses the resources or a chessboard. A chess player does not try to win by asking simply, "How do I win at chess?" Instead, the player asks, "How should I use my pawns, my rooks, my knights, my bishops, my queen, and even my king?" Similarly, each personal computer company should see itself as competing with other companies on design, on component manufacturing, on assembly of specific configurations, on software development, on marketing, on selling, on distribution, and on service support to the customer, and not simply as competing "in the personal computer industry."

Learning the Rules of the Game

Each activity in the business system adds perceived value to the product or service. Value[1], for the customer, is the perceived stream of benefits that accrue from obtaining the product or service. Price is what the customer is willing to pay for that stream of benefits. If the price of a good or service is high, it must provide high value, otherwise it is driven out of the market. If the value of a good or service is low, its price must be low, otherwise it is also driven out of the market. Hence, in a competitive situation, and over a period of time, the price customers are willing to pay for a good or service is a good proxy measure of its value.

The "game" is to create a disequilibrium between the perceived value offered and the price asked by either increasing the former or by reducing the latter. This modifies the terms of competition and potentially drives competitors out of the market. Competitors will have to respond by either offering more perceived value for the same price, or by offering the same value at a lower price.

At the same time, each activity in the business system is performed at a cost. Getting the stream of benefits that accrue from the good or service to the customer is thus done at a certain "deliv-

---

[1]"Value" is used here with the meaning it is given by economists in the utility theory.

ered cost" which sets a lower limit to the price of the good or service if the business system is to remain profitable. Decreasing the price will thus imply that the delivered cost be first decreased by adjusting the business system. As a result, the rules of the game may also be described as providing the highest possible perceived value to the final customer, at the lowest possible delivered cost.

In addition, the intrinsic logic of the business system must also be taken into account. This logic is dictated by the fact that the business-system activities must be coordinated to provide a specific final product. This requirement is best examined at the level of the resources needed for each activity: people, technologies, and money.

The personal computer industry again illustrates the point. Among the resources needed to perform the various activities of the business system, the technologies will be used as an example. Firstly, the final customers are not supposed to be computer experts. Their technological know-how might be in the areas of financial analysis, accounting, or text processing, not in programming or establishing communication protocols with peripherals. This implies technological choices at the level of product and software design that will make the machine user-friendly. It also implies that the technology required to service the machine and to assist customers, also selected at the time of product design, be compatible with the technology available in the distribution channels.

Similar consistency requirements could be observed with respect to the other resources: people and money. If these rules of the game were not respected, the business system could not deliver a product or service of desired perceived value. Laying out the activities of the business system and the resources required by each of them is thus necessary before the game can be played effectively.

Identifying the Other Players

"Players" in a business system do not consist only of competitors; they may be other participants in the business system that perform vital activities. For the provider of a product of service, managing the business system can be complicated by players up- and down-stream in the system. By playing an optimal game from their perspective, these other participants may suboptimize the whole business system and put pressure on other activities.

Consider, for example, the Swiss watch industry (Exhibit 2). As long as competition was limited, the Swiss watch manufacturers, who were essentially fragmented assemblers, enjoyed satisfactory margins, even though their value added was small relative to the entire business system. But the industry experienced intense global competition during the seventies and eighties, leading to sharp price decreases. The first reaction was to believe that competition among watchmakers was the source of these difficulties. Attempts were made to restructure the Swiss watch industry so as to obtain economies of scale similar to those of global competitors.

However, the business system shows clearly that competition among watchmakers was not the biggest problem. Producing cheaper watches was necessary, but not sufficient. The Swiss watchmakers were competing fiercely for the consumers' money with costly distribution channels whose added value was questionable for a fast-growing mass market. Developing a watch which would not only be inexpensive, but could also be sold through low-margin distribution channels with no service, such as the Swatch, was the way to effectively circumvent this form of competition.

Competitive Moves

Competitive advantages are built on the ability to utilize the business system to provide final customers with the desired perceived value, at the lowest delivered cost. However, not all the activities of a business system offer the same potential to build these competitive advantages. In addition, their choice is affected by the stage of development of the industry as well as by the moves of other competitors. This leads to the identification of a limited number of generic moves to gain competitive advantages.

EXHIBIT 2
The Swiss Watch Industry

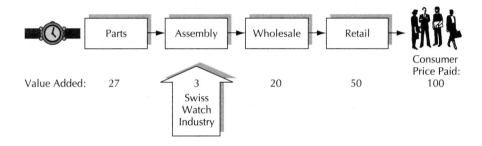

	Parts	Assembly	Wholesale	Retail	Consumer Price Paid:
Value Added:	27	3	20	50	100
		Swiss Watch Industry			

Competitive Advantages Offered by the Business System

Superior profitability requires either higher perceived value and/or lower delivered cost than the competition. This is achieved either through superior performance in at least one of the business-system activities, or through a creative and innovative combination of several activities. Such *competitive formulas* are the basis of all successful strategies.

For example, in the watch industry the main activities of the business system include design, manufacturing of movement parts, movement assembly, case manufacturing and assembly, wholesaling, and retail. Each of these activities can be performed to maximize the perceived value for the final user, or to minimize the delivered cost. Design, for example, can emphasize luxury and elegance, or it can ensure low-cost manufacturing. Traditional distribution channels through wholesalers and specialty stores will provide more perceived value, while mass distribution directly through low-margin outlets will contribute to a low delivered cost. A range of competitive formulas can thus be developed, combining the various activities of the business system in a manner that will provide the desired perceived value at the desired delivered cost.

Two observations, however, suggest that this range of possible competitive formulas is not very

wide. The first one is that there is an internal logic to each business system. The balance between perceived value and delivered cost cannot be established for one activity independently of the others. For example, it is not possible to use traditional distribution channels to distribute the Swatch. Because of the high distribution margins and of the limited volume, the delivered cost would be higher than the perceived value. This is indeed what is meant by a competitive formula. The various activities of the business system must combine high perceived value and low delivered cost in a coherent manner.

The second observation is that high perceived value and low delivered cost constitute the only possible generic competitive moves. Experience shows that there are no other possibilities. There are only variations around these two main themes, as allowed by the expectations of different market segments. Strategic advantages are obtained by combining them in a sequence, one being preferably implemented in a way that prepares the implementation of the other at a later time.

Many failures have been caused by the inability to put together coherent business systems, with respect to low delivered cost and high perceived value. This was exactly how the Swiss watch industry got into trouble, trying to compete in markets expecting low delivered cost with a business system designed for high perceived value. When the promoters of the Swatch saw that the biggest revolu-

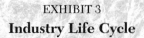

EXHIBIT 3
Industry Life Cycle

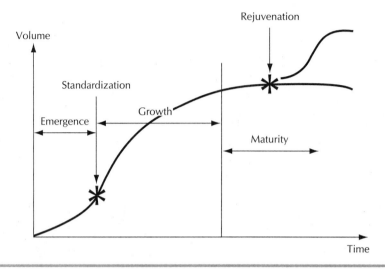

tion in the industry was not a technological one, but a distribution one, they engineered a fine-tuned competitive formula in which each business-system activity contributed to delivering a watch for less than SFr50 (about $25). Even though the Swatch is very precise and carries an element of snobbish appeal, the move was quite clearly a low-delivered-cost one, with a formula that provided maximum perceived value within the low-delivered-cost constraint.

Stage of Development of the Industry

Although it would be theoretically feasible to choose either of these two moves—high-perceived-value or low-delivered-cost—at any point in time, the actual possibilities are in fact strongly influenced by the stage of industry development. The personal computer industry will be used as an example of the inferences that can be drawn from an industry life cycle to assist in the diagnosis of potential competitive advantages.

Consider first the personal computer industry in the second half of the seventies. The characteristics of the product were in a state of flux, with many competing versions. The manufacturing process was not yet a matter of real concern, as the technology was still evolving. The business system of the industry had not stabilized. Competition was restricted to product innovation and development. These characteristics are typical of an *emerging industry* offering *high perceived value* to a limited market (Exhibit 3).

Consider now the personal computer industry after IBM's entry. Even though IBM's product was not regarded by seasoned users as particularly innovative on the technological side, it had the perhaps unintended advantage of embodying an acceptable common denominator of characteristics desired by a wide cross section of the market. Not the least of these characteristics was the image of IBM's reliability. The IBM PC was soon perceived as the industry standard.

Standardization marks the first important transition to another phase of industry evolution during which competitive advantages shift to *low delivered cost*. This new phase is characterized by *rapid market development*. The personal computer industry was no exception as it moved into a period of very rapid growth in unit sales. Attention had to be shifted to the production process, while most manufacturers were adopting the "IBM standard." Rather than further product development, resources were now directed towards the entire business system: process technology, market positioning, and distribution efficiency were key.

When IBM and others began to use prices strategically, many of the early competitors could not follow. Those who did survive had joined the industry-standard bandwagon and had the necessary resources to invest in the manufacturing process. The key competitors were now large, professional firms following a similar, low-delivered-cost industry discipline.

At the end of 1984 and in 1985, however, a new turn took place in the industry. Signs of industry maturity were appearing in the U.S., while activity was starting again on the side of product improvement. IBM itself launched its PC-AT and the need for networks were receiving increasing attention from competitors. Such renewed interest in the perceived value of the product is typical at this stage of an industry's evolution, often called rejuvenation (Exhibit 3). However, the entire process that made the business system work was still getting much attention. Resources were now channeled both to the process and to a new product generation: integrated computer networks. These developments were in the hands of a few large competitors who could be active on two fronts, process and product.

In a *maturing industry, rejuvenation* is the second important evolutionary transition. It marks the shift to product differentiation and innovation, in addition to cost reduction and process efficiency. At this stage, competitive advantages must be maintained on two fronts: *low delivered cost* and, again, *high perceived value.* As a result of this combination, however, perceived-value advantages can only be marginal and short-lived. This is a time when marketing activity is at its peak.

The effectiveness of high-perceived-value and low-delivered-cost advantages thus varies with the stage of development of the industry. The two generic moves that lead to these advantages must

be implemented at the right stage of development of the industry, either to accelerate its evolution, or to follow it.

Identifying Strategic Groups

The competitors in an industry can be positioned according to which generic moves they are making at a given time. The resulting mapping may be examined for signs of strategic groups of competitors.

Identifying strategic groups can serve several purposes. An important one is to assess how the moves of competitors may affect the evolution of the industry. The life cycle of an industry is not only pulled by changes in market expectations. It is also pushed by the move of some of the competitors. For example, IBM's entry in the personal computer industry accelerated the transition to market development. Subsequently, IBM's low-delivered-cost move accompanied with decreasing prices accelerated the transition to maturity. As we have seen, assessing the industry evolution is an important input in deciding which competitive move to implement next.

In addition, identifying strategic groups can serve two other purposes. Firstly, by observing how the key competitors play the business system to obtain their competitive advantages, it is possible to develop a better understanding of the business system and of the potential competitive advantages it offers. Secondly, identifying which competitive positions are occupied and by whom helps decide which competitors may be confronted or avoided. Although the movements of competitors can be assessed quantitatively, since both perceived value and delivered cost can be measured, an example of how it can be done qualitatively will be provided here. This example is based on the personal computer industry (Exhibit 4).

Three main groups could be unidentified in early 1986. The first group included the industry-standard competitors, of course led by IBM. A low-delivered-cost obsession was clear with this group, as indicated by the price decreases that marked 1985 and were continuing in 1986. In addition to IBM, the group included Compaq and Zenith, for example, in the United States; Sharp,

EXHIBIT 4
Strategic Groups: The PC Industry

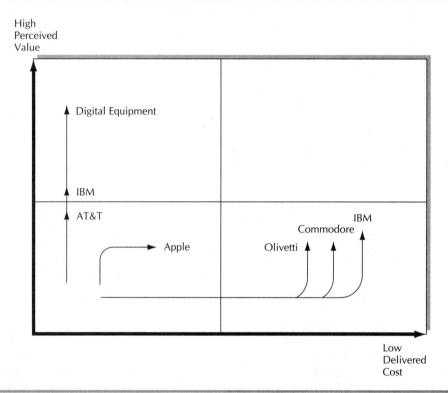

High
Perceived
Value

Digital Equipment

IBM

AT&T

Apple

Olivetti

Commodore

IBM

Low
Delivered
Cost

Epson and Toshiba from Japan; and Olivetti from Europe. All were offering basically the same commoditylike product. All were seeing low price as a necessary condition to stay in the game. However, and this is characteristic of a mature industry, all were also trying to offer something else in addition to low price, such as more speed, more capacity, more user-friendliness, wider distribution. But none of these features could yield a lasting advantage.

There was a second group that was trying to exploit the fact that the rules of the game could perhaps be changed. If networking of personal computers, with each other and with mainframes, became critical, which seemed to be the case, the personal computer would become a standard workstation in a decentralized data processing system. It would no longer be the "force de frappe," and future competitive advantages would accrue from the ability to provide communication hardware and software.

Among the companies competing effectively in this direction were Digital Equipment and other minicomputer vendors, such as Norsk Data of Europe, who had traditionally networked their machines. IBM was also trying to compete on this front, with its usual follower approach, but it was hampered by its traditionally centralized approach to data processing. AT&T and other telecommunication companies were other credible contenders. The strategies in this group were clearly on the side of high perceived value. The battle of communication standards that were taking place at that time was characteristic of these strategies.

There was finally a third group of those who were beginning to look as if they had missed the boat. Apple was still its most successful member, fighting with low prices and product uniqueness, but a uniqueness of increasingly questionable relevance. However, Apple's statements of intention concerning a future compatibility of the Macintosh with IBM's personal computer standard and with Digital Equipment's network architecture demonstrated some understanding of the emerging new rules of the game.

Generic Strategies

Two generic moves, leading either to high-perceived-value or to low-delivered-cost advantages, have been identified and their relevance at different stages of evolution of an industry has been discussed. Successful competitors, however, appear to be combining these moves within overall strategies that allow them to maintain a superior competitive position throughout the evolution of their industry. Two types of generic strategies can be identified:

- One-dimensional strategies, either high-perceived-value or low-delivered-cost.
- Outpacing strategies, either preemptive or proactive.

One-Dimensional Strategies

One-dimensional strategies rely on the continued repetition of one move, either a high-perceived-value one or a low-delivered-cost one. The situations where this seems possible are not numerous. Only in industries with very short life cycles, like fashion, is it possible to pursue indefinitely a high-perceived-value strategy. Only in industries with very long life cycles, like commodities, is it possible to stick continuously to a low-delivered-cost strategy. In other instances, one-dimensional strategies often hide an inability to implement a new move at the right time and lead to disasters.

The Japanese entry into Western automobile markets is an illustration. In the sixties, Western manufacturers were pursuing high-perceived-value strategies. In the United States, this led to yearly model changes. In Europe, ingenious, but overengineered small cars were being produced with rather primitive processes. In the late sixties, Japanese manufacturers began to sell basic and very inexpensive cars thanks to their highly efficient way of playing the business system, of which the manufacturing process was only a part. Success was almost immediate. Western manufacturers failed to see the need for a radical change in their competitive thrust and several were never able to respond.

However, this was not the end of the story. Under the price umbrella offered by Western manufacturers, the superior productivity of the Japanese allowed them to reinvest their cash-flow into product improvements and to offer more value for the same price. In Europe, this shift towards higher perceived value was welcomed because it brought new attraction to a standardized product entering the maturity stage. In the United States, it essentially met an unsatisfied need for a lower-value, lower-price car to which U.S. manufacturers could never respond. This is evidenced by the instant success achieved by Hyundai by providing the same value as a Japanese car maker, but for less money.

Outpacing Strategies

The example of the automobile industry showed clearly that the formulation of a successful strategy rarely relies on the repeated implementation of the same move to maintain a static position. Successful strategies generally consist of a planned sequence of moves from one position to another, at the right time. The sequential implementation of competitive moves should not be seen as strategy changes. It must be planned, one move creating the conditions for the implementation of the next. The dynamic nature of successful strategies is reflected in their description as *outpacing* strategies (Exhibit 5).

Outpacing strategies can be preemptive or proactive. A preemptive strategy is needed by an industry leader to prevent the occurrence of a situation such as the one in the automobile industry. If

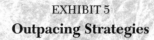

EXHIBIT 5
Outpacing Strategies

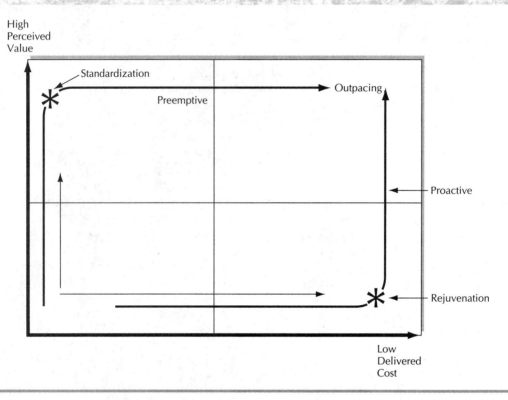

successful, this strategy will shift the industry life cycle from the emergence stage to the growth stage and thus impact on the industry life cycle. Its purpose is to prevent followers from developing secure low-price positions. This is achieved by adding at the right time a low-delivered-cost dimension to a high-perceived-value position. This will allow using prices tactically to retaliate against new entrants. This implies the establishment of a product standard as well as the development of a *pricing reserve*.

Establishing a standard is not only a matter of technology, as well demonstrated by the IBM Personal Computer. It is rather a question of business system: establishing a formula that meets the expectations of a larger number of potential cus-

tomers than do other competitive formulas. It is the desired outcome of a high-perceived-value move.

Developing a pricing reserve means investing in process improvements to enable the shift to a low-delivered-cost strategy, as soon as a standard is accepted. Experience shows that very few companies can make this shift effectively. It is nevertheless the condition for the tactical use of prices to prevent followers from generating the cash flow that will be necessary to go through the next industry transition, from low delivered cost, back to high perceived value, when the industry matures, if not to discourage them from entering at all. Such a strategy was followed by IBM, immediately after the IBM PC was accepted as a standard.

The timing of a preemptive outpacing strategy is clearly critical. Launched too early, considerable investments in process improvement will be started before the formula is accepted as a standard. Should another standard emerge rapidly, the company will not be able to write off its previous process investments. Launched too late, further investments will have been made into product improvements which the market will not be willing to pay for. This will make it difficult to defend market share against the lower-priced standards and will waste resources that would otherwise be needed for process investments.

Proactive outpacing strategies are required after the industry transition to lower growth and maturity. Their purpose is to escape the stalemate of maturity, so characteristic of many industries, where price wars often equate with self-destruction. Often implemented by followers, they consist of building a solid low-delivered-cost position from which to launch a high-perceived-value move. While a preemptive strategy focuses on a mass market, a proactive one focuses on selected market segments to which more perceived value can be offered through a range of possibilities, from simple formula differentiation to rejuvenation of the industry. All these possibilities imply essentially the same approach: changing the rules of the game of the business system.

This is done by "unbundling" the perceived value added by each activity of the business system: What does each activity really provide to the selected market segment, and at what cost? The process of unbundling will identify elements of perceived value that are not worth their delivered cost. Then, additional elements of perceived value, desirable for the market segment, can be included in the formula at an acceptable cost.

An example of this approach is the way in which the Swedish firm, Ikea, redesigned its business system in order to compete effectively in furniture mass distribution. Ikea eliminated or modified the activities that increased the delivered cost and did not add essential perceived value from the consumer point of view. Carefully monitored subcontracting of production to specialized manufacturers ensured quality at a lower cost. The furniture was no longer assembled, but flat-packed. It was not displayed in city-center stores, but in hyper-stores, outside cities. A trade-off was made between minimum inventories, to decrease the delivered cost, and immediate availability. Furthermore, by doing its own product design, Ikea could ensure a low-delivered-cost consistency throughout its business system.

On the other hand, perceived value was added where this could be done for a low delivered cost. A very wide range of home products was offered under the same roof and could be looked at and tried by the consumer in the display section of the stores, rather than only seen in different stores or in catalogues. The furniture was normally available immediately and could be taken back home by car. Doing its own design, Ikea could offer a homogenous, modular product range. The desirable image of Scandinavian furniture was skillfully exploited to add perceived value. Last but not least, by redesigning its entire business system, Ikea built an additional powerful competitive advantage: the know-how necessary to operate this formula.

Developing Competitive Advantage: An Intrinsic Part of Corporate Strategy

Analysis of competitive advantage is thus an intrinsic part of strategic management, rather than a separate exercise, as it is often presented. Indeed, it cannot be performed linearly in a way that leads to one end product, the "knowledge of the industry." It is performed through an iterative process, leading to hypotheses concerning possible strategies, testing them against the company's capabilities and against the positions of competition, and going back to the drawing board to assess other possibilities. This iterative process is the foundation on which each move can lead to sustainable competitive advantages by being part of an overall strategy to fight in the dynamic battlefield of an industry. Bringing this iterative process to life is a permanent responsibility of the general manager of a business unit.

Chapter 5

Business Marketing Intelligence: Analysis and Tools

This chapter discusses business marketing intelligence (BMI), an important activity because it links an organization to its external environment and makes it possible for management to develop informed and rational decisions about markets, competitors, and strategy. We first introduce BMI and explain why it is important. We distinguish BMI from marketing research and argue that BMI is much more than traditional marketing research. We then discuss different types of marketing intelligence: continuous and problem related. Then we address issues related to BMI system design, benchmarking, and sources of intelligence. We conclude the chapter with discussions about how to organize and manage intelligence efforts.

Intelligence and Information

The Importance of Business Marketing Intelligence

Intelligence is one of the most important business marketing functions. Intelligence activities of collecting and analyzing internal and environmental conditions are important to strategy formulation and operational conduct. BMI includes the gathering and understanding of market trends; customer needs, perceptions, attitudes, beliefs, and behavior; competitors' thinking, strengths and weaknesses; and all factors that influence business-to-business relationships. We view BMI intelligence as a broad set of activities, because success as a business marketer requires understanding the broader context of the market and the customers' strategic and operating environment.

BMI has three unique characteristics:

1. Business marketers usually deal with a smaller set of customers than consumer marketers do. Most business customers (and potential customers) are usually known to the business marketer. Therefore, intelligence activities often involve either the entire relevant customer population or much smaller samples than in consumer marketing.
2. Business marketing, as outlined in Chapter 3, involves multiple buying influences. These influences impact the reliability of the intelligence obtained from customers. Business intelligence information is often dependent on who is talking to the customer and who in the customer organization responds. To get a response that depicts a customer's organizational viewpoint, several customer sample points may be required.
3. The business marketing sales force usually has a close relationship with customers. This relationship represents a tremendous source of both customer and competitive information. A key issue in BMI is how to capitalize on the information the sales force has or can get.

The globalization of business has increased the need for broad-based intelligence systems. Even companies that consider themselves primarily local or regional find that an intelligence system based on a much broader geographical base is necessary. Technology often forces organizations to do extensive intelligence. For example, when new laser technology is developed and announced in Colorado, it does not take many hours before competing firms in Japan have all publicly available information reported to them by local consultants.

Entrepreneurial firms and firms in early stages of a product life cycle often need entirely different types of intelligence than firms in mature stages of the life cycle. A young entrepreneurial firm often needs market, product, and customer intelligence, while a firm operating in a mature oligopoly may need price and cost intelligence.

Business Marketing Intelligence Defined

Business marketing intelligence is the collection, analysis, and interpretation of relevant internal and external marketing information. It is a process that makes it possible for a firm to learn about, understand, and deal with new challenges. Marketing intelligence is therefore a future-oriented activity that helps an organization cope in the market. It includes all ways an organization acquires and uses information. It is comprised of all kinds of market and marketing research; the collection and analysis of internal data; competitive analysis; analysis and reverse engineering of competitors' products; understanding how and where to add value for customers; and the process of synthesizing large amounts of informally gathered information about the environment. Thus marketing intelligence can be as comprehensive or as narrow as a company may want it to be. In general, BMI consists of three important management activities. These activities are:

- Gathering internal and external data. The gathering of BMI data is a comprehensive task that includes activities ranging from collecting objective empirical market research data to recording subjective statements from salespersons. It may include activities such as periodic, detailed analysis of current data about customer sales gains and losses; recording employees' attitudes towards a particular customer or competitor; and scanning the trade press to assess events in the industry.

- Coding and interpreting the data collected. It is often very difficult to code and to provide valid and reliable interpretation of the broader dimensions of BMI. Over the last few decades, many firms have made substantial efforts to create centralized marketing information systems. Most of these efforts have failed due to the variety of data usually collected through BMI activities and to the lack of appropriate management and technology required to handle the complexity.

- Application of knowledge to produce useful information from data to be used in developing marketing strategy. An essential ingredient of BMI is the application of management knowledge and experience to marketing data collected. Only managers with the appropriate industry experience can assess the validity of BMI, translate it into a proper strategic context, and convert the knowledge into appropriate operating activities.

Table 5.1 shows examples of business marketing intelligence activities. BMI includes continuous and problem-oriented activities. Continuous BMI activities consist primarily of collection of data from secondary information sources and input from internal resources such as accounting, sales and cost data, technical standards, customer sales gains and loss data, and so on. Specific problem-related activities include market research, research related to product development,

TABLE 5.1
Examples of Business Marketing Intelligence Activities

Continuous	Problem Related
Secondary (desk) data analysis	Market potential analysis
Sales forecasting	Consept testing
Competitor analysis	Alpha-and beta testing
Market pricing analysis	Focus groups
Customer satisfaction surveys	

Management Experience and Judgment

establishment of target customer profiles, and specific assessment of market potential. A final activity is the integration of management inputs through informal observations, reports from meetings with external sources and management, opinions and experiences. Common to all this information is competitive data. The central component of the intelligence system is a function that conducts analysis of the data collected and provides integration. This includes synthesizing the information and preparing reports and recommendations to management. The intelligence is then integrated into strategy, planning, and implementation.

Many managers argue for the development of Marketing Decision Support Systems (MDSS). MDSS are formally structured computerized information systems that help managers make routine decisions. With current information systems technology this is possible. An MDSS can vary from sophisticated expert systems to simple sales variance analysis. If the company data bases and the necessary software are available, extensive "what if . . ." analysis may be possible. MDSS is usually best applied to repetitive and routine decision-making activities; for example, decisions related to order scheduling, field service, or order quantity discounts. MDSS is also used in sales reporting, customer service, and variance analysis related to product shipment. In general, the major portion of strategic marketing intelligence tends to be manual, and maybe difficult to get good return on very sophisticated MDSS in business marketing.

The Value of Business Marketing Intelligence

Marketing intelligence and the information it produces tends to create change. Marketing intelligence is driven by the marketplace and by competitors. As competitors change strategy and introduce new products, customers respond to these changes by changing their preferences and purchase behavior. Competing firms must therefore engage in intelligence work to understand exactly what is happening. As new intelligence emerges, competing firms find new ways of providing additional value to customers. They then deliver this new value to customers, which again produces change. This market-oriented information gathering is an ongoing process. Firms capable of learning by uncovering new information, and that can create knowledge through intelligence, are usually those that maintain their competitive position.

Marketing intelligence, like many other corporate functions, has changed dramatically over the last few years. Today marketing intelligence is global and very much influenced by changing customer behavior and new technology. Not only large multinational corporations, but also small- and medium-size firms are sourcing goods and services to a much greater extent across borders. The extent of sourcing varies from product to product and industry to industry. Sourcing is used extensively in the technology-related areas; for example, in electronics it is very common for smaller firms to establish alliances and source products, components, or assistance worldwide. This substantially increases the need for intelligence activities. It also influences the resources required to do intelligence work and the organization of such efforts. Even for small- and medium-size firms there is substantial negative opportunity cost if such efforts are not conducted satisfactorily. Many small- and medium-size firms' existence is threatened by developments taking place thousands of miles away. Failure to know about such developments, and to act appropriately, can have serious consequences for business performance.

Often the benefits and use of business intelligence are not recognized or fail because top management does not appreciate its value. Management often does not give this function the priority and/or resources that are required. The function is often staffed with low-level, inexperienced managers rather than experienced ones. Experienced managers who can help operating managers translate intelligence into strategy and implementation are often a scarce resource.

The Size of the BMI Activity

It is very difficult to estimate how important marketing intelligence is across world markets. However, it is clear that it tends to vary from industry to industry and across markets. BMI is growing in importance. One type of intelligence is market research. Table 5.2 shows market research revenue estimates for research agencies operating in all major regions of the world.

These agencies estimated that approximately $8.2 billion was spent on market research worldwide in 1992. SRG Research estimates that only 15 percent of this amount is business-to-business market research. This proportion may seem small, but this figure includes predominantly traditional qualitative and quantitative research. If the value of the broader definition of business intelligence is included, the resources used on business marketing intelligence are substantial. We estimate that between 60 percent and 90 percent of all business-to-business marketing intelligence is acquired through internal company resources. It is very difficult to estimate the size of this activity because it is conducted by company employees, and the amount of resources used on marketing intelligence are never publicly disclosed. However, the value of BMI efforts could be in excess of $5 billion worldwide. BMI is often conducted by managers in different functions and at several organizational levels and as a part-time endeavor. Therefore, many companies may not know themselves what resources are committed to marketing intelligence. Also, the cost and complexity of collecting and managing marketing intelligence influences the degree to which it is conducted. For example, in Europe, Japan, and the United States, extensive electronic information resources are available at modest costs. In many developing countries this is not so. Hence, the nature of marketing intelligence differs across world markets.

Culture and Business Marketing Intelligence

Culture influences the nature and role of marketing intelligence. For example, it is estimated that in Japan market research spending through agencies in 1992 was $600 million. This is a very small amount compared to the size of the Japanese economy and their economic and global success. Market research often has a different role in Japanese firms than in U.S. or German firms. Japanese marketing intelligence is primarily an internal company function.

TABLE 5.2
Marketing Research Expenditures in World Markets, 1992

Europe	*Market Research Revenue (in Million U.S. $)*
United Kingdom	$ 840
France	840
Germany	740
Italy	360
Spain	185
Netherlands	180
Belgium	105
Switzerland	88
Sweden	84
Austria	65
Finland	50
Denmark	40
Norway	33
Portugal	22
Greece	20
Other Europe	48
Total Europe	**3,700**
Asia Pacific	
Japan	600.0
Australia	100.0
New Zealand	30.0
Hong Kong	23.0
Korea	23.1
Singapore	12.3
Taiwan	9.2
Malaysia	10.0
Philippines	8.2
Indonesia	5.2
Other (China)	7.5
Total Asia	**835.0**
Americas	
United States	2,900
Canada	275
Other (Central and South America)	490
Total World	**$8,200**

Source: Esomar Market Study; SRG Research estimates.

When a Japanese company wants to learn about a particular aspect of business in Europe or the United States, it simply sends someone to live in the country for a period of time. Extensive, but often informal analysis is conducted, and all knowledge and raw data is forwarded to the main organization in Japan. This provides excellent insight and a broad base for the corporate staff to develop an effective marketing strategy. Swedish managers approach marketing intelligence differently. A study of Swedish and Japanese subsidiary managers in the United States showed that the Swedish managers were more self-confident than Japanese managers. Swedish managers did not view BMI as important as Japanese managers did. Swedish managers also tended to screen information more, forwarding only those facts they believed their superiors needed. Swedish managers seemed to have a completely different approach to marketing intelligence and the dissemination of results from that of the Japanese managers. This implies that the focus, organization, and reliance on BMI varies across cultures and that cultural norms may indicate management's use, willingness, and ability to use BMI in business development.

Business Intelligence and Opportunity Cost

Marketing intelligence provides some firms with significantly potential market and competitive opportunities. But information is useless and the cost of collecting data is wasted if firms are not able to take advantage of intelligence. Few companies make conscious efforts to include systematic approaches to marketing intelligence. In many firms marketing intelligence is an ad hoc and occasional activity. Only when a particular problem arises or a plan needs to be developed does marketing intelligence become an issue. For example, during the 1980s a European food processing firm prided itself on 15 percent annual growth in sales for most of the decade. At the end of the decade, when the company learned that its major competitor during the same period had grown 25 percent per year from a much larger base, the management decided to make changes in strategy. Unfortunately, the opportunity that was available in 1983–84 was not available at the end of the decade. At that point, the company had lost substantial relative position in the market and had eliminated both strategic market and product opportunities available earlier. The company still has not recovered from the error of not having adequate marketing intelligence.

There are numerous examples of managers who do not conduct business marketing intelligence or do not use knowledge that already has been acquired. During the 1980s, several surveys revealed that chief executive officers of U.S. firms did not believe that foreign competitors would pose much of a threat to U.S. companies in the twenty-first century. Such attitudes on the part of U.S. management have relegated competitive intelligence on foreign companies to a low priority in U.S. companies. We now know foreign competition is fierce and many U.S. companies are struggling to compete in many categories.

There are also numerous examples that illustrate the successful use of marketing intelligence. For example, Toshiba Corp.'s success in the 1M dynamic random access memory (DRAM) market was partially due to competitors' carelessness in gathering competitive intelligence. Toshiba, in contrast, mounted a formidable effort that resulted in significant support for the development project and a timely market launch. The Japanese takeover of the global videotape manufacturing business is another prime example of the successful application of marketing intelligence. This industry was characterized by fierce competition and a significant focus on production costs. Japanese intelligence programs of rapid reverse engineering of competitive products were key activities that brought them quickly to world-class level. Companies whose intelligence activities are unable to keep pace with competitor intelligence and development often quickly fall behind.

Types of Marketing Intelligence

Business marketing intelligence can be divided into two broad categories: (1) continuous intelligence that picks up signals, symptoms, and facts that can be used to assess performance or alert management to future problems, and (2) intelligence that focuses on solving a particular problem. Both types are important to a firm's total intelligence effort.

Continuous Marketing Intelligence

Continuous marketing intelligence efforts are broad activities often conducted by many people in the organization. This type of intelligence has an industry focus and often tries to identify unknown threats. The entire marketing, sales, and field service staff usually supports this effort in various ways. A market-oriented and inquisitive management culture often influences the effectiveness and quality of this type of intelligence and what can be done with it. In market-oriented organizations, nonmarketing employees are also involved in intelligence activity. This is particularly true for business organizations where engineers and R&D personnel are in frequent contact with customers. Continuous BMI efforts include market assessments and trend analysis, market potential estimation, product/market attractiveness analysis, market and customer profile analysis, customer gain-and-loss analysis, competitor assessment, competitive cost and pricing assessments, market share analysis, new technology assessment, and product and customer satisfaction analysis. Porter suggests a number of information items useful in conducting ongoing industry analysis, some of which are listed in Table 5.3.

Much of the data for ongoing intelligence usually comes from secondary published sources. This activity, referred to as desk research, is often overlooked in many companies. This type of BMI is particularly useful due to systems such as the Standard Industrial Classification (SIC) codes and standardized electronic data bases. Several industrial classification systems exist. In the United States the SIC code system is published by the Office of Management and Budget and is distributed by the U.S. Government Printing Office. The system divides economic activity into broad categories. The SIC codes consist of 9 digits (or more). The first two digits refer to a major product

TABLE 5.3
Areas of Continuous Market and Industry Intelligence

Macro Economic Environment

*Social, Political, and
Legal Environment*

Competitors
- Strategy
- Goals
- Strengths
- Weaknesses
- Assumptions

Innovation
- Types
- Sources
- Rates
- Economies of scale

*Distribution Channels
(Direct, Indirect, Infrastructure)*

Suppliers

Marketing and Selling
- Marketing segments and segmentation
- Marketing practices
- Success factors

Technology of Production and Distribution
- Cost structure
- Economies of scale
- Value added
- Logistics
- Labor

Growth
- Rate
- Pattern (seasonal, cyclical)
- Determinants

Substitute Products

Complementary Products

Product Lines

Adapted with the permission of The Free Press, an imprint of Simon & Schuster from *Competitive Strategy: Techniques for Analyzing Industries and Competitors* by Michael E. Porter. Copyright © 1980 by The Free Press.

group such as "Goods and Kindred Products" (Code 20). The next three digits refer to an industry subgroup. For example, the code for "canned and preserved fruits and vegetables" is 203. The last four digits refer to a specific industry. The code for "frozen fruits, fruit juices, and vegetables" is 2037. Thus, desk research on the SIC 20-203-2037 will yield data on this product category. It is also possible to go beyond the nine-digit codes. For example, SIC 20-203-20371 identifies "frozen fruit juices and ades" and SIC 20-203-20371-71 identifies "frozen concentrated orange juice." Over time, the SIC codes have become a consistent way of classifying data. Many private industrial research and intelligence organizations use the SIC code system. For example, American Business Information, Inc. in Omaha, Nebraska, provides prospect and mailing lists according to SIC codes.

Key sources of data for continuous marketing intelligence are financial reports, press releases, and trade magazines. Often firms subscribe to clipping services or newsletters that contain focused industry news or summaries of technology innovations. Other data sources include electronic data bases and electronic mail such as INTERNET, Dialog, and Dun and Bradstreet; internal accounting information; trade shows; reports from sales and service field forces; suppliers and customers; multiclient industry studies; omnibus and syndicated research; and industry experts. Marketing intelligence work may also include periodic customer satisfaction surveys and specific audit activities of suppliers and distributors. Availability and access to data vary from region to region. For example, in Europe multiclient industry studies, omnibus, and syndicated research are popular sources of information, while in Latin America multiclient studies are poorly developed.

Managing the continuous marketing intelligence effort is difficult. First, many managers do not understand the real value of this kind of intelligence work. Therefore, they tend to request it in spurts or when special projects require attention, requiring that employees and outside consultants often work overtime to make deadlines. Second, the ongoing marketing intelligence effort is usually placed relatively low in the organizational hierarchy and is staffed with relatively young and inexperienced employees. This approach is ineffective because analysis and interpretation of intelligence data often require extensive industry experience. The Quest International case describes how one company responded to these BMI management challenges.

Problem-Related Intelligence

The second type of intelligence is problem related. This type of intelligence is often initiated when a firm has a specific problem or need. The most common type of marketing intelligence is market research that collects primary data using qualitative or quantitative methods. Focus group and in-depth interviews are typical qualitative methods, and profiling target customers and defining the relative importance of product attributes are examples of quantitative intelligence. This ad hoc intelligence also includes such activities as benchmarking, reverse engineering, beta testing, and test marketing. Benchmarking is a systematic approach to comparing products and processes to the best firms in an industry. Later in this chapter we discuss some of the issues related to benchmarking. Reverse engineering is a technical laboratory study of competitive products. Beta testing is the testing of a prototype product in a customer's operating environment. In Chapter 7 beta testing is discussed in some detail.

Problem-related intelligence gathering is common, and it is easier to manage for several reasons. First, it is related to a particular problem, the answer to which leads directly to some concrete action by management. It is therefore easier for a manager to assess the value of the research work. Second, this kind of work is often perceived as essential and can therefore be more easily justified. It tends to reduce a manager's perceived risk, and reflects a "due-diligence" approach to top managers. Many middle managers, therefore, use market research to cover their bases before a decision is made. Third, this type of research is easier to manage because usually business firms hire a research manager who coordinates the work. This involves writing the research briefs, requesting bids, selecting a contractor, and presenting the results. Results from this ad hoc effort usually are produced quickly, and if managers are satisfied with the turnaround, quality, and results, problem-related intelligence is often easy to justify.

Benchmarking

Benchmarking is a concept that has become popular during the past decade. A commission set up by the Massachusetts Institute of Technology to report on the state of U.S. industry concluded in 1990 that most successful firms shared an emphasis on competitive benchmarking. In competitive benchmarking a firm's performance is measured against that of "the best-in-class" companies to determine how to achieve desired performance levels. Business functions are analyzed as processes that produce a good or service. Benchmarking can be applied to strategy, operations, and management support functions. Customers are the primary source for market and competitive benchmarking. Benchmarking should be a continuous process and should aim not just to match but to beat the competition. In 1979, Xerox, which dominated the market for high-technology copying machines, found that its market share had shrunk from 49 percent to 22 percent within a few years. Top managers were determined to meet this challenge and initiated several ambitious quality and productivity programs, one of which was competitive benchmarking.

In benchmarking a firm compares its own performance with products and processes of world leaders. Nonetheless, many Western firms are wary of looking too closely at companies they admire, fearing accusations of plagiarism or using competitors' or other leading firms' proprietary information or processes. Most firms take apart the products of firms they admire in the hope of discovering their manufacturing secrets. To supplement reverse engineering, firms use benchmarking. The technique involves several stages:

1. Determine which aspects of products, technology, or marketing the company may need to improve.
2. Identify a firm that is a world leader in performing the process.
3. Contact the company to find out exactly why it performs so well.

Often the ideal benchmark is a company in a different industry. Unlike the process of gathering competitive intelligence, benchmarking often involves the sharing of information about internal processes and then improving the process. It is important to distinguish benchmarking, which is a formal and rigorous process, from competitive intelligence. The difference is that benchmarking is entirely based on mutual agreement and between two firms. The information sharing is confidential and cooperative. For international companies, good benchmarking partners may or perhaps should be firms outside one's home market. For example, European and U.S. auto makers conduct extensive comparisons with Japanese auto makers to reduce their product development cycle time.

Some companies refuse benchmarking requests because their superb internal processes are sources of competitive advantage. As the popularity of benchmarking increases, obtaining good benchmarking data is becoming increasingly difficult. However, as indicated earlier in this chapter, there are legal and ethical ways to obtain nonconfidential information that will enable

TABLE 5.4
Sources of Information

Accounting records	Industry reports
Advertising agencies	Industry associations
Advertising messages	Industry surveys
Annual reports	International trade statistics
Bankers	INTERNET discussion groups
Census data	Investment companies
Classified advertisements	Mailing list providers
Competitors' products	Marketing research agencies
Competitor's customers	Multiclient studies
Consultants	News releases
Corporate directories	Original market research
Country export councils	Own customers
Country surveys	Patent and trademark offices
Country trade commissions	Public activities
Court documents	Security analyst research reports
Court records	State or country economic development offices
Credit records	Stock market data
Electronic data bases	Suppliers
Federal Procurement Centers	Tax records
Financial records	Trade directories
Focus groups	Trade magazines
General press	Unions
Government statistics	University/academic case studies
Handbooks	Yellow Pages
In-depth interviews	
Industry gurus	

effective benchmarks to be performed without the target company's direct knowledge. The objective of competitive benchmarking is to obtain as much valuable information as possible while giving away as little as possible about a company's own strengths and weaknesses.

Intelligence Sources

For organizations committed to establishing an intelligence system, there are many sources of information available. Some sources are listed in Table 5.4.

It is beyond the scope of this chapter to discuss each of these information sources. They are included merely as a checklist and to trigger thinking related to where firms may look to find symptoms of changes, competitive moves, price increases, and so on or answers to specific questions. Each company has specific needs and may find that some sources work better than others.

One source of intelligence data that deserves some attention is related to the intellectual property or patents of another company. Gathering patent information is primarily used by companies as a defensive mechanism to determine competitors' positions with regards to technology and product development strategy. Searches of patent, trademark, and copyright data bases are easy, and often help businesses avoid legal trouble from violating a competitor's intellectual property rights. But intellectual property files can also be used in a company's offensive strategy. The use of patent data bases for competitive intelligence and other business applications is growing in importance. It is particularly easy for non-U.S. firms to access U.S. patent information. In contrast, it is more difficult (and expensive) for non-Japanese companies to access similar data in Japan. Creative uses of these files enable firms to analyze technology, identify new business licensing opportunities, establish what the competition is doing, identify potential new competitors, and protect one's own intellectual property. An example of the aggressive use of patent information to circumvent existing patents and compete with an undisputed leader are the efforts of Intel's competitors in designing and producing cloned 386 and 486 computer chips.

Patents also have several advantages as a technology indicator. Patents provide a wealth of detailed information and comprehensive coverage of technologies. Some firms conduct statistical analysis of international patent records to assess and forecast technological activities of competitors. The results are often validated by comparison with expert opinion. Such analysis appears to be a valuable tool for corporate technology analysis and planning. Overall, results of patent analysis conform with the opinion of technology experts. This is particularly useful when such forecasts are combined with industry or product life cycle analysis.

Establishing an Intelligence and Information System

Much has been written about establishing marketing intelligence and marketing information systems. Proposals vary from formal computerized systems to informal manual systems. The system designed by Quest International described in Figure 5.1 indicates that effective marketing intelligence should contain both formal and informal components. The creation of a marketing intelligence system can be viewed as a strategic institutional change tool. Strategic and competitive intelligence systems should include management information systems, conventional decision support systems, and knowledge-based systems. Many companies have such systems and substantial amounts of internal intelligence information. What makes MI a significant competitive factor in the 1990s is the large number of well-conceived, flexible, and easy-to-use data base tools provided worldwide by firms such as Lotus, Oracle Inc., and IBM. Most firms have the necessary operating functions to integrate their own intelligence activities. In such

FIGURE 5.1
Management of MI at FMC Limited

FMC Limited, a wholly owned subsidiary of Sherer International, is one of the world's largest supplier of flavors and fragrances. FMC consists of many business units that operate as profit centers and are responsible for their own strategies and plans, and regional organizations that interface with customers. Customers range in size from small manufacturers of perfume to large manufacturers of detergents and food products. Some customers operate locally; other customers operate worldwide. Flavor and fragrance manufacturers are expected to work closely with customers to develop and supply flavors and fragrances that enhance customers' products. This requires active MI by FMC. The marketing research function was a corporate-level activity.

In 1993 FMC reviewed its approach to MI. It identified a number of issues and obstacles that needed to be addressed:

- The business units felt that the centralized marketing research function was bureaucratic and excessively costly. Those in the function were perceived to feel that they "owned" the data and that it was to be carefully doled out to the "less than bright" individuals in the business units.
- There was a "Kingdom of Information" attitude, as individuals used possession of information to achieve power in the organization.
- Timeliness was a problem, and in an effort to do all things, no one thing was done well.
- It was perceived that the system required the user to do all the work and that data were not available in the way information was used.
- Much of the research seemed to be interesting rather than relevant, raising questions in terms of value added.

In broad terms it was felt that it was important to make MI data widely available to the business units and the regions in a standardized form, to continuously update the data, to offer tools and templates to facilitate its use by the business units and regions, and to restrict analysis done centrally for "big picture" issues. Specifically FMC identified the following categories of MI data/information:

1. Competitive information, with data on more than 100 competitors.
2. Market information, with information on market volume growth rates, and so on.
3. Key customer information.

A key objective was to design a system that would accept data from many sources. The system, which is under development, also had to be designed to handle both structured and unstructured data. Structured data would include market, competitor, and financial information. Unstructured data would include a variety of information, including "comments" and input by members of the sales force and other employees.

A major source of the structured market data would be a market research firm in the United Kingdom, which agreed to provide information on volume and growth rates of food and other household products in some 40 categories from some 140 countries, together with population and gross domestic product figures. By applying appropriate conversion factors, FMC can translate these numbers into market potential for FMC products, calculate market share by country, and identify potential op-

(continued)

FIGURE 5.1 continued

portunities. The contract provided that the research company would bill FMC £120,000 per year for three years, and for this amount the company would continually update the information. Other structured data would come from company reports, industry reports, market research reports, and so on.

FMC would use Lotus Notes to access the various data bases. Several members of FMC's central marketing staff had been trained in writing programs for Lotus Notes, and they have started a major effort to develop a comprehensive and user-friendly system. It is estimated that the users of the system would be able to generate some 600,000 tables for analysis. In addition, the system would provide for ways to search the "comments" section using key words.

As with any MI system of this kind that contains proprietary information, there is the risk that the data may be used inappropriately. Restricting the access to the data, however, would limit its use and seem to defeat the purpose of the system. The present plan, therefore, would allow essentially unlimited access, but patterns of use would be monitored for possible abuse.

Source: Company records. Company name and some data have been disguised.

cases, all that is needed is to organize the effort following a well-designed set of information- and intelligence-handling procedures. This requires a company culture that supports marketing intelligence as well as broad-based management commitment and use that can best be accomplished through senior management example and leadership.

The nature of and need for intelligence varies by company, market, and industry. Therefore, characteristics of intelligence systems also vary. Some factors that influence the design of the intelligence system include:

- The complexity of the environment.
- Organizational environment and culture.
- The complexity of the business (products/markets).
- Cultural "transportability" of products across international markets.
- The rate of technological change.
- Stage in the product life cycle and growth rates.
- Competitive structure and market share.

The lesson corporate leaders must heed from the history of intelligence in business organizations is that, as the complexity of the environment and of their own organizations increases, their current intelligence activities may no longer suffice. With high business and environmental uncertainty, complexity increases and the need for a marketing intelligence system becomes vital. For example, changing customer demographics, industry innovation, the potential availability of product substitutes, the availability and new uses of technology, value changes, political instability, and shifts in public policy are factors that increase complexity and thus require marketing intelligence. Also, firms with many different product/markets must design their intelligence systems in such a way that relevant data are collected for each product/market combination.

Organizational structure impacts how and to what degree an organization conducts intelligence. Information flows from one organizational level to another and across organizational units. The organizational hierarchy and structure tend to influence the quality of intelligence and how intelligence information flows and is used throughout the organization. For example, in functionally organized companies, the integration and use of intelligence may be difficult across functions such as production, finance, and marketing because of entrenched cultures. This can particularly be true when marketing, rather than top management, initiates the intelligence efforts. On the other hand, when each function gathers and interprets intelligence data from different perspectives, the quality of the information gathered and how it is interpreted and converted into intelligence can be enhanced. Consequently, intelligence based on functional specialization provides depth of knowledge not found in organizations where all intelligence gathering and interpretation is conducted exclusively within the marketing department.

Organizing Intelligence Work

One of the most important but difficult aspects of business marketing intelligence is how BMI efforts are organized and managed. Often this important function only receives half-hearted commitment by senior executives and becomes a periodic task in the marketing organization. In this era of globalization, organizations need to incorporate new approaches in managing their intelligence processes. Several important factors include:

1. All key managers must agree that marketing intelligence is important and be committed to it. Managers must provide key strategic questions to guide the intelligence efforts and sufficient resources to accomplish required intelligence tasks.

2. Management must develop a company culture that encourages employees to search for intelligence and to question the validity and reliability of facts, assumptions, and conclusions in the spirit of organizational learning.

3. Management must assign the intelligence function to a visible position in the organization. By doing so it signals the importance of BMI to all managers. Management must also require the BMI function to produce and widely distribute useful documents.

4. Management must provide a communication climate that facilitates horizontal and vertical dissemination of intelligence. This flow should be from the bottom up and from the top down.

5. Management must select executives with substantial industry experi-

ence. This provides maturity and credibility to intelligence interpretation tasks. Good intelligence briefings require positioning to organizational context. Senior managers are more likely to listen to a manager they know has significant experience than to a manager with little industry experience. This prevents irrelevant recommendations and predictions sometimes provided by inexperienced employees.

It is difficult to recommend exactly how the marketing intelligence function should be organized and where it should be located. However, the function commonly reports to a marketing manager or vice president of marketing. The advantage of this approach is that the marketing function has this resource at its immediate disposal. Market and customer data can easily be collected and interpreted. The disadvantage of this approach is that it is often viewed as an exclusive tool for the marketing function. Other functions or departments may receive intelligence only on a need-to-know basis. This makes it difficult for other functions to become equal partners in intelligence gathering. As we stated previously, other functions such as research and development, engineering, field service, and manufacturing should be included as essential players in the intelligence gathering activities.

Another approach that appears to work is to disassociate the BMI activities somewhat from the day-to-day marketing operating activities. This can be done by establishing a marketing service organization that provides information and intelligence services to all departments. In practice this means that all functions receive intelligence and can request intelligence from this unit. Often when the marketing intelligence unit has such independent status, it also works closely with corporate and business management.

Demand Analysis

Defining the Market Potential and Its Components

One of the most common BMI activities is the determination of a company's potential in a particular market segment for a specific product. Figure 5.2 shows the various components of market potential. By understanding the nature and size of these components, it is possible to determine market potential in a company-specific context.

The top line in Figure 5.2 represents the total theoretical potential market. The theoretical market size is the size of the market if all customers would purchase a specific solution to solve their functional needs. For example, consider the business office market for personal computers. One could argue that all of a certain type of office worker could use a personal computer. However, it is not realistic to expect that this will happen in all offices worldwide. Therefore, the number we get by counting all office workers is just a theoretical number. This theoretical number is the theoretical market size for personal computers. Based on knowledge about the office market, we know that within a certain time only a proportion of office workers are likely to receive

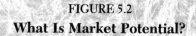

FIGURE 5.2
What Is Market Potential?

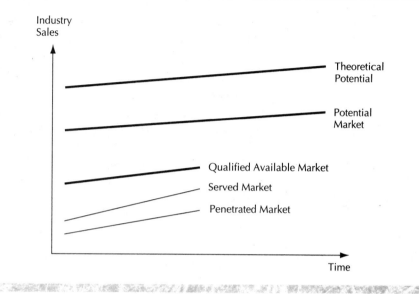

personal computers. The reasons for this include budget limitations, cultural barriers, executives unwilling to use computers, and the availability of a large pool of electric typewriters available. As a result, there will always be some office workers who will not have personal computers. Therefore, the question we need to answer is how many firms are likely to purchase personal computers within a given time period?

The answer to this question helps determine the size of the potential market, which needs to be broken down into smaller components. The next question is, what proportion of the potential market is available? Even though the market potential exists, the market infrastructure may be such that all potential customers may not be reachable. Many countries may have limited distribution or communications channels that restrict market penetration. Therefore, only a certain proportion of the potential market is available. This proportion is the available market or the level of likely penetration. The available market can be broken down into several components: the qualified market, the served market, and the penetrated market. The qualified market is the portion of the market for which a company with a given technology can qualify to compete. The served market is the portion of the market that the firm specifically targets. The penetrated market is that portion of the served market that the firm expects to reach with a particular marketing program.

TABLE 5.5

Arguments for Customer Satisfaction Research

- If you do not measure it, you can not improve it.
- Do not mistake silence for satisfaction.
- If you are not keeping score, you are only practicing.
- It costs five times more to get a new customer than it costs to keep a current customer.
- Increase in customer satisfaction = $ XXX increase in sales = $ XXX in company profits.

- More than 90 percent of unsatisfied customers do not complain.
- Satisfied customers tend to buy more and are more willing to pay premium prices.
- Satisfied customers are loyal customers, less likely to switch to competitive products.
- Companies can boost profits by almost 100% by retaining just 5 percent more of their customers.

It is very important for firms to go through an exercise similar to the one described above. It helps define what portion of the market is potential for the company. It may also reveal when a market potential represents an opportunity for a specific firm with a given solution.

Using Satisfaction Surveys to Understand Current Market Position

Many firms, particularly small- and medium-size companies, do not have a good understanding of their market position. In many international markets, market shares and market share growth figures are crude and inaccurate, which limits a firm's ability to accurately determine its competitive position. It is particularly important to obtain relative figures because they are the true measures of performance. A firm can have substantial aggregate growth but experience loss of its relative market position.

For this reason some business marketing firms conduct regular customer satisfaction studies. For example, the Diagnostic Division of Abbott Laboratories tracks customer satisfaction in 46 countries, a complex task that requires commitment and resources. To convince management that this was the appropriate intelligence approach, the MI group at Abbott used the arguments shown in Table 5.5.

For many of the reasons listed in the table, customer satisfaction measurement has become a popular intelligence activity. Although international customer satisfaction research is difficult to do, firms that can link satisfaction data to performance and evaluation may design customer satisfaction into their planning and reward systems.

Understanding Customer Requirements

Another essential BMI intelligence activity is gaining an understanding of customer needs. Many firms give "lip service" to this requirement; they push what they know best (are product oriented) without attempting to understand what the customer really needs. Business marketers that are market oriented know the customer requirements better than the customer. In such situations, selling is less important and persuasion becomes unnecessary. In Chapter 3 we discussed in detail the needs and motivation of business customers. Below are some of the key marketing intelligence aspects of customer requirements.

- Know the customer's operations and products in detail.
- Understand the customer's cost structure.
- Identify how the initial purchase enhances the customer's value versus its customers and how it impacts cost.
- Understand operating implications related to installation and startup.
- Understand the role of operating costs versus up-front investment.
- Find out how important product life cycle costs or cost of ownership are to the customer.
- Identify the customer's understanding of your product's relative benefits and the impact on the customer's cost structure and performance.

To determine customer requirements, business marketers must communicate directly with their clients. Much of the responsibility for intelligence gathering in many companies is given to the sales force. If used extensively, this can be an ineffective approach unless it is properly managed. Because salespeople may be biased toward the sale, they may not be objective assessors of what is in the best interest of the customer and the company in the long run. Consequently, it is important that other company employees such as marketing staff, product managers, engineers, researchers, and planners, communicate with the client organization. It is also common to use objective third parties, such as consultants and market research firms, to assist in the evaluation. Formal, problem-oriented market research is commonly used to identify customer requirements in addition to sales force recommendations. The nature of the research may vary from a survey to in-depth executive interviews. In Chapter 7 we discuss in more detail how a business marketer can use beta tests and conjoint analysis to determine and refine customers' product requirements.

Assessing Market Demand

In Chapter 3 we discussed how aggregate business market behavior often is a result of events in consumer or government markets. Business market behavior can therefore often be traced directly to changed behavior in these markets. Business market demand is often a derived demand. There is often a lag factor between changes in consumer demand and the impact that it has on business demand. Thus an extremely important intelligence activity for business marketers is to identify and monitor factors that influence changes and periodic fluctuations in demand.

Another important factor in analyzing demand for business products is demand elasticity. Demand elasticity, commonly discussed in relationship to pricing, reflects the positive and negative changes in demand as prices are reduced or increased. When the business marketer is selling a substitute product, in some markets and situations, this can result in quick changes in a firm's demand. However, it is not always that simple. In business marketing, relationships are important, and there may be substantial resistance to change even though there are economic incentives to use alternative suppliers. Personal relationships, service level, loyalty, and organizational culture are other important influences.

Product characteristics are another factor that influences demand fluctuations. Firms may use a simple but effective guideline: From the customer's point of view, does the product we provide contain attributes that are "like to haves" or are they "must haves"? If the firm provides a product with many of "like to have" features, it would expect that demand would fall as price increased. If the firm provides a product that has many "must have" features, it could expect demand to remain stable with price increases. From a marketing intelligence point of view, it is essential to determine the "must have" criteria. Failure to understand the difference between the two may have serious consequences. Many international companies through product development and delivery have incorporated a large number of "like to haves." But these efforts have had no influence on demand. They have only increased the firms' product and delivery costs.

Sales Forecasting

Although forecasting is not intelligence, one of the primary objectives of BMI is to provide the basis for the forecast. It is thus directly linked to intelligence efforts. The better the market intelligence, the better the forecast. We include a description of forecasting here because it is essential to the economic performance of any business organization. Forecasts are directly linked to company budgets and plans. Figure 5.3 shows the relationships between the forecast and various company budgets. The forecast requires extensive external inputs, and most of the activities conducted by BMI are directly linked to the quality of the forecast.

Forecasting is important because it directs the planning, allocation, and use of a business organization's resources. If a forecast is too high, a firm has overallocated resources and must go through the painful process of making cuts. If the forecast is too low, the firm usually has not allocated enough resources to satisfy the demand. This, of course, is also a problem, but a more pleasant one, because the firm may have to rush order materials, hire more labor, and so on. Forecasts should be on target. Therefore, many business-to-business marketers use rolling forecasts that are updated monthly. A forecast is not an objective or wishful thinking. A forecast is a commitment. It reflects what

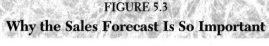

FIGURE 5.3
Why the Sales Forecast Is So Important

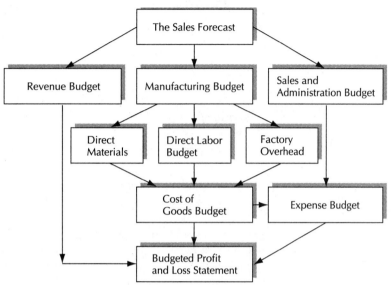

will be delivered in terms of sales. It is better to underestimate than to overestimate the sales forecast. Firms can choose from an extensive pool of methods and approaches developed to forecast sales. Below we describe some common approaches to forecasting.[1]

Forecasting techniques are often divided into two categories— qualitative and quantitative methods. The key qualitative methods are:

- *In-depth interviews* with customers regarding their buying intentions and purchase requirements. Due to the open-ended nature of this approach, it can contain significant bias. It is an excellent way of getting detailed information from important customers, and it allows for two-way interaction between the interviewer and the interviewee.

- *Jury of executive opinion* combines the average estimates of senior executives and knowledgeable individuals within the organization. The weakness of this method is that it strictly depends on the knowledge of executives. But because this method consolidates the knowledge of several people, it is less biased than the in-depth interview.

- *Sales force composites* are forecasts developed by salespersons for their respective territories. Salespeople may be biased. They may be either too optimistic, or, if they are paid a commission, salespersons may manipulate forecasts to plan their income stream. In spite of this weakness, this is still the most frequently used forecasting method in business marketing. It is easy to implement.

- *The Delphi method* is an extension of the jury of executive opinion approach. It is a group forecasting method that incorporates anonymity, forecast revisions, feedback to other forecasters, and consensus. It is time consuming to implement but usually unbiased due to anonymity.

Some quantitative forecasting methods are:

- *Survey of user needs* is similar to the in-depth interview, except that the customer fills out a questionnaire about buying needs and intentions. Because of ongoing negotiations, bias is likely to exist.
- *Time-series analysis* includes several methods—moving averages, trend fitting, exponential smoothening, least squares, and Box-Jenkins time-series analysis. All of these methods require historical data. Moving averages techniques use the average of recent periods to predict the next forecast period. Trend fitting and exponential smoothening tries to fit past data to a particular curve or adjusts the forecast with some proportional weight to predict sales for the next period. Box-Jenkins forecasting is a sophisticated computer model that allows the computer to pick a statistical time-series model that fits the data.
- *Regression analysis* involves identifying the variables that influence sales and building a model that can then be applied to historical data to determine the effect of each variable on sales. For maximum effectiveness regression analysis requires a large number of past observations and it is limited in its ability to identify major turning points. It is most useful for products in the mature stage of the product life cycle and for products where a constant set of variables, which can be accurately measured, have been identified.
- *Diffusion analysis* is very difficult to use, but it may work when a firm is trying to forecast sales for an entire product class. This category of forecasting models is also useful for forecasting sales of new products. It is quite problematic because it is a form of market simulation and requires significant market research to estimate parameters used in the analysis.
- *Input-output analysis* is an econometric technique that establishes links between sectors of one industry with sectors of another industry. This technique is complex and time consuming.
- *Product life cycle analysis* can be used when it is possible to estimate the parameters of the life cycle s-curve. Using this approach for forecasting requires knowledge of product acceptance rates.

By themselves, none of these methods may give an accurate forecast. A combination of methods integrated with sound intelligence and experience usually gives the best results. For mature businesses, with relatively stable patterns of competitive market shares, forecasting overall industry demand may be the most critical requirement, but estimates also need to be made of the relative marketing efforts of competitors. For firms introducing new products, forecasting becomes more uncertain. Sales paterns during previous introductions of similar products may provide guidance as can intelligence gathered from customers by the sales force. Regardless of the forecasting situation, it needs to be recognized that even the best forecasts deal with the future and so are inherently uncertain. However, the better management is able to estimate the future, the better it is prepared to deal with it. Good forecasts, therefore, require both management attention and resources.

How to Use Marketing Intelligence

Companies able to build intelligence and use systems that are better than their competitors often derive sustainable competitive advantage. It is the use of intelligence that represents an important asset. If the intelligence is not used, it is only a wasteful expense. How can companies incorporate market intelligence? Below are a few suggestions about how intelligence can be used.

- Publish internally the objectives of the marketing intelligence unit and explain who is responsible for what activity. Encourage managers to use the BMI resource.
- Periodically develop a presumed competitor business strategy document. Circulate this document to all managers and productively solicit updates and revisions.
- Provide periodic status reports on competitor and customer activities.
- Provide all managers with periodic technology updates.
- Provide an overview catalog or data base of available intelligence material. This might consist of a list of electronic data bases available, research reports on file, market statistics, and secondary resources.

How to Protect Intelligence and Business Secrets

It is essential that business intelligence is kept inside the organization. Intelligence should be treated as sensitive information and considered a trade secret. Such information is usually lost in three ways:

1. Accidental exposure by an employee entrusted with its possession.
2. Intentional theft by an unauthorized outside agent.
3. Internal theft by an ex-employee or a disgruntled worker who has access to the information.

Since there is no possible way to keep all intelligence information secret, management must create an awareness and responsibility program that informs and requires employees who work with BMI that it should not be disclosed to outsiders. Employees should be required to sign a statement related to disclosure of information. For example, throughout IBM, during its period of unparalleled success, a responsible and consistent approach existed among employees. Few employees divulged confidential information to outsiders. Internally, IBM was very "open," while to an outsider it appeared closed and little market intelligence was available to nonemployees.

Summary

Marketing intelligence is an important business marketing function. It represents a broad set of activities that supports strategy formulation and implementation. BMI is broader than marketing research and is conducted continuously by employees from a variety of company functions. Globalization of business has increased the importance of BMI and made it more taxing on resources and more difficult to conduct.

The BMI function is often ignored, poorly resourced, and inadequately staffed. This chapter distinguishes between problem-oriented and continuous BMI. Companies that conduct both well are often leaders in their field. Their managers are willing to change strategy as BMI requires.

Overview of Chapter Cases

✳ The MacTec case describes the situation of a Swedish manufacturer of equipment for use in water systems. The equipment was well received in Scandinavia and the firm was considering entry into the U.S. market. It provides the opportunity to consider the information the firm needed in order to make its decision and how it might go about obtaining the needed information.

✳ The Modern Plastics case describes the situation of a newly appointed sales manager required to forecast sales for his region. It provides the opportunity to consider the role of forecasts in a firm, the various methods that can be used to make a forecast, and how marketing efforts might vary the forecast.

✳ The Quest International case describes the situation of an international firm faced with hiring a new director of marketing research. It provides the opportunity to consider the role of marketing research in a multiproduct business and the relationship between the marketing research function and the product businesses.

Endnotes

1. For a good assessment of forecasting, see D.M. Georgoff and R.G. Murdick, "A Manager's Guide to Forecasting," *Harvard Business Review,* January 1986.

Lawrence B. Chonko
John F. Tanner Jr.
Ellen Reid Smith

Selling and Sales Management in Action: The Sales Force's Role in International Marketing Research and Marketing Information Systems

Many companies resist global markets because of seemingly insurmountable problems with these markets. Salespeople are often used successfully to gather market information. There is a wealth of market data that can be collected by a company's international sales force and distributors' sales force which can prove to be valuable in surmounting cultural and marketing barriers associated with global markets. The current paper discusses how and with what success U.S. multinational companies are using their international sales forces in gathering international marketing research data. ✳

Introduction

During the 1980s, top CEO's have learned that America's economic future lies in exports and that business needs to take a more global perspective. With varying degrees of success, great numbers of

At the time this article was written, Lawrence B. Chonko, who holds his Ph.D. from the University of Houston, was Chairman of the Marketing Department at Baylor University in Waco, Texas. Prof. Chonko has served as editor of the *Journal of Personal Selling and Sales Management.* His scholarly work has appeared in the *Journal of Marketing, Journal of Marketing Research, Academy of Management Journal, Journal of the Academy of Marketing Science, Journal of Business Ethics,* and other journals and edited volumes. John F. (Jeff) Tanner Jr. holds his Ph.D. from the University of Georgia. His industry experience includes marketing management with Rockwell International and sales and marketing management with Xerox Corporation. His work has appeared in the *Journal of Business Research, Journal of Business and Industrial Marketing, Journal of Personal Selling and Sales Management* and others. Ellen Smith was a graduate student in the Hankamer School of Business at Baylor University. *Source:* "Selling and Sales Management in Action: The Sales Force's Role in International Marketing Research and Marketing Information Systems," by Lawrence B. Chonko, John F. Tanner, Jr., and Ellen Reid Smith, *Journal of Personal Selling and Sales Management,* Vol. 11, No. 1, Winter, 1991, pp. 69–79.

American companies have entered foreign markets (Simon and Button 1990); however, many companies still resist global markets because of the seemingly insurmountable problems (Townley 1990).

Twenty-five years ago, Webster argued that the "use of the sales(person) for gathering information can be much more critical than [their] use for promotion" (1965, 78). More recently, Mellow (1989) observed that salespeople are a likely source of information about marketplace problems. There is a wealth of market data that can be collected by a company's international sales force and distributors' sales force which can prove to be valuable in surmounting such cultural and marketing barriers (Cavusgil 1985). How U.S. multinational companies are using their international sales forces in gathering international marketing research data, and with what success, is the subject of this paper.

Background

International marketing research is termed "comparative marketing research" by most authors with its principle focus being "the systematic detection, identification, classification, measurement, and interpretation of similarities and differences among entire national systems" (Boddewyn 1981, p. 61). Thus the terms "international" and comparative can be used interchangeably. Similar to domestic marketing research, comparative marketing research is required by the marketing manager to determine marketing mix decisions (Jeannet and Hennessey 1988). International marketing research has the added complexity of understanding a country's cultural norms, and its effects on the implementation of marketing policies, the consumer's purchasing behavior, and the reliability of secondary and primary data gathering techniques.

There are five main challenges a marketing manager faces in planning international marketing research: (1) understanding similarities across countries in order to define a target market; (2) a lack of accurate secondary information; (3) the high costs of conducting international research, particularly when primary data is desired; (4) coordinating marketing research across countries, which also involves losing control of not only the research process, but the translations as well; and (5) establishing comparability and equivalence in marketing research instruments (Jeannet and Hennessey 1988). It is the complexity of these five problems which significantly impact a company's decision to conduct international marketing research.

As Permut (1977) and Cavusgil (1985) noted, multinational companies do not use formal marketing research to any large extent. Instead, companies rely on secondary information, information that is often found by hiring outside consultants.

What's keeping companies from obtaining this information themselves? In addition to the five challenges cited earlier, there are problems of language barriers, contacts in the foreign data collecting offices, knowledge of governmental agencies, and most of all, having a person located in the foreign country to do data gathering footwork. In many cases, this person could be the foreign salesperson.

Based on a review of current literature, this research project is predicated on the following assumptions inferred from various sources (e.g. Cavusgil 1985; Hunt and Cooke 1990; Still 1981):

- Given the added political and economic risks involved when selling or operating in a foreign country, accurate and timely market information is even more important than in domestic marketing.
- International marketing research is often more difficult to perform in foreign countries. Its risk of unreliability is higher than in the United States, and the process is very costly. Consequently, companies are eager to find satisfactory alternatives to this risky and costly process.
- In many cases, salespeople are a company's only link to the customer, resulting in salespeople having (nearly) exclusive access to valuable customer data.

These assumptions provide the focus for this study, which is designed to assess the role international sales forces currently play in gathering market data from foreign countries. More specifically, the research is designed to find out what types of information are being gathered during each phase of the marketing cycle, how information is being communicated to the marketing offices, if salespeople are given the results of the marketing research, and if so, in what format. In addition, is the information system being used centralized or decentralized, and is the system being used formal or in formal? What problems do sales managers have in gathering and using marketing research data? How does the market data gathering process done by the sales force in foreign countries differ from that done domestically?

Method

The Sample

The sample consisted of companies who, according to *Standard and Poors Guide to Business* for corporations, had revenues of more than $2 million, who had international revenues, whose industry entailed personal selling, and who listed names of executives in an international division. This last requirement was needed for telephoning and asking for executives by name, thus assuring a higher respondent success rate.

No more than two corporations were chosen from the same type of industry, thereby preventing any industry bias in the collected data. Industries surveyed included: office products, pharmaceuticals, cosmetics, home care products, computer systems, raw metals, air travel and tours, foods, insurance, and several others. In addition, only those companies originating in the United States were chosen (i.e. foreign owned companies headquartered in or operating in the United States were not chosen). This procedure provided a sample of 26 corporations and resulted in 23 usable interviews and three refusals. Each executive was screened as to his or her knowledge of the international marketing practices of his or her firm and only appropriate, knowledgeable executives were included.

Measures

Phone interviews were chosen as the means for gathering data, as previous studies reported difficulty with mail surveys (e.g. Evans and Schlacker 1985). By contrast, success with personal interviews has been reported (e.g. Cavusgil 1985).

The data were gathered using a structured, in-depth telephone interview (see instrument at Appendix A). The instrument had ten open-ended questions, four of which had three parts each.

The questionnaire was designed to collect 6 types of information: (1) types of information gathered in each stage of the product life cycle; (2) types of systems used to gather and relay information; (3) types of problems encountered in gathering and using marketing information; (4) the role of expatriates in the information gathering process; (5) which types of decisions were made using the information gathered by the international sales force; (6) differences in using sales forces internationally versus domestically for gathering market data.

Results

Use of Data

Because of the necessity of a short questionnaire, the area which sales force information is used was narrowed to three types of decisions. According to the literature (Cavusgil 1985; Klompmaker 1980-81; Evans and Schlacter 1985; Wotruba 1976; Webster 1965), sales forecasting decisions were determined to be the most logical and frequent use of this information, product design a less frequent area, and company/product image making the least likely area for sales force input. It was hoped that the wide span could be used to judge the overall extent to which the sales force's input was used.

It was not surprising that 71 percent of the companies surveyed regularly used sales force information for sales forecasting. Only 35 percent, however, regularly used sales force information for product design, and 46 percent used sales force information for company or product image making. These last two findings are surprising because it was expected that fewer firms would use sales force information when making decisions concerning image.

Problems in Gathering and Using International Market Data

It is important to consider the problems which the sales manager faces in gathering and receiving marketing research data in order to understand how information systems should be designed to help minimize these problems. Problems in gathering market data from international salespeople can be classified as due to situational limitations or problems with the sales force. One-third reported difficulties due to situational limitations. Over 40 percent reported problems with the sales force such as resistance due to need to generate sales, non-response, lack of objectivity and accuracy, and inability to communicate data to management.

Using data collected by the sales force was reported to be limited by the difficulty in determining the quality of data. Several respondents reported concern that the data may not be accurate if the use of such data is perceived to negatively impact the sales force. Information is also seen as too broad or too local to be of value. These problems could be minimized by collecting specific data regularly, and not just when a decision is to

TABLE 1
Methods of Input of Market Information by International Sales Forces

Written Survey	32%
Informal Phone	26%
Continuous Communication	16%
Formal Phone Survey	21%
Written Sales Reports	21%
Field Visits	16%
Facsimile	16%
Quarterly Meetings	11%
Tiered Collection System	5%
Monthly Meetings	5%
Telex	5%

Sum is greater than 100% because respondents reported several methods.

be made. Salespeople who are used to providing specific data would be less likely to question the use of that data and would be conditioned to provide good data.

Information Collection and Dissemination

The methods used to collect information are shown in Table 1. The three most frequently used methods are written questionnaires (32 percent of the companies), informal phone conversations (25 percent), and continuous communication (written, telephone, and face-to-face) between the sales force and the marketing department (26 percent). As seen in Table 1, fax and telex are unpopular methods (11 percent and 5 percent), as are formal meetings (10 percent) and tiered collection systems (5 percent).

Companies provided marketing research findings to the sales force in many ways (see Table 2). Periodic written reports were mentioned most often (30 percent), but only one company used a monthly newsletter.

The format in which marketing research findings are presented is primarily as summarized data (30 percent) along with guidelines and sug-

gestions (30 percent). These findings are summarized in Table 3.

It was assumed that executives knew the best way to communicate marketing research findings to the sales force but may be unable to implement their system. Therefore, respondents were asked what they thought was the optimal technique for communicating research findings to the sales force. Their answers included both their currently used methods and future methods and are summarized in Table 4.

One of the primary factors for successful information gathering was felt to be the frequency with which data was relayed to the marketing office (even in non-volatile industries). Those with daily or weekly communication (telephone & telex) with salespeople reported receiving more timely information and expressed a feeling of understanding what was happening "on the front line."

Of those companies who felt their company's information system was good, their reasons were:

- Open communication between sales force and marketers.
- Regular working meetings between sales force and marketers.

TABLE 2
Methods of Relating Research Findings to International Sales Forces

Periodic Written Reports	32%
One-on-One Meetings	21%
Telephone	21%
Telex	21%
Product Seminars	16%
Word-of-Mouth	11%
Strategy Reports and Directives	11%
Facsimile	11%
Bulletins	11%
Quarterly Meetings	11%
Not Given to Sales Force	11%
Product and Competitive Information	11%
Monthly Newsletter	5%

TABLE 3	
Format of Research Findings Given to International Sales Forces	
Periodic Written Reports	32%
Guidelines/Suggestions (No Data)	32%
Analyzed Data (No Guidelines)	21%
Revenue Targets	11%
Directives	11%
Not Communicated	11%
Raw Data	5%

TABLE 4	
Optimal Methods of Relaying Research Findings to International Sales Forces	
Periodic Written Reports	16%
Meetings	16%
Telephone or Telex or Facsimile	11%
Seminars	11%
Monthly Newsletter	11%
One-on-One	5%
Electronically	5%
Brochure	5%
Customer Oriented Applications Reports	5%
Would Not Communicate	5%
Makes No Difference	5%

- Continuous exchange of information.
- Flexibility of system to meet changing market.
- Autonomy of sales force to make independent decisions.
- It's one of the best.
- We're good at it all.
- The sales force is our only touch with consumers.

Of those companies who felt their company's information system needed improvements, or was a poor system, their reasons given were:

- Information exchange is too infrequent.
- Not enough structure to system.
- Very rustic system, because not enough research by local consultants (not intention of increasing the use of the sales force).
- Need more money.
- Information exchange too slow.
- Not enough information to measure effectiveness of product, inventory, and distribution changes, or advertising and trade fair promotions.
- Poor system compared to competition.
- Not enough historical data.
- Not all data collected is correct, so must weigh all information with a grain of salt.
- System needs automating.

The Entry Phase

The sales force's role in the entry phase was considered particularly important to 18 of the companies interviewed because of the high costs associated with sending research teams to the foreign country or hiring consultants to evaluate new markets. Sales forces, or distributors in some cases, could assume the role of a specialized research team by collecting a substantial amount of information about market potential and entry logistics (price, package, distribution, and import regulations). Prior to market entry, these companies had their salespeople conduct secondary research, collecting all types of market statistics and information on government regulations obtained through published data and through sales experience in similar foreign markets.

Two companies included a salesperson on their five-person research teams which went to the new country to evaluate market potential. The team would be composed of a foreign country expert, an economist, a financial specialist, and a product manager or marketer, a lawyer, and a production expert. The teams were responsible for developing a plan for entry.

As is the case with U.S.-based sales forces, salespeople were often asked to gather competitor information. This included competitive price, product line, market share, number of salespeople, and customer perceptions of competitors' products, delivery, and service.

In the case of new product evaluation, four companies thought salespeople were the method of choice for new product trial research, customer expectations, market focus, and sales volume predictions.

In all cases, the salespeople's information was considered only in combination with data gathered from other sources. Two companies used both a formal research process and the sales force's information, but "surveys only formalized this (sales force's) information."

Essential market data which salespeople collected during the entry phase included:

- Competitor information.
- Government regulations.
- Entry logistics.
- Customers' needs and expectations.
- Customers' willingness to try product.
- Product trial implementation and results.
- Customers' awareness of company and product.
- Natural resource availability for production.
- Socio-economic climate and political stability.
- Data from local trade and industry publications.
- Data from government published statistics.
- Market volatility.

Growth Phase

The growth phase in this study was limited to growth within a foreign country, or within a set of very similar countries. An expanded product line, or growth into a new market segment, was still considered as growth and not entry, in order to assure uniformity of answer classification. Growth which involved entry into a new country, or new set of similar countries, was classified as the entry phase.

In the growth phase, companies use their salespeople for gathering information on the competition and any new market requirements. Of the two companies which felt this was the most important phase for using the sales force, the first company used salespeople primarily for gathering information on service needs and satisfaction once the product was in place. The second company concentrated on customers' likes or dislikes of its product and of competition. This information was used to detect a customers' intent to switch products.

One company's very sophisticated competitor intelligence system had the sales force gathering tactical information on competitors' moves. This included information about competitor pricing, sales force increases or decreases, increased/decreased advertising, changes in distribution, and plant expansions or alliances published in local journals. The sales force was also the eyes and ears for early detection of new market competition. Another company used sales volume statistics and predictions from the sales force to balance volume versus start-up costs to determine the size of growth which should be attempted.

Three of the companies changed from a centralized system of market research in the entry phase to a decentralized system in the growth phase so that information from the sales force was no longer available for consideration at the headquarters' office. More foreign office independence in the growth phase also resulted in less direct contact with the sales force.

Essential market data which salespeople collect during the growth phase include:

- Competitor information.
- New market requirements.
- Customer surveys.
- Product quality and features.
- Relationship of customer, with end consumer.
- Which areas are most profitable.
- Whether or not to expand.

- Volume vs. start-up costs to determine growth size.
- Distributor survey for customer satisfaction index.

Maturity Phase

Very few of the companies considered themselves in the maturity phase; however, information was gathered from those companies which had products in the maturity phase. For this reason, it is in this phase that the least amount of data was gathered from the respondents.

One company felt that using the sales force was most important in the maturity phase, and this was because of the significant amount of capital which had been invested up to that point. This sales force gathered mostly market information. The company felt that its increased risk warranted increased amounts of information from the salespeople. This company is in a supply driven market, meaning that the maturity phase requires assemblies working at full capacity and large inventories. No other company interviewed was in this situation, so a comparison was not possible.

One company with a very sophisticated intelligence system uses the sales force during product maturity as part of an "Early Warning System" to detect significant incoming competition. The salespeople are used to gather pre-specified key information which signals the competitive trend. Data collected by the salespeople include factors such as: salespeople being hired away, a change in the institutions which supply salespeople and technicians, and/or slack in product demand.

Essential market data which salespeople collect during the maturity phase include:

- Competitive information.
- Government data on product usage.
- Type of businesses using the product.
- Improved means of distribution.
- Customers' desire for product changes.
- New customer needs.
- What new products could replace mature product.
- Product weaknesses.

Structure of International Marketing Research Functions

The type of structures used to conduct international marketing research functions was mixed. Eight of the companies studied used a centralized structure, while five used decentralized approaches in their international marketing tasks. Three additional companies contacted but not included in research results used such decentralized systems that neither the international sales nor marketing departments could answer questions on the survey because they had so little knowledge of what went on in the decentralized marketing offices.

In some cases the current market stage which a company was in was a strong determinant in whether a centralized or decentralized approach was used. For example, three firms had gone from centralized marketing systems in the entry phase and then switched to decentralized systems once established in the foreign country and well into the growth phase. Only one company went from a decentralized system in the entry phase to a centralized system in the growth phase. In addition, one company used both systems and based it decision of centralization versus decentralization on economic climate and other situational factors within the foreign country.

Gestetner (1974) outlined two main factors determining a centrist versus decentrist sales management approach, which is closely transferable to this research analysis. First was the size of the home market:

> Companies with a large home market tend to be centrist, while those with a small home market tend to be noncentrist. If a company is successful in a large home market before it starts exporting, its management tends to assume that its approach to the domestic market must be effective in every market. Further, managers are often afraid to change methods they know and understand. (p. 103).

Since all the interviews were conducted with companies who were first successful in the home market (United States), this research does not support Gestetner's centrist theory.

Second, Gestetner (1974) found that the way a company began selling internationally affected the marketing management structure:

> Some companies start by making a definite decision to get into the export market. They usually adopt a centrist policy and set up an internal international division, which becomes a copy of the home selling division. (p. 107)

Although almost all companies interviewed had an international division, only about half have centralized approaches. This data does not support Gestetner's centrist theory of marketing management but supports a situational model based upon such factors as management structure, market cycle, product type, market type, market size, and knowledge or type of foreign culture.

As an interesting side note, Gestetner also found that "U.S. companies generally tended to be centrist, European companies noncentrist, and the Japanese companies combined these two approaches in a unique way." The fact that Gestetner studied U.S.-owned companies as well as foreign-owned companies could explain this discrepancy in findings.

Twenty companies responded to the question concerning formalization of information flow. An informal system is defined as a sporadic system, used without uniformity; whereas, a formal system conducted research on some sort of periodic bases and consistently used the same methods. Ten companies used informal programs, nine companies used formal programs, and one company entered the market using a formal system, but once in the growth stage, changed to an informal system.

There was not a pattern in the types of industries companies were in with respect to the use of formal or informal systems. Companies with very volatile markets were found to be using both formal and informal systems; however, almost all of these types of companies collected data daily. One of the companies surveyed whose market was very volatile had a marketing representative in each foreign country whose job was to collect information electronically on a daily basis but to relay research findings back to the sales force through sales quotas and sales suggestions in a one-on-one situation.

With one company, the method used, the extent of information gathered, and the frequency of reports are dependent upon the size of the sales contract and the country where the sale is taking place. Each sale is seen independently because of the type of product being sold.

International and Domestic Differences

Respondents were asked what they thought was the most significant difference, or the difference which they were most accustomed to dealing with, between international and domestic sales forces when gathering market information.

Five companies' executives commented explicitly that there was no difference in the "way" information was gathered and that the differences were in the "types" of information needed. These informational differences found in foreign countries included:

- Not as much information available.
- Information being harder to attain.
- Information being less reliable, resulting in the need for time consuming cross checking.
- Because of the many complexities and increased competition in a foreign market, there are more types of information needed.
- International sales depend more on relations, so there are more areas to monitor, and more representatives who need the information.
- Our U.S. strategy is to copy, but increased competition internationally necessitates the need for more market information and market research for more aggressive market strategies.

Other respondents noted that the differences lie in the sales force personnel. One respondent felt that international salespeople had a broader mentality and out of necessity were not culture bound. In direct contrast to this, one respondent felt that international salespeople, as well as their customers, were much less sophisticated. Another respondent felt that the problem was with management: "Although local salespeople understand customer and market needs, sales managers and marketers in the U.S. headquarters don't understand the different customer and market needs in the foreign country."

Accessibility of the sales force in a foreign market is quite different from the domestic market where the sales force is not only easily accessible, but so are the customers. Difficulties were attributed to the limited number of international salespeople as compared to the U.S. market, to the geographical accessibility of the sales force, and to language translation problems. Internationally, distributors or country sales managers are frequently seen as a barrier to directly contacting the sales force. Dealing with the sales force through these intermediaries caused the information gathered to not be as representative.

One respondent had experienced this phenomenon first hand when the company distributed a questionnaire to two groups of salespeople. The Canadian sales force was contacted directly, but the European sales force was contacted through a regional sales manager. The Canadian responses gave much more "creative solutions" and more "specific information" than the European sales force. The respondent attributed this problem to the European sales manager who distributed the questionnaire to only some of the sales force. Frequently, only subordinate sales managers were asked to complete the questionnaire, instead of giving the questionnaire directly to the salespeople.

Lastly, only four respondents mentioned cultural assumptions as part of the main differences between domestic and international data gathering by the sales force. One respondent noted that "after living in Asia for five years, and learning to speak the language, it was not enough to overcome the cultural barriers to gathering reliable data." Consequently, he recommended using only local salespeople for marketing research. Another company with a very successful intelligence system found that the key to overcoming cultural assumptions was to have a truly "global perspective" like his company did. He described this as not trying to compare each country with the United States for

differences, but to compare like countries for similarities in markets, customers, and competition.

Using a U.S. Expatriate

Of the companies surveyed, eight didn't use expatriates, one used all expatriates, and ten used both expatriates and foreign salespeople. Out of the ten companies who used both expatriates and local salespeople on their foreign sales forces, only three used both types of salespeople exactly the same to gather information. The majority of the companies employing both types of salespeople (six companies) used expatriates and local salespeople differently, and one company didn't have enough knowledge to answer the question.

One company felt that its expatriate salespeople gathered more detailed information because they were more used to marketing data techniques and the usefulness of the input. In contract, two companies felt that because of the cultural barriers an expatriate faced, information gathered by the expatriate tended to be less credible. Another company said that the effectiveness of using expatriates to gather market information depended both on the individual and the complexity of the foreign environment. While a local salesperson was better at gathering valid information because of his or her cultural advantages, the expatriate was typically felt to be better at communicating information to the headquarters' office.

In sum, the use of expatriates is not a universal process. The data indicate that many practices are in use.

Conclusions and Implications

Cavusgil (1985), in a study of U.S. export market research, reported that companies typically had information overload and information was frequently found to be conflicting. He concluded that the real task for his respondents, as is for this study's respondents, is to determine which information is more accurate, secondary information or that gathered by the salespeople. In many cases, the information gathered by salespeople was compared to data gathered by U.S. and foreign agencies to comb for discrepancies in the published data. Discrepancies were particularly prevalent for developing countries.

Evidence from the present study clearly shows that multinational companies frequently use international salespeople as sources for both marketing intelligence and marketing research data. Data gathered by international salespeople are consistently being used to make sales forecasts and company or product image decisions. As is true in domestic markets, data collected by salespeople are still not used routinely in product design decisions. Given the need for information by multinational companies regarding customer needs and preferences and the high cost of international research consultants, multinational companies should consider their salespeople more for product design in information than is currently the case.

Five of the companies interviewed appeared to be frequent collectors and users of data. This finding surfaced the "chicken or the egg" dilemma: were more decisions made because more timely data was available from the sales force, or was more information gathered because of the many decisions requiring this data? Empirical research on this subject is needed to clarify this relationship.

It was found that salespeople play a more significant role in the market entry stage than in the domestic marketing cycle, primarily because of their close proximity to the market, a position which is not easily attainable by marketers located outside the foreign country. Likewise, when market research teams are brought to the foreign country for market entry studies, it is not unusual to include salespeople for their invaluable input to the critical entry strategy formulation. Involving international salespeople in the entry phase could well be a catalyst for continued support from the sales force in subsequent marketing stages, but empirical research is needed in this area.

Beltramini (1988) addressed which methods should be used to disseminate marketing data to the sales force. Important to the effectiveness of any system is that it (1) be customer oriented; (2) be easily processed by the salesperson; (3) be relat-ed to the salesperson aiding in product development; (4) show corporate commitment to the customer, thereby demonstrating that the salesperson works for a company which has a consistent and strategic presence in the marketplace; and (5) involve direct interface with their organization's decision makers.

Therefore Beltramini recommends the implementation of:

- Time-saving summarizations.
- Explanations of how particular programs fit the "big picture."
- Innovative presentation formats.
- Matrix comparisons rather than narratives.
- On-line data bases.
- Video cassette briefings.

Although Beltramini's (1988) suggestions are targeted toward high-technology salespeople, many of the techniques apply to sales personnel in all type of industries.

Why should multinational companies rely more on their international sales force than their domestic sales force? "Lack of accessible information" is cited most often in the current international marketing research literature and is certainly supported by this study. However, more complex reasons for multinational companies to rely more on international sales forces than domestic sales forces for market data include:

- Foreign published data is often unreliable, necessitating primary information gathering for cross checking.
- U.S. management doesn't understand foreign customers or foreign sales techniques to make effective, educated decisions on marketing strategy.
- International sales in many countries rely more on relations so that more information areas need monitoring and more people in the marketing and sales process need the information.
- In a volatile market, close monitoring of the market may only be possible through use of the sales force, since by the time information was released, it would be obsolete.

- The increased complexity and competition in foreign marketing result in more information being needed to formulate successful marketing strategies.
- Too often, domestic strategy is copied, but increased competition in international markets necessitates the need for more information and marketing research by the sales force to design "aggressive" marketing strategies.

Despite the virtues of having marketing information gathered by the salespeople, the problems sales managers face in collecting data (primarily time information availability, and sales force resistance) must be addressed by multinational companies. Specific solutions to these problems were not addressed by this research. However, previous research (Churchill et at. 1985; Evans and Schlacter 1985) recommends keeping marketing information systems easy and clarifying these activities in a salesperson's job description. Reviews of effecting international sales force marketing information systems supported this recommendation.

The effectiveness of expatriates in international business continues to be a debated topic (Black and Mendenhall 1990). This study's findings on the effectiveness of expatriates in gathering market information is particularly timely. Multinational companies which use expatriates to gather primary market data involving personal interviews must be sure that cultural nuances (frequently misunderstood by an expatriate) do not distort the information gathered. However, in the collecting of secondary data and some tabulation-oriented observation studies, expatriates can be equally as effective as local salespeople and in some cases better.

We found that in some companies, the expatriates are better at gathering more detailed market data and communicating it more clearly and concisely. This advantage is attributed to their familiarity with these techniques in the domestic market. Since secondary data and market observations were found to be the most frequent kind of information collected during the entry stage and the salespeople were used the most during the entry stage, it serves

to reason that sending qualified expatriates for market information during the entry stage would prove effective, if not more effective than local salespeople. Conversely, during the growth and maturity stages when more "soft data" is collected, primarily by personal interview, local salespeople would be more effective in foreign countries.

Centralized and decentralized marketing management structures were used equally, as were formal and informal systems. Neither, however, was proven to determine the success of the marketing information system. What does tend to be an influencing factor is the ease and frequency of communication between the sales force and the marketing staff. For this reason it is recommended that multinational companies select the system which best facilitates good relations and timely communications between the sales force and the marketing staff. Regularly scheduled working meetings, field visits, and daily or weekly telephonic or electronic communication between the two groups should be one of the highest priorities in implementing any successful marketing information system. Marketing professionals should be careful to present marketing findings with this in mind. Data should be summarized and translated into sales guidelines and suggestions and electronically sent to the sales force.

Although structured research with sales and marketing executives of multinational companies has proven difficult, future empirical research on the effectiveness of these marketing information systems would greatly enhance the analysis of international marketing information and research systems. Likewise, research which included interviews with both U.S.-based marketing/sales executives and interviews with sales personnel in foreign countries would help define the intricate problems with these systems. Multinational companies clearly believe regular input from the international sales force is needed, and they benefit from the close working relationship between international salespeople and marketers.

References

Beltramini, Richard F. (1988), "High Technology Salespeople's Information Acquisition Strategies," *The Journal of Personal Selling & Sales Management,* Vol. 8, No. 1 (May), 37–44.

Black, J. Stewart and Mark Mendenhall (1990), "Cross-Cultural Training Effectiveness: A Review and Theoretical Framework for Future Research," *Academy of Management Review,* 15, 113–136.

Boddewyn, Jean J. (1981), "Comparative Marketing: The First Twenty-Five Years, " *Journal of International Business Studies,* Vol. 12, No.1 (Spring/Summer), 61–78.

Cavusgil, S. Tamer (1985), "Guidelines for Export Market Research," *Business Horizons,* Vol. 28, No. 5 (November–December), 27–33.

Churchill, Gilbert A., Neil M. Ford, Steven W. Hartley, and Orville C. Walker (1985), "The Determinants of Salesperson Performance: A Meta-Analysis," *Journal of Marketing Research,* Vol. 22, No. 5 (May), 103–118.

Evans, Kenneth R. and John L. Schlacter (1985), "The Role of Sales Managers and Sales People in a Marketing Information System," *The Journal of Personal Selling & Sales Management,* Vol. 5, No. 2 (November), 49–58.

Gestetner, David (1974), "Strategy in Managing International Sales," *Harvard Business Review* (September–October), 103–108.

Hunt, Sharyn and Ernest Cooke (1990), "Encouraging and Utilizing Sales Force Feedback," *National Conference in Sales Management,* J.B. DeConinck, ed., 129–133.

Jeannet, Jean-Pierre and Hubert D. Hennessey (1988), *International Marketing Management : Strategies and Cases,* Boston: Houghton Mifflin Company, 549–582.

Klompmaker, Jay E. (1980–81), "Incorporating Information from Salespeople Into the Marketing Planning Process," *Journal of Personal Selling & Sales Management,* (Fall–Winter), 76–82.

Mellow, Craig (1989), "The Best Source of Competitive Intelligence," *Sales & Marketing Management Magazine,* (December), 24–29.

Permut, Steven E. (1977), "The European View of Marketing Research," *Columbia Journal of World Business,* Vol. 12, No. 3 (Fall), 94–103.

Simon, Ruth and Graham Button (1990), "What I Learned in the Eighties," *Forbes,* (January 8), 100–102.

Still, Richard Ralph (1981), "Sales Management: Some Cross-Cultural Aspects," *Journal of Personal Selling & Sales Management,* Vol. 1, No. 1 (Spring–Summer), 6–9.

Townley, Preston (1990), "Global Business in the Next Decade," *Across the Board* (Jan.–Feb.), 13–19.

Webster, Frederick E. Jr. (1965), "The Industrial Salesman as a Source of Market Information," *Business Horizons* (Spring), 77–82.

Wotruba, Thomas R. (1976), "Sales Force Participation in Quota Setting and Sales Forecasting," *Journal of Marketing,* Vol. 40, No. 2 (April), 11–16.

Appendix A

Interview Questions

1. Is your international marketing research more centralized or decentralized? (Explain.) Does this policy of _____ change with the product life cycle?
   (A) Market Entry Period?
   (B) Market Growth Period?
   (C) Market Maturity?

2. What topics or kind of marketing information does your company's international sales force gather during:
   (A) Market Entry Period?
   (B) Market Growth Period?
   (C) Market Maturity?

3. In which stage of the marketing cycle is the sales force's role of collecting international marketing research data most important: Market Entry, Growth, or Market Maturity?

4. Does your company have a formalized plan for the exchange of marketing information between the sales force and sales management?

5. How does the sales force receive marketing research findings?

6. Are these findings presented as: raw data; statistically analyzed data; summarized data; or data interpreted into suggestions or guidelines?

7. How would you evaluate your company's international sales force market data gathering techniques?

8. Does your company's marketing information exchange differ when you use an expatriate sales force versus a local sales force?

9. What do you think would be the best way to communicate international marketing research data to the sales force?

10. What do you think would be a sales manager's most difficult problem in gathering international marketing research data?

11. What do you think would be a sales manager's most difficult problem in using international marketing research data?

12. Does your company's senior management consider information gathered by the sales force before making decisions in the areas of:
    (A) Forecasting sales?
    (B) Company/product image making?
    (C) Product design?

13. What are the main differences in sales forces conducting and using marketing research internationally versus domestically?

Paul A. Herbig

John Milewicz

James E. Golden

The Do's and Don'ts of Sales Forecasting

If there is any one function managers most despise, it is the art of forecasting. By its very nature it concerns guessing the outcome of future events. No matter how sophisticated computer-driven techniques and programs become, the future seems as elusive as ever to managers. In this paper the basics of forecasting and the problems involved with the art of forecasting are examined. A guide of do's and don'ts for managers is presented in an effort to promote more effective forecasting. ✳

When asked why he believed in the three-yards-and-a-pile-of-dust rushing attack, Woody Hayes, the famous Ohio State football coach, replied, "Because when you pass the football, three things can happen, two of which are bad." Managers have the same dread of forecasting that Woody had of the pass. Three things can happen when a manager forecasts, two of which are bad: One can overforecast or one can underforecast. In a rapidly changing economic environment, when they may need good forecasts more than ever, many managers downplay the importance of forecasts. One reason may be that, like many other things, when forecasts are right, they are not heard about. But when forecasts are wrong...

Forecasting is predicting, projecting, or estimating some future event or condition that is outside an organization's full control. Forecasting provides a basis for managerial planning. Organizations forecast so they can plan and help shape their future. Forecasting provides crucial input for planning: In a survey of 175 companies, 92 percent of the respondents indicated that the forecast was important for their companies' success. Forecasts are major components of the business decision-making process. When accurate, estimates of future economic activity associated with specific courses of action can correctly guide corporate strategy in an uncertain environment; when inaccurate, they can bankrupt or at the very least throw a company behind the industry power curve.

Managerial decisions at all levels in an organization are based explicitly or implicitly on some expectation concerning the future and some expectation that the future will act somewhat as the past has done. From these expectations, plans and policies are developed to respond to future opportunities and react to future threats. For a business to survive, it must meet its customers' needs at least as quickly as do its competitors. The better management is able to estimate the future, the better it should be able to prepare for it. Forecasting is the estimation of the future based on the past. If the future were certain, forecasting would not be necessary. The future is rarely certain, so some system of forecasting is necessary [1].

Forecasting plays an important role in every major functional area of business management.

At the time this article was written, Paul A. Herbig, John Milewicz, and James E. Golden were in the Department of Management/Marketing at the College of Commerce and Business Administration, Jacksonville State University, Jacksonville, Alabama. *Source:* Reprinted by permission of the publisher from *Industrial Marketing Management* 22, 49–57 (1993) © Elsevier Science, Inc., 1993.

More companies probably undertake some form of forward estimation of their markets and their sales than of any other aspect of their activities. The estimates produced may then be used in a variety of ways, such as in production planning, planning the sales force, setting advertising appropriations, estimating cash flow, assessing the need for innovation or diversification, and considering the general position of the company in the future. Unfortunately, although much of this forecasting is very good, a great deal of it is of poor quality and of doubtful value.

In the marketing area, forecasting is doubly important; not only does it have a central role in marketing itself, but marketing-developed forecasts play a key role in the planning of production, finance, and other areas of corporate activity. The importance of forecasting has become more widely acknowledged in the recent past as the result of substantial changes in the economic environment. The shortages and the increased inflation of the early 1970s, the oil shocks of the 1980s, and most recently the major recession of the early 1990s have focused renewed attention on forecasting and the benefits it can provide to an attentive manager.

Forecasting requires the making of judgments, often drawing on uncertain theory and evidence. Forecasting techniques range from simple to complex; all are designed to produce accurate, unbiased estimates of future activity in the presence of uncertainty. Applications of forecasting techniques can be improved as the forecaster gains experience and sophistication; however, there is always a risk that the forecaster's experience—expectations and hopes, among other things—may also introduce bias and error. Professional forecasters are most accurate when forecasting in areas in which they have prior experience. Forecasting demand for new, complex, and rapidly changing high-technology products is particularly difficult because of limited experience and a greater than usual number of unknowns.

Some useful generalizations about forecasting include the following:

1. Forecasts are almost always wrong.

2. The further out the forecasts, the less accurate they tend to be.
3. Aggregate forecasts for families or groups of products are usually more accurate than item forecasts.

A forecast is only an estimate of expected or potential demand; actual and forecasted demand cannot be expected to agree precisely. Forecasts are only ballpark figures that permit the planning function to commence. Frustration should not result from the inability to predict the future precisely. For all of the computer programs and statistical techniques, forecasting remains an art, not a science. Forecasting is an ongoing process that requires maintenance, revision, and modifications.

Forecasting: How Many Ways?

Forecasting is a form of inductive reasoning: One makes a set of observations in which certain trends or correlations occur. In addition, the assumptions of the planned marketing mix must be interjected. To generate predictions about future events, these observations must be interpreted and related to other knowledge. Some sort of theory must be formed to generate predictions, and if the theory fails, it must be revised or rejected. If the theory is wrong, then failure to detect this flaw early on could be extremely costly. In practice, it may be very difficult to assess the validity of a theory. A good example is the economic forecasting on which government policies are based. The frequent inaccuracies of such forecasts are usually attributed not to an error in the theory but to an error in its application to a complex situation. It is argued that certain assumptions upon which the forecast was based proved to be unsound. For example, who could have foreseen that a Gulf crises over Kuwait would arise in the summer of 1990 and very possibly set off a recession?

Patterns or relationships might change over time. A critical assumption for accurate forecasting is that patterns or relationships, once identified and measured, remain constant. People can influence future events. In the economic and business environment, predictions can become self-fulfilling or self-defeating prophecies, nullifying the forecasts.

The Time Horizons of Forecasting

The longer the time horizon of the forecasts, the greater the chance that established patterns and relationships will change, invalidating forecasts, and the more likely irregular nonpredictable events may happen. Specifically, the more time competitors have to react to predicted events or the predictions themselves, the more able they will be to influence future events for their own benefit. Thus, all else being equal, forecasting accuracy decreases as the time horizons increase. One of the greatest assets a firm can have is lead time (that time that one firm has the market to themselves before competition can react).

Technological Change

The higher the rate of technological change in a given industry, all other things being equal, the greater the chance that established patterns and relationships will change, and the greater the chance that competitors will be able to influence the industry through technological innovation. Excellent examples can be found in high-tech industries, where forecasting is almost impossible as firms strive to create the future according to their own conceptions. This is particularly true in young industries that do not have a significant industry history to analyze. By bringing out new technologies, they hope to shape the future in desired directions in order to achieve competitive advantage. Adequate reaction time may mean not just staying even with the competition, but it may mean the firm's actual survival. Thus, forecasting accuracy decreases as the rate of technological change increases.

Barriers to Entry

The lighter the barriers to entry and exit for firms within the industry, all other things being equal, the more inaccurate the forecasting. New competitors (both domestic and foreign) can drastically change established patterns and relationships in their quest to gain competitive advantage.

Dissemination of Information

The faster the dissemination of information, all other things being equal, the less the value of forecasting, as everyone with the same information, models, and assumptions can arrive at similar predictions. In such a case it becomes impossible to grain advantages from accurate forecasting since everyone else will have similar forecasts. This means accurate forecasts are not necessarily useful, a point that is not always understood or accepted, although examples abound. The growth in mainframes and microcomputers was correctly predicted, but few gains resulted because many companies that used such accurate forecasts went bankrupt.

Elasticity of Demand

The more elastic the demand, all other things being equal, the less accurate the forecasts. Thus, demand for necessities (for example, food items) can be predicted with a higher degree of accuracy than for non-necessities (such as vacationing). Obviously, people must eat and acquire necessities, which are given priority over other purchases in case of income reduction during periods of recession.

Consumer Versus Industrial Products

Forecasts for consumer products, all other things being equal, are more accurate than those for industrial products. Industrial products are sold to a few customers. If only one of those customers is lost, the resulting error can represent a substantial proportion of sales because of the large quantities, or sales value, such customers buy. Those customers are well informed and can receive offers of bargain terms from competitors because of the large quantities or value amounts they buy [2].

Variability

Forecasters can be somewhat more confident about a range of values than about a single-point forecast. A good forecast usually includes not only a single estimate but an estimate of the magnitude of likely deviations as a guide to the comparative reliability of the forecast. Deviation is usually expressed by developing the best single estimate (expected value) and then establishing limits above and below that indicate the range of likely variation. Forecasting the demand for a particular brand or model or component within a market is generally a far more hazardous task than forecasting the development of the market itself, because markets tend to move more slowly and less erratically than the individual products within them. In short-run forecasting, managers can benefit by extrapolating the inertia (momentum that exists in the economic and business phenomena). Seasonality can also be predicted fairly well. In the medium term, forecasting is relatively easy when patterns and relationships do not change.

Expenditures

Reducing forecast errors requires increasing expenditures on forecasting techniques and usually increases the time required to make the forecast. Eventually one reaches a point of diminishing returns—the value of project information would seldom justify the time and costs required to gain the information. Frequently, a much better investment is the development of operational and production flexibility that permits a rapid redeployment of resources in light of market changes.

Forecasting: Biases and Failures

Forecasting requires the making of judgments, often drawing on uncertain theory and evidence. There is always a risk that subjective biases may be introduced when forecasters add hopes and expectations, or secular, cyclical, or independent variables, to the forecasting mix. That risk is particularly prevalent when forecasters are inexperienced or caught up in human enthusiasms for the product or market in question.

Psychologists have undertaken many well-documented and replicable studies of such judgmental processes, and their findings point to many possible sources of error and bias in forecasting, such as a reluctance to seek possible falsifying evidence for assumptions or to see trends and patterns in random events [3]. Even when historical data are plentiful, however, the forecaster's judgment remains critical.

Experimental design, information gathering and interpretation, and assignment of judgmental probabilities are essential components of any competent forecast. New-product forecasts usually concentrate on trend, with all the attendant difficulties of defining an accurate trend line. Most new-product forecasts attempt to find the history of similar products that have previously been introduced.

Forecasters are vulnerable to hopes, expectations, and even hunches. The positive regency effect, popularly known as the gambler's fallacy, occurs when sequences of positive events, such as a string of winning craps rolls, are attributed to some benevolent spirit in the dice rather than seen as a chance event. Studies have shown that some forecasters—like gamblers—have been observed falsely inferring meaning from long runs of good or bad luck as a series of offsetting relationships between variables and outcomes that are purely illusion. And, at a very practical level, forecasters may find their clients happier, at least in the short term, with unrealistically rosy prognostications [4]. Thus, it severely impacts forecasting and one's ability to evaluate forecasts. Recommendations to overcome this bias include the following:

1. Know the market: Take the pulse of those who will actually buy and use the product.

2. Be independent, test your judgment and that of others, and do not be tempted to build on mistakes.

3. Deflate forecasts for a margin of safety, or at least test for the "goodness of the fit."

It has been determined from psychological studies that subjects receiving repeated reinforcement in the form of confirmed predictions become convinced of the correctness of their theories even when told they are wrong. There are numerous recorded instances in reasoning research where intelligence subjects maintain blatant self-contradictions and produce elaborate rationalizations to defend their forecasts. Research by social psychologists also shows that when beliefs are strongly held, people will seek to avoid evidence that contradicts them and seek to deny or devalue such evidence when it is encountered. This is one of the means by which prejudices are maintained.

Thus, the manner in which predictions are generated from hypotheses and beliefs—or, if you prefer, the manner in which hypotheses and beliefs are generated from data—may not be very efficient. People may choose to test hypotheses and predictions that are least likely to falsify their theories, or they may disregard falsifying evidence when it is encountered. Two factors that particularly affect this problem are the strength of belief in the theory and the complexity of the situation. The greater the number of factors involved, the more scope there is for rationalizing the outcome of faulty predictions [3].

Biases operate on every stage of forecasting. Because random events do not appear random, people perceive patterns and trends where they do not exist. This is turn affects their anticipations of the future. They tend to ignore base rates in the presence of specific evidence and generate predictions that are least likely to falsify their theories, and they tend to maintain beliefs in the face of contradictory evidence. Furthermore, subjective confidence in judgments is no guide to their accuracy, and people's abilities to draw correct inferences is highly dependent on the meaning and complexity of the evidence on which they are based. Attempts to forecast the future, however expertly based on knowledge and techniques, must often be vulnerable to these kinds of error. Intuitive biases are most likely to operate when there is much uncertainty and the events concerned are probabilistic in nature; when the situations are very complex, with many possible relevant factors to be considered; and when strong beliefs are held about the theories used to make forecasts. These conditions will frequently be met when attempts are made to forecast real-world events [3].

Biases of various kinds and incomplete understanding of the marketplace are often at their worst in forecasting demand for sophisticated, high-technology innovations. Not only is it likely that the forecaster does not understand the product well himself or herself, but it is a virtual certainty that the marketplace offers little useful experience with the product category from which the forecaster may extract essential relationships. Inaccurate forecasts of demand for high-technology products—personal computers, software, artificial intel-

ligence, cable television, fiber optics, satellites, telecommunications, genetic engineering, photovoltaics, robots, nuclear power, and many others—have been prevalent over the past 10 years. The vast majority of the forecasts have erred in the same direction and far too high: 5- and 10-year forecasts for many other technology-based products have been remarkably similar in their excessive optimism [4]. Most of the enthusiastic personal computer (PC) forecasts of the early 1980s were based on interviews with major manufacturers and vendors of PCs—a seemingly knowledgeable, though hardly unbiased, source. They identified a huge potential market. Unfortunately, the general market's intention to purchase was ignored. No one conducted research among potential users to determine whether they would actually buy the product. Exponential growth curves were used on early data without thorough consideration of inflation, fadism, third-party modifications, or upper limits to potential markets.

There is a tendency to jump on the bandwagon after seeing rosy numbers in print backed by the editorial credibility of a respected magazine. Few forecasters would want to offer the lowest or most negative predictions in an apparently booming industry since high-technology forecasters and their followers tend to be a tightly knit, homogeneous group, and there is a strong probability of excessive cohesiveness groupthink in their forecasting, which could be alleviated by the use of a broader base of data methodology and forecaster's expertise. There are several serious consequences of this widespread over-optimism, the most obvious being that businesses plan according to sales expectations that cannot be met. Companies borrow money, offer stock, issue bonds, build plants, establish distribution networks, and generally gear up with high hopes. Venture capitalists invest in new start-up companies. People are hired and trained. Then sales unexpectedly fall far below forecasts. In the past decade this pattern has regrettably been frequently repeated with an array of high-technology products. The vast majority of these forecasts shared several weaknesses: excessive optimism;

inadequate definition of markets, users, and year-to-year comparability; insufficient attention to price adjustments, inflation, revenues versus units sales, shipments to dealers versus retail sales, and the like; and failure to adjust for historical experience [4].

Three additional sources of bias include the postdecision audit bias reflecting a regression to the mean phenomenon since only those products that are forecasted to do well, including those with the most upward biased forecasts, are brought to market; the advocacy bias reflecting the tendency of product planners to champion their products by overpromising on forecasts; and the optimism bias resulting from the act of participating in planning activities. Because the forecast period is so long, those involved with the original preparation of the forecast rarely are associated with the forecast when the results are finally known; the results are subject to a wide range of uncontrollable events, and it is nearly impossible to assign accountability in the event of failure to live up to expectations [5].

Another very common reason for poor forecasting is failure to define the objectives of the forecasting exercise at the beginning. Different objectives demand different types of forecast based on different time periods and taking into account different sets of factors. For example, in forecasting market movements up to three months ahead for production planning or assessing short-term cash flows, any seasonal variations may be highly important, while a trend will normally be of far less significance during such a period and may frequently be ignored altogether. In forecasting the market for 12 months for budgeting purposes, such as assessing the size of the sales force or the advertising appropriation, seasonal variations will generally cease to be as important and considerations of trend will dominate, although resultant monthly appropriations may once again consider for seasonability. In forecasting even further ahead, the validity of the trend itself must be considered and other factors must be brought into the analysis, such as long-term economic or social changes, the rate of innovation in the market, and the possibilities of even more fundamental technological changes [1].

The Sales Force Composite

Forecasting is particularly critical to and an essential part of the lives of salespeople. Salespeople may give poor forecasts because they do not have enough information to make informed judgments. If salespeople have better information about the environment, better information about their customers, and better feedback about their own performance, they will make more informed and accurate forecasts. Therefore, salespeople should be provided with information about major factors that might affect their forecasts, such as economic conditions, political considerations, manufacturing constraints, customer profitability, change in corporate policy, and so on. By bringing these factors to the salespeople's attention, they may see how their particular customers will be affected. A manager should help salespeople maintain records to monitor their customers' past purchasing behavior; by examining customers' past pattern of purchasing under various conditions it might be possible to anticipate customers' future actions given the present conditions. Managers should provide feedback to salespeople about the results of their past forecasts as well as encourage salespeople to contact customers to determine customer expectations for future purchases. If a salesperson's propensity to deliberately over- or underestimate demand can be controlled, the accuracy of the sales composite technique would certainly improve.

Many times salespeople do not do a good job of forecasting because they do not allocate enough of their time for preparing forecasts; consequently, forecasts may be done haphazardly and at the last minute. Salespeople must be given enough time to provide well thought out forecasts. This means that management should start the forecasting process early enough to allow for sufficient preparation time. Salespeople must be reminded of when the process should start and when the forecasts are due (specific dates are suggested). The 80/20 rule should be used to make the best of salespeople's time used for forecasting. Salespeople can be encouraged to spend most of their forecasting time generating forecasts for their largest or most important customers and for the products with the greatest sales. In other words, salespeople can put the time in where it will be most critical to planning. A form for recording salespeople's forecast is helpful and will reduce the time needed to prepare the forecasts, will standardize data collection procedures, and will reduce the time it takes the salesperson to communicate the forecast.

Salespeople's job descriptions can include forecasting. A common complaint of salespeople is that they are required to generate forecasts in addition to their regular work. This attitude stems from the fact that salespeople do not appreciate that generating forecasts is a significant part of their jobs. They view their jobs solely in terms of making sales. A formal job description for salespeople that explicitly identifies forecasting as an important part of the job will indicate that time must be set aside to thoughtfully generate forecasts.

Salespeople need reinforcement to put more effort into generating better forecasts. This may be done with personal or financial incentives. Recommendations to increase the effectiveness of a salesperson's forecast include the following:

1. Formally record each salesperson's forecast and hold him or her accountable.

2. Provide a bonus to the salesperson's salary based on the accuracy of the forecast.

3. Improve the forecasting procedure used by salespeople. First, require salespeople to justify their forecasts in writing and/or orally (with the sales manager). Salespeople should enumerate the considerations they took into account when making the forecast (that is, their reasoning). This forces them to carefully consider the forecast they are generating. Second, encourage the use of interval or probability distribution forecasts, which would entail training for the salesperson who has limited knowledge or experience in those techniques and would allow them to express the confidence they have in their forecasts. An interval forecast might be: "I am 90 percent sure that sales for Customer A will be between $25,000 and $35,000."

4. Beware of overemphasizing a bonus for over-quota sales. This tends to bias the forecasts downward since the salesperson reasons that the quota is based on his or her forecast [6].

Forecasting Do's

Important considerations in choosing the most appropriate forecasting technique include the following:

1. *Time horizons.* Most managers will want the forecast results to extend as far into the future as possible. A manager must choose the right technique for the period of time desired, however.

2. *Technical sophistication.* The sophistication of the organization and the people who will be doing the forecasting must be matched with the technique used.

3. *Cost.* Greater accuracy has its price. How precise does the manager need to be? How much money is involved? How much has been allocated? How much can be afforded?

4. *Data availability.* How much data is available? How reliable, valid, or relevant is it? How much must be had to create a realistic, usable forecast? Before choosing a technique, the forecaster must consider the extensiveness, currency, accuracy, and representativeness of the available data. More data tend to improve accuracy, and detailed data are more valuable than those presented in the aggregate. Because a technique's ability to handle fluctuations is important to a forecast's success, the manager must match the sensitivity and stability of a technique to the random and systematic variability components of a data series.

5. *Variability and consistency of data.* Beyond changes that might occur in the company's structure or its environment, the manager must look at the kind of stable relationships assumed among a model's independent variables (represented by the "external stability" dimension).

6. *Amount of detail necessary.* While aggregate forecasts are easy to prepare, the manager will need specific information (including individual product classes, time periods, geographic area, or product-market groupings, for example) to determine quotas or allocate resources.

7. *Accuracy.* Is it satisfactory to be 95 percent accurate; 99 percent or 99.9 percent correct? Why is the forecast needed?

8. *Timing.* When will the forecast be used?

9. *Form.* Who will use the data?

Managers can improve their projection in the following ways:

- Combine forecasts.
- Simulate a range of input assumptions.
- Selectively apply judgment.
- Consider applying a deflator of 30 percent to 50 percent of any forecast used for substantial capital or manpower planning purposes for new, high-technology products [4].

Imaginative marketers who ask questions like "What things could cause this forecast to change dramatically?" produces the best estimates. They are most likely to identify potential risks and discontinuities developments in competing technologies, in customer industry competitiveness, and in supplier cost structures than those who do not. Once a baseline forecast is complete, the challenge is to determine how far it could be off target [7].

Forecasting Don'ts

The following are important "don'ts" to consider when using forecasting:

1. Don't delay reporting results to the owners of the forecast.

2. Don't assign quotas based on a salesperson's forecasts.

3. Don't separate accountability and responsibility for forecasts.

4. Don't consider any variable given: Always examine constants for any changes that may have occurred in the industry or environment.

5. Don't become overly dependent on computer analysis and algorithms. The best judgment for an uncertain future is the company's staff, not a machine.

6. Contingency planning needs to go hand in hand with forecasting efforts.

7. Don't become enamored with products or technology. Be subjective.

8. Don't rely on a single forecaster. Large numbers tend to be more accurate than individuals.

9. Don't rely on a single forecast or forecasting technique. Double check and compare using other methods.

10. Don't minutely forecast. The more micro the forecast is, the more prone it is to errors in magnitude.

Management Implications

Some generalizations concerning forecasting include the following:

1. More accurate forecasts are possible when a greater amount of data is available.

2. The higher the rate of technological change in an industry, the greater the chance that established patterns will change and the less certain forecasts become.

3. The lighter the barriers to entry, the more inaccurate the forecasting.

4. The faster the dissemination of information, the less useful the forecasting.

5. The more elastic the demand, the less accurate the forecasts.

6. Forecasts for consumer products are more accurate than those for industrial products, since the larger the number of customers or times involved, the smaller the effect of random forces and the higher the reliability of forecasting. Thus, firms selling to customers not only can forecast more accurately but can

know that the uncertainty of their forecasts is less than that of firms selling to industrial customers.

While each technique has strengths and weaknesses, every forecasting situation is limited by constraints like time, funds, competencies, or data. Balancing the advantages and disadvantages of techniques with regard to a situation's limitations and requirements is a formidable but important management task [8].

For the marketing manager, an important aspect of behavior challenge involves the interface between preparers of forecasts (specialists) and the users of forecasts (marketing managers). What is required is better knowledge, respect, and understanding of the role and value that preparers have for users and vice versa.

References

1. Davis, J., Techniques and Marketing Forecasting, *Management Decision* **25**(3), 62–71 (1987).

2. Makridakis, S. G., *Forecasting: Planning and Strategy for the 21st Century.* Free Press, New York, 1990.

3. Evans, J. St. B. T., Psychological Pitfalls in Forecasting. *Futures* **August**, 258–265 (1982).

4. Wheeler, D. R., Shelley, C. J. Toward More Realistic Forecasts for High-Technology Products, *Journal of Business and Industrial Marketing* **2**(3), 55–63 (1987).

5. Tyebjee, T. T., Behavioral Biases in New Product Forecasting, *International Journal of Forecasting* **3**, 393–404 (1987).

6. Cox, J. E. Jr., Approaches for Improving Salespersons' Forecast, *Industrial Marketing Management* **18**(4), 307–311 (1989).

7. Barnett, F. W., Four Steps to Forecast Total Market Demand, *Harvard Business Review* **July–August**, 28–35 (1988).

8. Georgoff, D. M., and Murdick, R. G., Manager's Guide to Forecasting, *Harvard Business Review* **January–February**, 110–120 (1986).

Chapter 6

Selecting Business Markets

F ew decisions a firm makes are more critical than market selection. Market growth rates indicate the commitment it must make to growth in its production and marketing capacity, and hence its need for capital, physical, and human resources. Customers' functional requirements dictate the required product characteristics. Purchasing policies and customer values dictate the nature of buyer–seller relationships and the communication effort. Levels of competition and customer sensitivity to price significantly influence pricing policies. Size of targeted customers and their preferences influence, and sometimes mandate, choice of distribution channels.

In this chapter we provide an overview of the issues involved in business market selection. We then outline the search process for potential market segments and describe criteria for their evaluation. We conclude with a discussion of a number of special issues that need to be considered in the market selection process.

An Overview of Business Market Selection

In broad terms a *market* can be defined as those potential customers who share a similar want or need and who are able and willing to commit their resources (usually money but sometimes barter or other media of exchange) to satisfy that want or need. Similar wants and needs, however, are subject to much variation. Having elected to participate in a given market, a firm must decide what portion, or segment, of the market it can serve feasibly with a given marketing strategy or mix, and to what extent marketing strategy needs to be varied in order to accommodate variation in the wants and needs of customers.

We define a *market segment* as a group of potential customers who are likely to respond similarly to one or more elements of marketing strategy. Market segmentation is the process of identifying segments that can feasibly be targeted and that represent profitable opportunities for the firm. In some instances, firms can achieve their aspirations for growth or financial performance by focusing on just one segment. In other instances, achievement of goals may require targeting several segments. In some instances this may require variation in just one element of marketing strategy—the promotional message, for example. In other instances this may require variation in all the strategy elements of product, price, promotion, and distribution.

Competitive forces and unique customer requirements argue for defining segments narrowly. Economies of scale, with respect to marketing as well as manufacturing, argue for broader definition of a segment, or aggregation of several segments. The final match of marketing strategy to a segment, or segments, depends on the particular situation of the firm. Hoover Universal, a diversified U.S. manufacturer with strong historical ties to the automotive industry, described its strategy as follows:[1]

> One final future direction concerns key customers. Industrial manufacturers such as Hoover exist to serve others. We design our products to fit the needs of our customers, to accommodate their timing and their geography, and importantly, to adjust to the dollars they have available. In a very real sense, our destiny is tied to our customers. Fortunately, or unfortunately, all customers are not equal. Some are more growth oriented and are prepared to make the serious commitments necessary to achieve that growth. It is imperative that we identify in our present markets the key customers who are making commitments. If we make the right identification, and if we find the way to build partnerships instead of simply a supplier relationship, then we can assure our future success. Or, said another way, if there are markets where we find that the key customer has already been usurped by one or more of our competitors, we must either find a way to displace a competitor or, failing that, cut our losses and move to another market. Happily for Hoover, we have strong relationships with key customers in most of our markets and are moving positively toward partnership relationships which can have such significant dividends in the future.

For Hoover the question of market selection was simplified by the existence of relatively few customers. But for most firms the issue is more complex. Consider, for example, Loctite Corporation, a U.S. manufacturer of high-performance adhesives and sealants. The company had developed Bond-a-Matic.® a new instant adhesive dispenser. Its studies indicated that 1,028,223 U.S. establishments, in 16 categories of SIC codes,[2] used adhesives. Depending on the SIC code, between 13 percent and 48 percent were either current or potential users of instant adhesives and so were potential customers for the new dispenser. Customers varied in the amount of adhesive they used, depending on the size of the firm and the nature of the manufacturing process. Some customers were sophisticated in their knowledge of adhesive technology, others were not. Some preferred to deal directly with the manufacturer, others preferred to deal with distributors, some of whom were very specialized. As Loctite developed its plan to launch Bond-a-Matic®, it was faced with a number of questions. Should it target all potential customers or a subset? Would one marketing plan be suitable for all customers? If not, should a number of plans be developed, each tailored for a particular set of homogeneous customers, or should it develop one plan, focused on one homogeneous segment? What characteristics would indicate homogeneity? Would the size of the firm or the nature of its product be sufficient indicators, or would it be necessary to take other variables into account?[3]

The notion of finding a market segment whose wants and needs are closely met, that responds more favorably to the firm's marketing strategy than to the strategies of competitors, and that is potentially profitable is intuitively attractive. The search for such segments, however, is highly situation specific. With new-to-the-world products, precise segmentation may be difficult and market selection may need to be broad, taking into account a wide range of possibilities. When Federal Express introduced Courier Pak, an overnight delivery service of packages of less than two pounds, it placed its introductory media messages in general business publications such as the *Wall Street Journal* and *Business Week* to reach organizations of all sizes and in all industries, rather than in more narrowly targeted trade journals. On the other hand, for Mid-Continent Computer Services, having successfully designed and produced a software system for its savings and loan parent, it was clear that its communications should be targeted just to other savings and loan institutions. In the growth stage of the product life cycle, major segments may emerge, requiring completely new strategies. This was the case in the personal computer industry when the corporate segment emerged a few years after initial introduction of personal computers by Apple Computer and Tandy Corporation, which focused principally on the school and consumer markets. By contrast, in mature industries the search for new segments may focus on narrow segments, requiring modification of only some part of marketing strategy. Micro Motion, for instance, initially dominated the worldwide mass flowmeter market with a proprietary, premium-priced, full-function product. As the market matured, a segment interested in less functionality at a lower price emerged.

Examples abound of firms that serve a particular segment successfully and some even dominate a segment to the exclusion of competitors. Given the variability in situations, is this the result of careful planning or of some fortuitous set of circumstances not particularly amenable to analysis? As we discuss in Chapter 7, failure rates of new products indicate that finding such segments is not an exact science. A number of approaches have been developed that can materially assist the search for characteristics that might identify customers who would respond favorably to a particular marketing strategy.

The Search for Business Market Segments

The process of selecting the market segment or segments to be served starts with the identification of potential segments. The second step in the process is to screen potential segments to identify those most likely to merit further evaluation. Finally, segments that merit further evaluation are analyzed on the basis of their feasibility for the firm and the likelihood that electing to serve them will meet the firm's financial or other objectives.

TABLE 6.1
Segmenting the Computer Market

Possible Variable	Possible Categories
Industry	Banking, retailing, manufacturing, shipping
Application	General purpose, process control, business computation, scientific research
Geography	United States, North America, Japan, Asia, France, Europe, Brazil, Latin America
Firm size/characteristics	Large multinational, large national, medium, small
Buyer behavior	Sealed bid from multiple sources, negotiated from sole source
Buyer culture	Innovator, follower
Intermediate levels	OEMs, VARs (value added resellers)
Benefits sought	Hardware characteristics, software availability, postsale service

Some firms segment a market on the basis of just one variable such as an industry or the size of the customer. This may be appropriate for certain broad decisions such as the type of product offerings to be made. For the development of comprehensive marketing strategy, however, it is necessary to take into account a wide variety of variables relevant to the many decisions associated with the strategy. The starting point of market segmentation, therefore, should be the identification of all possible segmentation variables. Generally variables are divided into macro and micro categories. Macro variables focus on the buying organization and include size, location, industry, market level (e.g., OEM or end user), or the end market served by potential customers. Micro variables focus on the decision-making unit and include individual characteristics of buyers, decision criteria, type of purchase situation, benefits sought, and perceived importance of the purchase. A list of possible variables and possible categories for segmenting the computer market is shown in Table 6.1. While many segmentation variables are reasonably obvious, some are not. For example, when Rolm Corporation introduced the first digital switch for use in telephone switching, it included the attitudes of state public utility commissions in

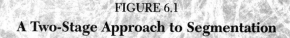

FIGURE 6.1
A Two-Stage Approach to Segmentation

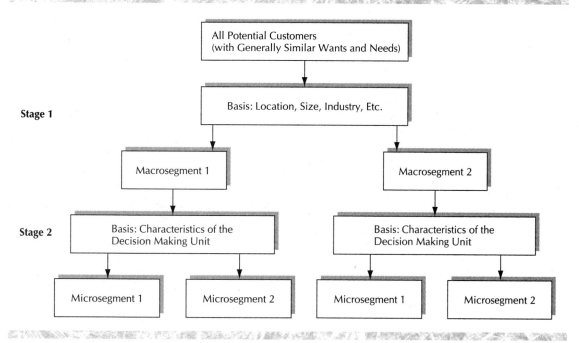

Source: "A Two-Stage Approach to Segmentation: (adapted) from *Marketing Decision Making: A Model Building Approach* by Gary L. Lilien and Philip Kotler, p. 311. Copyright © 1983 by Harper & Row, Publishers, Inc. Reprinted by permission of HarperCollins Publishers, Inc.

the United States toward AT&T as one of its segmentation variables. Rolm elected to enter markets only where it was felt that the regulatory bodies would favor increased competition for AT&T.

Segmentation Approaches

The most widely cited segmentation approach is the two-stage procedure shown in Figure 6.1. This starts with macrosegmentation, which is based on the characteristics of the buying organization. Within the macrosegments the focus of attention is on characteristics of the particular decision-making unit. This approach needs to be done with care. In particular, it should be noted that many microsegmentation variables are found in more than one macrosegment.

A nested, or multistage, approach to segmentation has been proposed by Bonoma and Shapiro.[4] Their classification scheme utilizes a number of categories. With some modifications, they are listed in Table 6.2 with subcategories and the kinds of questions that need to be asked. For the nested approach shown in Figure 6.2, the analysis might start with the outer nests—the general, easily observable segmentation variables, and then move to the inner nest—the

TABLE 6.2
Market Segmentation Variables for Business Markets

Geographic
- In country: Should we focus on local, regional, or national areas of the country?
- Regional: Should we focus on geographic regions that comprise several countries (e.g., Latin America or Scandinavia), geographic regions that cut across parts of several countries (e.g., the southern portions of European countries bordering the Mediterranean), free trade areas or common markets (e.g., the 15 countries in the European Union or the North American Free Trade Area)?
- Global: Should we select customers without regard to location?

Demographic
- Industry: What industries should we target? In some instances the industry will be defined broadly (e.g., financial services). In other instances, more specificity may be required (e.g., banks or insurance companies).
- Company size: Should we target large, medium, or small companies?
- Level: Should we target OEMs at various intermediate levels or end users?
- End product use: Should we take into account the use of our customer's end product?

Operating Variables
- Technology: Should we target customers who insist on components or capital equipment that utilize leading edge technology or those who prefer more proven technologies?
- User–nonuser status: Should we focus on heavy or light users of the product, on nonusers, or on users who buy from competitors?
- Customer capabilities: Should we target customers based on their need for services, their financial strength, or on the nature of their inventory control processes?

Purchasing Approach
- Purchasing organization: Should we target customers with centralized or decentralized purchasing departments?
- Power structure: Should we target customers where the purchasing or the engineering department dominates the decision-making process?
- Nature of relationships: Should we target customers who prefer a close working relationship with suppliers or those who prefer an arm's-length relationship?
- Purchasing policies: Should we target customers who lease, purchase, buy on bid, or negotiate?
- Purchasing criteria: Should we target customers for whom price, service, or functionality is the most important criterion?

Situational Factors
- Urgency: Should we target customers for whom fast delivery is critical?
- Specific application: Should we target customers based on application? Should a computer manufacturer, for instance, target a business application or a process control application?
- Size of order: Should we target customers who place large orders with one supplier or those who place many small orders with several suppliers?

Personal Characteristics
- Buyer–seller similarity: Should we target customers who are staffed by individuals whose values or other personal characteristics are similar to our own?
- Attitude toward risk: Should we target customers who are willing to take risks or those who are risk averse?

Adapted with the permission of Lexington Books, an imprint of Simon & Schuster from *Segmenting the Industrial Market* by Thomas V. Bonoma and Benson P. Shapiro. Copyright © 1983 by Lexington Books.

FIGURE 6.2
A Nested Approach to Segmentation

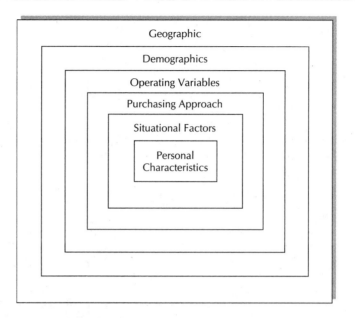

Reprinted with the permission of Lexington Books, an imprint of Simon & Schuster from *Segmenting the Industrial Market* by Thomas V. Bonoma and Benson P. Shapiro, p. 10. Copyright © 1983 by Lexington Books.

more specific, subtle, or hard-to-assess variables. Some caveats need to be observed with regard to using this approach. The notion of starting with the outer nests is based on the premise that they are easier to work with, not that there is a rigid sense of hierarchy to the analysis. In some situations it might be more appropriate to start at a middle point and work inward or even outward. In particular, it should not be inferred that a pattern of purchasing approaches, situational factors, or personal characteristics associated with one geographic, demographic, or operating category cannot be found in other categories.

Most recently, a three-stage, needs-based approach for segmenting business markets has been proposed.[5] It is designed to identify potential early adopters of new technologies by using organizational needs revealed in actual purchasing behavior, based on the assumption that past purchase behavior is a good predictor of future behavior. The first stage is macrosegmentation, designed to delineate firms that have broadly similar needs and to reduce the total market to generally manageable segments. The second stage is microsegmentation, designed to further segment the macrosegments based on benefits and/or needs. The authors argue that while needs are the most logical segmentation base, they provide managers with only part of the information necessary

TABLE 6.3
Use of SIC Codes in Selecting Business Markets

In Chapter 5 we briefly described the Standard Industrial Classification (SIC) system operated by the U.S. federal government. Its purpose is to segment business activity into fairly homogeneous categories and to provide information on the number of establishments and the revenues in each category. Each plant and business establishment in the United States is assigned a code, based on the primary product produced at that location. Data are then collected on such variables as sales, employment, investment, and value added.

Information from the SIC system can assist segmentation in two ways. First, the extensive list of industries coded can serve as an excellent guide or framework for considering target markets. At the four-digit level, for instance, some 450 specific industries are listed, at the five-digit level the system includes 1,300 industries, and at the seven-digit level the system contains 10,000 categories. Second, information can be used to estimate the purchases by firms in a particular category and then estimate the size of the segment. A manufacturer of magnet wire, for instance, can total the sales of transformer manufacturers (SIC3612), estimate the percentage of sales spent by these manufacturers on magnet wire, and then estimate the total purchases of magnet wire by firms in this SIC code.

Some caveats need to be observed. First, statistics for a particular plant are reported in just one category, the product with the highest value added, even though the plant may produce several products. The Census of Manufactures has developed two ratios that can be used to overcome this difficulty: the primary product specialization ratio, which indicates the percentage of total shipments of a given four-digit industry accounted for by its primary product; and the coverage ratio, which compares the shipments of a primary product by one four-digit industry to the total shipments of that product by all four-digit industries.

Second, the SIC code does not take into account variation in buying habits of reported firms or variations in product characteristics, either of products produced or of materials entering the product. This information needs to be obtained in other ways.

With these two caveats in mind, the SIC system can be extremely useful as a market selection tool. Data are readily and inexpensively available. Where specialization and coverage ratios are high, each SIC group should be reasonably homogeneous, especially with regard to manufacturing processes and components or raw materials used. SIC codes should facilitate searches for new customers in unserved categories.

for target market selection and development of marketing strategy. Hence, the third stage is to further describe microsegments in terms that can be directly linked to specific elemets of marketing strategy.

A number of considerations should be kept in mind when conducting a segmentation study:

1. The study should always be guided by its purpose. That is, as potential segments are considered, their usefulness should be tested by their relevance

to that aspect of marketing strategy at issue. In some instances, the purpose will be to develop a complete marketing strategy involving all elements of the marketing mix. We would expect such a study to describe potential segments extensively in terms of many segmentation variables. In other instances the purpose might simply be to develop an advertising campaign, with messages varied to most effectively communicate with significant groups of customers, or to develop a set of pricing strategies that take into account variations in pricing sensitivity of groups of customers. Such studies might be more limited in their use of segmentation variables.

2. Segmentation requires rigor and creativity. Secondary data abound on the size of markets based on geographical dimensions, SIC codes, or other classifications. (See Table 6.3 for a brief discussion of the use of SIC codes for selecting business markets.) Additional secondary data usually exist in company files, based on past order histories or other forms of marketing intelligence. In many instances these data lend themselves to various statistical methodologies such as cluster or factor analysis. There is, however, no set list of variables that definitively identify a market segment. As indicated in the Rolm example, the creative use of variables enhances insights for marketing strategy.

3. The process is, or should be, iterative. Identification of a microsegment in one macrosegment should be followed by consideration of its existence in others. Segmentation on the basis of needs or benefits are particularly likely to cut across several macrosegments.

Criteria for Initial Screening

The search for market segments is likely to reveal several segments of varying attractiveness. Some segments may not be real in the sense that they are not measurable. Others may not be reachable. Before extensive evaluation of potential segments, it is advisable to test them against the following broad characteristics:[6]

1. Measurability. We can hypothesize a number of variables that might influence how buyers respond to marketing strategies. However, unless they are measurable it would be impossible to use them to estimate the size of a particular segment. Prime Computer, for example, in its 1977 annual report, stated it estimated the size of its market based on two considerations: first, whether a Prime computer would satisfy a customer's requirements, and second, psychologically, whether customers would buy from a small company like Prime. While customers who bought from small companies could be identified after the fact, their prior identification on a psychological basis was highly problematic, raising serious questions about the accuracy of Prime's estimates of its market size.

2. Unique response. For a segment to be meaningful, it must respond differentially from another segment to at least one element of the marketing mix. If, for instance, large and small customers respond similarly to a

mail-order program for personal computers, then size would not be a useful basis for segmentation.

3. Substantiality. The aggregate demand of the customers making up the segment must be sufficient to cover marketing costs. Anticipated sales, taking into account not just the size of the segment but also expected market share, must generate sufficient contribution margin to cover the added cost of a specialized marketing program.

4. Accessibility. There must be a basis on which the firm can identify and hence reach a particular segment. With new products a firm may wish to reach customers who are innovators. But unless there is some characteristic that identifies the customer as an innovator, the firm is not likely to be able to reach this segment.

Dowling, Lilien, and Soni propose additional criteria for segments.[7] In particular, they emphasize that segments must ultimately be need based, as needs are the primary determinants of business purchase behavior, and they should be robust, meaning they should not be an artifact of the variability of a particular sample or a specific data analysis technique.

Evaluating Potential Segments

Of the identified segments that are real and reachable, some will represent a better profit opportunity or a better fit for the firm than others. While the ultimate objective in selecting a segment is profitability, there are many other considerations. The following suggest the kinds of questions that need to be answered before concluding to target a particular segment:

- How well do the requirements to successfully compete in the segment fit our distinctive competence? For example, does our sales force have the necessary skills in order to deal with a segment where intense negotiation characterizes the purchasing process?

- How well does the segment capitalize on the firm's current position? Can it be reached, for instance, with our present distributors?

- What are the growth prospects for the segment, either long or short term? Do they match our sales growth objectives?

- Are sales likely to be cyclical? If so, can we adjust our production and marketing efforts to the ups and downs of demand?

- Does a particular segment exhibit enough difference in response to justify its treatment as a separate segment with requirements for a separate marketing program? Would differences in buying behavior, for instance, require separate sales forces, or is the difference something we could reasonably expect the sales force to accommodate as part of its normal work?

- Assuming a successful marketing program for a particular segment, would it be defensible against competitive attack? How likely is it that a competitor could match our offering, and in what period of time? Are buyers likely to be loyal to a pioneer? What would be the switching costs for customers to change to a different supplier?

- Is it within the firm's resources to implement a marketing plan that effectively reaches and serves the segment? Merilab, a small manufacturer of wheel alignment systems for automotive production lines, believed it did not have the resources to reach customers in Europe and did not target them, despite the fact that these customers represented attractive opportunities.

- Will targeting this segment lead us in the direction we want to go? At IBM, the decision to target personal computer users was seen by many as an undesirable diversion from its traditional mainframe computer markets.

The final test of the attractiveness of a particular segment is the ability of the firm to develop an implementable marketing strategy. Other issues, however, should also be considered.

Additional Issues in Segmentation

Selecting a segment goes beyond simply identifying a potentially attractive segment. How the segment is defined may significantly influence competitor evaluation or future initiatives. Segments emerge, or become more clear, over the product life cycle, raising issues of timing. Finding niches or segments the firm can dominate to the exclusion of competitors is a special consideration, as is vertical segmentation. Finally, changes in the external environment constantly introduce new possibilities for segmentation variables as is particularly evident in considering opportunities outside of home country markets.

Defining the Market

While the segmentation process is used primarily to improve the likelihood of a favorable response to a given marketing strategy from a carefully selected set of customers, it should be recognized that the decision as to which segment, or combination of segments, to target defines the denominator in market share calculations. An excessively narrow definition of the served market—for example, a restrictive geographic definition—can result in overstating the firm's market share and misestimating the firm's competitive position. In the early stages of CT scanners, GE defined its market as hospitals in the United States, leading it to conclude it had a dominant position based on a 60 percent share of market. When GE redefined its market as hospitals worldwide, its market share dropped to less than 20 percent, leading to a significant reevaluation of its position. Segments, therefore, should be defined to include not just the customers the firm currently elects to serve but also customers with similar wants and needs that are being served by the firm's competitors in both domestic and foreign markets.

Timing

In the introductory and early growth stages of the product life cycle customer needs may not be clear or easily definable. Product concepts are new, early acceptance by some buyers may not indicate true market potential, and buyers may have little experience in developing definitive opinions about product features. As product concepts become better understood, new groups of buyers may emerge. Early commitment to one segment, therefore, has the potential to reduce the ability to serve other segments. Apple Computer, for instance, shortly after introducing its personal computer, committed strongly to sell only through distributors. This made it difficult for Apple to serve the corporate market, which, when it emerged, wanted to buy direct.

As more buyers gain experience, a better basis for specific need definitions is established and the late growth and mature stages of the product life cycle are characterized by the emergence of segments with differentiated needs. Failure to develop specialized offerings for these segments may result in competitive disadvantage. Prime Computer, for instance, with early successes in the minicomputer market, was reluctant to commit to any of a number of emerging segments. Subsequently it struggled through a number of reorganizations, each characterized by comments that Prime's biggest problem was its lack of focus. Unfortunately, by the time Prime did commit to a segment that it felt represented a good match between needs and its competence, the segment was crowded with other suppliers and Prime was not able to compete effectively.

Niche Markets

When products are beyond the introductory stage of the product life cycle, several firms may compete for share in the market. Within market segments, therefore, firms look for groups of customers, or niches, where a very specialized marketing strategy can establish a position not easily duplicated by competitors. Looking for such niches does not assure they will be found. For 10 years, Data Card Corporation had virtually cornered the market for the high-speed machines that emboss plastic credit cards. As growth slowed, the chairman said its strategy was to find narrow markets for specialized office machines that it could overwhelmingly dominate. Data Card's deliberate search for another lucrative niche proved disappointing.[8]

It would appear that Data Card's dominance of the machine market was the fortuitous result of product development at the right time, not the result of a methodological search. Segments can be evaluated, however, on the basis of customer loyalty to pioneers and switching costs. More particularly, good competitor analysis can evaluate the likelihood of competitor response or the timing of such response.

Vertical Segmentation

Unique to business marketing is the opportunity for firms to target markets at various levels. ALCOA, for example, having invented a new alloy with desirable properties for diesel engine bearings, had a number of options.[9] It could sell the alloy to bearing manufacturers, partially fabricate the alloy for sale to bearing or engine manufacturers, or make the complete bearing for sale to engine manufacturers or for sale in replacement markets. The value of the new alloy was most salient for purchasers of replacement bearings. But, ALCOA was not willing to make the commitment necessary to reach the replacement market and attempted to sell the alloy to bearing manufacturers. Despite the alloy's favorable characteristics, it was not a commercial success. Similarly, when the Graphics Division of Gould, Inc., introduced an electrostatic printer, the company was not willing to make the commitment necessary to sell the product to end-users, for whom the printer had great advantages. Rather, it attempted to rely on computer manufacturers, for whom the printer had little benefit, to sell the product and had disappointing results.

Selling to intermediate market levels, more easily reached than end users, is inherently attractive and, in many instances, such as components that completely enter the final product, there may be no alternative. As these examples illustrate, however, the decision to target intermediate market levels requires careful analysis of the potential benefits at each level.

Global Considerations

Despite country differences, the nature of business goods and services, with heavy emphasis on functionality, is such that foreign sales have long been important for most firms. Since World War II this importance has increased significantly. The work of GATT (General Agreement on Tariffs and Trade), culminating in the recently concluded Uruguay Round of negotiations, has dramatically reduced tariffs and other barriers to trade. Improvements in communication and transportation systems have further facilitated trade across national borders. For business marketers failure to consider foreign markets may result in missed opportunities that often may be more attractive than opportunities in the domestic market.

The traditional approach to foreign markets has been to segment on the basis of countries. Few segmentation variables would seem more straightforward. An atlas easily provides the basis for delineation of segments. In most instances, language, laws and currencies vary as a function of nationality. Business customs also may vary among regions and countries. As a result, firms tend to develop marketing strategies for individual countries. This so-called polycentric approach assumes that each country is so different as to require a unique marketing strategy.

The obvious differences between countries frequently obscure the many similarities that argue for global or regional strategies. Many firms, however, are developing strategies essentially common across countries except with regard to language and currency denomination. In the chemical industry, DuPont and Dow in the United States, Hoechst and BASF in Germany, Rhone-Poulenc in France, and Asahi in Japan all compete on a worldwide basis with essentially standardized products sold at world market prices. In the computer industry, IBM in the United States, Toshiba in Japan, Olivetti in Italy, and Bull in France compete on a worldwide basis with increasingly standardized products and prices that are slowly converging to a world level.

To the extent that strategies are less than global, many are being crafted for major economic regions such as the United States, Europe, or Asia. Numerous U.S. firms are consolidating their subsidiary operations in the various countries in Europe into centralized European operations. Electro Scientific Industries, Inc., a U.S. manufacturer of sophisticated manufacturing tools for the worldwide electronics industry has established a centralized operation in the Netherlands, where ESI Europe is the head sales and marketing office handling customer support, order processing, and distribution of spare parts.

For market segmentation purposes, this mandates consideration of other variables. One possibility is free trade areas or other forms of integrated economies, such as the European Union, the European Free Trade Area (soon to be merged into the European Union), the Andean Pact and the Mercado Sur in Latin America, the Association of Southeast Asian Nations (ASEAN) and, most recently, the North American Free Trade Area (NAFTA). Another possibility is countries that exhibit similarities along political or historical dimensions such as Scandinavia. Still another is the similarity of business customs, as might be found in the southern parts of European countries that border the Mediterranean or in the German-speaking countries of northern Europe. Still another might be to group countries that exhibit similar levels of political risk.

Summary

The fundamental objective of marketing strategy is to meet customer wants and needs more effectively than competitors and at a profit to the firm. The ultimate extension of the objective of meeting customer wants and needs would require a unique strategy for each customer. In some instances this indeed happens. Defense contractors supplying military needs in just one country frequently have just one customer. In markets with many customers, economies of scale with respect to production and marketing push firms in the other direction, with the extreme found with commodity products where there is essentially no attempt by sellers to determine individual customer's wants and needs. Most business marketers operate somewhere between these two extremes and are constantly faced with pressure either to aggregate segments, in order to achieve economies of scale or critical mass, or to further segment markets to better meet customer needs or respond to competitor threats.

As we have described in this chapter, the process of market segmentation is both analytical and creative. It is also dynamic, as changes in the firm's internal situation and the broader external environment change the context within which the process takes place. Flexible manufacturing, for instance, is increasing the ability of firms to respond to unique customer needs and so is increasing the number of segments a firm can feasibly target. Increasingly sophisticated marketing information systems are dramatically improving the ability of firms to more accurately identify customer needs and responses to marketing strategies and thereby capitalize on enhanced capabilities of the firm. In particular, segmentation processes need to take into account changing customer needs that, for business customers, develop from their strategies that similarly evolve from their efforts to adapt to their circumstances.

Finally, it should be remembered that the purpose of market segmentation is to improve the process by which firms decide which markets to pursue and which segments to target. These are the critical decisions. They must be accompanied by decisions that commit the firm's resources, talents, and energies. Without such commitment, even the best marketing strategy targeted at the most appropriate segment is not likely to succeed.

Overview of Chapter Cases

✹ The Machine Vision International case describes a company in a new high-tech industry. The case provides the opportunity to consider the firm's decisions as to product/market selection to capitalize on its new technology.

✹ In the Microsoft Corporation: The Introduction of Microsoft Works case we have the opportunity to consider the introduction of a new product in various markets, particularly the United States and Europe, and the extent to which the product should be modified to accommodate the views of the firm's subsidiary managers.

✹ The Toro: Industrial Flavors case describes the situation of a small Norwegian firm that had successfully entered the European market for flavor products but then found its organizational resources and competencies were stretched to the limit, requiring it to make some difficult market choices.

Endnotes

1. First Quarter and Annual Meeting Report, Hoover Universal, Inc., Ann Arbor, MI, November 26, 1980, 6–8.
2. Standard Industrial Classification codes: A system developed by the U.S. federal government to segment business activity into fairly homogeneous categories, based on products produced. Similar systems exist in most developed countries.
3. *Loctite Corporation: Industrial Products Group,* Harvard Business School, 9-581-066, Rev. 10/83.
4. This section draws heavily on Thomas V. Bonoma and Benson P. Shapiro, *Segmenting the Industrial Market* (Lexington, MA: Lexington Books, 1983).
5. Grahame R. Dowling, Gary L. Lilien, and Praveen K. Soni, "A Business Market Segmentation Procedure for Product Planning," *Journal of Business-to-Business Marketing,* Vol. 1 (4) (1993): 31–57.
6. Modified from Philip Kotler, *Marketing Management,* 8th ed. (Englewood Cliffs, NJ: Prentice Hall, Inc. 1994), 280–281.
7. Dowling, Lilien, and Soni, "A Business Market Segmentation Procedure for Product Planning."
8. *Business Week,* March 8, 1982, 88A.
9. As described in E. Raymond Corey, "Key Options in Market Selection and Product Planning, " *Harvard Business Review,* September–October, 1975, 119–128.

Thomas S. Robertson
Howard Barich

A Successful Approach to Segmenting Industrial Markets

Innovative market segmentation techniques that have been widely adopted by leading consumer products companies are now being imitated by many industrial firms.

Market segmentation is the act of dividing a market into distinct groups of buyers with similar requirements. It is the foundation of the marketing strategy process and the driver of resource allocation decisions. All other facets of strategy follow the selection of the targeted segments. Market segmentation enables the firm to recognize and meet the needs of the marketplace more precisely. By defining its segments, the firm serves the market more effectively, satisfies its customers, and fosters a flow of repeat business.

Surprisingly, the sophisticated market segmentation methods that power decision making for the consumer products businesses are often strikingly ineffectual in the industrial arena. Recently, in several industrial settings, market segmentation programs have shared a similar discouraging fate after passing through the same series of stages:

- The advocacy of innovative segmentation.

- The process of analyzing the markets.
- The introduction of the new system to top management and the sales team.
- And finally, its resounding rejection by the sales force. In a number of industrial firms, the failure of such programs has jeopardized the career of the manager championing the new strategic marketing techniques.

The History of a Doomed Initiative

Initially, the head of marketing sells top management on the need for a rational segmentation program and locates a consultant who has developed sophisticated segmentation analyses for consumer product companies. When the analysis is completed, the initial audience for the consultant's reconceptualization of the firm's markets is client Number One: senior management. Since a rationalization of markets from a strategic point of view offers top management considerable insight, such presentations often get high marks from influential senior managers.

A typical strategic segmentation study for one industrial firm was based on defining the product line's benefits to customers. The consultant's research identified nine separate categories of benefits, such as performance, service, and customized application. The types of customers most likely to be interested in each segment were also specified. For example, in the case in point, the customers most interested in performance tended to include small- and medium-sized accounts concentrated in manufacturing industries. The distinguishing char-

At the time this article was written, Thomas S. Robertson was the John and Laura Pomerantz Professor of Marketing at the Wharton School of the University of Pennsylvania. Howard Barich was Vice President of Marketing and Strategic Planning at Intersearch Corporation, Horsham, Pennsylvania. During the writing of this article he was a marketing advisor to senior management at IBM. In this article the authors report on results obtained in one leading industrial firm and on patterns they have observed in a number of industries. *Source:* Thomas S. Robertson and Howard Barich, "A Successful Approach to Segmenting Industrial Markets." This article is reprinted from *Planning Review* (November–December 1992), pp. 4–11, with permission from The Planning Forum, The International Society for Strategic Management and Planning.

acteristics for each segment are called "descriptors."

However, such a segmentation scheme plays to a much tougher audience when it's introduced to the company's account executives, systems engineers, and dealers. It's a tough sell for the head of marketing to make a presentation on an "intellectually intriguing" segmentation system to several hundred hard-bitten salespeople and dealers. In a number of firms, even though such an audience seemed to recognize some value in the innovative segmentation plan, that didn't mean that they would use it.

In fact, the feedback the head of marketing gets from the sales force is usually not overtly negative. Individual sales reps and systems engineers may well voice approval of the new process. However, while the new segmentation system may provide valuable insights for the best and brightest, it could prove difficult to institutionalize for the majority. Since the annual sales meeting assembles a demanding and unruly audience, the director of marketing may be glad to escape from the presentation with even lukewarm support.

Unfortunately, when follow-up studies on usage of the new system are done a year later, few if any adherents of the complex "Customer Benefit" method of segmenting the market are likely to be found. When the sales and operations managers in one firm were asked if they thought the bill for researching the segmentation systems should be charged to their budgets, 99 percent said, "No." If the CEO of the company believes in basing staff budget levels on the demand for services from operating people, then the head of marketing has genuine reasons to start having career anxiety.

One Size Doesn't Fit All

It's also the case that different managerial decisions within the firm may require different bases for segmentation. For example, in the design phase of innovative products, the R&D group may want to work closely with a segment of lead users. These ultra-sophisticated customers can help identify the future product features and capabilities that will be required.

Our focus here, however, is on marketing and sales. So, the crucial question is, "What form of segmentation is appropriate for the sales force?" In order to offer a segmentation approach that a firm's sales force and dealers will actually use, a number of criteria must be met. The resulting system must be:

- **Measurable**—Can the size, growth, and market potential of a segment be measured?
- **Profitable**—How profitable is the marketing effort likely to be? What is the payoff from each segment?
- **Accessible**—Can segments be identified and reached successfully?
- **Actionable**—Can effective marketing and sales programs be formulated for attracting and serving the segments?

Successful segmentation schemes must include a pragmatic business perspective. Elaborate computer and statistical results may be theoretically correct, but they may flunk the business judgment test. Overly complex segmentation schemes are not easily applied, especially when they form part of the sales process. Exhibit 1 outlines a set of common questions and answers for industrial segmentation.

A Tactical and Strategic System. Our segmentation approach is actionable at the account management level. It can be used easily and effectively by the sales representative or the agent or dealer assigned to an account. In many ways the role of the industrial sales rep is the ultimate form of segmentation—assessing and seeking to fulfill the unique needs of each account. However, sales reps can be even more effective if they're able to identify the customer's pattern of buying behavior—preferably before they make that sales call. The challenge for marketing and sales management is to help the salespeople segment the account base and

EXHIBIT 1
Segmenting Industrial Markets

Questions	Answers
• Why segment the market?	• To develop account priorities by knowing which accounts to target and which to ignore.
	• To allow the design of customized marketing programs in line with segment needs.
• Is segmentation always necessary?	• Only if the overall market is heterogeneous and segments can be identified with similar profiles of customer needs.
• How should segment priorities be developed?	• Based on the potential profitability of segments combined with the firm's competencies to serve particular segments.
• How is the segmentation of industrial markets different than the segmentation of consumer markets?	• The focus of executing a segmentation strategy will be on the sales force (direct or indirect) rather than on advertising.
• What criteria must be met to allow segmentation?	• Segments must be:
	—Measurable as to potential.
	—Profitable.
	—Accessible—they can be identified and reached.
	—Actionable—marketing programs can be designed that will be more effective than total market programs.
• What is the most common problem with industrial segmentation?	• It is not actionable at the sales force level, often because it is too complicated.

to provide the most effective sales programs for each segment.

Segmentation by Stage of the Purchase Decision Process

Recently, in the course of our work on the segmentation of industrial markets, we identified a highly effective segmentation approach. Its power lies in its simplicity since it can be easily used by the sales force or the company's dealers. The key is segmenting customers by the phase of the purchase decision process that they're currently experiencing. This approach identifies segments easily, characterizes different buying patterns, and suggests the benefits to emphasize in the sales call.

The purchase decision process can be thought of as a hierarchy through which a firm must move its customers. Although some very elaborate sequences have been proposed, we have found that a three-stage hierarchy encompasses everything needed for a meaningful segmentation approach to reach most industrial markets. Based on the purchase decision process, the key phrases are:

• **Segment 1: First Time Prospects:** These are accounts who see a possible need for your product and have started evaluating vendors—but they have not yet purchased.

• **Segment 2: Novices:** These are customers who have purchased the product for the first time within the last three months.

EXHIBIT 2
What Buyers of Industrial Products Look For

First-Time Prospects	Novices	Sophisticates
Dominant Theme:	***Dominant Theme:***	***Dominant Theme:***
"Take care of me."	"Help me make it work."	"Talk technology to me."
Benefits Sought:	***Benefits Sought:***	***Benefits Sought:***
• A sales rep who knows and understands my business.	• Easy-to-read manuals.	• Compatibility with existing systems.
• An honest sales rep.	• Technical support hot lines.	• Products customized to customer needs.
• A vendor who has been in business for some time.	• A high level of training.	• Track record of vendor.
• A sales rep who can communicate in an understandable manner.	• Sales reps who are knowledgeable about their products and services.	• Maintenance speed in fixing problems.
• A trial period.		• Post-sales support and technical support.
• A high level of training.		
What's Less Important:	***What's Less Important:***	***What's Less Important:***
• Sales rep's knowledge of products and services.	• An honest sales rep.	• Training.
	• A sales rep who knows and understands my business.	• Trial.
		• Easy-to-read manuals.
		• Sales rep who can communicate in an understandable manner.

• **Segment 3: Sophisticates:** These accounts have either purchased the product before and are now ready to rebuy, or have recently repurchased.

These three segments value different benefits, buy from different channels, and have varying impressions of providers.

Our results are drawn from a research study of an industrial product in which management was interested in becoming the leader among small- and medium-sized companies. The market was quite dynamic and heterogeneous, but it was highly fragmented among many competitors. There were many new company starts each year, as well as many failures. However, the company's product was innovative, and therefore the next step was an analysis of which customers were the leaders and which were the laggards.

Benefits Sought by Each Segment

The real value of any segmentation approach depends on its ability to separate potential buyers by the benefits they're seeking. If different benefit profiles have been established, then the sales call can focus on the most relevant motivators. In the industrial market we studied, the benefits sought by each segment showed strong differences (see Exhibit 2).

First Time Prospects: "Take Care of Me." These accounts want someone to take care of them. They are nervous and unsure of themselves. They require a gentle, guiding hand. Interestingly, they do not place a high value on the sales representative's knowledge of products and services. They do not want to be intimidated. What they do want is a sales rep who knows and understands their business and who they consider to be honest. They value a sales rep who can communicate with them in an understandable manner. They want a vendor who has been in business for some time. And they also want a trial period to test the equipment, and a high level of training.

The pattern that emerges is quite clear, as are the sales implications. These prospects need to develop a comfort factor if the sale is to be consummated. The sales approach must build a high level of trust in the vendor ("We'll be here tomorrow.") and in the company's sales representative. Customer training and trial will be critical determinants of whether the sale is concluded. Product features, functions, and performance take a back seat to personal needs for comfort and security ("We'll take care of you.").

Novices: "Help Me Make It Work." Those who have recently bought the product seek a different set of benefits. They are over the hurdle of uncertainty and are much less concerned with whether the sales rep understands their business or how honest that person is. Novices are more concerned with improving their utilization of the equipment. They want manuals that are easy to read, technical support hotlines, a high level of training, and sales reps who are extremely knowledgeable about the products and services they sell. The sales call on a novice buyer requires a very different approach than the sales call on a first time prospect. Selling the "warm fuzzies" has become a lot less important. Instead, the sales rep must build on the favorable initial experiences. These customers are driven by the need to make the equipment work for them, and they're looking for performance help—hotlines, training, and manuals.

Sophisticates: "Talk Technology to Me." Customers who have purchased one or more products are driven by long-term concerns. In considering new purchases, they seek compatibility with existing products, and new products that are customized to their needs. They evaluate the track record of the vendor and how quickly maintenance has fixed problems in the past. While post-sales support and technical support hotlines continue to be important, training, trial, and easy-to-read manuals are no longer very relevant.

Selling these accounts is based much more on product specifications—fit with existing systems and ability to customize. This is more of a technology sell than a personal relationship sell. These customers like to talk features and functions; they don't need to be hand held. They don't even value a sales rep who can communicate with them in an understandable manner.

Distribution Channels Used by Each Segment

Each of the segments seeks a different set of benefits. Based on its analysis of these customer benefits the firm must decide "how to get to market," or what distribution channels to use for each segment. Just as this purchase decision segmentation scheme is useful for the direct sales force in account management, it may also be useful in selecting appropriate channels of distribution that complement or substitute for the direct sales force.

We generally think of industrial markets as being reached by a direct sales force. However, alternative distribution channels are becoming increasingly important in industrial markets. For example, hybrid channels that include not only a direct sales force, but indirect dealers and distributors, as well as telemarketing, are becoming prevalent.

The movements to hybrid channels is driven by the potentially superior economics of indirect marketers. It may be more cost effective to use distributors or dealers as it reduces the fixed cost of the direct sales force, which is carried on the firm's books. Indirect channels may also provide access to a broader account base—especially smaller accounts. Indirect channels frequently have specialized industry knowledge that a direct sales force does not possess if it sells across industries. However, designing a hybrid system of direct and indirect channels is not easy, and all of the promised benefits may not materialize. Cost savings are sometimes illusory, conflict with the direct sales force may be inevitable, and indirect sales channels may also go after the big accounts rather than the hoped-for penetration of small accounts.

Nevertheless, in channel design—how the firm goes to market—the logic must always be to build channels compatible with customer segment needs. However, channels are constantly evolving and the firm must be sensitive to where channels are going. Many major firms make the mistake of locking in to existing channels. Merrill Lynch's key strategic asset may be its large and highly competent sales force, but this has also been a fixed commitment that has limited participation in the discount brokerage and direct marketing parts of the business. As a result, such firms as Schwab, Dreyfus, and Fidelity have chalked-up higher growth levels than Merrill Lynch and have frequently shown a higher return on investment.

Anticipate Shifts in Channels

The challenge for all firms—but most especially for industrial firms—is to anticipate where channels are going. Improving price/performance in the telecommunications industry, for example, has led to much broader channels of distribution for AT&T and Northern Telecom, who must now sell PBXs via a mix of direct and indirect channels.

Segmentation by the phase of the purchase decision process is again of value in understanding channel preferences. Based on the benefits that each segment seeks, here are some likely channel preferences:

• First Time Prospects prefer channels that provide lots of information, demonstration, training, and hand holding.

• Novices value channels that help make the product work. This includes customer training, and also back-up technical support and services.

• Sophisticates have a high level of confidence and seek channels that can talk technology as well as customize the product to their specific applications.

Indeed, our findings from the study of industrial buyers support these conclusions.

• First Time Prospects were interested in high value-added channels or in buying directly from the manufacturer. As would be expected, they were least likely to use catalog/direct mail, since this is a channel that usually does not provide much information or hand holding. They were also least likely to use a distributor who provides product customization.

• Novices were lowest in their preference for buying direct from the manufacturer—perhaps because their experiences in buying direct had not fulfilled their expectations. They were much more likely than first-time prospects to consider catalog/direct mail, and to use a distributor.

• Sophisticates were in the middle on preference for buying direct. However, they were the most likely of the segments to use mail order/catalog and to use distributors who provided product customization.

There is an interesting implication here about how channels are evolving. As the market matures, there are fewer and fewer first-time prospects and novices. Over time, therefore, the channels must reflect the preferences of sophisticates. This means that the firm's channels are not going to be stable, and that the appropriate channel configuration when a product or technology is first introduced will be quite different from the appropriate channel later in its life cycle. This is being demonstrated in the chemical industry today. Early life cycle sales for a new chemical require high information inputs since buyers are initially unsophisticated. Over time, however, as buyers develop knowledge and applications' expertise, they become less information sensitive and more price and service sensitive. Channels follow suit: from direct sales to fabricators, formulators, and distributors.

Manufacturers who lock into channels early in the life cycle, therefore, may have only a temporary advantage with a built-in major long-run disadvantage. GM may have had an advantage selling consumables for automobiles such as air filters and spark plugs through its dealer network early in the auto life cycle. Today's market, however, demands that these products be available from mass merchandisers, home centers, and even supermarkets. GM finally responded by taking its AC brand to Sears a couple of years ago, but not before years of delays and a great deal of consternation over dealer reaction.

Vendors' Images by Segment

An interesting question for firms is their marketing image. Many companies conduct image studies and build corporate identity campaigns. These studies and campaigns must be implemented at the segment level. A company must undertake formal image research if it wants to understand how customers view the company and its key competitors since its image influences buying decisions, which in turn affect the bottom line. An essential ingredient of image management is the ability to enhance the image among relevant market segments. A company must protect and enhance its image and engage in image tracking by segment.

In all phases of the buying decision, image or perceptions play a major role in customer decision making. It is important for a firm to understand the needs and wants and the perceptions of each segment. As was suggested in Exhibit 2, customers in each segment value different attributes. It is also important for the firm to understand how its strengths and weaknesses compare to its key competitors on the essential attributes for each segment.

In the course of researching a number of industrial products and services, we observed a curious phenomenon. As customers grow in sophistication, the images of their vendors tend to become less positive. We have been in more than one management meeting where there has been considerable justified concern over lower image ratings among the firm's more experienced customers. However, the information available to management was often myopic because it focused only on their firm, rather than taking into account the more general phenomenon in the marketplace. This often led to unconstructive overreaction.

It may very well be in the nature of things that more experienced customers are less accepting and more critical. This can be used to advantage to help assess future market needs. A number of observers have emphasized the value of working with lead users—generally highly experienced customers—to discover early indicators of new product needs. However, a key analysis for management is the level of image decline versus other vendors in the marketplace as we move from First Time Prospects to Novices to Sophisticates.

This decline is not surprising. Many industrial companies are notorious for over-promising and under-delivering. The first time prospect usually accepts the vendor's promises and has a high image of the vendor. But as customers move through the purchase decision phases, they develop more experience with vendors, often encountering disappointments. Thus, their images of vendors decline. In time, they become Sophisticates with even less faith in their suppliers. This is because most vendors, unfortunately, tend to promise more than they can deliver in an attempt to achieve competitive advantage.

As part of the research project, we developed some data on the levels of image decline within one industrial category. First of all, we observed the general phenomenon that image declined for almost all brands as we compared Prospects, Novices, and Sophisticates. Only one brand actually saw an improvement in image for more sophisticated customers. This was a brand that was sold primarily by direct mail and catalog so that it better fulfilled the evolving channel preferences of the Sophisticates.

Lost in the Pack Syndrome. However, another phenomenon occurred, one that we have also found in other product categories. The brands that showed the greatest decline in image were the ones that were stuck in the middle of the market share ranking. Among the eight brands we examined, brands three and four experienced the largest image decline. The next level of decline hit the top two brands. The lowest share brands in the market, six and seven, actually showed the least image decline—of course, they also had the least to lose!

Marketing to sophisticated or experienced customers is a very demanding task, since sophisticated buyers tend not to rely on the guidance of a manufacturer's sales force. They also rely less on image, and make more independent technology or product-based decisions.

What this suggests is that, as markets evolve and encompass a higher proportion of experienced customers, image advertising is probably of less value. Inexperienced accounts may value the prestige of the AT&T, Caterpillar, or Motorola names, but experienced accounts are looking for product performance and customization to their needs. It may well be that the best advertising focuses on product benefits rather than image, and that communication dollars are best spent on micro-marketing customized to the individual needs of accounts.

Purchase Decision Phase Segments as a Tracking Tool

The purchase decision phase segmentation scheme can also be a valuable diagnostic tool in tracking the performance of a new product. Often, after a new product is introduced, managers scan monthly sales reports and see increasing sales for the first few months. But then—in a pattern that repeats time after time—sales suddenly stall and decline.

Unfortunately, sales reports usually don't tell a company very much, especially if they're based on factory sales, a common practice in industrial markets. Initial sales may simply represent sell-in by the sales force to fill the distribution pipeline. And even if sales reports are based on deliveries to end customers, early sales often represent trial purchases that are never repeated. Eventually, the availability of trial customers dissipates and sales plummet.

The key to long-run product success is moving customers from Prospects to Novices to Sophisticates—in other words, to repeat purchasers. Yet, many industrial firms fail to track and to separate trial versus repeat sales. Thus, they miss out on valuable information on how to adjust their marketing program as the market evolves.

It is important to track product sales by the defined segments. Three negative scenarios or problems that may affect each of the defined segments might be:

• **The "Few Prospects" Scenario.** In this scenario, which is quite common, sales are being held back because of an inability to move the market to consider purchase. Rohm and Haas, for example, found this to be the case when it introduced a new biocide for small metalworking shops. The few prospects scenario usually suggests an awareness problem.

The remedy is generally to increase advertising/direct mail spending and sales force coverage. Advertising is usually more cost effective than using the sales force to create awareness and interest, but that of course depends on the number of potential customers. If the customer segment is small enough, sales force calls may be the local way to develop prospects. Schlumberger's market for oil-drilling rigs, for example, includes only about thirty major oil companies as clients. In this case, the sales force can cost-effectively undertake awareness building.

On the other hand, few prospects may also indicate that customers have not been given sufficient positive information. In such a case, the answer may lie in changing the communication campaign to emphasize the product's benefits or adding more sales force or trade demonstrations to present the new product's positive attributes.

• **The "Few Novices" Scenario.** Here the firm has been unsuccessful in moving the market to try its product. This may have been BAE's main problem in selling its short-haul jet to the world's airlines. Few first-time buyers may mean that the sales force has been emphasizing the wrong benefits. First-timers need to feel that they're being taken care of before they develop the confidence to try the product and thus move to the Novice segment.

It may also be that distribution or pricing is to blame. If customers have a positive attitude but haven't yet moved to a trial purchase, it often means that the product is not readily available or that the price is too high. Or, the advertising/direct mail campaign may be at fault. It may have focused on "reach" to develop prospects (exposure to many possible customers), while "frequency" (number of ad exposures per potential customers) is what it needs to convert Prospects to Novices. Finally, of course, a firm has to consider the possibility that its products might not meet customer needs in a superior manner in comparison with competitor's products.

• **The "Few Sophisticates" Scenario.** This is a troublesome case. It suggests that after the initial purchase, customers may have concluded that the technology did not fulfill its promise. Redesigning the product or repositioning it may be necessary. Another problem is that the customer's use of the first purchased technology may be so low due to lack of training, or support, or limited application packages that they see no reason to buy another of the firm's products. This suggests the need for follow-up sales support and application engineering to increase product usage.

In all markets, a company's future sales are dependent on the customer's success with the present product. This makes it absolutely critical not only to sell the product but to assist in every way with its integration into the customer's business process. Only a customer that uses the product successfully is likely to buy more of the company's products. It's only when Novices move to Sophisticates that sales efforts prosper in the long run. Otherwise, it runs out of the available set of potential first-time buyers and sales inevitably decline.

The Benefits of Segmentation

Segmenting industrial markets by phase of the purchase decision process can be a revealing and useful approach. It can make a crucial difference for the sales force in successfully engaging prospects and customers. In addition, an industrial firm can use the selection of appropriate distribution channels to measure its image and to track the performance of newly introduced products.

Segmenting industrial markets by phase of the purchase decision process has many advantages. It enables the sales force to identify segments easily, to characterize different buying patterns, and to know which benefits to emphasize in the sales call. This scheme is a combination of objective statistical methods and business judgments designed with sales calls in mind. The segments can easily pass the effective segmentation requirements of measurability, profitability, accessibility, and actionability.

This segmentation scheme helps management explore the firm's market position and the way the company is perceived by its customers relative to competition. It also enables management to monitor perception trends in the marketplace and to capture and understand the changes. This methodology is general enough to be applied to any firm, whether it focuses on products or services. Small, medium, or large firms can implement the analysis best suited for their objectives. It also allows management to implement actionable results and helps to make strategic market decisions.

Data from a nationwide sample of over 500 small and medium firms has pinpointed the product attributes most valued by each of the defined segments for one industrial product. These attributes may vary, of course, in other markets. In each segment, the channel preferences suggest using different distribution channels to match customer preferences. The differences by segment guide the firm in its "getting to market" decisions. Today, firms need to design hybrid channel systems to reach customers, since segments have varying support and service needs.

The tendency that we have observed in a number of industrial markets is that vendor images are highest among the Prospect segment and lowest in the Sophisticate segment. These customers are more discriminating and more demanding. They may also be reacting to the manufacturers' failure to keep its promises. These results should be cautionary to firms about overpromising in their quest for competitive advantage.

Finally, as companies try to become more market oriented, they must segment their markets to understand the needs and wants of customers. The concept of segments identified by phases of the purchase decision provides a practical approach to segmenting industrial markets.

James D. Hlavacek

B. C. Ames

Segmenting Industrial and High-Tech Markets

Segmenting a marketplace is one of the most important strategic moves that can be made by high-tech companies, industrial firms, and firms that sell services to other businesses. Yet technical-based businesses often miss out on opportunities by failing to divide their markets adequately and develop cohesive strategies to conquer and protect a market position. ✻

Market segmentation has enabled many industrial firms to concentrate their resources on one or a few customer groups so they can be more responsive to their particular requirements. Effective industrial market segmentation helps to capture a new business opportunity, protect a market position, and avert competitive threats. Conversely, the failure to segment a marketplace has resulted in missed opportunities, surprise competition, and even business failures.

Deere, a large farm equipment manufacturer, identified a market trend to fewer but larger farms that required large horsepower tractors and equipment. Deere designed and manufactured large horsepower machinery and subsequently captured a market opportunity. The existing market leader, International Harvester, was late to recognize and pursue the new and growing market segment and lost substantial market share as a result.

At the time this article was written, James D. Hlavacek was Professor and Director, The Institute for Executive Education, in the Babcock Graduate School of Management, at Wake Forest University. B.C. Ames was Chairman and CEO of Acme-Cleveland Corporation. He was previously President and CEO of Reliance Electric and a Managing Director at McKinsey & Company. *Source:* James D. Hlavacek and B.C. Ames "Segmenting Industrial and High-Tech Markets. This article is reprinted from *The Journal of Business Strategy*, vol. 7, no. 2 (fall 1986).

Xerox, the pioneer among photocopying machines, emphasized the high-speed segment for very large customers. The Japanese competitors were the first to identify and develop a desktop plain paper copier for a business's low-speed needs. It rapidly became the fastest-growing copier market segment. According to the president of Canon U.S.A., "It has been our strategy to identify a market demand and then create a product to fill that demand."[1] Xerox failed to resegment the marketplace and by so doing allowed Canon and other Japanese competitors to do it for them.

Both General Electric and RCA withdrew from the computer industry after unsuccessfully attempting to compete with IBM. The most successful entrants in the computer business concentrated their R&D, manufacturing, and marketing on one or a few select market segments. The chairman of Cray Research explains, "We avoided going head-on with IBM but rather focused in on the largest computers, where IBM was not as strong."[2]

Similar examples of successful computer market segmentation and strategic responses are

[1]"Copiers Still a Growth Industry," *High Technology*, May 1983, p. 54.

[2]Coel Ross and Michael Kami, *Corporate Management in Crisis: Why the Mighty Fall* (1973), p. 80.

NCR's concentration on retail store computer systems. Burroughs' emphasis on computers to meet the requirements of the banking industry, and Honeywell's successful focus on computers that control manufacturing processes.

Successful industrial or business-to-business segmentation can also be found in service industries. American National Bank rapidly became Chicago's fifth largest bank by exclusively focusing its capabilities on serving the highly profitable "middle market" of smaller-sized companies. After targeting the smaller companies, which were providing most of the economic growth in the region, American National carefully identified the unique financial services requirements of the segment. The identification and selection of a market segment determined the strategy and guided the development and packaging of financial services to effectively serve this group of customers with common requirements. American National was able to win over customers from even the largest competitive banks that had considerably less focused business strategies.

Foundation for Business Strategy

Over the past two decades, a number of industrial and high-tech companies have rediscovered Demosthenes' idea: "Small opportunities are often the beginning of great enterprises." Unable to compete broadly against entrenched competitors, the companies have adopted successful niches with a "divide and conquer" strategy. This involves identifying a market need, then focusing resources and energies on meeting that need better than anyone else.

The identification and selection of market segments is the most important strategic decision facing the industrial firm. The choice of which market segments to pursue is the key starting block for developing successful overall strategies and product/market plans for the technically based firm. Industrial market segmentation identifies the scope of the business in terms of products technology, and the respective competition in the segment. Only after it identifies a market segment and the customer's needs and specific requirements can the technical firm identify the relevant threats and opportunities. The identified market segment serves as a mirror for appraising the supplying firm's capabilities or strengths and weaknesses in meeting the segment's present and future requirements. The present or changing requirements of the segment determine what "your knitting" or business really is.

The strategic importance of market segmentation has been ignored by most staff planners and industrial economists who simply conduct macro "competitive analysis" exercises. Strategic planning formats that do not demand specific market segments when analyzing situations and developing strategies can easily become annual form-filling exercises. A "strengths and weaknesses" analysis that is not conducted up against the needs and requirements of an identified market segment is usually a total waste of time. Similarly, if planning and strategy development is done around the key success factor approach without considering the key success factors necessary to serve an identified market segment, the result will most likely be a macro analysis and a broad-based strategy that ineffectively tries to be something to everyone.

A well-thought-out division charter should define its business mission in terms of both products or technologies and key market segments served. Too many company or division charters simply describe products manufactured and some broad industry groups to which they are marketed. A clearly stated mission in terms of products and market segments served will focus the entire business unit on customer groups with common requirements. Such a clearly stated mission statement that focuses on market segments helps to answer the question, "What business are we really in?"

The identification and then selection of market segments determines the producer's customer mix, which business one is in, and who the competition is. The selection of an industrial segment(s) to concentrate on will significantly affect all of the functional areas of the firm. As Corey states:

All else follows. Choice of market is a choice of the customer and of the competitive, technical, political, and social environments in which one elects to compete. It is not an easily reversed decision; having made the choice the company develops skills and resources around the markets it has elected to serve. It builds a set of relationships with customers that are at once a major source of strength and a major commitment. The commitment carries with it the responsibility to serve customers well, to stay in the technical and product-development race, and to grow in pace with growing market demand. Such choices are not made in a vacuum. They are influenced by the company's background; by its marketing, manufacturing, and technical strengths; by the fabric of its relations with existing customers, the scientific community, and competitors.[3]

How an industrial or high-tech producer defines a market segment determines the boundaries of the business it is in. When the competitor's market segment definitions are the same, industrial market share measurement is clear and straightforward. The frequent difficulty of determining market boundaries and the resulting market shares is also at the heart of antitrust controversy. Naming the market a firm is dominating or in which it is restraining competition depends on how one segments and defines the market. The amount of product interchangeability among all customers helps to define the relevant industrial market segments. For example, IBM was accused by the U.S. Justice Department of "dominating the computer market." However, in the fastest-growing segments, mini and personal computers, IBM in 1981 did not have a strong position. The various market segments and IBM's *relative* strength in *each segment* helped in having the case dismissed.

Technical Manufacturers Often Don't Practice Segmentation

Market segmentation as a business practice has long been recognized and well-accepted in the consumer goods sector. Among technical manufacturing businesses, there has been no corresponding level of interest and rigor. In practice, industrial firms frequently have a product emphasis and little or no real market segmentation, identification, and selection. Many other industrial firms do not think as clearly as

they should about market segments before launching into the development of product and market plans. "Thinking segments" is not easy for many industrial marketing senior managers as the following statements show: "All our customers are unique and very different"; "You first must cover the territory well." As a result of this kind of thinking, many industrial companies tend to think of a market as one large unit that buys and uses similar products. At best, they might list their current customers by amount of annual purchases for an item. Larger accounts may be called "key accounts" but that is not market segmentation. Key account or sales "segmentation" schemes do not consider any differences or similarities among customers' requirements. Industrial market schemes that only partition customers by annual sales or distribution channels are simply sales analysis approaches that relate back to annual purchase volume for a specific item. These schemes, though useful in identifying users as heavy ("A" customers), medium ("B" customers), and light ("C" customers), do not identify groups of customers with common requirements or buying needs. Dividing market groups by geographic location is still another sales "segmentation" approach that may be useful for industrial sales territory alignment, but it does not address the grouping of customers' need for better focused and effective product/market strategies. A further analysis of one manufacturer's existing customers uncovered five segmentation findings that helped develop product/market strategies:

1. The product was being marketed to six end use market segments that they had not previously identified. They were:

   - Semiconductor equipment
   - Heavy-duty highway trucks
   - Fast-speed printing machinery
   - Surgical and medical instruments
   - Materials handling equipment
   - Robotics equipment

2. There were major differences among each of the six identified market segments relative to annual purchases, growth rates, long-term prospects, and profitability.

[3]E. Raymond Corey, "Key Options in Market Selection and Product Planning," *Harvard Business Review*, Sept.–Oct. 1975, p. 120.

3. The cost/benefit value added of the producer's high-performance component was the greatest in two market segments where the producer had little market penetration.

4. In some market segments it was competing with quite different products or technologies. In one low-performance segment, the company's product quality was far above the market segment's requirements.

5. There were different arrays of competitors in three of the six identified segments.

Sales- or product-focused industrial firms are usually not aware of any real market segments in their industry. At the other extreme, some sales-focused firms think in terms of one specific customer's needs rather than thinking of the common needs of customer groups. One medium-size plastic closure company that makes containers for consumer products manufacturers got 36 percent of its business from one large customer. This heavy dependency kept the company from thinking in terms of applying its capabilities to different groups of customers that had similar container closure problems. One of its most successful competitors, however, focused on child-resistant and tamper-proof pharmaceutical packaging applications. The need to "think segments" also appears to be difficult for many original equipment manufacturers (OEMs) and defense contract firms. In both OEM and defense situations, one or a few customers with similar requirements might constitute a market segment.

Consumer Goods Approaches

Most of the consumer goods approaches to market segmentation are of little or no value when segmenting a business-to-business marketplace. One reason is that consumer goods users are easily identified and the purchase decision makers are usually quite clear. The family or consumer household unit of one or two people does not buy so much on the basis of economic value as the industrial user. Household consumer buying is therefore segmented primarily on the basis of demographic and psy-

chographic factors. Entering a new consumer segment often translates into changing a product's packaging, brand, price, advertising program, or image. Segmentation in that context is often primarily psychological attribute segmentation. In contrast, industrial or business-to-business market segmentation must be based on common economic, application, or usage considerations. As a result, segmentation in consumer and industrial markets is as different as potato chips and integrated circuit chips. Some industrial or business-to-business firms have been misled by advertising agencies, consultants, or consumer goods marketers that eloquently tout the segmentation approaches that work well in the consumer goods world.

How to Segment Industrial Markets

Successful industrial high-tech business segmentation is both creative and judgmental. What will be an effective and profitable way to segment one market may not be a good method to segment another market. However, there are a number of essential and more advanced approaches to segmenting industrial markets that have proved to be successful.

Segment an Industry

Many industrial firms do not distinguish between industry and market segments *within* an industry. For example, one component manufacturer stated: "We serve the computer market with solid state connectors." But there are many kinds of computer market segments within the computer industry, and each segment has specific customer requirements. After analyzing the supplier's customer base, it would have been more useful for the division's charter to state: "We primarily serve the mainframe and microprocessor computer segments with solid state connectors."

In still another situation, an industrial firm's division charter simply stated: "The division is a supplier of hydraulic pumps and hoses to machinery markets." The division is defining a general industry, not market segments. A further analysis revealed that the division was primarily supplying certain types of farm equipment manufacturers, three kinds of construction machinery producers, and plastic injection equipment makers. An *industry* is a wide group of manufacturers producing a wide range of products. An industrial *market* segment is a much more distinct group of customers that have similar requirements. With the distinction made between an industry and a market, the manufacturer is now in a better position to identify target segments. Segmenting can be done by OEM and aftermarket, by four-digit SICs (standard industrial classification), by customer use (also called application), by common buying factors, and by buyer size.

Segment by OEM and Aftermarkets

The first level of industrial market segmentation is to classify a present or potential customer as an OEM or an aftermarket user. The OEM sale is usually a direct sale and if there is an aftermarket for the product, it often is served through distributors. The aftermarket or end user is sometimes called the maintenance, repair, and overhaul market (MRO). For farm tractors, Deere would be an original equipment manufacturer and the individual farmer would be the end user. The repair parts bought by the farmer would constitute the aftermarket. Deere's repair parts have both OEM and aftermarket segments. Component and equipment producer's products, therefore, always have both OEM and aftermarket customers. But materials like chemicals, metals, and adhesives, which are consumed in various product processes do not usually have both an OEM and aftermarket, but just OEM market segments. For example, a chemical firm will buy an ingredient to manufacture polyvinyl chloride plastic pipe. There is not an aftermarket for the plastic pipe ingredient. There are three industrial or high-tech product categories that have some distinct properties and uses that determine whether an OEM and aftermarket segments can be carved out:

1. *Components.* These are parts or items that are used to build and repair machinery and equipment. Components include items such as switches, integrated circuits, machine tool parts, connectors, and pistons. They are usually required by both the OEM and aftermarket segments.

2. *Systems and equipment.* These are end products used by those in industrial companies. Examples are machine tools, bulldozers, computers, laboratory instruments, and lasers. Systems and equipment require parts (components) for OEMs and for repair by end users, which creates both OEM and aftermarket segments.

3. *Materials.* These are consumed in the user's production process and include items such as chemicals, coolants, metals, herbicides, and adhesives. They do not usually have aftermarket segments.

Unfortunately, the OEM and broad aftermarket categories are the beginning and end of segmentation for many industrial producers. By not segmenting beyond this level, the producer typically lacks knowledge of which specific market segments are using its products a lot, some, or not at all. Firms that do not have segmentation beyond OEM/aftermarket are less likely to be positioned in the more attractive growth segments, will not know their competitive position in a segment, and therefore will tend not to develop competitor-based strategies. The OEM and aftermarket segmentation can sometimes be determined from existing sales records. But the existing sales records usually fail to reveal what SIC groups and end user application segments exist within the direct or distributor sales records.

Segment by SICs

The industrial producer should further segment his OEM and/or aftermarket customers by SIC. The U.S. Government Office of Management and Budget publishes a standard industrial classification manual that categorizes all business firms by the type of product or service they manufacture or sell. It classifies all businesses and plants by a four-digit classification system based on what is produced. An allied source to the four-digit SIC system for identifying and segmenting industrial markets is the *County Business Patterns*. This annual publication reports the number of employees and value of shipments by the same four-digit SICs. The four-digit SIC system, coupled with the *County Business Patterns,* helps the industrial producer identify and assess the size and location of more specific market segments. However, the existing SIC system does not have numbers assigned to, or categories for, the continuously emerging high-technology businesses and products. Therefore, leading manufacturers create their own numbers or codes for the newer technology businesses, which are developed as an extension to the existing four-digit SIC system.

Segmentation by OEM/aftermarket and four-digit SIC group is essential to sound industrial market segmentation. These two levels of segmentation should always be used by the producer of industrial products. Oftentimes, industrial firms do not have to segment beyond the OEM/aftermarket and four-digit SIC levels. However, some very successful industrial producers have creatively segmented one or two levels beyond OEM/aftermarket and SIC levels. Industrial segmentation beyond these two levels requires original field studies of present and potential customers to determine end use application market segments. New and emerging technologies or products that are not categorized by an SIC number must be segmented by these additional approaches.

Segment by Applications

Segmentation by use or application is one of the most useful approaches to capture a market opportunity successfully. It requires a careful analysis of where and how a group of customers uses the product. Industrial products frequently provide different economic value for different customer applications. The different economic value is a result of how the customer uses the product. Distinct market segments can emerge from different applications or uses of the same product. For example, a front-end equipment loader will have greater value to a customer who uses it eight hours a day in a mining operation than to a customer who occasion-

ally uses it two to three hours a day on a construction site. Operating costs usually differ sharply among applications.

A manufacturer of off-highway vehicles found that, on the average, its product had a purchase price and life-cycle cost disadvantage compared with that of a powerful competitor. This disadvantage was considerably alleviated by the discovery that for higher-tonnage, slower-speed application or use the fuel cost per ton mile of the company's vehicle had the advantage when operating at cruising speed with a light load. The company's marketing strategy was accordingly redirected at market segments who used the vehicle for short hauls. By selecting the key variables that explain most of the cost value of a customer's application, a supplier can come up with a creative market segmentation that yields an important strategic advantage.

Value analysis for each identified application helps to determine the economic value of the product for each application segment. A value analysis consists of identifying functions needed by the customers and then determining the customers' cost to perform the function. The solution to the problem or production need is what the industrial customer buys. Whatever product or technology provides the best cost/benefit to the problem will have a competitive advantage in that market segment. When conducting a market segment analysis by determining the customer's application, the producer must ask, "What function(s) does the customer want performed by this product?" The functions are the customer's needs in that application. The functions are also the benefits the customer receives from the product in that application. X-ray machines provide the customer function of diagnosing. In many applications, that function or requirement is fulfilled by a relatively simple machine. When the customer needs the functions of diagnosing *and* treatment therapy, a more sophisticated machine is needed for those end users. The identification of functional needs by applications requires in-depth studies and visits with customers.

The identification of functional needs by applications should include a consideration of substitute or potential substitute products that can perform the function. For example, Continental Can has found it necessary to consider the customer value of containers made of many different materials (metal, glass, fiber, plastic) for each application. This consideration helps Continental segment markets for its products creatively when the customer is currently using a different material than Continental produces. The evaluation of functional substitutes helps producers identify applications where their product has greater customer value. Many product-driven companies have difficulty breaking out of their pattern of only comparing their products with application segments using a very similar product. From the customer's viewpoint, a product or technology is only one solution to a problem. A simple two-dimensional matrix (Exhibit 1) helps one evaluate alternative products in each application and then determine the resulting customer value. If the resulting customer value from the product is significant, a possibly attractive market segment exists for the specific product or technology.

How, where, and how much the customer uses the product also helps (as shown in Exhibit 1) to determine the cost/benefit value by application. Value analysis costs include initial purchase, installation, operating expenses, and life-cycle costs. These costs should be used in determining cost/benefits by the end use application segment. The analysis should proceed as follows:

1. Evaluate the customer's cost/benefit of the product across a variety of customers in the applications.

2. Tentatively identify attractive market segments based on customer cost/benefit differences.

3. Further analyze more customers in each segment to verify those variables that underlie cost/benefit differences among applications.

When the value-in-use in an application segment is greater than the price of competitive substitutes, the producer will have a true market advantage in that application segment. Conversely, the value analysis may show that the producer has a competitive disadvantage in a specific segment. Application value analysis is a sound approach to

EXHIBIT 1
Product/Market Application Analysis

		Three Market Applications	
	1	2	3
Two Alternative A	Value	Value	Value
Products or			
Technologies B	Value	Value	Value

segmenting many industrial markets. It also provides a concrete methodology for developing promotional programs and sales presentations by the producer to show the demonstrable competitive advantage of its product to a defined market segment.

Segmenting by Common Buying Factors

A few industrial companies have successfully defined market segments by identifying groups of customers who share common buying characteristics. Most industrial and high-tech buying decisions hinge on five buying factors: (1) performance, (2) quality, (3) service, (4) delivery, and (5) price. Because common buying factors often cut across traditional market segments, this is often a difficult mode of market segmentation. For example, an electrical component manufacturing company had a complicated problem. In order to combat increasing price competition, it had spent two years trying to develop detailed segment strategies for its SIC market segments. The breakthrough came when it discovered that the customers could be grouped or aggregated into four strategic market segments based on common buying characteristics. Segment 1 consisted of large-lot buyers who were extremely price sensitive (because the component was a significant portion of their product cost), did their own applications engineering, required dedicated capacity to meet their demand for a standard product, demanded only a very basic quality standard, and cared little for features. At the other end of the spectrum, segment 4 was comprised of a host of small-lot buyers, mostly makers of specialty products, who insisted on high quality and special features, and who relied on the supplier for applications engineering. Because this group lacked buying clout, they were not noticeably price sensitive. Having redefined these market segments for the total market, the manufacturer was able to develop strategies for each segment. Top management chose to price itself "up and out" of segment 4 by raising prices 25 percent. As anticipated, the price increase stuck; none of the competitors wanted the specialty business. Next, top management launched a facilities study and found that it could meet the lower price and dedicated capacity requirements for the high-volume business in segment 1.[4] Industrial segmentation by similar buying features cannot be determined from sales analysis records alone. It is often the role of a professional and creative market researcher to identify and measure common buying factor segments.

Two Other Segmentation Approaches

Segmentation based on geographic considerations or account size are two other alternatives that are often used in industries, particularly when the business is based on commodity-type products that flow into a multiplicity of markets through a complex series of channels. Certainly, the first attempt should be to segment along the lines described previously to see if discrete and meaningful markets can be defined. However, if this turns out to be impractical for whatever reasons, there are generally advantages to be gained by segmenting around geographic boundaries and/or account size.

Sales managers are accustomed to grouping customers by geography or size for planning purposes, but until recently few top managers had thought to try developing niche strategies on this basis. Yet, the opportunity often exists.

An example of ingenious geographic market segmentation is the case of a midwestern commodity construction materials firm that found itself faced with over-capacity and unable to take share

away from its competition in its 200-mile trading area without starting a price war.[5] Company folklore maintained that because of high transportation costs, no producer could ship more than 300 miles from plant to customer and make money. This was true on an all-in cost basis; yet—as this company discovered—the fixed costs included in its all-in costs were so high that sales to customers as much as 700 miles away would still contribute to overhead. The results of its analysis was three strategic market segments: core markets (up to 200 miles distant); secondary markets (200 to 400 miles); and fringe markets (400 to 700 miles). Each of these segments had its own pricing strategy. In the core market, the strategy was business as usual; in the secondary markets, prices were cut to take a few selected bids away from competitors but not enough to provoke retaliation. With this strategy, the company tripled its volume in the first year. Although much of the added volume was from marginal business, its profits doubled. And the industry price structure remained intact.

Another approach is segmenting by account size. An electrical equipment manufacturer isolated 187 key accounts, accounting for 60 percent of the market, each of which bought direct and selected suppliers on the basis of price and sales coverage. These large accounts made up one strategic market segment. A second segment consisted of medium-sized OEM accounts that bought through distributors; a third comprised maintenance, repair, and operating supply accounts that required distributor servicing. Having identified these three strategic market segments, the company was able to develop programs (product pricing, distribution channels, and service policies) tailored to each.

Combine Segmentation Levels

When considering approaches to industrial and high-tech market segmentation, it is helpful to think in terms of levels of market segmentation as shown in Exhibit 2. The first three, OEM/aftermarket, four-digit SIC, and applications, nearly always occur in steps or a sequential order. The last

[5]R.A. Guarda, "How to Carve Niches in Industrial Markets," *Management Review,* August 1981, p. 19.

[5]Ibid.

EXHIBIT 2
Business Segmentation Approaches

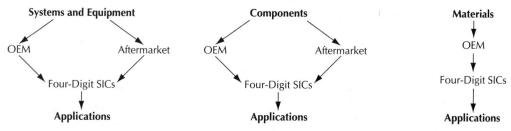

(The following may be considered with one or more of the above approaches)

Common Buying Factors	Common Buying Factors	Common Buying Factors
Geography	Geography	Geography
Buyer Size	Buyer Size	Buyer Size

Note: These analyses are intended to be completed for each country's geographic region within larger countries.

three, common buying factors, geography, and buyer size, do not necessarily follow any one of the first three segmentation steps. However, common buying factors and buyer size should be preceded by at least one of the other steps, such as the four-digit SIC or application. The situation should dictate which combinations in Exhibit 2 are coupled to form a visible segmentation approach.

Too Few or Too Many Segments

After conducting a segmentation analysis, many industrial firms experience one of two extreme situations. First, they may not have identified enough market segments. If the segmentation approach is not focused enough, a competitor will do it for them and zero in on a segment and gain a major part of the business. This happened to Xerox when it did not concentrate on the desktop copier market segment. It was then the smallest but fastest-growing segment. Niches, by definition, are at first relatively small acorns that can develop into large oak trees. Large corporations frequently segment the market into too few markets. Often, market segments are too broad. However, if large companies do not segment small enough, the competition will often do it for them. Smaller business units are usu-

ally more able to think, plan, and respond strategically in terms of small growing segments and position themselves within them to gain real competitive advantages.

At the other extreme, some industrial companies define the market into too many market segments. In one company, after investing in a seven-month study by a two-person team that produced mountains of data, the division's general manager stated: "They've segmented our market into twenty-eight segments. I've got a sneaking suspicion that's about one dozen too many. Even if it isn't, there's no way we can develop usefully competitive strategies for each one in less than five years, and we haven't got five years."

Some progressive industrial companies concentrate on a manageable number of product/market combinations in which their companies are involved and then design specific strategies for each segment. The results are often impressive. For example, a producer of electromechanical products captured the first position in its total marketplace by developing different strategies for *each* of eight product/market segments, while its prime competitors continued to treat all eight segments the same way. A materials supplier turned a losing division into a highly profitable one by pruning eight product lines to three and twelve market segments to four, thus focusing all its efforts on only four product/market segments.

Each identified and selected market segment requires a separate business or marketing plan and strategy. Parker Hannifin Corporation is the world's largest manufacturer of O-rings, which are used in fluid and air connections to seal against leaks. Parker Hannifin is a large industrial corporation effectively practicing a "divide and conquer" approach to business markets. Various sizes and forms of O-rings are used in literally hundreds of applications ranging from aircraft landing gears to cigarette lighters. Different sales and distribution channels are obviously required to serve each identified market segment effectively. Some of these products are standard catalog items; others are custom designed. To meet the unique selling requirements of the different market segments, Parker Hannifin has set up many full-fledged divisions that operate almost as totally separate businesses to serve the assigned markets.

Qualifying an Industrial Market Segment

To avoid having too few, too many, or unreachable market segments, there are some qualifying criteria to consider. If any one of the following seven criteria is not met, there is a strong possibility that the producer's segmentation approach is not operational or attractive enough to develop a strategy around. The seven validation criteria are the following:

1. Each identified segment should be characterized by a set of common customer requirements.
2. Each identified segment should have measurable characteristics (e.g., number of customers, annual purchases, and growth rate).
3. Each defined segment should have identifiable competitors.
4. Each identified segment should be "small enough" to reduce competition or to protect a position against competition.

5. Each identified segment should be served by a common sales or distribution channel.
6. For each identified segment, one should know the present and future key success factors necessary to serve the segment effectively.
7. For each identified segment, one should know what capabilities the company has or needs to develop or acquire to serve the segment profitably.

These criteria are by no means exhaustive or inclusive. However, they do help to determine if a segment does exist and whether it is attractive enough to consider further. After a segment is qualified, one would want to know existing, new, and lost accounts in the segment; value-added possibilities; and profit prospects. This additional information for each segment will help to rank segments and focus on them.

Segment and Resegment

Competitive activity and technological advances make industrial and high-tech market segmentation a dynamic activity. Kodak is the largest supplier of photographic film to most market segments. However, Du Pont concentrated on and achieved a large market share in the X-ray film market. Recently, developments in nuclear magnetic resonance (NMR) technology promise to replace a portion of the need for X-rays because the "picture" is "developed" electronically and shown on a computer screen. NMR scanners produce images similar to those made by CT scanners, but instead of using X-rays, the NMR machines use huge, powerful magnets. There is a need periodically to evaluate existing segments and consider new or different segmentation approaches. Business history is replete with cases in which an existing competitor saw market segment boundaries as static and did not identify new or emerging market segments.

The computer industry was at one time divided into fifteen segments. The finance industry was one of the fifteen segments and it was further segmented into (1) commercial banks, (2) brokerage and investment houses, (3) savings and loan institutions, and (4) other financial companies. These four applications had different data processing needs. With increased competition and new electronic capabilities, the computer market is periodically resegmented with viable new approaches. For example, the broad computer market was resegmented along a new and creative dimension called reliability and failsafe design. One small computer manufacturer noticed there was a type of customer that required high reliability. This type included banks, airlines, and other businesses where interrupted data response meant an immediate loss of customer revenue. To ensure uninterrupted service in these customer applications, most companies had to have backup computer or redundant systems that lay idle unless the on-line system failed. The manufacturer was able to design a failsafe computer that would not lose any data, as the other systems did, if any part of the system went down. As a consequence, the producer was allowed to have three years of excellent growth and considerable lead time before it had any real competitors in its newly defined market segment. So segmenting industrial and high-tech markets is a creative process; management should not allow ties to how markets were previously segmented to strangle new approaches to segmentation. In markets where there is rapid technological change, there is a need to resegment more frequently because new technologies blur segment boundaries.

Resegmenting and then focusing on selected segments can also prove to be a successful business strategy in a declining industry. By identifying such segments, one can maintain stable demand or slow decay while receiving high profit returns. Such resegmenting and refocusing allows a company to position itself strongly in one or a few segments while de-emphasizing or disinvesting from other segments.

General Manager's Responsibility

While many product managers and business planners are aware of the need to do a better job of segmenting the market, their enthusiasm or ability to do so is often blunted because of short-term sales and profit pressures demanded by top and general management. Far too many general managers still regard volume gains and relationships with key accounts as the most important factors in their business. To them, segmentation is some kind of theoretical exercise that is not worth much time and money, especially if it interferes with "bringing in or running the business." Segmentation requires a good deal of careful thought and creativity, and it is the primary responsibility of general management to make the money and resources available to ensure that it is done. Segmentation is not a theoretical exercise, and any general manager that skips over or short-cuts the need to define the discrete markets to be served is making a major strategic mistake. To ensure that the business is properly segmented, every general manager should be satisfied with the answers to the following questions:

1. How do we now segment the business?
2. Have we segmented enough?
3. Is there any evidence that competitors, especially small ones, have achieved an advantage by segmenting differently?
4. Have we defined the segments in the best way possible?
5. Which segments are most attractive for us to invest it?

If for any reason these questions are difficult to answer or cannot be answered at all, the chances are good that the business has not been properly segmented and that general management has fallen down on its job.

Implementing Segment Strategies

The most thorough analysis and soundest selection of the more attractive segments to pursue can be futile if cohesive action programs are not developed and implemented to serve the selected key segments effectively. Frequently, a staff group does the segmentation analysis and when it comes to action programs and execution across departmental lines, the results are often dismal. For the effective implementation of industrial market segment strategies, a cross-functional business plan, not just a marketing plan, must contain action programs in all functional departments to focus on supplying the needs and requirements of the targeted market segments. If the execution of the cross-functional plan is properly done, the result will be a truly market-led business unit.

Implementing a market segment emphasis begins with the business unit mission statement stating what the target market segments are. Action programs in R&D, manufacturing, and sales must be stated in the business plan to serve the mission statement's target segments effectively. R&D project selection and product development priorities should correspond to the segments being emphasized. Likewise, manufacturing and production planning must be informed of the requirements of the target segments so they can develop action programs to gear their operations efficiently to serve each segment successfully. If a specific technology, manufacturing process, or know-how does not now exist to serve the targeted product/market segments, the new capabilities must be developed and/or acquired and be shown as manufacturing action programs in the business plan.

Application stories should be developed for *each* target market segment. They should be written in the language of the respective segment and include cost/benefit information. Advertising copy, trade show selection, media selection, and sales letters must all be targeted to a specific market segment. Leads and inquiries generated by focused sales promotion and trade shows should be used to direct sales representatives and distributors to qualified prospects in the target segments.

Factory and distributor sales representatives must be provided with the appropriate application segment stories and selling aids. Sales representatives must be thoroughly trained to sell features and benefits as they apply to each respective target market segment. Sales incentives are often necessary to direct sales representatives' and distributors' selling time to the market being emphasized. Sales forces that are exclusively compensated on a commission basis are usually difficult to direct to new market applications that require more time to learn customers' requirements and build new relationships. New commissions structures, bonuses, or incentive programs tied to new accounts developed in the target segments are usually necessary to execute a segmentation emphasis through the sales force and to gain the target accounts in the segment. Market segmentation programs should be developed for specific geographic areas to capture the varying customer bases across the country. IBM develops U.S. business plans to executive target market programs in each branch office. Parker-Hannifin helps each of its key distributors develop a "localized" annual marketing plan that identifies the key products/markets to emphasize in each distributor's territory.

The training of field sales, distributors, and inside sales representatives in market segment applications is usually done poorly, if at all. The traditional product training, without concentrating on the target market applications, will not help implement segmentation strategies. Good in-depth application success stories are frequently the central focus of target market training sessions. Prime Computer has developed follow-up applications seminars for its three-week product training program. The Prime Computer market applications seminars feature company specialists in each segment and extensive use is made of successful customer case histories that Prime has developed for each target market segment. The Crawford Fitting Company developed VCR and audio cassettes application job stories for a sales representative to view and/or listen to before calling on an account in the respective segment.

Manufacturers that desire to sell their existing products in a new market segment with their existing sales representatives should develop case studies for each new market application and then conduct in-depth sales training sessions for their existing salesmen. Sometimes, a separate specialized manufacturer's sales force and different distribution networks must be recruited to penetrate effectively the newer segments being emphasized. Without application stories and sales force training in the new market segment, the result will be little or no additional penetration in the targeted markets. The manufacturer's product and market managers are logical people to conduct the market applications seminars. These managers are also in key organizational positions to couple annual operating programs to segmentation strategies.

Summary

Unable to compete broadly against entrenched competitors, threshold companies and those entering markets new to them have repeatedly adopted a "divide and conquer" or market-segmentation approach. A precise definition of a target market can lead to innovative product, price, distribution, and service strategies. Selective industrial or business market segmentation allows a company to marshal its R&D, engineering, production, and sales efforts toward specific areas rather than spread a little across a wider range of vulnerable marketplaces. At the same time, market segmentation and the selection of specific segments provide direction to the business unit as to which capabilities it must develop to serve the identified market segment effectively. Segmenting an industrial or high-tech marketplace is therefore one of the most important strategic weapons that should be used by technically based businesses. Segmentation defines which businesses the firm is in, identifies competitors, guides strategy development, and determines what programs are necessary in cross-functional departments of the firm. Since industrial and high-tech market selection is clearly a longer-term strategic decision that cannot be easily reversed, it is important that the general marketplace be first segmented into viable customer groups before any market selection and investment decisions are made.

Chapter 7

Business Product Management

The product or service produced by the firm lies at the heart of business and marketing strategy. When translated into customer benefits, it is the product or service that creates new markets or serves existing ones. Managing the processes by which new products are developed to serve emerging needs and existing products are modified to better serve existing needs is critical to the success of the firm.

In this chapter we discuss key product management concepts for business customers. We begin with concepts of product, product line, and how product management decisions are influenced by the nature of buyer–seller relationships. We then address the role of quality, product market choices (including global considerations), and new product development. We conclude with a discussion of positioning and branding.

The Concept of Product

Business customers use goods and services to directly or indirectly derive sales revenue and profit from their operations. Capital goods are major elements in the production process. Raw materials are critical to the production of many products. Components may be integral parts of an assembled product or bundled with another product or system and resold. Maintenance, repair, and operating supplies are necessary to keep the production process going. Similarly, a host of services are necessary to the production process and other functions of the firm. Despite the importance of the physical characteristics of products, customers look for benefits, not just physical properties. The product the customer buys is far more than just its physical attributes. In a very real sense, the

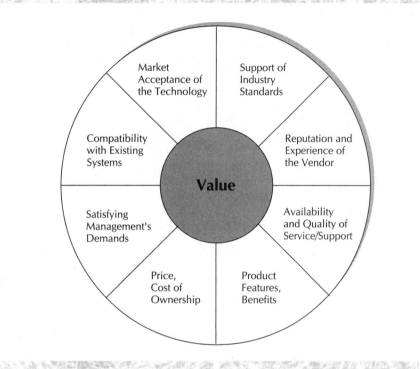

FIGURE 7.1
The Whole Product Approach to Value

Market Acceptance of the Technology

Support of Industry Standards

Compatibility with Existing Systems

Reputation and Experience of the Vendor

Value

Satisfying Management's Demands

Availability and Quality of Service/Support

Price, Cost of Ownership

Product Features, Benefits

Source: Adapted from a presentation made by Regis McKenna Inc., Summer 1994.

product is not what it is but what it does. Intimately linked with benefits is the concept of quality, a concept that transcends physical characteristics and takes into account the totality of the firm's offering. From the firm's standpoint, the product needs to be considered in terms of its role in the overall business strategy. Beyond its contribution to the firm's profits, what other objectives does the firm have for the product, how does the product relate to other products, and what is the impact of the product on the firm's operations?

Figure 7.1 shows the "whole product" the customer buys should be viewed as a bundle of tangible and intangible attributes from which customers derive benefit and value. The example is meant to be illustrative, not comprehensive. The attributes of importance vary among customers. For some customers joint product development is an important attribute, for others it is support of the firm's marketing effort. This suggests that the product is not a fixed element of marketing strategy. Rather, it is a variable whose attributes can be changed, depending on the needs of the particular customer or market segment. Where intermediate distribution is involved, the services provided by a distributor, such as availability and credit, are also part of the whole product. Even for commodity products, normally considered undifferentiable, the whole product concept suggests that opportunities exist for differentiation on such attributes as packaging, comprehensiveness of the product line, one-stop shopping convenience, or special services. For all products the core or generic attributes should be the starting point of development of a whole product from which consideration is given to other product features appropriate for particular customer needs.

The concept of quality is inextricably intertwined with the concept of product. Initially focused on manufacturing with Deming's emphasis on statistical approaches and Crosby's emphasis on conformance to specifications, the concept of quality has broadened to include all aspects of the firm's offering *as seen through the eyes of the customer.* The PIMS studies introduced the notion of relative quality, that is, quality as perceived by the customer *relative to competitors,* based on the principal tangible and nontangible attributes used by the customer in the buying decision. Despite evidence from the PIMS studies indicating that relative quality is a key determinant of a firm's profitability, it appeared to require competition from Japanese firms to convince the rest of the world of the importance of quality, the potential of quality programs, and, most importantly, that quality is not static but should be the focus of a constant and ongoing effort. Later we discuss the increasing imperative that those in marketing be involved in the firm's quality processes.

In addition to satisfying customer's wants and needs better than competitors, the concept of product also needs to assess its role for the firm, a role that almost always goes beyond just providing profits. The BCG approach described in Chapter 2, develops the role of cash cows as providers of cash to fund question marks, support R&D, fund dividends, and so forth, and the role of stars to establish dominant positions so that when growth slows stars can become productive cash cows. There are many other roles for products. One may be to support the sale of other, more profitable products, such as Bond-A-Matic®, Loctite adhesive dispenser introduced to increase sales of its adhesives. Other roles may be to defend against competitor attacks, to lead the way into new markets, to complement and facilitate the sale of existing products, or, perhaps inadvertently as in the case of the IBM PC, to pioneer a new organizational form.

The Product Line

As important as the product itself is the concept of product line, a group of products closely related by virtue of performing similar functions. Managing the product line is one of the most important product management tasks. While most firms start with a single product, or a very limited product line, almost inevitably the product line is expanded, raising a number of questions. Under what circumstances should we increase the variety of our product offerings? Should we add a product at the high end of the line? Should we add one at the low end? Should we extend our product scope into new arenas?

Increased variety, or depth, may respond to specific customer needs, enhance the firm's image as a full-line provider, or thwart competitor attack, but at the expense of increased complexity and added manufacturing cost. A large industrial firm, for instance, introduced a product consisting of five individually packaged components carefully selected, the firm thought, to meet the needs of the market. The package was offered as one catalog number. Within three years, customer requests for variations in the individual components that made up the package resulted in over 2,000 catalog numbers. In total, the packages were produced in high volume. Some catalog numbers, however, were sold in relatively small quantities, raising questions as to their profitability. Manufacturing and engineering departments complained that this kind of product line proliferation was unacceptable. Although extreme, this example indicates the problems that can arise in the name of responding to customer needs. For most firms, periodic pruning of the product line is a must to achieve balance between customer responsiveness and internal operations. Frequently described as the 80–20 rule, Pareto's law holds that a small percentage of a list of items represents a large percentage of value or impact. Analysis often reveals that the majority of the firm's profits is provided by a relatively small percentage of products. Judicious pruning of the product line can frequently improve profits and release engineering and manufacturing capacity without seriously affecting customer relations.

The product line may be lengthened. Adding products at the high end of the line may represent opportunities to achieve higher margins and enhance image, but it may also invite competitor retaliation, encounter customer resistance, and take the firm away from its basic competence. Products added to the low end of the line may thwart competitor attack, capitalize on the firm's image, and represent opportunities for increased volume, but it may also cannibalize the existing product line, negatively impact the firm's image, or take the firm away from its basic competence. GE's Medical Systems business, for instance, was faced with an attack on its CT scanners by a Japanese competitor that planned to market a smaller and less expensive machine. Introduction by GE of a similar machine might thwart the attack but it could also cannibalize sales of its larger and very profitable scanners. GE decided the new product was close to its competence and that it was better to cannibalize its own sales than to lose sales to the Japanese competitor. Other firms, however, have discovered that manufacturing low-end items is incompatible with a culture that has long focused on features, not cost.

Extending the scope or breadth of the product line may capitalize on existing competence, expand the firm's horizons, and establish major new opportunities, but it carries the risk of diverting managerial attention from the existing business and going beyond the firm's competencies. Exxon, for instance, which had developed a proprietary technology for variable speed motors, acquired Reliance Electric, a major player in variable speed drives, on the supposition that Reliance's experience could be used to commercialize the new technology. Exxon discovered that the promise of the new technology had been overestimated and that the challenges of managing a variable speed drive business were very foreign to its experience as a major producer and marketer of petroleum products. The venture was unsuccessful.

Buyer–Seller Relationships: A Key Contextual Element

The close relationship between business customers and their suppliers and their mutual dependency described in Chapter 3 strongly influences the product management process. Many new business products are developed at the specific request of customers. The nature of buyer–seller relationships can take many forms, and decisions with respect to these relationships can materially influence the product management process.

Increasingly buyers and sellers are moving toward closer relationships, sometimes taking on the nature of a partnership in which product decisions are made by mutual agreement. These relationships are particularly strong in Japan. Shikoku Kakokki, for example, a manufacturer of packaging machinery, has approximately 60 small, long-term vendors that provide the company with parts and components for its products. These suppliers are partners in the "Shikoku family." They not only provide Shikoku with machine parts, but they actively try to design new, innovative, and cost-saving solutions for the customer. Part of their motivation to continue these efforts is knowing that Shikoku will keep them as suppliers through good times and bad.

Close buyer–seller relationships that are the norm in Japan are also characteristic of business marketing in other countries, particularly in countries in Latin America and Europe and to a lesser extent in the United States. While close relationships have many desirable aspects, they need to be carefully managed. Large customers can significantly influence product development, but sometimes in a direction that may conflict with the supplier's ability to serve other customers. A large electric utility, for instance, worked closely with one manufacturer to develop a piece of equipment for use in underground electrical systems. As the market for these products matured, only this one customer continued to be interested in the design. In some instances, the customer may view a joint development as proprietary and attempt to restrict the supplier from offering the product to others. Manufacturers of paper machines who work closely with paper mills in developing new and improved designs usually agree to refrain from offering the improved designs for periods up to two years as a condition of being the mill's sole supplier. As relations become close, the potential exists for the customer to be the supplier's major, or only, source of orders. This has the potential to give the customer excessive bargaining power and ties the supplier to the customer's fortunes.

The Role of Quality

We previously discussed the increasing importance of quality. From the early interest in quality, with emphasis on manufacturing and conformance to specifications, we have seen the widespread adoption of some form of total quality management (TQM). Unfortunately, according to a recent survey most marketing managers do not fully understand the concept of quality nor its impact on profitability. The authors of the study argue that the concept of total quality, with its emphasis on quality as perceived by the customer, mandates that marketers become full-fledged members of the quality team, leading or cooperating as may be appropriate.[1]

In the United States, quality efforts have been widely publicized by means of the Malcolm Baldrige Award. Awards are determined using a 1,000-point scoring system to evaluate many quality-related factors. Of interest to marketers, the scoring system allocates 300 points to customer satisfaction, indicating the importance of marketing involvement in the quality process. A recent development in the quality arena of particular importance to business marketers is ISO9000, an international standard promulgated in 1987 by the International Organization for Standardization. ISO9000 and its various components provide business customers a well-defined way to specify quality processes to their suppliers, with the provision for compliance certification by outside auditors. Originally adopted in Europe, where conformance to ISO9000 is mandated for many products, interest has spread to the United States and Japan. First viewed by many non-European firms as a deliberately erected trade barrier to doing business in Europe, ISO9000 has since been accepted by many manufacturers as a valuable guide to quality processes. To date, more than 50 countries have adopted the ISO9000 system as part of their national standards. Thousands of companies worldwide have been certified as complying with the quality process requirements of ISO9000. Informed observers believe that ISO9000 will become the de facto starting point for the quality processes of most producers of goods and services in the next three to five years. Firms that adopt the standard ahead of competitors have an opportunity for significant competitive advantage. To fully capitalize on ISO9000, marketers need to be involved in the quality process to ensure that goods and services not only meet design specifications but also meet customer requirements better than competitors.[2]

Product/Market Choices

In Chapter 6 we discussed that market selection is fundamental to product decisions, posing an attendant number of questions. Can the one product design serve a number of segments? If not, should the firm attempt to serve just one, or a few, segments? Alternatively, should it modify the product to serve a number of segments, with the attendant complexity of proliferation of product designs?

For International Paper Company (IP), one of the largest paper firms in the world, a question was which of several opportunities should be considered for two recently acquired packaging systems. The Resolvo system, acquired from an Italian manufacturer, made it possible to package milk, juice, and other still drinks in flexible paperboard containers, to provide virtually unlimited shelf life. The Evergreen system, acquired from a U.S. manufacturer, was designed

TABLE 7.1
Product/Market Matrix Analysis of IP's Liquid Packaging

	Market/Application					
Product	**Flexible Packs**	**Metal Cans**	**Glass Bottles**	**Plastic Jugs**	**Folding Cartons**	**Bag-In-Box**
Alcoholic Drink						
Spirits			√	√		
Beers		√	√			
Wines	√R	√R	√R			√R
Nonalcoholic Drinks						
Carbonate		√	√	√		
Still juice	√R	√R	√R	√R	√R	√R
Fresh juice	√E		√E	√E	√E	√E
Noncarbonated mineral water	√E/R	√E/R	√E/R	√E/R		
Dairy Products						
Fresh milk	√E		√E	√E	√E	√E
Long-life milk	√R	√R	√R		√R	√R
Other	√E/R	√E/R			√E/R	√E/R
Culinary Products	√E/R	√E/R	√E/R	√E/R		√E/R

Note: √—indicates common method for packaging product; R—indicates a possible market application for the Resolvo system; and E—indicates a possible market application for the Evergreen system.
Source: This matrix was developed by Nils-Erik Aaby.

for fresh milk and juice products where limited shelf life was satisfactory. IP could develop a matrix, as shown in Table 7.1, based on products to be contained and present packaging approaches. The matrix indicates commonly used packaging methods for the various products and applications where IP might believe the Resolvo or Evergreen systems could successfully compete. Based on its knowledge of these applications, IP could develop a better view of opportunities where one or both of the products has a competitive advantage. Combined with other segment characteristics, the choice could then be narrowed to those representing the best opportunities for IP.

Unique to business marketing is the ability to vary the product on the basis of vertical market segments. Various horizontal segments might desire the same tangible attributes but different intangible attributes. Vertical segments present the business marketer with a different set of choices. As we previously indicated, ALCOA could provide its new aluminum alloy in ingot form to bearing manufacturers. Alternatively, it could provide a casting to bearing manufacturers or to diesel engine manufacturers. Finally, it could supply finished bearings to diesel engine manufacturers or to industrial supply houses for sale as replacements. Similar choices exist for many other products, requiring product adaptation to the needs of the chosen market. Computers, for instance, can be sold without application software to equipment manufacturers such as Rolm, who resell to end users, adding necessary software and other customizing features, but frequently computers must be sold with software if sales are to be made directly to end users.

Global Considerations

Almost without exception, major suppliers of business products and services do business globally. Boeing, McDonnell Douglas, and Airbus do business with airlines in every country. For many years, GE, Caterpillar, and other producers of industrial goods have been major exporters, making positive contributions to the U.S. balance of payments. Asea Brown Boveri (ABB), Hitachi, Komatsu, Ericsson, Alcatel, Siemens, Olivetti, and many other non-U.S. manufacturers similarly do business worldwide. The Big Six accounting firms have offices in every major city in most countries in the world, as do major consulting firms such as McKinsey, A.D. Little, and others. In the heavy construction industry, Bechtel, Ebasco, and CH2M-Hill are all major players on the global scene.

Despite the international participation of such well-known firms, large numbers of business marketers have not pursued global markets or have done so only on an opportunistic basis, usually when demand is slack in home markets. We first consider the circumstances that suggest attractive market opportunities and then identify options for product management.

In broad terms, most business goods, and many services, travel well across country borders. For many firms, foreign markets should represent profitable opportunities. The normal approach, nevertheless, seems to be to design new products to sell primarily in the domestic market. Only after the product is successfully introduced in the home market does the firm consider exporting either to neighboring countries or to world markets, preferably with a minimum of product modifications. In a study by Cooper and Kleinschmidt, this was the approach of 83 percent of the firms studied compared to 17 percent who initially designed products with world markets in mind. Interestingly, the 17 percent had a higher new product success rate and achieved higher profits *both at home and abroad.*[3] Apparently, the extra care taken in naming the product, choosing materials, designing its features, and so on, paid off in domestic markets and ensured that subsequent alterations for nondomestic markets, if necessary, would be less costly. In many instances, taking world markets into account can be as simple as designing dual voltage capability into electrical devices. Even in more complex situations, designing products for world markets pays off. Microsoft could have greatly simplified its introduction of Works had it considered programming requirements for various country markets during the product's early stages of development.

Clearly, world market opportunities are more attractive for some firms than others. Much depends on the managerial philosophy of the firm, as we discuss later, and management's comfort with world markets. Certain product and market characteristics strongly suggest the attractiveness of world markets. They include:

- High technology content
- High contribution margins
- High ratio of revenue to weight
- Customers with global views
- Global competitors
- Widely accepted international product standards
- Low tariff and nontariff barriers
- Export incentives (by the home country government)

Assuming world markets offer potentially attractive opportunities, what should be the firm's product strategy? Three general approaches are possible. The first, and simplest, is to export products with no adaptation. This approach may be successful for products that have enormous competitive advantage with respect to functionality or that can be offered at extremely low prices. It is usually associated with the so-called ethnocentric view of the world, a view that assumes the rest of the world is "like us." For most firms the choice is between a multidomestic strategy or a global strategy. The multidomestic strategy is usually associated with a polycentric view of the world, a view that assumes each country is sufficiently different to require a unique marketing strategy. In this case the firm makes extensive adaptations of the product and other elements of the marketing mix for each country in which it does business. Global strategies are usually associated with a geocentric view of the world, a view that holds there are more similarities across world markets than differences. In this case, the firm assumes products can be designed with a high degree of standardization and only modest adaptation to meet local requirements.

Much discussion has centered on which of these approaches works best. Ted Levitt has argued that technology is driving the world toward a converging commonality, that the globalization of markets is at hand, and that the objective of international marketers should be standardized products that can be offered at low cost.[4] Kenichi Ohmae, on the other hand, argues for an approach that involves extensive local adaptation of standardized products.[5] There is less difference in these points of view than would first appear. Both recognize that some modification of products is necessary to accommodate local preferences and practices. The point to be made is that decisions about the extent of adaptation need to take a host of circumstances into account. Standardization may be mandatory if economies of scale are important. Standardization may be appropriate where language is not a significant factor or where international standards prevail, such as for microelectronics components, chemical processes, and machine tools. Adaptation is a must where standards vary, as they do for some

> ## TABLE 7.2
> ## Key Issues for Product Development to the Year 2000
>
> 1. How can we improve the odds of success in new product development?
> 2. How can we better integrate the voice of the customer and convert this into better and more relevant new products?
> 3. How can we better leverage technology?
> 4. How can we speed up the entire product development process?
> 5. How can we better link various quality initiatives to new product development?
> 6. How can we better make new product offerings that are global?
> 7. How can we ensure faster, better, and cheaper new product development processes?
> 8. How can we better capitalize on outsourcing and strategic alliances?
>
> Source: Adapted from a seminar presented by Marketing Science Institute, Cambridge, MA 1994.

electrical devices or video equipment, or where products such as accounting and tax software meet country specific requirements.

New Product Development

Product development has long been a key element of product management. In recent years, with rapidly changing technologies and shortened product life cycles, the importance of new products has increased dramatically. During the 1980s, corporate profits derived from new products grew from one-fifth to one-third.[6] At 3M, products less than five years old now account for 25 percent of sales. A study of 700 industrial and consumer firms in Europe and the United States by Booz, Allen and Hamilton supported the importance of new products.[7] Senior executives in these firms indicated they expect to derive significant sources of revenue and profits from new products and new technology. This importance has stimulated research to find ways of improving new product development processes. The Marketing Science Institute (MSI) in the United States, a quasi-industry–academic research organization, recently announced that enhancement of product development processes is one of the highest priorities among its clients with key issues as shown in Table 7.2. The European Union has initiated a number of initiatives in support of research and development focusing on new technologies and products, including the European Strategic Program for R&D in Information Technology (ESPRIT), R&D in Advanced Communications Technology for Europe (RACE), and Basic Research in Industrial Technology for Europe (BRITE).[8] In Japan the Ministry of Internal Trade and Industry (MITI) organizes industrywide efforts to enhance Japan's capability through new products.

FIGURE 7.2
New Product Success Factors

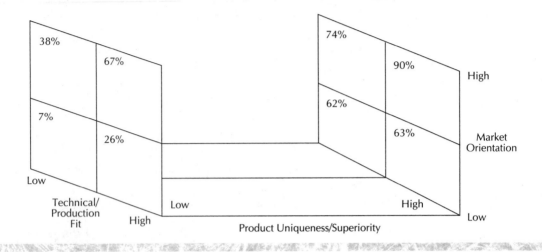

Source: Robert G. Cooper, "The Myth of the Better Mousetrap: What Makes a New Product a Success?" *Business Quarterly,*
Spring 1981, Volume 46, Number 1, pp. 79–81. Reprinted with the permission of *Business Quarterly,* published by the Western
Business School, The University of Western Ontario, London, Canada. Spring 1981 issue.

Despite the importance of new products and the interest in new product
development processes, for many firms new product development has been
largely fortuitous. In these firms new products are frequently the result of creative individuals taking a new idea and running with it, or a customer bringing a
new requirement to the right individual in the supplier's organization, rather
than the result of a well-managed process. Firms often seem to accept that the
development of new products is not amenable to normal management processes, and failures of new products are often justified with statements such as "90
percent of all new products fail." In fact, nothing like 90 percent of new products
fail. According to one study, only 24 percent of new industrial products failed.[9]
Other studies report similar numbers. More importantly, the success rate of
new products can be influenced by good management. In a study of industrial
firms in Canada, Cooper found that market orientation, product uniqueness, and
fit with the firm's technical/production processes were key success factors.[10] As
shown in Figure 7.2, when market orientation, product uniqueness, and fit were
high, the success rate was 90 percent. When all three factors were low, the success rate fell to 7 percent. The challenge, then, for business marketers is to
manage a process that effectively introduces products that are truly unique or
have competitive advantage and that have a good fit with the firm's manufacturing and other competencies. While research efforts continue, the last 20 years
have seen major advances in our understanding of how to do this.

The Product Development Process

Basic elements are common to all studies of the product development process. Crawford describes them in terms of the following five stages:[11]

Strategic Planning. Concerned with goals and guidance of the process, this stage takes inputs from the annual marketing plan, which may call for a particular feature to meet the encroachment of a new competitor; ongoing business planning, which will establish a sense of direction or market focus for product development; and special opportunity analysis, based on audits of relevant markets and internal resources. A key point is the development of a product innovation charter to provide guidance to the overall process and to ensure that developments are consistent with business goals and market choices.

Concept Generation. The creative part of the process requires establishment of a team or nucleus of individuals for ideation and screening, and a process to stimulate the input of ideas from customers, employees, universities, or other potential sources.

Pretechnical Evaluation. This stage focuses on concept development, testing, and screening, both for customer understanding and technical feasibility. It may involve a preliminary business analysis and development of a budget, based on preliminary marketing, technical, and operations plans.

Technical Development. In this stage the final concept is prepared, resources are gathered and teams are formed, prototype work is done, alpha tests (i.e., tests of the prototype within the firm) and beta tests (i.e., tests of prototypes with customers) are conducted, work starts on the development of a marketing plan, and a comprehensive business analysis is prepared.

Commercialization. In this stage the organizational structure necessary for production and marketing is put in place, initial product runs are made, marketing plans are further developed, market testing is done, primarily to test the elements of the marketing plan, plans are fine tuned, and the product is launched.

Aaby and Dicenza suggest that the product development process can also be thought of as a funnel, as shown in Figure 7.3. In the collaboration stage the approach is broad and open to new science and creative ideas. In this early stage, efforts are concerned with benchmarking (of science, technology, and competitors), idea generation, product/market choice, positioning, concept development, and testing. Cumulative investment of resources is low, and management involvement also tends to be low. However, at this stage concepts with little likelihood of success can be terminated with only modest financial consequences. Management's role should be to ensure disciplined choices and collaborative involvement of marketing, R&D or engineering, and manufacturing in the process. In the implementation stage the approach becomes more

FIGURE 7.3

The Product Development Process Funnel

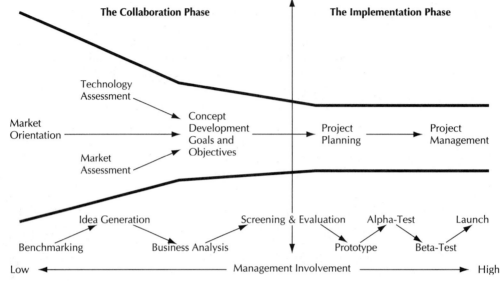

Source: Adapted from Nils-Erik Aaby and Richard Discenza, "Strategic Marketing and New Product Development: An Integrated Approach," *Journal of Business and Industrial Marketing,* 8 (2), 1993, 61–69. Reprinted with permission of MCB University Press.

narrowly focused and tightly controlled. During this stage costs escalate, suggesting the need at each step to review the decision to continue. Management becomes more involved in the process but, aside from termination, its role is limited to ensuring that all aspects of the process are carried out.

Lead Users

For business products, and especially for high-tech products, a frequent issue is market pull versus technology push. Ken Olsen, the founder of Digital Equipment Corporation, has been reported as being fond of saying that no amount of market research could have revealed the need for a mini-computer. On the other hand, when electrostatic printing technology indicated a promising approach to high-speed printers for computers, founders of Versatec spent six months talking to prospective customers before developing what turned out to be a highly successful product. In contrast, Gould Graphics developed its offering without customer input and the product was never a success.

In a sense the argument between market pull and technology push is inappropriate as technology must always match the needs of the market.

TABLE 7.3
Beta Test Questions

Problem Identification	Product Use	Improvement Opportunities
• Does the product function as planned?	• Which applications were expected/unexpected?	• What additional functions and/or features are required to meet minimal customer requirements?
• Does the product's performance meet design expectations?	• How often is the product used?	
• Does the performance meet user expectations?	• For how long and by how many people?	• What functions/features now appear unnecessary or optional?
• Are there differences between the firm's management and the user's management as to what adequate/superior performance is?	• What benefits do the users report? What drawbacks?	• Do the patterns of usage and/or applications suggest any changes in physical design of the product, user interface speed, capacity, or other functions?
	• What changes, if any, has the product made in work procedures?	
• Is the product's ease-of-use acceptable (i.e., interface, commands, operating instructions, control panel, easy to set up, etc.)?	• What changes in work habits or procedures, if any, does the product require of users?	• How can the product be made easier to install?
	• Who benefits the most/least from the product? Is anyone impacted negatively?	• How can the product be made easier to diagnose and/or repair?
• Do the required interfaces with other hardware, equipment, material, software, and communications media function properly? How easy was the product to install, initialize, troubleshoot, repair?	• What functions/features are used most/least?	• Should the product be offered in more/fewer models or configurations?
• Did the product malfunction, shut down, or perform unexpectedly?		• What lessons should be incorporated into the user manual?
• Were the causes identified?		

However, a unique aspect of development of goods and services for business markets is the extensive involvement of users, who have actually led the development of many of the successful new products commercialized by manufacturers. One study, for example, found users were the developers of 82 percent of all commercialized scientific instruments.[12] Studies of this kind suggest that analysis of needs and solution data from "lead users" can improve the productivity of new product development in fields characterized by rapid change. *Lead users* are those who face needs that will be general in a marketplace, but they face these needs months before others and are positioned to benefit significantly by obtaining a solution to those needs.

TABLE 7.4
Selecting Beta Test Sites or Firms

- Does the firm belong to one of the target segments?
- Does the firm have experience with the technology or product class?
- Is the firm known to have a potential need for the new product solution?
- Does the firm show evidence of using advanced technologies?
- Does the firm face stiff competition and new product time-to-market pressure that force it to be innovative?
- Does the firm make frequent changes in product lines such that all possible options can be tested?
- Is the company recognized as an industry leader?
- Is there an influential "high profile" person within the company who takes leadership and is willing and able to work with the suppliers?
- Will the individual/firm be willing to be used as a reference?

Beta Tests

Many aspects of the lead user concept apply to Beta testing, a key activity for field-testing prototypes—a requirement for effective launch of most industrial products. As elaborated in Table 7.3, Beta testing is used to identify problems in product design or function, to understand how the product is used, and to identify opportunities for improvements. As with lead users, a key to success is to find good Beta test sites, desirable potential early adopters, or customers who perceive the new product to have high incremental value. Some characteristics of good Beta test sites are indicated in Table 7.4

New Product Introduction

When introducing products to new customers or significantly different products to existing customers, business marketers need to take into account the fear, uncertainty, and doubt (FUD) that supplier changes or new products can foster, particularly in situations where the customer's ability to perform is highly dependent on the supplier's product. Small suppliers, with limited resources or unknown reputations, may particularly experience FUD. The introduction process, therefore, needs to recognize that FUD may prolong the customer's decision-making process. As shown in Figure 7.4, there are a number of ways to do this, particularly with performance proof and evidence of acceptance by industry leaders.

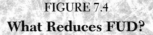

FIGURE 7.4
What Reduces FUD?

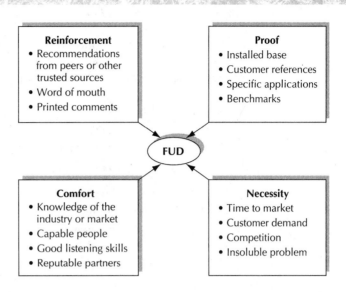

Positioning

Product positioning is concerned with the position the product holds in the customer's mind, based on perceived benefits as compared to those offered by competitors. Although the nature of the business purchasing process suggests comprehensive analysis of the benefits offered by various competitors, it is strongly influenced by customers' a priori perceptions which, in many instances, may be the major determinant of the buying decision. For years, for instance, customers' perceptions of IBM reliability and service were reflected in the comment "you can't go wrong buying IBM." Ultimately, of course, the position the firm occupies in the customer's mind will be the result of the customer's experience with the product. The objective of positioning is to influence product design, development, and customer interfaces to maximize the likelihood that this position corresponds to the firm's intent. As Dovel argues, positioning should be the backbone of product design and development and a key theme in the firm's business plan.[13]

We previously stated that a key element of product development is a positioning statement that clearly spells out the position the firm wants to occupy in the customer's mind. Most products will have a host of attributes, but the firm's position will be established on two or three attributes or benefits that are most important to the customers in the target segment. Hitachi, for instance, positioned its 256K integrated circuit chip on the core benefits of reliable and fast information storage and retrieval. This simple statement, easy to understand and expressed in terms that reflected the customer's perspective, guided subsequent product development work and became the basis for developing the communications program.

Conceptually straightforward, the development of a good positioning statement is a demanding but important exercise. A variety of processes have been proposed, most of which have steps similar to the following:

- Establish the target market.
- Ensure your product strategy is consistent with your business strategy.
- Understand the key attributes or benefits from customers' perspectives.
- Identify the relevant set of competitors.
- Understand their positions.
- Pick the position you want to, or can, occupy.
- Write your positioning statement.
- From the view of competitors, identify its weaknesses.
- Test the positioning statement against others, including peers, the sales force, and customers.

Concepts of product positioning also apply to companies. Consider the situation of Xerox. Firmly established as a copier manufacturer, Xerox purchased Scientific Data Systems to enter the computer business. The subsequent disappointing results were, at least in part, attributed to the market's refusal to recognize Xerox as a serious player in the computer business. Today Xerox positions itself as "The Document Company," a position that customers understand and that provides a strong sense of direction to the firm's product development efforts.

For international marketers there are additional issues. As we see in the Microsoft case, in its early years subsidiary companies had been allowed to tailor positioning strategies to individual countries, based on the needs of target markets within each country. With the advent of Works, and other products, it became clear that many products should be targeted at horizontal segments, that is, at segments that crossed country borders. For Microsoft, as for other companies in similar situations, this raised some difficult issues. Who, for instance, should be responsible for worldwide product positioning? Headquarters or individual subsidiary managers? Still further, what problems would be encountered if headquarters insisted on subsidiary companies repositioning their offerings? As we discussed in the section on global considerations, product planning that takes a global perspective initially can help to address such issues.

Once a desired position is determined, the firm must determine how to most effectively communicate the intended position to the marketplace. The nature of business marketing—with professional purchasing, very knowledgeable buyers, and close buyer–seller relationships—might suggest that this communication can be done exclusively in comprehensive technical or performance terms, and, in fact, much communication is done this way. Strongly associated with the marketing of consumer goods, brands can also play an important role in communication programs for business goods and services, either to identify the company, the product, or both.

Branding

According to the American Marketing Association, a brand is a name, term, sign, symbol, or design, or a combination of them, intended to identify the goods or services of one seller or group of sellers and to differentiate them from those of competitors. Used properly, brands can convey a number of meanings. At the company level, a brand can convey messages about the nature of the company, the kinds of products it makes, its level of reliability or service, and so forth. As we see in the Leykam Mürztaler case, in some markets the firm desired to establish a reputation for leadership, based on its new, leading-edge paper machine. In these instances, communication efforts focused on the company name, with little reference to products. At the product level, a brand can convey tangible or nontangible attributes or proposed customer benefits. Again referring to the Leykam Mürztaler case, in some markets the firm desired to establish a reputation for high-quality products in terms of benefits to printers. In these instances, communication efforts focused on its product brands for various grades of paper.

Establishing brands and deciding on how heavily to promote them raise a number of questions. For Leykam Mürztaler, the question was the extent to which a strong brand identity could develop product preference, resulting in higher prices or greater market share. For other firms, a brand identity can pave the way for initial calls by the sales force. Often a brand can provide a convenient way both to describe a particular product, such as the Intel series of 286, 386, 486, and now Pentium chips, and to convey their characteristics.

Frequently there are conflicting objectives with respect to brands. Schuller International, a subsidiary of Manville Corporation, sold most of its roofing and insulating products under the Manville brand, which, according to market research reports, was viewed very favorably by distributors and contractors. On the other hand, financial analysts advised Manville that use of the Manville name was adversely affecting its stock price because of the association of Manville with asbestos-related health problems, even though Manville no longer made asbestos products. In this case, the company rebranded its products under the Schuller name, recognizing that some customer goodwill or identification might be lost.

In general, it appears that selecting a brand name is more art than science. Firms are advised, for instance, that brand names should convey the use or function of the product and some do, such as Loctite's Bond-a Matic® adhesive dispenser. But there are many examples of well-recognized brands that do not, such as Apple's Macintosh® computers, Digital's Alpha® microprocessors, and AT&T's Merlin line of PBX systems. What is more important than the brand name, per se, is the message that accompanies the brand, with respect to the benefits or attributes the firm wants to be associated with the brand and the clarity and creativity with which the message is communicated.

Summary

Product management and new product development should be high on managers' lists of priorities. Traditionally the product is the most important element in the business marketing mix. However, development of individual new products is not sufficient to compete effectively. Firms that can manage the product mix in the context of correctly chosen markets and that can develop new products through effective development processes that increase new product success rates will have a competitive advantage over those that do not. The key to success will be the development of whole product solutions that satisfy a wide range of customer needs; management of the product line to ensure balance between customer needs and operational requirements; involvement of marketing in the firm's quality processes; and communication strategies that overcome fear, uncertainty, and doubt related to new technology and that increase the firm's ability to conduct effective product launches. This requires new and different organizational approaches, commitment of resources, enhanced collaboration with other functions, improved product development processes, effective new product testing, and comprehensive relationships with early adopter customers.

Overview of Chapter Cases

❋ The Machine Vision International case describes the situation facing a three-year-old firm in the robotics industry, still in its early stages of development. Each potential segment has different product needs, and the case provides the opportunity to assess product market fit and understand the selection process, which must decide on product variations to make and market.

❋ The Ohmeda Monitoring Systems case describes the situation of a firm that launched a new product with high hopes, only to experience disappointing results. The case provides the opportunity to consider what went wrong and what the firm should do next.

❋ The Microsoft case describes the situation facing Microsoft in the introduction of Microsoft Works. It provides the opportunity to consider the issues involved in adapting to differing country requirements and the impact of decisions on overall sales.

Endnotes

1. David W. Cravens, Charles W. Holland, Charles W. Lamb, Jr., and William C. Moncrief, III, "Marketing's Role in Product and Service Quality," *Industrial Marketing Management* (May 1988): 285–304.

2. H. Michael Hayes, "ISO9000: The New Strategic Consideration," *Business Horizons*, May–June 1994, 52–60.

3. Robert G. Cooper and Elko J. Kleinschmidt, *New Products: The Key Factors in Success* (Chicago: American Marketing Association, 1990), 35–38.

4. Ted Levitt, "The Globalization of Markets," *Harvard Business Review*, May–June 1983, 92–102.

5. Kenichi Ohmae, *The Borderless World: Management Lessons in the New Logic of the Global Marketplace* (New York: HarperCollins Publishers, 1991).

6. H. Takeuchi and I. Nonaka, "The New Product Development Game," *Harvard Business Review*, January–February 1986, 187.

7. Booz, Allen & Hamilton, *New Product Management for the 1980s* (New York: Booz, Allen & Hamilton, 1982).

8. It is of interest to note that these European programs are open to non-European firms. U.S. participants include Apple Computers Europe, Motorola, IBM Europe, and DuPont de Nemours.

9. Robert G. Cooper "New Product Success in Industrial Firms," *Industrial Marketing Management*, 1982, 215–223.

10. Robert G. Cooper, "The Myth of the Better Mousetrap: What Makes a New Product a Success?" *Business Quarterly*, Spring 1981.

11. C. Merle Crawford, *New Products Management*, 4th ed. (Homewood, IL: Richard D. Irwin, 1994).

12. E. von Hippel, "The Dominant Role of Users in the Scientific Instrument Innovation Process," *Research Policy*, 5 (1975): 212–239.

13. George P. Dovel, "Stake It Out: Positioning Success, Step by Step," *Business Marketing*, July 1990.

George P. Dovel

Stake It Out: Positioning Success, Step by Step

Positioning shouldn't be just a part of your strategy. It should be the backbone of your business plan.

Product positioning certainly has received its fair share of press in the past few years. But if you've actually tried to achieve a position in the marketplace, you know that the gulf between theory and practice can be distressingly wide.

Let's take a practical look at the steps you can take to develop a positioning statement, the cornerstone of the whole process. Work these steps into your product and promotion planning, and you can generate positioning statements systematically.

First Things First

Positioning applies to more than just products and services. A company's distribution channels, technologies and techniques all occupy positions in customers' minds. Particularly in technical and industrial marketing, it is critical to position not only your products, but your company, your distribution channel and frequently your technologies. Even if you're selling the product of the century, most customers will hesitate to buy it if they don't accept your company or your sales and support staff. Although this article focuses on product positioning, you also can apply its methods to those other positioning arenas.

First, a word of warning: Don't attempt positioning until you've segmented the market and

At the time this article was written, George P. Dovel, formerly a market development engineer for Hewlett-Packard Co., Everett, Wash., had recently founded the Dovel Group, which provides writing and consulting services for high-tech companies and is based in Snohomish, Wash. *Source:* Reprinted with permission from the 1990 issue of *Business Marketing.* Copyright, Crain Communications, Inc.

picked your targets. If you draft a positioning statement without identifying homogeneous user segments, you'll quickly find yourself with an unclear audience and an unclear message.

Once you've defined and selected your target segments, you can identify the position you want to occupy in them. Then you can develop the product or service that will give you legitimate claim to the position you want to occupy. When you've developed the product and prepared its introduction, you can implement the positioning program.

An important point in the last paragraph warrants restating: Positioning should be more than a part of your marketing strategy. It should be the backbone of your product design and development and a key thought in your business plan. Although it's possible to find a position for an already-designed product, it's much easier to define the position you want to achieve, and then design the product.

Communication Is Key

The promotional program is obviously an important vehicle for moving a product into a desired position, but it's not the only vehicle. Particularly with complex technical products sold through a direct sales force, the salesperson has as much or more impact on positioning success as do ads and promotional campaigns. That also can be true of a product that's not complex. With even the most common commodities, confidence in the supplier is critical.

Remember that any communication—in the broadest sense of the word—that potential customers receive contributes to or detracts from your positioning efforts. Packaging, shipping containers, invoices, Christmas cards, trash in your parking lot—they all affect the position you occupy.

What's more, customers aren't the only people who should receive your positioning message. You need to reach your own design staff, the distribution channel, the press and anyone else who might influence either your message or your ability to implement and support it.

Ultimately, the marketplace positions your product. Try as hard as you can to influence it, but a position resides in the buyer's mind, not in the seller's.

Why Bother?

The positioning statement is your path into the prospect's mind. You might use the statement directly as copy, or you can use it to develop other copy. It should be the guiding light for everything you do. Carve it into your desktop, put it under the pillow at night, stencil it onto the engineers' foreheads. The important thing is to generate a common vision, both inside and outside the company.

Keep a few guidelines in mind when you develop a positioning statement. Make sure that it:

- is worded in terms of customer benefits;
- defines your value proposition; and
- is very simple and instantly understandable.

We'll outline a few more criteria when we discuss how to test positioning statements; those three should start you on the right track.

Positioning is inextricably linked with several other marketing processes: segmentation, targeting and promotions. You can't define a good position until you've divided the market into its unique segments, then identified which ones offer a good chance for a high spot. And the most brilliant positioning statement in the world is nothing without effective execution. So, although the steps in this article should help you develop positioning statements, don't forget the important tasks you need to do before and after.

Here's a condensed version of the positioning process:

Step 1:   Recognize reality.

Step 2:   Compare your product strategy with your business strategy.

Step 3:   Understand what target customers care about.

Step 4:   Understand your competitors' positions.

Step 5:   Pick the position you want to occupy.

Step 6:   Write your positioning statement.

Step 7:   Attack yourself.

Step 8:   Test your positioning.

We'll discuss each step in terms of its purpose, results, comments and techniques.

Step 1: Recognize Reality

Purpose: To realistically characterize the task you're about to start; to make sure you take advantage of environmental influences whenever possible; to make sure you don't waste time and energy trying to move positions you can't influence. You can think of environmental influences as positions previously established in the market that are larger than you and largely out of your control. Nothing like starting with a cheerful step, is there?

Results: A list of environmental influences you identify in the market, with indications whether those established positions might hurt or help you.

Comments: You aren't positioning in a vacuum, and you'll rarely have full control over the process. If you're a marketing staff member deep inside a large company, you'll have precious little chance to reposition the entire company.

Other environmental influences include technologies (e.g., Unix is an operating system for serious users), locations (e.g., a company in the Silicon Valley must be high-tech) or people (e.g., Germans are highly methodical). All kinds of stereotypes can affect your positioning. In the interest of efficiency and effectiveness, recognize from the start what you can and cannot change.

In local contexts, you might affect the big positions. You won't reposition personal computers in general, but you might help reposition them in the specific area of computer-aided testing, for example.

Just remember that the average mind will reject your arguments if they threaten an established comfort zone or prejudice. If Jill Engineer believes microcomputers are no good for production line control, she'll look for evidence that supports her opinion, not evidence that makes her look like a buffoon.

Next, recognize how you can amplify your own position by exploiting the established environmental influences. Understand how your company is perceived, then use that thinking to your advantage. Catch the latest technological wave (microcomputers in engineering, surface mount technologies, computer-aided engineering, etc.). Like surfing, that's a balancing act. You want to ride the wave, not get swamped by it.

Techniques: They really depend on the situation at hand. Here are some suggested steps:

1. Identify organizational positions (e.g., Xerox = copiers).
2. Identify technological positions (e.g., Unix = serious users).
3. Identify social and geographical stereotypes/positions (e.g., Swiss = precision).

You'll probably need a two-step process to characterize each of the three kinds of positions and stereotypes: First, to find out what they are, then to find out how extensive they are. Use customer interviews and focus groups, and real current literature to see what concerns target customers have. Then you can use a quantitative survey to find out which issues are the most important.

Focus groups and depth interviews are good vehicles for identifying the range of issues. Just don't try to generalize what you hear.

For each environmental influence you identify, determine if it will affect your position positively or negatively. You can use concept testing with focus groups to learn that. Present your concept with and without visible linkage to the environmental influence (where possible), then compare the attendees' reactions. When it comes time to write, that insight will help you put the right spin on your copy.

For testing that relies on statistical comparison rather than judgment, use a technique such as conjoint analysis, and assign the environmental influence as one of the attributes.

Step 2: Compare Your Product Strategy with Your Business Strategy

Purpose: To verify that your product strategy supports your business strategy, and to make sure your product's success will be a success for your company.

Results: Nothing elaborate, just an awareness among members of your product development and marketing teams of the company's business objectives, and how the new product must fit into the overall strategy.

Comments: When you're scrambling to make a new product successful, it's too easy to lose sight of the company's overall situation. The potential for trouble appears whenever you have more than one product that sells into common markets, competes for distribution channel energy, or competes for support and administrative resources. You need to be sure that the success of one product doesn't hurt somewhere else in the company.

You might consider your business strategy one of the environmental influences discussed in Step 1. If your product strategy doesn't follow the direction your business is going, you'll lose on two counts: You won't take advantage of the company's larger positioning efforts, and you might have to divert energy explaining why you don't fit.

Techniques: No formal technique here; simply take a few minutes to compare your company's strategy with the marketing strategy for your new product. If they don't mesh, one of them should change.

Step 3: Understand What Target Customers Care About

Purpose: To identify the attributes customers use to differentiate products. You can shoot for an advantageous position only when you know the scorecard customers use.

Results: For each target segment, a list of differentiators customers use to select products. It might start as a long list of attributes, but you need to distill it down to two or three for effective positioning. Ultimately, you'd like to end up with a perceptual map or similar device.

Comments: If you don't understand your current and potential customers, that will become painfully clear in this step. There are two challenges here. Depending on the complexity of products and markets, they could be tough.

First, you need to understand all the decisions customers could possibly make when selecting products. For many product types, that's a long list, covering performance, physical dimensions, features, support, documentation, any warranties and so on. This part might be easy.

Second, you need to distill all that down to a map of one, two or three dimensions. Even if customers care about 50 different product attributes, they probably don't make purchase decisions based on that many. And you certainly can't explain 50 competitive advantages and hope to get your message across quickly. This part might *not* be easy.

Techniques: A common tool to use for this step is a perceptual map. That graphic device shows the dimensions customers use to differentiate products, together with how they perceive available products. You'd like to have a map for each target segment.

Of all the steps in positioning, this is the one in which theory and practice diverge the most. Theory says you should use some device to identify the dimensions in each segment and to understand the positions of all your competitors. A perceptual map can often do the job because of its ability to show what is important to customers and how well existing products meet their needs. "Perceptual" is the key word here; the map shows how customers *perceive* products that are available in the market.

But enter reality. Perceptual maps are not practical or possible in many situations because they require a fairly mature market, with a representative sample that readily understands existing products. That eliminates most emerging markets, and many others in which the products are dissimilar and/or very complex.

Instead, you could use some combination of qualitative research, judgment and guesswork. Don't think that's unscientific; you can be very systematic and rational using this method.

(And don't feel too bad about not having a perceptual map. They're not perfect, and what you're going to create is substantially better than the nothing you might have now.)

The "judgment map" looks just like a perceptual map. The difference is that it's based on a combination of customer opinions and your judgment, while the perceptual map is based on representative customer perceptions.

When all else fails, create a "guess" map. That's just what it sounds like: your guess as to what the various segments need and perceive. It's clearly a dangerous path to tread, but sometimes you don't have a choice. (If you're forced to take that route, you might want to think twice about proceeding with a product.)

Step 4: Understand the Positions of Existing Products

Purpose: Before you can differentiate yourself from competitors, you need to know who they are and how your target customers perceive them.

Result: Some device, verbal and/or graphic, that shows you where customers in target segments place the products your competitors offer. As in Step 3, a perceptual map is a good device to use.

Comments: Your method for this step depends on the complexity of the market situation and how much time and money you have. The better you understand each segment's needs, the better you can guess competitors' positions. Ideally, you'll have a perceptual map or other device based on information from real people in the market. Realistically, you may have a collection of opinions, guesses and qualitative fragments.

Techniques: You can use the same techniques here that you used to identify segment dimensions in Step 3: perceptual mapping, judgment mapping and guess mapping. If you can't generate a real map, you can rely on customer and sales force feedback and your own analysis of competitors.

Step 5: Pick the Best Position

Purpose: To identify the position you want to occupy in your target segments, so that you can start to work on the positioning statement itself.

Result: A verbal or graphic description of the position you want to occupy.

Comments: Remember that picking the ideal position can be hugely complicated because it requires an analysis of market structure, technologies, distribution channels and so on. As with choosing your target segments, picking a desired market position should be a strategic planning effort, with all the research and consideration that implies.

What if a competitor has already taken the best position? You have three choices:

• Forget it, and find another opportunity.
• Try to dislodge the current occupants.
• Try to reposition the current occupants.

The first option might be your only logical choice. If you've already developed the product, that won't be a popular recommendation.

However, the second option can be extremely difficult to achieve. As the journals amply document, the marketing path is littered with people who tried it. I mention it here because it has been done successfully, sometimes in a big way. (IBM Corp. displacing Apple Computer Inc. in the microcomputer market, for example.) But the wise marketer will take that approach with much nervousness.

The third approach can be particularly successful in emerging or evolving markets. Some products and applications are so complicated that you can alter customers' perceptions of the ideal product through education. That's one reason vendors of advanced-technology products spend so much time and money producing application notes and other such materials.

Let's say you've developed a product with a new technique for analyzing metal fatigue. If it could change the way customers work and you're the only vendor with it, you can try to reposition the competition as outdated. Your promotions can focus on the new technique's purpose and benefits, and stress that you're the only game in town.

If you convince the market that the new technique is now the best way to analyze metal fatigue, you become the leading edge. What you've done is modify the perceptual map by educating customers about a new parameter that should affect their decision making.

Techniques: Start by identifying desirable positions, through whatever combination of research, judgment, guesswork and divine insight you have at your disposal. If you have a perceptual map, you might consider gap analysis. Another technique is the customer panel, which includes clients or prospects who work with you to identify ideal positions. And there's always the brilliant-flash-in-the-middle-of-the-night technique.

When you find the position you'd like to occupy, ask yourself two questions:

• Can you achieve it? (Do you have the technology, market intelligence, money, time and management you'll need to create the product?)
• Can you gain access to it? (Once you develop the product, do you have the channels needed to sell and support it?)

If you can answer "yes" to both questions, continue to Step 6.

Step 6: Develop Your Positioning Statement

Purpose: To create a concise statement that embodies the position you want to occupy. You may or may not use the statement in your promotions. More important, it expresses the vision that drives everything you do.

Result: A positioning statement that communicates the position you want to achieve, using as few words as possible.

Comments: This could be the least analytical and most creatively demanding step in positioning. Your statement may be utterly obvious at this point, or you may have only a vague concept with no idea of how to present it.

Techniques: If writing comes easily to you and words flow out smoothly and naturally, throw this article away and get to work.

If you're more mortal, try the following six hints. To illustrate with an example, let's say you're building a portable fatigue-o-tron to analyze mental fatigue in the field. You've decided to position the product as offering the performance of laboratory units with the convenience of hand-held units.

1. Describe the position you want to occupy, in terms of the segment's dimensions (e.g., highest performance in smallest package).

2. Describe the problem you'll solve (e.g., infield fatigue analysis).

3. Describe the solution you offer to occupy that position (e.g., portable fatigue-o-tron).

4. Describe the people who should care about it (e.g., corn growers).

5. String it all together (e.g., "This portable fatigue-o-tron provides the highest performance in a portable package for corn growers who need in-the-field mental fatigue analysis.")

6. Simplify, simplify, simplify! Remove phrases that will be obvious when the message is taken in context (e.g., say "highest performance fatigue analysis" and show a picture of a corn grower out in the field with your equipment).

If you can't get the point across in one phrase, keep working on it. If you have trouble simplifying, analyze the stubborn areas and look for:

- big words. It's too easy to smooth over conceptual rough spots with inflated prose.
- self-centered phrases. If you're talking about yourself, you may be having trouble identifying

customers or customer needs. Explain, describe, promote—but don't boast or climb on a pedestal and scream, "Hey, look at me!"

Step 8 gives the criteria for evaluating your statement.

Step 7: Attack Yourself

Purpose: To identify weaknesses in your proposed positioning and to anticipate competitive responses.

Result: A list of vulnerable points in the position you want to achieve and a description of how you expect your major competitors to respond.

Comments: This can be a good way to throw your career into a power dive, but it is important. At this point, you've probably generated some momentum in your organization and people are starting to rally around the vision. Now stand up and list all of its weak points. Be sure to explain that it's better to hear about the weaknesses from an insider than from a customer or competitor.

Of course, your ability to anticipate competitive responses depends on how well you understand the competition. If you don't know how your competitors operate, you won't be able to predict how they'll respond.

Techniques: Pretend you're a product manager for a key competitor. Your task is to prepare a marketing response to the new product. Knowing what you know about both companies—their shares of awareness and preference, their histories, distribution, skill sets, operating styles, and so on—figure out how you'll respond. Look for weaknesses in the product, sales force, support staff, warranty, the company's stability—any aspect around which you can make a case.

Next, pretend you're a particularly nasty potential buyer who enjoys tormenting vendors. Have a colleague play the role of one of your salespersons. While he or she is pitching the product, counter with every weakness, real or imaginary, you can think up. Keep a list of how the seller responds to each point.

After those exercises, you might have a list of possible vulnerabilities. If there are some serious weaknesses, consider modifying your position statement to shield yourself. If you can't shield yourself or you don't think a weak point is serious enough to modify the statement, make sure you generate a reply for each weak point. Your sales channel will need those replies to survive in front of customers, and you'll need the replies to survive in front of your sales channel.

Step 8: Test Your Proposed Positioning

Purpose: To make sure you can effectively communicate the positioning statement.

Result: An assessment of how well the positioning statement will help you achieve your desired position. Depending on the technique used, you'll have a qualitative answer or a quantitative answer.

Comments: You've probably spent a lot of time developing your statement, and you're about to spend a lot of money communicating it to the market. Make sure it works first.

Techniques: Here are six possible techniques for testing your positioning statement. As you go from No. 1 to No. 6, the tests become more accurate. Alas, they also get a lot more expensive. Even if your company is wealthy, do them in order. If you do the free ones (Nos. 1 and 2) and cheap ones (Nos. 3 and 4) first, the expensive tests (Nos. 5 and 6) will be faster and more accurate.

1. Self Review: If you can look at your product and market objectively, a self review of your positioning can be quite helpful. Use the testing criteria described in a few paragraphs. However, if you can't look objectively, a self review might lead you over a cliff.

2. Peer Review: This can result in an analysis that's much more objective than is possible through self review, and it's still free. Test your positioning on your peers (and anybody else who can offer an intelligent opinion). Read them the positioning statement, and have them tell you the impression it makes. Then work with them through the positioning process starting with Step 1, explaining what

you did at each step. Your colleagues can check your techniques and the logic of your conclusions.

3. Sales Force Review: This technique can help in three ways.

First, salespeople and distributors monitor the market and know what customers are saying. They often know what competitors are saying, too. So the sales force can give you a reading about how well the message will fly in the marketplace.

Second, the sales force is responsible for getting the message across in front of customers. See if they can build selling propositions around the positioning. See whether they feel comfortable or embarrassed making the pitch.

Third, it's always a good idea to get your sales channel involved in decisions that affect its ability to succeed.

It's true that feedback from salespeople is often biased. But that's no reason not to listen. They have a unique and valuable perspective. Just remember that you're getting the sales force's assessment, not a general market survey. Use the sales group's feedback to check your other test data.

4. Customer Focus Groups: This is a good way to check for positive and negative issues associated with your positioning. It's also a good way to test alternative statements, if you've prepared any.

Just remember that, although focus groups are great for identifying issues, they're not terribly reliable for measuring the extent of those issues. You won't have enough samples, and you probably won't select them at random. But don't let statistical purists diminish the value of the customer focus group; it's a great way to find out what's going on in people's heads.

Focus groups aren't risk-free, however. In effect, you'll introduce your product to a small group of people. If secrecy is absolutely paramount, consider whether a possible leak is worth the insight you'll gain. By all means, have attendees sign nondisclosure agreements.

5. Customer Choice Modeling: Here, we shift from qualitative testing to quantitative testing.

Choice modeling simulates the selling and buying of products, both real and hypothetical.

The method isn't cheap, and it isn't foolproof. Buying a $100,000 system in 60 seconds in a marketing study is a lot easier than buying one in real life. But, given those limitations, it is the only way short of test marketing to get quantitative assessments of positioning alternatives.

6. Test Marketing: If you have the money, time and circumstances for test marketing, you're probably in the minority. I suspect that the development costs of most industrial and technical products outweigh their marketing costs. By the time they're ready, test marketing is out of the question.

If you are test marketing a product, however, try to assess the impact of positioning. If the test goes well, your position is probably good. If the test fails, the position may be part of the problem.

Meets the Test?

Now let's look at some criteria you can use to assess a positioning statement using self review, peer review or sales force focus groups:

Does it take the customer's perspective? Make sure that your solution's description uses the same vocabulary as the customer's description of his or her problem.

Is it easy to understand? When you're sitting at your desk explaining your positioning to a colleague, you can take as much time and as many different approaches as you like. But when your positioning vehicle (an ad, sales presentation, etc.) is out in the marketplace, you've probably got one quick shot at getting the point across. Even if you don't plan to use the actual statement in public, the message must be instantly understandable.

Does it encapsulate the value you offer? That is important in four areas.

First, the people designing the product need to know why they're making it. They need the same vision you have.

The second area is your sales channel. Salespeople and distributors will usually build their presentations and discussions around your message, so make sure the story you tell is complete and relevant.

Third, there's the press, consultants, and anyone else who might be an intermediary for your message.

And fourth, your customers. If they don't know why you made the thing, they won't get too excited.

Is it strategically compatible? If your message for a product supports your overall strategy, attaining the desired market position will be much easier. But if the product's strategy doesn't align well, you lose on two counts: You don't get a free ride on the larger message, and you have to spend time and energy explaining why you aren't in sync.

Is it culturally acceptable? Will people in the organization feel good about implementing the message? Does the position fit your operating style?

Is it honest? That means more than being honest with your customers; it also means being honest with yourself. Imagine that you're selling the product to your mother, using the proposed positioning statement. If you both feel good about it, you're probably on safe ground.

Is it promotable? Can you build an effective promotion around the message? (If your positioning is vague, that will become quite obvious here.) Try designing a few promotional vehicles (ads, brochures, sales training, etc.) that are based on your proposed message.

Use these criteria to see if your idea is promotable:

1. Can you create a logical sales proposition?
2. Can you explain your value proposition quickly?
3. Can you emphasize the solution, not the solution-provider?
4. Can you build a headline or graphic with stopping power?
5. Can you explain the benefits to the different buying influences (economic buyers, technical buyers, agents, end-users)?
6. Can you say anything original about the product benefits?

Getting Your Message Across

Now that you've got a positioning statement, how do you get the message across? I won't try to summarize the dozens of books and articles about effective promotions. Wander through the right aisle at the library, and you'll get plenty of advice on that topic.

Instead, as a reminder I'll provide a list of all the people to whom you should consider sending your positioning message. In the case of internal people—company staff, distributors or consultants—do more than just send the message; make sure they use the positioning statement as their guiding light:

- engineers
- designers
- programmers
- researchers
- finance and accounting
- everyone in marketing
- everyone in sales
- everyone in customer support
- applications engineers
- all managers with fingers in the pie
- reporters and writers
- editors and publishers
- consultants
- your ad agency
- your public relations agency
- other divisions in your company
- current customers
- potential customers.

That should keep you busy for a while.

It might seem like a lot of work to develop one little sentence. But everything you do—from developing the product to writing ad copy—will be much easier if you've nailed the positioning statement up front.

Cornelius Herstatt
Eric von Hippel

From Experience: Developing New Product Concepts Via the Lead User Method: A Case Study in a "Low-Tech" Field

Conventional market research methods do not work well in the instance of many industrial goods and services, and yet, accurate understanding of user need is essential for successful product innovation. Cornelius Herstatt and Eric von Hippel report on a successful field application of a "lead user" method for developing concepts for needed new products. This method is built around the idea that the richest understanding of needed products is held by just a few users. It is possible to identify these "lead users" and then draw them into a process of *joint* development of new product concepts with manufacturer personnel. In the application described, the lead user method was found to be much faster than traditional ways of identifying promising new product concepts as well as less costly. It also was judged to provide better outcomes by the firm participating in the case. The article includes practical detail on the steps that were used to implement the method at Hilti AG, a leading manufacturer of products and materials used in construction. ✳

Introduction

In a recent study of the market research preferences and practices of Swiss machinery manufacturers, Herstatt found that the firms viewed joint product development with users to be the most effective way to accurately understand user needs. At the same time, he found that the firms seldom employed this form of "market research," because they regarded it as being very complex, costly and difficult to implement.

Herstatt found no convincing reason *why* this form of market research would be inherently more complex or expensive than other, less-preferred

At the time this article was written, Cornelius Herstatt was a consultant with A.D. Little in Switzerland, and Eric von Hippel was Professor of Management of Technology at the Sloan School of Management. Reprinted by permission of the publisher from *The Journal of Product Innovation Management*, pp. 213–221. Copyright 1992 Elsevier Science, Inc.

methods, and so decided to conduct a "lead user" market research case study as a form of anecdotal research into the matter. In this article, we report on the procedures he used and the outcomes he obtained. As the reader will see, the method, which involves joint user-manufacturer development of new product concepts, was successfully applied in this case study. Further, anecdotal information provided by the firm participating in the case indicates that concept development with lead users was twice as fast as and half the cost of methods previously used.

What Is "Lead User" Market Research?

Traditional market research methods are designed to sample the needs of a relatively large group of users, analyze the data obtained and then present the findings to product developers. In many fields, however, the richest understanding of needed new products and services is held by just a few users. Von Hippel [4,5] developed a method that exploits this fact by prescribing that firms interested in identifying needs for new products and services begin by identifying a small sample of "lead users." These especially sophisticated users are drawn into a process of *joint* development of new product or service concepts with manufacturer personnel. Then, the likely commercial appeal of the concepts developed with lead users is tested against a population of more ordinary users.

"Lead users" of a novel or enhanced product, process, or service have been defined by von Hippel as those who display *both* of two characteristics with respect to it:

1. They face needs that will be general in a marketplace—but face them months or years before the bulk of that marketplace encounters them.

2. They expect to benefit significantly by obtaining a solution to those needs.

Thus, a manufacturing firm with a current strong need for a process innovation that many manufacturers will need in 2 years' time would fit the definition of lead user with respect to that process.

Each of the two lead user characteristics specified above provides an independent and valuable contribution to the type of new product need and solution data lead users possess. The first is valuable because, as empirical studies in problem solving have shown, users who have real-world experience with a need are in the best position to provide accurate data regarding it. When new product needs are evolving rapidly, as in many high-technology product categories, only users at the "front of the trend" will presently have the real-world experience that manufacturers must analyze if they are to understand accurately the needs that the bulk of the market will soon face.

The utility of the second lead user characteristic is that users who expect high benefit from a solution to a need can provide the richest need and solution data to inquiring market researchers. This is because, as has been shown by studies of industrial product and process innovations [2], the greater the benefit a given user expects to obtain from a needed novel product or process, the greater will be his or her investment in obtaining a solution.

In sum, lead users are users whose present strong needs will become general in a marketplace months or years in the future. Because lead users are familiar with conditions that lie in the future for most others, the lead user market research method can help manufacturers acquire need and solution information that will be useful in the development of "next generation" concepts for new products and services.

Four Steps in a Lead User Study

A lead user market research study involves four major steps, which are described in detail in articles by von Hippel [4] and Urban and von Hippel [3]. In brief summary, these are as follows. Step one involves specifying the characteristics lead users will have in the product/market segment of interest. That is, one must identify the trend(s) on which they lead the market, and also must specify indicators that show that they expect relatively high benefit from obtaining a solution to their trend-related needs. (One frequently useful proxy for expectations of high benefit is evidence of product development or product modification by users. As noted earlier, user investment in innovation, and user expectations of related benefit, have been found to be correlated.)

The second step is to identify a sample of lead users who meet both of the lead user criteria established in step one. Such a group will be both at the leading edge of the trend being studied and will display correlates of high expected benefit from solutions to related needs. The third step is to bring the sample of lead users together with company engineering and marketing personnel to engage in group problem-solving sessions. The outcome of these sessions is one or more "lead user" product or service concepts judged by session participants to be both responsive to lead user needs and responsive to manufacturer concerns regarding producibility, etc.

Finally, as the needs of today's lead users are not necessarily the same as the needs of the users who will make up a major share of tomorrow's predicted market, the fourth and final step in the lead user market research method is to test whether concepts found valuable by lead users also will be valued by the more typical users in the target market.

The Case Study

The company participating in this study was Hilti AG, a leading European manufacturer of components, equipment and materials used in construction. Hilti has major production facilities in Europe, the United States and Japan, and sells worldwide.

The product line we elected to concentrate on in our lead user case study was "pipe hangers"—a relatively "low-tech" type of fastening system often used in commercial and industrial buildings. Pipe hangers are assemblages of steel supports and pipe clamps and other hardware components used to securely fasten pipes to the walls and/or ceilings of buildings. Sometimes pipe hangers can be quite simple and support only a single pipe. Frequently, however, they are relatively complicated structures that simultaneously support and align a number of pipes of different sizes and types (Figure 1).

In the paragraphs that follow, we will describe how each of the four steps in a lead user study was carried out in this case.

Step 1: Specification of Lead User Indicators

Recall that lead users of a product, process or service are defined as those who display two characteristics with respect to it: they have needs that are advanced with respect to an important marketplace trend(s) and they expect to benefit significantly by obtaining a solution to those needs. To identify lead users of pipe-hanging hardware, a first step was to

identify important trends and users with relatively high benefit expectations related to these.

Identification of Trends

Identification of important trends in the evolution of user needs in pipe-hanging hardware began with a survey of experts. A brief analysis of the target market showed that people with expert knowledge in the relevant field would be found among "layout engineers," the specialists in charge of planning complex pipe networks in commercial and industrial buildings (layout engineers also are key decision makers with respect to determining which components will be bought and used for the pipe networks they design).

Expert advisors for this study were found in construction departments of technical universities, professional engineering organizations, and municipal departments responsible for approving the design of pipe networks. Some of these were already known to the Hilti R&D department; others were identified via recommendations. Ultimately, the panel of experts who provided information for this study consisted of eight leading layout engineers in Switzerland, Germany, and Austria; two researchers from the construction departments of the Swiss Federal Institute of Technology and the University of Darmstadt; one engineer from a professional organization in Bonn; and one engineer each from the municipal building departments in Bern and Berlin.

The trends identified as most important by the experts surveyed regarding pipe-hanger systems were as follows:

Trend 1: There is an increasing need for pipe-hanger systems that are extremely easy to put together—so easy that instruction booklets will not be needed. Such systems should have significantly fewer components than at present. They should adapt to a wide range of application conditions, and should be based on a simple, consistent construction principle.

Reason for trend: Education levels among installers are going down in many countries.

Trend 2: There is a need for rapidly actuated, positive, interlocking fasteners to connect pipe

A Conventional Pipe Hanger Configured to Support Several Pipes

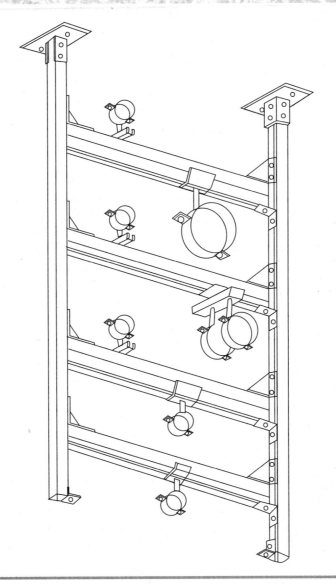

hanger elements together securely and to attach the completed hangers securely to building walls and ceilings.

Reason for trend: Safety standards in many countries are getting more stringent. Some of the multiple screws and bolts now used

to assemble hangers (see Figure 1) may be inadvertently overlooked by installers—with consequent risk of field failure.

Trend 3: There is a need for pipe hangers made from lighter, noncorrodible materials.

Pipe hangers should therefore increasingly be made of plastics rather than of the steel elements that are used almost exclusively today.

Reason for trend: Pipe-hanging systems made of steel are heavy and therefore difficult and dangerous to hang under some field conditions. In addition, steel is subject to corrosion and failure in wet environments or environments where chemicals are present.

Solutions that offered improvements with respect to these (somewhat overlapping) trends were expected to result in significant benefits for the users of pipe hangers. The skills required of installers would be reduced; fewer components would have to be stocked by users; the speed and safety of installation would be greatly increased; and the risk of field failures would be reduced.

Identification of High-Benefit Expectations

Expectations of innovation-related benefit on the part of users can be identified by survey, and this approach has been successfully applied elsewhere [3, 4]. However, as mentioned earlier, innovation-related *activity* by users also can serve as a proxy for expectations of benefit, and this is the approach used here.

Users showing innovation activity were identified by conducting telephone interviews with a sample of 74 interviewees. Because, as will be described in the next section, the same sample was screened to simultaneously identify users having *both* lead user characteristics (ahead with respect to identified trends and having high expected benefit), we will defer a detailed discussion of methods and findings with respect to user innovation activity until we describe how step 2 was carried out in this study.

Here, we simply note that users engaged in innovating were determined by questions such as "Do you/did you ever build and install pipe-hanger hardware of your own design? Do you/did you ever modify commercially available pipe-hanger hardware to better suit your needs?" We

also note that a high fraction of users interviewed (36 percent) were in fact found to display this characteristic.

Step 2: Identification of Lead Users

Once the trends and the user benefit characteristics were specified that would be used to identify lead users, the next step was to identify a lead user sample. This was begun by identifying, in cooperation with Hilti, a random sample of firms that buy and use pipe hangers. This sample was then screened to identify a subset of lead users within it.

The firms that install pipe-hanging systems are specialists in installing pipe networks in commercial and industrial buildings—for example, industrial plumbing firms. Installation of pipe hangers is a subtask in the larger task of pipe installation. The tradesmen who actually install pipe hangers comprised the group in which lead users would be identified. (Installers of pipe hangers have only a moderate-level technical education. In the countries from which our user sample was drawn—Switzerland, Germany, and Austria—these installers complete 8 years of general schooling, and then take a 2- or 3-year vocational training program in their particular trade. Finally, they pass a municipal examination and receive a license to practice.)

Hilti has a number of geographically based sales divisions with close and frequent customer contacts. The German, Austrian, and Swiss sales divisions (selected because of their geographical accessibility) were asked to provide the names of firms they thought were buyers of pipe-hanger systems made either by Hilti or its competitors. In this request no mention was made of either customer innovativeness or customer size. The three sales divisions eventually responded with the names of 120 firms they thought met the criteria.

Next, attempts were made to contact all 120 user firms for a telephone survey. Ultimately, 74 of these were in fact successfully contacted and judged suitable for and willing to undertake more detailed interviews (20 of the 120 were excluded

TABLE 1

Percent of Sample Found To Have Lead User Characteristics in Two Studies

	Sample of Pipe-Hanger Users	Sample of PC-CAD Users[a]
Users at front of selected trend(s):	30% (22)	28% (38)
Users who built own prototype products:	36% (27)	25% (34)

[a]Data source: Urban and von Hippel [3].

because they could not be reached after five telephone calls; 16 were excluded because they were found to be not currently using the product type at issue and ten were not included simply because they were not willing to participate in an interview).

In the instance of the 74 firms who were willing to participate in a telephone interview, interviewers sought to identify the most expert person on the products under investigation. To do this, the first contact at each firm was asked: "Whom do you regard the most expert person on pipe-hanger systems in your company, and can we talk to that person?" The interviewers were referred to expert "fitters"—employees who actually install pipe-hanging systems in the filed—in 64 of the 74 instances. In the remaining ten cases they were referred to direct supervisors of fitters, all of whom had moved into supervisory positions only after extensive experience in the field.

Interviews were next conducted with all 74 individuals. The interviews were aimed at identifying a subset of users in the total user sample who had both of the two lead user characteristics (being ahead on the trends identified by the experts and expecting high benefit from innovations along these dimensions).

The proxy used for "ahead on identified trends" was simply: (1) did the interviewees agree that advances along the trends that had been specified by the expert panel were in fact needed and important and (2) could the interviewees describe at least some technically interesting ideas regarding these trends? As we noted in our discussion of step

1 in a lead user study, the proxy used for "user innovation benefit expectations" was: had the users developed or modified pipe hangers in ways that they felt represented improvements with respect to the identified trends?

As a result of the interviews just described, a significant number of lead users of pipe-hanging hardware [22] were identified. Table 1 summarizes the findings on this matter and, as a matter of interest, compares these with data drawn from the Urban and von Hippel [3] study of PC-CAD (PC-computer-aided design) users. In both studies, there was a high overlap where users displayed the two lead user characteristics.

It is interesting to note that, as shown in Table 1, 27 (36 percent) of our random sample of users of pipe-hanging systems had designed, built and installed hangers of their own devising in one or more cases. This compares very favorable with the 25 percent of innovating users found in the technically sophisticated field of PC-CAD.

Step 3: Lead User Product Concept Development

A group of 22 lead users of pipe hangers had now been identified. The next task was to determine whether some of these lead users could be joined with expert Hilti personnel to produce novel product concepts that would be judged by Hilti marketing researchers and by routine users to be the basis of valuable commercial products, and that would be judged to be practicably manufacturable by Hilti engineers.

Selection of Lead User Concept Group

Recall that, in the method step described just above, a group of 22 lead users had been identified among a total user sample of 74 users. Two more tests were next applied to this sample to identify those few lead users who seemed to be most appropriate to invite to join with Hilti engineers and other experts in a 3-day concept generation workshop. These additional tests were intended to select the users most likely to be effective in such a workshop, and consisted simply of the judgment of the person who had interviewed the user on two matters: Did the interviewer judge that the user could describe his experiences and ideas clearly? Did the user seem to have strong personal interest in the development of improved pipe-hanger systems? Fourteen of the 22 lead users met these additional tests and were invited to join the workshop.

Twelve of the 14 lead users contacted—ten pipe fitters plus two supervisors of fitters—agreed to join the product concept development workshop. Interestingly, the two that did not were users who had patented their own pipe-hanger system designs. These two were not willing to present their ideas in a workshop, most probably because they were concerned about the diffusion of their proprietary-technical know-how.

All users who joined the workshop formally agreed that any inventions or ideas developed during the sessions would be the property of Hilti. As compensation, every participant was offered a small honorarium. Interestingly, most of the participants did not accept this; they felt sufficiently rewarded by simply attending and contributing to the planned workshop.

Three-Day Product Concept Generation Workshop

The goal of the product concept generation workshop sponsored by Hilti was to develop the conceptual basis for a novel pipe-hanger system with characteristics identified in the technical trend analysis described earlier. To most effectively meet this goal and to efficiently transfer the workshop findings to Hilti, the lead users at the workshop were joined by two of the expert layout engineers who had participated in the trend analysis segment of our study. Invitees from Hilti consisted of the marketing manager, the product manager, and three engineers who worked on the design of pipe-fastening systems.

The workshop was carried out over a 3-day period, and was organized as follows:

Day 1. The entire group conducted a review of important trends and problems in pipe-hanging systems. Next, five relatively independent problem areas were defined by the group, and a subgroup was established to work on each. The five subgroup topics were (1) methods of attaching pipe hangers to ceilings or walls; (2) design of support elements extending between the wall attachment and pipe clamp itself; (3) design of the pipe clamps; (4) design of the methods of attaching various system components to each other in the field; and (5) methods of conveniently adjusting length of supporting members at the field site. Membership in the subgroups was at the option of workshop participants, and shifts in membership were made from time to time to avoid the possible danger of premature fixation on individual problem-solving ideas championed by individual users. Each of the subgroups was assisted by technicians from Hilti or external layout engineers.

Day 2. The five subgroups worked on their problem areas in the morning, and in the afternoon all took a break from the specific problems at hand and participated in some general problem-solving and creativity exercises such as role-playing and team-building exercises. The purpose of these was both to lessen pressure on participants and to make them more comfortable with each other. After a short while, the workshop was in fact characterized by very strong group cohesion and intensive, cordial interaction.

Day 3. The subgroup ideas were presented to the entire group for evaluation and suggestions. As an aid to this evaluation effort, each of the subgroup ideas was evaluated on the three criteria of orginality (how revolutionary and novel is the solution from a technical point of view?), feasibility (how quickly can the solution be realized employing currently available technology?) and comprehensiveness of solution (does the idea represent a single solution or does it resolve several user problems simultaneously?). Next, membership in the subgroups was changed, work on the most promising concepts was continued and informal engineering drawings were produced by participants. Finally, these were critiqued and modified by the entire group and merged into one joint concept.

Results of Product Concept Generation Workshop

At the conclusion of the workshop, the single pipe-hanger system design was selected by the total group as incorporating the best of all the elements discussed in the subgroups, and this was the system recommended to Hilti.

After the workshop, the technical and economic feasibility of the new product concept proposed by the lead users was evaluated further by Hilti personnel. At the conclusion of this work, it was decided that the lead users had indeed developed a very valuable new pipe-hanger system. In the judgment of company experts it was well in advance of the offerings of competitors. Hilti, based in Lichtenstein, is a leading European manufacturer of components, equipment and materials used in construction. The firm's products range from fastening systems to drilling and cutting equipment to specialty chemicals. It has major production facilities in Europe, the United States and Japan, and sells worldwide. In 1990 the worldwide sales of Hilti were approximately 2 billion Swiss francs.

Step 4: Testing Whether Lead User Concepts Appeal to Ordinary Users

The fourth and final step in the lead user market research method involves testing whether typical users in a marketplace find the product or service concept developed by lead users to be attractive.

Because Hilti's internal evaluation showed the potential commercial value of the lead user concept to be very high, they were not willing to present it to a random sample of ordinary users for evaluation but instead decided to simply test the lead user product concept on a sample of 12 "routine" users.

The companies selected for this "routine user" sample were drawn from the sample of 74 interviewed companies. The selection criteria were that the telephone interview data showed them *not* to be lead users, and also that they must have had a long, close relationship with Hilti. (The latter requirement was added because the company wished to have confidence that these users would be willing to honor a request to keep the details of the new system secret.) The interviewees selected were buyers as well as users. They had the dominant role in the purchasing decisions of their own companies with respect to pipe hangers.

The 12 user–evaluators were asked to review the proposed pipe-hanger system in detail, noting particular strengths and weaknesses. Their response was very positive. Ten of the 12 preferred the lead user product concept over existing, commercially available solutions. All except one of the ten expressed willingness to buy such a pipe-hanger system when it became available, and estimated that they would be willing to pay a 20 percent higher price for it relative to existing systems.

Comparison of Lead User Method with Method Ordinarily Used by Hilti

The case study was, as reported above, very successful. Interestingly, Hilti personnel informally judged that the lead user method, beginning with a technological trend identification and ending with a novel product concept, was significantly faster and cheaper than the more conventional marketing research methods they normally used. Unfortunately, data needed to test this judgment carefully did not exist in the firm. However, it was possible to compare the time and costs expended in

TABLE 2
Anecdotal Time and Cost Comparison Between Two Product Concept Generation Efforts at Hilti

Concept Generation Method Employed	Time and Cost Expenditure for Concept Generation, Evaluation, and Acceptance by Hilti	
Lead user method	9	$ 51,000
Conventional method	16	$100,000

this first lead user study by Hilti with the time and costs expended on a project that they had recently conducted, and judged to be of very similar scope and complexity (Table 2).

The process Hilti conventionally used took a total (elapsed time) of 16 months from start to final agreement on the specifications of the product to be developed, and cost $100,000. The work began with marketing personnel collecting and evaluating data on needs and problems from customers (5 months; $56,000); then marketing explained to engineering what it had found, and these two groups jointly developed tentative product specifications (2 months; $5,000). Next, engineering went off on its own to develop technical approaches to meeting the agreed-upon specifications (4 months; $23,000). Then, engineering got together with marketing to evaluate and adjust these (3 months; $10,000). Finally, both engineering and marketing wrote up a formal product specification and submitted it to management for formal approval (2 months; $5,000).

In contrast, the lead user method took a total (elapsed time) of 9 months and cost $51,000 from the start of work to final agreement on the specifications of the product to be developed. In this instance, the major steps were all conducted by a project group headed by the manager of the pipe-hanger product line. The group membership consisted of two development engineers and two market specialists. One of the latter was responsible for pipe hangers specifically, and one was a market

research methods expert from Hilti's central market research group. The steps carried out by this group (and described in detail earlier in the article) were survey of experts (2 months; $9,000); telephone survey (2 weeks; $8,000); Lead User Workshop (3 days; $24,000); internal evaluation of lead user concept (3 months; $4,000); concept test on routine user group (2 months; $4,000); writing of formal product specification submission to management for formal approval (2 months; $2,400).

In sum, the lead user method consumed only 56 percent of the time used for the project put forward by Hilti as comparable. In our estimation and that of Hilti personnel, the reason for the time saving appeared to lie mainly in the systematic, parallel involvement of engineers, marketing people, and highly qualified users, as opposed to the serial involvement of these groups used in the earlier method. Because of this, time-consuming feedback loops or reconsiderations, often produced by misinterpretations or information-filtering in the serial method, were avoided.

The cost of the lead user process also was found to be significantly lower than market research methods previously used by Hilti (approximately 50 percent). An informal evaluation of the reasons for this, conducted by Hilti personnel, suggests that the cost saving had two principal causes. First, the costs for customer surveys were smaller in the lead user method (in the lead user project, only 12 selected users were involved in joint, face-to-face discussions; in the conventional project, approximately 130 interviews with a randomly selected group of users, each involving face-to-face visits by manufacturer personnel, were carried out in three different countries). Second, the solutions provided by the lead user group required less work on the part of Hilti technical departments than did the ideas provided by marketing researchers in the conventional method (in the lead user project, people from Hilti's technical departments had direct user contact and had been involved in concept development from the start; they therefore had richer data regarding user needs in the lead user project than they did in the conventional project).

Discussion

In this case study, the lead user method worked well in a relatively "low-tech" product category whose users were not characterized by advanced technical training. A significant fraction of all users sampled was found to have lead user characteristics. A group selected from among these proved very effective in working with company personnel on new product concept development. They did in fact develop a new system judged to be very valuable by both the manufacturer and a group of nonlead users. Also and importantly, study participants found participation to be both useful and enjoyable. Bailetti and Guild [1] report on a study that explicitly measured the responses of design engineers to visits with lead users. They also found that participants judged this experience to be very valuable.

An additional, unanticipated result of the lead user method was an observed improvement of teamwork within Hilti, manifested in a significant improvement in the level of cooperation between the technical and marketing groups in the company. One reason for this was apparently that the teamwork built into the lead user method had a carry-over effect. Also, as product and performance requirements of innovative users were immediately translated into language meaningful to *both* engineers and marketing people, a shared language was created that made further cooperation easier.

Although the lead user method worked well in this case study, the reader should note that it is still a very new method. Details of method application will appropriately differ from study to study—and we are all still learning.

References

1. Bailetti, Antonio J. and Guild, Paul D. Designers' impressions of direct contact between product designers and champions of innovation. *Journal of Product Innovation Management* 8(2): 91–103 (June 1991).

2. Mansfield, Edwin, *Industrial Research and Technological Innovation: An Econometric Analysis,* New York, NY: W.W. Norton & Company, 1968.

3. Urban, G. and von Hippel, E. Lead user analyses for the development of new industrial products, *Management Science* 34(5): 569–582 (May 1988).

4. von Hippel, E. Lead users: A source of novel product concepts, *Management Science* 32(7): 791–805 (July 1986).

5. von Hippel, Eric, *The Sources of Innovation,* New York, NY: Oxford University Press, 1988.

Related Readings

Biegel, U. *Kooperation zwischen Anwender und Hersteller im Forschungs- und Entwicklungsbereich,* Frankfurt/New York/Paris: 1987.

Foxall, G. User initiated product innovations, *Industrial Marketing Management* 18(2): 95–104 (May 1989).

Gemünden, H.G. *Investitionsguetermarketing, Interaktionsbeziehungen zwischen Hersteller und Verwender Innovativer Investitionsgueter,* Tübingen, 1981.

Geschka, H. Erkenntnisse der Innovationsforschung—Konsequenzen für die Praxis, *VD-Berichte* 724, Neue Produkte-Anstösse, Wege, Realisierte Strategien, Dusseldorf 1989.

Shaw, B. The role of the interaction between the user and the manufacturer in medical equipment innovation. *R&D Management* 15(4): 283–92 (October 1985).

Voss, C. The role of users in the development of applications software, *Journal of Product Innovation Management* 2(2): 113–21 (June 1985).

Chapter 8

Pricing for Business Markets

F ew marketing decisions have the apparent simplicity of the pricing decision. This simplicity is suggested by the fact that, in sharp contrast with other marketing decisions, the pricing decision can be made quickly, can be implemented almost immediately, and is viewed by many as no more than a matter of marking up an easily determined cost by some "fair" amount. Reality is that the pricing decision is one of the most complex decisions facing the marketer. More than any other marketing decision it has an almost immediate impact on sales volume and revenues, and thus on profits, often in unexpected ways. Because the price a customer pays reflects the customer's perception of the value of the product or service, all other marketing decisions come together in the pricing decision. That is, the price at which the firm elects to offer its good or service should represent the firm's belief as to the value of its offering to a particular target market and should, therefore, take into account all the benefits the customer may receive, including both tangible and intangible aspects of the product offering, how the product is made available, any value added by the sales force and, importantly, its appraisal of competitive offerings. Finally, to the extent that costs influence the firm's price, they seldom are easily determined and it is not at all clear what might be a fair markup.

In this chapter we review the considerations involved in making the pricing decision in business markets and in developing and implementing pricing policies.

The Economist's View of Price

Because most economics textbooks deal extensively with price, we feel it is useful to differentiate the views of economists and marketers on the subject. For the economist, price plays a major role in allocating resources among a host of competing uses. Economic theory, therefore, is concerned with how the price system operates in order to allocate resources and combine them to produce some optimum level and composition of output. In studying the pricing system, a principal objective is to answer questions such as "what determines the price of various commodities?" Implicit in such studies is the imperative to make simplifying assumptions about demand curves, marginal cost curves, and marginal revenue curves.

As a general observation, economic theory has been most successful at considering the question of price determination in markets where so-called perfect competition exists (i.e., markets where there are large numbers of buyers and sellers and products are essentially identical) or where monopoly exists. In markets characterized by this perfect competition we see the determination of price as the intersection of the familiar upward-sloping supply curve with the equally familiar downward-sloping demand curve. In markets characterized as monopolistic, with only one supplier, we see the determination of a profit maximizing price, associated with the quantity at the intersection of a firm's marginal cost and marginal revenue curves. In either case there is the notion that the demand curve, the marginal cost curve, and the marginal revenue curves are well known and that there is one right or optimum price for the conditions specified. This is seldom the case for marketing decision making.

Economic theory has been far less successful in considering the question of price determination in oligopolistic markets, characterized by a relatively small number of competitors who are keenly aware of each other and constantly strive to differentiate themselves through such things as product features, superior service, or personal relationships, and a relatively small number of customers who vigorously negotiate with suppliers or otherwise design their

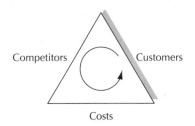

FIGURE 8.1
The Opportunity Range for Pricing Decisions

purchasing policies to achieve the best possible price. With few exceptions, theories such as the Chamberlin Model, the Kinked Demand Curve, and Game Theory have either been discredited or severely limited by their restrictive assumptions.[1] However, it is in these oligopolistic markets that the vast majority of firms strive for customer patronage, competitive advantage, and market share. Business marketers, therefore, have to look beyond economic theories in the pricing decision process.

The Marketer's View of Price

In sharp contrast to the notion of price as a fixed point, as conveyed by the intersection of supply and demand curves or marginal cost and marginal revenue curves, marketers see price as falling in an opportunity range—a range bounded by the three Cs of the firm's *costs, customers'* perception of value, and *competitors'* prices for similar goods or services, as depicted in Figure 8.1. In some instances the range may be large, affording the marketer considerable flexibility in price determination, as is the case for new products or those extensively differentiated from competitive offerings. In others there is little flexibility, as might be the case for mature products or those with little differentiation from competitive offerings. Even in these instances, however, the opportunity may exist to select market segments that allow a greater degree of pricing freedom.

The extent to which each of the three Cs influence the pricing decision also varies. For mature products, competitors' prices may be the predominant influence on price, and pricing decisions may be made in competitive terms such as premium, meet the competitive levels, or price below them. For new products, in the introductory stage of the PLC, intrinsic customer value and the expected future behavior of costs may be the predominant influences on price.

Beyond the three Cs, most marketers must also make their pricing decisions in the context of the firm's overall objectives for pricing policy. In the final analysis, of course, the objective of the firm is to produce a profit. Profit objectives, however, may be given to the marketer in a variety of ways. In some firms they may be stated in terms of return on investment or return on sales. In others they may be stated in terms of expected gross margin or profit contribution after marketing expense. Almost always there are other objectives such as attainment or maintenance of market share, avoidance of government antitrust actions, minimization of cannibalization of other goods or services, deterring competitive attacks, or leading the way into new markets.

In the following sections we first discuss the three Cs and then consider a number of other pricing considerations associated with pricing decisions and pricing objectives.

The Firm's Costs

Costs are clearly a major consideration in the pricing decision. While few firms rely solely on a cost-based approach to pricing, their costs are a major determinant of profit and set a finite lower bound for the pricing decision. It is important to distinguish among fixed, semifixed, and variable costs. Fixed costs do not vary as a function of volume produced. They include such items as physical plant and equipment, long-term leases, or interest on long-term debt. Semifixed costs do not vary as a function of volume produced but can be changed in the short term by management decision. They include such items as salaries of the sales force or other general administrative expenses, R&D expenses, or advertising commitments. Variable costs vary directly with the number of units produced. They include such items as raw materials, direct manufacturing labor, freight, and salespersons' commissions.

For pricing decisions there are a number of key aspects of cost that need to be taken into account. First, few firms make an investment in fixed costs that cannot be recovered in an appropriate time period. Breaking even is a must, but few firms are interested in simply breaking even. The price, therefore, must not only cover variable costs but must also result in sufficient volume so that the total contribution (revenue minus variable costs) covers all fixed costs and returns some desired level of contribution to profit, R&D, or investment in other opportunities. Second, even fewer firms price below variable costs. Hence, a firm's variable costs become a floor for the pricing decision. Third, it is important to recognize that the term *total cost* take on meaning only for a specific volume.

These relationships can be seen in a variation of the familiar break-even chart, as shown in Figure 8.2. A key concept is per unit contribution, or the difference between per unit revenue and per unit variable cost. Break-even volume, where revenue equals total cost (Q1), is calculated by dividing fixed costs by the per unit contribution. In this illustration, we show the situation where the desired profit contribution is constant, as might be the case with a target ROI. Here the required volume is where revenues equal total cost plus desired contribution (Q2). While most firms avoid pricing at a level that falls below what are considered total costs, there may be occasions when such a price will make a positive contribution toward fixed costs, even though they are not fully covered.

The relation of fixed to variable costs is a critical aspect of pricing. In high fixed cost industries (e.g., the chemical or paper industries), high contribution margins are necessary to cover fixed costs. In times of economic slowdown, when the level of fixed manufacturing capacity substantially exceeds industry demand, pressures to secure orders that provide at least some contribution margin frequently lead to price wars with large reductions in price that still do not fall below variable costs. In low fixed cost industries (e.g., most service industries, where personnel are the major element of cost), firms feel less pressure to secure orders at any cost and are more likely to respond to an economic slowdown through reductions in personnel or other variable costs.

For most firms, variable costs are not just a function of economies of scale but also can be expected to decline as the firm gains production experience. For some firms this experience curve effect is sufficiently large as to become the key determinant of pricing policy. In the semiconductor industry,

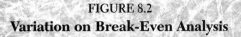

FIGURE 8.2
Variation on Break-Even Analysis

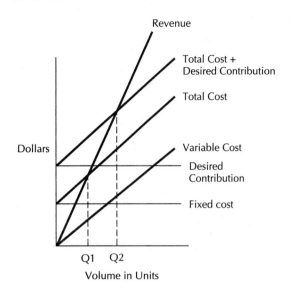

Q1 = Break-Even Volume = Fixed Cost/Contribution Margin
Q2 = Desired Contribution Volume = (Fixed Cost + Desired Contribution)/Contribution Margin

for instance, where experience curve effects as large as 25 percent (i.e., variable costs decline 25 percent for every doubling of cumulative volume) have been observed, industry observers have noted that Texas Instruments has introduced products at low prices associated with expected lower future costs that will result from the sales volume stimulated by the low price. This variation of a penetration strategy, which we discuss later in more detail, not only stimulates demand for its products but allows the firm to establish a preemptive high-share market position. Many Japanese firms employ a further variation of this approach by estimating a target price that will produce the desired volume and then working backwards to produce the product at a cost that will give an acceptable contribution.

Finally, we should note the impact of accounting practices on costs, particularly with respect to depreciation, inventory valuation, and fixed asset valuation. Where fixed costs include a depreciation component, accelerated depreciation schedules show higher costs. Firms that account for inventory using LIFO accounting (last-in, first-out) show higher variable costs than those using FIFO accounting (first-in, first-out). In some instances, firms require their businesses to value assets on a replacement cost basis rather than on an historical cost basis, resulting in higher depreciation charges and so higher fixed costs. As a result, the firm that bases its pricing decisions on these more conservative accounting practices may make its pricing decisions very differently from the less conservative firm.

The Firm's Customers

Perhaps the most salient aspect of pricing for business marketers is that customers are not passive entities in the exchange process. Rather, they are professionals who carefully analyze a firm's offerings in terms of their value, both intrinsically and relative to competitive offerings, consider the possibility of make or buy, and develop strategies designed to maximize value received by purchasing at the lowest possible price. Nevertheless, buying firms vary enormously with respect to their emphasis on price as a determinant of the purchasing decision.

This variation in emphasis on price comes in two ways. First is the variation in emphasis on price per se. Some firms indicate their objective is to receive a "fair" price as viewed by both buyer and seller. In the case of multiple sourcing, such firms typically solicit quotations or bids from suppliers and rely on the quotation or bid process to ensure fairness. Where sole sourcing is used, as might be the case where JIT is involved, buyers frequently require the supplier to provide cost information to justify a particular price and "fair" can become a matter for considerable debate, both with respect to cost calculations and profit margins. Other firms set aside any notion of fairness and work aggressively to extract the lowest possible price from a supplier. Typically such firms engage in extensive negotiation, frequently in connection with the bidding or quotation process, and do not hesitate to use their buying power or superior negotiating skill to their advantage. Still others, albeit in relatively small numbers, may be content to accept a supplier's price, even though it offers the supplier relatively more benefit than the buyer.

Second, firms vary in their view of required features or functionality. DuPont, for instance, has recognized this variation by offering a certain chemical at both a standard level and a premium level, where the latter includes several added benefits such as fewer impurities, quicker delivery, and high levels of customer support, for which DuPont charges a premium of 5 percent over the standard level.[2]

The Firm's Competitors

The pricing decision must take into account the presence of existing competitors or, in the case of new products, the existence of potential competitors. For the mature product, with existing competitors, the firm's pricing flexibility will depend on the extent to which customers perceive differences between competitive offerings. Combined with customers' concerns with price, this degree of pricing flexibility can be depicted as shown in Figure 8.3.

FIGURE 8.3
Pricing Flexibility in Competitive Markets

Customer Concern with Price

		Low	Medium	High
Relationship of Competitive Offers	Great Difference	Great	Substantial	Some
	Modest Difference	Substantial	Some	Little
	Indentical	None	None	None

Given significant competitive advantage and large numbers of customers not greatly concerned with price, the firm may elect a premium pricing strategy. Critical to the execution of such a strategy is the ability of the sales force to concentrate on the right customers and to communicate the inherent extra value in the firm's offering to its customers. Inevitably, however, there will be instances where customers become more price sensitive, where the sales force calls on price-sensitive customers or is unable to convince customers of extra value, or where additional volume may be sufficiently attractive as to require consideration of pricing at or below competitive levels. In such instances the firm may have to abandon its premium pricing policy or segment the market based on price sensitivity.

The presence of existing competitors, all with at least some knowledge of the actions of others, raises further issues. In an oligopolistic industry, for instance, how are overall price levels established, increased, or decreased? In many industries we find price leaders; that is, firms that by virtue of size, reputation, or past practice play a major role in determining the overall level of prices in the industry. In some instances, the price leader may take the lead in initiating price changes that are then widely followed by others in the industry. More frequently, and particularly with respect to price reductions, the initiative to change prices is taken by smaller firms, but it is the action by the price leader that legitimizes the new price level. The dynamics by which such moves occur are complex. In times of increased demand the opportunity may exist to increase industry prices, but some firms may elect to forgo price increases in an attempt to increase share. Similarly, in times of increasing costs the pressure may exist to pass cost increases on to customers, but, again, some firms may elect, instead, to forgo price increases in order to increase share. The role of the price leader, therefore, is not an easy one. Leading the way in raising prices may expose the leader to significant loss of market share. Leading the way in lowering prices results in loss of revenue and, if competitors quickly follow, will not result in an increase in market share. Despite these difficulties, oligopolistic industries tend to look for price leaders, recognizing the need for some kind of stabilizing force with respect to price levels.

For many firms, a key issue concerns the appropriate response to a competitor's move to make inroads on the firm's position with a valued customer, usually by offering a lower price. One policy is to match the competitor's offer. In many instances, however, the special offer may be conditional on not revealing its terms, or the opportunity to match it may not be available. A large European manufacturer of packaging materials, therefore, had a policy of responding to an attack on its positions by quickly making an extremely low price offer to a key customer of the competitor. The competitor could match the price offer, at a significant loss, or lose a significant amount of business, in either case experiencing some loss of profit. The firm's expectation, of course, was that knowledge of past retaliation would dissuade competitors from future attacks on the firm's positions.

Pricing Situations

Firms face two very different situations when making pricing decisions. First is the situation where a new product is being introduced, and second is the situation with respect to an existing product.

New Product Pricing

As we discussed in Chapter 7, the term *new product* has many meanings. It can mean products new to the world, products new to the firm, or products that are essentially just minor improvements over previous offerings. In this section we focus on products either new to the world or sufficiently different from existing products as to permit substantial flexibility in pricing.

The opportunity range for most new products is large. Its upper bound is the maximum price that at least some customers will pay, based on the product's value to them. The lower bound is normally close to variable costs. Cumberland Metals, for instance, when it introduced its curled metal pad for use in pile driving machines, felt the upper bound of its opportunity range might have been in excess of $1,000 and the lower bound as low as $50. Pricing at the high end of the opportunity range is known as skimming and attempts to maximize the per unit contribution. Skimming is often followed by "sliding down the demand curve," in which the product is introduced at a high price, but the price is gradually reduced after customers for whom the product has the highest value have bought. The personal computer industry is a classic example of using this skimming/sliding approach. Pricing at the low end is known as penetration pricing and attempts to maximize unit volume and to establish a pre-emptive market position.

Factors favoring one approach versus the other are shown in Table 8.1. The skimming approach is particularly appropriate where market demand con-

TABLE 8.1
Factors Influencing New Product Pricing

Skimming	Penetrating
Inelastic demand	Elastic demand
Uncertain demand	Experience curve effect
Strong patents	Economies of scale
Need for promotional dollars	Large capacity increments
Limited capacity	Ease of copying
Small capacity increments	No "elite" segment
Proprietary manufacturing	
New to the world products	
Few substitute products	
Price/quality inference	

ditions are uncertain or unknown, where strong patent positions or other factors would inhibit competitor responses, and where requirements for extensive promotion require high contribution margins. The rapidity with which one may slide down the demand curve is influenced by a number of factors, particularly customer demand and competitive response. The penetration approach is particularly appropriate where it is expected that low prices will result in high levels of demand, where the experience curve effect can be expected to result in dramatic cost reduction as volume increases, and where it is felt that a low price may deter competitors from entering the market or at least allow the firm to establish a leadership position with respect to market share and, hence, establish a favorable cost position.

Pricing Existing Products

Pricing existing products must take into account not only customer demand but also the competitive situation. This involves two considerations. First, how does the firm wish to position itself versus its competitors? It has three fundamental choices. It can elect to price at a premium over competitors, at the competitive level, or below competitors. As shown in Figure 8.3, premium pricing is a function of both customers' concerns with price and the firm's degree of competitive advantage. As we discuss in the Value/Quality/Price section, the firm also needs to consider the profitability of pricing above, at, or below its competitors and the customers' perception of its relative quality. In some instances, it may be more profitable for the firm to pursue a competitive price strategy, even when it has a competitive advantage.

The second consideration relates to how industry price levels and policies are established. As we have previously discussed, in many industries price levels

FIGURE 8.4
Leader and Follower Pricing Strategies
in Concentrated Industries

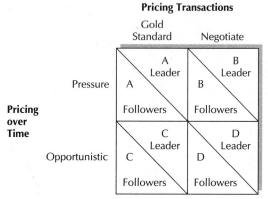

Only AA and DD (and rarely BB) have long term feasibility.

Source: Modified from Ralph G.M. Sultan, *Pricing in the Electrical Oligopoly*, Vol. 1 (Boston: Harvard University Press, 1974), 329 and 333.

and policies are established or significantly influenced by a price leader. According to Sultan, based on his monumental study of pricing in the electrical products industry, the price leader has the option of choosing a pricing strategy that can also be imposed on the leader's competitors.[3] Two considerations dictate the choice: (1) the pattern of pricing over time, as conditions of supply and demand fluctuate and (2) the pricing of individual transactions.

Over time the leader may choose pressure pricing and resist the psychological forces that permit a rapid upward movement in market prices during a period of surging demand or tight supply. In short, the leader holds the lid on any short-term price increases, thus maintaining a price-cost squeeze on its competitors and discouraging entry by new competitors. Alternatively, the leader may choose opportunistic pricing and, when business conditions are good, increase prices to the limit of customer goodwill and perceived fairness. While opportunistic pricing may increase profits, at least in the short run, there is the obvious risk of entry by new competitors, more aggressive moves by existing competitors funded by their short-term profit increases, and customer ill-will with increased likelihood of future loss of patronage.

Two options exist with respect to pricing individual transactions. Gold standard pricing refers to a policy under which *all* customers are quoted the same price, regardless of the competitive situation. For many years this typified IBM's pricing policy for mainframe computers and GE's pricing policy for turbine generators. The alternative is negotiated pricing, used here to mean that prices for various transactions may be established individually, taking into account the particular competitive and customer circumstances, including the customer's desire and ability to bargain. Gold standard pricing has certain attractions. It eliminates uncertainty among competitors and customers as to what is the market price. It has a certain element of fairness in that it treats all customers alike. Negotiated pricing has its attractions as well. For the firm, it may lead to higher profits and avoids the short-term losses of market position that may be associated with gold standard pricing. Additionally, large customers may feel they should receive preferential pricing treatment, and other customers very concerned with price may prefer a situation in which they can exercise their negotiating skills.

Possible combinations of the foregoing are shown in Figure 8.4. Strategy sets are designated by letters. Strategy A involves a combination of gold standard and pressure pricing, B is a combination of negotiated and pressure pricing, and so forth. Leader and follower strategies must be considered separately. Thus, A-B would mean an adoption of gold standard pressure pricing by the leader and negotiated pressure pricing by follower firms. For both the leader and the follower the question is which, if any, combinations are viable.

As a general rule, the leader firm cannot adopt a gold standard policy unless it is followed in that policy by its major competitors. This means that, in the long run, combinations A-B, B-A, C-D, or D-C are not feasible. There are exceptions, of course. For many years the A-B combination prevailed in the mainframe computer industry with IBM taking the gold standard approach and RCA, Honeywell, GE, and other competitors taking the negotiated approach. In most industries, however, if one major competitor is pricing on a negotiated basis, all others must do so as well, as was the case for electric watt-hour meters, which moved to negotiated pricing when just one player went off the gold standard. A second general rule is that C is not feasible for the leader because a gold standard price policy is incompatible with opportunistic pricing. A third general rule is that if the leader firm imposes pressure pricing, then follower firms must also adopt the same policy. Thus strategies A-C, A-D, B-C, and B-D are typically not feasible. A fourth general rule is that if the leader adopts an opportunistic approach, then the follower firms will do likewise.

As a result, there are only three strategy combinations that have long-term viability: A-A, B-B, and D-D. In fact, these forms of price behavior are most frequently observed in oligopolies. Which form should a firm choose? Examples of B-B are rare, probably because negotiating for maximum gain tends to be inconsistent with the philosophy of withholding price increases when they are feasible. The choice would seem to be between A-A and D-D. Gold standard pressure prices are more predictable, thus simplifying long-range planning and reducing risk, with the prospect of lower marketing and other costs. For A-A to work, however, requires either the willingness of followers to forgo the temptation of occasional deviations from the policy or the willingness of the leader to take aggressive downward price action when followers do deviate from the policy, or both. In many instances the cost to the leader may appear to be excessive. As a result, and because negotiated opportunistic pricing also has its advantages, D-D appears to be the most feasible strategy in oligopolistic industries.

Demand Concepts

The familiar downward-sloping demand curve suggests that the quantity demanded will increase if price is reduced. However, a unique aspect of business markets is derived demand, reflecting the fact that organizations buy only to support their efforts to supply the wants and needs of their customers. Hence, price may influence industry demand very differently from individual customer demand.

Industry Demand

Some products or services are directly related to the quantity of the customer's product or service being produced. In such situations demand is fundamentally determined by the level of the customer's demand, and total or industry demand for the product or service may not be influenced by price. In the automotive industry, for instance, the number of mufflers bought by car manufacturers to equip new cars is determined by the number of cars the industry sells. Changes in muffler prices, which represent only a minute portion of a car price, will have no impact on total demand for mufflers. In this case the price elasticity of industry demand for mufflers will be close to zero, with little incentive for muffler producers, collectively, to seek lower price levels for mufflers. On the other hand, in the personal computer industry, memory chips are a significant proportion of the total cost of a personal computer, and price reductions, if passed on to customers, are likely to significantly influence industry demand. In this case price elasticity of demand for memory chips will be something other than zero, and producers may have a collective interest in lower price levels for their products.

In the long run, demand for capital goods is also associated with the quantity of the customer's product or service being produced. Some capital goods have the potential to materially reduce the customer's costs. In the early years of the electric utility industry, for instance, lower prices per unit of output and improved efficiency of turbine generators allowed electric utilities to reduce electrical rates, thereby stimulating demand for electricity and thus for turbine generators. In this instance, manufacturers of turbine generators had a collective interest in lower prices for their products. Today, however, turbine generators appear to have reached their optimum size, and improvements in efficiency are increasingly difficult to achieve. Their demand, therefore, is more likely to parallel that of most capital goods—driven by the business cycle, with most customers buying for expansion purposes.

The foregoing suggests the difficulty of precisely estimating industry price elasticity of demand. Assumptions, however, can be made as to whether demand is in the elastic zone, in which case an industry price increase will result in a revenue decrease, or in the inelastic zone, in which case an industry price increase will lead to a revenue increase. These assumptions play a major role in determining price levels in an industry and can significantly affect responses to competitors' price moves.

Firm Demand

Although business marketers face many situations where industry demand is price inelastic, demand at the firm level is almost always highly cross elastic, either with respect to competitors' prices or with regard to prices of substitute materials. For products or services directly associated with the quantity of the customer's product or service being produced, the price paid is closely related to the firm's profits. While the Ford Motor Company is not likely to buy more mufflers if its suppliers reduce prices, it is certainly likely to buy more from Walker than from Hayes-Albion if Walker offers a lower price. Similarly, automotive manufacturers are not likely to buy more or less steel for bumpers, regardless of price. The price of engineered plastics, however, which have many desirable features as bumper material, can significantly influence steel purchases. For the supplier of products and services, knowledge of prices at the level of individual transactions, both for directly competing products and for substitutes, becomes critically important.

In many instances purchases of capital goods are not directly associated with the level of output. Rather, they are made to maintain or improve profitability by increased efficiency or to replace obsolete or functionally inadequate equipment. In these situations the purchasing decision may be highly discretionary. In some instances price will be important as customers carefully analyze costs, benefits, and the impact of the purchase on their profitability. In others, the emphasis may be on functionality, with less importance on pricing considerations, particularly in such industries as health care where for several years cost increases could easily be passed on to the final customer.

Value/Quality/Price Relationships

A major consideration for business marketers is the relationship between features and price. If, for instance, a firm has an advantage over its competitors with respect to functionality or service, should it charge a premium price and thus obtain higher margins, or should it price at competitive or below competitive levels and, presumably, enjoy a larger market share? Using the PIMS data base, Buzzell and Gale have framed this question in terms of relative quality, relative price, and value.[4] We emphasize here that relative quality in the PIMS conceptualization reflects the customer's perceptions of a firm *relative to its competitors* on all the attributes of the product or service, other than price, that affect customer buying decisions. Relative price is simply the firm's price level, relative to its principal competitors (i.e., the largest that compete in the same served market). Value is the relationship of relative price to relative quality.

As shown in Figure 8.5, a comparable quality for price curve can be constructed. Most firms fall along the constant value curve, offering the same value in either premium, average, or economy positions. Some firms, however, wind up off the curve and fall in the no price premium for superior quality

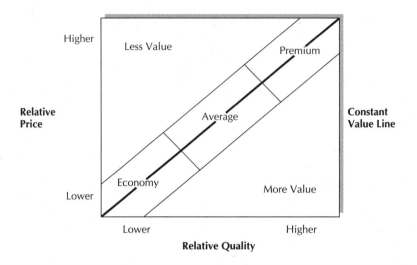

FIGURE 8.5
Value Map: Five Generic Relative
Price/Relative Quality Positions

Source: Adapted with permission of The Free Press, an imprint of Simon & Schuster from THE
PIMS PRINCIPLE: Linking Strategy to Performance by Robert D. Buzzell and Bradley T. Gale,
p. 112. Copyright © 1987 by The Free Press.

position (more value) or in the premium for less or the same quality position
(less value). According to Buzzell and Gale, offerings positioned along the
comparable value curve tend to hold share. Businesses in the premium position show, on average, the highest profitability. Somewhat surprising is that the
better value position (i.e., superior quality but no price premium) is nearly as
profitable. Apparently what is lost by not charging a premium is made up in
lower overall costs, stemming from the tendency to gain market share, and the
lower marketing costs incurred in selling a superior quality product at less
than a premium price.

Pricing the Product Line

So far we have discussed price determination as if the firm were producing a
single product. In fact, most firms offer a group of related products that may
differ in size or features or a group of products that are either substitutes or
complements. The pricing objective, therefore, is to maximize the profits for
this group of products. The basic approaches to pricing the product line are the
same as those used in pricing an individual product. Demand or value serves as
a ceiling and cost serves as a floor. A number of other factors, however, need to
be considered.

Demand Interdependence

If the products complement each other, they may sell in higher volume because they are offered together. In such instances it may be appropriate to offer one product at an attractive price to stimulate sales of the other. Loctite, for instance, needed to take this into account in pricing Bond-A-Matic®, its dispensing system for instant adhesives the firm offered, used to bond metals, plastics, rubber, and other materials in manufacturing operations.

Where products are potential substitutes for one another, prices need to be established so that demand for one product does not erode the sale of a more profitable product. DuPont, in the previously cited example, needed to consider this in establishing the price difference for its standard and premium products.

Cost Interdependence

Often costs are joint when products are produced together and marketed in a common line. A policy of setting individual product prices to reflect differences in full cost (i.e., variable costs plus an assigned allocation of fixed or joint costs) could ignore variations in competition faced or the role assigned to the product in the firm's marketing strategy. Certainly variable costs should set a floor for prices. If the product cannot support this minimum level, its contribution to the overall line is questionable. The extent to which the product is expected to contribute above variable costs needs to take into account not only competition faced and the product role but also customer demand and the profit of the overall line.

Products That Differ in Size or Capacity

Frequently the product line consists of products whose principal difference is size or capacity. An electric motor manufacturer, for instance, may offer a line of motors from 1 to 100 horsepower, or a manufacturer of disk drives may offer a line with models of several different storage capacities. What, then, should be the relationship of prices for products in the line? Two common approaches are to make them proportional to size or capacity, or to make them proportional to cost. These tend to be easy to compute and justify, but because they ignore both competitive offerings and customer demand, they are likely to miss significant profit opportunities.

Bundling

In many instances it may be advantageous for the supplier to bundle parts of the product line, either by offering a package combination at a lower price than if the components were offered separately or by tying the sale of components with little competitive advantage to those with significant advantage. The decision to bundle, or unbundle, is influenced by several factors. In some instances customers may pressure the supplier to unbundle the package because they do not want to purchase all the components in the bundle, as might be the case with training or special application assistance. In other instances tying the sale of a component with great competitive advantage to one with little advantage may by viewed negatively, not only by customers but also by regulatory authorities. The latter was the case when IBM was required by the U.S. Department of Justice to unbundle the sale of its mainframe computers and software.

Pricing When Distributors Are Involved

If the firm sells direct to its customers, it has complete control over the price at which it offers its goods or services. Where distributors or other intermediaries are involved, the price at which they offer the good or service must be taken into account in the price determination process. There are two key issues. The first is the distributor's margin, which should reflect the functions performed by the distributor. In most cases, a normal margin for a particular class of product sold to a particular industry evolves over time, reflecting industry experience and competitive practices. In the U.S. machine tool industry, for instance, margins for full service distributors range from 7.5 percent to 15 percent, depending on the product.

The second issue is the extent to which the manufacturer can control the price at which the distributor offers the good or service. In most industrialized countries, vertical price fixing (i.e., a specific agreement between manufacturer and distributor as to the price to be charged) is illegal. In theory, distributors are free to set prices at whatever level they choose, regardless of the normal margin. In practice, however, manufacturers can exert considerable influence over the distributor's price. In particular, it is usually legal for a manufacturer to indicate, if it so desires, that it expects its distributors to adhere to its suggested user prices. Distributors who do not do so may be terminated.

Price Administration

In this section we address three further considerations: (1) list versus net pricing, (2) discounts, and (3) transaction pricing.

For several reasons, manufacturers may elect to publish a schedule of prices in list and discount form rather than as net prices. Where distributors are involved, the list prices may indicate suggested user prices to be charged by distributors. The use of list prices, subject to some level of discount, facilitates price changes that can be implemented simply by changing the discount rather than by revising prices on an item-by-item basis. List prices also provide a basis for offering quantity discounts, a frequent business marketing practice. Finally, anecdotal evidence indicates that at least some purchasing agents prefer a list and discount approach, as they can report the discount as a saving achieved through aggressive purchasing practice.

Discounts are used in additional ways. As previously indicated, functional discounts to distributors reflect the level of service provided by a distributor, or the manufacturer's cost to serve a certain market. In a particular industry a limited-service distributor, providing only stocking and sales, might receive a discount of 20 percent whereas a full-service distributor, providing stocking, sales, and service, might receive a larger discount of 23 percent to 25 percent or, as frequently expressed, 20 and 5. Typically, large original equipment manufacturers receive additional discounts, perhaps another 5 percent, reflecting both functions performed and volume, frequently expressed as 20 percent, 5 percent, and 5 percent. In other instances discounts may be based strictly on volume as is the case in the steel industry where specific discounts are offered for carload quantities.

Closely related to list and discount pricing are terms of payment. While many products are offered on a net price basis, with a time stipulated for payment (e.g., terms are net 30 days), many firms offer a cash discount for prompt payment (e.g., terms are 2 percent 10 days or net 30 days). The decision as to what terms of payment schedule to offer needs to take into account industry practice as well as the firm's own situation. In the highly seasonal table radio business, for instance, speaker manufacturers frequently offer extended terms of payment to the radio manufacturers. In turn, magnet suppliers to speaker manufacturers also offer extended terms of payment. One large magnet supplier, hoping to standardize its terms of payments to all its customers, announced a change to net 30 days to speaker manufacturers. Despite an accompanying price reduction to reflect the savings associated with prompter payment, speaker manufacturers refused to accept the revised terms as alternative forms of financing were unavailable to them.

The nature of business marketing emphasizes the importance of considering the actual transaction prices at which goods and services are actually sold. As Marn and Rosiello point out, most firms are involved in hundreds or even thousands of customer- and order-specific pricing decisions daily, each of which has the potential to enhance or erode the firm's profitability.[5] They use the term "pocket price" to reflect the true price the supplier receives after taking into account trade discounts, prompt payment discounts, quantity discounts, volume bonuses, negotiated discounts, promotional support allowances, and freight. They reported ranges of pocket price bands of 70 percent for a computer peripherals supplier, 200 percent for a specialty chemicals company, and 500 percent for a fastener supplier. In some instances customers found ways to obtain quantity discounts associated with much higher than actual volumes. In others, sales representatives used pricing authority inappropriately. In still others, customers paid late but still took cash discounts. Frequently, customers perceived by management as profitable ended up at the low end of the band and those perceived as unprofitable at the high end.

Marn and Rosiello recommend that management needs to understand the price sensitivity of each element of what they call the price waterfall in setting policy and needs to carefully manage the administration of each element. In particular, the potential of the price waterfall makes the case for carefully thought out, well-understood price policies and clearly established pricing authority.

Special Issues

In this section we briefly describe a number of special pricing issues, including those associated with pricing across country borders.

Sealed Bidding

A unique aspect of business marketing is the frequent use of sealed bidding, in which buyers require formal quotations or bids, with no opportunity for subsequent negotiation. Some buyers will so completely specify the required product or service that the purchase decision can be make on the basis of price alone. More frequently, the decision is made on the basis of the "lowest and best bid," suggesting that some product or service attributes may be evaluated, either adding to or subtracting from the bid price. In the case of public procurement, the norm is for the bids to be publicly opened, affording bidders the opportunity to determine all aspects of competitive offerings. In the case of private procurement, practices vary but the norm is to reveal very little regarding competitive offerings.

In either case, price determination is challenging. A number of models have been proposed to assist in price determination, generally built around an expected value approach based on the following formula:

$$E(X) = P(X)Z(X)$$

where X = the bid price, $Z(X)$ = the profit at the bid price, $P(X)$ = the probability of an award at this price, and $E(X)$ = the expected profit of a bid. The assumption is that the price bid should be the one with the highest expected profit.

Empirical evidence indicates that such models are extremely limited in their application. In a study of the practices of general contractors, for whom sealed bidding is the norm, less than 10 percent of the respondents reported use of a statistical bidding model, payoff table, or probability model in preparing the bid.[6] This limited use reflects a number of problems in using such a model. Probability estimates are highly subjective, particularly in the absence of a long pattern of similar awards on which to base them. A number of other objectives beyond profit may influence the bid price, such as the prospect of follow-on work, maintaining a stable work force, size of the backlog, and so forth. Still further, the prices bid on one transaction may influence prices on future transactions, and bidders may use a sealed bid, particularly if publicly opened, as a way to communicate future pricing intentions.

Given this complexity, the final determination of the price to be bid or quoted will depend heavily on the experience and intuition of the manager. In appropriate circumstances, however, expected value models can assist this decision-making process.

Price Fixing

We have previously discussed the nature of price behavior and the role of the price leader in oligopolistic markets. The kind of stability suggested by firms following a price leader frequently vanishes in the face of profit pressures experienced in times of low demand and of aggressive moves by competitors to obtain orders that provide at least some contribution above variable cost. In many industries, this aggressive pricing has led to price wars, motivating managers to seek agreement with competitors on price levels or to look for other ways to eliminate price competition. In the United States such agreements violate the Sherman Antitrust Law. In the European Union, they violate Article 85 of the Treaty of Rome (the treaty that first established the European Economic Community). Additionally, most industrialized countries similarly prohibit such agreements, particularly those that prevent, restrict, or distort competition. In Germany, for instance, there is extensive anticartel legislation, administered by the Federal Cartels office, and in the United Kingdom the Competition Act of 1980 gives powers to the Director General of Fair Trading to investigate anticompetitive practices, including price fixing.

There is a fine line between the kind of stability suggested by the role of a price leader, generally followed by others in the industry, and price fixing. In the United States the Department of Justice has long been concerned with "conscious parallelism," a concept that holds that violation of the Sherman Act does not necessarily require a specific agreement to fix prices but can occur where competitors, simply by virtue of long association, have reached some common understandings about pricing that have the same effect on industry prices as overt collusion. As a result, the Department of Justice has frequently sought, and obtained, agreement on the part of firms to discontinue practices that facilitate conscious parallelism, such as price changes that all competitors in the industry make in a short period of time and in the same amounts. Announcements of aluminum price changes in the business press, for instance, were deemed to have been targeted more at competitors than at customers. The Department of Justice successfully obtained an agreement from major producers to discontinue the practice. Other actions have been more stringent. In one industry the major competitors were required to completely discontinue the use of published prices and to completely revise the basis on which prices had previously been calculated to ensure that quoted prices were arrived at independently.

The concern with price fixing, and the degree to which various activities may be illegal, varies around the world. In Switzerland, for instance, some forms of price agreements are still legal. Nevertheless, it behooves business marketers to fully understand and abide by provisions of antitrust legislation or competition policy.

Export Pricing

Pricing in export markets is subject to the same forces as in national markets, namely, customers' perception of value, prices of competitive offerings, and the firm's costs. Because at least first time exporters are less likely to have in-depth knowledge of customers and competitors, there is a tendency to rely more heavily on cost-based price determination when first entering a foreign market.

In this method, the exporter starts with the domestic manufacturing cost; adds for administration, research and development, overhead, freight forwarding, distributor margins, and profit; and denominates the transaction in the home currency or translates the cost of domestic items at the current exchange rate. If the export product has the same relative ex-factory price as a locally produced competitive product, the user price is likely to be considerably higher, particularly if the exporting country's currency is strong, thus resulting in lost sales. On the other hand, if the exporting country's currency is weak, the user price may actually be lower, resulting in lost profit opportunities.

The starting point, then, for export price calculation should be the determination of the customers' perception of value and the local competitive situation. For first time exporters there is a host of resources available to assist in such determination. In the United States, for instance, the U.S. Foreign and Commercial Service offers a wealth of useful services. With a target price established, the firm can work back through the cost chain, taking into account exchange rates, determine the level of contribution associated with foreign sales, and then evaluate the attractiveness of the opportunity.

Once prices are established, fluctuations in the rate of exchange are a matter of concern. Denominating a transaction in one's home country currency has the attractiveness of insulating the firm from the negative consequences of currency fluctuations, but at the expense of competitive position, particularly against local competitors. Caterpillar, with its dominant position in earth moving equipment and competing principally against U.S. and Japanese producers, is able to denominate its Mexican transactions in U.S. dollars. More common is denomination in local currency with some hedging of transactions or, in the case of multiproduct multinationals, a periodic calculation of worldwide transaction exposure with any hedging done at the corporate level. Finally, many firms have simply taken the position that, in the long run, profit fluctuations associated with currency fluctuations will balance out, accept this as a normal business condition, and make no provision with respect to currency fluctuation.

Transfer Pricing[7]

A transfer price is the internal price charged by a selling department, division, or subsidiary of a company for a material, component, or finished good or service that is supplied to a buying department, division, or subsidiary of the same company. Transfer pricing may be used both by firms that operate in only one national market and by firms that produce and sell their products in a number of national markets.

The need for establishing a transfer price arises principally where the buying and selling departments are SBUs, or components that are established as separate profit centers, and where the selling department also sells in external markets. The presumption, of course, is that the buying department should buy from the selling department rather than its competitors and that the selling department should sell to the buying department for a fair price, usually a market price less some credit to reflect the selling department's lower selling expense. Unfortunately, transactions between departments seldom go smoothly. The selling department frequently tends to assume the buying department is a captive customer and may not provide the same level of service as it does to external customers. At the same time, it may actually charge the buying department something above market prices, particularly when facing profit pressures. Buying departments, faced with what they feel is inappropriate treatment, may elect to do business with external suppliers, leading to strained internal relations and questions from customers. In many firms, these situations have led to the development of complex policies that recognize both the realities of the systems used to measure individual SBU performance and the firm's desire to optimize profits at the firm level. Such policies provide guidance, but the wide variety of approaches developed suggests that there is no easy solution to a very complex problem.

The problem becomes more complex when the buying and selling departments are in different countries and transfer prices need to take into account variations in tax rates between countries. From a tax standpoint, the firm would like to establish transfer prices that minimize the firm's worldwide tax liability by reporting high profits in low tax countries and vice versa. Recognizing the potential for tax avoidance of this behavior, many countries have introduced rules constraining aggressive behavior with respect to transfer prices, and there is general agreement among countries as to the need for an equitable system for profit and tax calculation. Even so, firms still have considerable leeway with respect to transfer prices that, if implemented just with respect to minimizing tax burden, has the potential to adversely affect managerial behavior. A large U.S. manufacturer, for instance, raised the transfer prices to its Swedish subsidiary to avoid the high Swedish corporate income tax rate. In doing so, it seriously penalized its Swedish country manager whose compensation depended heavily on subsidiary profits. For some firms this has led to two separate profit calculations or to rely on measures other than profit to measure managerial performance.

Dumping

The term *dumping* generally refers to the practice of selling a product in foreign markets at prices either below cost or below prices charged in the exporter's home market. The practice is attractive in situations of low demand or excess capacity in the home market because sales at low prices in foreign markets may make a positive contribution to fixed costs without running the risk of affecting prices in the home market. Dumping becomes an issue when a domestic producer claims injury because of lost sales due to the low prices of a foreign competitor.

Few issues have been more contentious with respect to trade policy between exporting nations than laws with respect to dumping. Manufacturers in all countries have vigorously sought protection against dumping. The line, however, between legitimate complaints of injury and efforts to seek protection from legitimate competitors is difficult to draw. Cost determination, as we have seen, is highly problematic. Nevertheless, most countries have antidumping laws that provide for the imposition of countervailing duties on foreign goods of firms found guilty of dumping.

Provisions with respect to dumping were one of the major issues in the recently completed Uruguay Round of the GATT (General Agreement on Tariffs and Trade), and a number of procedural and methodological changes have been included in the agreement. Complaints about country antidumping actions can be brought to the World Trade Organization (WTO), the successor to GATT. Manufacturers, however, are well advised to be familiar with the provisions of the Uruguay Round and the dumping laws in those countries in which they plan to do business.

Gray Markets[8]

Gray markets refer to circumstances in which goods bypass the normal channel of distribution and are then offered for sale below the prices offered by authorized resellers. This condition may arise in a variety of ways. Within a country, for instance, an original equipment manufacturer (OEM), to whom the manufacturer extends a large quantity discount, may overorder and then dispose of the excess goods at a small markup, resulting in a lower price than the normal price through distributors. Control Data experienced a variation of this problem with its disk drives when pseudo-OEMs emerged, purchased under the terms of an OEM agreement, and undercut the prices of distributors and other resellers. Across borders, the condition may arise when products are sold, in excess of demand, in one country at a lower price than in other countries, resulting in the surplus goods finding their way into other countries. A large pharmaceutical manufacturer, for instance, contracted through an agent in Hong Kong to sell a large quantity of a particular drug at a very attractive price to a customer in China. In this case, the order from China was fictitious and the agent in Hong Kong then offered the entire quantity at below normal prices in other countries, causing serious problems for the pharmaceutical manufacturer and its distributors.

It is unlikely that gray markets can ever be eliminated entirely. A number of steps can be taken to reduce their occurrence. Quantity discount schedules can be restructured to make overordering less attractive. Discount schedules to various classes of trade (e.g., OEMs, value added resellers (VARs), distributors) can be rationalized to more closely reflect the actual value of services performed. Sales of resellers can be monitored and discontinued to those who participate in gray markets. Warranty policies can require purchase only from authorized distributors. Perhaps most importantly, it needs to be recognized that performance measures that focus on volume or on profits from particular classes of customers versus optimizing profits across markets may induce behavior that encourages sales through gray markets.

Escalation Policies

Most transactions involving goods and services in business markets are completed in a relatively short period of time; hence, the quoted price is also the invoiced price. In many instances, however, the manufacturing cycle may be lengthy or a blanket order may cover a long period of time. In such instances there may be some provision for price adjustment, particularly in periods of inflation or where some of the supplier's costs are volatile in nature.

In situations where there is sufficient uncertainty about future costs, some manufacturers will quote prices "subject to adjustment to price in effect at time of shipment." While this protects the manufacturer against profit erosion, it shifts all the risk of cost changes to the buyer and raises questions about the nature of the supplier's price adjustment. As a result, most buyers vigorously seek to require the seller to quote firm prices, even in situations of cost uncertainty. In many industries compromise positions have developed in which the seller's price may be adjusted to reflect changes in the price of materials or labor, limited to changes in some third-party index. In the United States, for instance, it is common to use indexes calculated by the Bureau of Labor Statistics. Although these indexes may not reflect a particular manufacturer's cost changes, their impartiality and the fact that they may go down as well as up have given them some degree of acceptability.

Summary

The complexity of pricing decisions and the inherent uncertainty of their impact may lead some firms to avoid the kind of comprehensive analysis suggested in this chapter. However, the inherent potential for profit improvement in well-managed pricing practices, where as little as 1 percent improvement in price can result in as much as 10 percent improvement in operating profit, suggests the importance of such analysis.

Pricing decisions and price policies must take into account not only the firm's costs but also customer sensitivity to price and the competitive situation. Pricing situations vary enormously, but the first distinction to be made must be between new and existing products. For business marketers the concept of derived demand is of critical importance, influencing as it does both industry and firm demand. International pricing involves many of the fundamentals of domestic pricing but must also take into account issues of dumping, transfer prices, and fluctuation in exchange rates.

In sharp contrast to the notion of a "right" price that can be calculated as the intersection of a supply and a demand curve, we emphasize the importance of considering the pricing decision in the context of an opportunity range in which all but a few situations present the firm with a wide array of options. Consideration of these options should take into account not just the firm's external situation but also its objectives and the price relationship of products that make up a product line.

Good analysis is not enough, however. It must be accompanied by formulation of policies that are clearly communicated to those responsible for their implementation and managed to ensure that the policies are appropriately executed.

Overview of Chapter Cases

✻ The Cumberland Metals case describes the situation of a manufacturer whose new design of a cushioning pad for a pile driver provided tremendous cost savings over the traditional asbestos pad. Because of the low manufacturing cost of the new pad, Cumberland appeared to have an extraordinarily large opportunity range for pricing. The case provides the opportunity to consider what price Cumberland should actually quote.

✻ The Alias Research case describes the situation of a Canadian software producer faced with serious price competition in the California market, which Alias had targeted for penetration. The case provides the opportunity to consider whether or not to change its rigid pricing policy.

✻ The Texas Instruments: Global Pricing in the Semiconductor Industry case describes the pressure the firm was experiencing to move toward one world price rather than pricing at different levels in different markets. The case provides the opportunity to consider and evaluate the firm's options.

Endnotes

1. For a comprehensive treatment of the realities of oligopolistic pricing, see Ralph G.M. Sultan, *Pricing in the Electrical Oligopoly: Competition or Collusion*, Vol. 1 and 2 (Boston: Harvard University Press, 1974).

2. Philip Kotler, *Marketing Management: Analysis, Planning, Implementation and Control* 8th ed. (Englewood Cliffs, NJ: Prentice Hall, Inc., 1994) 501.

3. Philip Kotler, *Marketing Management: Analysis, Planning, Implementation and Control* 8th ed. (Englewood Cliffs, NJ: Prentice Hall, Inc., 1994) 501.

4. Robert D. Buzzell and Bradley T. Gale, *The PIMS Principles: Linking Strategy to Performance* (New York: The Free Press, 1987).

5. Michael V. Marn and Robert L. Rosiello, "Managing Price, Gaining Profit," *Harvard Business Review,* September–October 1992, 84–94.

6. Paul D. Boughton, "The Competitive Bidding Process: Beyond Probability Models," *Industrial Marketing Management,* Vol. 16, No. 2 (May 1987): 87–94.

7. For a short but comprehensive treatment of this subject, see Clive R. Emmanuel and Messaoud Hehafdi, *Transfer Pricing* (London: Academic Press, 1994).

8. For an excellent discussion of the gray market dilemma, see Frank V. Cespedes, E. Raymond Corey, and V. Kasturi Rangan, "Gray Markets: Causes and Cures," *Harvard Business Review,* July–August 1988, 75–82.

Michael H. Morris
Roger J. Calantone

Four Components of Effective Pricing

Industrial firms tend to manage prices in a fairly reactive and piecemeal fashion, with a heavy reliance on formula-based methods. This article introduces the concept of a strategic pricing program (SPP) to price determination. The program consists of four components: price objectives, strategy, structure, and levels. Each component is explained, relationships among them are established, and the program then is linked to corporate strategy. ✳

Introduction

Faced with stagnating sales growth, DEC decided to temporarily reduce the price of its VT 220 terminal by 27 percent. Such a move might seem commonplace in today's competitive environment, yet, pricing decisions such as this often are made arbitrarily and prove to be costly mistakes in the marketplace. Management may discover much later that the firm is sacrificing margins unnecessarily, alienating middlemen, confusing customers, and inviting aggressive responses from competitors.

Mistakes like these occur because management has no specific purpose in mind when reducing price, other than increasing sales. To better understand the problem, consider some of the potential underlying reasons for a price cut:

- An attempt to attract new users to the market.
- An effort to increase usage rates among existing customers.
- A method of taking customers away from competitors.

- A means of discouraging current customers from switching to competitors.
- An approach for encouraging customers to purchase now instead of later.
- A technique for discriminating among different types of buyers.
- A means of using the low price of one product to help sell other products in the line.

Each of these reasons represents an entirely different rationale for the pricing action. That is, the same price cut could be used for a number of distinct purposes.

To be effective, individual pricing moves should be part of a larger program of action. Management must identify a specific purpose for the price change, together with measurable goals for evaluating the effectiveness of the change. Otherwise, a company is, in effect, blindly taking a chance that a particular move is appropriate. This explains why managers are so frequently unsure as to whether or not they have made the correct pricing decision.[1]

The purpose of this article is to introduce the concept of a strategic pricing program (SPP) to those involved with industrial marketing. The components of this program are examined and then linked together. Relationships between the SPP and the industrial firm's marketing strategy are

At the time this article was written, Michael H. Morris, Ph.D., was an Associate Professor of Marketing at the University of Central Florida, Orlando, Florida. Roger J. Calantone, Ph.D., was Professor of Marketing at the University of Kentucky, Lexington, Kentucky. Reprinted by permission of the publisher from *Industrial Marketing Management* 19. 321–329 (1990) © Elsevier Science Inc., 1990.

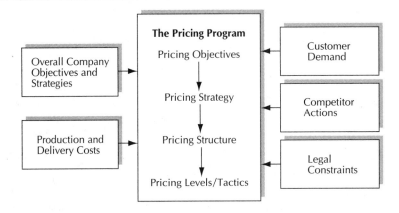

FIGURE 1

Company Pricing Program and Its Determinants

explored. Underlying determinants of the program are then discussed, and suggestions drawn for further research.

Strategic Pricing Program

The program of action that should guide pricing has four key components: objectives, strategy, structure, and levels (tactics). Each logically follows from the preceding component, as suggested in Figure 1. Of the four, the most important is objectives.

1. Role of Price Objectives

There is no one best price to charge for a given product. Once the need to set or change a price has been recognized, the manager must determine what he or she is trying to accomplish with this particular price. The answer might seem obvious: sell more products or services. However, this response is too general, and may not even be the case. In fact, companies can have a number of different pricing objectives.

Table 1 provides examples of some of these objectives. The ones cited are not mutually exclusive, and some could be used in combination. For instance, using price to accomplish a particular image, such as that of premier quality provider,

may also serve to maximize long-run profitability. On the other hand, certain of these objectives conflict with one another. An emphasis on long-term profits may come at the expense of short-term profits, and vice versa. Similarly, charging low prices to discourage market entry may serve to irritate middlemen or detract from the desired image of the firm. For example, although traditionally regarding itself as high quality, AT&T cut the prices of its PCs by up to 38 percent during the spring of 1987. This caused distributors to drop the line (low margins) and large corporate buyers to fear the technology was outmoded and to question the AT&T image.

Objectives should be measurable, which generally means they must be quantifiable. Otherwise, it becomes difficult to determine how well they are being accomplished, and whether or not the pricing program is working. In some cases, this is straightforward, such as with an objective of "increasing market share by two percentage points," or "increasing annual profitability by 3 percent." Others are more difficult to measure, such as "maintain middleman loyalty" or "be regarded as fair." Here, primary research may be necessary, such as surveys of middlemen or customers before and after the pricing action.

TABLE 1
Examples of 21 Pricing Objectives

1. Target rate of return on investment
2. Desired share of the market
3. Maximize long-term profit
4. Maximize short-term profit
5. Sales growth
6. Stabilize the market
7. Convey a particular image
8. Desensitize customers to price
9. Be the price leader
10. Discourage entry by new competitors
11. Speed exit of marginal competitors
12. Avoid government investigation and control
13. Maintain loyalty and sales support of middlemen
14. Avoid excessive demands from suppliers
15. Be regarded as fair by customers
16. Create interest and excitement for the item
17. Use price of one product to sell other products in line
18. Discourage others from lowering prices
19. Recover investment in product development quickly
20. Encourage quick payment of accounts receivable
21. Generate volume so as to drive down costs

Source: Adapted from Oxenfeldt, A. R., A Decision-Making Structure for Price Decisions, *Journal of Marketing* **37**, 50 (1973).

2. Establishing a Strategy

If objectives are the performance levels the manager wishes to achieve, then strategies represent comprehensive statements regarding how price will be used to accomplish the objectives. A pricing strategy provides a theme that guides all of the firm's pricing decisions for a particular product line and a particular period. Thus, it serves to coordinate all of the pricing activities related to the product line. By definition, the strategy adopts a longer-term time horizon, usually from 6 months to 2 years, and is flexible or adaptable to changing environmental conditions. To illustrate, the FMC fire apparatus division uses a pricing strategy that

can be characterized as premium pricing for its fire trucks. High prices and margins are charged, with relatively lower volume expectations. The central theme is excellence. Price is used to reflect the highest quality levels, and the firm is careful not to compromise its image with overly aggressive price deals or discounts.

Pricing strategies will generally fall into one of two groups: cost-based and market-based. Cost-based strategies usually rely on a formula in which costs are fully allocated to units of production, and a mark-up or rate of return is added to this total. Market-based approaches tend to focus either on the competition, customer demand, or both. Table 2 provides examples of specific pricing strategies.

Of these two groups, cost-based approaches are much more prevalent among industrial firms than are market approaches [2, 3]. This tendency is one of the great ironies of business, and reflects a general level of naiveté among managers responsible for pricing decisions. Price must be a reflection of value. It is a statement of what the customer is willing to pay. Value and customer willingness to pay are market-based considerations. Costs, alternatively, are frequently unrelated to the amount customers are willing to pay. They are primarily an indicator of company efficiency.

The popularity of cost-based strategies reflects the fact that they are easy to implement and manage. In addition, setting a price that covers costs and generates a fixed profit margin makes intuitive sense to the typical manager. Unfortunately, this price is often too high or low given current market conditions.

The actual strategy chosen should be based on a careful evaluation of a number of key factors, both internal and external to the company. These will be described later. The underlying philosophy, however, must be that every pricing consideration is examined from a customer perspective. The perceptions of customers represent the ultimate reality defining company success, mediocrity, or failure.

3. Developing a Structure

Once a pricing strategy has been selected, its implementation becomes the main concern. Imple-

TABLE 2
Types of Pricing Strategies

Cost-Based Strategies

a. Markup pricing—variable and fixed costs per unit are estimated, and a standard mark-up is added. The mark-up is frequently either a percentage of sales or of costs.

b. Target return pricing—variable and fixed costs per unit are estimated. A rate of return is then taken times the amount of capital invested in the product, and the result is divided by estimated sales. The resulting return per unit is added to unit costs to arrive at price.

Market-Based Strategies

c. Floor pricing—charging a price that just covers costs, usually in order to maintain a presence in the market given the competitive environment.

d. Penetration pricing—charging a price that is low relative to (a) the average price of major competitors, and (b) what customers are accustomed to paying.

e. Parity-pricing (going rate)—charging a price that is roughly equivalent to the average price charged by the major competition.

f. Premium pricing (skimming)—the price charged is intended to be high relative to (a) the average price of major competitors, and (b) what customers are accustomed to paying.

g. Price leadership pricing—usually involves a leading firm in the industry making fairly conservative price moves, which are subsequently followed by other firms in the industry. This limits price wars and leads to fairly stable market shares.

h. Stay out pricing—the firm prices lower than demand conditions require, so as to discourage market entry by new competitors.

i. Bundle pricing—a set of products or services are combined and a single lower price is charged for the bundle than if each item were sold separately.

j. Value-based pricing (differentials)—different prices are set for different market segments based on the value each segment receives from the product or service.

k. Cross-benefit pricing—prices are established so as to maximize profitability on an entire line of products or services, rather than on individual items. This sometimes involves loss leaders, products sold at little or no profit to help sell other items in the line.

---

mentation of a strategy requires that the manager develop a pricing structure and then a tactical plan.

The pricing structure is concerned with which aspects of each product or service will be priced, how prices will vary for different customers and products/services, and the time and conditions of payment. A number of the managerial questions to be addressed when establishing the price structure are identified in Table 3. Unfortunately, most of these issues are ignored entirely by those with pricing responsibility.

The simplest structure involves charging one standard price for a product or service, with no discounts or variations. This is relatively simple to administer, and easily understood by customers and middlemen. It does not suggest all customers or middlemen prefer such a one-price structure. Either may feel they deserve price breaks or special concessions for a variety of reasons, and both may be anxious to negotiate on price.

The biggest problem with such simple structures concerns their lack of flexibility as markets become more competitive, and as new profit opportunities arise for the firm. Consider the case of a fire extinguisher company that charges relatively moderate prices on its line of extinguishers. The firm is basically making a trade-off between the customers who perceive high value from these products, and those who perceive lower value. That is, high valuation customers (e.g., architects who rely on technical specs) would likely pay more than the firm is asking, whereas lower value customers (construction firms) may purchase less of the product than would be the case at lower prices because they are strongly cost-driven. Management may hope, in the process, to maximize revenue.

TABLE 3
Some Key Managerial Questions to be Addressed in Developing a Pricing Structure

1. Should a standard list price be charged for the product or service?
2. Should frequent or large customers be charged the same base price?
3. Can and should separate prices be charged for different aspects of the product or service?
4. How should time of purchase affect the price charged a customer?
5. To what extent should the price charged be varied to reflect the cost of doing business with a particular customer?
6. Should customers who value the product more be charged a higher price than other customers?
7. What is the nature of any discounts to be offered to the buyer?
8. When and where should title be taken by the buyer?
9. Is it realistic to offer a dual-rate structure, where the same customer has a choice between two pricing options for the same product or service?
10. Should the price structure involve a rental or leasing option?

However, consider the ways in which flexibility could be added by altering the price structure. Revenue might be enhanced by giving construction firms a 10 percent price discount, especially if they generally fall into the lower perceived value group of customers. Resources might be more completely utilized by charging less for certain extinguishers during low sales months, or a premium during peak months. The firm could offer 3 for 1 deals, or some form of quantity incentive. Or, alternatively, special "packages" might be put together for a single price, for example, when bidding for equipment or large office buildings. To facilitate source loyalty, repeat buyers might be given price breaks based on cumulative purchases, or told they can purchase on credit. The structural possibilities are virtually limitless if the manager is creative, and knows his or her customers.

As competition in an industry intensifies, price generally moves in the direction of costs, while demand is increasingly saturated. Both of these developments have implications for price structure. First, any differences in the cost positions take on significance as the price structure is modified to reflect a competitor's cost advantages or disadvantages. Second, competitors are apt to respond to market saturation with more aggressive market segmentation and targeting. One frequent result is price breaks for certain groups of customers.

Creative price structures are also critical for companies that do not sell a tangible product that can be inventoried indefinitely. This includes most service businesses, as well as those that sell perishable goods or products with short life cycles. Computer time-share companies as well as airlines, for example, sell asset use, not the asset itself. If a particular seat on a flight is not purchased during a particular period, revenue is lost forever. As a result, an airline may well vary price based on the distance to a destination, the popularity of that destination, the time of day, how long a person plans to stay, whether or not the customer is a regular patron (frequent flyer), how far in advance the reservation is made, and whether or not the customer will accept a "no cancellation" penalty. Many of these structural approaches have proved effective in reducing the number of unfilled seats on specific flights. The trade-off, however, is the complexity of administering such structures, and the potential for confused customers and antagonized middlemen.

4. Determining Price Levels and Related Tactics

Once established, strategies and structures may remain in place for a fairly long period. The day-to-day management of price focuses alternatively on setting specific price levels and using periodic tactical pricing moves. Price levels refer to the actual price charged for each product or service in the line, as well as the specific amount of any types of discounts offered. In determining exact levels, the manager's decisions must not only translate the firm's pricing strategy into specific numbers, but also must reflect a variety of practical considerations. Some of these issues include finding the acceptable range of price levels that convey the desired value perception, determining whether or not to charge odd prices (e.g., $197 instead of $200), ensuring price gaps between items within the same line are wide enough to convey meaningful differences in the items, and reflecting tax considerations in setting the final price.

Levels may require frequent modification in response to changes in production costs, competitor tactics, and evolving market conditions. For instance, costs of a key raw material may increase, a leading competitor may unexpectedly lower prices on a selective basis, supply conditions may change because a competitor has overproduced, or demand sensitivity (elasticity) may change within the current price range.

The ability to manage price levels effectively is heavily dependent on the manager's sense of timing. Price changes must not come across as arbitrary. Customers should sense a degree of consistency and stability in the firm's price levels over time. They must be able to justify, in their own minds, paying prices that are higher or lower than was previously the case. Otherwise, the company winds up sending conflicting signals regarding the value of its products or services, undermining customer confidence.

Beyond levels themselves, periodic tactical moves can include rebates, 2-for-1 price deals, a liberal trade-in policy, or any other creative means of temporarily varying price. These tactics are generally promotional in nature, and are usually part of special sales campaigns. They should be used with specific short-term objectives in mind, some of which may be communications-related objectives (e.g., creating product awareness, encouraging product trial). The pricing manager must ensure, however, that such tactics are consistent with the firm's overall pricing program.

Putting the Four Together

These four components of an effective pricing program are not independent, and should not be approached in an isolated fashion. Rather, they must be closely coordinated, with each element providing direction to the next. Consider two separate examples: Assume a local trucking company has entered the market positioning itself as a no frills, low-cost provider. Price objectives are set with an emphasis on high volume and revenue, low unit profits, and using price to convey a bargain image. To implement these objectives, the company selects a penetration strategy, in which price is set low relative to competitor prices and customer expectations. Structure is designed to include a low price per day and unlimited mileage for each of three classes of trucks plus drivers, with relatively small differences among each truck group. An even lower rate is offered to those who rent for 5 days or more, or over a weekend. Levels for the basic truck groups are established at $46.95, $69.75, and $85.75, respectively.

This pricing program may serve the company for a number of years. Pricing objectives and strategy may remain largely unchanged for an indefinite period. Structure may require periodic modification, such as addition of a "frequent renter" program, or special price deals for those who use the truck for particularly clean jobs or during certain seasons. Levels and tactics will require ongoing modification as competitor rates and tactics, production costs, and demand conditions fluctuate.

As a second example, a major manufacturer of quality copiers has found that unit costs have been falling while competition has intensified. At the same time, the product line has proliferated. Product life cycles have been getting shorter, as brief as one year for some models. In response, the firm has instituted an entirely new marketing strategy, of which price is a central component. The pricing objective in this case involves maximizing annual profitability across the product and service line. The strategic focus is on selective demand, where sales result from replacements/additions sold to the existing customer base, and by taking accounts away from competitors. The selected pricing strategy is parity pricing, with the firm attempting to charge base prices at or near the average competitive price. Structure is designed to be flexible, and salespeople are given some leeway in arriving at a final price. This is especially the case on mature products and those with the lowest manufacturing costs. The actual intent is to use the structure to place machines, but then to sell customers a service contract for which margins are considerably higher. In addition, significant discounts are provided to customers who purchase multiple machines. Finally, base price levels are established and adjusted monthly to reflect an index of the average prices of the three top selling machines in each major product category. A discount of 20 percent is provided for each purchase of three or more units.

Again, the four elements of the SPP are intimately tied to one another. Approached in this manner, price becomes an innovative variable with immense potential for affecting the strategic direction of the firm. Alternatively, if management approaches pricing as an afterthought, concerned only that costs be covered and the firm be reasonably competitive, opportunities are lost and mistakes are much more probable.

Linking Pricing Programs to Marketing Strategy

Up to this point, the need to systematically approach pricing as a strategic variable has been emphasized. Price is, however, only one of the strategic decision areas facing the manager. As such, it is essential that pricing programs be consistent with the decisions made in these other areas.

Because price is an indicator of customer value, the SPP should be designed in concert with other value-related activities of the firm, especially those activities that directly interface with customers. Of primary importance here are product programs, sales and promotion programs, and distribution programs. A high price can help convey a quality product image. A special price deal can be an integral part of the firm's promotional program. A trade discount can be an incentive for distribu-

tors to provide stronger support in pushing the company's products.

The focal point of all these activities should be the firm's overall marketing strategy. Marketing strategies attempt to define where the firm wants to be in the marketplace, and how it plans to get there. They provide the larger framework within which pricing and other programs are developed. Correspondingly, there should be a clear link between the strategies and the individual programs.

A large number of marketing strategies are available to any company. The appropriate choice requires considerable creativity, and keen insight regarding current and future marketplace conditions. One example of a fairly common marketing strategy is called differentiation. This is where the company attempts to create unique perceptions in the marketplace of its product offering relative to the offerings of all other competitors in the industry. For instance, IBM differentiates itself on the basis of customer service, whereas Caterpillar uses its outstanding dealer network as a source of differentiation.

If a company was pursuing a differentiation strategy, how might the pricing program be designed to reinforce this strategy? As a general rule, successful differentiation allows the manager to charge somewhat higher margins than competitors, reflecting the higher value being delivered to customers. In addition, differentiation encourages brand loyalty, frequently making customers less price sensitive. Customers are likely to perceive fewer acceptable substitutes. The more salient the source of differentiation is to customers, the more brand loyal they are likely to be.

Another marketing strategy is targeting or niching. This involves focusing on a particular market segment, such as a certain type of user, a specific product application, or a single geographic region. Square-D Corporation targets their "homeline" line of electrical distribution equipment to the low-end user, whereas Porter Paints are positioned solely to the professional painter. Using the Square-D example, price is set below that of conventional distribution equipment to convey the idea that the buyer is getting a reliable but lower quality product. This represents good value for the money to a sizable segment of the market.

Inconsistencies between overall market strategy and product or service pricing strategy frequently produces failure in the marketplace. The company that has positioned itself as a high-end or premium quality provider, but then drops prices when confronted with competitive pressures, is undermining its own market position, confusing customers, and giving away margins. Similarly, pricing strategies that focus on quickly recouping the initial investment in a product or service often result in escalated prices, given the firm's desired position in customer's minds.

Underlying Determinants of Pricing Program Decisions

When putting together the firm's pricing program, and subsequently managing the SPP over the stages of product or service life, the manager must continually evaluate a number of critical price determinants. These determinants fall into five categories: overall company objectives and marketing strategies, costs, demand, competition, and legal issues (Figure 1). Two of these determinants, overall objectives/strategies and costs, can be classified as internal company factors. The remaining three, demand, competition and legal issues, are external to the company.

Company objectives and strategies constitute a framework within which pricing decisions can be made. They effectively serve to define a role for the price variable. Costs indicate to the manager a minimum level for setting price in order to break even, and so represent a beginning point in pricing. Demand analysis seeks to determine customer perceptions of value, the relative importance of price when customers make purchase decisions, the size of the market, and the different quantities that are likely to be purchased at different price levels. Competitor assessments focus on evaluating market structure, estimating competitors' cost structures, identifying their current pricing strategy, deter-

mining their relative market advantages, and anticipating how they will respond to the various pricing moves of other companies. Lastly, many pricing actions raise serious legal questions and must be evaluated in this context. Unfortunately, jurisprudence is often quite vague in terms of the legality of specific price tactics. The manager's prime concern is to estimate how the use of a particular pricing method will affect the firm's competitive market position, and if it will create an unfair competitive advantage.

The ability to decipher each of these price determinants involves both art and science. For instance, certain skills are required to properly calculate unit costs, or to estimate customer price sensitivity (i.e., elasticity). These analyses can sometimes become quite sophisticated. At the same time, creativity is required in developing realistic estimates of figures for which no data is available, although both insight and experience are invaluable when making hard judgments regarding competitor actions and reactions, or assessing customer value perceptions.

The real challenge lies in putting these factors together and drawing implications for price decision. Consider the case of the Jefferson Chemical Company, a producer of specialty and commodity chemicals for industrial use, including muriatic acid.

Based on a decline in profits and market share over the past year, the product line manager has proposed that the firm either cut the price of its acid by 10 percent or increase sales and promotional support by $50,000. How would one go about evaluating the price component of this manager's suggestions?

The first step would concern product and company objective. What are the implications of the price reduction for the image of the product? How will the price cut affect other products in the line? What is the profit goal associated with such a price cut, and how does it relate to overall company profit objectives? Much of the remaining analysis follows from objectives in these areas. Assume the goal to be a 5 percent increase in profit, and that this increase is the sole objective of concern. The next step would involve examining costs. A logical approach would be to cover the lost unit revenue from the price cut (i.e., to break even on the price cut) plus the sales necessary to increase total contribution by 5 percent. This could be accomplished by determining how many dollars the product is currently contributing to overhead and profits after covering its own direct costs (before the price cut) and adding to this a 10 percent increase in contribution. This total figure then would be divided by the new profit margin (price-unit cost) resulting after the price cut. The result would be a required sales figure, from which current sales would be subtracted, leaving the required sales increase.

The required increase would next be expressed as a percentage of current sales. Assume it to be 20 percent. This brings us to demand analysis. The company requires a 20 percent increase in sales in response to a 10 percent price reduction, which suggests demand must be fairly elastic. Is this likely to happen? Based on experience and knowledge of the market, management must determine if customers are that price sensitive. The analysis here should raise questions about the importance of price compared with other product attributes, the strength of existing customer loyalties, and the extent to which market potential (both users and usage rates) had already been reached.

Finally, even if the research up to this point indicates the price cut makes sense, management must anticipate competitor reactions. How does the firm's cost structure compare with theirs? How dependent on cash flows from this product are they? How well-established are their customer ties in this product area? Do they view this market as growing, mature, or declining? The answers to these questions will provide insight into whether or not competitors will match the price cut.

Suggestions for Additional Research

The pricing area has received scant attention from industrial marketing scholars. Research efforts to date have been largely descriptive of current pricing practices [1, 3–6]. Significant advances are needed in the areas of theory development, formulation of hypotheses, and empirical testing. The strategic pricing program represents a useful framework for identifying priorities in this regard.

Each of the four components of the SPP lends itself to significant investigation. Specifically, research is needed to:

- identify, categorize, and establish hierarchies among various types of pricing objectives
- assess differences in profitability between industrial firms relying on cost-based versus market-based pricing strategies
- systematically identify the dimensions of price structure for products versus services and for categories of products (e.g., major equipment, accessory equipment, component parts, etc.)
- assess the effectiveness of various psychological pricing tactics (e.g., odd pricing, use of price anchors, pricing to reflect quality differences over the product line) when applied to organizational buyers

In addition, efforts should be devoted towards addressing more comprehensive questions regarding the overall nature and internal dynamics of strategic pricing programs. Key issues include:

- identifying major sources of conflict or inconsistency among the four components of the pricing program, and between SPPs and company marketing strategy
- determining types and causes of control problems in administering pricing programs including issues related to organizational structure, corporate policies and procedures, market structure, and degree of competitive turbulence
- establishing differences in the design and operation of pricing programs when price is determined by formal negotiation, competitive bidding, or establishment of standard list prices

Advances in these areas will enable managers to design and implement SPPs capable of generating greater profits while also bringing much needed flexibility to the price function. A better understanding of what works and why will help reduce the perceived risk in price decisions, and encourage managers to move away from traditional formula-based methodologies. In the process, price can become less a financial consideration and more a creative marketing tool.

References

1. Morris, M. H. and M. Joyce, How Marketers Evaluate Price Sensitivity, *Industrial Marketing Management,* **17**, 2, 169–176 (1988).

2. Morris, M., Separate Prices as an Industrial Marketing Tool, *Industrial Marketing Management,* **16**, 79–86 (1987).

3. Morris, M. and D. Fuller, Pricing an Industrial Service, *Industrial Marketing Management,* **18**, 139–46 (1989).

4. Abratt, R. and L. F. Pitt, Pricing Practices in Two Industries, *Industrial Marketing Management* **14**, 4, 301–306 (1985).

5. Day, G. S. and A. Ryans, Using Price Discounts for a Competitive Advantage, *Industrial Marketing Management* **17**, 1, 1–14 (1988).

6. Shapiro, B. and B. Jackson, Industrial Pricing to Meet Customer Needs, *Harvard Business Review,* November–December, 119–27 (1978).

7. Forgionne, G. A., Economic Tools Used by Management in Large American Operated Companies, *Business Economics,* April, 5–17 (1984).

Hermann Simon

Pricing Opportunities—And How to Exploit Them

Managers around the world continue to make poor pricing decisions despite discussion of new pricing techniques in both the academic and popular business press. Yet market saturation, overcapacities, quality standardization, and other developments are making price a more crucial factor than ever. Simon provides a number of examples that should convince managers to look again at how they set prices. He describes some of the new techniques for setting prices appropriately and strategically. Finally, he discusses the dynamics that make price-setting an ongoing concern, not a one-time decision. ❋

Have you had problems with your prices lately? You're not alone. Recently I conducted a study in which both U.S. and European marketing managers ranked price pressures at the top of the "sorrow scale."[1] Product quality and innovation came in second and third, respectively.

But beware! Quite likely your price problem isn't a "price problem." Price reflects a product's strengths and weaknesses—its value, competitive positioning, and distribution power. Never view price in isolation. Rather, consider it within the overall marketing mix and the competitive context. As E. Raymond Corey of the Harvard Business School says, "All of marketing comes to focus in the pricing decision."[2]

In this article I address the following issues:

- The increasing strategic importance of price;
- Sophisticated pricing methods that bridge the still large gap between theory and practice and,

thus, allow for better exploitation of profit opportunities; and

- Long-term competitive aspects of price strategies.

The gap between pricing theory and practice remains large despite price's increasingly critical role, the development of new, tested pricing methods, a vast body of literature, and numerous new MBA pricing courses. We still see little professionalism in pricing. Companies with specialized pricing groups (such as IBM and Daimler-Benz) are still exceptions. In most firms prices are determined by intuition, opinions, rules of thumb, outright dogma, top management's higher wisdom, or internal power fights. As recently as 1988, advertising guru David Ogilvy commented, "Pricing is guesswork. It is usually assumed that marketers use scientific methods to determine the price of their products. Nothing could be further from the truth. In almost every case, the process of decision is one of guesswork." Profit sacrifices and strategic damages are the results.

Consider the following pricing blunders:

In January 1983, Reemtsma Cigarettenfabriken cut the price of its West brand from DM 3.80 to DM 3.30, the first such move in the West German cigarette market since World War II. Within four months West's market share rocketed from .6 percent to 10 percent, corresponding to an annual sales gain of

At the time this article was written, Hermann Simon was Professor of Business Administration at Johannes Gutenberg University, Mainz, Germany. He chaired the Scientific Advisory Board of the UNIC University Connection Institute for Management and Marketing in Bonn, Germany, and wrote *Price Management* (New York: Elsevier Science Publishers, 1989).

more than DM 2 billion. A success? No—a disaster. Competitors retaliated, and the hitherto stable price structure collapsed. It took the industry four years to recover.

A company priced its new corrosion product at competitive levels although the product was superior. Management had been scared by intense price competition with its other, weaker products and was afraid to charge premium prices even for superior products. A thorough value analysis revealed that the product could bear a much higher price. About one-third of the product's profit potential had been sacrificed over several years.

A new consumer product entered the market with a price 40 percent below the incumbent leader's price. The leader responded by increasing advertising but maintaining the higher price. Within a year the leader's market share slipped 50 percent. Management's lack of experience with price competition led it to substantially underestimate price sensitivity and overestimate advertising effectiveness.

After a patent expired, more than twenty competitors entered the market, and some undercut the pioneer product's price by 50 percent. The pioneer attempted to defend its price position. But market share tumbled rapidly and the price had to be reduced in two steps by 50 percent. The product's annual contribution decreased by U.S. $25 million. In a different but similar situation, the pioneer cut its price by 20 percent six months before the patent expired and ran a heavy advertising campaign shortly before competitors entered the market. The product lost insubstantial market share, and the price didn't need to be further reduced.

An industrial components manufacturer sold seven product lines, each with hundreds of variants; this scope required simple pricing rules. The accounting department calculated unit costs and set prices by applying a standard markup. A detailed study revealed that only 40 percent of the products should have been priced with this markup. Profits increased 15 percent after management introduced differentiated markups.

In the notoriously inflationary Brazilian market, a German company tried to increase its market share by raising prices at a lower rate than inflation. To compensate for the smaller margin, the company reduced its advertising. The strategy was disastrous. The product even lost market share, and profits plunged.

What are the lessons from these cases?

- Price can have tremendous effects on market shares, profits, and market structures;
- Pricing blunders abound, and huge opportunities are missed;
- Intuition, instinct, experience, and even good accounting are insufficient for optimal price decisions; and
- Each case requires a sophisticated analysis. There are no simple rules.

Price and Its Dangers

Is price really that important relative to other marketing instruments? Yes! Price determines the economic "sacrifice" a buyer has to make to acquire the product. The buyer compares this sacrifice with the product's perceived value. Price and value are the cornerstones of every transaction. It follows that price elasticity is ten to twenty times higher than advertising elasticity. That is, a certain percentage price change has a ten to twenty times stronger effect on sales than the same percentage change in advertising outlays. A wrong price devastates profit.

As a marketing instrument, price is distinguished in other ways. Price changes, unlike product, advertising, or distribution changes, can be made quickly. The sales effect of a price change also shows up quickly, whereas other actions take time to affect sales. Thus aggressive pricing is popular during struggles for dominance, as when new products enter the market. However, competitors can react equally fast, and price can fire back like no other market device. For instance, time and again companies try to conquer a market through aggressive pricing without a cost advantage, as in the West case above. This reduces profits for all competitors. Price is, therefore, like the atomic bomb, an effective but dangerous competitive weapon. Think twice before you touch price.

Price is increasing in importance, primarily because of market saturation, overcapacities, and quality standardization. In 1988 General Motors spent $4.2 billion, or about $700 per car, on price concessions (cash backs, rebates, etc.). Consumers are becoming more price-conscious. In many markets, relative power is shifting from manufacturers to retailers; mass retailers are "price people." Virtually no segment of the market is immune to price attacks, not even premium categories, as the successful and aggressive pricing strategy for the Toyota Lexus shows. Often, aggressive pricing is the only choice for newcomers. Such entries induce a collapse of hitherto stable price systems.

And get prepared for the inflation of the 1990s. Inflation increases price awareness by making it more rewarding to shop around and compare prices.

Taken together, these developments indicate that managers must take a more sophisticated approach to pricing. They must seize the remaining opportunities in an increasingly price-conscious and price-competitive world by exploiting premium potentials, fine-tuning price to products' perceived value and competitive situations, using price differentiation and price bundling, and making shrewd timing decisions.

Price Decisions: An Example

A leading agrochemical company planned to sell a new insecticide called Netex to different segments in different countries. The Netex pricing process had started, as usual, with the accountants' cost estimates. It soon became apparent that the various functions involved differed on what the price should be.

Accountants and finance people, who traditionally had a strong influence on price decisions, thought and argued in cost plus and unit margin terms. Their remoteness from the customer made them uncomfortable with the "soft" information marketing provided. The product manager, a young man with ambitious market share goals, favored a low penetration price. On his side, though with a less radical position, was the sales manager. He saw price mainly as an obstacle to concluding deals. Any price above the competition made life difficult for his salespeople, particularly in developing countries. Therefore, he was opposed to price premiums. Too low a price, on the other hand, would

mean smaller commissions for his salesforce. Top management tended toward slight premiums, though smaller ones than the accountants wanted.

The difficulties in unifying these diverging views are obvious. This case was particularly complex because the product had several applications with different requirements, customer characteristics, and competitive structures. So each group could cite evidence that seemed to support its position. However, the product was the same across application segments; prices couldn't differ.

A number of questions emerged during the process: How important are price and product attributes—efficacy, spectrum, safety, delivery, and information—to farmers and dealers in the various segments? How does Netex's performance compare with that of competitors on these attributes? What are the values, in price terms, that Netex and competitive products deliver? How do farmers and dealers differ in purchasing volume, attribute importance ratings, perceptions, short lists of approved suppliers, preferences, price sensitivities, and so forth? What is the segment structure? Where are competitors positioned?

A narrow price analysis could not answer these questions. Rather, the situation required a full-fledged market and competitive analysis. Primary data was collected through personal interviews with farmers and dealers in several countries. A set of techniques such as conjoint measurement, multidimensional scaling, and regression (all well documented in textbooks but rarely used) were employed. Figure 1 gives an overview of the main issues and their interconnections. Such a framework is a far cry from economics textbook price theory. But it is much more likely to yield appropriate pricing and positioning.

How did the application of these methods affect the pricing decision? The availability of market data and objective analyses made the process more rational. Of course, each member of the team did not accept each finding, but the analysis provided a common base for further discussion. Deviating opinions had to be substantiated. The study increased the overall time to arrive at the decision, but it decreased the internal discussion

FIGURE 1
Frameworks for Consistent Pricing and Positioning

and implementation time. In this sense, management time was more efficiently allocated.

The price structure turned out to be complex, reflecting the market's intricacies. On average, the price was slightly above the competition. In fact there was no average price, but rather a set of highly differentiated price schemes. For example, in one major application, Netex's perceived value and thus the willingness to pay were markedly superior. This indicated a premium price. As it was not possible to sell the standard Netex at different prices, the company developed a slightly modified version called Netex-Forte to sell at a higher markup. In certain developing countries Netex's perceived value and the farmers' willingness to pay were far below average, mostly because the farmers did not appreciate the product's superior safety and environmental characteristics. The company did not introduce the product in these countries because the price attainable there could, via re-imports, jeopardize the price in other, more important markets. In another field Netex had to be used with a second, much cheaper product. By combining this agent with Netex to become Netex-Combi, the company saved farmers an additional spraying and raised the product's perceived value. The company could set a lucrative price for the combination. The study also influenced the overall price structure. The company found that light users were much less price sensitive than heavy users, so

it offered pronounced quantity rebates and a bonus system. It introduced a seasonal price scheme that reflected variations in orders.

With a few exceptions, the structural characteristics of the Netex pricing strategy were no surprise for the team members who were close to the market, but even the best experts were surprised about the extent of price and perceived value differentials. The profit potentials inherent in these differentials could not have been fully exploited without the analyses.

Such analyses are, of course, no guarantee for an optimal pricing strategy. Subjective considerations are always needed, but intuition and experience alone are shaky foundations for complex price decisions. It is crucial to look at as many different facets of price as possible (as shown in Figure 1) to secure a consistent and well-founded strategy.

The Systematic Price Decision

All price decisions should take into account the relationships depicted in Figure 2. These relationships suggest questions such as, "How does price affect sales volume or market share?" and "How do competitors react to our price moves?" Those nasty questions have to be resolved in order to set a price that yields maximum profit. Cost plus pricing neglects these aspects, as does an adjustment to competitors' prices. Both ignore vital relations in

FIGURE 2
Price Relationships That Affect Profit

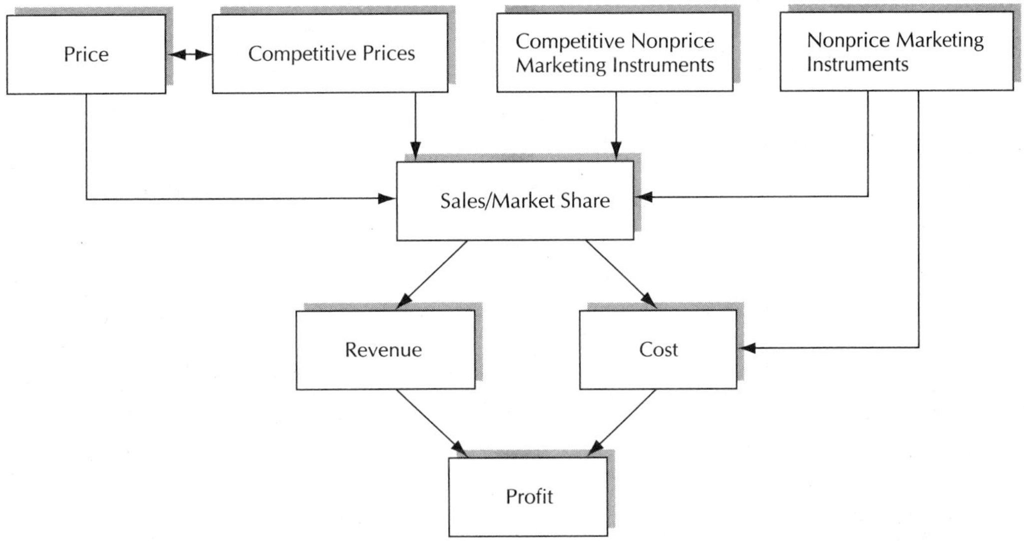

the system. Unless the relations in Figure 2 are quantified, pricing is guesswork.

All price decisions should have the goal illustrated in Figure 3: optimal pricing. I have talked to hundreds of managers about their understanding of the price–profit relationship. Almost two-thirds associate higher price with higher profit. They think in unit margins and not in trade-offs between margins and volumes.

Figure 3 shows that (1) there is always an optimal price. (2) The profit curve around this price is relatively flat. Thus, we need not search for the second digit behind the decimal point. What counts is the magnitude of the optimal price. (3) The more we deviate from the optimum, the steeper the downward slope of the profit curve becomes. If we are already off the mark, a further price move in the wrong direction is devastating (how often have you seen companies already pricing too high pushing that price even higher, such as the Western auto industry in recessionary times, or those already too low continue to slash prices, as in a typical price war?). (4) A price too low is as bad as

a price too high. In either case, profit is sacrificed. As a Russian proverb says: There are two fools in each market. One charges too little, the other charges too much.

The crucial question is, of course: How do we get information on the relations in Figure 2 and the resulting curve in Figure 3? There are only three rational ways: extracting expert knowledge, asking customers, and observing actual market behavior. Below I illustrate these methods and recommend ways to apply them.

Extracting Expert Knowledge

Managers usually have an intuitive understanding of customers and competitors. But they may have problems in ordering, structuring, and condensing their knowledge. By systemizing this knowledge, managers can quantify the relationships among price, sales, and profit.

A company was planning to introduce a pharmaceutical innovation in three major European countries. Certain constraints made a consumer

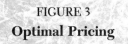

FIGURE 3
Optimal Pricing

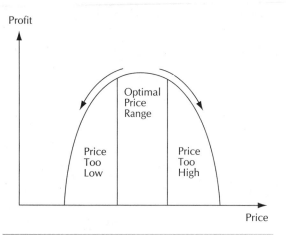

diverse in background and position in the hierarchy. Divergencies in the estimates are normal. Finally, discuss the results in a meeting of all responding experts and attempt to reach a consensus. This yields more valid results than a simple average of the individual estimates.

The managerial judgment approach has proved useful. The industrial components company with uniform markup discussed earlier used the method to develop specific markups for all product–market adjustments. Profit increased by about 15 percent. In another case the method was used with great success to develop preemptive pricing actions before a competitive entry.

The clarity of the decision structure and the expert quantification of price effects remove most of the ambiguity, subjectivity, and emotional

study of price infeasible. Instead, managers both in the countries and at headquarters were interviewed. Among other information, the managers provided the following estimates: the lowest realistic price and the sales expected at this price in the first year, the highest realistic price and the associated sales, and the sales they expected at the medium price.

Figure 4 shows the aggregated sales estimates and aggregated profits (the profit curve is calculated as profit = (price – unit costs) × sales volume). A price in the range of $1.25 to $1.35 yields the highest profit. A price of $1.50, which was strongly advocated by central marketing, would reduce annual profit from $55 million to $49 million. A profit reduction of similar magnitude would result from a price of $1.10, which was preferred by the sales subsidiaries.

To conduct this kind of analysis, a specialist must draft a case-specific questionnaire of five to ten pages that covers all realistic scenarios of customer and competitive reactions. A neutral outsider should conduct the interviews; price response estimates and pricing issues in general are highly political. Interview no fewer than 3 experts—more opinions improve reliability. Chose experts who are

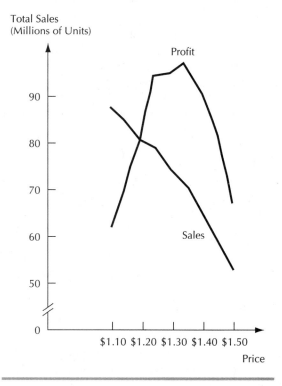

FIGURE 4
Price Setting via Expert Knowledge

issues so typical of pricing decisions. The method is particularly apt for new products and the anticipation of new competitive situations. It leaves enough room for the inclusion of nonquantitative aspects. Of course, it does not predict forecasting errors.

Asking Customers

Customers should know how they react to price. After all, they have to pay the bill. The obvious way to tap customers' knowledge is to ask them direct price-related questions: Would you buy this product at this price? How much would you be willing to pay? The main problem with this direct approach is that when customers view price in isolation, they become unrealistically price conscious. In reality, customers weigh price against product attributes, that is, they make a trade-off between price and product value.

Conjoint measurement captures this trade-off in a systematic way. Instead of answering direct questions about price, respondents choose among alternative product profiles that include price. They simply give their preferences for each product profile. From those answers a computer model can plot the effect of price and other product attributes. The sidebar, "Pricing the 'Tiger' with Conjoint Measurement" gives a case example.

Conjoint measurement is certainly the most important new tool to support price decisions. It allows us to answer seemingly unanswerable questions, such as: What is the relative value of a brand in price terms? What is the value of a technical feature (the costs of which are normally well known), a service, a faster delivery time, and so forth in price units? What happens to our market share if we change our price or a product feature? What is the effect of competitive price or product moves on our market share? Is it profitable to add or remove product characteristics if we can attain certain prices?

Conjoint measurement provides quantitative measures, in price terms, of perceived values. This is exactly the information needed to make adequate price decisions. I recommend the following:

- Apply conjoint measurement with great care and caution. Design and interpretation flaws are frequent.
- For the most accurate results, present highly realistic product profiles. Handmade actual products or photos of models can be very helpful.
- Confine numerical attributes to realistic levels and intervals—this is crucial.
- Use computer interviewing if possible. It allows the inclusion of many features, which is more realistic, and it motivates interviewees.

I have found conjoint measurement to be a valuable tool in a large number of applications. It is equally useful with consumer products, industrial markets, and services. As all analyses can be done for individual customers, conjoint also helps to segment a market.

Observing Market Behavior

Another source of price response information is actual customer behavior. We can either observe customers' responses to price variations in an experimental setting or use historic market data. Scanner technology is particularly apt for price experimentation. Each price and sale is automatically recorded, and price–sales relations can be computed quickly and cost-effectively.

In many markets, historical price and sales data are available but rarely used. In several of the cases reported at the beginning of this article the blunders could have been prevented if the companies had looked at the data more carefully. The truth was there, but nobody saw it. In the third case described at the beginning of this article, market data analysis revealed that price elasticity had been continuously increasing over several years, while advertising's effectiveness showed a corresponding decline. As corrective action the company reduced price by 20 percent

TABLE 1
Methods for Establishing Prices

Method	Expert Judgment	Customer Survey	Actual Behavior
Validity	Medium	Medium-High	High
Costs	Low	Medium	Medium-High
Applicable for New Products	Yes	Yes	Experiment: yes Market data: no
Overall	Useful for new products, new situations	Very useful for price value measurement	Particularly useful for established products

and advertising by 70 percent. Within a year the market share recovered from 40 to 55 percent. In the case of the Brazilian disaster, the message was hidden in the historic data but it took some sophisticated regression analysis to extract the information. Analysis showed that price elasticity was virtually zero. Extreme inflation had distorted consumers' ability to distinguish between cheap and expensive. The company raised prices up to the maximum allowed by the government and tripled advertising from 5 percent to 15 percent of sales. The product regained a modest level of profitability.

Follow these guidelines when using historic data to extract price information:

- Start with a visual inspection of the data.
- Make sure that the historic conditions under which the data originated prevail.
- Do not rely on one hypothesis but test many assumptions. Include nonprice marketing instruments if possible; they may distort the price effects.
- Remember that economic plausibility is as important as statistics.

These three methods of establishing prices are complementary. The more methods you use, the better. Table 1 summarizes the advantages and disadvantages of these methods.

Competitive Dynamics and Strategic Pricing

The dream of many price managers to establish a good price and retain it belongs to the past. IBM had to abandon this policy in the late 1970s, and pharmaceutical companies are just now learning that pricing strategies for innovative and for "me too" products have to be fundamentally different. Competitive and consumer dynamics make traditional stable price policies less and less tenable.

Skimming and penetration strategies are the classic qualitative options for new product pricing. While people talk a lot about these strategies, they rarely make clear what they mean in quantitative terms. A skimming price is close to or higher than the short-term profit-maximizing level, that is, a price usually perceived as relatively high. A penetration price is considerably lower.

In the skimming approach, a company often reduces the high introductory price over the course of the product's life cycle. With the penetration strategy, a company employs a low, often aggressive introductory price in order to drive up volume and market share quickly, to build a strong market position. And, if experience curve effects are strong, to drive costs down. The company refrains from maximizing short-term profits and, instead, invests in the product's future.

Pricing the "Tiger" with Conjoint Measurement

A German automobile company used conjoint measurement to set the price for its new "Tiger" model (name disguised). The managers involved in the decision raised questions like the following: What is the "price value" of our brand? How much is the customer willing to pay for a higher maximum speed? (No speed limit in Germany!) How does gasoline consumption relate to price acceptance?

The managers proceeded in the following steps:

• They determined that the most relevant product attributes were brand, maximum speed, gasoline consumption, and price.

• They chose characteristics for each attribute. They would test three brands—one German, one Japanese, and their own; three maximum speeds—200, 220, and 240 kilometers per hour; three levels of gasoline consumption—12, 14, and 16 liters per 100 kilometers; and three prices—DM 50,000; 60,000; and 70,000.

• They designed a questionnaire and collected data. The attributes and characteristics yielded eighty-one possible product profiles, but the company needed only nine profiles to answer their questions. Researchers developed the nine profiles and presented them to target group respondents in pairs, as shown below. Respondents, interviewed by computer, indicated whether they would buy A or B. Thirty-two such comparisons were presented.

• From the data, the company calculated "preference contributions"—numerical values that allow the preference for attributes to be compared. Preference contributions allow you to discover that, say, increasing car speed by 20 kilometers per hour generates the same increase in preference for the car as would decreasing the price by DM 10,000. Adding up the preference contributions results in an overall preference index.

The greater the difference between the lowest and the highest preference contribution within one attribute (that is, the greater the disparity between preference for, say, the most popular brand and the least popular brand), the more important is this attribute. These differences can be translated into percentage importance weights that add up to 100 percent. In this case:

Brand	35%
Maximum speed	30%
Price	20%
Gas consumption	15%

Thus customers in this target group were very interested in brand and maximum speed but less sensitive to price and gasoline consumption.

• Taking the known attribute levels for the Tiger model, the managers could calculate market shares and profits for alternative prices. They found that the optimal price was at the upper end of the price range; they set it slightly below DM 70,000.

Attribute	Profile A	Profile B
Brand	Tiger	Japanese
Maximum speed	200	240
Gas consumption	12	16
Price	50,000	70,000

An important recent trend is the shortening of both the quasimonopolistic time span of innovative products and of brand life cycles in general. In the pharmaceutical industry, effective patent life has decreased from sixteen years in 1964 to less than ten years in the late 1980s. As a consequence, prices in the early life cycle stages should be closer to the short-term profit maximum than traditionally. That is, skimming must be more pronounced in order to reduce the payoff period. A precondition is that the new product must offer superior value. Later on, prices may have to decrease faster and at a greater rate than they used to. The temporal distribution of profits shifts to the earlier life cycle stages. The same holds for shorter life cycles, which are down to a few months for products such as personal computers, consumer electronics, and sports shoes. The time to recover R&D and other investments is compressed; it is no longer worthwhile to invest in the long-term future of the brand or model, because there is no long-term future.[6]

In my work I have sometimes recommended setting introductory prices well above traditional levels. In one case, management's initial idea was to set the price a percent above current prices. Research showed that the market would bear a 50 percent price premium because of the product's superior benefit. Management at first hesitated but was convinced. Actual sales even exceeded the forecast. Compared to the initial plan, profits were at least 20 percent higher. In another case, the eventual price was twice as high as management's initial plan. But be careful when you make this kind of decision. Genentech's Activase (TPA), whose introductory price exceeded competitors' prices by a factor of ten, failed to sustainably penetrate the market. In March 1989, Boehringer Ingelheim, the company that markets TPA outside the United States, cut the price by 50 percent. When setting prices for new products, don't look at technical innovativeness but at customer benefit!

A company that skillfully plays the game of high prices for innovations is Bosch, the German automobile supplier. For its fuel injection and antilock brake systems, it applied pronounced and extremely profitable skimming strategies, supported by a smart patent policy. Hewlett-Packard is also good at this game. The Japanese, on the other hand, have difficulties with skimming. Take compact disc players. Says Kenichi Ohmae, undoubtedly an expert, "It was a perfect opportunity to move upscale with a 'Mercedes' compact disc player. What did the Japanese do? Corporate culture and instinct took over and they cut prices. This is foolishness—or worse." The Japanese are still adhering to pricing formulas that brought them past success. Today the Koreans and others are better equipped to play the low price game. Past success is the biggest enemy of change.

The value-oriented skimming approach must not prevent a company from slashing costs during periods of high prices. Costs have to be brought down by all means to secure survival in the competitive cycle's later stages.

When in the life cycle should price come down? Should the innovator cut the price before or after competitor entry? Or should a price level be defended as long as possible? Price cuts can sometimes prevent competitors from getting a foot in the door. In 1984, Cummins Engine slashed the prices for small diesels by 30 percent, at that time well below costs. Henry Schacht, Cummins' CEO, comments: "If you match the Japanese in price there is no way they get in."

Price is even more effective at redefining entry conditions. Newcomers typically use aggressive pricing to fight their way in. The incumbent has three options:

- Reduce price before competitors enter (proactive price cut);
- Reduce price after entry, usually after some market share losses (reactive price cut); or
- Maintain the high price and accept a market share erosion (harvesting strategy).

Harvesting can be profitable if the company wants to abandon the market or plans to introduce a successor product soon. With a loyal customer base, old products can live for a long time and be profitable.

Proactive and reactive price cutting are characterized by a strong antagonism between short- and long-term profit implications. In order to learn more about long-term effects, I have run hundreds of simulations. Under most realistic assumptions, proactive price cutting appears superior. It is the best compromise between short- and long-term profit maximization. While the seemingly premature price cut incurs short-term sacrifices, it is likely to yield higher long-term profitability. It also avoids the risk that customers feel cheated if price is reduced under the new competitive pressure. Proactive price cutting is,

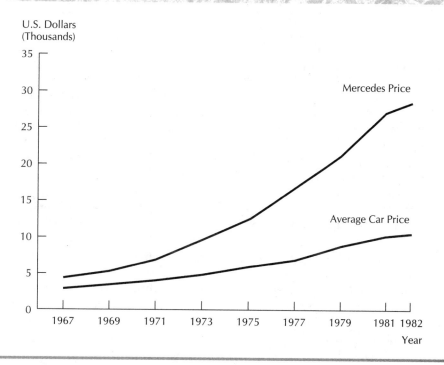

FIGURE 5

Penetration–Skimming Pricing: Mercedes in the U.S. Market

however; difficult to implement. Who likes to reduce price without actual competitive pressure? This may be the reason we see the reactive pattern more frequently.

For example, Olivetti and Olympia from Europe were the first to introduce electronic typewriters around 1980. They were reluctant to cut their high prices when Japanese companies entered about three years later. The Europeans' prices came down only after the bulk of the market had fallen into Japanese hands.

Gillette acted more prudently when Bic attacked the disposable razor market. Several months before Bic's entry, Gillette introduced a new model that was 31 percent cheaper than its established product and successfully defended its position. Gillette had learned a lesson from Bic's

earlier inroads in disposable pens and lighters, when it had cut prices reactively and lost market leadership.

Are penetration strategies for new products obsolete? Certainly not. For "me too" products and for international market entry by an unknown company, penetration is still the strategy of choice. One should, however, be aware that it is often necessary to raise prices later in the life cycle. This seems to become increasingly difficult. A classic example of this penetration–skimming approach is the long-term pricing policy of Mercedes-Benz in the U.S. market. In 1967 the Mercedes-Benz was priced close to the average car price, but by 1982 it was priced much higher than the average. Figure 5 shows the development of the average car price and the Mercedes price in

TABLE 2
New Product Pricing Strategies

Skimming	Penetration
• High short-term profits less affected by discounting	• High profit through fast sales growth and high volume
• For innovations, profits before competitive entry, quick recovery of R&D expenditures, and reduction of payoff period and risk	• Quick induction of trials and demonstrations
• Profits before obsolescence	• Reduction of short-term costs through large volume
• Room for future price reductions	• Reduction of long-term costs through fast growth of accumulated volume. Long-term competitive advantage
• Avoids, preempts price increases	• Better utilization of high fixed capacity in production or distribution
• Prestige and quality connotation at high introductory price	• Lower flop risk
• Avoids cut-throat competition if competitors are price followers	• Deterrence of entrants
• Lower volume—less demanding on capacities and financial resources	• Risk: Vicious cycle of declining prices

the United States. The Mercedes strategy clearly follows the penetration–skimming pattern, reflecting the initially weak position. The large Japanese automakers used the same strategy. Toyota's new luxury model, Lexus, seems headed in the same direction. The U.S. introductory price was below $40,000 (clearly a penetration price). It is unlikely that Toyota can make a profit with this price, and it has already raised the price substantially in 1991. Interestingly, in Germany, with a price tag well above $50,000, Lexus is priced much less aggressively.

Until a few years ago, IBM used similar strategies. Although the company nominally followed a strategy of constant prices, the continuous decline in competitive prices over time meant that the relative prices of IBM products started out on a (relative) penetration level and only later rose to a (relative) skimming level. Responding to a different competitive environment, IBM today follows a skimming strategy with substantial price slashes over time.

The most prominent traditional rationale for penetration pricing was the experience curve. Slashing prices early on to increase volume and bring costs down was a popular game in the 1970s

and early 1980s. But gone are the days of ads like the following from *Electronic Design Magazine* of October 25, 1980:

> Bubble price break! On August 11, 1980, Intel lowered its price for the BPK 72 Bubble Memory Kit by 40 percent to $995. By August 1981, the price will be an unprecedented $595. Not "projected," Not "expected." Guaranteed. One year later, the unit price will be $295—cutting the per bit price in half once more. Again, we guarantee it.

Too often, experience curve pricing has driven down prices faster than unit costs, and the expected profit never materialized. No longer can we believe in an automatic correlation between cumulative volume and unit costs. While the experience curve remains important in certain industries, managers must take greater caution with overly aggressive pricing. Even in the Cummins case, where prices for small diesels were cut by 30 percent to compete with the Japanese, it has been said recently that "doing the right thing has failed to pay off."

Table 2 summarizes both the more traditional and the more recent recommendations on skimming and penetration pricing.

How to Identify the Missed Opportunities

Promising as they are, there is no easy route to missed pricing opportunities. Identifying them requires both solid quantitative analysis of the structural relations and entrepreneurial anticipation of competitive and consumer dynamics. The usual grand strategy talk is too superficial. One has to dig deeper.

But much better digging tools are now available. Everyone concerned with price decisions should acquire some basic understanding of these tools, the core relations, and the information requirements. Unless this knowledge is broadly dissipated, cost-plus thinking and intuition will prevail. This becomes increasingly dangerous. In a more competitive world, prices must be fine-tuned according to the product's perceived value relative to the competition.

Managerial judgment, conjoint measurement, and market data analysis can generate the information required for price decisions. Specialists who can perform these analytical tasks are still rare but increasingly coming out of the universities. Managers should be demanding of these experts. They need information relevant to the price decision and not mountains of data. The data, the methods, the computers are there. The weak link is the application. And whether one likes it or not, pricing is mainly numbers work, though it is totally different from the number crunching accountants do. Most of the numbers are "soft," and the methods are complex. It is "price engineering" rather than "grand strategy" or "classical accounting."

While we have addressed the more amenable areas of pricing, there are many other opportunities. One particular promising area is nonlinear pricing. Here prices differ for each unit of the product. Forms include quantity discounts, "three for the price of two" offers, block tariffs, and frequent flyer programs. The fact that American Airlines called its frequent flyer program "the single most successful marketing tool we've ever had" points to the potential of such sophisticated price schemes. In studies for consumer products and telecommunication services, I have found possible profit increases of 20 percent to 50 percent. Another area with high potential is price bundling, in which several products (e.g., wine and cheese, hardware and software, machine and service) are offered together at one price. More sophisticated price differentiation across customers offers further profit opportunities. Ciba-Geigy's double-pronged approach on the U.S. pharmaceutical market under its own brand and the Geneva generic line is a good example. In general, price differentiation across customer segments is still in its infancy. Theoretically we know that huge opportunities are untapped. Although we do not yet know how to better exploit them, we make progress. The Japanese are exploiting pricing opportunities, too, as the new luxury car lines of Honda, Toyota, and Nissan prove.

Now when you set sails to better exploit the missed opportunities in pricing, remember it costs (almost) nothing. Price is the only marketing instrument without an upfront expenditure. Price pays for itself—any manager's dream.

References

1. H. Simon, *Price Management* (New York: Elsevier Science Publishers, 1989).

2. E. Raymond Corey, *Note on Pricing Strategy* (Cambridge, Massachusetts: Harvard Business School Press, 1982).

3. D. Ogilvy, *Ogilvy on Advertising* (New York: Vintage Books, 1988), p. 170.

4. See J. Lambin, *Advertising, Competition, and Market Conduct in Oligopoly over Time* (Amsterdam: North-Holland, 1976); and G. J. Tellis, "The Price Elasticity of Selective Demand: A Meta-Analysis of Econometric Models of Sales," *Journal of Market Research* 25 (1988): 331–341.

5. *Wall Street Journal*, 17 February 1989, p. B1.

6. For extensive simulations of long-term pricing strategies, see Simon (1989), chapter 6.

7. K. Ohmae, "Getting Back to Strategy," *Harvard Business Review*, November–December 1988, p. 149.

8. H. Schacht, "Leading a Company through Change," Harvard Business School seminar, 11 November 1988.

9. R. Henkoff, "The Engine That Couldn't," *Fortune International,* 18 December 1989, p. 86.

10. J. P. Newport, "Frequent Flyer Clones," *Fortune International,* April 1985, p. 113.

Chapter 9

Communicating with Business Customers: Personal Selling

The traditional purpose of communication, as part of the marketing mix, has been to inform, persuade, or remind. This may be appropriate for some products, but it falls far short of the purpose and nature of communicating with business customers. In this chapter we develop a more comprehensive framework for considering the purposes of communicating with customers and then address the role of personal selling in the communication process.

An Overview of Communication

Marketing strategies are designed to capitalize on the firm's strengths in order to exploit opportunities in selected markets or in target market segments. How well these opportunities are exploited is a function of both the appropriateness of the chosen strategies *and* the extent to which they are understood and accepted by enough customers to achieve the firm's objectives. Emerson's words about the builder of a better mousetrap notwithstanding, few products or services achieve success in the marketplace without an effective communication program—a communication program that has as its ultimate objective obtaining the customer's order. To achieve this objective, the communication program must also accomplish the following:

1. Ensure that the firm's communication efforts are targeted to those prospective customers whose needs most closely match the firm's product or service attributes.
2. Identify decision makers and important decision influences within the targeted customer organizations.
3. Create awareness and interest in the product or service.

4. Translate, or assist the customer to translate, product attributes into benefits.

5. Fine tune the product or service to more closely meet customer requirements.

6. Monitor the after-sale situation to assure customer satisfaction and to modify the marketing strategy with respect to future customer needs.

The effectiveness with which these elements of the communication program are implemented is critical to the success of the firm's marketing strategy. The nature of the business buying process, with a relatively small number of potential customers, the existence of multiple buying influences, and the frequent need for negotiation, plus the general technical complexity of products or services, is such that the predominant method of communication is personal selling. Nonpersonal methods of communication, particularly advertising, direct mail, telemarketing, and trade shows, also play an important role in communication strategy, either in support of the personal selling effort or as stand-alone methods to achieve communication objectives. In this chapter we first review the principal methods available to firms to communicate with customers and the concept of an integrated approach to communication. We then extensively discuss the nature of personal selling and its management.

The Methods of Business Communication

Traditionally advertising, personal selling, sales promotion, and publicity have been considered the principal methods of communication (or elements of the promotional mix). For business marketing we prefer the following more comprehensive classification scheme of communication methods:

- Personal selling: any face-to-face interaction with one or more prospective purchasers for the purpose of making a sale. Activities range from prospecting for customers, to providing information on the product or service, to order solicitation, to postsales service. Personal selling may be done by the firm's own sales force, by others in the firm who have some form of client or customer responsibility, by an agent of the firm (normally a manufacturer's representative), or by a distributor.

- Advertising: any form of paid, nonpersonal presentation or promotion of ideas, goods, or services by an identified sponsor in print or electronic media. In business marketing this tends to be principally in print media, oriented toward the business community in general or targeted to selected industry or occupational segments. In addition to providing information, advertising may be used to solicit a specific response such as a request for further information or, in some instances, an order for the product or service.

- Direct mail: any communication mailed to a specific, individual buying influence. As with advertising, direct mail may be used to provide information about a product or service or to elicit a specific response.

- Telemarketing: any contact made with a customer or prospective customer by phone. Growth in the use of this form of business communication has been explosive. From its original use as support for the personal selling effort, telemarketing has in some instances replaced personal selling as the principal method of order solicitation, and it is now widely used for lead qualifying, for marketing research, and for providing customers with ordering, service, or product information.
- Trade shows: any participation in an industry or trade show by means of an exhibit or other form of presence. Trade show participation is usually designed to inform customers about products or services, to identify prospective customers, or to identify prospective agents or distributors.
- Seminars, conferences/technical papers: any form of technical (i.e., noncommercial) presentation, usually by the firm's technical personnel regarding new products or their application. In some instances the presentation may be made by an industry-recognized expert outside the firm.
- Sales promotion: any use of samples, contests, catalogs, brochures, or other means to create interest or awareness of products not included above. Some sales promotion efforts, in particular contests, focus on the firm's sales force or on the sales force of its distributors and are designed to provide additional stimulus to the sales effort. In many instances contests are used very effectively to stimulate end-user interest in a product or service. (Note: The traditional definition of sales promotion usually includes trade shows and may include direct mail or telemarketing. For business marketing we believe these deserve separate identification.)
- Publicity: any effort to secure media attention to products or services, either as feature stories or short news items.

In addition to these categories, businesses communicate with customers in a number of other ways. Suppliers' engineers and customers' engineers interact at professional meetings or may jointly participate in standards meetings. Similar interactions take place between individuals in supplying and buying firms in other functional categories such as finance, production, or human resources and at various levels of management.

The variety of tools available to communicate with customers and the number of nonmarketing avenues of communication suggest the need for coordination of communication efforts. Much has been heard recently about integrated marketing communications (IMC), a concept of particular interest to consumer products companies but also of interest to business marketers. According to the American Association of Advertising Agencies, IMC has as its objective the combination of advertising, direct response, sales promotion, and public relations to provide clarity, consistency, and maximum communications' impact through the seamless integration of discrete messages.

The concept of coordinated communication efforts is hardly new. It has long been recognized that advertising or direct mail can support the personal selling effort by introducing the firm and its products to customers in advance of calls by the sales force or by reaching buying influences that the sales force cannot call on. Similarly, it has long been recognized that technical papers describing new products or their applications can play an effective role in the introduction and acceptance of new products. The current interest in IMC may reflect the fact that in many instances communication efforts have not been well coordinated. Sales promotion material, for instance, designed to support the efforts of the field sales force, frequently goes unused because the sales force does not feel it is effective. Similarly, leads developed by advertising messages may not be appropriately screened, with the potential for wasting the time of the sales force.

For business marketers, the imperative is a carefully coordinated communication program that effectively and economically utilizes all the tools of communication, that recognizes all the ways in which communications can take place between the firm and its customers, and that is well understood and supported by all who come in contact with the firm's customers. Given the role of personal selling as the most important element in the communications mix, we first discuss the role of the salesperson and management of the field sales force, both because of their importance, per se, and because understanding them is critical to understanding the role of other communication tools we discuss in Chapter 10, either to support personal selling or as substitutes for it.

The Role of the Salesperson

What, precisely, should the salesperson do and how should the sales force be managed? These are key questions for marketing strategy. Some years ago Drucker asserted, "There will always, one can assume, be need for some selling. But the aim of marketing is to make selling superfluous. The aim of marketing is to know and understand customers so well that the product or service fits them and sells itself."[1] To the extent that this statement is rooted in the view that the task of the salesperson is to sell things to people that they do not want or need, the assertion may be appropriate. It appears to assume, however, that products or services can be so precisely designed as to require no modification and so comprehensively explained in nonpersonal ways as to require no assistance in understanding their application—conditions that are seldom the case for business marketers. A more recent assertion is that "selling is dying."[2] The author explains what he means by this assertion is that selling in the future will be different, with emphasis on long-term affiliations and relationships that help people buy, a view that generally coincides with ours. We believe, however, a more appropriate view is that personal selling should reflect the firm's marketing strategy and that each firm should develop its own model of personal selling that fits its marketing strategy. In some instances this may be a variation of one of the many generic personal selling models that have been proposed. Hence, we start by examining three such models:

- Stimulus response. This model is based on the assumption that a standardized message delivered by a salesperson to a predetermined number of

customers will result in a predictable number of orders. Its key requirement is the salesperson's ability to get the opportunity to deliver the message. The model tends to have limited application in business selling as it is
appropriate principally for one-time sales, where there is one easily identifiable decision maker, or for very routine sales situations. It does, however,
have the merit of simplicity and is easily implemented.

- AIDA (Attention, Interest, Desire, Action). This model is based on the
  assumption that there are a number of standardized steps through which
  the salesperson should lead the customer: (1) get the customer's attention,
  (2) create interest in the product, (3) create desire for the product, and (4)
  get the order. The key requirement of this model is the salesperson's ability to determine when to move from one step to the next. The model, with
  somewhat broader application than the stimulus response model, suggests
  some of the dynamics involved in a sales call. But it also has limited applicability in business selling because it presumes there is a single decision
  maker and every sales call has the potential to result in an order. Also, evidence suggests it is difficult to determine when to move from one step to
  the next. AIDA generally is most useful as a starting point for consideration
  of additional task requirements.

- Consultative selling. This model is based on the assumption that high
  margin sales will result from focusing on improvement of customers' profits, resulting in customers willing to share their improved profits with the
  supplier.[3] While it takes into account the customer's most fundamental
  objective of profit improvement, it has been criticized for failing to recognize that many customers are not willing to enter into a relationship of the
  nature proposed by the model; that for many suppliers the opportunity is
  limited to significantly impact a customer's profit; and that it does not adequately consider the personal interactions between the salesperson and
  individuals in a customer's organization.

To the extent that these models are appropriate to a particular strategy, they may
be useful in suggesting the role of the salesperson, how he or she should be selected and trained, and how the sales force should be organized. As indicated, they
have serious limitations. For instance, both the stimulus response and AIDA
models fail to consider the customer, either with respect to the individual and his
or her characteristics or with respect to the customer's organization, its objectives,
and its way of doing business. In essence, the customer is seen as someone to be
manipulated by the salesperson. More broadly, all three models are generic. They
fail to incorporate the firm's marketing strategy and do not adequately connect
marketing strategy to the work of the salesperson. Still further, they do not suggest
the extent to which the customer's view of the supplier is influenced by the salesperson's behavior. As the purchasing manager of a large electric utility explained:

> Our view of a supplier changes substantially every time the supplier assigns a
> new salesperson. There is enormous variation in how they represent their prin-
> cipals. Some sell on personality, some sell on service. Some try to be the expert
> on every question. Others act more as conduits to connect us to those with spe-

cialized knowledge. In one situation, the salesperson was the only contact we ever had with the supplier. When he was transferred, the new salesperson introduced us to so many people in his firm we thought we were dealing with a different company.[4]

The key point is that marketing strategy should specify an appropriate model of personal selling. In a limited number of instances a generic model may be appropriate. In most instances, the model needs to be uniquely crafted to fit the firm's strategy and changed when the strategy changes. For example, at Ohmeda Monitoring Systems a new strategy lead to the development of a personal selling model, "The Ohmeda Way." It is used to guide all aspects of personal selling and sales force management, including training, selection, and compensation.

To provide the understanding necessary to the development of an appropriate model, we first introduce the concept of role as it applies to the salesperson's work. We next consider how the salesperson's role may be influenced by a number of situational factors . We then address issues in sales force management as well as the special issues associated with national or international accounts and the use of agents versus a firm's own sales force.

Role Concepts

In this chapter we use the term *role* to categorize a set of activities associated with a particular aspect of a sales position or assignment.[5] In some selling situations the salesperson may enact a single or limited number of roles, as might be the case in the routine sale of MRO items. In more complex selling situations, the salesperson may have a number of roles, as might be the case where the salesperson is expected to maintain relations with existing accounts, prospect for new accounts, introduce new products, secure orders from existing accounts and, in some instances, provide after-sales service. To enhance understanding of the salesperson's role we introduce a number of role concepts.

Role Set and Role Expectations. As salespersons enact the role specified by the marketing strategy, they relate directly or indirectly to individuals in other positions within their firm and in the customer's organization. These individuals make up the person's *role set*. At a minimum the role set includes the sales manager and key buying influences in customers' organizations. Because individuals in the role set depend on the salesperson's performance to some extent, they develop beliefs about what the salesperson should or should not do as part of his or her role. These prescriptions and proscriptions are designated as *role expectations*.

Role Conflict and Boundary Roles. *Role conflict* occurs when the expectations of one person in an individual's role set are at variance with the expectations of another. Such conflict is a fact of life in all social situations. Family expectations, for example, frequently conflict with those of employers. For the salesperson, role conflict is particularly acute. Salespersons occupy what are called *boundary positions*—positions that interface between two organizations. Such positions are particularly susceptible to role conflict, as a result of lack of power over persons in the other firm, from failure of others to understand the demands made on them, and from the great variation in objectives between organizations. The conflict between the firm's desire for a high price and the customer's desire for a low price, and the lack of the salesperson's authority to require the customer to buy, might exemplify this kind of conflict. Even within the firm, opportunities for role conflict tend to be greater for salespersons than for others, particularly in complex selling situations where the salesperson enacts a number of roles or represents products with significantly different marketing strategies. In such situations it is not unusual for product managers to have very different expectations as to appropriate sales approaches or to attempt to impose conflicting requirements as to time devoted to their products.

Role Ambiguity and Role Inaccuracy. Role ambiguity and role inaccuracy are related but arise very differently. *Role ambiguity* occurs when the nature of expectations of various members of the role set are unclear. Role ambiguity tends to be high for salespersons. The nature of personal selling, with many unanswered questions as to what makes for success, makes it difficult to clearly spell out all aspects of a salesperson's role. Boundary role positions exacerbate the problem as information about customer expectations may be difficult to obtain. *Role inaccuracy* occurs when the salesperson has an incorrect understanding of behavioral expectations with respect to some aspect of the job that is, in fact, specified by the job description or is clearly articulated by sales management or others who can legitimately prescribe the salesperson's behavior.

Role Repertory and Role Adjustment. Except for the simplest selling situations, salespersons are expected to have a *role repertory;* that is, they are expected to be able to enact a number of roles. As in more general social situations, large role repertories are generally associated with increased sales success. Adjustment from one role to another, however, is frequently difficult. The greater the required role repertory, the more likely the possibility for role conflict, ambiguity, and inaccuracy. As a result, many salespersons do not appropriately enact all required roles.

In summary, the salesperson must be able to enact a variety of roles in such a way as to be perceived by various constituencies in the firm as representing their interests *and* in such a way as to be perceived by the customer as representing the customer's interests. In enacting these roles, he or she will inevitably experience role conflict and is likely to experience role ambiguity, role inaccuracy, and problems in role adjustment. These problems cannot be eliminated. Managing them appropriately, however, is the key to sales success. The imperative for marketing strategy is to provide the framework within which the sales force is managed. This can be done only with a good understanding of the selling task, based on comprehensive understanding of the specific selling situation.

Understanding the Selling Situation

Most business selling situations share certain characteristics.

1. Relations between buying and selling organizations tend to be long term, as a result of either repetitive transactions or the length of the buying cycle.
2. Multiple buying influences are the norm.
3. Salespersons are generally assigned to call on specific accounts or to cover specific geographical territories.
4. Demand is derived. Hence, available business from individual accounts may be subject to substantial fluctuations.
5. Customer contact is primarily, and sometimes only, through the salesperson.
6. The salesperson's responsibilities usually include more than just selling.

A number of classification schemes have been developed to elaborate on these characteristics. In Chapter 3 we described the BUYGRID model, which suggests how the selling task may vary as a function of the buyer's situation in terms of the newness of the product to the buyer. The classification schemes described below provide further insights into the nature of the selling task in a particular situation.

Classification According to the Nature of the Product, Service, or Industry

The nature of the product, service, or served industry has a major influence in shaping the nature of the selling task. The tasks associated with selling a mainframe computer or a turbine generator, for example, which involve large expenditures and long buying cycles, vary significantly from those associated with the sale of highly standardized supply items. Similarly, the sales approach to contractor markets, with short-term relationships and emphasis on negotiation, is significantly different from the approach to the electric utility market, with its emphasis on long-term relationships and sealed bidding.

Product or service categories useful for consideration of the nature of the selling task include raw materials, components, capital goods, supplies, professional services, and maintenance services, each of which may suggest variations in the nature of the selling task. A complete list of categories where sales approaches vary would be quite lengthy, but the key is to recognize or identify the main aspects of the product, service, or industry that significantly influence the role of the salesperson.

Classification According to Selling Activities

A number of schemes have been proposed that consider the selling task in terms of the required activities. A now-classic study by Newton found sales forces organized around the following activities:[6]

- Trade selling. The principal activity focused on increasing business from customers by providing promotional assistance either to some element of the distribution channel or to a manufacturer purchasing for resale.

- Missionary selling. The principal activity focused on increasing business by providing a direct customer, such as a wholesaler, with personal selling assistance to indirect customers, such as small businesses, architects, or doctors.

- Technical selling. The principal activity focused on increasing business from existing customers by providing technical service and assistance.

- New business selling. The principal activity focused on increasing business by obtaining new accounts for the firm.

Classification According to Strategic Fit

The salesperson's job is to exploit the opportunity made possible by the supplier's strategy and marketing program. We define *strategic fit* as the match between the supplier's strategy and the wants and needs of individual customers. Achieving strategic fit is the purpose of market segmentation. Realistically, a high level of strategic fit with every customer in a targeted segment is difficult to obtain. Economy of scale considerations restrict opportunities to segment markets. Within narrowly defined market segments, business buyers are highly idiosyncratic in their business strategies as they strive for competitive advantage. Joint development efforts with one customer, for instance, may be seen as a competitive threat by another. Successful implementation of a pull strategy may interfere with at least some customers' efforts to achieve product differentiation with respect to their competitors. Even where competition between customers is not a factor, as may be the case with electric utilities or telecommunication companies, variation in their business strategies may make "a one marketing strategy fits all" difficult.

Finally, strategic fit is dynamic, not static. Economies of scale change as new technology influences manufacturing processes. Individual customer's strategies change as they pursue their changing market opportunities or respond to competitive threats. Environmental forces can influence the strategies of all or some of the firms within an industry. Some shifts may enhance strategic fit between supplier and customer. Others may detract from it.

In the long run, suppliers have the option to change their strategies to more nearly meet customer objectives or to attempt to influence favorable changes in customer strategies as ways to achieve strategic fit. The salesperson, however, solicits orders from assigned accounts in the short run and in the context of current strategies and programs. *The role of the salesperson is, therefore, materially influenced by current levels of strategic fit.*

High Level of Strategic Fit. Where strategic fit is high, the salesperson's opportunity is generally favorable. He or she enjoys significant competitive advantage or at least has competitive parity. Securing a large share of the customer's business is important, but success is assumed. The salesperson needs to understand the customer's decision-making process, but the nature of communications to individuals in the customer's organization is explanatory rather than persuasive. Equal emphasis is placed on management of the systems that support pre- and postorder activities. The salesperson develops an extensive network of contacts in the customer's organization, and close personal relationships may develop. The importance of continued strategic fit is recognized, and the salesperson is expected to monitor changes in customer strategy and needs and to use this knowledge to guide the supplier's continued fine-tuning of strategy and marketing programs. Competitive activity is monitored as a defensive tactic to guard against encroachment of the salesperson's favored position.

Low Level of Strategic Fit. Where strategic fit is low, the salesperson's role is very different. Opportunity is not as favorable. The competitive position is one of disadvantage. The salesperson is expected to get orders, but these expectations are not high. Understanding the buying decision process is important, but communications are persuasive rather than explanatory, as the salesperson attempts to influence change in the customer's evaluation system, objectives, or, in some instances, even the customer's strategy. The flow of orders is small or erratic, and systems to support pre- and post-order activity are modest or nonexistent. The salesperson's network of personal contacts is small, and the opportunity to develop close personal relationships is limited. Customer strategy is monitored primarily in hope of a change in a favorable direction. Competitive activity is monitored, but the emphasis is on identifying weakness in competitors' approaches or failure of competitors to respond to changes in the customer's strategy.

Although we have described the salesperson's role for two levels of strategic fit, in actuality strategic fit is a continuum, not a dichotomy. As a result, many variations are possible in the salesperson's role. Still further, in the case of a pooled sales force or a manufacturer's agent selling many products, strategic fit can vary not only by account but also by product within accounts. In some instances the salesperson will manage an ongoing relationship for one product and emphasize opportunistic positioning for another.

Personal Interaction between Salesperson and Buyer

We have described a number of classification schemes, or frameworks, to assist in better understanding the tasks and role of the salesperson. The essence of personal selling, however, is the one-on-one interaction with an individual in the customer's organization. In the final analysis, sensing how the prospect expects the salesperson to behave and how effectively the salesperson reacts to these expectations is a matter of the individual skill and personality of the salesperson. A number of classification schemes have been developed to assist the salesperson in thinking about the dynamics of this personal interaction. It is beyond the

FIGURE 9.1
Dimensional Model of Sales Behavior

Dominance

Q1. Dominant-Hostile

Customers don't buy
willingly. Salesperson
must impose his or her
will on the customer
through strength.
Selling is a struggle the
salesperson must win.

Q4. Dominant-Warm

Customers will buy if they can
satisfy a need. Salesperson must
show customer his or her product
will best satisfy customer's needs.
Selling is a win-win process for
customer, salesperson, and
company.

Hostility

Warmth

Q2. Submissive-Hostile

Customers buy when
ready. Little the
salesperson can do
to get them to buy.
Survive by taking
the order when the
customer is ready.

Q3. Submissive-Warm

Customers buy from friends.
The salesperson's job is to
make friends.

Submission

Source: Adapted from V.R. Buzzotta, R.E. Lefton, and Manuel Sherberg, *Effective Selling Through Psychology: Dimensional Sales and Sales Management Strategies* (St. Louis: Psychological Associates, Inc., 1991). Reprinted by permission of Psychological Associates, Inc., with corporate offices in St. Louis, Missouri, U.S.A. All rights reserved.

scope of this text to extensively explore the nature of this interaction. However, we briefly describe one classification scheme that suggests the complexity of possible interactions between salesperson and buyer.

The scheme developed by Buzzotta and his colleagues classifies the salesperson and the buyer on two dimensions: dominant–submissive and hostile–warm.[7] Using these dimensions, they then describe four sales approaches and four buying approaches, as shown in Figures 9.1 and 9.2. The value systems underlying the four sales approaches can be paraphrased as "make 'em buy" (dominant–hostile), "whatever will be, will be" (submissive–hostile), "you can't say no to a friend" (submissive–warm), and "get 'em committed" (dominant–warm). Similar value systems can be inferred for buyers. These can then be used to examine the nature of the interaction between the various categories of salespersons and buyers and to suggest how salespersons can adapt more effectively to individual buyers.

Managing the Sales Force

While marketing strategy should specify the major aspects of the selling task, directing the selling effort is the responsibility of the sales manager. A number of management tools can assist the sales manager in accomplishing this goal.

FIGURE 9.2
Dimensional Model of Sales Behavior

Dominance

Q1. Dominant-Hostile

Salespersons can't be trusted. They want to sell me something I don't want or need. I control them by being tough and resistant. The best defense is a good offense.

Q4. Dominant-Warm

I buy because I expect to benefit. I buy from salespersons who prove they can help me get more benefit than their competitors.

Hostility ——————————————————————— **Warmth**

Q2. Submissive-Hostile

Salespersons can't be trusted. They want to sell me something I don't want or need. To defend myself, I try to avoid them. If I can't, I try to stay uninvolved.

Q3. Submissive-Warm

Competitive products are all alike. Since it really doesn't matter which one I buy, I might as well buy from a salesperson I like.

Submission

Source: Adapted from V.R. Buzzotta, R.E. Lefton, and Manuel Sherberg, *Effective Selling Through Psychology: Dimensional Sales and Sales Management Strategies* (St. Louis: Psychological Associates, Inc., 1991). Reprinted by permission of Psychological Associates, Inc., with corporate offices in St. Louis, Missouri, U.S.A. All rights reserved.

Job Description: The Starting Point

The job description should be the starting point of sales force management. All else flows from a good understanding of selling objectives and how they are to be accomplished. It is not enough to say the objective is to get orders. The job description must spell out the firm's sales approach, the desired balance between new and existing accounts, the desired balance of product line sales, the desired activities beyond sales calls (e.g., participation in trade shows), the nature of the sales support, and how the salesperson is to use the resources of the firm. To guide the selection process the job description should also include the salesperson's qualifications.

Personnel Selection: The Critical Decision

Few aspects of sales force management are more critical than the selection process. Poor hiring decisions, quickly made, may take months to undo and in the process may excessively burden management resources. Unfortunately, there is no magic formula to guide the selection process. Despite countless studies, there is no evidence of a universal sales personality.[8] Good selection processes seem to rely on a number of techniques developed in the context of the firm's particular selling situation and taking into account the characteristics of successful salespersons in the firm. Multiple interviews that are carefully structured and done by individuals trained in interviewing and formal tests that are validated against the records of successful salespersons in the firm improve the selection process.

Training: The Ongoing Requirement

Training is a key aspect of sales force management. It has two principal dimensions:

1. Knowledge, with respect to the company and its strategy, processes, products, and procedures.
2. Skill, with respect to analyzing the customer situation, planning an account or call strategy, and handling the specific call.

Knowledge training is generally straightforward. Marketing managers can explain marketing strategy; product specialists can describe product or service features. Training in selling skills is more complex. Generic sales training programs can be used to introduce basic sales concepts. Sales training relevant to the marketing strategy, however, must be specially developed. Sales training for experienced salespersons must also be specially developed, taking into account both the experience of the salesperson and changes in the marketing strategy. As firms move to team selling, training in its unique requirements becomes particularly important.

Coaching: The Changing Element

Traditionally, coaching the salesperson has been an important element of the sales manager's job. This presumes that the sales manager makes calls with the salesperson, observes the sales approach and, subsequently, gives the salesperson feedback. As organizations flatten, increasing the number of the sales manager's direct reports, and as sales forces organize on other than geographic dimensions, the opportunity for the sales manager to make calls with the salesperson decreases. As a result, the nature of coaching is changing. Increasingly, there is emphasis on working with the salesperson to develop account or territory strategies, or to manage teams, with emphasis on how the team functions rather than on an individual's personal selling skill.

Sales Support

Few salespersons today can operate effectively without extensive support. Inside sales personnel backing up the salesperson are common. Computers are used increasingly to facilitate making the sales presentation, to enhance the ability of the salesperson to check order status, or to reduce the time required for administrative tasks. Telemarketing is used increasingly to reach small customers or to make customer contact between personal calls.

Compensation

Compensation is one of the most complex aspects of sales force management. Options include:

- Straight salary.
- Straight commission paid as a percentage of gross sales.
- Commission paid as a percentage of gross margin.
- Dollar bonuses or a percentage of salary paid on performance relative to quota.
- A combination of straight salary and some form of incentive payment.

In the United States, straight salary is common, but the predominant form of compensation is a combination of salary and incentive, usually based on performance with respect to quota. Typical combinations range from 50–50 (i.e., 50 percent salary and 50 percent incentive for meeting quota) to 80–20. The variation in compensation plans, however, is enormous. Cultural norms significantly influence plan selection. Firms in Northern Europe, for instance, tend to favor straight salary plans. Even within industries in the same country there is great variation. For many years Digital Equipment paid its sales force on straight salary, whereas the rest of the computer industry relied heavily on some form of incentive compensation.

While there are no rules for the "right" compensation plan, there are some guidelines:

- The plan should reflect the reality of the selling task. Incentive compensation tends to be less appropriate in long selling cycle situations or in situations where the salesperson is just one of many factors that may determine the order placement.
- The plan must be understandable. Incentive plans that attempt to pay for performance based on a large number of variables are generally too complex to be understood by the sales force and lose their ability to motivate.
- The plan should not attempt to be a substitute for good management. It is simply impossible to devise an incentive plan to guide or evaluate all dimensions of the salesperson's work.
- As firms move to more team selling, compensation planning must account for the impact of an incentive plan on all members of the team, both those in sales and those in support roles.
- The plan should be perceived as fair. Plans perceived as establishing arbitrary quotas or as penalizing the salesperson for events beyond his or her control will fail to motivate the sales force.
- The plan should take into account the values of those in the sales force. That is, to what extent are individuals in the sales force motivated by monetary incentives and how might this vary as a function of age or stage of career?

Career Pathing: Frequently Forgotten

Managing the sales force must take into account growth in sales competence, marketing personnel needs, and the future managerial needs of the sales force. It is important, therefore, to recognize the various career paths that salespersons may take within the firm. A typical career path to accomplish this might include the following assignments:

- A starting assignment at marketing headquarters, designed to acquaint the individual with the marketing strategy and the products and procedures of the firm.
- A low-level sales assignment followed by a mid-level sales assignment to demonstrate selling skills and leadership potential.
- A marketing headquarters assignment in a key activity such as pricing or field sales support.
- A high-level field sales assignment, possibly directing a sales team.
- A management position either in field sales or at headquarters.

Where the opportunity does not exist for an extensive array of assignments, changes in sales assignments with increasing levels of responsibility, combined with special assignments to new product development teams or to product introduction task forces, should be considered.

Special Issues

It is beyond the scope of this text to extensively treat all aspects of sales force management. Five issues, however, merit particular attention.

Use of Agents versus Own Sales Force

Traditionally, manufacturers' agents have been considered as part of a channel of distribution much in the same context as wholesalers. It has also been traditional to frame the decision to use agents principally in economic terms. That is, because they are not under the direct control of the manufacturer, they are thought appropriate just for small firms that cannot afford their own sales force or for large firms that cannot justify a full-time salesperson in new territories or other special situations.

We treat the topic here because it is more appropriate to think of a manufacturer's agent as a substitute for the manufacturer's own sales force. Consider the typical agent, either an individual or a small firm, that exclusively represents one manufacturer, or several manufacturers of complementary lines, in a specified geographic area. The agent does not take title to the product, does not handle invoicing, and sells at the manufacturer's price and in accordance with the manufacturer's policies. To earn the right to represent the manufacturer, the agent fields skilled salespersons who are both competent with respect to the product and knowledgeable with regard to their customers. In short, the agent performs almost the same functions as does a manufacturer's sales force.

The issue, then, of using agents is not simply a matter of economics, but should take into account the specialized knowledge or relationships of the agent and the ability of the firm to manage the agent. The economics of the decision are fairly straightforward. Commission expense paid to an agent can easily be weighed against the cost of a salesperson or the establishment of a sales office. In some instances, however, agents may have specialized knowledge or have relationships with customers that would be difficult to duplicate, whose value would transcend pure expense considerations. Finally, while agents are not directly under the control of their principals, it would be inappropriate to conclude that they are not responsive to their needs or desires. As with a manufacturer's sales force, agents' selling efforts can be influenced by a number of factors beyond just the commission rate. In particular, high levels of sales support can significantly increase an agent's effectiveness.

Organizing the Field Sales Force

How should the field sales force be organized? The difficulty in finding the correct answer to this question is indicated by the frequency with which sales forces are reorganized. For example, frequent reorganizations have characterized both IBM and AT&T, with changes from one general sales force selling all products and services to all industries, to various combinations of multiple sales forces selling limited lines of products to targeted industries. As late as 1993, it was still a key issue for Louis Gerstner, the new IBM CEO, who promised, "We're going to organize the sales force to give customers what they want. We're going to start with the customer."[9]

While giving the customers what they want is critical, this does not necessarily provide a clear path to the right organization. Some customers want to be called on by product specialists. Some want industry specialists. Others want "one-stop shopping" or an account executive who represents the total company. For small companies selling a limited product line to a restricted number of industries, the issue is relatively simple. One sales force organized on geographic lines can meet most if not all these requirements and, importantly, can assure the company that all product lines are well represented. As the firm expands its product line or elects to pursue new markets, it faces the choice of establishing several sales forces or, as is common, establishing a "pooled sales force" that represents a number of SBUs or product businesses. The choice is influenced by the ability of the sales force to sell to diverse markets, by its ability to have sufficient product knowledge to represent a variety of products, by the view of the SBU manager as to the adequacy of representation, and by customer desires. Inevitably the chosen form of organization represents a compromise between conflicting objectives. In particular, while pooled sales forces are widely used, SBU managers, as in the Ohmeda Monitoring Systems case, are frustrated by lack of direct control over the sales force. As with manufacturers' agents, one solution is to look for ways to increase the level of support provided to the sales force; in short, to make it easy for the sales force to sell the SBUs products.

Involvement in Marketing Research and Strategy Development

With few exceptions, business salespersons are knowledgeable about their customers' strategies, product needs, and buying practices. They are also likely to be knowledgeable about many aspects of competitive products and strategies. For the development of new products or changes in marketing strategy, the sales force represents a rich source of information but one that may be under-utilized unless formal processes are in place to ensure an appropriate flow of information. Systems need to be in place to encourage and reward salespersons who contribute customer and competitive information. At the least this requires (1) that the sales force knows what kind of information is desired and (2) that individuals who provide such information be recognized and rewarded for their contributions. When new products or changes in marketing strategy are being considered, members of the field sales force can make valuable contributions as members of task forces or planning teams.

National and International Accounts

We define a *national account* as one in which multiple buying influences are located in a number of locations within one country. *International accounts* are an extension of national accounts, with buying influences located in two or more countries.

Almost without exception, national accounts require some form of sales team to handle all the buying influences. Accounts are frequently large enough to require specialized sales support provided by individuals who are also often members of the sales team. We describe three key issues in the management of national accounts.

Sales Coverage. Options include coverage of all buying influences from a central office location, a dedicated national account team with salespersons strategically located throughout the country, or individuals in the regular sales force who may be assigned exclusively to national accounts or who may be assigned to a mixture of local and national accounts.

Teamwork. Historically, selling has been a highly individual activity. Customer relationships tend to be very personal. Information gained from key buying influences is closely guarded. The norm for most salespersons is "I got the order" not "we got the order." Teamwork, therefore, cannot be taken for granted. Extreme, perhaps, but illustrative is the experience of Kraft in the United States, which no longer hires experienced salespersons because of their difficulty in making the transition from operating as an individual to operating as a team member. Careful selection of team members, special training, and appropriate management practices are required if, in fact, salespersons are to operate as a team.

Sales Credit and Compensation. Where incentive forms of payment are involved, the importance of allocating sales credit is obvious. Even where members of the team are paid on straight salary, the issue of sales credit is still salient. Salespersons have budgets, and annual raises or promotions are influenced by performance relative to budget.

A variety of approaches to credit allocation have been used. The formula approach gives the office or individual receiving the order a specified percentage of the orders received credit, and the balance of the credit is evenly split among other salespersons assigned to the account, without consideration of the actual influence exerted. As we see in the Grasse Fragrances case, however, where the office receiving the order exerted no influence and, indeed, was unaware the order was coming, the formula approach would have led to serious inequities.

The drawbacks of the formula approach have led some firms to simply give each salesperson full credit for the order. In a sense this avoids the issue and, in any event, is generally not practicable if significant amounts of incentive compensation are involved. Some firms have attempted to assign management the responsibility to subjectively assess the share of influence exerted by members of the sales team. Management, however, may not be close enough to the situation to make an informed judgment. In situations where members of the sales team report to different managers, there is also the potential for bias and a manager's negotiating skill may outweigh the merits of a particular case.

Finally, there is the issue of nonselling personnel who are important members of the team but tend to be left out of incentive compensation schemes based solely on orders received.

One approach that holds promise is to establish a bonus pool for all members of the team based on the total volume of business or the profit contribution of the team. Shares in the bonus pool are then determined by the team members who allocate influence shares to other team members.

International Accounts. International accounts are an extension of national accounts, and share many of the same management issues. Other considerations include language and cultural differences, which add to the imperative for special training and management and to the cost of meetings and communication. GE Plastics, for instance, has for several years recognized the need for special attention to communication between far flung team members by establishing a computerized customer data base accessible by team members in any location in the world.

A special consideration in managing sales to international accounts is the firm's organizational structure. For firms with extensive operations outside of their home country, the most common form of organization is country based, with a country manager responsible for all activities of the firm within a particular country. In some instances, the country manager is essentially a sales manager, responsible only for sales and perhaps distribution activities. In other instances, the country manager is responsible for a number of additional activities including manufacturing and finance. In these instances, as we see in the Grasse Fragrances case, the interests and measurement system of the country manager must be taken into account.

Selling to Distributors

The role of the salesperson assigned to a distributor is significantly different from that of other sales jobs. The objective, of course, is to secure orders. Orders from distributors, however, result only if the distributor's customers place orders. Subject to the nature of the relationship the distributor elects to have with its suppliers, the role of the salesperson more nearly parallels that of a sales manager, albeit without any authority over the distributor. Keys to success include training or otherwise assisting the distributor's salespersons, sometimes making joint calls on distributor's customers; assistance to the distributor with respect to overall business planning; and general sales support to various parts of the distributor's organization. As in the case of Leykam Mürztaler, the effectiveness with which the assigned salesperson manages the relationship with the distributor can significantly increase the distributor's sales of the supplier's products.

Summary

Frequent reorganizations of field sales forces indicate a continuing quest for that right combination of marketing strategy and field sales efforts. Examples abound of product introductions that were not supported by the field sales force. Tensions between those in marketing and field sales are widely reported. Marketing strategy, therefore, must take into account not only how customers buy, but also how the sales force sells. Except in the most standardized situations, the success of the salesperson is determined by how well he or she orchestrates the firm's resources to connect the business and marketing strategy to the situation of an individual account. While personal selling is the predominant method of communicating with business customers, the efforts of the sales force can be supported and reinforced by a variety of nonpersonal selling methods that need to be coordinated with the personal effort.

Marketing strategy should establish the context within which the sales force operates, identify the target customers or specify their characteristics, and define the sales approach. Field sales management is the key to ensuring the connection of marketing strategy to the efforts of the sales force. Finally, marketing strategy should take into account the dynamic nature of personal selling and the extent to which the selling task changes as a result of changes in the external environment as well as marketing strategy. As we will discuss in Chapter 10, personal selling should be supported by and coordinated with a number of other methods of communication that also can be used for direct marketing.

Overview of Chapter Cases

❋ The Waters Chromatography case describes the marketing strategy and sales management practices of the firm and also describes in considerable detail the sales approach of one of the firm's sales representatives. It provides the opportunity to evaluate both the firm's sales management practices and to consider how the performance of the sales representative might be improved.

❋ The Grasse Fragrances case describes the situation of a French firm that revamped its internal marketing organization to adapt to changes in the international fragrances industry and now must consider how, or if, it needs to change its sales force management practices.

Endnotes

1. Peter Drucker, *People and Performance, The Best of Peter Drucker on Management* (New York: Harper & Row Publishers, Inc., 1977), 91.

2. Don Schultz, "Selling Is Dying," *Sales and Marketing Management,* August 1994, 82–84.

3. For a comprehensive treatment of the subject, see Mack Hanan, *Consultative Selling* (New York: AMACOM, 1985).

4. From a personal communication with H. Michael Hayes, July 1974.

5. This section draws heavily from Robert L. Kahn, et al., *Organizational Stress: Studies in Role Conflict and Ambiguity* (New York: John F. Wiley and Sons, Inc., 1964) and Orville S. Walker, Jr., et al., "Organization Determinants of the Industrial Salesman's Role Conflict and Role Ambiguity," *Journal on Marketing* (January 1975): 32–39.

6. Derek A. Newton, "Get the Most Out of Your Salesforce," *Harvard Business Review,* September–October 1969, 130–143.

7. V.R. Buzzota,. R.E. Lefton, and Manuel Sherberg, *Effective Selling Through Psychology: Dimensional Sales and Sales Management Strategies* (St. Louis: Psychological Associates, Inc., 1991).

8. Gilbert A. Churchill, Jr., Neil M. Ford, Steven W. Hartley, and Orville C. Walker, Jr., "The Determinants of Salesperson Performance: A Meta-Analysis," *Journal of Marketing Research,* Vol. XXII (May 1985): pp. 103–118.

9. *Sales & Marketing Management,* October 1993, 82.

Thomas R. Wotruba

The Evolution of Personal Selling

While personal selling positions have been categorized into taxonomies, a longitudinal view of how selling jobs change or evolve has not yet been provided. This article presents such a view, based on an inductive analysis from available literature on selling jobs, selling's history, and characteristics of competitive and market environments. Five stages in this evolution of selling are presented and discussed: provider, persuader, prospector, problem-solver, and procreator. Relationships to management practice and implications for future research efforts are also noted. ✳

The job category titled "personal selling" really encompasses a wide variety of positions and responsibilities. Many marketing students as well as others in the general public may not appreciate these variations, however, since their image of selling is conditioned by the stereotype portrayed in movies, television shows, and cartoons (Thompson 1972, Swan and Adkins 1980–81). This image, however misunderstood, presents a very narrow view of selling, thwarts the desirability of selling as a career, and reduces the appeal of a selling job as the start of a professional career path in marketing.

In fact, existent selling jobs encompass a wide range of duties, behaviors, and challenges. Various taxonomies of sales positions have been proposed to reflect the diversity in this job (McMurray 1961, Moncrief 1986, Newton 1973), while other studies have focused on job characteristics which differ among types of sales jobs (Moore, Eckrich, and Carlson 1986; Wotruba and Simpson 1990). These contributions are static in nature, however, and do not reflect how the selling process is changing or how the focus of selling behavior has evolved to outgrow those old stereotypes. Investigations of changes in behavior as individual salespeople progress through their careers represent a more dynamic analysis (Jolson 1974; Cron 1984) but consider changes in the job's incumbent only and not changes in the selling job itself.

Powers et al. (1987) described the historical origins and early practices of selling prior to 1900, and Powers, Koehler, and Martin (1988) continued this overview from 1900 to 1949. These perspectives showed distinct differences in the practice of selling in different time periods, particularly when they corresponded with changes in economic conditions and associated competitive and market variations. Dawson (1970) offered a view of how sales management evolved from the production era to a sales era, a marketing era, and will finally evolve to a human era, noting some changes associated with the typical salesperson at each stage as well.

At the time this article was written, Thomas R. Wotruba (Ph.D., University of Wisconsin, Madison) was a Professor of Marketing at San Diego State University. He has authored textbooks in sales management, marketing management, and marketing principles and has published numerous professional journal articles and research monographs. He has served as editor of the *Journal of Personal Selling & Sales Management,* and as a member of that journal's editorial board. His business experience involves ownership positions in both retail and manufacturing firms, as well as many consulting assignments for business and government organizations. The author thanks Linda Rochford, Massoud Saghafi, and Pradeep Tyagi for their comments on an early draft of this paper, and two *JPSSM* reviewers for their stimulating and constructive guidance in evolving this paper to its conclusion. *Source:* Reprinted by permission of the publisher from *Journal of Personal Selling and Sales Management,* Vol. II, No. 3, Summer 1991, pp. 1–12.

357

TABLE 1

Literature Related to Differences in Sales Jobs and the Evolution of Personal Selling

Author and Year	Primary Topics	Summary of Findings
McMurray (1961)	A taxonomy of sales positions	Identified and defined seven types of sales positions, from order-taker to creative.
Dawson (1970)	Evolution of sales management	Identified four eras for sales management: production, sales, marketing, and human; and noted characteristics of salespeople in each era.
Newton (1973)	Classification of sales positions	Narrowed down the McMurray taxonomy to four types: trade, missionary, technical, and new business.
Jolson (1974)	Salesperson's career cycle	Identified four phases in a salesperson's career: preparation, development, maturity, and decline.
Wotruba (1980)	Changes occurring in industrial selling	Described how the nature of industrial selling was becoming more professional and managerial in nature.
Jolson (1980)	Trends in the selling job	Discussion of environmental changes, their effect on the selling job, and implications for classroom and textbook coverage of this topic.
Cron (1984)	Salesperson's career stages	Related a salesperson's career objectives, personal challenges, developmental tasks, and psychosocial needs to each of four career stages.

(continued)

Fullerton (1988) disputed this categorization of eras, however, showing how marketing was an integral part of business success for numerous firms and industries during early periods termed the "production" era. Wotruba (1980) and Jolson (1980) discussed changes in the selling environment and how industrial selling was responding in terms of becoming more professional and managerial in nature. Schurr (1987) suggested that approaches to effective selling are evolving from closed and indirect techniques to consultative selling and finally to relational contracting. Cespedes, Doyle, and Freedman

TABLE 1 *(continued)*

Author and Year	Primary Topics	Summary of Findings
Moore, Eckrich, and Carlson (1986)	Competencies needed for successful sales performance	Study producing a hierarchy of importance among 82 sales competencies for three types of salespeople: company salespeople for manufacturers, manufacturers' agents, and distributors' salespeople.
Moncrief (1986)	Taxonomy of sales positions	Study identifying six types of industrial sales jobs based on frequency of occurrence of various sales activities.
Powers et al. (1987)	History of selling prior to 1900	Historical narrative of the early history of selling and its contribution to economic development.
Schurr (1987)	Evolution in sales approaches	Suggests an evolutionary pattern among three sales approaches: from closed or indirect techniques to consultative selling to relational contracting.
Powers, Koehler, and Martin (1988)	History of selling from 1900 to 1949	Historical narrative of the development of selling in the first half of the 20th century, focusing on the practices, philosophies, and events which have influenced the selling profession.
Fullerton (1988)	Role of marketing and selling in the production era	Disputes the view that marketing and selling were of little consequence in the production era (1870–1930).
Cespedes, Doyle, and Freedman (1989)	Changes in selling	Discussion and examples of a shift from individual salespeople to the use of selling teams, with management implications.
Wotruba and Simpson (1990)	The selling cycle	Relates various selling strategies and sales management practices to selling jobs with differing lengths of selling cycle.

(1989) noted and illustrated some major shifts in selling toward the use of selling teams. In comparison to the cross-sectional or static comparisons among sales positions, these latter efforts represent attempts at a longitudinal analysis of changes in the central character of selling. Table 1 presents a summary of these cross-sectional and longitudinal discussions and analyses involving both selling jobs and their incumbents and serves as the jumping-off point for this paper.

The purpose of this paper is to take a more detailed look at how the central character of personal selling changes as the seller's competitive and market environment changes. This paper's purpose does not include an analysis of the impact of specific models of competition or markets on selling or other marketing practices. That task has been attempted in Eliashberg and Chatterjee (1985).

The fundamental nature of selling evolves through a series of stages, though these stages are not necessarily related to specific calendar periods of time. The practice of selling may not be at the same stage at a given time in all industries, or in all companies in the same industry, or even in all components of the total sales organization within one company. The evolutionary pattern can be likened to Darwin's theory of natural selection, whereby the species best fitted to the contingencies of its environment will survive and prosper (Henderson 1983; Lambkin and Day 1989).

Firms relying greatly on personal selling for their marketing success will survive and prosper to the extent that they adjust their selling practices to "fit" the contingencies of the competitive and market environments they face. The most simple competitive environment is the *absence* of competition, a state typically followed by the *presence* of competition, then an enlarging *quantity* of competitors, and then an improving *quality* of competitor actions which provide increasingly effective responses to the market environment served. As firms adjust to these unfolding conditions in a particular market, some distinct stages appear in the conduct of personal selling taking place in that market. Its scope broadens and its nature becomes more elaborate. Selling evolves or else it becomes ineffective in the quest for business success and survival.

In many firms the evolution of selling is accompanied by a partitioning of their sales effort into components which are deployed into distinct market and competitive environments. This is done to allow the selling firm the opportunity to serve various environments with different kinds of selling effort—i.e., selling efforts positioned at different evolutionary stages of sophistication. Thus, a firm with one sales force that served all customers in essentially the same manner might find that, to remain effective with its largest customers, its selling effort must be upgraded, perhaps by using sell-

ing teams rather than individuals. But the firm might also determine that its smaller customers can be served with a different and less intensive type of selling effort, one which represents a less sophisticated stage of evolution, perhaps by using agents, distributors, or a simple telemarketing operation (Cardozo and Shipp 1987). Eventually, however, in response to changes in the characteristics of the smaller customer market and the competition faced in that market, the selling effort serving that market might have to evolve to remain effective. Further subdividing of this market might then be considered by management, followed by further partitioning of the firm's selling efforts, and the evolutionary pattern will continue.

The Evolutionary Process in Personal Selling

Five distinct stages in the evolution of personal selling can be induced from the identification of corresponding market and competitive states, reinforced by an analysis of the literature cited and supported by reports of company practices today. At any point in time, a cross-section of personal selling jobs will include some at each stage, however, because of the numerous competitive and market environments in which these salespeople and their firms operate. An overview of these stages and the characteristics associated with them can be seen in Table 2. The five stages and a brief description of each are as follows:

Provider stage: Selling is limited to accepting orders for the supplier's available offering and conveying it to the buyer.

Persuader stage: Selling involves attempting to convince any and all market members to buy the supplier's available offering.

Prospector stage: Selling includes seeking out selected buyers who are perceived by the salesperson to have a need for the supplier's available offering as well as the resources and authority to buy it.

Problem-solver stage: Selling involves obtaining the participation of buyers in identifying their problems which can be translated into needs, and

TABLE 2

Characteristics of the Stages in the Evolution of Selling

	Characteristics of Stages			
Stages and Description	**Customer Needs Are**	**Type of Market**	**Nature and Intensity of Competition**	**Examples**
1. Provider: accepting orders and delivering to buyer.	Assumed to exist; not a concern	Sellers'	None	Route salespeople–drivers; some retail sales clerks
2. Persuader: attempting to convince anyone to buy available offerings.	Created, awakened	Buyers'	Undifferentiated; slight intensity	Telemarketer for photography studio; many new car dealer salespeople
3. Prospector: seeking out prospects with need for available offering as well as resources and authority to buy.	Considered but inferred	Segmented	Differentiated; growing	Car insurance salespeople calling on new car buyers; office supplies sellers calling on small businesses
4. Problem-solver: matching available offerings to solve customer-stated problems.	Diagnosed, with attention to customer input	Participative	Responsive and counteractive with increasing resources	Communication systems salespeople for a telephone company; architectural services seller calling on a building contractor
5. Procreator: creating a unique offering to match the buyer's needs as mutually specified, involving any or all aspects of the seller's total marketing mix.	Mutually defined; matched with tailored offering	Coactive	Focused; growing in breadth of market and service offerings	Materials handling equipment salesperson who designs and sells a system to fit a buyer's manufacturing facility

then presenting a selection from the supplier's spectrum of available offerings that correspond with those needs and can solve those problems.

Procreator stage: Selling is defining buyers' problems or needs and the solutions to those problems or needs through active buyer–seller collaboration, and then creating a market offering uniquely tailored to match those specific needs of each individual customer.

Each stage will be discussed in detail. But as a foundation for that discussion, a look at some characteristics of the evolutionary process is in order.

The stages in the evolution of personal selling are cumulative. In other words, the selling job grows and enlarges, but does not discard the characteristics of the prior stage. Thus, the prospector must do some persuading and providing, and the procreator must engage appropriate prospects to define their problems prior to making a joint commitment with them to tailor a market offering to their needs. This cumulation of tasks represents selling strategy expanding in complexity, made necessary by a growing intensity of competition as well as an increasing sophistication of buyers in that particular marketplace. As a result, the incumbents of these sales positions must possess capabilities that increase in depth and scope from stage to stage.

Movement from one stage to the next also has cost implications. Each stage is more complex than its predecessor, and these complexities increase costs due to the additional time and talent needed to be effective. Movement from one stage to the next involves the need for greater attention to efficiency, especially since some of the strategies associated with the advanced stages are not always successful. For instance, problem-solvers might dig so long and deep for problems to solve that they fail to provide timely solutions to pressing needs of buyers (Dunn, Thomas, and Lubawski 1981). Later stages in the evolution, such as the problem-solver and procreator, also require focusing on customers with substantial sales potential to warrant the investment needed in the selling process to serve them. As firms advance their selling strategy upward in the evolution, it often becomes necessary to be more selective in which customers are to receive personal selling attention. A dramatic example involves an IBM salesperson who serves only one customer—a major New York City bank. This salesperson spends full time meeting with the many buying influences in that bank and coordinating a 21-person sales team from IBM dedicated to fulfilling the bank's requirements (Everett 1989).

Stages in the Evolution of Personal Selling

Stage 1: Provider. The provider stage is the earliest in the development of personal selling. Providers act simply as a contact point and do little more than supply a product to buyers. This type of selling occurs in a sellers' market where demand exceeds supply or in a monopolistic market where no true competition exists for a desirable good. Providers have no concern about recognizing buyers' interests. Their needs are assumed to exist as buyers beat a path to the seller's door. This "better mousetrap" situation is a marketer's dream, but when it occurs, it often causes its own demise by attracting competitors who also want to capitalize on the profits it generates. In today's world, examples of the provider include some public utilities (e.g., a water company), inbound telemarketers who take orders initiated by customers, and some route salespeople—drivers who supply restaurants, supermarkets, and bars with various beverages for which demand is largely advertising-driven. Sales clerks in some retail stores (especially self-service stores) also behave very much like providers.

Stage 2: Persuader. When a sellers' market changes to a buyers' market, the selling firm is faced with competition from other suppliers. Sales then occur through the action of the persuader, who attempts to create or "awaken" a need in marketplace members for the items being sold. The role of the salesperson as a promotional force is to persuade customers to purchase the seller's product rather than a similar product offered by a similar competitor. Salespeople in this stage make generalized attempts to convince anyone of a need for the seller's product. Characteristics of the persuader stage of selling include standardized sales presentations coupled with a broad repertoire of answers to objections and closing techniques (Yalch 1979). Underlying this philosophy may be the conviction that people are reluctant to buy even if they do want or need the product, and the salesperson's job is to coax a positive response from them which they really want to give anyway. Effectiveness in this job is often a function of how well the salesperson employs various influence techniques, and his/her training focuses on mastering these techniques (Cialdini 1984).

Salespeople fitting this category come from a wide range of businesses. Some (but certainly not all) insurance and automobile sellers behave this way, as do some outbound telemarketers and many of those very persuasive, hard-sell folks in carnival booths, as well as a few door-to-door sellers. In business-to-business markets, the persuader might be found selling highly undifferentiated, commodity-type products, relying on his or her charm and personality as a major influence effort. In some cases, the persuader role takes center stage when a salesperson is charged with getting rid of inventory that has piled up in the warehouse ("The Salesman as Marketer" 1984).

Stage 3: Prospector. The prospector realizes that persuasion works only with some but not all marketplace members. Business firms also realize that selling resources will be more efficiently used if salespeople seek out those who truly are qualified prospects for the product and quit wasting effort on the nonqualified "suspect." This realization is often a major breakthrough in sales organizations whose effectiveness has been stymied because they have lingered at the persuader stage for a long time period. Consider the statement of a major corporation's representative to a conference gathering not very many years ago:

> A given product and the way it's offered may not match the value structures of all potential customers. For example, the product may lack certain properties, the terms of sale may not be satisfactory, or traditional relationships between buyer and seller may not be to our advantage. If we eliminate prospects where opportunity is lacking and concentrate our finite resources on prospects where we do have an opportunity, we focus on those that are strategically important to the business (Coles and Culley 1986).

The prospector seeks to identify the most likely segments within the total market by inferring who has needs that the product or service can fulfill. This is the first stage in which the seller begins to consider what the needs of the buyer might be and how those needs match with the product characteristics being sold. Prospectors rely on their own sense of what the buyer needs, however, and still attempt to maintain control of the selling situation with a relatively "hard sell" strategy. Once successful in converting a prospect into a customer, the salesperson at this stage might attempt to maintain a "persuader" relationship with that customer (or even a "provider" relationship if he or she can manage it), offering sufficient attention and service to keep the customer's patronage and to have a good chance for selling his or her firm's new product offerings if they fit the customer's needs when they are introduced.

This stage occurs with the advent of differentiated competition, as competitors make small distinctions in their product lines. Sales presentations focus on product features, which are sometimes translated into benefits the seller assumes are of value to the customer. Comparison of the seller's product with those of competitors are also sometimes made, as long as the features compared are selected to provide a favorable picture.

The range of salespeople today who fit the prospector stage is very wide, including all those who generate or are supplied with selective leads but who monopolize the sales presentation time and minimize active participation by the customer. Some missionary salespeople also fit into this category. By the very nature of their job, missionaries do not immediately learn the sales outcome of their efforts with a customer, and without this feedback they operate in more of a one-way communication situation. Some manufacturers' representatives behave like prospectors as well. Reps are often selected by firms because they are active within specific and desired market segments. But if a rep treats his or her various product lines as simply a cafeteria from which the customer can make selections, that is prospector behavior. (Many reps fall into the next stage, however.)

Stage 4: Problem-Solver. The problem-solver is a salesperson whose sales approach is grounded in a true diagnosis of the customer's needs and concerns. Like the prospector, the problem-solver attempts to call on customers whose needs fit what the seller is offering. But unlike the prospector, the problem-solver actively engages the customer to participate in defining those needs. As a result, erroneous preconceptions on the part of the salesperson can be corrected, incomplete understanding of those needs will be filled in, and the customer will get a product or service which complements those needs most closely.

A number of selling strategies have been defined which fit this stage of evolution. One is adaptive selling, in which salespeople adjust their own behavior during a customer interaction to respond to the particular characteristics of that situation (Weitz, Sujan, and Sujan 1986). Another is consultative selling, a sales strategy which parallels the salesperson with a consultant serving clients (customers) with the aim of improving their overall business operation, not just selling them products or services (Hanan, Cribbin, and Heiser 1970). A third is negotiation, which is meant to signify that both parties to the transaction benefit as in a "win-win" outcome (Hanan, Cribbin, and Berrian 1977). Finally, there is relationship building in which seller and buyer make a commitment to a continuous stream of transactions over time rather than viewing each sale and purchase as an individual, isolated exchange (Jackson 1985). A major component of relationship building is gaining customer trust (Swan and Nolan 1985).

This stage in the evolution of selling blossoms as competing suppliers become more responsive to the smallest details in customer needs, thereby hoping to counteract each other's competitive advantage. As a result, the purchase decision may hinge on many small or subtle differences among competitive offerings. The problem-solving stage is also a response to the increased sophistication in the purchasing process, stemming from the involvement of more buying influences representing broader areas of expertise in the customer organization. To be competitively successful in these circumstances, the seller must listen a great deal more to these buying influences and fine-tune the final offering to satisfy as many of their concerns as possible—at least as many as other suppliers are able to satisfy. When done effectively, the buyer–seller "partnership" can extend over a long period of time to involve many transactions and a close association.

Selling in the problem-solving stage is usually complex and highly sophisticated. One mark of this sophistication is the use of specialized salespeople to call on only certain types of customers or to sell only a selected group of products from the company's total product line. Data General, for example, uses separate sales forces to sell to each of its major customer types, such as automotive, financial services, and aerospace firms (Beam and Buell 1985).

Team selling fits this stage of evolution as well. Selling teams are often assembled, made up of various specialists matching the buying influences in the customer's organization, so that communication with the buyer can be most effective (Hutt, Johnston, and Ronchetto 1985). In DuPont Electronics, for example, teams of salespeople, sales managers, research, engineering, and other management personnel all interact with customers (Tolson 1988). The selling cycle or negotiation period from first contact to final sale can be very lengthy, often running for many months. The dollar size of the sale can be very large, with corresponding sizable consequences to the buyer if a mistake is made. The consequences to the salesperson are likewise very large, and especially devastating if the sale is lost after so much time and effort. Further, the makeup of the total sales "package" is often larger than the core product or service itself, but may include many associated services such as special packaging, shipping arrangements, training of customer personnel, research of the customer's market, maintenance agreements, credit arrangements, inventory control systems, "hot line" access, and other managerial or technical assistance. The problem-solver salesperson who coordinates a selling team has indeed a most responsible, challenging, and often highly rewarding position.

Stage 5: Procreator. A procreator is defined in Webster's New International Dictionary as one who begets or brings forth. This term is used to describe the final stage in the evolution of selling because in that stage the salesperson creates a market offering tailor-made to the precise needs of the buyer, regardless of whether the seller's firm has all the needed components as standard offerings or available expertise. This is the ultimate in market segmentation, since the procreator is literally making an individual marketing mix to suit the unique needs of each buyer. As a result, this should also be the ultimate in need satisfaction, as competitors vie for that customer's business by focusing a microcosm of their total marketing effort on that customer alone. Customer requirements become evident through co-action with the seller. Buyer and seller work in concern to meticulously identify customer needs which become the compelling force behind the design of the seller's custom-tailored offerings.

As one writer noted, the salesperson in this situation has two selling jobs. He must find and sell to a customer that can be served by his firm's capabilities, but he must also go back to his company and sell to the internal people what needs to be changed or created in the total offering to serve the customer (Bragg 1986). For example, in Shuttleworth, Inc., a designer and producer of materials handling equipment, a team of applications engineers, product designers, software writers, control engineers, manufacturing, finance, quality control, assembly supervisors, and even warehouse managers might be called on as a relationship is being pursued and an offering designed for and with a prospect. In one of this firm's sales to Digital Equipment Corporation, 20 percent of Shuttleworth's employees were involved in the total selling effort (Tyler 1990).

The procreator does not only oversee the development of product offerings, but also has the ability to adjust other parts of the marketing mix. For instance, pricing and credit terms can be negotiated, promotional materials can be fashioned to communicate effectively with the particular set of buying influences in the customer organization, and delivery, storage, and inventory control programs can be established to meet that customer's needs. Systems selling is a term used to describe this comprehensive marketing strategy implemented by the sales organization (Dunn and Thomas 1986). National account management is another term defining an all-inclusive marketing approach to customers with complex needs encompassing multiple geographic locations and many departments and divisions in their organizations (Colletti and Tubridy 1987; Cardozo, Shipp, and Roering 1987). Thus, the procreator salesperson is really a marketing manager, adjusting all the marketing mix components to meet the needs of a target market in a competitively successful manner. That differs very little from what a marketing vice president does.

One sales organization which has evolved from stage 1 to stage 5 is found in PPG Industries Fiber Glass Reinforcement Products Division (Sullivan, Bobbe, and Strasmore 1988). A newly arrived sales manager characterized this sales organization as "a group of order-takers and goodwill ambassadors," a description somewhat like the provider stage of evolution. An immediate push was made to develop a call-frequency plan and implement time-management techniques, leading to expanded selling effort with prospects and customers as is typical in the persuader stage. The next part of this sales force transformation was a focus on developing account plans and learning how to recognize opportunities resulting from technology changes in the market, a key ingredient in the prospector stage. The PPG sales force next learned about preparing proposals or "work-plans" after consulting with their prospects and customer firms to understand their specific needs. This marked the problem-solver stage, which eventually progressed to the procreator stage as PPG established sales teams who worked with each customer's participation in creating and testing products which each customer would finally buy. As this evolution neared completion, the sales manager summed up the role of personal selling in his firm as follows: "The pivotal function of the sales organization is to exercise leadership with, and on behalf of, the customer. If the overall organization was to be truly customer-driven, the sales force had to assume this vital role" (Sullivan, Bobbe, and Strasmore 1988, p. 48).

Are there many such sales positions today? In various degrees, numerous selling jobs contain parts of the procreator stage. For instance, to provide a customer with a complete desired package, GM's Electronic Data Systems will now gather all the elements from whatever suppliers provide them and coordinate them into the final assemblage (Everett 1989). A customer of Owens-Corning characterized this supplier's salespeople as "well-trained, flexible, and aggressive, and willing to tailor marketing plans for individual companies to help them capitalize on sales" ("Owens-Corning . . ." 1986). A recent Forum Corporation study concluded that, in the near future, salespeople will manage direct mail and local advertising efforts ("Hail to the Salesperson-Manager" 1989). In fact, companies like Campbell Soup and Pepsi have experimented with training their field personnel so they could develop promotional programs suited specifically to their territories (*Sales & Marketing Management* 1987). Experiments with salespeople having pricing discretion have been going on for many years (Stephenson, Cron, and Frazier 1979; Kern 1989). The producer of automatic testing equipment regularly customizes its products to dovetail precisely with its customers' production processes and information networks (Cespedes, Doyle, and Freedman 1989). A well-known futurist speculated that customers will not only tell the marketer what they want, but will use home computers to punch in product specifications which the factory will then build ("Toffler on Marketing" 1985). It may be a number of years before customers start taking such action on their own, but it seems more likely that salespeople in some industries will have such capabilities to "order" tailor-made product specifications for their customers in the not-too-distant future.

As a company's sales force advances through this evolution, it also seems clear that the terms "personal selling" and "salesperson" are more and more unrepresentative of what this function and these people really are. While "selling" might be broadly interpreted as encompassing the various tasks of the problem-solver and the procreator, it is more likely that persons in those stages are taking on enlarged responsibilities typically included under the rubric of marketing and management. In this sense, advanced stages of personal selling are evolving into marketing and management positions as well, with their central mission to adjust the firm's output to benefit each buyer.

Relationship of Evolution of Selling to Sales Management Practices

As a firm's selling focus evolves from stage to stage, politics and procedures for managing the personal selling function will also change. The correspondence between evolutionary stage and sales management action also serves to provide face validity to the concept of evolution in personal selling, since most of the parallels discussed in the following sections represent accepted and popular sales management practice. The following summarizes how evolutionary stages impact some key sales management decision areas.

Organizational Design. Early stages of selling's evolution will be accompanied by relatively simple organizational structures, with little or no specialization, support personnel, staff specialists, or control mechanisms. When the prospector stage is reached, sales force specialization becomes attractive, allowing individual salespeople to concentrate on one or a limited number of market targets as defined by customer or product types. Later evolutionary stages will almost certainly require sales support personnel such as technical or after-sale service representatives (Fitz 1990). Staff specialists (e.g., training, engineering, financial analysis) within the sales organization, or easy access to such specialists in other parts of the salesperson's firm, become essential as the problem-solver and procreator stages are reached. Control mechanisms likewise become necessary as the selling process grows in complexity and intra-organizational relationships increasingly take on a matrix character. Electronic mail systems and computer networks are often matched to the organization structure as communication and reporting mechanisms providing control.

Recruiting and Selection. In the early stages of this evolution, salespeople are expected to close sales quickly, while later stages involve longer-term relationship building. Thus, the personality and background characteristics of persons successful in each stage will probably differ as well. A salesperson who fits best with early stage selling will probably possess strong ego drive, need for achievement, initiative, and a history of success in short-term tasks carried out independently and with great practice. Salespeople more suited to selling in the latter stages might possess greater need for affiliation, patience, flexibility, empathy, and greater analytical ability applied to their customers' business operations. For these salespeople, a history of success in lengthy projects and team situations seems appropriate. Thus, progression through the evolutionary stages may require a parallel shift in background and personality traits needed for success in each stage. Some evidence already exists that different hiring qualifications correspond to effective performance in selling jobs of different complexity (Avila and Fern 1986). Specific policies for each individual position in a given firm should be established through careful analysis, of course.

Training. Training for early stages in the evolution would most likely concentrate on the product, its characteristics or features, and perhaps its benefits. Training program content might then focus on steps in the traditional selling process, such as the "approach" or "closing" (e.g., Leigh 1987; Steinberg and Plank 1987). Later stages would be more concerned with diagnosis of customer needs through identification of who are the key buying influences (Mattson 1988) and establishing a solid relationship through mutual trust and social bonding (Turnbull and Wilson 1989). Problem-solvers and procreators also need training on internal company resources and how to effect coordination and cooperation among these resources, while persuaders and prospectors are more likely to learn how to rely on their own skills and initiative in generating orders.

Compensation. Progression through the stages is likely to be accompanied by a shift from variable cost to fixed cost types of compensation—from commissions to salary, for example. Commissions are more effective when the objective of the salesperson's work is relatively easy-to-define and measurable, and when the payoff from selling is more immediate and the product of one's individual effort. Thus, the persuader works alone and aims for a completed sale on each call, so pay by commission is appropriate to this stage. On the other hand, the procreator often works with a team (internally as well as making calls on the customer), and has many intermediate objectives to achieve with the customer prior to obtaining the actual purchase order. Some of these objectives might include reaching key buying influences, making product demonstrations, taking buyers to inspect

the product in action at other customer firms, completing a financial analysis projecting the benefits from using the seller's product, and so on (Taylor 1986). Because it is difficult to tie specific dollar values to the completion of these tasks, salary becomes the more reasonable method of compensation, with a bonus paid for a successful final outcome of obtaining the sale (Cespedes, Doyle, and Freedman 1989).

Control and Performance Evaluation. Some of the comments above regarding compensation apply here as well. For example, sales volume quotas used as a motivational or control device are more fitting to earlier stages in the evolution, and salespeople in those stages are more likely to be evaluated in terms of how well they met those quotas. Conversely, salespeople in later stages will more likely be evaluated on intermediate goal-achievement behaviors which will eventually lead to the desired outcome of a sale (Anderson and Oliver 1987). Success in these intermediate behaviors means successfully mastering the job itself, which is an intrinsic reward. It has been suggested that those with an intrinsic reward orientation are more likely to be successful in adaptive selling (Weitz, Sujan, and Sujan 1986). Those with an extrinsic reward orientation focus more on the outcome than the work itself, and thus would be more suited to selling in early stages of the evolution.

Other Implications and Conclusions

A look at this evolution should give college students a more realistic picture of the potential opportunities in selling as a career, especially as it takes on a stronger character of professionalism and managerialism. Many students identify selling with early stages in the evolution, based on their own encounters with salespeople in retail settings as well as the stereotypes portrayed in the media. By seeing how selling can and has progressed to higher stages, students will gain a better understanding of selling as a worthwhile and involving career experience. Indeed, classroom instructors should use this discussion of the evolution of selling as a vehicle to present that picture.

For the researcher, a detailed account of the stages in the evolution of selling can provide an additional basis for classifying personal selling strategy or philosophy. In turn, this classification could serve as a useful explanatory variable in sales-related research. For example, studies attempting to show relationships between personal characteristics and selling success might produce stronger results if stages in the evolution of selling were used as a moderating variable, since individuals with similar demographic or personality traits might not be equally successful in sales jobs at different evolutionary stages. This research might be modeled after studies which have found career stage to be such a moderator (Cron and Slocum 1986). Further, this classification might help to explain the success or failure of various selling strategies under different market and competitive conditions. A careful assessment of a firm's market and competitive characteristics might also help management determine whether a change in selling strategy should be made or planned for in the near future.

References

Anderson, Erin, and Richard L. Oliver (1987), "Perspectives on Behavior-Based Versus Outcome-Based Salesforce Control Systems," *Journal of Marketing*, 51 (October), 76–88.

Avila, Ramon A., and Edward F. Fern (1986), "The Selling Situation as a Moderator of the Personality-Sales Performance Relationship: An Empirical Investigation," *Journal of Personal Selling & Sales Management*, 6 (November), 53–63.

Beam, Alex, and Barbara Buell (1989), "Who's Breathing Down Whose Neck Now?" *Business Week*, November 25, 132–139.

Bragg, Arthur (1986), "Turning Salespeople Into Partners," *Sales & Marketing Management*, August, 82–84.

Cardozo, Richard N., and Shannon H. Shipp (1987), "How New Selling Methods Are Affecting Industrial Sales Management," *Business Horizons*, vol. 30 (September–October), 23–28.

Cardozo, Richard N., Shannon H. Shipp, and Kenneth J. Roering (1987), "Implementing New Business-to-Business Selling Methods," *Journal of Personal Selling & Sales Management*, 7 (August), 17–26.

Cespedes, Frank V., Stephen X. Doyle, and Robert J. Freedman (1989), "Teamwork for Today's Selling," *Harvard Business Review*, 89 (March–April), 44–58.

Cialdini, Robert B. (1984), *Influence, How and Why People Agree to Things*, New York: William Morrow and Company.

Coles, Gary J. and James D. Culley (1986), "Not All Prospects Are Created Equal," *Business Marketing*, May, 52–58.

Colletti, Jerome A. and Gary S. Tubridy (1987), "Effective Major Account Sales Management," *Journal of Personal Selling & Sales Management*, 7 (August), 1–10.

"Congratulations! It's a Field Marketing Manager" (1987), *Sales & Marketing Management*, March, 112.

Cron, William L. (1984), "Industrial Salesperson Development: A Career Stages Perspective," *Journal of Marketing*, 48 (Fall), 41–52.

Cron, William L. and John W. Slocum, Jr. (1986), "The Influence of Career Stages on Salespeople's Job Attitudes, Work Perceptions, and Performance," *Journal of Marketing Research*, 23 (May), 119–129.

Dawson, Leslie M. (1970), "Toward a New Concept of Sales Management," *Journal of Marketing*, 34 (April), 33–38.

Dunn, Dan T., Jr., and Claude A. Thomas (1986), "Strategy for Systems Sellers: A Grid Approach," *Journal of Personal Selling & Sales Management*, 6 (August), 1–10.

Dunn, Dan T., Jr., Claude A. Thomas, and James L. Lubawski (1981), "Pitfalls of Consultative Selling," *Business Horizons*, 24 (September–October), 59–65.

Eliashberg, Jehoshua, and Rabikar Chatterjee (1985), "Analytical Models of Competition with Implications for Marketing: Issues, Findings, and Outlook," *Journal of Marketing Research*, 22 (August), 237–261.

Everett, Martin (1989), "This is the Ultimate in Selling," *Sales & Marketing Management*, August, 28–38.

Fitz, Jane (1990), "Selling With Technical Support," *Training*, 27 (February), 53–59.

Fullerton, Ronald A. (1988), "How Modern is Modern Marketing? Marketing's Evolution and the Myth of the 'Production Era,'" *Journal of Marketing*, 52 (January), 108–125.

"Hail the Salesperson-Manager" (1989), *Sales & Marketing Management*, March, 18.

Hanan, Mack, James Cribbin, and Herman Heiser (1970), *Consultative Selling*, New York: AMACOM.

Hanan, Mack, James Cribbin, and Howard Berrian (1977), *Sales Negotiation Strategies*, New York: AMACOM.

Henderson, Bruce D. (1983), "The Anatomy of Competition," *Journal of Marketing*, 47 (Spring), 7–11.

Hutt, Michael D., Wesley J. Johnston, and John R. Ronchetto, Jr. (1985), "Selling Centers and Buying Centers: Formulating Strategic Exchange Patterns," *Journal of Personal Selling & Sales Management*, 5 (May), 33–40.

Jackson, Barbara Bund (1985), *Winning and Keeping Industrial Customers*, Lexington, MA: Lexington Books.

Jolson, Marvin A. (1974), "The Salesman's Career Cycle," *Journal of Marketing*, 38 (July), 39–46.

Jolson, Marvin A. (1980), "Business Courses Must Change to Reflect 'New Salesperson' of 1980s," *Marketing News*, 14 (July 25), 20.

Kern, Richard (1989), "Letting Your Salespeople Set Prices (Sort Of)," *Sales & Marketing Management*, August, 44–49.

Lambkin, Mary, and George S. Day (1989), "Evolutionary Processes in Competitive Markets: Beyond the Product Life Cycle," *Journal of Marketing*, 53 (July), 4–20.

Leigh, Thomas W. (1987), "Cognitive Selling Scripts and Sales Training," *Journal of Personal Selling & Sales Management*, 7 (August), 39–48.

Mattson, Melvin R. (1988), "How to Determine the Composition and Influence of a Buying Center," *Industrial Marketing Management*, 17 (August), 205–214.

McMurray, Robert N. (1961), "The Mystique of Super-Salesmanship," *Harvard Business Review*, 39 (March–April), 113–122.

Moncrief, William C., III (1986), "Selling Activity and Sales Position Taxonomies for Industrial Salesforces," *Journal of Marketing Research*, 23 (August), 261–270.

Moore, James R., Donald W. Eckrich, and Lorry T. Carlson (1986), "A Hierarchy of Industrial Selling Competencies," *Journal of Marketing Education*, 8 (Spring), 79–88.

Newton, Derek A. (1973), *Sales Force Performance and Turnover*, Cambridge, MA: Marketing Science Institute.

"Owens-Corning Calls on Its Customers' Customers" (1986), *Sales & Marketing Management*, June, 57.

Powers, Thomas L., Warren S. Martin, Hugh Rushing, and Scott Daniels (1987), "Selling Before 1900: A Historical Perspective," *Journal of Personal Selling & Sales Management*, 7 (November), 1–7.

Powers, Thomas L., William F. Koehler, and Warren S. Martin (1988), "Selling From 1900 to 1949: A Historical Perspective," *Journal of Personal Selling & Sales Management*, 8 (November), 11–21.

Schurr, Paul H. (1987), "Evolutionary Approaches to Effective Selling," *Advances in Business Marketing*, 2, 55–80.

Steinberg, Margery, and Richard E. Plank (1987), "Expert Systems: The Integrative Sales Management Tool of the Future," *Journal of the Academy of Marketing Science*, 15 (Summer), 55–62.

Stephenson, P. Ronald, William L. Cron, and Gary L. Frazier (1979), "Delegating Pricing Authority to the Sales Force: The Effects on Sales and Profit Performance," *Journal of Marketing*, 43 (Spring), 21–28.

Sujan, Harish (1986), "Smarter Versus Harder: An Exploratory Attributional Analysis of Salespeople's Motivation," *Journal of Marketing Research*, 23 (February), 41–49.

Sullivan, Kevin F., Richard A. Bobbe, and Martin R. Strasmore (1988), "Transforming the Salesforce in a Maturing Industry," *Management Review*, 77 (June), 46–49.

Swan, John E., and Robert T. Adkins (1980–81), "The Image of the Salesperson: Prestige and Other Dimensions," *Journal of Personal Selling & Sales Management*, 1 (Fall–Winter), 48–56.

Swan, John E., and Johannah J. Nolan (1985), "Gaining Customer Trust: A Conceptual Guide for the Salesperson," *Journal of Personal Selling & Sales Management*, 5 (November), 39–48.

Taylor, Thayer C. (1986), "Making Long-Term Sales Cycles Manageable," *Sales & Marketing Management*, August, 64.

Thompson, Donald L. (1972), "Stereotype of the Salesman," *Harvard Business Review*, 50 (January–February), 20–22ff.

"Toffler on Marketing" (1985), *Marketing News*, March 15, 1, 30–31.

"The Salesman as Marketer" (1984), *Industrial Distribution*, February, 39–43.

Tolson, Norris (1988), "Good Sales Team Knows Customers Inside and Out," *Marketing News*, November 21, 5.

Turnbull, Peter W., and David T. Wilson (1989), "Developing and Protecting Profitable Customer Relationships," *Industrial Marketing Management*, 18 (August), 233–238.

Weitz, Barton A., Harish Sujan, and Mita Sujan (1986), "Knowledge, Motivation, and Adaptive Behavior: A Framework for Improving Selling Effectiveness," *Journal of Marketing*, 50 (October), 174–191.

Wotruba, Thomas R. (1980), "The Changing Character of Industrial Selling," *European Journal of Marketing*, 14, (no. 5/6), 293–302.

Wotruba, Thomas R., and Edwin K. Simpson (1990), "The Selling Cycle: A Unifying Guide for Sales Management Decisions," in B. J. Dunlap (ed.), *Developments in Marketing Science*, 13, The Academy of Marketing Science, 81–83.

Yalch, Richard F. (1979), "Closing Sales: Compliance-Gaining Strategies for Personal Selling," in Richard P. Bagozzi (ed.), *Sales Management: New Developments From Behavioral and Decision Model Research*, Cambridge, MA: Marketing Science Institute, 187–201.

Madhubalan Viswanathan
Eric M. Olson

The Implementation of Business Strategies: Implications for the Sales Function

Utilizing existing conceptual frameworks in business unit level strategies and sales management activities, a set of propositions relating the sales department's role in the strategy implementation process has been generated. The focus of this conceptualization is at the functional level with specific attention on management of the sales force relative to three distinctive business unit strategies (prospector, differentiated defender, and low cost defender). ✳

W hether through a conscious decision process or by default, most firms adopt one or more strategies for competing in the marketplace. Because different competitive strategies generate different demands on a firm and the individual business units they are comprised of, it is important that those policies, programs, and structures most likely to facilitate the strategy's successful implementation be adopted. This is equally true for the sales function as it is for engineering, manufacturing, and other marketing related functions. However, with few exceptions (Strahle and Spiro

At the time this article was written, Madhubalan Viswanathan was an assistant professor in the Department of Business Administration at the University of Illinois, Urbana-Champaign. He has published in the *Journal of Product Innovation Management*. His primary research focus is in consumer information processing. Eric M. Olson was a doctoral fellow at the University of Minnesota and holds an MBA from Portland State University. He has ten years experience in selling and sales management with companies including AT&T and U.S. West. He has published in *Advances in Consumer Research*. His primary research focus is in the implementation of marketing strategy. The authors wish to thank Orville Walker, Jr. and two anonymous reviewers for their insightful comments on earlier drafts of this article and Christine Hanson for her editing assistance. *Source:* Reprinted by permission of the publisher from *Journal of Personal Selling and Sales Management*, Vol. 12, No. 1, Winter 1992, pp. 45-57.

1986; Strahle 1989), articles linking specific sales management activities with marketing strategies have been largely non-existent. Instead, the focus of past sales management research has been on tying prescriptive sales management activities to factors such as product characteristics (Harris et al. 1978) and distribution policies (Shapiro 1977a). The goal of this paper is to establish a framework that specifies how sales management programs and policies should differ between business units following different competitive strategies.

In establishing this framework, we have borrowed from existing frameworks of business unit level strategies (e.g., Walker and Ruekert 1987) and sales management activities (e.g., Churchill, Ford and Walker 1990). The first section of this paper consists of a brief review of these conceptual frameworks. The second section considers how three groups of sales management activities, namely: (1) specific sales force activities, (2) organizing the selling effort, and (3) evaluating sales performance, should be linked with specific business unit level strategies. A series of related propositions are generated for each. The last section consists of a discussion of managerial implications and proposals for future research.

Review of Conceptual Frameworks

Constructing a framework of sales management programs and policies appropriate for different strategies requires the clarification of three issues. The first consideration is the level of analysis within the firm. The second issue is differentiating between strategic options. The third issue is identifying appropriate measures of performance.

Level of Analysis

The strategic business unit (SBU) is deemed to be the appropriate level at which to consider sales management programs and policies for several reasons. First, as compared with corporate strategy where the emphasis is on determining what businesses to be in, the emphasis at the business unit level is on how to compete (Andrews 1987). As a consequence, separate SBUs within an organization can, and often do, pursue different competitive strategies. Second, SBUs are often designed to attain high levels of autonomy and self-containment, which means they often have dedicated sales forces. Finally, SBUs are usually charged with both sales and profit responsibilities (Aaker 1984).

While our analysis will focus on the business unit, our propositions would apply to joint sales forces for divisions or even subsidiaries following similar competitive strategies that sell complementary products or sell to similar customers. Emerson Electric provides a good example of this (Ruekert and Walker 1990). Indeed, synergies may well exist that more than compensate for potential shortcomings of a general sales force. However, attempting to address each of these potential contingencies is a topic for future study.

SBU Level Strategy

Two of the most influential typologies of business unit level strategies are those of Miles and Snow (1978) and Porter (1980). Both typologies provide a schema for categorizing ways in which individual firms compete. The primary conceptual difference between the two can be found in their locus of concentration. Whereas Porter focuses on competitive forces external to the firm, Miles and Snow focus on internal issues of intended levels of new product and/or new market development.

Walker and Ruekert (1987) capitalized on the strengths of both typologies by merging them. This generated six separate business unit level strategies: prospectors, differentiated analyzers, low cost analyzers, differentiated defenders, low cost defenders, and reactors. Walker and Ruekert (1987) indicate that the most distinctive of these strategies are: (1) prospectors, which are business units that seek a competitive advantage through product innovation and by being the first to introduce a new product to the marketplace, (2) differentiated defenders, which are business units that have an established base of customers and seek a competitive advantage by providing higher levels of customer service or product quality to their clientele, and (3) low cost defenders, which are business units that seek a competitive advantage by developing a cost leadership position.

Because pricing policy is a secondary concern to prospectors, Walker and Ruekert (1987) made no distinction between those pursuing a penetration versus a skimming strategy. Because low cost and differentiated analyzers represent an intermediate type of strategy whose actions can be expected to fall between those of prospectors and defenders, they were not considered in detail. Finally, reactors were not considered because of their failure to adopt any consistent competitive strategy. As shown in Figure 1, Walker and Ruekert (1987) adopted these three strategy types in order to derive implications for the marketing function. We adopted these strategy types in order to develop an initial link between business unit level strategies and the sales function.

Each of these strategies retained from the Walker and Ruekert typology can be differentiated from the others on the basis of its programs and policies. As first movers into new markets, prospectors typically have "broad and technically advanced product lines" (Walker and Ruekert 1987). Therefore, prospectors need to build awareness and primary demand for their products. This necessitates a policy of high spending on advertising and sales promotion (Walker and Ruekert 1987). While

FIGURE 1
A Hybrid Typology of Business Unit Strategy[a]

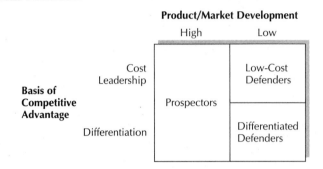

[a]Reproduced from Walker & Ruekert (1987), *Journal of Marketing*, 51, 17.

it is not suggested that customer service be ignored under any competitive strategy, prospectors gain advantage by introducing innovation and, as such, should place a lower emphasis on support than on generating market awareness and trial.

In contrast, both differentiated and low cost defenders tend to operate, or at least function best, in mature markets where product changes are typically incremental in nature. Differentiated defenders seek strategic advantage over their competitors by maintaining high product quality standards and/or providing superior levels of customer service for the relatively narrow line of products they typically offer. Therefore, differentiated defenders need to emphasize the satisfaction of existing customers over new product innovation. Consequently, their emphasis on new product development should be substantially less when compared to prospectors. Maintenance of a differential advantage in a mature market suggests a promotional policy involving a high emphasis on the sales force. As mentioned, differentiated defenders could focus on product quality or customer service, with each emphasis requiring a particular set of sales management activities for implementation.

In contrast, low cost defenders retain customers by offering prices substantially below that of the competition. Therefore, the emphasis of a low cost defender has to be on cost control. Customers who consider price as the most important criteria in making choices between brands or companies will demonstrate little loyalty when an acceptable but less expensive substitute becomes available. Consequently, low cost defenders, in keeping with their cost control focus, must limit expenditures on selling and promotional activities, customer services, and new product development.

Performance Measures

To achieve high performance on one measure usually requires forgoing high performance of another measure. As a consequence, Walker and Ruekert (1987) suggest it is important for a business unit adopting a specific strategy to also adopt the appropriate performance objectives. As both low cost and differentiated defenders have established products and customers, costs associated with new product development, locating customers, and introductory promotions should be substantially less than for prospectors. Consequently, the emphasis of defenders should be on efficient profit generation (e.g., ROI). Activities that promote significant and profitable revenues should be funded accordingly, while non-essential activities should be curtailed.

In contrast, as the primary focus of a prospector business unit is on the development of new products, its measures of success should reflect that emphasis. Appropriate measures of product development success are the percentage of sales generated by products introduced within a recent period of time, (e.g., five years) and the market share captured by a product. This does not mean that measures such as ROI are unimportant but merely that the determination of successful strategy implementation for prospectors is much less dependent on this measure than on the other two.

Implications for the Sales Function

The appropriate sales management activities for a specific competitive strategy are those that fit the strategy's primary competitive thrust and will enhance the performance dimension(s) of importance to that strategy. The key issue here is to understand the role of sales management under each of these distinctive strategies in order to assist in their successful implementation. In other words, how should SBU level strategies be translated into practical sales management activities. We focus specifically on three sets of sales management activities identified by Churchill, Ford, and Walker (1990): (1) selling activities and account management policies, (2) organizing the selling effort, and (3) evaluating the selling effort. The approach taken here is summarized in Figure 2. Propositions relating each business-level competitive strategy to these sales management activities can be found in Table 1.

Selling Activities and Account Management Policies

Key issues for sales managers to address in order to appropriately match sales activities and account management policies with specific business unit strategies include: (1) specifying the responsibilities of the sales force, (2) recruiting and selecting salespersons, (3) choosing the level and type of sales force training, and (4) determining the appropriate type of account relationship and sales approach (Churchill, Ford and Walker 1990).

Selling Responsibilities

Salespeople are expected to carry out a wide variety of sales related activities. But different organizations should place greater or lesser emphasis on specific activities relative to the strategic focus adopted by the business unit. Consequently, the responsibilities and activities that members of the sales force engage in may vary greatly across business units. Where a salesperson places his or her efforts should be dictated by the needs of the organization and will be influenced by the incentive system imposed on them.

Prospectors need to emphasize building consumer awareness, stimulating product trial, and developing primary demand for products. Under this strategy, a sales force should focus its activities on prospecting for new customers, making new product demonstrations, transmitting information about new products to customers, and identifying and transmitting new product ideas back to the R&D and/or design departments. While after-sales service may be important, it should not be emphasized at the expense of a prospector's primary objective of new product and/or market development. Functions closest to the customer are of importance to prospector businesses. Hence, personal selling in prospector businesses serve the function of staying close to the marketplace by keeping abreast of customer needs, obtaining new ideas from lead customers, and evaluating new product ideas with customers. A good example of this can be found in 3M's health care sector where the responsibilities of the sales force extend to identifying new opportunities for products consistent with the company's development expertise and capabilities.

Differentiated defenders need to focus on maintaining existing customer bases. Here, the emphasis of the sales force has to be on a broad range of direct and indirect sales activities. Direct selling activities such as conducting sales presentations to communicate product benefits, closing deals, and processing orders are required. Providing after-sales service, particularly if this is a source of differential advantage, may also be an

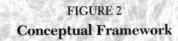

FIGURE 2
Conceptual Framework

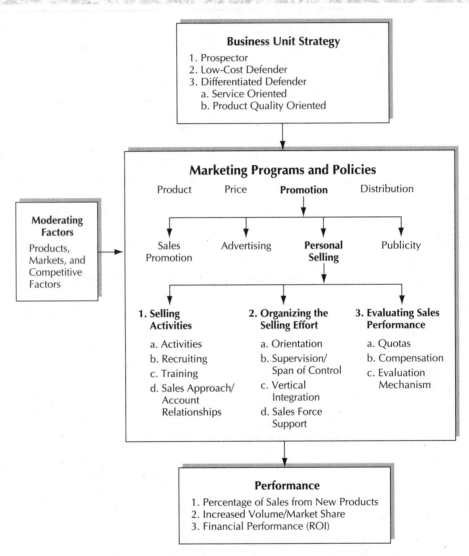

important sales function. Finally, the sales force is required to stay abreast of changing trends, customer needs, and competitive offerings in order to provide timely information relative to product modifications. Because of the great number of activities required under this strategy, the sales force is considered to be the most important component of the promotional mix. A noteworthy example of the adoption of this philosophy was the recent move by IBM to reallocate 20,000 employees from around the company to the sales force. By dramatically increasing the size of the

TABLE 1
Sales Force Management Propositions by Type of Competitive Strategy

Proposition 1: Prospectors will achieve superior performance on the critical measures of sales of new products and increased volume/market share when:

their selling activities and account management policies
a) focus on a relatively narrow range of activities such as new product presentations, prospecting for new customers, staying of market trends, and identifying new opportunities,
b) emphasize recruiting salespersons with high levels of technical skills,
c) place a moderate emphasis on sales training and a high emphasis on product training, and
d) reflect a system sales or major account management sales strategy, and encourage a customer oriented selling approach,

their organization of the selling effort reflects
a) a customer organization,
b) a moderate ratio of sales managers to salespersons,
c) a company sales force, and
d) a comparatively moderate level of sales support with an emphasis on technical support, telemarketing, and trial stimulation advertising,

and they evaluate the selling effort by
a) setting quotas for their sales forces based on new product sales volume and on activities such as new product presentations,
b) financially compensating their sales forces using a straight salary plan, and
c) adopting a behavior-based control system.

Proposition 2: Differentiated defenders will achieve superior performance on the critical dimension of financial performance when:

their selling activities and account management policies
a) focus on a broad range of activities such as direct selling, after-sales service, and staying abreast of market trends,
b) emphasize recruiting of salespersons with moderate technical skills and high selling skills,
c) place a high emphasis on sales and product training, and
d) reflect a relationship creation sales strategy (i.e., major account management or strategic account relationships), and encourage a customer oriented selling approach,

their organization of the selling effort reflects
a) a product organization in differentiated defenders with a product orientation or a customer or geographic organization in differentiated defenders with a service orientation,
b) a high ratio of sales managers to salespersons,
c) a company sales force, and
d) a comparatively high level of sales support with an emphasis on order processing, installation, repair service, missionary selling, and reinforcement advertising,

(continued)

TABLE 1 *(continued)*

and they evaluate the selling effort by

a) setting quotas for their sales forces based on volume and service related activities as well as financial considerations;

b) financially compensating their sales forces using a combination plan of salary and commission, and

c) adopting a combination of behavioral and outcome based controls.

Proposition 3: Low cost defenders will achieve superior performance on the critical dimension of financial performance when:

their selling activities and account management policies

a) focus on direct selling activities,

b) emphasize recruiting of salespersons with at least basic math and communication skills,

c) place a low emphasis on sales and product training, and

d) reflect a transaction sales strategy and encourage a stimulus-response selling approach,

their organization of the selling effort reflects

a) a geographic organization,

b) a low ratio of sales managers to salespersons,

c) an external sales force, and

d) a comparatively low level of sales support with the exception of logistical issues such as order processing and telemarketing,

and they evaluate the selling effort by

a) setting quotas for their sales forces based on profit margins and/or sales volume,

b) financially compensating their sales forces using a commission dominant plan, and

c) adopting an outcome-based control system.

---

sales force and by organizing it around customer segments, IBM has taken steps to improve contact with customers and maintain its market position.

In keeping with a policy of low costs and high efficiency, a comparatively low expenditure of resources on the sales force will be appropriate for low cost defenders. The primary focus should be on straight selling activities with little, if any, emphasis placed on non-sales activities. Adaptivity, awareness of changing customer needs, and knowledge about trends in the marketplace take a back seat to closing deals and processing orders in such a strategy. Firms such as Graybar Electric that compete in markets where products are often commoditylike in nature operate in this manner.

Recruiting and Selection Dynamics

Turnover is a fact of life in every sales force. However, because sales tasks are less complex in a typical low cost defender business, wages and salesperson qualification standards can also be lower. Salespersons in business units following this strategy typically do not require sophisticated skills and, hence, they are comparatively easy to replace. Lower wages engender within salespersons a lack of long-term commitment to the organization. Consequently, sales managers in business units following this strategy must constantly be considering or engaging in recruiting.

Because turnover in differentiated defender business units is typically lower, a greater emphasis on identifying and hiring high quality salespersons is important. The investment in each individual is comparatively high as are the consequences of a poor selection (Darmon and Shapiro 1980). Integrity and reliability are paramount personality requirements because of the importance of the relationship established between the firm and the client. In addition, because service is crucial the salesperson must be detail oriented. While differentiated defenders rely on a core of accounts for their prosperity, even they need to generate new sources of revenue. One way of securing new accounts without diluting the level of service to existing customers is through the establishment of a separate new prospect or missionary sales force.

Because the products developed and marketed by prospector business units are typically innovative and complex, a sales manager must recruit intelligent, creative salespeople. Specialized educational backgrounds (e.g., engineering, chemistry, etc.) are often essential. The person must not only understand the technology but be able to identify novel applications of it. In addition, the need to identify and develop new accounts necessitates a fairly aggressive individual.

Training

Salespeople require both product knowledge and selling skills to carry out specific selling activities and to be able to employ various selling approaches (Churchill, Ford and Walker 1990). Salespeople employed in differentiated defender organizations will require both extensive product knowledge and selling skills. Under a prospector strategy a salesperson requires extensive product knowledge. However, due to the nature of the salesperson's responsibilities, only moderate levels of selling skills are essential. Thus, training levels should be commensurate with these emphases. In contrast, because of the basic nature of the products they produce, the importance of keeping operating costs at a minimum, high turnover rates, and the emphasis their customers place on price, salespeople in low cost defender business units should generally be given comparatively less training on both product knowledge and selling skills.

As an example of this, newly hired account executives with AT&T receive upwards of 17 weeks of classroom training and six months of field training before they are assigned a territory. Classroom training consists of product knowledge, basic business skills, sales presentation skills, and specific industry familiarization. In contrast, salespersons in Premier Industrial Corporation are sent to a three-day training school and provided two days of supervisor "ride alongs" before assuming their territorial responsibilities.

Customer Relationships/ Sales Approaches

The sales approach employed by a salesperson should be consistent with the complexity of the product/situation and the relationship established between customer and company. Shapiro (1988) describes four sales relationships a firm may have with an account. These are: (1) transaction selling, which is a straightforward, reasonably quick sales approach where products are bought and sold on the basis of their benefits, availability, physical attributes and/or price, (2) system sales, which is a method similar to, but typically longer than, transaction selling, employed when the product is complex and requires input from a variety of sources (e.g., engineers, designers, service technicians, etc.), (3) major account management, which is a method where individual sales are secondary to the establishment of an ongoing, mutually beneficial relationship between important accounts and the firm, and (4) strategic account relations, which is an extension of major account management where a select customer in effect becomes a partner in a long-term joint venture. Consistent with this continuum are the level of expenses incurred in establishing and maintaining each type of customer relationship. Transaction selling is inexpensive but creates the least amount of codependency and goodwill. In contrast, strategic account relationships are very expensive but generate relationships that are intended to last well into the future.

Transaction selling is most appropriate for low cost defender units because their customers' major buying criterion typically is price. As specialized products or services are perceived by these customers to be of less value than their associated additional costs, a long-term contract between a buyer and a seller would be based predominantly on a perceived price advantage. The commoditylike nature of these products generally means significant alternative sources of product and customers are readily available therefore reducing the likelihood of a relationship.

In sharp contrast, relationship creation is of paramount importance to differentiated defenders who compete by investing in unique products or services. A long-term commitment from a customer serves to offset some of the costs and risks incurred in providing customized products or services. Firms such as Boeing whose products are very expensive and have long development and production lead times operate in this manner. In turn, the customer gains a sense of security knowing those products and/or services vital to their future prosperity will be of sufficient quality or made available in a timely manner to ensure their continued operation.

Finally, while relationship creation can be important to prospector business units, it is not as compelling an arrangement as it is for differentiated defenders. Prospectors sustain a competitive advantage through the talents of their innovators in the research and development, design, engineering, manufacturing, and marketing functions. Establishing long-term commitments may stifle creativity and potential gains in market share. On the other hand, relationships may be useful as a source of ideas as well as to evaluate ideas. Thus, a middle ground is suggested for prospector firms.

The type of relationship a firm has with its customers should influence the specific selling approach adopted by the sales force. A variety of different selling approaches can be employed (Churchill, Ford and Walker 1990; Gwinner 1968). Need-satisfaction and problem-solution approaches require extensive training, are relatively expensive to employ, and are used when a firm has a customer orientation. These approaches are considered most appropriate for prospectors because they facilitate quick responses to threats and opportunities and promote close contact with lead customers,

a major source of new product ideas (von Hipple 1989). An example of this is found in 3M's health care sector where the sales force must continuously seek the input of medical professionals in order to keep abreast of a rapidly changing industry.

The mental-states approach follows a formulated presentation which allows for tailoring messages to different prospects. This approach is appropriate for differentiated defenders because it allows for flexibility in making presentations. It may also be appropriate for a differentiated defender to use a customer-oriented approach for a number of reasons such as its adaptivity and allowance for customer input on product improvements. Salespersons from both IBM and AT&T adopt these approaches for several reasons. Products like mainframe computers or private branch exchanges (PBX) consist of both hardware and programmable software. Each system is designed to operate in a variety of settings but may require different hardware arrangements or software packages to address concerns unique to an industry or a specific company.

The stimulus-response approach requires minimal training and is used in selling standardized products due to its lack of flexibility. Because product lines are typically uncomplicated and sales force turnover rates are comparatively high in low cost defender firms, this is considered the most appropriate direct contact approach for their salespeople to adopt. Sales forces in firms such as Kroy, Inc. often rely on a scripted sales format in order to ensure presentation efficiency. Additional indirect contact approaches appropriate for low cost defender sales forces include telemarketing and automatic reordering.

Organizing the Selling Effort

The focus of this section is on the structural design of the sales function relative to the strategic alternative adopted by a business unit. Key aspects related to organizing the selling effort include: (1) orientation of the organization, (2) span of control/supervision, (3) vertical integration of the sales force, and (4) level of support afforded the sales force (Churchill, Ford and Walker 1990).

Organization Orientation

Three alternative approaches to organizing the sales force include geographic, product, and customer orientations (Churchill, Ford and Walker 1990). While these are addressed as separate alternatives, moderating factors such as breadth of product line, type of customer, and size of territory served can dictate the simultaneous adoption of two or more orientations.

Orienting a sales force around a geographical territory may make logistical sense for business units following any of the strategic alternatives described. However, the transaction orientation of a low cost defender business unit generates a greater logistical concern for sales managers of firms following this strategy than would be encountered by sales managers in either prospector or differentiated defender business units. Because of the fickle nature of customers whose buying criteria are driven largely by price, the sales force in a low cost defender business unit is typically required to have a greater number of contacts. The logistical issue of physically contacting those accounts coupled with the business unit's emphasis on cost control strongly indicate a geographic orientation. While some specialization may occur, a salesperson in a firm like Graybar Electric will typically have customers from a wide spectrum of industries. Because a salesperson or regional manager may be physically separated from company headquarters by large geographic distances, the organization should operate in a highly formalized manner. Decisions on important and/or non-routine issues should be made centrally.

In contrast, both product and customer organizations require greater levels of specialization and decentralized decision making than geographically designed organizations alone can provide. Sales forces oriented around specific product lines are most appropriate for business units whose focus is on adapting existing products to evolving customer needs. Because the product lines of product-oriented differentiated defenders are characteristically complex, a separate sales force for each product or group of related products is required. By estab-

lishing separate manufacturing facilities for different product groups, coordination between sales and production should be enhanced, leading to vital competitive advantages. Multi-industry firms such as G.E. and IT&T whose products and/or services are highly distinctive have established separate sales forces for different subsidiaries and/or products.

Sales forces oriented around major customers are most appropriate for prospectors or differentiated defenders with a service orientation. Large firms with a national or international focus such as AT&T and IBM will frequently establish national sales account teams or departments. In some situations a representative of the firm will actually have an office in the customer's building. As the focus of a prospector is on new product development, it might seem logical for a prospector to adopt a product-oriented structure. However, unlike differentiated defenders who emphasize incremental product change, prospectors seek out undeveloped product opportunities. A customer organization results in close contact with the customer, often leading to innovative ideas for new products (von Hipple 1989). Such an organization leads to specialized knowledge about markets and different selling approaches to fit with the idiosyncrasies of these markets. In comparison, differentiated defenders with a service orientation place less emphasis on new product development and more emphasis on prompt service and support. This necessitates vesting the individual salesperson with some decision-making authority and suggests that moderate levels of decentralization and specialization may be appropriate here. In order to provide high levels of service, firms such as IBM place considerable discretionary authority in the hands of their salespersons and managers.

Supervision/Span of Control

A second key structural issue is the design of the organization's sales management hierarchy. The vertical structure of a sales organization refers to the number of levels of management and the span of control (Shapiro 1977b). Because the activities of the sales force in a low cost defender business unit are comparatively routine, the amount of direct supervision by sales managers can be modest. Consequently, the number of salespeople a sales manager can oversee is fairly large, suggesting a comparatively flat organizational structure. Sales managers will typically be responsible for monitoring sales volume and number of account contacts made by individual salespersons, making periodic joint customer contacts, and recruiting and training new salespeople.

In direct contrast, differentiated defender business units place a high level of importance on each stable account. Sales managers must be familiar with these accounts in order to quickly adjust to customer demands and prevent small problems from growing into larger ones. Because of the importance of individual accounts, the need to react quickly to changing situations necessitates a high ratio of sales managers to the number of salespeople. This creates a pyramidal organizational structure consisting of multiple layers within the sales function.

Due to the comparatively narrow range of activities that the sales force is required to perform and the relatively less important nature of personal selling as an element of the promotional mix in prospector businesses, a moderate ratio of sales managers to salespersons is deemed most appropriate. However, since the sales force serves as a conduit for the transfer of information on evolving marketplace desires and trends as well threats in the environment, a large span of control is deemed inappropriate. Sales managers are responsible for passing this information along to the appropriate departments and individuals. In addition, sales managers need to assist in coordinating the schedules of personnel from the sales department and other functional areas required in joint sales contacts.

Vertical Integration

A third key organizational decision in managing the personal selling process is the choice of developing and maintaining a company sales force versus hiring independent agents (Anderson and Weitz 1983). Both economic and strategic criteria are used to make such a choice (Churchill, Ford and Walker 1990). The activities of independent agents are difficult to control. They may behave in an opportunistic manner with short-run orientations and refrain from performing non-sales activities such as cultivating new accounts, providing after-sale services, and making new product presentations (Anderson and Weitz 1983; Mahajan, Churchill, Ford and Walker 1983). This lack of control makes the enforcement of policies less effective. While external agents are likely to have industry-specific knowledge, they are less likely to have company-specific knowledge. Firms operating in ever changing markets, relying on their sales forces to serve as communication conduits between customer and company, and constantly developing new products may require their sales forces to anticipate and accept ongoing training sessions as a normal function of their position. This approach may not be feasible with external agents. The nature of selling activities required for prospector and differentiated defender units should make the use of a company sales force more appropriate. This approach is particularly relevant for differentiated defenders.

Due to the focus of low cost defenders on efficiency, economic criteria serve as the primary influences in their decision to employ either a company sales force or external agents. Fixed costs associated with external agents are lower than those associated with a company sales force (Churchill, Ford and Walker 1990). However, as sales volumes increase, external agents may prove more expensive since agents are often paid higher commissions than company sales personnel. Low cost defenders usually have narrow product lines which are not technically sophisticated. Such products could be handled by external agents since industry-specific knowledge may suffice for this purpose and extensive training would not be required. High turnover costs for a company sales force may be an additional reason for low cost defender business units using external agents.

The decision whether to build an in-house sales force or rely on agents and/or distributors can have a significant impact on a firm. An example of this was the attempt by Kroy, Inc. to augment their distributor network with an in-house sales force. The net result was a significant loss of dealer support and an erosion of the company's base clientele. This was eventually followed by a return to a predominantly dealer based sales arrangement due in part to a lack of new product offerings and the emergence of an innovative competitor.

Sales Force Support

The final organizational consideration is the degree of sales support provided to the sales force. A high level of sales support is required for differentiated defenders due to the importance of maintaining superior levels of service and the broad range of activities performed by the sales force. High quality and reliable order processing, installation, and repair service support are essential. Both IBM and AT&T have substantial system support to back up their products. Additional promotional support should come in the form of reinforcement advertising. Because differentiated defender business units will require some new accounts, it may be prudent for them to establish a new accounts sales force to augment the efforts of the key account sales force. This provides the firm with sources of incremental growth without reducing the level of service established customers expect.

In contrast, sales forces operating in low cost defender businesses require much lower levels of sales support. In firms such as Graybar Electric, delivery of the product generally constitutes the end of the transaction unless the product proves defective. Although it may be part of the salesperson's responsibilities, additional logistical support for the processing of orders and distribution of product may be required. Additional support may also come from telemarketing and/or automatic reordering services. In comparison, sales forces in prospector organizations should require moderate levels of sales support. Trial stimulation advertising is important for prospector business units seeking to generate product awareness. An inside sales force (telemarketing) can provide the firm with an eco-

nomical means of weeding out marginal accounts thereby freeing the field sales force to concentrate on the most potentially lucrative customers. Finally, additional technical support for novel applications or beta test sites may be required.

Evaluating the Selling Effort

In the absence of specific directives or incentives a salesperson may gravitate toward performing those activities he/she most enjoys and/or is especially adept at. Therefore, it is important that a business unit establish appropriate incentives to motivate members of the sales force to perform those additional activities necessary to ensure the successful implementation of a given strategy. Key activities associated with evaluating the performance of the sales force include (1) establishing quotas, (2) determining compensation, and (3) adopting evaluation mechanisms (Churchill, Ford and Walker 1990).

Quotas

Sales quotas provide an incentive to the sales force, serve as a basis for measuring sales performance, and act as a control over the sales program. A firm may be able to manipulate, to some degree, the activities of individual members of the sales force by placing greater or lesser rewards on certain activities. Those activities most important to the success of a given strategy should be emphasized through the adoption of the appropriate quota. Churchill, Ford, and Walker (1990) identified four types of sales quotas based on sales volume, margin, activities, and financial impact.

While each of these may be applicable in any given situation, some should have broader application under individual strategies. Sales volume is universally important but is of prime importance in a low cost defender business unit. However, an emphasis on volume must be tempered by the profit margin of the various products that make up the product mix. If the price is the paramount buying criteria emphasized by the customer, the sales force will focus on selling the most price competitive items. Consequently, a firm needs to identify those products most essential to generating significant cash flows and place greater emphasis on them. Thus, a margin quota is also appropriate for firms adopting this strategy. In order to ensure high sales volumes, Premier Industrial Corporation sets quotas based on dollar volume sold. However, in order to make sure the small accounts are not overlooked, they also establish a quota on number of sales.

Because prospector and differentiated defender oriented firms require substantially more from their sales force than just closing sales, activity quotas are important to both. This helps ensure that important market trends and opportunities are promptly communicated to the firm, less desirable activities of the sales function are carried out, and smaller accounts are not ignored. A firm trying to establish in-roads into a new product-market, such as AT&T with computers, will establish quotas on the type of product sold and the number of presentations/proposals made for a product line. Finally, financial quotas are most important to differentiated defender firms where the decision to either conduct an activity for an account or refrain from doing so may have long-term financial implications.

Compensation & Evaluation Mechanisms

Sales force compensations can be divided into two categories: financial and psycho-social. Financial incentives include salaries, commissions, and awards of significant monetary value such as trips, gifts, and bonuses. Psycho-social incentives are typically of modest monetary value and are designed to enhance the status of the individual and promote commitment to the organization. Examples of psycho-social awards include honorary titles, plaques, seniority pins, certificates, special privileges (e.g., parking), and special recognition (e.g., salesperson of the month).

The most important financial compensation issue for a firm is deciding between straight commissions, straight salaries, or a combination of the two. A key element in selecting a specific plan is identifying those sales activities of greatest importance to the implementation of an intended strategy (Churchill, Ford and Walker 1990). Anderson

and Oliver (1987) have considered conditions under which behaviorally based (largely subjective evaluations based on an individual salesperson's aptitude, skill, effort, attitude, and compliance with management's specific directives) versus outcome based (largely objective evaluations based on numerical data such as unit sales or gross revenue) control mechanisms are used in sales force management. They conclude, "Generally, environmental uncertainty, difficulty in the quantification or translation of sales outcomes, and risk averse, firm specialized, or intrinsically motivated salespeople argue for behavior control whereas small firms with high relative measurement costs and direct links between sales efforts and performance argue for outcome control." Their assertion supports a natural association between control mechanisms (outcome versus behavioral) and reward mechanisms (commission versus salary). Business units relying on direct outcome measures should reward salespeople on a commission basis. Business units relying on behavioral measures should compensate salespeople with a larger proportion of salary.

When a salesperson is required to conduct activities other than generating sales volume, when a salesperson's performance is difficult to assess in the short run, and when a salesperson has little control over generating sales volume, then a behavioral control system and a straight salary are considered appropriate. This plan appears appropriate for prospector businesses where the emphasis is on new product development and the sales force is required to perform non-sales activities. The sales force often has little control over the success of a new product and short-run performance may be difficult to assess. In contrast, an outcome control system and a straight commission are considered appropriate when the sales force is required to perform mainly direct selling and performance is clearly measurable in terms of sales volume. This type of compensation is appropriate for low cost defenders and represents the traditional method of compensating external agents. Combination plans are appropriate when an emphasis on both straight selling and non-sales activities are required of salespeople. Differentiated defenders, whose sales forces are required to perform a wide range of activities, may use such a combination plan to strike a balance in providing incentives for sales and non-sales activities. AT&T's incentive plans include a base salary to commission ratio of approximately 70:30 for those salespersons who reach their quotas. In contrast, the compensation policies for both Premier Industrial Corporation and Kroy, Inc. offer lower base salaries but higher commission rates to those members of the sales force who achieve a prespecified base level of sales in a given selling period (e.g., monthly).

The importance of psycho-social incentives depends on the situation. In low cost defender business units where turnover is typically high, attempting to foster a "family" environment of loyalty is of marginal value. However, as these awards are of marginal cost, even minimal increases in motivation may justify their use. When the financial needs of a salesperson are met, monetary incentives shrink in importance. Non-monetary compensations that provide a salesperson with an incentive to remain motivated then become increasingly important. This scenario is more likely to be reflective of a salesperson with many years in the business, such as is the case in a differentiated defender business unit where turnover rates are typically much lower. Perks and/or recognition for seniority are appropriate rewards. As the activities of a salesperson in a prospector business unit are often hard to evaluate in the short term, it is important that incentives be applied to motivate them to carry out those actions deemed important. In this scenario, contests for activities such as the number of contacts made, new accounts signed up, orders placed, most innovative solution to a customer's business problem, etc., are appropriate.

Discussion

The intention of this paper has been to provide a conceptual rationale for linking sales management activities and policies with specific business unit strategies. This has been a largely unexplored area

in both the sales force management and strategy implementation literature. Even though models of the sales management process, such as the one developed by Churchill, Ford, and Walker (1990), suggest that environmental factors influence marketing strategies, and subsequently that marketing strategies influence sales management activities, researchers have not focused on the relationship between different business unit strategies and sales management activities. By focusing on extreme strategy types we have attempted to initiate a bridge between business unit level strategy and sales management activities.

As this study represents an initial conceptualization of a framework linking marketing strategy with sales management activities, we have focused exclusively on extreme strategy types. We have not attempted to address hybrid strategies that may actually exist within individual businesses because of the large number of potential combinations. While a comprehensive evaluation of hybrid strategies is not undertaken, extreme strategy types can serve as reference points providing sales managers with a set of standards by which to evaluate the strategic focus of their own firms or business units. The closer the match between these extreme strategy types and the strategy adopted by the firm, the fewer modifications sales managers should need to consider. Another way of looking at the issues discussed here is in terms of the underlying dimensions of the strategy typology (i.e., rate of new product/market development and cost leadership versus differentiation). The relative position that a SBU seeks along each of these dimensions would moderate the propositions developed here about extreme strategy types.

We also note that moderating factors idiosyncratic to specific products, markets, and/or competitive situations may temper our propositions. However, identifying and evaluating the potential impact these factors may have on sales management activities is beyond the scope of this initial framework. Nevertheless, as Walker and Ruekert (1987) note, "Because a business strategy does set a general direction concerning how the unit will compete, it should at least have some impact on broad marketing policies that cut across products and product lines."

From a managerial perspective, this framework provides sales managers with a basis from which to consider and evaluate differences in sales management activities and policies relative to different strategies adopted at the business unit level. While not all business units will adopt one of the extreme strategies we have focused on, this framework can still serve as a template by which managers can compare and contrast differences in sales force design, activities, and performance measures, relative to their unique situations and hybrid strategies. While the focus here is on extreme strategy types, managers can consider the issues with respect to the two underlying dimensions of the hybrid typology: the rate of new product/market development and cost leadership versus differentiation. As an example, for SBU strategies which aim for higher rates of new prod-

uct/market development, propositions regarding prospectors would apply to higher degrees. Such inferences could be drawn from the rationale developed to support the propositions. Significant variances in experienced and prescribed policies coupled with low business unit performance may provide a signal to management that it is time to reassess the intentional strategy of the business unit and specifically the policies that govern the management of the sales force.

Two possible avenues of future research have emerged from this study. First, in order to enhance the validity of this framework, testing of the propositions needs to be conducted. Second, as noted earlier, factors such as specific products, markets, or competitive situations may moderate the propositions. Identification and evaluation of the impact these factors have on the implementation of specific strategies would provide a more complete understanding of the role of the sales force in the implementation of business unit level strategies.

References

Aaker, David A. (1984), *Strategic Market Management,* John Wiley & Sons, New York, NY.

Anderson, Erin M., and Barton A. Weitz (1983), "A Framework for Analyzing Vertical Integration Issues in Marketing," Report #3-110, Cambridge, Mass: Marketing Science Institute.

Anderson, Erin M., and Richard L. Oliver (1987), "Perspectives on Behavior-Based Versus Outcome-Based Sales Force Control Systems," *Journal of Marketing,* 51, (October), 76–88.

Andrews, Kenneth R. (1987), *The Concept of Corporate Strategy,* R. D. Irwin, Inc.: Homewood, IL.

Churchill, Gilbert, Neil Ford, Orville Walker (1990), *Sales Force Management: Planning, Implementation and Control,* R. D. Irwin, Inc.: Homewood, IL.

Darmon, Rene Y. and S. J. Shapiro (1980), "Sales Recruiting—A Major Area of Underinvestment," *Industrial Marketing Management,* 9, 47–51.

Gwinner, R. (1968), "Base Theories in the Formulation of Sales Strategy," *MSU Business Topics,* 37–44.

Harris, Clyde E., Richard R. Still, and Melvin R. Crask (1978), "Stability or Change in Marketing Methods," *Business Horizons,* 21, (October), 32–40.

Mahajan, Jayashree, Gilbert Churchill, Neil Ford, and Orville Walker (1983), "A Comparison of Organizational Climate on the Job Satisfaction of Manufacturers' Agents and Company Salespeople: An Exploratory Study," Working Paper #7-83-10, Graduate School of Business, University of Wisconsin.

Miles, Raymond E., and Charles C. Snow (1978), *Organizational Strategy, Structure, and Process,* McGraw-Hill, Inc.: New York, NY.

Porter, Michael E. (1980), *Competitive Strategy,* NY: The Free Press.

Ruekert, Robert W. and Orville C. Walker, Jr. (1991), "Shared Marketing Programs and the Performance of Different Business Strategies," in V. Zeithaml (ed.), *Review of Marketing,* 1990, Chicago: American Marketing Association, 4, 329–366.

Shapiro, Benson P. (1977a), "Improve Distribution With Your Promotional Mix," *Harvard Business Review,* 55, (March/April), 115–123.

—— (1977b), *Sales Program Management: Formulation and Implementation:* McGraw-Hill, New York.

—— (1988), "Close Encounters of the Four Kinds: Managing Customers in a Rapidly Changing Environment," HBS N9-589-015, *Harvard Business School,* Boston, MA.

Strahle, William M. (1989), "An Exploratory Study of the Relationship Between Marketing Strategy and Sales Strategy," unpublished dissertation, Indiana University.

————— and Rosann L. Spiro (1986), "Linking Market Share Strategies to Sales Force Objectives, Activities, and Compensation Policies," *Journal of Personal Selling and Sales Management*, 6, August, 11–18.

von Hipple, Eric (1989), "New Product Ideas From 'Lead Users,'" *Research Technology Management*, 32, no. 4, May/June, 1–4.

Walker, Orville C. Jr., and Robert W. Ruekert (1987), "Marketing's Role in the Implementation of Business Strategies: A Critical Review and Conceptual Framework," *Journal of Marketing*, 51, (July), 15–33.

Chapter 10

Communicating with Business Customers: Beyond Personal Selling

I n Chapter 9 we identified the principal methods of communication with business customers and then extensively considered the role of personal selling and its management. In this chapter we discuss the communication methods that either supplement personal selling or that, for many firms, carry the full burden of communication, including securing the customer's order. We conclude with a brief discussion of the cost of communication with business customers.

Supplementing Personal Selling

Personal selling efforts, no matter how extensive, can seldom accomplish all the communication objectives of marketing strategy. Personal calls on all buying influences may not be practicable. In what may be an extreme example, Xerox found that its salespersons selling photocopiers could see decision makers in only 1 out of 25 calls.[1] Buyers report relying extensively on a wide variety of sources for information about products, services, and their characteristics. According to one study, buyers in the machine tool industry actually rely more heavily on advertising than on salespersons as a source of information.[2] In many industries, trade shows are important sources of product information. In some instances, high-level management in the customer's organization, not actively involved in the purchasing decision, may influence supplier selection on the basis of overall perceptions of the supplier, based on advertising or other non-personal communications.

Reflecting the need to supplement the personal selling effort, a recent survey of industrial goods manufacturers in the United States by *Sales & Marketing Management* indicated that although they spent 11 percent of sales revenues on personal selling, they also spent 3 percent of sales on advertising and sales promotion. For these reasons, as well as others considered later, even communication programs that rely principally on personal selling need to consider the use of a wide variety of other communication methods.

Direct Marketing

The predominant role of personal selling in the communication program should not obscure the fact that for many firms the expense of personal selling by the firm's own sales force, an agent, or a distributor is either prohibitive or unnecessary. Therefore any discussion of communication with the customer by means other than the salesperson needs to take into account the concept of *direct marketing,* defined by the Direct Marketing Association as "an organized and planned system of contacts, using a variety of media, seeking to acquire or maintain a customer. It requires the development and maintenance of an information base to control targeting, manage the offer and maintain continuous contact."

For many firms, direct marketing constitutes the total communication effort. Dell Computer is perhaps the classic example of a firm that relies exclusively on direct marketing, but many other manufacturers and wholesalers communicate with customers and solicit orders only with advertising, direct mail, or telemarketing. Some firms use direct marketing to communicate with some segments and personal selling for others. In considering the use of the following methods of communication, the particular application needs to be taken into account.

Advertising

We defined advertising as any paid form of nonpersonal presentation of ideas, goods, or services by an identified sponsor. It includes the use of media such as magazines, newspapers, radio, TV, and billboards but does not include direct mail. Good use of advertising is rooted in a clear specification of its objectives, which can include:

- Introducing the firm to prospective customers to pave the way for the first sales call.
- Providing information about products to buying influences who cannot be reached by the salesperson or who cannot be reached in a timely manner.
- Generally enhancing the image of the firm, particularly with high-level buying influences.
- Generating sales leads by announcing new products.
- Directly soliciting the customer's order, either by mail or phone.

The starting point for developing an advertising campaign or strategy is the determination of objectives. In the case of Leykam Mürztaler, for instance, a brief to the advertising agency might have specified that the firm wished to reach a number of audiences, including printers and advertising agencies, to enhance the overall image of the company as a reliable, modern supplier and to position its brands as high-end products with superior printing qualities and color rendition.

In the ideal situation, business marketers use the objective-and-task method to guide advertising expenditures. That is, objectives of the nature indicated for Leykam Mürztaler are quantified, an economic analysis is made of the costs and expected benefits, and the results of the advertising campaign are measured and evaluated on a before-and-after basis. A recent study in the United Kingdom suggests that this approach is on the rise.[3] It is not without problems, however. Where the objective of advertising is to enhance the image of the firm, increase brand preference, or introduce the firm to prospective customers, establishment of an advertising budget inevitably involves subjective judgments as to benefits and measuring advertising effectiveness may be difficult. Faced with this subjectivity and difficulty, many firms simply determine advertising expenditures based on rules of thumb such as a historical percent-of-sales measure or industry norms. A more appropriate approach is to establish objectives and estimate benefits, even if rough, using past expenditures and industry norms as guides for advertising budgets, not as determinants.

Where the objective of advertising is to generate sales leads or solicit direct sales, establishment of objectives and measurement of effectiveness are far simpler. The value of a good lead can be reasonably estimated and the number of responses to an advertisement can be tracked, facilitating reasonably accurate cost–benefit estimates.

A salient characteristic of business advertising is the existence of specialized publications. In the United States alone, there are some 2,700 publications carrying business advertising. Some are vertical publications focused on a particular industry, such as *Electrical World*. Others are horizontal publications focused on a particular function, such as *Purchasing*. The business marketer faces choices between these specialized vertical or horizontal publications or more general business publications such as *The Wall Street Journal* or the *Financial Times*. Selection of the appropriate media must be consistent with the objective of the advertising.

Business marketers should not overlook radio advertising as a communication medium. In Detroit, for instance, radio messages by industrial firms reach large numbers of automotive engineers and purchasing agents in their cars during the morning rush hour.

Finally, for the multinational firm, the choice must be made between a standardized message worldwide or one that is tailored to specific markets. In some instances the answer is clear. Advertising messages directed to engineers in Germany must reflect their desire for extensive technical information. In other countries conceptual advertising may be more appropriate. Except for language, however, the nature of business markets suggests that standardized messages are appropriate in most situations.

Direct Mail

The nature of business marketing, with its relatively small number of fairly identifiable customers, emphasizes the potential usefulness of direct mail in the promotional mix. Key to its effective use is a good data base. We describe the use of direct mail for two categories of customers.

For existing customers, mailing lists can be developed from company records and kept up-to-date by the field sales force. Price changes can be transmitted simultaneously to all customers. New product or service announcements or extensive technical information can be transmitted to interested customers for subsequent follow-up by a salesperson. Catalogs or other promotional information can be mailed to key buying influences on a regular basis. Direct mail can also be used to reach key decision makers who cannot normally be contacted by the sales force. Beyond the need for mailing list accuracy and frequent updating, a key to success is creating messages that the sales force believes will assist their selling efforts.

For new customers, commercially available mailing lists can be used to introduce the company, to develop leads for subsequent follow-up by the sales force, or to solicit some other direct response. In the United States there are a number of list providers. Companies such as Dun and Bradstreet offer lists of upward of 10 million U.S. businesses, available for four-, six-, and eight-digit SIC codes. In addition to lists for U.S. businesses, Dun and Bradstreet offers international lists that include another 28 million names. Lists can be obtained just for mailing labels or with more comprehensive information such as years in business, company size, and credit history. Lists can be purchased for one-time use, suitable for a single mailing, or for multiple use, suitable for building a permanent data base. Keys to success are correct selection of mailing lists and careful screening of responses to ensure that leads are viable.

For most firms an extensive and accurate data base for direct mail, and for telemarketing as well, is a vital component of a marketing communication program. What needs to be recognized in building a data base of business customers is the existence of multiple influences. Not only does this require extensive knowledge of the names and positions of all the buying influences in the customer's organization, but it also may suggest ways in which the message needs to be varied, reflecting the functional interests of the individual. The impact of even the best message can be reduced if the customer's name is spelled incorrectly or the wrong title is used, further emphasizing the importance of accuracy in the data base. In his comprehensive handbook on building data bases in Europe, Rhind points out that it is not enough to translate messages into the customer's language, but that titles and forms of address also need to take local custom into account.[4]

Telemarketing

Contacting business customers by telephone has long been a staple of business communication. Salespersons phone customers for appointments and to communicate information in a timely manner. Inside sales personnel rely almost exclusively on the telephone in their work to support the sales force. Customers contact sales offices to request information and to place orders. What, then, is causing telemarketing to be recognized as a separate and distinct method of communicating with customers? Much of the growth reflects the number of ways the telephone can effectively be used to communicate with customers, including:

- Use as the principal method of communicating with customers (i.e., replacing the sales force).
- Use as a supplement to the sales force, to proactively stay in touch with customers, particularly small or remote customers called on infrequently in periods between sales calls.
- Providing customers a convenient way to place orders in response to direct mail.
- Generating and qualifying sales leads.
- Conducting market research.
- Conducting customer satisfaction surveys.
- Providing product/service information.

Facilitated by the use of 800 or other toll free numbers and the increase in the number of ways of use, overall growth in telemarketing has been explosive. It is estimated that business marketers in the United States spend almost $28 billion annually on telemarketing,[5] and it is forecasted that it will be one of the fastest-growing methods of business communication in the 1990s. This growth mandates that telemarketing be well organized and managed if it is to be effective. Often this means carefully integrating specialized personnel and procedures with the rest of the marketing effort. For example, one telemarketing operation designed to support the field sales force located all its personnel in a centralized location in the United States. To convey a "local feel," telemarketing personnel assigned to customers on the West Coast subscribed to West Coast newspapers so they could discuss local news with customers. As telemarketing operations grow, problems of coordination must be addressed to avoid situations such as that of a company running an ad with an 800 number without notifying the telemarketing center or the generation of leads without the knowledge or involvement of the sales force.

Trade Shows[6]

The trade show is one of the most important elements of the communication mix and yet is frequently overlooked in the formulation of communication strategy. Trade shows provide a unique opportunity for buyers and sellers to come together in an environment where buyers are actively looking for product information, new products, or new sources of supply. According to Trade Show Bureau estimates, 4,316 shows were held in the United States and Canada in 1994, of which 1,900 were open only to the trade, with attendance by invitation and requiring preregistration. At these shows some 723,900 firms exhibited their products and services to nearly 19,000,000 attendees. Some of these 1,900 shows exhibited consumer goods and were attended by wholesalers and retailers. Others, perhaps as many as half, focused on business markets. In 1992, for instance, the largest category of trade shows was manufacturing and engineering, with 633,720 attendees, and the top single show in the United States in terms of attendance was the International Manufacturing Technology Show, with 80,000 attendees.

Outside the United States trade shows attract even larger numbers of prospective buyers. The largest industrial trade show in the world is held annually in Hannover, Germany, attended by over 400,000 prospective buyers. The cities of Cologne, Dusseldorf, Essen, and Dortmund in the German state of Northrhine Westphalia are the homes of some 90 trade shows, of which 58 are international in scope and 40 are the largest worldwide in their specific sectors. The importance of trade shows in foreign trade is emphasized by the extensive help offered U.S. exporters by the U.S. Foreign and Commercial Service to participate in international trade shows, and by the help offered all exporters by the Japan External Trade Organization (JETRO) to participate in trade shows in Japan.

When exhibiting outside the United States, there is always the question of approach. In Europe the approach of European manufacturers to their exhibits has tended to be more conservative than that of U.S. manufacturers. Hence, when General Electric first exhibited its engineered plastics at a European trade show, with much emphasis on showmanship, many of the firm's competitors felt it had made a serious blunder. As it turned out, the showmanship was very effective and the company has since become one of the major players in the European market.

From 1989 to 1994 both the number of trade shows and the number of exhibiting companies in the United States grew by some 30 percent and, according to a Cahners Advertising Research Report, trade show expenditures (18 percent) are second only to business advertising (23 percent) as a percent of nonselling marketing costs. Driving this growth is the evaluation of trade shows as a top-rated source of purchasing information by buyers, attendance by individuals with significant levels of purchasing influence, and studies suggesting that closing a sale to a qualified trade show lead takes significantly fewer sales calls than if all calls are made in the field.

Despite the extensive use of trade shows, the high level of expenditures, the favorable reviews by purchasers, and the general evidence regarding their effectiveness, many executives still question participation in trade shows. Some view participation as a necessary evil, done only because competitors are there. Others view them as little more than vacations for participating personnel, particularly when they are held in attractive locations. More particularly, participation is questioned because of lack of specific evidence of their effectiveness and the high and rising cost of participation. For business marketers this suggests the need to have well-established objectives for trade show participation, to select trade shows carefully, to staff them appropriately, and to measure their effectiveness.

According to the Trade Show Bureau and others, companies exhibit at trade shows for a wide variety of reasons, including to:

- Generate sales.
- Generate qualified sales leads.
- Intensify awareness of the company and its products.
- Introduce a new good or service.
- Create a preference for products and the company.
- Find new distributors for their goods or services.
- Provide distributor support.
- Test prototypes and judge reaction to new products.
- Find new applications for existing products.
- Recruit sales representatives.
- Secure information about competitors.
- Provide technical staff the opportunity to interface with customers.

Selection of trade shows is facilitated by the segmentation that takes place by prospective customers, based either on their product or industry interest. Other factors to consider include the orientation of the show with respect to selling and the level of participants. Some trade shows are more selling oriented (i.e., orders are placed at the show), whereas others are more oriented to future or broader objectives. Some attract high-level managers with broad interests, while others attract technical personnel interested in technical detail.

Trade show exhibits often are staffed with relatively low-level, untrained personnel, reflecting the view of trade shows as a necessary evil. Effective use of trade shows, however, is enhanced by careful selection and preparation of personnel for their participation. In many instances, such participation is held out as a privilege that has the added benefit of improving morale.

A wide variety of measures can be used to evaluate effectiveness, depending on the objectives of the particular show. If the show is oriented toward selling, then sales generated is an easy and straightforward measure. Buying influence of attendees, or buying plans, can be measured through short questionnaires. Leads generated and sales generated from leads can be measured with relatively simple tracking systems. On a more subjective basis, customer attitudes can be measured as can the views of the trade show staff.

The use of trade shows is not limited to products. A Denver architect, for instance, specializing in designing sports centers, exhibited a model of one of his designs at a trade show, was contacted by a Japanese firm interested in building sports centers in Japan, and now is doing a thriving business designing sports centers for the Japanese market.

Seminars, Conferences/Technical Papers

Often overlooked in the communication mix, seminars, conferences, and technical papers can play an important role in business marketing. Attendance at seminars and conferences by both marketing and engineering/R&D personnel provides the opportunity to interact with buying influences in an environment conducive to open and informative discussion. In many instances, presentation of technical papers by suppliers comprise much of the program, affording suppliers the opportunity to communicate about their product developments or applications in a way perceived to have less bias than normal marketing communications. In some industries, such as health equipment, papers on favorable test results of a firm's product by a university researcher add further credibility to the supplier's performance claims and are frequently published in trade journals or used in a direct mailing.

Sales Promotion

In this text we have limited the definition of sales promotion to the use of samples, contests, catalogs, brochures, or other sponsored means to create interest or awareness of goods or services not included above. The use of contests merits particular attention. For the sales force, either that of the manufacturer, an agent, or a distributor, well-designed contests can materially enhance the sales effort. There are two basic approaches. The "sell harder" approach establishes incentives that reward sales personnel for additional sales, either in a certain period of time or of a particular product. Key to such an approach is to ensure that all participants have an equal opportunity to be rewarded and that many personnel will receive rewards. The "sell smarter" approach establishes certain goals that are steps along the path to a sale and rewards sales personnel for their achievement. More complex to administer than the sell harder approach, many firms have found this to be effective in enhancing communication between marketing and sales personnel.

Contests can also be used effectively with customers, either to stimulate product interest or to generate sales leads. A compressor manufacturer, for example, capitalized on interest in golf to mail a golf quiz to a mailing list of contractors. All respondents received a sleeve of golf balls and product information, and the winners were publicized in a subsequent mailing. From the manufacturer's view, the product interest thus stimulated far exceeded what would have been the result of a more traditional mailing.

Publicity

Publicity, perhaps the least expensive form of communication, can be an effective element of the communications mix. Relations with editors of trade journals enhance the likelihood of feature stories on the firm or its products. In many instances, trade journals will report on, or even publish, technical papers referred to above. Many trade journals include new product and personnel sections. News releases focusing on these new product sections, including how to get further information, can be very effective in generating leads for further selling effort. News releases about personnel changes can be effective in keeping the firm's name before its customers.

The Cost of Communication

Cost is clearly a major consideration in developing and implementing an appropriate communication program, increasingly so as organizations reengineer, downsize, or take other steps to improve productivity and meet competitive pressures. What, then, is the "right" amount for the firm to budget for its communication programs?

In the final analysis the budget for communications must take into account the unique situation of the individual firm. Products in the early stage of the product life cycle, for instance, require greater expenditures on communication than those in the mature or decline stage. As referred to in the pricing chapter, firms that adopt a greater value pricing strategy (i.e., more features per dollar) may be able to achieve revenue goals with relatively lower expenditure on communication. Uncomplicated products usually require less communication effort than complex ones. Compensation levels of personnel vary widely among industries, reflecting necessary skill levels and availability of personnel. Pressures on communication costs reflect the firm's profit situation. The variation in these situational aspects suggests there is no "right" amount to be spent on communication programs. It is useful, however, to consider how the budget process should be approached and the experience of other firms or firms in other industries.

We previously referred to the recommended objective-and-task approach for determining advertising expenditures. Conceptually, the same approach is appropriate for the entire communication program. In essence, the budget can be built based on estimates of the expense of each element of the program, as determined by its objectives and what is required to achieve them. For example, estimates can be made for the number of sales calls necessary to achieve certain revenue objectives, and these estimates can be used to size and cost out the required sales force. In most instances, however, budgets are not built from the bottom up. Rather, programs are ongoing, and last year's budget is usually the starting point for the next, modified to reflect changes in objectives and strategies. In either case, some sense of industry norms is helpful to check on the reasonableness of the firm's budget.

Considerable aggregated data are available, such as the previously mentioned study by *Sales & Marketing Management* that reported industrial goods companies spent 11 percent of sales on selling expenses and 3 percent on advertising and other promotional expenses, compared to service companies, which spent 15.3 percent on selling and 3.4 percent on advertising and other promotional expenses.[7] There have been fewer comprehensive studies that provide information by industry on all elements of communication. One such study

TABLE 10.1

1992 Compensation and Expenses by Industry

	Industrial Goods			Services		
	Compensation	T&E Expenses	Total	Compensation	T&E Expenses	Total
Sales trainee	$30,552	$ 9,855	$40,407	$28,078	$ 5,255	$33,333
Mid-level salesperson	$46,571	$15,118	$61,689	$42,311	$ 8,128	$50,439
Top-level salesperson	$65,610	$16,748	$82,358	$63,672	$ 9,822	$73,494
Sales supervisor	$71,012	$19,713	$90,725	$65,947	$14,021	$79,968

Compensation includes base salary, commission, and bonus.
T&E expenses includes travel, entertainment, food, lodging, and other related expenditures.
Source: Adapted from *Sales & Marketing Management,* June 1993, 62.

indicated total marketing costs ranging from a high of 15.2 percent of sales for electronic computing equipment to a low of 4.7 percent of sales for transportation equipment.[8] This study confirmed that direct selling was the major component of total marketing costs, ranging from 2.9 percent of sales for transportation equipment to 9.5 percent of sales for instruments and related products. In aggregate, the industries studied reported direct selling costs as 5.9 percent of sales, sales promotion costs as 1.0 percent of sales, advertising costs as 0.6 percent of sales, and direct mail costs as only 0.1 percent of sales. While the levels of expenditures reported are at variance with other studies, the key point to be recognized is the variation of total marketing expenditures by industry. Similar patterns were shown in a more comprehensive study undertaken by the Conference Board in the 1970s that reported total marketing costs ranging from 29.3 percent of sales for office equipment, of which 22.6 percent was direct selling, to 3.5 percent for pulp and paperboard products, of which 2.6 percent was direct selling.[9]

These data need to be used with caution. The nature of industry studies, with all the difficulties of sampling and different ways in which firms report data, is such that reported percentages should be taken as no more than general indicators. Still further, it is highly likely that reported percentages have changed over time and across industries. They do, nevertheless, along with other reports of marketing costs and data gleaned from annual reports of competitors, provide background useful for development or analysis of the communication budget.

Sales & Marketing Management also publishes frequent estimates of the cost of a sales call and the compensation of sales personnel in the United States. For industrial goods firms, they estimate the cost of a 1992 sales call for industrial goods at $227.27, up from $217.92 in 1988. For service firms, the 1992 estimate was $213.64, up from $200.87 in 1988. As shown in Table 10.1, annual salesperson compensation, including travel and entertainment, ranged from a low of $33,333 for trainees in service firms to $82,358 for top-level salespersons in industrial goods firms. As with the industry percentage expenditures above, these numbers need to be used with care. Costs per sales call vary as a function of the number of calls made per year and the compensation level of the salesperson. Compensation levels of salespersons vary considerably across industries and from firm to firm within an industry. Used with care, however, they can be very helpful in developing or analyzing the personal selling component of the communication budget.

Summary

Business marketers have a number of communication methods available to support the personal selling effort or to implement direct marketing programs. Advertising, direct mail, telemarketing, and trade shows are the principal methods, but participation in conferences and seminars, use of contests, brochures, and catalogs, as well as publicity should all be considered in developing a communication program. Whatever methods are used, coordination is imperative. Sales aids that are not used by the sales force, advertising that solicits calls to an unprepared 800 number, and sales leads that are not properly qualified before being given to the sales force are all examples of uncoordinated efforts that are economically wasteful and sometimes counterproductive.

The cost of the communication program is the major portion of total marketing expense. For most business marketers the cost of personal selling is the major portion of the communication program. Careful control of these costs, taking into account the objectives of each element of the communication program, is increasingly important. Although each firm will develop a budget appropriate to its own unique marketing strategy, industry figures can be very useful as checks on the reasonableness of the firm's expenditure on communication.

Overview of Chapter Case

✳ The Leykam Mürztaler case describes the situation of a firm considering ways to establish a brand identity and preference for its high-quality printing paper, a product many consider a commodity. It provides the opportunity to consider how, or if, this objective can be achieved and what might be an appropriate communication program.

Endnotes

1. Peter Finch, "Xerox Bets All on New Sales Groups," *Business Marketing*, July 1986, 21.
2. Charles H. Patti, "Buyer Information Sources in the Capital Equipment Industry," *Industrial Marketing Management*, 6 (1977): 259–264.
3. James E. Lynch and Graham J. Holley, "Industrial Advertising Budget Approaches in the U.K., *Industrial Marketing Management*, 18 (November 1989): 266.
4. See Graham R. Rhind, *Building and Maintaining a European Direct Marketing Database* (Hampshire, England: Gower Publishing, 1994).

5. George E. Belch, and Michael A. Belch, *Introduction to Advertising and Promotion Management* (Homewood, IL: Richard D. Irwin, 1990), 647.

6. This section draws heavily on *A Guide to the U.S. Exposition Industry* (Denver, CO: Trade Show Bureau, 1994); Thomas V. Bonoma, "Get More Out of Your Trade Shows," *Harvard Business Review,* January–February 1983, 75–83; and Paul Herbig, Brad O'Hara, and Fred Palumbo, "Measuring Trade Show Effectiveness," *Industrial Marketing Management,* 23 (1994): 165–170.

7. *Sales* & *Marketing Management,* June 28, 1993, 65.

8. *Laboratory of Advertising Performance Report No. 8015.8* (New York: McGraw-Hill Research Department, 1985).

9. Earl L. Bailey, *Marketing Cost Ratios of U.S. Manufacturers: A Technical Analysis* (New York: The Conference Board, Inc., 1975).

Byron G. Quann

How IBM Assesses Its Business-to-Business Advertising

Whenever the subject of measuring advertising comes up in business-to-business marketing circles, we all say, of course, it's something we do with great precision, utilizing the most advanced scientific techniques, enabling us to prove conclusively the value of our advertising would it were so.

But I guess it's only fair to tell you that at IBM, we can't do that.

Can anyone? By its very nature, advertising quality and effectiveness are extremely difficult to measure. And even when we have statistical data it must be carefully analyzed and presented with the proper perspective.

From our perspective, Information Systems Group (ISG) is responsible for all of IBM's marketing and service in the U.S. Of our three marketing divisions, two are national marketing divisions with direct sales forces. Another marketing division manages sales through third parties. ISG also includes one nationwide service division, as well as a number of small start-up ventures in new business areas for IBM, called independent business units, which ISG advertising supports.

Yet ISG is responsible for only a portion of what the public perceives as "IBM" advertising. Our portion comprises the bulk of IBM product advertising. Our mission is to complement the field sales force in the two major marketing divisions, as well as to enlarge the business through the other channels of distribution.

At the time this article was written, Byron G. Quann, based in Rye Brook, N.Y., was group director of communications for the Information Systems Group of International Business Machines Corp. His article is adapted from his presentation to the Advertising Research Foundation. Reprinted with permission from the 1985 issue of *Business Marketing*. Copyright, Crain Communications, Inc.

Personal computer advertising is done by our Entry Systems Division in Boca Raton, Fla., which is responsible for manufacturing and development of the personal computer product line. Their mission is to create interest and product identity in the consumer marketplace and also to support the large dealer network that we've established.

Beyond the personal computer dealers, a separate organization handles channel advertising to support our IBM-owned retail stores and third-party resellers.

And there's corporate advertising, responsible for enhancing the perception that the general public and the business community has toward the company.

As a result, we are one of the largest advertisers, promoting as wide a variety of products as we do under a single brand name.

That's both good news and bad. The good news is that because we are very well known and highly regarded, there is a real benefit to having the IBM name on every product. The bad news is that we have many products which are very similar in appearance, function and application. And because each has the same brand name they are extremely difficult to differentiate.

It is also very difficult to measure the singular effect of one piece of advertising because the IBM name washes over everything we do. Having created ads for so many of our products, we have the potential to create our own clutter. For example, the average customer, when asked what product Charlie Chaplin represents, might well say, "I remember Charlie Chaplin, he's the guy that sells IBM typewriters." But in fact, he's associated strictly with our Personal Computer line and its related software.

FIGURE 1
Campaign Research Measurement Model

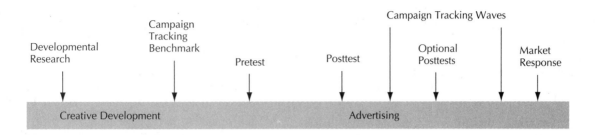

Those circumstances make goal-setting difficult and measurement of the results expensive. As a result, over time we have evolved into campaigns by business area rather than doing individual ads.

Setting Advertising Levels

The second aspect of our strategy is, within each business area, to determine our advertising level based on three factors:

1. Our current participation in the marketplace.
2. The competitive levels of advertising among our major competitors.
3. Our current year's sales objectives for the products that are in that business area.

In addition, we select new business areas for special emphasis.

Of course, we try to target our advertising to specific audiences. Because the buying cycle for our products is long, and the cost is nontrivial, there can be many people involved in the purchase decision. Consequently, we not only try to appeal to the decision maker who will ultimately decide to purchase the IBM product, but also to the key decision influencers.

On that point about competitive levels, in the past we tried to track our competitor's advertising but found ourselves dissatisfied with the usefulness of publicly available information. Finally we realized that to get meaningful information on our industry, we had to develop our own tracking system.

We now track both the print and TV advertising of more than 300 of our competitors. The analysis groups the ads within the same 19 business areas that we group our products. Two different outside firms do the bulk of the data collection work. The first provides a press clipping service scanning 200 magazines and 130 newspapers. The other tracks radio and TV, including the three major networks, cable, syndicated channels in major cities and local stations in a number of selected cities.

From them we get a wealth of information and reports quarterly. They tell us the total dollars spent by each competitor, grouped by business area and itemized by medium. We also receive a comparative spending ranking which ranks IBM along with each of the competitors tracked in each of our business areas.

A Model in Action

Our ideal approach to research and measurement is the model shown in Figure 1. We use it for major campaigns from the very beginning of the creative development process through the life of the campaign itself.

The actual vehicles that we use to do the research are the same ones that business marketers often use: post-testing, pre-testing, Gallup & Robinson and Starch, tip-ins, tracking studies, impression studies and focus groups. However, time and money usually prevent all of us from using all of them for everything we do. The key point is that we try to use as many as we can for major campaigns.

Here's a recent example of how we used the model for a key business area—the typewriter. That product presents some very real problems that advertising can address.

In the fall of each year, we assess each of our business areas in terms of where we stand in the marketplace versus our objectives, and then put together a plan for the following year. In the fall of 1983, we went through that exercise for the typewriter business area. We found that our lead position was being challenged by more than two dozen increasingly capable competitors.

Therefore, our objective for 1984 was to maintain the leadership position that we currently held.

A survey in 1983 told us that the IBM typewriter was, in the minds of decision makers and users, the preferred typewriter in the marketplace. Therefore, our communications strategy was to maintain those preference levels throughout the year. And do it by emphasizing individual product features, all within the umbrella theme of the typewriter of preference. We aimed the campaign to both decision makers and secretaries.

We geared our copy points to stress preference, quality, ease of use and a wide range of features. We developed a broad media coverage plan including print, radio and TV. And we used most of the measurement techniques mentioned above.

Print and TV ads were then developed to capitalize on this theme of preference. For example, an IBM ad stating "Some of our best salespeople work for someone else," stresses the fact that people who often do the best job of selling our product are not our own people, but those who have experience in using our product and experiencing its benefits. And TV with the same theme

airing during the first quarter of 1984 turned out to be the highest scoring commercial we have ever tested. It received a day-after-recall score of 53 versus our norm of 29, and an industry norm of 23.

During the second quarter of 1984, we identified a need for more continuity in our typewriter ads. We took a look at what we had, both in print and TV and felt that while individually each was fine, there was not much continuity between them.

So we felt that we needed a campaign theme and one that would work with both print and TV. One which would conjure up the theme of preference, and at the same time be warm, light and upbeat, taking advantage of our leadership position.

Departures

Our agency, Doyle Dane Bernbach, came up with a theme, "We're your type," and a number of supporting concepts. The theme was "We're Your Type." The proposed campaign involved some fairly radical ideas, at least from an IBM point of view.

For instance, the TV commercial used a jingle—new for us. The print ads used almost the entire ad to show nothing but a single typewritten character, magnified hundreds of times to fill a page. The copy block was short and to the point— stressing preference. And we also wanted a typewriter ad without any picture of the product. Those concepts were so different for us that testing was a must to make sure that we weren't heading off the deep end.

The first thing we did was to test that ad, our biggest concern being that people would find the ad to be too whimsical. We were pleased to find that less than 25 percent of the group interviewed did not like the ad. Of those that didn't like it, 80 percent felt the copy was condescending. Rewriting the copy was an easy fix.

We also asked those who we interviewed about the message they got. More than a third said that they thought that the ads conveyed that IBM makes the best typewriter, of the highest quality. And more than a quarter said it's the typewriter secretaries prefer most. Two messages that we wanted to convey.

FIGURE 2

	1983			1984					1985	
2Q	3Q	4Q	1Q	2Q	3Q	4Q		1Q	2Q
Preference survey			Aired straight preference commercial Reaction test	Created development pretest *Newsweek* ad—split run test Survey: first tracking benchmark Broke the campaign: TV and print Added music to the commercial	Ran revised Miss Tomkins commercial	Revalidate preference claim			Survey: first tracking wave

We also wanted to determine how an ad without a picture of a product would fare versus one with a picture. So in the same time frame, we did a split run test in *Newsweek*. The test showed that the ad with the picture of the typewriter had less stopping power than the one without.

We also tested the initial TV commercial for the new "We're Your Type" campaign. A major concern was whether people might find the music somewhat offensive or think it inappropriate for IBM. But through testing we found that less than 20 percent of the people who saw the commercial disliked it. And the reasons were not at all music-related. Criticisms like 'not informative enough,' 'doesn't tell me what the features are,' 'doesn't hold my attention.' But despite our concern, there was no negative reaction to the music.

When we asked the group what was communicated in the commercial, close to half said the product could be used by many businesses. The next most common message cited was the fact that many different kinds of people can use IBM type-writers. And the third most consistently reported message was the fact that the product is versatile.

We were so pleased with the results of our testing, that we went back and retrofitted the commercial, focusing more on the secretary appearing in it as an implicit spokeswoman for the product.

To review the chronology of our research, we did the creative development pre-test on the print and TV concept, and also ran the split-run test for the ads with and without the pictures of the typewriter. Also during the second quarter of the year, we ran our first tracking benchmark survey. Based on the results of the testing, we decided to go ahead and break the campaign both in TV and print. And in that same time frame, we altered the TV commercial for third quarter airing.

In the next few months, we plan to do another survey to revalidate the preference claim. Lastly, during the second quarter of this year, we will conduct our first tracking wave survey.

Figure 2 summarizes how we used research to develop and tune the campaign.

Assessing Sales Impact

How did we measure the impact of advertising on product sales? Of course, it's very difficult to establish a direct relationship between advertising and sales volumes in business-to-business markets.

It's even more difficult for us primarily because of the many possible actions a viewer of our ads might take. The reader can go to four different places in response to our print advertising. He can contact an IBM product center, contact an authorized IBM typewriter dealer, dial a toll-free number that's listed in the ad or, should he have one, call his IBM representative.

It's also very difficult to know what activity levels in each of those four information channels are directly related to people having seen our advertising. In addition, there is the problem of using one brand name for all products.

Nonetheless, we still go out of our way to try to track activity in each of those areas and, where we can, identify some correlation between our advertising and the activity levels it may generate. We track the number of calls that come into our 800 numbers, we track dealer activity through surveys,

and we do periodic tracking surveys to determine how the market's perception changes over time. And naturally we do measure our sales volumes.

But I should stress that we are very careful in assuming any correlations between absolute sales volumes and advertising because of the number of factors that influence decisions to buy our products.

The typewriter campaign was new in 1984, so the results aren't in yet. But if the test results and the early response from our dealers is any indication, we may have a winner.

This year we're introducing a new typewriter line featuring advanced technology. Much of what we learned in last year's research is helping us formulate our communications strategy for the new line.

Despite our considerable progress in the area of advertising research and measurement, we at IBM are not at all complacent or comfortable with where we are today. We have quite a long way to go.

However, we have built a fairly extensive research and measurement data base which is growing rather dramatically and we will continue to expand its use.

Paul Herbig
Brad O'Hara
Fred Palumbo

Measuring Trade Show Effectiveness: An Effective Exercise?

The trade show is an event that seems to be well accepted in marketing circles. However, despite their growing numbers, trade shows do have their downsides and critics. Part of this problem may be due to the fact some marketers fail to answer the basic question of trade show effectiveness. Thus, in an effort to bring some focus to this issue, we examine findings and research to date with respect to trade shows and highlight some areas that marketers might consider in assessing the effectiveness of these events. ✻

Introduction

Trade shows, trade fairs, expositions, scientific/technical conferences, conventions—the names may vary, but the basic function of the activity represents a major industry marketing event. Essentially, trade shows "bring together, in a single location, a group of suppliers who set up physical exhibits of their products and services from a given industry or discipline"[2].

Trade shows represent a considerable investment on the part of marketers. For example, in 1988, over 100,000 firms in the United States alone exhibited at some 11,000 business trade shows and spent over $9 billion. This represents a tremendous rate of increase when compared to 1982 figures: 91,000 firms exhibited at some 8,000 trade shows at a cost of $7 billion. Further, in the 10-year period

At the time this article was written, Paul Herbig was Professor at College of Commerce and Business Administration, Jacksonville State University, Jacksonville, Alabama. Brad O'Hara was Professor at Southeastern Louisiana State University, Hammond, Louisiana. Fred Palumbo was Professor at College of Business, Yeshiva University, New York, New York. Reprinted by permission of the publisher from *Industrial Marketing Management 23*, 165–170 (1994) © Elsevier Science Inc., 1994.

from 1980 to 1990, the number of trade shows shot-up from 4,500 to 10,000.

Although it appears, based on these industry figures, that the trade show is an important component of American business practice, the question of their effectiveness remains unanswered to some [12]. Many individuals remain unconvinced about the role of trade shows in the overall marketing plan of the firm because many trade show proponents have neglected this basic issue. Although trade show marketers, for the most part, have done a good job in promoting these events externally, it appears that they have failed to market these functions internally. Perhaps part of the solution to this problem lies in identifying what specifically to measure/report about trade show performance and how to go about measuring these variables. Thus, through an extensive review of the nature of trade shows, we will shed some light on this fundamental issue. Our goal is to outline several trade show components in which senior managers might be interested and to define experience to date. Hopefully, consideration of these various measures will demonstrate that measuring trade show effectiveness is an effective exercise!

Two Sides of Trade Shows

That the trade show is a tool which marketers use extensively remains without question. Trade shows accounted for 22–25 percent of the typical U.S. business market promotional budget, second only to personal selling activity and ahead of print advertising and direct mail. In aggregate, American businesses spend annually an approximate $9 billion on exhibitors' travel and labor costs and $12 billion for actual exhibit costs. In concert with these astounding figures, the Trade Show Bureau estimates that the industry itself generates $50 billion per annum.

Associated with these impressive expenditure figures are some other equally important numbers. First, growth of exhibit space averaged nearly 15 percent annually during the 1970s, while slowing to a sustainable 7–8 percent annually during the 1980s. Early reports for 1992 show that this growth rate averaged 3–4 percent, tumbling primarily due to the recession. Second, according to trade show industry reports, participation figures have also been increasing. The number of firms exhibiting at the 200 largest trade shows grew by 7.7 percent between 1986 and 1987. During the 1970s, the number of new exhibitors increased at an average annual increase of 3–4 percent, while in the 1980s it exceeded 7 percent annually [10]. Concomitantly, show attendance at the major trade fairs increased at an average of 3 percent per year during the 1970s, rising to more than 6 percent during the 1980s.

With respect to trade show attendees, it is reported that nearly 44 percent of trade show visitors travel more than 400 miles to shows and that the average individual spends approximately $1,000 per visit on travel, accommodations, and meals. These attendees are typically "important" individuals to exhibitors, as 85 percent of these visitors play some role in the buying decision. This, combined with the fact that the cost per visitor (which includes space rental, construction costs, booth personnel travel, living expenses, and salaries) is one-third of a personal sales call [16], makes the trade show a cost-effective vehicle when viewed in this light. Additionally, trade show proponents point to the fact that it takes approximately 0.8 sales calls on average to close a sale initiated by a trade show lead, while most estimates place the number required in the field to be about five visits.

Other advantages of using trade shows abound. Industry advocates point to the fact that the marketing message is generally well received at these events. As most attendees have buying influence or have a specific interest in the product(s) being displayed, the trade show can be ideal for the introduction of new products to large numbers of people. Additionally, potential customers may be uncovered, while at the same time the ability to enhance goodwill with existing clients presents itself. Generally, salespeople have the opportunity to perform all elements of the personal selling process at trade shows: (1) identifying prospects, (2) servicing current accounts, (3) introducing products, (4) improving corporate image, (5) gathering competitor information, and (6) selling [3, 8]. This accounts for the finding that for buyers, trade show activities play a major part in vendor evaluation and recognition [1b, 11].

Despite these appealing statistics, trade shows do have their downside. For one, costs can be exorbitant: for example, the cost of exhibit space, which is typically 15 percent of a company's total trade show budget, can range up to $39 or more per square foot. This cost has more than doubled over the previous decade. Other negatives, which some individuals associate with trade shows, are common: (1) these events take salespeople away from their territories, (2) large shows are sometimes cluttered, crowded, and confusing, (3) labor problems and unions occasionally "flare up" and (4) there sometimes are an excessive number of sightseers at these events.

However, the biggest problem with respect to the trade show is that they lack substantive quantitative research. This probably accounts for the fact that only a handful of executives think trade show effort is very effective. All too often, a substantial number of corporate marketing executives perceive trade shows as a nonselling activity, or at best a social affair for those employees that attend [12]. Part of this problem might be rooted in an apparent lack of direction: only 56 percent of firms participating in trade shows set specific objectives before participating in a given show [5]. This may also be compounded by the fact that 56 percent of exhibitors do not train the people staffing their trade show booths and that 78 percent of participants do not promote their exhibit prior to the show. Perhaps this accounts for the disheartening statistic revealed in an SMU study, which found that more than 40 percent of all first-time trade show exhibitors were one-time trade show users!

In addition to the lack of goal setting for trade shows, many marketers have also failed to quantify several other important aspects of trade shows. Lead qualification, tracking, and return on investment evaluation remain relatively unexplored by most exhibitors (only 14 percent claim they track lead conversations to sales, while barely 17 percent of all exhibitors provide their management executives with ROI data [10]). With the millions spent on trade shows each year, coupled with the apparent lack of follow-up on basic trade show issues, is it any wonder that many executives question the value of trade shows?

Evaluating the Trade Show Effort

The outcome of establishing the existence of two trade show "camps"—the "pros" and the "cons"—demonstrates a need to better define and evaluate the trade show effort. Thus, in an effort to shed some light on this matter, we review the literature in order to solidify our knowledge base about trade shows and outline various measures that are being used to evaluate trade shows.

First, from the exhibitor side of the fence, we note various patterns. Although more than 50 percent of trade show exhibitors attend five or more trade shows each year, trade shows are not for everybody. Generally, the larger the company, the higher the number of trade shows exhibited at annually. Further, the greater the number of products in a company's product line, the more trade shows the firm tends to exhibit at. Typically, companies which exhibit at trade shows market complex products, do business in industries where sales are high, charge a premium price for their product, and usually sell to firms where many people are involved in the decision process [9]. Spending levels for trade shows tend to be higher when a company markets goods early in the stages of the product life cycle, its sales are high, its customer concentration is low, and the firm has aggressive product plans. There also appears to be a direct relationship between market share and trade show participation, as firms with greater than 20 percent market share average nearly twice as many shows per year than those with less than 5 percent market share [7].

Generally, firms participate in trade shows to identify prospects [4]. This, however, is not the only reason for exhibiting at these events. Other sales-related reasons include servicing current customers, introducing new or modified products, testing new products, gathering competitive information, and selling. Nonselling reasons may also prompt trade show participation, such as enhancing corporate image and improving/maintaining corporate morale [8].

As to participating in a particular show, trade show exhibitors are primarily concerned about audience quality and numbers. Specifically, they are interested in the proportion of decision makers in the audience, the proportion of visitors relating to the company's target market, screening of show visitors, total show attendance in previous years, and the extent of promotion by show organizers to generate attendance. In addition to these audience characteristics, display booth location and other logistical aspects are also important to the participation decision [6]. This includes booth position/location on the floor relative to traffic flow patterns, ability to specify/negotiate booth size and location, aisle traffic density, easy registration/preregistration, security, and moving in/moving out assistance and facilities. Show amenities such as an exhibitors' lounge, eating facilities, and visitor parking are not that critical to this decision.

Fortunately, much is known about trade show attendee audiences. From a general perspective, we know that buyers attend trade shows to (1) find solutions to known problems, (2) decide on or finalize vendor selection for postshow purchases,

(3) identify new methods, (4) meet with technical experts, and (5) assess technical directions [10]. The Trade Show Bureau [15] reports that 50 percent of attendees go to trade shows to see new products, services, and developments. In any particular show, 16 percent of the audience is interested in seeing a specific product, and 6 percent is actually planning to buy a specific product. Fifty-seven percent of all attendees expect to buy one or more of the products at that event.

Swandby and Cox [13, 14] have also extensively examined this aspect of trade shows. (Their findings represent an attempt to quantify trade show participation and thus would be of interest to trade show and marketing managers alike.) They have found, for example, that with respect to net buying influence, the percentage of the show audience that has the final say or makes recommendations for purchase of one or more of the products/services exhibits is significant and has remained relatively constant at 85 percent in 1987 to 86 percent in 1988 to 84 percent in 1989. Concerning purchase intentions or total buying plans, the percentage of the audience planning to buy one or more of the products/services displayed at the show within the next 12 months has remained constant at a somewhat appealing 60 percent in 1987 and 61 percent in 1990. Finally, an audience interest factor demonstrates that buyers are somewhat active at trade shows, as they solicit information from exhibitors. The percentage of the trade show audience that visits at least 20 percent of the exhibits in their field of interest has been tending slightly upwards from 45 percent (1987) to 48 percent (1990). This is an aggregate score over many trade show types; generally, the more narrowly focused the trade show, the higher the audience interest factor tends to be. Interestingly, trade show size has a depressing effect on this measure. Although a trade show may be "improved and expanded" with more exhibitors and more space, decreases in audience interest are usually noted as visitors did not see proportionally more exhibits. Future research is needed in this area to pinpoint the impact of pre-event advertisements and publicity on this factor.

In addition to these three audience measures, there are other benchmarks that may be of interest to senior managers. First, the average time spent at each exhibit, which is calculated by dividing the average hours spent at exhibits by the average number of exhibits visited, has been relatively constant during the past 10 years, at 20 minutes. Related to this statistic is the finding that attendees typically spend 7.8 hours viewing exhibits over a 2-day period and stop at an average of 21 booths during this time. Traffic density is another measure that allows one to compare different trade show sites. Overall, the average number of visitors who could theoretically occupy every 100 square feet of exhibit space during the time trade shows were open was approximately 3.2 visitors in 1990. Throughout the past 20 years, this factor has ranged between 3 and 4. A density factor of 6 is quite high and highly congested, while a factor of 1 means traffic is extremely light.

Obviously, audience measures are important to selling trade shows and to determining their effectiveness. However, audience measures are not the only statistics that managers are interested in hearing about. A summary of several audience and other exhibit performance measures that may be of interest to senior management includes the following:

- **Potential Audience:** Potential audience is the percentage of the total trade show audience with a high interest in seeing a company's products/services. Obviously, this is a pre-trade show measure that might be a critical factor in choosing to participate in one of these events.

- **Exhibit Efficiency:** This represents the percentage of the potential audience that receives person-to-person contact at the company's exhibit. As a global measure of American trade shows, this performance factor was 62 percent in 1990. This rate has been relatively constant in the nearly 30 years it has been calculated at around 60 percent.

- **Personnel Performance:** Various measures could be employed here; measures should be generated in light of trade show objectives. For example, if the firm were concerned with lead generation, an indication of personnel performance might be to divide the number of booth personnel into the number of contacts generated. Further, if the trade show has a selling orientation, personnel performance could be determined by the amount of sales achieved per trade show representative.

- **Product Interest:** Product interest represents the percentage of booth visitors who said they were interested in seeing the company's type of products/services. This measure would be determined during or after interaction with booth personnel.

- **Buying Influence:** Another measure that would be indicative of the quality of booth visitors would be a buying influence measure. This is a percentage calculation based on the number of visitors who claimed a buying influence for its products/services relative to total trade show attendance.

- **Buying Plans:** This concerns the percentage of an exhibit's visitors who said they were planning to buy specific products/services as a result of what they saw at the show.

- **Memorability:** One interesting measure of trade show effectiveness concerns memorability. Memorability is determined by calculating the percentage of visitors who stopped at an exhibit and remember doing so eight to ten weeks after the show. In 1989, global memorability statistics averaged 71 percent. For management, low memorability can be caused by poor personnel performance, insufficient corporate identification, poor pre-event publicity, and failing to follow-up on inquiries. Memorability statistics can focus in on the overall exhibit, a particular product or demonstration, product literature, and other promotional tools.

- **Cost per Visitor:** For many managers, effectiveness means getting the "biggest bang for the buck." Thus, cost measures will probably be part of the trade show effectiveness story. One widely used measure is the cost per visitor (CVR) statistic, which is calculated by determining total trade show costs and dividing this figure by the number of visitors stopping by your booth. These figures averaged nearly $90 in 1989, and have been steadily increasing over the years.

- **Top Performing Exhibit:** Within trade show circles, an exhibit that reaches at least 70 percent of its potential audience at a CVR of less than the show average is deemed to be a top performing exhibit. Top performers usually average less than half of the CVR average.

- **Number of Leads Generated:** This is a number that can be easily determined by counting the number of prospects generated from trade show activities. Trade show exhibitors are required to keep basic prospect information such as name, firm, address, and phone number.

- **Sales Generated from Leads:** Another tracking statistic is to determine the number of sales generated from the prospects obtained at a trade show. In some cases, this sales figure might be determined immediately (if selling occurred at the show), or months after the fact, in the case of selling complex items which require several sales calls and much follow-up activity.

- **Cost per Lead Generated:** Perhaps a more effective statistic than the CVR value would be to determine the cost per lead generated. For management, this probably represents a more accurate reflection of the value obtained from the costs invested in a particular trade show.

Although these statistics present a broad-based overview of trade show performance, they do not represent the entire list of indicators that can be used to measure effectiveness of these events. Additional effectiveness measures might be generated in light of company trade show objectives. For example, if the firm were concerned about disseminating information about a new product, they might wish to track the number of brochures distributed to visitors.

Regardless of how many trade show measures are generated, it appears that we can group these statistics in three areas: audience quality indicators (i.e., potential audience, net buying influence, total buying plans, and audience interest factor), audience activity indicators (i.e., average time spent at exhibit, traffic density), and exhibit effectiveness indicators (i.e., CVR, cost per lead generated, memorability, and sales generated) [1]. These measures have two general thrusts, as they assess audience characteristics/activities and exhibitor characteristics/activities. In order to assess trade show effectiveness, both audience and exhibitor measures are necessary.

Conclusion

Measuring trade show effectiveness can be an effective exercise, if the proper tracking mechanisms are established and management makes a commitment to monitor performance. Various effectiveness measures can be generated, focusing on the audience and on the activities of the exhibitor. The development and tracking of measures can go a long way in fighting the battle that occurs in some firms between trade show believers and trade show skeptics.

Although addressing the question of trade show effectiveness is a necessary one, perhaps a more challenging exercise to trade show exhibitors is to consider the issue of how to improve effectiveness. Obviously, once effectiveness measures are in place, the impact of pre-event advertisements, in-show promotional items, additional booth personnel, larger booth space, etc., can be determined with the objective of getting a better return for the trade show dollar.

References

1a. Bellizzi, J. A., and Lipps, D. J., Managerial Guidelines for Trade Show Effectiveness, *Industrial Marketing Management* **13**, 49–52, (1989).

1b. Bello, Daniel C., and Barczak, Gloria J., Using Industrial Trade Shows to Improve New Product Development, *Journal of Business and Industrial Marketing* **5**, 43–56 (1990).

2. Black, R., *The Trade Show Industry: Management and Marketing Opportunities*, Trade Show Bureau, East Orleans, Massachusetts, 1986.

3. Bonoma, T. V., Get More Out of Your Trade Shows, *Harvard Business Review* **61**, 75–83 (1983).

4. Cavanaugh, S., Setting Objectives and Evaluating the Effectiveness of Show Exhibits, *Journal of Marketing* **40**, 100–103 (1976).

5. Donald, B., Show and Sell by the Numbers, *Industrial Marketing* **March** 70–75 (1980).

6. Faria, A. J., and Dickinson, J. R., Behind the Push to Exhibitat Trade Shows, *Business Marketing*, **Aug.**, 98–102 (1985).

7. Faria, A. J., and Dickinson, J. R., What Kinds of Companies Use Trade Shows Most—and Why, *Business Marketing* **71**, 150–153, 155 (1986).

8. Kerin, R. A., and Cron, W. L., Assessing Trade Show Functions and Performance: An Exploratory Study, *Journal of Marketing* **51**, 87–94 (1987).

9. Lilien, G. L., A Descriptive Model of the Trade Show Budgeting Process, *Industrial Marketing Management* **12**, 25–29 (1983).

10. Mee, W. W., Trade Shows: This Marketing Medium Means Business, *Association Management* **40**, 50–55 (1988).

11. Moriarty, R. T., Jr., and Spekman, R. E., An Empirical Investigation of the Information Sources Used During the Industrial Buying Process, *Journal of Marketing Research* **21**, 137–147 (1984).

12. Skolnik, R., Getting the Brass to Take Trade Shows Seriously, *Sales and Marketing Management* **139**, 99–102 (1987).

13. Swandby, R. K., and Cox, J. M., How Trade Shows Served the '70s, *Industrial Marketing* **April**, 72–78 (1980).

14. Swandby, R. K., and Cox, J. M., Trade Shows Poised for 1990s Growth, *Business Marketing* **May**, 46–52 (1990).

15. Trade Show Bureau, Attitudes and Opinions of Computer Executives Regarding Attendance at Information Technology Events, Study no. 1080, 1988.

16. Trade Show Bureau, Exhibit Management Practices—Setting Objectives and the Evaluation of Results, Study no. 2010, 1986.

Judith J. Marshall
Harrie Vredenburg

Successfully Using Telemarketing in Industrial Sales

Telemarketing has steadily increased in use in industrial sales organizations. Management faces the difficult problem of successfully implementing this tool. This research surveyed industrial sales and marketing managers involved in telemarketing operations to determine how successful their telemarketing operations were and how telemarketing was implemented in their companies. ✳

Introduction

Telemarketing has become a very popular catchword in marketing circles in recent years. It has been called "a new weapon in the arsenal" [16], "a great idea whose time has come" [18], and "the answer to the rising costs of cold calls" [2], in various business journals and publications. Statistics indicate that about 20 percent of industrial firms in the United States are now using telemarketing [14]. Annual sales revenue generated by telemarketing is close to $100 billion and users of telemarketing are increasing by 25 percent per year [4].

So much has been written about the advantages of telemarketing as a marketing communications tool that there is a tendency to see telemarketing as the great panacea—the way to solve a variety of sales problems. Moreover, so much emphasis has been placed on telemarketing success stories that there is also a tendency to view telemarketing as an *easy* solution to sales problems:

> Many people believe telemarketing's purported benefits of increased sales, cost reduction and market

share enhancement are virtually *automatic*. . . . However, for every success in telemarketing, there are probably failures—or at least marginal results [3].

It is critical to recognize the world outside the rosy picture of telemarketing success we read so much about. It is difficult to estimate how many telemarketing operations are failures, but, senior management in a major telecommunications company has estimated that almost 40 percent of companies who have tried telemarketing discontinue or quit [13]. There appear to be some very difficult problems in implementing telemarketing successfully in industrial sales organizations [3, 11, 13, 14, 17]. In response to these problems, the purpose of this article is to explore the level of success achieved in industrial sales organizations that adopt telemarketing, to describe the implementation practices followed by firms that adopt telemarketing, and to try to assess whether success is associated with particular implementation practices.

The Literature

In the marketing and sales literature, telemarketing is generally viewed as a marketing communication system where trained specialists utilize telecommunications and information technologies to conduct marketing and sales activities [5, 6, 14, 16]. Because telemarketing can be used in many ways, ranging from disseminating new product informa-

At the time this article was written, Judith J. Marshall was an Assistant Professor of Marketing in the School of Business at Carleton University, Ottawa, Canada. Harrie Vredenburg was an Assistant Professor of Marketing in the Faculty of Management, McGill University, Montreal, Canada. Reprinted by permission of the publisher from *Industrial Marketing Management* 17, 15–22 (1988) © Elsevier Science, Inc., 1988.

tion, to selling to marginal accounts, the term actually encompasses multiple approaches to communication. However, telemarketing is routinely categorized as (1) incoming (calls originate with the customer), or (2) outgoing (calls originate with the firm employing telemarketing). Most industrial telemarketers operate both incoming and outgoing telemarketing [73.5 percent], but, outgoing telemarketing is viewed as offering the largest future growth potential [9, 16]. Outgoing telemarketing, in particular, offers firms an alternative to the increasingly expensive personal sales visit. As such, it represents an extremely attractive option for complementing or even supplanting the personal sales visit as the premier sales tool.

A review of the trade and marketing research literature revealed a strong interest in, but comparatively little research on telemarketing. The trade literature is characterized by case examples and recommendations from telemarketing consultants and practitioners based upon their professional experiences with telemarketing. These articles outline reasons for telemarketing failure and contain numerous prescriptions for increasing telemarketing success. Many of the reasons for failure involve problems with the implementation of telemarketing. For example, Bencin argues that a major reason for telemarketing failure is lack of expertise in managing such operations [3]. Other reasons for failure include lack of commitment in telemarketing, improper facilities, lack of use of format scripts, defective human resource planning and so on. Other writers have also offered advice for telemarketing success, arguing that proper sales training for telemarketing representatives is critical [8], that telemarketing representatives should be paid commissions, that special facilities are required for telemarketing [17], that informal scripts work better for business audiences [10], and that formal scripting is necessary for successful telemarketing [3]. While many of these prescriptions are useful to marketers responsible for managing telemarketing operations, it should be noted that they are sometimes contradictory, they may be case specific and they are based on anecdotal evidence which, for the most part, has not been substantiated by empirical research.

A review of the research literature revealed that relatively few researchers have studied industrial telemarketing. Several descriptive papers have outlined how to apply telemarketing to achieve marketing and distribution objectives [16], how to use telemarketing to supplement face-to-face selling [6], how telemarketing centers function, and how telemarketing can serve as a strategic tool for marketers [5]. One study documented the current selling practices of industrial distributors noting the roles and responsibilities of both inside and outside sales reps [12]. Based on a mail survey combined with personal interviews, Narus and Anderson report that the role of outside reps in distributor firms is to find new customers, get products specified, distribute catalogues, and gather market information. The inside representatives were responsible for more routine and recurring sales tasks including negotiating price, checking inventory, and order follow-up. The authors project that the outside salesforce will continue to become more specialized and the inside salesforce will assume new responsibilities and increased status in the next few years.

Empirical research on telemarketing in consumer markets is equally rare. One study surveyed 489 respondents to investigate possible side effects of telemarketing on company image [15]. The study reported that conventional live telemarketing messages did not adversely affect respondents' perceptions of the company sponsoring the message, while a computerized message was viewed as not considerate or friendly and "disguised" messages (ones that pretend to be surveys then switch to being sales calls) were viewed as inconsiderate, dishonest, and unfriendly.

One can conclude that strong interest exists in how telemarketing can be used successfully in industrial marketing, but no research articles were identified that focused specifically on the success achieved and the implementation practices followed in industrial sales organizations using telemarketing. With the current high cost of personal selling, it is likely that telemarketing will become even more attractive to industrial sales organizations in the future. An understanding of the factors associated with success and failure in the implementation of this practice is taking on greater importance.

The Study

Given the exploratory nature of the research, the researchers began by conducting three case studies of firms which had implemented telemarketing. Included in the case studies were (a) an industrial firm that had little success with telemarketing and had discontinued it, (b) an industrial firm that had achieved great success with telemarketing and had expanded it, and (c) a firm that viewed its success with telemarketing as moderate. Based on the information gained in the case studies and from the literature, a telephone interview was designed to survey a large number of respondents about their salesforces' experiences with telemarketing.

The sample for the study consisted of 385 sales and marketing managers in industrial firms that had implemented outgoing telemarketing programs to perform sales support or actual sales functions in the salesforce. The sample was randomly selected from a list of all firms in the manufacturing, wholesaling, and distribution sectors that had purchased a telemarketing package consisting of necessary telecommunications equipment as well as telemarketing expertise from a major marketer of telecommunication equipment and telemarketing expertise.

Telephone interviews were conducted with 249 respondents—representing a response rate of 64.6 percent. The respondents represented the entire range of marketing and sales positions. Slightly more than half the respondents (58 percent) were senior managers, such as national sales managers, marketing vice presidents, and so on. The remaining 42 percent occupied more junior positions in divisional sales management, telemarketing management, and sales. All respondents had been involved in the decision to use telemarketing in their company.

Participating companies were in manufacturing and wholesaling/distribution industrial sectors. The majority of companies were small to medium in size, with average sales of $15 million per year, employing a median of 60.5 employees. The type of products sold varied from packaging and art supplies to computer and electronic equipment. Paralleling this variation in products was a wide range in product price. The average product price was $900.

Data on company size, sales, geographical location, and use of telemarketing were gathered from the sampling frame to use in checks for nonresponse bias. No significant differences between responding and nonresponding firms were found. Respondents were asked a number of questions related to their use of telemarketing, the level of success achieved, and the implementation of telemarketing in their company.

Use of Telemarketing

Most companies view telemarketing as supplementing rather than supplanting the work done by outside sales representatives. Exclusive use of telemarketing was highly unusual for firms in the study. Almost all companies (94.4 percent) had their own outside sales force. Only two companies sold their products exclusively by telemarketing. The major uses of outgoing telemarketing included qualifying sales leads (73.6 percent), supporting field sales representatives (73.2 percent), generating sales leads (73.1 percent), and handling marginal accounts (70.0 percent). Relatively few firms used telemarketing for full account management (40.0 percent) and opening new accounts (15.4 percent).

The type of telemarketing systems found in the sample companies was extremely varied, ranging from large, very formal telemarketing centers employing 15–20 full-time sales representatives, to smaller, more informal telemarketing centers employing only three or four reps. When beginning telemarketing, the average number of telemarketing representatives employed was 3.8.

Level of Success

Three measures were used to assess the level of success achieved with telemarketing in industrial sales organizations. First, respondents were asked to rate the overall success of telemarketing in their company on a 7 point scale ranging from "very successful" to "not at all successful." Respondents were also asked whether use of telemarketing had increased, decreased, or stayed about the same since they had introduced it in the company. Thirdly, respondents were asked to report the number of telemarketing sales representatives hired to perform telemarketing tasks when telemarketing was first adopted in the company and also to report the number employed at the time of the interview. From these responses, a third measure of success was calculated—the change in the number of telemarketing sales representatives employed since the adoption of telemarketing. It would have been useful to measure the success of telemarketing by measuring the sales attributable to it, but, because telemarketing is often a sales support function, it was not possible for respondents to place a dollar figure on the sales directly attributable to it.

Table 1 shows the results of the success measures. Given the strong advocacy of telemarketing in the trade and marketing literature reviewed in this article, it is reassuring to note that most firms that implemented telemarketing were successful with it. Table 1 suggests that only about 20 percent of respondents perceived their telemarketing operation as an unsuccessful venture, whereas more than one-third (37.3 percent) rated their telemarketing operations as successful. The largest portion (41 percent) experienced moderate success. This high proportion of moderate success is difficult to interpret but tends to suggest that even though respondents would not rate their operations as failures, they perceive that there is room for some improvement.

Table 1 also shows the proportions of respondents reporting whether overall use of telemarketing had increased, decreased, or stayed about the

TABLE 1
Success of Telemarketing

Overall Level of Success	Percent of Respondents (n = 249)
Very Successful	37.3%
Moderately Successful	41.0%
Not Very Successful	21.7%

Change in Use of Telemarketing Since Adoption

Increased	39.7%
Stayed About the Same	38.2%
Decreased	22.1%

Change in the Number of Telemarketing Sales Representatives Since Adoption

Increased	42.3%
Stayed the Same	38.1%
Decreased	20.6%

same since telemarketing first had been adopted and whether the number of telemarketing sales representatives had increased, stayed the same, or decreased since telemarketing was first adopted. Roughly the same proportions of respondents indicated that they had achieved success (37.3 percent), as had increased use of telemarketing (39.7 percent), as had increased the number of telemarketing sales representatives (42.3 percent). This pattern of similar proportions of respondents is also evident (a) for those reporting moderate success, keeping telemarketing operations at about the same level, and keeping the same number of telemarketing sales reps; and (b) for those reporting "not very successful" telemarketing, decreasing use of telemarketing, and decreasing the number of telemarketing sales reps.

One would expect that more successful firms would increase their use of telemarketing or that at least it would stay about the same. The findings showed that this was indeed true. There was a high correlation between overall success ranking and

TABLE 2
Extent of Planning for Telemarketing

	Very Successful	Moderately Successful	Not Very Successful	Total
		(n = 249)		
Specific Goals Had Been Set	80.6%	75.9%	59.8%	71.0%
Specific Goals Were Not Set	19.4%	24.1%	40.2%	28.9%
$x^2 = 10.7$ P = .005				
Had Formulated Clear Cut Plan	81.7%	56.9%	57.4%	66.3%
Little or No Planning Done	18.3%	43.1%	42.6%	33.7%
$x^2 = 15.9$ P = .000				

changes in extent of use of telemarketing (Spearman R = .53; P = .00); between success ranking and change in the number of telemarketing reps (Spearman R = .52; P = .00); and, between changes in the extent of use of telemarketing and changes in the number of telemarketing representatives (Spearman R = .68; P = .00). The more successful firms increased their use of telemarketing and increased the number of telemarketing sales representatives; the less successful decreased use or discontinued it altogether.

Implementing Telemarketing to Achieve Success

Previous research on the management of change in organizations suggests that careful implementation involves planning for the change and making certain that the group responsible for carrying out the change have the ability and motivation to perform the new behavior [1, 7]. This research focused on these issues in examining how telemarketing was implemented in the salesforce under study. Tables 2 through 6 examine the extent of planning done before implementing telemarketing, the level of specialization of telemarketing representatives, the compensation system established for telemarketing representatives, office arrangements provided for telemarketing representatives, and script

use. After crosstabulating the level of success with each of these implementation steps, it became apparent that firms operating the more successful telemarketing systems carefully planned for and managed their implementation of telemarketing.

Table 2 shows the extent of goal setting and planning done by firms implementing telemarketing. The good news is that relatively high proportions of respondents reported setting goals (71 percent) and formulating plans (66 percent) for telemarketing before implementing it. Table 2 also shows that there is a significant difference in both goal setting and planning between the less successful and the more successful firms. Over 80 percent of the respondents claiming very successful telemarketing operations indicated that specific goals were set. These goals included dollar sales, number of calls to be placed per hour, number and type of accounts to be called, and so on. In addition, over 80 percent of respondents operating very successful telemarketing systems stated that they had formulated clear cut plans before implementing telemarketing in their organizations. Planning included specifying the sales tasks that telemarketing would be used for, who would be hired, who would supervise, how performance would be monitored, how telemarketing work would be integrated with work of outside sales representatives, and what role telemarketing would play in various types of accounts.

TABLE 3
Level of Specialization of Telemarketing Representatives

	Very Successful	Moderately Successful	Not Very Successful	Total
		(n = 249)		
Telemarketing Is Major Part of Rep's Job	80.2%	52.0%	42.3%	60.5%
Telemarketing Is Minor Part of Rep's Job	19.8%	48.0%	57.7%	39.5%
$x^2 = 25.0$ P = .000				

Respondents in moderately successful companies reported less planning and goal setting and respondents in "not very successful" firms reported the least amount of both goal setting (40 percent) and planning (42.6 percent).

Table 3 looks at the level of specialization of telemarketing representatives at the time telemarketing was first introduced. Respondents were asked whether telemarketing representatives were dedicated exclusively to telemarketing or whether employees combined other duties with their telemarketing ones. The last column of the table shows that at the time of adoption of telemarketing, 60.5 percent of respondents indicated that telemarketing representatives in their company were hired to work exclusively in telemarketing. However, it was not unusual for telemarketing sales representatives to have other company responsibilities. Of respondents, 39.5 percent indicated that telemarketing representatives in their company had been assigned other major responsibilities in addition to telemarketing. It appears that this sizable proportion of companies attempted to implement telemarketing by spreading telemarketing tasks among a number of employees who hold other responsibilities as well. This approach is quite different from the usual picture of telemarketing described in the literature where telemarketing representatives have full-time telemarketing responsibilities. The remaining columns of Table 3 examine the implications of having employees specialize in telemarketing versus doing telemarketing along with other tasks.

A significant different in success between firms where telemarketing representatives are employed full time on telemarketing duties and those where telemarketing representatives spend only part of their time on telemarketing duties was observed. Of very successful companies, 80 percent made telemarketing a major part of the telemarketing rep's job, whereas over half (57.7 percent) of the "not very successful" group included telemarketing as one of a number of tasks an employee was expected to perform. This finding suggests that even if a company is implementing a small telemarketing operation, it is probably a better strategy not to spread telemarketing responsibilities too thinly, but to make telemarketing tasks a major part of the job for one or two people who can then become telemarketing specialists.

The question of whether to pay telemarketing representatives salary only or some form of bonus or commission has been hotly debated in the trade and business press. Table 4 looks at the compensation system established to motivate the telemarketing sales representatives to perform their duties. The last column of the table shows that slightly more than half the respondents in the study reported paying salary only (53.8 percent) while the other half (46.2 percent) paid bonus or commission in addition to a base salary. The table also shows that there is a significant difference in success achieved between companies paying salary only and those incorporating a bonus or commission into the remuneration package. A

TABLE 4
Compensation System Established for Telemarketing Representatives

	Very Successful	Moderately Successful	Not Very Successful	Total
		(n=249)		
Paid Bonus or Commission	54.8%	50.0%	24.1%	46.2%
Paid Salary Only	45.2%	50.0%	75.9%	53.8%

$x^2 = 12.8$ P = .001

TABLE 5
Office Arrangements for Telemarketing Representatives

	Very Successful	Moderately Successful	Not Very Successful	Total
		(n=249)		
Provided Special Telemarketing Office Arrangements	52.7%	31.4%	31.5%	39.4%
Provided No Special Telemarketing Office Arrangements	47.3%	68.6%	68.5%	60.6%

$x^2 = 11.05$ P = .004

higher percentage reporting very successful telemarketing paid some salary/bonus combination—54.8 percent compared to 45.2 percent who paid salary only. A very high proportion of "not very successful" companies paid salary only (75.9 percent). Interestingly, the moderately successful companies were split evenly between the two types of reward systems.

Two additional questions facing managers implementing telemarketing include whether special office arrangements are needed and whether scripting is a good idea in business-to-business applications. Tables 5 and 6 show the results of these analyses.

Respondents were asked whether special telemarketing office arrangements were provided for the telemarketing reps. The last column of Table 5 shows that only about 40 percent of respondents indicated that special telemarketing facilities had been arranged. Special facilities included using private offices or headphones in an environment to minimize distractions. The remaining 60 percent or so reported that telemarketing reps were given desks similar to those occupied by individuals in sales or clerical positions in open-office arrangements. Table 5 also shows that there were significant differences between the successful and unsuccessful telemarketing systems and provision of special telemarketing facilities. Less successful and moderately successful operations were less likely to have provided special facilities for the telemarketing reps. It appears that special office

TABLE 6
Provision of Scripts for Telemarketing Representatives

	Very Successful	Moderately Successful	Not Very Successful	Total
		(n=249)		
Written Script Provided	45.2%	43.1%	53.7%	46.2%
Written Script Not Provided	54.8%	56.9%	46.3%	53.8%
Not Significant Difference Was Found				

arrangements minimize distractions for the telemarketing reps and this is important in achieving success. Many respondents indicated that distractions were a real problem for the telemarketer. Co-workers stopping by for a chat or to ask questions interfered significantly with call-making.

To script or not to script is a major question for telemarketers. Advocates of scripting argue that it is both efficient and effective, while others argue that it might be inappropriate in industrial selling where the buyer is often a professional and a telemarketing call should be more similar to a personal sales call. Slightly less than one-half (46.2 percent) of the respondents reported that scripts were used in their telemarketing operation. Fifty-four percent did not provide formal written scripts. Table 6 shows that there does not appear to be any significant difference in success whether scripts are used or not. This suggests that it is probably much too simplistic to argue (as much of the writings on telemarketing have done) that scripting is either always appropriate or never appropriate. The appropriateness of scripts depends on the products, the type of customer, and a myriad of other factors. Appropriateness of scripting can only be decided on a case-by-case basis.

Conclusions

An interesting picture of telemarketing success and of the telemarketing implementation process in industrial sales forces emerged from this exploratory research. It is exciting to note that a large proportion—about 40 percent of respondents—reported achieving a high degree of success with telemarketing. This relatively high degree of success can be considered encouraging for those considering adopting telemarketing in industrial firms. At the same time, one should not lose sight of the fact that at least 20 percent of respondents reported that their firms had not been very successful with telemarketing. Although telemarketing can be considered a powerful sales tool, the results of the research show that success is certainly not automatic. One cannot simply assign some employees to the telephone and expect to reap the advantages that telemarketing offers.

Taken together, the findings show that successful firms were significantly more likely to have carefully managed the implementation of telemarketing in their sales forces. Firstly, companies that established specific goals and had clear-cut plans before beginning telemarketing were more likely to be successful. This suggests that managers considering adopting telemarketing as adjuncts to their sales forces would benefit from setting goals for and planning carefully for the use of telemarketing in their own organizations. Although this is a basic part of good, general management practice, it needs to be stressed here, because there is a tendency to expect that telemarketing is easy. There is still a need to plan for what accounts will be targeted by the telemarketers, what selling tasks will be performed by the telemarketers, how many telemarketing reps will be employed, how they will be supervised, and so on. As part of the planning process, managers need to establish specific goals for telemarketing within their companies.

Making certain that those hired as telemarketing sales representatives had the ability and motivation to perform their jobs appeared to be very important in achieving success. The research showed that successful firms were significantly more likely to use dedicated, specialized telemarketing representatives, to incorporate a bonus or commission into their compensation package, and to provide telemarketing reps with special facilities to enable telemarketing reps to conduct their responsibilities effectively. Even if one is implementing a relatively small telemarketing operation, it appears to be a better strategy to hire only one or two full-time representatives than to spread telemarketing responsibilities among several employees who are assigned other company responsibilities.

It is also important to provide special telemarketing facilities—set up a private quiet environment free from distractions to enable telemarketing representatives to do their jobs effectively. Many respondents indicated during the course of the interviews that their companies had originally expected telemarketing reps to perform telemarketing responsibilities in standard, open-office environments, but this proved too distracting and unsuitable.

The matter of scripting does not appear to be clear cut. Since no significant difference in success was found between companies who had scripted and those who had not, it appears that companies can be successful either way. Those implementing telemarketing should assess their own situations and own preferences regarding the use of scripts in industrial sales. Future research is required on the use of scripts in industrial telemarketing to provide guidelines on their use for management.

Lastly, in drawing these implications for sales and marketing managers, it is critical to note the non-experimental nature of the study. Because the research was exploratory and cross-sectional in nature, no definite casual links can be drawn between managerial action and success of telemarketing. However, it is believed that even these preliminary implications can be used given the current rate of adoption of telemarketing and the accompanying need for guidelines for marketing managers attempting to manage telemarketing systems in their sales forces.

References

1. Beckhard, R., and R. Harris, *Organizational Transitions: Managing Complex Change,* Addison-Wesley, New York, 1977.

2. Bencin, R. L., Telemarketing: The Answer to Rising Costs of Cold Calls, *Direct Marketing* **44**, Dec. (1981).

3. Bencin, R. L., The Trouble With (Some) Telemarketers, *Business Marketing* **80**, Aug. (1986).

4. Bower, S., Telemarketing: An Intimate Instrument, *European Research* **71** May, (1987).

5. Coppett, J. C. and Voorhees, R. D., Telemarketing: A New Weapon in the Arsenal, *Journal of Business Strategy* **40** (4), (1983).

6. Coppett, J. C. and Voorhees, R. D., Telemarketing: Supplement to Field Sales, *Industrial Marketing Management* **14** (1985).

7. Deutscher, T., Marshall, J., and Burgoyne, D., The Process of Obtaining New Accounts, *Industrial Marketing Management* **11** (1982).

8. Franco, J. J., Ring Up More Telephone Sales With Well-Trained Personnel, *Business Marketing* **84** (Aug 1986).

9. Gage, J. J., Telephone Rings in the Last Frontier, *Advertising Age* **51** (Jan 21, 1980).

10. Higgins, K. T., Telemarketing Focuses on Recruiting, Training, *Marketing News* **1**,10 (Ap 25, 1986).

11. Higgins, K. T., Rep's Fears of Telemarketing Present Management Hurdle, *Marketing News* (April 25, 1986).

12. Narus, J. A. and Anderson, J. C., Industrial Distributor Selling: The Roles of Outside and Inside Sales, *Industrial Marketing Management* **15**, 55–62 (1986).

13. Personal Interviews with Telecom Canada Management (1982).

14. Roman, M. and Donath, B., What's Really Happening in Business/Industrial Telemarketing, *Business Marketing,* 82–89 (Ap 1983).

15. Schneider, K. C., Telemarketing as a Promotional Tool—Its Effects and Side Effects, *Journal of Consumer Marketing,* 29–38 (1985).

16. Vorhees, R. and Coppett, J., Telemarketing in Distribution Channels, *Industrial Marketing Management* **14**, 213–216 (1985).

17. Webster, G., *Telephone Selling—The Essential Tool For Improving Sales Productivity,* Riverview House Publication, Beaufort, South Carolina (1980).

18. Wingis, C., Telemarketing: A Great Idea Whose Time Has Come, *Industrial Marketing,* 71–79 (Aug. 1981).

Chapter 11

Business Distribution Management

I n Chapters 9 and 10 we discussed communication with customers, primarily from the perspective of a firm doing business directly with its customers. In practice, however, most firms rely at least to some extent on intermediaries to communicate with customers and to perform many of the other functions necessary to satisfy customer wants and needs. In this chapter we first outline the major issues related to channel selection and management. We then describe some of the most common intermediaries and the functions they perform and discuss some of the major changes taking place in distribution channels. We next discuss channel design and issues related to managing intermediaries. We conclude with a discussion of the role of logistics and physical distribution.

Issues in Distribution Management

Decisions with respect to the use of intermediaries are among the most important business marketing managers make. In some circumstances firms elect direct distribution. These firms communicate with customers through their own sales forces or some form of direct marketing, accept orders directly from customers, ship products directly to customers from factories or company-owned warehouses, bill customers directly, and provide their own after-sales service. Most firms, however, use some form of indirect distribution, either exclusively or to supplement direct distribution.

For firms using indirect distribution, the importance of decisions with respect to the desired pattern of distribution and the relationships firms have with intermediaries cannot be overemphasized. As Corey has observed:

419

A distribution system, which consists of some combination of agents, jobbers, and distributors, is a key *external* resource. Normally it takes years to build, and it is not easily changed. It ranks in importance with key internal resources such as manufacturing, research, engineering, and field sales personnel and facilities. It represents a significant corporate commitment to large numbers of independent companies whose business is distribution—and to the particular markets they serve. It represents, as well, a commitment to a set of policies and practices that constitute the basic fabric on which is woven an extensive set of long-term relationships.[1]

As the foregoing suggests, decisions with respect to the use of intermediaries are of two very different kinds. At one level, decisions are strategic, concerned with the overall pattern of distribution. These decisions focus on the structure of the channel, the number of levels between the producer and the customer, and the use of mixed patterns of distribution. In particular, should the firm use its own sales force or manufacturers' agents and should it distribute directly or indirectly? These decisions tend to have long time horizons and are changed only infrequently. At another level, decisions are more tactical and are concerned with how the channel should be managed. These decisions address how channel members communicate and relate to each other, and consider cooperative efforts, trade discounts, inventory levels, responsibility for promotion, information sharing, and so forth. Although the basic pattern of these decisions may have a long time horizon, the associated activities are usually important elements in implementation of the annual marketing plan.

Types of Business Distribution Channel Members

The term *channel of distribution* has a sense of orderliness about it, suggesting that goods flow from producer to customer in a precise and easily described manner. In fact, channels of distribution are made up of an incredibly diverse and constantly changing set of intermediaries. The structure of channels of distribution varies depending on the industry. Within a particular industry, functions of intermediaries will vary, as will the terminology used to describe them. As we will subsequently discuss, forces in the external environment are reshaping many distribution channels and the roles of intermediaries. There are, however, broad categories of intermediaries and general patterns of channel flows that provide a useful framework for considering the issues of concern to management.

In Figure 11.1 we show the principal elements of business distribution channels, together with a general pattern of channel flows. While some definitions of channels include sales branches (i.e., a manufacturer's sales office and warehouse) as a channel element, it is our view that it is more useful to limit the definition of a channel intermediary to entities independent of the producer, thus requiring management or influence without direct control. These intermediaries perform some or all of the following functions:

FIGURE 11.1

Principal Elements of Business Distribution Channels

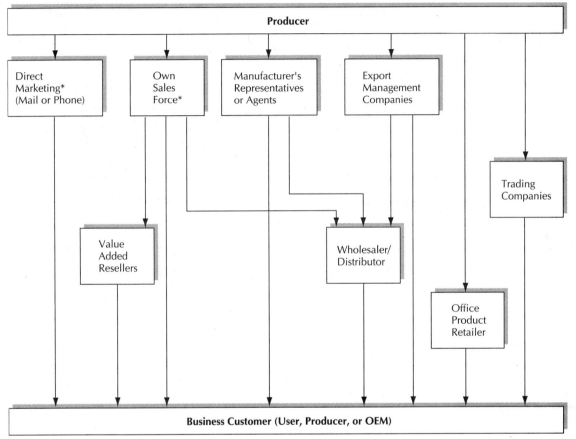

* Not normally considered an intermediary.

- Promotion.
- Stocking.
- Order solicitation and handling.
- Pre- or postsales service.
- Market research.
- Sales financing.
- A variety of value-adding activities.

In broad terms, channel members can be thought of in two categories: (1) agent middlemen, whose principal function is to promote the manufacturer's products or services but who do not take title to goods, and (2) merchant middlemen, who perform a wider variety of functions and do take title to goods. Within these categories are a wide range of specialized firms that serve various markets.

Agent Middlemen

The key characteristic of agent middlemen is that they do not take title to goods. They vary significantly, however, on a number of other dimensions, both with respect to the functions they perform and the nature of the relationship they have with their principals. For business marketers, the two principal types of agent middlemen are manufacturers' agents (or representatives) and export management companies.

Manufacturers' Agents (or Representatives). In business marketing, the most frequent form of agent is an individual or firm with a formal agreement to represent the producer of a good or service. As we discussed in Chapter 9, such an agent in many ways is analogous to a manufacturer's own sales force, whose principal function is promotion but who also may be extensively involved in product planning, marketing research, or development of marketing strategy. The agent may be an individual operating in a limited area and representing a limited number of products to a limited number of customers. Alternatively, the agent may be a firm with large numbers of salespersons representing a larger number of products and operating in a large geographic area, with sales responsibility for large numbers of customers.

As a general rule, agents specialize by product or market classifications. In the United States, the 1995 Directory of Manufacturers' Sales Agencies lists agents in 108 separate market classifications, of which the vast majority are oriented to business markets.[2] Typically, the agent is paid on commission for all orders received from a specified geographical area or a specified set of customers. In some instances the agent represents only one principal, but more frequently the agent represents a number of noncompeting products, usually complementary in nature.

In the United States, the terms of the relationship between manufacturer and agent are usually governed by a formal agreement that stipulates the responsibilities of each party. A major bone of contention between manufacturers and their agents is the basis on which agreements may be terminated by the manufacturer, frequently with little notice and little or no recognition of the work of the agent to develop a given set of accounts or a territory. Outside the United States, termination of agreements between manufacturers and agents tends to be more difficult. In many European countries legal stipulations mandate payment to the agent in case of termination. In Japan, where long-term relations are highly prized, termination of an agreement may be viewed very negatively by customers or other prospective agents.

Export Management Companies. An export management company (EMC) is a specialized form of agent that normally functions as the exclusive export department for several allied but noncompeting manufacturers. As such, it conducts business in the name of each manufacturer it represents. It negotiates in the name of the manufacturer, and all quotations and orders are subject to confirmation by the manufacturer. An EMC frequently does market research for its principals and may play a significant role in formulation of marketing strategy.

There are many variations of this basic model. EMCs may represent agricultural producers, as is the case in Norway where salmon farmers have joined forces to promote and distribute products internationally, or they may represent an industry, as is the case in Denmark where the office furniture industry has extensive cooperative distribution organizations. Normally paid on a retainer and commission basis, some EMCs buy the goods and take title to them, in which case they act more as merchant middlemen.

Other Agent Middlemen. Beyond the agents described above are a host of other agents, usually of a very specialized nature. We briefly describe a few of the more common ones. Brokers are agents with a wide network of contacts who bring buyers and sellers together, usually on an individual transaction basis with more emphasis on knowledge of particular markets and less on specific products. We particularly find brokers operating in the insurance industry but also in specialized fields such as used equipment. Selling agents are similar to manufacturers' agents but generally perform a broader range of functions for their clients, sometimes actually serving as the clients' entire marketing department. Commission merchants receive products on consignment and negotiate sales in their own names. Purchasing agents are firms that specialize in representing buyers, generally for a limited number of clients and for a limited set of products.

Merchant Middlemen

The salient characteristic of merchant middlemen that distinguishes them from agents is that they buy from the producer, take title to the goods, and then resell them. As with agents, merchant middlemen vary greatly on a number of other dimensions. Some act principally to buy commodities in bulk and resell them in small quantities, a role that requires little promotion or service. Others provide an extensive array of services, including promotion, warranty and other after-sales service, and, increasingly, engage in a variety of value-adding activities. We describe four major categories of merchant middlemen for business products.

Distributors (or Wholesalers). The most common type of merchant middleman is the full-function or full-service firm, most frequently referred to as a distributor. At a minimum, the distributor stocks and resells goods, principally to users or OEMs but also to other resellers. Given the nature of business marketing, with its reliance on personal selling, most distributors field their own sales forces and may provide extensive product information or application assistance. In some industries, such as the machine tool industry, distributors may also provide equipment installation and warranty and other forms of after-sales service.

As with agents, distributors specialize by product, market, or both, with an almost limitless variety of classifications—abrasives, construction equipment, electrical equipment, janitorial equipment and supplies, MRO items, uninterruptable power systems, and well drilling equipment, to name just a few. In the United States, distributors may be local, regional, or national and may be independent or captive. In the electrical industry, for instance, Graybar Electric is a national independent distributor serving utility, contractor, and manufacturing markets with a broad array of products. General Electric Supply, on the other hand, which serves the same markets, is owned by GE and sells both GE and non-GE products. In the United States the trend appears to be away from captive distributors. Westinghouse, for instance, recently divested itself of Westinghouse Electric Supply. In Europe, on the other hand, as we see in the Leykam Mürztaler case, paper producers have been aggressively acquiring independent paper merchants (the industry term for distributors).

Increasingly, industry specialization has led distributors to serve international markets. The U.S. firm Medtronics, for instance, a large manufacturer of medical equipment, distributes its products and the products of other manufacturers to hospitals internationally. Unitor, a Norwegian firm that provides specialized services to the shipping industry, has a global network through which manufacturers of maritime products can distribute equipment.

Value-Added Resellers. Value adding has long been a characteristic of merchant middlemen. Steel distributors, for instance, buy coils of steel strip from steel mills and then slit and cut the steel to meet the requirements of small customers. The term *value-added reseller (VAR)*, however, has emerged from the computer industry to describe intermediaries who buy and resell computer hardware or software and add specialized software or other customizing features. Lotus Development Corporation, for example, has its own sales force of some 400 but has 4,000 "business partners," many of whom are value-added resellers (others are distributors, consultants, and system integrators) who buy and customize Lotus Notes and other company products for specific clients or market segments.

Closely related to the notion of value-added resellers is the concept of value-added logistics, which goes beyond the value added by virtue of making goods available at the right time and place and actually involves modifications to the product while it is in the distribution channel. In its bid to become a distribution center in Europe, the Netherlands has advocated establishing value-added logistics facilities there that can modify products before being reshipped to other countries in Europe. Computer manufacturers, for instance, can stock computers without electrical plugs and then add plugs in the warehouse to meet the requirements of the country of destination.

Trading Companies. Trading companies are a specialized form of merchant middlemen, generally involved in import/export activities. Although we find trading companies in most industrialized countries, it is in Japan where the current form of a trading company has developed as a unique and admired model.

Large Japanese general trading companies, also known as *sogo shosha*, such as C. Itoh, Mitsui, and Mitsubishi, engage in a far wider range of commercial activities than simply trade and distribution. They play a central role in such diverse areas as shipping, warehousing, finance, technology transfer, planning resource development, construction and regional development (for example turnkey projects), insurance, consulting, real estate, and deal-making in general (including facilitating investments and joint ventures of others).[3] They have established global sales networks consisting of branch offices overseas, or wholly-owned subsidiaries, but also are heavily involved in domestic distribution. A key to the success of many of the large Japanese trading companies is that they belong to a *keiretsu,* a uniquely Japanese institution with large numbers of closely linked firms with significant manufacturing and financial resources that operate with some degree of common interest and coordination. Mitsui, for instance, is part of the Mitsui Group, which recently included some 2,300 member firms.

Stimulated by the success of Japanese trading companies, the United States passed the Export Trading Company Act of 1982, designed to encourage U.S. manufacturers to export by offering exporters greater protection from U.S. antitrust laws and permitting banks to own and control export trading companies. A number of export trading companies were formed. Several failed or had disappointing results, raising serious questions as to suitability of this type of intermediary to the needs of the average U.S. exporter. Nevertheless, the successful use of trading companies around the world, including many examples in the United States, suggests that trading companies should receive serious consideration in developing a distribution strategy.

Office Product Retailers. Few aspects of the dynamic nature of distribution are more evident than changes in the distribution of office products. Once typified by small stores selling mostly stationery products, office product distribution in recent years has changed with the development of chains of large office stores selling not just stationery products but also business machines and accessories, computers, printers and their accessories, office furniture, and a host of other products for large and small businesses.

In the United States, Office Depot with over 400 stores and OfficeMax with just under 400 stores are typical of such chains. Operating coast to coast, these stores stock some 500 product categories of supplies, software, computers, business electronics, and furniture. In addition to extensive in-store sales, both chains feature catalog sales and direct delivery to offices. Corporate Express, on the other hand, a relatively new player in office product retailing, is moving away from retail stores, as the firm has decided to focus on large corporations. It now has 35 warehouses and offices in 110 cities in the United States and Canada and envisions a national network of regional warehouses from which companies could order office products from a single national vendor and receive reliable, next-day service. Corporate Express already operates in

Australia, and Jirka Rysavy, the firm's founder, believes the concept will be viable in Europe and Latin America. According to Rysavy, "We are competitive, but we really don't sell products. We sell service. We sell relationships."[4]

The Changing Environment of Business Distribution

The long-term relationships that characterize many channels of distribution may suggest that the structure of channels and functions of intermediaries are stable and unchanging. In fact, forces in the external environment are exerting a profound influence on patterns of distribution throughout the world. There is concern, however, that many manufacturers and distributors are resisting adapting to this changing environment. This was the conclusion of "Facing the Forces of Change 2000: The New Realities of Distribution," a 1993 study in the United States sponsored by the Distribution Research & Education Foundation of the National Association of Wholesaler-Distributors (NAW).[5] Reasons for resistance include:

- Strong commitment to original and traditional distribution channels.
- Lack of understanding about new roles and requirements of customer relationships.
- Inability and/or unwillingness to evaluate new operating alternatives.
- Desire to avoid conflict that might threaten testing of market position.
- A strong concern that if distribution channel changes are made competitors might take over the existing channels.

While the study found resistance to change, it is also clear that many firms have recognized the forces of change and are successfully adapting their distribution strategies to them.

Few industries have seen as much change as the information technology industry, where new technology, shifts in customers needs, increased competitiveness, and the changing orientation of key players have forced every information technology supplier to rethink and, in many instances, radically change distribution strategy. Virtually all the players have come to embrace multichannel approaches to the market. IBM, for example, uses multiple and nontraditional channels to distribute its hardware and software. Its "business partner" program has existed for more than 20 years, but in 1992 sales of $2.5 billion broke records. In addition, sales through a new original equipment manufacturers (OEM) program reached $1.25 billion in revenue in 1992, up 65 percent from 1991.[6] The use of intermediaries for software sales for personal computers has grown enormously. In 1994, 94 percent of software sales went through intermediaries, in sharp contrast to the 1980s when the bulk of software sales went directly to end users.[7]

Technology is also changing the nature of distribution. The rampant pace of communication technology is facilitating more direct communication with customers through electronic data interchange (EDI) and electronic mail.

According to a 1994 Survey of Distributor Operations, the percentage of distributors using EDI between 1991 and 1993 nearly doubled, from 26 percent to 51 percent. Significantly, of those distributors using EDI, nearly 70 percent are doing so at the request of their customers.[8] Satellite communications, video telecommunications, and digital cellular technology are increasing the ability of distributors to communicate with distant customers at the same time that changes in logistics, warehouse automation, and better inventory control procedures are increasing the ability of distributors to offer greater value to larger geographical areas.[9]

A major trend in the United States is the growth in the size of some distributors through mergers or acquisitions. For smaller distributors this has posed a competitive threat, met in many instances by the formation of consortiums such as Integrated Suppliers Alliance, a group of eight distributors supplying the automotive industry, or by alliances such as the Industrial Supply Division of Affiliated Distributors, a group of 50 industrial and electrical distributors doing $4.5 billion in annual sales. In many instances large distributors or consortiums have elected to represent several competing manufacturers, acting more as purchasing agents for their customers than as representatives for a manufacturer. For manufacturers, these changes, combined with changes in distributor–customer relationships resulting from technology, are having profound effects on their relationships with distributors.

The emergence of large and sophisticated office product retailers has been accompanied by their use by many manufacturers who previously sold direct or through wholesalers. In the field of computer products, for instance, IBM and Compaq computers and Hewlett-Packard and Canon printers are widely available through office product retailers. Not all manufacturers of computer products have been successful in selling through office product retailers. In 1991, Dell Computer Corporation, widely hailed for its successful use of direct mail and direct sales, signed agreements with many office supply stores to display and sell Dell products. But interchannel conflict led Dell to terminate the arrangements. However, for many hardware and software firms, as well as manufacturers of office furniture and other products, the use of office product retailers has become an integral part of their distribution strategy.

The increase in world trade and the emergence of regional trading blocs are also having a major influence on distribution channels. We have already mentioned the Export Trading Company Act of 1982, passed in the hope that it would stimulate the formation of export trading companies in the United States. Where it was once necessary to have significant distribution facilities in each of the 15 countries in the European Union, the move to a single market within the union has made it possible to consolidate many distribution operations. It is likely that the recently passed North American Free Trade Agreement will have a similar impact in the United States, Canada, and Mexico.

The emergence of new markets in China, Eastern Europe, and Latin America will require substantial attention to distribution issues. In contrast to more developed markets, distribution channels in these markets are not well defined. In China, for instance, the approach to many markets is not clear. For one thing, China is not one market, but several large markets with regional barriers that discriminate against producers in other regions as well as foreign producers and block distribution of certain goods. Many types of middlemen do not yet exist. In addition, the physical distribution channel infrastructure is poorly developed and bottlenecks stifle the flow of goods. The experiences of Shanghai Ingersoll-Rand Compressor Ltd. (SIRC) and Xerox of Shanghai suggest how barriers can be overcome. Instead of trying the almost impossible task of finding existing agents, SIRC and Xerox built their own direct sales teams utilizing Chinese nationals.

A very different situation exists in Japan, which has a long-established, unique, and complicated distribution system often controlled by well-established domestic manufacturers. For many non-Japanese companies the nature of the distribution system and the differences in ways of conducting business have made it difficult to penetrate the Japanese market. Alliances with Japanese companies, particularly members of a keiretsu, are often essential to build successful distribution in Japan.

As we have previously mentioned, many business marketers are being asked to follow their customers as they pursue global strategies. Leprino Foods, a major supplier of mozzarella cheese to chains of pizza restaurants in the United States, is now considering the challenge of distributing its products to U.S. pizza chains operating in Europe. Patterns of distribution that have worked in the United States will have to be modified to take into account distribution structures in Europe.

In this section we have identified and discussed a few of the many forces influencing distribution channels, and some of the changes taking place. It is essential that business marketers understand the changes and the forces influencing channels in their industries.

Developing a Channel Structure

Despite the complexity of distribution channels, certain fundamental questions, when addressed properly, can guide the development of an appropriate structure. For most firms, the first question concerns the use of manufacturers' agents or its own sales force. Unless the firm has elected direct marketing, as described in Chapter 10, it must have personal selling capacity to contact end customers, channel intermediaries, or both. The second question concerns the use of other intermediaries. Assuming the firm elects to use merchant middlemen, the third question concerns the use of mixed patterns of distribution.

Agents versus Own Sales Force

For small firms, the question is often purely an economic one. In the early stages of the firm's existence, agents may be the only viable way to establish personal selling capacity. The traditional view holds that, as the firm grows, it should make the transition to its own sales force when the cost of sales through agents exceeds the cost of operating its own sales force. There are, however, other considerations that might favor the continued use of agents.

- Use of agents, paid on a commission, ensures that selling costs are variable. For many firms this is an attractive alternative to the fixed costs associated with the firm's own sales force. Still further, in many instances where pure economics might indicate transitioning to one's own sales force, there is the possibility of renegotiating the agent's commission rate.
- Use of agents avoids much of the management complexity associated with a firm's own sales force and may be attractive for firms that find it difficult to effectively manage a sales force.
- Many agents have unique skills, market knowledge, or strong customer relationships that cannot be easily replicated.
- Agents may be used to supplement the firm's sales force either by selling to small customers or by taking over account maintenance after the firm's sales force has introduced a new product.
- Although not subject to direct control, agents can be effectively influenced through appropriate processes, similar to those used by large firms with pooled sales forces, where SBU managers do not have direct control of the sales force.

Direct versus Indirect Distribution

The second question, to a considerable extent independent of the first, is the use of other intermediaries (i.e., merchant middlemen) versus direct distribution. It is important to understand that no matter which alternative is chosen, major operating activities must be performed for either scenario. The starting point for analysis, therefore, is to identify the necessary activities. Some of the activities that always need to be accomplished are:

- Initiate and maintain contact with customers in local market.
- Promote the product, usually by personal selling.
- Forecast sales and order products for stock.
- Stock the product in local inventories.
- Receive and process customers' orders.
- Arrange for transportation, insurance, and delivery.
- Collect, analyze, and transmit market information.
- Handle warranty claims.

If the firm chooses a strategy of direct distribution, it basically elects to perform all the necessary activities to move the product from the point of production to the customer. If the firm decides to use an indirect channel, it elects to delegate some of the activities to an intermediary. The key is to delegate those activities

TABLE 11.1
Factors Influencing Distribution Decisions

Factor	Direct	Indirect
Sales cycle	Long	Short
Required product knowledge	Extensive	Modest
Nature of the selling task	Complex	Simple
Personal relations	Close, long term	Impersonal
Product line	Broad or extensive	Narrow or limited
Target market(s)	Homogeneous	Segmented
Customer location	Concentrated	Dispersed
Product development	Extensive end-user involvement	Limited end-user involvement
Order size	Large	Small
Order placement	Infrequent	Frequent
After-sales service	Specialized or limited	Extensive
Management resources	Extensive	Limited
Financial resources	Extensive	Limited

that a distributor can accomplish more effectively than the firm can. The delegation decision involves asking at least four questions:

- Of the required activities, which are we willing to (or qualified to) handle internally?
- How do these activities vary depending on the market segments we intend to reach?
- How extensive a distribution effort is required?
- How important is it that we have complete control over the necessary activities?

Table 11.1 lists factors that influence the decision. Another consideration that merits special attention is the matter of customer preference based on nontask variables. A large computer manufacturer, for instance, identified what it called "strategically important" customers for direct handling, with all others to be handled by distributors or VARS. A number of customers, however, were highly offended when told they were not strategically important, even though they were to receive the same level of service. Smaller customers, on the other hand, may prefer intermediaries over large suppliers simply because they are uncomfortable in situations where there is an obvious imbalance in relative power.

Mixed Patterns of Distribution

Some firms elect one mode of distribution and adhere to it over long periods of time. For over 40 years, Thomas and Betts, a U.S. manufacturer of electrical and electronic connectors, sold its products only through electrical distributors, despite severe pressure from many customers, including the U.S. government, who wanted to do business directly. Dell Computer, having experimented with selling through office product retailers, has returned to its original strategy of selling directly.

The exemplar of a firm that has stayed with one mode of distribution is Caterpillar, Inc. (CAT). With 1994 sales of $13.9 billion, CAT dominates the construction industry market worldwide. According to a recent report, its distribution system, consisting of over 65 U.S. dealers and 122 foreign dealers, is its most important asset.[10] In fact, CAT frequently points out that the net worth of its dealers exceeds its own. For example, in 1994 dealer net worth was $4.57 billion compared to CAT's net worth of $2.9 billion. With the exception of Russia and certain other countries where dealers do not exist, CAT has fostered, developed, and protected its dealers when necessary, making them a primary vehicle for CAT's success. In sharp contrast to many firms who seem to begrudge a distributor's financial success, CAT has reportedly said its objective is to make the owners of CAT dealerships rich.

The CAT example suggests the degree of success that can be achieved by using intermediaries. Most firms—except those that elect to serve only a very homogeneous market or produce a limited product line—use both forms of distribution and many use multiple forms of intermediaries. For example, Eastman Kodak Co.'s Business Imaging Systems Division has established multiple channels for microfilm, supplies, and imaging systems and software.[11] These channels include an organization with direct sales representatives, a set of independent brokers and distributors, and a components marketing organization that markets system components to systems integrators and value-added resellers. The VARs are responsible for more complex systems, such as Kodak mainframe software and optical disk records management systems, products involving long sales cycles and requiring extensive product knowledge and after-sales service.

The extent to which a firm uses a mixed pattern of distribution is influenced by the degree to which competition between the direct and indirect channels can be avoided. Agreements with agents can clearly stipulate the customers or territories to be served, avoiding any conflict with the manufacturer's own sales force. Agreements with distributors are another matter. Although a distributor may be selected on the basis of the industry or territory served, U.S. antitrust laws provide that after a distributor buys a product from a manufacturer, the distributor is free to sell the product to any customer, regardless of size, industry, or location, thus raising the possibility of competing with either the manufacturer or some other distributor.

Competition between channel members cannot be totally avoided. Firms can, however, take steps to reduce the potential for conflict. Distributor agreements can indicate what markets the distributor is expected to serve. Firms can limit the product lines handled by distributors. Ingersoll-Rand, for instance, sells its large compressors direct but sells smaller compressors through distributors. Firms can establish prices based on volume rather than function so large customers can buy at the same price as a distributor, a typical practice in the steel industry.

An interesting variation of the mixed pattern of distribution is the "virtual distribution" channel. In this approach various distribution operating activities are unbundled to independent organizations that are highly efficient in one specialized area of distribution. For example, a firm may use one company to sell and take orders, another company to handle the physical movement of products (which may include packaging as well as transportation), and a third company to handle after-sales service.

The foregoing discussion suggests that distribution decisions are complex and are likely to become more complex. They must take into account the processes by which firms find, select, and manage intermediaries.

Finding and Selecting Agents and Distributors

Finding and selecting the right channel intermediaries is crucial to the success of the marketing strategy. Unfortunately, too many stories of problems indicate the lack of sufficient attention to channel selection. For example, a senior executive of an international mining equipment supply company reported that of 100 distributors worldwide, his company replaced approximately 30 distributors annually. This high turnover raises questions not only about the firm's selection process, but also about its relationships with its distributors and the impact of turnover on prospective distributors.

With over 400,000 merchant wholesalers and thousands of manufacturers' agents in the United States alone, the magnitude of the search and selection process may seem overwhelming. An organized approach can assist the process. We suggest a five-step approach.

1. Establish a profile of what the intermediary is expected to do. We previously listed some of the activities necessary to move goods from producer to customer. Table 11.2 provides a more comprehensive list of dimensions on which to establish such a profile.

2. Locate distribution prospects. Potential domestic and international agents and distributors can be identified from many sources. Current or potential customers can identify intermediaries they respect. Trade associations and organizations such as the Manufacturers' Agents National Association can provide lists of members and advice on how to ensure a good match. Trade shows are excellent venues in which to meet and evaluate prospective intermediaries. Internationally, export and trade organizations are often helpful in identifying potential candidates. In the United States, the Department of Commerce sponsors several activities designed to link U.S. firms with international distributors. We have previously referred to JETRO, which can be a valuable source of assistance for

TABLE 11.2
Business Distributor Characteristics

- Accounting systems
- After-sales service
- Bank relations
- Collections
- Commitment
- Cooperativeness
- Credit
- Customer complaints
- Customers
- Customer relations
- Exclusivity
- Experience
- Geographical coverage
- Government relations
- Inventory control procedures
- Language abilities
- Legal actions

- Marketing capabilities
- Market research
- Organization
- Packaging
- Physical facilities
- Pricing strategy
- Products handled
- Promotions
- Reputation
- Risk carrying
- Sales force
- Size
- Specialization and focus
- Storage requirements
- Technical services
- Track record
- Transportation

locating representatives in Japan. The Compass series of directories, published by country, includes most industrialized countries and provides substantial details about potential agents and distributors. International trade shows are excellent sources for identifying potential distributors, particularly in Germany and Japan. Additional sources for finding overseas partners are listed in Table 11.3.

3.   Screen and evaluate prospective agents or distributors against the established profile and reduce the list to three or four prospects for personal interviews.

4.   Conduct personal interviews. The personal interview should be used both to ensure that a certain level of personal comfort can be established between the parties and to identify the principal dimensions on which the agreement is to be based.

5.   Select the preferred candidate and negotiate an appropriate agreement. The agreement should be as clear and comprehensive as possible. Potential elements of such an agreement are shown in Table 11.4.

Managing Relationships with Intermediaries

Finding and selecting intermediaries and negotiating agreements with them are the starting points of a successful distribution strategy. Channels of distribution

TABLE 11.3
Ways to Find Overseas Trading Partners

- Ask potential customers who is the best representative.
- Examine trade publications.
- Talk to trade show attendees.
- Enlist the help of international freight forwarders.
- Contact trade associations in the targeted market for membership lists.
- Consult the World Trade Index.
- Consult the American Export Register.
- Place ads in local papers or trade journals.
- Contact foreign embassies, consulates, and trade offices.
- Use the Department of Commerce's Trade Opportunity Program.
- Use the Department of Commerce's Agent-Distributor Service.
- Contact overseas chambers of commerce.

involve dynamic relationships among many independent organizations with diverse objectives, conflicting motivations, various operating characteristics and forms, managed by individuals with different personalities and cultural backgrounds. How, then, should firms work together in this dynamic relationship to best achieve the collective objectives of all channel members? We consider this from two aspects.

In broad terms, relationships within a channel of distribution can be considered in terms of four concepts: channel leadership, channel control, channel conflict resolution, and channel cooperation. In most channels, members look to some entity to provide leadership. The leader, often called the channel captain, is expected to influence other members of the channel to act in ways that are advantageous to all members of the channel. The leader may be a manufacturer, as in the case of Caterpillar, or a large wholesaler, as in the case of Graybar Electric. In either case the leader is expected to determine the basic nature of relationships among channel members and to ensure that there are clear-cut rules adhered to by all participants. Large manufacturers, for instance, are expected to minimize competition between intermediaries by careful selection of intermediaries or through policies with respect to pricing, service requirements, and so forth. Leadership suggests the ability to influence, or control, the behavior of channel members. Sources of ability to control can be economic or noneconomic. Economic control comes principally from the provision of financial incentives to other channel members.

TABLE 11.4
Elements of a Distributor Agreement

I. General

- Identification of the contracting parties
- Duration of the agreement
- Conditions for cancellation
- Definition of covered products
- Definitions of territory
- Sole or exclusive rights
- Arbitration or resolution of disputes

II. Rights and Obligations of the Seller

- Conditions of termination
- Protection of sole and exclusive rights
- Sales and technical support
- Tax liability
- Conditions of sale
- Delivery of goods
- Prices
- Order refusal

- Inspection of distributor's books
- Trademarks and patents
- Information to be provided to the distributor
- Advertising and promotion
- Responsibility for claims and warranties
- Inventory requirements

III. Rights and Obligations of the Distributor

- Safeguarding the supplier's interests
- Payment arrangements
- Contract assignment
- Consignment arrangements
- Competitive lines
- Customs clearance
- Observance of conditions of sale
- Inventory requirements
- After-sales service
- Information to be provided to the supplier

Noneconomic control is related to the reputation of the leader based on such factors as past leadership, superior products, and technical competence. Regardless of how well a channel leader manages, there is likely to be channel conflict. Major reasons for channel conflict include competition, variation in objectives and approach, differing perceptions, and unclear roles among the channel leader and other channel members. To prevent channel conflict, channel members establish formal channel cooperation. Channel cooperation may be formalized through industry associations and implemented through mutually beneficial programs. Channel members have the option of exercising or following leadership, depending on their situations, or of operating independently on the assumption that it will serve their interests better than some form of cooperation.

Regardless of the leadership situation, individual manufacturers are faced with the challenge of effectively managing relationships with each member of the channel. Their ability to effectively do so depends to a large extent on the attitude of individual intermediaries, some of whom expect to have close relationships with suppliers and feel their interests are best served by actively representing the supplier, while others operate on an arm's-length basis, believing

---

TABLE 11.5

Factors That Tend to Improve Distributor Performance

- Frequent personal contact by salespersons or management.
- Frequent follow-up contacts by phone or mail.
- Requests for monthly or quarterly reports on sales, service, and competitive activity.
- Visits by distributor personnel to headquarters or production facilities.
- Incentive programs with monetary rewards and prizes.
- Recognition programs.
- Regional or international distributor conferences.
- Training programs, technical and business assistance.
- Joint customer visits.
- Joint development of objectives.
- Distributor involvement in strategy development.
- Distributor participation in advisory boards.

---

their best interests are served by acting more as a purchasing agent for their customers. The majority of intermediaries fall in the first category; their relationships with suppliers and the effectiveness with which they represent them can be materially enhanced by an active program of support. Table 11.5 lists some of the activities suppliers can engage in to create an effective support program. By virtue of such activities, Parker-Hannifin, a major U.S. producer of fluid power systems, electromechanical controls, and related components, has been hailed as a firm that has been able to establish an unusual level of rapport with its distributors. One indication of this mutual trust is that PH distributors share complete information with PH on their monthly sales of the firm's products. PH then uses the information to assist its distributors in developing more effective selling strategies.

Issues Related to Physical Distribution

We conclude this chapter with a brief discussion of physical distribution. Once viewed simply as a matter of shipping goods direct from factory to customer or from factory to warehouse for reshipment to customers, physical distribution has come to be recognized as a major element of marketing strategy, with significant potential for creating competitive advantage, and as a major element of controllable cost, with significant potential for improving the firm's profitability.

FIGURE 11.2
Cost/Service Relationship

How Much Should you Spend to Improve Service?

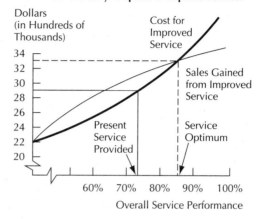

Note: How much should a firm spend on customer service in order to gain extra sales? Graph shows how much a typical firm can improve its share of market for each $100,000 spent. Indicated too is the point of diminishing returns at which additional expenditures will exceed the value of increased sales. Though the graph suggests a breakpoint of about 85 percent, a company can determine its own figure only by studying specific conditions in its field. The nature of the product, geographic circumstances, transport characteristics, and other factors all affect the optimum service point.
Source: "Does Your Customer Service Program Stack Up?" *Traffic Management* (September 1982), 55. Reprinted with permission of *Traffic Management* magazine. © by Cahners Publishing Company.

It is beyond the scope of this text to extensively address the many aspects of physical distribution.[12] There are, however, a number of key considerations that business marketers should take into account in designing distribution strategies.

The starting point is to recognize the need to balance logistics costs against the competitive advantage to be obtained by virtue of high levels of delivery performance. For example, rail freight or low levels of inventory may be less expensive than some forms of motor freight and higher inventory levels, but they may not provide the desired level of customer service. On the other hand, shipment by air, backed by extensive stocks, may provide outstanding levels of customer service but not enough competitive advantage to permit the firm to price at a level that will recover its costs. Conceptually, these trade-offs are shown in Figure 11.2. In the example, sales gained by improving the service level from 74 percent to 85 percent justified an additional expenditure of some $500,000. This approach suggests an optimum service level with benefits in terms of increased sales estimated by marketing and costs controlled by those responsible for warehousing and transportation.

TABLE 11.6
Some Physical Distribution Activities

- Production planning
- Material procurement
- Inbound transportation
- Receiving
- In-plant warehousing
- Sales forecasting
- Distribution planning
- Packaging
- Outbound transportation

- Field warehousing
- Inventory management
- Order processing
- Shipping
- Insurance
- Documentation
- Customs clearance
- Customer service

While conceptually attractive, the notion of an optimum service level, easily calculated, is not without problems. Competitive pressures and the moves by many firms to just-in-time manufacturing are forcing firms to continually raise their level of customer service as a matter of competitive survival. In many instances, improvements in transportation methods such as container vessels, logistics systems provided by specialists such as Federal Express, improved information systems, closer working relationships with distributors, and value-added logistics are enabling firms to improve levels of customer service with modest or no increase in cost. In these situations, service levels tend to be moving targets requiring constant attention.

For business marketers, a key question concerns the extent of their involvement in physical distribution activities and the determination of customer service levels. Responsibility for physical distribution activities and the definition of what a physical distribution activity is vary among firms. Table 11.6 lists some common physical distribution activities, many of which are outside the scope of marketing. Nevertheless, marketers need to be involved in the determination of customer service levels and work closely with channel intermediaries to ensure their appropriate involvement in physical distribution.

Summary

The design and management of channels of distribution is one of the most important activities of the business marketer. During the last decade, channels of distribution have become increasingly important as more firms go to market through distribution. Decisions about the design of a channel include choosing between direct and indirect distribution while taking into account the functions required, the types of intermediaries, the markets they serve, and the availability of intermediaries to the firm. Decisions about the management of intermediaries need to take into account the relationships of channel members, their aspirations, and their attitudes toward their suppliers. International distribution involves the same basic considerations but has the added complexity of different distribution structures and different cultural and legal systems. A business channel relationship requires significant management resources to motivate independent intermediaries to behave in ways consistent with the business marketer's strategy. Finding and selecting intermediaries is a key management activity that can contribute to successful channel strategies. Business marketers must be involved in physical distribution, even where they do not have direct responsibility for physical distribution activities. Perhaps most critical to the overall success of distribution strategies is recognizing the changes taking place in distribution channels, understanding the forces driving these changes, and modifying distribution strategy to respond to them.

Overview of Chapter Cases

✳ The Leykam Mürztaler case describes the situation of a firm considering ways to establish a brand identity and preference for its high-quality printing paper, a product that many consider a commodity, and how this product strategy comes into conflict with its distributors' use of private brands. It provides the opportunity to consider the role of distributors and how potential conflict might be resolved.

✳ The Curtis Automotive Hoist case describes the situation facing a Canadian manufacturer of surface automotive hoists as it considered opportunities in the European Community. The company had been successful in expanding sales into the U.S. market but was considering the possibility that Europe offered a more attractive opportunity. The case provides the opportunity to evaluate entry options available to the firm.

✳ The Dell Computer Corporation case describes the situation facing Dell after its decision to use indirect distribution and issues relating to its entry into the notebook market. It provides the opportunity to consider channel selection, channel conflict, and channel management.

Endnotes

1. E. Raymond Corey, *Industrial Marketing: Cases and Concepts* (Englewood Cliffs, NJ: Prentice-Hall, Inc., 1976), 263.
2. The Directory of Manufacturers' Sales Agencies is published by the Manufacturers' Agents National Association, headquartered in California. It lists some 6,300 agents in the United States and Canada.
3. Gerald Albaum, Jesper Strandskov, Edwin Duerr, and Laurence Dowd, *International Marketing and Export Management* 2nd ed. (Reading, MA: Addison-Wesley Publishing Company, 1994), 180.

4. *Rocky Mountain News,* July 9, 1995, 114A.

5. John F. Monoky, "New Realities of Distribution," *Journal of Industrial Distribution,* 1993, 82 (6), 93.

6. Tim Clark, "Marketing Alliances Starting to Pay Off," *Journal of Business Marketing,* 1993, 78 (5), 46.

7. Lee Levitt, "Why Software Companies Should Direct Market Too," *Brandweek,* 1993, 34 (39), 93.

8. "Getting Wired for Global Business," *Industrial Distribution,* May 1995, S8–S10.

9. Louis W. Stern, F. D. Sturdivant, and G. A. Getz (1993), "Accomplishing Marketing Channel Change: Paths and Pitfalls," *European Management Journal,* 11 (1) 1–8.

10. *Caterpillar, Inc.,* a CS First Boston report by John E. McGinty, June 21, 1995.

11. Thomas E. Ferguson, "Customers' Diverse Needs Require Diverse Channels," *Journal of Business Marketing,* 1992, 77 (3), 64–66.

12. For a comprehensive discussion of physical distribution, see James E. Johnson, and Donald F. Wood, *Contemporary Physical Distribution and Logistics* 4th ed. (New York: Macmillan Publishing Company, 1990).

W. Benoy Joseph

John T. Gardner

Sharon Thach

Frances Vernon

How Industrial Distributors View Distributor–Supplier Partnership Arrangements

This nationwide survey reports distributors' perspectives of their relationship with a core supplier. The survey reports on elements of partnership, expectations, outcomes, and satisfaction relating to the relationship's position on a continuum between arm's length and close partnership styles. ❋

Introduction

The formation of manufacturer–distributor partnerships has recently emerged as a significant trend in marketing channel relationships. Both academic and practitioner-oriented literature have drawn attention to the potential of these working relationships as a means of gaining significant competitive advantage. Impressive examples of partnership achievements, along with numerous prescriptions for building successful partnerships, have appeared in the popular press.

Partnership-style relationships are characterized by a high degree of coordinated effort and planning, and full sharing of information. Narus and Anderson [16] have stated that a successful partnership is characterized by mutual cooperation, objectives, strategies, and tactics. Mutual interdependence has been identified as a key to successful partnerships [11]. However, partnerships are not necessarily exclusive or contractual relationships, and they must not be confused with the legal business structure called "partnership" [3]. Through mutual cooperation, the partnering firms are able to enjoy many of the benefits of vertical integration such as economies of scale, cost reduction, improved market intelligence, and spreading of risk without the associated disadvantages of large capital expenditures, loss of flexibility, and costly management infrastructure [9, 22]. Formation of the relationship may be motivated by a desire to improve customer service, or by competitive pressures. Partnerships, however, are not necessarily ideal for every business relationship. Dependence upon a few customers or suppliers can obviously pose a substantial risk to any business [7]. Furthermore, in order to build the relationship, firms may have to invest in what Williamson [24, 25] has termed "specific assets," such as specialized communication software or employee training that are not easily transferable to other business uses.

It is generally agreed that partnering arrangements require careful attention and nurturing.

At the time this article was written, W. Benoy Joseph was Marketing Department Chair at the Nance College of Business Administration, Cleveland State University, Cleveland, Ohio. John T. Gardner was Assistant Professor of Marketing at SUNY College-Brockport, Brockport, New York. Sharon Thach was Associate Professor of Marketing in the College of Business, Tennessee State University, Nashville, Tennessee. Frances Vernon was a doctoral student in marketing at Cleveland State University, Cleveland, Ohio. *Source:* Reprinted by permission of the publisher from *Industrial Marketing Management* 24, 27–36 (1995) © Elsevier Science Inc., 1995.

Indeed, Shapiro [20] warns firms not to dissipate managerial energy by establishing too many partnerships. Furthermore, he urges potential partners to consider the compatibility of their respective corporate cultures.

Literature Review

Current investigations suggest that partnering or strategic alliances result from expectations of mutual benefits in such arrangements [3, 4, 9]. Successful partnerships between manufacturers and distributors include planning and information sharing [19] and investments in specialized information exchange systems such as electronic data interchange [5, 12, 21]. Success is also predicated upon the level of commitment both firms make to the relationship and their understanding of mutual needs [14, 15, 16].

A firm's expectations, prior to forming a partnership arrangement, may influence the eventual outcome of the relationship. In studying joint ventures, Harrigan [10] attributed a large number of failures to one or more of the following causes: unclear objectives; failure to properly match the capabilities of the respective partners; and unrealistic expectations.

Williamson's [24, 25] three critical dimensions of transactions—uncertainty, frequency of transactions, and specificity of assets—have been examined in a variety of settings as factors influencing the development of partnering agreements [1, 11, 17, 18, 23]. Dependency and conflict have also been studied within existing relationships. For example, Anderson and Narus [1] examined manufacturer–distributor partnerships from the perspective of both parties. Their model, however, focused upon the structure of the relationship rather than the relationship-building process. In this study, as well as in other previous research, factors that may have influenced the choice of relationship style and the nature of the post-choice relationship have not been investigated in a systematic manner.

Other research streams have investigated potential components of partnership arrangements.

Macneil [13] identified seven components of contractual relationships between firms: (1) commencement, duration, and termination provisions; (2) measurement and specificity; (3) planning; (4) sharing versus dividing benefits and burdens; (5) interdependence, future cooperation, and solidarity; (6) personal relations and numbers; and (7) power, both unilateral and bilateral. However, after reviewing Macneil's schema, Dwyer, Schurr, and Oh [6] suggested that the number of dimensions be reduced to make this framework useful for research on channel relationships.

Gardner, Cooper, and Noordewier [7] reduced Macneil's set to five behavioral dimensions:

1. *Extendedness.* The strength of the long-term commitment between the parties; extendedness encompasses loyalty and the commitments to each other made over time.

2. *Sharing of benefits and burdens.* This dimension is a measure of both parties' willingness to share short-term losses as well as gains in an equitable manner.

3. *Planning.* Encompasses the coordination of the two firms through both horizontal and vertical communication links in order to achieve the goals of both firms.

4. *Systematic operational information exchange.* Involves building joint information systems such as EDI, bar coding, or other types of similar systems.

5. *Operating controls.* Mechanisms which allow for mutual verification of all operations in both firms which could potentially affect the key dimensions of the relationship.

Gardner and his colleagues [7] found support for the five dimensions with data from a nationwide survey of more than 200 logistics service suppliers. Their framework can be applied to a broad range of partnering relationships.

Despite the widespread interest in partnering agreements, there appears to be little agreement on the method for identifying the dimensions or key elements of successful relationships. Furthermore, there have been few attempts to determine what factors influence the formation of partnerships, the degree of coalition achieved, and the outcomes of these arrangements. Our study attempts to examine these issues from the perspective of the industrial distributor.

A dyadic study, assessing both distributor and supplier perspectives, has obvious merit. However, we elected to limit our investigation to the industrial distributor because this permits more distributor-specific issues to be explored. This approach was driven also by practical considerations (e.g., availability of lists, limited budget), methodological concerns (e.g., getting matched samples of distributors and suppliers, adequate sample sizes), and conceptual choices (e.g., studying perceptions versus concrete evidence of partnerships). Furthermore, distributor perceptions are significant because if a partnership is perceived to exist, the distributor will act as if there is a partnership.

Research Objectives

Our principal objective was to investigate the industrial distributor's perspective on partnership-style arrangements with suppliers. Specific objectives were to identify:

- Distributor's perceptions, attitudes, experiences, and satisfaction concerning the style of their relationship with a core supplier.
- The conditions that led to or triggered partnership-style arrangements.
- The expectations that distributors had in entering into such arrangements and the outcomes realized.

Methodology

The Industrial Distributors Association's U.S. membership list served as the sampling frame for the selection of 1,000 distributors. IDA's membership represents a wide cross-section of industries. However, a majority of its members serve automotive, construction, metal working, electrical/electronic, aircraft, chemicals, and institutional markets.

The survey instrument was developed from previous findings in the literature and from a theoretical model of the structure and process of relationship-building between distributors and suppliers [8]. The general objective was to study distributors' perceptions of the antecedents and consequences of distributor–supplier partnership arrangements. The instrument was pretested with five distributors and two experienced consultants serving the industrial distribution industry.

Surveys were mailed to distributors and followed three weeks later with a reminder postcard. A final sample of 221 completed surveys was obtained, a response rate of 22 percent.

Who Responded

The sample consisted of a representative cross-section of IDA members nationwide. Service areas and annual sales of distributor respondents are summarized in Table 1. A profile of the sample shows:

- Nearly nine out of ten distributors surveyed (87 percent) operate within a multicounty or multistate area.
- More than half (54 percent) have annual sales of less than $5 million; 24 percent sell $5 to $10 million; 20 percent sell between $10 and $50 million; and 2 percent sell more than $50 million.
- The number of customers served ranges from 10 to 28,000 with a median of 900.
- The number of product lines carried ranges from 3 to 25,000 (median: 75; mean: 275). The median number of stock keeping units (SKUs) or items carried is 10,000.

Findings

How Common Are Partnership Arrangements?

Respondents were asked to choose a "core" supplier (one who was important but not necessarily their largest supplier) and describe the style of their relationship with this supplier on a seven-point scale (1 = strong partnership style to 7 = very "arm's-length" style).

TABLE 1
Characteristics of Distributor Respondents

	Total Sample	Strong Partnership	Arm's-Length Relationship
Territory served by distributor			
Metro area	8%	8%	6%
Multicounty	56%	57%	56%
Multistate	31%	29%	33%
National	2%	2%	2%
International	3%	3%	2%
	$n = 218$	$n = 163$	$n = 47$
Annual sales			
$1,000,000 or less	4%	4%	6%
$1,000,000–5,000,000	50%	49%	51%
$5,000,000–10,000,000	24%	23%	23%
$10,000,000–50,000,000	20%	21%	19%
$50,000,000–100,000,000	1%	1%	0%
More than $100,000,000	1%	2%	0%
	$n = 212$	$n = 163$	$n = 47$

Nearly eight out of 10 distributors surveyed (79 percent) described their relationship styles with their core suppliers as being moderate to strong partnership (with scores of 4 or less on the seven-point partnership scale). This evidence empirically confirms the growing popularity of partnership-style arrangements in distribution channels.

Factors Influencing Partnership Styles

Distributors were asked to rate the importance of the factors that had influenced the style of the relationship arrangement with their core suppliers when the relationship was "initiated, reviewed, or revamped." Importance ratings were obtained on a seven-point scale (1 = very important to 7 = very unimportant).

Table 2 shows that long run survival and competitive pressures were rated as important by all distributors, regardless of their relationship style with their core supplier. However, when respon-

dents were forced to name one factor as the primary influence, long run survival (36 percent) and customer demands (30 percent) were cited most frequently among distributors with strong partnership styles (Table 2). Among distributors in arm's-length style relationships with core suppliers, customer demands were rated as most important.

Elements of Partnership

Distributors were asked to identify the elements of their business relationship with core suppliers by agreeing or disagreeing with 18 relationship statements (e.g., "There is much mutual loyalty between our firms") and indicating if five practices (e.g., "The supplier monitors our systems to ensure overall efficiency") were present in their relationship. Agreement items were assessed with a seven-point scale (1 = strongly agree to 7 = strongly disagree). Presence of certain practices (e.g., sharing of

TABLE 2
Influencing Factors When the Relationship
Was Initiated, Reviewed, or Revamped

	Strong Partnership		Arm's-Length Relationship	
	Mean	SD	Mean	SD
This relationship was [a]				
The result of demands of our customers	3.50	1.87	3.17	1.57
The result of demands by this [core] supplier[b]	4.02	1.79	4.45	1.69
Necessitated by competitive pressures	2.86	1.60	2.70	1.20
A requirement for our long run survival	2.06	1.20	2.08	1.22

	Total Sample	Strong Partnership	Arm's Length
Which *one* of the above was the primary influence?			
Our customers	32%	30%	40%
This supplier	17%	18%	13%
Competitive pressures	16%	13%	21%
Long run survival	32%	36%	21%
Other	3%	3%	2%
	100%	100%	100%

[a]The responses to the items in this section were code as 1 (very important) to 7 (very unimportant).
[b]Means are significantly different between the two groups at $p < .05$.

market forecasts or customer information) was assessed with a different seven-point scale (1 = always to 7 = never).

What are the business relationship elements that distributors believe to be present in strong partnerships? Which elements correlate with general satisfaction with the core supplier? Table 3 answers these questions, reporting the correlations between business relationship elements and various measures. The results are classified into four correlation levels: strongest ($r = .4$ or more), moderate ($r = .2$ to .39), weak ($r < .2$), and not measurable (not statistically significant).

The Strongest Elements. Distributors in strong partnership-style arrangements view the presence of mutual loyalty between them and their core sup-

pliers as a strong characteristic of their relationship ($r = .72$). Other strong elements of partnership include the expectation that partners will help each other in difficult situations, and that more joint planning is done.

The Weakest Elements. Contrary to expectations, some arrangements are uncorrelated or weakly correlated with the presence of strong partnerships. For example, compatible software, computer-to-computer links, and long-term contracts—elements one would expect in partnership arrangements today—were uncorrelated with the strength of the partnership style. This leaves an open question as to how certain information linkages influence partnership building. Some possible explanations are that industrial distributors have

TABLE 3

How Strength of the Partnership with Supplier and Satisfaction with the Relationship Are Correlated with Elements of the Business Relationship

Business Relationship Elements	Correlation with Partnership	
	Strength (*n* = 221)	Satisfaction (*n* = 221)
Strongest relationships		
There is much mutual loyalty	.72	.79
The supplier will help in a difficult situation	.58	.66
We do more joint planning	.48	.48
We are more likely to help this supplier	.48	.51
We expect a long-term relationship	.43	.55
We have more face-to-face communications	.42	.42
Supplier will favor our prime customers	.42	.39
We balance supplier production with our inventory needs	.40	.40
Moderate relationships		
We share market information with one another	.38	.39
We share customer information	.38	.35
We will support this supplier's products during shortages	.34	.27
We have more joint task forces than with other suppliers	.31	.28
Supplier shares risks	.28	.27
We have developed joint information systems	.28	.32
We coordinate value added steps	.21	.19
We monitor the supplier's systems	.20	.15
We use specific goals to monitor this relationship	.20	.25
Weak relationships		
Supplier has financial commitment to our firm	.16	.14
Long-term contract present	.16	—
Supplier monitors our system	.13	—
No measurable relationships		
This relationship offers a broader range of products than usual	—	—
We have many computer-to-computer links	—	—
We use compatible software	—	—

All Pearson correlation coefficients shown are significant at the .05 level. Partnership strength is coded as 1 (strong partnership) to 7 (very arm's length). Distributor's satisfaction with current core supplier relationship is coded as 1 (very satisfied) to 7 (not at all satisfied).

found alternative information systems (e.g., fax-based), or that such technologies may be common among all styles of relationships, or may not have penetrated this environment sufficiently. Indeed, our survey found that compatible software and computer-to-computer links were not common.

Weak correlations were also noted for three elements. These were financial commitments by

TABLE 4

Relationship Expectations of Distributors in Strong Partnerships versus Arm's-Length Relationships

	Strong Partnership		Arm's-Length Relationship	
	Mean	SD	Mean	SD
This relationship would[a]				
Yield better customer service for our customers[b]	2.04	1.13	3.06	1.58
Yield lower total costs for our customers[b]	3.53	1.88	4.00	1.69
Yield an improved range of products for our customers	2.95	1.74	2.69	1.60
Yield improved overall quality for our product offering	2.84	1.58	2.98	1.52
Yield lower prices for our customers	4.31	1.86	4.35	1.88
Yield increased customer satisfaction with our offering[b]	2.11	1.15	2.74	1.61
Protect our investment in assets specific to this account (e.g., special equipment or systems)[b]	3.15	1.77	3.98	1.87

[a]Responses to these items were coded as 1 (very likely) to 7 (very unlikely).
[b]Means are significantly different between the two groups at $p < .05$.

the supplier, presence of long term contracts, and supplier monitoring of the distributor's system.

Satisfaction with the Relationship

The survey assessed global satisfaction with the relationship with a single measure (1 = very satisfied to 7 = not at all satisfied). The second column in Table 3 reports correlation coefficients between individual elements and global satisfaction. The findings suggest that the strongest partnership elements were also the strongest influences on satisfaction with the relationship.

Notable for their high correlations were elements such as mutual loyalty, supplier helping in a difficult situation, and expectations of a long-term relationship. In notable contrast is the much lower correlation between satisfaction and helping suppliers during shortages. Understandably, it is much more satisfying to receive than to give.

Expectations and Outcomes

The correspondence between expectations and outcomes is important in understanding the dynamics of

partnership building. Early in the survey, distributors were asked to rate their expectations for the relationship with the core supplier when it was initiated or revamped. Toward the end of the survey, outcomes were assessed. Expectation and outcome items, by design, were not identical in order to minimize response bias. Expectation questions were more specific whereas outcome questions were more global.

Expectations. Table 4 summarizes the likelihood of specific expectations being met (1 = very likely to 7 = very unlikely). The results are reported for two groups: Distributors in strong partnership style versus those in arm's-length relationships.

Distributors with strong partnerships expected customer service improvements, protection of specific assets, and increased customer satisfaction to a greater degree than those with arm's-length relationships. In contrast, partnership style did not appear to influence expectations of improved overall quality, improved range of products, or lower prices.

Outcomes. The results achieved with the relationship were measured by six items covering prof-

TABLE 5
Results Achieved in Relationship with Core Supplier for Distributors in Partnership versus Arm's-Length Relationships

Results Achieved[a]	Strong Partnership		Arm's-Length Relationship	
	Mean	SD	Mean	SD
This supplier account allows us to make more profit from complementary lines of trade[b]	3.00	1.41	4.23	1.61
This account enables our managers to manage our business more efficiently[b]	3.27	1.42	4.67	1.46
This account expends more managerial effort and time than a typical account[b]	3.24	1.60	4.02	1.95
This account is more profitable than other accounts we have[b]	2.96	1.34	4.52	1.65
Working with this supplier has a negative impact on relations with other suppliers[b]	5.64	1.47	4.92	1.60
Working with this supplier has had a negative impact on relations with our customers[b]	6.37	1.05	5.56	1.53

[a]Responses to these items were coded as 1 (strongly agree) to 7 (strongly disagree).
[b]Means are significantly different between the two groups at $p < .05$.

itability, efficiency, and external relationships (see Table 5). Distributors in strong partnership arrangements, in contrast to those in arm's-length relationships, realized more profits from the core supplier's account and complementary lines of trade. Strong partnership distributors also experienced more managerial efficiencies but applied more managerial effort and time to the core supplier account.

Partnership arrangements appear to influence distributor relationships with other suppliers and with customers. Strong partnership-style distributors report more negative impact on their relations with other suppliers. This is understandable because competing suppliers will be at a disadvantage when their distributor-customer has formed strong ties with another supplier. On the other hand, strong partnership appears to improve a distributor's relations with its customers.

When compared with their expectations, distributor-reported experiences (outcomes) reveal interesting insights about the way partnerships evolve. In initiating or revamping a relationship, distributors expected partnerships to yield better customer service and increased customer satisfaction. These expectations appear to be realized in improved customer relations. Also, expectations about specific asset protection square with more profitable outcomes reported by strong partnership distributors.

How Satisfied Are Distributors with Supplier Partners?

In order to permit comparison between distributors in partnership versus arm's-length–style relationships with their core supplier, we divided the sample into two groups: Partnership-style distributors (those who rated their relationship with their core supplier as 4 or less; $n = 171$) and arm's-length–style (those with self-ratings greater than 4; $n = 48$). The two groups were compared on a seven-point global measure of satisfaction with their core supplier (1 = very satisfied to 7 = not at all satisfied).

Results showed that partnership-style distributors are significantly more satisfied with their core supplier (mean = 2.1) than are distributors in arm's-length relationships (mean = 4.1; p <.001). This is not surprising. As Table 5 shows, distributors in partnership-style relationships with their core suppliers realize many benefits that distributors in arm's-length relationships do not.

Implications and Conclusions

Implications for Distributors

Perception of customer needs and demands seem to be the most influential factor in determining the style of relationship between distributor and supplier. However, those with stronger partnering arrangements report more pressure toward close ties in order to ensure survival. This indicates that future research should explore the difference in either circumstance or perception that leads to a difference in the relationship style. The connection between customer demands and partnership for survival is also worthy of further exploration. It is possible to speculate on industry reorganization having an effect on all members of the channel, so that customer expectations are generated by the outcomes of various distributive arrangements and these in turn feed perceptions of customer needs, which require a certain type of structure. The reported movement toward closer relationships may reflect changes in all participants' expectations, thus generating more pressure toward change.

Although a majority of distributors reported more partnering-style relationships, the actual activity reported suggests that the relationship is manifested more in distributor attitudes than in actual behaviors. For example, the strongest relationships with partnering were for items reflecting goodwill and beliefs about potential support. Far weaker correlations were reported for activities such as information sharing, coordinating value-added steps, and development of joint information systems.

This dichotomy between words and deeds suggests that either trust is a precursor of specific activities and that these relationships are too new for the implementation of shared business operations, or that many managers feel pressures toward having "modern" business arrangements and have simply changed their perceptions but not their practices. The importance of facilitating technology is also important. Integrated planning and information sharing may be dependent on certain technologies that themselves are not accepted, valued, or needed. Change in technologies or their use may not occur until the need to invest in the relationship forces a reevaluation. Alternatively, the availability of technological support may lead to deeper levels of shared activity. The consistency of satisfaction correlations with partnership correlations supports the attitudinal explanation more than the technological one.

Implications for Suppliers

Suppliers wishing to explore the potential for partnering relationships with their distributions or review existing relationships should consider the following actions suggested by the results of our survey.

Express Loyalty Through Actions. Distributors value loyalty among partners. Suppliers should nurture desirable partnerships with special relationship-enhancing strategies, actions, and symbolic gestures (e.g., preferred delivery schedules, allowances, discounts, and personal contacts) that send clear messages to distributor partners that they are special. When distributor partners encounter difficulties or setbacks, the supplier should take reasonable steps to help them.

Strengthen Partnerships to Deter Competitors. Our results suggest that a strong partnership-style relationship weakens a distributor's relations with other suppliers. Hence, strengthening ties with a strong distributor can translate into a competitive advantage.

Assess Internal Capabilities. Suppliers must assess their readiness to undertake the relationship-building process and willingness to commit necessary resources. Our survey indicates that partnerships demand more management time and attention and more joint planning with suppliers than do arm's-length relationships. Distributors also said they expected the partnering arrangement to improve customer service and satisfaction. Unless the supplier can demonstrate how such a relationship will achieve these objectives, it is unlikely that the distributor will want to forge a closer relationship with that supplier.

Evaluating and Terminating Current Distributor Partnerships. Regular evaluations can reveal if the partnership is meeting distributor as well as supplier expectations. Periodic assessments of customer as well as distributor satisfaction with various dimensions of the product or service can provide the supplier with early warnings of potential problems that can undermine the partnership. For example, improved customer service ratings by end-use customers can mean that the partnership arrangement is succeeding.

But not all partnerships are worth preserving. When key indicators of partnership well-being show weaknesses (e.g., unilateral actions by distributor that impact on supplier's business; erosion of mutual loyalty and trust), a more careful review of the partnership is warranted. Whereas long-term relationships should be terminated only after careful analysis, preserving such relationships are counterproductive if the distributor's goals and expectations are no longer compatible with those of the supplier.

Scope and Limitation of Study

The empirical methodology of this study featured objective assessment of the nature of distributor–supplier relationships. The IDA membership list provided a sampling frame that included a wide range of industries and sizes of firms in industrial distribution. This permits broader generalizations to be made from this study, compared to case studies and informal observations. However, because our survey was limited to U.S. distributors, caution must be exercised in drawing conclusions about global distribution practices.

A substantial body of research has explored power and conflict issues in partnership building [e.g., 2]. Whereas this approach is valid, alternative paradigms need to be explored. Our study utilized

Macneil's relational contract concept [13] and Williamson's transaction cost approach [24, 25].

Major Contributions of the Study

This study assessed distributors' views on the partnership-building process. The national survey identified the principal influencing factors, expectations, elements of partnership, and outcomes. Differences between strong and weak partnerships were explored across the partnership-building process.

Survey results offer distributors and suppliers a differentiated list of potential partnership-building concerns. For example, in choosing elements to incorporate into a partnership, our study revealed that face-to-face communications were consistently related to strong partnerships, whereas computer-to-computer links were not.

Future Research

This study examined the distributor's perspective. An alternative approach would be to simultaneously examine the partnership-building process from the perspective of each value chain member. Going beyond the dyadic approach, which examines the supplier's and distributor's perspectives, the value chain approach would also include the customer's perspectives. Another possible avenue for further study would be an analysis of how distributors choose between partnership opportunities, and what strategies they might choose in building a portfolio of relationships. Alternative managerial models of relationship portfolio building could be developed (e.g., what mix of arm's-length versus strong partnership style is optimal, and under which conditions would some styles flourish).

Conclusion

Building good quality business relationships are vital to successful channel management and business success. A high quality relationship is one that matches the needs of both parties as well as the demands of the value chain. This relationship may be arm's length, extremely close, or somewhere in between. Getting it right is the issue.

References

1. Anderson, E., and Weitz, B. A., Make or Buy Decisions: Vertical Integration and Marketing Productivity, *Sloan Management Review* **27**, 3–19 (1986).

2. Anderson, J. C., and Narus, J. A., A Model of Distributor Firm and Manufacturer Firm Working Partnerships, *Journal of Marketing* **54**, 42–58 (1990).

3. Bowersox, D. J., Logistical Partnerships. In *Partnerships: A Natural Evolution in Logistics,* Logistics Resource, Inc., Cleveland, 1988.

4. Bowersox, D. J., and Murray, R. J., Logistics Strategic Planning for the 1990s. Annual Conference Proceedings, Council of Logistics Management, 231–243 (1987).

5. Davis D., WINS is On-Line, *Distribution* **83**, 94 (November 1984).

6. Dwyer, R. F., Schurr, P. H., and Oh, S. Developing Buyer-Seller Relationships, *Journal of Marketing* **51**, 11–27 (1987).

7. Gardner, J. T., Cooper, M. C., and Noordewier, T. G., Understanding Shipper-Carrier and Shipper-Warehouser Relationships: Partnerships Revisited, *Journal of Business Logistics* **15**, 121–144 (1994).

8. Gardner, J. T., Joseph, W. B., and Thach, S., Modeling the Continuum of Relationship Styles Between Distributors and Suppliers, *Journal of Marketing Channels* **2**, 1–28 (1993).

9. Johnston, R., and Lawrence, P. R., Beyond Vertical Integration—The Rise of the Value-Adding Partnership, *Harvard Business Review* **88**, 94–108 (1988).

10. Harrigan, K. R., *Strategies for Joint Ventures,* Free Press, 1985.

11. Heide, J., and John, G., The Role of Dependence Balancing in Safeguarding Transaction-Specific Assets in Conventional Channels, *Journal of Marketing* **52**, 20–35 (1988).

12. Lorincz, J. A., Getting There with EDI, *Purchasing World* **29**, 58, 60 (November 1985).

13. Macneil, I. R., Economic Analysis of Contractual Relations: Its Shortfalls and the Needs for a Rich Classifactory Analysis, *Northwestern University Law Review* **75**, 1018–1063 (1981).

14. Narus, J. A., and Anderson, J. C., Turn Your Industrial Distributors into Partners, *Harvard Business Review* **64**, 66–71 (March–April 1986).

15. Narus, J. A., and Anderson, J. C., Distributor Contributions to Partnerships with Manufacturers, *Business Horizons* **30**, 34–42 (September–October 1987).

16. Narus, J. A., and Anderson, J. C., Strengthen Distributor Performance Through Channel Positioning, *Sloan Management Review* **29**, 31–40 (Winter 1988).

17. Noordewier, T. G., and John, G., and Nevin, J. R., Performance Outcomes of Purchasing Arrangements in Industrial Buyer-Vendor Relationships, *Journal of Marketing* **54**, 80–93 (1990).

18. Palay, T., Comparative Institutional Economics: The Governance of Rail Freight Contracting, *Journal of Legal Studies* **13**, 6–17 (1984).

19. Reddy, N. M., and Marvin, M. P., Developing a Manufacturer-Distributor Information Partnership, *Industrial Marketing Management* **15**, 157–163 (1986).

20. Shapiro, B. P., Close Encounters of the Third Kind: The Latest Selling Revolution. Unpublished Manuscript, Harvard University, Boston (1985).

21. Skagen, A. E., Nurturing Relationships, Enhancing Quality with Electronic Data Interchange, *Management Review* **78**, 28–32 (February 1989).

22. Thackray, J., America's Vertical Cutback, *The McKinsey Quarterly* **74**, 41–51 (1986).

23. Walker, G., Strategic Sourcing, Vertical Integration, and Transaction Costs, *Interfaces* **18**, 62–73 (1988).

24. Williamson, O. E., The Economics of Organization: The Transaction Cost Approach, *American Journal of Sociology* **87**, 548–67 (1981).

25. Williamson, O. E., *The Economic Institutions of Capitalism,* The Free Press, New York, 1985.

N. Mohan Reddy
Michael P. Marvin

Developing a Manufacturer–Distributor Information Partnership

The growing importance of industrial distribution calls for increased emphasis on cooperative arrangements between manufacturers and distributors. This article focuses on what is perhaps the most crucial and sensitive element in developing such a partnership: sharing and use of market information. A case study details the developmental effort of such a partnership by a large manufacturer and explains the benefits that both parties can accrue. ✳

A ccelerating direct sales costs, prohibitive inventory carrying costs, intensifying domestic and foreign competition, and higher levels of service demands by customers are but a few factors that have contributed to a growing reliance on industrial distributors by manufacturers [1, 2]. Manufacturers, thus, are under increasing pressure to foster cooperative arrangements with their distributors to enhance the effectiveness of their operations.

This article's focus is on a key dimension of the manufacturer–distributor relationship: sharing and use of market information. The case study presented provides guidelines on how an effective manufacturer–distributor partnership can identify, collect, share, and use market information to formulate marketing plans.

Importance of Industrial Distributors

Environmental and competitive trends are forcing manufacturers to rethink channel strategies with

industry analysts predicting a greater proportion of industrial products moving through distributors in the coming decade [3, 4]. A recent study of industrial distributor problems [5] showed that distributors ranked problems associated with suppliers well below those associated with economic conditions, competition, and internal operations. The implication of this finding for the manufacturer is fairly clear—the distribution community is more concerned with its customer base and operations than with ensuring a source of supply. With manufacturers' growing reliance on distributors, the time has come for the manufacturers to step in and strengthen the manufacturer–distributor relationship by helping its distributors better manage their marketing and operational functions. Only by engaging in this partnership mode of behavior will the manufacturer–distributor relationship evolve and achieve mutually profitable goals.

This call for a "channel partnership" perspective is something marketing academics have stressed from time to time [6, 7]. Bonoma [8], in a recently concluded study, notes the fact that the best implementers of formulated plans tended to view maintenance of a partnership with their distributors as a primary objective. As Hlavacek and McCuistion [9, p. 101] note:

At the time this article was written, N. Mohan Reddy was Assistant Professor of Marketing at the Weatherhead School of Management, Case Western Reserve University. Michael P. Marvin was Manager of Marketing Research at Parker Hannifin Corporation. *Source:* Reprinted by permission of the publisher from *Industrial Marketing Management* 15, 157–163 (1986) © Elsevier Science Inc., 1986.

A good distributor network is often the key to market leadership and overall business success. Because it takes many years of continuous attention to develop and maintain, a sound producer–distributor organization is often a high barrier to competitors. Without a solid network, even a manufacturer with a superior product can fail in the marketplace. A producer that recognizes the importance of distributors has a major competitive advantage that can reap attractive profits for itself and its distributors.

Though the importance of distribution and distributors has rarely been denied, the primary emphasis of the marketing literature remains—selection, evaluation, and control of distributors from the manufacturer's perspective. The case study that follows is an example of a successful channel partnership in information sharing with implications for both participants: manufacturers and distributors. Development of, and benefits from such an endeavor, it is argued, are inextricably tied to the level of involvement exhibited by both parties. A well-managed system as shown can considerably enhance the competitive standing of manufacturer and the distributor organizations by making available market information to both parties that may not otherwise be possible.

A Successful Partnership

The Parker Hannifin Corporation (P-H) manufactures an extensive line of fluid power components and systems for industrial, automotive, aviation, and marine applications. Its product lines number over 320, totaling 10,000 catalog items serving over 800 diverse industries. Given the range of products and diversity of industries, P-H's reliance on independent distributors is extensive. About 1,000 direct salespeople support 9,300 franchised distributors worldwide. It is estimated that approximately 50 percent of P-H's sales of $1.5 billion go through independent distributors. P-H views its distribution network as a critical resource and management of it as a profitable partnership. The Industrial Distribution Marketing System (IDMS) recently established and discussed in the following pages is one more step in cementing this partnership. The IDMS has two basic interrelated components: (i) sharing and use of market information, and (ii) manufacturer's support services. This supports the participants' contention that manufacturers and distributors are privy to information that could be more meaningfully shared. In addition, the translation of this information sharing into actionable decisions in the marketplace demands that support services be in place to guide manufacturer and distributor decision makers.

Sharing and Use of Information

The cornerstone of the IDMS is the "reporting" agreement P-H has been able to reach with many of their distributors. The case study in this article deals with the Industrial Sector, one of the four Sectors of P-H which accounts for sales of about $817 million. Twenty-nine hundred distributors are the primary outlet for the Industrial Sector's products, with about 500 of these distributors accounting for 90 percent of sales. These 500 are reporting distributors. These reporting distributors send in copies of all invoices detailing their customer transactions. P-H's marketing research department is charged with the responsibility of collecting and coding these on a monthly basis. This coding of each invoice enables identification by end use customer, product, territory, and industry. The distributor's sales information is then merged with each division's direct sales information. This file, which forms a comprehensive picture of all product line sales to end customer, is titled the *customer file*.

The customer file is an indication of P-H's current market situation. Corporate marketing research's generated company file details the population for P-H's products. End user industries identified in the customer file are used as the starting point to generate the company file. This company file contains over 250,000 purchasing locations in 454 industries throughout North America. The compilation and updating of the company file utilizes primary and secondary data sources. Information gathered by surveys and direct sales reports is coupled with secondary data sources, including on-line data bases to generate the file which lists *all* organizations who may be potential customers for P-H products.

FIGURE 1
Distributor Information System

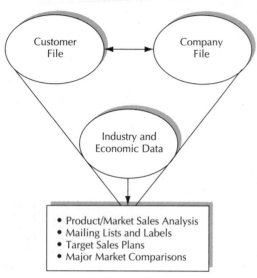

- Product/Market Sales Analysis
- Mailing Lists and Labels
- Target Sales Plans
- Major Market Comparisons

The customer file and the company file are used to generate the product/market sales analysis reports and to compare an existing distributor's customer base within each industry to the total population of plants for a specific geographic area, thus pinpointing potential target accounts by industry, name, and location. The potential plant locations can be broken down further by size of employment, sales territory, and by sales to an OEM (original equipment manufacturer) or MRO (maintenance, repair, and overhaul) account. The PMSA, in addition to providing the distributor with a current situation analysis, forms important input for the formulation of target market plans. Distributors, upon receipt of this information, are often surprised that they served as diverse a range of industries and have such potential available to them. As one distributor summed up:

> The initial reaction of our field salespeople has been very positive. They recognize that there is far more potential available to them than they are willing to admit and that there are potential customers right in their own areas and in the very same business as some of their best accounts.

It is the interaction of the customer file with the company file and information on regional industry and economic data which forms the starting point for some specific product/market reports. Figure 1 provides an overview of the system.

Product/Market Sales Analysis (PMSA)

Figure 2 is an example of a product/market sales analysis for XYZ distributor. This report shows a distributor's product line sales by market segment (SIC), number of customers by market segment, and number of potential new customers by market segment. Though the example uses 4-digit SIC codes for identification, the reports also use Parker Industrial Codes (PIC). PICs provide more detail within each 4-digit SIC code, thus overcoming the aggregation problems inherent in most 4-digit SIC codes. An example of a PIC would be 7699A Hydraulic Repair Shops, which is much more actionable than the 4-digit SIC classification 7699 (Repair Shops and Related Services, nec).

Detailing Potential Accounts

The PMSA provides an aggregate picture of existing potential. Effective targeting demands that more specific information be provided to the distributor. The PMSAs are complemented by mailing lists of potential customer accounts detailing size, nature of business (OEM/MRO), and contact person. Using these mailing lists, distributors have often uncovered customers who used to buy from them but were lost due to territory realignments or plain neglect.

A further extension to the PMSA's end mailing lists is the development of a suggested sales strategy by P-H for each distributor territory (Figure 3). These target market plans are developed for individual distributors by product line, geographic area, and by market segment. Regional economic forecasts of industry growth rates, manufacturing employment, and other economic indicators are incorporated into each target market plan,

FIGURE 2

XYZ Distributor Product/Market Sales Analysis

SIC	# Of Cust.	Total Mfg. Pit. Pop.	Air Cylinders	Air Valves	SIC Total	$ Of Total
3541	10	99	$ 8,000	$ 2,000	$ 10,000	10%
3542	5	9	10,000	10,000	20,000	20%
3544	83	146	15,000	35,000	50,000	50%
3545	2	20	10,000	0	10,000	10%
3549	10	60	0	10,000	10,000	10%
35xx	110	334	$43,000	$57,000	$100,000	100%
Percent of Totals			43%	57%	100%	

thus reflecting local economic conditions instead of the more aggregate and less useful national economic indicators. Distributors have utilized these to establish sales incentive programs, invest in telemarketing systems to qualify MRO accounts, and more importantly, rethink marketing resources allocation to geographical territories. To quote a pleasantly surprised distributor:

> . . . . one of the most dramatic impacts we see so far is distorted distribution of new potential. We may end up with territory realignments to enable us to dedicate manpower to the concentration of potential.

Thus far our discussion has been with distributors and their territories. Given the rate of technological change it is important that distributors be kept informed of changes currently taking place outside their region which may have a lagged effect on them. A good starting point is to feed back to the distributor a comparison of markets for each product. Figure 4 shows a comparison of a distributors' major markets with those of P-H. A distributor, by comparing these statistics, and often on a product line basis, can isolate regional and national occurrences that may influence his market. This comparison enables distributors to better understand their market and competition, by exploring the dimensions that account for the differences on an ongoing basis.

Manufacturer Support Functions

Early in the design of the P-H IDMS, a key concern that surfaced was that of a distributor's ability to fully utilize the information that was fed back to it. This concern resulted in the design of a continuing education program for distributors. This program titled *Distributor Marketing Information Program* explains the use of the various reports described earlier. P-H employees travel the country meeting with groups of distributors for a day or two at a time. Distributors' attendance and participation has been nothing short of enthusiastic. Distributor statements indicate that this program has proven helpful in their ability to undertake actionable decisions on the information fed back to them.

Two recent additions to the support services include the *Distributor Marketing Management Program* and a *Telemarketing Program*. The Distributor Marketing Management Program is a 4-day executive development course offered to P-H distributor management personnel. The course is a natural linkage and extension to the distributor marketing information program as the course was designed to be a step-by-step guide for developing and implementing product/market plans for industrial distributors.

A few years ago P-H management realized the growing importance telephone sales could play

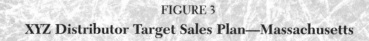

FIGURE 3
XYZ Distributor Target Sales Plan—Massachusetts

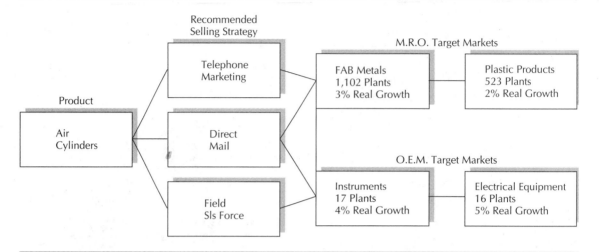

in helping reduce the costs of the ever increasing direct sales call, and improving its service to the small MRO accounts. Based upon the desires of its distributors, P-H initiated a Telephone Marketing Skills Training Course for inside and outside distributor sales personnel. Though recent in origin, the telemarketing consultants at P-H are actively used by distributors.

Though not formally used as a feedback tool, a possible extension to further enhancing the manufacturer–distributor relationship is the "two way" evaluations that P-H actively subscribes to.

Two-Way Evaluations

Performance evaluations in Industrial Distribution Channels have more often than not taken a one-sided perspective, with the manufacturer doing all of the evaluating. P-H's acknowledgment of the importance of its distribution structure is reflected in its two-way perspective to performance evaluation.

The distributors' performance evaluation by P-H, in addition to sales quotas, considers net addition to customer base and development of new markets. P-H takes the responsibility of estimating

market demand for a particular product by market segment and geographic area. As most of this information is unavailable from secondary sources, it is generated through primary marketing research and used to establish sales territories, location of new distribution points, and sales goals. All the other distributor performance factors can be generated from the customer file and the company file.

Traditionally, a manufacturer's performance evaluation by its distributors has been largely ignored, often meeting with active resistance by operating management. Needless to say, top management's commitment is crucial for this system of "reverse" evaluation to work. P-H has an active evaluation program (How We're Doing Survey) based on key performance factors that are likely to affect the distributors' competitive stance in the marketplace. The distributors rate specific product divisions on criteria related to product quality, manufacturer sales and sales support, and responsiveness. The aggregated information from the surveys is fed back to the distributors and to the participating divisions. The benefits of this type of evaluation program are most beneficial when conducted on an annual basis enabling comparison of

FIGURE 4

XYZ Distributor Pneumatic Products—Highest Ranking Market Segments—Parker/XYZ Distributor

Description	Parker's Major Mkts (SIC)	XYZ Distr Major Mkts (SIC)	Description
Spec. Ind. Machy.	3559	3545	Mach. Tool Access.
Conv. & Conv. Eqp.	3535	3511	Steam, Gas & Hyd. Turb.
Mach. Tools, M.C.	3541	3315	Steel Wire Drawing
Motor Veh. Pass Car	3711	3494	Valves & Pipe Ftgs.
Gen. Ind. Machy.	3569	3569	Gen. Ind. Machy.
Paper Ind. Machy.	3554	3535	Conv. & Conv. Eqp.
Truck & Bus Bodies	3713	3079	Misc. Plastics Prods.
Mach. Tools, M.F.	3542	3313	Steel Mills
Paper Mills	2621	3554	Paper Ind. Machy.
Mach. Tool Access.	3545	3599	Machy. Exc. Electrical

changing conditions and strategies. The most important benefit, however, is a marked improvement in the distributor–manufacturer relationship due to improvement in the overall communication in the channel. The manufacturer, in addition, gains valuable market information in terms of perceived problem areas, product line gaps, and new marketing ideas.

Discussion

The Industrial Distributor Marketing System presented in this article acknowledges the basic premise that channel expertise is not the exclusive domain of either the manufacturer or the distributor. Sharing of market information, based on mutual trust, is bound to enhance the effectiveness of both partners.

On a more prescriptive note, we are hard pressed for specific steps to follow that build the underlying trust which makes a system such as this possible. The presentation of this article seems to suggest that the distributor give up the most sacred of his assets—the market knowledge which is internal to him, the market knowledge that gives him the leverage to obtain favorable terms from the manufacturer. The prospective of being "cut out" of the business with the manufacturer going direct is a major concern to the distributor and one that the manufacturer needs to address first. P-H distributors who subscribe to the reporting agreement receive a high degree of manufacturer support services. An additional factor that has aided implementation of the reporting agreement is the fact that a proportion of these distributor organizations are headed by Ex-Parker-Hannifin employees, people well steeped in the partnership mode of thinking.

Reassuring the distributor is not enough; suggesting that they start with a single product may lower resistance. Experimenting with a single product would expose both sides to the benefits that accrue from information sharing laying the path for more extensive involvement. The system we have presented is not a quick fire prescription (few channel decisions are) for a more effective distribution arrangement. It is a system that is the outcome of a way of thinking about industrial markets—the partnership mode. The P-H Industrial Distributor Marketing System is off to a good start and well subscribed to. The critical dimension that will determine its longevity is the ability of the partners to uphold their respective commitments and trust fostered in the system.

A well-managed system (IDMS) should clearly result in more efficient allocation of resources by pinpointing attractive pockets of potential to target. The distributors' search for new accounts is made more efficient. The manufacturer gains not only from the increased sales, and hence market share, but also from the standpoint of early

warning signals that he might pick up on from a "partner" who is closer to the market. The notion of the manufacturer as the channel captain has long been dead. We need to wake up to the fact that a trusting, dependent relationship in the channel is the most effective means of managing it. Channel relationships do not have to be tenuous, adversarial, and time consuming. A well-tuned IDMS can provide the manufacturer–distributor partnership with a distinct competitive edge in the marketplace to achieve common goals but still enable each partner flexibility in developing local business plans and marketing strategies.

References

1. Arthur Anderson, Inc., *Future Trends in Wholesale-Distribution*, Distribution Research and Education Foundation, Washington, D.C., 1983.

2. Morgan, James, (ed)., Distribution '82: An Overview, Bigger Opportunities and Obstacles, *Purchasing* **93**, 45–48 (Sept 9, 1982).

3. Industry Markets Goods Through Dual Channels, Says McGraw-Hill Study, *Industrial Distribution* **74**, 15 (April 1985).

4. Price, Margaret, Distributors: No Endangered Species, *Industry Week* (Jan 24, 1983), pp. 47–50.

5. Narus, James, Reddy, N., Mohan, and Pinchak, George L., Key Problems Facing Distributors, *Industrial Marketing Management* **3**, 139–148 (1984).

6. McVey, Philip, Are Channels of Distribution What the Text Books Say? *Journal of Marketing* (1960), pp. 61–64.

7. Webster, Jr., Frederick, The Role of the Industrial Distributor in Marketing Strategy, *Journal of Marketing* (July 10–16, 1976).

8. Bonoma, Thomas, V., Making Your Marketing Strategy Work, *Harvard Business Review* (March–April 1984), pp. 69–76.

9. Hlavacek, James D. and McCuistion, Tommy J., Industrial Distributors When, Who and How? *Harvard Business Review* (March–April 1983), pp. 96–101.

Cases

Case Relation to Chapter

Case	Locale	Product	1	2	3	4	5	6	7	8	9	10	11
1 Alias Research	US	Software								✳			
2 Cumberland Metal	US	Specialty								✳			
3 Curtis Automotive Hoist	Can/Europe	Hoists		✳				✳					✳
4 Dell Computer	US/Global	PC		✳								✳	✳
5 DIPROD	Canada	Chemical			✳								
6 Du Pont	US	Fibers		✳					✳		✳	✳	
7 Ethical Situations	Global	Ethics		✳	✳		✳		✳	✳	✳	✳	✳
8 Grasse Fragrances	Europe	Flavors & frag.		✳							✳		
9 Japanese Construction	Japan	Contracting				✳							
10 Leykam Mürztaler	Europe	Paper							✳			✳	✳
11 Lussman-Shizuka	Japan	Medical			✳								
12 Machine Vision	US	Robots		✳				✳	✳				
13 MacTec Control	Sweden/US	Instruments					✳						
14 Microsoft	US/Global	Software						✳					
15 Modern Plastics	US	Plastic bags					✳						
16 Ohmeda	US/Global	Medical equip.						✳	✳				
17 Quest	Neth/Global	Flavors & frag.					✳						
18 RNL Design	US	Architecture	✳	✳	✳			✳					
19 Texas Instruments	US/Global	Semiconductor								✳			✳
20 Toro: Indus. Flavors	Europe	Flavors	✳					✳	✳				
21 Van Moppes IDP	UK	Machine tools		✳				✳	✳				
22 Waters Chromatography	US	Instruments		✳							✳		
23 West European Car Rental	Europe	Car rental				✳							
24 World Flavor Industry	Neth/Global	Flavor & frag.				✳							

Alias Research, Inc.

Douglas Snetsinger

Susan Spencer

"I can't believe they did it again!" exclaimed Isaac Babbs, district sales manager for the southwestern United States for Alias Research, Inc. For the fourth time in 1990 he had lost a sale to Wavefront, his major competitor in the animation software market. He had worked on this sale for a month, and he felt confident that the prospective customer was ready to buy Alias' $100,000 software. But Wavefront had stepped in at the last moment, cut their price from $55,000 to $25,000, and obtained the sale. Wavefront, a California-based company, seemed determined to dominate the region, while Alias, based in Toronto, was at least equally determined to make further inroads into the California market. "How does Toronto expect me to compete it they won't give me some flexibility on pricing?" Babbs lamented as he thought about Alias' rigidly enforced policy of not permitting any price discounting on its products. With a sigh of resignation, he reached for the phone to call Toronto and let them know that another sale was lost to a price-cutting competitor.

The High-End Graphics Market

Alias Research, Inc., a software company located in Toronto, was a recognized market leader in high-end, three-dimensional (3D) computer graphics. Its product, ALIAS, was used in film animation, industrial design, architecture, education, medical and scientific visualization, packaging and product design, flight or space simulation, and a number of other applications. Seventy percent of the world's automobile manufactures used ALIAS in their design processes. Some of its customers in other industries included Goodyear, Timex, Kraft, Motorola, Northern Telecom, Johnson & Johnson, and Industrial Light and Magic. Alias had sales offices in Boston, Princeton, Los Angeles, Chicago, and Detroit, as well as in France and Germany. The corporate officers for Alias are listed in Exhibit 1.

The total size of the market served by Alias was estimated at $81 million (U.S.) in 1990, of which Alias held a 15% share. Industry experts had forecast that the market would increase to $300 million by 1992. Virtually all of the growth was in the field of industrial design, which currently accounted for 40%

This case was prepared by Douglas W. Snetsinger, Executive Director, Institute of Market Driven Quality, and Susan Spencer of the University of Toronto. Copyright © 1990 by Douglas Snetsinger. Reproduced by permission.

EXHIBIT 1
Alias Research, Inc.—Executive Officers and Directors

Name	Age°	Position
Stephen R. B. Bingham	40	President, Chief Executive Officer, and Chairman of the Board of Directors
Susan I. McKenna	31	Executive Vice-President and Director
William J. McClintock	38	Vice-President Finance, Secretary, Treasurer, and Chief Financial Officer
Arthur W. Bell	34	Vice-President Marketing
Martin I. Tuori	38	Vice-President Research and Development
Gregory S. Hill	35	Vice-President Business Development
David N. Macrae	34	Vice-President Sales
Brian J. Conway	31	Director
William S. Kaiser	34	Director
Barry L. Stephens	50	Director

°Ages are as of July 1990.

of the market. The remaining 60% was in the animation field, which was growing at a rate of only 1% each year. The animation market was saturated with a variety of competing products.

Alias' three main competitors were Wavefront Technologies, Thompson Digital Image (TDI), and Evans and Sutherland Computer Corporation (E&S). Originally a private customer software builder, Wavefront entered the video animation market in 1985 at approximately the same time as Alias. It had recently modified its package to provide some industrial design capability. However, Wavefront's product did not easily translate into manufacturable designs, and it required extensive training before any of its advanced tools could be properly used. Wavefront's major advantage was that its product could be run on many different types of computers, as opposed to Alias', which could only be run on Silicon Graphics hardware or IBM workstations.

Based in Paris, France, Thompson Digital Image (TDI) was Alias' principal competitor in the European market. TDI was a subsidiary of the Thompson Group, though 56% of TDI was owned by the French government. TDI's primary market, accounting for 80% of sales, was the video animation market. It was estimated that TDI had approximately 20 clients in the video post-production industry. TDI was also pursuing industrial design customers and had been successful with some leading French firms including Renault, the automobile manufacturer. TDI was currently overhauling its design software based on a similar technology to the Alias product.

Evans and Sutherland (E&S) was a large, multidivisional computer hardware and software company with total sales of $129 million (U.S.). Based in Salt

Lake City, they were engaged in the development of interactive super-computers for large-scale scientific and technical computations, modeling, and simulations. The Graphics Products Group designed and built high-performance three-dimensional graphics hardware and specialized software. E&S's closest product to ALIAS was the Conceptual Design and Rendering System, a turnkey, computer-aided design system that was introduced in 1988. The system was developed in partnership with Ford and Chrysler. It was based on Alias-type technology and was priced at $200,000 (U.S.) to $250,000 (U.S.) and ran only on proprietary hardware manufactured by E&S.

Alias History

The Beginning

Alias Research, Inc., was founded in 1983 by Stephen Bingham, Nigel McGrath, Susan McKenna, and David Springer. With few resources, they borrowed $500,000 of computer graphic equipment from McGrath's company and rented an office in an old elevator shaft for $150 per month. Though starting small in scope, the owners of this fledgling company had a big dream: to create an easy-to-use software package that would produce realistic 3D video animation for the advertising industry post-production houses.

Many companies in this industry had difficulty raising start-up funds, and Alias was no exception. The problem was that it required substantial time and effort to develop software to the point where it was "debugged" and ready to be sold to customers. As much as 150 person-years of research and development effort might go into making the first working piece of software. Thus, investors were reluctant to provide funds on promises, as opposed to finished products.

However, Alias was able to obtain a $61,000 grant from the National Research Council, which, when combined with the limited funds of the founders, allowed work to begin. Other financial support was gained from the federal government through Scientific Research Tax Credits (SRTCs). A SRTC was actually a contract that allowed an investor to hire Alias to do a specified amount of research, in return for which the investor would get a tax credit for his or her own company. This sort of arrangement yielded two benefits for Alias. It provided much needed start-up funding and it allowed the four founders to maintain control of the company. It also allowed Alias to earn money by doing the research that was required for its own project.

Development of the software continued until mid-1985. One of the early decisions made was building the software based on a relatively new form of modeling technique which used cardinal splines rather than traditional polygonal lines.[1] Silicon Graphics, a small hardware firm based in California, pro-

---

[1] A cardinal spline is based on the first derivative of the modeling equation, while polygonal lines are based on the actual equation. The results that were achieved from cardinal splines, in terms of computer graphics, were a much smoother, more realistic line or surface than had been possible from a polygonal line.

duced a workstation that was specifically designed to work with spline technology. Silicon Graphics soon became a staunch supporter of Alias as they saw the opportunity for enhanced applications for their workstation.

The product, ALIAS, was unveiled at the Special Interest Group on Graphics (SIGGRAPH) show in July 1985. The annual SIGGRAPH show was attended by many people who were involved in design (for example, designing products, labels, packages) and by many people who could help the designers (for example, software companies like Alias). For a company like Alias, the SIGGRAPH show provided an important opportunity to introduce and market new products. Many of the Alias group would attend the show and work long hours to generate leads for the ALIAS system. In fact, sales of ALIAS could often be traced to an initial meeting at the SIGGRAPH show.

The first sale, to a post-production house, came on July 15th. Then the unexpected occurred; General Motors Inc. (GM) expressed an interest in buying a system. GM was looking for a system that was compatible with their spline-based computer-aided-design (CAD) systems, and ALIAS was the only spline-based system available. Initially, the Alias group were reluctant to enter this new market; industrial design applications had not been part of the corporate objective and seemed too distant from their animation market. Further, GM wanted the package to run on basis-splines (b-splines),[2] which would require yet another significant investment by Alias in research and development (R&D). However, when GM kept dropping broad hints about 20 systems, potentially representing millions of dollars of revenue, Alias decided to go ahead and, in November 1985, the deal with GM was signed.

Once again, money was required to finance the research. However, Alias now had a major customer, more or less in hand, which reduced the risk of the venture in the eyes of potential investors. Early in 1986, Crownx, a venture capital company associated with Crown Life, invested $1.2 million for a 20% stake in Alias.

By early 1986, the company had sold ALIAS to a number of firms. Most of the sales were to small production houses in the video animation market, but sales were also made to Kraft, Motorola, and NASA. By the middle of 1986, there were 70 people working for the company, of whom 40 were programmers, morale was high and the employees were beginning to see the fruits of their labors in print and on video. The work environment was flexible and relaxed—purposely designed to facilitate and simulate creativity. Improvements and upgrades to the original package were constantly being developed, and a new release of the software (with a b-spline base) was planned for mid-1986. Staff increased to 80 in April 1987, with the opening of three sales offices in the United States. In the same year, almost $3 million in new venture capital was received from two American companies. Everything was moving quickly and the people at Alias were looking forward to a promising future.

---

[2]B-splines are based on the second derivative of the modeling equation and were generally regarded as producing the smoothest lines and surfaces available in computer graphics.

The Downturn

The development of ALIAS/2 (using b-splines) took much longer than had been expected and the product was not released until late in 1986. Initial sales were strong, but a problem was discovered with the new system. The final rendered picture was not matched to the original design on a consistent or reliable basis. While Alias could fix the bug on the installed systems on a patchwork basis, the sales force would find it next to impossible to sell new installations of ALIAS/2 until the problem was solved. The company immediately pulled members of the marketing and R&D staff together with a product management group to fix the software.

The first half of 1987 saw the beginnings of what was to become a major downturn in the animation industry as a whole. Premium, high-end systems, like those of Alias, were particularly affected by the slump. At the same time, personnel changes and budget cuts at GM had reduced the number of systems purchased from the expected number of 20 to only 4. Some of the new investors in Alias were dissatisfied with the company's performance and were demanding cuts in investment, particularly on R&D spending and personnel. Bingham and the other original owners still retained control and resisted the pressure. However, by late summer 1987, Alias was forced to lay off 12 employees from marketing and administration.

The Recovery

Following the layoffs, quarterly company meetings were instituted in which the status of the company as a whole, plans for the future, and the past quarter's performance were reviewed with all employees. Day-long meetings of the management team (vice-president level and above) were held monthly. Efforts at clearing the lines of communication between departments were made to build a more cohesive team atmosphere than had existed previously. Although the culture of the company remained informal, the methods of control and the way of doing business became more formalized, with more attention being paid to earnings and profit. Although Alias experienced an operating loss in fiscal 1989, it was considerably less than in fiscal 1988 (the corporate year end is January 31).

In the summer of 1989, for the first time in two years, the company began to hire people for new positions. A new vice-president of finance, Bill McClintock, took over the financial aspects of the company and tightened the purse strings on all expenditures. Staff were added to R&D, customer support, and marketing. For over two years, marketing of ALIAS had been handled primarily by the vice-president of marketing and communications, Arthur Bell. People were now hired to fill the positions of product manager, CAD marketing manager, distributor marketing manager, and communications manager. These people came from a variety of different backgrounds, not necessarily in computer-related industries. Bell, who was very enthusiastic about his new recruits, commented:

EXHIBIT 2
Alias Research, Inc. — Consolidated
Statement of Operations ($000 U.S.)

	1988	1989	1990	First Three Months of Fiscal 1991
Revenue:				
Products	5,709	6,466	10,962	3,106
Maintenance and services	451	744	1,044	271
Total revenue	6,160	7,240	12,006	3,377
Costs and expenses:				
Direct cost of products°	2,861	2,131	1,810	336
Direct cost of maintenance and services	448	509	615	198
General and administration	842	910	1,956	533
Sales and marketing	1,716	2,172	3,527	1,100
Research and development	1,150	954	973	525
Depreciation and amortization	480	500	560	145
Total costs and expenses	7,497	7,176	9,441	2,837
Operating income (loss)	(1,337)	64	2,565	540
Interest income (expense)	(39)	(20)	134	73
Other income (expense)	13	(9)	163	13
Income (loss) before income taxes	(1,363)	35	2,862	626
Provision for (recovery) income taxes	(43)	0	1,229	258
Net income (loss)	(1,320)	35	1,633	368

°Hardware purchased for resale.

So often, people who market software come directly out of R&D, or they are engineers. They are way too "techi" for most of our customers, who are designers. I wanted people who understood marketing, but who did not necessarily know computers. Peter Goldie [formerly senior brand manager for Crisco at Procter & Gamble] understands shelf space and everything that leads up to getting that shelf space. No one knows it better. He knows how to market, no matter what, and he can do that for us.

Perhaps most important of all were the changes made to the software itself. Because of all the "bugs" in ALIAS/2, R&D immediately went to work on a "bug-fix" version, known as ALIAS/2.1. Other versions followed, which in some cases included only bug-fix material and in other cases included new applications or improved processes. By the summer of 1989, Version 2.4.2 was being used by most Alias customers. At that time, Alias had $3 million in the bank. The income statements for 1988 to 1990 are provided in Exhibit 2.

Alias Culture

The culture at Alias was by design relaxed and informal. Everyone, from the programmer in the R&D department to the president, appeared in jeans most of the time. Suits were worn only when people were expected from outside the company. In the words of Bill McClintock: "There are very few 'ties' around here, never mind 'suits,' and that is the way it should be." Friday was known as "shorts day," and throughout the summer, anyone not wearing shorts on a Friday had better have been expecting company.

Employees referred to themselves as "Alians," and the term was expressed with affection and pride. A friendly rivalry existed between the R&D and administrative sides of the company, each housed in a separate section of the office. Employee birthdays were celebrated by all, with cake, drinks, and the occasional Elvis impersonator supplied by the company. Team spirit abounded, and everyone regarded it as a great place to work. This was reflected in an article that appeared in the August 1990 *Report on Business Magazine* which described the company, its culture, and the software industry (Exhibit 3).

Alias Marketing

In many ways, marketing software is unlike marketing any other product. For example, security is a serious problem. Once the product has been sold, it is always possible that the product will be copied or even copied and resold. Once the product has been purchased, customers have to be kept up-to-date on new developments. When new versions and developments occur, the decision needs to be made whether current customers should be given free upgrades or not. Selling expenses are very high in the industry. Customers are geographically dispersed, and sales are often achieved over an extended period and with the support of a number of individuals. As was the case with the Isaac Babbs sale that fell through or the GM installations that were slow in coming, significant resources were invested in a potential sale which might evaporate at the most inopportune time.

Having a professional marketing and sales team was critical. As well, knowing how much to spend on marketing and in what areas was a perplexing task. Another difficult task was deciding how much R&D should be spent and on what projects. The company needed to determine how much customer service and support to provide and what price, if any, to charge for that support and service. The potentially crippling problem of bugs needed to be considered and what actions were to be taken if, and when, they occurred. How should the product be priced in the first place? Should all the R&D, marketing, and overhead be factored into the price? How flexible should the company be with its pricing strategy?

The ALIAS Product

When a data tape containing the ALIAS product left Toronto, it contained a "hole" or a missing line of code which must be filled in before the software would operate. This line of code, called an *encryption string*, was twelve digits

EXHIBIT 3
Excerpts of an Article in *Report on Business*
***Magazine*, August 1990**

- Unlike cars or clothes or bread, no raw material is required to manufacture software. It is purely a creation of the mind, which is why it [Alias] attracts people that include a former comedian, a French horn player, and a former cabinetmaker.

- When the Honda Accord became the first car made by a foreign manufacturer to head the U.S. best-seller list last year, it was more than just another triumph for Japanese industry. Only a few insiders knew that it was also a triumph for Alias. All of Honda's cars, like those of BMW and Volvo, are designed on three-dimensional graphics software created at Alias.

- Canada produces almost no original industrial designs; there is no such thing as a Canadian-designed car—but the eccentrics at Alias have created a wonderful tool for industrial designers. Until their software was developed in 1985, these designers did their work the old-fashioned way—with pencil and paper and clay models. Now the designers for such Alias customers as Timex, Motorola, Mitsubishi, British Telecom, and Goodyear can create moving, three-dimensional designs on their computer screens. The models are so realistic that a designer can see how light will reflect off a watch face or a car body long before the actual objects exist. Using Alias software can shave precious months, even years, off the time it takes to create a product.

- Good software is a living thing, constantly growing and adapting to meet its users' needs. That means long nights in front of computer screens. The Alias office contains two eating areas because software developers don't have time to go out for lunch or dinner. On a typical evening, the company will order in large quantities of chicken or pizza. Then the denizens of the factory might amuse themselves for a while playing the latest computer games or reading. A favorite writer at Alias is Vancouverite William Gibson, who writes science fiction novels about "cyberpunks" with computer chips embedded in their brains.

- In the software industry, tiny companies can grow into billion-dollar giants like Lotus and Microsoft almost overnight. That's exactly the sort of future the president, Stephen Bingham, has in mind for Alias, and he is off to an impressive start. Sales were just $12 million last year, but more than a third of those sales were to the Japanese—not known to deal with bantam-weights unless they have very good reasons to do so. The company even managed to forge a strategic alliance with mighty IBM. But for all its successes, there is no guarantee that Alias will make it. In fact, the odds are stacked against it. Software companies in Canada are starved for capital. Without money they can't grow, and in this business if you don't grow fast, you're dead.

- The sale is only part of the story. After you sell someone a $150,000 hardware and software package, you don't just wander off in search of the next customer. Software must be continually enhanced, and most of the enhancements are suggested by the users. Alias personnel meets regularly with their biggest customers. Investing in software is a commitment, and customers are anxious to know where the company is going long term. Several have visited Alias's offices. "The Japanese were impressed that we can turn out so much new technology so quickly," Mr. Bingham says. "A visitor from Honda said we had 20 people doing the work of 200."

- Alias got early support from Montreal "angel" Jim Muir, a friend of one of the partners, and Crownx Inc. of Toronto. Two Boston-based venture capitalists who specialize in high-tech also chipped in. But the company's growth has been largely financed through its own sales. Banks have so far refused to offer more than a small line of credit,

(continued)

EXHIBIT 3 *(continued)*

saying they do not wish to finance foreign receivables which are the only kind Alias has. Banks also like to have collateral in case a loan goes sour—and by collateral they mean some real estate or a yard full of steel ingots. They don't mean a numeric code on a computer disc—software—which is where the wealth of a company like Alias resides.

• It's not hard to understand why lenders shy away from technology companies. Just look at the record of those high-tech darlings of the '70s—companies like Mitel and Lumonics. More recently, Canada's biggest software firm, Cognos, lost $17 million in fiscal 1990 after several years of good earnings. From an investor's viewpoint, the problem is the rapid rate of change. One banker notes: "In a traditional borrowing relationship, you might analyze the company's record over the last five years. With high-tech companies, I look at the last five quarters. They go through the same cycles as a traditional firm but they do it at an accelerated pace. The products they were selling two years ago are now all obsolete and they've got new products."

Source: Daniel Stoffman, "Big Dreams, No Backers," *Report on Business Magazine,* August 1990, pp. 47–51.

long and could contain numbers, punctuation marks, and upper- or lowercase letters. The string was unique to one tape of software and to the one piece of hardware upon which it would run. In other words, the same data tape could not be used to start up several different machines.

When customers purchased the software, they purchased customer support for that software. Phone support was provided 12 hours a day, as well as free upgrades and bug fixes for a period of one year. The support contract had to be renewed each year by the customer if continuing support was to be received. No services were provided until the contract was renewed and payment was received.

A major advantage with the ALIAS system over other software was that ALIAS was easy to learn and easy to use. See Exhibit 4 for a comparison of Alias and Wavefront products. Those who were not computer literate, and even those who regarded computers with suspicion, were able to make use of most of the system's tools after only a few days of training. Like Apple products, ALIAS was menu-driven, and most "drawing" was done with the aid of a mouse. Once the design, or "modeling" process was finished, the information could be sent to a variety of media. The information could be fed to a plotter, which gives a flat wireframe picture of the object, or it could be directly linked to a CAD machine, which was then used to construct the object from the computerized data. Other options included creating a surface and background for the object and outputting the picture or pictures to slides or videotapes, or even to a stereolithography vat[3] where a plastic prototype is created. In any case, ALIAS shortened

---

[3]A stereolithography vat is a vat filled with molten plastic and equipped with a pinpoint laser. The path that the laser takes is determined by the instructions in ALIAS. The result is a perfectly proportioned, solid, three-dimensional plastic model of the original computerized design.

EXHIBIT 4
A Comparison of Wavefront and Alias

Dimension	Wavefront	Alias
Ease of use	Not easy Requires substantial training to use advanced functions	Pioneer in the development and improvement of making the product easy to use
Price	Negotiable Approximately U.S. $55,000 Discounts as much as 50% to make a sale	Fixed Base price is approximately U.S. $65,000 Discounts to educators and co-developers only
Primary market	Animation Some industrial features recently added	Industrial design but also has found wide application in animation
Basic technology	Polygonal lines	Basis splines
Hardware	Runs on many different kinds of hardware	Dedicated to Silicon Graphics and IBM workstations (industry standards)

Source: Company records.

the time between the conception of an idea and its appearance on the market, be that idea a car, a building, a piece or jewelry, or a special effect for a movie.

Customers, in general, had responded favorably to the flexibility and ease of use of ALIAS and its convenient access to a wide range of powerful options. Designers had liked the way ALIAS reduced the time between the conception of their ideas and having prototypes built, as well as having the capability of examining more interations, improvements, and changes at the early stage of product development. Engineers had found that ALIAS provided a precise reading and measurement of designers' concepts and took advantage of its ability to directly link into CAD/CAM systems.

The fundamental source of ALIAS's strength had been as a communication tool. It had given designers and engineers a common language to speak and, in the process, sped up the design-to-market cycle. The enthusiastic response of designers and engineers had let to the steady shift of Alias' revenue from animation into industrial design markets (Exhibit 5). While this trend was expected to continue, there are no plans to abandon the animation market.

Marketing and Sales

Alias promoted its products through participation in trade shows like SIG-GRAPH, an annual world demonstration tour, articles and advertisements in industry publications, live demonstrations, television advertising, and sponsorship of cultural events. These activities were augmented by print and videotape

EXHIBIT 5
Alias Research, Inc.—Sales History by
Line of Business ($000 U.S.)

	1987	1988	1989	1990
Industrial design market				
Sales	790	3,374	5,320	10,186
Percent of revenue	17%	55%	73%	85%
Animation market				
Sales	3,970	2,786	1,920	1,820
Percent of revenue	83%	45%	27%	15%
Total sales	4,760	6,160	7,240	12,006

sales support materials. A direct sales force was employed in North America and Europe. This group, which also managed Alias' distributor and dealer network, consisted of 19 people. There were sales offices in five cities in the United States, as well as in France and Germany. Alias' network of 16 dealers and distributors represented the product in 11 countries. This network generally specialized in design and engineering hardware and software complementary to the ALIAS product.

Pricing the Product

As is shown in the consolidated income statement for 1990 (Exhibit 2), the direct costs of sales amounted to only 20% of revenue. Almost all of the direct costs were for hardware purchased for resale, for maintenance, and for other services. The direct cost of the software was negligible. Using a cost-based approach to pricing would give Alias substantial room to maneuver on price; however, that was not their approach.

The approach used was to price the software at parity to the hardware upon which it was mounted. For example, a Silicon Graphics Personal IRIS Workstation cost the customer approximately $100,000 (U.S.). The ALIAS tape installed on that workstation would cost another $100,000 (U.S.). This method of pricing put ALIAS at or near the top of what the market would bear. A stripped-down version of ALIAS could sell for as little as $65,000 (U.S.), while the version with every option could run as high as $150,000 (U.S.). Once a system was installed, further options could be added at a cost of $10,000 (U.S.) to $30,000 (U.S.) per option. Customer support was provided on a two-tier pricing schedule. The first tier, which included software release updates and installation only, was provided for an annual fee equal to 10% of the then current software price. A second tier, in addition to incorporating the services of the first tier, provided hotline support and could be purchased for an annual fee of 15% of the then current software price. Training and consultant services were provided on a per day or per task rate (usually about U.S. $500 per person per day).

Back to the Field

As Isaac Babbs drove down Highway 1 on the California coast to meet a new prospect at Boeing, his thoughts wandered back to his telephone call with Arthur Bell. Arthur had expressed his disappointment over the lost sale but had refused to make any changes in the pricing policy.

Isaac Babbs had a lot of confidence in the company. Alias' management had made some tough calls over the history of the company and been proven right. However, Toronto was a long way from California, and he felt he knew his customers better than anyone did. He disliked losing any sale, and he was still smarting from this last one. He understood why Alias had not engaged in price-cutting in the past, but he was unsure if he could continue to compete against aggressive price-cutters like Wavefront. Maybe it was time for a change. How many times had he heard about what a flexible company Alias was, he thought. Perhaps the pricing policy was the correct one, but he could not help worrying over the long-term implications of this rigid policy.

Arthur Bell had been disappointed to have received the news from Babbs. Babbs was one of his best field representatives and had been very successful in cultivating the lucrative southwestern market. Arthur Bell respected Babb's opinions and was not pleased to hear about his concern over the lost sales and the inflexible pricing policy. The morale and commitment of any member of the sales force could not be treated lightly. Bell wondered if he came across as too intransigent on the issue of pricing. Perhaps it was time to review the pricing policy and bring it forward at the next management meeting. As he began preparing the memo, Stephen Bingham, the president, walked by. Arthur told him about the California incident and his interest in putting the pricing policy on the agenda. "Sure, let's take a look at the issue," said Stephen. "I think our current pricing policy is just fine, but I am prepared to listen. However, I don't think we can look at price in isolation from the other marketing policies. It would be more useful if it was in the context of a review of the entire marketing program."

Cumberland Metal Industries: Engineered Products Division

Jeffrey J. Sherman

Benson P. Shapiro

R obert Minicucci,[1] vice president of the Engineered Products Division of Cumberland Metal Industries (CMI), and Thomas Simpson, group manager of the Mechanical Products Group, had spent the entire Wednesday (January 2, 1980) reviewing a new product CMI was about to introduce. (See Exhibit 1 for organization charts.) The room was silent, and as he watched the waning rays of the sun filtering through the window, Minicucci pondered all that had been said. Turning toward Simpson, he paused before speaking.

> Curled metal cushion pads seem to have more potential than any product we've ever introduced. A successful market introduction could as much as double the sales of this company, as well as compensate for the decline of some existing lines. It almost looks too good to be true.

Simpson responded, "The people at Colerick Foundation Company are pressing us to sell to them. Since they did the original test, they've been anxious to buy more. I promised to contact them by the end of the week."

"Fair enough," Minicucci said, "but talk to me before you call them. The way we price this could have a significant impact on everything else we do with it."

The Company

Cumberland Metal Industries was one of the largest manufacturers of curled metal products in the country, having grown from $250,000 in sales in 1963 to over $18,500,000 by 1979. (Exhibit 2 shows CMI's income statement.) It origi-

---

[1]Pronounced Minikuchi.

Jeffrey J. Sherman, research assistant, prepared this case under the supervision of Professor Benson P. Shapiro as a basis for class discussion rather than to illustrate either effective or ineffective handling of an administrative situation. It was made possible by a company that prefers to remain anonymous. All data have been disguised.

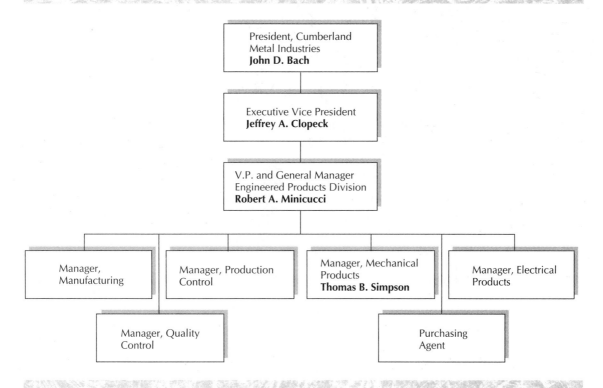

EXHIBIT 1a
Engineered Products Division Organization Chart

President, Cumberland Metal Industries
John D. Bach

Executive Vice President
Jeffrey A. Clopeck

V.P. and General Manager
Engineered Products Division
Robert A. Minicucci

Manager, Manufacturing

Manager, Production Control

Manager, Mechanical Products
Thomas B. Simpson

Manager, Electrical Products

Manager, Quality Control

Purchasing Agent

nally custom fabricated components for chemical process filtration and other highly technical applications. Company philosophy soon evolved from selling the metal as a finished product to selling products that used it as a raw material.

The company's big boost came with the introduction of exhaust gas recirculation (EGR) valves on U.S. automobiles. Both the Ford and Chrysler valve designs required a high temperature seal to hold the elements in place and prevent the escape of very hot exhaust gases. Cumberland developed a product that sold under the trademark *Slip-Seal*. Because it could meet the demanding specifications of the automakers, the product captured a very large percentage of the available business, and the company grew quite rapidly through the mid-1970s. Company management was not sanguine about maintaining its 80% market share over the long term, however, and moved to diversify away from a total reliance on the product and industry. Thus, when a sales representative from Houston approached CMI with a new application for curled metal technology, management examined it closely.

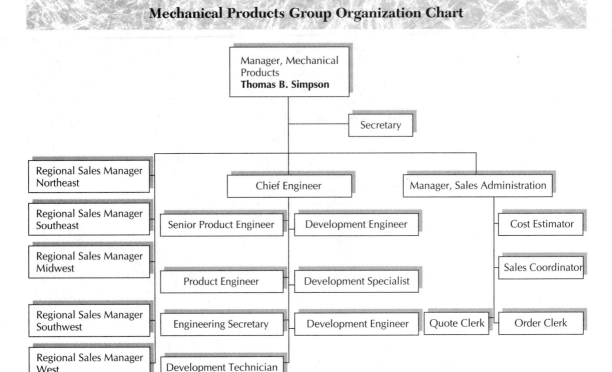

EXHIBIT 1b
Mechanical Products Group Organization Chart

The Product

Background

The product that Minicucci and Simpson were talking about was a cushion pad, an integral part of the process for driving piles.[2] Pile driving was generally done with a large crane, to which a diesel or steam hammer inside a set of leads was attached. The leads were suspended over the pile for direction and support. The hammer drove the pile from the top of the leads to a sufficient depth in the ground (see Exhibit 3).

The cushion pads prevented the shock of the hammer from damaging hammer or pile. They sat in a circular "helmet" placed over the top of the pile and were stacked to keep air from coming between striker plate and ram, as shown in Exhibit 3. Of equal importance, the pads effectively transmitted energy

---

[2]Piles were heavy beams of wood, concrete, steel, or a composite material which were pushed into the ground as support for a building, bridge, or other structure. They were necessary where the geological composition could shift under the weight of an unsupported structure.

EXHIBIT 2
Income Statement

EXHIBIT 2
Income Statement

December 31	1979	1978
Net sales	$18,524,428	$20,465,057
Costs and expenses		
Cost of sales	11,254,927	11,759,681
Selling expenses	2,976,396	2,711,320
General and administrative expenses	2,204,291	2,362,528
	16,435,614	16,833,529
Income from operations	2,088,814	3,631,528
Other income (expense)		
Dividend income	208,952	—
Interest income	72,966	186,611
Interest expense	(40,636)	(31,376)
	241,282	155,235
Income before income taxes	2,330,096	3,786,763
Provision for income taxes	1,168,830	1,893,282
Net income	1,161,266	1,893,481
Net income per share	$ 1.39	$ 2.16

from the hammer to the pile. A good cushion pad had to be able to transmit force without creating heat, and still remain resilient enough to prevent shock. With an ineffective pad, energy transmitted from the hammer would be given off as heat, and the pile could start to vibrate and possibly crack.

Despite the importance of these pads to the pile-driving process, little attention had been paid to them by most of the industry. Originally, hardwood blocks had been used. Although their cushioning was adequate, availability was a problem and performance was poor. Constant pounding quickly destroyed the wood's resiliency, heat built up, and the wood often ignited. The blocks had to be replaced frequently.

Most of the industry had shifted to asbestos pads (normally ¼-inch thick) which were used most often and seemed to perform adequately, or stacks of alternate layers of ½-inch-thick aluminum plate and 1-inch-thick micarta slabs. (These were not fabricated, but simply pieces of micarta and aluminum cut to specific dimensions.) Both pads came in a variety of standard diameters, the most common being 11½ inches. Diameter was determined by the size of the helmet, which varied with the size of the pile.

Curled Metal and the CMI Cushion Pad

Curled metal was a continuous metal wire that had been flattened and then wound into tight, continuous ringlets. These allowed the metal to stretch in both length and width and gave it three-dimensional resiliency. Because it

EXHIBIT 3
Typical Steam- or Air-Operated Pile Driver with Helmet and Cushion Pad

A schematic diagram of typical pile driver

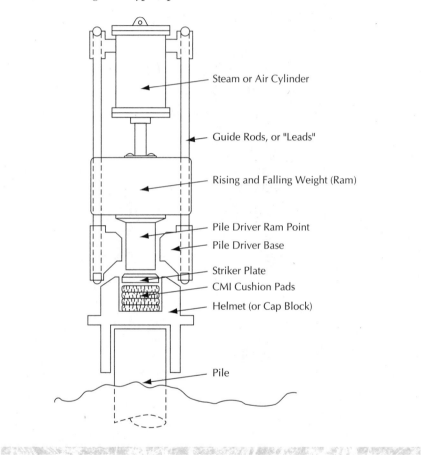

could be made of various metals (such as copper, monel, and stainless steel), curled metal could be made to withstand almost any temperature or chemical. Stacking many layers could produce a shock mount, an airflow corrector, or a highly efficient filter. Tightly compressed curled metal could produce the Slip-Seal for exhaust systems applications or, when calendered and wound around an axis, a cushion pad for pile driving.[3]

Cumberland purchased the wire from outside vendors and performed the flattening and curling operations in-house. The CMI pad started with curled metal calendered to about one inch thick and wound tightly around the center

---

[3]In calendering, curled metal ringlets were compressed between rollers to make a smooth, tight band.

of a flat, metallic disk until the desired diameter had been reached. A similar disk was placed on top, with soldered tabs folded down to hold it all together. The entire structure was then coated with polyvinyl chloride to enhance its appearance and disguise the contents.[4]

The advantage of this manufacturing process was that any diameter pad, from the standard minimum of $11^{1}/_{2}$ inches to over 30 inches for a custom-designed application, could be produced from the same brand of curled metal.

Comparative Performance

The Colerick Test

After struggling to find a responsible contractor to use the product and monitor its performance, CMI persuaded Colerick Foundation Company of Baltimore, Maryland, to try its pads on a papermill expansion in Newark, Delaware. The job required 300 55-foot piles driven 50 feet into the ground. The piles were 10-inch and 14-inch steel H-beams; both used an $11^{1}/_{2}$-inch helmet and, thus, $11^{1}/_{2}$-inch cushion pads. The total contractor revenue from the job was $75,000 ($5 per foot of pile driven).

Colerick drove a number of piles using the conventional $^{1}/_{4}$-inch thick asbestos cushion pads to determine their characteristics for the job. Eighteen were placed in the helmet and driven until they lost resiliency. Pads were added, and driving continued until a complete set of 24 were sitting in the helmet. After these were spent, the entire set was removed and the cycle repeated.

The rest of the job used the CMI pads. Four were initially installed and driven until 46 piles had been placed. One pad was added and the driving continued for 184 more piles. Another pad was placed in the helmet, and the job was completed. Comparable performances for the entire job were extrapolated as follows:

	Asbestos	CMI
1. Feet driven per hour while pile driver was at work (does not consider downtime)	150	200
2. Piles driven per set of pads	15	300
3. Number of pads per set	24	6
4. Number of sets required	20	1
5. Number of set changes	20	1
6. Time required for change per set	20 mins.	4 mins.
7. Colerick cost per set	$50	Not charged

---

[4]The managers at CMI were concerned that other manufacturers might discover this new application for curled metal and enter the business before CMI could get patent protection. The company had a number of competitors, most of whom were substantially smaller than CMI and none of whom had shown a strong interest or competence in technical, market, or product development.

Although the CMI pads drove piles 33% faster than the asbestos and lasted for the entire job, Simpson felt these results were unusual. He believed that a curled metal set life of 10 times more than asbestos and a performance increase of 20% were probably more reasonable, because he was uncertain that the CMI pads in larger sizes would perform as well.

Industry Practice

Industry sources indicated that as many as 75% of pile-driving contractors owned their hammers, and most owned at least one crane and set of leads. To determine the contractors' cost of doing business, CMI studied expenses of small contractors who rented equipment for pile-driving jobs. These numbers were readily available and avoided the problem of allocating the cost of a purchased crane or hammer to a particular job.

Standard industry practice for equipment rental used a three-week month and a three-day workweek.[5] There was no explanation for this, other than tradition, but most equipment renters set their rates this way. The cost of renting the necessary equipment and the labor cost for a job similar to that performed by Colerick were estimated as shown in Table A.

Hidden costs also played an important role. For every hour actually spent driving piles, a contractor could spend 20 to 40 minutes moving the crane into position. Another 10% to 15% was added to cover scheduling delays, mistakes, and other unavoidable problems. Thus, the real cost per hour was usually substantially more than the initial figures showed. Reducing the driving time or pad changing time did not usually affect the time lost on delays and moving.

All these figures were based on a job that utilized 55-foot piles and $11\frac{1}{2}$-inch pads. Although this was a common size, much larger jobs requiring substantially bigger material were frequent. A stack of $11\frac{1}{2}$-inch asbestos pads weighed between 30 and 40 pounds; the 30-inch size could weigh seven to eight times more. Each $11\frac{1}{2}$-inch CMI pad weighed $15\frac{1}{2}$ pounds. The bigger sizes, being much more difficult to handle, could contribute significantly to unproductive time on a job. (See Exhibit 4.)

Most contracts were awarded on a revenue-per-foot basis. Thus, contractors bid by estimating the amount of time it would take to drive the specified piles the distance required by the architectural engineers. After totaling costs and adding a percentage for profit, they submitted figures broken down into dollars per foot. The cost depended on the size of the piles and the type of soil to be penetrated. The $5 per foot that Colerick charged was not atypical, but prices could be considerably greater.

---

[5]This means that a contractor who rented equipment for one calendar month was charged only the "three-week" price, but had the equipment for the whole calendar month. The same was true of the "three-day week." Contractors generally tried to use the equipment for as much time per week or per month as possible. Thus, they rented it on a "three-week" month but used it on a "4.33-week" month.

TABLE A
Equipment Rental, Labor, and Overhead Costs

	Per Standard			Average Cost
	Month	**Week**	**Per Hour**	**per Real Hour**[a]
1. Diesel hammer	$4,500–7,200	$1,500–2,400	$ 62.50–100.00	$ 34
2. Crane	8,000–10,000	2,667–3,334	111.00–140.00	52
3. Leads @ $20 per foot per month (assume 70 feet)	1,400	467	19.44	8
4. Labor[b]—3 laborers @ $6–8 per hour each			8.00–24.00	21
1 crane operator			8.00–12.00	10
1 foreman			12.00–14.00	13
5. Overhead[c] (office, trucks, oil/gas, tools, etc.)			100.00	100

(Casewriter's note: Please use average cost per real hour in all calculations, for uniformity in class discussion.)

a. These costs were calculated from a rounded midpoint of the estimates. Hammer, crane, and lead costs were obtained by dividing standard monthly costs by 4.33 weeks per month and 40 hours per week.
b. Labor was paid on a 40-hour week, and a 4.33-week month. One-shift operation (40 hours per week) was standard in the industry.
c. Most contractors calculated overhead on the basis of "working" hours, not standard hours.

Test Results

The management of CMI was extremely pleased by how well its cushion pads had performed. Not only had they lasted the entire job, eliminating the downtime required for changeover, but other advantages had become apparent. For example, after 500 feet of driving, the average temperature for the asbestos pads was between 600°F and 700°F, which created great difficulty when they had to be replaced. The crew handling them was endangered, and substantial time was wasted waiting for them to cool. (This accounted for a major portion of the time lost to changeovers.)

The CMI pads, in contrast, never went above 250°F and could be handled almost immediately with protective gloves. This indicated that substantial energy lost in heat by the asbestos pads was being used more efficiently to drive the piles with CMI pads. In addition, the outstanding resiliency of the CMI product seemed to account for a 33% faster driving time, which translated into significant savings.

In talking with construction site personnel, CMI researchers also found that most were becoming wary of the asbestos pads' well-publicized health

EXHIBIT 4
Curled Metal Cushion Pad Standard Sizes

Diameter (inches)	Thickness (inches)	Weight (pounds)
11 ½	1	15 ½
14	1	23
17 ½	1	36
19 ¾	1	48
23	1	64
30	1	110

dangers. Many had expressed a desire to use some other material and were pleased that the new pads contained no asbestos.

The CMI management was quite happy with these results; Colerick was ecstatic. Understandably, Colerick became quite anxious to buy more pads and began pressing Tom Simpson to quote prices.

A Second Test

To confirm the results from the Colerick test, CMI asked Fazio Construction to try the pads on a job in New Brighton, Pennsylvania. This job required 300 45-foot concrete piles to be driven 40 feet into the ground. Asbestos pads (11½ inches) were again used for comparison. Total job revenue was $108,000, or $9 per foot, and Fazio would have paid $40 for each set of 12 asbestos pads used. The results from this test are shown as follows:

	Asbestos	CMI
1. Feet driven per hour while pile driver was at work (does not consider downtime)	160	200
2. Piles driven per set of pads	6	300
3. Number of pads per set	12	5
4. Number of sets required	50	1
5. Number of set changes	50	1
6. Time required for change per set	20 mins.	4 mins.
7. Fazio cost per set	$40	Not Charged

The Market

Projected Size

There were virtually no statistics from which a potential U.S. market for cushion pads could be determined, so Simpson had to make several assumptions based on the information he could gather. A 1977 report by *Construction Engineering* magazine estimated that approximately 13,000 pile hammers were owned by companies directly involved in pile driving. Industry sources estimated that another 6,500 to 13,000 were leased. He assumed that this total of 19,500 to 26,000 hammers would operate about 25 weeks per year (because of seasonality) and that they would be used 30 hours per week (because of moving time, repairs, scheduling problems, and other factors).

Simpson further assumed that an average actual driving figure (including time to change pads and so on) for most jobs was 20 feet per hour, which amounted to between 290 million and 390 million feet of piles driven annually. To be conservative, he also assumed that a set of curled metal pads (four initially installed, plus two added after the originals lost some resiliency) would drive 10,000 feet.

Purchase Influences

In the pile-driving business, as in other parts of the construction industry, a number of entities participated in purchases. The CMI management was able to identify six types of influences.

1. *Pile hammer manufacturers.* A number of manufacturers sold hammers in the United States, although many were imported from Western Europe and Japan. The leading domestic producer in 1979 was Vulcan Iron Works of New Orleans, whose Model #1 had become the standard used by architectural engineers specifying equipment for a job. Simpson did not feel these manufacturers would purchase a large dollar volume of cushion pads, but they could be very influential in recommendations.

2. *Architectural/Consulting engineers.* Pile driving required significant expertise in determining the needs of a construction project. Thorough stress analysis and other mathematical analyses were necessary. Because of the risks in building the expensive projects usually supported by piles, the industry looked to architectural/consulting engineers as the ultimate authorities on all aspects of the business. Consequently, these firms were very detailed in specifying the materials and techniques to be used on a project. They always specified hammers and frequently mentioned pads. The CMI management felt that, although no sales would come from these people, they could be one of the most important purchase influences.

3. *Soil consultants.* These consultants were similar to the architectural/consulting engineers, but were consulted only on extraordinary conditions.

4. *Pile hammer distributing/Renting companies.* This group was an important influence because it provided pads to the contractors. In fact, renting companies

often included the first set of pads free. CMI management felt that these companies would handle the cushion pads they could most easily sell and might even hesitate to provide pads that enabled a contractor to return equipment faster.

5. *Engineering/Construction contractors.* The contracting portion of the industry was divided among large international firms and smaller independents. The former almost always participated in the bigger, more sophisticated jobs. Companies like Conmaco and Raymond International not only contracted to drive piles, but also designed jobs, specified material, and even manufactured their own equipment. It was clear to Simpson that if he was to succeed in getting CMI pads used on bigger, complex construction projects, CMI would have to solicit this group actively on a very sophisticated level.

6. *Independent pile-driving contractors.* These contractors represented the "frontline buying influence." Their primary objective was to make money. They were very knowledgeable about the practical aspects of pile driving, but not very sophisticated.

No national industry associations influenced this business, but some regional organizations played a minor part. Contractors and others talked freely, although few were willing to reveal competitive secrets. The company was unsure how important word-of-mouth communication would be. Very little was published about the pile-driving industry, although construction-oriented magazines like *Louisiana Contractor* occasionally reported on pile-driving contractors and their jobs. These magazines featured advertising by suppliers to the trade, mostly equipment dealers and supply houses. One industry supplier, Associated Pile and Fitting Corporation, sponsored professional-level "Piletalk" seminars in various cities, bringing designers, contractors, and equipment developers together "to discuss practical aspects of installation of driven piles."

Another potential influence was Professor R. Stephen McCormack of Pennsylvania A&M University. He had established a department to study pile driving and had become a respected authority on its theoretical aspects. Sophisticated engineering/construction firms and many architectural consultants were familiar with his work and helped support it. Cumberland management felt that his endorsement of the operational performance of CMI cushion pads would greatly enhance industry acceptance. The company submitted the pads for testing by Dr. McCormack in the fall of 1979, and although the final results were not yet available he had expressed considerable enthusiasm. Final results were expected by early 1980.

Competitive Products and Channels of Distribution

The pile-driving industry had paid very little attention to cushion pads before CMI's involvement. Everyone used them and took them for granted, but no one attempted to promote pads. No manufacturers dominated the business. In fact, most pads came unbranded, having been cut from larger pieces of asbestos or micarta by small, anonymous job shops.

Distribution of pads was also ambiguous. Hammer sales and rental outlets provided them, heavy construction supply houses carried them, pile manufacturers sometimes offered them, and a miscellaneous assortment of other outlets occasionally sold them as a service.[6] The smaller pads sold for $2 to $3 each; larger ones sold for between $5 and $10. Three dollars each was typical for $11\frac{1}{2}$-inch pads. The profit margin for a distributor was usually adequate—in the area of 30% to 40%—but the dollar profit did not compare well with that of other equipment lines. Most outlets carried pads as a necessary part of the business, but none featured them as a work-saving tool.

The CMI management felt it could be totally flexible in establishing an organization to approach the market. It toyed with the idea of a direct sales force and its own distribution outlets, but eventually began to settle on signing construction-oriented manufacturers' representatives,[7] who would sell to a variety of distributors and supply houses. The company feared an uphill struggle to convince the sales and distribution channels that there really was a market for the new pad. Management expected considerable difficulty in finding outlets willing to devote the attention necessary for success, but it also felt that once the initial barriers had been penetrated, most of the marketplace would be anxious to handle the product.

The Pricing Decision

Simpson had projected cost data developed by his manufacturing engineers. Exhibit 5 shows two sets of numbers: one utilized existing equipment; the other reflected the purchase of $50,000 of permanent tooling. In both cases, the estimated volume was 250 cushion pads per month. Additional equipment could be added at a cost of $75,000 per 250 pads per month of capacity, including permanent tooling like that which could be purchased for $50,000.

Both sets of numbers were based on the assumption that only one pad size would be manufactured; in other words, the numbers in the $11\frac{1}{2}$-inch size were based on manufacturing only this size for a year. This was done because CMI had no idea of the potential sales mix among product sizes. Management knew that $11\frac{1}{2}$ inches was the most popular size, but the information available on popularity of the other sizes was vague. CMI accounting personnel believed these numbers would not vary dramatically with a mix of sizes.

Corporate management usually burdened CMI products with a charge equal to 360% of direct labor to cover the overhead of its large engineering staff. Simpson was uncertain how this would apply to the new product, because little engineering had been done and excess capacity was to be used initially for manufacturing. Although it was allocated on a variable basis, he thought he

---

[6]Supply houses were "hardware stores" for contractors and carried a general line of products, including lubricants, work gloves, and maintenance supplies. Distributors, in contrast, tended to be more equipment oriented and to sell a narrower line of merchandise.

[7]Manufacturers' representatives were agents (sometimes single people, sometimes organizations) who sold non-competing products for commission. They typically did *not* take title to the merchandise and did *not* extend credit.

EXHIBIT 5
Two Sets of Projected Manufacturing Costs

	Size					
	11½"	14"	17½"	19¾"	23"	30"
Estimates per Pad with Existing Equipment						
Variable						
Material	$ 15.64	$ 20.57	$ 31.81	$ 40.39	$ 53.16	$ 95.69
Labor	28.80	33.07	50.02	57.07	69.16	118.36
Total variable	44.44	53.64	81.83	97.46	122.32	214.05
Fixed factory overhead @ 360% direct labor	103.68	119.05	180.07	205.45	248.98	426.10
Total manufacturing cost	$148.12	$172.69	$261.90	$302.91	$371.30	$640.15
Estimates with Purchase of $50,000 of Permanent Tooling						
Variable						
Material	$ 15.64	$ 20.57	$ 31.81	$ 40.39	$ 53.16	$ 95.69
Labor	11.64	15.25	21.85	26.95	30.57	56.09
Total variable	27.28	35.82	53.66	67.34	83.73	151.78
Fixed factory overhead @ 360% direct labor	41.90	54.90	78.66	97.02	110.05	201.92
Total manufacturing cost	$ 69.18	$ 90.72	$132.32	$164.36	$193.78	$353.70

Note: Estimated volume was 250 cushion pads per month.

might consider the overhead "fixed" for his analysis. Corporate management expected a contribution margin after all manufacturing costs of 40% to 50% of selling price.

Simpson was enthusiastic about the potential success of this new product. The Engineered Products Division was particularly pleased to offer something with such high dollar potential, especially since in the past, a "large customer" of the division had purchased only about $10,000 per year.

He was still uncertain how to market the pads and how to reach the various purchase influences. Advertising and promotion also concerned him because there were no precedents for this product or market.

For the moment, however, Simpson's primary consideration was pricing. He had promised to call Colerick Foundation Company by the end of the week, and Minicucci was anxious to review his decision with him. He hoped other prospects would be calling as soon as word about the pads' test performance got around.

Curtis Automotive Hoist

Gordon H.G.
McDougall

I n September 1990, Mark Curtis, president of Curtis Automotive Hoist (CAH), a Canadian company, had just finished reading a feasibility report on entering the European market in 1991. CAH manufactured surface automotive hoists, a product used by garages, service stations, and other repair shops to lift cars for servicing. The report, prepared by CAH's marketing manager, Pierre Gagnon, outlined the opportunities in the European Community and the entry options available.

Mr. Curtis was not sure if CAH was ready for this move. While the company had been successful in expanding sales into the United States market, Mr. Curtis wondered if this success could be repeated in Europe. He thought, with more effort, that sales could be increased in the United States. On the other hand, there were some positive aspects to the European idea. He began reviewing the information in preparation for the meeting the following day with Mr. Gagnon.

Curtis Automotive Hoist

Mr. Curtis, a design engineer, had worked for eight years for the Canadian subsidiary of a U.S. automotive hoist manufacturer. During those years, he had spent considerable time designing an above-ground (or surface) automotive hoist. Although Mr. Curtis was very enthusiastic about the unique aspects of the hoist, including a scissor lift and wheel alignment pads, senior management expressed no interest in the idea. In 1980, Mr. Curtis left the company to start his own business with the express purpose of designing and manufacturing the hoist. He left with the good wishes of his previous employer who had no objections to his plans to start a new business.

Over the next three years, Mr. Curtis obtained financing from a venture capital firm, opened a plant in Lachine, Quebec, and began manufacturing the marketing hoist, called the Curtis Lift (*Exhibit 1*).

From the beginning, Mr. Curtis had taken considerable pride in the development and marketing of the Curtis Lift. The original design included a scissor

At the time of this writing, Gordon H.G. McDougall was a professor at the School of Business and Economics at Wilfrid Laurier University, Waterloo, Ontario, Canada.

27

EXHIBIT 1
Examples of Automotive Hoists

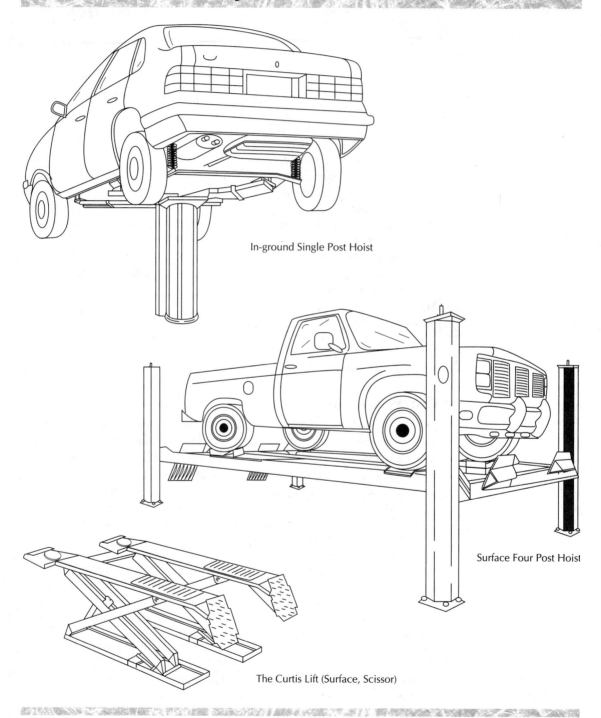

In-ground Single Post Hoist

Surface Four Post Hoist

The Curtis Lift (Surface, Scissor)

lift and a safety locking mechanism that allowed the hoist to be raised to any level and locked in place. As well, the scissor lift offered easy access for the mechanic to work on the raised vehicle. Because the hoist was fully hydraulic and had no chains or pulleys, it required little maintenance. Another key feature was the alignment turn plates that were an integral part of the lift. The turn plates meant that mechanics could accurately and easily perform wheel alignment jobs. Because it was a surface lift, it could be installed in a garage in less than a day.

Mr. Curtis continually made improvements to the product, including adding more safety features. In fact, the Curtis Lift was considered a leader in automotive lift safety. Safety was an important factor in the automotive hoist market. Although hoists seldom malfunctioned, when they did, it often resulted in a serious accident.

The Curtis Lift developed a reputation in the industry as the "Cadillac" of hoists; the unit was judged by many as superior to competitive offerings because of its design, the quality of the workmanship, the safety features, the ease of installation, and the five-year warranty. Mr. Curtis held four patents on the Curtis Lift including the lifting mechanism on the scissor design and a safety locking mechanism. A number of versions of the product were designed that made the Curtis Lift suitable (depending on the model) for a variety of tasks, including rustproofing, muffler repairs, and general mechanical repairs.

In 1981, CAH sold 23 hoists and had sales of $172,500. During the early years, the majority of sales were to independent service stations and garages specializing in wheel alignment in the Quebec and Ontario market. Most of the units were sold by Mr. Gagnon, who was hired in 1982 to handle the marketing side of the operation. In 1984, Mr. Gagnon began using distributors to sell the hoist to a wider geographic market in Canada. In 1986, he signed an agreement with a large automotive wholesaler to represent CAH in the U.S. market. By 1989, the company sold 1,054 hoists and had sales of $9,708,000 (*Exhibit 2*). In 1989, about 60% of sales were to the United States with the remaining 40% to the Canadian market.

Industry

Approximately 49,000 hoists were sold each year in North America. Typically, hoists were purchased by an automotive outlet that serviced or repaired cars including new car dealers, used car dealers, specialty shops (for example, muffler shops, transmission, wheel alignment), chains (for example, Firestone, Goodyear, Canadian Tire), and independent garages. It was estimated that new car dealers purchased 30% of all units sold in a given year. In general, the specialty shops focused on one type of repair, such as mufflers or rustproofing, while "non-specialty" outlets handled a variety of repairs. While there was some crossover, in general CAH competed in the specialty shop segment and, in particular, those shops that dealt with wheel alignment. This included chains such as Firestone and Canadian Tire as well as new car dealers (for example, Ford) who devote a certain percentage of their lifts to the wheel alignment business and independent garages who specialized in wheel alignment.

EXHIBIT 2
Curtis Automotive Hoist—Selected Financial Statistics
(1987–1989)

	1987	1988	1989
Sales	$6,218,000	$7,454,000	$9,708,000
Cost of sales	4,540,000	5,541,000	6,990,000
Contribution	1,678,000	1,913,000	2,718,000
Marketing expenses°	507,000	510,000	530,000
Administrative expenses	810,000	820,000	840,000
Earnings before tax	361,000	583,000	1,348,000
Units sold	723	847	1,054

Source: Company records.
°Marketing expenses in 1989 included advertising ($70,000), four salespeople ($240,000), marketing manager and three sales support staff ($220,000).

The purpose of a hoist was to lift an automobile into a position where a mechanic or service person could easily work on the car. Because different repairs required different positions, a wide variety of hoists had been developed to meet specific needs. For example, a muffler repair shop required a hoist that allowed the mechanic to gain easy access to the underside of the car. Similarly, a wheel alignment job required a hoist that offered a level platform where the wheels could be adjusted as well as providing easy access for the mechanic. Mr. Gagnon estimated that 85% of CAH's sales were to the wheel alignment market to service centers such as Firestone, Goodyear, and Canadian Tire and to independent garages that specialized in wheel alignment. About 15% of sales were made to customers who used the hoist for general mechanical repairs.

Purchase Behavior

Firms purchasing hoists were part of an industry called the automobile aftermarket. This industry was involved in supplying parts and service for new and used cars and was worth over $54 billion at retail in 1989, while servicing the approximately 11 million cars on the road in Canada. The industry was large and diverse; there were over 4,000 new car dealers in Canada, over 400 Canadian Tire stores, over 100 stores in each of the Firestone and Goodyear chains, and over 200 stores in the Rust Check chain.

The purchase of an automotive hoist was often an important decision for the service station owner or dealer. Because the price of hoists ranged from $3,000 to $15,000, it was a capital expense for most businesses.

For the owner/operator of a new service center or car dealership the decision involved determining what type of hoist was required, then what brand would best suit the company. Most new service centers or car dealerships had multiple bays for servicing cars. In these cases, the decision would involve what types of hoists were required (for example, in-ground, surface). Often more than one type of hoist was purchased, depending on the service center/dealership needs.

Experienced garage owners seeking a replacement hoist (the typical hoist had a useful life of 10 to 13 years) would usually determine what products were available and then make a decision. If the garage owners were also mechanics, they would probably be aware of two or three types of hoists but would not be very knowledgeable about the brands or products currently available. Garage owners or dealers who were not mechanics probably knew very little about hoists. The owners of car or service dealerships often bought the product that was recommended and/or approved by the parent company.

Competition

Sixteen companies competed in the automotive lift market in North America: four Canadian and twelve United States firms. Hoists were subject to import duties. Duties on hoists entering the U.S. market from Canada were 2.4% of the selling price; from the U.S. entering Canada the import duty was 7.9%. With the advent of the Free Trade Agreement in 1989, the duties between the two countries would be phased out over a ten-year period. For Mr. Curtis, the import duties had never played a part in any decisions: the fluctuating exchange rates between the two countries had a far greater impact on selling prices.

A wide variety of hoists were manufactured in the industry. The two basic types of hoists were in-ground and surface. As the names imply, in-ground hoists required that a pit be dug "in-ground" where the piston that raised the hoist was installed. In-ground hoists were either single post or multiple post, were permanent, and obviously could not be moved. In-ground lifts constituted approximately 21% of total lift sales in 1989 (*Exhibit* 3). Surface lifts were installed on a flat surface, usually concrete. Surface lifts came in two basic types, post lift hoists and scissor hoists. Surface lifts, compared to in-ground lifts, were easier to install and could be moved, if necessary. Surface lifts constituted 79% of total lift sales in 1989. Within each type of hoist (for example, post lift surface hoists), there were numerous variations in terms of size, shape, and lifting capacity.

The industry was dominated by two large U.S. firms, AHV Lifts and Berne Manufacturing, who together held approximately 60% of the market. AHV Lifts, the largest firm with approximately 40% of the market and annual sales of about $60 million, offered a complete line of hoists (that is, in-ground and surface) but focused primarily on the in-ground market and the two post surface markets. AHV Lifts was the only company that had its own direct sales force; all other companies used (1) only wholesalers or (2) a combination of wholesalers and a company sales force. AHV Lifts offered standard hoists with few extra features and competed primarily on price. Berne Manufacturing, with a market share of approximately 20%, also competed in the in-ground and two post surface markets. It used a combination of wholesalers and company salespeople and, like AHV Lifts, competed primarily on price.

EXHIBIT 3
**North American Automotive Lift Units Sales, By Type
(1987–1989)**

	1987	1988	1989
In-ground			
Single post	5,885	5,772	5,518
Multiple post	4,812	6,625	5,075
Surface			
Two post	27,019	28,757	28,923
Four post	3,862	3,162	3,745
Scissor	2,170	2,258	2,316
Other	4,486	3,613	3,695
Total	48,234	50,187	49,272

Source: Company records.

Most of the remaining firms in the industry were companies that operated in a regional market (for example, California or British Columbia) and/or offered a limited product line (for example, four post surface hoists).

Curtis had two competitors that manufactured scissor lifts. AHV Lift marketed a scissor hoist that had a different lifting mechanism and did not include the safety locking features of the Curtis Lift. On average, the AHV scissor lift sold for about 20% less than the Curtis Lift. The second competitor, Mete Lift, was a small regional company with sales in California and Oregon. It had a design that was very similar to the Curtis Lift but lacked some of its safety features. The Mete Lift, regarded as a well-manufactured product, sold for about 5% less than the Curtis Lift.

Marketing Strategy

As of early 1990, CAH had developed a reputation for a quality product backed by good service in the hoist lift market, primarily in the wheel alignment segment.

The distribution system employed by CAH reflected the need to engage in extensive personal selling. Three types of distributors were used: a company sales force, Canadian distributors, and a U.S. automotive wholesaler. The company sales force consisted of four salespeople and Mr. Gagnon. Their main task was to service large "direct" accounts. The initial step was to get the Curtis Lift approved by large chains and manufacturers and then, having received the approval, to sell to individual dealers or operators. For example, if General Motors approved the hoist, then CAH could sell it to individual General Motors dealers. CAH sold directly to the individual dealers of a number of large accounts including General Motors, Ford, Chrysler, Petro-Canada, Firestone, and Goodyear. CAH had been successful in obtaining manufacturer approval from the big three automobile manufacturers in both Canada and the United States. As well, CAH had also received approval from service companies such as Canadian Tire and Goodyear. To date, CAH had not been rejected by any major account, but, in some cases, the approval process had taken over four years.

In total, the company sales force generated about 25% of the unit sales each year. Sales to the large "direct" accounts in the United States went through CAH's U.S. wholesaler.

The Canadian distributors sold, installed, and serviced units across Canada. These distributors handled the Curtis Lift and carried a line of noncompetitive automotive equipment products (for example, engine diagnostic equipment, wheel balancing equipment) and noncompetitive lifts. These distributors focused on the smaller chains and the independent service stations and garages.

The U.S. wholesaler sold a complete product line to service stations as well as manufacturing some equipment. The Curtis Lift was one of five different types of lifts that the wholesaler sold. Although the wholesaler provided CAH with extensive distribution in the United States, the Curtis Lift was a minor product within the wholesaler's total line. While Mr. Gagnon did not have any actual figures, he thought that the Curtis Lift probably accounted for less than 20% of the total lift sales of the U.S. wholesaler.

Both Mr. Curtis and Mr. Gagnon felt that the U.S. market had unrealized potential. With a population of 248 million people and over 140 million registered vehicles, the U.S. market was over ten times the size of the Canadian market (population of 26 million, approximately 11 million vehicles). Mr. Gagnon noted that the six New England states (population over 13 million), the three largest mid-Atlantic states (population over 38 million), and the three largest mid-eastern states (population over 32 million) were all within a day's drive of the factory in Lachine. Mr. Curtis and Mr. Gagnon had considered setting up a sales office in New York to service these states, but they were concerned that the U.S. wholesaler would not be willing to relinquish any of its territory. They had also considered working more closely with the wholesaler to encourage it to "push" the Curtis Lift. It appeared that the wholesaler's major objective was to sell a hoist, not necessarily the Curtis Lift.

CAH distributed a catalogue type package with products, uses, prices, and other required information for both distributors and users. In addition, CAH advertised in trade publications (for example, *Service Station & Garage Management*), and Mr. Gagnon travelled to trade shows in Canada and the U.S. to promote the Curtis Lift.

In 1989, Curtis Lift sold for an average retail price of $10,990 and CAH received, on average $9,210 for each unit sold. This average reflected the mix of sales through the three distribution channels: (1) direct (where CAH received 100% of the selling price), (2) Canadian distributors (where CAH received 80% of the selling price), and (3) the U.S. wholesaler (where CAH received 78% of the selling price).

Both Mr. Curtis and Mr. Gagnon felt that the company's success to date was based on a strategy of offering a superior product that was primarily targeted to the needs of specific customers. The strategy stressed continual product improvements, quality workmanship, and service. Personal selling was a key aspect of the strategy; salespeople could show customers the benefits of the Curtis Lift over competing products.

The European Market

Against this background, Mr. Curtis had been thinking of ways to continue the rapid growth of the company. One possibility that kept coming up was the promise and potential of the European market. The fact that Europe would become a single market in 1992 suggested that it was an opportunity that should at least be explored. With this in mind, Mr. Curtis asked Mr. Gagnon to prepare a report on the possibility of CAH entering the European market. The highlights of Mr. Gagnon's report follow.

History of the European Community

The European Community (EC) stemmed from the 1957 "Treaty of Rome" in which six countries decided it would be in their best interest to form an internal market. These countries were France, Germany, Italy, Belgium, Luxembourg, and the Netherlands. By 1983, the EC consisted of 12 countries (the additional six were Denmark, Greece, Ireland, Portugal, Spain, and the United Kingdom) with a population of over 325 million people.[1] In 1992, virtually all barriers (physical, technical, and fiscal) in the EC were scheduled to be removed for companies located within the EC. This would allow the free movement of goods, persons, services, and capital.

In the last five years many North American and Japanese firms had established themselves in the EC. The reasoning for this was twofold. First, these companies regarded the community as an opportunity to increase global market share and profits. The market was attractive because of its sheer size and lack of internal barriers. Second, in 1992, companies that were established within the community were subject to protection from external competition via EC protectionism tariffs, local contender, and reciprocity requirements. EC protectionism tariffs were only temporary, and would be removed at a later date. It would be possible for companies to export to or establish in the community after 1992, but there was some risk attached.

Market Potential

The key indicator of the potential market for the Curtis Lift hoist was the number of passenger cars and commercial vehicles in use in a particular country. Four countries in Europe had more than 20 million vehicles in use, with France and West Germany having the largest domestic fleets of more than 30 million vehicles followed by Italy and the United Kingdom (*Exhibit 4*). The number of vehicles was an important indicator because the more vehicles in use

---

[1]As of September 1990, West Germany and East Germany were in the process of unification. East Germany had a population of approximately 17 million people.

EXHIBIT 4
Number of Vehicles (1988) and Population (1989)

Country	Vehicles in Use (000s)		New Vehicle Registrations (000s)	Population (000s)
	Passenger	Commercial		
West Germany	28,304	1,814	2,960	60,900
France	29,970	4,223	2,635	56,000
Italy	22,500	1,897	2,308	57,400
United Kingdom	20,605	2,915	2,531	57,500
Spain	9,750	1,750	1,172	39,400

meant a greater number of service and repair facilities that needed vehicle hoists and potentially the Curtis Lift.

An indicator of the future vehicle repair and service market was the number of new vehicle registrations. The registration of new vehicles was important as this maintained the number of vehicles in use by replacing cars that had been retired. Again, West Germany had the most new cars registered in 1988 and was followed in order by France, the United Kingdom, and Italy.

Based primarily on the fact that a large domestic market was important for initial growth, the selection of a European country should be limited to the "Big Four" industrialized nations: West Germany, France, the United Kingdom, or Italy. In an international survey companies from North America and Europe ranked European countries on a scale of 1 to 100 on market potential and investment site potential. The results showed that West Germany was favoured for both market potential and investment site opportunities while France, the United Kingdom, and Spain placed second, third, and fourth, respectively. Italy did not place in the top four in either market or investment site potential. However, Italy had a large number of vehicles in use, had the second largest population in Europe, and was an acknowledged leader in car technology and production.

Little information was available on the competition within Europe. There was, as yet, no dominant manufacturer as was the case in North America. At this time, there was one firm in Germany that manufactured a scissor-type lift. The firm sold most of its units within the German market. The only other available information was that 22 firms in Italy manufactured vehicle lifts.

Investment Options

Mr. Gagnon felt that CAH had three options for expansion into the European market: licensing, joint venture, or direct investment. The licensing option was a real possibility as a French firm had expressed an interest in manufacturing the Curtis Lift.

In June 1990, Mr. Gagnon had attended a trade show in Detroit to promote the Curtis Lift. At the show, he met Phillipe Beaupre, the marketing manager for Bar Maisse, a French manufacturer of wheel alignment equipment. The firm, located in Chelles, France, sold a range of wheel alignment equipment throughout Europe. The best-selling product was an electronic modular aligner that enabled a mechanic to utilize a sophisticated computer system to align the wheels of a car. Mr. Beaupre was seeking a North American distributor for the modular aligner and other products manufactured by Bar Maisse.

At the show, Mr. Gagnon and Mr. Beaupre had a casual conversation in which each explained what their respective companies manufactured, they exchanged company brochures and business cards, and both went on to other exhibits. The next day, Mr. Beaupre sought out Mr. Gagnon and asked if he might be interested in having Bar Maisse manufacture and market the Curtis Lift in Europe. Mr. Beaupre felt the lift would complement Bar Maisse's product line and the licensing would be of mutual benefit to both parties. They agreed to pursue the idea. Upon his return to Lachine, Mr. Gagnon told Mr. Curtis about these discussions, and they agreed to explore this possibility.

Mr. Gagnon called a number of colleagues in the industry and asked them what they knew about Bar Maisse. About half had not heard of the company, but those who had, commented favourably on the quality of its products. One colleague, with European experience, knew the company well and said that Bar Maisse's management had integrity and would make a good partner. In July, Mr. Gagnon sent a letter to Mr. Beaupre stating that CAH was interested in further discussions and enclosed various company brochures including price lists and technical information on the Curtis Lift. In late August, Mr. Beaupre responded stating that Bar Maisse would like to enter a three-year licensing agreement with CAH to manufacture the Curtis Lift in Europe. In exchange for the manufacturing rights, Bar Maisse was prepared to pay a royalty rate of 5% of gross sales. Mr. Gagnon had not yet responded to this proposal.

A second possibility was a joint venture. Mr. Gagnon had wondered if it might not be better for CAH to offer a counter proposal to Bar Maisse for a joint venture. He had not worked out any details, but Mr. Gagnon felt that CAH would learn more about the European market and probably make more money if they were an active partner in Europe. Mr. Gagnon's idea was a 50-50 proposal where the two parties shared the investment and the profits. He envisaged a situation where Bar Maisse would manufacture the Curtis Lift in their plant with technical assistance from CAH. Mr. Gagnon also thought that CAH could get involved in the marketing of the lift through the Bar Maisse distribution system. Further, he thought that the Curtis Lift, with proper marketing, could gain a reasonable share of the European market. If that happened Mr. Gagnon felt that CAH was likely to make greater returns with a joint venture.

The third option was direct investment where CAH would establish a manufacturing facility and set up a management group to market the lift. Mr. Gagnon had contacted a business acquaintance who had recently been involved in manufacturing fabricated steel sheds in Germany. On the basis of discussions with his acquaintance, Mr. Gagnon estimated the costs involved in setting up a plant in Europe at: (1) $250,000 for capital equipment (welding machines, cranes, other equipment), (2) $200,000 in incremental costs to set the plant up, and (3) carrying costs to cover $1,000,000 in inventory and accounts receivable. While the actual costs of renting a building for the factory would depend on the site location, he estimated that annual building rent including heat, light, and insurance would be about $80,000. Mr. Gagnon recognized these estimates were guidelines but he felt that the estimates were probably within 20% of actual costs.

The Decision

As Mr. Curtis considered the contents of the report, a number of thoughts crossed his mind. He began making notes concerning the European possibility and the future of the company.

- If CAH decided to enter Europe, Mr. Gagnon would be the obvious choice to head up the "direct investment" option or the "joint venture" option. Mr. Curtis felt that Mr. Gagnon had been instrumental in the success of the company to date.
- While CAH had the financial resources to go ahead with the direct investment option, the joint venture would spread the risk (and the return) over the two companies.
- CAH had built its reputation on designing and manufacturing a quality product. Regardless of the option chosen, Mr. Curtis wanted the firm's reputation to be maintained.
- Either the licensing agreement or the joint venture appeared to build on the two companies' strengths; Bar Maisse had knowledge of the market and CAH had the product. What troubled Mr. Curtis was whether this apparent synergy would work or would Bar Maisse seek to control the operation.
- It was difficult to estimate sales under any of the options. With the first two (licensing and joint venture), it would depend on the effort and expertise of Bar Maisse; with the third option, it would depend on Mr. Gagnon.
- CAH's sales in the U.S. market could be increased if the U.S. wholesaler would "push" the Curtis Lift. Alternatively, the establishment of a sales office in New York to cover the eastern states could also increase sales.

As Mr. Curtis reflected on the situation he knew he should probably get additional information—but it wasn't obvious exactly what information would help him make a "yes" or "no" decision. He knew one thing for sure—he was going to keep his company on a "fast growth" track—and at tomorrow's meeting he and Mr. Gagnon would decide how to do it.

Dell Computer Corporation Reformulation Strategy

Robert A. Peterson

Marisa Manheimer

"Well, I'm certainly glad that's behind us," Michael Dell muttered to himself as he walked back to his office. "Now it's time to really concentrate on the future of the company and achieve our 50 percent sales growth goal this fiscal year."

Michael Dell, Chairman and Chief Executive Officer of Dell Computer Corporation, had just released his firm's second-quarter financial results. For the period May–July, 1993, Dell Computer had record revenues of $701 million, but the company experienced a first-ever quarterly loss of $75.7 million, and gross margins declined 16.2 percent (22.7 percent to 6.5 percent) compared to the second quarter of the previous fiscal year. Much of the loss was due to a one-time restructuring charge, but even without the restructuring charge the company would not have been profitable.

Dell Computer Corporation had closed out its 1993 fiscal year January 31, 1993, as the world's fifth-largest personal computer (PC) company, with sales in excess of $2 billion and profit of more than $100 million. Even so, the downturn in the world economy was beginning to take its toll and the marketing activities of major competitors in late 1992, such as IBM and Compaq, began to undermine Dell's competitive position by early 1993. These uncontrollable events, when combined with certain product-line gaps, lack of inventory control, and a shortage of experienced upper-level managers, together with rapid international growth, culminated in the company's first-ever quarterly loss. As Joel Kocher, Dell President of Worldwide Sales and Marketing, so aptly noted, competition in the PC industry is no longer limited to technology. Instead, partly because of impending market saturation for desktop computers, the focus is on "inventory, execution, and supply." Indeed, due to the industry's adoption of open standards (essentially initial standard industry components popularized by IBM), few proprietary technologies exist anymore with respect to desktop personal computers.

This case was prepared by Professor Robert A. Peterson, of the University of Texas at Austin, with the assistance of Marisa Manheimer, as a basis for class discussion and is not designed to illustrate effective or ineffective handling of an administrative situation. Unless otherwise indicated, the case describes the situation at Dell and for the industry as of late 1993.

EXHIBIT 1
Dell Computer Corporation's Net Sales, Fiscal Years 1985–1993[a] (Thousands of Dollars)

	1985[b]	1986	1987	1988	1989	1990	1991	1992	1993
Domestic	$6,195	$33,685	$69,450	$153,074	$218,204	$300,257	$358,877	$566,392	$1,283,899
International	—	—	—	5,963	39,606	88,301	187,358	323,547	730,025

[a]Fiscal years generally run February through January.
[b]May 1984–January 31, 1985.
Source: Annual reports of the company.

The Company

The story of Dell Computer Corporation is the story of Michael Dell and his strategic vision. As a college freshman in 1983, Michael Dell began selling personal computer disk drive kits and related parts to enthusiasts at local meetings of PC users. Within a few months, he was selling "gray market" IBM PCs out of his dormitory room. By April 1984, Dell had dropped out of college and was devoting all of his energies to his burgeoning business. Operating out of a small storefront, he began to manufacture and market some of the first IBM "clones" under the brand name PC's Limited. By 1986, PC's Limited had grown to 400 employees and reached $69.5 million in annual revenues.

In 1988, at the age of 23, Dell took his company public. By the end of January 1990, annual sales had reached $388.6 million (see Exhibits 1 and 2 for pertinent sales and operating information), and Michael Dell was named *Inc. Magazine's* Entrepreneur of the Year. The following year *Fortune* listed Dell Computer Corporation as one of the 100 fastest-growing companies in the United States. During 1992 the company continued to expand both in the United States and internationally. By the end of 1992, Dell Computer employed approximately 4,700 people worldwide and had achieved sales as shown below. Also in 1992, Dell had its first "3 for 2" stock split and made the Fortune 500 list of top industrial corporations in the United States.

	Dell Computer Sales (in millions)	
Customer Group	**F1992**	**F1993**
Major corporate, government, and education accounts	$416	$ 953
VARs and systems integrators	137	274
Medium/small businesses and individuals	337	787
Total	$890	$2,014

Source: Company records.

EXHIBIT 2
Dell Computer Corporation Operating Results, Fiscal Years 1987–1993[a]

	Percentage of Net Sales						
	1987	**1988**	**1989**	**1990**	**1991**	**1992**	**1993**
Net sales	100.0%	100.0%	100.0%	100.0%	100.0%	100.0%	100.0%
Cost of sales	76.9	68.5	68.5	71.8	66.7	68.3	77.7
Gross profit	23.1	31.5	31.5	28.2	33.3	31.7	22.3
Operating expenses							
Marketing and sales	10.2	13.0	15.0	16.0	16.2	16.1	11.0
General and administrative	4.6	4.2	4.8	4.5	4.8	4.4	2.3
Research, development, and engineering	2.3	3.5	2.8	4.4	4.1	3.7	2.1
Total operating expenses	17.1	20.7	22.6	24.9	25.1	24.2	15.4
Operating income	6.0	10.8	8.9	3.3	8.2	7.5	6.9
Other expenses	0.4	1.3	0.7	1.2	3.2	1.8	1.9
Income before taxes	5.6	9.5	8.2	2.1	5.0	5.7	5.0

[a]Fiscal years generally run February through January.
Source: Annual reports of the company.

The Strategic Vision

According to analysts who follow the company, the success of Dell Computer Corporation can be traced to Michael Dell's strategic vision of a high-performance/low-price personal computer marketed directly to end users. Dell computers were not designed to be the most powerful or the most technically advanced. Instead, they were intentionally designed to be of higher-than-average quality and very reliable. Likewise, Dell computers were not designed to be the lowest-cost PCs available. The key strategic concepts of Michael Dell can be stated as "relatively high performance" and "relatively low price" combined in such a fashion as to produce exceptionally high value for buyers.

However, perhaps more important than the high-performance-to-price ratio was the manner in which Dell Computer marketed its products. Rather than marketing its computers through one of the currently existing (indirect) distribution channels—traditional dealers, value-added resellers (VARs), and so forth—or by means of a sales force, Dell Computer initially marketed its computers directly to end users by means of direct-response advertising in selected computer magazines. Later it added telemarketing activities, an indirect sales force, and field sales representatives. Initially all products were distributed directly from the Dell factory to the end user by UPS or Airborne Express. This provided a single source for complete computing solutions, and total account-ability to customers. No intermediaries, wholesalers, or retailers were utilized in the initial distribution channel. The industry recognized Dell as the pioneer of a unique form of direct-relationship marketing.

Interestingly enough, Michael Dell's direct marketing approach did not spring full-grown from his imagination. At age 13, he had already experimented with a mail-order stamp-collecting business.

As Dell Computer grew rapidly through its manufacturer-direct market-ing strategy, its strategic vision evolved to include three key elements: main-taining a direct relationship with the end users of its products, developing high-quality products that are custom-configured and sold at reasonable prices, and providing industry-leading service and support.

The first key element, maintaining direct relationships with the end users of its products, is standard in all distribution channels used by Dell. For exam-ple, even the newer indirect channel (added in 1991), through which Dell sells PCs to end users by means of mass merchandisers, requires that all end-user buyers register their computers with Dell at the time of purchase. This process enables Dell to enter the new buyer into its catalog/mail-out database and immediately begin a direct relationship with the buyer.

The second key element of Dell Computer's success is its commitment to developing high-quality products that are custom-configured and sold at rea-sonable prices. The company prides itself on providing the highest-quality com-ponents and testing standards in the industry, and through innovative market segmentation, it offers a combination of competitively priced products and pro-motional bundles targeting specific market segments.

The final key aspect of Michael Dell's strategic vision that contributed to the success of Dell Computer Corporation is the unrelenting emphasis on the customer. Since customer satisfaction is dogma at Dell Computer, industry-leading warranty packages, installation, maintenance, repair services, and user support have always been first priority. Dell was the first company in the indus-try to offer manufacturer-direct toll-free, 24-hour technical support service and next-day, on-site, service programs that have become standard in the industry.

Distinctive Competency

The distinctive competency of Dell Computer in its early years resided in its innovative direct selling model more than anything else. Indeed, in several interviews in the 1980s, Michael Dell stressed his belief that the company's dis-tribution channel was *the* most efficient way to market personal computers. Even the company's advertising reflected Dell's belief. For example, in the mid-1980s, company print advertisements contained a picture of a computer store with a red X drawn through it and featured the line "and you don't have to go there to buy it." (See Exhibit 3 for an example of a Dell Computer Corporation advertisement used in 1990.)

The success of the Dell selling model opened the door to literally hun-dreds of small PC manufacturers who found they only needed a telephone

EXHIBIT 3
Dell Computer Corporation Print Advertisement in 1990

HERE'S OUR NEW STORE, SO YOU'LL NEVER HAVE TO GO TO THEIR STORE AGAIN.

When you go out to buy computers, here's what you usually get:

A beefy mark-up.

Pressure to buy something you don't want.

That crummy feeling of not knowing what you're getting, because the salesman isn't sure what he's selling.

And, when there are problems, some stranger with a screwdriver taking your computer apart.

When you call Dell, on the other hand, here's what you get:

A frank talk with computer experts about what you need, and a recommendation about the best overall package for you.

$1749

THE DELL SYSTEM 316SX 16 MHz 386™SX.
The perfect low profile mainstream computer.

• Intel 80386SX microprocessor running at 16 MHz. • Standard 1 MB of RAM, optional 512 KB, 640 KB or 2 MB of RAM • expandable to 16 MB (8 MB on system board). • Page mode interleaved memory architecture. • LIM 4.0 support for memory over 640 KB. • Socket for Intel 80387™SX math coprocessor. • 5.25" 1.2 MB or 3.5" 1.44 MB diskette drive. • Enhanced 101-key keyboard. • 1 parallel and 2 serial ports. • 3 full-sized 16-bit slots. • 12-month On-Site Service Contract provided by Xerox.◊
Commercial Lease Plan. *Lease for as low as $82/month.* ◊Xerox Extended Service Plan pricing starts at $220.
40MB VGA Color Plus System $2,199
Price listed includes 1 MB of RAM. 20, 40, 80, 100 and 190 MB hard drive configurations available. | AD CODE 11X24 |

TO ORDER, CALL
800-283-1490
IN CANADA, CALL 800-387-5752

FOR NETWORK/UNIX•INFO
800-678-UNIX
HOURS: 7 AM-7 PM CT M-F 9 AM-4 PM CT SAT

Customer configuration, with a long list of options including monitors, memory sizes, software, accessories and peripherals.

Service—often voted the best in the industry—by computer experts who know our computers inside and out.

A variety of financing and leasing◊ options.

A firm promise to build your computers, a configured systems test, and shipment by two-day air standard.

A 30-day, no questions asked, money back guarantee.

A one-year limited warranty.

And a great price, with no mark-up.

Call us now. Why waste a trip when everything you need is right in front of you?

**DELL
COMPUTER
CORPORATION**

Above and beyond the call.

number and/or a post office box to enter the marketplace. Ultimately Dell Computer's success prompted even its largest competitors to expand into this direct channel. In 1992 both IBM and Compaq began offering new PC lines through direct distribution channels. IBM created a direct sales operation in late 1992 called Ambra, whereas Compaq created Compaq Direct in attempts to "Dell-ize" their selling methods.

What currently keeps Dell Computer competitive in the PC market is its ability to efficiently deliver new value-added services. Because it is becoming more difficult to distinguish among personal computers based on technology alone, and customers expect more value at lower prices, Dell approaches the PC desktop market, which has effectively become a commodity market due to the industry's adoption of open standards, with an array of custom-made products and services, which clearly sets the company apart from its competitors.

In mid-1993, Dell Computer launched a unique marketing campaign to further its market leadership in producing customized computing solutions for individual needs. This campaign was based on a new segmentation scheme wherein customers are profiled according to their "techno-type." Based on extensive research into customer computing needs and concerns, PC-use environment, and decision-making factors, Dell Computer structured the market for personal computers along two dimensions: extent to which advanced PC features are required and extent of connectivity (networking) requirements.

Company Sales Organization

As of mid-1993, Dell Computer Corporation had approximately 5,500 employees. The sales organization consists of Dell North America and Dell International. Although the majority of sales revenues are derived from the North American operation, significant growth is also occurring internationally. In the first quarter of the 1994 fiscal year (February–April 1993), international sales represented 36 percent of total company revenues. This compared with 23 percent in the first quarter of fiscal year 1990. By the end of 1992 Dell was marketing personal computers in 95 different countries, either through selected distributors or wholly owned and operated subsidiaries. For example, international subsidiaries exist in Canada, France, Sweden, Germany, the United Kingdom, Australia, Japan, Asia, the Caribbean, and Central and South America. Through its manufacturing facility in Limerick, Ireland, Dell Computer supplies virtually all of its products sold in Africa, Europe, and the Middle East.

Over time the company has evolved from relying solely on direct marketing to employing account teams—groups of individuals that focus on potentially large orders. The purpose in doing so is to expand the initial customer base of small businesses and individuals (some of whom are called "hackers") to large corporations, government agencies (federal, state, and local), and medical and educational institutions. Whereas small businesses and individuals tended to purchase from Dell because of its low prices (and typically purchased only a small number of low-margin computers), large corporations, government agencies, and medical and educational institutions were believed to offer a much larger market for higher-priced (and high-margin) computers.

The Dell North American sales organization consists of four distinct entities: (1) commercial, (2) government, medical, and education, (3) direct sales, and (4) indirect sales. The commercial division focuses on Fortune 1000 firms and large privately held corporations, often employing account teams and field representatives. The government, medical, and education division markets Dell products to government entities and medical and educational institutions in much the same way as does the commercial division. The direct sales division specializes in small/medium businesses and the household/small or home office (SoHo) market through direct-response advertising, mailouts, and telemarketing. Although the direct sales division still accounts for approximately 40 percent of domestic revenues and represents the traditional Dell approach to distribution, its revenue growth has been relatively flat in recent quarters and is predicted to remain so.

It was the direct sales division's flat revenues that prompted Michael Dell to create the indirect sales division in 1991. Dell Computer entered the indirect market through the retailer CompUSA with a new brand name called Precision— a product line similar to that sold through the direct marketing channel. The Precision line is preloaded with the most current software on the market and is parity-priced with other value-line products offered in this channel. Since initiating the relationship with CompUSA, Dell has carefully formed alliances with distributors that have very low overheads and are extremely efficient. By 1992, Dell had expanded its presence in the indirect channel through retailers such as Sam's Club, Wal-Mart, Price Club, Costco, Staples, and Best Buy.

In addition to such mass retailers, the indirect sales division concentrates on marketing to value-added resellers, such as Falcon Micro Systems (a government reseller), original equipment manufacturers, and systems/network integrators, such as Andersen Consulting and EDS, often employing field sales representatives and account executives similar to the commercial division. While the creation of this division signaled a major change from Dell's traditional marketing strategy, the division has been relatively successful. Even so, nearly four-fifths of the company's revenues derive from its direct marketing efforts.

Selling Environment

Oversimplifying somewhat, there are two major markets for personal computers, businesses and households. Each of these markets consists of numerous submarkets, segments, and niches. Business submarkets, for example, range from government entities to large publicly held firms (such as Fortune 500 companies) to small businesses with only a few employees. Overall, however, the business market is more heterogeneous than the household market. For instance, it consists of niches (for example, scientific laboratories) with very specialized performance needs with cost a secondary concern as well as government entities whose purchase decisions are based primarily on price. Even so, the household market is becoming less homogeneous as the growing SoHo market has very specialized needs.

Hence, as might be expected, the two major markets generally have different buying requirements. The household market consists of consumers using a computer for basic word processing and games as well as small/home office applications requiring complex financial and graphics software. The business market (medium to large-sized firms) requires sophisticated, powerful personal computers that are frequently networked (linked or connected together) to provide a variety of functions such as information sharing. The household market, on the other hand (except for "hackers" and the SoHo segment), is not as concerned with computing power or system capability. One of the primary concerns of the household market is cost. In general, personal computers sold to medium/large businesses tend to be on the high end of the price continuum and have higher margins. Exhibit 4 presents estimated domestic personal computer sales for selected application segments for the years 1993–1996.

Technology

Computer manufacturers such as Apple and Compaq respectively spend approximately 8 percent and 4 percent of their annual revenues on research and development. These funds are spent on new technology such as Pentium-based (586 mhz) systems, notebooks, subnotebooks, hand-held communications, and pen-based technologies. As the new Pentium technology increases the processing speed of PCs much like the 486 systems greatly improved upon 386 performance, computer companies are scrambling to master the technology and be the first to ship systems containing this high-speed microprocessor.

Notebook computers are portable (that is, battery-powered) PCs weighing from four to seven pounds that are capable of a wide variety of computing functions and frequently possess advanced communication capabilities. They took their name from the fact that their outside dimensions roughly correspond to those of a standard ring-binder notebook. Subnotebooks weigh a maximum of four pounds, about two to three pounds less than their counterpart full-sized notebooks, and often feature a pen-based technology. Typically they have a longer battery life but fewer capabilities than a full-sized notebook. Computer firms are scrambling to win over price-sensitive buyers who want the ability to take their office home with the new subnotebook products. Hewlett-Packard's Omnibook, Northgate's ZXP-XL2, Toshiba's Portege, and Compaq's Contura are all subnotebooks reaping profits from early entry into this market. Similarly, hand-held computing technology, which integrates standard business tools such as a cellular phone, personal computer, fax machine, and personal organizer, is finding its own place in the market. AT&T's EO and Apple's Newton are in direct competition in this market. In general, a growth rate of nearly 90 percent per year is predicted for mobile computing technology.

Industry Sales Trends

By the end of 1992, more than 40 million personal computers had been sold in the United States. And, by the end of 1992, the total number of PCs sold to businesses and governmental and educational agencies cumulatively surpassed

EXHIBIT 4

Estimated U.S. Personal Computer Sales by Application Segment

Sales

Application Segment	1993		1994		1995		1996	
	Units (Thousands)	Dollars (Millions)	Units (Thousands)	Dollars (Millions)	Units (Thousands)	Dollars (Millions)	Units (Thousands)	Dollars (Millions)
Business/professional	9,507	$17,181	10,269	$18,295	10,754	$19,233	11,100	$20,574
Home/hobby	1,070	598	1,124	580	1,142	579	1,063	559
Scientific/technical	1,347	5,735	1,465	5,984	1,528	6,200	1,579	6,622
Education	1,294	1,446	1,380	1,503	1,424	1,571	1,443	1,707
Total	13,218	$24,960	14,238	$26,362	14,848	$27,583	15,185	$29,462

Source: Company records.

46

the number sold to households. Industry data show that small businesses and home offices (the SoHo segment) are the fastest-growing customer groups in the 1990s, even though sales to large businesses are still experiencing some growth. Sales to the former groups are expected to grow at an average annual rate of 25 percent through 1996, whereas sales to large businesses are expected to grow about 5 percent annually during the same time period.

The fastest-growing personal computer in the 1990s is expected to be the notebook. In 1990, fewer than 20,000 notebook computers were sold. By 1991, sales of portable/notebook computers in the United States were about $2 billion. By 1998 industry experts forecast annual notebook sales in the United States alone to be in excess of $25 billion, and worldwide sales to total $50 billion. At the present time, none of Dell Computer's major competitors are able to meet the demand for their notebook computers. Unlike desktops, most notebook technology is proprietary, and designing and building them require special skills beyond simply inserting chips and cards into motherboards.

Competition

Dell Computer Corporation's competitors vary from well-known firms such as IBM, Compaq, and Apple to nearly 200 "no-name" firms, many of which consist of only one or two entrepreneurs assembling personal computers in garages or storefront locations. It is common in the industry to refer to IBM, Apple, Compaq, and Dell as "tier 1" firms in terms of their sales. In 1992 IBM's personal computer sales totaled $7.7 billion; Apple's were $5.4 billion; Compaq's were $4.1 billion; and Dell's were $2.0 billion. "Tier 2" competitors consist of firms such as Gateway and AST. There is a third tier of firms, such as Zeos and Austin Computer, each with sales of up to $100 million annually. In the past few years there has been considerable consolidation occurring in the industry through both bankruptcies and acquisitions. For example, in July 1993 AST purchased Tandy Corporation's PC business, overnight boosting its sales to more than $2 billion.

In 1992 the top ten PC manufacturers in the United States collectively held a 58 percent market share. This represented an increase of 6 percent from the comparable figure of 52 percent in 1990. Despite this consolidation, though, gross margins in the industry are relatively anemic and average slightly less than 30 percent.

Historically, firms such as IBM, Apple, and Compaq have possessed relatively high brand awareness. Even so, the brand awareness of non-tier 1 firms has steadily risen. Moreover, the price decline of PCs generally has not only squeezed the margins of all firms. It has greatly reduced the price advantages formerly held by second- and third-tier firms. Compaq and IBM in particular have become very aggressive in their marketing and created low-cost, low-price lines of PCs with brand names such as Compaq's Proline and IBM's ValuePoint to meet the demand of the fast-growing segment of price-conscious customers who are not concerned with advanced features. Partly as a consequence of industrywide price-cutting, once-successful PC manufacturers such as CompuAdd filed for bankruptcy.

A major trend began in the industry in 1991 and gained momentum in 1992 and early 1993. This was the tendency for firms that were fierce competitors to form strategic alliances and partnerships to both develop and market new products. For instance, Packard Bell and Zenith Data Systems agreed to jointly design and manufacture desktop and notebook computers, although each would be free to modify them for its particular markets. Likewise, IBM and Toshiba established an alliance to co-develop new portable computers. Motorola, IBM, and Apple partnered on the development of a new microprocessor called the Power PC, a direct competitor for the industry standard Intel microprocessor chip found in Dell and most other personal computers. Compaq, Intel, Microsoft, and VLSI Technology, Inc. formed an alliance for a mobile companion series that hooks into existing desktop networks. Apple and Siemens AG Private Communications Systems Group collaborated on the development of Notephone—a PC with fax and telephone capabilities.

Distribution Channels

Personal computer manufacturers use five primary channels to reach end users: (1) dealers/value-added resellers, (2) direct marketing, (3) mass merchandisers, (4) direct sales, and (5) systems/network integrators. Exhibit 5 contains estimated personal computer sales for several distribution channels through 1996.

Dealers/Value-Added Resellers

The traditional channel used to reach personal computer buyers is the storefront dealer. Dealers are retailers that focus on selling personal computers and peripheral equipment to both the business and household markets. Some PC manufacturers sell exclusively through dealers. Generally, dealers operate out of facilities of 3,000 to 5,000 square feet and assume the marketing, servicing, and support functions for a manufacturer. Consequently, PCs sold through this channel tend to be on the high end of the price continuum. (Gross margins average 35–40 percent for dealers.) Major dealer chains include Computerland and Businessland. A subcategory of dealers consists of value-added resellers such as Microage. VARs are dealers that specialize in a particular market niche (often a vertical market such as educational institutions) and offer specialized services to that niche, such as complete hardware and software systems or special expertise in an application area.

Another type of dealer that merits special mention is the manufacturer-owned outlet. Although this dealer type is decreasing in popularity, some PC manufacturers market their computers through wholly owned company stores, usually in the range of 5,000 square feet or less. This permits considerable control over the distribution and selling process. The manufacturer-owned outlet can "showcase" the manufacturer's products because it does not have to share space with competing brands. Also, the manufacturer does not have to rely on intermediaries for sales, servicing, and support functions. As Exhibit 5 shows, in 1993 dealers accounted for the largest proportion of personal computer sales. A

EXHIBIT 5

Estimated U.S. Personal Computer Sales by Channel

Sales

Channel	1993 Units (Thousands)	1993 Dollars (Millions)	1994 Units (Thousands)	1994 Dollars (Millions)	1995 Units (Thousands)	1995 Dollars (Millions)	1996 Units (Thousands)	1996 Dollars (Millions)
Dealer								
Dealers	5,533	$10,955	5,859	$10,793	5,802	$10,669	5,521	$10,811
VARs	1,635	3,408	1,731	3,765	1,934	3,903	1,982	4,158
	7,168	$14,363	7,590	$14,558	7,736	$14,572	7,503	$14,969
Direct marketing								
Direct response	1,761	$ 3,165	1,731	$ 3,012	1,658	$ 2,862	1,699	$ 3,049
Direct outbound	503	974	400	1,004	414	1,041	425	1,109
Mail order	377	730	400	753	553	1,041	651	1,275
	2,641	$ 4,869	2,531	$ 4,769	2,625	$ 4,944	2,775	$ 5,433
Mass merchandise								
Mass merchants	1,006	$ 1,704	1,199	$ 2,008	1,243	$ 2,082	1,416	$ 2,495
Consumer electronics	604	1,169	692	1,305	760	1,431	807	1,580
Superstores	755	1,217	799	1,506	829	1,561	849	1,386
	2,365	$ 4,090	2,690	$ 4,819	2,832	$ 5,074	3,072	$ 5,461
Other	101	$ 195	266	$ 502	276	$ 520	425	$ 832
Total	12,275	$23,517	13,077	$24,648	13,469	$25,110	13,775	$26,695

Source: Company records.

major issue facing manufacturers using this channel is the amount of shelf space available for both new and existing brands.

Direct Marketing

Dell Computer Corporation pioneered the use of the direct-marketing channel. Personal computer manufacturers marketing through this channel typically use direct-response advertisements in computer magazines, direct mailings (catalogs, brochures, etc.), and both inbound and outbound telemarketing to reach potential customers and communicate with current customers. Firms marketing through this channel traditionally have competed on the basis of price and have offered "mainstream" personal computers, often known as "boxes" because of their simplicity and lack of features. Manufacturers using this channel have tended to spend little on research and development. Of the five primary distribution channels, this one has probably attracted the most competition because of the ease of entry and lack of capital requirements. According to industry forecasters, over the long term the market share of this channel will decrease somewhat. This likely decline is due to a variety of reasons, including both intense competition and shifting market conditions.

Mass Merchandisers

Until recently, relatively few personal computers were sold through mass merchandisers. However, as Exhibit 5 suggests, this distribution channel may become dominant in the near future, especially for the SoHo market segment. The term *mass merchandiser* is a bit misleading because it covers a variety of different types of retailers. For example, this distribution channel encompasses traditional retailers such as Sears and Dillards, which sell IBM personal computers among others, as well as specialized consumer electronics stores.

Perhaps the most important development among mass merchandisers is the "superstore" or "category killer." Based on the model of Toys R Us and Home Depot, several companies such as Computer City and CompUSA have opened large personal computer "supermarkets." These superstores typically range in size from 25,000 to 50,000 square feet and carry up to 5,000 different computer-related items. They operate on the principle of high volume, low prices, low margins (generally in the neighborhood of 10 percent or less), and minimal service and support. Most of the projected growth in sales among mass merchandisers can be attributed to an increase in the number of superstores, several of which offer their own brand of personal computers (for example, CompUSA's Compudyne brand).

Direct Sales (Field Sales)

The direct sales channel is typically used by manufacturers trying to reach businesses and government agencies. Since it is a relatively expensive channel because of the costs associated with supporting a field sales force, this channel type is typically not used for other than large corporate customers and/or major government agencies. Its advantages are flexibility, person-to-person contact, and the ability to work closely with a customer to solve unique computing problems and to target specific organizations and even individuals within an organization. Because of its size, IBM tends to dominate this distribution channel. Although exact sales figures are not available for this channel, it is believed that the channel had decreased in importance in recent years as PCs have become more user-friendly, prices have declined, and individuals at all levels of business and government have become more computer-literate.

Systems/Network Integrators

The fifth distribution channel is one of the fastest growing. This channel consists of what is termed "systems" or "network" integrators. Integrators are consulting firms that work with both personal computer manufacturers and end users to ensure that the end user purchases the right hardware (personal computers) and software for its specific needs. They may also help install a particular computer system or assist an end user in changing from one computer system to another. Systems/network integrators offer large corporate and government accounts a single hardware/software source and turnkey solutions to their computing problems. The largest integrators are Andersen Consulting and EDS. Since corporate and government end users frequently seek the advice of an integrator for personal computers, more and more computer manufacturers are trying to form alliances with them, especially because there is a trend toward systems/network integrators purchasing personal computers from a manufacturer and reselling them to an end user.

September 1993

Following the release of his company's second-quarter financial results, Michael Dell began to draft an agenda for the upcoming strategy session of his senior management team. As he did so, his mind focused on the major issues that had to be addressed. Although he strongly believed that the company was well-positioned to meet the challenges facing it, he knew that to reestablish the momentum lost due to the second quarter's financial performance and regain the confidence of the marketplace, the company would have to act quickly and decisively. This meant squarely facing the two primary marketing issues that were appearing more and more to be firm albatrosses: notebooks and distribution. It also meant that the firm would have to decide if it wanted to position itself as a "manustributor," a company that simultaneously is a hybrid manufacturer and distributor.

The Notebook Decision

During the past eight years Dell Computer has met the challenge of developing products that kept up with the ever-changing computer industry. The current desktop product line that Dell offers takes advantage of industry-leading technology; however, its portable line has fallen short of industry standards.

In February 1992, Dell Computer entered the notebook market with a new color notebook based on the 25-megahertz Intel 386 SL microprocessor.

This notebook was followed by the 320 SLi in June and the 325 SLc in December. Unfortunately, the notebook line was plagued with technical problems, one of which would result in a product recall. As a consequence of quality problems and the inability to design a notebook line that would be leading edge and incorporate the newest technologies, the company decided to phase out notebook computers in the first half of 1993. At the present time, less than 6 percent of Dell Computer revenues were derived from notebook sales, down from 17 percent in the summer of 1992 and considerably less than the 20–25 percent of revenues that other PC manufacturers were experiencing.

By the middle of 1993 notebook computers were the fastest-growing segment of the PC market. Hence, given customer demand and industry trends, it was clear that the company would have to replace its notebook line as quickly as possible. Unfortunately, determining the proper strategy to successfully bring a new notebook line to market was not so clear. The proper strategy would quickly close the existing product-offering gap due to the lack of a notebook and stem the direct loss of revenues (with customers possibly diverting to competitors) while simultaneously guarding against possible product quality and corporate image problems if the new notebook line was less than successful due to a forced and premature reentry. In brief, if Dell Computer is to maintain its growth momentum, it is necessary to introduce a new high-quality notebook line quickly. But a major question existed: How? As Michael Dell and his chief lieutenants discussed the notebook issue, it seemed as though at least seven different actions were possible.

The company could simply go back to the recently phased-out line and provide whatever enhancements would make it competitive. Or it could market other manufacturers' brands of notebooks simply to complement other Dell products. Either of these strategies would minimize the "downtime" of not having a notebook line in the marketplace.

Some managers favored licensing the appropriate technology from other firms as another alternative to minimize the length of time it would require the company to produce a new Dell notebook. Others argued that Dell should develop a strategic alliance with a current notebook manufacturer or another "technology-wise" company and through some sort of partnership co-develop a new notebook line. Still other managers argued that Dell should simply find a contract manufacturer to produce notebooks under the Dell name so as not to lose its brand franchise. (Until June 1993, a sizable percentage of the Dell product line had been produced by SCI in Huntsville, Alabama.) One manager suggested that Dell simply purchase another company.

Finally, although there was wide agreement with respect to moving quickly, there was also considerable sentiment for Dell not to "rush into" a potentially bad situation by moving too rapidly. Rather, there was sentiment that Dell should assemble its own design team and design and manufacture its own notebook line. The company had recently hired John Medica as Vice President for Portable Products. Medica, who had engineered the Apple Computer Powerbook, was very experienced in the notebook area (in its first year of exis-

EXHIBIT 6
Estimated PC Shipment Percentages by Channel in 1992

Channel	Percentage of Company Shipments			
	Dell	**Apple**	**Compaq**	**IBM**
Dealers	0	63	68	65
Value-added resellers	15	5	15	8
Direct marketing	74	15	0	7
Systems integrators	3	5	6	5
Other (including mass merchandisers)	8	12	11	15

Source: Company records.

tence, the Apple Powerbook achieved more than 400,000 unit sales) and it was his job to develop Dell's notebook strategy.

The Distribution Decision

There was virtual consensus among Dell's senior management team that to remain competitive the company must diversify its direct-centric distribution strategy. According to Dennis Jolly, Group Vice President of Indirect Sales, the company needed a balanced portfolio of channels, one that was not overly dependent on direct marketing. The question was how to achieve such an objective. (See Exhibit 6 for comparative PC shipment information for Dell and its major competitors.)

Although Dell Computer owed its early success to individual buyers, by 1993 the majority of its customer base (approximately 61 percent) consisted of large businesses. The remainder consisted of small/medium businesses and individuals. While large businesses account for the greatest proportion of company sales, and the computers they purchase have large gross margins, they must produce approximately 25 percent more revenue to generate the same profit margins as small/medium businesses and individuals. This is because of the higher marketing costs associated with selling to large businesses, such as the costs of maintaining account executives and field representatives, the need for evaluation units (try before you buy), and required volume discounts. These higher costs, when combined with projected segment growth rates, led Dell, as well as other PC manufacturers, to search for markets and distribution channels that would produce sustainable and profitable revenue growth. For example, in a significant strategy shift, Compaq Computer Corporation began offering its Presario line to consumers and home office users through mass retailers including Montgomery Ward, Service Merchandise, and Best Buy in August 1993.

Currently, Dell Computer markets its products through large retail chains such as Wal-Mart and Best Buy. However, several individuals in the company believe that Dell's position in the mass-merchandiser channel is still one of underdistribution as compared with IBM and Compaq, which are thought to be overdistributed. In 1992, for instance, IBM obtained 96 percent of its personal computer revenue through indirect distribution, whereas Compaq obtained 83 percent of its revenue through this channel. At the same time, the indirect channel accounted for only about 20 percent of Dell Computer's sales.

The vertical reseller segment consists of firms that target particular markets and develop software applications to meet the specific needs of these markets. For instance, many accounting firms that need industry-specific software often look to resellers to provide them with a "total solution" of both hardware and software. Recently Dell Computer has attempted to build partnerships with VARs and resellers through an aggressive advertising program (see Exhibit 7).

Systems and network integrators combine hardware, software, and peripherals—most often in a client/server environment—as a total package for a turnkey solution to customers. Because it is a relatively new channel to Dell, the company is not as well represented in it as are Compaq and IBM.

One channel where Dell Computer is conspicuously absent is the traditional dealer channel. Despite being the largest distribution channel, it is an enigma for Dell (partially because of its financial condition the company is not able to offer dealers the margins they traditionally require). In an interview published in the August 23, 1993, issue of *Computerworld*, the Chairman of Computerland stated that his company was not interested in marketing Dell computers because "we want to commit to someone who wants to be our partner. Dell doesn't really want to do that. They want to run the business and then try to find some cracks and crevices they can use us for, but whenever possible they want to go to the direct channel."

EXHIBIT 7
Dell Computer Corporation Reseller Advertisement

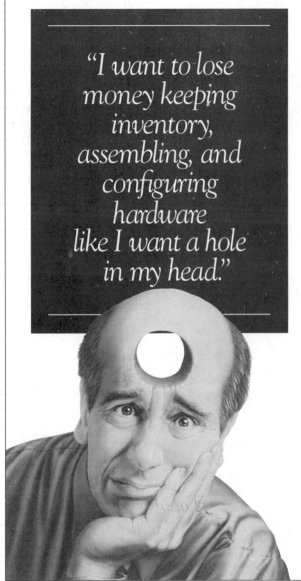

"*I want to lose money keeping inventory, assembling, and configuring hardware like I want a hole in my head.*"

DELL INTRODUCES A PARTNERSHIP THAT FILLS THE VOID.

Finally, someone's come along with a partnership that can get rid of headaches and help you focus on the profitable parts of your business. Someone who's done it for hundreds of other VARS and Resellers already. And that someone is Dell.

We'll preconfigure systems to your customers' specifications at the factory. These systems come with Dell's exclusive compatibility guarantee.* You'll get unique programs like ReadyWare,℠ which let you choose from over 200 applications pre-installed for one low $15 fee per system. And we also have a flexible nationwide service and support program that can be custom-fit to your organization.

We even reduce your inventory costs (a.k.a. being burdened with warehouses of systems and parts) by maintaining a "virtual inventory" for you, easily accessed around the country.

Dell takes care of other pains, too. Pains like your administrative and support tasks. We'll direct ship to the user, saving you time and handling costs. Heck, we've even prepared competitive leasing options and will handle lease administration.

Just call Dell for an application kit. Because anybody who would ignore help like this should probably have their head examined.

D∉LL

TO ORDER, CALL
800-553-5982

HOURS: MON-FRI 7AM-9PM CT SAT 10AM-6PM CT SUN 12PM-5PM CT
IN CANADA,* CALL 800-668-3021. IN MEXICO CITY,* 228-7811. #11ML3

*Guarantees available in USA only for registered owners of Dell Performance Series systems purchased after 7/1/93. For a complete copy, please call our TechFax℠ line at 1-800-950-1329 or write Dell USA L.P., 9505 Arboretum Blvd., Austin, TX 78759-7299. Attention Guarantees. The Intel Inside logo is a registered trademark of Intel Corporation. Dell disclaims proprietary interest in the marks and names of others. ©1993 Dell Computer Corporation.

DIPROD (R)

Michael Leenders

O n June 15, Brent Miller, raw materials buyer, had to prepare his recommendation for DIPROD's annual hexonic acid requirements. Four suppliers had submitted substantially different bids for this annual contract to commence August 1. Brent knew his recommendation would involve a variety of policy considerations and wondered what his best option would be.

Company Background

DIPROD (Canada) was the Canadian subsidiary of a large international chemical company. The company sold both consumer and industrial products and had over the years established an excellent reputation for quality products and marketing effectiveness. This was evidenced by a very substantial growth in total sales and financial success. Total Canadian sales were approximately $800 million and after-tax profits were $40 million. Raw material and packaging costs were about 50 percent of sales.

Purchasing

Brent Miller, a recent graduate of a well-known business school, knew that purchasing was well regarded as a function at DIPROD. The department was staffed with 24 well-qualified persons, including a number of engineering and business graduates at both the undergraduate and masters levels. The department was headed by a director who reported to the president. It was organized along commodity lines and Brent Miller had recently been appointed raw materials buyer reporting to the manager of the chemicals buying group. The hexonic acid contract would have to be approved by the immediate supervisor and the director of the department.

Brent was aware that several DIPROD purchasing policies and practices were of particular importance to his current hexonic contract decision. The pur-

The basic objectives for the DIPROD purchasing department are:

A. *Assurance of Material Availability*
The major objective of purchasing must be the guarantee of sufficient supply to support production requirements.

B. *Best Value*
DIPROD recognizes that value is a combination of price, quality, service, . . . and that maximum profitability can only be obtained through the purchase of optimal value on both a short- and long-term basis.

C. *An Ethical Reputation*
All dealings must respect all aspects of the law and all business relationships must be founded on a sound ethical approach.

D. *Gathering of Information*
Purchasing involves a constant search for new ideas and improved products in the changing markets. A responsibility also exists to keep the company informed on industry trends including information on material supply and costs.

chasing department had worked very hard with suppliers over the years to establish a single-bid policy. It was felt that suppliers should quote their best possible offer on their first and only quote and all suppliers should be willing to live with the consequences of their bid. Long-term supplier relations with the best possible long-term opportunities were considered vital to the procurement strategy. Assured supply for all possible types of market conditions was also of prime concern. Multiple sources were usually favored over single sources where this appeared to be reasonable and where no strong long-term price or other disadvantages were expected. Frequent supplier switching would not be normal, although total volumes placed with suppliers might change depending on past performance and new bids. Brent recognized that any major departure from traditional practice would have to be very carefully justified. Exhibit 1 shows the four prime objectives of the purchasing department and Exhibit 2 contains excerpts from the company's familiarization brochure for new suppliers.

Hexonic Acid—Recent Market History

DIPROD expected to use approximately 3,000 tons of hexonic acid in the following year. Requirements for the past year amounted to 2,750 tons and had been supplied by Canchem and Alfo at 60 and 40 percent.

Hexonic acid was a major raw material in a number of DIPROD products. Its requirements had grown steadily over the years and were expected to remain significant in the years to come. The availability of this material in the marketplace was difficult to predict. The process by which it was produced

EXHIBIT 2
Excerpts from Brochure for New Suppliers

The purpose of the information contained herein is to give our suppliers a better understanding of certain policies and practices of DIPROD. We believe it is important that we understand our suppliers and, in turn, that they understand us. As you know DIPROD believes in free enterprise and in competition as the mainspring of a free enterprise system. Many of our basic policies stem from a fundamental belief that competition is the fairest means for DIPROD to purchase the best total value. However, the policies and practices we want to outline here for you relate to DIPROD business ethics and the ethical treatment of suppliers. In brief, fair dealing means these things to us:

1. We live up to our word. We do not mislead. We believe that misrepresentations, phantom prices, chiseling etc., have no place in our business.
2. We try to be fair in our demands on a supplier and to avoid unreasonable demands for services; we expect to pay our way when special service is required.
3. We try to settle all claims and disputes on a fair and factual basis.
4. We avoid any form of "favored treatment," such as telling a supplier what to quote to get our business or obtaining business by "meeting" an existing price. In addition, all suppliers that could qualify for our business are given identical information and an equal opportunity to quote on our requirements.
5. We do not betray the confidence of a supplier. We believe that it is unethical to talk about a supplier with competitors. New ideas, methods, products, and prices are kept confidential unless disclosure is permitted by the supplier.
6. We believe in giving prompt and courteous attention to all supplier representatives.
7. We are willing to listen to supplier complaints at any level of the buying organization without prejudice concerning the future placement of business.

We also do not believe in reciprocity or in "tie-ins" which require the purchase of one commodity with another.

We believe that supplier relationships should be conducted so that personal obligations, either actual or implied, do not exist. Consequently, we do not accept gifts and we discourage entertainment from suppliers. Similarly, we try to avoid all situations which involve a conflict of personal interest.

The above comments cover the main DIPROD buying policies on both corporate and personal ethics. We sincerely want our relationships with suppliers to be built on respect and good faith, which grow from mutual understanding. Please feel free to discuss with us any points that need clarification.

---

yielded both hexonic and octonic acids and the market was, therefore, influenced by the demand for either product.

Two years previously there had been major shortages of hexonic acid due to strong European and Japanese demand. Furthermore, capacity expansions had been delayed too long because of depressed prices for hexonic and octonic over the previous years. During this period of shortage both of DIPROD's

EXHIBIT 3
Recent Hexonic Acid Purchases

Period	Total Volume Purchased	Percent Supplier Delivered Cost	Percent Supplier Delivered Cost
Three years ago	1,800 tons	50% Canchem $414/ton	50% Alfo $414/ton
Two years ago	2,200 tons	50% Canchem $588/ton	50% Alfo $542/ton
Last year	2,750 tons	60% Canchem $692/ton	40% Alfo $646/ton

suppliers, Alfo and Canchem, were caught by the market upsurge. Alfo had just shut down their old Windsor plant and had not yet brought their new Quebec City plant up to design capacity. At the same time, Canchem was in the midst of converting their process to accommodate recent chemical improvements and they, too, found themselves plagued with conversion problems. Both companies were subsidiaries of large American multinational firms. Both were large multiplant companies in Canada and had supplied DIPROD for many years. The parent companies of both Alfo and Canchem had been faced with too high a demand in the United States to be able to afford any material to help meet the Canadian commitments of their subsidiaries. As a result, both Canadian suppliers were forced to place many of their customers on allocation. However, through considerable efforts both were able to fulfill all of DIPROD's requirements. The increased prices charged throughout this period fell within the terms of the contracts and were substantially lower than those that would have been incurred if DIPROD would have had to import offshore material. Quotations on such imports had revealed prices ranging from $960 to $1,440 per ton.

The past year was relatively stable with both producers running almost at capacity. DIPROD again had contracted its requirements with Alfo and Canchem, both of whom continued to perform with the same high quality and service to which DIPROD had become accustomed over the years.

For the past year Brent's predecessor had recommended a split in the business of 60 percent to Canchem and 40 percent to Alfo based on a number of factors. Important to the decision at that time was the start-up of the new Alfo plant. The Alfo quotation of $600 per ton offered a lower price per ton than Canchem's at $646 per ton, but it had been uncertain whether the new plant would be able to guarantee more than 40 percent of DIPROD's hexonic requirements. Currently, however, Alfo had brought their plant up to capacity and could certainly supply all the 6 million pounds required, if called on (see Exhibit 3 for a recent history of hexonic acid purchases).

Brent thought that recently the hexonic acid cycle had turned around. Hexonic demand had eased and now it was octonic acid which was in high demand by the booming paint industry. Recent plant expansions by a number of suppliers had been completed. The overall result seemed to be a building of excess hexonic inventories. Brent believed this would be reflected in a buyer's market in the coming year and looked forward to aggressive quotes from all potential sources.

Meetings with Hexonic Suppliers

An important part of the buyer's job at DIPROD was to become an expert in the materials purchased. Among other things, this meant keeping an open ear to the market and building strong relationships with suppliers. It was the buyer's responsibility to assure that all information between buyer and seller would be completely confidential. The director of purchasing believed it was important to build a reputation that suppliers could trust DIPROD purchasing personnel.

On May 14, Brent had mailed the hexonic inquiry (see Exhibit 4) to the four suppliers he believed had a chance of quoting competitively on the needs of the Hamilton plant. The two current Canadian suppliers, Alfo and Canchem, were included as well as two American sources. The deadline for bids was June 7, at 4 P.M.

Brent knew that on receipt of the inquiry, supplier salesmen would be eager to discuss it. Actually, he had two contacts before the inquiry was mailed out.

Meeting with Alfo

Mr. Baker, sales representative of Alfo, met with Brent on April 20. He said that Alfo had unfilled capacity at its new Quebec City plant and he appeared eager to receive an indication of DIPROD's future hexonic requirements. Mr. Baker informed Brent that he was aware of low-priced hexonic on the European market but also made sure to emphasize that it would be uncompetitive in the Canadian market after the costs of duty and freight were added. Brent said it was a published fact that inventories were building in the United States as other hexonic users showed signs of easing their demands. The meeting ended with the assurance from Brent that Mr. Baker would again receive an invitation to quote on the next period's business when it was reviewed in June.

Phone Call by Michigan Chemical

Mr. Wallace, sales representative of Michigan Chemical, assured Brent over the telephone on April 30 that his company would be a contender this year. He said that Michigan Chemical would be represented by their Canadian distributor, Carter Chemicals, Ltd., located in Niagara Falls, Ontario. Brent remembered that Michigan Chemical had a good record with DIPROD (U.S.). According to the U.S. raw materials buying group, Michigan Chemical had supplied close to 99 percent of their commitment in the recent period of shortage. Brent emphasized to Mr. Wallace over the telephone that the present suppliers held the advantage and that he would have to offer better value in order for DIPROD to swing any business away from them. Brent said at the end of the call that Michigan Chemical would receive an inquiry and that their quote would be seriously considered.

EXHIBIT 4
Hexonic Acid Inquiry

P.O. Box 372, Terminal "A"   Toronto, Ontario

May 14

Dear Sir:

Subject: Hexonic Acid

We invite your best quotation to supply all or part of our requirements of Hexonic Acid for the month period beginning next August 1. Please use the attached quote sheets in preparing your reply for the following material:

DIPROD Specification No. 87831 (attached), purchased in tank cars or tank trucks. The total requirement for our Hamilton, Ontario, plant is estimated to be 3,000 tons.

Prices

Provide pricing for spot purchases; in addition, indicate any special price arrangement you would offer if we were to agree to purchase this material on a contractual basis. We consider firm prices to be a significant element of value.

If your material is of other than Canadian origin and if Canadian Customs clearance would be the Buyer's responsibility, please include the appropriate fair market value (FMV) within the terms of the Canadian Customs Regulations. Note that the FMV and the selling price can quite properly be different.

In addition to your proposal on the above, we encourage any other proposals which might offer us better value and so enhance your competitive position. We are willing to consider proposals of both a chemical or commercial nature.

Use of the attached quote sheet ensures that we receive the basic information that must be contained in every quote. This format is not intended to restrict your quotation in any way. Please feel free to attach any other additional information that will help us clearly identify the value your company is offering.

To receive consideration your quotation must be in our hands by 4:00 P.M. June 7.

If you have any questions, please don't hesitate to call me at 416-366-5859.

Yours very truly,

B. W. Miller
Buying Department

BWM/em
Att'd.

Meeting with Canchem

On June 3, Mr. Aldert, sales representative for Canchem, personally brought in his company's quotation and presented the terms to Brent with a distinct air of confidence (see Exhibit 5). Mr. Aldert explained that although his price of $646

EXHIBIT 5
Hexonic Acid Quote Sheet

For all or part of DIPROD's requirements of 3,000 tons for the period beginning August 1 to be shipped to our Hamilton plant.

Pricing:

(A)   On our desired shipment size of tank trucks only.

      (a)   spot price   <u>$646.00/ton</u>

            (i)   do you perceive this price to be stable?

                       <u>short-term yes</u>

            (ii)   if not: expected increase

                       <u>8% during 2nd or 3rd quarter</u>

                       expected decrease

                       <u>   </u>

      (b)   contractual purchase price <u>$646.00/ton</u> with <u>30 day</u> price adjustments with <u>30</u>   days prior notice of change in price.

          (i)   minimum period (if any): 1 year

          (ii)   minimum volume (if any): 1,000 tons

Fair Market Value (if applicable):

Manufacturer of this material is confirmed as

                       <u>that of Canchem Ltd</u>

This material will be shipped from   <u>Kingston, Ontario (plant/warehouse)</u>

Normal inventory of this material that will be carried at any time, <u>500 tons</u>

FOB point: Kingston, Ontario

Freight terms: Freight Collect

Cash terms and discounts: Net 30

Lead time for delivery from receipt of purchase order: 2 weeks

Planned shutdowns: None

Union affiliation at manufacturing plant: Oil & Chemical workers

        (i)   Union contract expires: August 28, next year.

Material supplied against this quotation will be in accordance with DIPROD Specification No.: 87831

Signed: <u>   </u>   Name of Company <u>Canchem Ltd.</u>

Date: <u>June 3</u>

per ton was the same as that which DIPROD was currently paying for Canchem material, it remained a competitive price. Brent could not help showing his disappointment to Mr. Aldert and he said that he had expected a more aggressive quote. However, he assured Mr. Aldert that every consideration would be given to Canchem once all the quotations were in by the June 7 deadline.

Meeting with American Chemical Inc. (AMCHEM)

On the morning of June 7, two representatives from AMCHEM delivered their hexonic quotation and explained its contents to Brent. AMCHEM had recently completed a plant expansion at their Cleveland plant and clearly had the ability to supply many times DIPROD's total requirements. Brent thought their quote of $480 per ton appeared very attractive and noted that the price per ton depended on the specific volume allocated to AMCHEM. The price of $480 applied to an annual volume of 1,050 tons. For a volume of 2,250 tons per year the price would be lowered to $474.80. A 15 percent duty would have to be added to the cost of AMCHEM material as well as freight.

When the representatives had left, Brent searched the hexonic material file for any information about past dealings with AMCHEM. He found that DIPROD had been supplied with AMCHEM hexonic seven years previously. At that time AMCHEM apparently had quoted a price below Canchem and Alfo and, as a result, had been allocated a portion of the business. This had the result of sparking aggressiveness into the two Canadian suppliers during the next inquiry. Both fought to gain back the tonnage that had been taken away from them. Apparently, neither Canchem nor Alfo had been aware who their competitor was at the time.

Brent also telephoned the purchasing department of DIPROD (U.S.) in an effort to draw any information about their experience with AMCHEM. Supplier information like this flowed quite freely within the corporation on a need-to-know basis. The U.S. buyer informed Brent that AMCHEM did at one time supply the parent with hexonic and that quality and service were excellent. However, he did caution Brent that during the recent period of shortage AMCHEM did place DIPROD (U.S.) on allocation and as a result fell short of their commitment by a considerable extent.

Meeting with Alfo

Mr. Baker, sales representative of Alfo, presented his company's quote to Brent at 3 P.M., the afternoon of June 7. He explained that the contractual terms and $600 price offered were the same as those under the current contract with Alfo. Brent thanked Mr. Baker for his quotation and told him he would be informed in late June when a decision had been made.

Quotation by Carter Chemical

The quotation from Carter Chemical arrived in the afternoon mail on June 7. The $634 per ton FOB Hamilton plant quote was a pleasant surprise to Brent. He thought that Michigan Chemical had been right when they had said that their distributor would make an aggressive offer. Brent now had received two quotes that offered a better laid-down cost than the two current suppliers.

Visit of Canchem

At 3:45 P.M. on June 7, Brent received another visit from Mr. Aldert of Canchem, who had apparently been disheartened after his earlier meeting on June 3. He had obviously gone back to his management, for he now had a new quotation prepared. His new quote offered DIPROD hexonic on a three-year contract for $550 per ton. With freight added, this price appeared to be equal to the lowest that had been received. Brent realized that he had probably inspired Mr. Aldert to resubmit his quotation by the feedback he had given him during their June 3 meeting. With this in mind, Brent was wary of accepting this quotation for fear he would be setting a bad precedent. He told Mr. Aldert that he might not be in a position to accept his bid, but would let him know subsequently. The following day Brent discussed the situation with his superior, Mr. Williams. Mr. Williams retraced the steps Brent had gone through. It had been normal practice at DIPROD to open quotes as they were received. It had also been standard policy not to give suppliers any feedback on their quote until all quotes had been received. Mr. Williams told Brent to think the situation over in his own mind and to make a recommendation on how Canchem's second bid should be treated as part of his hexonic acid contract deliberations.

Quote Summary

Brent prepared a quote summary to put all bids on an equal footing (see Exhibit 6). To be able to compare quotes fairly, it was necessary to examine the laid-down cost of each of the four options. Items like duty and freight could make a significant difference. Brent realized that his final recommendation would have to be based on his calculations as well as his objective view of the current suppliers. He did not have much time left and the unusual situation surrounding Canchem's second bid gave him further concern. Mr. Williams was expecting his written analysis and recommendation no later than June 17.

EXHIBIT 6
Quotation Summary: Hexonic Acid

	Price			Terms
	Spot	**Contract**		
1. Alfo:				
FOB Quebec City	600.00/ton	600.00/ton		Min. period: 1 year
Freight (equal	46.00	46.00		Min. volume: —
on Kingston)	646.00/ton	646.00/ton		Price protection: 90 days
				Notice: 15 days
2. Canchem:				
		(2nd proposal, June 6)		
FOB Kingston	646.00/ton	550.00/ton		Min. period: 3 years
Freight	46.00	46.00		Min. volume: 1,000 tons
	692.00/ton	596.00/ton		Price protection: 30 days
				Notice: 30 days
3. American Chemicals		*Min. 1,050 tons*	*Min. 2,250 tons*	
FOB Cleveland	659.00/ton	480.00	474.80	Min. period: 1 year
Duty @ 15%	98.86	72.00	71.20	Min. volume: Stated
Freight	46.00	50.00	50.00	Price protection: Firm
	803.86	602.00	596.00	Notice: —
4. Carter Chemicals: (Michigan Chem material)				
		Min. 750 tons		
FOB our Hamilton Plant	634.00/ton	634.00/ton		Min. period: 1 year
				Min. volume: 750 tons
				Price protection: 90 days
				Notice: 15 days

E. I. Du Pont de Nemours & Co., Inc.

Jonathan Guiliano

Cornelius A.
deKluyver

David T. Blake, marketing director for the Spunbonded Division in the Textile Fibers Department of Du Pont, reviewed the 1984 marketing plan as he thought about the 1985 plan, which was due in a few weeks. The overall strategy for Sontara fiber in the surgical gown and drape market and for Tyvek fiber in the construction industry had already been formulated; now he wondered whether the budget proposals on his desk fit the strategies.

Company Background

Du Pont, with 1983 sales of $35.4 billion, ranked seventh in the Fortune 500 list of companies. Comprising 90 major businesses and operating in more than 50 countries, Du Pont organized its more than 1,700 products in eight industry segments: biomedical products; coal; petroleum exploration and production; industrial and consumer products; polymers; agricultural and industrial chemicals; petroleum refining, marketing, and transportation; and fibers (see *Exhibit 1*).

The fibers segment (1983 sales: $4.8 billion) marketed the world's most extensive offering of man-made fibers, including fiber products for apparel, carpets, tire and aircraft component reinforcement, road support, packaging, protecting clothing, and medical apparel. The company sold the fiber products to textile and other manufacturers that processed them into consumer goods. Four groups made up this segment of the business: apparel fibers, carpet fibers, industrial fibers, and spunbonded products.

The Spunbonded Products Division

The Spunbonded Division (1983 sales: ca. $500 million) produced and marketed four products:

    REEMAY®—spunbonded polyester

    TYPAR®—spunbonded polypropylene

    TYVEK®—spunbonded olefin

    SONTARA®—spunlaced fabrics

EXHIBIT 1
Industry Segments: E. I. Du Pont de Nemours & Co., Inc.

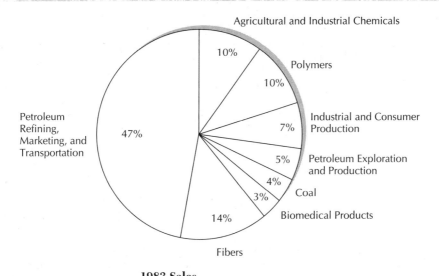

Industry Segment	1983 Sales (billions)	Products
• Petroleum refining, marketing, and transportation	16.8	Gasoline, jet fuel, diesel fuel, heating oil, fuel oil, asphalt, petroleum coke, natural gas liquids
• Fibers	4.8	Man-made fibers
• Agricultural and industrial chemicals	3.5	Fungicides, herbicides, insecticides, pigments, organic chemicals, fluorochemicals, petroleum additives, mineral acids
• Polymer products	3.4	Plastic resins, elastomers, films
• Industrial and consumer products	2.5	Photographic products, electronic products, analytical instruments, explosives, nonstick coatings, sporting firearms and ammunition
• Petroleum exploration and production	1.9	Crude oil, natural gas
• Coal	1.4	Steam coal, metallurgic coal
• Biomedical products	1.1	Clinical instruments, biomedical instruments, prescription pharmaceuticals, radio pharmaceuticals

Manufacturing the first three of these generally involved a continuous process of spinning, bonding, and finishing, as diagrammed in *Exhibit 2*; the process to make Sontara involved fiber entanglement and related steps.

Reemay®, a polyester, was a lightweight, hygienically safe, heat-resistant fiber that was used as apparel interliner, coverstock (e.g., to cover diapers),

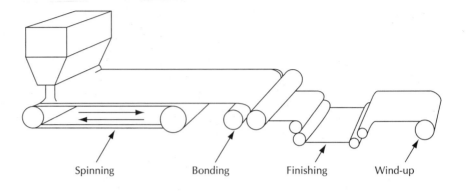

EXHIBIT 2
Spunbonded Product Manufacture

Spinning   Bonding   Finishing   Wind-up

and agricultural crop cover. Typar® was a strong, stable, low-cost polypropylene used as a primary carpet backing, as a geotextile (to provide drainage under roads), and in furniture as a replacement for burlap. Tyvek®, a strong and opaque olefin with a protective barrier, was used for envelopes, disposable apparel, sterile packaging, bookcovers, tags and labels, and "housewrap" (material to provide a barrier against air infiltration). Sontara® structures were noted for softness, absorbency, and comfort, and were used in curtains, bedspreads, and surgical gowns and drapes.

The Spunboded Division was managed by a division director. Reporting to him were a technical director, a manufacturing director, and a marketing director, David T. Blake. Reporting to Mr. Blake were a number of marketing managers responsible for various end-user markets for the division's products; each marketing manager was assisted by several marketing and technical representatives. Throughout the Spunbonded Division, managers used a communications network through personal computers, on which they also ran their own software for analysis and control. The Spunbonded Division was one of the first divisions to use computer networking at Du Pont.

Marketing managers submitted annual budget proposals to the marketing director, who reviewed and usually approved them. If Mr. Blake thought a proposal was unreasonable, he asked the marketing manager to modify it and then combined the various proposals into an overall marketing plan for consideration by the division director.

Sontara Spunlaced Products

Sontara, introduced in 1975, was a sheet structure of entangled fibers. It looked and felt like a conventional textile, and was made from 100 percent polyester, or a blend of polyester and rayon, or from a wood pulp/polyester blend. This last

EXHIBIT 3
U.S. Surgical Gown and Drape Market Trends

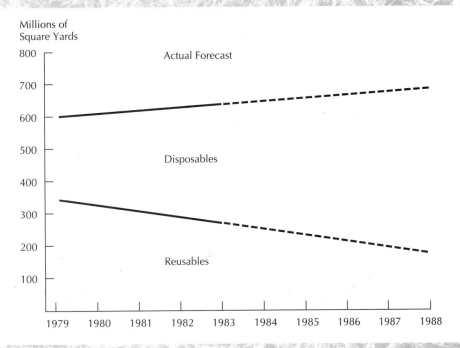

The U.S. market for surgical gowns and drapes in 1983 was approximately 637 million square yards, and its annual growth rate was about 2 percent. The market was divided into two parts: reusable fabric, or cotton; and disposable fabrics, such as Sontara. The benefits of cotton, such as comfort, absorbency, and in the short term, cost, were increasingly becoming outweighed by the advantages of disposables—principally, convenience and infection-barrier qualities. Market share for disposables was 55 percent in 1983 with a forecast annual growth rate of 8 percent for the next few years (see *Exhibit 3* for market trends). It was thought unlikely that more than 90 percent of the market would ever switch to disposables. Fabric manufacturers, or fabric suppliers, in the disposables market, made the fabric and sold it to firms that made the gowns and drapes and sold them to hospitals. Unlike Du Pont, several companies were

was used primarily for disposable surgical gowns and drapes in hospital operating rooms; the gowns were worn by operating personnel and the drapes were used for patient apparel and to cover objects. Sontara accounted for about 17 percent of all division sales in 1983.

The Surgical Gown and Drape Market

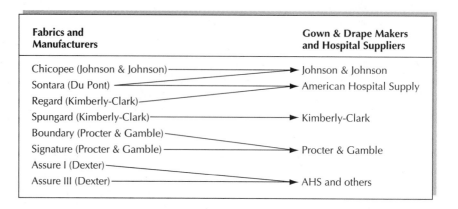

EXHIBIT 4
**Relationships Among Companies in the U.S.
Surgical Gown and Drape Market**

Fabrics and Manufacturers	Gown & Drape Makers and Hospital Suppliers
Chicopee (Johnson & Johnson)	Johnson & Johnson
Sontara (Du Pont)	American Hospital Supply
Regard (Kimberly-Clark)	
Spungard (Kimberly-Clark)	Kimberly-Clark
Boundary (Procter & Gamble)	
Signature (Procter & Gamble)	Procter & Gamble
Assure I (Dexter)	
Assure III (Dexter)	AHS and others

both fabric manufacturers and gown and drape makers and suppliers, as shown in *Exhibit 4*. Du Pont sold Sontara to Johnson & Johnson (J&J) and to American Hospital Supply (AHS). J&J also manufactured a fabric, Chicopee, or Fabric 450, which it made into gowns and drapes and sold to hospitals. AHS sold gowns and drapes of both Sontara and Regard, a Kimberly-Clark (K-C) product. Besides Regard, K-C, the first company in the disposables market, also manufactured Spunguard, a fabric which K-C made into gowns and drapes and sold to hospitals. Procter & Gamble (P&G) manufactured two fabrics, Boundary and Signature, made them into gowns and drapes, and sold them to hospitals.

Among companies selling gowns and drapes to hospitals, AHS held a dominant position, with J&J and P&G a strong second and third. Among disposable materials used for the gowns and drapes, Sontara barely trailed the two K-C products combined, as shown in *Exhibit 5*. Du Pont's Tyvek also held a 1 percent share of all gown and drape fabric sales. *Exhibits 6* and 7 provide additional information on the U.S. surgical and drape market.

Competition, which had already eroded gown-maker profit margins, was widely expected to grow more intense. Du Pont's main competitors were K-C, P&G, and J&J's Chicopee Division. K-C (1983 total sales: $3.3 billion), though steadily losing market share, had begun to consolidate its position as a fully integrated supplier to the medical apparel market; it had recently added production capacity and expanded its sales force. K-C's Regard continued to lose share to Sontara at AHS; of course, because K-C also supplied hospitals with gowns and drapes made of its Spunguard, AHS both bought from K-C

EXHIBIT 5
A: Market Shares of Companies Selling Directly to Hospitals

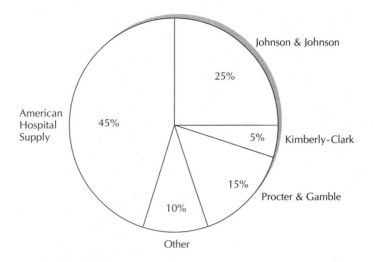

B: Market Shares of Materials Used by Hospitals

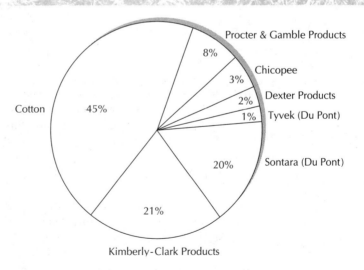

and competed against it. P&G (1983 sales: $12.5 billion) had entered the market several years ago as a vertically integrated supplier and touched off protracted price competition. To strengthen its position, P&G had reorganized its highly visible medical apparel sales force, a few years previously. Like P&G, J&J (1983 sales: $6.0 billion) recently had invested heavily in

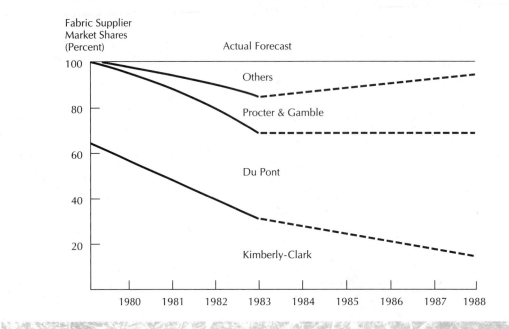

EXHIBIT 6
U.S. Surgical Gown and Drape Market

research and development. Production costs at Chicopee were now high, but because of J&J's large volume, it was expected that the company would move quickly down the experience curve and costs would drop. J&J's Chicopee was much softer than Sontara, but was therefore also more difficult to process. J&J often sold gowns and drapes made of Sontara and later substituted Chicopee, which was relatively simple to do because neither J&J nor AHS used the Sontara name on their products.

In addition to these complex company rivalries and relationships, there were still others of possible significance. K-C, for example, also competed against Sontara in the home furnishings, furniture, and bedding market, and against Tyvek in the industrial apparel market. Although a competitor of Du Pont, P&G was also a customer; P&G used Du Pont's spunbonded fabric Reemay as a coverstock for disposable diapers. And although the Spunbonded Products Division was engaged in sales of Sontara only to hospital suppliers and not in sales of Sontara apparel to hospitals, Du Pont did have sales forces that sold other Du Pont products directly to hospitals.

Cost, "barrier," and "flexural rigidity" were the three most important qualities used to compare surgical gowns and drapes. "Barrier" referred to how well the fabric protected against infection, and "flexural rigidity" defined the material's comfort and wear. *Exhibit 8* diagrams the relative positions of the

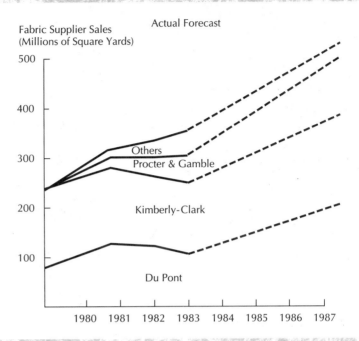

EXHIBIT 7
U.S. Surgical Gown and Drape Market

competing fabrics in terms of each of these three qualities; the fabrics most directly comparable and competitive with Sontara were P&G's Boundary and J&J's Chicopee.

Strategy and Tactics for Sontara

The future of Sontara involved several problems. First, because of increasing price competition, R&D was needed to lower unit production costs. Second, end-user brand awareness for Sontara was relatively low, primarily because J&J and AHS never identified the Sontara name. Third, hospitals, under government pressure to reduce costs, were becoming more price sensitive, and purchase decisions were increasingly made by administrators rather than by operating room nurses who used the gowns and understood Sontara's value. Fourth, every hospital had its own accounting system, so it was difficult to prove the long-term cost-effectiveness of Sontara products. Fifth, because hospitals would rarely admit to incidences of post-operative infection, it was also difficult to demonstrate Sontara's ability to reduce such infections. Sixth, disposables threatened to become commodities as more hospitals switched from cotton to disposable products. Finally, Du Pont

EXHIBIT 8
Key Fabric Properties of Surgical Gowns and Drapes

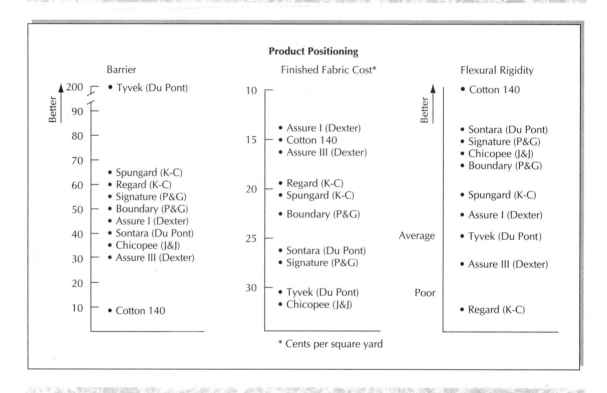

Product Positioning

| Barrier | Finished Fabric Cost* | Flexural Rigidity |

Barrier

Better →

- 200 • Tyvek (Du Pont)
- 90
- 80
- 70
- 60 • Spungard (K-C)
  • Regard (K-C)
  • Signature (P&G)
- 50 • Boundary (P&G)
  • Assure I (Dexter)
- 40 • Sontara (Du Pont)
  • Chicopee (J&J)
- 30 • Assure III (Dexter)
- 20
- 10 • Cotton 140

Finished Fabric Cost*

- 10
- 15 • Assure I (Dexter)
  • Cotton 140
  • Assure III (Dexter)
- 20 • Regard (K-C)
  • Spungard (K-C)
  • Boundary (P&G)
- 25 • Sontara (Du Pont)
  • Signature (P&G)
- 30 • Tyvek (Du Pont)
  • Chicopee (J&J)

Flexural Rigidity

Better →

• Cotton 140

Average

Poor

- • Sontara (Du Pont)
  • Signature (P&G)
  • Chicopee (J&J)
  • Boundary (P&G)
- • Spungard (K-C)
- • Assure I (Dexter)
- • Tyvek (Du Pont)
- • Assure III (Dexter)
- • Regard (K-C)

* Cents per square yard

faced potentially severe capacity limitations, which impeded the company's ability to compete aggressively.

Despite these problems, the market offered opportunities as the preference for disposable fabric increased, as professional groups, such as the Association of Operating Room Nurses (AORN), made statements favoring disposables as more clinical proof of Sontara's efficacy became available, and as new uses for Sontara, such as for scrub suits, developed.

In view of these circumstances, Du Pont's two principal strategic objectives for Sontara were (1) to at least maintain market share over the next two years, without further price erosion, until the capacity problems had been resolved, and (2) to convince garment makers that Du Pont could support them in promoting Sontara to end-users and would remain a strong force in the disposable fabric business. At the same time, the company planned to continue R&D to lower production costs as a hedge against further price reductions and to restore profit margins.

To implement this strategy, the 1984 budget for Sontara had consisted of $450,000 for the sales force and $92,000 for advertising and promotion.

Advertising and promotion were principally targeted toward operating room nurses, who traditionally decided what garments and drapes to buy. About $50,000 of this amount was spent on repeating the "Scrubby the Surgical Bear" campaign at the next annual AORN conference. Nurses had to listen to a 10-minute presentation about Sontara by a mind reader to receive a small teddy bear dressed in Sontara surgical garb and enclosed in a Tyvek sterile package. Scrubby had become a favorite at the conferences, and many nurses would stop by "Bear Mountain" to hear Scrubby's message:

> Hi!
>
> I'm Scrubby the Surgical Bear! I'm wearing soft, single-use surgical garments made with SONTARA spunlaced fabric from Du Pont. SONTARA keeps me cool and comfortable, and helps prevent infections in my patients.
>
> Notice that my package has a tough lid of TYVEK spunbonded olefin from Du Pont. Sterile packing of TYVEK gives me superior protection. It keeps out water and bacteria, resists punctures and tears, peels open cleanly and has proven shelf life.
>
> Take good care of me, just as SONTARA and TYVEK take good care of you and your patients in the O.R.!
>
> Love,
> Scrubby

The costs of the bears was $20,000. Brochures depicting Scrubby were $10,000. Du Pont also sent direct mail material (shown in *Exhibit 9*) to AORN nurses at a cost of $7,000, and ran advertisements (shown in *Exhibit 10*), at a cost of $5,000, in the AORN Journal (circulation 50,000) to give away big Scrubbies (*Exhibit 10*). Du Pont estimated that over the past two years, this program had put Sontara in touch with 25 percent of the 55,000 operating room nurses in the U.S.

The sales force allocation for Sontara was an estimate. It assumed that the marketing division assigned the equivalent of four and one-half people to the gown and drape market, and that each person represented about $100,000 in total cost. Tentative plans for 1985 called for the same sales force expenditure and an increase of 25 percent for each item in the advertising and promotion budget.

Tyvek

Tyvek spunbonded olefin was a sheet of extremely fine, high-density polyethylene fibers. It was a high-strength, high-barrier, low-weight structure, resistant to tearing, puncturing, shrinking, and rotting. One of the many uses for Tyvek was as "housewrap," an air infiltration barrier for homes, introduced in 1981. U.S. sales for Tyvek housewrap in 1983 were $2.8 million, or 800,000 pounds, while international sales were $0.8 million, or 400,000 pounds. Total Tyvek sales in 1983 were in excess of $100 million.

Tyvek housewrap was stapled to the sheathing of a home under construction before siding was put up. An average house required 16 pounds of Tyvek; the cost of Tyvek to the home builder averaged less than $200, including

EXHIBIT 9
The Du Pont Bear Lair

Sample of mailer sent out to 6,000 preregistered O.R. nurses prior to the 1984 A.O.R.N. Congress in Atlanta. Mailer tied together the "bear theme," also made it easier for nurses to find Du Pont booth among the hundreds they could visit, and promoted the annual Du Pont Vacation Sweepstakes (which helps pull traffic to the booth).

Make Tracks
for the Du Pont Bear Mountain

•Scrubby the Surgical Bear
•The Amazing Zellman, Psychic Perceptionist
•The Du Pont 1984 AORN Vacation Sweepstakes

THE

DU PONT

BEAR

LAIR

labor, for a conventional wood frame house. In a National Association of Home Builders study, Tyvek was reported to reduce heating costs by an average of 30 percent and air conditioning expenses by approximately 10 percent. The Tyvek wrap covered cracks and seams, thereby enhancing or protecting the effectiveness of a home's insulation.

The market for Housewrap sales were directly related to new housing starts. As interest rates declined in 1983, starts for one-family houses soared to 0.9 million, and Tyvek housewrap sales exceeded forecasts by 60 percent. The 1984 forecast for new one-family homes was 1.0 million. It was estimated that Tyvek housewrap sales in the U.S. would reach 2.3 million pounds in 1984 (see *Exhibit 11*).

Tyvek's only direct competitor as a housewrap was 15-pound felt, or tar paper, which was thick, heavy, and difficult to install because it tore easily. Although tar paper's price was about one-third less, Tyvek cost less overall because of labor savings during installation.

Because of the size of the market, and despite numerous patents on Tyvek, Du Pont expected competition for housewrap to increase significantly in the near future. Among potential competitors were Boise Cascade (1983 sales: $3.5 billion), Certain-Teed (1983 sales: $1.0 billion), Georgia-Pacific (1983 sales: $6.5 billion), and Kimberly-Clark (1983 sales: $3.3 billion).

Du Pont sold Tyvek to 42 leading building supply distributors with 83 warehouses throughout the U.S. These distributors, carefully selected by Du Pont, sold to dealers, who in turn sold to home builders. In some areas, the distributor's sales force called directly on home builders.

Just answer these easy questions about SONTARA® spunlaced fabric for single-use O.R. gowns and drapes.

You may be one of 75 lucky O.R. nurses who'll win a 3-foot high "Scrubby the Surgical Bear" dressed in cap, mask, and gown of SONTARA.° SONTARA is the *soft* gown and drape fabric . . . the one with over 10 years' proven O.R. experience. And made only by Du Pont, a leader in health-care product research.

You're always a winner if you ask for SONTARA by name . . . from such leading O.R. gown and drape manufacturers as American Converters, Surgikos, Kendall, and Mars.

Now . . . answer the questions, and qualify to win a giant "Scrubby" bear. Use either this form or a reasonable facsimile.

	Yes	*No*
• SONTARA is the most cloth-like, single-use O.R. fabric.	☐	☐
• SONTARA is remarkably strong, light, and comfortable.	☐	☐
• SONTARA is a proven barrier material.	☐	☐
• SONTARA lints less than reinforced paper or cotton.	☐	☐
• SONTARA fabric is available in gowns and drapes from leading manufacturers.	☐	☐

Winners will be selected at random from all entries received before March 1, 1984. You must be an O.R. nurse to win. Send your completed entry form to:

"Scrubby" Contest, Du Pont Company, Room X40201, Wilmington, DE 19898

Name _____   Title _____

Hospital _____   Address _____

City, State, Zip _____

°Du Pont registered trademark. Du Pont makes SONTARA® spunlaced fabric, not gowns and drapes.

Builders were the key buying influence for housewrap. Secondary influences included architects, government agencies, city and state building code officials, and energy conservation specialists at public utilities. Home buyers, increasingly energy-conscious, were also becoming more important.

Strategy and Tactics for Tyvek

Du Pont's principal objective for Tyvek was to achieve maximum market penetration in the shortest possible time. The 1985 strategy for Tyvek, therefore, was to continue to gain visibility, to strengthen the distributor network, and to promote the product as effectively as possible.

The 1984 budget for Tyvek housewrap consisted of $250,000 for the sales force and as listed in *Exhibit 12*, $475,000 for advertising and promotion. Ads, such as the one shown in *Exhibit 13* on page 80, were placed in trade and professional magazines to reach home builders and architects. Sales aids were developed for distributors, dealers, and home builders; and a direct mail campaign was mounted to buyers of blueprints for house designs from certain companies.

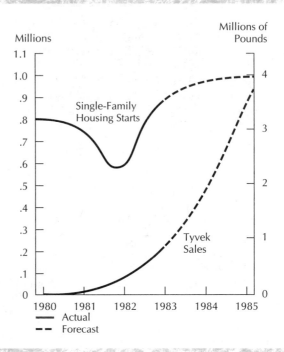

EXHIBIT 11
Sales of Tyvek Housewrap

(See *Exhibit 14* on page 81 for a Tyvek direct-mail piece.) In addition, the division had initiated co-op advertising with distributors, and made information about research findings on Tyvek's ability to conserve energy available to various publications through press releases. Finally, the budget covered trade shows, such as Du Pont's exhibit at the National Association of Home Builders' annual convention. Tentative budget plans for 1985 kept the sales force expenditure at the current level and increased advertising and promotion by 50 percent, with allocations similar to those of the 1984 plan.

The 1984 Budget Review

In considering how the 1985 budget proposals fit his strategies for Sontara and Tyvek, Mr. Blake had several questions. How would each product's push and pull emphasis change in 1985? How did the marketing mix affect push and pull, and how did the elements of the mix interact? What results would the various elements cause at different expenditure levels? He wondered how competitors' marketing strategies affected Sontara. He also thought about buyer behavior: How well would each product do in a use test at the current price? Of the total

EXHIBIT 12
Tyvek 1984 Advertising and Promotion Budget

Advertising	
Builder magazine, 8X	$ 55,000
Professional Builder, 8X	53,000
Multi-Housing World, 8X	28,00
Progressive Architecture, 8X	16,000
Sweet's 1985	8,000
Test publications	5,000
Preparation	12,000
Du Pont magazine	1,000
Total	$178,000
Sales Aids	
Builder Support:	
Model home display	$ 3,000
Homebuyer sell sheet	2,000
"Wise Builder" certificate	4,000
Mailing to *Home Planners* and *Home Magazine* plan buyers	10,000
Retailer Support:	
Literature	50,000
Co-op support	110,000
Co-op merchandising	1,000
Distributor Support:	
Distributor sales meeting	9,000
Distributor handbook	2,000
Sweet's brochure	8,000
LaBelle presentation	7,000
Masthead mailings	6,000
NAHB exhibit	20,000
Multi-Housing World exhibit	20,000
Regional shows	12,000
Manufactured-home support	12,000
Inquiry handling	1,000
Postage/freight	1,000
Store room	1,500
List maintenance	500
Total	$280,000
Product Information	
Press release production	$ 8,000
Press release distribution	3,000
Cost Saving release	4,000
Photography	2,000
Total	$ 17,000
Total advertising and promotion 1984	$475,000

EXHIBIT 13
Tyvek Housewrap

New test proves TYVEK Housewrap cuts heating costs 29%. And that sells homes.

Give yourself a competitive edge and a faster sale by offering homebuyers the extra value of TYVEK Housewrap.

The NAHB Research Foundation determined that there is a 29% reduction in heating costs in a home wrapped with TYVEK°. Placed over sheathing, TYVEK seals cracks and seams and significantly reduces interior air exchange rate.

It also keeps air out of the wall cavity, preserving insulation R-value and reducing heat loss through walls. And because it passes moisture vapor, it won't cause in-wall condensation.

It costs under $200 to wrap an average-size house. That includes labor. Two workers can put up 1,800 square feet in less than two hours with just a knife and staple gun.

TYVEK helps homes sell faster, and Du Pont helps you get the word out with free literature and model display.

Order TYVEK Housewrap—made only by Du Pont—from your building supply dealer. And for free test data literature and the name of your nearest distributor, call (302) 999-5088. Or write Du Pont Company, Room G-39982, Wilmington, DE 19898.

°Before-and-after test on a conventionally constructed 2-by-4 wood-frame home with R-11 insulation in walls. Your savings may be more or less depending on climate and construction.

TYVEK Housewrap is a Du Pont trademark for its air infiltration barrier.

value that buyers of Sontara and Tyvek received, how much of that value was built into the product and how much was added by marketing? Which mix elements contributed the most value? To find answers to these questions, he talked with the Sontara and Tyvek marketing managers.

John Murray, marketing manager for Sontara in the surgical gown and drape market, described the emphasis behind the 1984 budget as push rather than pull. He estimated that 75 percent of the current effort was push and that the percentage should go unchanged until he had something with which to launch a cost-effective pull campaign. For example, Sontara was under clinical study for the next two or three years, after which he could put the findings in professional journal ads and in direct mail to doctors, nurses, hospital administrators, and others. With this type of campaign, the push/pull percentage could approach 50/50.

Mr. Murray believed that it was misleading to identify specific budget items in the 1984 advertising and promotion budget as mix elements. It was more accurate, he said, to think of the overall budget as one-third advertising activity and two-thirds trade support. He said that the difference between the two was that the intent of advertising was to create a favorable image for the product, and the intent of trade support was to assist indirectly the sales effort of Du Pont customers. Because all budget items were part advertising and part trade support, it was more useful to look at the total budget rather than at each item. The $92,000

EXHIBIT 14
Tyvek Housewrap

Energy-saving air infiltration barrier.

A simple, inexpensive way to improve energy efficiency and make your homes more appealing.

Cold air infiltration consumes up to 40% of home heat. At the same time, cold air passing through insulation significantly reduces R-value. Housewrap of TYVEK spunbonded olefin seals cracks and seams in sheathing and at plates and sills. It keeps cold air out of insulation, so insulation delivers its full R-value. And it keeps cold air out of the house and warm air in.

TYVEK reduces heat loss.

Tests on an NAHB research home showed a 29% reduction in heating costs after applying TYVEK. That's the kind of energy-savings home buyers are looking for. And it costs very little to add to your homes.

TYVEK won't cause condensation build-up.

It's a durable sheet of high-density polyethylene fibers. It's not a film or paper. It allows moisture vapor to pass through (94 perm), so there's no danger of in-wall condensation. It's lightweight, tear-resistant, and will never rot or shrink.

TYVEK is easy to install.

Start at one corner and roll over the entire wall, wrapping around corners and over doors and windows. One man rolls, the other follows, applying staples or roofing nails.

When house is wrapped, go back and x-out windows and doors, pulling TYVEK in over window frame.

TYVEK comes in two sizes: 3 ft. wide rolls covering 999 sq. ft. and 9 ft. rolls covering 1,755 sq. ft. One 9 ft. roll covers an average-size house and weighs only sixteen pounds.

Two men can do a typical house in less than two hours, so labor cost is minimal. Find out from your building dealer how little it costs to add this important energy-saving feature to your homes.

advertising and promotion expenditure in 1984, he said, was in effect $31,000 for advertising and $61,000 for trade support. He thought that the same proportion was appropriate for the 1985 proposal of $115,000: $40,000 for advertising, and $75,000 for trade support. So, with $450,000 for the sales force, the three general mix elements were sales force, advertising, and trade support.

As he looked at the market, however, Mr. Murray found that these three elements did not fully capture the marketing activity of both Du Pont and its competitors. He believed that the sales force actually involved two functions: to maintain the current sales effort, and to do missionary sales. He said that he could make the same distinction concerning trade support, and that he could divide advertising between advertising to intermediate-users (i.e., gown and drape makers) and to end-users (i.e., hospitals). The 1985 proposal, he said, thus involved six mix elements: $450,000 in sales force/maintenance, $0 in sales force/missionary, $75,000 in trade support/maintenance, $0 in trade support/missionary, $10,000 in advertising/intermediate-users, and $30,000 in advertising/end-users.

Mr. Murray believed that the effective level of competitors' marketing spending was $900,000 sales force/maintenance, $100,000 sales force/missionary, $150,000 trade support/maintenance, $75,000 trade support/missionary, $25,000 advertising/intermediate-users, and $100,000 advertising/end-users.

The effectiveness of the marketing mix elements was interrelated. Examined individually, spending on sales force/maintenance, trade support/maintenance, and advertising/intermediate-users exhibited decreasing (concave) returns to scale. The market share response curve for the other elements was S-shaped: little effect of low spending, with first increasing and then decreasing returns to scale as spending increased.

The weighted-average price for Sontara was $.26 per square yard, and the variable cost was $.12. Sontara's relatively high price did not discourage purchases, he thought; for example, he said, in a use test, roughly 30 percent of the respondents said they would buy Sontara on the next occasion.

Mr. Murray described the effect of budget changes on sales in terms of three scenarios: (1) sales expected with the proposed budget, (2) the effect on sales of raising one mix element to its maximum reasonable expenditure level while holding the others constant at the proposed level, and (3) the impact of reducing one mix element to zero while holding the others at their proposed spending level.

With the current proposal of $565,000, he estimated that 1985 sales could reach 210 million square yards. This represented 32 percent of the total market or 50 percent of the smaller disposable market. If sales force/maintenance expenditures were to be raised from the proposed level of $450,000 to a maximum reasonable expenditure level of $550,000 while holding other spending to what had been proposed, Mr. Murray thought market share could reach 33 percent of the total market. Similarly, if the other mix elements were increased to their maximum reasonable levels while holding the remaining expenditures at their proposed levels, he thought market share increases would be likely as well, although not as dramatically. Specifically, if $200,000 were to be spent on sales force/missionary instead of the proposed $0, he thought market share would increase to 33 percent; if trade support/maintenance would be increased to $100,000, a 33 percent market share would result; if $100,000 would be spent on trade support/missionary, market share would be 33 percent; if advertising to intermediate-users were to be increased to $50,000, the net effect would be a 1 percent increase in market share; while an increase in advertising to end-users to $300,000 would also result in a 1 percent share gain.

Reductions in spending were thought to have the opposite effect. Reducing sales force/maintenance expenditures to zero while holding other spending at the proposed level was thought to reduce share to 22 percent of the total market during the next 12 months. Similarly, reductions to zero spending for sales force/missionary expenditures, trade support/maintenance, support/missionary, advertising to intermediaries, and advertising to end-users were thought to reduce expected market share to 32, 27, 32, 31, and 28 percent respectively.

As a validity check on the above estimates, Mr. Murray described what he thought would happen if all mix elements were to be raised simultaneously to their maximum reasonable expenditure levels, or if all support were to be withdrawn from the product. With maximum effort he thought a 39 percent share could be realized, although he was not sure how viable such an aggressive strategy would be for the long run. If all support were to be withdrawn, he estimated that market share would drop to 22 percent in the next 12 months before declining further.

Glenn White, marketing manager for Tyvek housewrap, said his marketing emphasis was mostly push, but increasingly pull. The push/pull percentage was 95/5 in 1984, he believed, and would become 65/35 in 1985, and 50/50 in 1986.

Mr. White categorized his marketing plan in terms of seven mix elements: sales force, advertising/end-users, advertising/intermediate-users, press releases, builder support, retailer support, and distributor support. He believed that interactive effects could occur among the mix elements, though he did not know what they were or how to account for them. For advertising/end-users, he believed that the effectiveness of additional expenditures followed an S-shaped curve, and that for the other elements the curve was concave.

The current price for Tyvek housewrap was $3.60 per pound, and the variable cost was about $1.50. In a use test, Mr. White estimated that between 20 percent and 25 percent would purchase the housewrap on the next occasion.

Mr. White, like Mr. Murray, described the effects of budget changes on Tyvek sales in terms of a number of scenarios: (1) sales expected from the baseline proposal, (2) the effects of item-by-item budget increases, and (3) the effects of item-by-item reductions as well as what would happen if all budget elements were increased to their maximum reasonable expenditure levels or if all support for the product would be withdrawn.

Specifically, Mr. White thought the proposed budget of $250,000 for the sales force, $0 for advertising to end-users, $230,000 for advertising to intermediaries, $25,000 for press releases, $35,000 for builder support, $225,000 for retailer support, and $195,000 for distributor support would result in sales of 3.6 million pounds, which translates into a 23 percent market share.

Raising the budget on an item-by-item basis was thought to have the following effects: sales force expenditures to $800,000, a 4 percent share increase; advertising to end-users of $1,100,000—a pull campaign—an 8 percent share increase; more advertising to intermediaries (to $460,000), an additional 2 share points; increased builder support (to $100,000) or retailer support (to $325,000), a 1 percent share gain; additional funds for press coverage (to $50,000), 1 percent share increase; and finally, additional distributor support (to $300,000), a 1 percent share increase. In similar fashion, reduction of the above mix elements to zero was thought to reduce market share for sales force expenditures to 20 percent, for advertising to end-users to 23 percent, for advertising to intermediaries to 20 percent, for press releases to 21 percent, for builder support to 22 percent, for retail support to 17 percent, and for distributor support to 19 percent.

In judging the overall effects of budget adjustments, Mr. White thought that if all elements were increased to their maximum reasonable expenditure limits, market share could reach 33 percent. On the other hand, if all support was withdrawn, a likely market share of 13 percent would result.

Conclusion

As he listened to the various arguments and estimates, Mr. Blake wondered about their consistency and what their implications would be for the 1985 budget. Should the Sontara and Tyvek budget proposals be revised? If so, how?

Ethical Situations in Marketing and Personal Conduct

H. Michael Hayes

The nature of marketing, with its responsibility for interfacing with customers, frequently places marketing and other personnel in situations where there is considerable conflict between the objectives and policies of their firms and the objectives and policies of their customers. We believe it is important to recognize the nature of such conflicts and how they might impact policy or personal decisions. The following situations provide a basis for discussion of how you as an individual might handle them.

1. You're the president. Your firm's sales manager went to jail for six months, convicted of being engaged in a price fixing conspiracy. The marketing manager was not indicted but should have been suspicious of the conspiracy. You state that neither you nor the marketing manager started the conspiracy or participated in it and that you will not censure a successful executive for not running around seeking possible law violations of her people.

2. You're the president of a large defense contractor. Department of Defense (DOD) regulations prohibit officials from accepting any kind of gratuity from defense contractors. You concede that you knew about entertainment of DOD officials by your firm but assert that it was not improper to offer such "hospitality"—only improper for the DOD officials to accept it.

3. The new product sold very well when it was introduced. Subsequently, problems developed. Sales in the U.S. declined to a point where you decided to withdraw the product from the U.S. market, pending a "fix" of the problems. In Europe, customers had learned to live with the problems, and sales were holding up reasonably well.

4. In exchange for your agreement to manufacture Product X in a foreign country, the government granted your firm exclusive rights to sell the product in their country. At the time of the agreement you built the product to the same specifications as in the very competitive U.S. market. Subsequently, the U.S. version of the product has been improved significantly.

These situations were developed by Professor H. Michael Hayes, University of Colorado at Denver, based on discussions with a number of marketing managers, sales managers, field sales personnel, and reviews of marketing and purchasing literature.

5. You have been appointed marketing manager for a large producer of commodities. Shortly after assuming the position and moving your family to a new city, you become aware that your firm has been engaged in price fixing activities with its competitors, that this practice is supported by top management, and that you are expected to participate in it. You decide to bring the matter to the attention of the Department of Justice and agree to tape record some of the price fixing sessions.

6. You're the marketing manager for a large manufacturer. Many of your customers have published policies prohibiting gift giving by suppliers at Christmas, or any other time. You know, however, that many of your competitors give gifts to key middle managers. You instruct your sales force to meet the competitive practice.

7. The ABC Company is one of your best customers. Traditionally they have bought from your firm on a sole source basis, with assurances that the price you quote them is as good a price as you would bid in a competitive situation. ABC placed its annual order with you two months ago. In the last month you have had to reduce your prices in a number of instances to meet competitive situations, sometimes as much as 10%.

8. A certain product has had a high failure rate. Two previous "fixes" did not eliminate the problem. Manufacturing and engineering tell you they now have a fix they are confident about. It comes to your attention that some of the field sales people are insisting on extensive detail on the fix so that they can "decide whether or not to recommend the product to their customers." You write a letter to the field sales force telling them that it is the factory's job to make the product and that their job is to sell it, not to review designs for their suitability or reliability.

9. Most of your customers have published policies stating they will not reveal details about competitors' bids. Details about competitors' bids are most important, however. You instruct your sales force to get this information, regardless of customers' policies.

10. You have just seen a study made by the National Association of Purchasing Management indicating the frequency with which "favors" are offered, their acceptability and the frequency of acceptance (see table below). You conclude that any item falling below 50% acceptability will not be offered by your firm.

Item	Offered by Vendors	Rated Acceptable	Actually Accepted
Lunches	98%	90%	87%
Advertising Souvenirs	96	92	87
Dinners	90	70	76
Tickets (Sports, Theater)	86	60	19
Christmas Gifts	85	50	19

(continued)

Item	Offered by Vendors	Rated Acceptable	Actually Accepted
Trips to Vendor Plants	83%	51%	34%
Golf Outings	74	47	33
Food and Liquor	65	29	9
Discounts for Personal	46	21	9
Small Appliances	33	6	5
Vacation Trips	26	2	1
Clothing	15	3	3
Large Appliances	13	1	–
Loans	3	1	–
Automobiles	2	1	–

1,184 responses, as reported in *National Purchasing Review,* January–February 1979.

11. Due to an old tool, one of your products is not meeting all its specifications. It is highly unlikely that this will cause a problem, however, as few customers have applications that are sensitive to the particular deficiency. Replacement of the tool will mean coming in under profit budget for the quarter, with extensive need for explanation to higher ups. You tell the manufacturing people that you concur in their decision to postpone the purchase of the tool until next quarter.

12. Your authorized distributor bids your product to a local government. The low bid is from an out-of-state distributor on a competing product (although this distributor is also authorized to sell your product). The out-of-state distributor offers you the order if you will meet the price of the competing product. Note: Your local distributor also has access to the competing product.

13. You return from vacation with a beard. Your customers, who have known you for a long time, kid you about it but you don't detect any negative reaction. Your boss tells you to shave it off.

14. You prefer not to drink at lunch. Frequently you take your customers to lunch at restaurants where drinks are not served. Your boss feels that a drink or two at lunch establishes a much more relaxed climate, one of which facilitates communication with customers. He insists you encourage your customers to have a drink at lunch.

15. The customer tells you the order is yours if you can improve the shipment from 52 to 42 weeks. The factory tells you that 52 weeks is the absolute best estimate they can make and that, if anything, shipment might be a little longer than 52 weeks. The commission on the order is in the neighborhood of $10,000. Shipping promises in this industry are frequently missed.

16. Your firm has a very strict set of "Terms and Conditions of Sale." You have been working on a very large order. The customer tells you the order is yours, if you will accept their "Terms and Conditions of Purchase." You know these are not acceptable to your firm. You also know that it is very rare for problems to arise where the terms are the basis for settlement. The order will actually go through a distributor which means your firm would not have to know of the terms in the customer's order (although in a court of law they probably would be binding).

17. Your customer has a published policy stating they will not reveal details about competitors' bids. Your factory tells you that details about competitors' bids are most important. You have found a source in the customer's organization who will make most of the details available to you.

18. Your customer has published a code of buyer-seller relations that, among other things, prohibits any form of entertainment other than a business lunch. Those in the purchasing department scrupulously adhere to this provision. In other parts of the customer's organization the code is not adhered to strictly. Your competitors continue to entertain individuals in the engineering department. You are concerned that specifications will start to favor your competitors.

Grasse Fragrances SA

H. Michael Hayes

G rasse Fragrances, headquartered in Lyon, France, was the world's fourth largest producer of fragrances. Established in 1885, the company had grown from a small family-owned business, selling fragrances to local perfume manufacturers, to a multinational enterprise with subsidiaries and agents in over 100 countries.

For Marketing Director Jean-Pierre Volet, the last few years had been devoted to building a strong headquarters marketing organization. In February 1989, however, he was returning to France after an extensive tour of Grasse sales offices and factories, and a number of visits with key customers. As the Air France flight touched down in Lyon Airport, Jean-Pierre Volet was feeling very concerned about what he had learned on the trip. "Our salesforce," he thought, "operates much as it did several years ago. If we're going to compete successfully in this new environment, we have to completely rethink our salesforce management practices."

The Flavor and Fragrance Industry

Worldwide sales of essential oils, aroma chemicals, and fragrance and flavor compounds were estimated to be around $5.5 billion in 1988.

Five major firms accounted for something like 50% of the industry's sales. The largest, International Flavors & Fragrances Inc. of New York, had 1988 sales of $839.5 million (up 76% from 1984), of which fragrances accounted for 62%. The company had plants in 21 countries, and non-U.S. operations represented 70% of sales and 78% of operating profit.

Quest International, a wholly owned subsidiary of Unilever, was next in size with sales estimated at $700 million, closely followed by the Givaudan Group, a wholly owned subsidiary of Hoffman-LaRoche with sales of $536 million, and Grasse Fragrances with sales of $480 million. Firmenich, a closely held

Swiss family firm, did not disclose results but 1987 sales were estimated at some $300 million.

Grasse produced only fragrances. Most major firms in the industry, however, produced both fragrances and flavors (i.e., flavor extracts and compounds mainly used in foods, beverages, and pharmaceutical products). Generally, the products were similar. The major difference was that the flavorist had to match his or her creations with their natural counterparts, such as fruits, meats, or spices, as closely as possible. On the other hand, the perfumer had the flexibility to use his or her imagination to create new fragrances. Perfumery was closely associated with fashion, encompassed a wide variety of choice, and products had to be dermatologically safe. Development of flavors was more limited, and products were required to meet strict toxicological criteria because the products were ingested.

Markets for Fragrances

While the use of perfumes is as old as history, it was not until the 19th century, when major advances were made in organic chemistry, that the fragrance industry emerged as it is known today. Focusing first on perfumes, use of fragrances expanded into other applications. In recent years manufacturers of soap, detergents, and other household products have significantly increased their purchases of fragrances and have represented the largest single consumption category. Depending on the application, the chemical complexity of a particular fragrance and the quantity produced, prices could range from less than FF40 per kilogram to over FF4,000.[1]

Despite its apparent maturity, the world market for fragrances was estimated to have grown at an average of 5–6% during the early 1980s, and some estimates indicated that sales growth could increase even further during the last half of the decade. New applications supported these estimates. Microwave foods, for instance, needed additional flavorings to replicate familiar tastes that would take time to develop in a conventional oven. In laundry detergents, a significant fragrance market, the popularity of liquids provided a new stimulus to fragrance sales, as liquid detergents needed more fragrance than powders to achieve the desired aroma. Similarly, laundry detergents designed to remove odors as well as dirt also stimulated sales, as they used more fragrance by volume.

The New Buying Behavior

Over time, buying behavior for fragrances, as well as markets, had changed significantly. Responsibility for the selection and purchase of fragrances became complex, particularly in large firms. R&D groups were expected to ensure the compatibility of the fragrance with the product under consideration. Marketing groups were responsible for choosing a fragrance that gave the product a competitive edge in the marketplace, and purchasing groups had to obtain competitive prices and provide good deliveries.

---

[1]$1.00 = approximately FF6.00 in 1988.

Use of briefs (the industry term for a fragrance specification and request for quotation) became common. Typically, a brief would identify the general characteristics of the fragrance, the required cost parameters as well as an extensive description of the company's product and its intended strategy in the marketplace. Occasionally, a fragrance producer would be sole sourced, generally for proprietary reasons. Usually, however, the customer would ask for at least two quotations, so competitive quotes were the norm.

Grasse Fragrances SA

Background

The company was founded in 1885 by Louis Piccard, a chemist who had studied at the University of Lyon. He believed that progress in the field of organic chemistry could be used to develop a new industry—creating perfumes, as opposed to relying on nature. Using a small factory on the Siagne River near Grasse, the company soon became a successful supplier of fragrances to the leading perfume houses of Paris. Despite the interruptions of World Wars I and II, the company followed an early policy of international growth and diversification. Production and sales units were first established in Lyon, Paris, and Rome. In the 1920s, company headquarters were moved to Lyon. At that time, the company entered the American market, first establishing a sales office and then a small manufacturing facility. Acquisitions were made in England, and subsequently the company established subsidiaries in Switzerland, Brazil, Argentina, and Spain.

Faced with increased competition and large capital requirements for R&D, plant expansion, and new product launches, the Piccard family decided to become a public company in 1968. Jacques Piccard, oldest son of the founder, was elected president and the family remained active in the management of the company. Assisted by the infusion of capital, Grasse was able to further expand its business activities in Europe, the United States, Latin America, and the Far East.

In 1988 total sales were $450,000,000, up some 60% from 1984; 40% of sales came from Europe, 30% from North America, 10% from Latin America, 5% from Africa/Middle East, and 15% from Asia/Pacific. In recent years the company's position had strengthened somewhat in North America.

By the end of 1988, the company had sales organizations or agents in 100 countries, laboratories in 18 countries, compounding facilities in 14 countries, chemical production centers in 3 countries, and research centers in 3 countries. Employment was 2,500, of whom some 1,250 were employed outside France.

Products

In 1988, the company's main product lines were in two categories:

- Perfumery products used for perfumes, eau de cologne, eau de toilette, hair lotion, cosmetics, soaps, detergents, other household and industrial products.

- Synthetics for perfume compounds, cosmetic specialties, sunscreening agents and preservatives for various industrial applications.

According to Jacques Piccard:

> From the production side, flavors and fragrances are similar, although the creative and marketing approaches are quite different. So far we have elected to specialize in just fragrances, but I think it's just a matter of time before we decide to get into flavors.

Following industry practice, Grasse divided its fragrances into four categories:

- Fine Fragrances
- Toiletries and Cosmetics
- Soaps and Detergents
- Household and Industrial

Marketing at Grasse

In 1980, Jean-Pierre Volet was appointed Marketing Director after a successful stint as country manager for the Benelux countries. At the time, the headquarters marketing organization was relatively small. Its primary role was to make sure the salesforce had information on the company's products, send out samples of new perfumes that were developed in the labs, usually with little customer input, and handle special price or delivery requests. As Volet recalled:

> In the 1940s, 1950s, and 1960s, most of our business was in fine fragrances, toiletries, and cosmetics. Our customers tended to be small and focused on local markets. Our fragrance salesman would carry a suitcase of 5 gram samples, call on the customer, get an idea of what kind of fragrance the customer wanted, and either leave a few samples for evaluation or actually write an order on the spot. It was a very personal kind of business. Buying decisions tended to be based on subjective impressions and the nature of the customer's relation with the salesman. Our headquarters marketing organization was designed to support that kind of selling and buying. Today, however, we deal with large multinational companies who are standardizing their products across countries, and even regions, and who are using very sophisticated marketing techniques to guide their use of fragrances. Detergents and other household products represent an increasing share of the market. When I came to headquarters, one of my important priorities was to structure a marketing organization which reflected this new environment.

The marketing organization in 1988 is shown in Exhibit 1. In addition to the normal administrative activities such as field sales support, pricing, and budgeting, Volet had built a fragrance creation group and a product management group. More recently, he had established an international account management group.

The fragrance creation group served as a bridge between the basic lab work and customer requirements. It also ran the company's fragrance training center, used to train both its own salesforce and customer personnel in the application of fragrances. The product management group was organized in the four product categories. Product managers were expected to be knowledgeable about everything that was going on in their product category worldwide and to

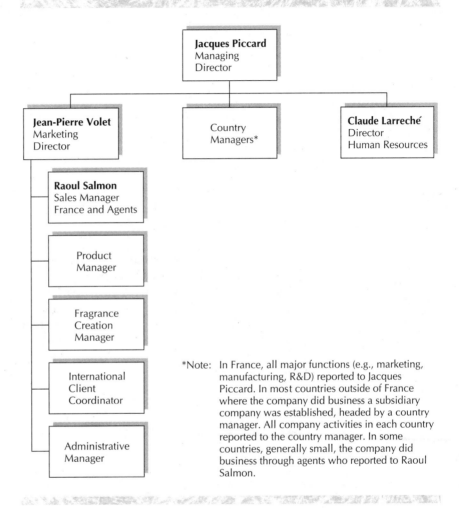

EXHIBIT 1
Partial Organization Chart

Jacques Piccard
Managing
Director

Jean-Pierre Volet
Marketing
Director

Country
Managers*

Claude Larreché
Director
Human Resources

Raoul Salmon
Sales Manager
France and Agents

Product
Manager

Fragrance
Creation
Manager

International
Client
Coordinator

Administrative
Manager

*Note: In France, all major functions (e.g., marketing, manufacturing, R&D) reported to Jacques Piccard. In most countries outside of France where the company did business a subsidiary company was established, headed by a country manager. All company activities in each country reported to the country manager. In some countries, generally small, the company did business through agents who reported to Raoul Salmon.

use their specialized knowledge to support field sales efforts as well as guide the creative people. It was Volet's plan that international account managers would coordinate sales efforts.

Field sales in France reported to Piccard through Raoul Salmon, who was also responsible for the activities of the company's agents, used in countries where it did not have subsidiaries or branches. In recent years, use of agents had declined, and the company expected the decline to continue.

Outside France, field sales were the responsibility of Grasse country managers. In smaller countries, country managers handled only sales, thus operating essentially as field sales managers. In other countries, where the company had manufacturing or other non-selling operations, the norm was to have a field sales manager reporting to the country manager. Although individual sales representatives reported to the field sales managers, it was understood that there was a dotted line relationship from the sales representatives to the ICCs and the product managers.

The company relied extensively on its field salesforce for promotional efforts, customer relations, and order-getting activities. There were, however, two very different kinds of selling situations. As Salmon described them:

> There are still many customers, generally small-scale, who buy in the traditional way where the process is fairly simple. One salesperson is responsible for calling on all buying influencers in the customer's organization. Decisions tend to be based on subjective factors, and the sales representative's personal relations with the customer are critically important.
>
> The other situation, which is growing, involves large and increasingly international customers. Not only do we see that people in R&D and marketing as well as in purchasing can influence the purchase decision, but these influencers may also be located in a number of different countries.

In either case, once the decision had been made to purchase a Grasse fragrance, the firm could generally count on repeat business, as long as the customer's product was successful in the marketplace.

On occasion, however, purchase decisions were revised, particularly if Grasse raised prices or if the customer's product came under strong competitive price pressure, thus requiring that a less expensive fragrance be considered.

The Quotation Procedure

For small orders, the quotation procedure was relatively simple. Popular fragrances had established prices in every country, and the salesforce was expected to sell at these prices.[2] In some instances, price concessions were made, but they required management approval and were discouraged.

For large orders, it was the norm to develop a new fragrance. Increasingly, customers would provide Grasse with extensive information on their intended product and its marketing strategy, including the country or countries where the product would be sold. To make sure the fragrance fit the customer's intended marketing and product strategy, Grasse was expected to do market research in a designated pilot country on several fragrances, sometimes combined with samples of the customer's product. According to Volet:

> Once we have found or developed what we think is the best fragrance, we submit our quotation. Then the customer will do his own market research, testing his product with our fragrance and with those of our competitors.

---

[2]Subject to approval by marketing headquarters, each Grasse producing unit established a transfer price for products sold outside the country. Country prices were established, taking into account the country profit objectives and the local market conditions. Transfer prices were usually established for a year. Adjusting transfer prices for fluctuations in exchange rates was a matter of ongoing concern.

Depending on the outcome of the market research, we may get the order at a price premium. Alternatively, we may lose it, even if we are the low bidder. If, on the other hand, the results of the market research indicate that no fragrance supplier has an edge, then price, personal relationships, or other factors will influence the award.

Because of the extensive requirements for development and testing, headquarters in Grasse was always involved in putting a quotation together, and close coordination was vital between headquarters and the branch or subsidiary. When buying influencers were located in more than one country, additional coordination of the sales effort was required to ensure that information obtained from the customer was shared and also to have a coherent account strategy.

Coordination of pricing was also growing in importance. Many large customers manufactured their products in more than one country and looked for a "world" price rather than a country price. In these situations, country organizations were expected to take a corporate view of profits, sometimes at the expense of their own profit statements. The lead country (i.e., the country in which the purchasing decision would be made) had final responsibility for establishing the price. Increasingly, however, this price had to be approved in Lyon.

Submitting quotations in this environment was both complex and expensive. According to Volet:

> Receiving a brief from a customer starts a complex process. We immediately alert all our salespeople who call on various purchasing influencers. Even though the brief contains lots of information on what the customer wants, we expect our salespeople to provide us with some additional information.
>
> The next step is for our creative people to develop one or more fragrances which we believe will meet the customer's requirements. They are aided in this effort by our product managers who know what is going on with their products worldwide. If additional information is needed from the customer, our international account people will contact the appropriate salespeople.
>
> After creating what we think is the right product or products, we may conduct our own market research in a country designated by the customer. This is usually done under the direction of our product manager, working closely with our market research people. Throughout this process, our salesforce is expected to stay in close touch with the customer to give us any changes in his thinking or any competitive feedback. Based on the results of this effort, we then submit our proposal which gives the customer the price, samples, and as much product information as possible.
>
> With some customers, there is little further sales effort after they receive our quotation, and the buying decision is made "behind closed doors." In other instances, we may be asked to explain the results of our research or to discuss possible modifications in our product and, sometimes, in our price. Frequently we find that the customer is more concerned with our price policy (i.e., how firm the price is and for how long) than with the price quoted at the time of the brief.
>
> When you make this kind of effort, you obviously hate to lose the order. On the other hand, even if we lose, the investment made in development work and market research is likely to pay off in winning another brief, either with the original customer or with another customer.

International Accounts

In 1988 about 50% of the firm's business came from some 40 international accounts. Looking to the future, it was expected that the number of international accounts would grow, and some estimated that by 1994 as much as 80% of the firm's business would come from international accounts.

As of 1988, 18–20 international accounts were targeted for coordination by International Client Coordinators (ICCs) in Lyon. The principal responsibility of each ICC was to really know assigned customers on a worldwide basis and put that knowledge to use in coordinating work on a brief. The rest were followed in Lyon, but coordination was a subsidiary responsibility. In either case, it was the view at headquarters that coordination was critical. As Volet described it:

> We rely extensively on account teams. European teams may meet as often as once a quarter. Worldwide teams are more likely to meet annually. For designated accounts, the ICC takes the lead role in organizing the meeting and, generally, coordinating sales efforts. For others, the Parent Account Executive (the sales representative in the country selling the customer component with the greatest buying influence) plays the lead role. In these situations, we hold the Parent Account Executive responsible for all the ICC's daily coordinating work with the customer. We also expect him to be proactive and already working on the next brief long before we get a formal request.
>
> Here in Lyon, we prepare extensive worldwide "bibles" on international accounts which are made available to all members of the team. We also prepare quarterly project reports for team members. Our next step will be to computerize as much of this as possible.

Sales Management Practices

In 1988, salesforce management practices were not standardized. Selection, compensation, training, organization, etc. were the responsibility of subsidiary management. Even so, a number of practices were similar.

Sales representatives tended to be compensated by a salary and bonus scheme. A typical minimum bonus was 1.5 month's salary, but could range up to 2.5 month's salary for excellent performance. The exact amount of the bonus was discretionary with sales management and could reward a number of factors.

Sales budgets were established from estimates made by sales representatives for direct orders (i.e., orders that would be placed by their assigned accounts). These estimates were developed from expectations of sales volume for fragrances currently being used by customers, in which case historical sales were the major basis for the estimate, and from estimates of sales of new fragrances. While historical sales of currently used fragrances were useful in predicting future sales, variations could occur. Sales activity of the customer's product was not totally predictable. In some instances, customers reopened a brief to competition, particularly where the customer was experiencing competitive cost pressures.

Predicting sales of new fragrances was even more difficult. Customers' plans were uncertain, and the nature of the buying process made it difficult to predict the odds of success on any given transaction. Grasse Fragrances, nevertheless, relied heavily on these estimates. The sum of the estimates was expected to add up to the company budget for the coming year. When this was not the case, sales managers were expected to review their estimates and increase them appropriately.

The company had recently introduced, company-wide, its own version of management by objectives. Each sales representative was expected to develop a personal set of objectives for negotiation with his or her sales manager. Formal account planning, however, had not been established, although some subsidiaries were starting the practice.

Sales training had two components. Product knowledge tended to be the responsibility of headquarters, relying heavily on the fragrance training center. Selling skills, however, were principally the responsibility of the subsidiary companies.

Selection practices were the most variable. Some subsidiaries believed that company and product knowledge were key to selling success and so tended to look inside the company for individuals who had the requisite company and product knowledge and who expressed an interest in sales work. Others believed that demonstrated selling skills were key and so looked outside the company for individuals with good selling track records, preferably in related industries.

Sales Management Issues

A number of sales management practices were of concern, both in headquarters and in the subsidiaries.

Influence Selling

Ensuring appropriate effort on all buying influencers was a major concern. According to Salmon:

> Our sales representatives understand the importance of influence selling, but we have no formal way of recognizing their efforts. A number of our large accounts, for instance, have their marketing groups located in Paris, and they have lots of influence on the buying decision. If we win the brief, however, purchasing is likely to take place in Germany or Spain or Holland, and my sales representative will not get any sales credit.

In a similar vein, Juan Rodriquez, sales manager for a group of countries in Latin America, commented:

> We have a large account that does lots of manufacturing and purchasing in Latin America but does its R&D work in the U.S. The customer's people in Latin America tell us that without strong support from R&D in the U.S., it is very difficult for them to buy our fragrances. The sales representative in New York is certainly aware of this, but his boss is measured on profit, which can only come from direct sales in the U.S., so he's not enthusiastic about his sales representative spending a lot of time on influence business.

In some instances, the nature of the buying process resulted in windfalls for some sales representatives. Commenting on this aspect, Salmon observed:

> It can work the other way as well. Our Spanish subsidiary recently received an order for 40 tons of a fragrance, but the customer's decision to buy was totally influenced by sales representatives in Germany and Lyon. Needless to say, our Spanish subsidiary was delighted, but the people in Germany and Lyon were concerned as to how their efforts would be recognized and rewarded.

While there was general recognition that influence selling was vital, it was not clear how it could be adequately measured and rewarded. As Salmon pointed out:

> In some instances (e.g., the order in Spain) we're pretty sure about the amount of influence exerted by those calling on marketing and R&D. In other instances, it is not at all clear. We have some situations where the sales representative honestly believes that his calls on, say, R&D are important but, in fact, they are not. At least not in our opinion. If we come up with the wrong scheme to measure influence, we could end up with a lot of wasted time and effort.

Incentive Compensation

Compensation practices were a matter of some concern. The salary component was established at a level designed to be competitive with similar sales jobs in each country. Annual raises had become the norm, with amounts based on performance, longevity, and changes in responsibility. The bonus component was determined by the immediate manager, but there was concern that bonuses had become automatic. Still further, some held the view that the difference between 1.5 and 2.5 times the monthly salary was not very motivating, even if bonus awards were more performance driven.

Whether merited or not, sales representatives expected some level of bonus, and there was concern that any change could cause morale problems. At the same time, there was growing recognition of the increasing importance of team selling.

Overall responsibility for compensation practices was assigned to Claude Larreché, Director of Human Resources. According to Larreché:

> Some of our sales managers are interested in significantly increasing the incentive component of salesforce compensation. It has been my view, however, that large incentive payments to the salesforce could cause problems in other parts of our organization. Plus, there seems to be considerable variation in country practice with regard to incentive compensation. In the U.S., for instance, compensation schemes which combine a fixed or salary component and an incentive component, usually determined by sales relative to a quota, are common. To a lesser degree, we see some of this in Europe, and somewhat more in the South, but I'm not sure that we want to do something just because a lot of other companies are doing it.
>
> We're also thinking about some kind of team incentive or bonus. But, this raises questions about who should be considered part of the team and how a team bonus should be allocated. Should the team be just the sales representatives, or should we include the ICCs? And what about the customer service people without whom we wouldn't have a base of good performance to build on?

Allocation is even more complicated. We're talking about teams comprised of people all around the world. I think it is only natural that the local manager will think his sales representative made the biggest contribution, which could result in long arguments. One possibility would be for the team itself to allocate a bonus pool, but I'm not sure how comfortable managers would be with such an approach.

Small Accounts

Despite the sales growth expected from international accounts, sales to smaller national accounts were expected to remain a significant part of the firm's revenues and, generally, had very attractive margins. According to one country sales manager:

> With the emphasis on international accounts, I'm concerned about how we handle our smaller single country accounts. Many of them still buy the way they did 10 and 20 years ago, although today we can select from over 30,000 fragrances. Our international accounts will probably generate 80% of our business in the years to come, but the 20% we get from our smaller accounts is important and produces excellent profits for the company. But I'm not sure that the kind of selling skills we need to handle international accounts are appropriate for the smaller accounts. Personal and long-term relationships are tremendously important to these accounts.

Language

In the early 1980s, it had become apparent to Grasse management that French would not serve as the firm's common language. In most of its subsidiary countries, English was either the country language or the most likely second language. With considerable reluctance on the part of some French managers, it was decided that English would become the firm's official language. Personnel in the U.S. and England, few of whom spoke a second language, welcomed the change. There were, however, a number of problems. As the Italian sales manager said:

> We understand the need for a common language when we bring in sales representatives from all over Europe or the world. And we understand that English is the "most common" language in the countries where we do business. All of my people understand that they will have to speak English in international account sales meetings. What they don't like, however, is that the Brits and Americans tend to assume that they are smarter than the rest of us, simply because we can't express ourselves as fluently in English as they can. It's totally different when my people talk to someone from Latin America or some other country, where English is their second language, too.
>
> A related problem is the attitude that people from one country have towards those of another. This goes beyond language. Frequently, our people from Northern Europe or North America will stereotype those of us from Southern Europe or Latin America as disorganized or not business-like. My people, on the other hand, see the Northerners as inflexible and unimaginative. To some extent, these views diminish after we get to know each other as individuals, but it takes time and there is always some underlying tension.

Language also influenced decisions on rotation of personnel. It was Volet's view that there should be movement between countries of sales managers and marketing personnel. Still further, he felt that sales representatives who aspired to promotion should also be willing to consider transfers to another country or to headquarters in Lyon. As he pointed out, however:

> Customer personnel in most of our international accounts speak English. Hence, there is a temptation to feel that English language competency is the only requirement when considering reassignment of sales personnel. In fact, if we were to transfer a sales representative who spoke only English to Germany, for instance, he would be received politely the first time, but from then on it would be difficult for him to get an appointment with the customer. It has been our experience that our customers want to do business in their own language, even if they speak English fluently.
>
> An exception might be an international account whose parent is British and which transfers a lot of British personnel to another country. Even here, however, there will be lots of people in the organization for whom English is not a native tongue.
>
> Therefore, we require that our salespeople speak the language of the country and are comfortable with the country culture. Local people meet this requirement. The real issue is getting all, or most, of our people to be comfortable in more than one language and culture.

Sales Training

One of the most perplexing issues was what, if any, changes to make with regard to sales training. At headquarters there was considerable sentiment for standardization. As Volet put it:

> I really don't see much difference in selling from one country to another. Of course, personal relations may be more important in, say, Latin America or the Middle East than in Germany, but I think that as much as 80–85% of the selling job can be harmonized. In addition, it's my view that our international accounts expect us to have a standardized sales approach. Sales training, therefore, should be something we can do centrally in Lyon.

This view was supported by those in human resources. According to Claude Larreché, Director of Human Resources:

> We no longer see ourselves as a collection of individual companies that remit profits to Lyon and engage in occasional technology transfer. Our view of the future is that we are a global company that must live in a world of global customers and markets. I think this means we must have a Grasse Fragrance culture that transcends national boundaries, including a common sales approach, i.e., this is the way Grasse approaches customers, regardless of where they are located. A key element in establishing such a culture is sales training here in Lyon.

Others disagreed with this point of view, however. Perhaps the most vociferous was the U.S. sales manager:

> I understand what Jean-Pierre and Claude are saying, and I support the notion of a common company culture. The fact is, however, that selling is different in the

U.S. than in other parts of the world. Not long ago we transferred a promising sales representative from Sweden to our office in Chicago. His sales approach, which was right for Sweden, was very relaxed, and he had to make some major adjustments to fit the more formal and fast-paced approach in Chicago. I don't see how a sales training program in Lyon can be of much help. Plus, the cost of sending people to Lyon comes out of my budget, and this would really hit my country manager's profits.

In fact, I think we ought to have more flexibility with regard to all our sales management practices.

As Jean-Pierre Volet waited for his bag at the Lyon Airport, he wondered how far he should go in making changes with regard to the salesforce. Whatever he did would be controversial, but he was convinced some changes were necessary.

The Japanese Construction Industry—1992

Naoko Ochiai

Per V. Jenster

Overview

In 1992, the Japanese construction industry was entering a period of tremendous strategic upheaval. Four factors were precipitating this change. Firstly, severe financial losses from their venture businesses had placed a heavy burden on management. During the 1980s, construction companies had started to venture outside their traditional scope of activities by making extensive speculations in land as well as in the stock market. But, by the beginning of the 1990s, the anticipated profits from these investments still had not materialized. Also, the recession had worsened the huge financial burden being faced by these companies. The first six months of 1992 showed a 15.6% drop in orders compared to the same period in 1991, due to the drastic decline in new construction orders from the private sector, which comprised over 60% of the industry.

Secondly, the major—i.e., the largest—construction companies actually employed very few people, as they principally relied on a network of subcontractors to perform the on-site work. Due to the aging demographic profile of Japanese society and subcontractors' increasing bargaining power, the cost of managing a large subcontractor network was curbing the industry's growth.

Thirdly, their clients' changing needs were forcing these companies to re-evaluate their marketing and sales approach. Clients were demanding more services and financial support—e.g., asking the construction companies to share in the investment of joint projects.

It was becoming increasingly clear to the senior executives of the larger construction companies that new perspectives had to be applied to improve financial deficits, reduce costs, and restructure the operational and marketing focus of their organizations.

This case was prepared by Research Associate Naoko Ochiai, under the supervision of Professor Per V. Jenster, as a basis for class discussion rather than to illustrate either effective or ineffective handling of a business situation.

Fourthly, industry had been hit by probes and allegation of bribery. This front-page attention did not help industry leaders keep a strong focus on the strategic issues of the business.[1]

Growth and Market Fluctuations

The market size of the Japanese construction industry in 1991 was estimated to be at ¥83.7 trillion ($642 billion)[2] and was the second largest in the world. (Refer to Exhibit 1.) The market had expanded 62% over the five years between 1986 and 1991. (Refer to Exhibit 2.) This expansion had occurred mainly in the market sourced by the private sector which increased its ratio to the whole market. (Refer to Exhibit 3.)

The Japanese Research Institute of Construction and Economics predicted that a low growth trend of 2.3% would continue in the construction industry throughout the '90s. The public works and housing sectors were still expanding (market segments are described in a later section). Regional development was also expanding, although the economy were experiencing difficult times. The civil engineering works was stable due to the government's plan to invest ¥430 trillion in mainly local civil engineering projects, where local and small-sized construction companies were strong. The private non-housing sector was declining due to the economic recession. It was anticipated that these trends would remain constant until the year 2000. Following the hypothesis that the Japanese construction industry had a fluctuation cycle of eight years, the next surge of demand was expected in 2000. (Refer to Exhibit 4.)

Demographic Trends

In 1991, Japan's population was increasing at a rate of only 0.35%. At the same time, however, the proportion of those over 64 years of age, which had been only 7.1% in 1970, had increased to 12.6% by 1991. As a result, 31.5% of the employees in the construction industry were over 50, which meant that it was becoming harder to secure young human resources. (Refer to Exhibit 5.)

---

[1]In June 1993, the biggest series of scandals in the construction industry started with the arrest of top executives from HAZAMA (the chairman and the president), from SHIMIZU (the vice-president), from MITSUI Construction (the vice-president), and from NISHIMATSU Construction (the vice-president). They were suspected of having bribed the city mayor of Sendai (located 300 km northeast of Tokyo) in order to win a public works contract. On September 20th, Mr. Yoshino, Chairman of SHIMIZU and Chairman of the powerful Federation of Construction Contractors, was arrested on suspicion of having bribed Fujio Takeuchi, the prefectual governor of Ibaragi (northeast of Tokyo), allegedly so that SHIMIZU would be given favorable treatment in a construction project decision. Two days later, SHIMIZU was shaken again by the arrest of another two top executives, a vice-president and a senior director. On October 4th, Mr. Hashimoto, a vice-president of TAISEI and the strongest candidate to be the next president, was arrested on suspicion of having bribed the prefectual governor of Miyagi (300 km northeast of Tokyo). On October 26th, Mr. Kiyoyama, a vice-president of KAJIMA, was also arrested on suspicion of having bribed the Sendai mayor. During these four months, the widening scandal led to the arrests of two prefectual governors, two big city mayors and 26 officials from the top management of three of the giant companies.

[2]¥130 = US $1.00 in 1991.

EXHIBIT 1
Construction Investment by Countries

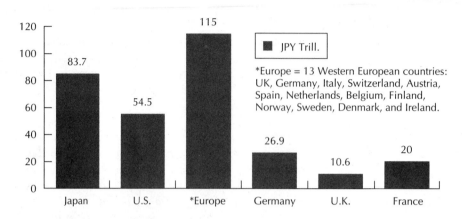

*Europe = 13 Western European countries: UK, Germany, Italy, Switzerland, Austria, Spain, Netherlands, Belgium, Finland, Norway, Sweden, Denmark, and Ireland.

Source: Japan Ministry of Construction, U.S. Department of Commerce and Euroconstruct Conference, 1991.

EXHIBIT 2
Trends in Domestic Market Size in Japan 1986–1991

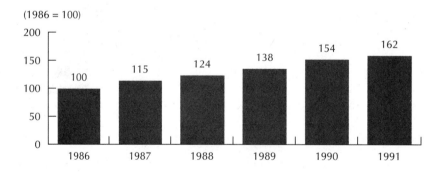

Market Segments

The market typically was divided into three segments by product type: civil engineering and building construction; housing construction; and non-housing projects. (Refer to Exhibit 6.)

One-third of all construction investment was in civil engineering. Civil engineering consisted of industrial facilities, roads, railroads, and land preparation. The largest player engaged in civil engineering was **KAJIMA** (the major

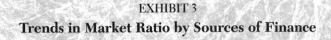

EXHIBIT 3
Trends in Market Ratio by Sources of Finance

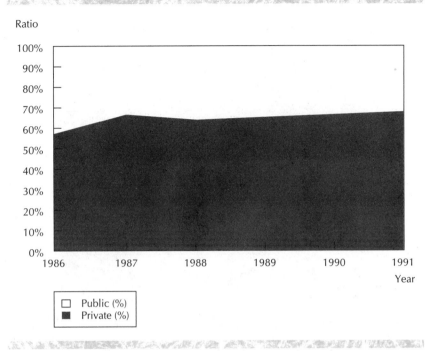

Ratio

□ Public (%)
■ Private (%)

firms are described in a later section). SEKISUI-House, not included among
the giant companies, was the largest player in the housing area, although all
major companies participated in the housing segment. Non-housing projects
included office, factory and warehouse space, and commercial facilities such as
department stores, hotels, schools and hospitals. The largest company in non-
housing was SHIMIZU.

Segmentation by the source of financial investment for the project was an
equally important factor. (For construction companies, "financial source"
referred to the client.)

The public sector provided approximately one-third of the investment in
construction, with 80% going to civil engineering projects—as they provided
the infrastructure necessary to society. (Refer to Exhibits 7A and 7B.)

The remaining two-thirds came from the private sector, with 85% of that
investment being earmarked for building construction (housing and non-housing). The private sector—which included companies from industries such as
land development, insurance, banking, trading, etc.—mainly supported building
construction, especially in non-housing projects. In housing, the private sector
invested more heavily than the public sector. (Refer to Exhibit 7C.) However,
the public sector invested more consistently in housing than the private sector,

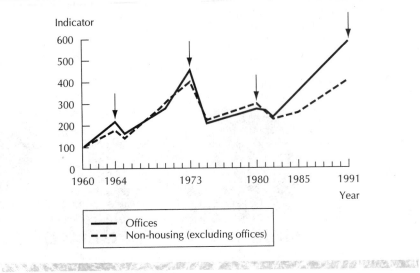

EXHIBIT 4

Trends in Total Area under Construction by Building Type

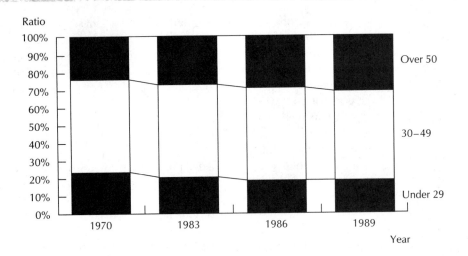

EXHIBIT 5

Trends in the Average Age of Employees in the Japanese Construction Industry

EXHIBIT 6
Market Segments by Product Type and Source of Finance

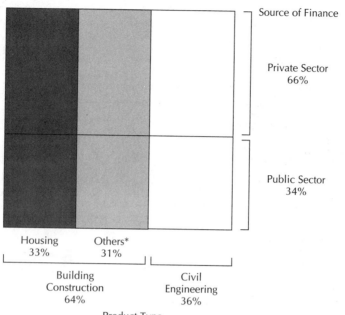

Source of Finance

Private Sector
66%

Public Sector
34%

Housing
33%

Others*
31%

Building
Construction
64%

Civil
Engineering
36%

Product Type

* Others (= non-housing) include offices, factories, warehouse
space, commercial facilities, hotels, schools, and hospitals.

EXHIBIT 7

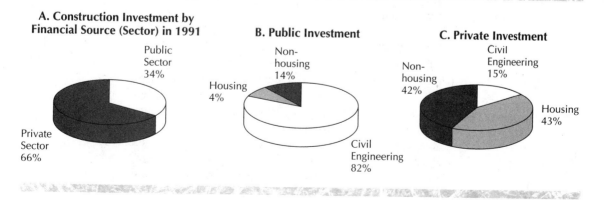

A. Construction Investment by Financial Source (Sector) in 1991

Public Sector 34%

Private Sector 66%

B. Public Investment

Non-housing 14%

Housing 4%

Civil Engineering 82%

C. Private Investment

Civil Engineering 15%

Non-housing 42%

Housing 43%

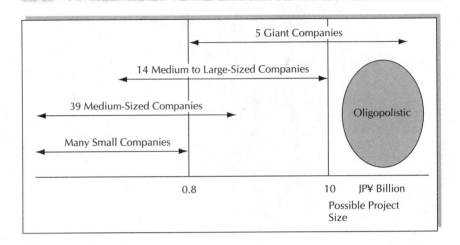

EXHIBIT 8

Price Segmentation and Possible Project Size by Size of Construction Company

because its social welfare policy ensured having housing that was not affected by economic recession continuously available.

Price segmentation also led to clustering of the projects. The largest projects (over ¥10 billion) consisted of high-rise buildings, regional development projects, larger civil engineering projects, etc. This cluster tended to be oligopolistic because of the high level of technological skills needed, as well as the ability to manage the subcontractor network and obtain the necessary financial resources. Mid-sized projects ranged from ¥.8 billion to ¥10 billion, while the smallest projects—usually private homes—were under ¥.8 billion and were priced competitively. (Refer to Exhibit 8.)

Geographical Considerations

The Japanese construction industry was firmly rooted in Japan; less than 10% of all sales occurred in foreign markets. In the domestic market, 34.1% of the 1989 building construction market (cost based) was concentrated in Tokyo and its suburbs. Construction projects often occurred intensively within certain districts, because construction investment was motivated by increasing commercial land values due to new traffic networks. Local companies were used on local projects. The construction company and the subcontractors were unwilling to send their site workers far from their base district because of moving expenses. Moreover, local companies tended to give their construction orders to local construction companies because of the relationships which existed within the district.

EXHIBIT 9
Largest Regional Development Project Being Planned

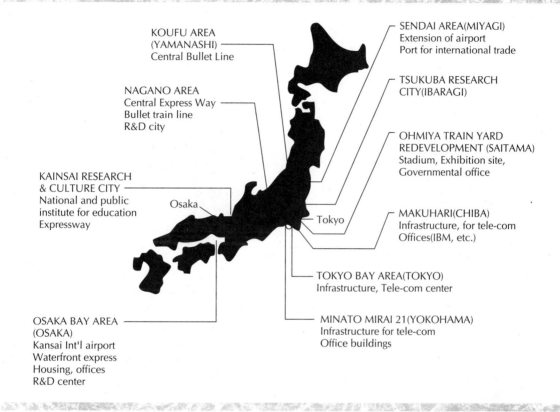

KOUFU AREA
(YAMANASHI)
Central Bullet Line

NAGANO AREA
Central Express Way
Bullet train line
R&D city

KAINSAI RESEARCH
& CULTURE CITY
National and public
institute for education
Expressway

Osaka

Tokyo

OSAKA BAY AREA
(OSAKA)
Kansai Int'l airport
Waterfront express
Housing, offices
R&D center

SENDAI AREA(MIYAGI)
Extension of airport
Port for international trade

TSUKUBA RESEARCH
CITY(IBARAGI)

OHMIYA TRAIN YARD
REDEVELOPMENT (SAITAMA)
Stadium, Exhibition site,
Governmental office

MAKUHARI(CHIBA)
Infrastructure, for tele-com
Offices(IBM, etc.)

TOKYO BAY AREA(TOKYO)
Infrastructure, Tele-com center

MINATO MIRAI 21(YOKOHAMA)
Infrastructure for tele-com
Office buildings

Geographically, growth was predicted to be concentrated in suburban areas where enhanced traffic access had created new opportunities. (Refer to Exhibit 9.) In the center of Tokyo, the construction market was almost saturated. Every major company was shifting its target to the suburban areas of Tokyo.

Industry Structure

Over 90% of the companies in the construction industry were small, i.e., had less than 19 workers. (Refer to Exhibit 10.) Typically, these small companies were working mainly as subcontractors, which meant that they were highly dependent on the larger main contractor companies and vulnerable in a downward economy. However, the five major companies together employed more than 10,000 workers. In addition, each of the major companies had its own network of over 100 subcontractors. These companies usually selected subcontractors from their own registered lists. Subcontractors consisted of two types:

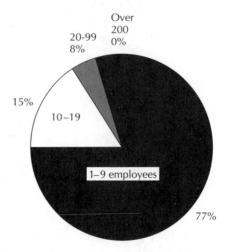

EXHIBIT 10
Percentage of Companies by Size of Personnel

specialized construction workers (excavators, plasterers, plumbers, carpenters, etc.) and general construction workers. Normally, site workers were hired by the subcontractors and machinery was offered either by the subcontractor, the main contractor, or by leasing companies. Economies of scale existed for the entire industry—i.e., larger companies were more profitable than smaller ones. However, among the top 20 companies, profitability varied greatly and size was not unilaterally a source of above-average returns. Return on equity ranged from 3.3 to 16.0. (Refer to Exhibit 11.)

Project Financing

Japanese companies generally contracted for work based on a total cost agreement or lump-sum payment. Payment was made either on the accumulated estimates of each completed project or by determining a fixed price and timeframe. The latter, also known as "partition payment," was the more popular method. Partition payment gave contractors the opportunity to gain or lose interest according to the time difference between receiving cash from the clients and paying the subcontractors.

All the major construction companies made finance a priority in order to compete in the land development market and in R&D. The land development market was very attractive, not only because of its growth potential, but also because it utilized a company's competencies. Furthermore, success in land development strengthened the company's social reputation and dominance.

EXHIBIT 11
Sales and ROE

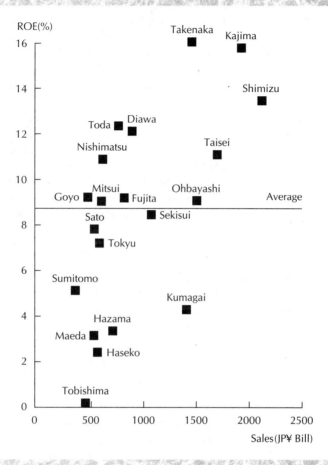

Companies also could take advantage of land speculation. They usually financed land purchases from their profits, borrowing from banks or by issuing corporate bonds.

Expanding into land development investment was also an attractive option for the client companies of construction companies. Due to escalating land values, most client companies which had vast unutilized land easily received strong financial support from the banks to enter the regional redevelopment business. Even individual clients were beginning to think of construction as an investment. Client companies and individual clients hastened to learn the skills of construction project management and to develop these skills even further through information exchange.

Contracting Issues

Two procedures, *bidding* and *tokumei*, were used to obtain the contractors who would carry out the projects. All publicly financed projects were required to choose contractors through *bidding*, a contract system based on price competition using cost estimates. In addition, there were two types of bidding processes: open bidding and designated bidding. The latter was mainly used in Japan as it was in the United Kingdom, as an easy way to exclude incompetent companies in advance. Normally, several firms were designated and invited to submit estimates, and the firm with the most reasonable estimates was selected. However, this form of bidding was severely criticized by the U.S., because the standards and the process for determining the companies to be designated was very unclear and illegal confidential exchanges among contractors—so-called *dango*—could easily take place. *Tokumei*, used only for private projects, was a discretionary contract system whereby the contractor was chosen after a negotiation process between the client and the contractor, which considered not only the estimate price but also the type of project and its specific needs.

The government had three major roles other than making a public investment in construction. Firstly, the government issued every construction company's business license. In Japan, for private or public sector projects, firms interested in obtaining construction contracts in Japan were required to obtain a contractor's license as specified by the Construction Business Law. Secondly, the government maintained the Construction Disputes Committee (CDC), an organization affiliated with the Ministry of Construction. This was a quasi-judicial organ established by the Construction Business Act to settle disputes concerning construction work contracts. Thirdly, the government dealt with international issues—such as whether the Japanese market should open up to overseas construction companies and to foreign workers.

The Japan-U.S. Construction Talks was playing a vital role in solving these international issues. This conference had been held on a regular basis since 1986, when the office of the U.S. Trade Representative (USTR) proposed international bidding for the Kansai Airport project in Japan. In 1992, the USTR was insisting that designated bidding be abolished and that open bidding be the only form of bidding used—as in the U.S.

The issue of how to deal with foreign workers needed to be considered by the Japanese government. Under the present Immigration Law, a work permit was never given to foreign workers unless they had a high level of expertise, knowledge and experience. Yet, in actuality, there were many foreigners already working illegally in Japan. Although the labor force was in short supply in some industries—such as construction and service, the government was still not strongly in favor of opening up the employment market, because of the low social receptiveness to foreign residents and the fear of discouraging the driving forces for innovation in less labor-intensive processes.

In addition, Japanese regulations required that an agreement be reached between the construction investors and the people living near the construction

EXHIBIT 12
Top 10 Contractors Worldwide

Ranking	Name	Country	Orders Received (A)	Overseas Orders (B)	% of Overseas Business (B)/(A)
1.	Fluor Daniel, Inc	U.S.	21,376	4,980	23.3
2.	Shimizu Corp.	Japan	19,165	1,279	6.7
3.	Bechtel Group	U.S.	18,339	11,630	63.4
4.	Taisei Corp.	Japan	17,750	390	2.2
5.	Kajima Corp.	Japan	17,683	1,029	5.8
6.	Takenaka Corp.	Japan	16,264	812	5.0
7.	Ohbayashi Corp.	Japan	14,635	1,248	8.5
8.	John/Brown/Davy	U.K.	14,334	8,844	61.7
9.	The M.W. Kellog Co.	U.S.	13,127	9,786	74.5
10.	The Parsons Corp.	U.S.	13,100	5,000	38.2

Unit: Millions of U.S. dollars
Source: ENR in 1991

site. Investors usually asked the construction company to help by persuading the residents to be tolerant about noisy machinery, heavy truck traffic and certain environmental changes.

Major Players in the Industry

The U.S. trade journal, *Engineering News Record*, identified five Japanese construction companies among the top ten companies worldwide in 1991. (Refer to Exhibit 12.) The five giant companies, which together had approximately a 20% share of the domestic market, received domestic orders worth ¥10.28 trillion in 1990, a 26% increase over 1985 sales. These five companies participated in all product sectors and in all major foreign countries in Asia, Europe and the Pacific. (Refer to Exhibit 13.)

SHIMIZU

SHIMIZU was the largest company in the whole construction market (revenues of ¥2.1 trillion in 1992). (Refer to Exhibit 14.) Founded by a carpenter in 1804, the company, based in Tokyo, had expanded rapidly in recent years. Its overseas sales were 4% of total sales, with its main overseas clients being its own subsidiary in the real estate business or other Japanese companies. It was the strongest one in the private sector and in non-housing construction, especially office buildings—the most dominant segment in non-housing. (Refer to Exhibit

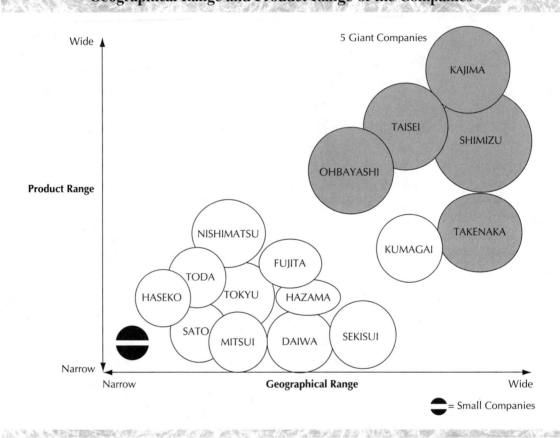

EXHIBIT 13
Geographical Range and Product Range of the Companies

15.) The company was known for being aggressive and for excelling in quick decision making and comparatively low delivery costs among major players. SHIMIZU was currently focusing on entering the smaller-sized project market. Its relationship with subcontractors was strongly developed, through strategic distribution of work, cheap transfer of computer software and training its subcontractors' employees.

SHIMIZU's target for the remainder of the 1990s was to obtain 60–70% of its total sales from the domestic construction market and 30–40% from land development, engineering, diversified business, and the overseas construction market. Its main challenge was to develop the domestic *"kansai"* market (the western metropolitan region of Japan whose center was Osaka, the second largest city in Japan), where the company had been weak compared to the *kansai*-based companies OHBAYASHI and TAKENAKA.

EXHIBIT 14
Financial Result of Five Major Companies

	Shimizu	Kajima	Taisei	Ohbayashi	Takenaka
ROE (%)	13.4	15.7	11	9	16
Sales (JP¥ trillion)	2,130	1,951	1,717	1,509	1,480
Cost (JP¥ trillion)	1,868	1,705	1,497	1,334	1,300
Cost/Sales (%)	88	87	87	88	88
Margin (JP¥ trillion)	263	246	221	175	181
Margin/Sales (%)	12	13	13	12	12
Operating Income	137	127	102	69	70
Other Income	−12	−3	−6	−16	7
Income Before Tax	124	124	96	53	77
Ranking of Market Share by Building Type					
Building Construction	1	3	4	5	2
(Housing)	4	6	7	8	N.B.
(Offices)	1	2	3	4	N.B.
(Factories etc.)	2	1	4	3	N.B.
Civil Engineering	4	1	2	3	N.B.

°Data; 1992

KAJIMA

KAJIMA, founded in the 19th century, was the second largest company (revenues of ¥1.9 trillion in 1992). Like SHIMIZU, the company was located in Tokyo. It emphasized civil engineering and regional development projects, and sold the largest amount in both segments. KAJIMA was a family business and had a "traditional" image in the construction industry. It had a technology-oriented culture, and its top management consisted of only elite people graduated from Japan's most prestigious university, Tokyo University. The company was also well connected in the social strata of society: its Chairman of the Board was also the chairman of the Japanese Chamber of Commerce and Industry in 1992. KAJIMA was the only company with a diversified organization structure; its areas of business comprised four independent departments: Construction Management, Design and Engineering, Land Development and New Business. Its ¥20 billion expenditure for R&D was the largest in the construction industry. The company was also perceived as the technological leader in the industry due to its quick commercialization of new products such as high-rise buildings. (Refer to Exhibit 16.)

EXHIBIT 15
Portfolio of Shimizu Corporation

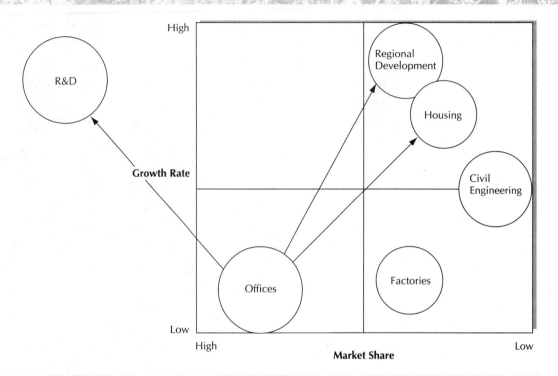

TAISEI

TAISEI, the third largest company (revenues of ¥1.7 trillion in 1992) was founded in 1873. It was known as the most diversified company, its 77 subsidiaries,
ranging from financial services to tourism, produced a revenue equal to 18% of
that achieved by the parent company (the highest among the major companies).
Mr. Satomi, the Chairman of the Board, said, "We follow up on every challenging possibility for diversification related to the construction business so that we
will grow increasingly global as a company group." Among the industry players,
TAISEI was the only company which regularly employed foreigners as office
workers. Its product and geographical segment were similar to KAJIMA.

OHBAYASHI

OHBAYASHI, a family business founded in 1892, was the fourth largest company (revenues of ¥1.5 trillion in 1992). The company was located in Osaka.
In 1992, OHBAYASHI was the third largest in the civil engineering market
after KAJIMA.

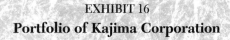

EXHIBIT 16
Portfolio of Kajima Corporation

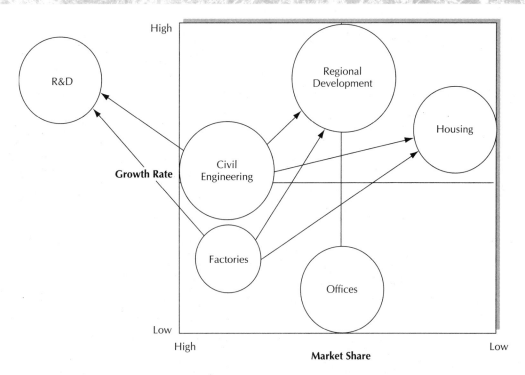

The company also emphasized land development and, of the five major companies, was the most profitable in this market. However, a poorly conceived financial management strategy had resulted in a loss of 23% of its total income in 1992. The company gained 32% of its revenue from the *kansai* market, which the larger companies—SHIMIZU and KAJIMA—were beginning to target.

TAKENAKA

TAKENAKA, a privately held company that had been founded in 1610, was the fifth largest company (revenues of ¥1.4 trillion in 1991). Like OHBAYASHI, the company was located in Osaka and was a family business. Of the five major companies, TAKENAKA was the only company which focused solely on building construction, particularly prestigious buildings. It also competed strongly with the largest company, SHIMIZU, in the building construction market. The *kansai* market provided 35% of its revenues. The company was known for high technology and good design, and was perceived to offer excellent value.

EXHIBIT 17
Ranking of Japanese Construction Companies by Sales[*]

	Sales	Assets	Income	ROE	ROA
1. Shimizu	2,130	2,806	124	13.4	4.4
2. Kajima	1,951	2,884	124	15.7	4.3
3. Taisei	1,717	2,344	96	11.0	4.1
4. Ohbayashi	1,509	2,229	53	9.0	2.4
5. Takenaka	1,480	1,709	77	16.0	4.5
6. Kumagai	1,405	1,813	38	4.2	2.1
7. Sekisui House	1,077	1,361	89	8.7	6.6
8. Daiwa House	882	1,059	91	12.1	8.5
9. Fujita	820	1,362	44	9.1	3.2
10. Toda Const.	780	890	48	12.3	5.4
11. Hazama	697	845	33	3.3	3.9
12. Nishimatsu Const.	622	638	26	10.9	4.1
13. Tokyu Const.	591	768	22	7.2	2.8
14. Mitsui Const.	580	768	23	7.2	2.8
15. Sato Kogyo	543	901	18	7.8	2.0
16. Haseko	529	1,161	25	2.7	2.2
17. Goyo Const.	501	567	14	9.1	2.5
18. Maeda Const.	501	648	15	3.2	2.3
19. Tobishima Const.	461	650	−44	N.B.	N.B.
20. Sumitomo Const.	360	408	8	5.1	1.8
Average of ROE, ROA				9.0	3.6

[*]JP¥ trillion

Several other companies were also well known throughout Japan and were competitive with the five giants. (Refer to Exhibit 17.) The best positioned among this group were SEKISUI-House and DAIWA-House, experts in housing construction and cost containment. Other highly competitive companies included TODA Construction, FUJITA, NISHIMATSU Construction, HAZAMA, TOKYU Construction, and MITSUI Construction.

EXHIBIT 18
Core Activities

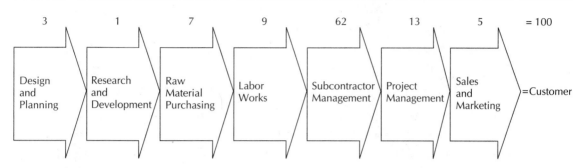

Core Activities

The core business activities of the Japanese construction industry consisted of Design and Planning, Research and Development, Raw Materials Purchasing, Labor Works, Subcontractors Management, Project Management, and Sales and Marketing. (Refer to Exhibit 18.)

Design and Planning

Design and planning added 3% to the total cost paid by the client for the project. Each of the five major companies employed 400–800 highly talented architects internally. Undertaking both the design and the construction was allowed in Japan, although it was prohibited in some European countries (e.g., France). The governments of these countries thought that consumers should be protected from the possibility of collusion—such as padding bills, careless technical checks, or ambiguity about responsibility—which could occur when the architect and contractor belonged to the same company. However, integrating the design and construction was believed to improve the quality of a building as it enhanced having more effective internal communication.

Research and Development

Research and development was considered essential for the development of new products and better manufacturing methods, both of which could significantly change the construction industry. However, research and development added only 1% to the client's cost. The amount of R&D spending by major companies in 1992 ranged from ¥10 billion to ¥20 billion, nearly 1% of their total yearly gross sales. Each major company employed approximately 200 researchers in their respective laboratories. Smaller companies could not afford

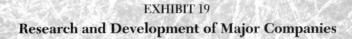

EXHIBIT 19
Research and Development of Major Companies

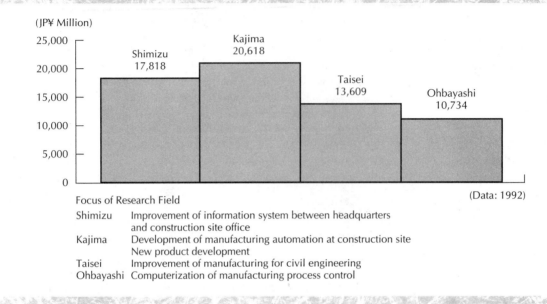

Focus of Research Field

Shimizu	Improvement of information system between headquarters and construction site office
Kajima	Development of manufacturing automation at construction site New product development
Taisei	Improvement of manufacturing for civil engineering
Ohbayashi	Computerization of manufacturing process control

R&D laboratories due to their limited budgets and lack of human resources. The three major areas of research consisted of greater automation in manufacturing, new product development, and development of information systems. (Refer to Exhibit 19.)

Manufacturing automation referred to large projects which required various repetitive manufacturing processes. More automation was expected to solve the decreasing human resource supply and to reduce labor management costs. However, its cost per unit was higher than non-automated work due to the lack of volume necessary for obtaining economies of scale. New product development was expected to produce high perceived value. Although no drastically new products were developed during the 1980s, it was unclear whether this trend could continue in the next decade. Information systems development was thought to lower construction site management costs, the communication costs at headquarters, and between the sites and headquarters.

The R&D emphasis differed from one major company to another. SHIMIZU strongly focused on information networks in order to manage a greater number of sites without increasing the number of managers and to strengthen the subcontractor networks. KAJIMA was eager to develop new products (the latest was the "Urban Slalom," an artificial roof-covered skiing site located in the center of the city). TAKENAKA was also active in new product development (especially known for its commercialization of the inflated dome stadium). TAISEI emphasized civil engineering technology. (Refer to Exhibit 19.)

Raw Materials Purchasing

Raw materials added 9% to the project's value. Cement, steel and wood were the primary raw materials used in the industry. These materials were usually purchased through a manufacturer/retailer distribution system (e.g., trading companies). Cement, iron and steel were mainly purchased from big trading companies (e.g., MITSUBISHI or SUMITOMO) or big steel companies (e.g., Nippon Steel or NKK). The price was dependent on market conditions, but could sometimes be arranged through negotiation for the volume buyer for a long period. The construction industry players tended to have a weak negotiating power due to being the minor buyer. In the housing construction segment of the industry, the top 20 construction companies succeeded in lowering costs by integrating raw material suppliers and project management. Some of these companies had started as subsidiaries of raw material suppliers. They developed light construction materials and patterns which drastically cut down on human labor and costs at the construction site.

Subcontractors Management

The major construction firms depended heavily on subcontractors. Subcontractors employed the site workers and owned most of the engineering equipment. Inevitably, the construction company and its subcontractors tended to be close partners. As subcontractors consumed 62% of the resources of a turnkey project, they were an increasingly powerful component. Subcontractors normally were small family businesses that were experts in excavating, piling, building structures, plumbing, interior finishing, etc. They also often purchased the raw materials.

The subcontractors were responsible for labor resource management under the supervision of a project manager from the main contractor. A good relationship between this project manager and the subcontractors was critical. A large construction company would choose the subcontractors according to their experience with the company. Mutual experience decreased communication time and improved overall communication with fewer misunderstandings. It was the project manager who ultimately would choose the subcontractors. A good relationship between the project manager and the subcontractors easily became a long-term relationship, because both the project manager and the subcontractors tended to stay with the same job/position throughout the years until retirement. However, such a long-standing relationship sometimes became too closed and stagnant, creating disadvantages for the business by lowering the driving force to improve and neglecting to make essential changes in technology, for environmental reasons or to meet customers' needs.

The relationship with subcontractors varied with the economic situation. In a time of economic growth, subcontractors became stronger and more than equal partners due to the tight supply of site workers. They could freely choose amongst orders from several major contractors. During a recession, their bargaining power became weaker, as they were more dependent on the construction company for obtaining projects.

Another important factor which affected this relationship even more was the technological progress being made in manufacturing automation. It was believed that the subcontractors' role would be greatly limited if site workers were replaced by factory machines and robots. However, industry observers thought that the replacement of site workers by automation would occur only gradually over the next decade, due to limited financing for further technical improvement and more site workers available than in the late 1980s.

Project Management

The core activity of the construction company was management of the project. Project management costs were estimated to be 13% of a project's value. The project manager was responsible for controlling quality, budget, time lines and safety, and was the key player on site because he was the one who was able to gain substantial profits through efficient management. (In large companies, the project manager was generally equal to a senior executive.) Prices were established using estimates that included some margin, then were set in a fixed contract before construction started. However, the actual margin was determined after completion of the construction by calculating the difference between the estimated price (stated in the contract) and the actual costs incurred. If the project manager raised the margin of a ¥1 billion project by 5% through his efforts, he produced ¥50 million for his company.

The project manager had two basic ways to decrease the actual cost of a project: reducing the estimated cost, or reducing the subcontractors' margins. Of course, they tried to maintain tight control of unit costs and the amount of raw materials, site workers and leasing equipment used. But, a more skillful way to cut on-site costs was to manage several sites at the same time, thus the project manager was generally in charge of several sites. (Refer to Exhibit 20.) Sharing not only the site office and equipment but also the site workers could reduce costs considerably. Moreover, the merit of sharing among several construction sites enhanced the ability to negotiate with the local administration offices, each of which had various criteria and restrictions for construction. Reduction of the subcontractors' margins was the most direct way to increase the contracting company's profit, but this approach could be risky. Forcing subcontractors to work on slim margins could tempt them to cut corners or seek out other projects with competing firms.

In Japanese construction companies, a competent project manager was highly respected and often promoted to the level of director after a long career as a project manager.

Sales and Marketing

The sales and marketing function was divided into two categories: by customer type—i.e., public or private (which was further broken down by company or individual); and by construction purpose—i.e., construction only or also with other various types of special needs (e.g., purchasing land, making specific financial arrangements, requiring a feasibility study of the real estate business,

EXHIBIT 20
Project Manager in Charge of Several Sites

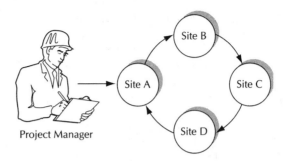

EXHIBIT 21
General Supporting Service Offered by Construction Company

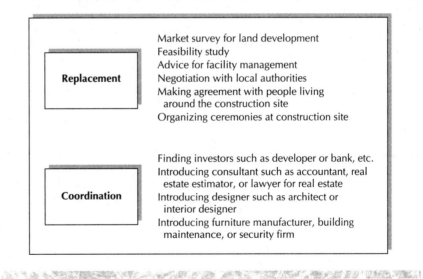

Replacement	Market survey for land development Feasibility study Advice for facility management Negotiation with local authorities Making agreement with people living around the construction site Organizing ceremonies at construction site
Coordination	Finding investors such as developer or bank, etc. Introducing consultant such as accountant, real estate estimator, or lawyer for real estate Introducing designer such as architect or interior designer Introducing furniture manufacturer, building maintenance, or security firm

finding end users for the floor of a building, etc.). (Refer to Exhibit 21.) In the major companies, 70% of the salesmen were designated for private clients; 20% for public clients and 10% for clients with special needs. Traditionally, each sales manager had his own roster of client companies which he visited daily. Occasionally, the client asked a question which the sales manager would refer to the section for "special needs" and would then relay the answer back to the client. However, this kind of approach was changing. As business increased and the competition became more severe, clients were beginning to expect the construction companies to provide additional support and greater expertise—such as planning the strategy for facility management, regional development management, etc. The construction companies had to reconsider the tasks and structure of the sales teams. In response to these challenges, the "Key Account Manager" was introduced. (Refer to Exhibit 22.) The key account manager was responsible for managing the entire client account, including coordinating the necessary resources from both inside and outside the company to produce a competitive proposal. About 5% of the total corporate staff were key account managers. It was estimated that a total of 5% of sales was spent on marketing and sales activities.

Although, on the one hand, clients seemed to be exercising greater influence on the construction companies, at the same time some clients continued to stay faithfully with certain construction companies. For example, tradition still tended to be strong in certain areas which affected sales and marketing. Many Japanese clients trusted older, established companies more than new companies. They would select a "traditional" company without even receiving any sales promotion material, basing their decision on social reputation and satisfaction with previous construction work. In such cases, price was believed to be a secondary consideration. Because clients did not have the resources to oversee the contractors' prices and quality, they depended on the construction company's integrity. Another reason for being highly dependent on the construction company was that the investment was seen as a memorial or as an artistic endeavor by some company. Being known and well perceived by already completed projects contributed to good will, which then carried over into other areas—such as facilitating financing and securing subcontractors.

Future Challenges

During the period when every major construction company was rushing into the real estate business, firms were also trying to utilize surplus assets by seeking to develop overseas expansion, an overall trend stimulated by Japan's prosperous domestic market and available seed money for future regional development. By 1992, however, the real estate business had lost its luster, and much of the construction industry was burdened with bank debts for the substantial investments in land purchasing both in Japan and overseas. Thus, the major companies were now re-evaluating the amount of risk they could assume, repositioning themselves in the market, and deciding what to do with their devaluated land—to keep it or sell it. SHIMIZU had already sold most of its real estate property in the U.K. and Australia after deciding that the land development business in these countries was no longer affordable. It was also considering downsizing that business in the U.S.

After experiencing failure in land development, the top executives in every company realized the difficulties of running a diversified business and the importance of enhancing their competitive position in their original business:

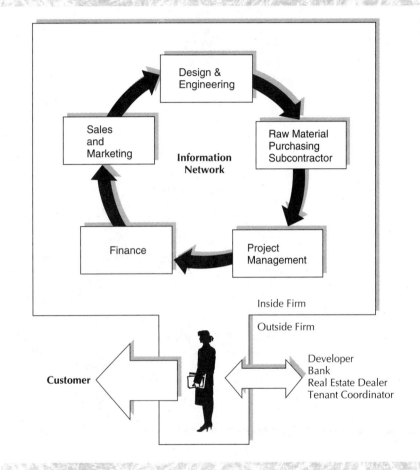

EXHIBIT 22
Role of Key Account Manager

construction. For the rest of the 1990s, the Japanese construction industry would have to compete differently from before; companies would need a more thorough cost focus, a reorganization of sales and marketing, and more strategic research and development activities.

According to an estimation by the Japan Research Institute, the per unit cost for construction could be decreased by 30%. A more thorough cost focus obviously related to the management of subcontractors. Construction companies would have to decide whether to maintain the same relationship with their subcontractors or to introduce new manufacturing systems—including the factories to perform the manufacturing, which would be likely to replace some subcontractors. Cutting the relationship with subcontractors, a most important business resource for many many years, would have to be a gradual process that was carefully handled by the major companies. Small family businesses would inevitably be excluded from the industry. As well, the small family business segment feared that lower-cost foreign companies would take their place if the Japanese market completely opened to foreign contractors. One way to decrease this kind of conflict would be to have contractors re-educate subcontractors as robot operators or in-factory workers. In order to launch a new manufacturing system, they would need to work together also with raw material suppliers.

In addition to subcontractor management, raw material purchasing could also be rationalized—e.g., by switching to direct purchasing instead of using intermediate companies or by importing directly from foreign countries in Asia. Regarding opportunities to save *inside* the company, the bureaucratic structure of the larger companies, and their high personnel and R&D budgets, put them at a cost disadvantage.

The reorganization of sales and marketing would be critical for several reasons: more demanding customers; an expanding regional development market; a geographical shift of customers—from urban central cities to local cities; and a change in customer type—from companies to individuals. The key account manager system would be one solution for demanding customers, but this system could create a conflict between being centralized (in order to utilize highly integrated and speedy communication) and the decentralization required to shift to local areas and to handle an enormous number of individual customers. The optimal solution would be to enhance the communication system between the company human intelligence at the central office and the local salespeople. The number of salespeople could be increased by re-positioning office workers.

Strategic research and development activities would also be important. Major construction companies thought that R&D was still risky but worthy, because the number of players which could afford R&D was limited and, if commercialized, would be likely to reap the original investment many times over. However, the target result of all R&D efforts should be determined; they should be more market oriented and cross-boundary oriented so as to optimize state-of-the-art engineering technology, and fulfill the ever-more complicated and demanding needs of consumers.

These three key levers—cost focus, re-organization of sales and marketing, and strategic research and development—were strongly related. R&D and subcontractor management should collaborate in the development of increased automation in manufacturing. With regard to commercializing these efforts, R&D and sales and marketing should work together to promote automated manufacturing in order to obtain enough clients for economies of scale. Also, suggestions from sales and marketing to R&D was seen as important for developing customer-oriented products.

However, the top executives of the giant companies were still not sure what the status of the construction industry would be in the year 2000 or how to enhance their competitive position. The one thing that was clear was . . . the need to change.

Leykam Mürztaler

H. Michael Hayes

I n February 1989, Dr. Gertrude Eder, Marketing Manager for Leykam Mürztaler AG, was reviewing a problem that had occupied her thoughts a great deal during the past few months. Although Leykam Mürztaler, like the paper industry in general, had been doing well in recent years, it was her opinion that it was time to think about ways to strengthen the company's ability to prosper as industry growth inevitably began slowing down. In particular, she was considering what recommendations to offer the Executive Board regarding the firm's branding strategy.

Leykam Mürztaler AG

The past few years had been good for the Leykam Mürztaler Group. Paralleling the industry's increased sales, the firm's total sales had risen from ASch4,842 million[1] in 1983 to ASch7,100 million in 1988, an increase of 47%. For Leykam Mürztaler AG, the principal operating component of the Group, 1988 revenues had reached ASch6,300 million, an increase over 1986 of 41%, enhanced by the successful start-up of a new production line and by above average growth in demand for high-grade coated woodfree printing papers, the firm's main sales segment.

Leykam Mürztaler AG, together with its predecessor companies, had been a producer of paper for over 400 years. Headquartered in Gratkorn, Austria, the firm produced coated woodfree printing paper and newsprint, with integrated pulp production. Principal mills and offices were located at Gratkorn and Bruck, Austria. Export sales offices for coated woodfree paper were headquartered in Vienna.

In 1988, woodfree papers represented approximately 80% of sales, newsprint 13% and pulp 7%. Twenty-two percent of revenues came from

---

[1]ASch12.48 = $1.00 in December 1988.

This case was written by Professor H. Michael Hayes as a basis for class discussion rather than to illustrate either effective or ineffective handling of an administrative situation.

EXHIBIT 1

Highlights of the Development of the Leykam Mürztaler Group

	1987	1988	Percentage
Production (in Tons)			
Printing and Writing Papers	272,900	340,900	+24.9
Newsprint (Bruck)	98,200	99,200	+ 1.0
Paper Total	371,100	440,100	+18.6
Chemical Pulp	209,500	204,500	− 2.4
Mechanical Pulp	30,900	32,100	+ 3.9
Deink Pulp	58,900	62,700	+ 6.4
Total Sales (Gross, in ASch mn)			
Leykam Mürztaler AG	5,234	6,300	+20.4
Export Share	4,056	5,100	+25.7
Exports in %	78	81	—
Leykam Mürztaler Group	5,906	7,100	+20.2
Capital Expenditure and Prepayments			
for Fixed Assets (in ASch mn)	1,418	1,500	+ 5.8
Cash Flow (in ASch mn)	1,020	1,500	+47.1
Employees (Excluding Apprentices)			
as of 31 December	2,825	2,865	+ 1.4

Source: Annual Report

Austria, 56% from Western Europe and 22% from exports to the rest of the world (including Eastern Europe). The highest share of exports was for coated woodfree papers at approximately 90%.

(Production volumes in 1987 and 1988 are shown in Exhibit 1.) The large increase in production of printing and writing paper in 1988 (to 340,900 tonnes) reflected successful selling of the output of the new coated woodfree paper machine at Gratkorn, with a capacity of 138,000 tonnes per year. The decline in pulp production reflected a change in product mix. External sales of pulp were declining as the company's pulp production was further integrated into the company's own paper production.

With the addition of the new production line, the company had become the European market leader in coated woodfree papers, with a market share of 8–10%. In December 1987 the Supervisory Board approved a project to establish a new production line at Bruck to produce mechanical coated printing papers (LWC) for magazines, catalogues and printed advertising materials. Planned capacity was 135,000 tonnes, to be put into operation at the end of 1989.

EXHIBIT 2
Financial Results

	1983	1984°	1985°°	1986	1987
Total Sales (Gross, in AS m)	4,842	5,367	5,420	5,187	5,906
Export Sales (AS m)	2,973	3,413	3,537	3,331	4,062
Export Share of Leykam Mürztaler AG (%)	69	72	74	74	78
Capital Investment (AS m)	313	253	444	2,461	1,518
Total Depreciation (AS m) Thereof: Reducing-Balance Depreciation (AS m)	374 —	344 —	337 —	476 125	1,064 674
Cash Flow (AS m)	373	1,025	959	871	1,020
Profit for the Year (AS m)	1	422	81	101	67
Personnel Expenditure (As m)	1,096	993	1,046	1,076	1,231
Number of Employees (Excluding Apprentices) as of 31 December	2,918	2,424	2,364	2,578	2,825
Dividend and Bonus (AS m)	—	54	81	101	67
(%)	—	4 + 4	4 + 8	4 + 8	8

°excluding Niklasdorf Mill
°°excluding Frohnierten Mill from 1 April 1985
Source: Annual Report

Despite the increased level of investment, financial results were very good. In 1987, the last year for which complete financial details were available, profit was down slightly from the previous year (see Exhibit 2), reflecting the greatly increased depreciation charges associated with the new paper machine and the decision to use the reducing-balance method of depreciation for it and some other equipment. Cash flow, however, was close to an all-time record, results were "clearly better than originally forecast," and operating profits were near the top of the European woodfree paper producers, on a percent of sales basis. Preliminary indications were that financial results for 1988 would be still better.

The company marketed its coated products under its MAGNO series brand (e.g., MAGNOMATT, MAGNOPRINT, MAGNOMATT K) principally through wholly owned merchants in Austria and other merchants throughout Western Europe. In addition, it sold to other kinds of merchants in Austria as well as to some printers and publishers directly. Paper merchants were contacted by sales representatives in Vienna and Gratkorn, sales subsidiaries in Germany, Italy and France, and sales agents in other European countries. Some of its products were sold on a private brand basis to certain large merchants.

Although Leykam Mürztaler served paper markets on a worldwide basis, and planned to enter the LWC market, this case focuses on coated woodfree papers for printing applications in Western Europe.

The Pulp and Paper Industry in Western Europe[2]

Despite its maturity, the pulp and paper industry was undergoing major change. Characterized by high breakeven volumes, small fluctuations in demand could significantly impact profits, and there was some evidence that capacity was outgrowing demand. Despite the sophistication of paper-making technology, product differentiation was increasingly difficult to achieve. Some paper makers were integrating backwards to control the cost or assure the supply of pulp. Others were integrating forward, buying paper merchants in order to have better control of marketing. Still others were integrating horizontally to have a more complete product line.

Other changes were affecting the industry as well. Customers were being merged, acquired or reorganized, thus changing established purchasing patterns. Changes in advertising were impacting traditional usage patterns. Paper merchants were merging to gain economies of scale. Some were emphasizing private brands to reduce their dependence on paper makers. Markets were fragmenting as new, small businesses were forming at a record rate. Consumption patterns were changing. In Europe, consumption ranged from 233kg per capita in Sweden to 60 in Portugal, but growth rates ranged from a high of 29.4% in Greece to a low of 2.4% in Denmark. There was some uncertainty about the implications of Europe's move toward a true common market in 1992, although trade barriers were not a significant factor in the industry.

Printing and Writing Paper

In the pulp and paper industry, the major and high growth segment was printing and writing papers. Both coated and uncoated papers were produced from mechanically or chemically processed pulp to form four broad categories: coated woodfree, mechanical coated[3], uncoated woodfree and mechanical uncoated. To be defined as coated, a paper had to have a surface coating of at least 5 grams per square meter (gsm).

Coated woodfree papers represented the highest quality category, in terms of printability, gloss, feel, ability to reproduce color and many other characteristics. Grades of coated woodfree papers were not precisely specified, but the industry had established further categories such as cast coated, art paper, standard and low coated. (See Exhibit 3 for categories and prices.) The standard grade represented the bulk of sales. Within this category, however, there were many gradations—the amount of whiteness, brightness, stiffness and other characteristics. Leykam Mürztaler competed principally at the high end of the standard grade, but was planning to enter the art paper segment also.

---

[2]Western Europe included the countries in the European Community plus Finland, Norway, Sweden, Austria and Switzerland.

[3]Designated LWC or MWC, depending on the weight, although the dividing line was not precise.

EXHIBIT 3

Prices per Tonne (in $) of Woodfree Printing and Writing Papers in Western Europe (2nd Quarter 1987 Delivered)

Grade	West Germany	UK	France	Netherlands
Cast Coated, Sheets	2,734	2,324	2,588	2,480
Art Paper, Sheets	1,897	1,660	1,837	1,736
Standard, Sheets	1,283	1,212	1,235	1,166
Standard, Reels	1,199	1,145	1,169	1,091
Low Coated, Sheets	1,172	1,130	1,136	1,066

Note: Cast coated paper was estimated to represent 5% of the coated woodfree market, Art paper 7–8%, Standard coated 70% and Low coated less than 20%. Within the standard coated category, actual transaction prices could vary as much as 25% as a function of quality and as much as 10% due to competitive or other factors.

Source: EKONO Strategic Study, September 1988

Coated woodfree was the smallest printing and writing paper segment (17.8% of total consumption), but it was also the most dynamic, with an average growth rate of 8.4% from 1980 to 1987. Expectations were that 1988 consumption would exceed three million tonnes.

Markets for Printing and Writing Paper

Principal markets for printing and writing paper were magazines (33%), direct mail (17%), brochures and general print advertising (15%), copy paper (11%), other office paper (9%) and books (5%). For coated woodfree papers, it was estimated that advertising, direct and indirect, accounted for 85–90% of consumption.[4]

On a country by country basis, there was significant variation in the mix of advertising expenditures, however. In the UK, for instance, the bulk of advertising expenditures went to newspapers and TV, whereas in Germany advertising expenditures were split somewhat evenly among newspapers, magazines, catalogues and direct mail.[5] Major uses for coated woodfree papers were direct mail, brochures, annual reports, etc. The dynamic growth of coated woodfree papers in recent years was largely fueled by the rapid increases in "non-classical" advertising. Changes in this mix could significantly affect country consumption patterns for coated woodfree papers.

Despite cost pressures and shifts in individual markets and end uses, coated woodfree papers were benefiting from demand for more and better four-color printing as advertisers sought ways to improve the impact of their messages.

---

[4]ECC International, Limited, 1987.

[5]Papis Limited.

The Printing Industry

The vast majority of orders for coated woodfree paper were placed by printers, either on the merchant or directly on the mill. In some instances, however, for very large orders, the order would be placed by either the printer or the publisher, depending on which seemed to have the strongest negotiating position with the supplier.

Selection of paper grade and manufacturer was a complex process that varied significantly according to end use, size of order, and sophistication of both the printer and the specifier or user. Almost without exception, the printer had the final say in the selection of paper make and could significantly influence the grade of paper as well. The specifier (ad agency) or user (advertiser, publisher, mail order house, etc.) influenced paper selection, particularly with respect to grade, and could also influence selection of make, subject to final agreement by the printer.

For the printer, key paper characteristics were printability and runability. Surface characteristics, whiteness and brightness were also important. Price was always important, especially when deciding between two suppliers with similar offerings or where paper costs represented a significant portion of the total cost of the printed product. Complaint handling, emergency assistance, speed and reliability of delivery were key service components. Sales representative knowledge was also important. Within limits, relative importance of decision criteria varied from one country to another. In Italy and the UK, for instance, price and quality tended to be equally important, whereas quality and service factors tended to predominate importance rankings in Switzerland. There was some favoritism given producers for patriotic reasons, but seldom at the expense of quality or price.

The user or specifier considered many of the same characteristics as the printer. Printability and delivery were usually at the top of the list, but the major concern was the paper's suitability for the particular advertising message, within the constraints of the overall advertising budget.

Despite the apparent similarity of products offered by different mills, there was substantial variation in runability, which could only be determined by actual trial. According to one printer:

> The final test is how well the paper prints on our presses. This is a matter of "fit" between paper, ink and press characteristics. We find there are variations between papers that meet the same specifications, which can only be determined by actual trial. This is not cheap as a trial involves printing 3,000 sheets. Because the paper characteristics cannot be completely specified, we like the idea of a mill brand. One time we tested two merchant brands that we thought were different. Then we found out that the paper came from the same mill, so we really wasted our time on the second test.
>
> The merchant's sales representative is important, but we don't need him to call all that frequently. We like to talk to him about trends or problems we're having, but when we need something quickly, we call the merchant.
>
> Once we have selected a paper, it is critically important that its quality be consistent. Most suppliers are pretty good. Except for obvious flaws, however, we find they tend to want to blame problems on the ink or the press.

EXHIBIT 4
Transaction Characteristics: A Comparison of the Roles of Manufacturers and Merchants

Characteristics	Manufacturer	Merchant
Order Size (kg)	>1,500	200–500
Items Carried	Small	2,500–5,000
Fixed Costs	High	Low
Stock Level (kg)	>2,000/item	500–1,750
Delivery	Often slow	24 hours
Service	None	Possible
Cash Flow	Low	Low

Source: The European Printing and Writing Paper Industry—1987.

Over the past several years, the number of printers remained relatively constant, at about 15–20,000, with decreases from mergers and acquisitions offset by a growth in instant print outlets. In the last 10 years, the number of commercial print customers doubled to over 500,000, half of whom used instant print outlets.

As the number of small businesses and the use of desktop publishing continued to grow, it was suggested that within 10 years traditional printers would perhaps only handle longer-run full color work. Monochrome and spot color work would be produced in customers' offices, with the paper buying decision being made by people with little knowledge about paper or printing.[6] In-plant printing, however, was not expected to have a significant impact on the coated woodfree market.

Paper Merchants

Printers and publishers were reached in two principal ways: direct sales from the mill and sales from the mill through merchants, either independent or mill-owned. Direct sales were more common for high volume products sold in reels, such as newsprint and LWC magazine paper. The pattern of distribution was influenced by characteristics of the transaction (see Exhibit 4) and the pattern varied significantly from one country to another (see Exhibit 5). For coated woodfree papers it was estimated that 70–80% of sales went through merchants.

As with all wholesalers, stocking to provide quick delivery in small quantities was a principal merchant function. Fragmentation of the fastest growing market segments (business and small printers) had decreased the average order size and increased demand for a wide choice of paper grades, making it more difficult for mills to directly access these customers.

---

[6]By BIS Marketing Research Limited.

EXHIBIT 5
Market Shares per Distribution Channel (%)

	Country			
Form of Distribution	**UK**	**France**	**Germany**	**Italy**
Paper Mills	48	50	59	80
Mill-owned Merchants	52	50	—	20
Independent Merchants		—	41	

Source: The European Printing and Writing Paper Industry—1987.

In warehousing, larger merchants had introduced expensive computer-controlled logistical systems, which reduced delivery times and the cost of preparing orders for delivery. Predictions were made that electronic interchange of information between merchants and their suppliers and larger customers would be the norm within the next few years. Merchants in the UK were spearheading an initiative to achieve industry standards for bar codes throughout Europe.

Changes in end user profiles and new customer needs had forced merchants to expand the scope of their activities and customer support functions. As a result, the merchants' role broadened to include a number of additional services, including technical advice on paper choice and broader printing problems.

Private branding, supported by advertising, had long been used by some merchants to differentiate their products and service. Some large merchants had also invested in testing apparatus, similar to that found in mills, to check conformance to specifications and to support their desire to become principals, with full responsibility for product performance.

Merchant margins varied with location, type of sale and nature of the transaction. For sales from stock, margins ranged from a low of 12% in Italy and 15% in Germany to 25% in France and Switzerland. Margins reduced to about 5%, or less, when a merchant acted as the intermediary solely for invoicing purposes.[7] (A typical income statement for a paper merchant is shown in Exhibit 6.)

Patterns of merchant ownership also varied from one country to another (see Exhibit 7). In the UK, for example, Wiggins Teape, a paper producer established in 1780, became a merchant in 1960 when existing merchants resisted introducing carbonless copy paper in the market. The company opened a network of offices to stimulate demand and provide technical support for the product. Between 1969 and 1984, the company acquired control of several major

---

[7]The European Printing and Writing Paper Industry—1987, IMEDE Case No GM 375.

EXHIBIT 6
Typical Income Statement: Paper Merchant

	Percentage
Sales	100.0
Cost of Goods Sold	75.0
Contribution	25.0
Other Costs	23.0
Net Profit	2.0
Depreciation	.5
Cash Flow	2.5

Source: The European Printing and Writing Paper Industry—1987.

EXHIBIT 7
Paper Merchants: Ownership and Concentration per Country

Country	Merchants Totaling 80% of Country Sales	Ownership
Sweden	2	Mill-owned
Denmark	3	Mostly mill-owned
Netherlands	5	Mill-owned
Belgium	5	Mill-owned
Switzerland	5	Mostly mill-owned
Austria	2 (70%)	Mill-owned
France	6	Mill-owned
West Germany	7	All independent
UK	Few big and many small ones	Partly mill-owned Mostly independent

Source: Paper Merchanting, the Viewpoint of Independent Merchant.

merchants operating in the UK, France, Belgium, Italy and Finland. In 1984, sales of $480 million made Wiggins Teape the largest merchant in Europe.

On the other hand, Paper Union, one of the two largest merchants in Germany (turnover of $142 million and market share of 12% in 1984), was an independent merchant. It was formed in the early 1960s, from three smaller merchants, in an attempt to reach the critical size of 100,000 tonnes per year. Due to low margins in Germany, Paper Union had emphasized reducing operating costs and consistently fast delivery. Plans were being made, however, to introduce further services and advertising in an attempt to add value and increase customer awareness.

The move toward company-owned merchants was not without controversy. According to one independent merchant:

> We believe that independent merchants are very much in the best interest of paper mills. We're aware, of course, that many mills are integrating forward, buying merchants in order to maintain access to distribution. It is our view, however, that this will cause a number of problems. No one mill can supply all the products that a merchant must offer. Hence, even mill-owned merchants must maintain relations with a number of other mills, who will always want to supply their full range of products to the merchant, including those which compete with the parent mill. This will create serious tensions and frequently will put the merchant in the position of having to choose between corporate loyalty and offering the best package to the customer. The parent can, of course, impose restrictions on the merchant with respect to selling competing products, but the sales force would have serious problems with this.
>
> Our strong preference is for exclusive representation of a mill. This is particularly important where there are strong influencers, such as advertisers, to whom it is important for us to address considerable promotional effort. Also when we are an exclusive merchant, we provide the mill with extensive information on our sales, which allows the mill to do market analysis that both we and the mill find very valuable. We certainly would not provide this kind of information if the mill had intensive distribution. In a country like Switzerland, we can give the mill complete geographic and account coverage, so it's not clear to us why the mill needs more than one merchant. In our view, intensive distribution creates a situation where there is much more emphasis on price. While this first affects the merchant, it inevitably affects the mill as well.
>
> If we do sell for a mill that has intensive distribution, we prefer to sell it under our brand, although we identify the mill in small print. This is somewhat an historical artifact, going back to the days when mills did not attempt to brand their products, but if we're going to compete for business with another merchant, selling for the same mill, we feel having our name on the product helps us differentiate ourselves from the competitor.
>
> At the same time, we should point out that we don't sell competing brands. There are about five quality grades within standard coated woodfree, and we handle two to three brands.

One industry expert predicted significant changes in distribution patterns.[8]

> Looking to the future, it is predicted that there will be an increase in the number of paper grade classifications, moving from 4 just a few years ago to 20 or more. There will be an increasing number of different types of middlemen and distributors, and merchants will move into grades traditionally regarded as mill direct products (e.g., newsprint and mechanical grades) to bring these grades to the smaller customers.
>
> Just as we have seen a technological revolution hit the traditional printing industry, we must now see a marketing revolution hit the traditional paper indus-

---

[8]From a paper presented by BIS Marketing Research Limited.

try. Selection of the correct channel of distribution and the development of an active working relationship with that channel will be vital.

Competition in Coated Woodfree Papers

In varying degrees, Leykam Mürztaler encountered at least 10 major European firms in the markets it served in Europe. Some, like KNP and Zanders, competed principally in coated woodfree papers. Others, like Stora and Feldmühle, produced a wide range of products, from coated woodfree papers to tissue to newsprint.

There was considerable variation in competitive emphasis among producers. Zanders, for instance, generally regarded as the highest quality producer, mostly produced cast coated and premium art paper, competed only at the top end of the standard coated range and was relatively unusual in its extensive use of advertising. Hannover Papier was particularly strong in service, offering fast delivery. PWA Hallein, which had tended to emphasize price over quality, had recently improved its quality but was keeping prices low in an apparent effort to gain market share. Arjomari, the biggest French producer, owned the largest merchant chain in France and had recently purchased merchants in the UK and Southern Europe. It had recently entered the premium art paper segment, generally regarded as difficult to produce for. Burgo, a large Italian conglomerate, concentrated principally on the Italian market. (See Exhibit 8 for a report on the image of selected suppliers.)

Rapid growth in the coated woodfree market had stimulated capacity additions by existing producers and was also stimulating conversion of facilities from uncoated to coated. Nordland of Germany, for instance, switched 100,000 tonnes of capacity from uncoated to coated by adding a coater in October 1988. Excellent in service, there was, however, some question about its ability to produce high quality.

Branding was a relatively new aspect of the industry. All the major producers had established brand names for major products or grades. To date, however, only Zanders had actively promoted its brand to the trade or to advertisers.

Marketing at Leykam Mürztaler AG

Marketing activities at Leykam Mürztaler were divided between the Sales Director, Wolfgang Pfarl, and the Marketing Manager, Gertrude Eder. Pfarl, a member of the Executive Board, was responsible for pricing as well as all personal selling activities, both direct and through merchants. Eder was responsible for public relations, advertising and sales promotion, and marketing research. As a staff member, she reported to Dr. Siegfried Meysel, the Managing Director.

Coated Woodfree Products and Markets

In coated woodfree papers, Leykam Mürztaler offered a comprehensive product line of standard coated papers under the MAGNO brand, for both sheet and web offset printing. These were produced in a wide variety of basis

EXHIBIT 8
Major Mill Reputation

Company	Comments on Reputation
Zanders (Germany)	• Mercedes Benz in coated woodfrees • Excellent service • Strong promotion • Marketing activities have also been directed to advertising agencies, who can influence on choice of brand.
Leykam Mürztaler	• Reliable supplier • Good service
Arjomari (France)	• Strong positions in France due to its own merchants
Condat (France)	• Good and stable quality
Feldmühle (Germany)	• Stable quality • Rapid deliveries and good stocking arrangements
KNP (Netherlands)	• Flexible supplier, also accepts small orders • Good service
PWA Hallein (Germany)	• Competes with price
Scheufelen (Germany)	• Good and stable quality • Reliable deliveries
Stora Kopparberg (Sweden)	• Reliable deliveries • Quality and service OK

Source: EKONO Strategic Study, September 1988.

weights, ranging from 80–300 grams per square meter depending on the particular application. The firm targeted the high quality end of the standard coated category by offering higher coat weights, better gloss and print gloss, and better printability.

Using Austria as its home market, Leykam Mürztaler focused its principal efforts on countries in Europe. The majority of sales revenues came, in roughly similar amounts, from Austria, Italy, France and the UK, with somewhat higher sales in Germany. Belgium, Holland, Switzerland and Spain were important but smaller markets.

The firm also sold in a number of other countries, including the United States. Penetration of the U.S. market by the European paper industry had been assisted by the favorable exchange rates during the early 1980s. The firm's policy, however, was to maintain its position in different countries despite currency fluctuations. As Gertrude Eder explained:

We believe our customers expect us to participate in their markets on a long-term basis and to be competitive with local conditions. This may cost us some profits in the short term, as when we maintained our position in the UK despite the weak pound, but now that the pound is strong again, this investment is paying off. If we had reduced our presence when the exchange rate was unfavorable, it would have been very difficult to regain our position.

Channels of Distribution

Over the years, Leykam Mürztaler had sold most of its output through merchants. To some degree the method of distribution was influenced by the country served as the firm tended to follow the predominant trade practice in each country. In Switzerland, Germany and the UK, all its business was done through merchants. In France, Italy and Austria, there was a mixed pattern of distribution, but with a strong merchant orientation.

Merchants were carefully selected, and the firm did business only with stocking merchants who competed on service rather than price. In some countries (e.g., Holland) it used exclusive distribution, but this was not the normal pattern. Gertrude Eder explained:

As a large producer, we have a volume problem. In the larger countries, one merchant simply can't sell enough product for us, plus we believe it is risky to commit completely to one merchant.

Similarly, Wolfgang Pfarl commented:

In Germany, for instance, we could go to one merchant only, but to get the volume of business we need would require going into direct business with some non-stocking merchants, and that is something that neither we nor our stocking merchants want to happen.

To date, the trend toward mill ownership of merchants had not adversely affected the firm's ability to get good merchant representation. There was some concern, however, that with changing patterns of mill ownership, some merchants might be closed off to firms like Leykam Mürztaler in the future.

Service was also seen as a key to merchant relations. In this connection, the firm felt its computerized order system and new finishing facilities at the Gratkorn mill, highly automated, permitting flexibility in sheeting and packaging, and able to handle the total output of the new paper machine, provided great service capability and gave it a competitive advantage. As the mill superintendent put it:

From a production standpoint, the ideal scenario is one in which we can run one grade of paper all year and ship it to customers in large reels. Reality is that meeting customer needs is critical, and I believe we have "state-of-the-art competence" in our ability to meet a tremendous variety of customer requirements efficiently.

Pricing

Pricing practices in the paper industry had a strong commodity orientation and, for coated woodfree papers, industry prices tended to serve as the basis for arriving at transaction prices. (See Exhibit 3 for information on industry prices and paper grades.) For sales to merchants, Leykam Mürztaler negotiated price lists, using the industry prices as a starting point, with final prices taking paper quality and other relevant factors into account. Price lists then remained in effect until there was a change in industry price levels. Routine orders were priced from the established price list. Large requirements, however, usually involved special negotiation.

According to one Leykam Mürztaler sales manager:

> We have some interesting discussions with our merchants about price. The customer knows we make a high quality product, so his principal interest is in getting it at the lowest possible price. In Europe there is no uniform classification of coated papers, as there is in the USA and Japan, so a standard approach is to try to get me to reclassify my product to a lower grade, and so a lower price. To some extent, though, my customer's preoccupation with price simply reflects price pressures he is experiencing from his customers. Still, it is frustrating because we believe we offer a lot more than just price and a good product. But I think we do a good job for the firm in getting the highest price possible.

Branding

In recent years, Leykam Mürztaler had followed the industry practice of branding its principal products. It did, however, supply products to certain merchants for private branding, a practice that was established when mill branding was not the norm. In 1988, some 30% of sales carried a merchant brand, largely reflecting the volume from Germany and the UK, where private branding was customary. Recently, however, the firm had started to identify most of its products by using a typical Leykam Mürztaler packaging, even for private labels.

Brands had been promoted primarily by the sales force, in direct contact with customers, using brochures and samples, and by packaging. More recently, a series of superb visual messages was commissioned, using the theme, "Dimensions in Paper," to suggest ways that high quality paper combined with printing could produce more effective communication. The script accompanying the visual messages was designed to appeal to both the advertisers, with emphasis on communication, and printers, with emphasis on paper finish, touch, color, absorption, contrast and other key paper characteristics. On a limited basis, these messages had appeared in selected magazines and in brochures for customers. (See Exhibit 9 for a copy of the text in a MAGNOPRINT promotional piece. The piece included a surrealistic picture of a tuning fork, done in vivid color.)

There was general agreement within the firm that more emphasis needed to be placed on branding as a way to achieve product differentiation and convey the desired high quality image. There was less agreement on how much to spend promoting the brands or how to deal with merchants who were now

EXHIBIT 9
MAGNOPRINT Promotional Piece (text)

Dimensions of Sound

*MAGNO***PRINT**

Photographed for Leykam Mürztaler by Willi Langbein, Vienna.

Only when looking at the picture more closely does one realize how the artist interprets "dimensions of sound."
It is not the tuning fork that produces the sound but the impact of the melting metal on the water surface.

With this extraordinary photographic interpretation of the "sound" dimension we cannot only demonstrate the outstanding quality of MAGNOPRINT but also the reproduction of the finest color shades, the brilliance of the print; or, for example, the smoothness of the paper which brings out the contrast between the metallic light effects and the dark, calm water surface in the best possible way.

For the highest demands in printing. The woodfree high-gloss double-coated MAGNOPRINT is among the most widely used brands of Leykam Mürztaler and is mainly used for art printing, ambitious advertising and annual reports. Areas of application which fully bring out the qualities of MAGNOPRINT:

- high-gloss and smoothness
- brilliant printed results
- high-contrast reproduction
- snow-white — therefore exact color reproduction, even in the most delicate shades.

The MAGNO range for the highest demands:

- woodfree coated papers and boards
- velvet or high-gloss finish
- sheets and reels
- substance range 80 gsm up to 300 gsm.

buying Leykam Mürztaler products for sale under the merchants' labels. According to Gertrude Eder:

> Over the past few years we designed the corporate logo and corporate graphics and established blue, black and white as the colors for all corporate communication. We have worked hard to establish a consistent presentation of our corporate identity. Feedback from customers and the sales department indicates that this has helped improve our visibility and image. Nevertheless, we are currently spending considerably less than 1% of sales on advertising. Zanders, on the other hand, a firm of about our size, has been spending a lot of money on advertising for years and as a result has better visibility than we do, particularly with advertising agencies, as well as an enviable reputation for quality and service.
>
> I don't know what the right number is for us, but we will need to spend substantially more if we are to establish the kind of brand awareness and image we desire. I think that to have any significant impact would take a minimum of ASch3–4 million for classical advertising (i.e., advertising in trade publications, in various languages) and ASch8–10 million for promotions, including brochures, leaflets and trade fairs. In Western Europe we have to advertise in at least four to five languages, and sometimes more. In addition, the nature of the ads varies. In

private brand countries, our ads emphasize the company name and focus on the Dimensions in Paper theme as well as the company's experience and modern production facilities. In other countries we emphasize the MAGNO brand.

We are convinced that printers want to know what mill brand they are buying. Also, we believe that there is some subjectivity in selecting paper, particularly by the advertiser, and we want to convince the advertiser that his message will come across better on Leykam Mürztaler paper.

The decision on supplying Leykam Mürztaler products for private branding was even more complex. As Wolfgang Pfarl commented:

> I understand the position of the merchants who want to offer a private brand. The fact remains, however, that it is the mill that determines product characteristics and is responsible for meeting specifications. It is really a question of who is adding the value. In my view the merchant ought to emphasize those things which he controls, such as local stocks, good sales representation and service. Putting a merchant label on paper produced by Leykam Mürztaler misrepresents the value added picture. Don't get me wrong. Our firm strongly believes in merchants. In fact, we avoid direct business wherever there are strong stocking merchants. It's just that we think mills and merchants have distinct roles to play, and they should not be confused.
>
> Currently, we will still produce for a merchant's label, but we have started to insist that it also is identified as Leykam Mürztaler. The merchants aren't very happy about this, but we think it's the right thing to do.

Nevertheless, the situation with respect to existing merchants was difficult. As one of the senior sales managers said:

> We have been supplying some of our merchants with paper to be sold under a private label for a long time, and they have invested substantial sums of money in establishing their own brands. I completely support the company's position on this, but I don't know how we can get the practice to change. If we insist on supplying products only under our own brand, there are a lot of competitors who would, I think, be happy to step in and take over our position with some merchants. If we can't convince a merchant to switch over to our brand, we could lose a lot of business, in one or two instances as much as 6,000 tonnes. On the other hand, if we aren't uniform on this, we will not be able to really exploit the potential of developing our own brands.

In addition to questions about branding policy, it was not clear how to capitalize on increased brand preference, if indeed it were achieved. As Wolfgang Pfarl said:

> We might want to think in terms of higher prices or increased share, or some combination. Exactly what we would do could vary from market to market.

Personal Selling

Contact with merchants and with large, directly served accounts in Europe was mainly made by the company's own sales force headquartered in Vienna, by sales representatives in subsidiary companies in Germany, Italy and France, and by sales agents in other markets (e.g., the UK). Direct sales representatives numbered 20. Including clerical staff, Leykam had some 60 individuals in its sales department, most of whom had direct contact with customers.

The major activity of the sales force was making direct calls on large customers and on merchants. In addition, sales representatives made occasional calls on a merchant's customers, generally accompanied by the merchant's sales representative. Objectives usually included negotiating long-term contracts, "selling" the existing product line, new product introduction and a review of customer requirements for products and service.

It was the firm's belief that its sales force was a major asset and that sales representatives could significantly influence relations with merchants. A major objective for all Leykam Mürztaler representatives was to do everything possible to develop close relations with assigned merchants. According to Wolfgang Pfarl:

> The average age of our sales force is between 35 and 40, and most of the individuals have spent their entire career in sales with Leykam Mürztaler. They are really committed to serve the customer, with on-time deliveries or any other aspect of our relationship, and the customer really respects their high level of service. In addition, they are good negotiators and represent Leykam effectively during contract negotiations. They do not need to be technical experts, but they make sure that our technical people provide technical information as required. Also, they monitor shipping performance, make presentations to merchants, and may make joint customer calls with merchant sales representatives.

Mathias Randon, one of the Vienna based sales managers, made the following comments:

> In total we call on about 100 merchants in Europe. I work with our sales offices in Italy, France and Belgium and handle 5 merchants personally in the UK, in cooperation with our representative there. I call on the merchants two to three times a year and have extensive phone contact with our sales offices and representatives from Vienna.
>
> In general, the customer wants to talk about quantity, price and service. We have conversations about private labelling. The new merchants would like us to give them private labels, but I think they know they can't get it. On the other hand, the ones to whom we are currently providing private labels don't want to give it up. The problem varies from country to country. In France, for instance, it's not such a big problem.
>
> One of my objectives is to encourage more stock business versus indent (merchant orders for direct mill shipment to the customer). This means we have to give them better service and provide back-up stocks.
>
> Some merchants handle mill brands that compete directly with Leykam Mürztaler, but most tend to do this under a private label.
>
> From time to time we work to develop a new merchant, but generally we work on building long-lasting relationships with existing merchants. We encourage trips by merchant personnel to the mill. I will make short presentations to merchant sales representatives when I call on the merchant, but generally they are pretty knowledgeable about paper. We've tried contests and other incentives with merchants and are still thinking about it, but I'm not sure if that's what we should do.
>
> From a quality standpoint, I try to stress whiteness, opacity, printability/runability and consistency. Lots of customers ask for lab figures, but I don't think you can

rely just on lab reports. We have trial print runs every week by an independent printer to check our consistency. I think most printers feel the same way.

We tend to have lots of small problems rather than any one large problem. Branding, for instance, pricing, friction when we appoint a new merchant and country variations with regard to ways of doing business. I think branding will be important in all countries, but how we capitalize on it may have to vary.

After Sales Service

Problems in printing could arise due to a number of circumstances. There might be variations or flaws in the paper or in the ink. Presses could develop mechanical problems. Even changes in temperature and humidity could negatively affect printing quality. Because of the complexity of the printing process, the cause of a problem was not always clear, and reaching an equitable settlement could be difficult.

When problems did arise, the printer turned to the merchant or mill for technical advice and frequently wanted financial compensation for lost production. According to Wolfgang Pfarl:

> When the printer encounters a production problem, it is important for us to be able to give him technical advice and work with him to solve the problem. Sometimes the sales representative can do this. More often, we have to involve one of our technical people from the mill. All too often, however, the printer is just looking for someone to compensate him financially, and we have to be very tough or we're likely to find ourselves paying for a lot of other people's mistakes.

Future Issues

Looking to the future, the firm was focusing its attention on managing "through the business cycle." As Wolfgang Pfarl put it:

> Our real challenge is to strengthen our market position in Western Europe. Most of our coated woodfree paper goes into advertising. We have seen extraordinary growth in this market in the last few years, but we have to expect there will be a significant downturn in one or two years and that advertisers will then look intensely at their costs. In many cases this means the printer will suggest a lower cost grade as a substitute for coated woodfree. Our task is to differentiate MAGNO from the generic category and position it as "a paper for all seasons," so to speak. In other words, we want our customers to think of MAGNO as the "right" paper for high quality advertising, separately from coated woodfree.
>
> In general, this means strengthening our corporate identity, being partners of the strongest merchants and encouraging our merchants to support the MAGNO brand.

In a similar vein, Gertrude Eder commented:

> This is a business where the impact of the business cycle is made worse by the tendency of merchants to overstock in good times and destock in bad times. Our objective, I think, should be to position Leykam as the last mill the merchant or printer would think of cancelling in a downturn.

Lussman-Shizuka Corp.

Dominique Turpin

Joyce Miller

It was 6:00 pm on June 22, 1991, and Rudolf Richter, President of Lussman-Shizuka Corp., could see several photographers and journalists representing Osaka's major newspapers gathered outside on the street 20 floors below. Richter sighed and glanced nervously at his secretary who was signalling him that yet another reporter was on the telephone wanting his view of the allegations recently made against the company. Four hours earlier, the Japanese authorities had arrested three of Richter's employees and accused them of bribing university professors to win orders of the company's products. In his entire 25-year career with Lussman Pharmaceuticals, Richter had never faced a more difficult situation.

Lussman in Japan

Located near Osaka, Lussman-Shizuka Corp. was a 50:50 joint venture between Lussman Pharmaceuticals based in Düsseldorf and Shizuka Corp., a Japanese chemical firm. Formed to produce and distribute anti-cancer drugs in Japan, the venture had operated since 1971 in what Richter called "one of the toughest, most competitive markets in the world." Richter had headed Lussman-Shizuka for the pat six years and was the only foreigner working in the joint venture. Although he had begun learning Japanese, his ability to handle a business discussion was still limited. Consequently, most meetings were conducted in English. Two executives from Shizuka Corp., Hiroshi Shibuya and Yasumi Kato, served as vice presidents of Lussman-Shizuka and were involved in the daily operations of the joint venture. They both had a reasonably good command of English.

For many years, Japan had kept foreign products out of its national market with what Richter described as "high tariffs and complex production and import procedures." Through negotiations with the European Community, these trade barriers had gradually been dismantled, but importing goods into Japan was still cumbersome in Richter's view. Lussman Pharmaceuticals had entered the

This case was prepared by Professor Dominique Turpin, with the assistance of Research Associate Joyce Miller, as a basis for class discussion rather than to illustrate either effective or ineffective handling of a business situation. Research for this case was made possible by a grant from Egon Zehnder.

145

market by tying up with a leading Japanese company. The venture represented a rare success for a European company in Japan. Lussman-Shizuka sold quality products at competitive prices, serviced through a national distribution network. Technological leadership had given the venture its initial edge in the fight for market share. Currently, the company manufactured 10% of its products in Japan and imported the remainder from a Lussman factory in Germany.

Over-the-counter drugs in Japan were primarily available through doctors rather than pharmacists. Japanese physicians typically charged low fees for clinic visits, relying on the sale of drugs for the bulk of their income. Doctors had a great deal of influence over their hospitals' buying decisions as well as the drug purchases of their former students now working in other medical institutions.

The Lussman-Shizuka Affair

Three weeks earlier, five doctors who worked at prominent university hospitals in Osaka had been arrested for accepting improper cash payments from Lussman-Shizuka. Two doctors, who had previously purchased Lussman products, had reportedly received $22,000 for entertainment expenses. Another was arrested for accepting $31,000 from Lussman-Shizuka for attending an academic conference in the United States. Two other professors in a major Japanese university were each accused of receiving $18,000 from Lussman-Shizuka, but prosecutors had not yet released their names. Shortly after this incident, the Ministry of Health, together with the Ministry of Education, advised all state university hospitals against purchasing drugs from Lussman-Shizuka for an unspecified period of time, a move that could have devastating consequences for Lussman's business in Japan.

Dr. Yutaka Hayashida, an Osaka physician, observed, "Pharmaceutical companies commonly court doctors to buy their drugs because it is such a competitive market. Salesmen will do almost anything to get access to the most influential practitioners. They'll give them presents, buy drinks, pay for trips, even help their kids get into the best universities." Dr. Hayashida added that he had made a personal decision to turn down all such offers, although there was no hospital requirement to do so. He continued, "Low-paid university professors and newly established doctors are particularly vulnerable to such offers. The Lussman-Shizuka affair is just the tip of the iceberg. Most companies and most doctors do the same thing. In fact, much of the competitive bidding that does happen in hospitals is meaningless, because the doctors have decided in advance which drugs they want to buy and the specifications are set so that only those products will be accepted."

The Reaction from Shizuka Corp.

Yasumi Kato, a director in the Japanese parent company who was also a vice president in the joint venture, offered his view of the situation:

> The fact that Lussman-Shizuka is an outsider makes the company especially vulnerable to exposure. Furthermore, in Japan, stability is very important. We

brought attention to ourselves by marketing aggressively. Within less than a decade of its founding, Lussman-Shizuka moved to the top ranks in the industry in its particular specialty. Our share of the market did not come cheap. Where most Western companies in Japan will seek a small position and focus on maintaining high profits, Lussman-Shizuka wanted to be at the top in anti-cancer drugs, and the company matched Japanese discounts blow for blow. Now we are paying the price.

Richter knew that the venture's quick climb had created a lot of tension among the competitors. In fact, his Japanese partners had warned him of the danger of disrupting the market with an aggressive sales policy. Industry leaders had frequently complained that prices had fallen too low. Now, the venture's Japanese staff speculated that a competitor had leaked inflammatory information to the press. Richter was aware that scandals typically broke in the Japanese press after reporters were fed information aimed at undercutting foreigners who were seen to be undermining the status quo.

Why was Lussman-Shizuka singled out? According to Richter,

In some respects, the company has been too honest. When investigators raided our office last week and demanded to see the company's accounts, we had only one set of books with a straightforward accounting of our activities. Many local companies have two sets of books or, at a minimum, they have couched the payments to doctors in vague terms, such as cooperative research. The reality in this industry in this country is that you are not a fully-fledged salesman until you have reached the point where a doctor will accept your gifts and agree to meet with you.

Hiroshi Shibuya, a vice president in the joint venture, felt that what had gotten the company into difficulty was its effort to woo university professors. Investigators had told the press that Lussman-Shizuka had compiled a list of influential doctors to be regularly targeted by its salesmen.

Where to Go Next

Richter had to decide how to proceed, and quickly. He could not help thinking that a scandal now would jeopardize his forthcoming retirement. His wife had already moved back to Bavaria, and Richter himself was scheduled to leave Japan permanently at the end of December. Now, the Japanese authorities had forbidden him to leave the country, and he could face a long trial if convicted.

While his Japanese partners tended to blame Richter openly for the consequences of aggressive selling, Richter felt they also shared some responsibility for the current situation. Although he knew that "gift-giving" was a long-standing Japanese tradition and standard industry practice, Richter felt that the salespeople may have overdone it.

While Richter had been mulling over his alternatives, the crowd outside the office building had grown considerably. And, there were likely to be more waiting for him at his home, all with the same questions. Should he talk to the press and give his own version of the story, or should he try to avoid the media at all costs? Since Japanese doctors and the salespeople considered the alleged actions as acceptable industry practice, should he follow the advice of one of his managers to meet with the competition to work out some common actions? Should he also ask for assistance from his government, as one of his German business associates had suggested? Should he try to get help from his European headquarters?

Machine Vision International®

Constance M.
Kinnear

Thomas C. Kinnear

Our industry is very much like a newly found gold mine. Each vein in the mine is a different market opportunity. We're entering the main mine shaft, digging first in the directions our research shows will contain the largest ore deposits, those in the automotive and electronics industries. We'll use the knowledge we gain in those shafts of the mine to tunnel to other veins, finding gold deposits in other markets. This is our approach.

Richard P. Eidswick
Chairman and CEO, MVI

As 1985 came to a close, Machine Vision International (MVI) was completing its third year of operations. Only two years earlier, MVI had had only 37 employees. By the end of 1985, MVI had expanded greatly. The company now had three sales divisions and was selling products for very diverse applications in many varied industries. However, the financial results for 1985 showed that MVI was not yet making a profit. The question being asked was whether MVI had expanded into too many markets too quickly for a company in a fast-growing, quickly changing industry.

The Machine Vision Industry—a Definition

A machine vision product is a high-technology, computer-based image processing system enabling a machine or other device to "see." The use of this technology permits automation of industrial tasks involving the interpretation of the work scene or the controlling of work activity.

Machine vision may be understood by way of analogy to human vision. A human eye captures an image, which is then transmitted to the brain via the optic nerve. The brain processes those parts of the image most important to the situation; it ignores parts of the image which are irrelevant. The brain then tells other parts of the body what actions to take. In machine vision, the camera (eye) captures an

This case was prepared by Constance M. Kinnear, Research Associate, with the assistance of Thomas C. Kinnear, Professor of Marketing, both at the Graduate School of Business Administration, The University of Michigan.

Copyright © 1986 by the authors. This abridged version was prepared, with permission of the authors, by Adrian B. Ryans and Terry Deutscher, faculty at Western Business School, University of Western Ontario.

image and transmits it to the controller (brain) via a coaxial cable (optic nerve). The controller sorts relevant from irrelevant data and instructs the machine tool, conveyor, or robot what action to take.

MVI's Prospectus
September 18, 1985

There were many potential application areas for machine vision in the industrial workplace. Data received by a computer from television cameras viewing an assembly area could be almost instantaneously analyzed so that task performance guidance commands could be sent to a robot. Vision systems could be used in quality control processes to check work in process against required product parameters, which were stored in the system's computer. A vision system could, therefore, check during production for the proper dimensions and shape of the product, for the presence of all features or parts, and for its general condition including surface flaws. Deviations from acceptable parameters could be brought to the attention of supervisory staff before they caused a substandard product to be produced. Because vision systems could recognize different shapes or identifying markings, production parts could be sorted, facilitating the movement, processing, or assembly of parts. The goals in the use of vision systems were to increase product quality, increase product rates and industrial efficiency, and provide labor savings.

The Market for Machine Vision Products

The machine vision industry did not exist in 1980. In 1981, total industry sales were $7 million. Between 1981 and 1984, sales more than doubled each year, so that by 1984 industry sales totalled $80 million. A compound average growth rate of 60 percent per year had been estimated for the industry as a whole for the period from 1984 to 1990. Estimated sales for 1985 were $125 million. For 1990, the total market was estimated to reach between $750 and $800 million.

Despite all the optimistic estimates for growth in the market, not one competitor in machine vision had consistently made a profit by 1985. Between 70 and 100 competitors were vying for the industry's total sales of $125 million in that year, in literally thousands of different applications. The bulk of this revenue was shared among 20 companies. The major competitors in the industry and their sales for the period 1983–85 are shown in Exhibit 1. In 1984, none of these competitors made a profit in this industry.

Analysts of the machine vision industry were hard pressed to pick which companies would survive the early growth years. For one thing, the technologies in the industry were not yet perfected. There were many technologies applicable to vision applications, and these technologies were still very much in the developmental stage. Possible applications of machine vision could be found in almost any industrial setting where part inspection, part identification, or automated assembly processes were used. These usually came from large-volume sales or repeatably manufacturable products. The market was often uneducated or unrealistic about the true capabilities of machine vision.

EXHIBIT 1
Competitive Sales Figures (millions)—1983–85

Company	1983 Sales	1984 Sales	Expected 1985 Sales	Type of Financing
Applied Intelligent Systems, Inc. (1976)	$ 0.4	$ 1.4	$ 5.0	Private
Automatix	6.3	17.3	27.0	Public
Cognex Corp.	2.0	5.0	6.0	Private
Diffracto Ltd. (1973)	3.7	5.1	7.3	Private
International Robomation/Intelligence	1.0	2.3	8.0	Public
Itran Corp. (1982)	0.2	1.1	2.2	Private
Machine Vision International	0.5	4.0	10.0	Public
Perceptron, Inc. (1981)	1.0	5.5	15.0	Private
Robotic Vision Systems, Inc. (1977)	1.0	5.1	10.0	Public
View Engineering (1976)	7.5	15.0	19.0	Private
All Others	11.4	18.2	15.5	
Total Market	$35.0	$80.0	$125.0	

Competitors were finding it very difficult to determine all the variables that had to be satisfied and solved to make the products work in an actual, operating industrial environment.

One development with great potential impact on the machine vision industry was the involvement of General Motors. GM became very interested in production automation. This interest was spurred by the results of several automobile industry studies, which found that the Japanese had a sizable cost advantage, ranging between $1,500 and $1,800 per car, over U.S. producers in 1985. Also, it was estimated that it took approximately three times as many labor-hours for U.S. automobile manufacturers to produce a car than it did their Japanese competitors. Studies predicted that U.S. car manufacturers would have to reduce their costs by about 25 percent between 1985 and 1990 to remain competitive in the industry. Of possible automation alternatives, it was determined that the use of robotics and machine vision was a key strategy to solve the problem. Forty-four thousand machine vision applications were identified within GM alone by GM analysts.

Taking action on these findings, GM entered into a joint venture with Fanuc Ltd. of Japan, forming GMF, a highly respected robotics firm. To back its belief that vision was also key to automation, GM invested in five machine vision companies in 1983 and 1984. These were Applied Intelligent Systems (AIS), Automatix, Diffracto Ltd., Robotic Vision Systems (RVS), and View Engineering. The full impact of these investments on the machine vision industry was yet unknown.

The Customers for Machine Vision Products

Though the machine vision market was very fragmented and very new, some information about the buyers of these products was provided by a study entitled *Vision Systems Survey of End Users*, conducted by Prudential-Bache Securities and published on February 6, 1985.

The report showed several interesting characteristics of present and potential machine vision customers. Sixty-seven percent of the companies surveyed achieved annual gross revenues of greater than $1 billion. Eighty-four percent of the companies had annual gross revenues of greater than $100 million. Fifty-seven percent of the companies interested in vision were located in the Midwest. Another 19 percent were located in the Northeast, with 9 percent on the West Coast. The end users surveyed were in the following industries:

Industry	Percentage of Study
Automotive	35%
Electrical/electronics	35
Aerospace	12
Construction	3
Pharmaceutical	1
Other°	14

°Ranges from paper products to metal fabricators.

Ninety-seven percent of the end users surveyed indicated that vision was an important factor in the overall manufacturing process. Sixty-four percent had an actual capital budget for vision system purchases.

Decision makers in the purchasing of vision systems were located in many different levels of the companies surveyed. Sixteen percent responded that the purchase decision was made at the corporate level only, while 29 percent said that the decision was made at the division level. Another 37 percent responded that vision system purchase decisions were made at the department level, with the remaining 17 percent of those surveyed answering that the decision involved more than one level within the company.

The lengths of present and anticipated future buying cycles for vision systems were as follows:

Buying Cycles	Present	Future
Less than 3 months	13%	31%
6–9 months	47	41
9–12 months	23	18
Over a year	8	6

Many customers believed that machine vision systems would not only be installed for production work applications but also for internal development work on automation processes. Nineteen percent of respondents had installed vision systems for development work only, while 54 percent said that they had or planned to install vision systems for both production work and development work.

Fifty-nine percent of survey respondents purchased their vision systems through the direct salesforces of the suppliers. Twenty percent used only OEMs, while 8 percent purchased through distributors. The remaining 13 percent used more than one channel for their purchases.

Vision companies most often mentioned as possible suppliers were Automatix, View Engineering, Machine Vision International, and Perception. The factors most important to purchasers of vision systems, in their order to importance, were technology, service and support, applications engineering, user friendliness, reputation of vendor, expendability, and price.

The end users were also asked to list areas of application or vision systems in both the present and the future. The responses were:

Applications	Present	Future
Inspection	84%	93%
Gauging	44	60
Sorting	21	35
Process Control	37	63
Robot Guidance	40	45

The Technologies Employed in Machine Vision

There were four main technologies employed in machine vision systems. These were signal processing, mathematical morphology, statistical pattern recognition, and artificial intelligence. These four and the significant characteristics of each are displayed in Exhibit 2.

To more fully understand these technologies, it is useful to see how each is used in a given application. MVI had a 3-D robot guidance product in which vision was used to direct the robot's placement of windshields in a car moving along an assembly line at the pace of 60 cars per hour. All four technologies were employed in this application. Lighting was used to produce a very sharp, mirrorlike image of the car as it came into the work area. The bouncing of the light off the car surface to produce this image employed signal processing, a technology developed from radar technology. However, this light reflected off more than just the edge of the car body needed to be seen to perform the window insertion task; mathematical morphology allowed the computer control to extract from the image reflected only the part of the image needed for the task, and eliminated the rest from consideration. That was done through complex computer programs that directed the computer to search the image for the

EXHIBIT 2
Vision Systems Technologies and Their Characteristics

	Image Based	Object Based	
How is the processing done?	**Signal Processing** High speed Simple discrimination Requires special hardware	**Statistical Pattern Recognition** Low speed Simple discrimination No special hardware required	Arithmetic computations
	Mathematical Morphology High speed Complex discrimination High hardware requirements	**Artificial Intelligence** Low speed Very complex discrimination Can require special hardware	Logical computations

What is being processed?

exact shape needed for analysis. Statistical pattern recognition was used to take measurements of window position and orientation, since the actual opening size and the position of the car body on the assembly line could vary slightly from car to car. Thus, this technology made use of another set of computer algorithms to take statistical measurements of the pertinent areas of the problem in question. Artificial intelligence software was used to answer such questions as "Is the window opening the right shape for the windshield that is here?" and "Can the robot reach the opening from its present position?" These questions could all be answered logically; they were either true or false. If corrections were necessary, the computer controls could command the robot to move and change position before actual insertion commands were given.

Exhibit 3 takes the example given above one step further, showing which technologies were necessary to perform the most common applications of vision systems currently on the market. Many applications required the use of only one of the technologies available, while others required multiple technologies. It was estimated that between 50 percent and 60 percent of the applications in the market in 1985 used signal processing. Between 20 percent and 30 percent of applications made use of statistical pattern recognition. The remaining 15 percent of the applications relied on mathematical morphology to perform the desired task.

Exhibit 4 shows how many of the current competitors in the vision systems market were positioned along technology lines. Most competitors used only one technology. MVI was unique in the employment of all four technologies. MVI began as a mathematical morphology company; then it consciously developed the use of the other three technologies in order to be able to handle

EXHIBIT 3
Technologies Used in Machine Vision Applications

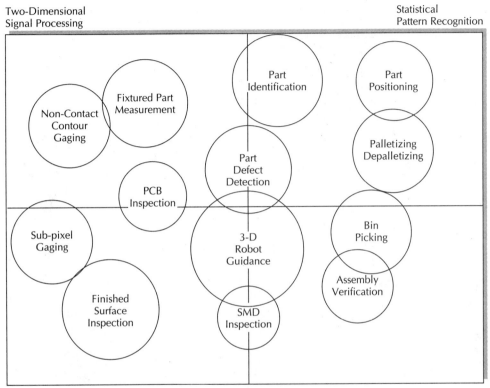

Two-Dimensional
Signal Processing

Statistical
Pattern Recognition

Non-Contact Contour Gaging

Fixtured Part Measurement

Part Identification

Part Positioning

Palletizing Depalletizing

PCB Inspection

Part Defect Detection

Sub-pixel Gaging

3-D Robot Guidance

Bin Picking

Assembly Verification

Finished Surface Inspection

SMD Inspection

Mathematical Morphology

Artificial Intelligence

more difficult industrial problems and to give itself a technology edge over its competition. This was explained in the company's prospectus, as follows:

> The company specializes in mathematical morphology, which it believes is the most suitable technology for application in machine vision. Moreover, the company is complementing its capabilities in mathematical morphology by establishing capabilities in pattern recognition, signal processing, and artificial intelligence, and believes that the combination of these technologies will enhance the applications of the company's systems. It is the advanced application of mathematical morphology and the move toward a combination of technologies to complement mathematical morphology that the company believes differentiates it significantly from its competitors.

Dr. Sternberg explained why it is important to use all the available technologies. He said:

EXHIBIT 4

Industry Competitors' Technology Positions

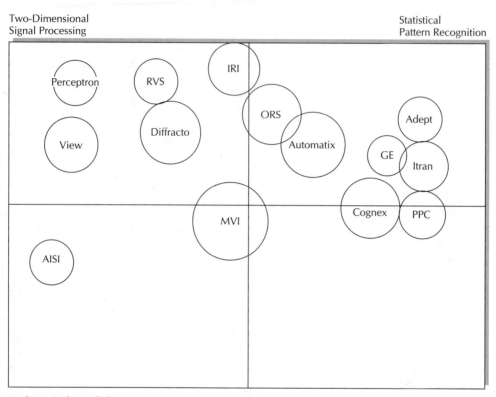

You can force a solution using just one tool, but you end up working 10 times harder than if you use the right tool for the right part of the job. You can find a way to change the spark plugs on your car with just a hammer, but it will take you a lot longer to do it this way than if you had all the right tools for the job.

Machine Vision International—History

MVI was founded in June 1981 by Dr. Stanley R. Sternberg. Dr. Sternberg had previously worked at the Environmental Research Institute of Michigan, where he was instrumental in the development of the technology of mathematical morphology. Dr. Sternberg's idea was to develop products based on this technology that could be used for measurement, inspection, and control in manufacturing processes. In the fall of 1982, Dr. Sternberg joined with Richard P. Eidswick to develop strategy to bring this technology to market. Prior to joining

MVI, Mr. Eidswick was senior vice president and director of Comshare, Inc., an international computer services company.

To fund the company, nearly $9.5 million of equity capital was raised through private offerings of MVI securities. Approximately $5 million of these funds were raised through the sales of common stock to Safeguard Scientifics, Inc. As of November 5, 1985, MVI was a public company, with its shares traded in the over-the-counter market.

As its strategy in the vision industry, MVI chose to focus on three business areas and three specific applications of machine vision. The business areas were automotive, electronics, and general industrial. The applications were three-dimensional robot guidance, surface inspection, and surface-mounted electronic component inspection. The principal component of all systems sold by MVI was the image flow computer (IFC), an image processing computer that used MVI's proprietary operating software, BLIX, to perform the mathematical calculations necessary for image analysis.

MVI marketed its products primarily through direct sales groups dedicated to end users in the three business areas. It also marketed its products to original equipment manufacturers (OEMs) who specified MVI products in their systems, and through certain specialized sales representatives. Through September 1985, MVI had manufactured and sold approximately 100 machine vision systems for an aggregate sales price of nearly $12 million. Financial statements for MVI are presented in Exhibits 5 and 6.

Market Approach

An organizational chart for MVI is shown in Exhibit 7. The sales function within MVI was divided along market segment lines. The three current sales divisions—automated systems, electronic systems, and manufacturing technology—mirrored those markets pointed out by the Prudential-Bache survey as the major customers interested in machine vision products.

The Automated Systems Division (ASD)

MVI began its search for applications in the automotive industry, where executives were already talking about putting resources into finding vision solutions to solve automation problems. Mr. Jake Jeppesen, who joined MVI in June 1983 to head the Automated Systems Division, found a group at GM that had been talking for two years to various vision companies about the possibility of using vision to automate auto glass insertion. The other companies had failed to develop a product that worked. Mr. Jeppesen convinced them to try again with the mathematical morphology technology that MVI offered. The first order for the window insertion product was received by MVI in December 1983. A prototype was working in a GM lab in March 1984, and the first plant installation was made in June 1984. See Exhibit 8 for a representation of how this product worked.

Even though the first vision applications taken on by MVI showed themselves to be successfully working projects within the automotive industry,

EXHIBIT 5
Machine Vision International Corporation—Statements of Operations

	June 25, 1981– Dec. 31, 1983	Jan. 1– Dec. 31, 1984	First Six Months	
			1984	1985
Net sales	$ 541,058	$ 4,011,730	$ 760,807	$ 4,481,476
Cost of sales	338,921	2,536,398	555,891	2,021,068
Gross profit	$ 202,137	$ 1,475,332	$ 204,916	$ 2,460,408
Operating expenses:				
Product development	$ 318,961	$ 1,733,667	$ 610,836	$ 1,354,943
Selling	360,601	1,979,102	652,364	2,011,329
General and administration	542,101	904,272	420,356	365,184
Total operating expenses	$ 1,221,663	$ 4,617,041	$ 1,683,556	$ 3,731,456
Loss from operations	$ (1,019,526)	$ (3,141,709)	$ (1,478,640)	$(1,271,048)
Other income (expense):				
Interest expense	$ (5,076)	$ (105,089)	$ (15,697)	$ (116,207)
Other	23,342	67,895	64,858	19,410
Total other income (expense)	$ 18,266	$ (37,194)	$ 49,161	$ (96,797)
Net loss	$ (1,001,260)	$ (3,178,903)	$ (1,429,479)	$(1,367,845)
Loss per share	$ (.41)	$ (.56)	$ (.28)	$ (.18)
Weighted average number of shares	2,458,495	5,714,391	5,164,775	7,457,460

the sales process for ASD remained a very complicated one. The division maintained an ongoing educational sales effort, selling everyone from the executive level to plant production people on who MVI was and what the company and machine vision were capable of doing. Automotive executives and manufacturing research staff personnel were interested in the technology involved and its advantages over existing or alternative assembly automation techniques. However, manufacturing staff were interested in finding ways in which higher-quality cars could be built better, cheaper, and faster. Plant production staff were generally interested in improvements in product quality, but were mainly concerned with production speed so that their quotas could be met. To this group, a product's reliability on the assembly line was of the utmost importance. Since orders within automotive companies came most often from the manufacturing staff or the plant production people, it was the goal of the sales process to give these people confidence that MVI's product

EXHIBIT 6

Machine Vision International Corporation—Balance Sheet

	December 31, 1983	December 31, 1984	June 30, 1985 (unaudited)
Assets			
Current assets:			
Cash and cash equivalents	$ 104,117	$ 191,361	$ 151,601
Receivables	272,945	2,095,875	3,255,081
Inventories	238,772	1,964,951	3,749,191
Prepaid expenses and deposits	8,689	34,961	34,228
Total current assets	$ 624,523	$4,287,148	$7,190,101
Property and equipment			
Computer and other equipment	$ 221,274	$ 972,614	$1,213,574
Office furniture and equipment	91,436	171,737	249,738
Leasehold improvements	6,520	91,665	102,232
	$ 319,230	$1,236,016	$1,565,544
Less: accumulated depreciation	31,154	275,087	470,087
Net property and equipment	$ 288,076	$ 960,929	$1,095,457
	$ 912,599	$5,248,077	$8,285,558
Liabilities and shareholders' equity			
Current liabilities:			
Current portion of long-term debt	$ 42,500	$ 74,823	$ 118,000
Note payable	—	675,000	500,000
Accounts payable	246,058	993,292	1,887,677
Accrued liabilities	104,540	407,842	633,709
Total current liabilities	$ 393,098	$2,150,957	$3,139,386
Long-term debt, less current portion above	$ 118,365	$1,671,775	$1,205,073
Shareholders' equity			
Common stock, no par value, stated value $.001	4,018	6,509	8,214
Paid-in capital	1,398,378	5,598,999	9,480,893
Accumulated deficit	(1,001,260)	(4,180,163)	(5,548,008)
Total shareholders' equity	$ 401,136	$1,425,345	$3,941,099
	$ 912,599	$5,248,077	$8,285,558

EXHIBIT 7
Corporate Organization Chart

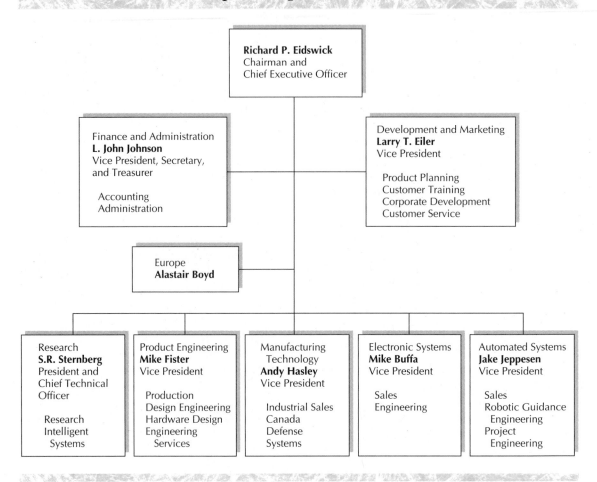

"will do what we say it's going to do forever, first time every time, and never fail," as Mr. Jeppesen put it. These groups were not interested in machine vision for its technology; they wanted their task performed in the most reliable, fastest way possible.

Since this sales effort was so educational in nature, the decision was made to approach the market on a direct basis; MVI did not want to entrust this type of basic technology and company-image selling to a third party. The ASD was currently selling products for two applications in the automotive industry. These

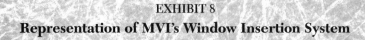

EXHIBIT 8
Representation of MVI's Window Insertion System

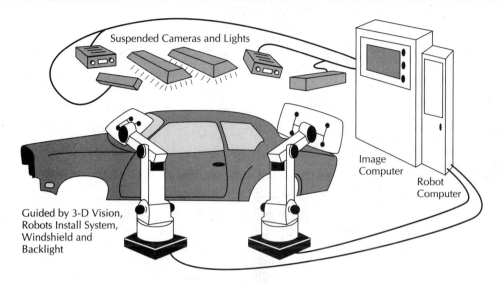

Suspended Cameras and Lights

Image Computer

Robot Computer

Guided by 3-D Vision, Robots Install System, Windshield and Backlight

were 3-D robot guidance for window insertion and other applications, and surface paint inspection.

The window insertion product had a selling price of approximately $450,000 per installation. It was only a part of an entire window insertion system that included robots, body handling equipment, material handling equipment, and controls supplied by other vendors. This total system cost in the neighborhood of $5 million. The surface paint inspection product was currently used only to inspect finished paint surfaces; it sold for approximately $500,000 per system. MVI had received seven orders for window insertion systems and one for a paint inspection system.

Though relatively few orders for these products had been received to date, the markets for these products were very large. Mr. Jeppesen saw many potential application areas for both MVI's 3-D robot guidance and paint surface inspection products. 3-D robot guidance could also be employed to automate such tasks as automobile wheel and cockpit loading, to apply paint stripes, and to control many fluid fill operations. Although paint inspection systems were currently used only for finished product inspection, the market could be expanded to include inspection of bare metal after frameup, phosphate coating before priming, primer coats, and other checkpoints during automobile production. In total, Mr. Jeppesen currently foresaw 10 application possibilities for 3-D robot guidance and 6 application areas for surface inspection in each automobile plant. In 1985, there were 73 automobile assembly plants operating in the United States, and many of these operated with more than one assembly line per plant.

At the time, no other vision company even claimed to be able to supply a product that could perform surface inspection. Mr. Jeppesen listed three companies as major competitors in the 3-D robotics business: GMF Robotics, ASEA Robotics, and Automatix. In this area, Mr. Jeppesen said that many companies claimed to be able to perform this task, but they really did not have the necessary capabilities. As a result, there was a great amount of confusion in the marketplace, but Mr. Jeppesen believed that this confusion would soon be dispelled as competitors tried to supply the market and failed.

The Electronics Sales Division (ESD)

The electronics market was very different from the automotive area. Therefore, the sales strategy and marketing positioning employed in the electronics market were unique to it. The sales process for the ESD began with marketing research to find out the vision needs in the electronics industry and was subsequently combined with a concerted effort to get to know the decision makers within that industry. In this effort, MVI marketing personnel attended electronics industry meetings, where they got to know the technology leaders within the industry. Thus they gained firsthand knowledge of the industry's technology trends as well as the strategies of the major electronics firms.

In 1985, the U.S. electronics industry was currently undergoing a great change in production procedures. Ninety percent of electronics assembly was being done on lead-through boards. However, overseas, and especially in Japan, nearly 95 percent of electronics assembly was being done on higher-quality, more reliable surface-mounted boards. It was believed that U.S. production would shift to surface-mounted boards very rapidly. This type of production would be highly compatible with automated assembly techniques since the components on surface-mounted boards were much smaller and required greater production sensitivity than lead-through boards.[1]

The total market for surface-mounted inspection systems was divided into three segments by MVI's market researches. The two in which MVI thought it could successfully compete were: (1) low-speed, high-precision inspection of a broad range of components, and (2) high-volume, low-precision inspection of a limited range of components. For these areas, MVI made the following total market size projections.

---

[1]Surface mount technology (SMT) was an electronic manufacturing method in which miniaturized, prepackaged components were assembled on the top (hence surface) of a circuit. In lead-through assembly, the components had conductors or leads that were inserted through holes that are drilled or punched through the board. These leads were folded or clinched on the back of the board to provide mechanical component attachment. In SMT manufacturing, the components were placed on the board by an automatic mechanism and then soldered in place.

Year	Segment 1 Total Number of Vision Systems	Segment 1 Total Dollar Market (in Millions)	Segment 2 Total Number of Vision Systems	Segment 2 Total Dollar Market (in Millions)
1984	30	$ 3.6	7	$ 1.05
1985	65	7.8	20	3.00
1986	90	10.8	130	19.50
1987	125	15.0	340	51.00
1988	350	42.0	525	78.75

MVI had spent two years developing a product that could use vision to control the assembly process and provide inspection for this automated production. MVI believed that the contrast and complexity of the components used in this process required the capabilities of the company's mathematical morphology technology. An effective product for this market had to be able to perform three tasks: (1) determine if the correct component (chip, diode, resistor, or capacitor) was present; (2) determine if each part was in the correct position relative to the other components; and (3) check the solder used to attach parts to the board for voids and excess solder material. MVI's vision technology was capable of solving the first two tasks. The third task required a low-level X-ray capability, which MVI did not currently have but was working to achieve.

Unlike ASD sales, ESD sales were technology sales. ESD's personnel talked to technical processing engineers, not the traditional purchasing departments within the electronics firms. MVI people talked to these technical people to determine their automation needs and to educate them as to the capabilities of MVI's product. The goal was to get to know the people who would use the system and get their support before there was a quotation request made on the part of the electronics firm.

By the end of the third quarter of 1985, MVI had three working surface-mounted inspection systems in the field. The company expected to make deliveries on nine or ten more orders before the end of the year. Prices on these systems ranged from $80,000 to $200,000. The hardware used in these systems was priced to match closely the prices of MVI's competition. The software used was specific to each application and, therefore, was priced to be the profit margin producer for the company.

Competitors in this market were View Engineering, International Robomation/Intelligence (IRI), and Automatix. IRI was specifically mentioned as an aggressive price competitor. IRI's system that competed with MVI was priced between $75,000 and $125,000.

The Manufacturing Technology Division (MTD)

MVI's Manufacturing Technology Division comprised two sales groups, the Industrial Sales Group (ISG) and the Aerospace Sales Group (ASG). This division had as its goal finding new markets for the products developed by the other sales divisions. Manufacturing technology sales groups were to take on applications that required extensions of existing technology or new combinations of what had already been developed by MVI's R&D and engineering personnel. The MTD was headed by Mr. Andrew Hasley.

Industrial Sales Group. MVI received between 250 and 300 inquiries each month through its marketing work, by its presence in several vision shows, and through references from its present customers. Many of these inquiries did not come from people within the automotive or electronics industries. Leads from these other nonspecialized industries were turned over to the Industrial Sales Group, which was under the direction of Mr. John Kufchock.

Mr. Kufchock used three initial criteria to determine whether MVI would pursue these inquiries. The lead had to come from a Fortune 500 company; thus, the company would have considerable funds to spend on capital investments. The application being pursued had to involve the use of technology already developed by MVI; thus, sales of the ISG were meant to produce a multiplier effect on sales for MVI. Furthermore, the inquiry had to come from a company that had an established engineering group capable of understanding both the technology involved and the advantages of MVI's technology over competitors.

The ISG had made sales in many industries, all of surface inspection products that performed very diversified tasks. For example, in the food industry, surface inspection was used to identify foreign objects in produce coming from the fields as well as produce of less than acceptable grade, so that these could be eliminated from further processing. In the lumber industry, surface inspection was used to check plywood as it was produced so that its grade and sales quality could be determined. In the rubber industry, tires were checked for flaws. By the end of 1985, the ISG had placed more than 20 systems in the industrial workplace. Mr. Kufchock expected to have nearly 50 more systems on the market in the first six months of 1986. He predicted that ISG could sell over 100 systems per year from a total of only 20 different customer corporations.

The sales process for the ISG usually began with an inquiry from a prospective customer. Qualified leads were turned over to one of Mr. Kufchock's two sales-oriented application engineers. Through talking with and visiting the prospect, the application engineer studied the customer's vision needs to determine whether MVI's technology could meet the requirements of the task. The application engineer also identified the right people to deal with in the customer's organization. These included those who would understand the technology, those who would use the product, and those who would actually make the purchase decision. All those involved in the decision process had to be "put on the team" if the sales process was to be successful. When this had been completed, a test of MVI's product on the prospect's material would be made at ISG's own lab. When the test was successful, the application engineer contacted the customer, asking that they send people to see the test results. Then, a trip was made to the customer's business to determine the actual conditions under which the system had to perform and to talk to all the decision makers involved, getting their input on a preliminary sales proposal. Then a final proposal was drawn up and sent to the purchasing department of the customer. This entire selling process took between three and nine months.

The ISG also sold its products to other firms that needed vision to make their large automation systems work for their customers. MVI called these firms strategic partners because often significant development work had been done by MVI's engineering staff to make the vision products work successfully for this partner. These strategic partners had market knowledge that MVI did not possess. Often, the vision portion of the systems sold by these partners comprised less than 20 percent of the entire system's selling price.

Prices on vision systems sold through the ISG ranged from $45,000 to $75,000 each. These prices included the hardware and software necessary for the application plus training. Fees for engineering services at the customer's plant to get the system up and running were charged separately at an established per diem rate. In the first applications, it was common for MVI to find this engineering support taking more time than expected. This resulted in profit margins less than what had been predicted.

Aerospace Sales Group (ASG).   The Aerospace Sales Group was established in mid-1985. It was spun off from the ISG when it was believed that there was enough business in this area alone to support a dedicated sales effort. The first sales made in the aerospace industry were made by the ISG group.

This group sold products for many different applications involving the different technologies developed by the ASD and ESD. These included 3-D robot guidance systems, small parts inspection systems, surface inspection products, and combinations of small parts inspection and 3-D robot guidance in which the system would recognize, inspect, and control the handling of parts. Current applications included turbine blade inspection, surface-coating inspections on space shuttle booster rockets, and 3-D robot guidance used for assembling wiring harnesses in aircraft.

The defense supply industry had different requirements for vision products than did the other industries MVI sold to. Here speed was of less concern than it was in other industrial environments. What was important here was the complexity of the parts to be inspected or assembled. As a result, the systems sold by the ASG were complicated and averaged in price from $400,000 to $500,000.

Major competitors were Robotic Vision Systems, IRI, and View Engineering. As in the automotive industry, no other competitor even claimed to be able to perform surface inspection. Also, MVI believed there was little competition in the area of parts inspection. In discussing the competitive environment, Mr. Hasley, director of the Manufacturing Technology Division, said,

> In a lot of cases, we don't find we're competing directly with anybody. We still make a lot of cold calls. Selling here is a market development problem really. It's just getting the application defined. Can you do this? Can you do that? It involves a lot of education on what vision can do.

Commonalities of Sales Approach

Though each of MVI's three divisions sold to different markets and to different groups of people within customer firms, each application's real bottom-line sales approach was similar. What MVI was really selling was improved return on investment (ROI). In some sales, MVI's salespeople were showing how their product could reduce warranty claim costs. This was especially true in automobile paint inspection, since paint flaws were the industry's fourth-largest warranty claim cost. Thus, improving paint finish quality was a paramount goal for these firms. In others, it was improved product quality that resulted from the use of vision equipment. For yet other applications, the main purpose of the vision equipment was to reduce the costs of inspection. For example, Mr. Kufchock pointed out that the plywood inspection system in one facility replaced the use of eight inspectors each earning $21 per hour.

Production

For each first-time application, MVI built whatever hardware and software were needed to make the project work for the customer. For further similar applications, MVI looked for a supplier for the necessary components of the system. Thus, for all of MVI's multiple applications, it purchased the optics, hardware, circuit boards, cables, communications devices, and other material handling equipment from outside suppliers. The role of production then became that of packaging the optical equipment, the hardware, the software, and the communications materials so that the application worked for the customer.

The Future Goals for MVI

Mr. Eidswick, MVI's chairman and CEO, established the company's goal of being a dominant supplier in the machine vision industry. This goal translated into obtaining a 15 percent share of this market within five years and then sustaining that 15 percent share.

Mr. Eidswick also set achievement goals for each sales division. The ASD and the ESD were to be specialized divisions and, as such, technology and market share leaders within their industries. Here, there would be a continuing effort to take on new projects that had a strategic purpose. The groups within the Manufacturing Technology Division were to have multiplier strategies; their sales were to come from extensions of products developed by the ASD and ESD. The MTD groups were also to seek out strategic partners, finding companies who needed vision in their products and who already had market knowledge and a strong customer base. For this type of customer, MVI would sell its products at a discount from the prices quoted to direct end users since the strategic partners would take over much of the selling process for MVI.

Mr. Eidswick prepared sales expense breakdowns for the company's two types of sales, those direct to end users and those made through strategic partners. These expense breakdowns, expressed as percentages of sales revenue, are shown below. The third column shows the breakdown of expenses as percentages of sales for MVI's sales for the first half of 1985.

	End User	Strategic Partner	First Six Months of 1985
Revenue	100%	100%	100%
Cost of Goods Sold	35	55	45
Gross Margin	65%	45%	55%
Selling Expense	25	9	45
R&D and Engineering	10	10	30
Corporate Expenses	10	6	8
Total Expenses	45%	25%	83%
Profit before Taxes	20%	20%	(28%)

MVI had not made a profit to date; however, no competitor in the vision industry had been consistently profitable. MVI had bid each project, even the first one for each of its applications, at a price that the company thought would be profitable. However, the number of engineering, selling, and application development hours that these early applications needed to achieve systems capable of working in real industrial environments and to educate customers on the use of the products had been hard to estimate. These problems led to the higher than desired selling, R&D, and engineering expenses to date. Mr. Eidswick was most concerned about the high selling-expense figure. He was not so concerned about the R&D and engineering expense, since this was to be expected in a new, high-technology industry. MVI needed, as Mr. Eidswick saw it, to find ways to reduce it selling expense.

The Question of Focus

Some vision companies have chosen to be very specialized. They believe that an emerging company cannot afford to spread itself too thin. It must establish a market niche, exploit that niche, make some money, and then go out and spread itself. Others say that this is a new market. No one understands it. What may be a niche one day might just disappear. Some competitors are very specialized. Others are all over the place. Some of each have failed. Why? For the specialized firms, perhaps the market never appeared or the task they chose proved too difficult. For those who were in all markets, each project was different and they had no repeat sales.

Dr. Sternberg

Multiple orders of the same kind of things, that's the kind of result we want to have. We want more repeat orders for the same product, the same application . . .

less customization. That way we don't have to keep reinventing the wheel, inventing new technology, and engineering new software for every order that we get.

Mr. Eiler

Mr. Eidswick believed that the fact that MVI had "so much going on, in so many markets, with so many different applications" was the company's biggest problem. But he explained that "we have to do this if we want to find the applications that will provide repeat business, applications that will establish us as an industry leader."

Mr. Eiler pointed out that the company had purposefully chosen only very difficult applications, a strategic approach he called "a tough jobs positioning." That product positioning, along with what Mr. Kufchock called the company's credo that "There is no unhappy customer," was designed to build a strong company image for MVI as "the company that makes products that work," as Mr. Eiler put it.

MVI had not found that it was easy to get a vision application job even after another competitor had failed to provide a product that worked. Often customers who had spent thousands and thousands of dollars on vision equipment wanted to protect that investment by giving their supplier another chance to succeed. Other customers turned away from vision after initial system failures, waiting for the technology to mature and for the market winners to appear rather than give another company a chance at that time.

The prospectus published by MVI at the time of its stock offering to Safeguard Scientifics shareholders stated that MVI focused on three applications. These were three-dimensional robot guidance, surface inspection, and surface-mounted electronic component inspection. Dr. Sternberg believed that, in looking at the company, one should be careful not to confuse its technological diversity with its market position. He said, "MVI is focused; we are working toward three standardized products."

MacTec Control AB

James E. Nelson

"The choices themselves seem simple enough, " thought Georg Carlsson. "Either we enter the U.S. market in Pennsylvania and New York, we forget about the U.S. for the time being, or we do some more marketing research." The difficult part was the decision.

Georg was president of MacTec Control AB, a Swedish firm located in Kristianstad. Georg had begun MacTec in 1980 along with his wife, Jessie. MacTec had grown rapidly and now boasted of some 30 employees and annual revenues of about $2.8 million. Since 1985, MacTec had been partly owned by The Perstorp Corporation whose headquarters were located nearby. Perstorp was a large manufacturer of chemicals and chemical products, with operations in 18 countries and annual revenues of about $600 million. Perstorp had provided MacTec with capital and managerial advice, as well as chemical analysis technology.

MacTec's Aqualex System

MacTec's product line centered about its Aqualex System, a design of computer hardware and software for the monitoring and control of pressurized water flows. Most often these water flows consisted of either potable water or sewage effluent as these liquids were stored, moved, or treated by municipal water departments.

The System employed MacTec's MPDII microcomputer (see Exhibit 1) installed at individual pumping stations where liquids are stored and moved. Often these stations were located quite far apart, linking geographically dispersed water users (households, businesses, etc.) to water and sewer systems. The microcomputer performed a number of important functions. It controlled the starts, stops, and alarms of up to four pumps, monitored levels and available capacities of storage reservoirs, checked pump capacities and power consumptions, and recorded pump flows. It could even measure amounts of rainfall entering reservoirs and adjust pump operations or activate an alarm as needed. Each microcomputer could also be easily connected to a main computer to allow remote

This case was written by Professor James E. Nelson, University of Colorado. This case is intended for use as a basis for class discussion rather than to illustrate either effective or ineffective administrative decision making. Some data are disguised. © 1989 by the Business Research Division, College of Business and Administration and the Graduate School of Business Administration, University of Colorado, Boulder, Colorado, 80309-0419.

EXHIBIT 1
MacTec's MPDII Microcomputer

The Aqualex System is based on the MPDII which controls and monitors the pumping stations

An MPDII microcomputer is installed at a pumping station and works as an independent, intelligent computer. When required, it can go online with the central computer and report its readings there.

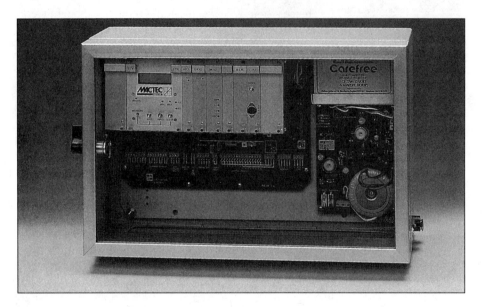

Here are some of the functions of the MPDII

___ It governs the starts, stops, and alarms of up to four pumps, controlled by an integrated piezo-resistive pressure-level sensor.

___ It checks the sump level.

___ It checks pump capacity and changes in pump capacity.

___ It activates an alarm when readings reach preset deviation limits.

___ It registers precipitation and activates an alarm in case of heavy rain.

___ It constantly monitors pump power consumption and activates an alarm in case of unacceptable deviation.

___ It registers current pump flow by means of advanced calculations of inflow and outfeed from the sump.

___ It can register accumulated time for overflow.

___ It switches to forward or reverse action, even by remote command.

___ It stores locally the last nine alarm instances with time indications. These may be read directly on an LCD display.

___ It can be remotely programmed from the central computer.

An MPDII does a great job, day after day, year after year.

control of pumping stations and produce a variety of charts and graphs useful in evaluating pump performance and scheduling needed maintenance.

The Aqualex System provided a monitoring function that human operators could not match in terms of sophistication, immediacy, and cost. The System permitted each individual substation to: control its own pumping operations; collect, analyze, and store data; forecast trends; transmit data and alarms to a central computer; and receive remote commands. Alarms could also be transmitted directly to a pocket-sized receiver carried by one or more operators on call. A supervisor could continually monitor pumping operations in a large system entirely via a computer terminal at a central location and send commands to individual pumps, thereby saving costly service calls and time. The System also reduced the possibility of overflows that could produce disastrous flooding of nearby communities.

MacTec personnel would work with water and sewage engineers to design and install the desired Aqualex System. Personnel would also train engineers and operators to work with the System and would be available 24 hours a day for consultation. If needed, a MacTec engineer could be physically present to assist engineers and operators whenever major problems arose. MacTec also offered its clients the option of purchasing a complete service contract whereby MacTec personnel would provide periodic testing and maintenance of installed Systems.

An Aqualex System could be configured a number of ways. In its most basic form, the System would be little more than a small "black box" that monitored two or three lift station activities and, when necessary, transmitted an alarm to one or more remote receivers. An intermediate System would monitor additional activities, send data to a central computer via telephone lines, and receive remote commands. An advanced System would provide the same monitoring capabilities but add forecasting features, maintenance management, auxiliary power back-up, and data transmission and reception via radio. Prices to customers for the three configurations in early 1989 were about $1,200, $2,400, and $4,200.

Aqualex Customers

Aqualex customers could be divided into two groups: governmental units and industrial companies. The typical application in the first group was a sewage treatment plant having some four to 12 pumping stations, each station containing one or more pumps. Pumps would operate intermittently and—unless an Aqualex or similar system were in place—be monitored by one or more operators who would visit each station once or perhaps twice each day for about a half hour. Operators would take reservoir measurements, record running times of pumps, and sometimes perform limited maintenance and repairs. The sewage plant and stations typically were located in flat or rolling terrain, where gravity could not be used in lieu of pumping. If any monitoring equipment were present at all, it typically would consist of a crude, on-site alarm that would activate whenever fluid levels rose or fell beyond a preset level. Sometimes the alarm would activate a telephone dialing function that alerted an operator some distance from the station.

Numerous industrial companies also stored, moved, and processed large quantities of water or sewage. These applications usually differed little from those in governmental plants except for their smaller size. On the other hand, there were a considerably larger number of industrial companies having pumping stations and so, Georg thought, the two markets often offered about identical market potentials in many countries.

The two markets desired essentially the same products, although industrial applications often used smaller, simpler equipment. Both markets wanted their monitoring equipment to be accurate and reliable, the two dominant concerns. Equipment should also be easy to use, economical to operate, and require little regular service or maintenance. Purchase price often was not a major consideration—as long as the price was in some appropriate range, customers seemed more interested in actual product performance than in initial outlays.

Georg thought that worldwide demand for Aqualex Systems and competing products would continue to be strong for at least the next ten years. While some of this demand represented construction of new pumping stations, many applications were replacements of crude monitoring and alarm systems at existing sites. These existing systems depended greatly on regular visits by operators, visits that often continued even after new equipment was installed. Most such trips were probably not necessary. However, many managers found it difficult to dismiss or reassign monitoring personnel that were no longer needed; many were also quite cautious and conservative, desiring some human monitoring of the new equipment "just in case." Once replacements of existing systems were complete, market growth would be limited to new construction and, of course, replacements of more sophisticated systems.

Most customers (as well as noncustomers) considered the Aqualex System to be the best on the market. Those knowledgeable in the industry felt that competing products seldom matched Aqualex's reliability and accuracy. Experts also believed that many competing products lacked the sophistication and flexibility present in Aqualex's design. Beyond these product features, customers also appreciated MacTec's knowledge about water and sanitation engineering. Competing firms often lacked this expertise, offering their products somewhat as a sideline and considering the market too small for an intensive marketing effort.

The market was clearly not too small for MacTec. While Georg had no hard data on market potential for western Europe, he thought that annual demand here could be as much as $9 million. About 40% of this came from new construction while the rest represented demand from replacing existing systems. Industry sales in the latter category could be increased by more aggressive marketing efforts on the part of MacTec and its competitors. Eastern European economies represented additional, new potential. However, the water and sewer industries in these countries seemed less interested than their Western counterparts in high technology equipment to monitor pumping operations. Additionally, business was often more difficult to conduct in these countries. In contrast, the U.S. market looked very attractive.

MacTec Strategy

MacTec currently marketed its Aqualex System primarily to sewage treatment plants in Scandinavia and other countries in northern and central Europe. The company's strategy could be described as providing technologically superior equipment to monitor pumping operations at these plants. The strategy stressed frequent contacts with customers and potential customers to design, supply, and service Aqualex Systems. The strategy also stressed superior knowledge of water and sanitation engineering along with up-to-date electronics and computer technology. The result was a line of highly specialized sensors, computers, and methods for process controls in water treatment plants.

This was the essence of MacTec's strategy, having a special competence that no firm in the world could easily match. MacTec also prided itself on its being a young, creative company, without an entrenched bureaucracy. Company employees generally worked with enthusiasm and dedication; they talked with each other, regularly, openly, and with a great deal of give and take. Most importantly, customers—as well as technology—seemed to drive all areas in the company.

MacTec's strategy in its European markets seemed to be fairly well decided. That is, Georg thought that a continuation of present strategies and tactics should continue to produce good results. However, an aspect that would likely change would be to locate a branch office having both sales and manufacturing activities somewhere in the European Community (EC), most likely the Netherlands. The plan was to have such an office in operation well before 1992, when the 12 countries in the EC (Belgium, Denmark, France, Greece, Ireland, Italy, Luxembourg, the Netherlands, Portugal, Spain, United Kingdom, West Germany) would mutually eliminate national barriers to the flow of capital, goods, and services. Having a MacTec office located in the EC would greatly simplify sales to these member countries. Moreover, MacTec's presence should also avoid problems with any protective barriers the EC itself might raise to limit or discourage market access by outsiders.

Notwithstanding activities related to this branch office, Georg was considering a major strategic decision to enter the U.S. market. His two recent visits to the U.S. had led him to conclude that the market represented potential beyond that for western Europe and that the U.S. seemed perfect for expansion. Industry experts in the U.S. agreed with Georg that the Aqualex System outperformed anything used in the U.S. market. Experts thought that many water and sewage engineers would welcome MacTec's products and knowledge. Moreover, Georg thought that U.S. transportation systems and payment arrangements would present few problems. The System would be imported under U.S. Tariff Regulation 71249 and pay a duty of 4.9%.

Entry would most likely be in the form of a sales and service office located in Philadelphia. The Pennsylvania and New York state markets seemed representative of the U.S. and appeared to offer a good test of the Aqualex System. The two states together probably represented about 18% of total U.S. market potential for the System. The office would require an investment of some $200,000 for inventory and other balance sheet items. Annual fixed costs would total upwards of $250,000 for salaries and other operating expenses—Georg thought that the office would employ only a general manager, two sales technicians, and secretary for at least the first year or two. Each Aqualex System sold in the U.S. would be priced to provide a contribution of about 30%. Georg wanted a 35% annual return before taxes on any MacTec investment, to begin no later than the second year. At issue was whether Georg could realistically expect to achieve this goal in the U.S.

Marketing Research

To this end, Georg had commissioned the Browning Group in Philadelphia to conduct some limited marketing research with selected personnel in the water and sewage industries in the city and surrounding areas. The research had two purposes: To obtain a sense of market needs and market reactions to MacTec's products and to calculate a rough estimate of market potential in Pennsylvania and New York. Results were intended to help Georg interpret his earlier conversations with industry experts and perhaps allow a decision on market entry.

The research design itself employed two phases of data collection. The first consisted of five one-hour interviews with water and sewage engineers employed by local city and municipal governments. For each interview, an experienced Browning Group interviewer scheduled an appointment with the engineer and then visited his office, armed with a set of questions and a tape recorder. Questions included:

1. What procedures do you use to monitor your pumping stations?
2. Is your current monitoring system effective? Costly?
3. What are the costs of a monitoring malfunction?
4. What features would you like to see in a monitoring system?
5. Who decides on the selection of a monitoring system?
6. What is your reaction to the Aqualex System?

Interviewers were careful to listen closely to the engineers' responses and to probe for additional detail and clarification.

Tapes of the personal interviews were transcribed and then analyzed by the project manager at Browning. The report noted that these results were interesting in that they described typical industry practices and viewpoints. A partial summary from the report appears below:

> The picture that emerges is one of fairly sophisticated personnel making decisions about monitoring equipment that is relatively simple in design. Still, some engineers would appear distrustful of this equipment because they persist in sending operators to pumping stations on a daily basis. The distrust may be justified because potential costs of a malfunction were identified as expensive repairs and

cleanups, fines of $10,000 per day of violation, lawsuits, harassment by the Health Department, and public embarrassment. The five engineers identified themselves as key individuals in the decision to purchase new equipment. Without exception, they considered MacTec features innovative, highly desirable, and worth the price.

The summary noted also that the primary use of the interview results was to construct a questionnaire that could be administered over the telephone.

The questionnaire was used in the second phase of data collection, as part of a telephone survey that had contacted 65 utility managers, water and sewage engineers, and pumping station operators in Philadelphia and surrounding areas. All respondents were employed by governmental units. Each interview took about 10 minutes to complete, covering topics identified in questions 1, 2, and 4 above. The Browning Group's research report stated that most interviews found respondents to be quite cooperative, although 15 people refused to participate at all.

The telephone interviews had produced results that could be considered more representative of the market because of the larger sample size. The report had organized these results about the topics of monitoring procedures, system effectiveness and costs, and features desired in a monitoring system:

> All monitoring systems under the responsibility of the 50 respondents were considered to require manual checking. The frequency of operator visits to pumping stations ranged from monthly to twice daily, depending on flow rates, pumping station history, proximity of nearby communities, monitoring equipment in operation, and other factors. Even the most sophisticated automatic systems were checked because respondents "just don't trust the machine." Each operator was responsible for some 10 to 20 stations.
>
> Despite the perceived need for double-checking, all respondents considered their current monitoring system to be quite effective. Not one reported a serious pumping malfunction in the past three years that had escaped detection. However, this reliability came at considerable cost—the annual wages and other expenses associated with each monitoring operator averaged about $40,000.
>
> Respondents were about evenly divided between those wishing a simple alarm system and those desiring a sophisticated, versatile microprocessor. Managers and engineers in the former category often said that the only feature they really needed was an emergency signal such as a siren, horn, or light. Sometimes they would add a telephone dialer that would be automatically activated at the same time as the signal. Most agreed that a price of around $2,000 would be reasonable for such a system. The latter category of individuals contained engineers desiring many of the Aqualex System's features, once they knew such equipment was available. A price of $4,000 per system seemed acceptable. Some of these respondents were quite knowledgeable about computers and computer programming while others were not. Only four respondents voiced any strong concerns about the cost to purchase and install more sophisticated monitoring equipment. Everyone demanded that the equipment be reliable and accurate.

Georg found the report quite helpful. Much of the information, of course, simply confirmed his own view of the U.S. market. However, it was good to have this knowledge from an independent, objective organization. In addition, to learn that the market consisted of two apparently equally sized segments of simple and sophisticated applications was quite worthwhile. In particular, knowledge of system prices considered acceptable by each segment would make the entry decision easier. Meeting these prices would not be a major problem.

A most important section of the report contained an estimate of market potential for Pennsylvania and New York. The estimate was based on an analysis of discharge permits on file in governmental offices in the two states. These permits were required before any city, municipality, water or sewage district, or industrial company could release sewage or other contaminated water to another system or to a lake or river. Each permit showed the number of pumping stations in operation. Based on a 10% sample of permits, the report had estimated that governmental units in Pennsylvania and New York contained approximately 3,000 and 5,000 pumping stations for waste water, respectively. Industrial companies in the two states were estimated to add some 3,000 and 9,000 more pumping stations, respectively. The total number of pumping stations in the two states—20,000—seemed to be growing at about 2% per year.

Finally, a brief section of the report dealt with the study's limitations. Georg agreed that the sample was quite small, that it contained no utility managers or engineers from New York, and that it probably concentrated too heavily on individuals in larger urban areas. In addition, the research told him nothing about competitors and their marketing strategies and tactics. Nor did he learn anything about any state regulations for monitoring equipment, if indeed any existed. However, these shortcomings came as no surprise, representing a consequence of the research design proposed to Georg by the Browning Group some six weeks ago, before the study began.

The Decision

Georg's decision seemed a difficult one. The most risky option was to enter the U.S. market as soon as possible; the most conservative was to stay in Europe. In between was the option of conducting some additional marketing research.

Discussion with the Browning Group had identified the objectives of this research as to rectify limitations of the first study as well as to provide more accurate estimates of market potential. (The estimates of the numbers of pumping stations in Pennsylvania and New York were accurate to around plus or minus 20%.) This research was estimated to cost $40,000 and take another three months to complete.

Microsoft Corporation: The Introduction of Microsoft Works

Thomas J. Kosnik

In July of 1987, Bruce Jacobsen, the product manager for *Microsoft Works for the IBM PC and Compatibles* (Works), and Ida Cole, the Director of Microsoft's International Products Group, were preparing for a presentation to Microsoft's country managers. Works was a new, integrated software product that included a spreadsheet, word processor, graphics program, database, and communications program. The country managers were the chief operating officers of Microsoft's international subsidiaries. The purpose of the presentation was to outline Works' design and tentative positioning strategy, and to ask for questions and suggestions from the field.

The upcoming meeting was an important one for Works. In 1986, over 41% of Microsoft's sales dollars were to countries outside the United States. It was critical to win the support of the country managers for the marketing strategy to increase the chances of the new product's success.

Cole and Jacobsen were aware that two issues were likely to fuel a lively debate during the meeting. The first involved requests to modify the design of Works. Microsoft's strategy was for a standard version of Works to meet a set of common needs around the world. That philosophy allowed for limited "localization," whereby the program and the documentation were translated into local languages, and small changes were made to accommodate local conventions for currency, time and date formats, etc. However, the programs that provided spreadsheet, word processing, and other functions remained unchanged. Several country managers had asked for features to meet the needs of their markets that would require redesign of Works' programs. Microsoft had to decide how to respond to the requests.

The second issue was Works' product positioning strategy. Jacobsen was planning to position Works as an easy-to-learn, easy-to-sell product for the

This case was prepared by Assistant Professor Thomas J. Kosnik as the basis for class discussion rather than to illustrate either effective or ineffective handling of an administrative situation. Certain information has been disguised.

home and small business market. Ida Cole believed that the U.S. positioning strategy might not be appropriate in a number of countries.

Jacobsen sent an electronic message to Jabe Blumenthal, the Program Manager and designer for Works, inviting him to drop in on the discussion. Then he turned to Ida Cole. "Well, Ida, what are we going to say to the country managers?"

The Worldwide Market for Microcomputer Software

The microcomputer software industry emerged in the United States during the mid 1970s, as a number of enterprising individuals left more conventional pursuits to develop programs for the first generation of microcomputers. Bill Gates, Chairman of Microsoft, was among those industry pioneers. As a freshman at Harvard University, Gates developed a BASIC programming language for micros. He dropped out of Harvard to found Microsoft in 1975.

Microcomputer Software Categories

By 1987, most observers divided the fledgling industry into different segments based on the products sold. The first category was *systems software*. One group of systems software products included operating systems such as Microsoft's Disk Operating System (MS-DOS). Operating systems provided a layer of communication between individual software programs and the computer itself. Another type of systems software included programming languages such as BASIC, PASCAL, and COBOL. Such high level languages were used to write programs to perform functions for the computer user.

The second software category was *application software*. It included horizontal applications and vertical applications. Horizontal application software performed broad functions that were used by different customers for a variety of tasks. Microsoft Works and Lotus 1-2-3 were examples of horizontal applications. Vertical applications performed a narrower set of functions to support a specific set of tasks. Examples included accounting software for law firms and sales force management systems.

In 1986, the microcomputer software industry was over $5 billion in retail sales, with 14,000 companies offering over 27,000 different products around the world. Industry observers divided the $5 billion total into sales of $250 million for systems software, $2.25 billion for horizontal applications, and $2.5 billion for vertical application software.

Leading Competitors in the Microcomputer Software Market

Microcomputer software was sold both by hardware companies, such as IBM and Apple, and by "independent" software companies whose products ran on a variety of computer hardware. The leading independent microcomputer software companies in 1986 are shown in Exhibit 1. All of the largest microcomputer software companies were headquartered in the U.S. However, two of Microsoft's largest competitors were aggressively expanding their international

EXHIBIT 1
Leading Independent Microcomputer Software Vendors (sales in millions of $)

Company Name	Worldwide Sales in 1986°	Name(s) of a Few Leading Products	Category of Software Products°°
Lotus Development Corp.	$283	1-2-3	GP Spreadsheet
		Symphony	GP Integrated
		Jazz	GP Integrated
Microsoft Corp.	$260	DOS	SS Operating System
		Excel	GP Spreadsheet
		Microsoft Word	GP Word Processor
Ashton-Tate	$203	DBase III	GP Database
		Framework	GP Integrated
		Multimate	GP Word Processor
Word Perfect	$ 52	WordPerfect	GP Word Processor
		WordPerfect Executive	GP Integrated
Autodesk	$ 50	AudoCad	SP Computer Assisted
		CAD Camera	Design Products
Borland	$ 38	SideKick	GP Organizer
		TurboPascal	SS Language
Micropro	$ 36	Wordstar	GP Word Processor
		Wordstar 2000	GP Word Processor
Digital Research	$ 26	CP/M	SS Operating System
		GEM	SS Operating Environment
Software Publishing	$ 26	PFS: Write	GP Word Processor
		PFS: File	GP Database
		First Choice	GP Integrated

°Sales for based on the period from January 1–December 31, 1986. In the first half of 1987, Microsoft sales exceeded Lotus Development Corp.'s
°°GP = General Purpose Application Software; SP = Special Purpose; SS = System Software

sales. Twenty-four percent of Lotus Development Corp.'s 1986 sales were outside the U.S., compared with 14% a year earlier. Ashton-Tate international sales comprised 20% of its 1986 total.

Two companies were the most likely to compete with a product like Works on the IBM PC. Software Publishing, which had dominated the market for easy-to-learn, inexpensive products with its PFS series, had recently introduced an integrated product called "First Choice." It was priced at $179, and included word processing, spreadsheet, communications, and limited database functions for the first-time computer user. Some industry watchers predicted that Software Publishing would have an improved version of the product ready for release by the autumn of 1987. Borland, which had a reputation for clever, easy-to-use products at very low prices, marketed a best-selling product called "SideKick" for $59, to support telephone lists, light calculations, and other tasks. It was rumored that Borland might enhance SideKick to compete with Works.

Microsoft Corporation

Overall Leadership

Microsoft was a leader in the micro software industry. The company chairman, Bill Gates, was an avid programmer-turned-entrepreneur whose vision for Microsoft was "to make the software that will permit there to be a computer on every desk and in every home." His hard-driving style pervaded the company. Microsoft's President, Jon Shirley, a former executive at Tandy Corporation (Radio Shack), brought a wealth of experience about marketing of microcomputer products to the top management team. Both men were hands-on managers who delegated responsibility but demanded outstanding performance and attention to detail.

Much of Microsoft's success had come through a combination of timing and skill in managing alliances with leading hardware manufacturers. One example of the importance of timing for Microsoft was a story that had become an industry legend. In 1980, IBM approached Gates to have Microsoft design the operating system for the new personal computer it was planning. Gates first sent IBM to Digital Research, who already had an operating system. When IBM was rebuffed by Digital Research's attorney, they called Gates back, and he seized the opportunity. Microsoft's Disk Operating System (MS-DOS) became an industry standard. As other hardware manufacturers introduced PC Clones, they turned to Microsoft to develop a version of MS-DOS for their machines. By 1986, Microsoft had supplied operating systems for over 300 different models of microcomputers.

Microsoft also made an early commitment to the emerging "second standard" in microcomputers, the Macintosh computer from Apple. Several Microsoft application software products, including Word, Excel, and Works for the Macintosh, enjoyed a leadership position among Macintosh users.

International Marketing Strategy

Timing and hardware alliances were important facets of Microsoft's international marketing strategy as well. The company began its efforts in the international arena in 1982. Microsoft entered a number of countries with local language versions of its products a year or two before most of its competitors. In addition to being first with local language software, Microsoft formed alliances with leading computer companies in Europe and Asia. Through a series of Original Equipment Manufacturer (OEM) arrangements, the sales forces of hardware OEMs sold Microsoft products like Multiplan (spreadsheet) and Word (word processing) along with their microcomputers to large corporations in many countries.

As a result of early entry and strong OEM alliances, Microsoft's Word and Multiplan products were market leaders in a number of countries in Europe and Asia. In 1986, the International Division had over 350 employees and international sales were over $106 million. However, that leadership position was being challenged by Lotus, which had recently introduced a local version of 1-2-3 in Japan and had 200 employees outside the U.S. and over $67 million in international sales in 1986.

Organization

Exhibit 2 shows part of Microsoft's corporate organization chart. In addition to serving as Chairman, Bill Gates was also the acting Vice President of Applications Software, the division where Bruce Jacobsen worked as a product manager. Gates' keen interest in the application software side of Microsoft's business had led him to assume that role until the right person could be found to fill the position. Bruce Jacobsen reported to Mike Slade, the Works Group Product Manager, who reported to Jeff Raikes, the Director of Applications Marketing, who in turn reported to Gates. However, the informal management style and heavy use of electronic mail in decision making led to a great deal of direct communication between product managers, like Jacobsen, and Bill Gates and Jon Shirley.

Exhibit 3 shows the organization of the International Division. Jeremy Butler had responsibility for International. Ida Cole reported to Butler, as did three other directors responsible for international operations in Europe, Asia, and Intercontinental (the rest of the world).

Financial Performance

Exhibit 4 contains a five-year summary of Microsoft's financial performance. The company's growth and earnings record had made it a favorite of many Wall Street analysts. Its 1986 return on sales was the highest of any company in the *Datamation 100*, an annual review of the largest companies in the computer hardware and software industries. In the first half of 1987, Microsoft's sales surpassed Lotus Development Corp.'s, making it the largest microcomputer software company in the world. Microsoft's 1986 sales by product line were: systems software and languages = 53%; applications software = 37%; hardware and books = 10%.

Segmenting the Software Market

At Microsoft, four dimensions were considered in analyzing market segments for software products: the computer hardware environment; the usage situation; the level of the customer's needs; and the country/language.

Segmenting by Computer Hardware Environment

Microsoft developed application software products to meet the needs of customers who bought the most popular "standard" types of computer hardware. The first major standard in IBM-compatible microcomputer technology was established with the introduction of the IBM PC in 1981 and extended with the more powerful IBM AT in 1984. A number of companies around the world

EXHIBIT 2
Microsoft's Corporate Organization Chart

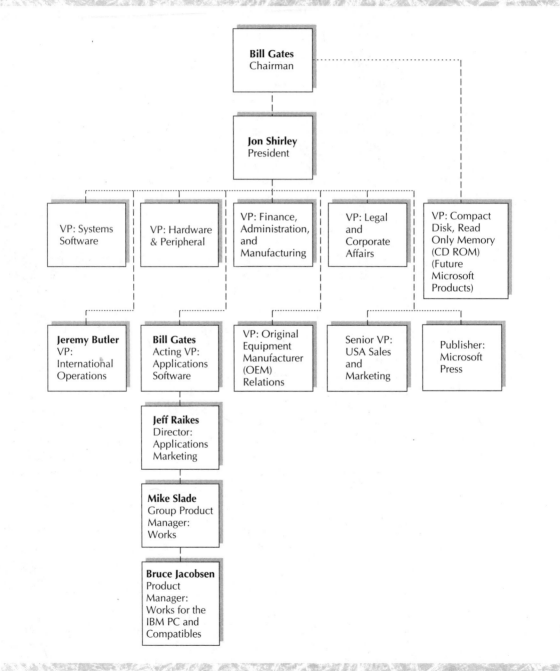

Source: Microsoft Corporation internal records

EXHIBIT 3
Organizational Chart for Microsoft's International Operations

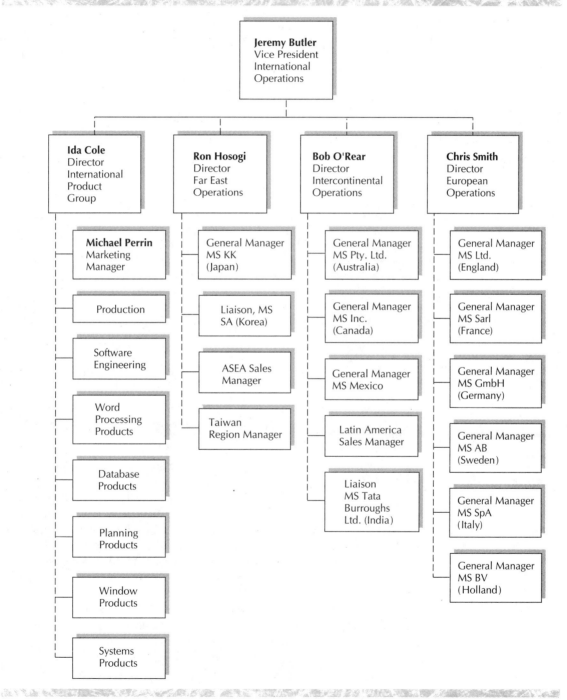

Jeremy Butler
Vice President
International
Operations

Ida Cole
Director
International
Product
Group

Ron Hosogi
Director
Far East
Operations

Bob O'Rear
Director
Intercontinental
Operations

Chris Smith
Director
European
Operations

Michael Perrin Marketing Manager	General Manager MS KK (Japan)	General Manager MS Pty. Ltd. (Australia)	General Manager MS Ltd. (England)
Production	Liaison, MS SA (Korea)	General Manager MS Inc. (Canada)	General Manager MS Sarl (France)
Software Engineering	ASEA Sales Manager	General Manager MS Mexico	General Manager MS GmbH (Germany)
Word Processing Products	Taiwan Region Manager	Latin America Sales Manager	General Manager MS AB (Sweden)
Database Products		Liaison MS Tata Burroughs Ltd. (India)	General Manager MS SpA (Italy)
Planning Products			General Manager MS BV (Holland)
Window Products			
Systems Products			

EXHIBIT 4
A Summary of Microsoft's Financial Performance: 1983–1987*

	1983	1984	1985	1986	1987
Net Revenues	$50,065	$97,479	$140,417	$197,514	$345,890
Cost of Revenues	15,773	22,900	30,447	40,862	73,854
Gross Margin	34,292	74,579	109,970	156,652	272,036
Research and Development	7,021	10,665	17,108	20,523	38,076
Sales/Marketing	11,916	26,027	42,512	57,668	85,070
General and Administrative	4,698	8,784	9,443	17,555	22,003
Income from Operations	10,657	29,103	40,907	60,906	126,887
Non-Operating Income (loss)	407	(1,073)	1,936	5,078	8,638
Stock Option Bonus					(14,187)
Income before Tax	11,064	28,030	42,843	65,984	121,338
Income Tax	4,577	12,150	18,742	26,730	49,460
Net Income	$ 6,487	$15,880	$ 24,101	$ 39,254	$ 71,878
Total Assets	$24,328	$47,637	$ 65,064	$170,739	$287,754
Stockholders' Equity	$14,639	$30,712	$ 54,440	$139,332	$239,105
Earnings per Share	$ 0.15	$ 0.35	$ 0.52	$ 0.78	$ 1.30
Number of Employees	367	608	910	1,153	1,816

Source: Microsoft Corporation Financial Statements
*Microsoft's fiscal year ran from July 1st to June 30th.

introduced PC-compatible computers—also known as "PC Clones"—that used the same software and functioned the same way as the IBM PC but offered slight enhancements and lower prices. These "clone makers" moved even more quickly to imitate the IBM AT.

The average price of a PC Compatible dropped from almost $3,000 in 1983 to below $1,000 in 1987. IBM lowered its prices as well, but continued to lose market share to the "act-alike" vendors. Exhibit 5 shows unit sales from IBM and the clone makers. In 1987, IBM introduced the Personal System 2 (PS/2) family—a "second generation" of IBM machines with greater power and graphics capabilities that had the potential to overthrow the standards it had created with the IBM PC and AT.

Although Microsoft Works was technically capable of running on both the old and new generations of IBM computers, its primary target hardware was any IBM PC or PC compatible. The more mature, "low end" IBM-Compatible hardware was selected for Works because simple, inexpensive software was needed for the millions of customers who were planning to purchase inexpen-

EXHIBIT 5

**Unit Sales of IBM PC-Compatible Microcomputers
in Two Technology Families (in thousands of units)**

Type of Technology	1981	1982	1983	1984	1985	1986
U.S. Market Only:						
IBM PC & XT	35	190	590	1,553	1,287	1,009
PC Compatibles from clone makers	0	2	108	367	839	1,270
TOTAL PC COMPATIBLE	35	192	698	1,920	2,126	2,279
IBM AT				22	261	384
AT Compatibles from clone makers					132	490
TOTAL AT COMPATIBLE	0	0	0	22	393	874
Worldwide Market (Includes U.S.)						
IBM PC & XT	35	195	670	1,855	1,961	1,538
PC Compatibles from clone makers		2	113	427	1,069	1,610
TOTAL PC COMPATIBLE	35	197	783	2,282	3,030	3,148
IBM AT				22	330	572
AT Compatibles from clone makers					151	641
TOTAL AT COMPATIBLE	0	0	0	22	481	1,213

Source: International Data Corp. reports on the microcomputer market

sive machines for use in homes and small businesses. Other Microsoft products including Word (word processing) and Excel (spreadsheet) were targeted at the purchasers of AT compatibles and PS/2 computers.

Exhibit 6 is a forecast of the unit sales of "low-end" IBM machines and PC Clones in selected country markets. There was considerable controversy about the potential impact of the new IBM PS/2 computers on the sales of the older models of IBM-compatible PCs. Some experts speculated that the market for the less powerful models would decline, as customers migrated to newer, easier-to-use models. Others argued that most new computer users would purchase the older, less expensive products, because in most cases the benefits of the new technology were not worth the cost. The debate heightened uncertainty about future growth of the older IBM products, PC Clones, and the software that ran on them.

Segmenting by Usage Situation

Microsoft, following most commercial market research reports, identified four major segments by customer usage of microcomputer products: business/professional, home/hobby, scientific/technical, and education.

EXHIBIT 6
Forecast Sales of Low-End IBM-Compatible Microcomputers in Selected Countries (thousands of units)

Country	1986 Population (in 000)	1986 Estimated Unit Sales	1987 Forecast Unit Sales	1988 Forecast Unit Sales
U.S.A.	240,856	2,279	2,000	1,500
England	56,458	170	225	220
Canada	25,625	106	120	110
Australia/New Zealand	19,098	34	45	40
France	55,239	139	160	155
West Germany	60,734	136	145	120
Italy	57,226	83	115	130
Netherlands	14,536	46	60	55
Portugal	10,095	2	5	10
Sweden	8,357	39	45	40
Spain	39,075	16	30	50
Japan	121,402	50	50	30
TOTAL	708,701	3,100	3,000	2,460

Note: Sources: A variety of International Data Corp. (IDC) market research studies from 1986 and 1987. Data have been disguised.
The figures above included IBM PCs, XTs, and computers from other manufacturers that were compatible with those IBM microcomputers.
They do NOT include IBM ATs, IBM PS/2s, or computers from other manufacturers that were compatible with those IBM microcomputers.

The business/professional segment consisted of people who used microcomputers for a variety of functions in organizations. While the specialized applications depended on the industry in which a company operated, the general applications of word processing, spreadsheet, graphics, database, and communications were used in most businesses to provide automated support for office functions. Within Microsoft, the business professional market was further divided into large and small organizations. Large companies tended to have extensive data processing capabilities, more formal buying procedures for computer products, and more sophisticated requirements for computer support. Small businesses tended to have few, if any, employees with data processing expertise, a less-structured buying process, and simpler needs.

The home/hobby segment was comprised of individuals and families who used a computer for practical and recreational purposes in the home. Customers in the home/hobby segment tended to buy smaller, less expensive computer systems than did those in the business professional marketplace.

The scientific/technical segment consisted of scientists and engineers who used computers for tasks that ranged from analysis of laboratory experiments to computer aided design (CAD) and computer aided engineering (CAE). Members of this segment often needed powerful, expensive computer hardware for special scientific programs. They also used word processing, spreadsheet, database, graphics, and communications software.

The education segment included students, teachers, and administrators in schools, colleges, and universities. Administrators used microcomputers for planning and fund-raising, and faculty were introducing computers into their curricula. Students used word processing, spreadsheet, and graphics for term papers, presentations, and examinations. Many customers in this segment needed simple, inexpensive computers, but some required the power and sophistication typically demanded in scientific/technical environments.

Segmenting by Customers' Depth and Clarity of Software Needs

Jeff Raikes divided the office productivity software market into "breadth customers" and "depth customers." Breadth customers were professionals or managers who did a little bit of everything, and needed a combination of spreadsheet, word processing, database, graphics, and communications. They were likely to want low price and simplicity in software that supported those functions, as well as "integration," which provided the ability to move information between spreadsheets, databases, and word processing documents. Depth customers were specialists who made heavy use of at least one function, like writers using word processing or financial analysts using spreadsheets. They were likely to be less price sensitive, more willing to learn a complex product, and driven by the need for power and sophistication to do all that they demanded.

Raikes believed that people buying low-end PC compatibles in the future—especially first time buyers—were likely to be breadth customers: "the kind of people who come into a store to buy a computer but aren't sure why." In his mind, Works was ideal for breadth customers, because it met a variety of needs at a relatively low price. Bill Gates agreed, calling Works "the macho integrated product for the first time user."

Segmenting by Country and Language

It was necessary to translate software into the local language to establish a significant presence in any particular country. At Microsoft, the process of creating a local-language version was called localization.

A major distinction existed between countries with languages based on an alphabet, like the U.S. or Western European countries, and those which used hieroglyphic symbols, like Japan and other Asian countries. One letter in the alphabet required a single byte of computer memory for storage purposes. However, a character in a language like Japanese Kanji required two bytes of computer memory. As a result of this difference, programs written in "two-byte" languages like Japanese had to be designed differently from those written in "one-byte" languages like English, French, and German.

Ida Cole stressed that there were differences among "one-byte" languages as well:

> German is 29% longer than English. That means it takes 29% more space to translate a phrase from English to German. As a result, messages in English that might fit on one line of an 80-character computer screen might be too long for the line when translated into German. That could change the way the screen looks to the users. Programs that might fit onto one diskette in English might require two diskettes in German. If that happens, it requires writing a different user's manual, because German users need to insert different disks for various functions. The ripple effects can be enormous. Germany isn't alone. French is 10% longer than English, and there are problems in other languages, too. We in International try to get the Program Managers to think of these differences between languages when they first design a product so that what the user sees on the screen or in the manual is essentially the same around the world.

Some at Microsoft believed that other than translating into the native language, very little was needed for "localization" in various countries. Jeff Raikes asserted that "The office productivity market is pretty similar worldwide." However, many in Microsoft's International Division believed that there were substantial differences between countries. Profiles of several European country-markets are summarized in Exhibit 7.

Differences in Hardware

Because "compatible" rarely meant identical, the hardware sold by leading PC Clone manufacturers in various countries had implications for localization. For example, there were slight differences in the keyboard layouts to accommodate the use of non-English characters such as tildes and accent marks. As a result, software documentation that showed a diagram of the keyboards from leading PC Clone manufacturers in France was different from the documentation for Italy, Holland, or Germany. The leading printers used in each country also varied, leading to slight differences in the set of printing programs (called the printer drivers) and user manuals.

Differences in Microsoft's Competitive Position and Corporate Image

There were also differences in the relative position of competing software products in various countries. For example, in countries like Italy and Holland where Lotus 1-2-3 was the market share leader for spreadsheet software, Microsoft country managers wanted to label Works' spreadsheet columns with letters and rows with numbers, creating an "A1" reference number for the cell in the first row and column. That labeling made it easier for those familiar with 1-2-3 to use Works. However, in France and Germany, Microsoft's Multiplan was the leading spread-sheet product. Those countries wanted Works' cell in the first row and column to be labeled "R1 C1," making it easier for Multiplan users to learn Works.

EXHIBIT 7
A Comparison of Market Conditions in Selected Country-Markets

Comparative Criteria	France	Germany	Holland	Italy
Leading IBM-Compatible Hardware Manufacturers Ranked Roughly in Descending Order of 1986 Unit Sales of Low-End PC Clones	IBM Bull Goupil Olivetti	IBM Schneider/Amstrad Olivetti Siemens	IBM Olivetti Tulip Phillips	Olivetti IBM Sperry Commodore
Estimated Position of Microsoft Products:				
Multiplan Spreadsheet	Market Leader	Market Leader	In the Top 4	In the Top 3
Microsoft Word	Market Leader	Market Leader	In the Top 5	Tied for #2
Microsoft Corporate Advertising Theme	"The Software of the Simple Life"	"Software with a Future"	"Pioneers in Compatibility"	"Power and Simplicity Together"
Number of Dealers Surveyed Reporting Sales of Microsoft Products to the Following Market Segments:				
Public Accounting	15	47	21	22
Banking	35	27	12	
Financial Services	36	23	19	
Architecture	8	40	18	
Construction	38	50	14	
Engineering	29	47	20	
Medical/Dental	5	44	8	
Legal	9	39	5	
Home	19	46	8	1
Other	66	52	15	4
Total Number of Dealers Responding to the Survey	71	70	32	27
How important is a low price for success of software like Works?	Somewhat Important	Not Very Important	Very Important	Very Important

Sources: Information on leading hardware manufacturers is from International Data Corp. All other information is from Microsoft internal records.

Even in countries like France and Germany in which Microsoft products were market leaders, the positioning of Microsoft as a company—which might affect how customers perceived its products—was not the same. For example, in France, much had been made of the "ease of use" of Microsoft application products. French advertisements had a corporate "tag line" after the Microsoft name that roughly translated as "software for the simple life." A butterfly was displayed as the Microsoft logo in French ads.

In Germany, the Microsoft corporate "tag line" was "Software with a Future." According to International, the German customer was not worried about ease of learning so much as ensuring that the software would not become technologically obsolete as new generations of hardware made it possible for the software to become more powerful. Microsoft's corporate logo in Germany was a series of cartoons by the German poet Wilhelm Busch. The cartoons were quite popular in Germany, but meant nothing to people in other countries who were unfamiliar with Busch's work.

Differences in the Importance of Target Market Segments

Data on the relative potential of market segments in various countries were difficult to obtain. Exhibit 7 contains the results of a survey of retail dealers of Microsoft software in France, Germany, Holland, and Italy. Each dealer was asked whether he sold a significant number of Microsoft office productivity products in each of ten market segments.

Differences in Price Sensitivity

Some at Microsoft believed that there were national differences in price sensitivity. The suggested retail prices for localized versions of Microsoft products varied from 10% higher to 40% higher than the price of the U.S. version. England was the lowest, with a 10% increase. Holland was 15% higher, and Italy averaged 25% higher. France was 30% more and Germany 40% higher. Since Microsoft headquarters charged the same price per unit of software to each subsidiary, some speculated that the variation was due to country-by-country differences in the perceived relationship between price and quality. One European country manager explained: "In the U.K., customers want the lowest possible price for software. They are always shopping for a bargain. In France and Germany, people look at software the way they do wine. If it doesn't cost a lot, it can't be good quality."

Others argued that the price differences arose because the channels of distribution varied by country. Price discounting of software occurred in countries that had a well developed direct mail channel, or that had mass merchandisers (discount department stores) carrying computer software. For example, while Bruce Jacobsen was planning a recommended retail price of $195 for Works in the U.S., he estimated that discounting activities due to direct mail software distributors was likely to drive the "street price" of the product to around $140. England had both a direct mail and a mass merchandiser channel, with some retailers offering computers at very low prices.

International believed that the "street price" for Works in England might go as low as $110. In Germany, which had no direct mail distribution channel for software and a higher proportion of sales via an OEM channel to large companies, the street price was rarely more than 20% lower than the recommended retail price.

Other Differences among Countries

Some inter-country differences were the result of local habits and customs. For example, countries like France and Germany used the metric scale for distance, while England used feet and inches. This affected the spacing when printing text from a word processor or spreadsheet. The standard size of paper also changed from country to country. The formats for currencies and for time and date varied around the world.

National attitudes about copyright restrictions caused software copy protection to be essential in some countries to keep unauthorized pirating of software to an acceptable level. Microsoft did not use copy protection in the U.S. The aggravation it caused customers and the added cost and quality problems it raised in the production process were a bigger headache than the loss of revenues from "pirated" copies. But some country managers demanded copy protection. One electronic mail message to Jacobsen said:

> We may need a copy protection scheme applied for certain countries. We don't need it in Germany and Switzerland, and hopefully, we can talk France out of it. But Italy and South America will probably insist, as they would only sell one copy in each language otherwise.

While some cross-cultural differences required a change in the software itself, others affected the packaging and documentation. Mary Oksas, the Localization Manager for Works, recounted an example:

> We were trying to come up with a good story line to use in the training manual for Works around the world. First the U.S. documentation team suggested a "health club" theme . . . figuring that the potential market for Works were young, affluent, and would probably be into fitness and health. That was before we told them that in a number of European countries, dieting and health clubs have a very negative connotation. Then the U.S. team decided to go with a "stockbroker" theme, until we let them know that stockbrokers in London and in Japan don't perform exactly the same functions as their counterparts in the States. Now they are suggesting a travel agency or a pet shop theme, in hopes that attitudes about vacations and animals are pretty similar around the world. The jury's still out on that suggestion.

The tradeoffs in viewing the target market segments for Works globally, rather than on a country-by-country basis, were significant. Establishing a worldwide standard product with only minor variations to accommodate national differences reduced the time required to develop localized versions of the software. In an industry where early entrants in a product category enjoyed a substantial advantage over latecomers, the benefits of reducing the localization timetable were potentially great. A global standard also reduced the cost and time needed to develop enhanced versions of a software product, which were typically rolled out every twelve to eighteen months after the initial product launch.

On the other hand, if the standardized software did not meet the needs of a particular country, the product was unlikely to succeed in that market. Moreover, it generally took longer to design a global product than it did to develop a product for the U.S. market. The relentless pressure to launch a new product in the U.S., either to pre-empt competition or to ensure availability during the heavy year-end buying season, often caused Microsoft development teams to resist requests for features that were important for global markets, but unnecessary for the U.S.

Key Roles and Activities in the Development of Works

The Application Software Division

The U.S. version of Works was being developed through the cooperative efforts of Bruce Jacobsen, the product manager, responsible for marketing, Jabe Blumenthal, the program manager, responsible for product design, and Tony Cockburn, the development manager, who led the team of programmers who wrote the software. In addition, a team from User Education was responsible for developing the manuals and Computer Based Training (CBT) for Works.

The International Product Group

The International Product Group, located in Microsoft Headquarters in Redmond, Washington, was responsible for creating localized versions of Works. Ida Cole maintained liaison with the country managers, provided information about Works, solicited their requests for product features, and developed the suggested international strategy for pricing, positioning, and advertising. Michel Perrin, Microsoft's International Marketing Manager, was responsible for coordinating the efforts of the marketing managers in the international subsidiaries, who reported directly to their respective country managers. Mary Oksas, Works' localization manager, ensured that the software, documentation, and computer based training (CBT) were translated into various languages, oversaw testing of the local-language versions of the software, and designed the packaging for each country.

The International Product Group was planning to develop localized versions in seven non-English languages: French, German, Swedish, Italian, Dutch, Spanish, and Portuguese. The investment to localize Works was estimated at $84,000 per country, assuming that there were no major changes to the programs. Microsoft planned to charge the same price per unit ($68) to subsidiaries for localized versions of the product. Exhibit 8 is a forecast of unit sales and retail prices of Works in each country.

While the International Products Group was developing the localized versions of Works for Europe, Japan was responsible for its own localization.

EXHIBIT 8
Forecast Monthly Sales of Works English and Localized Versions

Country	Forecast of Monthly Unit Sales of PC Works English Version (1)	Forecast of Monthly Unit Sales of PC Works Localized Version (1)	Forecast Suggested Retail Price Per Unit of Localized Version (2)
U.S.A.	6,000	0	$195
England	1,000	0	$215
Canada	500	0	$215
Australia and New Zealand	380	0	$215
France	0	650	$254
West Germany	200	500	$273
Italy	50	160	$244
Netherlands	80	200	$224
Portugal	25	80	$220
Sweden	100	200	$234
Spain	50	200	$234
	8,385	1,990	

Sources: (1) Preliminary forecasts by Country Managers of Microsoft's International Subsidiaries made in June, 1987.
(2) Estimates by Microsoft International Product Support Group based on past experience with other products.
Notes: For planning purposes, it was assumed that Microsoft subsidiaries' selling prices to the channels of distribution would be approximately 50% of the Suggested Retail Prices in their respective countries.
Localized versions for subsidiaries were manufactured in Ireland and sold to all subsidiaries for 35% of the U.S. Suggested Retail Price. Import tariffs were not considered in this analysis.

Technical complexities of the two-byte architecture and the unique issues in adapting products for the Japanese market led Microsoft to establish a separate group in the Japanese subsidiary to develop its own products and localize software developed in Redmond for Japan.

Country Managers in Microsoft's International Subsidiaries

Soon after his arrival at Microsoft, Bruce Jacobsen had been told by another product manager about how the international subsidiaries operated:

> The country managers are kings. They and the marketing managers who work for them exercise a lot of autonomy in most marketing decisions. For example, Microsoft Redmond typically recommends a worldwide retail selling price for a product, and suggests a positioning strategy and communications theme. But the management in each subsidiary ultimately decides what price to charge, what distribution channels to use, what advertising to employ, and what market segments to attack.

When Jacobsen recounted the conversation to Ida Cole, she reminded him of the ways in which they really could have an impact:

> The country managers and their marketing managers are focused on tactical issues in their day-to-day operations. They are driven by the goals of selling existing Microsoft products. As a result, during a new product launch, they tend to rely on us to conduct market research, think about the longer term issues, and present an overall marketing strategy. They won't go along with everything we suggest . . . They'll use it as a starting point, and tell us the things that don't make sense based on the realities of their local markets.

The Debate over the Design of Works

Microsoft planned to develop the U.S. version of Works, incorporating as many of the features required for other countries as possible, given limited programmer availability and project deadlines. The U.S. version would be launched in mid-September. One month later, after minor changes, the International English version would be released. That version was the baseline product that would be translated into different languages.

Microsoft had received requests from country managers for two additional features in Works. First, France and Germany wanted a software "toggle switch" that would let the customer choose whether Works' cell references appeared as "A1," like Lotus 1-2-3, or as "R1 C1," like Multiplan. This feature would let a customer decide whether he wanted the spreadsheet in Works to "look like" either Lotus 1-2-3 (A1) or Multiplan (R1 C1). That way, a person who used Lotus at the office and was buying a home computer could make Works look like 1-2-3, greatly reducing the time required to learn Works. A person who had used Multiplan at the office could choose to make the Works spreadsheet look like Multiplan, thereby minimizing learning time. In the U.S., where 1-2-3 had a dominant market share position and very few customers had seen Multiplan, Microsoft planned to make Works look like Lotus 1-2-3 (A1 format), and the toggle switch feature was not important. In Europe, where both Multiplan and 1-2-3 were widely used, the toggle switch might have particular value to customers.

Second, country managers had asked that additional programs be written so that Works files could be converted to the Multiplan file format. Conversion programs allowed the exchange of information between Works and other spreadsheet products. If a person made a spreadsheet using Multiplan at the office and wanted to bring it home to continue working on evenings or weekends, she could convert it to use on Works and then back again. Conversion programs also allowed a person with Works to share data with colleagues using Multiplan. Works was originally designed only to allow data exchange with Lotus 1-2-3. Like the toggle switch option, file conversion programs might be particularly useful in some European countries due to the widespread use of Multiplan.

If Microsoft incorporated the two changes in the U.S. version, the introduction of Works in the U.S. would be delayed by two months. The additional time was needed to develop documentation and CBT showing both the A1 and

R1 C1 displays, and to write several new programs. It would still take one month to go from the U.S. to the International English version.

If the programmers developed the U.S. version without the two requested changes, and then tried to add the features to the International version, a major redesign would be required. Substantial portions of the programs for the U.S. version would have to be re-written, and the elapsed time required for the International version would increase from one month to five months.

Several country managers had informed Ida Cole that without the toggle switch and conversion programs, Works was unlikely to be successful in their markets. They were also concerned that without the changes, Works might even undermine the market position of Multiplan by promoting the Lotus 1-2-3 user interface and file formats.

However, Jabe Blumenthal argued strongly against changing the design because of the adverse effects of missing the target U.S. launch date. The introduction of Works was set for mid-September, which allowed retailers just enough time to order the product and train their people how to sell it before the end of October. That timetable was critical because November and December were a period of heavy buying activity for computer products, as the home market made purchases for Christmas and some businesses bought at the end of the year for tax reasons. Retailers were likely to resist or ignore a new product launch in the midst of their busiest season. Missing the September launch date would also increase the risk that Software Publishing's First Choice or a new product from Borland might establish a leadership position in the segment targeted for Works.

The labor and direct overhead costs of keeping the development team on Works was $50,000 per month. However, there was also an opportunity cost. A month spent on Works was a month that was unavailable for other software products, and programmers were in critically short supply. Assessing the impact of the decision on future sales was difficult, since unit sales forecasts for the U.S. were based on a September 15th launch date, and for the other countries assumed that Microsoft would make the two modifications.

Works' Positioning

Jacobsen was planning to position Works as an easy-to-learn, easy-to-sell, integrated solution to the productivity needs of "breadth users" in homes and small businesses who were buying their first computer. Tentative advertising plans were to use a Swiss Army Knife as an internationally recognizable symbol of an easy-to-use tool with multiple functions.

Microsoft had a family of application software designed to meet the needs of "depth users" and "breadth users" on IBM-compatible computers and on the Apple Macintosh. Exhibit 9 identifies a few of those products. One of the challenges in positioning Works was to distinguish it from the other Microsoft products, thereby minimizing customer confusion and the risk that Works might cannibalize sales of other software.

In discussing Jacobsen's positioning, Ida Cole pointed out the concerns of several country managers. First, throughout most of the world, the home and

EXHIBIT 9
Selected Products in the Microsoft Family of Software

Product Name	Description	U.S. Recommended Retail Selling Price of the Product on the:		
		Apple Macintosh	IBM PC/XT/AT & Compatibles	IBM PS/2 & Compatibles
PRODUCTS FOR DEPTH USERS:				
Multiplan	Sophisticated spreadsheet for quantitative analysis. Graphics available as a separate product. Key competitor: Lotus 1-2-3	$295	$195	N/A
Word	Sophisticated word processor. Key competitor: WordPerfect	$395	$450	$450
Excel	New and very advanced product for spreadsheet, graphics, and data management. Key competitor: Lotus 1-2-3	$395	$395 (Only on IBM ATs & Compatibles)	$395 (Launch was planned for one month after Works)
PRODUCTS FOR BREADTH USERS:				
Works	Integrated, easy-to-use product for: – Spreadsheet – Word processing – Graphics – Data management – Communications Key competitor: Software Publishing's First Choice	$295	$195	$195

small business markets for IBM-compatible machines were much smaller than in the U.S., making his positioning difficult to execute on a global basis. Second, in European countries where Multiplan and Word were market leaders, the financial risk of cannibalization was greater than in the U.S.

Plans for the Launch

Jacobsen was developing the details for an introductory U.S. marketing communications campaign with a price tag of $2.8 million, and a target launch date of September 15th. With a suggested list price of $195, trade margins averaging

50% of retail selling price, and cost of goods just over $18, Microsoft's unit contribution for Works was approximately $79. Jacobsen was confident that the projected U.S. volume of 6,000 units a month would more than offset the costs of the introductory campaign.

Conclusion

As they continued working on the presentation, Jacobsen silently wondered how he should respond to country managers' suggestions about design changes to make Works more attractive for their local markets. He saw merit in both Blumenthal's and the country managers' arguments, and knew he needed to formulate a position on that topic for the meeting. In addition, there might well be other requests for design modifications, and he and Ida Cole needed to develop an approach for handling them if they arose.

Jacobsen also pondered how, if at all, he could modify his product positioning for Works to make it more effective as the foundation for communications strategy for the product around the world.

Cole interrupted his reverie: "Earth to Bruce . . . Let's put together a slide or two with our major recommendations, and then brainstorm about the reactions we're likely to get from the country managers."

Modern Plastics

Kenneth L.
Bernhardt

Tom Ingram

Danny N.
Bellenger

Institutional sales manager Jim Clayton had spent most of Monday morning planning for the rest of the month. It was early July and Jim knew that an extremely busy time was coming with the preparation of the following year's sales plan.

Since starting his current job less than a month ago, Jim had been involved in learning the requirements of the job and making his initial territory visits. Now that he was getting settled, Jim was trying to plan his activities according to priorities. The need for planning had been instilled in him during his college days. As a result of his three years' field sales experience and development of time management skills, he felt prepared for the challenge of the sales manager's job.

While sitting at his desk, Jim recalled a conversation that he had a week ago with Bill Hanson, the former manager, who had been promoted to another division. Bill told him that the sales forecast (annual and monthly) for plastic trash bags in the Southeast region would be due soon as an initial step toward developing the sales plan for the next year. Bill had laughed as he told Jim, "Boy, you ought to have a ball doing the forecast, being a rookie sales manager!"

When Jim had asked what Bill meant, he explained by saying that the forecast was often "winged" because the headquarters in New York already knew what they wanted and would change the forecast to meet their figures, particularly if the forecast was for an increase of less than 10 percent. The experienced sales manager could throw numbers together in a short time that would pass as a serious forecast and ultimately be adjusted to fit the plans of headquarters. However, an inexperienced manager would have a difficult time "winging" a credible forecast.

Bill had also told Jim that the other alternative meant gathering mountains of data and putting together a forecast that could be sold to the various levels of Modern Plastics management. This alternative would prove to be time-consuming and could still be changed anywhere along the chain of command before final approval.

This case was written by Kenneth L. Bernhardt, Georgia State University, Professor Tom Ingram, University of Kentucky, and Professor Danny N. Bellenger, Texas Tech University. Copyright © 1990 the authors.

Plastic Trash Bags—Sales and Pricing History, 1987–1989

	Pricing Dollars per Case			Sales Volume in Cases			Sales Volume in Dollars		
	1987	1988	1989	1987	1988	1989	1987	1988	1989
January	$6.88	$ 7.70	$15.40	33,000	46,500	36,500	$ 227,000	$ 358,000	$ 562,000
February	6.82	7.70	14.30	32,500	52,500	23,000	221,500	404,000	329,000
March	6.90	8.39	13.48	32,000	42,000	22,000	221,000	353,000	296,500
April	6.88	10.18	12.24	45,500	42,500	46,500	313,000	432,500	569,000
May	6.85	12.38	11.58	49,000	41,500	45,500	335,500	514,000	527,000
June	6.85	12.65	10.31	47,500	47,000	42,000	325,500	594,500	433,000
July	7.42	13.48	9.90°	40,000	43,500	47,500°	297,000	586,500	470,000°
August	6.90	13.48	10.18	48,500	63,500	43,500	334,500	856,000	443,000
September	7.70	14.30	10.31	43,000	49,000	47,500	331,000	700,500	489,500
October	7.56	15.12	10.31	52,500	50,000	51,000	397,000	756,000	526,000
November	7.15	15.68	10.72	62,000	61,500	47,500	443,500	964,500	509,000
December	7.42	15.43	10.59	49,000	29,000	51,000	363,500	447,500	540,000
Total	$7.13	$12.25	$11.30	534,500	568,500	503,500	$3,810,000	$6,967,000	$5,694,000

°July–December 1989 figures are forecast of sales manager J. A. Clayton, and other data comes from historical sales information.

Clayton started reviewing pricing and sales volume history (see Exhibit 1). He also looked at the key account performance for the past two and a half years (see Exhibit 2). During the past month Clayton had visited many of the key accounts, and on the average they had indicated that their purchases from Modern would probably increase about 15–20 percent in the coming year.

Schedule for Preparing the Forecast

Jim had received a memo recently from Robert Baxter, the regional marketing manager, detailing the plans for completing the 1990 forecast. The key dates in the memo began in only three weeks:

August 1	Presentation of forecast to regional marketing manager.
August 10	Joint presentation with marketing manager to regional general manager.
September 1	Regional general manager presents forecast to division vice president.
September 1–September 30	Review of forecast by staff of division vice president.

EXHIBIT 2
1989 Key Account Sales History (In Cases)

Customer	1987	1988	First Six Months 1989	1987 Monthly Average	1988 Monthly Average	First Half 1989 Monthly Average	First Quarter 1989 Monthly Average
Transco Paper Company	125,774	134,217	44,970	10,481	11,185	7,495	5,823
Callaway Paper	44,509	46,049	12,114	3,709	3,837	2,019	472
Florida Janitorial Supply	34,746	36,609	20,076	2,896	3,051	3,346	2,359
Jefferson	30,698	34,692	25,044	2,558	2,891	4,174	1,919
Cobb Paper	13,259	23,343	6,414	1,105	1,945	1,069	611
Miami Paper	10,779	22,287	10,938	900	1,857	1,823	745
Milne Surgical Company	23,399	21,930	—	1,950	1,828	—	—
Graham	8,792	15,331	1,691	733	1,278	281	267
Crawford Paper	7,776	14,132	6,102	648	1,178	1,017	1,322
John Steele	8,634	13,277	6,663	720	1,106	1,110	1,517
Henderson Paper	9,185	8,850	2,574	765	738	429	275
Durant Surgical	—	7,766	4,356	—	647	726	953
Master Paper	4,221	5,634	600	352	470	100	—
D.T.A.	—	—	2,895	—	—	482	—
Crane Paper	4,520	5,524	3,400	377	460	566	565
Janitorial Service	3,292	5,361	2,722	274	447	453	117
Georgia Paper	5,466	5,053	2,917	456	421	486	297
Paper Supplies, Inc.	5,117	5,119	1,509	426	427	251	97
Southern Supply	1,649	3,932	531	137	328	88	78
Horizon Hospital Supply	4,181	4,101	618	348	342	103	206
Total Cases	346,007	413,217	156,134	28,835	34,436	26,018	17,623

October 1	Review forecast with corporate staff.
October 1–October 15	Revision as necessary.
October 15	Final forecast forwarded to division vice president from regional general manager.

Company Background

The plastics division of Modern Chemical Company was founded in 1965 when Modern Chemical purchased Cordco, a small plastics manufacturer with national sales of $15 million. At that time the key products of the plastics division were sandwich bags, plastic tablecloths, trash cans, and plastic-coated clothesline.

Since 1965 the plastics division has grown to a sales level exceeding $200 million with five regional profit centers covering the United States. Each regional center has manufacturing facilities and a regional sales force. There are four product groups in each region:

1. Food packaging: Styrofoam meat and produce trays; plastic bags for various food products.

2. Egg cartons: Styrofoam egg cartons sold to egg packers and supermarket chains.

3. Institutional: Plastic trash bags and disposable tableware (plates, bowls, etc.).

4. Industrial: Plastic packaging for the laundry and dry cleaning market; plastic film for use in pallet overwrap systems.

Each product group is supervised jointly by a product manager and a district sales manager, both of whom report to the regional marketing manager. The sales representatives report directly to the district sales manager but also work closely with the product manager on matters concerning pricing and product specifications.

The five regional general managers report to J. R. Hughes, vice president of the plastics division. Hughes is located in New York. Although Modern Chemical is owned by a multinational oil company, the plastics division has been able to operate in a virtually independent manner since its establishment in 1965. The reasons for this include:

1. Limited knowledge of the plastic industry on the part of the oil company management.

2. Excellent growth by the plastics division has been possible without management supervision from the oil company.

3. Profitability of the plastics division has consistently been higher than that of other divisions of the chemical company.

The Institutional Trash Bag Market

The institutional trash bag is a polyethylene bag used to collect and transfer refuse to its final disposition point. There are different sizes and colors available to fit the various uses of the bag. For example, a small bag for desk wastebaskets is available as well as a heavier bag for large containers such as a 55-gallon drum. There are 25 sizes in the Modern line with 13 of those sizes being available in 3 colors—white, buff, and clear. Customers typically buy several different items on an order to cover all their needs.

The institutional trash bag is a separate product from the consumer grade trash bag, which is typically sold to homeowners through retail outlets. The institutional trash bag is sold primarily through paper wholesalers, hospital supply companies, and janitorial supply companies to a variety of end users. Since trash bags are used on such a wide scale, the list of end users could include almost any business or institution. The segments include hospitals, hotels, schools, office buildings, transportation facilities, and restaurants.

Based on historical data and a current survey of key wholesalers and end users in the Southeast, the annual market of institutional trash bags in the region was estimated to be 55 million pounds. Translated into cases, the market potential was close to 2 million cases. During the past five years, the market for trash bags has grown at an average rate of 8.9 percent per year. Now a mature product, future market growth is expected to parallel overall growth in the economy. The 1990 real growth in GNP is forecast to be 4.5 percent.

General Market Conditions

The current market is characterized by a distressing trend. The market is in a position of oversupply with approximately 20 manufacturers competing for the business in the Southeast. Prices have been on the decline for several months but are expected to level out during the last six months of the year.

This problem arose after a record year in 1988 for Modern Plastics. During 1988, supply was very tight due to raw material shortages. Unlike many of its competitors, Modern had only minor problems securing adequate raw material supplies. As a result the competitors were few in 1988, and all who remained in business were prosperous. By early 1989 raw materials were plentiful, and prices began to drop as new competitors tried to buy their way into the market. During the first quarter of 1989, Modern Plastics learned the hard way that a competitive price was a necessity in the current market. Volume fell off drastically in February and March as customers shifted orders to new suppliers when Modern chose to maintain a slightly higher than market price on trash bags.

With the market becoming extremely price competitive and profits declining, the overall quality has dropped to a point of minimum standard. Most suppliers now make a bag "barely good enough to get the job done." This quality level is acceptable to most buyers who do not demand high quality for this type of product.

Modern Plastics versus Competition

A recent study of Modern versus competition had been conducted by an outside consultant to see how well Modern measured up in several key areas. Each area was weighted according to its importance in the purchase decision, and Modern was compared to its key competitors in each area and on an overall basis. The key factors and their weights are shown below:

	Weight
1. Pricing	.50
2. Quality	.15
3. Breadth of line	.10
4. Sales coverage	.10
5. Packaging	.05
6. Service	.10
Total	1.00

As shown in Exhibit 3, Modern compared favorably with its key competitors on an overall basis. None of the other suppliers were as strong as Modern in breadth of line nor did any competitor offer as good sales coverage as that provided by Modern. Clayton knew that sales coverage would be even better next year since the Florida and North Carolina territories had grown enough to add two salespeople to the institutional group by January 1, 1990.

EXHIBIT 3
Competitive Factors Ratings (By Competitor*)

Weight	Factor	Modern	National Film	Bonanza	South-eastern	PBI	BAGCO	South-west Bag	Sun Plastics	East Coast Bag Co.
.50	Price	2	3	2	2	2	2	2	2	3
.15	Quality	3	2	3	4	3	2	3	3	4
.10	Breadth	1	2	2	3	3	3	3	3	3
.10	Sales coverage	1	3	3	3	4	3	3	4	3
.05	Packaging	3	3	2	3	3	1	3	3	3
.10	Service	4	3	3	2	2	2	3	4	3

Overall Weighted Ranking†

1. BAGCO	2.15		6. Southeastern	2.55
2. Modern	2.20		7. Florida Plastics	2.60
3. Bonanza	2.25		8. National Film	2.65
4. Southwest Bag (Tie)	2.50		9. East Coast Bag Co.	3.15
5. PBI (Tie)	2.50			

*Ratings on a 1-to-5 scale with 1 being the best rating and 5 the worst.
†The weighted ranking is the sum of each rank times its weight. The lower the number, the better the overall rating.

EXHIBIT 4
Market Share by Supplier, 1987 and 1988

Supplier	Percent of Market 1987	Percent of Market 1988
National Film	11	12
Bertram	16	0°
Bonanza	11	12
Southeastern	5	6
Bay	9	0°
Johnson Graham	8	0°
PBI	2	5
Lewis	2	0°
BAGCO	—	6
Southwest Bag	—	2
Florida Plastics	—	4
East Coast Bag Co.	—	4
Miscellaneous and Unknown	8	22
Modern	28	27
	100	100

°Out of business in 1989.
Source: This information was developed from a field survey conducted by Modern Plastics.

Pricing, quality, and packaging seemed to be neither an advantage nor a disadvantage. However, service was a problem area. The main cause for this, Clayton was told, was temporary out-of-stock situations which occurred occasionally, primarily due to the wide variety of trash bags offered by Modern.

During the past two years, Modern Plastics had maintained its market share at approximately 27 percent of the market. Some new competitors had entered the market since 1987 while others had left the market (see Exhibit 4). The previous district sales manager, Bill Hanson, had left Clayton some comments regarding the major competitors. These are reproduced in Exhibit 5.

Developing the Sales Forecast

After a careful study of trade journals, government statistics, and surveys conducted by Modern marketing research personnel, projections for growth potential were formulated by segment and are shown in Exhibit 6. This data was compiled by Bill Hanson just before he had been promoted.

Jim looked back at Baxter's memo giving the time schedule for the forecast and knew he had to get started. As he left the office at 7:15, he wrote himself a large note and pinned it on his wall—"Get Started on the Sales Forecast!"

EXHIBIT 5
Characteristics of Competitors

National Film	Broadest product line in the industry. Quality a definite advantage. Good service. Sales coverage adequate, but not an advantage. Not as aggressive as most suppliers on price. Strong competitor.
Bonanza	Well-established tough competitor. Very aggressive on pricing. Good packaging, quality okay.
Southeastern	Extremely price competitive in southern Florida. Dominates Miami market. Limited product line. Not a threat outside of Florida.
PBI	Extremely aggressive on price. Have made inroads into Transco Paper Company. Good service but poor sales coverage.
BAGCO	New competitor. Very impressive with a high-quality product, excellent service, and strong sales coverage. A real threat, particularly in Florida.
Southwest Bag	A factor in Louisiana and Mississippi. Their strategy is simple—an acceptable product at a rock bottom price.
Sun Plastics	Active when market is at a profitable level with price cutting. When market declines to a low profit range, Sun manufactures other types of plastic packaging and stays out of the trash bag market. Poor reputation as a reliable supplier, but can still "spot-sell" at low prices.
East Coast Bag Co.	Most of their business is from a state bid which began in January 1984 for a two-year period. Not much of a threat to Modern's business in the Southeast as most of their volume is north of Washington, D.C.

EXHIBIT 6
1990 Real Growth Projections by Segment

Total Industry	+5.0%
Commercial	+5.4%
Restaurant	+6.8%
Hotel/Motel	+2.0%
Transportation	+1.9%
Office Users	+5.0%
Other	+4.2%
Noncommercial	+4.1%
Hospitals	+3.9%
Nursing Homes	+4.8%
Colleges/Universities	+2.4%
Schools	+7.8%
Employee Feeding	+4.3%
Other	+3.9%

Source: Developed from several trade journals.

Ohmeda Monitoring Systems

H. Michael Hayes

Brice Henderson

Looking out his office window at the magnificent Front Range of the Colorado Rockies, Joseph W. Pepper, General Manager of Ohmeda Monitoring Systems, was deep in thought concerning the future of Finapres®, a relatively new Ohmeda product. Introduced in 1987, the product had not lived up to its expectations. Now, in mid-June 1990, Pepper was considering a number of options. His choice, he knew, would have a significant impact on Ohmeda Monitoring Systems.

Background

Finapres (the name was derived from its use of finger arterial pressure) was the only product on the market providing *continuous non-invasive blood pressure monitoring* (CNIBP). As such it was the only unique product that Ohmeda could offer in 1990.

Originally introduced to the market in 1987, initial results had been disappointing. Its introduction in the U.S. had been generally unsuccessful. Results in Europe, and internationally, had been somewhat better but still had failed to meet the firm's expectations. Concerns about the product had led Ohmeda to stop shipments on May 1, 1990, pending a review of product problems and the overall situation.

At an all day meeting on May 23, 1990, marketing research, field sales, and R&D had presented information on the status of Finapres. In particular, R&D had given its assessment as to the likelihood that proposed product changes and improvements would solve some of the product's shortcomings.

The specter of the disappointing initial introduction, and the uncertainty that R&D could improve the product sufficiently to satisfy all the concerns, hung over the decision to commit more funds to the product. An unsuccessful reintroduction would further hurt Ohmeda's credibility, both with customers

This case was prepared by Professor H. Michael Hayes and Research Assistant Brice Henderson as a basis for class discussion, rather than to illustrate either effective or ineffective handling of an administrative situation.

and with the field sales force. On the other hand, successful reintroduction of Finapres would ensure a strong, and possibly dominant, position in the non-invasive blood pressure monitoring market; plus the possibility of increased sales of other monitoring products, as Finapres was combined with other Ohmeda products into packaged systems.

Subsequently, Pepper had many discussions with his key managers regarding their views of Finapres. In early June he visited a number of Ohmeda customers and distributors in Japan, many of whom were very interested in Finapres. Although there were several unanswered questions, it was up to Pepper to make the key decisions concerning Finapres.

BOC/Ohmeda

Ohmeda Monitoring Systems was a business unit of The BOC Group, a multinational firm, headquartered in Windlesham, Surrey, England. The Group had an international portfolio of what it described as "world-competitive" businesses; principally industrial gases, health care products and services and high vacuum technology. The Group operated in some 60 countries and employed nearly 40,000 people.

Health care products and services were provided by BOC Health Care for critical care in the hospital and in the home. Their equipment, therapies and pharmaceuticals were used in operating rooms (OR), recovery rooms (PACU), intensive care (ICU) and cardiac care (CCU) units throughout the world. Divisions of BOC Health Care were organized around *pharmaceuticals*, *home health care*, *intravascular devices*, and *equipment and systems*.

Ohmeda Health Care, providing equipment and systems, was an autonomous division of BOC Health Care. It was made up of five major business units, plus a field operations unit. The five business units manufactured products for *suction therapy*, *infant care*, *respiratory therapy*, *anesthesia*, and *monitoring systems*. Field operations provided field sales and sales support, worldwide, on a pooled basis to all the business units. (See Exhibit 1 for a partial organization chart of Field Operations.)

A 1985 reorganization had put all business decisions in the hands of the business general managers, and established profit of the business unit as a major performance measure. In 1990, the managers of the business units, and the manager of field operations, reported to the President of Ohmeda Health Care, Richard Leazer, who, in turn, reported to the Managing Director of BOC Health Care, W. Dekle Rountree.

Ohmeda Monitoring Systems

Ohmeda Monitoring Systems (headquartered in Louisville, Colorado) designed, manufactured and sold (through the field operations unit) monitoring equipment for a number of segments of the health care industry. It focused its business activities on three classes of products:

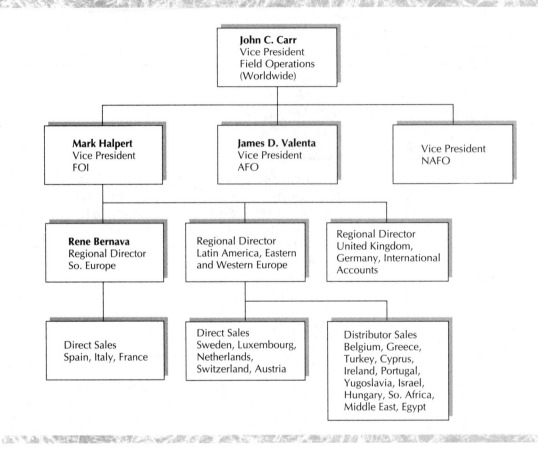

EXHIBIT 1
Partial Organization Chart Field Operations

- Oximetry products, used to measure oxygen content in arterial blood.
- Gas analysis products, used to measure a patient's respiratory gas levels.
- Non-invasive blood pressure measurement products.

Applications for these products were found in a wide variety of departments within hospitals and other health care facilities. Products were usually sold to the health care facility, either directly by the field sales force or by a distributor. Some products, however, were also sold to equipment manufacturers (OEMs) for incorporation in a larger measurement package.

Most Ohmeda oximetry and Finapres products consisted of a "box," containing the hardware, software and a display unit, and a probe, or cuff, to allow a non-invasive way to measure the parameter of interest. These were of two types, disposable or reusable, and were designed to be attached to the patient's toe, foot, finger, hand or ear, depending on the application.

Ohmeda had access to Finapres technology by virtue of a worldwide exclusive license, obtained from Research Unit Biomedical Instrumentation TNO (Amsterdam, The Netherlands). Many other technologies had also been acquired, either by license or outright purchase.

Ohmeda estimated the non-invasive monitoring market was $1.2 billion worldwide, with 60% of the market in the United States. Overall, its market share was some 15% of those segments it served. In selected categories, however, its market share was considerably higher. With considerable variation by country and specific product, Ohmeda estimated the growth rate of its served market at 5–10% per year.

The competitive picture for Ohmeda was complex. Its main competitors were U.S.-based firms. Many of its products, however, faced strong competition from European firms. In oximetry there were an estimated 25 competitors, although only four had significant shares. Major competitors and estimated market shares were:

Nellcor (U.S.)	50%
Ohmeda (U.S.)	30%
Criticare (U.S.)	10%
Novametrix (U.S.)	8%

In respiratory gases there were an estimated 12 competitors. Major competitors and estimated market shares were:

Datex (Finland)	16%
Ohmeda	15%
Siemens (West Germany)	14%
Hewlett-Packard (U.S.)	12%

In blood pressure measurement only five companies competed. With an 80% share, Critikon (U.S.) dominated the non-invasive market with its oscillometric, or non-continuous, product. Ohmeda's sales of its non-invasive products represented just 2% of this market.[1]

Based on pre-tax operating profits in 1989, Ohmeda's financial situation appeared to be very healthy. There were concerns, however. As Pepper observed:

We tend to be more financially driven than market driven. Also, we have not been investing heavily in R&D. As a result, our product line is relatively mature

[1]Market shares were for the U.S. market.

and I don't know how much longer we can count on present products for high contribution margins.

Finapres is the only major new product that is close to ready to go. Perfecting Finapres, and successfully reintroducing it, would not only produce direct sales but its uniqueness could also benefit our other monitoring businesses, through integrated packages that included a technology available nowhere else. The sales force in Europe, and also in Asia, is very excited about the product, even with its present deficiencies, and believes that with reasonable improvement it could become a major contributor to sales and profits. In the U.S. there is not the same excitement. There is agreement that if all the product deficiencies could be corrected, we would have a real winner, but R&D can't give us any guarantees.

Field Operations

Following the 1985 reorganization of Ohmeda Health Care, from a functional organization to the five therapy units, the firm had considered how to organize its field sales operations. Given the complexity of the five product lines, and some desire on the part of the therapy unit managers to have more direct control over the sales forces that represented them, there was considerable support to establish specialized sales forces. There was also support for direct sales, as opposed to extensive use of distributors or dealers. Selling anesthesia equipment, it was argued, was very different than selling patient monitors and other Ohmeda products, both because of product differences and customer buying procedures. Many of Ohmeda's competitors (e.g., Siemens and Hewlett-Packard) relied heavily on direct sales, feeling that distributors or dealers could not provide the required level of technical knowledge and service.

Arguing against specialized selling was the belief that it was far more efficient, in terms of time, travel expense and customer knowledge, to have one salesperson calling on a hospital, rather than three, as was contemplated in one proposed form of organization. Still further, there was great concern about the consequences of terminating distributors or dealers, some of whom had been associated with Ohmeda (or its predecessor companies) for over 70 years. Finally, Ohmeda was aware that Baxter-Travenol, the largest medical supplies and equipment company in the world, had specialized its sales force in 1981 but had subsequently gone back to a general sales organization.

After extensive study, it was decided to continue with a pooled form of sales organization, together with pooled product service, customer service and finance, all reporting to the Vice President of Field Operations. As of early 1990 Field Operations had three principal regional components: NAFO, responsible for sales and service in North America (the U.S. and Canada); FOI, responsible for sales and service in Europe, the Middle East and Latin America; and AFO, responsible for sales and service in Asia, including Japan. Depending on the particular country, sales were all direct, a combination of direct and dealer, or totally through dealers.

Ohmeda recognized the need for making specialized product knowledge, beyond the expertise of the local salesperson, available quickly to the customer. In

NAFO it was assumed that such specialized knowledge could be provided by specialists from manufacturing locations. In FOI and AFO it was deemed impractical for specialists to travel from the U.S. and Product Champions were appointed in the major countries. Paid principally on salary (as opposed to the salespeople who were paid on a salary and commission basis), the Product Champions supported the sales force, for their assigned products, in a variety of ways. They were available to call on customers with the salespeople. They held product seminars, either for salespeople or for customer groups. In some instances they acted as missionary salespeople, soliciting orders from new customers. In all instances, they provided a focused communication channel between the field and headquarters marketing. It was Ohmeda's view that the Product Champions had played a major role in assisting the introduction of Finapres in Europe. There was also some concern that not enough manpower was available from headquarters to provide similar support to the field sales force in the U.S. and Canada.

Health Care Markets

The health care industry was one of the largest, and most rapidly growing, segments of the world economy. While growth was occurring worldwide, the potential for Ohmeda products was greatest in the U.S., Europe, Japan, and, generally, in the developed countries of the world. With certain exceptions, the U.S. tended to lead the world in the development and use of technologically sophisticated health care products. U.S. manufacturers of such products generally felt that the rest of the world followed the U.S. lead in acceptance and use, with countries in Europe following in as little as six months but with longer delays in other parts of the world.

Hospitals were the principal buyers of Ohmeda products. With some variation, due mainly to government regulations, purchasing practices were very similar in the developed countries of the world. All purchases of medical equipment required budgetary approval of the hospital administration. Their purchasing influence, however, was generally inversely related to the complexity of the item. Purchase decisions of disposable supplies and gases, for instance, were generally made solely by the hospital purchasing agent, based on the lowest price. By contrast, capital equipment was invariably selected by the hospital's medical specialists and clinical area end-users. Because any machine malfunction was potentially life-threatening, medical specialists were especially concerned with precision, reliability and safety. In addition, both the sophistication of clinical procedures and the technical expertise and interest of medical specialists were increasing. As a result, the product and clinical knowledge required to sell medical equipment was also increasing.

Ohmeda segmented its market by hospital department or application, as follows:

- OR/PACU (Operating Room/Post Anesthetic Care Unit or Recovery Room)
- ICU/NICU/CCU (Intensive Care Unit/Neo-natal Intensive Care Unit/ Coronary Care Unit)

EXHIBIT 2
U.S. Market Size: Sales Potential (in units) 1990–1992

Segment	Potential Sites°	Oximetry	Gas Analysis	Blood Pressure	Saturation
OR/PACU	60,000	26,000	31,000	15,000	HI
ICU/NICU/CCU	78,000	20,000	15,500	9,750	HI
L&D	57,000	10,000	0	4,000	MED
Floors	800,000	15,000	0	2,000	LO
Non-Hosp	65,000	10,500	0	200	MED

°Number of physical locations.

- L&D (Labor and Delivery)
- FLOORS (Basically patients' rooms in hospital wards)
- NON-HOSPITAL (The growing non-hospital segment, which included ambulances, surgicenters, physicians' offices, dental and homecare, for oximetry and blood pressure products.)

Sales potential varied substantially, depending on the particular segment and the product, as shown in Exhibit 2. Segments outside the U.S. generally had lower saturation levels than in the U.S. As was pointed out, however, saturation levels were not always the best indicator of sales potential. In many instances the replacement markets offered high potential as well.

In the operating room the physician (generally the anesthetist) was the key buying influence for all products. In all other segments decision making was a shared responsibility, as indicated in Exhibit 3. Key buying influences were thought to be influenced by different factors, in order of importance as indicated below:

Physician	Nurse	Technician
Technology	Ergonomics	Serviceability
Ergonomics	Relationship	Technology
Relationship	In-service	
Price/Value	Technology	

Administrator	Financial Officer	Material (Purchasing)
Company Reputation	Leasing Options	Price/Value
Price/Value	Total Package Cost	Total Package Cost
Revenue Generation	Reimbursement	Serviceability

EXHIBIT 3
Buying Influences

	OR	ICU	NICU	PACU	CCU	FLOORS	L&D
Probes	P	NTM	NT	NT	NTM	NTM	NT
Blood Pressure	P	PNM	PN	PN	PNM	PNM	PN
Gas Analysis	P	PTM	PT	PT	—	—	PT
Oximetry	P	NTM	NT	NT	NTM	PNTM	NT

Legend:

P = Physician   OR = Operating Room

N = Nurse   ICU = Intensive Care Unit

T = Technician   NICU = Neo-Natal Intensive Care Unit

A = Administrator   PACU = Post Anesthetic Care Unit

F = Financial Officer   CCU = Coronary Care Unit

M = Materials (Purchasing)   L&D = Labor and Delivery

Personal contact with key buying influences, by direct sales representatives or distributors, was an essential ingredient to securing an order. Key to success, however, were favorable results from experimental trials, particularly of new products, as reported in medical journals. Manufacturers worked closely with the medical community, worldwide, to identify opinion leaders interested in equipment who were willing to experiment with it and then publish their results in scholarly journals. Most such experiments were reported in English language journals, but these were widely read in non-English speaking countries.

Finapres®

Modern medicine viewed measurement of arterial blood pressure as essential in the monitoring of patients, both during and after surgery. Traditional monitoring techniques have included both invasive and non-invasive methods. Arterial line monitoring provided continuous measurement but invasion (meaning surgical insertion of a long, small bore catheter into the radial or femoral arteries) involved the risk of thrombosis, embolism, infections and nerve injuries. These risks were acceptable when arterial blood samples had to be taken regularly but otherwise were to be avoided.

An oscillometric monitor, such as Criticon's Dinamap, was non-invasive. As commonly used, such a device provided readings automatically every 3–5 minutes, or on demand. It could provide readings more frequently but this involved considerable patient pain or discomfort. As normally used, therefore, it could miss vital data due to the time lag of the readings. (Ohmeda sold a non-invasive blood pressure monitor of this type, manufactured for them, but had not promoted it heavily.) Manual methods were non-invasive but were highly dependent on the skill of the clinician and the application of the correct size arm cuff and involved even more time lag.

Finapres Technology

In 1967 a Czech physiologist, Dr. Jan Peñaz, patented a method with which it was possible to measure finger arterial pressure non-invasively. (See Exhibit 4 for a detailed description of the method.) In 1973 the device was demonstrated at the 10th International Conference on Medical and Biological Engineering at Dresden. Subsequently, a group of engineers at the Research Unit Biomedical Instrumentation TNO in the Netherlands became interested in the technology and constructed, first, a laboratory model and then a model which they felt was clinically and experimentally useful and commercially viable. In 1983 Ohmeda acquired an exclusive license for the Finapres technology.

Finapres and Ohmeda

Although TNO had produced a working model of Finapres, Ohmeda had invested between two and three million dollars in R&D in order to develop a manufacturable box and cuff and to recode the software to conform to Ohmeda protocols. The resultant design could be built largely on existing equipment, although some $100,000 was required for tooling for the cuff. Prior to commercial introduction, extensive work was done with opinion leaders to establish the credibility of the product. Favorable test results of clinical studies of Finapres were reported in medical journals, and were widely distributed to the medical profession. Cost of this work, and other market development expenditures, was roughly equivalent to the cost of R&D.

Ohmeda introduced a commercial design of Finapres in 1987 in the U.S. and in 1988 in Europe and other world markets. The initial offering consisted of a box, a patient interface module which attached to the patient's hand, and three reusable cuffs. It was positioned to compete against invasive measuring products. Although it was expected it would ultimately be offered to the OEM market it was originally introduced directly to the OR market. Priced at approximately $9,500, it was expected to return a contribution margin in excess of 70% (generally typical for new and unique products in the health equipment industry). Some price resistance was experienced and the U.S. price was reduced to $8,500, six months after introduction. Disappointingly, U.S. sales through 1989 totalled only 200 units.

In 1988 the product was introduced internationally, at a U.S. equivalent price of $9,600. In contrast to the U.S. introduction, the product was targeted, for direct sale, at a number of segments in hospitals. As in the U.S., price resistance was encountered and by 1989 the price had been reduced to approximately the U.S. equivalent of $5,000.

To some extent low sales in the U.S. were blamed on tactical marketing errors, such as the positioning and price of the product at introduction. There

EXHIBIT 4
Principles of Operation

Arteries transport blood under high pressure to the tissues. The artery walls are strong and elastic; that is, they stretch during systole (when blood is forced onward by contraction of the heart) and recoil during diastole (dilation of the heart when its chambers are filling with blood). This prevents arterial pressure from rising or falling to extremes during the cardiac cycle, thus maintaining a continuous uninterrupted flow of blood to the tissues. The volume of blood inside the artery increases when it expands and decreases when it contracts. This change in volume is the key phenomenon on which the Peñaz/Finapres technology was based.

In the Finapres system, a cuff with an inflatable bladder was wrapped around the finger (see diagram below). A light source (LED) was directed through the finger and monitored by a detector on the other side. This light was absorbed by the internal structures according to their various densities. The emitted light was an indication of blood volume in the artery. Through a complex servo-mechanism system, the cuff was inflated, or deflated, to maintain the artery size at a constant level. Thus, cuff pressure constantly equalled arterial pressure and was displayed on the monitor as an arterial waveform and also digitally.

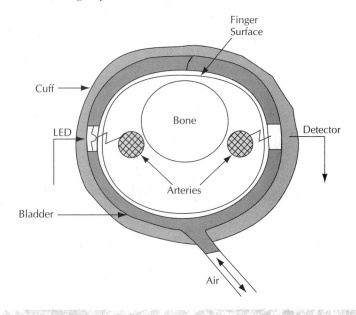

were also some technical problems with the system. Some were cosmetic in nature and easily fixed. Others were more serious, both for the clinicians using the equipment and for Ohmeda.

Major problems were the difficulty in applying the cuff properly in order to get an accurate reading, and drift in readings that occurred after several hours of continuous use, a particularly serious problem in OR. Another problem was the inability of the equipment to accurately monitor patients with poor blood circulation.

Results were more promising in Europe. The European medical community had been anxious to get access to Finapres. Much had been written about the Peñaz methodology and the system developed by TNO in the European medical press. The non-invasive aspect of Finapres was particularly attractive. European doctors were less comfortable with arterial line methodology than were their American counterparts. In addition, they tended to be more willing to invest time and effort to learn new technologies and there was less preoccupation with patient throughput than in the U.S.

News of the problems experienced in the ORs in the United States had made penetration of the OR segment in Europe difficult. With its broader contacts, the sales force was able to introduce the product to other segments, particularly in CCU and physiology in teaching hospitals, where stability over long periods of time was either not as critical as in OR or where continuous blood pressure monitoring was of paramount importance. With this approach, supported by the willingness of the sales force to train medical personnel in application of the cuff, the company experienced much greater success, selling a total of 700 units in these markets through 1989.

Commenting on results through 1989, Melvyn Dickinson, International Marketing Manager, observed:

> There are significant differences between the hospital markets in the U.S. and Europe, and in how our sales forces sell to them. In the U.S., for example, anesthetic machines, made by one of our sister therapy units, are sold by the same field sales force that sells our monitoring equipment. The U.S. machines are made to more stringent requirements and are much more expensive than those sold in Europe. In addition, they tend to be replaced on a 5-year cycle, compared to 10–15 years in, say, Italy. As a result, our sales force in the U.S. tends to really concentrate on the OR market, whereas in Europe the sales force takes a broader approach.
>
> It's also important to recognize that the key influence for OR purchases is an anesthesiologist, for whom blood pressure is just one of many concerns. In other segments of the hospital, the situation is very different. In the CCU, or the cardiac operating theater, blood pressure is of paramount importance. Not all procedures are lengthy, and even where they are many cardiologists saw value in CNIBP, even though there was drift. For physiological measurements in research hospitals, or in hypertension units, there were even fewer drawbacks, plus the clinicians in these situations were much more inclined to take extra care with application of the cuff.
>
> Beyond these differences, we misread the market in general. It had been our assumption that arterial lines (the term for invasive systems) were the major competitors for Finapres. We priced and positioned Finapres accordingly. Unfortunately, our promotion didn't get this position established in the minds of our customers. As it turned out, many customers viewed the oscillometric machines as our major competitor. For these customers, our original price involved too large a premium, versus the less expensive oscillometric machines. Now there is some real question about going back to the original positioning strategy.

The two years following the introduction of Finapres were characterized by indecision about its future and lack of significant support for the product. Once introduced, Ohmeda required it to be self-supporting, with product improvements made on an ongoing basis, financed out of current revenues. When the sales force began to report complaints from the clinicians in the field it was felt that the major problems were cosmetic, concerning the size of the box and the readability of the screen. Complaints regarding inaccurate readings were thought to result from misapplication of the cuff. Despite some modifications, complaints continued and sales declined. As 1990 began, it was apparent that decisions as to the future of Finapres needed to be made.

Reassessment

Reassessment of Finapres had started with the development of the 5-year plan for Ohmeda Monitoring Systems. Subsequently, concerns on the part of the sales force about the commitment to Finapres indicated the desirability of a meeting involving sales force management, product management and R&D. On May 23, 1990, Joe Pepper convened a meeting of representatives of all three groups, as well as headquarters marketing. The main points that emerged from the meeting were as follows:

• There was general agreement that the market potential for CNIBP was large. There was, however, considerable disagreement as to its exact size. Some estimates of the U.S. market were as large as 7,740 units per year. International estimates were considerably lower. There was general agreement that the largest market segments for Finapres were OR and ICU/CCU. It was the view of Ohmeda's product managers, however, that the focus of the NAFO sales force on the OR market made selling to the ICU/CCU segment difficult.

• It was emphasized that the diffusion of innovation in many instances took a long time. Acceptance of some currently standard medical equipment came only after a number of years. Oximetry, for example, took 14 years, echocardiography took 10 years and, as it was emphasized, capnometry (CO_2 gas analysis) took 40 years to become accepted. However, if Finapres was to ultimately succeed, investment was necessary not only in technological development, but in market development as well.

• The following reasons for lack of success to date were identified:
  • drift in readings over time
  • not accurate for average clinician
  • not easy to use
  • inadequate alert for misapplied cuff
  • no alerts for problems with poor circulation
  • no toe/pediatric/neo-natal/thumb cuffs

- Concerns were expressed about:
  - lack of a research culture
  - bottom line/short term focus
  - R&D research shortage
- R&D gave its assessment of time and cost to develop fixes, and their likelihood of success:
  - The cause of drift was not certain, but there was a high probability that the problem could be fixed with changes in software, probably in 1990. If this fix worked, the cost would be relatively modest.
  - Assessing the present cuff as offering 30% of ideal requirements, currently contemplated modifications could be expected to improve performance to 40% by January 1991, again with relatively modest cost. With a more substantial effort, it was expected performance could be improved to 80% in two years.
- Non-invasive oscillometric blood pressure machines were not likely to be "thrown out" in favor of Finapres. It was more likely they would be replaced on a normal schedule.
- On the positive side, a number of strengths were identified:
  - patents lasting past the year 2000 (except UK and Germany)
  - strong distribution, particularly in OR
  - technical expertise
  - head start over competition

Following extensive discussion, four options were presented:

I. Stay on the present course. Make sufficient modifications to make it possible to carefully reintroduce the product in selected markets. This approach was estimated to cost $307,000 in R&D expense, generate sales of 820 units through 1994 and have a net present value of $30,000.

II. Stop the project. Taking into account writing off current inventory costs and possible return costs, this approach was estimated to have a negative NPV of $160,000.

III. Make a significant investment in R&D and marketing (including going forward with a mini-Fini, a much smaller version of Finapres that would be targeted at the OEM market). This contemplated a 50% penetration of the OR market by 1995, a 50% penetration of the ICU market by 1998, and significant penetration of the OEM market. Cumulative sales estimates for this approach were 7,700 units in the U.S. and 4,000 internationally (through 1995). With projected revenues of $40 million, investment in R&D of $2 million, investment in marketing of $1.2 million, the net present value of this approach through 1995 was estimated to be $2,200,000.

IV. Sell the business. There was considerable discussion of this option but the general view was that it was not likely Ohmeda could find a buyer willing to pay any significant amount for the business. In any event, it was unlikely that top management at BOC would approve such a step.

Management Views

Subsequent to the May 23 meeting, a number of views were expressed by Ohmeda managers. As John Carr, Vice President of Field Operations, saw it:

> The international experience with Finapres was more successful for a variety of reasons. The original technology was developed by a European company (TNO) so the European medical community was familiar with the concept. The sales force is more balanced in its approach to the market. Hence, it was able to exploit niche markets where the device worked very well. The initial sales built confidence. The real key was the use of product champions. The product was given support and attention that it did not receive in the states.
>
> Finapres represented a once in 5 to 10 years type of opportunity. It was a significant new technology which didn't seem to fit Ohmeda's culture or annual financial cycle. If the initial effort had been followed by product enhancements, Finapres would have been successful. From here, the only two decisions I see are sell or go.

Similar views were expressed by James Valenta, Vice President for Asia (AFO):

> Finapres is a great product, which, from my view in the Asian markets, has significant customer appeal. It seems that things were stacked against the product from the beginning. Soon after Finapres was purchased, Ohmeda reorganized. The individual who had pushed to buy the technology moved on to other assignments which resulted in some lost momentum. Finapres never really had a home, which compounded the problems with the system itself. Had there been a quicker response to feedback from the international sales force, most of what was discussed at the meeting today, the drift issue and the cuff, could have been resolved some time ago. Ohmeda had trouble accepting the fact that there was a problem. The feedback domestically was focused more on cosmetic rather than substantive issues. Changes were made without knowledge of the impact to other parts of the system.
>
> Japan is more technologically oriented, they grasped the idea of the system quickly and easily. Maybe its just that invasive technology isn't as advanced overseas as in the U.S. The doctors in Japan seem more interested in learning about new technology than in the states.
>
> If Ohmeda doesn't want to continue with Finapres, I'll buy it and produce it. I believe in the product that much.

A somewhat different perspective was given by René Bernava, Regional Director for Southern Europe:

> Europe was ready for Finapres. The medical community, especially in Germany, was excited about the studies and papers written about the product. As a whole, European doctors were much less comfortable with arterial monitoring than their American counterparts. Finapres should have been a dazzling

success in Europe but there were problems, both with the product and the way it was marketed.

The technology for Finapres was purchased but not improved. The early version did not work. The project had software problems and lacked leadership. The original plan was to make an inexpensive disposable cuff. With this focus, a cuff that really worked regardless of cost was never developed. Also, the product was introduced at a premium price. That philosophy did not work.

The international sales force felt we had the top technology and wanted to go ahead. The meeting today occurred because we were the most vocal. I went to Dekle (President Dekle Rountree) some time ago and asked him to investigate the product, renew agreements with TNO, and put some money into the project. Some money was forthcoming but it wasn't a continuing process.

As Mark Halpert, Vice President for FOI, saw the situation:

There are several reasons Finapres was more successful in Europe and overseas than in the United States. The sales force in Europe sells many products whereas in the U.S. the sales force only sells Ohmeda products. With the large product line, we developed customer expertise. We know what the customer wants, and we use technical support to help conclude the transactions.

The organization of the medical community in Europe is different also. Anesthesia and monitoring are the same customer. In the U.S. there are more specialists. The sales force, with its broader coverage and experience, went after other niches rather than anesthesia, where the product had failed in the U.S.

The key difference internationally was the product champions. Internationally, the product champion was part of the sales force, thus closer to the customers. In the U.S., management served this role. Europe is still enthusiastic about the product. In Germany, just with the 1991 cuff, the product will be a success.

Bonnie Queram was Manager—Sales Programs and Administration in NAFO and reported to the Vice President of Sales. As she recalled:

Everyone was enthusiastic when Finapres was introduced. It looked easy to sell, although the box was big and clunky. Initially there was a high level of sales activity and orders. Unfortunately, when problems surfaced we tended to focus on cosmetic fixes and sales tapered off in the U.S. In contrast, sales held up well in Europe. I developed a questionnaire to find out why. The responses indicated there is a major difference in clinical practice between the U.S. and Europe. The physicians, for instance, are more down to earth there. In contrast to the U.S., they are very patient and want to work with the manufacturer, particularly on a new product. The anesthesiologists will spend lots of time in pre-op making sure things like the cuff are OK, whereas in the U.S. they are very impatient. For these reasons, and a number of others, I concluded that the European experience wouldn't transfer to the U.S. Our normal assumption is that we can develop our products for the U.S. market, and then go abroad with the same strategy. This is the one case in a hundred where this assumption doesn't apply.

Bill Belew, a Senior Product Manager in Louisville, had a somewhat different view. According to Belew:

The product problems in Europe and the U.S. are identical. The only difference is the sales approach. What we need is a complete fix. That will cost in the neighborhood of $2 million, but once we have it we can go after the OR/ICU markets anywhere in the world.

He went on to say:

The May 23 meeting was both good and bad. The potential for the product was reiterated and we heard the product would not be killed. On the other hand, it didn't sound as if we were going to make the kind of commitment the potential justified. And this was despite information that Nellcor might introduce a CNIBP product in September.

The enthusiasm for Finapres was shared by Lloyd Fishman, Director of Marketing. He had a number of concerns, however:

I've been watching Finapres evolve since joining Ohmeda 2½ years ago. I think the product has potential to represent as much as 10% of our sales, but I was concerned that there was no sense of purpose, no vision, about the product. We were doing lots of little "fixits" without any real sense of our markets or what the product should be. I called the May 23 meeting to see if we couldn't develop such a sense of purpose or vision.

There's no question that we face a complex situation. The markets in the U.S. and international are very different. The financial orientation of the doctors in the U.S. rubs off on our sales force and they're much less inclined to sell concept products than in Europe, where the doctors like to work with us on new developments.

Ray Jones had recently joined Ohmeda as R&D Group Manager, and was responsible for the Finapres R&D effort. As he put it:

I think Finapres has lots of potential but we need to resolve a number of critical issues. For instance, we use finger pressure as a measure of central blood pressure, but we're not sure how closely finger pressure simulates central pressure or how accurately we're measuring finger pressure.

Management would like us to give some performance guarantees but that's not the nature of R&D. We can, however, identify the key technical and physiological issues and identify milestones with the expectation that we can get data to indicate if the issue is resolvable.

One of the things that would really help would be for marketing to give us some better performance criteria.

Finally, Joe Pepper reflected on his thoughts subsequent to the May 23 meeting, his various discussions with his managers and his visit to Japan:

I know the people in the organization feel we don't spend enough on R&D. But it's a question of balance. We have been spending over 6% of sales on R&D, plus the corporation has a major research facility at Murray Hill, N.J., where we do the riskier, blue sky R&D. In the past our competitors have spent a higher percent of sales on R&D. We estimate that Nellcor, for instance, spent over 10% during the last four years. However, we also estimate that they will reduce this in the next four years.

The May 23 meeting was valuable and we got a lot of opinions on the table. One option that was not looked at, however, was to go exclusively with OEMs.

In Japan the product is selling well. The physicians appear more willing to fiddle with the product to make it work. Based on what's going on in Japan, and what is going on in Europe, I wonder if we might not be able to bootstrap their experience to back into the U.S. market.

Part of our problem is our whole development process. We've hired some new people, Ray Jones as Product Development Manager and Nick Jensen as a research scientist, but it's going to take them some time to sort out the problems and establish better procedures.

I know John Carr wants us to go with a product that will sell in the U.S. Part of the question, though, is how much faith do I put in the numbers.

Quest International: Industrial Market Research

David Hover

Per V. Jenster

Jan de Rooij, the director of the flavor center at Quest International, contemplated the early retirement request of the director of market research and strategic development, Hans Dieperink, that was on his desk. Jan was not surprised by the request; he had known Hans was approaching retirement age but he had been counting on a couple of more years before having to face the music and find a replacement. Hans was a one-man phenomena and would be missed, he mused. Yet his departure opened up the opportunity to reevaluate the company's approach to market research. In the competitive world-wide industrial flavors business, market knowledge was an important asset, but was Quest going about it the right way? The industry was changing and mis-steps were increasingly dangerous. "What we know, we know well," noted Jan, "But I still feel vulnerable. What really scares me is what we don't know, we don't know."

Quest International, a division of Unilever, developed and manufactured flavors, fragrances and, recently, food ingredients for end consumer product companies throughout the world. Traditionally strong in both flavors and fragrances, Quest management believed that food flavors and ingredients were going to become increasingly important as the market for processed foods became more international and competitive.

World Flavor Industry

The term "flavors" is applied to any of a number of chemical products added to processed foods or beverages to impart taste and aroma. Flavors were usually classified as either natural, nature identical or artificial depending on the production method used. A flavor was classified as natural if it was extracted from animal or vegetable products using physical means including standard

This case was prepared by Research Associate David Hover, under the supervision of Professor Per V. Jenster, as a basis for class discussion rather than to illustrate either effective or ineffective handling of a business situation.

Copyright © 1991 IMD. International Institute for Management Development, Lausanne, Switzerland. IMD retains all rights. Not to be used or reproduced without written permission directly from IMD, Lausanne, Switzerland.

kitchen activities like cooking, heating, boiling, etc. Flavors produced through fermentation were generally considered natural flavors. Nature identical flavors or enzymology consisted of synthesized substances but which occurred naturally in food. Artificial flavors were substances derived from any source which did not occur naturally in food.

Traditionally, the manufacturers of flavors, known as flavor houses, had also supplied fragrances (for perfumes, personal hygiene products, soaps, detergents, etc.) because both flavors and fragrances were extracted from raw materials using the same fractionation and distillation processes. However, the changing market and technology were eroding many of the synergies between the two businesses. Not only was demand for flavors increasing as the food processing industry became more competitive, but the food industry also demanded more sophisticated flavors, able to withstand the rigorous food processing procedures and meet government and end consumer standards. The market conditions made creating suitable flavors much more difficult and technologically demanding than creating fragrances. As one executive noted, "Everyone knows what green peas taste like—coming up with the exact same flavor is challenging. However, with fragrances you can be more creative." At the same time the market for fragrances became stagnant.

The impact of the market changes was felt in the performance figures of the industry. (Please see Exhibits 1, 2 and 3 for an overview of the competitors and market forces.) Until the late 1970s, the world flavors and fragrances (F&F) industry had shown consistently strong results. Industry profitability approximated 15% of sales in the mid to late 1960s and 10% in the 1970s. In the 1980s, however, slower growth and increased competitive pressures had reduced profitability to about 6–7% industry-wide and real sales growth averaged 5–6% per year, reaching an estimated $6.7 billion in 1990. Projections into the 1990s estimated growth rates to remain in the 5% range. Flavors comprised nearly 45% of the total F&F market and were valued at approximately $3.1 billion in 1990. Western Europe and the United States were the largest regional markets, together accounting for 63% of world flavor sales. Japan was the third major market. Consumption in the rest of the world was significantly lower. However, Eastern Europe and the Far East were identified as having significant growth potential.

Quest International

Quest International was formed in 1986 when Naarden International was purchased by Unilever and merged with Unilever's existing flavors division, PPF International. Since the merger, approximately 7 other companies had been purchased and incorporated into Quest's operations, including Biocon Biochemicals (Ireland) and Sheffield Products (USA), both manufacturers of natural food ingredients. These later mergers were intended to increase Quest's knowledge or expertise in specific fields such as biotechnology and improve its ability to offer complete food systems. Financially, Quest had grown quickly during the late 1980s. In 1989, the division reported a

EXHIBIT 1
Top 15 Flavor Houses by Flavor Sales
(Market Share in Parentheses)

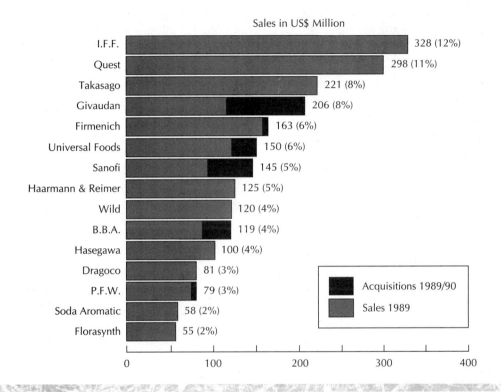

Sales in US$ Million

Company	Sales
I.F.F.	328 (12%)
Quest	298 (11%)
Takasago	221 (8%)
Givaudan	206 (8%)
Firmenich	163 (6%)
Universal Foods	150 (6%)
Sanofi	145 (5%)
Haarmann & Reimer	125 (5%)
Wild	120 (4%)
B.B.A.	119 (4%)
Hasegawa	100 (4%)
Dragoco	81 (3%)
P.F.W.	79 (3%)
Soda Aromatic	58 (2%)
Florasynth	55 (2%)

Legend:
- Acquisitions 1989/90
- Sales 1989

Source: Quest International

turnover of US$ 702 million. (Refer to Table 1 for a summary of the division's performance.)

Quest's parent company, the British-Dutch end consumer and industrial products giant, Unilver, was one of the world's largest companies with 1989 sales in excess of US$ 34 billion. Unilever owned such famous brands as Lipton Teas, Ragu Sauces, Iglo Frozen Foods, Lux Soaps, and Elizabeth Arden Cosmetics. Besides Quest, Unilever had a number of other industrial product divisions including Lever Industrial (detergents and cleaning supplies) and National Starch and Chemicals (adhesives and starches). Unilever's industrial divisions operated relatively autonomously. They were not guaranteed in-company business and were required to find external markets for their products. Conversely, divisions such as Quest did not feel constrained from conducting business with competitors of Unilever's end consumer products groups.

EXHIBIT 2
Food Ingredient Sales of Flavor Houses: Sales and Market Shares

Food Ingredient Sales (in US$ million)	1989	% Share	Including '89/90 Acquisitions	% Share
Sanofi	412	14%	414	14%
Haarman & Reimer	—	0%	231	8%
Quest	98	3%	158	5%
Universal Foods	67	2%	83	3%
R.F.W.	75	3%	75	3%
Takasago	68	2%	68	2%
Subtotal	720	24%	1029	34%°
Others	2280	76%	1971	66%
Total	3000	100%	3000	100%

°Acquisition effect: 43%
Source: Quest International

EXHIBIT 3
Example of Sources of New Entries from Other Industries

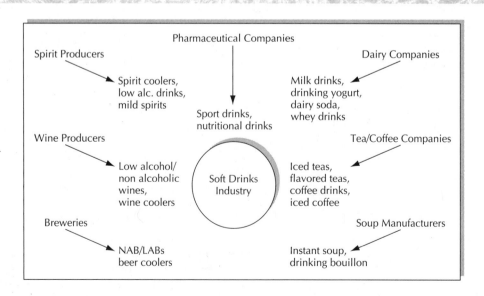

Source: Quest International

TABLE 1
Quest International Financial Data

	1988	1989
Sales	$625MM	$702MM
R&D Expense	$ 39MM	$ 48MM
Capital Expense	$ 31MM	$ 38MM
Operating Profit	$ 71MM	$ 72MM

The Marketing Organization

Quest had three main business areas: flavors, fragrances, and food ingredients. Because of similarities between their client bases, the flavors and food ingredients units were merged in 1990. Initially, the process experienced some teething difficulties but management was confident the synergies would soon become apparent. The flavor center (as the flavor and food ingredients unit was called) was organized into five nodes, each reporting to the director, Jan de Rooij. (Refer to Exhibit 4.) Operational contact with clients (although not sales) was through the 4 individual business development groups: beverages, savory, tobacco, and confectionery/bakery and dairy. Each area was directed by a Business Development Manager (BDM), assisted by a marketing and technical contingent which varied in size depending on the nature of the particular product group. Savories, for example, had the largest technical support staff with 12 people and 4 marketing people. Beverages had 5 marketing people and 9 technical people.

Each BDM team was responsible for servicing the clients' needs in terms of marketing, product support, product development, and applications for the specific product area. The BDM team, however, did not handle the actual sales. The BDMs worked closely with the marketing research group when gathering information and interpreting market signals. For managers at Quest, the market was the fundamental driving force of the company.

Sales Process. Sales at Quest, as with Unilever in general, were the responsibility of individual country sales forces for most products. The beverages and tobacco areas were notable exceptions. Beverages had been recently reorganized as a single unit for all of Europe in anticipation of the unified market. The small number and global nature of tobacco organizations obviated the need for diversified sales support.

Sales were generated in two ways: 1) clients issued a detailed description (called a brief) of the concept they were looking for and then held a competition among the proposals made by the flavor houses or 2) flavor houses submitted unsolicited proposals detailing either new product ideas or product

EXHIBIT 4
Quest International: Flavor Center Organization

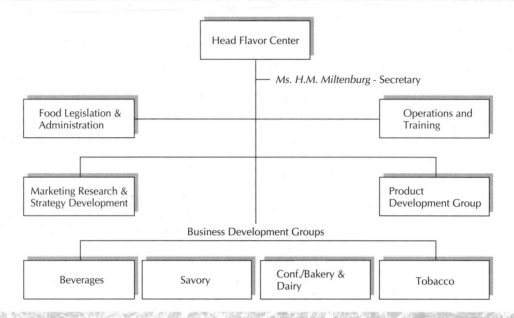

Source: Quest International

enhancement features of their flavors versus the flavors the client was then purchasing. Clients looked for a variety of features in any briefs submitted including the quality of the flavor, the price of the raw materials, suitability to processing techniques, etc.

Clients occasionally changed suppliers to either find lower prices or reduce their dependence on a particular supplier. Quest found it difficult to systematically identify potential switchers and, generally, did not consider the opportunities attractive. Instead, the firm favored building strong relationships with existing clients and seeking out new clients only when new product opportunities were evident.

Quest had three types of clients (large international, large national and medium size national), each requiring different types of services. For example, international clients included international service coordination, which Quest provided from their host countries. Although contradictory for the country-based sales organization, the internationalization of some major clients was inescapable. The new demands on coordination required Quest units which had previously not worked closely together to team up. National clients were served through the country-based Business Industry Managers (BIMS).

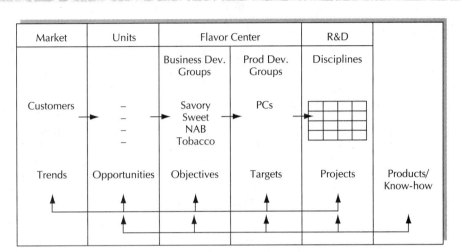

Market	Units	Flavor Center		R&D	
		Business Dev. Groups	Prod Dev. Groups	Disciplines	
Customers	– – – –	Savory Sweet NAB Tobacco	PCs		
Trends	Opportunities	Objectives	Targets	Projects	Products/ Know-how

To permit the necessary flows between product areas, client demands, and R&D, Quest had adopted a matrix organization. Client interaction was active primarily at the BIM and BDM levels. When the BDM groups were unable to manage a specific client need they went to the product development group also located at the Naarden flavor center. The project coordinators in Product Development focused on special topics (there were 8 in 1991) such as flavor delivery systems, natural flavors, and process flavors (flavors produced during cooking). When project coordinators required special technical knowledge, for example, expertise in physical chemistry, they contacted the Research and Development group. In some instances, clients asked Quest to develop specific products. In other cases, R&D on its own initiative could develop new products for market applications. (Refer to Exhibit 5.)

Market Research Function

In all of Quest's activities, knowledge of market conditions was believed to be important. Data on market conditions came in part from the sales force, although the most important contribution came from the marketing research group. The director of market research, Hans Dieperink, whose early retirement request had put Jan de Rooij's mind on the subject, described his unit's function:

> There are three layers of the market research support function in an industrial marketing company: market research, marketing research and business strategy development. Market research looks specifically at the end product level and covers areas such as the market size, segments, growth rates, maturity, level of captured or tied demand, price levels, trends and so on. Marketing research

provides management with the information necessary to analyze the company on its strengths and weaknesses. Things like market share, client relations, the image the company has among competitors and clients, the technology capability of competitors, product lines and so on. Business strategy development involves analyzing the total business approach of the company which includes everything from technology to financial status to profitability.

It was believed within Quest that only when all three of these fields were adequately covered would the company be able to remain one of the industry pacesetters. Hans Dieperink discussed the importance of complete market research:

> Your current competitive position is a function of your past strengths and weaknesses. If you want to develop your competitive position in a particular segment you have to look at all of the relevant information, not just the advantages of your new products. It also involves looking at the technology, prospects for the segment, competitors and the clients. Everything I mentioned before. In our group, we have work in all of these areas.

Funding of Market Research.   Conducting market research was not free. The market research department at Quest was provided a budget of 600,000 Dutch guilders (Fl) by the division. Financing the function through the division was preferred to having the operational units pay for the services they received. Management felt units would be reluctant to use the services of market research if they had to pay for it out of their budgets. Under the existing system any unit could request assistance from the market research group. Mr. Romkes, the BDM for savory, added, "Marketing research should know which requests are important to look at and support." Recently, however, market research had received an influx of requests from the food ingredients managers. Market research was hesitant to accept these requests because of budget limitations and a staff shortage.

The market research budget allowed the purchase of a wide range of information sources both regularly and as necessary to complete individual reports. Data was also collected in-house from press clippings, brokerage reports, annual reports, etc. Quest maintained a large database on clients, competitors and markets. Some of the information was regularly circulated to management. Gathering the information from such a broad range of sources required a well-trained documentation staff with good industry knowledge.

Organization.   Quest's Market Research and R&D group operated as central functions. Conversely, the sales and marketing units were very decentralized to encourage maximum authority, accountability and responsibility. Some Quest managers wanted market research to be more decentralized, reaching as far down as the level of the sales force. Others argued this was difficult or even inappropriate operationally. Not only was it believed to be more expensive as various efforts would be duplicated, but the sales force would have to be retrained in information collecting. The nature of Quest's client base was thought to be a critical issue. Hans Dieperink explained:

We have a relatively complicated and diverse client base. Because of that we have to do more market research. If you look at our largest competitor, for example, they don't have a large market research department. There are two reasons for that: 1) they have strategically concentrated on retaining only the largest clients and 2) they have a very competent and highly experienced sales force with a high retention rate.

IFF has mostly market leaders as their clients. They don't need to do extensive market research because their clients are the market and their sales force is excellent! If we were willing to spend that kind of money on getting the best of the best we would probably be able to reduce the efforts of the central market research group. That's not how we have organized ourselves, though, and for us a centralized market research group is critical to the competitiveness of the firm.

Role in Strategy Formulation and Product Development

The market research group actively participated in strategy formulation. Quest had designated three strategic areas of concentration: beverages, savories, and dairy. In 1989, Quest had completed a series of studies on the beverages and savories areas. This, together with the company's good market position, gave the company the ability to "freewheel" for a couple of years in those fields and concentrate its energies elsewhere. It was apparent the company had limited market knowledge on the dairy industry and consequently made a substantial investment to explore the market.

Quest relied on market research to provide justification for new product development and to act as an indicator of potential new product demands in the market place. Occasionally, Quest scientists developed new technologies which were not immediately accepted by clients. In this situation, managers looked to market research findings to determine if the new product was too early and the market was not yet ready. If so, a new product might be kept in the product portfolio for release when market conditions improved.

Market research also exposed gaps in the portfolio. For example, if market research indicated a strong end-consumer interest in a fat-free beef flavoring for frying oils, management would consider the desirability of starting a development project to create a suitable product.

Defining the Market. A recent internal report at Quest had outlined the differences between the tied and untied markets. Tied markets were those for products such as Coca-Cola where the product was jealously guarded by the manufacturer and flavor houses were only able to sell raw materials. The untied market in which manufacturers frequently relied on outside suppliers to handle everything from flavor development to supplying the prepared ingredients was considered more lucrative in terms of future business for Quest.

Periodically, market research reported on competitive trends. Management used the reports in analyzing Quest's performance, in developing strategic plans and in reporting to the board of directors. One such report had dealt exclusively with the effect of the recent spate of acquisitions in the industry and the motivation for them. The report carefully detailed the impact of the acquisitions on relative market shares and new entrants in flavors by food ingredient companies and vice versa.

The information was important because of the wide diversity of national market characteristics even within Europe. For example, Quest was relatively weak in beverages in Germany but also did not see the market as particularly interesting because of the high level of competition there. The UK, where there were a large number of smaller competitors, offered a number of opportunities.

Hans Dieperink commented on the degree of market research necessary:

> To determine how much marketing research you must do you have to decide what phase you are in and what kind of company you are. Some of our competitors do almost no market research. For example, IFF does almost none. It was traditionally a fragrance company. Fragrances are more marketing driven and the technology is much more mature.
>
> Because of that and their market position, market research is not so important. For us that isn't the case.
>
> We need market research to provide information on market size and the level of innovation to local sales management. They have to make choices and the information helps the decision making process, how you want to compete, what markets you want to be in and so on. We have to find out what our clients are looking for and then tell managers so they can make a decision as to where to focus our energies. Should we stay in the snack market, for example. How do you guide management in setting the right marketing mix?
>
> Each market segment has something different going on and we have to ask ourselves what will be our role there. For example, we are already in the North American meat flavor market but with the US-Canadian Free Trade Agreement the whole market will change.

Quest always began segment studies by looking at the market and Quest's position within the market. Then the company's strengths and weaknesses were evaluated as were profitability and technology contribution. When the particular market study was complete, a picture of the segment was available. S. Romkes noted:

> That's the time for a decision, do you want to do something in the market or do you want to leave it as it is? Once you know that you can determine your research programs, product development and so on. Maybe we don't want to go into that market, but we don't know that until we have the market research.

Hans Dieperink added,

> Our task is solving the problems of uncertainty for the business managers.

Not everyone at Quest agreed with the value placed on market research at Quest. Robert Sinke argued:

> We spent months putting reports together with tremendous amounts of detail but if you look at what we do with it is relatively limited. By working in Europe this last year, I can tell what the market is doing. My question is, do we really need all the market research we are doing?

Role in Market and Client Selection

Determining how and why a client should be approached in the first place was important and seen by many at Quest as the primary function of market research. According to Jan de Rooij:

> Previously we chased everything that moved everywhere. We have a wide range of flavor products and were able to do that, but it probably wasn't the most efficient. Now we are in almost all markets but they aren't always served the way they should be served.

Quest did not have the resources to pursue every potential client given the large number of candidates. Pursuing clients was expensive and the cost of failure high. The role of market research here was twofold: discovering 1) the potential of a client in terms of demand for flavors and food ingredients and 2) the ability of the client to succeed in the market place.

From the units there was considerable demand for information on various subjects. The need for some strategy to filter the demands was necessary and a constant struggle. Generally, however, the qualifying need was in identifying the primary clients.

> We need that guidance about what is going on in the market. Although very often, I feel, market research is looking too much at the past and not enough into the future. We need to be at the frontier of development. Our clients are anticipating market developments and we have to do that even more,

explained Mr. Romkes. He continued:

> My major requirement from market research is identifying, for each major client, what his needs are for the next few years. Where he is going for instance. If they are building a new factory, what will the factory be producing? You have to know from market research that this segment will be really important for your client in the future.

Clients were evaluated based on their prospective volume of business and the likelihood of getting the contract. The sources of information used to analyze clients were very diverse. Frequently, the starting point for analyzing sales was the annual reports or press releases of the clients or industry newsletters. Quest researchers also looked at market share figures either as published or, if public information was not available, through extrapolating from competitors' shares, factory size or any other method of estimating a potential's output. The information was supplemented with any internal data available at Quest. By comparing the various figures Quest was able to generate at least a rough approximation of how much a company was producing. From Quest's knowledge of flavor technology they could then estimate a company's potential demand for flavors. If the purchases were estimated to be large enough, Quest would explore the relationships between the potential clients and their current suppliers.

Using the sales force as a conduit for information, Quest evaluated the strength of a potential client's relationship with its existing suppliers. If the situation was felt to be conducive for Quest either because of weak links with existing suppliers or interest in the potential for new sources, Quest would add the company to its target list. The process of evaluating potential clients was complex and as much of an art as the rest of market research.

Role in Sales Support

Market research findings were often an effective sales tool. Quest frequently found that it had better market knowledge than some of its clients. In fact, one manager noted, "Sometimes we know more about a client's product offerings world-wide than he does." Increasingly, as the food processing companies focused more on marketing, they looked to the flavor houses to provide input into what was happening in their markets, what new products were being introduced and what trends were influencing the market. Occasionally, the clients were unaware of fast breaking product developments and welcomed Quest's suggestions for new products. Quest placed a lot of emphasis on tracking new product launches throughout the world. Most of the time, however, the clients were informed about market trends, but nevertheless appreciated Quest's interest and understanding of their business. Managers at Quest believed this was an important part of their sales effort.

The new product introduction and market condition information Quest provided clients was not, however, expressly charged to the client. It was assumed that the costs of providing the services would be recovered through the higher margins Quest was able to command. Not all of the managers at Quest believed this was realistic. Robert Sinke, assistant to the director, commented, "The clients are getting a lot of very expensive information from us free. It would be interesting to see at what price they value the information." Quest conducted the market research for internal purposes as well but Robert added, "That doesn't prevent us from charging clients for it when we turn the information over to them."

Market research, of course, also assisted sales in obtaining existing contracts from competitors. For example, after completing a study of strawberry flavorings in the dairy industry in Europe, Quest approached the client of one of its competitors. Quest told the manufacturer, "Do you know your competitor is saving money by using one flavor all across Europe? Why are you not doing it? In each country you have a different profile which is adding to your costs." Quest then offered a flavor profile which could be used by the client all over Europe with only a little modification and won the contract. Entering existing markets, however, was difficult and not a priority. Clients demanded that the new supplier match the existing flavor and offer lower prices or better service. The complex character of flavors was difficult (and very expensive) to match and there were better opportunities for Quest in new product introductions.

Hans Dieperink, the director of market research and strategy development, had been at Quest since 1975. "Yes," thought Jan de Rooij, "his early retirement in February was going to promulgate some reevaluations at Quest about market research and who we want to replace him." Quest traditionally had brought people up through the ranks and abhorred bringing outsiders into the company. Mostly it was believed that the detailed and complex nature of the flavors business required having people with a long history of experience.

When asked to comment on his departure, Hans Dieperink reflected: "They usually think that anybody can do the job and that's not true. Handling and getting the information is important. You need to have someone with the ability to always get information and to interpret it. You don't build market knowledge quickly."

Rogers, Nagel, Langhart (RNL PC) Architects and Planners

H. Michael Hayes

It was August 1984. John B. Rogers, one of the founders and a principal stockholder in RNL, had just completed the University of Colorado's Executive MBA program. Throughout the program John had tried to relate the concepts and principles covered in his courses to the problems of managing a large architectural practice. In particular, he was concerned about the marketing efforts of his firm. As he put it, "Marketing is still a new, and sometimes distasteful, word to most architects. Nevertheless, the firms that survive and prosper in the future are going to be those which learn how to market as effectively as they design. At RNL we are still struggling with what it means to be a marketing organization, but we feel it's a critical question that must be answered if we're going to meet our projections of roughly doubling by 1989 and we're giving it lots of attention."

RNL

With 1984 sales (design fees) of approximately $3,300,000 RNL was one of the largest architectural firms in Denver and the Rocky Mountain region. The firm evolved from the individual practices of John B. Rogers, Jerome K. Nagel, and Victor D. Langhart. All started their architectural careers in Denver in the 1950s. The partnership of Rogers, Nagel, Langhart was formed from the three individual proprietorships in 1966 and became a professional corporation in 1970.

In 1984 the firm provided professional design services to commercial, corporate and governmental clients, not only in Denver but throughout Colorado, and, increasingly, throughout the western United States. In recent years it had designed a wide range of buildings, including offices, schools, condominiums, parking garages, laboratories and vehicle maintenance facilities. In addition to basic architectural design services, three subsidiaries had recently been formed:

- Interplan, which provides pre-architectural services, programming, planning, budgeting, scheduling, and cost projections, utilized in corporate budgeting and governmental bond issues.

- Denver Enterprises, formed to hold equity interests in selected projects designed by RNL and to take risk by furnishing design services early in a project and by participating in the capital requirements of a project.

- Space Management Systems, Inc. (SMS), which provides larger corporations with the necessary services (heavily computer system supported) to facilitate control of their facilities with respect to space, furnishings, equipment and the cost of change.

In 1984 the firm had 72 employees. John Rogers served as the Chairman and Vic Langhart served as President. Nagel had retired in 1976. (See Exhibit 1 for an organization chart.) Development of broad based management had been a priority since 1975. The firm had seven vice presidents. Two of these vice presidents, Phil Goedert and Rich von Luhrte, served on the Board of Directors, together with Rogers and Langhart.

Growth was financed through retained earnings. In addition, a plan to provide for more employee ownership, principally through profit sharing (ESOP in 1984), was initiated in 1973. Rogers and Langhart held 56% of RNL stock and 66% was held by the four board members. The Colorado National Bank Profit Sharing Trust held 12% in its name. The remaining 22% was controlled by 23 other employees, either personally or through their individual profit sharing accounts. It was a goal of the firm to eventually vest stock ownership throughout the firm, in the interest of longevity and continuity.

The firm's principal assets were its human resources. Rogers and Langhart, however, had significant ownership in a limited partnership which owned a 20,000 square foot building in a prestigious location in downtown Denver. In 1984 RNL occupied 15,000 square feet. Use of the remaining 5,000 square feet could accommodate up to 30% growth in personnel. Through utilization of automation and computers, RNL felt it could double its 1984 volume of work without acquiring additional space.

Architectural Services

architecture: the profession of designing buildings, open areas, communities and other artificial constructions and environments, usually with some regard to aesthetic effects. The professional services of an architect often include design or selection of furnishings and decorations, supervision of construction work and the examination, restoration, or remodeling of existing buildings. (Random House Dictionary)

Demand for architectural services was closely tied to population growth and to the level of construction activity. The population in the Denver metropolitan area grew from 929,000 in 1960 to 1,620,000 in 1980 and it was

EXHIBIT 1
Organization

Note: RNL does not have a formal organization chart, as such. The following was developed by the case writer to portray the general nature of work assignments and reporting relationships in the firm. As a general rule, project managers report either to John Rogers or Vic Langhart. Most administrative staff functions report to Vic Langhart. At the operational level, Interplan and SMS projects are handled similarly to RNL projects.

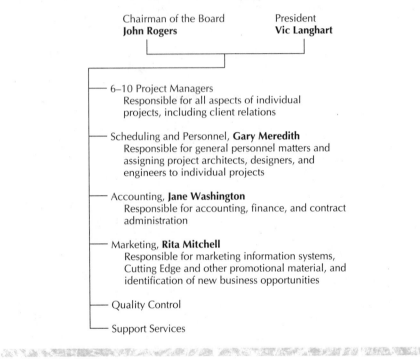

Chairman of the Board
John Rogers

President
Vic Langhart

— 6–10 Project Managers
Responsible for all aspects of individual projects, including client relations

— Scheduling and Personnel, **Gary Meredith**
Responsible for general personnel matters and assigning project architects, designers, and engineers to individual projects

— Accounting, **Jane Washington**
Responsible for accounting, finance, and contract administration

— Marketing, **Rita Mitchell**
Responsible for marketing information systems, Cutting Edge and other promotional material, and identification of new business opportunities

— Quality Control

— Support Services

estimated to grow to 1,958,000 by 1990. Denver's annual population change of 3.4% in the decade 1970–1980 ranked tenth for major American cities (Dallas and Phoenix ranked one and two). The projected population growth for the Denver metropolitan area from 1978 to 1983 ranked third in the nation and Colorado was predicted to be one of the ten fastest growing states during the 1980s.

Commercial construction permits grew from 340 in 1970, with an estimated value of $70,818,000, to 1,235 in 1980, with an estimated value of $400,294,000. This growth was not steady, however. Year to year changes in dollar value of commercial construction varied from 0.2% to 91.6% and the number of permits dropped from a high of 2,245 in 1978 to 1,235 in 1980. Similar patterns of growth and variation characterized industrial construction.

Translating construction growth into estimates of demand for architectural services was difficult. One rule of thumb held that each additional person added to the population base required 1,000 square feet of homes, schools, churches, offices, hospitals, manufacturing facilities, retail and shopping facilities and transportation facilities. In the Denver Metro area alone this could mean 338,000,000 square feet. At $50 average per square foot, total construction expenditure over the decade could reach $16,900,000,000 involving as much as $845,000,000 in design fees during the 1980s.

The past and projected growth in demand for architectural services was accompanied by a significant growth in the number of architects in Colorado. From 1979 to 1982, the number of state registrations of individual architects grew from 1,400 to 3,381, an increase of 141.5%. Over 100 architectural firms competed actively in the Denver market. (Over 500 architects were listed in the Yellow Pages of the Denver Metro Area phone directory.) In recent years a number of national firms (e.g., Skidmore, Owens and Merrill) had opened offices in Denver. Other major firms came to Colorado to do one job and then returned to their home offices (e.g., Yamasaki for the Colorado National Bank Office Tower, TAC for Mansville World Headquarters, etc.). Of the 26 major firms working on 38 selected jobs in Denver in 1983, 16, or 61.5%, were Denver based. Of the other ten, which had headquarter offices elsewhere, all but two had offices in Denver.

Major categories of customers for architectural services include:

Industrial

Commercial

    Owner

    Developer

Government

    Federal

    State

    Municipal

Residential (Note: RNL did not compete in this market)

Within these categories, however, not all architectural work was available to independent firms and not all architectural work on a project was awarded to one architect. A recent Denver survey, for example, indicated that of 49 commercial jobs under construction with a known architect, 11 were handled by an "inside" architect. Of the remaining 38 jobs, 20 included shell and space design whereas 18 involved space design only. In the 18 space designs only 50% were actually done by architects.

The rapid growth in the construction market in Denver came to an abrupt halt in February 1982. Triggered by the broad realization that the oil boom was over, or had at least slowed significantly, project after project was put on hold. Construction of office space literally came to a halt. Of particular concern to RNL, which had just completed negotiations for a $1,000,000 contract with Exxon, was the Exxon announcement of the closure of its Colorado Oil Shale activities at Parachute, Colorado.

It was against the backdrop of these changes that RNL felt the pressing need to review its marketing activities.

Marketing of Architectural Services

The basis of competing for architectural work had changed dramatically over the past several decades. As John Rogers recalled:

> At the beginning of my practice in 1956, you could establish an office, put a sign on your door, print calling cards and have a "news" announcement with your picture in the *Daily Journal* that you had established a new practice of architecture. Beyond that, it was appropriate to suggest to friends and acquaintances that I was in business now and I hoped that they might recommend me to someone they knew. The Code of Ethics of the American Institute of Architects, like many other professions at the time, prohibited any kind of aggressive marketing or sales effort as practiced in recent times.
>
> In fact, after convincing one School Board member (an artist) in Jefferson County that design was important, and then being awarded a commission to design an elementary school, which led to another and another, it was not surprising to read in the *Daily Journal* that the School Board had met the previous evening and had selected me to design a new junior high school, one that I hadn't even known about. I called and said, "Thank You." Marketing expense was zero with the exception of an occasional lunch or courtesy call here and there.
>
> Today, the situation is vastly different. We have to compete for most jobs, against both local firms and, increasingly, large national firms. Clients are becoming more sophisticated regarding the purchase of architectural services (see Exhibit 2 for a brief description of buyer behavior). Promotion, of some kind, and concepts such as segmentation have become a way of life.

During the 1960s, development of an architectural practice was a slow process, characterized by heavy reliance on word of mouth regarding professional experience and expertise. Overt communication about an architect's qualifications was limited to brochures. Personal acquaintances played a significant role in the development of new clients. Personal relations between principals and clients were an important part of continuing and new relations. This method of practice development tended to favor local firms, whose reputation could be checked out on a personal basis, and small firms, whose principals could provide personal management and design of client projects.

As Denver grew, the market changed. The advantage of being a successful, local architect and knowing the local business community diminished. Newcomers to Denver tended to rely on relationships with architects in other

EXHIBIT 2
Buyer Behavior

Purchase of architectural services is both complex and varied. Subject to many qualifications, however, there seem to be several steps that most buying situations have in common:

- Development of a list of potential architects.
- Identification of those architects from whom proposals will be solicited for a specific job. (Usually called the "short list.")
- Invitations to submit proposals.
- Evaluation of proposals and screening of final candidates.
- Selection of a finalist, based on proposal evaluation, or
- Invitations to finalists to make oral presentations to an evaluation group.

From a marketing standpoint, the focus of interest is the process of getting on the short list and the process by which the final selection is made.

The Short List

Prospective clients find out about architects in a variety of ways. Those who are frequent users of architectural services will generally keep a file of architects, sometimes classified as to type or practice. Additions to the file can come from mailed brochures, personal calls, advertisements, press releases or, in fact, almost any form of communication. When a specific requirement develops the file is reviewed for apparent fit. With many variations, a short list is developed and proposals are solicited.

Those who use architects infrequently tend to rely on various business or social networks to develop what is in essence their short list. In either case, a previously used architect is almost always on the short list, provided the past experience was satisfactory.

As the largest single customer for architectural services, agencies of the federal government follow a well defined series of steps, including advertisement in the *Commerce Business Daily* and mail solicitation of local firms.

The Selection Process

The selection process is significantly influenced by the nature and scope of the work and its importance to the firm. Architect selection on major buildings is usually made at the highest level in the organization; by a principal or the president in a private organization or by various forms of boards in not-for-profit organizations such as churches. In some instances the principal, president or board are actively involved in all phases of the process. In others the management of the process is delegated to those who develop recommendations to the decision makers. On smaller jobs, and those of an ongoing nature (e.g., space management), the decision is usually at lower levels and may involve a plant engineer or facilities manager of some kind.

Regardless of the level at which the selection process is made there seem to be two well defined patterns to the process. The first, and predominant one, evaluates the firms on the short list, taking into principal consideration non-price factors such as reputation, performance on previous jobs and current work load. Based on this evaluation one firm is selected and a final agreement is then negotiated as to the scope of the work, the nature of the working relationship, the project team and specific details as to price. The second, and of limited but growing use, attempts to specify the requirements so completely that a firm price can accompany the proposal. In some instances the price and the proposal are submitted separately. Evaluation of the proposals includes a dollar differential and these dollar differentials are applied to the price quotation to determine the low evaluated bidder.

Regardless of the process, there appear to be three main criteria on which firms are evaluated:

- The ability of the firm to perform the particular assignment. For standard work this assessment is relatively easy and relies on the nature of past work, size of the organization, current backlogs and so forth. For more creative work the assessment becomes more difficult. Much importance is put on past work but the proposal starts to

(continued)

EXHIBIT 2 *(continued)*

take on additional importance. Sketches, drawings and sometimes extensive models may be requested with the proposal. In some instances there may actually be a design competition. Much of this evaluation is, perforce, of a subjective nature.

• The comfort level with the project team that will be assigned to do the work. For any but the most standard work there is recognition that there will be constant interaction between representatives of the client's organization and members of the architectural firm. Almost without exception, therefore, some kind of evaluation is made of the project team, or at least its leaders, in terms of the client's comfort level with the personalities involved.

• Finally, there is the matter of cost. While direct price competition is not a factor in most transactions, the cost of architectural services is always a concern. This has two components. First, there is concern with the total cost of the project, over which the architect has great control. Second, there is growing concern with the size of the architect's fee, per se.

At least some assessment of the reputation of the architect with respect to controlling project costs is made in determining the short list. Once final selection is made there is likely to be much discussion and negotiation as to the method of calculating the fee. The traditional method of simply charging a percentage of the construction price seems to be on the wane. Increasingly, clients for architectural services are attempting to establish a fixed fee for a well defined project. The nature of architectural work, however, is such that changes are a fact of life and that many projects cannot be sufficiently defined in the initial stages to allow precise estimation of the design costs. Some basis for modifying a basic fee must, therefore, be established. Typically this is on some kind of direct cost basis plus an overhead adder. Direct costs for various classes of staff and overhead rates obviously become matters for negotiation. In the case of the federal government the right is reserved to audit an architect's books to determine the appropriateness of charges for changes.

cities. For local architects there wasn't time to rely on traditional communication networks to establish relationships with these newcomers. The size of projects grew, requiring growth in the size of architectural staffs. Personal attention to every client by principals was no longer possible.

Concomitantly, there was a growing change in the attitude toward the marketing of professional services. New entrants in the fields of medicine and law, as well as architecture, were becoming impatient with the slowness of traditional methods of practice development. A Supreme Court decision significantly reduced the restrictions that state bar associations could impose on lawyers with respect to their pricing and advertising practices. In a similar vein, the American Institute of Architects signed a consent decree with the Justice Department which prohibited the organization from publishing fee schedules for architectural services.

Perhaps of most significance for architects, however, was the start of the so-called "proposal age." Investigations in Maryland and Kansas, and other states, had revealed improper involvement of architects and engineers with state officials. Financial kickbacks were proven on many state projects. Formal proposals, it was felt, would eliminate or reduce the likelihood of contract awards made on the basis of cronyism or kickbacks. Starting in the government sector the requirement for proposals spread rapidly to all major clients. In 1984, for example, even a small church could receive as many as 20 detailed proposals on a modest sized assignment.

Marketing at RNL

In 1984, RNL was engaged in a number of marketing activities. In addition to proposal preparation, major activities included:

- Professional involvement in the business community by principals which provides contacts with potential clients. This included memberships in a wide variety of organizations such as the Downtown Denver Board, Chamber of Commerce, Denver Art Museum, etc.
- Participation in and appearances at conferences, both professional and business oriented.
- Daily review of the *Commerce Business Daily* (a federal publication of all construction projects) along with other news services that indicate developing projects.
- Maintenance of past client contacts. (RNL found this difficult but assigned the activity to its project managers.)
- Development of relationships with potential clients, usually by giving a tour through the office plus lunch.
- VIP gourmet catered lunches for six invited guests, held once a month in the office. These involved a tour of the office and lively conversation, with some attempt at subsequent follow-up.
- Participation in appropriate local, regional or national exhibits of architectural projects.
- Occasional publicity for a project or for a client.
- The "Cutting Edge."[1]
- An assortment of brochures and information on finished projects.
- Special arrangements with architectural firms in other locations to provide the basis for a variety of desirable joint ventures.

RNL participated in a number of market segments which it identified as follows, together with its view of the required approach:

---

[1]The Cutting Edge is an RNL publication, designed to inform clients and prospects about new developments in architecture and planning and about significant RNL accomplishments (see Exhibit 3 on page 244 for a typical issue).

EXHIBIT 3
RNL Publication

The Cutting Edge

Computer Usage Enhances Client Services

The combined use of Computer Aided Design (CAD) and a Hewlett Packard 250 computer are enabling RNL/Interplan to enhance its client services in a variety of ways.

The CAD system significantly increases productivity where drawings are essential. While the productivity increase varies from project to project, RNL Vice President Gary Merideth states that, overall, the computer is three times as fast as drawing by hand.

"This speed provides a number of advantages," says Merideth. "Additional time can be given to the design phase, as well as being spent in coordination of all building elements. The overall result is better service to the client, and a better end product at a lower cost."

Improved drawing accuracy results from the CAD system's use of geometric coordinates, and its several automated functions.

Because the screen can show different layers in a plan, the CAD system also permits rapid analysis of any potential conflicts between building systems. For example, a plan layer showing lighting, affords the architects the opportunity to check lighting levels at all work stations.

The net result to the client is overall savings in construction time and costs.

Merideth explains that the CAD system can be extremely beneficial to clients expanding in a number of locations using a prototype design. The CAD system can rapidly modify the basic prototype to satisfy the requirements of each new location.

Five functions available on the Hewlett Packard 250 will allow RNL/Interplan to assist clients in developing logical, long-term facility management plans, and to avoid crisis facilities and space management.

The space projections software element allows for definition of area space and personnel equipment needs within a sin-

gle department, or a department within a department, with five individual projection years. Information on furniture needs can also be incorporated into the program to aid in developing furniture budgets.

Using trend analysis software, past growth data and future projections can be compared together or individually to verify business or industry trends.

Computer Aided Design (CAD) allows RNL/Interplan to produce drawings which rapidly translate into usable spaces. For American Home Video, this meant the ability to open 60 new units within six months.

Interrelationships between departments can be examined with the vertical stacking software applications. This allows for the most advantageous placement of departments with a facility, enabling departments to function most effectively together in the future.

In the area of rental site decisions, lease modeling software allows RNL/Interplan's clients to closely compare different building or location alternatives on a wide range of criteria including cost per square foot, gross rentable area and available dates.

The net result is a tool for improved decision making and long-range facilities management, a critical cost tool for clients.

A Publication of   RNL Interplan

1576 Sherman Street   Denver, Co. 80203   (303)832-5599

Segment	Approach
Government	
City and County Governments	Personal selling, political involvement.
School Districts	Personal selling (professional educational knowledge required).
State Government	Political involvement, written responses to RFPs (Requests for Proposals, from clients), personal selling.
Federal Government	Personal selling, very detailed RFP response, no price competition in the proposal stage.
Private Sector	Personal selling, social acquaintances, referrals, Cutting Edge, preliminary studies, price competition.
Semi-private Sector (includes utilities)	Personal selling, Cutting Edge, referrals, continuing relationships, some price competition.

Net fee income and allocation of marketing expenses by major segments is given in the following table. The general feeling at RNL was that there is a lapse of 6 to 18 months between the marketing effort itself and tangible results such as fee income.

	1982		1983		1984 (est.)		1985 (est.)	
	Net Fee	Marketing Expenses	Net Fee	Marketing Expenses	Net Fee	Marketing Expenses	Net Fee	Marketing Expenses
Government	$ 800	$104	$1,220	$101	$1,012	$150	$1,200	$140
Private	1,376	162	1,261	140	1,200	195	1,616	220
Semi-private	88	11	118	24	100	25	140	30
Interiors	828	40	670	30	918	100	1,235	110
Urban Design	95	20	31	10	170	30	220	40
Total	$3,187	$337	$3,300	$305	$3,400	$500	$4,411	$540

Salient aspects of budgeted marketing expenses for 1985, by segment, were:

- **Government**. Heavy emphasis on increased trips to Omaha (a key Corps of Engineers location), Washington, and other out of state, as well as in state, locations plus considerable emphasis on participation in municipal conferences.

- **Private**. Personal contact at local, state and regional level with corporations, banks, developers and contractors plus local promotion through

Chamber of Commerce, clubs, VIP lunches, Cutting Edge, promotion materials and initiation of an advertising and public relations effort.

- **Semi-private**. Increased level of personal contact and promotional effort.
- **Interiors**. Major allocation of salary and expenses of a new full-time marketing person to improve direct sales locally plus other promotional support.
- **Urban design**. Some early success indicates that land developers and urban renewal authorities are the most likely clients. Planned marketing expense is primarily for personal contact.

Additional marketing efforts being given serious consideration included:

- A more structured marketing organization with more specific assignments.
- Increased visibility for the firm through general media and trade journals; paid or other (e.g., public relations).
- Appearances on special programs and offering special seminars.
- Use of more sophisticated selling tools such as video tapes, automated slide presentations, etc.
- Increased training in client relations/selling for project managers and other staff.
- Hiring a professionally trained marketing manager.
- Determining how the national firms market (i.e., copy the competition).
- Expansion of debriefing conferences with successful and unsuccessful clients.
- Use of a focus group to develop effective sales points for RNL.
- Training a marketing MBA in architecture versus training an architect in marketing.

RNL Clients

RNL described its clients as:

1. Having a long history of growing expectations with respect to detail, completeness, counseling and cost control.
2. Mandating the minimization of construction problems, including changes, overruns and delays.
3. Having an increased concern for peer approval at the completion of a project.
4. Having an increased desire to understand and be a part of the design process.

Extensive interviews of clients by independent market researchers showed very favorable impressions about RNL. Terms used to describe the firm included:

- Best and largest architectural service in Denver.
- Innovative yet practical.
- Designs large projects for "Who's Who in Denver."
- Long-term resident of the business community.
- Lots of expertise.
- Designs artistic yet functional buildings.

RNL's use of computer aided design systems was seen as a definite competitive edge. Others mentioned RNL's extra services, such as interior systems, as a plus, although only 35% of those interviewed were aware that RNL offered this service. In general, most clients felt that RNL had a competitive edge with regard to timeliness, productivity and cost consciousness.

Two major ways that new clients heard about RNL were identified. One was the contact RNL made on its own initiative when it heard of a possible project. The other was through personal references. All those interviewed felt advertising played a minor role and, in fact, several indicated they had questions about an architectural firm that advertises.

Clients who selected RNL identified the following as playing a role in their decision:

- Tours of RNL's facilities.
- Monthly receipt of the Cutting Edge.
- Low-key selling style.
- RNL's ability to focus on their needs.
- Thoroughness in researching customer needs and overall proposal preparation and presentation.
- RNL's overall reputation in the community.
- Belief that RNL would produce good, solid (not flashy) results.

Clients who did not select RNL identified the following reasons for their decision:

- RNL had less experience and specialization in their particular industry.
- Decided to stay with the architectural firm used previously.
- Decided to go with a firm that has more national status.
- Other presentations had more "pizazz."

Overall, clients' perceptions of RNL were very positive. There was less than complete understanding of the scope of RNL services but their current approach to clients received good marks.

Marketing Issues at RNL: Some Views of Middle Management

Richard von Luhrte joined RNL in 1979, following extensive experience with other firms in Chicago and Denver. In 1984 he led the firm's urban design effort on major projects, served as a Project Manager and participated actively in marketing. He came to RNL because he said the firm "fits my image." He preferred larger firms that have extensive and complementary skills. He commented on marketing as follows:

> RNL has a lot going for it. We have a higher overhead rate, but with most clients you can sell our competence and turn this into an advantage. I think RNL is perceived as a quality firm but customers are also concerned that we will gold-plate a job. I'd like to be able to go gold-plate or inexpensive as the circumstances dictate. But it's hard to convince a customer that we can do this.
>
> For many of our clients continuity is important and we need to convey that there will be continuity beyond the founders. RNL has done well as a provider of "all things for all people" and our diversification helps us ride through periods of economic downturn. On the other hand, we lose some jobs because we're not specialized. For instance, we haven't done well in the downtown developer market. We're starting to do more but if we had targeted the shopping center business we could have had 7 or 8 jobs by now. One way to operate would be to jump on a trend and ride it until the downturn and then move into something else.
>
> There's always the conflict between specialization and fun. We try to stay diversified but we ought to be anticipating the next boom. At the same time, there's always the problem of overhead. In this business you can't carry very much, particularly in slow times.
>
> I like the marketing part of the work but there's a limit on how much of it I can, or should, do. Plus, I think it's important to try to match our people with our clients in terms of age and interests, which means we need to have lots of people involved in the marketing effort.
>
> Oral presentations are an important part of marketing and we make a lot of them. You have to make them interesting and there has to be a sense of trying for the "close." On the other hand, I think that the presentation is not what wins the job, although a poor presentation can lose it for you. It's important that the presentation conveys a sense of enthusiasm and that we really want the job.

As Comptroller, Jane Washington was involved extensively in the firm's discussions about its marketing efforts. As she described the situation:

> There is little question in my mind that the people at the top are committed to developing a marketing orientation at RNL. But our objectives still aren't clear. For instance, we still haven't decided what would be a good mix of architecture, interiors and planning. Interiors is a stepchild to some. On the other hand, it is a very profitable part of our business. But it's not easy to develop a nice neat set of objectives for a firm like this. Two years ago we had a seminar

to develop a mission statement but we still don't have one. This isn't a criticism. Rather, it's an indication of the difficulty of getting agreement on objectives in a firm of creative professionals.

One problem is that our approach to marketing has been reactive rather than proactive. Our biggest marketing expenditure is proposal preparation and we have tended to respond to RFPs as they come in, without screening them for fit with targeted segments. From a budget standpoint we have not really allocated marketing dollars to particular people or segments, except in a pro forma kind of way. As a result, no one person is responsible for what is a very large total expenditure.

Another problem is that we don't have precise information about our marketing expenditures or the profitability of individual jobs. It would be impractical to track expenditures on the 500–1,000 proposals we make a year but we could set up a system that tracks marketing expenditures in, say, 10 segments. This would at least let individuals see what kind of money we're spending for marketing, and where. We also could change from the present system which basically measures performance in terms of variation from dollar budget to one that reports on the profitability of individual jobs. I've done some studies on the profitability of our major product lines but those don't tie to any one individual's performance.

Rita Mitchell, who had an MS in Library Science and Information Systems, joined RNL in 1981. Originally her assignment focused on organizing marketing records and various marketing information resources. In her new role as New Business Development Coordinator she had a broader set of responsibilities. According to Rita:

We definitely need some policies about marketing, and these ought to spell out a marketing process. In my present job I think I can help the board synthesize market information and so help to develop a marketing plan.

I do a lot of market research based on secondary data. For instance, we have access to Dialog and a number of other on-line databases, using our PC. Based on this research, and our own in-house competence, I think I can do some good market anticipation. The problem is what to do with this kind of information. If we move too fast, based on signals about a new market, there is obviously the risk of being wrong. On the other hand, if we wait until the signals are unmistakably clear they will be clear to everyone else and we will lose the opportunity to establish a preeminent position.

With respect to individual RFPs, our decision on which job to quote is still highly subjective. We try to estimate our chances of getting the job, and we talk about its fit with our other work but we don't have much hard data or policy to guide us. We don't, for instance, have a good sense of other RFPs that are in the pipeline and how the mix of the jobs we're quoting and the resulting work fits with our present work in progress. The Marketing Committee (consisting of John Rogers, Vic Langhart, Phil Goedert, Rich von Lurhte, Dick Shiffer, Rita Mitchell and, occasionally, Bob Johnson) brings lots of experience and personal knowledge to bear on this but it's not a precise process.

We have a number of sources of information about new construction projects: *The Commerce Business Daily* (a federal government publication), the *Daily Journal* (which reports on local government construction), the Western Press Clipping Bureau, Colorado trade journals and so forth. Monitoring these is a major activity, and then we have the problem of deciding which projects fit RNL.

Bob Johnson, a Project Manager and member of the Marketing Committee, commented:

The way the system works now we have four board members and 12 project managers, most of whom can pursue new business. They bring these opportunities before the Marketing Committee but it doesn't really have the clout to say no. As a result, people can really go off on their own. I'd like to see the committee flex its muscles a little more on what jobs we go after. But there's a problem with committing to just a few market segments.

Right now we're involved in something like 30 segments. If we're wrong on one it's not a big deal. But if we were committed to just a few then a mistake could have really serious consequences.

For many of us, however, the major problem is managing the transfer of ownership and control to a broader set of individuals. Currently the prospective owners don't really have a forum for what they'd like the company to be. My personal preference would be to go after corporate headquarters, high tech firms, speculative office buildings and high quality interiors. But there probably isn't agreement on this.

Marketing Issues: The Views of the Founders

Vic Langhart started his practice of architecture in 1954 and had taught design in the Architecture Department of the University of Colorado. He was instrumental in developing new services at RNL, including Interplan and SMS, Inc., and was heavily involved in training of the next level of management. In 1984 he supervised day-to-day operations and also served as President of Interplan and SMS, Inc. Looking to the future, Vic observed:

Our toughest issue is dealing with the rate of change in the profession today. It's probably fair to say there are too many architects today. But this is a profession of highly idealistic people, many of whom feel their contribution to a better world is more important than dollars of income and so will stay in the field at "starvation wages." We wrestle with the question of "profession or business?" but competition is now a fact of life for us. The oil boom of the 1970s in Denver triggered an inrush of national firms. Many have stayed on and we now have a situation where one of the largest national firms is competing for a small job in Durango. We're also starting to see more direct price competition. Digital Equipment recently prequalified 8 firms, selected 5 to submit proposals that demonstrated understanding of the assignment and asked for a separate envelope containing the price.

Our tradition at RNL has been one of quality. I think we're the "Mercedes" of the business and in the long haul an RNL customer will be better off economically. A lot of things contribute to this; our Interplan concept, for instance, but the key differentiation factor is our on-site-planning approach.

In 1966–1968 we were almost 100% in education. Then I heard that they were closing some maternity wards and we decided to diversify. Today we have a good list of products, ranging from commercial buildings to labs and vehicle maintenance facilities. In most areas the only people who can beat us are the super specialists and even then there's a question. Our diversification has kept our minds free to come up with creative approaches. At Beaver Creek, for example, I think we came up with a better approach to condominium design than the specialists. Plus, we can call in special expertise, if it's necessary.

Over the past several years we've had a number of offers to merge into national, or other, firms. We decided, however, to become employee owned. Our basic notion was that RNL should be an organization that provides its employees a long time career opportunity. This is not easy in an industry that is characterized by high turnover. Less than 10% of architectural firms have figured out how to do it. But we're now at 35% employee ownership.

I'm personally enthusiastic about Interplan. It has tremendous potential to impact our customers. In Seattle, for instance, a bank came to us for a simple expansion. Our Interplan approach, however, led to a totally different set of concepts.

We've had some discussion about expansion. Colorado Springs is a possibility, for instance. But there would be problems of keeping RNL concepts and our culture. We work hard to develop and disseminate an RNL culture. For example, we have lots of meetings, although John and I sometimes disagree about how much time should be spent in meetings. A third of our business comes from interiors and there is as much difference between interior designers and architects as there is between architects and mechanical engineers.

In somewhat similar vein, John Rogers commented:

In the 1960s RNL was primarily in the business of designing schools. We were really experts in that market. But then the boom in school construction came to an end and we moved into other areas. First into banks and commercial buildings. We got started with Mountain Bell, an important relationship for us that continues today. We did assignments for mining companies and laboratories. In the late 1960s no one knew how to use computers to manage office space problems and we moved in that direction which led to the formation of Interplan. We moved into local and state design work. One of our showcase assignments is the Colorado State Judicial/Heritage Center.

In the 1980s we started to move into federal and military work and this now represents a significant portion of our business. We have done some developer work but this is a tough market. It has a strong "bottom line orientation" and developers want sharp focus and expertise.

As we grow larger we find it difficult to maintain a close client relationship. The client wants to know who will work on the assignment but some of our staff members are not good at the people side of the business.

Currently we're still doing lots of "one of a kind" work. Our assignment for the expansion of the Rocky Mountain News building, our design of a condominium lodge at Beaver Creek, our design of a developer building at the Denver Tech Center are all in this category. A common theme, however, is our "on-site" design process. This is a process by which we make sure that the client is involved in the design from the start and that we are really tuned in to his requirements. I see this as one of our real competitive advantages. But I'm still concerned that we may be trying to spread ourselves too thin. Plus, there's no question that there is an increased tendency to specialization. "Shopping center architects," for example.

We need to become better marketers but we have to make sure that we don't lose sight of what has made us the leading architectural firm in Denver: service and client orientation.

Case 19

Texas Instruments: Global Pricing in the Semiconductor Industry

Per V. Jenster

B. Jaworski

Michael Stanford

Mr. John Szczsponik, Director of North American Distribution for Texas Instruments' Semiconductor Group, placed the phone back on its cradle after a long and gruelling conversation with his key contact at Arrow, the largest distributor of Texas Instruments' semiconductors. With a market-leading 21.5% share of total U.S. electronic component distributor sales in 1994, Arrow was the most powerful distribution channel through which Texas Instruments' important semiconductor products flowed. It was also one of only two major American distributors active in the global distribution market.

Arrow's expanding international activities had made it increasingly interested in negotiating with its vendors a common global price for the semiconductors it sold around the world. In the past, semiconductors had been bought and sold at different price levels in different countries to reflect the various cost structures of the countries in which they were produced. Semiconductors made in European countries, for example, were usually more expensive than those made in Asia or North America, simply because it cost manufacturers more to operate in Europe than in the other two regions. Despite these differences, large distributors and some original equipment manufacturers were becoming insistent on buying their semiconductors at one worldwide price, and were pressuring vendors to negotiate global pricing terms. Szczsponik's telephone conversation with Arrow had been the third in the past month in which the distributor had pushed for price concessions based on international semiconductor rates:

> Yesterday they discovered that we're offering a lower price for a chip we make and sell in Singapore than for the same chip we manufacture here in Dallas for the North American market. They want us to give them the Singapore price on our American chips, even though they know our manufacturing costs are higher here than in the Far East. We can't give them that price without losing money!

This case was developed by Profs. Per V. Jenster, CIMID, B. Jaworski, USC, and Michael Stanford as a basis for classroom discussion rather than to highlight effective or ineffective management of an administrative situation.

In anticipation of increased pressure from Arrow and other large distributors, Szczsponik had organized a meeting with Mr. Kevin McGarity, Senior Vice President in the Semiconductor Group and Manager of Worldwide Marketing, to begin developing a cohesive pricing strategy. They were both to meet with Arrow executives in four days, on February 4, 1995, to discuss the establishment of common global pricing for the distributor.

Szczsponik knew that he needed to answer some basic questions before meeting with Arrow:

> Global pricing might make Arrow's job of planning and budgeting a lot easier, but our different cost structures in each region make it difficult for us to offer one price worldwide. How do we tell Arrow, our largest distributor, that we aren't prepared to negotiate global pricing? Alternatively, how can we reorganize ourselves to make global pricing a realistic option? And what implications will a global pricing strategy have in relationship to other international customers?

With only two hours to go before his meeting with McGarity, Szczsponik wondered how they could respond to Arrow's request.

The Semiconductor Industry

Semiconductors were silicon chips which transmitted heat, light and electrical charge and performed critical functions in virtually all electronic devices. They were a core technology in industrial robots, computers, office equipment, consumer electronics, the aerospace industry, telecommunications, the military and the automobile industry. The majority of semiconductors consisted of integrated circuits made from monocrystalline silicon imprinted with complex electronic components and their interconnections (refer to Exhibit 1 for the key categories of semiconductors). The remainder of semiconductors were simpler discrete components that performed single functions.

The pervasiveness of semiconductors in electronics resulted in rapidly growing sales and intense competition in the semiconductor industry. Market share in the industry had been fiercely contested since the early 1980s, when the once-dominant U.S. semiconductor industry lost its leadership position to Japanese manufacturers. There followed a series of trade battles in which American manufacturers charged their Japanese competitors with dumping, and accused foreign markets of excessive protectionism. By 1994, after investing heavily in the semiconductor industry and embarking on programs to increase manufacturing efficiency and decrease production costs, American companies once again captured a dominant share of the market (refer to Exhibit 2 for the Top Ten Semiconductor Manufacturers).

In 1994, total shipments of semiconductors reached $99.9 billion, with market share divided among North America (33%), Japan (30%), Europe (18%) and Asia/Pacific (18%). The industry was expected to reach sales of $130 billion in 1995, and $200 billion by the year 2000. To capture growing demand in the industry, many semiconductor manufacturers were investing heavily in

EXHIBIT 1
Key Semiconductor Categories

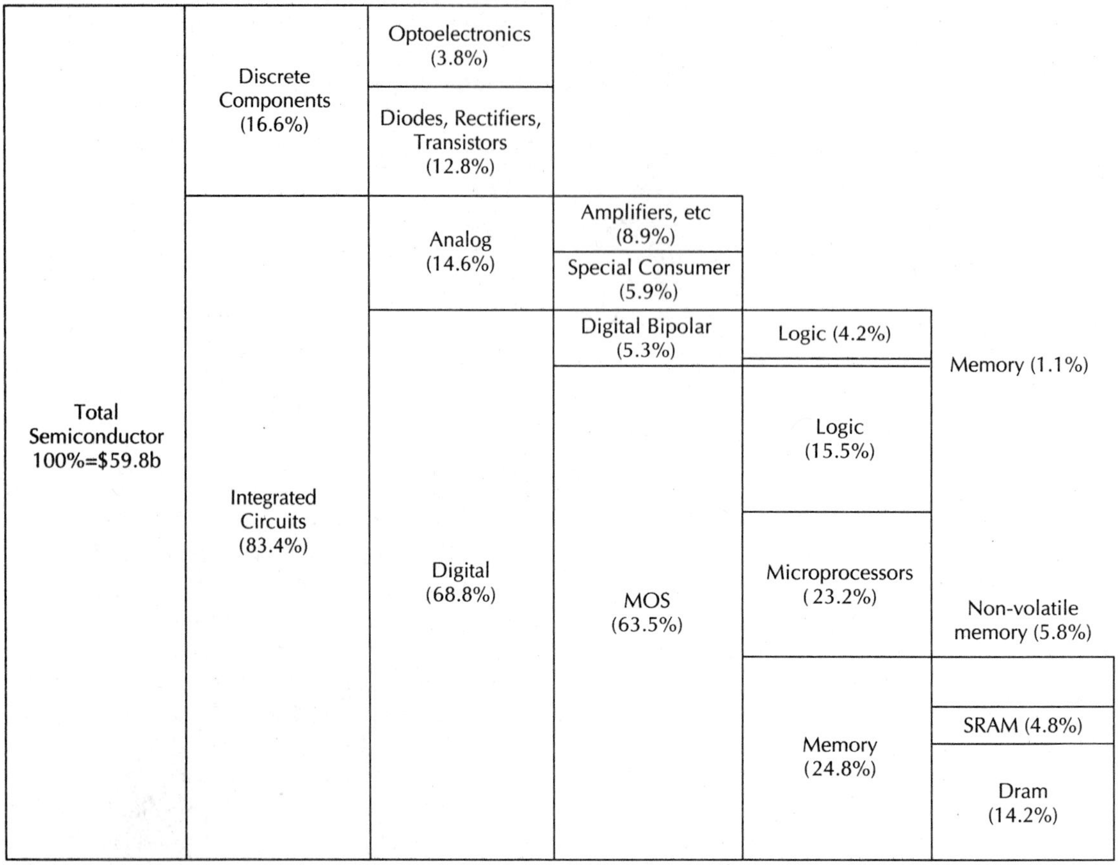

Total Semiconductor 100%=$59.8b	Discrete Components (16.6%)	Optoelectronics (3.8%)			
		Diodes, Rectifiers, Transistors (12.8%)			
	Integrated Circuits (83.4%)	Analog (14.6%)	Amplifiers, etc (8.9%)		
			Special Consumer (5.9%)		
		Digital (68.8%)	Digital Bipolar (5.3%)	Logic (4.2%)	Memory (1.1%)
			MOS (63.5%)	Logic (15.5%)	
				Microprocessors (23.2%)	Non-volatile memory (5.8%)
				Memory (24.8%)	SRAM (4.8%)
					Dram (14.2%)

Source: Analysts' Reports

increased manufacturing capacity, although most industry analysts expected expanding capacity to reach rather than surpass demand. Combined with record low inventories in the industry and reduced cycle times and lead times, a balancing of supply and demand was causing semiconductor prices to be uncharacteristically stable. The last three quarters of 1994 had brought fewer fluctuations and less volatility in the prices of semiconductors (refer to Exhibit 3 for a History of Semiconductor Price Stability) despite their history of dramatic price variations.

Regardless of price stability, most semiconductor manufacturers were looking for competitive advantage in further cost reduction programs, in devel-

EXHIBIT 2
Top Ten Semiconductor Manufacturers

	1980		1985		1990		1992	
	Company	**Sales $**	**Company**	**Sales $**	**Company**	**Sales $**	**Company**	**Sales $**
1.	Texas Instruments	1,453	NEC	1,800	NEC	4,700	Intel	5,091
2.	Motorola	1,130	Motorola	1,667	Toshiba	4,150	NEC	4,700
3.	Philips	845	Texas Instruments	1,661	Motorola	3,433	Toshiba	4,550
4.	NEC	800	Hitachi	1,560	Hitachi	3,400	Motorola	4,475
5.	National	745	National	1,435	Intel	3,171	Hitachi	3,600
6.	Intel	630	Toshiba	1,400	Texas Instruments	2,518	Texas Instruments	3,105
7.	Hitachi	620	Philips	1,080	Fujitsu	2,300	Fujitsu	2,250
8.	Fairchild	570	Intel	1,020	Mitsubishi	1,920	Mitsubishi	2,200
9.	Toshiba	533	Fujitsu	800	Philips	1,883	Philips	2,041
10.	Siemens	525	Advanced Micro Devices	795	National	1,730	Matsushita	1,900

Source: Analysts' Reports

oping closer relationships with their customers, and in creating differentiated semiconductors which could be sold at a premium price. Integrated circuits were readily available from suppliers worldwide, and were treated as commodity products by most buyers. Any steps manufacturers could take to reduce their production costs, build stronger relationships with customers or create unique products could protect them from the price wars usually associated with commodity merchandise.

Texas Instruments Incorporated

Established in 1951 as an electronics company serving the American defense industry, by 1995 Texas Instruments was a leading manufacturer of semiconductors, defense electronics, software, personal productivity products and materials and controls. Its 1994 sales of $10.3 billion, a 21% increase from the previous year, was split among components ($6.8 billion), defense electronics ($1.7 billion), digital products ($1.66 billion) and metallurgical materials ($177 million). 1994's profits of over $1 billion came almost entirely from its components business. Components made a profit of $1.1 billion, while defense electronics made $172 million (refer to Exhibit 4 for Income Statements).

1994's performance was record-breaking for Texas Instruments. It marked the first time the company exceeded sales of $10 billion and over $1

EXHIBIT 3
History of Semiconductor Stability

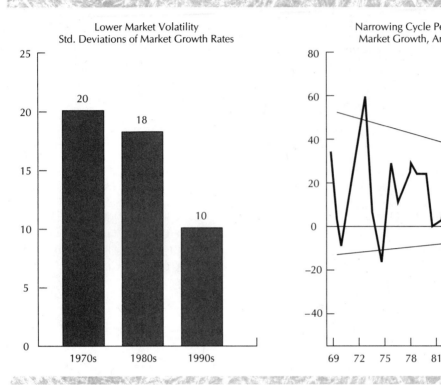

Lower Market Volatility
Std. Deviations of Market Growth Rates

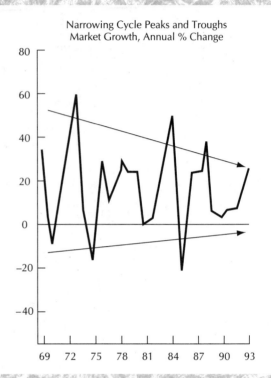

Narrowing Cycle Peaks and Troughs
Market Growth, Annual % Change

EXHIBIT 4
Income Statements

Texas Instruments Key Financial Numbers

	1994	1993	1992	1991	1990
Sales ($M)	10,200	8,523	7,049	6,628	6,395
Operating Margin (%)	17.5	16.8	9.1	5.0	0.7
Net Profit ($M)	715	459	254	169	0.7
Working Capital ($M)	1,800	1,313	961	813	826
Long-Term Debt ($M)	800	694	909	896	715
Net Worth ($M)	2,975	2,315	1,947	1,955	2,358

billion in profit, and followed a history of volatile financial results. Although Texas Instruments was often considered the pioneer of the American electronics industry—it was one of the first companies to manufacture transistors and developed the first semiconductor integrated circuit in 1958—it struggled to maintain its position in the electronics industry through the intense competition of the 1980s. After receiving market attention with its development of such innovative consumer products as the pocket calculator and the electronic wrist watch, Texas Instruments lost its business in both markets to cheap Asian imports. Meanwhile, it struggled to keep up with orders for its mainstay business in semiconductors through the 1970s, only to see demand for its pioneer semiconductors shrink during the recession of the early 1980s. Faced with heavy losses in many of its core areas, Texas Instruments reorganized its businesses to foster innovation and embarked on a program of cost-cutting. By 1985, the company had refocused its efforts on its strengths in semiconductors, relinquishing market dominance in favor of greater margins. While the company continued to grow its technological leadership, it also sought to build stronger relationships with its customers.

By 1995, Texas Instruments had developed a strong position in the electronics industry, despite its reputation as a technological leader rather than a skilled marketer of its products. The company continued to remain powerful in the semiconductor industry, in part because it was the only American company that continued to manufacture dynamic random access memory chips in the face of fierce Japanese competition in the 1980s. The company had manufacturing sites spread throughout North America, Asia and Europe, and was pursuing its strategy of increasing manufacturing capacity and developing manufacturing excellence.

The Semiconductor Group

In 1958, Texas Instruments engineer Jack Kilby developed the first integrated circuit, a pivotal innovation in the electronics industry. Made of a single semiconductor material, the integrated circuit eliminated the need to solder circuit components together. Without wiring and soldering, components could be miniaturized and crowded together on a single chip. Only a few years after Kilby's invention, electronics manufacturers were demanding these integrated circuits, or chips, in smaller sizes and at lower costs, a move that led to unprecedented innovation in the electronics industry. Soon chips became a commodity, and chip manufacturers relied on high-volume, low-cost production of reliable chips for success. Only a few manufacturers had strong positions in the production of differentiated semiconductors.

Forty years after its discovery, Texas Instruments still remained dependent on its semiconductor sales, which fell primarily in integrated circuits. The Semiconductor Group, a part of the Components Division, had total sales of $2 billion in 1994, the third consecutive year in which Texas Instruments' semiconductor revenues grew faster than the industry. The company's return to financial success in the early 1990s was based on its strong performance in semiconductor sales and profits, both of which were at record levels in 1994. Management in the company expected semiconductor sales to continue to grow strongly, and were planning heavy capital expenditures on new or expanded plants in the United States, Malaysia and Italy to increase the company's capacity.

The Semiconductor Group divided its business into two segments: standard products and differentiated products. Standard semiconductors, which accounted for 90% of the Group's sales, included products which could be substituted by competitors. Standard semiconductors performed in the market much like other products for which substitutes were readily available. Texas Instruments, like its competitors, competed for market share in these commodity products based primarily on the price it offered to original equipment manufacturers and distributors. The remaining 10% of the company's semiconductor business came from differentiated products, of which Texas Instruments was the sole supplier. Because substitutes for these products were not available on the marketplace, differentiated products commanded higher margins than their standard counterparts and were receiving greater strategic emphasis on the part of Group management. While the company continued to hold a strong position in standard semiconductors, it was searching for a strategy that would allow it to achieve a higher return on development and manufacturing investments. Managers at Texas Instruments believed that higher returns were possible only by developing more successful differentiated semiconductors.

Electronics Distribution Market

Texas Instruments sold its semiconductors through two channels: directly to original equipment manufacturers or through a network of electronics distributors. Szczsponik estimated that 70% of the Group's U.S. customers dealt directly with Texas Instruments. The remainder bought their semiconductors through one or more of the seven major semiconductor distributors that served the North American market (refer to Exhibit 5 for information on the Top Electronics Distributors). Whether an original equipment manufacturer dealt directly with Texas Instruments or bought from a distributor depended on the manufacturer's size. The largest original equipment manufacturers were able to negotiate better prices from semiconductor manufacturers than were the distributors and therefore bought directly from the manufacturers. Because mid-sized and small original equipment manufacturers were fragmented, and thus more difficult to serve, these customers were served more efficiently through the distribution channel. Szczsponik explained:

> The semiconductor market can be divided into three tiers. Fifty % of our sales in semiconductors go to the top tier of perhaps 100 large electronics manufacturers who deal with us directly. The next 46% of sales come from 1,400 medium-sized companies at the next level, half of whom deal directly with us and half of whom buy through distributors. The remaining 4% of sales are to 150,000 smaller companies at the bottom tier in the market, who deal only through distributors. Distributors have a clearly defined role in servicing mid-sized and small buyers.

EXHIBIT 5
Top Electronics Distributors

Company		1994	1993	1992	1991	1990
Arrow Electronics	Sales ($b)	3.973	2.536	1.622	1.044	.971
	Share (%)	21.5	17.4	14.8	11.0	10.2
Avnet	Sales ($b)	3.350	2.537	1.690	1.400	1.429
	Share (%)	18.1	17.4	15.4	14.8	15.0
Marshall Industries	Sales ($b)	.899	.747	.605	.563	.582
	Share (%)	4.8	5.1	5.5	6.0	6.1
Wyle Laboratories	Sales ($b)	.773	.606	.447	.360	.359
	Share (%)	4.2	4.2	4.1	3.8	3.8
Pioneer Standard	Sales ($b)	.747	.540	.405	.360	.343
	Share (%)	4.0	3.7	3.7	3.8	3.6
Anthem	Sales ($b)	.507	.663	.538	.420	.408
	Share (%)	2.7	4.6	4.9	4.4	4.3
Bell Industries	Sales ($b)	.395	.308	.282	.257	.239
	Share (%)	2.1	2.1	2.6	2.7	2.5

Source: Lehman Brothers, "Electronic Distribution Market," December 22, 1994

Distributors were considered to be clearinghouses for the semiconductor industry. Each distributor dealt with products from all the major semiconductor manufacturers. For example, Arrow Electronics sold semiconductors manufactured by Motorola and Intel as well as those made by Texas Instruments. The distributors specialized in handling logistics, material flows, sales and servicing for electronics manufacturers who were either too small to negotiate directly with the major semiconductor manufacturers or lacked sufficient expertise in logistics management. In addition, the distributors sometimes kitted packages of different products together for the smaller original electronics manufacturers as an added service. Some also performed varying scales of assembly operation.

The electronics distribution network had originally consisted of a large group of smaller companies. By 1995, however, industry consolidation had left almost 40% of the distribution market in the hands of its two largest competitors, Arrow Electronics and Avnet. The seven largest distributors captured 58% of sales in the market (refer to Exhibit 6 for the Sales and Market Shares of the Top Distributors). This trend toward consolidation had had a major impact on the nature of the relationships among semiconductor manufacturers and the distributors through which they sold their products. According to Szczsponik:

Fifteen years ago, 30 distributors were active in the industry and it was clear that the semiconductor manufacturers controlled the distribution network. With the consolidation of the distribution network into only 7 or 8 powerful players,

EXHIBIT 6
Total Sales and Market Share of Top Distributors

		1994	1993	1992	1991	1990
Industry Total	Sales ($b)	16.22	12.95	10.18	9.06	9.17
Top 25	Sales ($b)	13.41	10.69	8.11	7.10	7.20
	Share (%)	82.7	82.5	79.7	78.4	78.5
Top 7	Sales ($b)	10.75	8.42	6.36	5.05	5.00
	Share (%)	58.0	57.9	57.9	53.5	52.5
Top 2	Sales ($b)	7.32	5.07	3.31	2.44	2.40
	Share (%)	39.6	34.8	30.2	25.8	25.2

Source: Lehman Brothers, "Electronic Distribution Market," December 22, 1994

however, power is shifting. It's hard to say if we are more important to them or they are more important to us.

Price Negotiations and Global Pricing Issues

Since the vast majority of semiconductors were considered commodity products, the buying decisions of distributors were based almost entirely on price. Distributors forecasted the demand for the various semiconductor products they carried and negotiated with vendors for their prices. Since semiconductor prices were notoriously volatile, the price levels negotiated between manufacturers and distributors played a vital role in the distributors' profitability. The Semiconductor Group at Texas Instruments combined the practices of forward pricing and continuous price negotiations to set prices with its distributors.

Forward Pricing. The cost of semiconductor manufacturing followed a generally predictable learning curve. When a manufacturer first began producing a new type of chip, it could expect only a small percentage of the chips it produced to function properly. As the manufacturer increased the volume of its production, it both decreased the costs of production and increased the percentage of functioning chips it could produce. This percentage, termed "yield" in the industry, and the standard learning curve of semiconductor manufacturing together had a large impact on the prices semiconductor manufacturers set for their products (refer to Exhibit 7 for the Price Curve of Semiconductor Products). This yield was important to TI; a 7% increase in overall yield was equivalent to the production of an entire Wafer Fab, an investment of $500 million.

According to Jim Huffhines, Manager of DSP Business Development in the Semiconductor Group, managers could predict with considerable accuracy the production cost decreases and yield improvements they would experience as their production volumes increased:

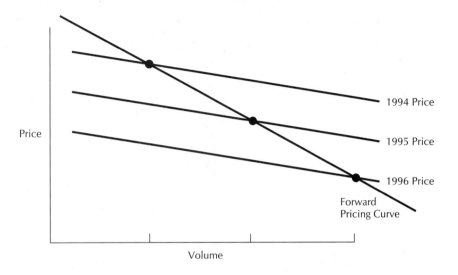

EXHIBIT 7
Forward Pricing Curve

We know the manufacturing costs for any given volume of production. We also know that these costs will decrease a certain percentage and our yields will increase a certain percentage each year. These predictions are the basis of the forward prices we set with both original equipment manufacturers and distributors.

Continuous Price Adjustments. Production costs and yield rates were not the only contributing factors to price levels for standard semiconductors: market supply and demand also played a powerful role in establishing prices. As a result of volatile prices caused by shifts in supply and demand, distributors often held inventories of semiconductors that did not accurately reflect current market rates. To protect distributors from price fluctuations, most semiconductor manufacturers offered to reimburse distributors for their over-valued inventories. Szczsponik explained:

> Semiconductor prices have fallen by 15% over the past 9 months. If Arrow bought semiconductors from me for $1.00, 9 months ago, they are worth only 85¢ now. Arrow is carrying a 15% "phantom" inventory. If Arrow sells those semiconductors now, we give it price protection by agreeing to reimburse it the 15¢ it has lost per semiconductor over the past three quarters.

At the same time, distributors had at their disposal sophisticated systems for monitoring semiconductor prices from each of the major manufacturers, and were constantly in search of price adjustments from vendors when placing their orders. Szczsponik continued:

Distributors have access to the prices of products from all the semiconductor manufacturers at any given time, and some anywhere in the world. The largest distributors have a staff of 20 to 30 people shopping around continuously for the best prices available for different types of semiconductors, add to this group a staff of accountants managing the price adjustment transactions. For example, they may call us to say that Motorola has quoted them a certain price for a semiconductor, and ask us if we can beat their price. In total, we get close to 150,000 of these calls requesting adjustments from distributors a year, and do over 10% of our sales through price adjustments. I have 10 people on my staff who negotiate price adjustments for distributors: 5 answer their calls, and 5 work with our product managers to make pricing decisions. These decisions are critical: if we make a mistake in our pricing, we lose market share in a day that can take us 3 months to recapture. At the same time, through our negotiations with distributors, we capture masses of data regarding the pricing levels of our competitors and the market performance of our different products. This data is critical to our ability to set prices.

As the distribution network consolidated into a small number of powerful companies, Szczsponik had begun to notice that his price negotiations were increasingly focused not only on beating the competition in North America, but on beating prices available around the world, including those of TI in other regions. With distributors becoming more active in the global market, they were more often exposed to semiconductor price levels from Europe and Asia. Industry analysts expected North American distributors to become more active in global markets as they pursued aggressive expansion campaigns in Europe and Asia. Although Texas Instruments' current contracts with its distributors prevented them from selling semiconductors outside of the region in which they were purchased, distributors were becoming insistent on access to freer global supplies and markets. While the concept may have appeared reasonable to the distributors, it was somewhat more complicated for Texas Instruments. Kevin McGarity elaborated:

> Because business is different everywhere in the world, our international distribution channels have evolved independently. They aren't subjected to the same costs, and don't operate under the same methods and calculation models. In the United States, for example, we offer a 30-day payment schedule for our customers. If they don't pay us within 30 days, we cut off their supply, no matter who they are. Italy operates under a 60-day schedule. Europeans include freight in their prices; we don't in North America. Finally, the cost of producing semiconductors varies by country. Europe tends to be more expensive than North America or Asia, simply because their infrastructure is more costly. So when one of our large distributors phones with the Singapore price for semiconductors manufactured in Düsseldorf, he is crossing boundaries that may be invisible to him but are very real to us.

Preparing for the Meeting with Arrow

With sales of almost $4 billion in 1994, Arrow Electronics was the largest semiconductor distributor in North America, of which TI products accounted for approximately 14%. Its aggressive growth had taken the company into global markets, and had given it increased exposure to fluctuating price and exchange levels in different international markets. Seeking to minimize its costs, Arrow had begun to pressure semiconductor manufacturers to set standard global prices for each of their products. Motorola, one of Texas Instruments' largest competitors in the semiconductor industry, was rumored to be preparing for global pricing. Management at Texas Instruments, however, was unsure of the wisdom of moving toward global pricing. According to Szczsponik, the pros and cons to global pricing seem unevenly balanced:

> The large distributors want global pricing to reduce their costs and simplify their planning. But does it make sense for us? Right now our organization, calculation systems and costs in each country are too different for us to offer standard global prices. There are other things to consider as well. If we set global prices, we will no longer continue our price adjustment negotiations with the distributors. This may save us the cost of staffing our negotiations team, but it also takes away from us a powerful tool for gathering information on our customers' prices and our product performance. As soon as we stop negotiating price adjustments, we lose our visibility into the market.

To prepare for his discussion with McGarity and forthcoming meeting with Arrow Electronics, Szczsponik knew TI had to make some fundamental decisions regarding global pricing. Who held the power in the relationships Texas Instruments had with its distributors? What was the source of the negotiating strength each party would bring to the meeting? Finally, what position should the Semiconductor Group take with its distributors regarding global pricing? And what organizational implications would such a decision imply?

Toro: Industrial Flavors

Per V. Jenster

Bethann Kassman

On a crisp fall morning in October 1990, Jan Emil Johannessen, strategic planner for the Toro division of Rieber & Son, sat in his Bergen office looking out at the fiord as he contemplated the analysis work on his desk. The firm's decision to formally enter into the industrial sales of flavor products had been a challenge to its traditional capabilities in consumer culinary products. In August 1987, management had decided to follow up a 1985 entrepreneurial effort to pursue international opportunities in the industrial flavors business more rigorously (refer to Exhibits 1, 2a, and 2b). By early 1990, however, they realized that the firm's organizational resources and competencies were already being stretched to the limit. As Jan Emil Johannessen stood reflecting on the European industrial flavor market, he had to acknowledge that some tough decisions needed to be made regarding Rieber & Son's future strategy in culinary products and the international industrial strategy in particular.

Company Background

Rieber & Son A/S

The history of Rieber & Son A/S began in 1817 when the Rieber family from the Kingdom of Wurtemberg set off from Amsterdam aboard the sailing vessel "De Zee Ploeg." Their destination was Philadelphia, but fate led them to Norway instead. During a terrible storm, their ship was wrecked off the Norwegian coast, but they were towed to safety into the harbor of the small town of Bergen.

In 1839, one of the sons of the Rieber Family, Paul Gottlieb, founded the company Rieber & Son A/S, which engaged in various activities, particularly in the building materials sector.

This case was prepared by Professor Per V. Jenster and Research Assistant Bethann Kassman as a basis for class discussion rather than to illustrate either effective or ineffective handling of a business situation. This case was developed as part of an Institutional Project on the Management of Internationalization, and conducted in collaboration with the Industrial Development Authority of Ireland.

EXHIBIT 1
Meeting Notes
Rieber & Son A/S
Bergen 21.10.85

Action Program—Marine Powders

Objectives:

Primary: To be the world's leading producer of natural marine powder products.

Secondary: Within marine powder, we will aim to have an assortment of products which cover the main needs of our customers.

We will aim always to be able to deliver products when needed.

We must be competitive with respect to price and quality of our products.

Budget:

	1986	1987	1988	1989
Turnover (NOK mn.°)	7.5	9.5	12.0	15.1
(actual sales)	6.5	9.0	13.5	15.0

°SF1.00 = NOK 4.50
Source: Company records

Building materials became the mainstay of the company for the following 100 years. By 1990, Rieber & Son A/S was a professionally managed Norwegian Group with a turnover of approximately NOK 3,200 million and 2,850 employees. The key business areas were Food, Packaging Materials, Road Surfacing Materials and Building Materials. (Financial data is presented in Exhibit 3.) The company's activities ranged from industrial production to purely commercial operations. Each division had its own business concept and, likewise, separate strategies for reaching its objectives.

Over and above the ordinary advantages of group structure, such as management, availability of resources and systems common to all members of the group, there initially seemed to be few points of contact between the individual divisions within the company. Yet, the firm stressed that there was, in fact, commonality in financial management and, to a certain degree, corporate philosophy. Nevertheless, day-to-day synergies among the divisions were limited due to the highly diversified nature of the overall Group.

Strategy and Future Outlook

Rieber & Son's attention had been directed towards the domestic markets with 80% of the company's sales taking place in Norway. Overseas sales were made within defined niches and were mainly linked to the packaging sector

Status:

We have a solid point of departure in our own production of dried food products to a discerning market. This has forced us to develop a large degree of proprietary processes and semifinished products of high quality.

With this in mind, we have developed sales of NOK 20 mn., with a satisfactory/good profitability.

The selling process is largely characterized as technical sales to a target group consisting of the technical decision makers in flavor houses and other food producers.

Marine Products

Product/Markets:

- 2 fish powders (one high end, another somewhat lower in costs)
- Crab powder
- Lobster powder
- Shrimp powder
- Oyster powder

Strategic Position:

High quality of powders, with some brought forth with own proprietary processes based on natural raw materials. The emphasis is on long shelf life for these products.

Critical Success Factors!   Raw materials and replication of recipes of consistent nature.

Future Possibilities:

As of now, our customers have primarily been flavor houses. This has been a good fit with our pure taste systems, without formulated mix combinations, e.g., hydrolysate spices, starches. However, we assume that the food producers are demanding products with a higher value-added dimension.

Thus, we see a need for

- less expensive products, e.g., shrimp products
- mixed raw materials (different levels of value added)
- developing other extract products in collaboration with universities
- possibly looking for acquisition candidates producing similar or complementary powder products.

Bouillon (Hydrolysate)

Sales 1987—NOK 9 mn.
Budget 1988—NOK 12 mn.

Product/Markets

Internationally, we sell formulated bouillon, that is, hydrolysate with meat extract, spices, etc. Here, our main clients are in the U.K.

EXHIBIT 2a

Although we do not have strong competitive advantages in pure hydrolysate, we have developed talent in formulating end products. Thus, we have been functioning as a flavor house, and are offering our products in formulated condition to our customers.

Strategic Perspective

We have strong talent in formulating products vis-a-vis end producers, based on our own experience in vacuum-based products.

Future Developments

We believe that further efforts in this area should follow the direction pursued in the U.K. This will be emphasized after the purchase of our British agent. Such opportunities may be pursued elsewhere.

Meats

Status

Our own developments in meat-based products, particularly for use in micro ovens, are very encouraging. However, as of yet no international sales have been made, partly due to our cost disadvantage created by import restrictions.

Future Developments

Viewed in light of our effort in bouillon, we see certain possibilities which are being pursued.

Budgets

As per attachment.

Source: Company records

EXHIBIT 2b
Forecast in NOK

	Growth	1987	1988	1989	1990	1991	1992	1993	1994
Existing Marine powders	10%	9.2	12	14	16	18	20	22	24
Formulated Marine powders			1	3	5	7	8	10	12
Acquired mixes			12	13	14	15	16	17	18
Total Marine			25	30	35	40	44	49	54
Dried meats			3	6	9	12	15	18	21
Peas, lentils			1	2	3	4	4	4	4
Flavour blends	7%		200	214	228	245	262	280	300
Boullion			9	12	17	22	27	32	37
Total			238	264	292	323	352	383	416

EXHIBIT 3
Financial Information on Main Areas

(Figures in NOK mill.)	Food		Packaging Materials		Road/ Asphalt		Building Materials		Joint Costs/ Elimination		The Group	
	1989	1988	1989	1988	1989	1988	1989	1988	1989	1988	1989	1988
Income Statement												
Net sales	697	657	691	645	654	551	1,102	1,032	− 2	− 15	3,142	2,870
Of which, exports etc., represent	51	49	331	320	24	29	243	163	—	—	649	561
Contribution from sales and other income	424	399	336	315	306	265	383	376	6	2	1,455	1,357
Operating costs	−152	−143	− 86	− 78	− 80	− 67	−132	−139	− 10	3	−460	−424
Wages/social security costs	−135	−133	−166	−147	−154	−132	−170	−159	− 35	− 36	−660	−607
Depreciations	− 22	− 27	− 31	− 29	− 30	− 28	− 21	− 18	− 4	− 4	−108	−106
	115	96	53	61	42	38	60	60	− 43	− 35	227	220
Balance Sheet												
Net operating capital[1]	38	63	68	57	9	− 27	242	209	−142	−120	215	182
Capital assets	180	183	200	196	125	111	178	173	223	161	906	824
Net working capital	218	246	268	253	134	84	420	382	81	41	1,121	1,006
Key Figures												
Yield ratio[2]	46%	37%	20%	25%	31%	33%	16%	19%	—	—	22%	24%
Turnover rate[3]	2.8	2.5	2.6	2.6	4.7	4.6	2.8	3.0	—	—	2.7	2.7
Profit margin[4]	17%	15%	8%	10%	7%	7%	6%	6%	—	—	8%	9%
Average Number of Employees	578	573	735	701	524	517	884	884	79	78	2,800	2,753

[1] Net operating capital
   Receivables plus stock less interest-free credits.
[2] Yield ratio
   Operating result plus financial revenues in percent of average net working capital.
[3] Turnover rate
   Net sales divided by average net working capital.
[4] Profit margin
   Operating result plus financial revenues in percent of net sales.
The average net working capital used in the calculation of the key figures appears as a weighted average of the consumption of capital throughout the whole year, and is thus not directly comparable with the above net working capital which is obtained from the balance sheet at 31 December.

and natural stone products. Rieber & Son had concentrated its efforts on growth within sectors often considered "established areas."

The company's strategy was twofold. On the one hand, it was working for a logical further development of all 10 divisions both nationally and internationally. This strategy included both the growth of the divisions' own products, the acquisition of companies well suited to fit into existing divisions and the achievement of competitive advantage through strategic alliances. On the other hand, the firm was seeking further development by taking over various companies in areas where it could achieve a sounder strategic position through the takeover.

Toro

In 1948, Rieber & Son laid the foundation for its current food division, Toro Foods, by introducing Bouillon Cubes, rapidly followed by related dehydrated food products. By 1989, sales of Toro Foods had reached NOK 697 million (refer to Exhibit 3 for the division's financial results). Toro Foods was the most profitable of the 10 Rieber divisions.

With production concentrated in Norway, the firm was proud of its expanding plant outside Bergen, equipped with sophisticated technology for the production of dried products. Air and vacuum dehydration processes were used in internal production while raw materials processed by freeze, drum and spray drying techniques were acquired. By early 1990, annual production had exceeded 11,000 tons of dehydrated foods and ingredients for consumers, catering markets and other food producers.

The firm could proudly point to significant domestic success, despite the presence of large multinational producers, such as Nestlé (Maggi), CPC (Knorr), and Unilever (Lipton). The Toro brand brought the Rieber organization impressive market share results in the Norwegian culinary retail sector with the following products:

Soups	87%
Stews	95%
Sauces	86%
Casseroles	99%
Bouillons	75%

In catering, the firm held similarly strong positions with an overall estimated market share of 70%. (Refer to Exhibit 4 for details of the Toro Organization.)

Introduction of Dehydrated Fish Soup

Historically, Toro was a major world player in the whale extract market. The extract was dehydrated and used to add flavor to processed food products. When whaling declined during the 1950s and 1960s, Toro used the knowledge

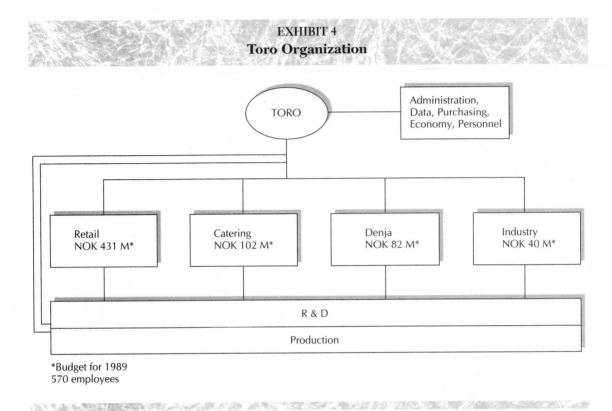

EXHIBIT 4
Toro Organization

TORO

Administration,
Data, Purchasing,
Economy, Personnel

Retail
NOK 431 M*

Catering
NOK 102 M*

Denja
NOK 82 M*

Industry
NOK 40 M*

R & D

Production

*Budget for 1989
570 employees

gained in the whaling industry and applied it to other food ingredients. Real success came in 1959 when Toro developed and launched dried soups in sachets. Four years later another breakthrough came when Toro produced dehydrated fish soups. Dehydration, the oldest form of conservation, was actually a fairly simple idea. Water, removed at the beginning of the process, was then added at the time of preparation, without losing any of the product's major nutritive value. The problem was to retain the finer flavors of the raw materials. It was this problem that Toro solved and marketed, initially to the Norwegian market, followed shortly by entry into the Scandinavian market.

Catering

The Toro Catering Division was created as a specialized organization responsible for developing the catering product range, and for sales and marketing in the Norwegian catering market. The division achieved total sales of NOK 102 million in 1989. Despite a decline in the total market, Toro's Catering Division enjoyed an increase in volume. The product line was expanded to include products produced in Toro's factory as well as products from several Norwegian and foreign suppliers of dried, canned, chilled and frozen foodstuffs.

Toro's Catering Division's strategy was to combine high quality with labor saving properties for the user and advantageous prices. The products were specially developed for and adapted to use in catering establishments. The end users of these products included all types of catering establishments such as hotels, restaurants, transport companies and the armed forces. Distribution took place through wholesalers and ships' chandlers.

Expanding to Other Markets

Toro was the undisputed retail market leader in Norway with 90% of the market in dehydrated foods comprising a wide range of products—soups, casseroles, stews, sauces, etc. The quality of these dehydrated foods was perceived to be very high. In addition, Toro had adapted its products to Norwegian tastes.

With the successful launch of its dehydrated fish soup in the 1960s, Toro decided early on to expand into the neighboring Scandinavian market. Through an informal process, the other four Nordic countries (Sweden, Finland, Denmark, Iceland) were targeted. Toro embarked on a niche strategy using distributors and local people to test the market, then tailor the product to the demands of the broader Scandinavian marketplace. Considerable money was spent, especially in Sweden as it was the largest and most attractive market, but the outcome was less successful than had been anticipated.

For 25 years, the market had been dominated by three big players: Unilever, Nestlé, and CPC. These players had the resources to stay in the market long enough to become profitable, had successfully covered the market for many years and had a product line similar to Toro's. Thus, Toro made the decision to retreat from the branded products market in all the other Scandinavian countries except Iceland.[1] In both Sweden and Denmark, however, Toro's name had become recognized, a fact the firm used to its advantage by producing private label products for two of the largest chains in both countries. Toro sold through the Swedish Cooperative Society in Sweden under the Foodia name and in Denmark under the IRMA label. Toro's experience in the Nordic market did not discourage the company from trying to enter the wider European market with export of branded retail lines. The strategy was to develop unique products in Norway and exploit them with niche marketing on the Continent.

In the early 1970s, Toro had developed a range of seafood specialties through a specific process technology for producing tastier fish powder. These products were believed to be superior to those available in Europe. The strategy objective was to introduce the product into as many countries as possible in order to achieve volume through market penetration (in contrast to its first international effort where Toro targeted only the "home market," Scandinavia). However, it soon became apparent that there were many issues which needed to be addressed in order to succeed in the Continental European markets.

---

[1]In Iceland, a market equivalent in size to the city of Bergen, Toro was able to maintain the dominant position.

First, Toro faced Unilever, Nestlé, and CPC, which together accounted for 80–85% of the market share in dehydrated foods worldwide. These competitors commanded considerable resources and, through sheer volume, were able to bring economies of scale to their product development and market maintenance costs which Toro could not match. In other than fish soups, Toro was at a cost disadvantage because it imported raw ingredients for use in its products and then often exported the finished products to the same countries that the ingredients had come from. In addition to being unable to meet a vast set of packaging requirements, Toro received little support from distributors and agents, who were largely selected using the simplest criteria. This resulted in inconsistent marketing plans which varied from country to country and were insufficient to penetrate the Continental market.

Sales remained flat for 10–15 years while production problems increased due to packaging requirements and small order runs. By 1985 Toro had decided that the Continental niche was too small and required excessive effort for too little profit. It decided to stop selling to the retail market in most European countries, but to keep a presence in those countries where it had the best agents and the highest sales volume. Thus, Toro increased its marketing in Spain, the United Kingdom and the United States, while moving more into private label sales for specific stores in Continental Europe.

By 1986, Toro found at this point in time that the retail market for its products was declining in both absolute and relative terms. Private label sales were largely sold through cooperatives, which were also losing business. Therefore, Toro decided to discontinue its strategy of entering new retail markets in the dried and dehydrated product lines, and to confine its retail food sales primarily to the Norwegian market. Meanwhile, the company discovered an emerging market for expansion—wholesale flavors to the larger European community.

Dabbling in Industrial Ingredients

In the late 1980s, sales remained flat in the finished product sector but continued to rise in the raw materials market. Toro management looked at these results and realized that, over the years, the firm had developed a unique knowledge in the production of seafood and fish powders. Toro also had a strong research and development base in the process and product technology for dry foods, especially relating to taste. Management concluded, therefore, that Toro not only had a role as supplier of finished culinary products to major retailers, but it also had a viable role helping other producers with product formulation and process expertise. To larger firms, Toro offered its special knowledge in fish products, and, to smaller companies, research and development support.

In addition, Norway suffered from a tariff burden on the shelf ready products it exported to the EEC, so it made sense for Toro to sell its knowledge and raw materials to others. During a large strategy meeting in 1988, management decided to limit retail sales to the Nordic market and treat Europe as its industrial market. Having made this decision, Toro withdrew from the finished product sector so as not to compete directly with its potential industrial customers. It was felt that the product segment where Toro had an advantage over its competitors was in the development of natural savory products related to seafood. Consequently, this was the area that Toro targeted for expansion within the European industrial flavors market.

The strategy quickly became a challenge to the various functional disciplines within the organization, partly due to its broad scope. Over the next year and a half, as experience increased, the strategy narrowed down to focus on different distribution methods in various countries and on a more limited product range specifically geared to convenience foods, dried and frozen foods. Using advanced technology and a combination of available first class raw materials, Toro produced a powder with high quality taste. Its R&D unit produced flavor systems which were sold to other culinary companies for use in their products. As demand increased, the majority of powders and granulates of various fish were exported either as semi-manufactured goods, such as stocks and sauces, or as raw material. By the end of 1989, 50% of industrial sales were direct sales to convenience food producers, with the remaining 50% to flavor houses and mixers.

Worldwide Flavor Industry

Because flavors and fragrances used similar materials and technology in production, most producers made both types of products, customarily called the Flavors and Fragrances (F&F) industry. However, the market dynamics (i.e., driving forces for growth) and the bases for competition differed between the flavors and fragrances segments. Fragrances included combinations of natural and/or synthetic raw materials, whereas flavors tended to be less exotic and were usually based on something found in nature.

Growth and profitability of the flavors segment (retail and industrial) had to be viewed in the context of the F&F industry as a whole. Until the late 1970s, the world F&F industry was seen as an extraordinarily high performer. Industry profitability approximated 15% of sales in the mid- to late 1960s and 10% in the 1970s. Since that time, slower growth and increased competitive pressures had reduced profitability to about 6–7% industry-wide. For the past 10 years, real sales growth averaged 5–6% per year, reaching $5.8 billion in 1987. Because of widely fluctuating world currencies, especially the dollar, actual growth was difficult to estimate; however, expected growth was projected to be roughly 5% per year through 1992.

Valued at nearly $2.6 billion in 1987, flavors comprised nearly 45% of the total F&F market, with 15% of the total flavor market from savory flavors. Western Europe and the United States were the largest regional markets, together accounting for 63% of world flavor sales. Japan was the third major market. Consumption in the rest of the world was significantly lower. However, the USSR and the Far East were identified as having the greatest growth potential.

Industry Trends

In the 1960s, artificial flavors accounted for 75% of the market, while natural flavors accounted for 25%. These percentages were reversed by the late 1980s. Although natural flavors were more costly to develop and could not withstand all techniques of food processing, most of the major flavor houses oriented their development programs to meet the growing demand for natural flavors. As the costs of flavor ingredients continued to rise and product development became costly and complex, strategic acquisitions became an important means of company growth. Most of these acquisitions were made for market reasons: to gain a base in a particular regional market, to acquire a market niche, to allow for R&D expansion in an area, or to acquire a talented flavorist or a key food account.

Despite the high level of merger and acquisition activity, the world flavor industry remained highly fragmented. This was not expected to change, although Arthur D. Little, a management consulting firm, predicted that an acquisition slowdown would occur through the early 1990s. Continued success in the industry required an enhanced working relationship with customers in order to understand their changing needs better and thus be able to offer more applications research and technical service.

Companies in the F&F business spent significantly more on R&D than did most participants in their end-use markets. R&D spending varied by company size; the large multinationals spent 7–12% of sales on R&D, while the smaller companies spent 2–5%. Heavy investments in biotechnology focused on developing ways to produce better quality natural flavors at a lower cost. Major research was also conducted to develop more stable natural flavor systems to protect against the effects of processing, packaging, and ingredient interaction. High temperature short-time (HTST) food processing, retorting and microwave cooking, in particular, presented challenges and opportunities to the flavor houses. New techniques to further improve the stability and shelf life of flavors was also being investigated.

In the industrial flavor segment of the market, the growth of processed foods as a percentage of total food consumption was expected to continue through the 1990s, with particularly strong growth in Northern Europe. An increase in sales of savory flavors was anticipated as well. Because of the high cost of research and development, product development would continue to be contracted out to flavor houses, mixers, and raw material suppliers. Overall, ingredients were seen as a profitable area of activity since they did not demand the heavy marketing expenditure required to promote food products to the retail trade. Furthermore, the considerable increase in demand for convenience foods was likely to continue to grow throughout the 1990s, creating new opportunities to expand the market.

Industrial Competitors

The largest producers of seafood products were the Japanese; however, industrial sales from Japanese companies were concentrated almost exclusively in the Far East. In Europe, competition was confined to a limited number of small

EXHIBIT 5

Companies with 1987 Flavor and Fragrance Sales of $100 Million or More

Company/Parent	Headquarters	1987 World Sales (MM$)
International Flavors & Fragrances (IFF)	United States	745
Quest International/Unilever	United Kingdom/Netherlands	635
Givaudan/Hoffmann-La Roche	Switzerland	480
Takasago Perfumery	Japan	440
Haarman & Reimer/Bayer	West Germany	350
Firmenich	Switzerland	240
Dragoco Gerberding	Germany	350
Bush Boake Allen (BBA) Union Camp, U.S.	United Kingdom	140
Florasynth-Lautier	France	130
Fritzsche Dodge & Olcott/BASF	Germany	130
PFW Division/Hercules	United States	120
Universal Group/Universal Foods	United States	110
Roure	France	100
Hasagawa	Japan	100
Total		3,870

Note: In today's world monetary system of fluctuating currencies, all calculations in current U.S. dollars, or any other currency, are subject to considerable exchange rate distortions. Thus, the dollar sales for each of these companies do not necessarily reflect the company's true size or position relative to the other major players.
Sources: Annual reports and Arthur D. Little, Inc., estimates.

niche players, primarily located in Norway and France. Of these companies, only one (Isnard Lyraz located in France) produced a high quality product similar to that produced by Toro.

Toro's major competitors in the retail sector (Maggi, CPC, Unilever) were not direct competitors with Toro in the industrial seafood powder area. Although there were areas where some competition existed (HVP and bouillons), by and large, these flavor houses as well as others were Toro customers who purchased and reprocessed Toro's products.

The top 15–20 participants in the F&F industry accounted for the majority of flavor sales; 14 of these companies had sales of $100 million or more (refer to Exhibit 5). The remaining sales were dispersed among some 100 other major producers and nearly 1,000 smaller companies around the world. Thus, in spite of the concentration of sales at the top, fragmentation of the industry was not reduced, primarily because many of the hundreds of small flavor houses were not vulnerable to takeover and because many new companies had entered the business due to the low entry barriers.

Buying Process

Flavor was one of the major differentiating factors among various brands within a food product category. Safety, nutrition, convenience and price were also important, but taste acceptance by the consumer was essential to the creation of brand loyalty. In spite of the importance of flavors to the food industry, food processors exerted considerable pressure on suppliers of food additives. These pressures included demand for natural ingredients, high quality but low cost products, and product diversity to meet the varied tastes of the increasingly sophisticated consumer.

Responding to buyer influence led to tremendous growth in new product introduction (according to Productscan/Marketing Intelligence Service, more than 8,000 new food products were introduced to the European markets in 1987). The trend towards an expanding product market was expected to continue. All of which required a corresponding development in the area of new flavor systems. Product obsolescence—caused by changes in consumer preferences, habits and lifestyles—also occurred at a higher rate in the industry. These factors, combined with the competitive pressures stemming from the food industry, forced flavor suppliers to increase their internal capabilities in product application, basic research and development, technical service, and marketing.

The eruption of more freedom in Eastern Europe and the Soviet Union foreshadowed economic opportunities comparable to the period of international business expansion in the 1950s and 1960s. The internationalization of tastes and increasing health concerns among consumers in all countries presupposed heavy investments in research to keep pace with innovation, or changing the focus to a compounder or blender. As the costs of producing innovative flavors increased, more producers looked to others in the industry for product development, technical expertise and market knowledge.

Many flavor houses predicted that the 1990s would bring a continuation of the flavoring fads of the 1980s—exotic flavorings, natural flavorings and easy to prepare foods. However, the area receiving the greatest interest was in natural flavorings and "healthy" foods. Toro had a fairly large advantage in this area in that all its products were 100% natural, unlike the Japanese whose products were mixed with enhancers and additives. In essence, Toro's processing consisted of taking the frozen blocks of fish filet, crushing and boiling them, drying and milling them. Although this process sounded simple on paper, its technology was quite advanced for the complex production of seafood.

Toro's Initial Efforts in Industrialization

Until 1986, Toro had grown through retail sales and finished products. The decision to enter the European industrial market required a change in sales, distribution and production. Staff that had been working with retail sales and technology was quickly shifted to serve the requirements of an industrial market. It soon became evident that the organization had difficulty with this transition. The staff was not trained to deal with the different requests from industrial customers; specific recipes had to be developed and sold, creating an impact on both R&D and sales; new country-specific regulatory requirements had to be incorporated into the product specifications; and production had to be adjusted to accommodate short runs. There were, however, a number of key strengths which Toro built upon as it entered this new environment. Backward integration (the processing of its own raw materials) continued to be handled by the processing department. The vertical integration allowed Toro to take raw ingredients, process them to specification, and produce a finished product for sale to the marketplace similar to the way it had done in the retail market. Its large, well-staffed research and development department was already familiar with developing a wide range of formulations, and Toro's presence in the retail market lent credibility to its entry into the industrial market.

Sales Department

Focusing on the industrial market required specific sales tasks and behavior which differed from those used in the retail market. Initially, Toro went in with its standard products, but discovered that the customer wanted tailored or specially developed products within short time frames. The salesmen were not prepared to deal with the technical issues raised by industrial clients and were unfamiliar with the amount of effort required to meet these demands, particularly by the research and development department. It was felt that a sales force with technical skills was needed. To meet this new demand, R&D staff were teamed with the sales staff. In addition, one technical sales manager was recruited from the factory and one was hired from the outside. This new staff and technical focus allowed for greater communication between the client and R&D at an earlier stage in the customer relationship, and eliminated basic misunderstandings as to availability of products and the time frames required for production. It raised, however, a different problem—taking research and development staff away from its other tasks. In-house education as well as attendance at seminars helped enhance the skills of both the sales staff and the R&D staff. In fact, one individual from research and development was moved into the sales department to enhance the technical understanding of this unit.

Export sales were split 50/50—half on finished goods for the consumer and half on semifinished product and raw material. Rieber/Toro's biggest markets for selling fish powders were West Germany (25%), Benelux (20%), the USA (10%) and France (10%). Spain, as a large fish-eating nation, was on the verge of becoming a big market for the company, with sales running at 10% of total industrial turnover. The rest of the sales went to the Far East, Australia and Scandinavia. In Europe, the products were sold through agents; in the Nordic countries, the product was sold directly. In 1989, Rieber/Toro's decision to apply a model of direct sales representation in the UK which added an additional 10% of sales. An English staff of two salespeople and a technical person were obtained when a small distributor was purchased in an effort to gain a better understanding of the English customers' requirements. Small distributors were usually selected in the various countries, because they were more responsive to

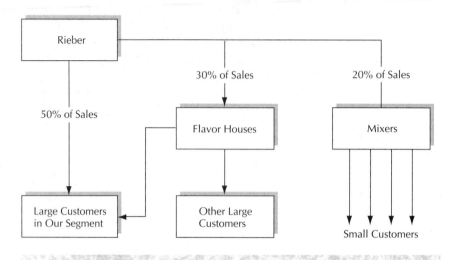

EXHIBIT 6
Sales to End User

Toro's needs than were the larger distribution houses, which were perceived to be less loyal. As a common sales strategy, the largest producers and mixers were targeted priorities for both the agents and the sales force.

Large food producers buying directly from Toro accounted for 50% of sales. Selling directly enhanced Toro's ability to offer advice on usage and to provide blended products. Direct sales to flavor houses accounted for 30% of sales. The flavor houses made a living out of extracting taste from raw materials and selling it to the customer at a high markup. Also, the flavor houses had access to an international market which Toro neither knew nor understood. The remaining 20% of sales were to mixers who serviced smaller companies and other industries, such as those in meat-based products (refer to Exhibit 6).

Research and Development

With a budget equivalent to $2.4 million invested each year (representing 2.6% of total turnover), the company was proud of its applied developmental work. The R&D department was responsible for dealing with a customer's technical questions as well as formulating new products and controlling existing ones. With 45 staff members working in its development laboratories and pilot plant, the company was continually testing new methods and ways of handling ingredients.

An industrial market focus, however, strained the R&D department's resources. Used to having one to two years' lead time to develop products for the company to sell, the department's position had reversed—it now had to produce products to demand as well as develop new products. As the company focused its emphasis more on the industrial component, staff who had been working in the retail area were moved to the industrial area. Most of these people needed time and education in order to understand the new business focus as well as to deal with the new regulatory requirements demanded by the various countries in which Toro was now selling. Ensuring quality also needed additional resources to comply with the changing requirements of data and documentation. But, perhaps the biggest change was that, as orders came in, products had to be tailor made, reformulated and produced under very tight time lines to meet customer demand. This situation created a lot of internal pressure.

To deal with these new demands, R&D focused on building up its staff to deal professionally with individual customers. Technical staff were assigned to travel with the sales staff and to communicate directly with clients. By being on the scene, the technical staff were able to lay out the product requirements and to identify problem areas early in the process. Within the company itself, increased communication with all departments, but particularly with sales and manufacturing, was emphasized.

Being located so far from the market made it imperative that Toro do everything possible to facilitate communication and product delivery. This strategy required a large investment in new equipment, as well as in personnel training and continually helping the staff to adapt. There were, however, some economies of scale which surfaced. Some recipes were able to be used across borders and, in some cases, industrial projects provided the testing ground for retail products. The research and development department had faced the challenge of being responsive to the developmental needs of the industrial environment well. Nevertheless, continuing the effort to maintain a strong research focus was of some concern to the department manager.

Production

Production problems centered around the difficulties created by small runs as opposed to the larger runs common for products in the retail market. This change affected scheduling and equipment as well as the process used. R&D staff were often needed in the factory to provide hands-on expertise during small trial runs. The short timetables requested by customers exacerbated the issues. To meet these new production requirements, specific small batch, dedicated equipment was purchased. R&D staff continued to be involved in production runs, particularly pilot runs which focused on developing products. The buying department found alternative sources for shellfish in order to have the necessary resources on hand for production to meet client demand. Although communication among the various departments had improved, the increased interaction among the departments involved in production required having constant communication about, and evaluation of, the problem areas.

A New Way of Working

The development of flavorings and natural additives for the international food market forced many changes in the day-to-day operations and the overall aspects of the business. The need for technical and production staff to be located closer to the clients—especially those smaller companies located in Europe—was acknowledged. A strategy was developed which included acquisition of a network of smaller companies already in the industrial market in Continental Europe. Distribution networks were expanded and staff requirements in R&D, Export, and Manufacturing were under constant review. Contacts with flavor houses and agents were expanded. This intense evaluation involving the entire Toro division was geared to speed up and facilitate entry into the industrial market.

With over 40 years of retail marketing and a strong presence in the Norwegian market, Toro had consistently relied on its technical formulation and product expertise. The changing retail environment and the opening of international borders implied that Toro would have to use those strengths to face the many challenges which lay ahead. Jan Emil Johannessen was optimistic that Toro would meet the challenges and succeed in its new industrial environment.

Van Moppes-IDP Limited

H. Michael Hayes

In November 1983, after a turbulent turnaround year, Ian W. Marsh, Managing Director of Van Moppes-IDP Limited (VMIDP), was considering the next steps needed to build on the past year's work and to position the firm for future growth and profitability. In particular, he was considering an offer by corporate staff to take advantage of PIMS (Profit Impact of Market Strategy), a program which, it was felt, might help in developing and implementing the firm's business strategy.

Background

Formed in 1981 by a merger between L.M. Van Moppes Limited and Impregnated Diamond Products Limited, the firm was a leader in ultra-hard technology products for cutting, grinding, sawing and drilling equipment for the engineering, glass processing and construction industries. Despite bright hopes for its prospects, the new company had not done well. Hard hit by a worldwide recession and a severe decline in diamond prices, the firm sustained severe losses in 1981 and 1982. When Ian Marsh was appointed Managing Director in November 1982, he had a clear sense that if the firm could not be turned around, its parent, Foseco Minsep, would seriously consider selling the business or shutting it down.

As a total stranger to the ultra-hard technology business, the first year was not an easy one for Marsh. In his first few weeks he was faced with a number of difficult personnel decisions in order to establish his own team, while at the same time making sure that key expertise was retained. Simultaneously, he had to take immediate steps to stem the losses and to learn the business. Personally convinced that the business could be turned around, a key challenge for Marsh was to convince members of the organization that it could survive, if it did the right things.

This case was written by Professor H. Michael Hayes as a basis for class discussion rather than to illustrate either effective or ineffective handling of an administrative situation.

Copyright © 1989 by IMEDE, Lausanne, Switzerland. The International Institute for Management Development (IMD), resulting from the merger between IMEDE, Lausanne, and IMI, Geneva, acquires and retains all rights. Not to be used without written permission from IMD, Lausanne, Switzerland.

By November 1983, the picture had brightened. Losses had been stemmed and the personnel situation had stabilized. Serious problems remained, however. According to Marsh:

> I was convinced that we were not focusing on the customer as we should and that we had serious product and service quality problems. The problem was how to get the organization more customer and quality oriented and how to insure that this orientation got translated into appropriate action.

At this time, corporate staff informed Marsh that it had become a member of the Strategic Planning Institute (SPI) and that they would fund his use of the PIMS (Profit Impact of Market Strategy) data base and SPI consulting services if he decided on their use. Marsh knew, generally, that the PIMS data base represented the detailed experience of some 3,000 businesses and that many businesses had found this data base useful in their strategic planning. He was not sure, however, just how the data base or SPI consultants might be used to help VMIDP. He had heard that the concepts were quite sophisticated and that he and his staff would have to devote a lot of time to working with PIMS.

In evaluating the offer from corporate headquarters, he tried to weigh his need for help in formulating the right strategy for the business against the time he and his staff would have to commit, and the relative uncertainty about the benefits a PIMS study would provide.

The Ultra-Hard Technology (UHT) Industry

Major markets for diamond products were the aircraft, motor vehicle, glass processing, general engineering and civil engineering industries. In the manufacturing industries, few components were produced without involving the industrial diamond at some stage. In the aircraft industry, for instance, engine components such as rotor shafts, guide vanes and turbine blades were all precision ground, with grinding wheels formed by single point, multipoint or rotary type diamond dressers. With more carbon fibre, resin compacts and glass-filled materials, diamond type drills and diamond plated bandsaws were increasingly required. In the motor vehicle industry, engine components were precision ground, turned or bored with diamond tools. In the glass industry, spectacle lenses were production milled, and all kinds of flat glass was edged, bevelled or drilled using diamond wheels and tools. In the construction and mining industries, a wide variety of diamond impregnated drills and saws were used to cut or machine concrete, granite, marble or other rock formulations.

Historically, these markets had been served by a host of small specialized firms, making an extensive array of products, sold in relatively small volume. While some products could be standardized (e.g., saws for the construction industry), products for engineering businesses were sometimes actually designed for a specific machine tool in one customer's plant. Principal product categories were diamond tipped tools, diamond impregnated grinding wheels and devices, and diamond impregnated saws and drills. (See Exhibit 1 for a list of VMIDP products.)

EXHIBIT 1
Partial List of VMIDP Products

Application	Type of Product	Brand Name
Machining	Diamond Boring Machining Tools	DIATIPT
Dressing	Dragoon Type Diamond Dressers	DRAGOON
Grinding	Single Point Diamond Wheel Truers	DIATRU
Measuring	Diamond Indenters, Gauge Anvils, and Tracer Points	DIATEST
Lapping	Laboratory Graded Diamond Powder	DIADUST, DIALAP
Profiling	Adjustable Head Production Turning Tool	DIAPAK
Truing	Magazine Type Diamond Wheel Truers	DIATRIM
Truing	Multi-Point Dressing Tools	COMMANDO, CENTURION

Many firms were closely associated with, or grew out of, diamond merchants. In the early days of the industry, international expansion was the norm as diamond merchants looked for markets for the growing accumulation of industrial diamonds produced by diamond mining companies. In some instances only the sale of industrial diamonds was involved. In others, manufacturing operations were established. The product's high value to weight ratio facilitated participation in export markets. Specialized requirements, however, tended to emphasize local production and sales. Thus, the predominant pattern in recent years was to manufacture locally for local markets.

For many years the price of the final product was dominated by the diamond content. With a continuing rise in diamond prices, there was little emphasis on manufacturing economies. With the introduction of artificial diamonds, first by GE and then by DeBeers, and then a decline in natural diamond prices, industry economics were significantly changed. It appeared, however, that many firms had still not adapted to the new situation. While diamonds continued to be the principal element used for UHT cutting and grinding, silicon carbide was also being used, and cubic boron nitride (CBN) appeared to have great potential as a superabrasive material.

Van Moppes-IDP Limited

VMIDP was an operating company of Foseco Minsep, an international specialty chemicals group manufacturing and selling a wide range of products and services, mainly to industrial customers, worldwide. Headquartered in Birmingham, England, Foseco Minsep had a 1987 profit on ordinary activities before tax of £35.2 million on a turnover of £515.1 million. The group was comprised of over 100 operating companies spread across 35 countries. Management control of these diverse operations was exercised by a Group Executive, with operating companies reporting through to members of the Executive on a predominantly regional basis.

Foseco Minsep had three principal operating sectors: FOSECO, which supplied chemical products to the world's foundry and steel industries; Fosroc, which supplied chemical products for the building, construction, mining and tunnelling industries; and Unicorn, with specialized expertise in hard materials technology for applications of natural and synthetic diamonds for industrial use, abrasive products and systems, as well as drilling systems and equipment for ground investigation and extraction.

Unicorn began to take its present form in the 1960s when two leading British abrasive manufacturers, the Universal Grinding Wheel Company Limited and English Abrasives Limited, merged. Shortly afterward, they were joined by international diamond merchants and diamond tool manufacturers L.M. Van Moppes & Sons Limited. Expansion continued and operations were developed in North and South America, Europe, Scandinavia and Japan. In 1980 Unicorn became part of Foseco Minsep. By 1989, Unicorn comprised three principal groups: Diamond Products[1]; Bonded Coated and Abrasives; and Electro-Minerals & Media.

L.M. Van Moppes & Sons Limited was founded by Louis Meyer Van Moppes in 1893 shortly after his arrival in London from Amsterdam. Founded principally as a diamond merchant, the firm moved gradually into the manufacturing of diamond tipped tools. In 1950 its headquarters were established at Basingstoke, England. By 1970, when the firm was acquired by Unicorn, it had a worldwide network of sales offices and manufacturing activities.

Impregnated Diamond Products Limited (later IDP) began in Antwerp, Belgium, in 1932 when Peter Neven invented and patented a process for manufacturing an abrasive for the stone, optical and engineering industries. This process involved mixing crushed industrial diamonds with iron and other metal powders, heating the mixture to the sintering point and pressing. In the early part of World War II, the plant was "spirited" to Gloucester where it played an important role in the war effort. In 1959 it was acquired by Universal Grinding Wheel, one of Unicorn's predecessors.

In May 1981 the UK diamond tools business of L.M. Van Moppes Limited was merged with IDP. Already, for a number of years, the two companies had been sharing marketing and sales resources and had jointly contributed to the funding of the R & D Laboratory at Gloucester. The relocation of another Unicorn company, which had shared the Gloucester manufacturing site with IDP, made space available in Gloucester for the diamond tools business, and the Basingstoke operation was shut down.

---

[1]The Diamond Products Group included the Belgian Tool Company in Belgium, Precidia SA in France, LM Van Moppes & Sons in Italy, Nippon Van Moppes, Ltd. in Japan, Svenska Unicom AB in Sweden, and Indimant in West Germany.

EXHIBIT 2
Financial Results 1982 and 1983 (£ 000)

	1982	1983
Total sales	6,481.5	5,827.5
Cost of sales	4,738.5	4,134.0
Gross margin	1,743.0	1,693.5
Distribution	78.0	78.0
Royalties	21.0	36.0
Selling and technical	1,249.5	946.5
Administration	511.5	484.5
Operating profit	(117.0)	148.5
Interest (receivable)/payable	474.0	82.5
Non-operating (income)/expense	99.0	295.5
Net profit before tax	(690)	(229.5)
Factored sales	1,812.0	1,659.0
Factored materials	1,228.5	1,195.5

November 1983

As Ian Marsh recalled:

> When I came here in late 1982, it was clear we were facing serious problems. Losses in 1981 had been £1.5 million, on sales of around £5 million. Predictions for 1982 were not quite as bad, £0.7 million (see Exhibit 2 for the December 1982 profit and loss statement), but the situation was still very bleak.
>
> Foseco had bought Unicorn in 1980. When diamond prices dropped by half, it was discovered that much of the stock was redundant or very slow moving. Normal group accounting policies required writing off redundant inventory after a year, but an exception had been made for diamonds, on the premise that "diamonds were forever." It was clear that our policy had to change and, in 1981 and 1982, we took some large write-offs to reflect the realities of the situation. Much of this effort was led by John Cowley who, as acting managing director, was my predecessor. John also had started the process of analyzing products for their growth potential. He had another full-time job, however. There was a real limit on what he could do, and it was obvious that much more needed to be done.
>
> It was generally felt that the management team lacked credibility, both with the work force and the head office in Birmingham. Some of the products that had been transferred from Basingstoke turned out to be money losers, even though they had been making money at Basingstoke. We had serious productivity problems and morale was terrible. Although the predominant view was that there was no chance of turning the business around, there seemed to be little sense of urgency about the situation. The managing board was still having its customary gin and tonic every day at lunch.

I knew I was going to have to take a number of actions which were going to inflict considerable pain. At the same time, I had to give everybody as much good news as possible, although there wasn't much good news to give.

My first step was to restructure my management team. I moved, or replaced, the directors for technical, sales and marketing, finance and production. We first focused our attention on the high scrap rates and low productivity. This resulted in a number of confrontations with the unions, but we made it clear to them that we had no choice. We didn't have time to figure out what the problems were with the Basingstoke products, so we closed one or two of them down and subcontracted their manufacture. We gave no wage increases the first year. In 1984 we tied the wage increase to agreements that gave us considerable more flexibility in work practices. We put much tighter controls on ordering material.

At the same time, we started a program of company briefings once a month, department by department. I felt it was critical for everyone in the organization to understand our situation and know what progress we were making. For instance, we made sure that everyone in the plant knew when we made a customer breakthrough. It was also important to get lower management levels to buy into what we were doing. Involving them in the communication process forced them to accept the "responsibilities of management." As soon as possible, we established a profit sharing scheme.

My view was that we needed to think of the turnaround in four stages. Stage one involved stemming the losses. Stage two involved consolidating, or trimming back. My goal for stage three was to achieve a 30% return on capital employed (ROCE) and a 10% return on sales (ROS). A real dilemma during these first three stages was how far could we go in cost cutting without hurting our ability to move into stage four—where I wanted to focus on growing the business. My basic assumption, however, was that we could preserve the core strengths of the business, so our real challenge was to devise an appropriate strategy and then organize ourselves to focus on doing the right things in the right way. If we were successful, I was convinced we could meet some aggressive sales and profit goals.

Products and Markets

The best way to organize the company was a complex question. As Table 1 shows, the firm served a variety of markets with a diverse product line.

Diamond products were also used in a wide array of other industries. Diamond wire dies, for instance, were used by lighting equipment manufacturers, and diamond knives were used by eye surgeons. Over time, VMIDP had developed products for these applications and a host of others.

When Marsh first joined VMIDP, the company was organized along functional lines. Although there was some sense of different markets, profits were calculated only for the total business. The salesforce tended to be organized along industry or market lines, but within the plant there was little or no industry or market focus. As Marsh put it:

> I had a feeling that we needed to reorganize the company, but I wasn't sure along what lines or how far to go. After all, we are a small organization and the idea of splitting still further seemed to have many problems.

TABLE 1
Principal Markets and Products

Markets	Products
Aircraft industry Automotive industry	Dressers, drills, bandsaws, truers, turners, indenters, grinding wheels
Glass industry	Grinding wheels, milling tools, diamond powder, smoothing pellets
Construction industry Mining industry	Segmental saws, core drill bits

We had another problem. Although we didn't keep books that way, it was my view that some parts of the business were less profitable than others. I wasn't sure whether we should prune back those businesses that were unprofitable now or those which had less profit potential in the long run.

Rotary truers, for instance, were going downhill fast. We had serious quality and productivity problems, and turnover had dropped to less than £200,000. Mining, by contrast (the firm's term for a group of products for which it acted principally as a reseller for products made by others), was doing well. Sales were holding steady, margins were good and, since we were buying and reselling, we didn't have any manufacturing problems. Our products for the stone and construction businesses and our general line of superabrasive products fell somewhere in between.

If current profitability were the criterion, then it looked as though we should stay in mining, get out of rotary truers and try to turn stone and construction and superabrasives around. There was some thought that PIMS could help with this decision, but I wasn't sure. I had heard of PIMS but it sounded very theoretical, the kind of thing used in very large companies by strategic planners. Besides, my staff was really spread thin and I wasn't at all sure that we could justify the time it might take to work with PIMS.

PIMS

The PIMS program originated at General Electric in the early 1960s. It was further developed at the Harvard Business School, in cooperation with the Marketing Sciences Institute, and is now housed at the Strategic Planning Institute (SPI), a not-for-profit business research and consulting organization located in Cambridge, Massachusetts. (See the Appendix on page 291 for a brief description of PIMS.)

Foseco became a corporate member of SPI in 1983. In January 1984, Keith Roberts, a senior consultant in the London office of SPI, met with C.W.N. Ward, Managing Director of Unicorn, and Peter Welch, Group

Financial Director. At that meeting it was decided that VMIDP might represent an interesting opportunity for evaluating PIMS in a turnaround business situation. If Ian Marsh agreed, Keith would work with VMIDP but the costs would be borne by corporate headquarters.[2]

As Keith Roberts recalled:

> I called Ian and introduced myself. I told him a little about our meeting and about PIMS. I also told him that I felt the best way to proceed was for me to come to Gloucester and meet with him and some of his people. At that meeting, which I thought would take a day or two, we would make a fairly comprehensive presentation on PIMS, show him what kind of data we need and what kind of information we could provide about his business, after we had data on it entered in the computer. I suggested that he evaluate what he heard on the first day and then make a decision on whether or not to go further.
>
> He agreed, and I met with him, Carol Spiller, then Marketing Director, Morris Edmonds, then Finance Director, and some of the technical people. I made a formal presentation that gave an overview of PIMS, with particular emphasis on its use as a framework for thinking about business units, performance measurement, investment intensity and marketing issues.
>
> We then had a substantial discussion about his business and ways to reorganize. The guidelines for defining a business are reasonably straightforward—a well-defined external market, a clear-cut competitor, or set of competitors, control over all resources and so forth. Applying them is another matter. At first we got bogged down in trying to come up with good definitions, but finally we simplified it to High Tech (rotary truers), Stone and Construction, Mining and Me Too, a term we coined for their wide array of miscellaneous abrasives. Although some of their business came from abroad, we also decided to focus on just the UK market.
>
> We then jumped right into a discussion of the PIMS concept of quality. I explained our view that it is the customer's judgment that defines quality, not the supplier's; that quality includes all the non-price attributes that count in the purchase decision; and that quality should be measured relative to competitors. Value then, or what the customer gets for his money, is a combination of relative quality and relative price. (See Exhibit 3 for a graphical depiction of this relationship of relative price, relative quality and value.) We then spent a lot of time trying to identify the key product and service related attributes for each of the four businesses and, finally, to assess how VMIDP stacked up against its major competitors. (See Exhibit 4 for the form used to score competitive position.)

At the end of the first day, it still was not clear to Marsh whether or not he should go ahead with PIMS. The normal PIMS data forms required information on some 160 variables, many of which would be difficult for VMIDP to obtain. Roberts had suggested that SPI could first do a so-called "LIM analysis," which needs data on only 18 variables, but it was not clear how useful such an analysis would be.

---

[2]Cost of membership in SPI varied as a function of the firm's size. The membership fee covered the cost of assistance by the SPI staff to fill out the original set of data forms which comprehensively described the firm's business. Subsequent services were billed on a time and expense basis.

EXHIBIT 3
Value Map (5 Generic Price/Quality Positions)

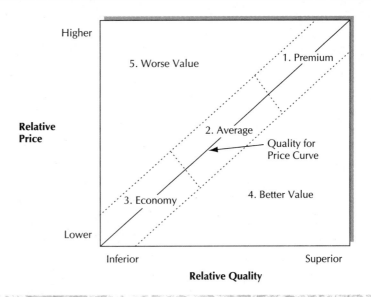

Source: The PIMS Principles

According to Marsh:

It had been a useful and interesting day. I was impressed by our discussion of how to define or organize our businesses and felt that the quality discussion was valuable. But I had some concerns about the additional staff time that would be required if we decided to go ahead. Many of the assumptions we made about our quality and our competitors needed further checking, much of the information PIMS wanted simply wasn't available or could only be estimated, and the financial information on the businesses as we had defined them was going to take considerable time to prepare. In addition, my staff was not very sophisticated. At the time, for instance, we had only a few university graduates. I wasn't sure what their reaction would be to PIMS.

I was concerned that defining our market as just the UK could be misleading, given that some of our competitors had a much larger served market. Also, some of my staff said, PIMS focuses on what we are doing, not necessarily on what we should be doing. That is, it doesn't identify the key "order getting" ingredients.

Finally, I really wondered what I would do if the PIMS analysis suggested a different set of conclusions from those I was leaning toward. For instance, Keith told me that one of the outputs of the report would be a comparison between actual ROI and PAR ROI (a PIMS concept that developed an expected ROI, based on the firm's strategic position). What if the businesses I thought we should stay in showed up poorly in the PIMS analysis?

EXHIBIT 4

Scoring Our Competitive Position

Business _____ Year _____

Customer Group (Name) _____ Importance (%) _____ Date _____

Quality (non-price) Attributes (Key Purchase Criteria)	Relative Importance to Customers (%)	Comp. A 0-10	Comp. B 0-10	Comp. C 0-10	Comp. D 0-10	Our Business 0-10	Our Business		
							Super	Equiv	Inter
Product-Related Attributes									
1 _____									
2 _____									
3 _____									
4 _____									
5 _____									
6 _____									
Service-Related Attributes									
1 _____									
2 _____									
3 _____									
4 _____									
5 _____									
6 _____									
Totals:	100%								

Market Share					
Price (relative to ours)					100
Direct Cost (relative to ours)					100
Technology (relative to ours)*					equal

*Ahead, equal, behind

Importance of quality vs. price in purchase decision

quality	
Price	

100%

Source: © 1983 The Strategic Planning Institute

VAN MOPPES-IDP LIMITED APPENDIX

PIMS (Profit Impact of Market Strategies)[1]

The PIMS research program was initiated in 1960 as an internal project at the General Electric Company (US). The basic concept was to examine a wide variety of businesses for the factors which explained, or predicted, superior operating performance. Using return-on-investment (ROI) as a measure of performance, regression models were constructed that "explained" a substantial part of the variation in ROI. These models identified those factors that related most strongly to ROI and provided an indication of their relative role as explanatory variables.

Under the direction of Sidney Schoeffler, development of the models continued throughout the 1960s and early 1970s, first at GE and later at the Harvard Business School and the Marketing Science Institute. At that time the project was expanded to other corporations beyond GE. The Strategic Planning Institute, a non-profit corporation governed by its member companies, was formed to manage the PIMS program. As of 1987, around 450 corporations had contributed annual data, for periods ranging from 2 to 10 years, on some 3,000 product divisions or strategic business units.

PIMS Concepts

The fundamental concept underlying the PIMS approach to business analysis is that a business can learn from the experiences of strategy peers, as opposed to industry peers. That is, for instance, low market share companies in one industry can learn more about successful ways to compete from successful low market share companies in another industry than from analysis of a high market share company in one's own industry.

The architecture of the PIMS data base is built on two concepts: the business unit and its served market. Business units can be defined in a variety of ways. The PIMS definition is a division, product line, or other profit center of a company that:

- Produces and markets a well-defined set of related products and/or services;
- Serves a clearly defined set of customers, in a reasonably self-contained geographic area; and
- Competes with a well-defined set of competitors.

A firm's served market is a combination of customers for whom the product is suitable and to whom a marketing effort is made. Good identification of served market is important because:

---

[1]This section draws heavily on a number of PIMS publications; and on Buzzell, Robert D. and Gale, Bradley T., *The PIMS Principles*, New York: The Free Press, 1987.

- A business unit's market share is measured in relation to its served market.
- Market growth rates are measured or estimated for each unit's served market.
- The identity and market shares of leading competitors are determined by the scope of the served market.
- Assessments of the relative quality of a business unit's products and services are made in relation to competitors in the served market.

Factors that influence performance are generally grouped in three main categories:

- Those associated with the market environment (e.g., market growth rate, importance to end users, marketing expenditures, etc.);
- Those associated with competitive position (e.g., relative quality, market share, patent protection, etc.);
- Those associated with the capital and production structure (e.g., investment intensity, capacity utilization, vertical integration, etc.).

Twenty-two "major" profit influences explain about 40% of the difference in ROS and ROI among the PIMS businesses. A more complete model (the PAR ROI model) explains over 70%.

The PIMS Data Base

Each participating company supplies more than 160 data items on various aspects of its strategic and financial position. Data that might make it possible to identify an individual company or business are disguised (by use of ratios, or multipliers) and elaborate precautions are taken to otherwise protect the confidentiality of information in the data base.

Many different industries, products, markets and geographic regions are represented in the PIMS data base. In 1985 some 90% of the businesses were in manufacturing, versus 10% for service. About one-third produced consumer products, 20% produced capital goods, and the remainder were material suppliers. About two-thirds marketed their products/services in North America. The data base included about 400 businesses in the UK and Western Europe.

On average the data base tends to include the more mature, large and profitable businesses. Even so, there is great variation in performance and strategic situations. Average pre-tax ROI, for instance, has been around 21%, but ROI for individual businesses has ranged from −25% to +80%. Similarly, the data base contains start-up as well as mature businesses and also businesses well under $10,000,000 in sales.

PIMS Applications and Tools

According to PIMS, a successful strategic analysis of a business unit yields:

- A clear and precise definition of the business, its market, and its competitors;
- An understanding of the current strategic situation, including strengths and weaknesses relative to competitors, threats and opportunities;
- A program for getting the most out of the business in its current position, over the near term, consistent with:
  - A specific strategy to be followed over the long term, to gain the maximum improvement in strategic position;
  - Identification of tactics required to successfully implement the strategy, in enough detail to be easily translated into functional plans and budgets.

  Major PIMS Tools include:

- **The PAR ROI Model**: Calculates the expected or "normal" profitability for a business based on approximately 30 of its structural and operating characteristics;
- **Contribution Ratio Analysis**: Separates business profitability into Operating Effectiveness components and a Strategic Position component;
- **Operating PAR Models**: Determine expected or "normal" levels of employee productivity, working capital, marketing, etc. based on various characteristics of the business and its market;
- **The Strategy Model**: Assesses the feasibility and expected financial results of major changes in the structural characteristics of a business, including the likely competitive dynamics of such changes (for example, growth in market share);
- **The Report on Look-alikes**: Focuses on structurally similar businesses in the data base to identify short-term opportunities and tactics for improving the performance or defending the current position of a business;
- **The Productivity Tracking System**: Identifies effects on profits of price/cost movements and changes in input/output relationships, providing normal or benchmark rates of change for each;
- **The Business Start-Up Model**: Gives an objective assessment of the marketing tactics and future prospects of start-up ventures, using a special data base of businesses in their first few years of operation;
- **Portfolio Models**: Examine diverse businesses within a portfolio to provide guidelines for resource allocation and tactical focus, in light of corporate constraints and priorities;

- **Limited Information Models (LIM)**: Permit analysis of competitors, acquisition candidates or associates, where data are not freely available;
- **PIMS OASIS Data Base**: Developed jointly with Hay Associates and the University of Michigan to study links between human resource issues, competitive strategy and business performance.

Waters Chromatography Division: U.S. Field Sales

Thomas V. Bonoma

Shirley M. Spence

> The cornerstone of our business—and a big part of the Waters culture—is "The Waters Difference."

William (Bill) Shippey, president of the Waters Chromatography Division of the Millipore Corporation, explained further:

> Waters was considered a pioneer in high-performance liquid chromatography [HPLC], which is a relatively new technique for separating complex chemical mixtures into their individual components. In the early years, there was limited expertise in the industry, and many of the people who knew HPLC worked at Waters. We built our business by helping customers with their separation problems. We would send in application specialists to show them how to use HPLC—and our products—for their particular task. With this application-oriented approach, Waters essentially created the market for HPLC.

Chane Graziano, vice president of worldwide business operations, agreed: "Technical expertise and strong customer support are the basis of our differentiation in the marketplace, and our premium price. That's why our field organization is staffed by expert chemists with experience in HPLC—not typical sales representatives."

Rod Bretz, regional sales manager for New England, interjected:

> It's not always that easy to make a technical person into a salesperson. They sometimes get caught up with the technology and don't close the order as soon as they might. Also, a salesperson must be flexible, and highly technical people sometimes tend to be inflexible and thus not responsive to customer needs. Selling, though, is a skill that can be learned. Salespeople with a technical background have a

---

much better chance for success because we sell solutions to problems, and a technical background very often is needed to deal with our customers' problems.

Industry Background

HPLC Technology

The objective of HPLC was to separate a complex chemical mixture into its individual components. Essentially, an HPLC system consisted of a reservoir of solvent, a pump, an injector, a steel or plastic column tightly packed with microscopic particles, a detector, and a recorder. The HPLC separation process involved a three-way chemical interaction among the sample, the solvent, and the column packing material. Depending on the nature of the sample, specific solvents and column packings were selected from the wide array of available HPLC chemical products. (Exhibit 1 shows the basic components of a system for performing HPLC, and describes the separation process.)

Competitive Environment

The worldwide market for HPLC was estimated at approximately $350 million in 1984, and was expected to grow 15% annually through the rest of the decade. Waters was the world leader in HPLC, with a market share at least double that of its nearest competitor. Competitive pressures varied by geographic area, as reflected in Waters's regional business performance (see Table A).

The HPLC market could be divided into two broad segments: (1) instruments, which included pumps, injectors, detectors, and data and control units, and (2) chemical products, which included the packed columns and other disposable supplies and accessories used in HPLC systems. Both market segments were dominated by Waters, who competed directly against other premium-priced vendors (Hewlett-Packard, Varian, Perkin Elmer, Beckman, and IBM in instruments; Du Pont and Altex in columns) and also faced growing pressure from smaller, low-cost manufacturers.

Company Background

History

Waters was founded in 1962 to develop, manufacture, and market HPLC-based products used for the analysis and purification of fluids in critical applications. A 10-year "boom period" of fast growth and big profits ended in the mid-1970s as competitive pressure mounted. Sold by founder James Waters in 1980, the company became a largely autonomous operating unit of the Millipore Corporation—the world leader in membrane separation technology. Projections for 1984 showed worldwide sales of the Waters Chromatography Division at $142 million, which represented approximately 43% of Millipore's total net revenues. (Exhibit 2 shows the Waters income statement.)

EXHIBIT 1
Liquid Chromatography: Components of an HPLC System

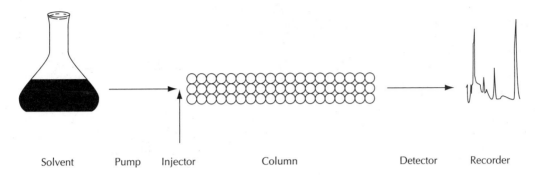

| Solvent | Pump | Injector | Column | Detector | Recorder |

Separation Process

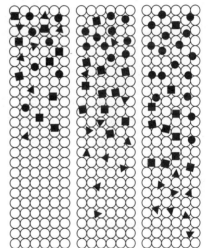

When a sample is injected into a liquid chromatography column, its various components are uniformly distributed. The components move at different speeds through the column packing material.

Their different rates of progress tend to separate the components into bands in the column which exit separately. As they exit, the components of the sample can be detected and quantified.

Chromatogram

The chromatogram at right results from the HPLC separation of a common headache tablet. A comparison of the positions and heights of peaks derived from known standards allows an identification and quantitation of the four components of the tablet.

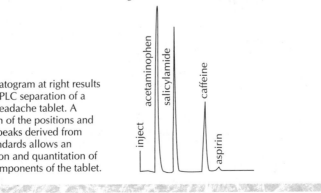

Source: Waters Chromatography Division

TABLE A
Waters Regional Business Results 1984 Forecast ($ in millions)

	U.S.	Canada	Europe	Pacific	Total
Sales	$70.0	$5.7	$40.8	$25.5	$142.0
Market share (%)	48%	60%	36%	30%	40%

EXHIBIT 2
Waters Income Statement ($ in millions)

	1983 (Actual)	1984 (Forecast)
Sales	$120.0	$142.0
Gross Margin	72.0	85.2
% of sales	60.0%	60.0%
Selling, General and Administrative	48.0	54.0
% of sales	40.0%	38.0%
Research and Development	9.0	10.7
% of sales	7.5%	7.5%
Operating Expense	57.0	64.7
% of sales	47.5%	45.6%
Corporate Contribution	$ 15.0	$ 20.5
% of sales	12.5%	14.4%

Source: Waters Chromatography Division

Products

Waters offered a complete line of HPLC instruments, accessories, columns, and supplies. In 1984, instrument sales represented over 62% of total Waters revenues, with the balance largely accounted for by sales of chemical products and revenues from spare parts and service, i.e., preventive maintenance contracts, repair fees, customer "HPLC Schools" (see Table B).

A Waters instrument system was assembled from a choice of standard modules (pumps, injectors, detectors, and other accessories), as shown in Exhibit 3. Modules could be facility-installed as part of a complete new system, added to an existing system, or sold separately to customers wishing to assemble their own system. A complete system cost between $10,000 and $40,000, depending on the choice of modules. Waters also offered dedicated systems tailored for specific applications (e.g., the Sugar Analyzer I for analyses of corn, beet, and cane sugars).

TABLE B
Waters Sales by Product Line ($ in millions)

	1983 (Actual)		1984 (Forecast)	
	$	% Change	$	% Change
Instruments	$ 75.7	7.2%	$ 88.5	16.9%
Chemical Products	23.1	1.8	26.3	13.9
Spare Parts and Services	18.7	28.1	22.6	20.9
Other[a]	2.5	78.6	4.6	84.0
Total Sales	$120.0	9.8%	$142.0	18.3%

[a]Products purchased from original equipment manufacturers for resale to Waters customers

The Waters chemical products line encompassed a total of 380 items, including a variety of packed columns for use in Waters or competitive instrument systems. Chemical products prices ranged from $175 to $750 per item, with an average customer order amounting to $900.

Customers

Waters served a technical customer base in a variety of research and industrial settings, focusing on specific application niches within each customer market. In 1984 the company's largest markets were (1) pharmaceuticals, a large and mature business base, and (2) life sciences/biotechnology, a new and rapidly growing segment. Other important markets included polymers, industrial chemicals, food/agriculture, and electronics. The four broad application areas targeted by Waters were analytical laboratories, research laboratories, clinical laboratories, and quality control laboratories. Virtually all Waters sales were made directly to end users by the division's own sales force.

Marketing Strategy

Waters's overall marketing objective was to grow the business at least 20% annually by maintaining market share in existing markets and by developing new market areas via the aggressive marketing of existing products, the timely introduction of new products, and a broadened applications emphasis.

Organization and Management

The Waters Chromatography Division, which employed 1,485 people in 1984, was organized into functional departments: manufacturing, human resources, marketing, research and development, and worldwide business operations (field sales and service). Department heads were based at the divisional headquarters in Milford, Massachusetts, and reported directly to Bill Shippey. Shippey, who held

EXHIBIT 3
Waters Instruments

Source: Waters Chromatography Division

an engineering degree and had a background in sales, joined Waters in 1981 as general manager of U.S. business operations and was named president in 1983.

Waters Sales and Service Organization

As vice president of worldwide business operations for Waters, Chane Graziano was responsible for the company's domestic and foreign field organizations, and also supervised three staff groups located at divisional headquarters. (See Exhibit 4 for a partial organization chart.) Graziano, whose background included a position as a laboratory chemist at Procter & Gamble as well as 10 years in sales management with a major HPLC competitor, had been recruited by Waters in 1979 for a U.S. sales management position. In his current role, he had profit and loss responsibility for Waters's U.S. business and its foreign subsidiaries.

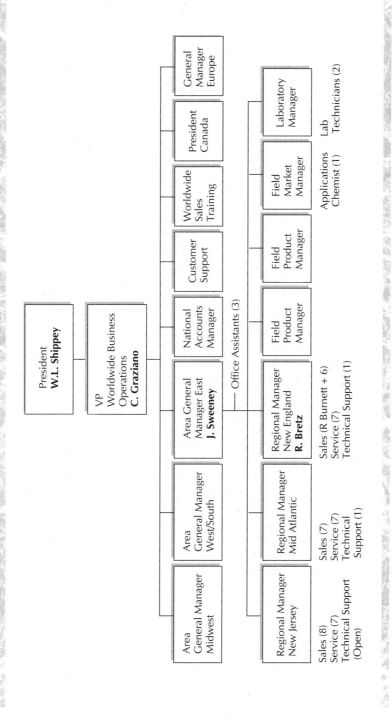

EXHIBIT 4
Waters 1984 Partial Organization Chart

President
W.L. Shippey

VP
Worldwide Business
Operations
C. Graziano

Area
General Manager
Midwest

Area
General Manager
West/South

Area General
Manager East
J. Sweeney

National
Accounts
Manager

Customer
Support

Worldwide
Sales
Training

President
Canada

General
Manager
Europe

— Office Assistants (3)

Regional Manager
New Jersey

Regional Manager
Mid Atlantic

Regional Manager
New England
R. Bretz

Field
Product
Manager

Field
Product
Manager

Field
Market
Manager

Laboratory
Manager

Sales (8)
Service (7)
Technical Support
(Open)

Sales (7)
Service (7)
Technical
Support (1)

Sales (R Burnett + 6)
Service (7)
Technical Support (1)

Applications
Chemist (1)

Lab
Technicians (2)

Note: Numbers in parentheses indicate staff positions filled as of November 1984
Source: Waters Chromatography Division

301

Headquarters Staff

Headquarters staff for worldwide business operations consisted of a national accounts manager, two worldwide sales training personnel, and a 31-person customer support group.

National Accounts Manager (NAM). The NAM position involved the management of 40 U.S. customers who collectively represented about 45% of Waters's total dollar volume. These included U.S. government agencies (e.g., the Food and Drug Administration) and major university and industrial accounts such as Hoffman LaRoche, Eli Lilly, Dow Chemical, the Massachusetts Institute of Technology, Procter & Gamble, and Monsanto. With each of these accounts, Waters conducted annual contract negotiations in which customer spending commitments were made in exchange for special terms. Waters management tried to institute high-visibility programs that provided value to the end user, as opposed to price discounts seen only by the purchasing agent. As an example, for the $2 million Monsanto account, Waters offered a $200,000 package that included a full-time service engineer plus a 5% discount, rather than an equivalent cost 10% discount.

The NAM position had evolved over time. Until recently, contract negotiations, order monitoring, and the handling of other major account program details had been assigned to a trained national accounts administrator. In 1984 Graziano decided to convert the job to a training position for senior sales representatives on track for regional management posts. Responsibilities would include managing Waters's existing base of national accounts and establishing 10 to 20 high-potential target accounts. Graziano was considering restructuring the NAM compensation package—which offered a flat salary of $40,000—to include a base salary plus a commission linked to growth within target accounts. As of late 1984, the new NAM position had not yet been filled.

Worldwide Sales Training. The director of worldwide sales training was responsible for planning and implementing Waters's standardized training program for new field sales personnel. The program consisted of six week-long courses designed for 20 to 25 participants each. Course topics were (1) chemistry, (2) chromatography, (3) HPLC hardware, (4) basic selling, which taught a consultant-style approach, (5) competitive selling, and (6) S-4, which described four basic social styles (expressive, amiable, driver, analytical) and taught sales representatives to recognize and adapt to the individual customer's preferred style. A new sales recruit was sent immediately to the first four courses of the series, and then attended the remaining two courses sometime over the next few years.

Customer Support. The primary goal of the customer support group was "to get the right people doing the right thing when a customer calls."[1] This effort

---

[1]This group also provided secretarial support for special field sales activities (e.g., a mailer for a seminar).

occupied a staff of 31 people, and involved three major activities: (1) telephone support for customers needing technical assistance with application or equipment problems, (2) response to customer requests for information, and (3) telephone order-taking. Management estimated that 75%–80% of instrument orders and virtually all chemical products orders were placed by mail or telephone. Instrument orders usually were based on a quotation prepared by a field sales representative, whereas chemical products and small parts typically were ordered by the purchasing agent from Waters's published price list. Field sales representatives received weekly order reports for their respective territories.

The customer support department also included a six-person telephone-lead screening group staffed by sales trainees. Prospective customers requesting information were taken through a series of questions listed on a "qualifier" sheet, which then was forwarded to the appropriate field sales representative for follow-up.

U.S. Field Operations

Since 1981, U.S. field operations had been divided into three areas (Midwest, West/South, East), each operating as a profit center. Each area had its own branch sales office and applications laboratory facilities for running customer samples. Overall responsibility for each area rested with its general manager, who reported directly to Chane Graziano. Area general managers earned approximately $75,000 in salary and were eligible to participate in company stock benefit plans.

In addition to the 3 area general managers, the 1984 U.S. field organization included a total of 8 regional managers, 57 sales representatives, 53 service representatives, and 26 sales support personnel. The Eastern area's reporting structure (see Exhibit 4) was similar to that of the two other areas. Its general manager, J. Sweeney, directly supervised an applications laboratory manager, 3 field marketing managers,[2] and 3 regional managers. Each regional manager, in turn, directly supervised 7 or 8 sales representatives and also was responsible for 7 service representatives and a technical support person.

The Regional Manager

The regional manager (RM) typically had come up through the sales ranks, where he or she had demonstrated good selling skills and the ability to manage a territorial business effectively. The RM was charged with maximizing revenues from an assigned geographic region, and managed a regional budget that included service as well as sales expenses. RM compensation consisted of a salary of $40,000–50,000 plus $10,000–20,000 in commissions, based on regional sales volume growth.

The RM was considered a "front line manager" whose primary responsibility was managing the sales force. The RM was expected to spend at least

---

[2]Field marketing managers, who focused on specific products or markets according to the area's needs, conducted promotional activities (e.g., seminars, direct-mail campaigns) designed to generate leads for sales follow-up.

60% of his or her time in the field, helping sales representatives with skills development and customer calls. At the beginning of every year, the RM worked with each salesperson to construct a territorial business plan, which they reviewed together on a quarterly basis. The RM also conducted annual performance reviews, which included career development planning. Hirings and terminations were handled by RMs, with the approval of the area general manager.

In performing their sales supervisory duties, regional managers relied primarily on personal observation of salespeople's activities and on quote conversion rates (i.e., a comparison of quotations issued versus actual orders, which afforded a measure of lost business). Chane Graziano explained his views on performance standards as follows:

> I leave it up to the regional managers, some of whom are interested in calls per day. I'm not. I believe you should concentrate on the input (i.e., skills development) and the output (i.e., quotations and orders), not the number of calls. The key thing is productive time. If I know the number of leads sent to a rep, how many prospects he or she has, the dollar value of quotations issued, and the actual order figures, then I can calculate productive time and the success of the individual.

The regional manager's direct supervision of field service and technical support personnel was limited. The service group was managed internally by a regional service manager.[3] Field service representatives were responsible for prepurchase demonstrations, installation of equipment, customer training on new instruments, preventive maintenance for service contract customers, and repair work. Service representatives received about $24,000 in base salary, and could earn $3,000–5,000 extra through an incentive plan based on service billings and contracts, and sales of spare parts, accessories, and chemical products. Technical support staff, who handled customer training programs ("HPLC schools") and provided service for customers' technical problems, earned $25,000–35,000 per year, with no incentive plan.

When not working directly with the sales force, the regional manager was occupied with administrative duties such as signing expense accounts, tracking quotations and orders, preparing sales forecasts, and writing monthly reports. The RM, who was authorized to discount prices up to 8.9% in competitive situations, also was responsible for good business practices on the part of Waters field personnel.

The Sales Representative

Field sales representatives sold all Waters products to all customer markets in their assigned geographic territories, and also conducted technical seminars on various HPLC topics. Each salesperson had a dollar-volume quota, and was

---

[3]Regional service managers indirectly reported to the vice president of products, projects, and services, who was part of the Waters marketing department.

expected to devise and implement a business plan to achieve that goal. In 1984 a salesperson managed from 2 to 100 customer accounts (the average was 40 accounts) and generated $1.3 million in total sales.

Over the 1980–1984 period, Waters added 27 new field sales positions to meet the needs of its rapidly growing business. The typical new recruit was 25 to 30 years old with two or three years of laboratory experience. Waters management explained that there had been a shift first away from and then back to the tradition of fielding a technically trained sales force:

> By the mid-1970s, the HPLC market had matured to the point where there was a substantial base of experienced chromatographers who were more interested in instrument features and options than in application support. Our competitors were quick to capitalize on this, taking the approach: "You already know how to use HPLC, customer; now buy this fancy new gear." We were losing hardware business because we couldn't sell competitively. Our technically trained reps just couldn't handle it and began to fall out, so we hired the competition to fill the gaps. When we did a study on the backgrounds of our top-performing salespeople, we found that the competitive hires were the most productive over the short term, but generally stayed only 12 to 18 months. Part of the problem was that they were from companies where HPLC was just one of five or six product lines sold, so they weren't expected to be expert in HPLC. Also, they liked to get the order and move, and didn't want to spend a lot of time with each customer. In the early 1980s, we returned to our policy of recruiting expert chromatographers for field sales.

New field sales representatives usually were drawn from the telephone-lead screening group at Waters headquarters, or were recruited directly from Waters application laboratories and from among Waters customers. New sales hires usually spent their first month attending sales training courses in Milford, and then moved to the field. The regional manager would help the new salesperson develop a territorial business plan and set up a call schedule, and usually spent a minimum of one week making calls with the representative.

The sales representative's compensation package included a base salary, a sales incentive program, an expense account, and the use of a company car. In 1983 the average Waters salesperson earned $34,000 in salary and commission, while about 10% of the sales force earned $60,000 or more. In addition, Graziano accompanied 40 salespeople and their spouses to Hawaii on a vacation trip earned by increasing territorial volume by $300,000 or more.

In 1984, base salaries, which included an annual merit increase tied to U.S. inflation rates, ranged from $24,000 for a new hire to $42,000 for a salesperson with 10 years of experience. The Waters 1984 incentive program was linked to achievement of territorial sales quota and had two broad components: (1) an annual plan linked to a 12-month quota calculated by adding $300,000 to the territory's base business (i.e., the previous year's volume), and (2) a quarterly plan linked to quarterly goals, which were seasonally adjusted percentages of the annual quota. (Incentive plan descriptions and a sample calculation of a salesperson's 1984 bonus appear in Exhibit 5).

EXHIBIT 5
Waters 1984 Sales Incentive Program

Program Description

Under the *annual plan*, sales representatives were paid a 4% commission on the first $300,000 in territorial growth versus base business and a 10% commission on any sales in excess of that quota figure. Under the *quarterly plan*, Waters paid a $500 bonus for achieving the quarterly volume goal plus approximately $300 commission on each instrument system sold. (For purposes of the incentive program, Waters defined an instrument system as either *pump plus injector plus detector* or *two pumps plus control unit*.)

Quarterly plan earnings were paid at the end of each 3-month period, and were retained whether or not annual plan quotas were met. For sales representatives who did achieve their annual plan quotas, these quarterly plan payments were considered a draw against the annual plan, i.e., total earnings from the quarterly plan were deducted from the sum earned under the annual plan. Earnings from the 1984 annual plan (minus quarterly draw) would be paid to sales representatives in a single sum in February of 1985.

Sample Calculation of Sales Representative's 1984 Bonus

Performance:	Base business (1983) sales = $1.0 million	
	1984 quota = $1.3 million	
	1984 actual sales = $1.4 million	
	Sold 20 systems (5 per quarter)	
	Met all quarterly goals	
Annual Plan Earnings:	4% on $300,000	= $12,000
	10% on $100,000	= 10,000
	Total	$22,000
Quarterly Plan Earnings:	By quarter	
	5 systems @ $300	= $ 1,500
	Goal @ $500	= 500
	Total	$ 2,000
	Total year	$ 8,000
Total 1984 Bonus:	Annual plan earnings	= $22,000
	Less quarterly draw	= −8,000
	Net earnings	$14,000

Source: Waters Chromatography Division

At the time of hire, 70% of sales representatives did not plan a career in sales but rather saw it as a route to a marketing position at the home office. In reality, only 10% eventually did follow that path, while the others decided to remain sales representatives, opted for a sales management track, or left the company. Management estimated annual field sales turnover at 10%–20%, and the cost in lost orders of each turnover at $260,000.

EXHIBIT 6
Ray Burnett's Schedule: November 14, 1984

A.M.

9:00–10:00[a]	Drove from home to the Harvard Business School (HBS) for 10:00 A.M. pickup of casewriter. Arrived early so made phone calls from pay phone for about half an hour.
10:00–10:30	Drove to Everett, Mass., for an 11:00 A.M. appointment with the Quality Control/Assurance manager at the Teddie Peanut Products, Inc., factory.
10:30–11:00	Talked with casewriter.[b]
11:00–11:30	First personal call.
11:30–12:00	Drove to Cambridge, Mass., to drop off replacement instrument part at Otis Clapp (second personal call).

P.M.

12:00–12:15	Left part and note at Otis Clapp.
12:15–12:30	Drove to Massachusetts General Hospital where had a 3:00 P.M. appointment with Chief of Cardiac Surgery. Parked at hospital and walked to nearby restaurant.
12:30–1:45	Lunch.[c]
1:45–2:45	Made phone calls from restaurant pay phone.
2:45–3:00	Walked back to Massachusetts General Hospital for appointment, and went to Cardiac Lab. Brief conversation with another hospital staff client on elevator.
3:00–4:00	Third personal call.[d]
4:00–4:45	Made phone calls from hospital lobby pay phone.
4:45–5:00	Walked to another Massachusetts General Hospital building for appointment with Radiation Lab technician to check equipment breakdown.
5:00–5:30	Fourth personal call.
5:30–6:30	Drove casewriter to HBS, and headed home.

[a]Ray had spent approximately an hour the previous night planning calls.
[b]Normally, Ray would have used this time to make phone calls.
[c]Lunch was longer than usual due to the presence of the casewriter.
[d]Call was probably longer than would have been in the absence of the casewriter since the customer was interested in discussing Waters with the casewriter.

Waters Sales—A Day in the Field

On November 14, 1984, a casewriter spent a day making customer calls with Ray Burnett, a Waters field sales representative. An accounting of this day follows background descriptions of Ray Burnett and his supervisor, Rod Bretz. (A summary of the day's activities is also provided in Exhibit 6.)

Ray's Background

Ray grew up in New England and also attended college there, earning a degree in biology. He joined Waters in 1975 as an applications laboratory chemist, and subsequently moved to the position of telephone-lead screener at the Milford home office. In 1977 he was assigned to a sales territory in St. Louis,

Missouri, where he built up a successful sales record over the next three years. Ray then decided to return to New England and requested a transfer, which was granted. He purchased a home in a seaside Massachusetts town about 40 minutes by car from downtown Boston and 60 minutes from Milford. Ray, his wife, and two young children were still living there in 1984.

Since returning to the New England region, Ray had managed three different sales territories. Upon his arrival in late 1981, he had been given a choice of two territories: (1) an industrially oriented area that was enjoying good growth, or (2) Boston, where Waters business was biology-based and less strong. Ray chose Boston, and had a relatively poor year in 1982. In 1983 Ray was assigned a new territory that included downtown Boston and the Massachusetts Medical Center. That year he generated $1.4 million in sales, earning $26,000 in commissions. In 1984, territorial boundaries shifted once again. Ray's new territory included part of his previous area plus some new accounts.

Ray's Supervisor

Ray reported directly to Rod Bretz, the New England regional manager. Bretz, who held a business administration degree, had come from a regional sales manager's position at a pharmaceutical company to be a field sales representative for Waters in 1973. In 1975 he was transferred from his Louisiana territory to a management position at Waters headquarters. Five years later, he decided to return to field sales: "It wasn't any fun inside anymore. For a salesman, getting the order is all the fun, and I'm a salesman."

During Bretz's subsequent four years as regional manager for New England, that region's sales climbed from $2.4 million in 1980 to $9.5 million in 1984, its field organization grew from six people to sixteen, and the number of sales territories doubled. To Bretz, establishing territorial boundaries had been an immediate and ongoing challenge. He explained:

> When a territory's volume base gets too big, you have to divide it up. The big question, though, is: Who divides it? When I took over New England, I could see there had been gerrymandering: people had been setting up territory boundaries so as to get and keep the best accounts. I believe in fair play, though, so each time there was a personnel shift, I'd readjust the territories with the objective of giving each salesperson a business base that would allow him or her to be successful.

According to Bretz, the salesperson's job was "to go out and get orders." Noting that new recruits typically had strong chemistry backgrounds but no field sales experience, he added:

> A lot of people here think of salespeople as used-car hucksters. We're always arguing over what's more important—technical or selling skills. I say it's a 49%–51% split, with the extra 2% going either way. You don't have to be a Ph.D. in chemistry, though it makes it easier. I believe the salesperson must know a certain amount about the product but that, essentially, he or she is a broker for the technical know-how of our applications laboratory people and service engineers. It's my job to make sure my salespeople get that technical support . . . and anything else they need to be successful.

Bretz maintained substantial contact with customers through his frequent participation in sales representatives' calls and his involvement in service management issues. On average, Bretz spent three days a week in the field and two days at home, where he had an office. He prioritized his field time against inexperienced salespeople, but had frequent telephone interaction with all his sales representatives. Bretz estimated that over the past year he had spent 12 days in the field with Ray and had spoken with him by telephone at least once a week.

Ray Burnett's Job

Ray defined his field sales position as "using my technical background to help people solve their problems." He also compared his job to "running my own little business." He had full responsibility for building volume in his territory, and a large measure of control over his time and activities. He estimated that 25%–30% of his time was spent on direct selling, with much of the balance devoted to customer service and the conducting of seminars on various HPLC topics. Ray said he usually got home around 8:00 P.M., often because he would "get stuck helping someone in a lab." He did weekly call reports only sporadically, preferring to spend the time on call planning.

Ray covered a geographic area that included parts of downtown Boston, some northern suburbs, and central Massachusetts. In 1983, about 80% of that territory's $1.4 million business had been generated by only 20% of its accounts: the Massachusetts General Hospital, the Massachusetts Institute of Technology, the University of Massachusetts medical area, the New England Nuclear Corporation, and the Polaroid Corporation. In planning his calls, Ray concentrated first on his existing customer base. He allocated calls roughly according to the percentage of business represented by each account, but tried to see each customer at least twice a year.

Ray also tried to allocate some time to new business development. For instance, if time permitted, he could "cold call" any one of a number of companies along his route, i.e., get into its research and development or quality control laboratory, speak with someone about potential applications for HPLC, and get a sample for a "trial run" at a Waters laboratory. Ray felt there were many new business opportunities in his territory, but found he had little time to pursue them.

Ray's sales quota for 1984 was $1.7 million, which represented a 21% increase over his 1983 base business. He expected to sell 25 instrument systems and generate about $1.5 million in total sales in 1984. In general, Ray felt he did "pretty well" financially as a Waters sales representative, but had some concerns about the company's sales incentive program:

> When I started with Waters there was no bonus plan. They started one in 1980 and have changed it every year since then. The current program is largely based on volume growth. The problem with this program, I think, is that it encourages a "sell and run" attitude. It says, "Don't worry about support and service"—which is not how this company became successful. I personally feel that we ought to have an uncommissioned sales force.

Recently, Chane Graziano had contacted Ray to set up a meeting to discuss an opening for the position of national accounts manager. Ray had mixed feelings about the idea of leaving field sales for a home office position. On the one hand, he was tired from the long hours and hectic pace of his field sales job. On the other hand, he would miss the freedom of working out of his home, and also had some questions about the financial implications of the move.

Ray was looking forward to the next day's meeting with Graziano, both to learn more about the NAM position and to see whether his field-based perceptions of the business matched those of management. Ray felt that, in general, HPLC customers made their instrument purchase decision based on three considerations: (1) equipment capabilities (i.e., instrument features), (2) service and support, and (3) price. Ray had noticed an increasing price sensitivity in the market, and found that Waters was perceived as high priced: "Some of our instrument systems are less expensive and more capable than the competition, yet customers don't call because they think they can't afford us." Ray also found that whereas Waters once dominated the chemical products business, the impression now among customers was that Waters had not "kept up."

Ray Burnett's Customer Calls, November 14, 1984

Teddie Peanut Products, Inc. (Everett, Massachusetts). Ray's first appointment was at 11:00 A.M. with the quality control (QC) manager at the Teddie Peanut Products processing plant. In the car, Ray explained to the casewriter that Teddie Peanut Products was a marketing-generated lead. Joe, Teddie's QC manager, had seen some Waters promotional materials and had called the company for more information on HPLC systems to be used for aflatoxin analysis.[4] His name had been forwarded to Ray, who had followed up by telephoning for an appointment and mailing some informational materials: a 12-page color brochure on Waters instrument systems, a Waters technical bulletin on "Rapid High Sensitivity Determination of Aflatoxins in Peanut Products by HPLC," and a sample chromatogram from an aflatoxin analysis.

The factory was off the highway but relatively easy to find. The otherwise nondescript building was topped by a huge billboard cutout of a teddy bear. At 10:55 A.M., Ray asked the receptionist in the front lobby to tell Joe that "Ray from Waters" had arrived. In a few minutes, Joe came down to escort his visitors up to a small, crowded office on the second floor.

Ray first asked Joe how he had heard about Waters. In response, Joe pulled out a magazine to show Ray the Waters advertisement that had prompted his call. Joe then explained that his monitoring of aflatoxin levels involved testing incoming batches of raw peanuts as well as samples of the processed product. At present, the samples were sent to a local laboratory and the results telephoned to Joe, who logged them in a book and used them for quality control decisions.

---

[4]Aflatoxins were carcinogenic compounds produced naturally by fungi in many agricultural products, including peanuts. In the United States, the Food & Drug Administration (FDA) had established maximum aflatoxin levels for raw and finished peanut products.

Joe said he was interested in in-house alternatives to the laboratory contract service. When probed as to his specific needs, he indicated that speed and cost were important factors. He also asked about help with equipment installation. Ray assured him that Waters would provide assistance in installing the system and "debugging" his application.

When asked if he was familiar with HPLC techniques, Joe said he had a basic understanding from his university studies but had never used the method himself. Ray then reviewed the sample chromatogram with Joe, who seemed a little puzzled. Upon asking about Joe's staffing situation, Ray learned that doing the aflatoxin analysis work in-house would require hiring a new, technically qualified person.

Ray brought out the quotation sheet he had prepared the previous evening and reviewed it in detail with Joe. For Joe's needs, there were two instrument system options: (1) a less expensive ($13,000) basic package that could be automated at an incremental cost and, if desired, could be expanded to provide additional application capabilities, or (2) a dedicated system ($21,000) that was easier to operate but was specific to aflatoxin analysis. Joe seemed most interested in the basic package option, since he was anticipating FDA regulations that would require the monitoring of additional substances. He said that he would, however, need to look at cost considerations more closely and present the issue to his management. Joe accepted Ray's offer to telephone in a few weeks for further discussion, and the meeting ended.

Back in the car at 11:30, Ray commented that the promise of technical support by Waters was especially important to new HPLC users like Joe. Following up on that promise, however, was the challenge. In Joe's case, Ray probably would get a sample from him and take it to the Waters laboratory for analysis. There was supposed to be support staff for running samples, but Ray found the turnaround time slow and often did it himself. If Joe ultimately did buy a system, Ray would have to get an already overextended Waters service person to do the installation and initial training, or do the two-day job himself. The danger, though, was that the salesperson could easily end up "doing it all": finding the customer, running samples, selling instruments, starting up equipment, training, and servicing.

Otis Clapp (Cambridge, Massachusetts). At noon, Ray arrived at Otis Clapp, a medical supply company located in the warehouse district. Otis's laboratory manager had called Ray about an instrument breakdown, and Ray wanted to drop off a replacement part. Ray told the casewriter:

> Customer loyalty depends on rapport. They'll remember me at Otis. It takes one to three years to build up a relationship but eventually it pays off. Yet, I've changed territories every year, because business growth calls for splitting one territory into two or because the company wants to vary reps' mix of accounts. I think continuity is critical, but we've had pretty high turnover in field sales over the past three years.

After climbing the two flights of stairs to the main office, Ray was told that the laboratory manager was at lunch but should be back in twenty minutes. Ray asked if he could use the telephone to catch up on calls, but was told that all telephones were out of order. About five minutes later, Ray decided to leave the part, along with a note telling the laboratory manager to call if the replacement piece didn't fix the equipment problem.

Massachusetts General Hospital, Cardiac Research Laboratory (Cambridge, Massachusetts). In the elevator, on the way to a 3:00 P.M. appointment with Dr. Michael Margolis, chief of Cardiac Surgery, Ray encountered a Waters customer from another laboratory area. The technician had a question about a new Waters instrument. Her question was only partially answered by the time her floor was reached. Ray offered to stop by later to see her, but she said she could get any other needed information from the Waters brochure on the instrument.

Dr. Margolis had been a Waters customer for a number of years. He had called Ray to ask him to stop by, but had not specified the purpose of the meeting. Since Ray was a few minutes early, he made a quick tour of the cardiac research laboratory and chatted briefly with the laboratory research assistant. The laboratory had three Waters HPLC systems, one of which was very old and one of which included some components from other manufacturers. The laboratory assistant subsequently joined Dr. Margolis and Ray in a meeting held in the doctor's office.

Dr. Margolis began by explaining that he recently had attended a Waters symposium and had some questions about Waters's new data and control system and its amino acid analyzer. The ensuing discussion was lively, relaxed, and technically detailed. Dr. Margolis clearly was knowledgeable not only about HPLC technology but also about various competitors' products and services. He took notes throughout the meeting, and frequently asked his laboratory assistant for his opinions. Ray handled questions about cost and instrument capability easily and without referring to technical publications.

Dr. Margolis first asked Ray to tell him about the Waters 840 Work Station. Ray explained that the system, which included a Digital benchtop computer plus Waters software plus instrument interface units plus a printer, could handle the data management and system control needs of up to four HPLC instruments. Ray estimated the cost of a Waters 840 capable of handling the cardiac research laboratory's three instruments at about $30,000. He also advised Dr. Margolis that the next availability date for the Waters 840 would be in March of 1985.

There was considerable discussion of the logistics and cost of incorporating the Waters 840 into the laboratory's existing facilities. For instance, Dr. Margolis wanted to know if Waters would give a trade-in allowance on the laboratory's present data and control system.[5] He also had concerns about who would be responsible for repairs, citing problems in the past with two vendor-warranty arrangements. Ray explained that Digital would be responsible for servicing the

---

[5]Waters had a buy-back policy based on 20% depreciation per year of use.

computer hardware, but assured him that Waters would stand behind the equipment. Last, Dr. Margolis asked where he could see a Waters 840; Ray told him that there was one presently in use in the radiation biology laboratory.

Dr. Margolis then turned to the subject of the new Waters amino acid analyzer, asking Ray who was using it and what had been published about it. Ray answered, "Ever since the *Science* magazine blurb about it, the phones have been ringing off the hook." He invited Dr. Margolis to come to see the new system at Waters in Milford.

As they walked to the elevator, Dr. Margolis advised Ray that the Waters 840 purchase was a long-term issue, and that in 12 months or so he would be ready to buy. He had raised the issue with Ray now because he was trying to decide whether or not to sell his existing Waters data and control module to an interested buyer. In the elevator, Ray explained that this situation was not unusual: research customers usually first decided to buy the instrument and then found the money.

Massachusetts General Hospital, Radiation Biology Laboratory (Cambridge, Massachusetts). At 5:00 P.M., Ray was scheduled to see Bill, a radiation biology researcher who had come to the Massachusetts General Hospital to work with his present supervisor. One of Bill's responsibilities was to start up a newly purchased Waters HPLC system. Ray had been working with him on that task and the two had become quite good friends, sometimes going out for a drink after work.

When a problem with the new system had arisen, Ray had brought in his own instrument as a temporary substitute. That replacement was now malfunctioning, and Bill had called Ray for help. Ray spent about 15 minutes poking around the system before identifying the problem. He also checked another Waters instrument, which was awaiting a spare part from Service. Ray promised to follow up on the replacement part. He also offered to come in and explain to Bill's supervisor why the new system start-up had been delayed. The offer was accepted by Bill, who then escorted Ray to the parking lot. At 5:30, Ray headed home.

Telephone Calls. Between personal calls, Ray would find a pay phone, usually in the lobby of his last or next appointment, and make as many calls as possible. In the hour between lunch and the meeting with Dr. Margolis, for example, Ray made nine telephone calls and talked to fifteen people on a range of topics: a customer interested in a rental program needed help with financing, and Ray was trying to make the necessary arrangements through a bank in Chicago; another customer had an instrument problem; one prospect was almost ready to buy and wanted to talk to Ray; Romicon offered him a job in marketing. A large percentage of Ray's calls involved problem solving. Ray's favorite calls, however, were those that occurred late in the afternoon and culminated in a customer commitment to buy a $60,000 instrument system.

The West European Car Rental Industry

Manuel F.
Colcombet

Per V. Jenster

By 1990 the revenue of the West European car rental industry[1] was expected to reach £3,1 billion ($5 billion), 12% more than the previous year (refer to Exhibit 1). The year 1989 had been an exciting one for the major players in the business. Hertz, the largest worldwide car rental company, had dramatically ensured its presence in the UK by reaching exclusivity agreements with British Rail (representation at 2,500 stations) and with British Airways through their BABS reservation system. Avis, the second largest worldwide operator, showed a 31% increase in pretax profits for its European car rental network. Budget, the third worldwide operator, had increased its European fleet by 38% over a 12-month period. Europcar, by merging with Interrent in January 1989, had become the largest European operator with an overall 13% market share.

Market Segments

There were two dimensions of customer usage patterns which industry executives viewed as important market segments: 'usage scope' and 'usage purpose.'

Usage Scope

The first dimension referred to the location where the car was booked and where it would be used. 'Local usage' was when the car was booked and used in the same city; 'incoming' rental was when the booking was made in a different city. Industry operators realized that serving incoming customers required a different infrastructure and commercial approach than what was needed to serve local customers.

One manager explained:

> For the 'incoming' customers, the most important sites of car rental outlets were airports, where more than 30% of European car hires were generated. Travellers

[1]Short-term car rental in Europe, excluding Warsaw Pact countries, and excluding commercial vehicles.

This case was prepared by Manuel F. Colcombet, IMD MBA Research Assistant, and Professor Per V. Jenster as a basis for class discussion rather than to illustrate either effective or ineffective handling of a business situation. It is based on industry sources and the work of: Laurent Bachmann, Regina Erz, Gustavo Fernandez Bonfante, Barbara Lauer, and Manuel Ordas Fernandez.

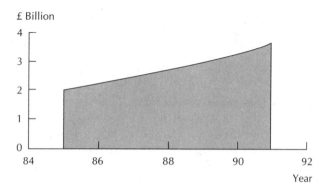

EXHIBIT 1
Market Size

Sources: Budget, ECATRA, industry estimates

also required outlets at major railway stations and hotels. Stations were expected to increase in importance with the expansion of high speed rail lines and the completion of the Channel Tunnel projected for 1993. The supra-local customers were eager to be able to book the car in their home country and even pay for the service with their own currency. These customers were keen to avoid anything going wrong in a city that they might not know well; therefore, they would choose the operator that instilled the most confidence from among the ones they managed to contact.

Local renters looked for convenience and price. These customers knew the place, managed the environment, and were aware of the other means of transportation that could substitute for car rental such as taxis and public transportation. Finding a telephone book was nearly all they needed to price shop, check proximity and the opening time of outlets.

Usage Purpose

The second dimension was divided into the following categories: business, car replacement and repair, and tourism. The relevance of each segment varied among countries and seasons, but the business segment was the most important with 50% of the overall market value, 30% for replacement and local traffic, and tourism 20%.

The demand for rental cars for business purposes was higher on work days, especially Mondays to Thursdays, and throughout the year from September to June. The industry viewed business people as emphasizing the following factors: reliability, convenience, image and status. They expected to have no hassles, speedy delivery, easy check-ins and rapid check-outs. To attract this segment, car operators constantly made efforts to improve their service standards. As part of this program, they issued personal cards such as Budget's

'Rapid Action' and Hertz's 'Number One Card' (7 million in circulation). Avis had established a self-imposed standard maximum check-in-to-rent time of five minutes. At certain airport locations like London's Heathrow where customers had to go elsewhere to collect their vehicles, this was obviously not always possible. In an effort to increase convenience, Hertz had experimented with 'Travel-pilot,' an in-car electronic vehicle navigation system.

Industry sources stated that, in selecting a car rental company, half of the business people were restricted to using the operator that had a corporate account relationship with the employer. Additionally, these sources mentioned that secretaries would make all the travel arrangements in one out of five occasions.

Tourism and leisure was a particularly active segment in summer. Tourists welcomed reliability and convenience; however, if the consumer were young, price mattered more. In the UK, 60% of those under 34 years of age shopped around for a 'better deal,' but only 40% of those over 45 years old bothered to do so. In choosing a car rental company, customers preferred those which offered all inclusive rates, eliminating surprises on tax and mileage expenses.

The car replacement segment was particularly active at the beginning of every week, as Monday was the day people most often took their car in for repair. In some countries, like Germany, this segment was important because insurance companies were compelled to offer a replacement for cars damaged in an accident. In recent years, this segment was declining because there were fewer car accidents, and car insurance companies were attempting to reduce costs by compensating people who did not rent a replacement. In the early 1970s, consumers who were replacing cars that were out of order or hiring an extra car for short-term usage represented 60% of the German car rental business; in the late 1980s this figure was approximately 40%.

In selecting a car rental company, the garage owner exerted some influence, particularly if his garage offered a replacement service. This service tended to be 'free' or included in the repair bill.

Main Geographical Markets

More than 70% of the West European car rental revenue was generated in six countries, the biggest market being West Germany, followed by the UK, France, Italy, Sweden and the Netherlands. (Refer to Exhibit 2.) Prices tended to vary across borders, according to the following index (UK = 100):

Netherlands	135
Sweden	131
Italy	123
France	110
UK	100
Germany	97

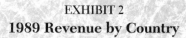

EXHIBIT 2
1989 Revenue by Country

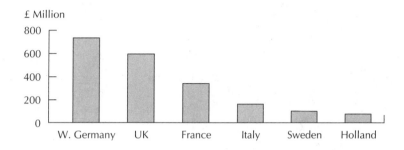

Sources: Budget, ECATRA, industry estimates

Usage also varied. In Britain, customers typically rented a car for four days (versus an average of three days on the Continent), predominantly for private use. In Northern France and in Germany, business and replacement were the main segments with one-way rentals constituting 30% and 23%, respectively, of all rentals; these were the highest in Europe. In the Mediterranean area, foreign visitors (both tourists and business people) were the main client groups, representing over 40% of the market; the average driven rental distances covered were the largest in Europe.

Industry operators also studied differences in consumer attitudes across countries. For example, for Germans the car's characteristics such as model, luxury, maintenance, and cleanliness were important in addition to the speed of service. British customers were viewed as price shoppers; their interests also focused on convenient locations (pick-up points) and all inclusive rates. The French generally viewed the industry with skepticism and, therefore, preferred all inclusive rates (as opposed to base rates plus additional charges for distance, insurance, tax, etc.). Payment mode, one-way rentals and having a selection of models to select from were also considered relevant in the French market.

There were also notable differences according to gender. In Europe, France had the highest rate of cars being rented by women, with 24% of the market. In the UK, even though women represented only 6% of the rental market, they were believed to play an important role in the purchasing decision; for example, it was found that women made half the inquiries about car rental in the leisure market.

Market Outlook

Industry observers expected the market to continue growing by 10–13% over the next three to five years, up from a 7% growth rate in previous years, due to these factors:

- General growth of the overall economy (based on a moderately strong increase of 4% for GNP). Improved business conditions would generate more business travel; increased income would expand the leisure industry, and growing car ownership would also increase replacement rentals because of more trips and breakdowns.

- The '1992' phenomenon was also seen as a factor which would stimulate rental, because cross-border trade would be easier in a single market.

- Car rental executives also saw business opportunities coming from industry consolidations. A range of factors was contributing to more growth—such as better reservation systems, better services, different pricing, new products such as cabriolet cars. Industry members resisted disclosing the financial results due to the new products. But, one Central European operator increased business by 10% just from luxury cars and evening hire. Another area where operators were seeking new opportunities was in car ownership replacement.

One Budget executive reached the following conclusions after an extensive analysis of the UK market:

> For town or country dwellers, car rental is also an efficient alternative to owning a second car which might be idle most of the time but still incurring tax, insurance and maintenance costs. With many car rental companies able to deliver a car to the doorstep, the rental alternative offers good value and convenience. An Escort, for instance, could be rented for 134 days a year, including delivery and collection, within a 15-mile radius of an office at the same cost as owning it. If the second car is actually used less than 134 days a year, renting as needed offers significant savings.

Several industry experts based their outlook on comparisons with the U.S. market. They expected that the single market would result in a narrowing of differences between Europe and North America. Cross-border differences in car taxation and car rental taxation were expected to disappear. One-way cross-border rentals would not be restricted. Air transportation was going to be deregulated, thus providing additional opportunities for car rental firms.

Alan Cathcart, chairman and chief executive of Avis Europe, clearly expected greater prosperity from a unified Europe:

> The USA is an excellent precursor of what 1992 could lead to in Europe. Consider the following statistics: less than 5% of the European drivers has ever rented a car, compared to 10–20% of U.S. adults. Further, there are only 1.5 rental vehicles per 1000 Europeans, compared to 5.5 for every 1000 Americans.

Others felt, however, that the U.S. market would not necessarily be replicated in Europe. The differences in distances, lifestyle and the European transportation system were sufficient reasons to explain this point of view (i.e., in Europe only 30% of the car rental business was generated at airports, compared to 70% in North America). (Refer to Exhibits 3 and 4 for key country indicators and size of the private and rental car fleets.)

EXHIBIT 3
Country Indicators: Population, Number of Cars and Rental Cars

Country	Population (Millions)	Cars (Millions)	Rental Cars (Thousands)
Belgium	9.9	3.6	7
Denmark	5.1	1.6	5
France	55.9	22.5	90
Germany (West)	61.5	29.2	80
Greece	10.0	1.4	12
Ireland	3.5	0.8	10
Italy	57.5	23.5	45
Luxemburg	0.4	0.2	2
Netherlands	14.8	5.3	17
Portugal	10.3	1.4	23
United Kingdom	57.2	21.3	140
Spain	38.9	10.5	30
Total EC	325.0	121.2	461
Austria	7.6	2.8	3
Sweden	8.5	3.5	23
Switzerland	6.5	2.7	9
USA	247.0	140.0	1380

Sources: Eurostat, ECATRA, industry estimates

Industry Structure

Even though global competitors dominated the market, there was no clear market leader. Large local markets with regional differences in preferences, rental patterns, taxation, historic development and low barriers to entry were seen as key reasons for significant market fragmentation. Traditionally, firms had entered the car rental business as a sideline to auto retail or gas station operations, where the overhead costs could be kept to a minimum through operational synergies. Garages handling car repairs were an excellent example of the local company that competed within the replacement segment. The garage owner could keep a few cars on hand which he then rented out to a customer having repairs made.

Another reason for fragmentation was that national borders prevented the global competitors from fully exploiting their relative size. Economies of scale through volume discounts on car purchases and insurance were not always possible because of frontiers. In addition, country regulations significantly

EXHIBIT 4

Per Capita Country Indicators: Income, Number of Cars and Rental Cars

Country	GDP per Capita (°)	Cars per 100 Persons	Rental Cars per 1000 Persons
Belgium	16	36	0.7
Denmark	17	31	1.0
France	17	40	1.6
Germany (West)	18	47	1.3
Greece	9	14	1.2
Ireland	10	21	2.9
Italy	16	41	0.8
Luxemburg	19	40	5.0
Netherlands	16	36	1.1
Portugal	9	14	2.2
United Kingdom	17	37	2.4
Spain	12	27	0.8
Total EC	16	37	1.4
Austria	16	37	0.4
Sweden	19	41	2.7
Switzerland	21	42	1.4
USA	25	57	5.6

(°) Gross domestic product per capita at current prices and purchasing power parities.
Sources: Eurostat, ECATRA, industry estimates

increased the cost of cross-border rentals because the car had to be returned to the country of origin at the company's or the consumer's expense.

Some local operators (licensees) had franchise agreements whereby they could use the brand name of global players. This arrangement benefitted both parties. The licensees enjoyed the benefit of using a recognized name, won access to computer reservation systems and to international clients. As the licensees supplied themselves with outlets and vehicles, these agreements enabled the licensor to extend its presence with little capital expenditure and to benefit immediately from a 3–4% fee on gross licensee sales. Additionally, the licensor enjoyed the strategic advantage of penetrating an area that might not have been accessible to him. Another way of extending coverage without too much increase in fixed costs was by establishing agencies; that is, independently owned firms that operated the outlets, received a commission, but did not own the hired cars.

The existing market structure was far from static. A growing number of mergers as well as many new entrants indicated that this industry was undergoing significant changes. The previously mentioned Europcar-Interrent merger was only one example of the industry's restructuring. Increased concentration was also occurring as local firms joined global companies or departed from the industry. In 1989 alone, almost 1,000 companies (12%) left the industry (i.e., discontinued the business or were absorbed). The primary reason appeared to be the fight for market share by the international companies. In an effort to increase their business base, these firms tried hard to enter new regions and to approach new customer sub-segments. Using the U.S. as a comparable single market, major companies clearly expected gaining from 1992. The top four companies in the U.S. had an 80% market share versus only 43% in Europe. With this comparison in mind, an industry marketing director asserted that the 'big four' would command 70–75% of the European market by the year 2000. Yet, Europe still faced new entrants coming from the U.S.: Eurodollar, Alamo, and Thrifty were looking for a stake in the market before the consolidation process ended. All three companies had entered the market through partnerships or franchising, and had competed in the U.S. on a price platform. Some operators feared that Japanese car rental companies, backed by the powerful vehicle manufacturers of that country, would also try to enter the market.

Sales and Marketing

The industry used a wide range of channels to maximize the speed and availability with which customers could book their services, including travel agents, corporate accounts arrangements and dedicated sales people. Travel agents accounted for 20% of the bookings. In return for their selling services, travel agents and tour operators received a commission, ranging from 5% to 25%. The highest fee corresponded to the sale of a full rate car rental package.

CRS Systems

Travel agents would either call the car rental company or use their computer reservation system (CRS). When receiving a telephone reservation, the larger car rental companies immediately booked the reservation on their in-house CRS. These CRS systems were continuously developed and improved. Avis asserted that its World-Wide Wizard system enabled the company to offer improved service, because customers could 'check out' (rent a car) in just two minutes, and 'check in' (return it) in only one minute.

When a travel agent reserved directly on a CRS, it was generally through an 'outside' system, to which the car rental firms did not have direct access. However, changes were taking place for some industry participants. Budget was proud to claim that it was the first international car rental company to sign up with both the Amadeus and Galileo airline reservation systems. These two systems, Amadeus and Galileo, founded by the major airlines, were backed by groups of European carriers.

Commenting on the effects of CRS systems, Robin Gauldie, editor of *Travel Trade Gazette*, stated:

There is no doubt that these systems will become vital to the survival of the travel agent in the complex environment of post-1992 Europe. They will give agents an enhanced sales tool, will speed up their reaction time to fare changes and, importantly, in view of the threat of increased paperwork, provide them with a vastly more powerful back office facility, as well as faster and more comprehensive reservation facilities. Agents who adopt the new technology are likely to become increasingly hostile to principals who are not themselves accessible through CRS, a move which will have profound implications for tour operators, hoteliers and other travel service providers.

Robin Gauldie's forecast implied that small car rental operators would encounter an increasingly tough environment, as these systems would not be able to carry more than 20 car rental companies.

The range of alliances was extending beyond the airlines and travel intermediaries. Railways were willing to provide selling services to the car rental industry and, on some occasions, signed agreements providing exclusivity. Examples included a contract between the SNCF in France and Avis, and between British Rail and Hertz. In another type of arrangement, the car and hotel CRS CONFIRM had a development agreement with Budget as an equity partner along with Hilton, Marriott and AMR.

Corporate Accounts

Industry sources estimated that corporate accounts represented nearly one-fifth of the car rental industry. In some countries, such as France, Germany and Italy, this segment represented nearly 30% of all car rentals. To obtain these agreements, car rental companies offered discounts between 10% and 40%. In France, where a price war was raging for corporate accounts, these discounts reached 30% in 1990. In return, the car rental companies received first choice on all rentals and thus were ensured a non-seasonal captive market. These corporate accounts, in addition to favoring the market share of a particular operator, could increase the size of the rental market by providing a corporate fleet.

Gentlemen's Agreements

Industry operators often maintained informal agreements with automobile mechanics and hotel receptionists, who served as sales intermediaries by referring clients. These intermediaries could receive a commission of 10%, or even 20%, for a full rate sale. Regarding this type of sale, global companies did not show any sizeable advantage over local companies.

'Walk-in' and Telephone Sales

Direct contact between the car rental company and the consumer, where telephone reservations were made by the customer directly, accounted for more than half of total sales. To attract the customer's attention, firms relied on good advertisements in telephone books and on billboard postings in multiple urban locations.

EXHIBIT 5
Price List for International Customers
Budget 1990 Rent A Car

	Unlimited Mileage Tariff, per Day			Unlimited Mileage Tariff
	1–3 Days, 4–6 Days, 7 Days and More			Friday 12:00 to Monday 9:00
	Special Offer–Not Discountable			
OPEL Corsa	142.-	108.-	96.-	182.-
VW Golf OPEL Kadett	195.-	152.-	136.-	213.-
OPEL Kadett Stationw.	196.-	157.-	137.-	215.-
OPEL Kadett, Autom.	210.-	161.-	147.-	223.-
OPEL Vectra TOYOTA Corolla Wagon 4x4	227.-	182.-	167.-	247.-
OPEL Vectra Autom.	205.-	205.-	180.-	285.-
OPEL Omega	268.-	207.-	181.-	310.-
OPEL Omega Stationw.	323.-	250.-	225.-	385.-
VW Microbus ISUZU Bus	375.-	315.-	275.-	400.-
BMW 316i OPEL Vectra 4x4	379.-	316.-	285.-	430.-
MERCEDES 190 E. Autom. BMW 525i Autom. (sunroof)	281.-	230.-	199.-	550.-
MERCEDES 230 E. Autom. A/C	512.-	440.-	385.-	590.-
MERCEDES 300 SE Autom. A/C	583.-	496.-	436.-	670.-

Source: Company Price List 1990

In this area, local operators had the same advantages as global players, especially when there were synergies with existing businesses, such as when garages rented replacement cars to customers having repairs done. The major companies were slowly gaining market share by offering affiliated garages repair and maintenance work on the operator's fleet, as well as a commission of 10% for referring clients.

Pricing

Car rental rates varied by country, city, season, day of the week, rental length and mileage requirement. Prices were also affected by the booking mechanism and the predelivery booking period, creating complex pricing schedules which even employees found difficult to manage and apply. The extra cost options and insurance charges made pricing even more complicated. (Refer to Exhibits 5

EXHIBIT 6
Price List for Local Customers
Budget Rent A Car

	Local Tariff		1990		
	Unlimited Mileage, per Day			**Week-end Tariff**	
	1–3 Days,	**4–6 Days,**	**7 Days and More**	**2 Days**	**3 Days**
	Special Tariff				
OPEL Corsa	71.-	54.-	47.-	119.-	156.-
VW Golf					
OPEL Kadett	91.-	73.-	63.-	146.-	188.-
OPEL Kadett Stationw.	94.-	74.-	65.-	147.-	190.-
OPEL Kadette Autom.	96.-	76.-	66.-	157.-	203.-
OPEL Vectra					
TOYOTA Corolla Wagon 4x4	115.-	89.-	81.-	175.-	224.-
OPEL Vectra Autom.	124.-	97.-	87.-	188.-	244.-
OPEL Omega	136.-	112.-	97.-	207.-	270.-
OPEL Omega Stationw.	182.-	147.-	133.-	259.-	339.-
VW Microbus					
ISUZU Bus	195.-	159.-	142.-	302.-	392.-
BMW 316i					
OPEL Vectra 4x4	184.-	146.-	132.-	278.-	359.-
MERCEDES 190 E Autom.					
BMW 525i Autom. (sunroof)	233.-	188.-	170.-	336.-	435.-
MERCEDES 230 E					
Autom. A/C	290.-	236.-	214.-	419.-	541.-
MERCEDES 300 SE					
Autom. A/C	361.-	293.-	267.-	499.-	651.-

Source: Company Price List 1990

and 6 for a typical tariff structure for one company in one country.) Pricing had little relation to operating costs, in part because the cost related to a particular hire was difficult to allocate, and because pricing was a tool used to attract different segments and increase the utilization of the rental fleet.

The pricing policies of the various competitors in the industry were also designed to charge, when possible, as much as the 'market will bear.' As in other service industries, one way to support this marketing policy was by rewarding the employees when clients chose higher margin products from the firm's portfolio, i.e., upgrading, ordering additional options, or selecting a more luxurious car. For example, customers perceived that rental rates corresponded to the prices for different new car models, even though the operator's costs did not correlate proportionally. A customer might also walk into an outlet in a

EXHIBIT 7
USA-Europe Rate Comparison

Region	Subcompact	Compact
Germany	440	580
UK	430	575
Spain	335	415
New York	290	315
Florida	160	180

Note: Prices in U.S. dollars including taxes, unlimited mileage and insurance
Source: AVIS Supervalue weekly rates at April 90 exchange rates

hurry and with no advance booking, and be willing to take a more expensive model, even if initially attracted to that contract claiming a special offer. (The simplified pricing example occurred below provides an illustration.)

	Regular	Contract°	Weekday	Weekend
Business	100	80	100	80
Tourist	100	70	100	70

°Corporate account contracts were arranged through the head office. Reservations were booked in advance.

Prices also varied significantly amongst the European countries, although they were always much higher than those in the U.S. (refer to Exhibit 7). Tax differences explained only a small part of the difference (refer to Exhibit 8).

Other Marketing Tools

Creating brand awareness through advertising was considered important to attract the cross-border traveller. It was estimated that global companies spent around 2% of sales on advertising. Achieving the right spending balance posed continued problems, as advertising was not uniformly recognized as an order winner. One industry observer commented that Budget Switzerland had difficulties in 1987 and was subsequently sold, largely because of its belief that it could win increased sales only through heavy advertising and promotion.

In addition to pricing discounts, most large companies were willing to spend more than 5% of sales on various promotional activities. The main objectives were to:

EXHIBIT 8
Value Added Tax by Country

Country	On Short-Term Car Rental (%)	On Car Purchase (%)	On Car Insurance (%)
Belgium	25	25 to 33	(°)
Denmark	22	22	—
France	25 to 28	25	—
Germany	14	14	7
Greece	16	6	(°)
Ireland	10	25	NIL
Italy	19 to 38	19 to 38	12.5
Luxemburg	12	12	12
Netherlands	20	18.5	(°)
Portugal	17	17	—
UK	15	15 to 25	NIL
Spain	12	33	NIL
Austria	20	32	10
Sweden	23.5	—	—
Switzerland	NIL	6.2	—
USA	6 to 12	6 to 12	—

Note: This list does not include import duties and other special taxes on vehicle.
(°) The value added tax is replaced by a specific tax.
Sources: Hertz, ECATRA

- Maintain an information flow about the company's products to the market, that is, point of sales offerings, brochures, maps, etc.
- Meet clients' expectations and attract the repeat client segment by offering free gadgets, better service, etc. Some operators also launched so-called "internal promotions," such as training programs for personnel.

Outlet Management

Outlet management involved the ongoing management of the rental outlets, including activities such as 'checking out,' 'checking in,' invoicing, car cleaning, and staffing. Selection of the site and the people were considered the key factors because of their promotional impact. The main outlet costs (totaling 35% of revenues) were maintaining properties (offices and garages) in key locations, and supporting a trained staff with long working hours (e.g., Avis's location in Amsterdam Airport employed over 120 people).

Airport administrations, aware of their control at key locations and having only limited space, charged car rental firms a premium of 10% of their sales for an outlet on the premises. Some companies, in an attempt to avoid this charge, established outlets just outside the airports and relied on a shuttle service to transport their customers (e.g., Heathrow) with resulting delays.

Major companies carried an extensive network of outlets in order to meet the needs of the supra-local traveller and to fully capitalize on their established brand names (e.g., Hertz had more than 150 locations in Germany). In addition, these companies regarded increased distribution as a way to gain market share. To help reduce investments and swap fixed costs for variable costs, they relied on subcontracting in less critical locations. In contrast, local firms minimized outlet costs through synergies with other lines of business such as car sales or repairs.

Car Control

Ensuring that a given car was in the right place at the right time was considered critical for the large firms in order to obtain high utilization rates. This was not easy, considering the amount of one-way travelling, the need to wash and service the cars, and the industry's practice of not penalizing clients who did not respect their reservations.

All international companies made extensive use of information technology to optimize car utilization. By considering booked reservations and historical sales figures, they determined the mix and number of cars at any given outlet. When adding the expenses of redistribution of vehicles and staff needed, 10% of revenues were typically spent performing this operation. In smaller firms, this activity was either limited or unnecessary.

Fleet Management

Fleet management represented up to 30% of revenues. It involved the purchase of the vehicles, maintenance and repair of the fleet, as well as insurance and, eventually, resale. The large rental companies were important customers for the vehicle manufacturers. An estimated 4–7% of all new cars were purchased by the car rental industry. In addition, car rental represented an important test opportunity for potential new car buyers. The large volume of cars purchased resulted in significantly reduced prices for the car rental companies. The importance of these firms as customers had led to acquisitions by the car companies. For example, Avis was partially owned by General Motors, Europcar by VW, Hertz by Ford and Volvo.

New cars were purchased and resold every 6 to 12 months by the large companies. Market conditions within the new car and resale market tended to move together. Thus, if the resale market were soft, the new car market would also be soft, offsetting any arbitrage risk for the rental companies.

Repair and maintenance costs tended to be minimal for the larger companies, because their cars were generally sold within the normal warranty

EXHIBIT 9
Profile of Major Competitors in Western Europe

	Avis	Budget	Europcar	Hertz
Market Share (%)	12	7	13	11
Fleet (000 cars)	80	35	75	70
Outlets	1,700	1,200	1,850	1,600(°)
Airport Market Share (%)	25	10	20	25

(°) Plus 3,300 railway representations
Sources: Company brochures, company directories, press releases, industry literature and estimates

period. In addition, the companies tended to contract insurance only for damages to third parties, thereby self-insuring their own fleet. Local rental companies tended to keep their car fleet longer, thus reducing their acquisition costs, but increasing maintenance and resale expenses.

Main Competitors

The industry could be divided into three groups of competitors: the 'big four,' the other international firms, and the local operators.

The 'Big Four'

This group consisted of Avis, Hertz, Budget and Europcar. The first three had started operating in the U.S. and now enjoyed market leadership positions in that country; Europcar was, as its name suggests, European and owned by major European car manufacturers. The 'Big Four' could be called Pan European in the sense that they were present in all West European countries. Their market share, size and structure differed somewhat (as indicated in Exhibit 9). In some countries (West Germany, France, the Netherlands, Spain, and the UK), their presence was diluted by the existence of hundreds of competitors. In other countries like Sweden and Italy where competition was concentrated, the 'Big Four' managed to control well over half the market. (Refer to Exhibits 10a and 10b.)

In the most rewarding segment, 'the walk-in customer,' the major companies enjoyed large shares (approximately 80%), but the percentage was even higher in the commercial traveller segment. Such high shares were the result of efforts made by this group of competitors to cater to these customers at every airport and to capitalize on the selling power of their international network. Industry observers named Hertz as the most successful in following this strategy, with nearly two-thirds of their turnover generated at airports. Hertz

EXHIBIT 10a
EXHIBIT 10a
Market Share and Number of Competitors by Country

| | Market Share | | |
	Big Four (%)	Others (%)	Number of Competitors
Germany	46	54	○○○
UK	39	61	○○○
France	46	54	○○○
Italy	67	33	○
Sweden	60	40	○
Netherlands	34	66	○○

Notes on number of competitors: (orders of magnitude)
°Italy, Sweden: a hundred
°°Netherlands: around 3 hundred
°°°Germany: a thousand
UK & France: more than a thousand

EXHIBIT 10b
Market Share by Major Competitors by Country

	Avis (%)	Budget (%)	Europcar (%)	Hertz (%)
Germany	10	9	19	8
UK	9	8	12	10
France	14	4	15	13
Italy	27	5	15	20
Sweden	10	13	19	18
Netherlands	10	9	6	9
West Europe	12	7	13	11

Sources: Budget, ECATRA, industry estimates

was supposed to be closely followed by Avis, then Europcar and, finally, Budget where less than one-third of the turnover was generated at airports (refer to Exhibit 10b).

For all these companies, the segments reached and the strategies being used varied from country to country. As a result, price positioning also varied. Observers perceived that Avis was situated at premium price points followed by Hertz and Europcar, with Budget having the lowest prices among this group (refer to Exhibit 11).

EXHIBIT 11

Examples of Car Rental Prices in £ [All prices valid on March 31, 1988 (VAT included); one day's rental of a category A car, 200 km and CDW]

	Avis	Budget	Europcar[1]	Interrent[1]	Hertz	Local°	Local°°	Local°°°
B	98.41	86.93	98.41	91.53	99.56	75.76		
DK	106.74		83.77	82.26	108.74	73.74		
D	89.55	67.33	83.61	83.55	89.09	72.78		
GR	54.03	49.77	49.77	50.98	69.50	44.71		
E	63.57	60.56	64.98	61.13	63.77			
F	111.19	106.06	111.71	105.64	111.15	87.74	99.61	84.17°°°
IRL	96.93		85.55		101.06°°	38.76	34.23	
I	134.72		147.41	135.08	137.14	134.06	100.38	130.37
L	87.68		86.62	56.81	105.86			
NL	96.63		94.11	85.21	98.17			
P	43.13	41.83	42.45	51.18	43.00	33.92	37.71	41.08
GB	92.57		84.82					
A	113.63	93.10	100.87	101.09	83.75	91.92	79.86	
CH	114.57	105.04	111.39	95.56	112.57			
YU	50.34		43.11	52.01	59.80			

[1]Europcar and Interrent have merged
°Locally owned firms
°°Becomes 115.26 when driver is under 23 years of age (CDW more than doubles)
°°°PAI included as well
Source: BEUC, car rental price survey, 1989

Avis Europe

In 1988 this company became public and independent of its parent, Avis US. By the end of 1989, however, it returned under parent control of Avis Inc., Lease International S.A., and General Motors. Throughout the period of independence, Avis Europe had continued to use Avis's reservations and marketing network.

Avis Europe's 1989 annual report revealed that its short-term rental operations had increased profits by 31% despite an 8% price drop and only 19% increase in revenue. Employee morale was high (70% owned company shares). The company was known for its slogan 'We *try harder*' and enjoyed an 'international,' 'upmarket' and 'good service' reputation.

Though already enjoying a dense location network with more than 1,700 outlets, industry observers were expecting Avis to 'buy more market share.' The goal was: 'to grow ahead of hungry opposition' and at the same time meet its objectives of being present in all communities of over 50,000 inhabitants. It was felt that one of the key issues for Avis was to rethink its international pricing policies.

Hertz Europe

Hertz was the largest worldwide car rental company, with about half of its fleet in the U.S. Represented in 120 countries, Hertz had a network of around 400,000 vehicles in 4,700 locations. Its major strength was the control of the airport market and the consequent share of visitors to Europe, particularly those coming from North America.

The ownership of Hertz had continued to change. In 1987 the Ford Motor Company took control of Hertz. By 1989, Ford had sold 26% of its stake to Volvo North American Corporation and 5% to Commerzbank. The Hertz management team owned 20%, with Ford's remaining share amounting to 29%.

In the industry, it was believed that Hertz was performing well and was consolidating its presence in the European market. Hertz's West European network consisted of around 1,600 locations of which 350 were served on a contract basis or operated on a reduced schedule (i.e., seasonal outlets open for holiday periods, reduced hour outlets for low traffic airports). Hertz had also made an effort to be present at railway stations, in addition to its traditional airport locations. Hertz obtained 3,300 representations resulting from its agreements with British Rail and the Swiss rail system. Hertz was permanently installed at 140 airports, but was also present at another 210 airports, some of which largely served private aviation.

With Hertz's caption, '*Number one,*' it held a market perception of being 'big,' 'American,' and 'upmarket.' One industry observer commented that Hertz's management was faced with an organization which risked becoming bureaucratic because of its size. On the other hand, it was credited with excellent media advertisement and positioning.

Europcar/Interrent

On January 1, 1989, Europcar, a French operator with an international network, and Interrent, also international but mostly German, merged to create the largest European network. By the end of 1989, the combined organization had more than 1,800 locations in Western Europe. The merged company was then controlled by Wagons-Lits and by Volkswagen, a German car manufacturer.

The intent of the merger was to build strength through:

- An extensive coverage and a clear leadership position in the major European markets: Germany, the UK and France;
- The alliances built by Europcar with 'National Car Rental' in the Americas and the Pacific, 'Tilden Rent a Car' in Canada, 'Nippon Rent a Car' in Japan and the Pacific;
- Their established name and reputation;
- Synergies from operations.

An industry observer noted that the integration of the two operations was slow to come, because of cultural differences, differing goals of the shareholders, and different management and operating systems. Another asserted that the companies would have been stronger if they had remained separate.

> Merged operations will mean reduced desk occupancy at the airports, and half the offerings on the CRS screens of travel agents and airline personnel. Also, there is the risk of redundant personnel and that subcontractors will migrate to the competition. Remember what happened to Hertz when it restructured its German operations in the mid-'70s; Interrent and Europcar profited from that opportunity.

Because much work still had to be done to complete the merger, Europcar's results were quoted as being poor, and the fruits of the merger were yet to be seen.

Budget

Budget was the most recently founded company of the big four (Los Angeles, 1958). In October 1988 Ford Motor Company financed a management buyout of the company. By 1989, its worldwide operations served 3,400 locations with 200,000 cars. The European network consisted of 1,200 locations, with a majority held by licensees and their agents. Budget made extensive use of franchising. The result was that the company was less homogeneous than its major competitors in most areas—from marketing practices to operating performance. One example of this heterogeneous approach was the situation at the Madrid Airport. In contrast to all the other major European airports, Barajas Budget only offered a 'pick-up' service from the airport. Budget's franchising policy, however, provided a network of highly motivated entrepreneurial companies, such as Sixt/Budget in Germany. This strategy had resulted in a growth of 38% over recent years.

Every country had to adhere to the overall strategy of providing '*Good value for the money.*' Hence, Budget was well regarded, especially in the leisure segment of the market. Some felt, however, that it relied too much on this particular segment. Yet, Budget claimed that it was getting the highest operating performances in the industry with utilization rates above 70%, in contrast to the industry average of 60%. In general, Budget used less media advertisement than its competitors, but this savings was compensated by more discounts and promotion (internal and external).

Other International Firms

A series of other companies were trying to establish themselves as pan-European, or even international. In pursuing that objective, they joined forces with other European or North American players.

Thrifty, regarded as number five in the U.S. and clearly competing on price, had moved into the UK, France, Greece, Belgium, Spain, Portugal, Italy, Ireland and Scandinavia. In Germany, it had reached an agreement with **PROcar**. But, industry observers considered that, after achieving this network, Thrifty had become somewhat 'stretched' and 'coverage was very thin.'

Dollar, another U.S. operator, had been able to merge with **Swan** (UK) and also signed convenient licensing and franchising agreements on the Continent. The resulting network operated 11,000 cars in UK and 4,000 on the Continent.

Another kind of alliance was 'reciprocal marketing and representation agreements' which, for example, had been achieved between **General** (Florida) and **Kenning** (UK).

Industry observers pointed to **Ansa International** as the most successful medium-sized company operating in more than 50 countries worldwide. Its shareholders were 40% American, 40% EC, 10% Swiss, and 10% Pacific based.

Local Companies

The overwhelming majority of these companies were small independent concerns operating at a regional or purely local level. For these firms, renting cars was generally an ancillary activity to vehicle repair and sales. Not generally 'geared up' for the businessman, these local operators received most of their turnover from accident replacement rentals and had suffered from the contraction of this market. Their relative inflexibility, the debilitating effects of insurance companies' cost-cutting on the industry and increasing competition from the multinational rental leaders also contributed to the continuous rationalization process which had occurred. Nevertheless, some of them benefitted from the major players' appetite and sold their telephone numbers and client accounts for healthy amounts. Thus, the local company's client would be referred to the major one. Still others continued the operation as a strong contributor to the profitability of their main business.

The World Flavor Industry

David Hover

Per V. Jenster

The term "flavors" is applied to any of a number of chemical products added to processed foods or beverages to impart taste and aroma. Flavors were usually classified as either natural, nature identical, or artificial depending on the production method used. A flavor was classified as natural if it was extracted from animal or vegetable products using physical means including standard kitchen activities like cooking, heating, boiling, etc. Flavors produced through fermentation were generally considered natural flavors. Nature identical flavors or enzymology consisted of synthesized substances but which occurred naturally in food. Artificial flavors were substances derived from any source which did not occur naturally in food.

Traditionally, the manufacturers of flavors, known as flavor houses, had also supplied fragrances (for perfumes, personal hygiene products, soaps, detergents, etc.) because both flavors and fragrances were extracted from raw materials using the same fractionation and distillation processes. However, the changing market and technology was eroding many of the synergies between the two segments. Not only was demand for flavors increasing as the food processing industry became more competitive, but the food industry also demanded more sophisticated flavors, able to withstand the rigorous food processing procedures and meet government and consumer standards. The market conditions made creating suitable flavors much more difficult and technologically demanding than creating fragrances. As one executive noted:

> Everyone knows what green peas taste like—coming up with the exact same flavor is challenging. However, with fragrances you can be more creative.

At the same time the market for fragrances was static and in the case of designer perfumes actually declining.

The impact of the market changes was felt in the performance figures of the industry. Until the late 1970s, the world flavors and fragrances (F&F) indus-

This case was prepared by Research Associate David Hover, under the supervision of Professor Per V. Jenster, as a basis for class discussion rather than to illustrate either effective or ineffective handling of a business situation.

Copyright © 1991 IMD. International Institute for Management Development, Lausanne, Switzerland. IMD retains all rights. Not to be used or reproduced without written permission directly from IMD, Lausanne, Sitzerland.

try had shown consistently strong results. Industry profitability approximated 15% of sales in the mid to late 1960s and 10% in the 1970s. In the 1980s, however, slower growth and increased competitive pressures had reduced profitability to about 6–7% industry-wide and real sales growth averaged 5–6% per year, reaching an estimated $6.7 billion in 1990. Projections into the 1990s estimated growth rates to remain in the 5% range. Flavors comprised nearly 45% of the total F&F market and were valued at approximately $3.1 billion in 1990. Western Europe and the United States were the largest regional markets, together accounting for 63% of the world flavor sales. Japan was the third major market. Consumption in the rest of the world was significantly lower. However, Eastern Europe and the Far East were identified as having significant growth potential.

In the flavor segment of the market, the growth of processed foods as a percentage of total food consumption was expected to drive up demand through the 1990s. An increase in sales of savory flavors (25% of the total flavors market) was anticipated as well. Because of the high cost of research and development, the food processing companies were increasingly contracting product development out to flavor houses, seasoning houses, and ingredient suppliers, further strengthening demand. The considerable increase in demand for convenience foods was also likely to continue to grow throughout the 1990s, creating new opportunities to expand the market.

Other developments had also influenced the industry in the late 1980s, including changing customer profiles, evolving competitive environment, and more sophisticated end-consumers. Together, these factors acting on the industry were forcing flavor houses to reevaluate the way they did business.

Importance of Flavors

Although the flavor component usually represented only a small fraction of the total cost of a food product, its benefit to the final product was very large. Price, image, nutrition, convenience, and texture were also important, but taste acceptance by the consumer was essential to the creation of brand loyalty. Food processors placed considerable pressure on flavor houses to deliver consistent, high quality flavors at low costs.

Major research was also conducted to develop more efficient delivery systems. The natural and nature identical flavors favored by the producers were difficult to protect from degradation in processing, packaging, and reactions with other ingredients. High temperature short-time (HTST) food processing, restoring and microwave cooking, in particular, were harsh environments for the delicate flavors. The price premiums paid for the natural products also increased demands for efficient delivery systems. New techniques to enhance stability and shelf life were also important. The leading edge technologies such as micro encapsulation were expensive to develop and tailor to different types of applications. The high capital costs associated with many of these technologies necessitated large end user markets frequently only possible through a global presence.

End product consumers were also changing their demands. Natural healthy foods, low cholesterol, low fat, low sodium, high fiber, and low sugar were increasingly in demand and able to command a price premium. As the population in most of the developed world aged, tastes became more sophisticated. Rising interest in tea flavored drinks was one of the manifestations of this development. Convenience (largely related to the microwave) was also a major interest of consumers, despite their otherwise increasing demand for natural ingredients. Furthermore, the flavor houses had to work with the packaging companies so that the combination of ingredients, flavors, and packages would have the flavor, texture, browning ability (appearance), and shelf life demanded by the consumer. For the flavor houses each of these trends placed demands on the R&D activities of the flavor houses.

Labelling and Regulation

The distinctions between natural, nature identical and artificial flavors were frequently subtle and no firm international standards existed. For example, flavors which were non-declarable (nothing had to be mentioned on the label) in some countries might have to be labelled or were even prohibited in other countries. Few international standards existed on acceptable ingredients. Until recently, German brewers, for example, were unable to use any additives in beer. Other countries were much less restrictive in potential ingredients. Individual product requirements forced flavor houses to reconfigure their product lines for some countries. With the exception of some EC regulations coinciding with the realization of the European common market in 1992, industry experts did not anticipate comprehensive coordination of national food regulations.

Emphasis on natural products by end-consumers was having its own impact on product rationalization. In response to the changing market and regulatory trends, most major flavor houses had reoriented their development programs to focus on natural flavors. Natural flavors, however, were more technologically demanding. Artificial and nature identical flavors generally cost less to manufacture and were more able to withstand the modern food processing techniques such as ultra high temperature (UHT) and industrial scale microwaving which degraded many natural flavors. Despite the advantages of artificial flavors, they were increasingly shunned by the market and the market share of artificial flavors had fallen from 75% in the 1960s to 25% by the late 1980s.

Competitors

In 1990, International Flavors and Fragrances (IFF) was the largest flavor house with 12% of the world-wide market. Quest was a close second with 11% market share. (Refer to Exhibit 1.) The market share of the two companies, however, differed from market to market. Quest was market leader in a number

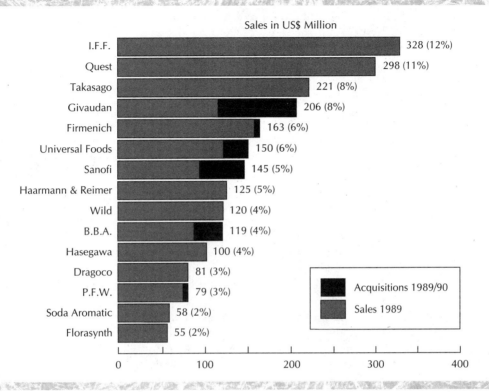

EXHIBIT 1
Top 15 Flavor Houses by Flavor Sales (Market share in parentheses)

Sales in US$ Million

Company	Sales (Market share)
I.F.F.	328 (12%)
Quest	298 (11%)
Takasago	221 (8%)
Givaudan	206 (8%)
Firmenich	163 (6%)
Universal Foods	150 (6%)
Sanofi	145 (5%)
Haarmann & Reimer	125 (5%)
Wild	120 (4%)
B.B.A.	119 (4%)
Hasegawa	100 (4%)
Dragoco	81 (3%)
P.F.W.	79 (3%)
Soda Aromatic	58 (2%)
Florasynth	55 (2%)

■ Acquisitions 1989/90
■ Sales 1989

Source: Quest International

of smaller European countries while IFF's market leadership was primarily a result of its dominant position in the U.S. In other countries, notably Japan and Germany, neither IFF nor Quest had significant market shares.

In the F&F industry overall, 14 companies had sales of $100 million or more. The remaining sales were dispersed among some 100 other major producers and nearly 1,000 smaller companies around the world. Most of the smaller companies were very specialized and closely held. New entrants were constant. It was relatively easy for companies to enter the market (especially in fragrances) as niche players in specialized products or for individual producers. As new product development became more costly and complex, strategic acquisitions had become an important means of company growth in the flavor industry. Acquisitions were also made for other reasons: accessing a base in a particular regional market, acquiring a market niche, expanding R&D in a particular field, or retaining a talented flavorist or a key food account.

Despite the high level of merger and acquisition activity, the world flavor industry (and the F&F industry in general) remained highly fragmented in the early 1990s. This was not expected to change. Arthur D. Little, a management consulting firm, even predicted a slowdown in the rate of acquisitions in the first part of the decade. Continued success in the industry required an enhanced working relationship with customers and mergers and acquisitions were one way for flavor houses to obtain the necessary range of products and knowledge to meet customer demands.

Customers

Competitive strategies and changes in the flavor industry were partly in response to the fast pace of change in the food processing industry, the primary flavor market. Concentration and globalization, frequently through mergers and acquisitions, were the dominating trends as the food processors tried to enhance their competitive position. The search for global products and associated economies of scale was motivated by such factors as the emergence of free trade areas like the European Community and the U.S.-Canadian Free Trade Association, and increased interest in ethnic foods. In Europe, the industry was responding more slowly to the market trends than in Japan or the U.S., but already the aggressive European producers had begun to establish a European-wide (and occasionally global) base of operations.

One result of the new industrial order was an increased level of competition. In the past, regional political and physical boundaries had sheltered many companies from outside competition. The gradual erosion of many of these barriers had allowed companies to expand into new markets more efficiently. As in the flavor industry, meeting the new competitive challenge frequently meant acquisitions either for additional market share, national presence, or product range extension. With many of the acquisitions, however, also came increased debt loads which put pressure on the companies to allocate funds away from such "investment" areas as R&D. Because of the cutbacks in R&D spending at many of the food processors and greater cost efficiency, the flavor houses came to spend significantly more on R&D than their customers. R&D spending varied by company size: the large flavor houses spent 7–12% of sales on R&D, while the smaller companies spent 2–5%.

Global branding had an impact on the food processing industry. Food products companies, interested in reducing costs, continuously searched for product concepts that could be applied trans-culturally. Although David Stout, the head of Unilever's economics department, claimed, "There is no such thing as an edible Walkman," some products were more suitable to global branding and marketing than others. Many beverages, snacks, fast food and some dairy products were relatively easy to sell across national borders. Despite sharing the same product concept, the product inside the can or package was frequently modified (sometimes substantially) from country to country to satisfy local tastes, cooking habits, and/or cultural norms.

The structural changes in the food industry had led to increasing polarization between the very large multiproduct companies (Kraft, itself a division of Philip Morris, CPC International Nestlé, BSN) and the small, highly specialized niche players. The large multinationals strove to enlarge their market shares while the remaining niche players further specialized. Medium sized companies, if they were to survive, found themselves forced either to expand or specialize. As the food processing companies went international they wanted their flavor suppliers to be there with them.

Providing international service to their customers was not easy for the flavor houses. Because of the extensive resources needed, it was important to identify which customers were going to be successful in the 1990s and the decades beyond. Limited resources did not allow all options with each customer to be pursued. Working hard and expending limited resources to maintain extensive relations with a customer unable to compete in the long-term was potentially disastrous for a flavor house. Consolidation in the food processing industry also reduced the number of potential alternative customers, further increasing the risk associated with a failing customer.

Declining numbers of customers, besides increasing the proportion of business associated with one customer, changed the nature of the sales relationship. Fewer sales people were needed but the necessary level of expertise and interaction increased. Sales personnel had to interact with managers and technicians at many levels and functional areas including R&D, production, operations, purchasing offices and marketing. These interactions had to be managed carefully: each area had different interests, needs and concerns which had to be addressed if the relationship was to work effectively. Effectiveness was also dependent on a complete understanding of the customer's business needs. It was no longer sufficient to just sell a product; the supplier also had to know how it integrated with the rest of the customer's operation.

Flavor Industry Developments

In the latter part of the 1980s a number of notable trends were becoming apparent in the flavors industry which had long-term implications for industry players. The trends included more emphasis on flavor systems, high rates of new product introduction and the breakdown of traditional distinctions between competitors in different segments.

Total Food Systems

As they concentrated internal activities on marketing, food processing companies were increasingly interested in flavor houses which were able to offer solutions to particular problems rather than just individual flavors. The development of low-fat, low-calorie ice cream was a typical example of the services food processors wanted from their suppliers. Removing fat from ice cream was technically not difficult. However, the fat was the basis for both the taste and mouthfeel of the product. Creating the same sensation the customer experienced when eating ice cream but without the fat required developing a complete system comprised of flavors, food ingredients and additives. Companies that had previously operated only as suppliers of specific products like emulsifiers, colors, or preservatives began to find that their customers, lacking the ability to develop flavors systems on their own, wanted more than just the basic product.

A total food system combined various products (flavors, food ingredients, and additives) to create an end product with certain desired flavor, texture, and appearance qualities. Food ingredients, to replace bulk or assist in product enhancement, were a fundamental part of many systems although the actual costs of the flavor or ingredients frequently only constitute 5% of the final and consumer product price. Few flavor houses had the necessary expertise and production facilities in ingredients yet they had to begin adding food ingredients and additives (such as fats, fat substitutes, emulsifiers, preservatives, etc.) to their product range.

In 1990, however, only six flavor houses were serious players in food ingredients and together held only 34% of the market. Their share, worth $1.029 billion, was, however, growing quickly (it had increased 42% from 1989) primarily through acquisitions. (Refer to Exhibit 2.) Many in the industry believed the best way to get the necessary expertise in ingredients was through acquisitions. Quest and others in the industry believed the ability to offer complete systems was more and more a prerequisite to remaining a world-wide competitor in the industry.

Previously, food ingredients had been produced by specialty chemical companies. Just as flavor houses began investing in food ingredients, food ingredient manufacturers began investing in flavors. Many chemical companies had found food ingredients a natural outgrowth of their specialty chemicals operations. Grindsted and Gist Brocades had made investments with varying levels of success in the area of flavors.[1] It was becoming apparent that the successful flavor houses and food ingredient companies would be those that could provide global one-stop services or particular niche products.

Product Innovation

Redoubled efforts to reach new consumers had caused a significant jump in the number of new food product introductions. According to Productscan/ Marketing Intelligence Service, more than 8,000 new food products were introduced in European markets in 1987. The trend towards expanding product

[1]Biotechnology was another industry which was encroaching on the flavor houses. While flavor houses had spent considerable sums in developing the technology themselves, companies with a biotechnology background were still at an advantage in applying the technology to the production of natural flavors. (Most regulations treated flavors made through enzymology or fermentation as natural as long as the flavor met the other requirements.)

EXHIBIT 2
Food Ingredient Sales of Flavor Houses:
Sales and Market Shares

Food Ingredient Sales (in US$ million)	1989	% Share	Including '89/'90 Acquisitions	% Share
Sanofi	412	14%	414	14%
Haarman & Reimer	—	0%	231	8%
Quest	98	3%	158	5%
Universal Foods	67	2%	83	3%
P.F.W.	75	3%	75	3%
Takasago	68	2%	68	2%
Subtotal	720	24%	1,029	34%°
Others	2,280	76%	1,971	66%
Total	3,000	100%	3,000	100%

°Acquisition effect: 43%
Source: Quest International

offerings was expected to continue, and in turn, increase the demand for new flavors and flavor systems. Many flavor houses predicted that the 1990s would bring a continuation of the flavoring fads of the 1980s—exotic flavorings, natural flavorings and easy to prepare foods. However, the area receiving the greatest interest was in natural flavorings and "healthy" foods. Product obsolescence, due to changes in consumer preferences, habits, and lifestyles was also occurring faster than before. Together, combined with the competitive pressures stemming from the food industry, these factors were forcing flavor suppliers to improve their customer service in product application, research and development, technical assistance, and marketing.

Extended Product Lines

Blurring of the distinctions between different fields in the industry was also having a major impact on the competitive structure of the food industry and created an excellent opportunity for flavor houses. Companies were expanding existing product lines utilizing either existing technological expertise in a particular area (such as chocolate or tea) or a successful brand image (such as Mars Bars or Lipton). The occurrence of blurring industry definitions was especially marked in the area of soft-drinks. Companies from many previously unrelated fields were becoming interested in obtaining a piece of the market. For example, the "healthy-athletic" trend in parts of North America, Japan, and northern Europe had prompted pharmaceutical companies to

EXHIBIT 3
Example of Sources of New Entries from Other Industries

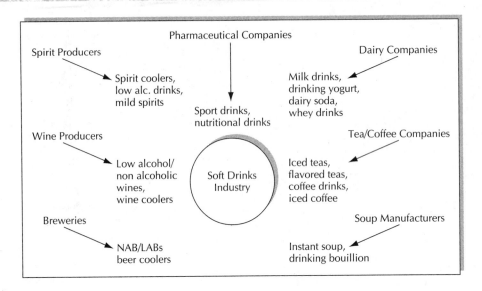

Source: Quest International

develop nutritional and "sport" drinks as alternatives to traditional soft-drinks. Also, as soft-drinks like Coca-Cola were increasingly marketed as alternative morning beverages to coffee, coffee producers tried to develop iced coffee as an alternative to soft-drinks for consumption throughout the day. (Refer to Exhibit 3.)

Index

Note: C indicates page number for cases, located in the last half of the text
        n indicates footnote

I-1